IEEE INFOCOM'97

The Conference on Computer Communications

Volume 3

Proceedings Volume 3

IEEE INFOCOM'97

The Conference on Computer Communications

Sixteenth Annual Joint Conference of the IEEE Computer and Communications Societies

Driving the Information Revolution

April 7–12, 1997
Kobe, Japan

Sponsored by

IEEE Computer Society
Technical Committee on Computer Communications
IEEE Communications Society

In cooperation with

IEICE (the Institute of Electronics, Information and Communication Engineers) Japan
IPS (Information Processing Society) of Japan
ORS (The Operations Research Society) of Japan

IEEE Computer Society Press
Los Alamitos, California

Washington • Brussels • Tokyo

IEEE Computer Society Press
10662 Los Vaqueros Circle
P.O.Box 3014
Los Alamitos, CA 90720-1264

IEEE Computer Society Press Order Number PR07780 (Three-volume set)
IEEE Order Plan Catalog Number 97CB36034
ISBN 0-8186-7780-5
IEEE Order Plan ISBN 0-8186-7782-1
Microfiche ISBN 0-8186-7781-3
ISSN 0743-166X

Additional copies may be ordered from:

IEEE Computer Society Press
Customer Service Center
10662 Los Vaqueros Circle
P.O. Box 3014
Los Alamitos, CA 90720-1314
Tel: +1-714-821-8380
Fax: +1-714-821-4641
Email: cs.books@computer.org

IEEE Service Center
445 Hoes Lane
P.O. Box 1331
Piscataway, NJ 08855-1331
Tel: +1-908-981-1393
Fax: +1-908-981-9667
misc.custserv@computer.org

IEEE Computer Society
13, Avenue de l'Aquilon
B-1200 Brussels
BELGIUM
Tel: +32-2-770-2198
Fax: +32-2-770-8505
euro.ofc@computer.org

IEEE Computer Society
Ooshima Building
2-19-1 Minami-Aoyama
Minato-ku, Tokyo 107
JAPAN
Tel: +81-3-3408-3118
Fax: +81-3-3408-3553
tokyo.ofc@computer.org

Editorial production by Penny Storms
Printed in the United States of America by Braun-Brumfield, Inc.

The Institute of Electrical and Electronics Engineers, Inc.

Table of Contents

Message from the General Co-Chairs

Toshiharu Hasegawa **Raymond L. Pickholtz**

INFOCOM'97 comes at a critical juncture in networking. While the Internet's growth now threatens to exhaust address space and create congestion and extreme slowdowns, if not deadlock, new technologies, architectures and protocols are becoming available "just in time." Among these are high speed ATM networks at gigabit rates, a new IP protocol with enlarged address space and streamlined header processing, multi-gigabit optical links and more-versatile routers and switches. As a result of these developments, convergences of networking and services are occurring. We are beginning to see "cells in frames," gigabit Ethernet, gigabit ATM/SONET, gigabit switching, routing and protocols. The need for innovative design and the opportunities that this will open will engage researchers world-wide for decades. Most exciting are the potential applications that are difficult even to imagine at this time. The applications will likely go beyond our current framework of multimedia interactive communications, information access, and entertainment.

In the corporate world, new giants are forming such as BT/MCI and others to come. The brave new world of ultra high speed global networking will include untethered wireless communication and universal personal access with security.

The challenge is such that we envy our younger colleagues who will make the most-significant contributions to this enterprise. INFOCOM'97 starts the process with a program that clearly has the seeds of this revolution in networking. The conference committees have worked hard to insure this objective with a careful paper screening process, outstanding and up-to-date tutorials, a special Gigabit Workshop, keynote addresses by Vinton Cerf, VP of MCI and one of the visionaries of the Internet, and Toshiharu Aoki, Executive VP of NTT. We thank all of them. We also thank the host city of Kobe for making INFOCOM'97 a completely rewarding experience. As Kobe has seen a rebirth since the recent earthquake, so with similar ingenuity and vision, the participants of INFOCOM'97 in Kobe will initiate a rebirth in networking. We welcome you to INFOCOM'97, the networking conference in the beautiful new Kobe, where east, west, north and south will converge in April of 1997.

Message from the Technical Program Co-Chairs

Hideo Miyahara

Tatsuya Suda

Greetings to everyone.

Welcome to the 16th annual IEEE INFOCOM'97 conference. This year, the INFOCOM'97 conference theme is "Driving the Information Revolution," and the technical program was created to advance our knowledge in computer communications and networking. It offers 42 technical sessions, 3 panels and 6 tutorials, all addressing the most recent advances in the field.

A number of people have contributed, creating a strong technical program. First of all, we received a large number of paper submissions — 524 to be exact. This is the second highest number of paper submissions in INFOCOM's history. Papers were submitted from all over the world: 250 from the North America, 171 from the Asia Pacific, 80 from the Europe, and 23 from other parts of the world. Second, a number of researchers served on the INFOCOM'97 Technical Program Committee; it has 127 members, 13 of whom served as area coordinators. They helped to evaluate paper submissions in a rigorous and fair, yet timely, manner and contributed significantly to the strength of the technical program. The excellent quality of this year's technical program is a reflection of the strong efforts of the researchers who submitted papers, the TPC members, and the area coordinators.

We employed a rigorous and fair review process with layers of check points, evaluating and re-evaluating the technical merits of the paper submissions. Paper submissions were first reviewed by at least 3 experts, including a TPC member, who were assigned the paper. In many cases, 4 to 6 experts reviewed a paper. Reviews and the TPC members' recommendations were then submitted to the corresponding area coordinators, who read all the paper submissions in their areas and integrated their evaluations into the review results. The recommendations of area coordinators were then discussed extensively at the TPC meeting in order to arrive at the 167 papers accepted to the conference.

The acceptance ratio for INFOCOM'97 this year was approximately 30% (167 papers accepted out of 524 submissions). Due to the competitive nature of this year's submission process, we were unable to accommodate a number of technically solid and qualified papers. We hope that the authors of these submissions will find other high quality conferences and journals in which to publish their fine results.

We would like to express our deep appreciation for the efforts of those who helped with the various administrative duties of the INFOCOM'97 TPC. They include Jaime Bae Kim, Duke Hong, Brett Vickers, Carlos Oliveira, Celio Albuquerque, George Lin, Larry Chen, Huy Phan, Sang Ahn, Leslee Xu, Hayato Ishibashi, Shinji Shimojo and Bernie Bender. Their aid was indispensable.

Finally we thank the conference attendees, whose engaging discussions with researchers will certainly make this year's conference a rousing success.

This year, INFOCOM'97 is held in Kobe, Japan, making this the second time in INFOCOM's history that the conference has been held abroad. April is considered one of the best times of the year to visit Japan. We are certain that the technical program will be thoroughly engaging and enjoyable, but we also hope that conference attendees allot some time to delight in Japan's springtime beauty.

INFOCOM'97 Organizing Committee

General Co-Chairs
Toshiharu Hasegawa, *Kyoto University*
Raymond L. Pickholtz, *The George Washington University*

Technical Program Committee Co-Chairs
Hideo Miyahara, *Osaka University*
Tatsuya Suda, *University of California at Irvine*

Local Aarrangements Co-Chairs
Masayuki Murata, *Osaka University*
James Kurose, *University of Massachusetts at Amherst*

Treasurer
Tetsuya Takine, *Osaka University*
Jing-Fei Ren, *Texas Instruments*

Publicity Co-Chairs
Yuji Oie, *Nara Institute of Science and Technology*
Henning Schulzrinne, *Columbia University*

Internet Arrangements Co-Chairs
Shinji Shimojo, *Osaka University*
Kazuhiro Ohtsuki, *Kobe University*

Publications Co-Chairs
Miki Yamamoto, *Osaka University*
Joseph Bannister, *USC/Information Sciences Institute*

Tutorials Co-Chairs
Kiyoshi Nosu, *NTT Optical Network Systems Labs*
Tom LaPorta, *Bell Labs, Lucent Technologies*

Panel Sessions Co-Chairs
Shuji Tasaka, *Nagoya Institute of Technology*
Roch Guérin, *IBM T.J. Watson Research Center*

Standing Committee Chair
Harvey Freeman, *LANWORKS, Inc.*

International Advisory Committee

Chair
Toshiharu Hasegawa, *Kyoto University, Japan*

Members
Hisashi Kobayashi, *Princeton University, USA*
Kojiro Watanabe, *NEC U.S.A., Inc., USA*
James Kurose, *University of Massachusetts at Amherst, USA*
Mark Karol, *Bell Labs, Lucent Technologies, USA*
Celia Desmond, *Stentor Resource Center Inc., Canada*
Hiromasa Ikeda, *Osaka University, Japan*
M. Naim Yunus, *VXL Holdings Sdn Bhd, Malaysia*
Tomonori Aoyama, *NTT, Japan*
Lye Kin Mun, *National Univ. of Singapore, Singapore*
Guy Pujole, *University of Versailles, France*
Seung-Taik Yang, *Electronics and Telecommunications Research Institute, Korea*
Tak-Shing Yum, *Chinese University, Hong Kong*
Lin-Shan Lee, *Academica Sinica, Taiwan*
Tetsuya Miki, *The University of Electro-Communications, Japan*
Koichi Matsuda, *NTT, Japan*

Japan Local Committee

Chair
Hideo Miyahara, *Osaka University*

Members
Masayuki Murata, *Osaka University*
Tetsuya Takine, *Osaka University*
Yuji Oie, *Nara Institute of Science and Technology*
Kazuhiro Ohtsuki, *Kobe University*
Naoto Miyoshi, *Kyoto University*
Ken-ichi Aihara, *NTT*

INFOCOM'97 Technical Program Committee

Co-Chairs

Tatsuya Suda, *University of California at Irvine*
Hideo Miyahara, *Osaka University*

Area Technical Program Coordinators

Joe Bannister, *USC/ISI*
Luigi Fratta, *Politecnico di Milano*
Roch Guérin, *IBM T.J. Watson Research Center*
Mark Karol, *Bell Labs, Lucent Technologies*
David Lee, *Bell Labs, Lucent Technologies*
Kin K. Leung, *AT&T Laboratories*
Biswanath Mukherjee, *University of California at Davis*
Shojiro Nishio, *Osaka University*
Giovanni Pacifici, *IBM T.J. Watson Research Center*
Guru Parulkar, *Washington University*
George Polyzos, *University of California at San Diego*
Hiroshi Saito, *NTT*
Lixia Zhang, *University of California at Los Angeles*

Technical Program Committee Members

Ian F. Akyildiz, *Georgia Tech.*
Harmen R. van As, *Vienna University of Technology*
Abhaya Asthana, *Bell Labs*
Mohammed Atiquzzaman, *Monash University*
Ender Ayanoglu, *Bell Labs, Lucent Technologies*
Anindo Bagchi, *Bellcore*
Victor Bahl, *Digital Equipment Corporation*
Krishna Bala, *Bellcore*
Subrata Banerjee, *Stevens Institute of Technology*
Sujata Banerjee, *University of Pittsburgh*
Joe Betser, *The Aerospace Corp.*
Nicola Bléfari-Melazzi, *Univ. of Rome at Tor Vergata*
Michael S. Borella, *DePaul University*
Imrich Chlamtac, *Boston University*
Song Chong, *Sogang University*
Kee Chaing Chua, *National University of Singapore*
John N. Daigle, *University of Mississippi*
Rajiv Dighe, *NEC USA*
Christos Douligeris, *University of Miami*
Patrick W. Dowd, *University of Maryland*
Anwar Elwalid, *AT&T*
Anthony Ephremides, *University of Maryland*
Deborah Estrin, *University of Southern California*
Michael J. Ferguson, *Université du Québec*
Andrea Fumagalli, *Politecnico di Torino*
J.J. Garcia-Luna, *University of California at Santa Cruz*
Dipak Ghosal, *University of California at Davis*
Fengmin Gong, *MCNC*
Sanjay Gupta, *Illinois Institute of Technology*
Zygmunt J. Haas, *Cornell University*
Chao-Ju Jennifer Hou, *Ohio State University*
Tony Hsiao, *Sun Microsystems*
Pierre A. Humblet, *Eurecom Institute*
Toru Ishida, *Kyoto University*
Raj Jain, *Ohio State University*
Feiling Jia, *Optivision, Inc.*
Ahmed E. Kamal, *Kuwait University*
Dennis Karvelas, *New Jersey Institute of Technology*
Tohru Kikuno, *Osaka University*
Hyong S. Kim, *Carnegie Mellon University*
Jaime B. Kim, *California State University at Northridge*
Belka Kraimeche, *The Cooper Union*
Arvind Krishna, *IBM Research*
Jim Kurose, *University of Massachusetts at Amherst*

Reviewers

Bob Aaron
Mohamed Abdelaziz
Tarek F. Abdelzaher
Arup Acharya
Abdelnaser Adas
Ron Addie
Yehuda Afek
Charu C. Aggarwal
Ehud Aharoni
Nima Ahmadvand
Masaki Aida
Nail Akar
Humayun Akhtar
Bora Aydin Akyol
Fouad Al-Hallel
Murat Alanyali
M. Mehmet Ali
Mohammad Ali Arad
Kevin Almeroth
Hussein M. Alnuweiri
Kemal Altinkemer
Onur Altintas
Eitan Altman
Mostafa Ammar
Nikos Aneroussis
P.N. Anirudhan
Nirwan Ansari
Rohan Aranha
Gerald R. Ash
Yukio Atsumi
Valery Augais
Cristina Aurrecoechea
Ra'ed Y. Awdeh
Daniel O. Awduche
Yossi Azar
Murat Azizoglu
B.R. Badrinath
Anantaram Balakrishnan
Mario Baldi
Ilia Baldine
Dhritiman Banerjee
Majid Barazande-Pour
B. Basch
Richard Barry
Jochen Behrens
George Benke
Lotfi Benmohamed
Jon Bennett
Brahim Bensaou
Arthur Berger
Randall A. Berry
Steven Berson
Maged Beshai
Riccardo Bettati
Pravin Bhagwat
Samrat Bhattacharjee
Partha P. Bhattacharya
Andrea Bianco
Subir K. Biswas
Gordon S. Blair
Chris Blondia
Raffaele Bolla
Christian Bonnet
Alberto Bononi
Maurizio A. Bonuccelli
Vanu Bose
Eric Bouillet
Raouf Boutaba
David Boyer
Lawrence S. Brakmo
Oliver Brand
Torsten Braun
Greg Brewster
Dale Buchholz
Jim Burns
Mehmet Ufuk Caglayan
Franco Callegati
Ken Calvert
Pietro Camarda
Jiannong Cao
Jeffrey Capone
Olga Casals
Christos G. Cassandras
Dirceu Cavendish
Mun Choon Chan
Shiu C. Chan
Y. Chandramouli
Cheng-Shang Chang
Chung Ju Chang
Henry Chang
Jonathan H. Chao
Anna Charny
Hemant Chaskar
Hao Che
Biao Chen
Cheng C. Chen
Chien Chen
David Chen
Geping Chen
Hsiling Chen
Tom Chen
Wai Chen
Wen-Shyen E. Chen
Yao-Min Chen
Zhigang Chen
Chi-Chung Cheung
Kwan F. Cheung
Michael Cheung
Shun Yan Cheung
Marco Chiani
Franco Chiaraluce
Steve Chiu
Jinwoo Choe
Manhoi Choy
Hao-hua Chu
Hon-Wai Chu
John Chu
Anthony Chung
Israel Cidon
Reha Civanlar
Kimberly Claffy
John G. Cleary
Rosangela Coelho
Reuven Cohen
Blair Collier
Marco Conti
Adrian Conway
Giovanni E. Corazza
M. Scott Corson
R. Mitchell Cox
Brian P. Crow
Rene Cruz
Francesca Cuomo
Matteo D'Ambrosio
Walid Dabbous
Pankaj K. Das
Brian DeCleene
Amir Dembo
Sanjeev Deora
John Desmond
George Develekos
Michael Devetsikiotis
Jayanta Dey
Jason Ding
Tien V. Do
Matthew B. Doar
Wlodek Dobosiewicz
B.C. Domzy
Michael J. Donahoo
Lakshminath Dondeti
Pamela Drew
Oswald Drobnik
Alain Dupuis
Amitava Dutta
Deborah Dyson
Zbigniew Dziong
Viktoria Elek
Georgios Ellinas
Khaled Elsayed
Mike Erlinger
Cem Ersoy
Ted Faber
Sonia Fahmy
M. Faloutsos
Ruixue Fan
Romano Fantacci
Serge Fdida
Anja Feldmann
Kerry Fendick
Fang Feng
Wu-chi Feng
Wu-chun Feng
Gerhard P. Fettweis
J. Andrew Fingerhut
Stefan Fischer
Allan Fisher
Sally Floyd
Nelson L.S. Fonseca
Daniel Friedman
V.J. Friesen
Imed Frigui
Satoshi Fujita
Errin Fulp
Cathy Fulton
Toshitsugu Futagami
Maurice Gagnaire
Dominique Gaiti
Alexei A. Gaivoronski
Aura Ganz
Rodrigo Garces
Roberto Gaudino
Paul Gauthier
Constant Gbaguidi
Pawel Gburzynski
N. Georganas
Ori Gerstel
Nasir Ghani
J. Ghosh
Paolo Giacomazzi
Andre Girard
Aniruddha Gokhale
Andrea Goldsmith
Jamal Golestani
Jie Gong
Ramesh Govindan
Shri Goyal
Pawan Goyal
Rohit Goyal

Shri Goyal
Marcel Graf
J.-Ch. Grégoire
Albert G. Greenberg
Enrico Gregori
Wayne D. Grover
Fabrice Guillemin
Amit Gupta
Anil K. Gupta
Jun Han
Ibrahim Habib
Hisaya Hadama
Yaiche Haikel
Bruce Hajek
S. Louis Hakimi
Yukihiro Hamada
Babak Hamidzadeh
J. Han
Janelle J. Harms
Tim Harrison
Felix Hartanto
Kaname Harumoto
Hossam Hassanein
John Heidemann
Ahmed Helmy
Enrique J. Hernandez-Valencia
Meir Herzberg
Daniel P. Heyman
Manabu Higashida
Teruo Higashino
Atsushi Hiramatsu
Miwa Hiroyoshi
Gisli Hjalmtysson
Joseph Ho
Ricky Ho
David Hoffmeister
Markus Hofmann
Tad Hofmeister
Michael Honing
Steve Hotz
Chao-Ju Jennifer Hou
Yiwei Thomas Hou
Henry Houh
Fahad Hoymany
Scott Hrastar
Deh-Phone K. Hsing
Po-Chi Hu
Nian-Chi Huang
Jean-Francois Huard
Frank Huebner
Lucas Hui
Zbigniew Hulicki
Eoin Hyden
Chih-Lin I
Steve Iatrou
Noboru Iida
Chinatsu Ikeda
Jason Iness
Ichiro Inoue
Kenji Ishida
Fumio Ishizaki
Hiroyasu Itoh
Rauf Izmailov
X. Jia
Jonathan Jiang
Shengming Jiang
Shantigram Jagannath
Bjorn Jager
Prashant Jain
Andrzej Jajszczyk
Gabriel Jakobson
Ju-wook Jang
Anura Jayasumana
Predrag Jelenkovic
Seong-Ho Jeong
Hongbin Ji
Feiling Jia
Xiaohua Jia
Hong Jiang
S.M. Jiang
Song Jiang
David B. Johnson
Robert D. Johnston
H. Jonathan
Scott Jordan
Anupam Joshi
Y. Frank Jou
Jinoo Joung
Jason Jue
Youki Kadobayashi
Lampros Kalampoukas
C.R. Kalmanek
Shivkumar Kalyanaraman
Sanjay Kamat
Anshul Kantawala
Ezhan Karasan
Kamal Karlapalem
Shoji Kasahara
Irene Katzela
Fred Kaudel
Richard Kautz
Kenji Kawahara
Haruko Kawahigashi
Ryutaro Kawamura
Kai-wei Ke
S. Keshav
G. Kesidis
Asad Khamisy
Irfan Khan
Bhumip Khasnabish
Samir Khuller
Robert Kibler
Hyong S. Kim
Jeong Geun Kim
S.-C. Kim
Yonghwan Kim
Yasuhiko Kitamura
Hideo Kitazume
Masaru Kitsuregawa
John G. Klincewicz
Edward W. Knightly
Kazutomo Kobayashi
Ulf Koerner
Daniel Kofman
Aleksandar Kolarov
Takis Konstantopoulos
Willard Korfhage
Milan Kovacevic
W. Kreutzer
K.R. Krishnan
Ram Krishnan
Santosh Krishnan
Heiko Krumm
Marwan Krunz
Paul Krzyzanowski
Oguz Kucur
Seiya Kudoh
Vitaly M. Kuleshov
Lalita A. Kulkarni
Lakshmana N. Kumar
Srikantha Kumar
Joy Kuri
Seok-Kyu Kweon
Koenraad Laevens
Richard O. LaMaire
Yael Lapid
George Lapiotis
K.L. Eddie Law
Jean-Yves Le Boudec
Byoung-Joon Lee
Hung-Ju Lee
Kuo-Chun Lee
Ming-Jeng Lee
Tony T. Lee
Robert C. Lehr
William Lehr
Wolfram Lemppenau
Emilio Leonardi
Ian Leslie
Stefan Leue
Victor Leung
Charles Levert
Brian Neil Levine
Hanoch Levy
Yoni Levy
Bo Li
Chengzhi Li
Chih-Peng Li
Chung-Sheng Li
Junyi Li
Tony Li
Soung C. Liew
F. Joe Lin
Yow-Jian Lin
Ting-Li Ling
Marco Listanti
Kuo-Hui Liu
Te-Kai Liu
Wei Liu
Yao-Ching Liu
Zhao Liu
F.L. Lo
F. Lo Presti
Edwin Loecherbach
Alfio Lombardo
Steven Low
Steven Lowen
Chien-Chun Lu
Kevin W. Lu
Walter Lucchesi
Dante De Lucia
Qingshan Luo
Wenjun Luo
Bryan Lyles
Qingming Ma
Michelle MacRae
U. Madhow
Naoki Makimoto
Sam Makki
Nicholas Malcolm
Manu Malek
David A. Maltz
Dragos Manolescu
Weizhen Mao
Bill Marcus
Brian L. Mark
Doug Marquis
Saverio Mascolo
Lorne Mason
Rudolf Mathar
Ibrahim Matta
Jean McManus
D.C. McNickle
Aref Meddeb
Gopal Meempat
Marialuisa Merani
Zoran Miljanic
Frank Miller
Robert F. Miller
Jelena Misic
Sumita Mishra
Sanjay Mithal
Danny J. Mitzel

Naoto Miyoshi
Ahmed Mokhtar
José A.S. Monteiro
Robert Moose
Daniel Mossé
Hussain Mouftah
Andrew Muir
Sarit Mukherjee
Sumedh Mungee
Toru Murase
Shree Murthy
Nagi Naganathan
Shin'ichi Nagano
Ramesh Nagarajan
Erich Nahum
Philippe Nain
Hajime Nakamura
Masahide Nakamura
Sanjiv Nanda
Mahesan Nandikesan
Seffi Naor
Srinivas Narayan
B. Narendran
Tapas K. Nayak
Arnold L. Neidhardt
Tho Le Ngoc
BoFriis Nielsen
Ioanis Nikolaidis
Arne Nilsson
Joerg Nonnenmacher
Katia Obraczka
Toshikane Oda
Yoram Ofek
Richard Ogier
Nagao Ogino
Chang-Hwan Oh
Yoshihiro Ohba
Hiroyuki Ohsaki
Chikara Ohta
Masataka Ohta
Kazuhiro Ohtsuki
Yuji Oie
Sema Oktug
Lyndon Y. Ong
Luis Orozco-Barbosa
Timucin Ozugur
A.R. Pach
Leon Paley
Rajesh K. Pankaj
Daniela Panno
Christos Papadopoulos
M. Papamichail
Shyam Parekh
Jin-Soo Park
Gerard Parr
Sanjoy Paul
Rajesh S. Pazhyannur
Carlos M. D. Pazos
Jon M. Peha
Frank A. Pellegrino
Dimitrios E. Pendarakis
Wuxu Peng
Vinod Peris
Jim Perreault
Harry Perros
Hussain Pezeshki-Esfahani
Niki Pissinou
Gregory P. Pollini
Phil Porras
Greg Pottie
Balaji Prabakhar
Sharat C. Prasad
Robert L. Probert
Ramon Puigjaner
Hung Keng Pung
Irfan Pyarali
Kun Qian
Sonrong Qian
Yi Qian
Chunming Qiao
Lintian Qiao
R.Venkateswaran
Nabi Rafie
C. S. Raghavendra
Amitava Raha
Mahfuzur Rahman
Cynthia D. Rais
Gokul Rajaram
Byrav Ramamurthy
Rajiv Ramaswami
Ramachandran Ramjee
Nol Rananand
Sampath Rangarajan
Ramesh Rao
S. Rao
Anoop Reddy
Douglas S. Reeves
Kiran M. Rege
Amy R. Reibman
Peter Reiher
Martin Reisslein
Qiang Ren
Jennifer Rexford
Ronn Ritke
Charles E. Rohrs
Allyn Romanow
Zvi Rosberg
Oliver Rose
Jonathan Rosenberg
Kurt Rothermel
H. Rudin
John Rulnick
Chester Ruszczyk
Bong Ryu
Debanjan Saha
Anirudha Sahoo
Prescott Sakai
Charbel M. Sakr
Vijay K. Samalam
J.M. Didier Samfat
Pedro I. Sanchez
Huzur Saran
Chandramouli Sargor
Arvind Sathi
Stephen Schwab
Ahmet Sekercioglu
Abhijit Sengupta
Yetik Serbest
Srinivasan Seshan
Adarshpal Sethi
Sanjeev Setia
Faisal Shad
N. Shankar
Puneet Sharma
Jacob Sharony
Yuval Shavitt
Showi-Min Shen
Scott Shenker
Prashant Shenoy
Stephen Shew
Clay Shields
Cheul Shim
Nahum Shimkin
Shinsuke Shimogawa
Shinji Shimojo
N. Shivakumar
Adam Shwartz
Ikhlaq Sidhu
Rainer Siebenhaar
James Sienicki
Jim Sienicki
Sushil da Silva
Sundeep Singatwaria
Inderjeet Singh
Suresh Singh
Mukesh Singhal
Nishith Sinha
Rupam Sinha
H.R. Sirisena
Kumar N. Sivarajan
Vijay Sivaraman
Donald Smith
Kazem Sohraby
Cormac J. Sreenan
A. Srinivasan
Santhanam Srinivasan
K. Sriram
Mani Srivastava
Jerrold F. Stach
Mark Stahl
Pat Stakem
David Starobinski
James Stepanek
Donpaul C. Stephens
Dimitrios Stiliadis
Burkhard Stiller
Kris Struyve
Suresh Subramaniam
Dan Keun Sung
Hiroshi Suzuki
V. Swaminathan
Nina Taft-Plotkin
Masahiro Taka
G. Takahara
Yukio Takahashi
Yoshitaka Takahashi
Rajesh R. Talpade
Qiang Ming Tan
Ahmed N. Tantawy
Leandros Tassiulas
Daisuke Teratani
David Thaler
Chen-Khong Tham
Hideki Tode
Tom Tofigh
C-K Toh
Ozan K. Tonguz
Don Towsley
Ljiljana Trajkovic
John Trotter
Sophia Tsakiridou
Jason L. Tsay
David Tse
Kent H. Tseng
Thierry Turletti
Jonathan S. Turner
Hung-ying Tyan
Sathyadev V. Uppala
Huseyin Uzunalioglu
R. Vaidyanathan
Pravin Varaiya
Emmanouel Varvarigos
Gustavo de Veciana
Malathi Veeraraghavan
Paul A. Veitch
Nalini Venkatasubramanian
R. Venkateswaran
Dinesh Verma
Rajiv Vijayan
Yannis Viniotis
M. Vishnu
Krzysztof Wajda

Yasushi Wakahara
Bin Wang
Kuang-Yeh Wang
Kuochen Wang
Qiong Wang
Weiping Wang
Weyl K. Wang
Y.T. Wang
K. Watanabe
Kojiro Watanabe
Bernard M. Waxman
Gosse Wedzinga
Liming Wei
Martin Weiss
Ward Whitt
Jeffrey E. Wieselthier
Kenneth A. Williams
Sabine Wittevrongel
Ralph Wittmann
Joel Wolf
Kwok-Yee Michael Wong
P.C. Wong
Dallas E. Wrege
Fuxiang Wu
Gang Wu
Guo-Liang Wu
Tsong-Ho Wu
Geoffrey Xie
Shimpei Yagyu
Shalini Yajnik
S. Yalamânchili
Atsushi Yamada
Miki Yamamoto
Hideaki Yamanaka
O. Yang
Tao Yang
Keiichi Yasumoto
David Yates
Jennifer Yates
David K. Yau
Yi Ye
Uri Yechiali
Wei Yen
Liu Hui Yeo
Kwan L. Yeung
Makoto Yokoo
Kiroyuki Yokoyama
Jay Yoo
Masatoshi Yoshikawa
Chaoyu Yue
Jens Zander
Ali Zaringhalam
Pamela Zave
Ofer Zeitouni
Hui Zhang
Yongbing Zhang
Yaling Zhou
Moshe Zukerman

Volume 3

Technical Sessions 8A – 11D

Multicast ATM Switches Using Buffered MIN Structure : A Performance Study *

Yijun Xiong
Dept. of Electrical & Computer Eng.
Louisiana State University
Baton Rouge, LA 70803

Lorne Mason
INRS-Telecommunications
16 Place du Commerce
Verdun, Quebec, Canada H3E 1H6

Abstract

A (large) multicast ATM switch with external structure of output queueing and internal structure of buffered MINs (multistage interconnection networks) is considered, where the buffered MIN (also called switching network) is composed of switching elements with shared buffer output queueing. Cell replication while routing scheme is used in the switch to implement multicast function. In this paper, we study the performance of the switch with multicast traffic, mainly via computer simulations. The multicast traffic can be random and bursty. From our study we found that for multicast traffic with truncated geometric distribution of cell fanouts it has only a slightly worse impact on the performance of switching elements in isolation or in the last stage of the switching network. The multicast traffic has no worse effect on the switch output buffer behavior and cell delay in the switching network. Moreover, traffic splitting can substantially improve the switching network performance for highly bursty traffic. Some analytical approximations are given which could be useful in the dimensioning of switching networks.

1 Introduction

Cell replication and copy routing are additional issues in the design of multicast ATM switches. Several cell replication schemes have been proposed in the literature, which can be roughly classified into three categories : (1) *cell replication before routing* [1, 2, 3], (2) *cell replication while routing* [4, 5] and (3) *cell recycling* [6, 7]. It is likely that switches with various architectures will choose different schemes or a combination to implement multicast function [13].

Previous study reveals that for small (point-to-point) ATM switches (e.g., 8x8, 16x16 or even 32x32), shared buffer output queueing gives the best delay/throughput performance [8]. Many manufactures have adopted this queueing strategy in their switch design [9, 10]. By adding a multicast tree table, the switch with shared buffer output queueing can be readily extended to a multicast ATM switch [11, 12], which still yields the best delay/throughput performance. In such a multicast switch, cell replication is performed via table lookup (*cell replication while routing* scheme). To build a large ATM switch from those small switches, probably the most cost-effective way is to use the multistage interconnection network (MIN) structure. It is clear that the second cell replication scheme is very suitable for this buffered MIN structure in providing multicast function [4]. Under this scheme, cell replication is easily and efficiently performed in each stage of MIN via table lookup, as one will see in Section 2.

The purpose of this paper is to study the performance of the multicast switch using buffered MIN structure and cell replication while routing scheme. Due to the complexity of multicast traffic and shared buffer queueing, we mainly resort to computer simulation in our study. Based on simulation results, we develop some simple analytical approximations which are useful in the dimensioning of switching networks. Performance analysis of multistage switches has been conducted before, for instance in [14, 15, 16], however, only for unicast traffic.

The rest of the paper is organized as follows. In Section 2, we will describe the multicast ATM switch under study in more detail and illustrate how multicast cells are stored and replicated inside the switch. The multicast traffic model is given in Section 3. Performance of the multicast switch is thoroughly studied in Section 4.

2 The multicast ATM switch

To be clear, let us start with an ATM switch with shared buffer output queueing. In such a switch, multicast cells can be easily replicated via table lookup as depicted in Fig. 1 where an incoming multicast cell is copied to switch outlets 0,1 and 3. Note that we only need to store the incoming multicast cell instead of all its copies in the shared buffer memory (SBM) and send the address of the multicast cell to address queues connected to the switch outlets that receive copies. So the memory space requirement of a switch can be reduced to its minimum. The last copy leaving the switch will erase the multicast cell and release the occupied buffer space. For unicast cells, we still use the self-routing principle.

In Fig. 1, the multicast tree table contains bit mapping of multicast trees where each entry has 4 bits in this example. The multicast tree reference number

*This work was supported under contract by General DataComm.

0-8186-7780-5/97 $10.00 © 1997 IEEE

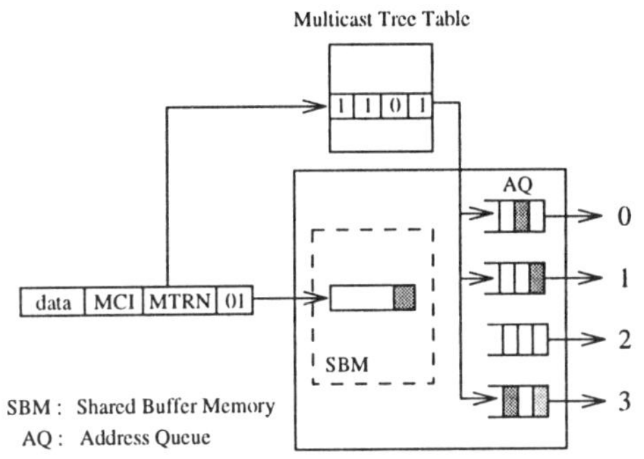

Figure 1: Cell replication in a 4x4 switch.

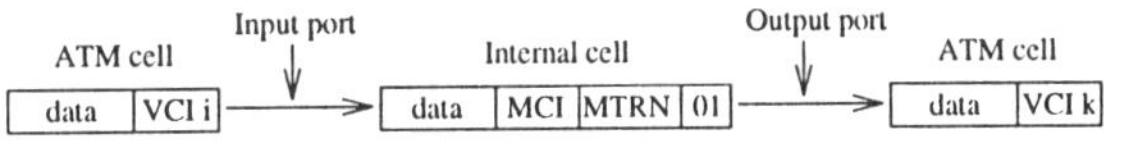

Figure 2: Cell header translation at input and output ports of the switch.

(MTRN) in the cell header is used to distinguish different multicast trees, and the multicast connection identifier (MCI) is used to identify different multicast connections in the switch which must be unique at any instant. In general, the MTRN can be defined by the subset of switch outlets which will receive copies. It is clear that a multicast connection can be uniquely identified by the MTRN and MCI. One important feature of MTRN is that different multicast connections which have the same subset of switch outlets can share one multicast tree. Hence, the number of entries in the multicast tree table is drastically reduced.

Multicast cell label translations at input and output ports of the switch are shown in Fig. 2. The MTRN is used by the switch to generate copies and route them to their destinations. The MCI is used at switch outputs to convert copies back to ATM cells via table lookup. It is worth mentioning that the above cell replication approach is also suitable for switches with (separate buffer) output queueing [17].

To build a large multicast ATM switch, we use the MIN structure and one will see that the above cell replication procedure is still applicable. As an example, Fig. 3 shows a 3-stage switching network (SN) which is composed of 4x4 switches called switching elements (SEs) hereafter. This SN is a nonblocking network. To avoid handling call setup stage by stage inside the SN, we use the multipath self-routing principle [11]. In this concept, the first stage of the SN is called the distribution network (DN) which distributes/randomizes the input traffic evenly among its outlets. The second and third stage are the routing network (RN) which replicate multicast cells and route the copies to their destinations. The operation of SEs in the RN is exactly the same as in Fig. 1, except that

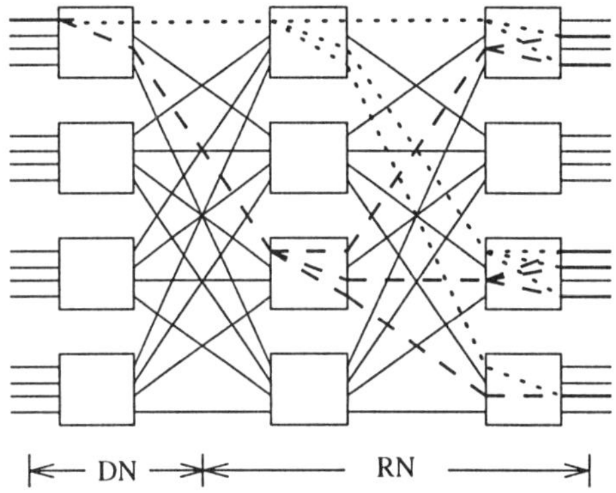

Figure 3: A 3-stage switching network composed of 4x4 switching elements.

the multicast tree table in each SE now contains tree branch information. Because of the DN, cells belonging to the same connection may take different paths through the network, as illustrated in Fig. 3.

In general, for an NxN SN composed of SxS SEs, there are $2K-1$ stages ($K = log_S N$) where the first $K-1$ stages belong to the DN and the last K stages belong to the RN. The multicast tree branch table in a SE of the RN needs S bits for each entry. To support M multicast trees, we need MS bits in the tree branch table. The cell header for supporting multicast is SK bits. Note that as multicast connections having the same subset of outlets of the SN in fact share one multicast tree, the number of multicast connections being supported simultaneously by the SN is not limited by the number of multicast trees M. Due to the regular interconnection network architecture (see Fig. 3), the maintenance of a multicast tree (e.g., to add or delete one connection) can be easily done in a parallel/distributed fashion. Especially, when a multicast tree changes to an existing one, nothing need to be done except to update the MTRN at the input port of the switch.

There are at least two possible operation modes for SEs in the DN: (1) shifting-operation mode and (2) cyclic-operation mode [23]. As the effects of these two modes on the performance of RN are almost identical, we consider the shifting-operation mode, where SEs in the DN operate independently and arriving cells to a SE are evenly distributed among its outlets in a shifting manner. Specifically, suppose at the beginning of slot n, the shifting pointer of a tagged SE is at outlet i ($0 \le i \le S-1$), and there are j cell arrivals, $1 \le j \le S$. The j cells will be sent out on SE outlets i, $((i+1) \bmod S)$, ..., $((i+j-1) \bmod S)$ and the shifting pointer will move to outlet $((i+j) \bmod S)$. The movement of the shifting pointer (sp) is calculated recursively from $sp_{n+1} = (sp_n + e_n) \bmod S$, where e_n denotes the number of cell arrivals to the SE in slot n.

The block diagram of a whole multicast ATM switch is given in Fig. 4, where the internal structure in general can have G (≥ 1) parallel SNs. As cells from

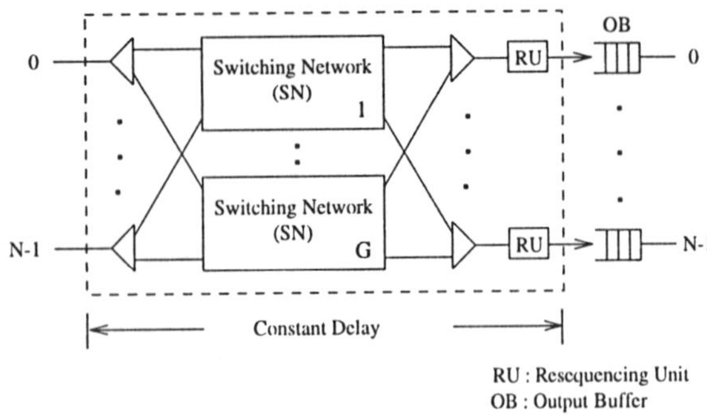

Figure 4: The internal structure of an ATM switch.

a virtual circuit will take different paths within a SN (see Fig. 3) as well as among different SNs, they may experience different delays in the SNs and arrive at the switch outlet out of sequence. Resequencing units (RUs) are required at switch outlets to guarantee the cell sequence. The RU is usually designed to compensate variable cell delays such that cells enter the switch at same time will leave the RU simultaneously. In other words, cell delays inside the switch are constant instead of variable (caused by internal buffers). Consequently, the whole switch shown in Fig. 4 could be regarded as a single large switch with (separate buffer) output queueing.

3 Multicast traffic model

Here we consider two types of multicast input traffic: random and bursty traffic. For random input traffic, cell arrivals on each inlet of the switch are independent and identifically distributed (i.i.d.) from slot to slot. In a given slot, there is a cell arrival on a switch inlet with probability σ and no cell arrivals with probability $1-\sigma$, where σ is the average traffic load of the switch inlet. Using the term *fanout* to denote the number of copies of a multicast cell to be generated by the switch, we assume that fanouts of arriving cells to the switch are also i.i.d. Here we take a truncated geometric distribution for the cell fanout, i.e., an arriving cell having fanout i with probability

$$\Pr[cell\ fanout = i] = \left(\frac{1-\gamma}{1-\gamma^N}\right)\gamma^{i-1}, \qquad 1 \le i \le N. \tag{1}$$

Different destinations of the i copies are *uniformly* distributed among N outlets of the switch. From the above expression, the mean cell fanout F equals

$$F = \frac{1}{1-\gamma} - \frac{N\gamma^N}{1-\gamma^N}. \tag{2}$$

We also assume that cell arrivals on different inlets of the switch are i.i.d. Due to the uniform assumption for copy destinations, it is clear that the average traffic load ρ on each outlet of the switch is given by

$$\rho = \sigma F. \tag{3}$$

Note that unicast traffic is a special case of multicast traffic with mean cell fanout $F = 1$.

For bursty input traffic, cell arrivals on each inlet of the switch are in bursts. The burst lengths are i.i.d. and assumed to have a geometric distribution with mean L,

$$\Pr[burst\ length = i\ cells] = (1-\alpha)\alpha^{i-1}, \qquad i \ge 1, \tag{4}$$

where $\alpha = 1 - \frac{1}{L}$. After a burst or an idle slot, a new burst may arrive with probability β and no new burst arrivals with probability $(1-\beta)$, i.e.,

$$\Pr[idle\ period = i\ slots] = \beta(1-\beta)^i, \qquad i \ge 0.$$

The average idle period $I = \frac{1-\beta}{\beta}$ slots. From the mean burst length L and the average idle period I, the average traffic load σ of a switch inlet is obtained as

$$\sigma = L/(L+I). \tag{5}$$

Similar to the random input traffic, the fanouts of bursts are i.i.d. and have a truncated geometric distribution given in (1). The destinations of copies of a burst are uniformlly distributed among different outlets of the switch. Traffic on different inlets of the switch are also i.i.d. It is clear that the average traffic load ρ on each switch outlet satisfies (3).

The random and bursty traffic described above are two extreme cases of input traffic. It is easy to see that in fact the random traffic is also a special case of the bursty traffic when the average burst length $L = 1$. The random traffic model could be used to describe the multiplexed traffic sources which have very low bit rates (e.g. 64 Kbits/s) compared to the link rate (e.g. 150 Mbits/s or 600 Mbits/s) of the switch, and it is often used in the performance evaluation of multicast ATM switchs of various kinds [12, 19, 20]. The bursty traffic, on the other hand, could be used to model high speed data traffic. The above bursty traffic model was used in [21] to analyze the switch performance with unicast traffic.

4 Performance

4.1 Switch output buffer behavior

Consider the multicast ATM switch shown in Fig. 4 where all the inlets and outlets are slotted in time. One slot is the time interval to carry exactly one cell. As cell delays inside the switch are constant, we could neglect the internal switching fabric when analyzing the switch output buffer behavior. In other words, each output buffer of the switch can be modeled as a discrete-time single-server queue where cell arrivals to the queue are determined directly from the cell arrivals to the switch. Note that the performance of address queues in Fig. 1. is equivalent to the switch output buffer behavior.

For random input traffic with mean cell fanout F, it is not difficult to verify based on the uniform assumption for copy addressing that for each arriving cell to the switch, an (tagged) output buffer will receive a copy with probability $\frac{F}{N}$ and no copies with

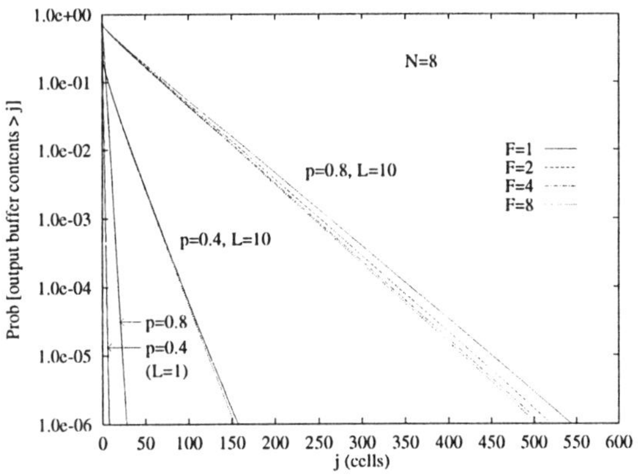

Figure 5: Buffer-contents distributions of an NxN switch with random ($L = 1$) and bursty ($L = 10$) input traffic and mean cell fanout $F = 1, 2, 4$ and 8.

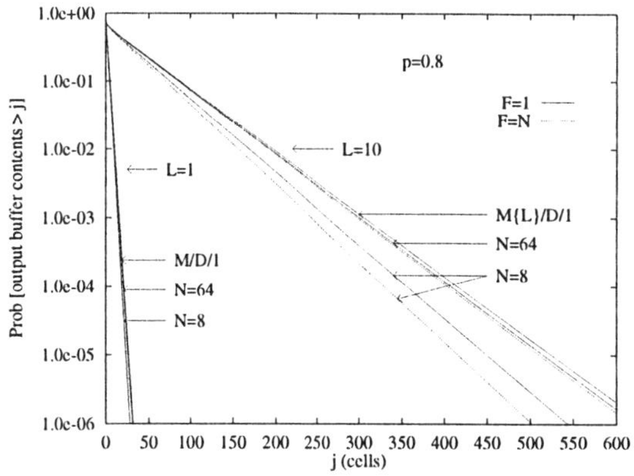

Figure 6: Impact of switch size N on the buffer-contents distributions.

probability $1 - \frac{F}{N}$. Since there is a cell arrival on a switch inlet per slot with probability σ, it is obvious that each switch inlet will send a cell (or its copy) to the tagged output buffer per slot with probability $\sigma\frac{F}{N} = \frac{\rho}{N}$ and no cell is sent with probability $1 - \frac{\rho}{N}$. So the switch output buffer can be analyzed using the $Geo(N)/D/1$ queueing model in which N independent Bernoulli traffic sources with parameter $\frac{\rho}{N}$ are multiplexed. The solution of $Geo(N)/D/1$ can be found in the literature and we will not repeat it here. From the above discussion, we observe an important phenomenon: for random input traffic the switch output buffer behavior only depends on the traffic load ρ and is *independent* of cell fanout distributions.

In the bursty input traffic case, similarly as above, each arriving burst to the switch will be copied to the tagged output buffer with probability $\frac{F}{N}$ and not with probability $1 - \frac{F}{N}$. As cells in a burst have the same destination, cell arrivals to the tagged output buffer are highly correlated. In this case, the output buffer behavior can be described by a 3-dimensional Markov chain which is solved by using the solution technique described in [22]. We found that given the traffic load ρ and average burst length L, the switch output buffer behavior only depends on the mean cell fanout F and is irrelevant to the distributions of cell fanout.

Some numerical examples are given in Figs. 5 and 6. As expected, the buffer-contents distributions are identical for random input traffic with same traffic load ρ but different mean cell fanout F. We observe from Fig. 5 that the switch output buffer behavior under multicast bursty traffic ($1 < F \leq N$) is better than that under unicast bursty traffic ($F = 1$). However, the buffer-contents distributions are not very sensitive to the mean cell fanout F, and their differences are getting even smaller when the switch size N increases (see Fig. 6). It is illustrated in Fig. 6 that when $N \to \infty$, the distributions of buffer contents converge to the buffer-contents distribution of $M^{\{L\}}/D/1$ queueing model which is independent of mean cell fanout F. The notation $M^{\{L\}}/D/1$ represents a single-server queue with Poisson train arrivals where the average train length is equal to L. A recursive algorithm is decribed in [23] to calculate the buffer-contents distribution of the $M^{\{L\}}/D/1$ model. From Figs. 5 and 6, we also see that bursty traffic has worse effect on the switch performance.

In [23], we have explained why multicast bursty traffic leads to better switch output buffer behavior than unicast bursty traffic. From Figs. 5 and 6, one may conclude that for switches with output queueing, multicast traffic has no worse effect on the switch output buffer behavior. Further, using the general relationship between distributions of buffer contents and cell delay [24], it is readily seen that the multicast traffic has also no worse impact on cell delay.

4.2 Switches with shared buffer

An SxS multicast ATM switch with shared buffer output queueing, as shown in Fig. 1, is considered. The number of cells in the SBM is called *shared buffer contents*. As only the original multicast cells are stored in the SBM, to obtain analytically the distribution of shared buffer contents is very difficult. So in the following we use simulation in our study.

At first glance, it appears to us that the effect of multicast traffic on the switch performance is not intuitive. On one hand, multicast traffic is more bursty than unicast traffic, because each arriving cell may generate several copies. Cell arrivals in multicast traffic could be regarded as a kind of *bulk* arrivals with average size F. But on the other hand, only the original cells instead of their copies are allowed to store in the SBM, which will reduce significantly the total number of cells in the SBM. However, a multicast cell in the SBM may stay longer than an unicast cell because it must wait until its last copy has left the SBM. Putting all together, it is really difficult to tell what will be the impact of multicast traffic on the switch perfor-

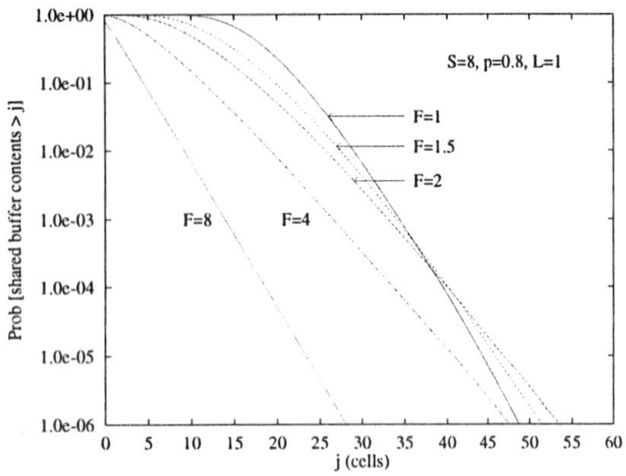

Figure 7: Distributions of shared buffer contents of an SxS switch with random input traffic of various mean cell fanouts.

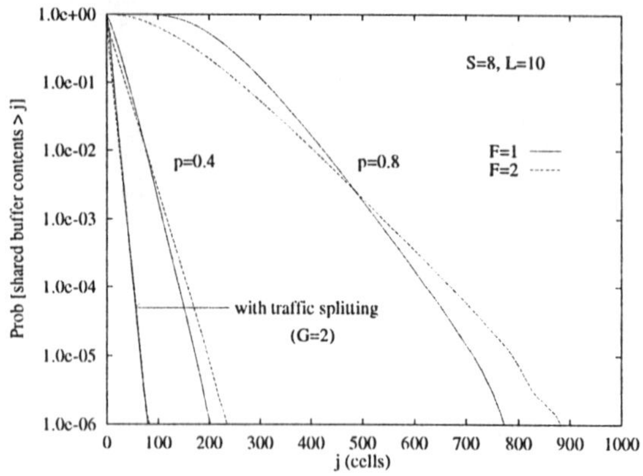

Figure 8: Distributions of shared buffer contents of SxS switches with bursty input traffic, without and with traffic splitting.

mance. Below we present and discuss some simulation results based on an 8x8 multicast switch. The simulation times are 10^9 slots for unicast traffic ($F = 1$) and $5x10^8$ slots for multicast traffic ($1 < F \leq S$). Note that in all numerical examples, we use the average traffic load ρ on each switch outlet to denote the traffic load of the switch.

Fig. 7 shows the distributions of shared buffer contents for random input traffic with load $\rho = 0.8$ and various mean cell fanouts. We see that for small mean cell fanout F (e.g., $F = 1.5$ and 2), in the low probability region (starting roughly from 10^{-4}), the shared buffer overflow probability is larger than that of unicast traffic ($F = 1$). A possible explanation is as follows. From the previous subsection, we know that the steady-state statistical characteristics of address queues in the switch of Fig. 1 are identical. But the correlation between these address queues increases from small to 100% when F increases from one (unicast traffic) to S (broadcast traffic), which is due to the *bulk* arrivals in the multicast traffic. Therefore it is clear that the sum X_m of lengths of S address queues in the multicast traffic case is often much larger than the sum X_u of lengths of S address queues in the unicast traffic case. The probability exists, though rather small, that even substracting all the duplicated addresses D_m from X_m which yields the shared buffer contents, we may still have $X_m - D_m > X_u$. As F gets large enough, the correlation between address queues increases and such probability becomes even smaller as shown in Fig. 7. In the extreme case of broadcast traffic, all S address queues are 100% correlated and the shared buffer behavior is exactly the same as the output buffer behavior ($Geo(S)/D/1$ model). Consequently, the shared buffer behavior in broadcast traffic case is always better than that in unicast traffic case. From the above, it also becomes clear that cell fanout distributions will have some impact on the switch performance.

Similar results are observed for different traffic load ρ and also for multicast bursty traffic, as shown in Fig. 10. It is clearly illustrated in Fig. 10 that from performance point of view, using two parallel switches and splitting input traffic among them is better than simply reducing the load of input traffic. This is because traffic splitting reduces not only the load of input traffic but also the burstiness of input traffic. Moreover, using traffic splitting, the shared buffer overflow probability is not very sensitive to the mean cell fanout.

4.3 The switching network

Next, we investigate the impact of multicast traffic on the SN in Fig. 4. As the function of DN is to distribute/randomize input traffic uniformally among its outlets, no buffers are really required in SEs of the DN. The SN performance is determined by the performance of the RN. It is assumed that all SEs of the SN are synchronized on a slot basis. The SBM of a SE in the RN is observed in each slot. For the input traffic described in Section 3, it is readily seen that the performance of SEs in a given stage of the RN are identical. So we only need to think of one SE in each stage of the RN. In our simulation, the run time is sufficiently long such that the distributions of shared buffer contents of SEs in the RN are stable at least above 10^{-3}.

4.3.1 Mean cell fanouts in the SN

Let F_k ($1 \leq k \leq K$) denote the average number of copies of a multicast cell to be generated by a SE in stage k of the RN. It is clear that the mean cell fanout $F = \prod_{k=1}^{K} F_k$. The load of multicast traffic increases stage by stage in the RN, which equals $\sigma \prod_{i=1}^{k} F_i$ in stage k where σ is the traffic load on each inlet of the RN. F_k can be obtained from

$$F_k = \begin{cases} \bar{o}_k/\bar{o}_{k+1}, & 1 \leq k \leq K-1, \\ \bar{c}_k, & k = K, \end{cases}$$

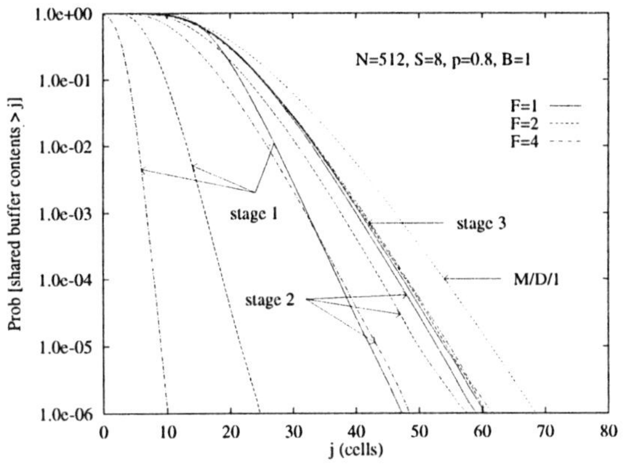

Figure 9: Distributions of shared buffer contents of SEs in a 3-stage RN under random input traffic.

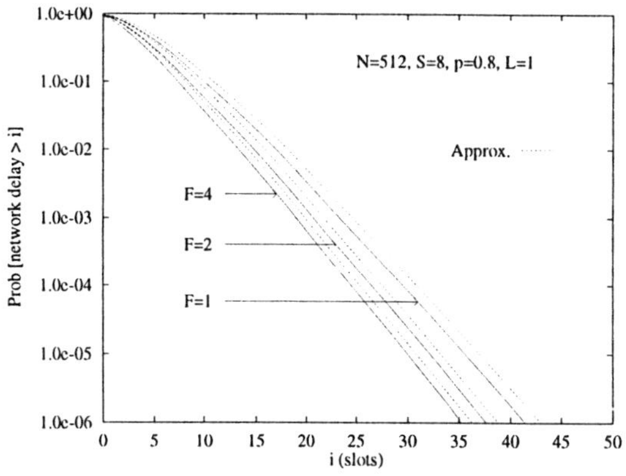

Figure 10: Cell delay distributions and approximation in a 3-stage RN under random input traffic.

where $\bar{c}_k$ is the expected value of c_k, the total number of copies of a multicast cell *before* stage k and to be generated in the remainder of the RN. Let $c_k(i)$ be the distribution of c_k. $c_1(i)$ is given by (1) and $c_{k+1}(i), 1 \leq k < K, 1 \leq i \leq S^{K-k}$, can be obtained as [23]

$$c_{k+1}(i) = \sum_{j=0}^{S^{K-k}(S-1)} \frac{\binom{S^{K-k}}{i}\binom{S^{K-k}(S-1)}{j}}{\binom{S^{K+1-k}}{i+j}} \frac{c_k(i+j)}{SUM},$$

$$SUM = \sum_{i=1}^{S^{K-k}} \sum_{j=0}^{S^{K-k}(S-1)} \frac{\binom{S^{K-k}}{i}\binom{S^{K-k}(S-1)}{j}}{\binom{S^{K+1-k}}{i+j}} c_k(i+j).$$

4.3.2 Random input traffic

Fig. 9 shows the distributions of shared buffer contents of SEs in a 3-stage RN with load $\rho = 0.8$ and mean cell fanout $F = 1, 2, 4$ and 8. We see that the performance of SEs in stages 1 and 2 under multicast traffic is better than that under unicast traffic. This is because the multicast traffic load in stages 1 and 2 ($=\sigma F_1$ and $\sigma F_1 F_2$, respectively) are less than the unicast traffic load ρ ($= \sigma F$). For instance, when $\rho = 0.8$ and $F = 4$ ($\sigma = 0.2$), the traffic load in the first two stages are equal to 0.583 and 0.768, respectively. Further, we observe that the tail distribution of shared buffer contents of SEs in stage 3 under multicast traffic is slightly larger than that under unicast traffic. In stage 3 of the RN, the traffic load equals ρ for both unicast and multicast traffic. But the average number of cells F_3 to be generated in this stage is usually small (for $F = 4$, $F_3 = 1.041$). From the previous subsection, we learn that for multicast traffic with small mean cell fanouts, it has a bit worse impact on the tail distribution of shared buffer contents (see Fig. 7), which seems also true for the SEs in the last stage of the RN, as illustrated in Fig. 9.

In general, for a given mean cell fanout F, as F_K decreases when K, the number of stages, increases, the SE performance in the last stage of the RN becomes less sensitive to F and will quickly converage to a limit, which can be well bounded by the S-fold convolution of the buffer-contents distribution of $M/D/1$ model (labeled "M/D/1" in Fig. 9).

Fig. 10 shows the distributions of cell delay in the RN. It tells us that unicast traffic leads to the worst cell delay distribution, which is understandable as the cell delays in the first two stages, especially in stage 1, of the RN are smaller under multicast traffic, due to the lower load in these stages. The approximations in Fig. 10 are obtained by doing convolutions on the delay distributions of $M/D/1$ model. The traffic load used in the $M/D/1$ model is $\sigma \prod_{i=1}^{k} F_i$ for stage k ($1 \leq k \leq 3$) of the RN. One can see from Fig. 10 that the $M/D/1$ model can compensate for correlation of cell delays in different stages and give a good upper bound for the distributions of cell network delay.

4.3.3 Bursty input traffic

Similar results are observed when the input traffic to the SN is bursty traffic ($L > 1$). As an example, we show in Fig. 11 the performance of SEs in a 2-stage RN for bursty traffic with average burst length $L = 10$ cells. Because of the DN, the performance of SEs in stage 1 is greatly improved and made less sensitive to the input traffic. Without the DN, the performance of SEs in stage 1 would be identical to the performance of an isolated SE shown in Fig. 8. However, as the DN transforms the correlation of cell arrivals from time into space (among different outlets of the DN), it will not improve the performance of SEs in stage 2 (last stage) of the RN, as illustrated in Fig. 11. Comparing Fig. 11 with Fig. 8 reveals that the performance of SEs in the last stage of the RN is worse than the performance of a SE in isolation. This is clear because in a given slot more bursts may be destined to the same SE in the last stage of the RN. The curve labeled "$M^{\{L\}}/D/1$" is drawn from the S-fold convolution of

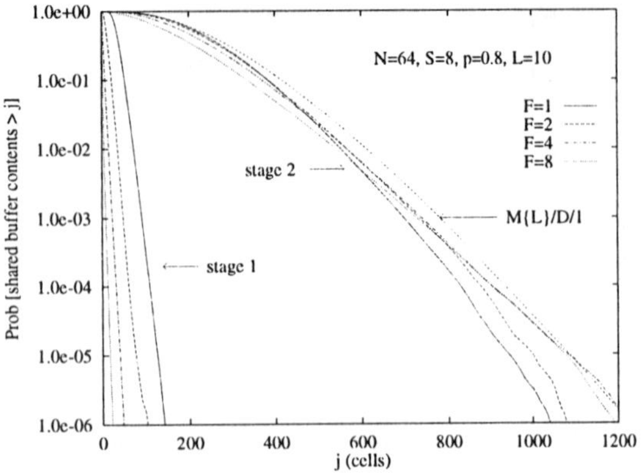

Figure 11: Distributions of shared buffer contents of SEs in a 2-stage RN under bursty input traffic.

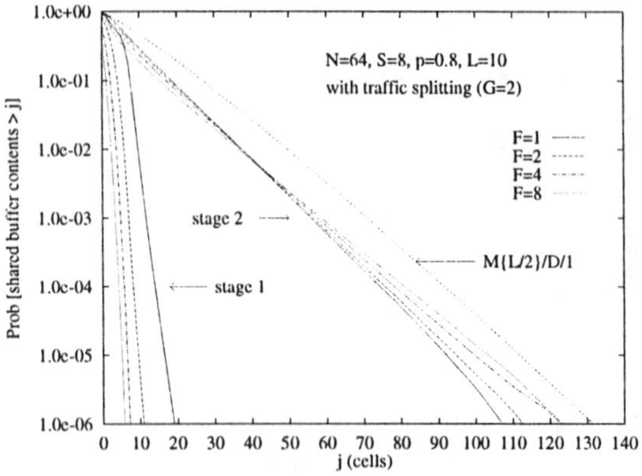

Figure 12: Impact of traffic splitting on SE performance of the 2-stage RN.

the buffer-contents distribution of $M^{\{L\}}/D/1$ model, which gives a good approximation though it is difficult to see whether it is an upper bound or not as the simulation results are not stable in the low probability region.

To reduce the worse impact of bursty traffic on the SE performance, traffic splitting is an effective approach as illustrated in Fig. 8. In the remainder, we consider the switch shown in Fig. 4 with two parallel SNs (i.e. $G = 2$). As arriving cell streams to the switch are split evenly among SNs, the performance of the two SNs are in fact identical. With traffic splitting, the load of each SN is now equal to $\frac{\rho}{2}$ and the average number of cells in a burst is reduced to $\frac{L}{2}$ cells. Further, there is a gap of one slot between two consecutive cells in a burst. Fig. 12 depicts the SE performance of a 2-stage RN with traffic splitting. Compared to Fig. 11, it shows that with traffic splitting, the SE performance in the RN, especially in the last stage of the RN, can be substantially improved. Also, the $M^{\{L/2\}}/D/1$ model leads to a reasonable good approximation (possibly upper bound) for the performance of SEs in the last stage of the RN (see Figs. 12 and 13).

Fig, 13 shows the performance of SEs in a 3-stage RN when using traffic splitting. Similar to Fig. 9, we also find that for bursty input traffic, the SE performance in the last stage of the RN is not sensitive to the mean cell fanout F. As the total cell network delay in the RN is mainly determined by the cell delay in the last stage of the RN, the cell network delay distributions are also not sensitive to the mean cell fanout F, as depicted in Fig. 14. The approximation shown in Fig. 14 is obtained by modeling cell delays in the first two stages of the RN as $M/D/1$'s and cell delays in the last stage as $M^{\{L/2\}}/D/1$. The traffic load in each stage of the RN is 0.4 (unicast traffic). It is obvious that the SN performance can be further improved if we add one more SN (i.e. $G = 3$).

To summarize, in this section we have shown that

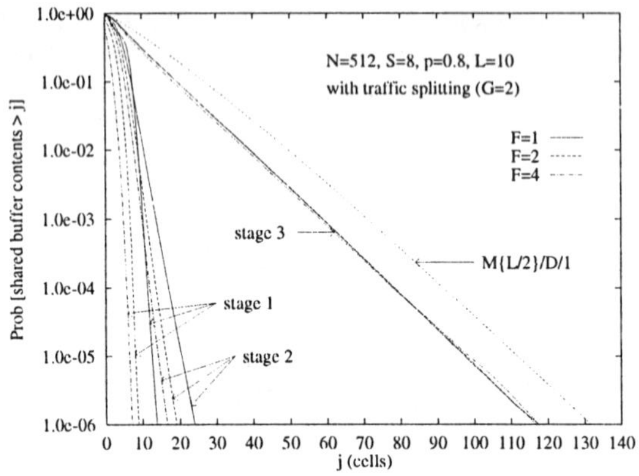

Figure 13: Performance of SEs in a 3-stage RN under bursty input traffic, with traffic splitting.

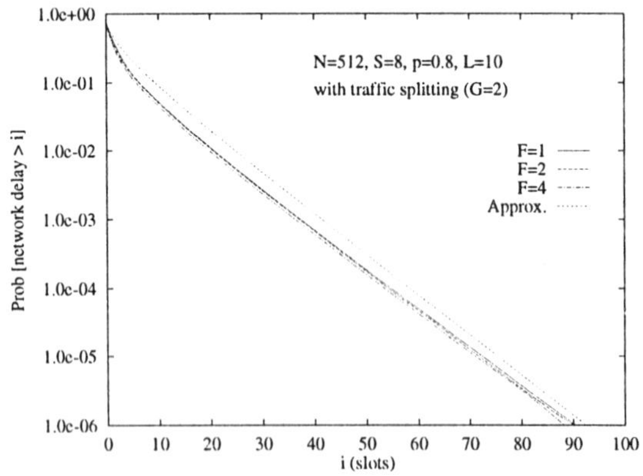

Figure 14: Cell network delay distributions and their approximation in the 3-stage RN.

multicast traffic has slightly worse impact on the tail distribution of shared buffer contents of SEs in the last stage of the RN, but no worse effect on the cell network delay distribution. Using traffic splitting can significantly improve the performance of SNs with highly bursty input traffic.

5 Further study

In the paper, we have only considered the truncated geometric distribution for the cell fanout. For the SE with shared buffer output queueing and the SN which is composed of SEs, their performance may also depends on the distributions of cell fanout which remains for further study.

References

[1] J. Turner, "Design of a broadcast packet switching network", *IEEE Trans. Commun.*, vol. 36, 1988, pp. 734-743.

[2] T. Lee, "Nonblocking copy networks for multicast packet switching", *IEEE J. Select. Areas Commun.*, vol. 6, 1988, pp. 1455-1467.

[3] S. Shimamoto, W. Zhong, Y. Onozato and J. Kaniyil, "Recursive copy networks for large multicast ATM switches", *IEICE Trans. Commun.*, vol. E75-B, 1992, pp. 1208-1219.

[4] K. Schrodi, B. Pfeiffer, J. Delmas and M. De Somer, "Multicast handling in a self-routing switch architecture", Proc. of *ISS'92*, pp. 156-160.

[5] J. Chao and B. Choe, "A large-scale multicast output buffered ATM switch", Proc. of *GLOBECOM'93*, pp. 34-41.

[6] R. Cusani and F. Sestini, "A recursive multistage structure for multicast ATM switching", Proc. of *INFOCOM'91*, pp. 1289-1295.

[7] J. Turner, "An optimal nonblocking multicast virtual circuit switch", Proc. of *INFOCOM'94*, pp. 298-305.

[8] H. Kuwahara, N. Endo, M. Ogino, T. Kozaki, Y. Sakurai and S. Gohara, "A shared buffer memory switch for an ATM exchange", Proc. of *ICC'89*, pp. 118-122.

[9] Special issue on large-scale ATM switching systems for B-ISDN, *IEEE J. Select. Areas Commun.*, vol. 9, no. 8, Oct. 1991.

[10] K. Eng, M. Pashan, R. Spanke, M. Karol and G. Martin, "A high-performance prototype 2.5Gb/s ATM switch for broadband applications", Proc. of *GLOBECOM'92*, pp. 111-117.

[11] M.A. Henrion, G.J. Eilenberger, G.H. Petit and P.H. Parmentier, "A multipath self-routing switch", *IEEE Communications Magazine*, vol. 31, no. 4, April 1993, pp. 46-52.

[12] H. Saito, H.Yamanaka. H. Yamada, M. Tuzuki, H. Kondoh, Y. Matsuda and K. Oshima, "Multicast function and its LSI implementation in a shared multibuffer ATM switch", Proc. of *INFOCOM'94*, pp. 315-322.

[13] P. Newman, "ATM technology for corporate networks", *IEEE Communication Magazine* vol. 30, no. 4, April 1992, pp. 90-101.

[14] Y. Xiong, G. Petit and H. Bruneel, "Performance study of an ATM self-routing multistage switch with bursty traffic : simulation and analytic approximation", *European Trans. Telecom. (ETT)*, vol. 4, 1993, pp. 443-453.

[15] S. Montagna, R. Paglino and J. Meyer, "Delay performance of a multistage ATM switching network", Proc. of *ITC'14*, pp. 623-634.

[16] M. De Marco and A. Pattavina, "Performance analysis of ATM multistage networks with shared queueing under correlated traffic", Proc. of *ITC'14*, pp. 601-610.

[17] K. Kou, A. Arutaki and S. Iwasaki, "The architecture and implementation of ATM switch for broadband ISDN", Proc. of *GLOBECOM'93*, pp. 8-13.

[18] K. Eng, M. Karol and Y. Yeh, "A growable packet (ATM) switch architecture: design principles and applications", *IEEE Trans. Commun.*, vol. 40, 1992, pp. 423-430.

[19] W. Zhong, Y. Onozato and J. Kaniyil, "A copy network with shared buffers for large-scale multicast ATM switching", *IEEE/ACM Trans. Networking*, vol. 1, 1993, pp. 157-165.

[20] B. Choe and J. Chao, "Performance analysis of a large-scale multicast output buffered ATM switch", Proc. of *INFOCOM'94*, pp. 1472-1479.

[21] M. Karol and K. Eng, "Performance of hierarchical multiplexing in ATM switch design", Proc. of *ICC'92*, pp. 269-275.

[22] B. Steyaert and Y. Xiong, "Analysis of a discrete-time queue with general three state Markovian traffic sources", *Performance Evaluation*, vol.24, 1996, pp. 277-294.

[23] Y. Xiong and L. Mason, "Multicast ATM switches using buffered MIN structure : a performance study", INRS *Internal Report*, 1995.

[24] Y. Xiong, H. Bruneel and B. Steyaert, "Deriving delay characteristics from queue length statistics in discrete-time queues with multiple servers", *Performance Evaluation*, vol.24, 1996, pp. 189-204.

Design and Performance Analysis of a Growable Multicast ATM Switch

Kuochen Wang and Ming-Howe Cheng

Department of Computer and Information Science
National Chiao Tung University
Hsinchu, Taiwan 30050, ROC
Email: kwang@cis.nctu.edu.tw

Abstract

In this paper, we design and analyze a growable multicast ATM switch. It can grow to a large size since both cell routing and contention resolution are designed to distribute over switch elements, and the switch structure is modular. The output ports are partitioned into groups to permit sharing of routing paths. The concept of group routing helps reduce an order of magnitude of switch elements. A two-stage switch architecture is described to illustrate our design principle. The switch can be easily expanded to a larger size by using more stages. The performance analysis of the switch in terms of cell loss rate, cell delay, mean queue length, mean waiting time, and throughput is conducted using the M/Geom/1 model. Experimental results show that the proposed ATM switch not only meets the ATM performance requirements either for unicasting or multicasting but also uses fewer switch elements and has less delay than other comparable switches.

1 Introduction

The asynchronous transfer mode [1], based on the fast packet switching [2][3], has been standardized and is likely to become the switching and multiplexing technique for B-ISDN. An ATM switch has to meet the following requirements: high throughput, low delay, and small cell loss rate [4][5][6]. Besides these, the capability of modular growth of an ATM switch is equally important. Several proposed multicast ATM switches have a size limitation because of a centralized processing unit for replication and routing [7], a shared medium for transmission [8][9], or an irregular interconnection network for switching [2][3]. Straightforward interconnection of small switch elements creates several stages of queuing delay and may result in performance degradation if congestion occurs at intermediate stages [10].

For the capability of modular growth, there are two methods to fulfill [11]: (1) using the Knockout principle: generalization from a single output to group outputs [12] and (2) using the interconnection fabric: concept of multistage interconnection networks [13]. For a unicast switch [14], self-routing and output port contention resolution should be performed in a distributed way so that the centralized processing will not become a bottleneck to construct a large switch. Multicast routing can be performed by broadcasting incoming cells to all output ports and filtering at each output port [15], or replicating into several copies and each sent to the corresponding output port [16]. Several multicast switches have been proposed [7][17]-[20]. The switches in [17][18] have high complexity for translation tables. The copy network in the Gauss multicast switch [20] employs an adder for overflow control. It causes large delay time since cells from an upper input port must pass through the cell processing units of all other inputs that are below to it. The multicast switch in [21] would not have high throughput because of input-queuing. The centralized multicast switch in [7] replicates cells over a crossbar network. It results in a limited switch size.

This paper presents a growable multicast ATM switch. Our switch is based on the generalized Knockout principle. By including input controllers between stages, we design the proposed switch with multicast capability. Performance analysis in terms of cell loss rate, delay, mean queue length, mean waiting time, and throughput is conducted and experimental results are shown.

2 Structure and operation of the proposed ATM switch

2.1 Overall architecture

A two-stage architecture of our proposed growable multicast ATM switch is shown in Fig. 1 for illustration [22]. For expansion, it can be easily extended to more than two stages. It consists of three parts: input port controllers (IPC_1, IPC_2), grouping networks (GN_1, GN_2), and output port controllers (OPC). Each IPC (IPC_1 or IPC_2) accepts arrival cells, uses the arrival routing information (VCI) to look up the routing table, and attaches new routing information to the front of the cell to route it in the grouping network. A GN (GN_1 or GN_2) sends multicast cells to

0-8186-7780-5/97 $10.00 © 1997 IEEE

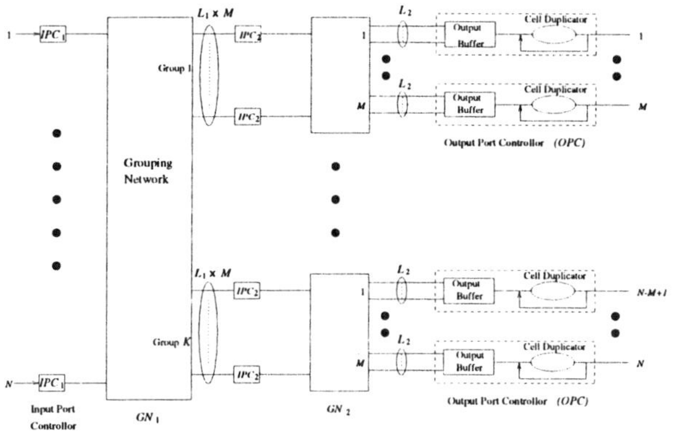

Figure 1: Overall architecture of the growable multicast ATM switch.

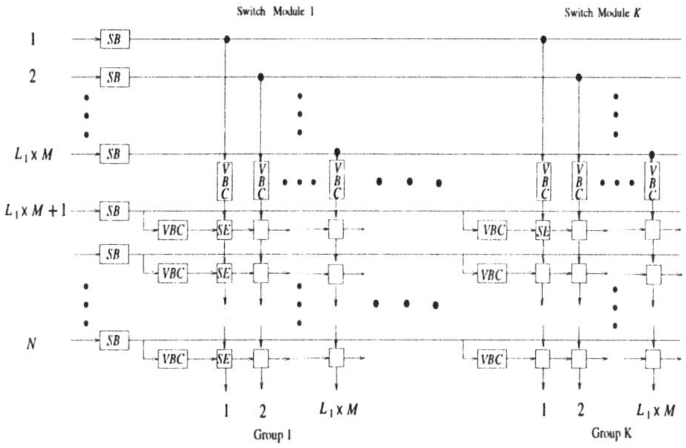

Figure 2: Grouping network.

broadcast buses, and the cell will be sent to all output groups. The output groups of the GN will decide whether to accept these cells or not by checking the multicast patterns. An output port controller stores arrival cells in the output buffers, replicates multiple copies with a cell duplicator, looks up the multicasting table to attach new VCI to the front of outgoing cells, and finally sends the cells to output ports.

As shown in Fig. 1, a set of M output ports of GN_1 forms a group at the first stage [22]. Each output port is dispatched L_1 links. So, there are a total of $L_1 \times M$ routing links in each output group. If there are more than $L_1 \times M$ cells arriving at the same group in a given time slot, the additional cells will be discarded. There are K output groups ($K=N/M$) in total. Up to L_2 cells may be time division multiplexing and are stored in the output buffer, and then are read out sequentially. We can engineer L_1 or L_2 (called a group expansion ratio) to meet the required cell loss rate.

2.2 Grouping network

Fig. 2 shows a modular structure of a grouping network at the first stage. The grouping network consists of N *skew buffers* (SB) and K ($K=N/M$) *switch modules*. A switch module at the first stage consists

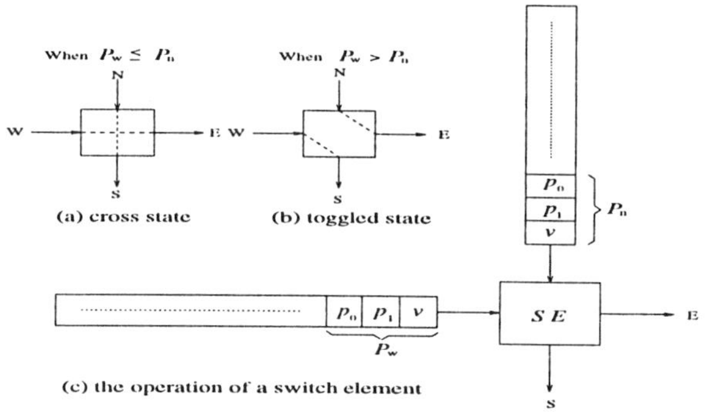

Figure 3: The two states and the operation of a switch element.

of N *valid bit controllers* (VBC) and a *switch array*. A switch array consists of $(L_1 \times M) \times (N - L_1 \times M)$ switch elements. Since the structure and operation of a grouping network are applicable to both stage 1 and stage 2, we will only discuss the grouping network at stage 1. As shown in Fig. 2, each switch module accepts at most N cells from N broadcast buses and sends out at most $L_1 \times M$ cells through the $L_1 \times M$ links. These routing links are shared by these cells that will be sent to the same output group. The routing information attached to an arrival cell may be a multicast pattern. The multicast pattern is a bit map for all output groups in the grouping network. Each bit represents whether the cell will be sent to this corresponding output group or not. If more than one bit of the multicast pattern are set to 1, the cell will be sent to more than one corresponding output groups. A *valid bit controller* (VBC) monitors whether there is an arrival cell in a time slot. We use a valid bit (v) to check whether a cell is valid or not and two priority bits (p_0p_1) for contention resolution in an output group. If there is no arrival cell, the VBC will send an empty cell, with the lowest priority ($p_0p_1 = 11$) and the valid bit value of 1 ($v = 1$), to the switch array. If there is an arrival cell, but the arrival cell is not destined for this output group, the VBC will also set the valid bit of the cell to 1 as an invalid cell and send it to the switch array. The first ($L_1 \times M$)-th VBCs will send cells to the north side of the switch array by vertical links. The other VBCs will send cells to the west side of the switch array by horizontal links.

A switch element has two states, *cross state* and *toggled state*, as shown in Fig. 3(a) and Fig. 3(b), respectively [22]. The switch element accepts two cells coming from the west and the north, respectively, as shown in Fig. 3(c) [22]. The state of the switch element depends on the comparisons result between priority levels P_w and P_n only. A priority level is used for contention resolution. The smaller value of the priority level is, the higher priority of the cell is. Initially, the switch element is set to *cross state*. When the west's priority level (P_w) is lower than or equal to the north's (P_n), the switch element is at *cross state*, as shown in Fig. 3(a). When the west's priority level

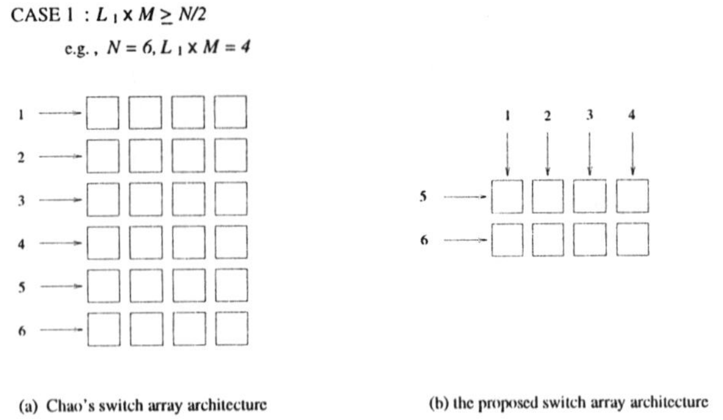

Figure 4: On the condition of $L_1 \times M \geq N/2$ at the first stage.

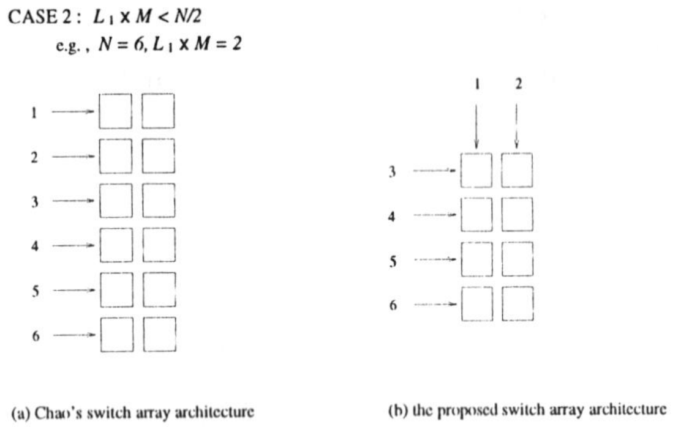

Figure 5: On the condition of $L_1 \times M < N/2$ at the first stage.

(P_w) is higher than the north's (P_n), the switch is at *toggled state*, as shown in Fig. 3(b). Each switch element causes 1 bit delay when a cell passes through it. To adjust cell timing, a cell of the ith input port is first skewed $(i-1)$ bits as $i \leq L_1 \times M$, or $i-(L_1 \times M+1)$ bits as $i > L_1 \times M$ by using SBs before it is delivered to the corresponding VBC. The operation of SBs will be detailed later. By using our approach, if $L_1 \times M = N/2$ for the first stage, we can reduce one half of switch elements in the switch array than the design by Chao [22]. Our approach also lowers one half of cell delay in the switch array than the design by Chao [22]. If $L_1 \times M \geq N/2$ for the first stage, e. g., N=6, $L_1 \times M$=4, our design as shown in Fig. 4(b), can reduce two thirds of switch elements in the switch array than the design by Chao as shown in Fig. 4(a) [22]. Similarly, we can also lower two thirds of cell delay in the switch array. If $L_1 \times M < N/2$, e. g., N=6, $L_1 \times M$=2, our design shown in Fig. 5(b), can reduce one third of switch elements and lower one third of cell delay in the switch array than the design in Fig. 5(a) [22]. In sum, we can reduce switch elements and cell delay by a factor of $(L_1 \times M)/N$ than the design in [22].

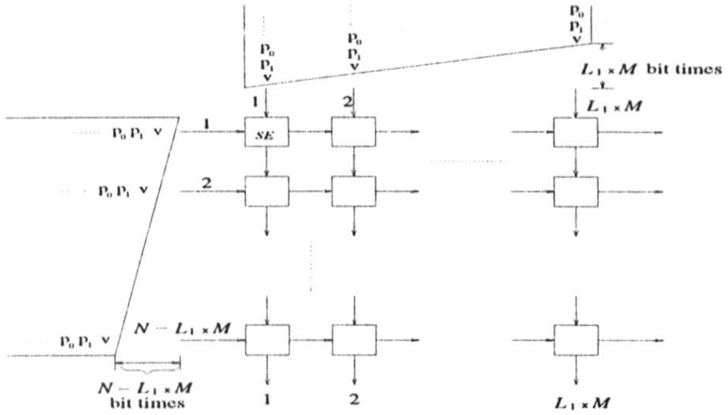

Figure 6: The operation of skewed buffers.

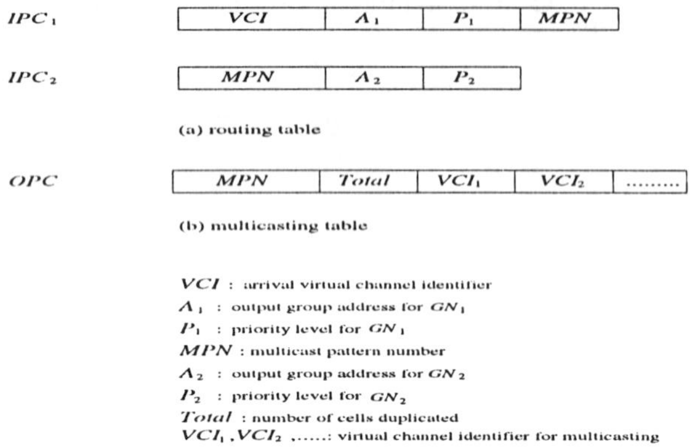

Figure 7: The routing table and the multicating table.

2.3 Cell sequence maintained

For a switch array to work properly, we need to adjust the timing between cells at the vertical links and horizontal links of the array. An arriving cell before entering the switch array will be skewed properly by skewed buffers (SB), as shown in Fig. 6 [22]. The arrival cells may be routed to different paths in the array. It may cause the problem of cells out of sequence. Two cells that originate from the same source may be routed to the left-most and the right-most links of the array, respectively. In this situation, the cell sequence may not be guaranteed. The two cells may have a timing difference of $C-(L_1 \times M - 1)$ bit times, where C is the cell length. To guarantee the cell sequence, $C-(L_1 \times M - 1)$ must be greater than zero.

This means the cell length has to be greater than the number of routing links in an output group.

2.4 Unicast and multicast

The routing tables in the IPC_1 and IPC_2 contain information for properly routing or multicasting in the grouping network, as shown in Fig. 7(a). The multicasting table in the OPC contains all virtual channels identifiers that a source wants to multicast in the OPC, as shown in Fig. 7(b). A multicast pattern number (MPN) is used to identify each multicast call. In other words, all the multicast cells in the switch use

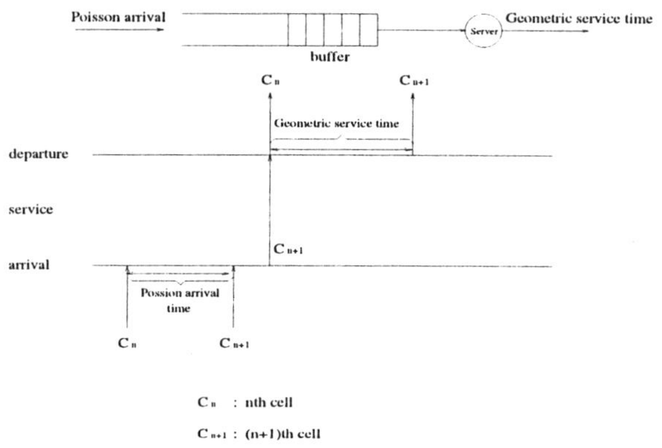

Figure 8: Queuing model for an OPC.

MPN to check if they come from the same source. When a cell arrives at the switch, its VCI is used to look up the routing table in the IPC_1. The IPC_1 will attach the output grouping network address A_1 for the first stage, a valid bit for checking if the cell is valid, two priority bits for contention resolution in the switch array at the first stage, and an MPN for identifying a multicast call. A valid bit controller (VBC) of the nth switch module will check if the nth bit of A_1 is set to 1. If the bit is not set to 1, the VBC will set the valid bit to 1 representing an invalid cell since the arrival cell is not destined for this output group. Before a cell leaves the VBC, the A_1 of the cell will be removed from the header. When a cell arrives an OPC, its MPN is used to obtain a new VCI for each duplicated copy which is produced by the corresponding cell duplicator.

3 Performance analysis of the switch

3.1 Analysis of queuing model with infinite buffers

An OPC can be modeled by the $M/Geom/1$ queuing model as shown in Fig. 8. We want to solve the *distribution function of the buffer occupancy* ($F^*_{\tilde{q}}(z)$), *mean queue length* ($\overline{N_q}$), *mean waiting time* ($\overline{W}$), and *throughput* (Th) when the buffer size is infinite. Assume the number of arrival cells for an OPC has a Poisson distribution with a rate λ', the number of arrival cells for an IPC has a Poisson distribution with a rate λ , the OPC has geometric distribution service time with parameter σ which depends on the number of multicast cells generated, and c_n represents the nth cell. Let's define some random distribution variables as follows:

$\tilde{q}_n$: number of cells left behind by the departure of c_n from service

$\tilde{v}_n$: number of arrival cells during the service time c_n

$\tilde{q}$: $\tilde{q}_n$ as $n \to \infty$

$\tilde{v}$: $\tilde{v}_n$ as $n \to \infty$

We have the following relation between $\tilde{q}_{n+1}$ and $\tilde{q}_n$,

$$\tilde{q}_{n+1} = \tilde{q}_n - \Delta_{\tilde{q}_n} + \tilde{v}_{n+1} \tag{1}$$

where

$$\Delta_k = \begin{cases} 1 & \text{if k} = 1, 2, \ldots \\ 0 & \text{if k} \leq 0 \end{cases}$$

In equation 1, we first take square on both sides, then take the expected value on both sides, and let $n \to \infty$. We have,

$$E[\tilde{q}] = \frac{E[\tilde{v}] + E[\tilde{v}^2] - 2(E[\tilde{v}])^2}{2(1 - E[\tilde{v}])} \tag{2}$$

Based on the derivation of $F^*_{\tilde{v}}(z)$ in [23], we have

$$E[\tilde{v}] = \frac{\partial}{\partial z} F^*_{\tilde{v}}(z)|_{z=1} = \frac{\lambda'}{\sigma} \tag{3}$$

$$E[\tilde{v}^2] = \frac{\partial}{\partial z} F^*_{\tilde{v}}(z)|_{z=1} + E[v] \tag{4}$$

$$= \left(\frac{2\lambda'^2}{\sigma^2} - \frac{\lambda'^2}{\sigma}\right) + \frac{\lambda'}{\sigma} \tag{5}$$

Thus,

$$E[\tilde{q}] = \frac{\frac{\lambda'}{\sigma}(2 - \lambda')}{2(1 - \frac{\lambda'}{\sigma})} \tag{6}$$

Since the $M/Geom/1$ queuing model is a birth-death system and has Poisson arrivals [24][25], the mean number of cells ($\overline{N}$) in the OPC is

$$\overline{N} = \frac{\frac{\lambda'}{\sigma}(2 - \lambda')}{2(1 - \frac{\lambda'}{\sigma})} \tag{7}$$

And the mean queue length ($\overline{N_q}$) is

$$\overline{N_q} = \overline{N} - \frac{\lambda'}{\sigma} \tag{8}$$

Based on the Little's result [24][25], the mean waiting time ($\overline{W}$) in the OPC is

$$\overline{W} = \frac{\frac{1}{\sigma}(2 \quad \lambda')}{2(1 - \frac{\lambda'}{\sigma})} - \frac{1}{\sigma} \tag{9}$$

Throughput (Th) can be expressed as

$$Th = 1 - p(\tilde{q} = 0)p(\tilde{v} = 0) \tag{10}$$

where

$$p(\tilde{q} = 0) = 1 - \frac{\lambda'}{\sigma} \quad (see\ [23]) \tag{11}$$

$$p(\tilde{v} = 0) = \sum_{c=1}^{\infty} p[\tilde{v} = 0 | \tilde{x} = c]\, p[\tilde{x} = c]$$

$$= \frac{\sigma e^{-\lambda'}}{1 - e^{-\lambda'}(1 - \sigma)} \tag{12}$$

Therefore,

$$Th = 1-(1-\frac{\lambda'}{\sigma})(\frac{\sigma e^{-\lambda'}}{1-e^{-\lambda'}(1-\sigma)}) \quad (13)$$

Let the expected replication of a multicast cell be $\overline{M}_1$ for a GN_1, $\overline{M}_2$ for a GN_2, and $\overline{M}_3$ for an OPC. In the grouping networks (GN_1, GN_2), if the number of output groups that an incoming cell is multicast to has the geometric distribution with parameter $\rho = 1-q$, then we can figure out $\overline{M}_1$ and $\overline{M}_2$, where

$$\overline{M}_1 = \sum_{j=1}^{N/M} jP_{m1}(c=j) \quad (14)$$

$$\overline{M}_2 = \sum_{j=1}^{M} jP_{m2}(c=j) \quad (15)$$

With $\lambda' = \lambda\overline{M}_1\overline{M}_2$,
the mean queue length ($\overline{N}_q$) is:

$$\overline{N}_q = \frac{\frac{\lambda\overline{M}_1\overline{M}_2}{\sigma}(2-\lambda\overline{M}_1\overline{M}_2)}{2(1-\frac{\lambda\overline{M}_1\overline{M}_2}{\sigma})} - \frac{\lambda\overline{M}_1\overline{M}_2}{\sigma} \quad (16)$$

the mean waiting time ($\overline{W}$) is:

$$\overline{W} = \frac{\frac{1}{\sigma}(2-\lambda\overline{M}_1\overline{M}_2)}{2(1-\frac{\lambda\overline{M}_1\overline{M}_2}{\sigma})} - \frac{1}{\sigma} \quad (17)$$

and the throughput (Th) is:

$$Th = 1-(1-\frac{\lambda\overline{M}_1\overline{M}_2}{\sigma})(\frac{\sigma e^{-\lambda\overline{M}_1\overline{M}_2}}{1-e^{-\lambda\overline{M}_1\overline{M}_2}(1-\sigma)}) \quad (18)$$

3.2 Analysis of cell loss rate

To analyze the cell loss rate, we assume the duplicated cells of a multicast cell are uniformly delivered to all output groups and the arrival cells at different input lines are statistically independent. Note that the probability that a cell arrives at an input port in a time slot is λ.

3.2.1 Cell loss rate in GN_1

The probability (a_i) of i arrival cells at an output group of GN_1 in a time slot is

$$a_i = \binom{N}{i}(\frac{\lambda\overline{M}_1}{K})^i(1-\frac{\lambda\overline{M}_1}{K})^{N-i} \quad (19)$$

As $N \to \infty$, we have

$$a_i = \frac{e^{-\lambda\overline{M}_1 M}(\lambda\overline{M}_1 M)^i}{i!} \quad (20)$$

The cell loss rate (P_1) in GN_1 is

$$P_1 = \frac{1}{\lambda\overline{M}_1 M}\sum_{i=L_1\times M}^{N}(i-L_1\times M)\binom{N}{i}(\frac{\lambda\overline{M}_1}{K})^i \times(1-\frac{\lambda\overline{M}_1}{K})^{N-i} \quad (21)$$

As $N \to \infty$, we have

$$P_1 = [1-\frac{L_1\times M}{\lambda\overline{M}_1 M}][1-\sum_{i=0}^{L_1\times M}\frac{(\lambda\overline{M}_1 M)^i e^{-\lambda\overline{M}_1 M}}{i!}] + \frac{(\lambda\overline{M}_1 M)^{L_1\times M}e^{-\lambda\overline{M}_1 M}}{(L_1\times M)!} \quad (22)$$

3.2.2 Cell loss rate in GN_2

The probability (T_j) of j arrival cells at an output group of GN_2 in a time slot is

$$T_j = \begin{cases} a_j & \text{if } j < L_1\times M \\ \sum_{j=L_1\times M}^{N} a_j & \text{if } j = L_1\times M \end{cases}$$

Under the condition of j arrival cells at GN_2, the probability of i arrival cells at an output group is

$$b_{i|j} = \binom{j}{i}(\frac{\overline{M}_2}{M})^i(1-\frac{\overline{M}_2}{M})^{j-i} \quad (23)$$

Then the probability of i arrival cells at an output group is

$$b_i = \sum_{j=i}^{L_1\times M} b_{i|j}T_j \quad (24)$$

The cell loss rate (P_2) in GN_2 is thus

$$P_2 = \frac{\sum_{L_2+1}^{L_1\times M}(i-L_2)b_i}{\lambda\overline{M}_1\overline{M}_2(1-P_1)} \quad (25)$$

3.2.3 Cell loss rate in OPC

If we have a finite buffers of size b in each OPC [23], the cell loss rate (P_3) in an OPC can be expressed as

$$P_3 = q_b(1-a_0) \quad (26)$$

3.2.4 Total cell loss rate of the switch

With the cell loss rates in IPC_1, IPC_2 and OPC, the total cell loss rate can be computed by summing them up:

$$P_{total}(loss) = \frac{KP_1\overline{M}_2\overline{M}_3 + NP_2\overline{M}_3 + P_3}{N\lambda\overline{M}_1\overline{M}_2\overline{M}_3} \quad (27)$$

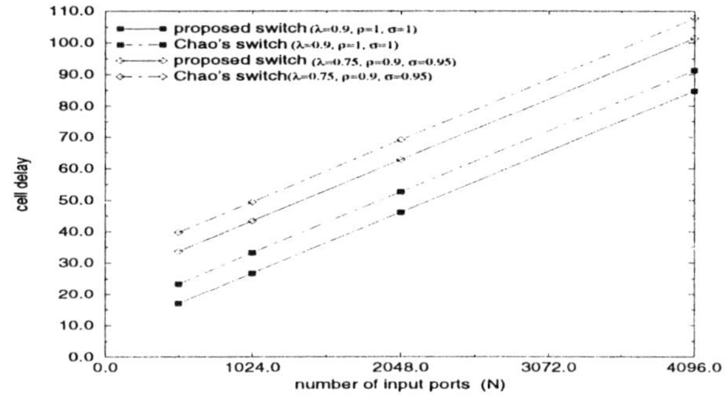

Figure 9: Comparison with Chao's switch in cell delay for $M = 256$.

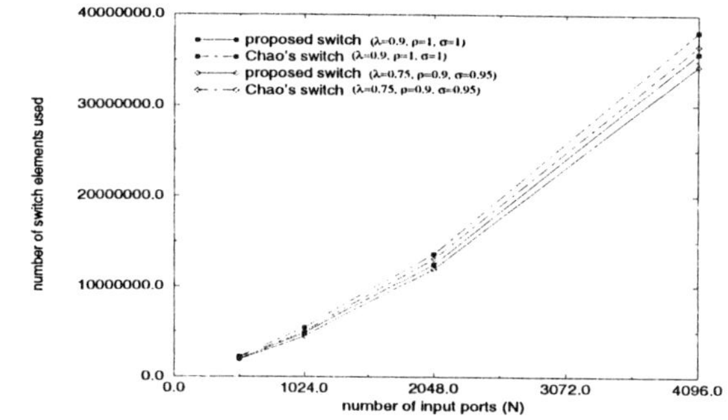

Figure 10: Comparison with Chao's switch in number of switch elements used for $M = 256$.

4 Experimental results

4.1 Comparison with Chao's switch

We will compare our switch with Chao's switch [22] in terms of cell delay and number of switch elements used. We use a two-stage switch architecture for comparison. For a large-scale switch with more than two stages, our results will be even better. Because the cell delays in a VBC is similar to that in an MPM (Multicast Pattern Masker) of Chao's switch [22], we only compare the main cell delays resulted from other components. For a switch array, the complexity of an address broadcaster along with MPMs in Chao's switch is also comparable to that of VBCs in our switch. So, we only compare the number of switch elements used, which is the main difference between the two schemes.

4.1.1 Cell delay

We use two traffic conditions: (1) unicasting for $\lambda = 0.9$, $\rho = 1$, and $\sigma = 1$; (2) multicasting for $\lambda = 0.75$, $\rho = 0.9$, and $\sigma = 0.95$, and group sizes: $M = 256$ for comparison. For the group size $M = 256$, as shown in Fig. 9, our switch always reduces $5 \sim 7$ cell delays than Chao's for either unicasting or multicasting. For example, when the switch size $N = 1024$, we reduce 6.50 cell delays for unicasting and 6.02 cell delays for multicasting. Our switch always performs better than Chao's switch in term of cell delay under different group sizes and different traffic conditions.

4.1.2 Number of switch elements used

Now we will compare our switch with Chao's switch [22] in terms of number of switch elements used. We use the same traffic conditions and group sizes as above to illustrate. For the group size $M = 256$, as shown in Fig. 10, our switch reduces 12% of number of switch elements used than Chao's as $N = 1024$ and 14% as $N = 512$, for either unicasting or multicasting. Our switch uses fewer switch elements than Chao's switch under any group size and traffic condition.

5 Conclusions

This paper proposes a recursive modular architecture for a multicast ATM switch which is growable. This switch has the following key features : (1) cell replication is achieved by broadcasting incoming cells to each switch array; (2) cell filtering and cell contention are distributed over switch elements arranged like a crossbar architecture; (3) the function of address broadcaster is distributed over small valid bit controllers; (4) the output ports are partitioned into groups for sharing routing paths; (5) Output queueing with cell duplication capability is to achieve the best possible delay/throughput performance. This switch has a regular and uniform structure. In addition, our switch is very cost-effective, which has fewer switch elements and less cell delay than Chao's switch under any group sizes and traffic conditions. The performance analysis in terms of cell loss rate, cell delay, mean queue length, mean waiting time and throughput shows that our ATM switch meets the ATM performance requirements either for unicasting or multicasting.

Acknowledgment

This research was supported in part by the National Science Council, ROC under Grant NSC85-2213-E-009-120.

References

[1] P. Jonet, J. P. Coudreuse, and M. Servel, "Implementation of Asynchronous Transfer Mode Concepts: Main Results of the Prelude Experiment," *GLOBECOM '87 Conference Record,* pp. 1871-1875, Nov. 1987.

[2] H. Ahmadi and W. E. Denzel, "A Survey of Modern High-Performance Switching Techniques,"

IEEE J. Selected Areas Commun., vol. 7, no. 7, pp. 1091-1103, Sep. 1989.

[3] A. R. Jacob, "A Survey of Fast Packet Switches," *ACM Computer Communication Review*, vol. 20, no. 1, pp. 54-64, Jan. 1990.

[4] J. Y. Hui, "Switching and Traffic Theory for Integrated Broadband Networks," *Kluwer Academic Publishers*, 1990.

[5] R. Handel, M. N. Hunber, and S. Schroder, "ATM Networks: Concepts, Protocols, Applications," *Addison Wesley*, 1994.

[6] C. Partridge, "Gigabit Networking," *Addison Wesley*, 1992.

[7] K. Y. Eng, M. G. Hluchyj, and Y. S. Yeh, "Multicast and Broadcast Services in a Knockout Packet Switch," *Proc. INFORCOM '88*, pp. 29-34, Mar. 1988.

[8] H. Suzuki, et al., "Output-Buffer Switch for Asynchronous Transfer Mode," *IEEE ICC '89*, pp. 99-13, Jun. 1989.

[9] A. Itoh, et al., "Practical Implementation and Packaging Technologies for a Large Scale ATM Switching System," *IEEE J. Selected Areas Commun.*, vol. 9, no. 8, pp. 1280-1288, Oct. 1991.

[10] Y. C. Jung and C. K. Un, "Banyan Multipath Self-Routing ATM Switches with Shared Buffer Type Switch Elements," *IEEE Trans. Commun.*, vol. 43, no. 11, pp. 2847-2857, Nov. 1995.

[11] K. Y. Eng, M. J. Karol, and Y. -S. Yeh, "A Growable Packet (ATM) Switch Architecture: Design Principles and Applications," *IEEE Trans. Commun.*, vol. 40, no. 2, pp. 423-430, Feb. 1992.

[12] M. J. Karol and C. -L. I, "Performance Analysis of a Growable Architecture for Broadband Packet (ATM) Switching," *IEEE Trans. Commun.*, vol. 40, no. 2, pp. 431-439, Feb. 1992.

[13] J. Hui and T. H. Lee, "A Large Scale ATM Switching Network with Sort-Bayan Switch Modules," *GLOBECOM '92 Conference Record*, vol. 1, Dec. 1992.

[14] Y. S. Yeh, M. G. Hluchyj, and A. S. Acampora, "The Knockout Switch: A Simple Modular Architecture for High Performance Packet Switching," *IEEE J. Selected Areas Commun.*, vol. SAC-5, no. 8, pp. 1274-1283, Oct. 1987.

[15] M. J. Karol and M. G. Hluchyj, "The Knockout Switch: Principles and Performance," *Proc. 12th Conf. Local Comput. Networks*, pp. 16-22, Oct. 1987.

[16] X. Liu and H. T. Mouftah, "Design of a High Performance Nonblocking Copy Network for Multicast ATM Switching," *IEE Proc. Commun.*, vol. 141, no. 5, pp. 317-324, Oct. 1994.

[17] T. T. Lee, "Non-Blocking Copy Networks for Multicast Packet Switching," *IEEE J. Selected Areas Commun.*, vol. 6, no. 9, pp. 1455-1467, Dec. 1988.

[18] J. S. Turner, "A Practical Version of Lee's Multicast Switch Architecture," *IEEE Trans. on Commun.*, vol. 41, no. 8, pp. 1166-1169, Aug. 1993.

[19] C. L. Tarng and J. S. Meditch,"A High Performance Copy Network for B-ISDN," *Proc. INFORCOM '91*, pp. 171-180, Apr. 1991.

[20] R. J. F. De Vries, "ATM Multicast Connections Using the Gauss Switch," *Proc. GLOBECOM '90*, pp. 211-217, Dec. 1990.

[21] N. Mckeown and B. Prabhakar, "Scheduling Multicast Cells in an Input-Queued Switch," *IEEE INFORCOM '96*, pp. 271-278, Mar. 1996.

[22] H. J. Chao and B. S. Choe, "Design and Analysis of a Large-Scale Multicast Output Buffered ATM Switch," *IEEE/ACM Trans. Networking* , vol. 3, no. 2, pp. 126-138, Apr. 1995.

[23] M. H. Cheng "Design and Performance Analysis of a Growable Multicast ATM Switch, *Master Thesis*, National Chiao Tung University, 1996.

[24] L. Kleinrock, "Queuing Systems, Vol. 1: Theory," *New York: Wiley*, 1975.

[25] J. N. Daigle, "Queuing Theory for Telecommunications," *Addison-Welsey*, 1992.

Performance Analysis of a Multicast Switch based on Multistage Interconnection Networks*

Jaehyung Park, Lillykutty Jacob, and Hyunsoo Yoon
Dept. of Computer Science and Center for Artificial Intelligence Research,
Korea Advanced Institute of Science and Technology
373-1, Kusong-Dong, Yusung-Gu, Taejon 305-701, Republic of Korea

Abstract

In this paper, we study multicasting in the self-routing multistage interconnection networks (MINs) for asynchronous transfer mode (ATM) switch architectures. Many B-ISDN applications require multicast connections in addition to conventional point-to-point connections. This paper presents a novel approach to support multicast connection, on the basis of a restricted address encoding scheme which constructs a short fixed-size multicast header and a recursive scheme that recycles a multicast packet one or more times through the network to send it to the desired destinations. The proposed two-phase multicast algorithm provides deadlock-free multiple multicast connections in MIN-based ATM switches. The emphasis is on analyzing the performance of an unbuffered MIN-based switch using the multicast algorithm in terms of network throughput. The proposed algorithm can be easily applied to buffered MIN-based ATM switches.

1 Introduction

The broadband integrated services digital network (B-ISDN) should support a wide variety of services including video communication, hifi sound, graphics application, and high speed data communication. For supporting these services efficiently, the asynchronous transfer mode (ATM) has been widely accepted as a well-suited transmission and switching principle. The ATM switching technique allows the integration of various services with different bandwidth requirements in an efficient manner since the information transfer is based on a short fixed-sized packet (*cell*).

Most of the services have been provided in the last decade typically between two end users, that is as point-to-point services. As video services are playing the key role of the broadband services, it is important for B-ISDNs to provide point-to-multipoint (*multicast*) services as well [10, 9, 15]. The multicast service, in which the same message is delivered from a source to an arbitrary number of destinations, includes one-to-all (*broadcast*) service as a special case. For various broadband applications such as terrestrial broadcasting, teleconferencing, and video-on-demand (VOD) services, the capability of handling multicast services is demanded in designing ATM switch architectures [3, 10, 15, 17].

Many of the ATM switch architectures which support broadband services efficiently employ multistage interconnection networks (MINs), either buffered or unbuffered, as routing networks. To provide the multicast capability in these ATM switches, there are two alternative approaches. The first is to add a copy network at the front of a routing network, which replicates the cell to obtain the number of copies requested by a given multicast connection. Those copies will be transmitted through the routing network to the desired destinations. The design of copy network may be quite different from that of routing network, and requires extra complexity of componentry [4, 12, 18].

Instead of designing an additional copy network, the second approach is to exploit the inherent multicast capability of a routing network by recycling the cells from the outputs of a routing network to its inputs to generate extra copies. This approach is known as *recursive scheme*, since it simulates the function of a copy network by using the routing network recursively. This approach has the advantage that it does not require extra hardware. The simplicity of the network control algorithm and hardware implementation makes this scheme more attractive.

Many multicast routing algorithms based on such a recursive scheme have been proposed [5, 6, 7, 13, 16]. The algorithm in [6] employs header encoding scheme which is based on a *multi-address encoding scheme*, in order that a source node directly sends a multicast message to all destination nodes at a time. However, such a multi-address encoding scheme is not suitable for ATM switches handling fixed-sized cells, because of the need for constructing variable-sized headers. Other algorithms [5, 7] which employ a *restricted address encoding scheme* and construct a fixed-sized multicast header suffer from the large number of passes for one multicast connection and deadlock which radically degrades the switch performance for multiple multicast connections. Also performance of these multicast algorithms are not analyzed for the case of several multicast connections, but evaluated in terms of the number of recycling passes for the case of one multicast connection.

In this paper, we propose a novel recursive multi-

*This work is supported by *Samsung Group* under the project of *Fundamental Research on Multimedia Engines*.

0-8186-7780-5/97 $10.00 © 1997 IEEE

cast algorithm which provides deadlock-free multicast connection in the wrap-around MIN and is based on the restricted address encoding scheme. The proposed algorithm exploits the intrinsic nonblocking properties of the MIN. The performance of the multicast switch using the algorithm has been analyzed for the unbuffered MIN in terms of network throughput, where several multicast connections are considered. The proposed multicast algorithm can be easily applied to MIN-based ATM switches, such as Phoenix switch [11], Adaptive Corporation ATMX [1], and Fore Systems ASX-100 [8].

The structure of this paper is organized as follows. Section 2 describes the intrinsic nonblocking properties, the header encoding scheme, and the related works. In Section 3 a recursive multicast algorithm is proposed which is based on the restricted address encoding scheme. We analyze the performance of the multicast switch in Section 4. Section 5 concludes the paper.

2 System Model and Related Works

This section describes the basic architecture under consideration, the nonblocking property of the banyan networks, and the header encoding schemes. It also briefly reviews some algorithms for MIN-based ATM switches.

2.1 Basic Architecture and Nonblocking Property

The banyan network under consideration has $n = \log_2 N$ stages. Each stage contains $N/2$ (2×2) switching elements (SEs). The stages are labeled in a sequence from $(n-1)$ to 0 with $(n-1)$ for the first stage. The N input/output ports at each stage are labeled using n bits $(a_{n-1}a_{n-2}\cdots a_0)$, within each stage starting from the top. Similarly, the SEs at each stage are labeled using $(n-1)$ bits $(a_{n-1}a_{n-2}\cdots a_1)$ starting from the top. When we refer to one of the two input ports of a specific SE, then we use the bit a_0 to represent that input port for simplicity. We consider butterfly interconnection patterns between stages, and a perfect shuffle interconnection pattern between input controllers and stage $(n-1)$. The formal definitions of these connection patterns are as follows:

Definition 1 The *interconnection function* for the output ports at stage i in the banyan network under consideration, for $n-1 \geq i \geq 0$, and that for the outputs of the input controllers are respectively defined by

$$IC_i[(a_{n-1}\cdots a_{i+1}a_ia_{i-1}\cdots a_0)] = (a_{n-1}\cdots a_{i+1}a_0a_{i-1}\cdots a_i),$$
$$IC_n[(a_{n-1}a_{n-2}\cdots a_1a_0)] = (a_{n-2}a_{n-3}\cdots a_1a_0a_{n-1}),$$

where the right hand side labels are that of the input ports of the next stage [6].

Though we consider a special class of banyan networks with the interconnection patterns as described above, the results we obtain hold for all the networks that are topologically equivalent to this network.

A broadcast banyan network is a banyan network with SEs which are capable of packet replications. A packet arriving at each broadcast SE can be either routed to one of the output ports, or it can be replicated and sent out on both ports. Figure 1 illustrates the basic wrap-around MIN which is constructed from a $\log_2 N$-stage broadcast banyan network. In a wrap-around MIN, outlets are connected to inlets through external links in order to recycle packets.

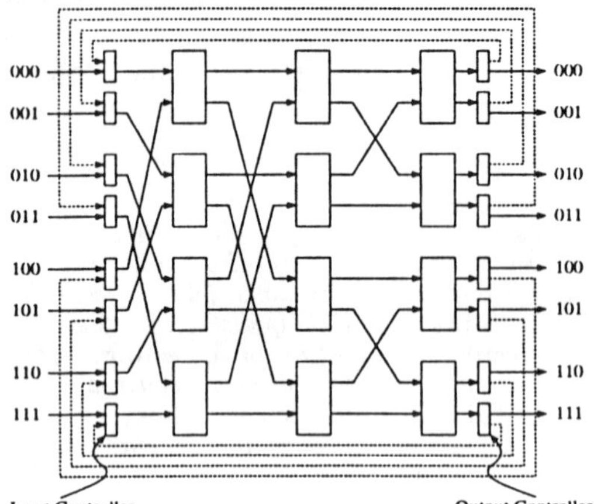

Figure 1: The basic architecture based on the broadcast banyan network, where $N = 8$

The banyan network itself is a blocking network. However, it is known that if the incoming packets with distinct destinations are arranged in an ascending or a descending order of their destination port numbers and the active sources are all connected to consecutive input links then the banyan network becomes nonblocking [2, 12].

2.2 Header Encoding Schemes

The restricted address encoding scheme constructs a multicast routing tag from reachable destinations which are restricted into a single cube or a single region in the MINs.

As one of the restricted address encoding scheme, a cube encoding specifies arbitrary destinations forming a single cube C. The multicast routing tag for the cube encoding scheme is specified by $\{R, M\}$, where $R = r_{n-1}\cdots r_1r_0$ contains the routing information and $M = m_{n-1}\cdots m_1m_0$ contains the multicast information [5, 7]. To handle the multicast tag $\{R, M\}$, an SE at stage i $(0 \leq i \leq n-1)$ examines r_i and m_i. If m_i is 0, the normal unicast routing is performed according to r_i. If m_i is 1, r_i is ignored and the broadcast is performed. Figure 2 shows routing paths for the destinations which form a cube $C = 1x0x$; corresponding M is 0101 and R can be any one of the destination addresses belonging to the cube C.

Other restricted address encoding scheme is a region encoding scheme which specifies arbitrary consecutive destinations forming a single region [12]. The multicast routing tag for the region encoding scheme indicates the *minimum* and *maximum* addresses of

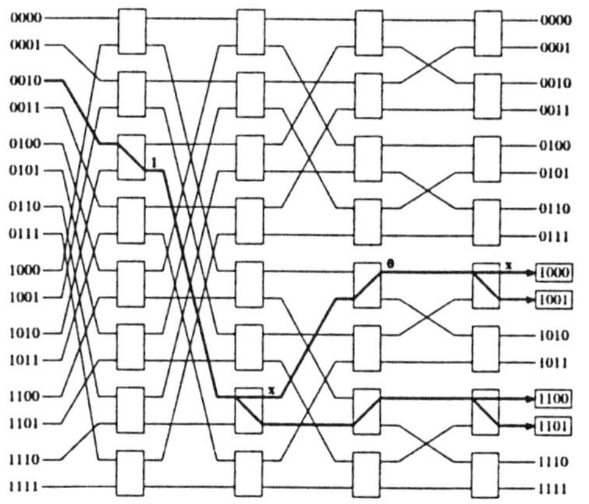

Figure 2: An example of self-routing based on the cube encoding scheme

consecutive destinations. Suppose that an SE at stage i received a packet with the header containing the two addresses: $\min_{i+1} = m_{n-1} \cdots m_1 m_0$ and $\max_{i+1} = M_{n-1} \cdots M_1 M_0$, where the argument $(i+1)$ denotes an SE at stage $(i+1)$ from where the packet came to stage i. The decision for packet routing and replication is as follows:

- If $m_i = M_i = 0$ or $m_i = M_i = 1$, then send the packet out on port 0 or 1, respectively.
- If $m_i = 0$ and $M_i = 1$, then replicate the packet, modify the headers, and send both packets out on both ports.

These rules that $m_{i'} = M_{i'}$, $i < i' \leq n-1$ hold for every packet which arrives at stage $i, 0 \leq i \leq n-1$. The modification of a packet header at stage i is done according to the following recursion:

- For the packet sent out on port 0, $\left.\begin{array}{l} \min_i = \min_{i+1} = m_{n-1} \cdots m_1 m_0, \\ \max_i = M_{n-1} \cdots M_{i+1} 01 \cdots 1 \end{array}\right\}$,
- And for the packet sent out on port 1, $\left.\begin{array}{l} \min_i = m_{n-1} \cdots m_{i+1} 10 \cdots 0, \\ \max_i = \max_{i+1} = M_{n-1} \cdots M_1 M_0 \end{array}\right\}$.

Figure 3 illustrates an example of routing paths through the MIN for a multicast packet with routing tag containing an address interval specified by 0100 and 1000.

The size of multicast routing tag for the above two restricted address encoding schemes is fixed to $2n$ bits.

2.3 Related Works

An algorithm considering the blocking effect among several constituent copies of one multicast packet at any pass is proposed in [5], which uses the cube encoding scheme. This multicast algorithm checks whether any two constituent copies of one multicast packet can be routed without conflict or not. As any two constituent copies which cause conflict in being routed cannot be sent at the same pass, this algorithm prevents blocking. This algorithm generates a multicast tree which models the sequence of recycling through the network for routing a multicast packet to all destinations. In the multicast tree, a parent node sends

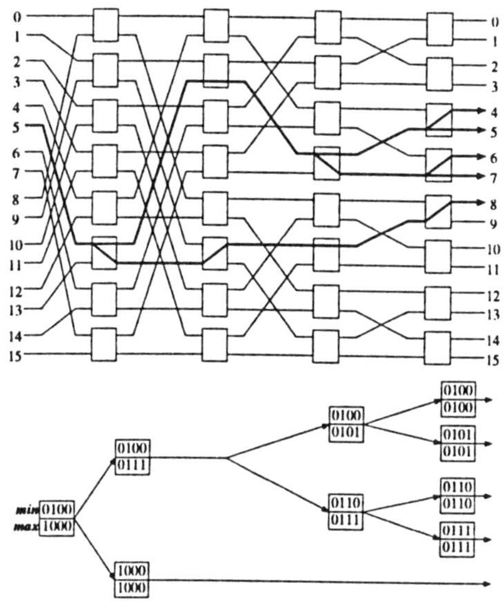

Figure 3: An example of self-routing based on the region encoding scheme

a copy with one multicast routing tag to its children. Figure 4 shows the generated nonblocking multicast tree and the multicast routing example, where source 5 sends a packet to destinations $\{3, 4, 6, 7, 9, 11, 13\}$. However, the algorithm has $O(f^2)$ time complexity to construct the nonblocking multicast tree for the given f destinations of one multicast packet. This algorithm also delivers the packet to the desired f destinations in f passes in the worst case.

Raghavendra, et al. [16] proposed a two-phase multicast algorithm, which guarantees nonblocking between any two constituent copies at the same phase. Because other outputs which are not included in the multicast destinations can receive and send a copy, this algorithms has the advantage that it can easily minimize the number of passes for one multicast packet across the MIN. This algorithm constructs nonblocking multicast tree as in [5]. However, while the region encoding scheme is used in the first phase, the cube encoding scheme is used in the second phase. Since the SE's structure of handling the multicast routing tag in the second phase is different from that of handling it in the first phase, it needs an additional hardware cost for processing the two encoding schemes.

Thus, these proposed multicast algorithms require excessive network resources such as very complex SEs and/or large number of internal links. Furthermore, they do not consider the deadlock that may occur among multiple multicast packets.

3 A Recursive Multicast Algorithm in Wrap-Around MINs

In this section we describe a new recursive multicast algorithm in wrap-around MINs which is based on the restricted address encoding scheme. The proposed

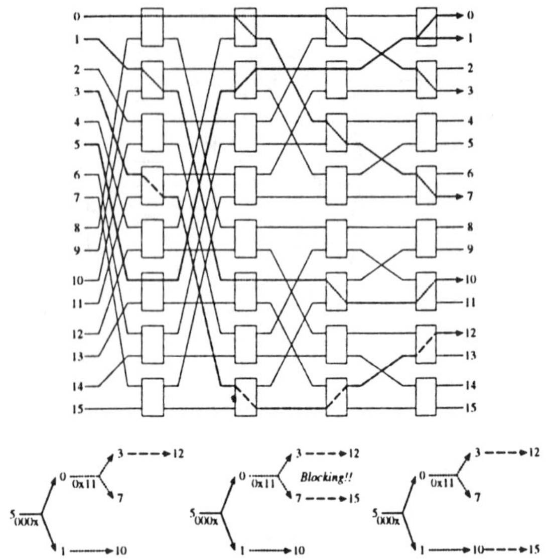

Figure 4: A multicast routing example

algorithm avoids blocking effect among constituent copies of a multicast packet by exploiting the intrinsic nonblocking properties of the MIN as described in Section 2.1. We also consider the occurrence of deadlock among multiple multicast packets and present a scheme for deadlock-free multicast connection.

3.1 Two-Phase Multicast Algorithm

This algorithm routes a multicast packet to arbitrary f destinations in two phases, which are copying and routing phases. During a copying phase, a source sends a multicast packet to f consecutive outputs where the minimum address is randomly selected. The multicast routing tag is constructed using the region encoding scheme. In the second phase, the recycled packets from these f consecutive outputs are sent to the desired destinations. The two-phase multicast algorithm with the region encoding is described as follows:

Assume that the f arbitrary destinations for a multicast packet are sorted in the ascending order as $D_0, D_1, \ldots, D_{f-1}$.

Phase 1: Copy from the source to f consecutive outputs through the MIN. The f consecutive outputs are addressed as $s, s+1, \ldots, s+f-1$ where s is randomly selected. Region encoding scheme is used to copy the packet to f consecutive outputs.

Phase 2: Route the recycled copy from the output $(s+l)$ to the destination D_l, where $0 \leq l \leq f-1$. The routing tag of the packet from input $(s+l)$ contains D_l.

In Figure 5, an example of the second phase is shown, where source 5 sends a multicast packet to destinations $\{3,4,6,7,9,11,13\}$. During the copying phase, source 5 sends a copy to outputs $\{4,5,6,7,8,9,10\}$, where the minimum address 4 is selected randomly.

Theorem 1 *In the two-phase multicast algorithm, blocking does not occur among any constituent copies.*

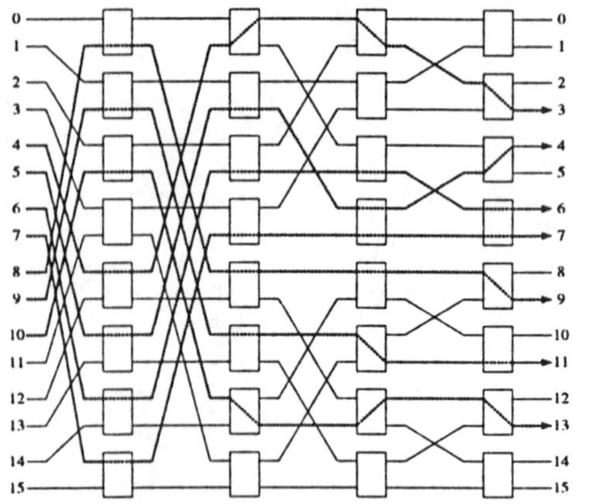

Figure 5: An example of the routing phase in the multicast algorithm

Proof : In the first phase, it is trivial because packet is copied from a single inlet to f consecutive outlets. On the contrary, in the second phase these f copies move from multiple inlets to the corresponding destinations through the MIN. However, active inputs which receive the copies at the end of the first phase are concentrated on inlets $s, s+1, \ldots, s+f-1$ and the output addresses satisfy the monotonicity property, i.e., $D_0, D_1, \cdots, D_{f-1}$ are in the ascending order. Thus the constituent copies pass without blocking. ■

Theorem 1 guarantees that a multicast packet that is destined for any arbitrary set of destinations is sent to the desired destinations in two passes across the broadcast banyan network.

3.2 Deadlock Avoidance

These multicast algorithms suffer from potential deadlock due to multiple multicast packets in the unbuffered MIN. In the MINs using distributed control, one packet which is copied at stage i for a multicast packet does not know whether other copied packets for the multicast packet are forwarded or dropped at stage j ($j > i$) due to other multicast packets. As a result, it is not guaranteed that all copied packets for a multicast packet arrive at the desired destinations. This is the situation of deadlock occurring among multiple multicast packets. Figure 6 shows an example of deadlock situation in a multicast algorithm given two multicast packets $5 \rightarrow \{5,6,7,8,9,10,11,12\}$ and $15 \rightarrow \{4,5,6,7,8,9,10\}$. One packet from source 5 collides with another from source 15 at SE μ and at SE ν. As shown in Figure 6, at SE μ the packet from source 5 is randomly selected to be broadcasted to two output ports and at SE ν the packet from source 15 is randomly selected to be broadcasted to the two output ports. As a result, the packet from source 15 is dropped at the SE μ and the packet from source 5 is dropped at the SE ν, assuming a packet dropping policy at the SEs. Thus, at the beginning of the second phase we have neither all the copies of packet from source 5 nor the copies of packet from source 15 at

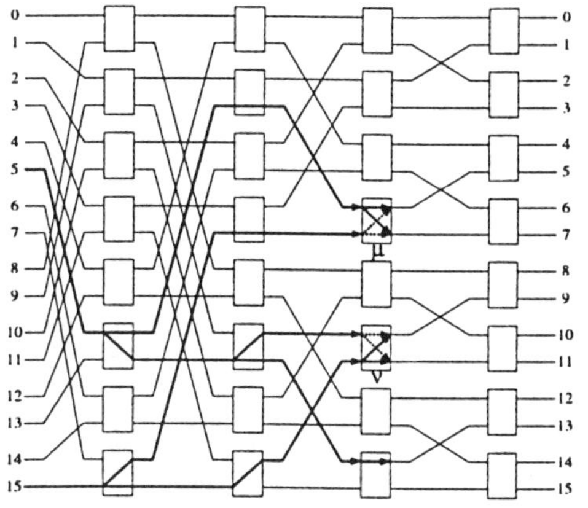

Figure 6: An example of deadlock situation

consecutive input lines. Hence, a deadlock occurs.

In order to avoid deadlock, SEs must use some arbitration mechanism for multiple multicast packets. One scheme in which global unique time is added to all packets at the source is the most intuitive approach [6]. This scheme, however, is centralized and it is difficult to maintain global unique time. We present a simple scheme, the *upper input port first scheme*. This arbitration method, which chooses the packet from the upper input port, is a distributed scheme.

Theorem 2 *In multicast algorithms, the upper input port first scheme guarantees a deadlock-free transmission through the broadcast banyan network.*

Proof : In the two-phase multicast algorithm, all multicast packets simultaneously request output port(s) on one or more SEs at the same stage i, $0 \leq i \leq n-1$. Assume that the source address and the multicast routing tag of a multicast packet are $s_{n-1}\cdots s_0$ and $\{m_{n-1}\cdots m_0,\ M_{n-1}\cdots M_0\}$. The address of the input port at stage $(n-1)$ into which this multicast packet enter is $s_{n-2}\cdots s_0 s_{n-1}$ by Definition 1. Using our notation described in Section 2.1, the label of the particular SE is then $s_{n-2}\cdots s_0$ and the specific input port of this SE is identified by the bit s_{n-1}. Similarly, the address of the input port(s) at stage i, $n-2 \geq i \geq 0$, into which the packet copies enter are $m'_{n-1}\cdots m'_{i+1}s_{i-1}\cdots s_1 s_0 s_i$. Note that $m'_{i'} = M'_{i'}$, for $n-1 \geq i' \geq i+1$, and they are the modified bits of the routing tag of the packets (see Section 2.2). Again using our notation described in Section 2.1, the label(s) of the specific SE(s) are then $m'_{n-1}\cdots m'_{i+1}s_{i-1}\cdots s_1 s_0$ and the specific input port(s) of these SE(s) are identified by the corresponding bit s_i. Thus, the position of the input port(s) at any stage i at which the multicast packet(s) arrive from a particular source depends only on the source address. Therefore the copies of a multicast packet that request output port(s) at one or more SE(s) at any stage have got the same priority and hence the upper input port first scheme renders deadlock-free multiple multicast connections. ∎

4 Performance Analysis of the Multicast Switch

In this section, we analyze the performance of the MIN-based switch using the proposed recursive multicast algorithm in terms of network throughput, where several multicast connections are considered.

4.1 Assumption and Modelling

Given the rate of packets at input controllers, network throughput is represented by the number of packets accepted per time slot. A packet is said to be accepted only if it is successfully transmitted to the requested multiple outputs. Performance is analyzed on the basis of the following assumptions.

- Each input controller generates random and independent packets; the packet destinations are uniformly distributed over all outputs.
- At the beginning of every time slot, each processor generates a new packet with a probability ρ. And $m\rho$ is the average number of multicast packets with fixed fanout f which are generated per time slot by each input controller, where $0 \leq m \leq 1$.
- The packets which are not accepted are ignored to reenter the switch from the corresponding input controller ports later; the packets issued at the next time slot are independent of these blocked packets.

Assume that an $N \times N$ wrap-around MIN is constructed from 2×2 SEs. In the copying phase, the minimum for the address interval in the routing tag at the input controller is randomly selected. And for the subsequent stages, the corresponding bits of the routing tag are modified according to the scheme mentioned under region encoding scheme. In each time slot, a SE at any stage i will be in one of the possible configurations shown in Figure 7. In (a) and (b) each, there is only one packet and $m_i = M_i$ for that packet. In (c) and (d) there are two packets with $m_i = M_i$ for both packets. However they have distinct output port requests. In (e) there are two packets with $m_i = M_i$ and both the packets have the same output port requests. The packet from upper input port is selected. In (f) and (g) each, again there is only one packet, but $m_i \neq M_i$ and hence broadcasted to both output ports. In (h), (i), and (k) there are two packets with the packet from the upper input port to be broadcasted. Following the upper input port first scheme, copies are generated for the packet from the upper port and the packet from the lower input port is ignored. In (j) the packet from the upper input port is to be unicasted to the upper output port and the packet from lower input port is to be broadcasted. Though the lower output port is idle, no copies of the packet from the lower input port are generated. This means that the multicast packet to be copied in the SE is either generated into two copies or is not generated into any one. That is, there is no case that the multicast packet to be copied is generated into a single copy. Note that we consider only those configurations in which a packet is passed on to the upper output port of the SE.

For a multicast packet with fanout f, let c_i be the copy rate, i.e. the probability that the packet is copied at stage i in the wrap-around MIN, where $0 \leq i \leq n-1$.

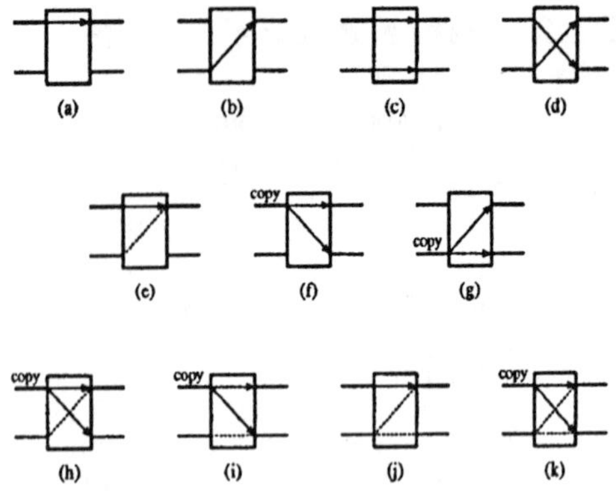

Figure 7: SE's configuration where a packet is passed on to the upper output port

Given the packet rate ρ_i, multicast rate m_i, and copy rate c_i at each of the two inputs of a 2 × 2 SE at stage i, the expected number of packets, both unicast and multicast, that it passes to the upper/lower output port in each time slot is given by;

$$\rho_{i-1} = \rho_i(1+m_ic_i) - \frac{1}{4}\rho_i^2(1+m_ic_i)^2 - \frac{1}{2}\rho_i^2 m_ic_i(1-m_ic_i). \quad (1)$$

The above expression is obtained by listing the probabilities of the possible configurations shown in Figure 7 which lead to the transmission of a packet to the upper output port, and then by simplifying it. Because of the symmetry, the same expression holds for lower output port. Note that the expression is equated to ρ_{i-1} since the packet rate from an output port of a SE at stage i is the packet rate at an input port of a SE at stage $(i-1)$.

And the expected number of unicast packets that it passes per time slot is

$$u_{i-1} = \rho_i(1-m_i) - \frac{1}{4}\rho_i^2(1-m_i)(1+m_ic_i). \quad (2)$$

From the relation that $\rho_{i-1} = u_{i-1} + m_{i-1}\rho_{i-1}$, where $0 \le i \le n-1$, the probability that a given packet at stage $i-1$ is a multicast packet is given by;

$$m_{i-1} = 1 - u_{i-1}/\rho_{i-1}.$$

For any stage of the wrap-around MIN, the output rate of packets is a function of its input packet rate, multicast rate, and copy rate. Since the output rates of a stage are the input rates of the next stage, one can recursively evaluate the output rates of any stage starting with stage $(n-1)$. We have $\rho_{n-1} = \rho$ and $m_{n-1} = m$. Let ρ' be the expected number of both unicast and multicast packets that a SE at the final stage (i.e., stage 0) passes on to the upper/lower output port and u' be the corresponding number of unicast packets alone. Note that ρ' and u' are obtained from Equations (1) and (2) respectively, for stage 0. Then the throughput per output port of the switch η is given by

$$\eta = \frac{\rho' - u'}{f} + u'.$$

4.2 Numerical Results

To evaluate the throughput for the wrap-around MIN, first the copy rate c_i for a multicast packet with fanout f is computed at stage i, where $0 \le i \le n-1$. We consider two cases. In case (a), the start address s for the f consecutive destinations in the copy phase is always selected as $s_{n-1}s_{n-2}\cdots s_k\overbrace{00\cdots0}^{k}$ where k is the minimum integer such that $f \le 2^k$. In case (b), the start address s is randomly selected from N destinations as mentioned in the description of the two-phase algorithm. These results are depicted in Figure 8.

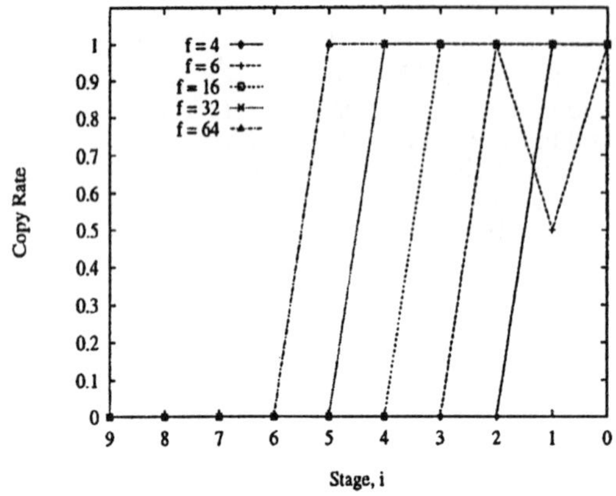

(a) Fixed Start Address

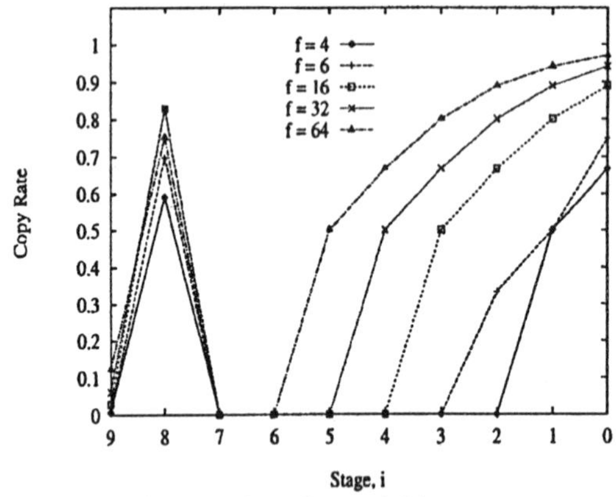

(b) Random Start Address

Figure 8: Comparison of copy rates c_i for various fanouts, where $n = 10$

The offered load that is plotted on the x-axis of Figures 9 - 11 is $(1-m)\rho + m\rho f$. In Figures 9 - 11, solid lines represent the fixed start address case and dotted lines represent the random start address case.

Figure 9 shows the throughput η for n equals to 10 and m equals to 50%. The throughput behaviour is

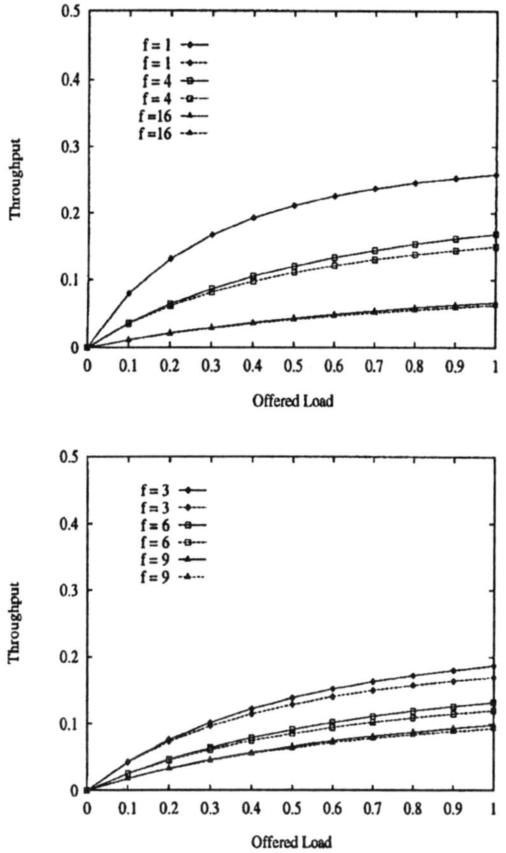

Figure 9: Throughput η vs. offered load, where $n = 10$

identical to that reported in [14] when the fanout f of the multicast packets is one. The throughput of the switch in the case of the fixed start address outperforms that in the case of the random start address.

Figure 10 shows the throughput η for n equals to 10 and with m varying.

In Figure 11, the throughput of the multicast switch using the algorithm is shown varying with network size n. Different curves are shown for various values of multicast rate and fanout. System's offered load is 1.0, that is $(1-m)\rho + m\rho f = 1.0$. In all the cases, the throughput of the switch using multicast algorithm with the fixed start address outperforms that with the random start address. This may be attributed to the behaviour of the copy rates with the random start address and the fixed start address as shown in Figure 8.

5 Conclusion

In this paper, we have considered the issue of multicasting in the MIN for high performance ATM switches. To support multicast connection efficiently, a two-phase multicast algorithm is proposed on the ba-

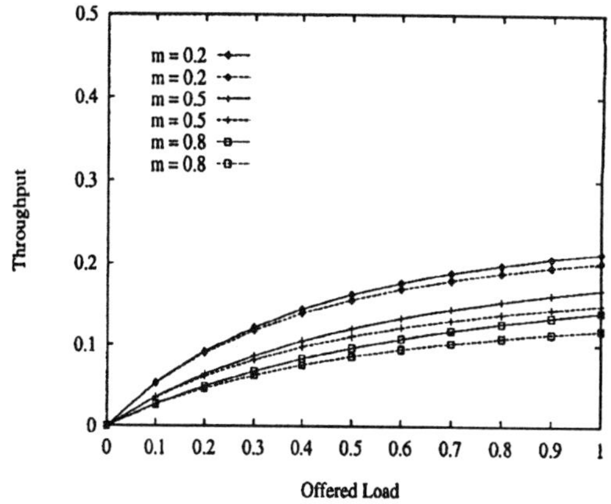

(a) $f = 4$

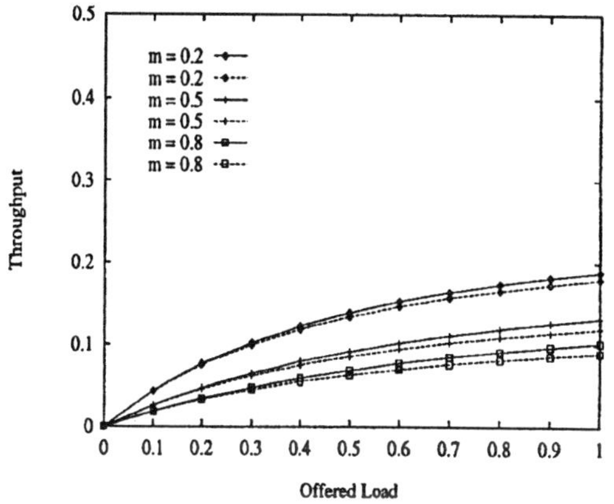

(b) $f = 6$

Figure 10: Throughput η vs. offered load, where $n = 10$

sis of the restricted address encoding scheme and the recursive scheme which recycles a multicast packet one or more times through the network to send it to the desired destinations. The algorithm prevents deadlock among multiple multicast connections in ATM switch architectures based on the unbuffered MIN. The performance of the multicast switch using the proposed algorithm is analyzed in terms of the switch throughput, where several multicast connections are considered. The proposed algorithm can also be easily applied to buffered MIN-based ATM switches.

References

[1] ADAPTIVE CORPORATION. *ATMX Broadband Switch, Release 1.2.* Network Equipment Technologies Inc., 1993.

[2] BATCHER, K. E. Sorting Networks and Their Applications. In *AFIPS Proc. of the Spring Joint Computer Conference* (1968), pp. 307–314.

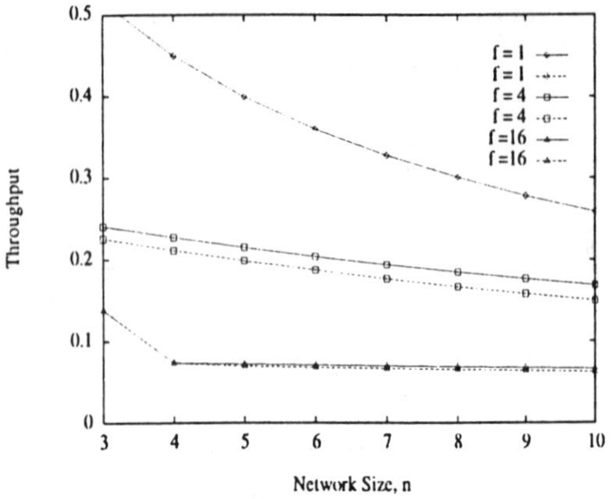

(a) $m = 50\%$

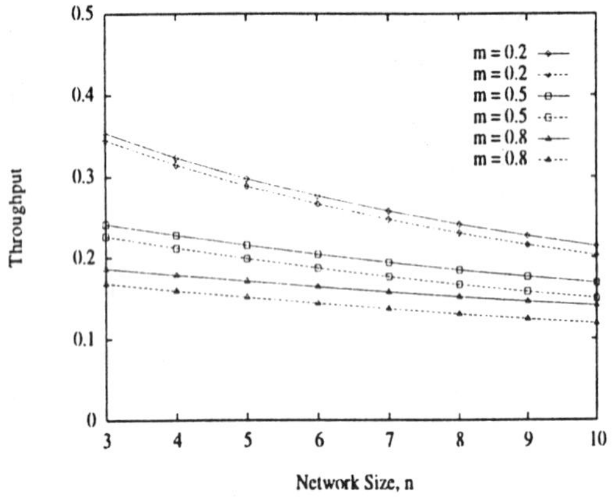

(b) $f = 4$

Figure 11: Switch throughput η vs. network size

[3] BUFORD, J. F. K. *Multimedia Systems.* Addison-Wesley Publishing Company, 1994.

[4] CHEN, D. X., AND MARK, J. W. Multicasting in the SCOQ Switch. In *Proc. of IEEE Infocom* (Apr. 1994), pp. 290–297.

[5] CHEN, X., AND KUMAR, V. Multicast Routing in Self-Routing Multistage Networks. In *Proc. of IEEE Infocom* (Apr. 1994), pp. 306–314.

[6] CHIANG, C.-M. *Multicasting in Multistage Interconnection Networks.* PhD thesis, Dept. of Comp. Sci., Michigan State Univ., East Lansing, MI, 1995.

[7] CUSANI, R., AND SESTINI, F. A Recursive Multistage Structure for Multicast ATM Switching. In *Proc. of IEEE Infocom* (Apr. 1991), pp. 1289–1295.

[8] FORE SYSTEMS INC. *ForeRunner^{TM} ASX-100 ATM Switch Architecture Manual.* 1992.

[9] GIACOMAZZI, P., AND PATTAVINA, A. Providing Multicast Services by the ATM Shuffleout Switch. In *Proc. of IEEE Globecom* (1994), pp. 1483–1489.

[10] HÄNDEL, R., AND HUBER, M. N. *Integrated Broadband Networks: An Introduction to ATM-Based Networks.* Addison-Wesley Publishing Company, 1991.

[11] KUMAR, V. P., KNEUER, J. G., PAL, D., AND BRUNNER, B. Phoenix: A Building Block for Fault Tolerant Broadband Packet Switches. In *Proc. of IEEE Globecom* (Dec. 1991).

[12] LEE, T. T. Nonblocking Copy Networks for Multicast Packet Switching. *IEEE Journal on Selected Areas in Communications 6*, 9 (Dec. 1988), 1455–1467.

[13] PARK, J., YOO, D., YOON, H., AND MAENG, S. R. Efficient Two-Pass Multicast Algorithms in ATM Switches based on Multistage Networks. In *Proc. of the Int'l Conf. on Systems Engineering* (Jul. 1996), pp. 55–60.

[14] PATEL, J. H. Performance of Processor-Memory Interconnections for Multiprocessors. *IEEE Transactions on Computers C-30*, 10 (Oct. 1981), 771–780.

[15] PRYCKER, M. D. *Asynchronous Transfer Mode: Solution for BISDN.* Ellis Horwood Ltd., 1991.

[16] RAGHAVENDRA, C. S., CHEN, X., AND KUMAR, V. P. A Two Phase Multicast Routing Algorithm in Self-Routing Multistage Networks. In *Proc. of Int'l Conference on Communications* (Jun. 1995), pp. 1612–1618.

[17] TOBAGI, F. A. Fast Packet Switch Architectures for Broadband Integrated Services Networks. In *Proc. of IEEE* (Jan. 1990), pp. 133–167.

[18] TURNER, J. S. Design of a Broadcast Packet Switching Network. *IEEE Transactions on Communications COM-36*, 6 (Jun. 1988), 734–743.

Performance and Complexity of Multicast Cross-Path ATM Switches

Raymond H. Lin Cheuk H. Lam Tony T. Lee
Department of Information Engineering, The Chinese University of Hong Kong

Abstract - A newly proposed large-scale ATM switch called cross-path switch has been shown to be capable of handling multirate traffic efficiently. In this paper, we will study two replication approaches to enhance the switch to support multicasting. The first approach replicates multicast cells at both input and output stages, while the second one replicates cells at the input stage only. A feasible configuration for each scheme is considered and the effect of multicast traffic on the switch performance in terms of throughput and cell loss probability is studied. We observed that, to achieve the same throughput and loss requirement, the second architecture may require fewer switching elements than the first one.

Keywords - multicasting, cross-path switch, bipartite graph, copy network, knockout switch, ATM, cell replication, Clos network

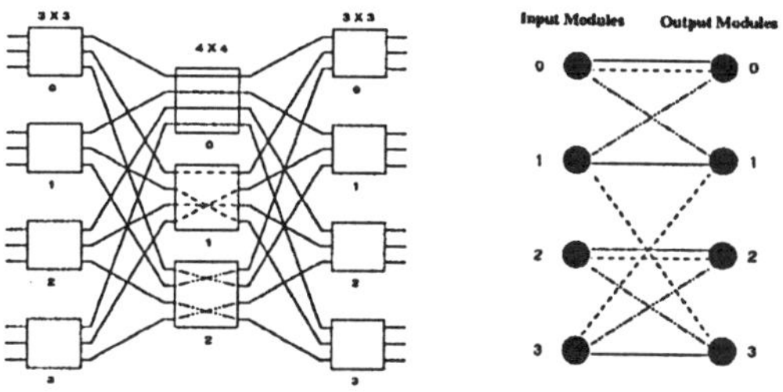

Fig. 1. Correspondence between middle-stage connection pattern in a Clos network and edge-coloring of regular bipartite multigraph

I. Introduction

Recently, a new switching concept called *path switching* implemented on a new switching architecture called *cross-path switch*, a statistical three-stage Clos network, was proposed in [9]. Path switching is a quasi-static routing scheme in the sense that connection pattern in the middle stage of the network is repeated periodically. By considering each input and output module as a node, the connection pattern in the middle stage of the Clos network can be represented by the edge-coloring of a bipartite multigraph as illustrated in Fig. 1 [9].

The number of edges between node I_i and node O_j denotes the number of cells that can be routed from input module i to output module j in one time slot, which determines the capacity of the virtual path between this pair of modules. The scheduling procedure of path switching is to find the capacity of each virtual path satisfying the bandwidth requirement and then convert the capacity to a desirable periodic central-module connection pattern by edge-coloring of the corresponding regular bipartite multigraph based on the time-space interleaving principle [9]. The connection pattern will be updated only if the traffic statistics changes significantly, so that the slot-by-slot route assignments needed in dynamic cell switched routing schemes can be avoided. In addition, the cross-path switch implements look-ahead selection at the input stage to resolve head-of-line blocking and output queueing at the last stage to resolve packet contentions. Local route scheduling is still allowed in each smaller input and output module to exploit the statistical multiplexing gain that is lacking in static circuit switched routing schemes. Therefore, even for multirate traffic, the cross-path switch can easily achieve high throughput and low loss rate.

With some modifications, the cross-path switch can be enhanced to support point-to-multipoint communications such as teleconferencing and video on demand. Two multicast approaches originally proposed in [11] for the growable packet (ATM) switch [4] are adopted in the implementation of the multicast cross-path switches. The first scheme performs replication at both the first and the last stages, while the second scheme only replicates cells in input modules. We do not consider multicasting at the middle stage, because the capacity provided by some point-to-multipoint connection pattern in the central modules will be affected by the time-varying replication requests and it is not appropriate for the capacity assignment of the cross-path switch.

With the same number of central modules, one would intuitively expect higher throughput in the first scheme. However, as it requires cell replication at the last stage, the complexity of output modules will be higher. On the contrary, by using more central modules in the second multicast scheme, the same throughput can also be attained. Since both schemes have their own advantages, it is necessary to evaluate the

0-8186-7780-5/97 $10.00 © 1997 IEEE

trade-off between the performance and the complexity.

The objectives of this paper are to investigate the performance of the multicast cross-path switch under different fanout distribution, and to compare the complexity of the multicast schemes described above. The remaining content of this paper is organized as follows. Section II is the details of the enhanced multicast cross-path switch. Section III is the evaluation of the throughput and cell loss performance of the switch, while Section IV compares the two multicast approaches and provides the overall complexity estimations. Finally, the conclusions are given in Section V.

II. Multicast Schemes and Capacity Allocation

The multicast cross-path switches can be classified into the following categories:

1. Scheme 1 - Cell replication performed at both input and output stages
   As shown in Fig. 2a, scheme 1 replicates cells in both input and output modules. A cell waiting at the input stage is first replicated. The number of copies replicated at this stage is equal to the number of destined output *modules* of the cell. These copies will be routed by the central modules to their destined output modules. Each copy arriving at the last stage will be further replicated if it is destined for more than one output port within that output module.

2. Scheme 2 - Cell replication performed only at the input stage
   In this scheme, cells will not be replicated at the output stage. Therefore, all the replications must be performed within the input modules, as shown in Fig. 2b. In contrast to the first multicast scheme, a packet that has different destined output ports within the same output module needs to be replicated in the first stage and the resulting copies will be routed independently through different central modules.

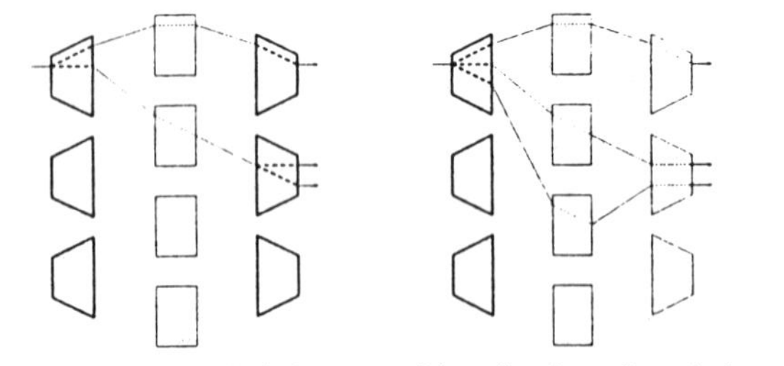

(a) replicating cells in both input and output stage (b) replicating cells only in the input stage

Fig. 2. Two multicast schemes in cross-path switch

In the original unicast cross-path switch, the capacity allocation is based on the traffic load and the effective bandwidth of each virtual path at the middle stage to guarantee the QoS requirement. For multicast traffic, the middle-stage traffic load will be affected by the cell fanout distribution and the replication schemes used. The modified capacity assignment procedure is described below.

Let i_u, o_v, I_i, O_j be the sets of the call requests on input link u, output link v, input module i and output module j respectively. We assume that the traffic load (before replication) ρ_r, in unit of cell/slot, the effective bandwidth (before replication) α_r and the cell fanout number y_r of call request r are given at the call setup, and they satisfy the following constraints to fulfill the cell level QoS requirement.

1. Input link load constraint

$$\sum_{r \in i_u} \rho_r \leq 1, \ \forall u.$$

2. Output link capacity constraint

$$\sum_{r \in o_v} \alpha_r \leq 1, \ \forall v.$$

We say that $r \in i_u$ when the call request r comes from input link u, and $r \in o_v$ when one of the destinations of r is output link v.

Define λ_{ij} to be the total traffic load of the virtual path connecting input module i and output module j. For scheme 1, in which a call request has only one copy routed in the middle stage for each destined output module,

$$\lambda_{ij}^{(1)} = \sum_{r \in I_i, \ r \in O_j} \rho_r.$$

In contrast, the traffic load of call request r at the middle stage of scheme 2 is expanded y_r times, and $y_r(i,j)$ of them will be routed through the virtual path from I_i to O_j. Then the total traffic load of this virtual path is given by

$$\lambda_{ij}^{(2)} = \sum_{r \in I_i, \ r \in O_j} \rho_r \cdot y_r(i,j).$$

Similarly, the aggregate effective bandwidth β_{ij} of a virtual path connecting I_i and O_j in two multicast schemes are given respectively as follows

$$\beta_{ij}^{(1)} = \sum_{r \in I_i, \ r \in O_j} \alpha_r, \qquad \beta_{ij}^{(2)} = \sum_{r \in I_i, \ r \in O_j} \alpha_r \cdot y_r(i,j).$$

The capacity assignment is to find the capacity C_{ij} for the virtual path connecting I_i and O_j such that the following constraints are satisfied.

$$\begin{cases} C_{ij} & \geq & \beta_{ij} & \forall i,j; \\ \sum_i C_{ij} & = & m & \forall j; \\ \sum_j C_{ij} & = & m & \forall i, \end{cases}$$

where m is the number of central modules.

An optimal assignment requires establishing an objective function such as minimizing total weighted delay z [1, 7, 9] after each virtual path is modeled as an $M/M/1$ queue.

$$z = \sum_{i,j} \frac{\lambda_{ij}}{C_{ij} - \lambda_{ij}}.$$

III. PERFORMANCE EVALUATIONS

In this section, we will study how the multicast traffic affects the throughput and the packet loss probability in an 1024×1024 cross-path switch. Adopting the notations in [9], the dimensions of an input module, a central module and an output module are $n \times m$, $k \times k$ and $m \times n$ respectively. The performance analysis is based on two assumptions. Firstly, the traffic distribution among input ports and output ports is homogeneous, a packet is equally likely to be destined for any output port. Secondly, the arrival process at each input link is Bernoulli, i.e. the probability that there is a packet arriving in each time slot is identical and independent.

A. Route scheduling

Details of the route scheduling are given in [9], we just briefly explain the main procedures here. In order to convert the capacity assignment to a desirable middle-stage connection pattern, a frame size f was introduced to extend the route scheduling of the m central modules in one time slot to the scheduling of totally mf "central modules" in f time slots, such that the capacity assigned for a virtual path is always an integer. In other words, the frame size f should be chosen to make $g = \frac{mf}{k}$ an integer, where g denotes the number of central modules assigned for each virtual path during every f time slots. For unifrom traffic, the connection pattern in the central modules is given by the *Latin Square* assignment shown in Table 1. In the table, each A_i, $0 \leq i \leq k-1$, represents

Table 1. Latin square assignment

	O_0	O_1	O_2	$\cdots$	O_{k-1}
I_0	A_0	A_1	A_2	$\cdots$	A_{k-1}
I_1	A_{k-1}	A_0	A_1	$\cdots$	A_{k-2}
$\vdots$	$\vdots$	$\vdots$	$\vdots$	$\ddots$	$\vdots$
I_{k-1}	A_1	A_2	A_3	$\cdots$	A_0

a set of g distinct central modules ranging from 0 to $fm-1$, i.e.

$$\begin{cases} A_0 &= \{0,\ 1,\ \cdots,\ g-1\}; \\ A_1 &= \{g,\ g+1,\ \cdots,\ 2g-1\}; \\ & \vdots \\ A_{k-1} &= \{(k-1)g,\ (k-1)g+1,\ \cdots,\ kg-1\}. \end{cases}$$

The assignment a can be translated to a pair (t, s) by

$$a = s \times f + t,$$

where s and t are the quotient and the remainder when a is divided by f, which means that central module s will connect input module i to output module j in the tth slot of every frame.

B. Fanout distribution and middle-stage traffic load

In order to characterize the effect of multicast traffic, we consider three fanout distributions to make comparisons. Let Y be the random variable of the fanout number, and M be its maximum.

1. *Constant distribution*

   $$\Pr\{Y = M\} = 1.$$

   Mean $E[Y] = M$, and variance $Var[Y] = 0$.

2. *Uniform distribution*
   Suppose the requested fanout is uniformly distributed from 1 to M. In other words,

   $$\Pr\{Y = y\} = 1/M, \qquad 1 \leq y \leq M.$$

   Thus $E[Y] = \frac{M+1}{2}$ and $Var[Y] = \frac{M(M+1)}{6}$.

3. *Truncated geometric distribution*

   $$\Pr\{Y = y\} = \frac{(1-q)q^{y-1}}{1-q^M}, \qquad 1 \leq y \leq M.$$

   The mean is given by

   $$E[Y] = \frac{1}{1-q} - \frac{Mq^M}{1-q^M}.$$

   This distribution is often used in the literature for modeling the fanout distribution [8, 6]. By fixing M equal to the switch size $N = 1024$, the parameter q can be calculated for a given mean fanout $E[Y]$.

Multicast traffic load at the input stage is different from that at the output stage because multicast cells are replicated inside the switch. Let ρ_{in} and ρ_{out} denote the traffic load of each *input* link at the *input* stage and the traffic load of each *output* link at the *output* stage respectively. Then, the ratio of these two quantities is given by

$$\frac{\rho_{out}}{\rho_{in}} = E[Y],$$

which is the mean cell fanout number.

We also define the middle-stage traffic load ρ_{mid}, such that ρ_{mid}/ρ_{in} is equal to the ratio of the amount of traffic in the *middle stage* to that in the *input stage*. It can be viewed as a reference load of the switch, which reflects some difference between the two schemes. In table 2, we provide some numerical figures

Table 2. The middle-stage traffic load in multicast cross-path switches for different fanout distributions

Module Size	Multicast Scheme	Fanout Distribution	Mean Fanout $E[Y] = 2$	$E[Y] = 4$	$E[Y] = 8$
n=16	S1	Geometric	0.9855	0.9578	0.9064
		Uniform	0.9902	0.9712	0.9345
		Constant	0.9927	0.9782	0.9501
n=16	S2	G/U/C	1		
n=32	S1	G	0.9706	0.9165	0.8242
		U	0.9800	0.9416	0.8712
		C	0.9849	0.9554	0.9000
n=32	S2	G/U/C	1		
n=64	S1	G	0.9419	0.8438	0.6978
		U	0.9596	0.8857	0.7620
		C	0.9692	0.9113	0.8087
n=64	S2	G/U/C	1		

S1 - replicating cells at both input and output stages
S2 - replicating cells at input stage only

of ρ_{mid} by fixing $\rho_{out} = 1$. Details of the calculation procedure are given in Appendix A.

C. Throughput

Since output queueing implemented in output modules ensures 100%-throughput at the last stage, the throughput of the whole switch is limited only by the head-of-line blocking in input modules with look-ahead selection. In this subsection, we will only focus on the throughput at the input stage.

In a cross-path switch, the throughput of an input module is mainly characterized by the window size w of the input queues and the group size m/k. The window size in look-ahead selection is defined to be the number of packets waiting at each input queue that will be checked in one time slot, and it is limited by the module size n and the processing speed. For multicast cells, the window size is defined to be the number of copies instead of cells. On the other hand, the group size represents the maximum number of packets that can be delivered to an output port in one time slot. For an $n \times m$ input module in cross-path switch, the real destination of a packet is one of the k *output* modules, thus the average group size is m/k. The window size is used to release the head-of-line blocking, while the group size can be regarded as the output capacity provided by each destination. Increasing either of them will certainly result better throughput, but there is a trade-off. The processing speed limits the product of the window size w and the module size n, thus a smaller n is desirable. On the contrary, when n is larger, the statistical multiplexing gain is higher. We choose the median size $n = 32$ in this paper.

We itemize the factors affecting the throughput as follows.

1. *The expansion factor m/n*
   In a cross-path switch, the ratio m/n is called the expansion factor [9]. One can think that it is the average capacity per input link. As shown in Fig. 3, the throughput is increasing with the expansion factor. Nearly 100%-throughput can be achieved by a sufficiently large expansion factor. The saturation speed is relatively faster in scheme 1 or with a larger mean fanout.

2. *The mean fanout $E[Y]$*
   To see the multicast effect, we first focus on the first moment of multicast traffic, i.e. the mean fanout. The throughput versus $E[Y]$ is plotted in Fig. 4. It can be observed that the throughput is higher when the mean fanout is larger. The reason is that the copies from the same packet have distinct destinations, thus the output contention at the head-of-line is reduced, compared with the case of having the same total number of unicast cells waiting. In conclusion, the look-ahead throughput performance is more favoured to multicast traffic.

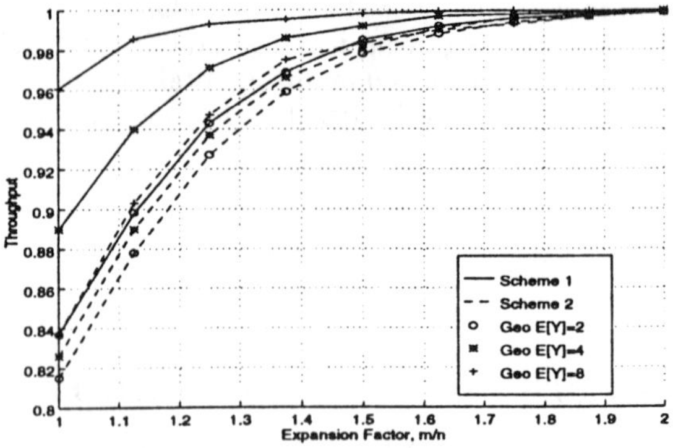

Fig. 3. Throughput increase with expansion factor m/n

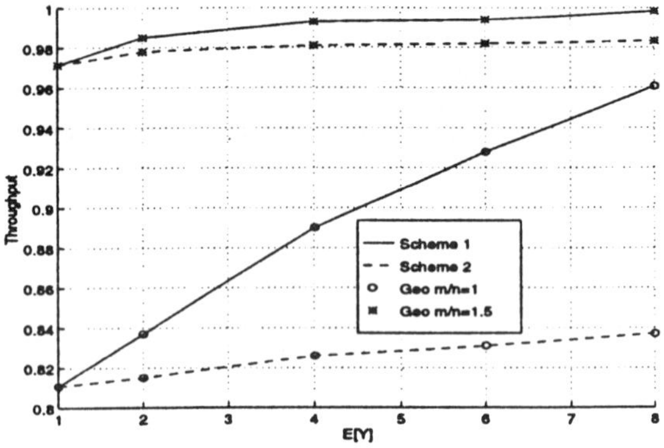

Fig. 4. Throughput increase with mean fanout number E[Y]

3. *The fanout distribution*
   Even with the same mean fanout number, the throughput still varies for different fanout distributions as shown in Fig. 5 and 6. The throughput discrepancy is larger in scheme 1 because the middle-stage traffic load ρ_{mid} is different for different fanout distributions, as shown in Table 2. The larger the ρ_{mid}, the more congested the switch and the smaller the throughput. It helps to explain why the highest throughput is attained when the cell fanout is geometrically distributed.

   Conversely, the throughput discrepancy in scheme 2 is smaller because the middle-stage traffic load ρ_{mid} is the same as ρ_{out} for all fanout distributions. However, since the geometric fanout distribution has the largest variance, its performance is the worst. This is similar to other switching systems that the performance is probably better in handling traffic with less fluctuations.

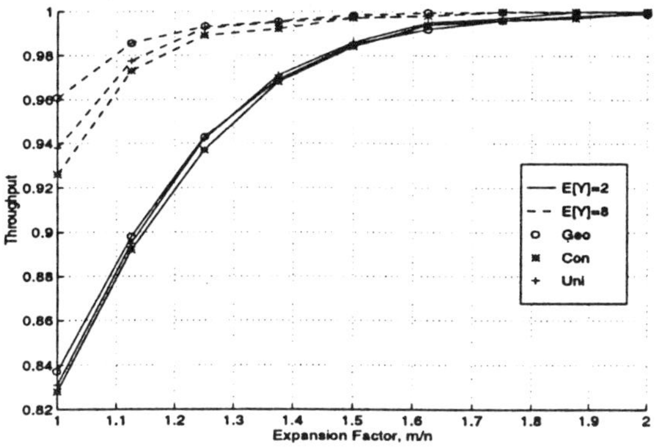

Fig. 5. Throughput varying with fanout distribution in scheme 1

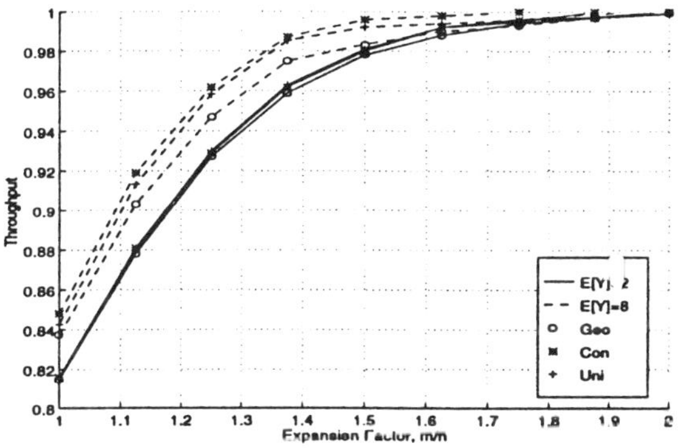

Fig. 6. Throughput varying with fanout distribution in scheme 2

D. Loss Probability

The overall loss probability of the switch can be well approximated by the knockout loss at the output stage, provided that the buffer size of each input link is sufficiently large and thus the cell loss at the input stage is negligible.

Consider an output module of size $m \times n$. Since the cells of the m input links may come from different input modules and the pattern is varying from time to time, we need to simulate all k input modules and totally $N = 1024$ links in order to obtain the loss probability. However, we devise a procedure in order to obtain this value more easily. Since there is no buffering at the input links of the output modules, the time correlation between the arrival process of the input links is not necessary to be taken into consideration. Although we still need the simulation data to capture the "space" correlation among the active neighbouring input links connected from the same input module in order to calculate the loss probability, it is sufficient to simulate only one input module and collect the statistics of the packets delivered to the specific output module. The procedure is presented in Appendix B and the numerical results are presented below.

1. *The group size G*
   First, we demonstrate the function of group size G in output modules in Fig. 7 and Fig. 8. The group size G is defined to be the number of packet-copies that can be delivered to each output port during one time slot. The larger the group size, the smaller the loss probability but the higher the complexity. Arbitrarily small loss probability can be achieved by a sufficiently large G. In addition, the discrepancy in the loss probability is not so significant with different parameters such as the number of central modules m and the mean fanout number $E[Y]$. In other words, it is mainly characterized by the group size G.

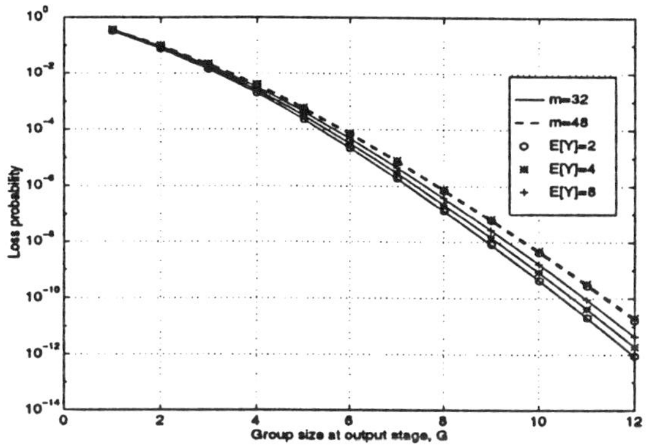

Fig. 7. Loss probability decrease with group size G in scheme 1

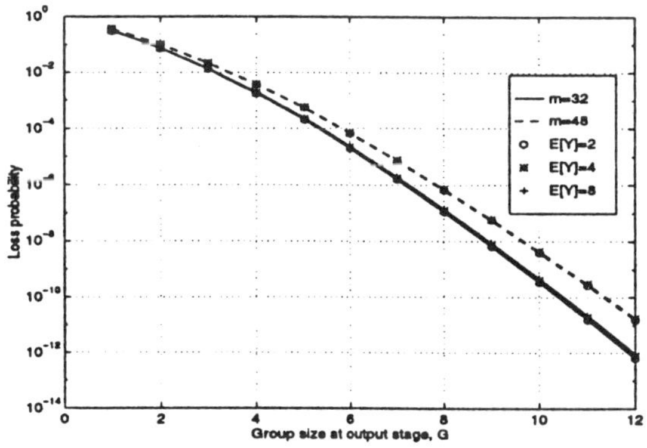

Fig. 8. Loss probability decrease with group size G in scheme 2

2. *The expansion factor*
   As shown in Fig. 9, the loss probability is also

varying with the expansion factor m/n. When the number of central modules is large, the number of active packets allowed to be simultaneously delivered to an output module tends to be more uniformly distributed, and thus a higher loss probability is expected.

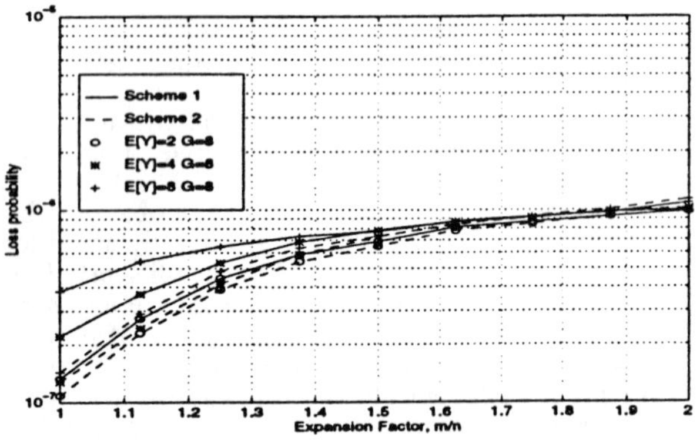

Fig. 9. Loss probability increase with expansion factor m/n

3. *The mean fanout number*
The effect of multicast traffic on the loss probability is not so significant. As shown in Fig. 10 with fixed group size $G = 8$, the expansion factor m/n dominates the trend of the loss probability. It changes only a little when the mean fanout number $E[Y]$ increases, except that if the expansion factor is small ($m/n = 1$) in scheme 1 due to the dramatic increase in throughput. Please refer to Fig. 4.

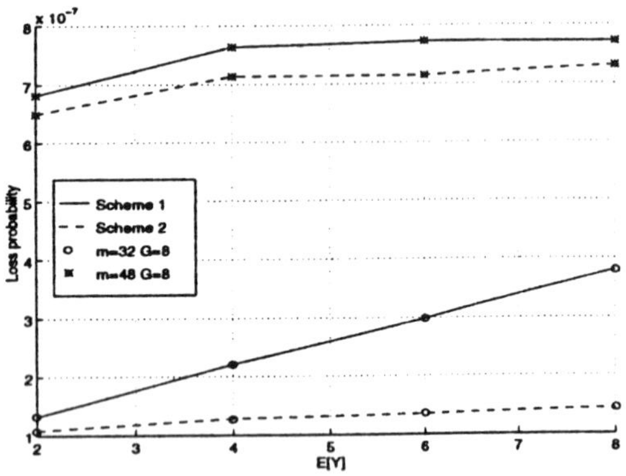

Fig. 10. The little change of loss probability with mean fanout E[Y]

IV. Overall Complexity Measurements and Comparisons

We have considered feasible designs for each multicast schemes to implement the multicast cross-path switch. In this section, we will estimate their complexity in terms of the number of switching nodes used, under certain performance requirement.

The input modules and the central modules in both schemes will be the same. Since the central modules are required to be rearrangeably nonblocking only, so that every connection pattern of the route assignment can be realized, Benes networks are suitable and sufficient. Its complexity is given by

$$C_{cm} = k(\log_2 k - \frac{1}{2}),$$

where k is the size of a central module, i.e. the number of input modules. Then the complexity of the middle stage consisting m central modules is

$$C_{mid} = mk(\log_2 k - \frac{1}{2}).$$

Since cell replications are necessary at the input stage, a copy network [8] cascaded with a point-to-point switch is sufficient. The copy network is estimated as two banyan interconnection fabrics, each with complexity $C_{cn} = \frac{m}{2}\log_2 m$, while the point-to-point switch consists of a Batcher-banyan and its complexity is given by

$$C_{pp} = \frac{m}{4}\log_2 m(\log_2 m + 1) + \frac{m}{2}\log_2 m.$$

Then the overall complexity of the input stage is $C_{in} = k(C_{cn} + C_{pp})$.

At the last stage, two different switches are used. For scheme 1 where cell replications are still needed in the output modules, a knockout switch [16, 3] with broadcast buses can be used. Since each concentrator with group size G has the complexity

$$m+(m-1)+(m-2)+\cdots+(m-G) = mG-\frac{G(G+1)}{2},$$

we need $C_{knock} = n[mG-G(G+1)/2]$ switching nodes to build up one knockout switch and totally $C_{out1} = kC_{knock}$ for the whole output stage [16]. For scheme 2, a Batcher-banyan [5] switch with channel grouping can be used in the output module. This switch consists an $m\times m$ Batcher-sorting network, an $m\times m$ concentrator and G parallel banyan networks. The total complexity of the output stage for scheme 2 is given by

$$C_{out2} = k\cdot\left[\frac{m}{4}\log_2 m(\log_2 m + 1) + \frac{m}{2}\log_2 m + G\cdot\frac{n}{2}\log_2 n\right].$$

The complexity measures of the switch architectures are shown in Fig. 11 and Fig. 12 respectively. The trade-off between performance and complexity of scheme 2 is superior to scheme 1 because of the huge complexity in establishing the broadcast knockout switches.

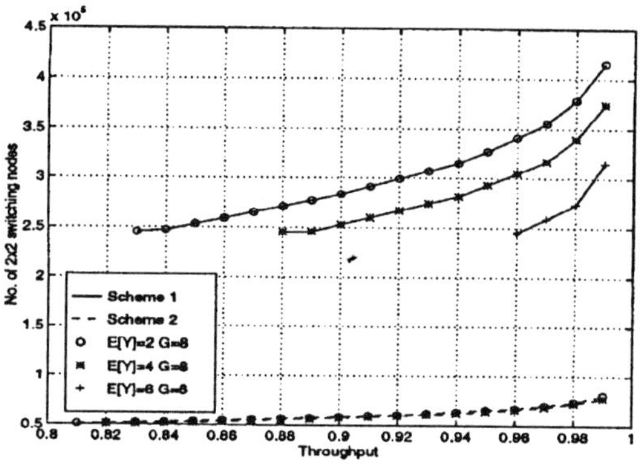

Fig. 11. The complexity comparison between two multicast schemes for different throughput requirement

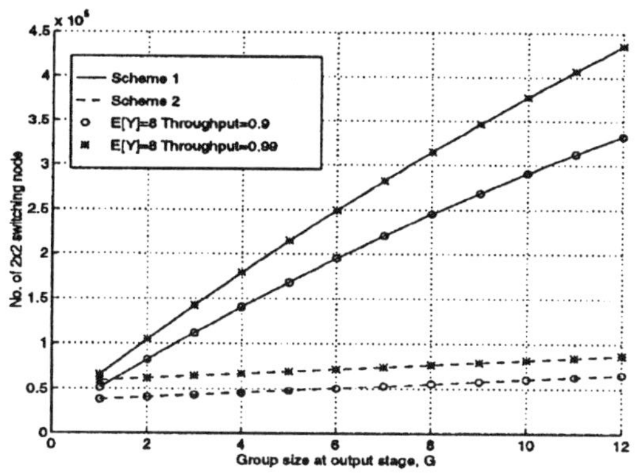

Fig. 12. The complexity comparison between two multicast schemes for different order of loss probability requirement

V. Conclusions

In this paper, we have studied the performance of multicast cross-path switches. We found that the throughput increases as the mean fanout becomes higher. In contrast, the loss probability is mainly determined by the group size of the output modules and is not sensitive to the fanout distribution of multicast traffic. We also presented the complexity comparison between two feasible implementation of the multicast schemes. The results show that, when the mean fanout of the system is not large compared with the switch size, the second scheme has a lower complexity and it can still achieve the same throughput and loss rate requirement as the first scheme. Therefore, we concluded that it might not be worth implementing multicast switching at the output stage of the cross-path switch.

Appendix

A. Calculation of middle-stage traffic load

Let X be the number of copies of a packet that are replicated at input stage, which is also the number of distinct output modules that the packet is destined for. Then $\rho_{mid} = \rho_{in} \cdot E[X]$. For scheme 1, in which there is cell replication at both the input and the output stages, $E[X]$ varies for different fanout distributions. In order to evaluate $E[X]$, we first notice that the probability that a packet has no copy destined for a specific output module is given by

$$p_0 = \sum_{y=1}^{M} \frac{\binom{n}{0}\binom{N-n}{y}}{\binom{N}{y}} \cdot \Pr\{Y = y\}.$$

Then the average of the total number of copies of a packet replicated at the input stage is $k \cdot (1 - p_0) = E[X]$. For scheme 2 without replication in output modules, $E[X] = E[Y]$, thus $\rho_{mid} = \rho_{out}$.

B. Procedures of calculating loss probability

1. Consider all m input links of an output module. And let A be the random variable of the number of active links. In order to calculate the loss probability, we first need to obtain the probability distribution of A. Define $G_A(z) = \sum_{a=0}^{m} \Pr\{A = a\} \cdot z^a$ be the generating function. Suppose m_i of the m input links are connected from input module i, $0 \le i \le k-1$; $\sum_{i=0}^{k-1} m_i = m$. Similarly, we define A_i be the number of corresponding active links among the group of m_i links. Since the traffic from different modules is independent, it follows that

$$G_A(z) = \Pi_{i=0}^{k-1} G_{A_i}(z).$$

   Also since the traffic statistics from any input module is independent and identically distributed, we can obtain the probabilities $\Pr\{A_i = a\}$, $0 \le a \le m_i$, $\forall i$, by simulating only one input module and collecting the departure statistics. For example, we demonstrate the calculation of $G_A(z)$ for the case that $m = 36$ and $E[Y] = 2$. The frame size is equal to $f = 8$, and $g = \frac{mf}{k} = 9$, indicating that there are totally 9 links connected from an input module to an output module during 8 time slots. The statistics of the packet delivered from any input module to the specific output module is summaried in Table 3. The $m = 36$ input links of an output module can be partitioned into four groups, each has 9 links with statistics as given in Table 3. By convolution, the generating function of the probability distribution of the number of active packets arriving at an output module is given by

$$[G0(z)G1(z)G2(z)G3(z)G4(z)G5(z)G6(z)G7(z)]^4 .$$

2. Let Y_o be the random variable of the fanout number of a packet arriving at the output module.

Table 3. The statistics of the number of packets leaving from an input module for an output module

Time slot	C	Pr {x links are active}			The corresponding generating function
		$x = 0$	$x = 1$	$x = 2$	
0	2	0.1589	0.2474	0.5937	$G0(z) = 0.1589 + 0.2474z + 0.5937z^2$
1	1	0.2286	0.7714	-	$G1(z) = 0.2286 + 0.7714z$
2	1	0.2109	0.7891	-	$G2(z) = 0.2109 + 0.7891z$
3	1	0.1973	0.8027	-	$G3(z) = 0.1973 + 0.8027z$
4	1	0.1850	0.8150	-	$G4(z) = 0.1850 + 0.8150z$
5	1	0.1795	0.8205	-	$G5(z) = 0.1795 + 0.8205z$
6	1	0.1710	0.8290	-	$G6(z) = 0.1710 + 0.8290z$
7	1	0.1682	0.8318	-	$G7(z) = 0.1682 + 0.8318z$

C: Number of links connected to the specific output module

Consider a packet (at the input stage), the average number of the copies destined for the specific output module is obviously $E[Y]/k$, including the case that no copy of the packet is destined for the output module. Then

$$\frac{E[Y]}{k} = p_0 \cdot 0 + (1 - p_0) \cdot E[Y_o],$$

where p_0 is the probability that no copy of the packet is destined for the output module. Thus,

$$E[Y_o] = \frac{E[Y]}{k(1 - p_0)} = \frac{E[Y]}{E[X]}.$$

3. Consider the probability that one copy of a packet arriving at the output module is destined for a particular output port, which is simply $p = E[Y_o]/n$. In scheme 1, this probability is independent from link to link, because no two packets arriving at the output module come from the same original cell. In scheme 2, since there may be the case that more than one packet simultaneously arriving at the output module is generated from the same original cell, this probability is dependently distributed over the links from the same input module. This dependence here is beneficial to having less loss because the copies generated from an original cell will not be destined for the same output port, resulting in less output port contention. We make the independence assumption in the following computation is therefore producing an upper bound for the loss probability of scheme 2. When k is sufficiently large or m/n is small, the bound is expected to be tight.

4. Consider a particular output port. Let L be the random variable that the number of packet-copies destined for the port in one time slot. Its generating function is given by

$$G_L(z) = \sum_{a=0}^{m} (1 - p + pz)^a \Pr\{A = a\},$$

where $p = E[Y_o]/n$ and $\Pr\{A = a\}$ is the probability that a of the m links are active. Thus

$$\Pr\{L = l\} = \sum_{a=l}^{m} \Pr\{A = a\} \cdot \binom{a}{l} (1 - p)^{a-l} p^l.$$

And the loss probability is

$$\frac{1}{p_{out}} \sum_{l=G+1}^{m} (l - G) \Pr\{L = l\},$$

where G is the group size of an output module.

References

[1] D. Bertsekas and R. Gallager, "Data Networks" 2nd ed., *Prentice-Hall International*, 1992.

[2] C. Clos, "A study of Non-blocking Switching Network", *Bell System Tech. J.*, vol. 32, pp. 406-424, 1953.

[3] K. Eng, M. Hluchyj, and Y. Yeh, "A Knockout Switch for Variable-Length Packets", *IEEE JSAC*, vol. 5, no. 9, Dec. 1987.

[4] K. Y. Eng, M. J. Karol, and Y. S. Yeh, "A Growable Packet (ATM) Switch Architecture: Design Principles and Applications", *Proc. Globecom '89*, pp. 32.2.1-32.2.7.

[5] A. Huang and S. Knauer, "Starlite: A Wideband Digital Switch", *Proc. Globecom '84*, pp. 121-125.

[6] Joseph Y. Hui and Thomas Renner, "Queueing Analysis for Multicast Packet Switching", *IEEE Trans. Commun.*, vol. 42, no. 2/3/4, Feb./Mar./Apr. 1994, pp. 723-731.

[7] A. Kershenbaum, "Telecommunications Network Design Algorithm", *McGraw-Hill* 1993.

[8] Tony T. Lee, "Nonblocking Copy Networks for Multicast Packet Switching", *IEEE JSAC*, vol. 6, no. 9, pp. 1455-1467, Dec. 1988.

[9] Tony T. Lee and Cheuk H. Lam, "Path Switching - A Quasi-static Routing Scheme for Large-Scale ATM Packet Switches", to appear in *IEEE JSAC*.

[10] F. T. Leighton, "Introduction to Parallel Algorithms and Architectures: Arrays · Trees · Hypercubes", *Morgan Kaufmann* 1992.

[11] Daniel J. Marchok and Charles E. Rohrs, "First Stage Multicasting in a Growable Packet (ATM) Switch", *Proc. ICC '91*, pp. 1007-1013.

[12] R. J. McEliece, R. B. Ash and C. Ash, "Introduction to Discrete Mathematics", *McGraw-Hill*, 1989.

[13] K. J. Schrodi, B. Pfeiffer, J. M. Delmas and M. De Somer, "Multicast Handling in a Self-Routing Switch Architecture", *Proc. of ISS '92*, Yokohama 1992, pp. 156-160.

[14] J. S. Tuner, "Design of a Broadcast Packet Switching Network", *IEEE Trans. Commun.*, vol. 36, no. 6, June 1988, pp. 734-743.

[15] R. J. Wilson, "Introduction to Graph Theory", *Academic Press, New York*, 1972.

[16] Y. S. Yeh, M. G. Hluchyj, and A. S. Acampora, "The Knockout switch: A simple, modular architecture for high-performance packet switching", *IEEE JSAC*, vol. 5, pp. 1274-1283, Oct. 1987.

PSD-based Neural-net Connection Admission Control

Chung-Ju Chang, Song-Yaor Lin, Ray-Guang Cheng, AND Yow-Ren Shiue

Department of Communication Engineering
Center for Telecommunications Research
National Chiao Tung University
Hsinchu, TAIWAN 300
Republic of China
cjchang@cc.nctu.edu.tw

Abstract

ATM (asynchronous transfer mode) systems can support services with bursty traffic. An ATM system needs a sophisticated and real-time connection admission controller not only to guarantee the required quality-of-service (QoS) for existing calls but also to raise the system efficiency. Input process has a power-spectral-density (PSD) which explicitly contains the correlation behavior of input traffic and has a great impact on the system performance. Also, a neural network has been widely applied to deal with traffic control related problems in ATM systems because of its self-learning capability. In this paper, we propose a PSD-based neural-net connection admission control (PNCAC) method for an ATM system. Under the QoS constraint, we construct a decision hyperplane of the connection admission control according to parameters of the power spectrum. We further adopt the learning/adapting capabilities of the neural network to adjust the optimum location of the boundary between these two decision spaces. Simulation results show that the PNCAC method provides a superior system utilization over the conventional CAC schemes by an amount of 18%, while keeping the QoS contract.

I. Introduction

Due to the demand for all kinds of communication services such as video, voice, and data, high speed networks have increasingly received high attention. ATM (Asynchronous Transfer Mode) is considered to be the ground on which broadband integrated services digital network is built [1, 2]. The advantage of ATM systems is the flexibility of accommodating the diverse mixture of traffic which possess different traffic characteristics and service requirements. A set of traffic control functions must be provided by the ATM network to ensure QoS of each service and to raise efficiency of the system.

One of the most important traffic control function for an ATM system is connection admission control (CAC). CAC is defined as "the set of actions taken by the network at the call set-up phase in order to establish whether a VC/VP connection can be accepted" [3]. A new VC/VP connection is accepted only if sufficient network resources are available and the required performance can be maintained. However, an effective CAC strategy is still to attain high system utilization.

However, the bandwidth requirements for services are various in an ATM system. In order to enhance the system utilization as high as possible, the system should have information about traffic characteristics of current connected users. For this sake, traffic parameters which contain the anticipated traffic characteristics are provided by users. The traffic parameters should be convenient for users to specify and their conformity with load should be easy for the network provider to monitor.

Several CAC schemes for ATM networks have been proposed. The simplest scheme is the peak rate allocation. In this scheme, a new call will be accepted only if the sum of all existing calls' peak rates and the new call's peak rate does not exceed the system capacity. In the peak rate allocation, the quality of the service is always guaranteed because the aggregate bit rate will never exceed the system capacity. However, it leads to a low system utilization. Guérin et. al. [4, 5] proposed an equivalent capacity method to estimate the required bandwidth according to a desired QoS for individual or aggregate connections. Saito [6] proposed a CAC scheme to infer the upper bound of cell loss probability from the traffic parameters specified by users. However, the estimation error will be accumulated in these schemes. Gallassi et. al. [7] gave a simple bandwidth assignment policy by classifying all traffic sources. However, it would fail if there is a new traffic source not belonging to any predefined traffic class.

All above-mentioned studies mainly focus on time-domain analysis. Li [8, 9, 10, 11] has studied the queueing performance of an ATM network from the standpoint of frequency-domain of input traffic. The power-spectral-density (PSD) function in frequency domain, which is the Fourier transform of the auto-correlation function of the input process, can capture the correlation and the burstiness features of the in-

0-8186-7780-5/97 $10.00 © 1997 IEEE

put process in time domain. From their studies, it is known that the low-frequency band of input PSD has a dominant impact on queueing performance and the high-frequency band can be neglected to a large extent. This is because the low frequency component of PSD contains the correlation component. The more the low frequency component is, the burstier the traffic source will be. Also, the information of input traffic in frequency domain can be easily collected by using DSP chips in practice. The study on traffic control mechanisms for ATM networks from the standpoint of power spectrum of traffic would be a valuable alternative.

On the other hand, neural networks have been widely applied to deal with the traffic control problems for ATM systems [13, 14, 15, 16, 17]. The major feature of neural networks is the self-learning capability which can be utilized to characterize the relationship between the input traffic and the system performance. In [13], Hiramatsu proposed a CAC scheme using a neural network. This neural network connection admission controller used offered traffic characteristics, QoS requirement, and performance measures of actual network operation to decide whether to accept or reject a new call. The results showed that the neural network learned a complicated boundary for call acceptance decision. In [14], Tran-Gia and Gropp investigated different aspects concerning possible use of neural network to perform CAC. The numbers of active connections of each traffic class were selected as the inputs of the neural network for connection acceptance decision. Numerical results showed that the neural network approach had significant benefits. In [15], they proposed a call admission controller for ATM networks. A neural network is trained to compute the effective bandwidth required to support MPEG-1 VBR video calls with different QoS requirements. They showed that the adaptability of the neural network controller to new traffic situations had been achieved by adopting a hierarchical approach to the design. We proposed a neural fuzzy connection admission control (NFCAC) scheme and a neural network connection admission control (NNCAC) scheme for an ATM traffic controller in [16] and [17]. In [16], the NFCAC scheme combined the linguistic control capabilities of a fuzzy logic controller with the learning abilities of a neural network to automatically construct the rule structure and the membership functions by learning from training examples. In [17], the NNCAC scheme used three pre-processed input parameters to simplify the training process and to improve the controlled performance. Simulation results revealed that both NNCAC and NFCAC schemes had an improvement of system utilization by an amount of 20% improvement over Hiramatsu's neural network CAC scheme, 10% over the fuzzy-logic-based CAC [18], while maintaining QoS contracts.

In this paper, we propose a PSD-based neural-net connection admission control (PNCAC) method for an ATM system. A decision hyperplane of the connection admission control is constructed under the constraint of QoS, according to parameters of the power spectrum. The decision hyperplane splits the sample space

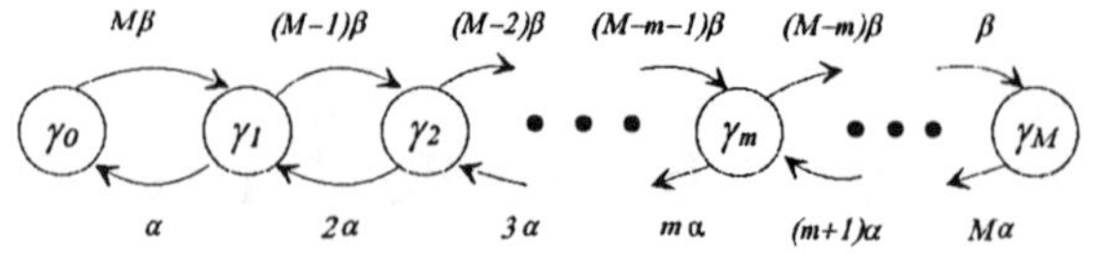

Figure 1: The (M+1)-state MMPP source model

into two — one is for "accept" and the other is for "reject." New originating call will be accepted only if it is located on the "accept" space. Otherwise, it will be rejected. We will adopt the learning/adapting capabilities of the neural network to adjust the optimum location of the boundary between these two decision spaces (i.e. use the back-propagation training algorithm to adjust the link weights of PNCAC to optimum values). Simulation results show that PNCAC has a superior system utilization over the conventional CAC scheme.

The rest of the paper is organized as follows. Section II describes the power spectrum of input processes and proposes a concept of "equivalent half-power bandwidth." In section III, we describe the system configuration and address how to design the proposed PNCAC. In section IV, we illustrate some simulation examples to justify the feasibility of PNCAC. Concluding remarks are presented in section V.

II. Power Spectrum of Input Process

We assume that any input rate process $a(t)$ can be modeled as an $(M+1)$-state MMPP. As shown in Fig. 1, MMPP can be represented as $(Q, \vec{\gamma})$, where Q is the state transition rate matrix and $\vec{\gamma} = [\gamma_0, \gamma_1, ..., \gamma_M]$ is the vector representing the mean arrival rate at each MMPP state. We denote the stationary probability vector of state by $\vec{\pi} = [\pi_0, \pi_1, ..., \pi_M]$ and obtain it by solving equation of $\vec{\pi}Q = 0$ and $\vec{\pi}\vec{e} = 1$, where $\vec{e}$ is an unit column vector. The average input rate $\bar{\gamma}$ is then given by

$$\bar{\gamma} = \sum_{i=0}^{M} \gamma_i \pi_i. \tag{1}$$

Q is diagonalizable; by spectral decomposition, Q can be represented as [8]

$$Q = \sum_{l=0}^{M} \lambda_l \vec{g}_l \vec{h}_l, \tag{2}$$

where λ_l is the l-th eigenvalue of Q, and $\vec{g}_l$ and $\vec{h}_l$ are the associated right column and left row column eigenvectors of Q with respect to λ_l, respectively.

The autocorrelation function of MMPP, defined as $R(\tau) = \overline{a(t)a(t+\tau)}$, and the corresponding PSD, denoted by $P(\omega)$, which is the Fourier transform of $R(\tau)$ are given by [8]

$$R(\tau) = \bar{\gamma}\delta(\tau)+\psi_0+\sum_{l=1}^{M}|\psi_l|e^{Re\{\lambda_l\}|\tau|}\cos(Im\{\lambda_l\}|\tau|+arg\{\psi_l\}) \tag{3}$$

and

$$P(\omega) = \bar{\gamma} + 2\pi\psi_0\delta(\omega) + \sum_{l=1}^{M} b_l(\omega), \tag{4}$$

where

$$\delta(\omega) = \begin{cases} \infty & \text{for } \omega = 0 \\ 0 & \text{elsewhere}, \end{cases} \tag{5}$$

where $Re\{\cdot\}$, $Im\{\cdot\}$, and $arg\{\cdot\}$ denote the the real part, imaginary part, and the phase of the argument, respectively; ψ_0 is the DC component, given by

$$\psi_0 = \bar{\gamma}^2; \tag{6}$$

and $b_l(\omega)$ is the bell-shaped function with respect to λ_l, given by

$$b_l(\omega) = \frac{-2\psi_l Re\{\lambda_l\}}{(Re\{\lambda_l\})^2 + (\omega - \omega_l)^2} \tag{7}$$

$$= \frac{\psi_l B_l}{(B_l/2)^2 + (\omega - \omega_l)^2}, \quad \text{for } \lambda_l \neq 0, \tag{8}$$

and

$$\frac{1}{2\pi}\int_{-\infty}^{+\infty} b_l(\omega)d\omega = \psi_l, \tag{9}$$

where ψ_l is the average power contributed by λ_l, given by

$$\psi_l = \sum_i \sum_j \pi_i \gamma_i \gamma_j g_{li} h_{lj} \quad \text{for } 1 \leq l \leq M, \tag{10}$$

and g_{li} and h_{lj} are the i-th and j-th entities of the vector $\vec{g}_l$ and $\vec{h}_l$, respectively, $B_l = -2Re\{\lambda_l\}$ is the half-power bandwidth, and $\omega_l = Im\{\lambda_l\}$ is the central frequency of the bell-shaped function $b_l(\omega)$.

From Eq. (4), it can be found that PSD is constituted by white noise $\bar{\gamma}$, DC component $2\pi\psi_0\delta(\omega)$, and a set of bell-shaped functions $b_l(\omega)$ described by the average power ψ_l, the half-power bandwidth B_l, and the central frequency w_l with respect to the l-th eigenvalue of Q. The white noise is contributed by Poisson local dynamics. From the result showed in [8, 9] that the influence of the white noise on system performance can be neglected. Hence, we do not consider the white noise component in the study. Also, from Eq. (8), we can see that the bell-shaped function $b_l(\omega)$ is located at the central frequency $\omega_l = Im\{\lambda_l\}$ and weighted by the average power ψ_l. The half-power bandwidth $B_l = -2Re\{\lambda_l\}$ determines the shape of $b_l(w)$. Since the eigenvalues of a birth-death MMPP are all real, the bell-shaped functions are zero-centered. An input PSD with a single bell-shaped function centered at zero frequency is shown in Fig. 2.

Therefore, a traffic source can be described by a PSD with power spectrum parameters of the DC component ($\bar{\gamma}$), the half-power bandwidth (B), and the average power (Ψ) of the bell-shaped function. The higher the $\bar{\gamma}$ is, the higher traffic load in the network will be; the smaller the B is, the more input power will be concentrated in the low-frequency band; and

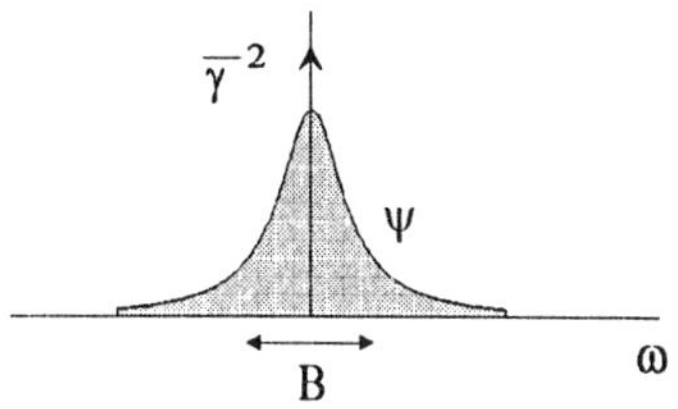

Figure 2: A zero-centered power spectrum.

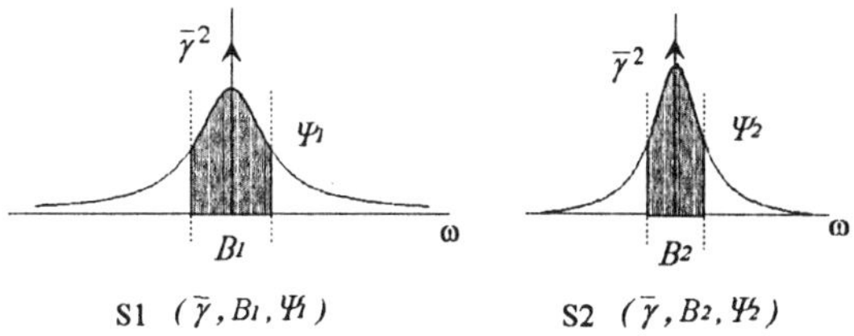

Figure 3: Two sources with the same QoS

the higher the Ψ is, the larger the input rate variance will be. The three power-spectrum parameters $(\bar{\gamma}, B, \Psi)$ of a traffic source plays important factors on the queueing performance. We once proposed a power-spectrum based table-lookup scheme for CAC using the three parameters $(\bar{\gamma}, B, \Psi)$. The method is rather effective has a disadvantage that the CAC table is infeasible implemented when the ATM system is large.

Assume that source $S1$ with power-spectrum parameters $(\bar{\gamma}, B_1, \Psi_1)$ and source $S2$ with $(\bar{\gamma}, B_2, \Psi_2)$, as shown in Fig. 3, have the same DC component and the same system performance. If $B_1 > B_2$ ($B_1 < B_2$), the fact that Ψ_1 must be larger (smaller) than Ψ_2 is obvious. This fact implies that given a source with power-spectrum parameters $(\bar{\gamma}, B, \Psi)$, an equivalent source that will have the same QoS can be found [12]. B_e and Ψ_e denote the equivalent half-power bandwidth and equivalent average power for the source $(\bar{\gamma}, B, \Psi)$. Without loss of possibility, if B_e is chosen to be fixed and less than B, the transformation from (B, Ψ) to (B_e, Ψ_e) can be regarded as a process of lowpass filtering. Refer to Fig. 4, if we choose a low pass filter with an appropriate cut-off frequency [19], we can get Ψ_e. Notice that the original source $(\bar{\gamma}, B, \Psi)$ will have the same system performance as the source $(\bar{\gamma}, B_e, \Psi_e)$. Ψ_e can be obtained by

$$\Psi_e = \frac{1}{2\pi}\int_{-\omega_c}^{+\omega_c} [P(\omega) - 2\pi\bar{\gamma}^2\delta(\omega) - \bar{\gamma}]d\omega. \tag{11}$$

Since we have fixed B_e, the power-spectrum parameters for a traffic source can be simplified from $(\bar{\gamma}, B, \Psi)$ to $(\bar{\gamma}, \Psi_e)$. The half-power bandwidths of all practical traffic sources generally fall in the range of 10^{-6} to 10^{-2} [12], therefore we choose $B_e = 10^{-6}$

III. PSD-based Neural-net Connection Admission Controller

Fig. 5 shows the functional block diagram of the PSD-based neural-net connection admission con-

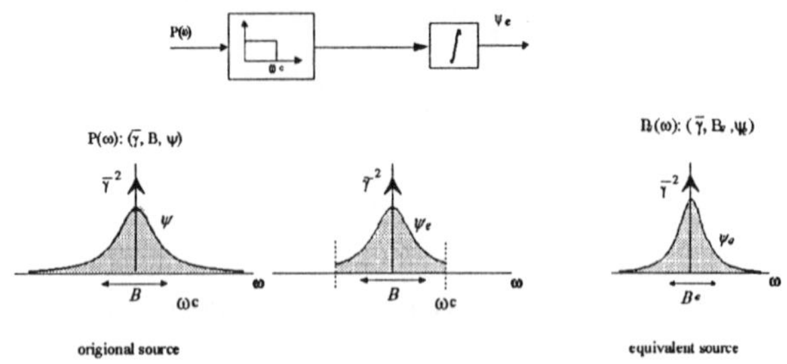

Figure 4: Low pass filtering to get the equivalent bell-shaped function

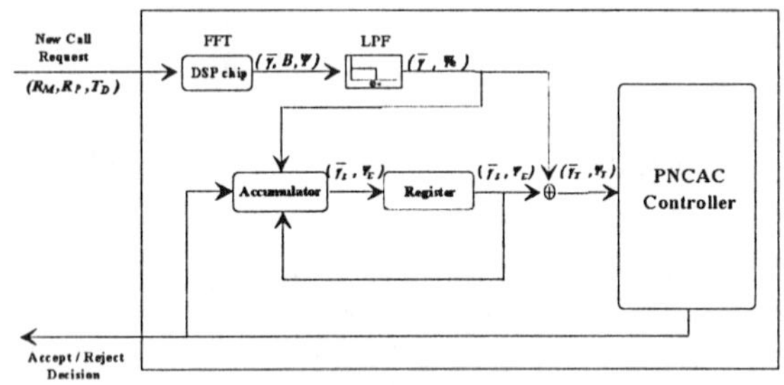

Figure 5: The functional block diagram of the PSD-based neural-net connection admission controller

troller. It mainly contains a PNCAC controller, a DSP chip, a lowpass filter, a register, and an accumulator. As a user wants to make a new call, it would provide traffic parameters such as peak cell rate (R_P), mean cell rate (R_M), and peak cell rate duration (T_D) in the call-request packet. The three input traffic parameters (R_P,R_M,T_D) are transformed into a corresponding PSD with power-spectrum parameters ($\bar{\gamma}, B, \Psi$) [11, 12] by the DSP chip. Through a process of lowpass filtering described in the previous section, the three power-spectrum parameters ($\bar{\gamma}, B, \Psi$) are transformed to ($\bar{\gamma}, \Psi_e$). The register records traffic parameters ($\bar{\gamma_E}, \Psi_E$) of total existing connections, where $\bar{\gamma_E}$ is the sum of the average input rates and Ψ_E is the the sum of the average powers, of the total connections. Since PSD has additive property [12]; two sets of parameters: ($\bar{\gamma}, \Psi_e$) of the new call and ($\bar{\gamma_E}, \Psi_E$) of the existing calls, can be added to form a new set of parameters ($\bar{\gamma_T}, \Psi_T$). This new set of parameters is fed into the PNCAC controller, and the PNCAC controller will decide whether to accept or reject this new call request using the neural-net control logic.

If the decision is to accept the new call, the accumulator sums ($\bar{\gamma}, \Psi_e$) of the new call to ($\bar{\gamma_E}, \Psi_E$) of the existing calls and restores the updated ($\bar{\gamma_E}, \Psi_E$) in the register. If the decision is to reject the new call, no accumulation and updating procedure is needed. Notice that the subtraction of the ($\bar{\gamma}, \Psi_e$) from ($\bar{\gamma_E}, \Psi_E$), when a call is disconnected, is needed but not shown here.

Fig. 5 shows a block diagram of an ATM network element. Input traffic to ATM network is classified into two types. Type-1 traffic such as voice and video

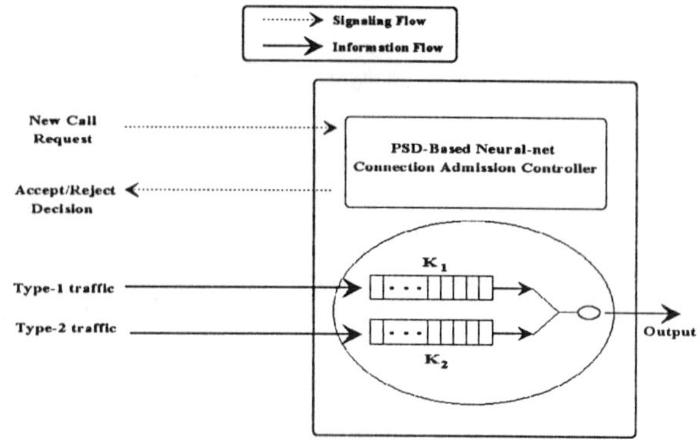

Figure 6: A block diagram of an ATM network element

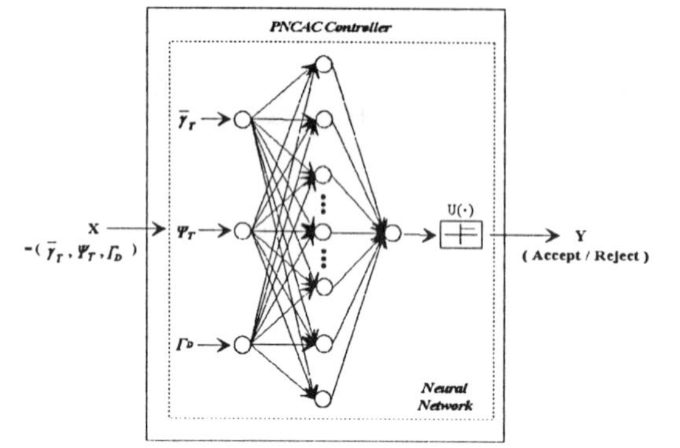

Figure 7: The basic structure of the PNCAC controller

is real-time, and type-2 traffic such as data is non-real-time. The type-1 traffic source is modeled by an MMPP, while type-2 traffic source is modeled by an independent Poisson process. As shown in Fig. 7, the PNCAC controller is designed as a three-layer feedforward neural network. The neural network possesses capabilities of approximation to a perfect connection acceptance decision function from input/output data pairs $\{X, Y\}$. In our feedforward PSD-based neural network **PNCAC**(X, W), X = ($\bar{\gamma_T}$, Ψ_T, Γ_D) represents an input vector, where $\bar{\gamma_T}$ denotes the total average input rate of type-1 traffic, Ψ_T denotes the total average power of type-1 traffic, and Γ_D denotes the total input rate of type-2 traffic, and W represents a set of weights updated by some learning rules; $Y = f(X)$ denotes the call acceptance decision function. From [20], it is known that **PNCAC**(X, W) can be trained to asymptotically approach $f(X)$ as much as possible. In other words, the CAC problem in the PNCAC controller can be treated as a pattern recognition problem: upon recognition of the input pattern X = ($\bar{\gamma_T}$, Ψ_T, Γ_D), an accept/reject connection request decision Y has to be made.

Based on the system model described above, we constructed a set of training data containing the performance measures of type-1 and type-2 traffic for different sets of $(\bar{\gamma}_T, \Psi_T, \Gamma_D)$. Note that the cell delay and cell delay variation in the QoS requirements can be restricted to a desired value if we have properly designed the buffer size and scheduling policy for this system. Thus, we only consider the performance measure of the cell loss ratio (CLR) in the collection of the training data. Denote $CLR1(\bar{\gamma}_T, \Psi_T, \Gamma_D)$ and $CLR2(\bar{\gamma}_T, \Psi_T, \Gamma_D)$ as the type-1 and type-2 traffic CLRs, respectively, for sources with traffic parameters $(\bar{\gamma}_T, \Psi_T, \Gamma_D)$. The procedure for constructing the set of training data is described below:

Step 1 Initialize the values of $(\bar{\gamma}_T, \Psi_T, \Gamma_D)$

Step 2 Set the desired range of $(\bar{\gamma}_T, \Psi_T, \Gamma_D)$

Step 3 Set the desired increments of type-1 traffic load $\Delta\bar{\gamma}_T$, the equivalent average power $\Delta\Psi_T$, and type-2 traffic load $\Delta\Gamma_D$,

Step 4 Generating a set of training data

```
For γ̄ within the desired range of type-2
traffic load
  For Ψ_T within the desired range of type-1
  traffic load
    For Γ_D within the desired range of the
    equivalent average power
      Obtain CLR1(γ̄_T, Ψ_T, Γ_D) and
      CLR2(γ̄_T, Ψ_T, Γ_D)
      If both CLR1 and CLR2 satisfy the
      QoS contract
      Then
        Set the call as an accepted one
      Else
        Set the call as a rejected one
      Increase Γ_D by ΔΓ_D
    EndFor
    Increase Ψ_T by ΔΨ_T
  EndFor
  Increase γ̄_T by Δγ̄_T
EndFor
```

Based on the procedure described above, a set of training data is obtained. One should note that the accuracy of decision made by the PNCAC controller is depended on the granularity of the desired increments used in the procedure. The training data was here selected such that a wide spectrum of traffic with different characteristics could be learned by the neural network. A back-propagation learning algorithm [21] is used to train a neural network for solving such a CAC problem. Let X_i denote the input of the PNCAC controller randomly sampled at time instant t_i, let $\mathrm{PNCAC}(X_i, W) = \hat{Y}_i$ denote the respective output, and let $f(X_i) = Y_i$ denote the desired output. The objective of the back-propagation learning algorithm is to minimize a decision error E by recursively adjusting its weight in each layer, where E is defined as

$$\begin{aligned} E &= \frac{1}{2}||PNCAC(X_i, W) - f(X_i)||^2 \\ &= \frac{1}{2}(\hat{Y}_i - Y_i)^2. \end{aligned} \quad (12)$$

In the three-layer feedforward neural network for the PNCAC controller, each layer has a number of processing elements called neurons which are fully interconnected via adaptive weights. In the learning phase, the PNCAC controller is trained to approximate the accurate decision function (or equivalently, to obtain a set of optimum weight W^*) from training data via back-propagation learning algorithm. It is trained to capture characteristics of any possible combinations of the power spectrum parameters and their resulted QoS. The input/output mapping function learned by the PNCAC controller is accordingly used as the call acceptance decision function. Through many learning trials, the PNCAC controller implicitly learns the call acceptance decision function.

IV. Simulation Results

In this section we illustrate some simulation examples to justify the feasibility of the proposed PNCAC method. The block diagram of an ATM network element has been shown in Fig. 6. This ATM network element may be an ATM multiplexer, or an ATM hub, etc. The users' information are transported through the network element. Before a new user begins its information transfer, a call establishment procedure must be performed. In the call establishment procedure, a new call request is issued through a signalling channel to the PNCAC controller. The accept or reject decision will be delivered by the PNCAC controller to the user and the call establishment procedure is completed.

All the input messages are segmented into fixed-length ATM cells. The service time for each ATM cell is constant and equal to a slot time. Here, we use two separate buffers, one for type-1 traffic and the other for type-2 traffic with buffer sizes K1 and K2, respectively. One buffer space can accommodate one ATM cell. The cells stay in the user buffer and wait for transmission. When the buffer is full, new coming cells are then blocked and lost.

In the simulations, the buffer sizes K1 and K2 are all taken to be 100 cells; the link capacity is assumed to be 150 Mbps. Because of the different QoS requirement for these two types of traffic, the cell loss probability is set to be 10^{-5} for type-1 traffic and 10^{-6} for type-2 traffic. The voice source is modeled by a two-state on-off Markov chain; the video source is modeled by a modified Markov process addressed in [12]; and the data source is modeled by Poisson process. The numbers of video interframe and intraframe are assumed to have five states. The traffic parameters for voice and video sources are shown in Table 1, and the mean rate for data source is 1M bps. The mean holding time of voice and video are assumed to be exponentially distributed. The call arrival processes are assumed to be independently Poisson distributed.

We consider several simulation examples that a system accepts only video calls and a system accepts voice, video and data calls. In order to reveal the effectiveness of this PNCAC method, we compare the results with the system adopting the scheme of equivalent capacity proposed by Guérin et al. [4].

Traffic Parameters	Peak Rate	Mean Rate	Peak Rate Duration
Voice	64 kbps	27.6 kbps	1.366 sec
Video	5.7 Mbps	1.9 Mbps	0.033 sec

Table 1: Traffic source parameters

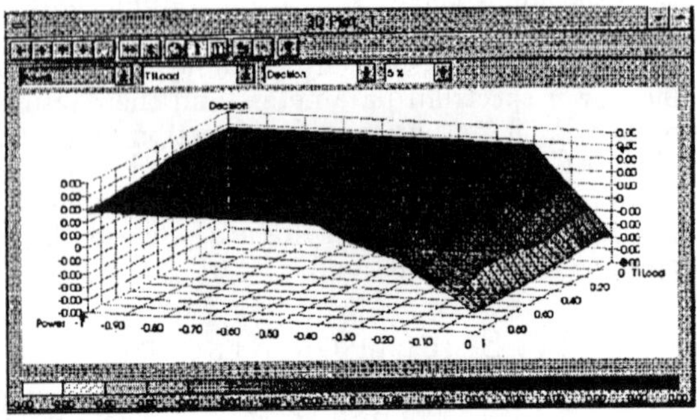

Figure 8: The decision hyperplane constructed by using the PNCAC method.

For the simulation example of the system that accepts only video calls, the call arrival rate is assumed to be 0.2 calls/sec and the mean holding time for a call is assumed to be 5 minutes. This is a system with load 0.83. The decision hyperplane constructed by the PNCAC controller via learning from training data is shown in Fig. 8. In Fig. 8, the labels 'Decision,' 'Power,' and 'T1Load' in the 3-D plot represent the decision of the PNCAC method y, the total power Ψ, and the type-1 traffic load $\bar{\gamma}$, respectively. We can find that a new call tends to be rejected when Ψ and $\bar{\gamma}$ increase. Fig. 9(a) shows the number of accepted video calls versus time. We find that the maximum number of accepted video calls can achieve 51 by using PNCAC method, while the maximum number of accepted video calls is only 33 by using equivalent capacity scheme. Fig. 9(b) shows the call blocking probability versus time. This figure reveals that our PNCAC method has less call blocking probability than equivalent capacity scheme. Fig. 9(c) shows the system utilization versus time. The result shows that the system utilization of our PNCAC method has an amount of 19% higher than that of the equivalent capacity scheme. The cell loss probabilities of type-1 traffic and type-2 traffic are zero for both PNCAC method and equivalent capacity method, which we do not show here. The QoS requirements of type-1 traffic and type-2 traffic are both satisfied for both methods. For a system that accepts voice, video and data calls, the call arrival rate for voice is 15.4 calls/sec with mean holding time 1 minutes, the call arrival rate for video is 0.082 calls/sec with mean holding time 5 minutes, and the call arrival rate for data is 3.2 calls/sec with mean holding time 20 seconds. The decision hyperplane constructed by the PNCAC method is shown in Fig. 10. Here, the hyperplane constructed under the condition that the data load $\Gamma_D = 0.5$ is shown as an example. One should mention that the hyperplane shown in Fig. 8 is the case with $\Gamma_D = 0$. Similarly, a new call tends

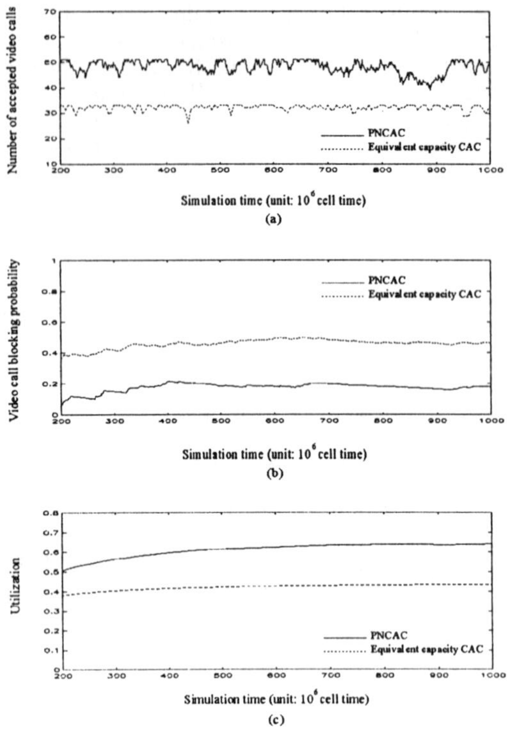

Figure 9: The simulation results of a system that accepts only video calls. (a) The number of accepted video calls versus time, (b) the video call blocking probability versus time, (c) the system utilization versus time.

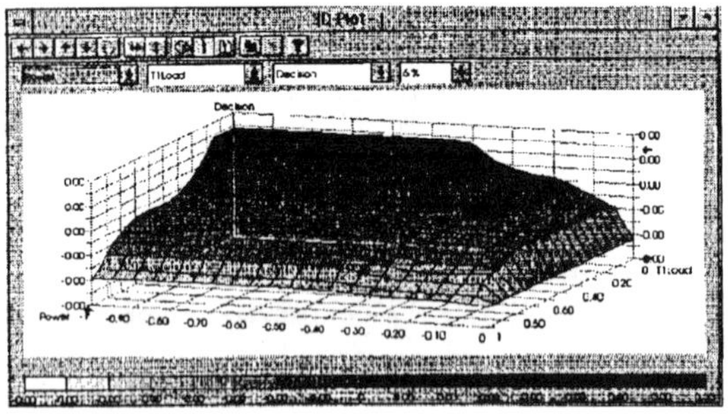

Figure 10: The decision hyperplane constructed by using the PNCAC method with data load=0.5

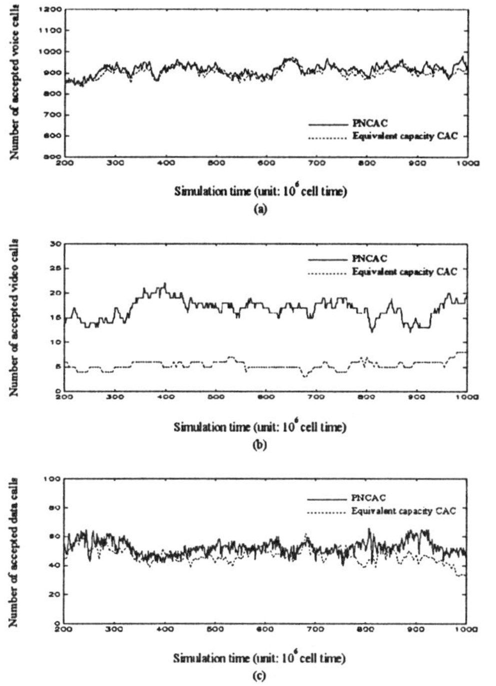

to be rejected when Ψ and $\bar{\gamma}$ increase. In Figs. 8 and 10, we further find that a new call tends to be rejected if Γ_D increases. From Fig. 11(a), we see that the number of accepted voice calls is similar for both methods. However, the PNCAC method can accommodate more video and data calls than the equivalent capacity scheme as shown in Fig. 11(b) and (c). From Fig. 11(d), (e) and (f), we also find the system using the PNCAC method has less voice call blocking probability, video call blocking probability, and data call blocking probability than the one using equivalent capacity method. From Fig. 11(i), we see that the PNCAC method can improve the system utilization by an amount of about 18% over the one using equivalent capacity scheme. The cell loss probabilities of type-1 traffic and type-2 traffic are zero for both PNCAC method and equivalent capacity method, which we do not show here. The QoS requirements of type-1 traffic and type-2 traffic are both satisfied for both methods.

V. Concluding Remarks

In this paper, we propose a PSD-based neural-net connection admission control (PNCAC) method for an ATM system. According to power-spectrum parameters of the input process, a decision hyperplane of the connection admission control is constructed under the constraint of QoS. We further adopt the learning/adapting capabilities of the neural network to adjust the optimum location of the boundary between these two decision spaces. Simulation results show that the proposed PSD-based neural-net connection admission controller highly improves the system utilization while maintaining QoS contract over the conventional equivalent capacity scheme. The PNCAC method is a promising approach to design a simple and

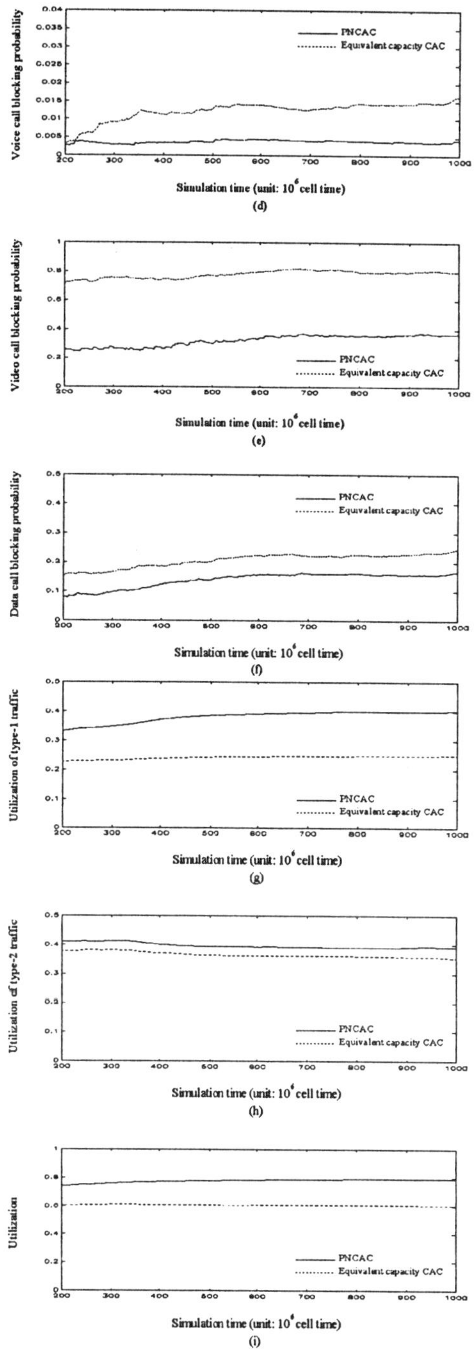

Figure 11: The simulation results of a system that accepts voice, video, and data calls. (a) The number of accepted voice calls versus time, (b) the number of accepted video calls versus time, (c) the number of accepted data calls versus time, (d) the voice call blocking probability versus time, (e) the video call blocking probability versus time, (f) the data call blocking probability versus time, (g) the utilization of type-1 traffic versus time, (h) the utilization of type-2 traffic versus time, (i) the overall system utilization versus time.

fast connection admission controller for ATM systems.

The designed PSD-based neural-net connection admission controller does not consider system performance parameters such as the queue-length, the change rate of queue-length, and the cell loss ratio, as we did in [16, 18]. It is believed that a PNCAC method adopting both power-spectrum parameters of input traffic and performance parameters of system would have much better performance.

References

[1] R. Händel, M. N. Huber and S. Schröder, "ATM networks: concepts, protocols, applications," Addison-Wesley, 1994.

[2] ITU-T: Recommendation I.121. "Broadband aspects of ISDN," Geneva, 1991.

[3] ITU-T: Recommendation I.371. "Traffic control and congestion control in B-ISDN," Geneva. 1993.

[4] R. Guérin, H. Ahmadi, and M. Naghshineh, "Equivalent capacity and its application to bandwidth allocation in high-speed networks," *IEEE J. Select. Areas Commun.*, Vol. 9, No. 7, pp. 968-981, Sep. 1991.

[5] R. Guérin and L. Gun, "A unified approach to bandwidth allocation and access control in fast packet switched networks," *IEEE INFOCOM '92*, pp. 1-12, 1992.

[6] H. Saito, "Call admission control in an ATM network using upper bound of cell loss probability," *IEEE Trans. Commun.*, Vol. 40, No. 9, pp. 1512-1521, Sep. 1992.

[7] G. Gallassi, G. Rigolio, and L. Fratta, "ATM: bandwidth assignment and bandwidth enforcement policies," *IEEE GLOBECOM '89*, pp.1788-1793, 1989.

[8] S. Q. Li and C. L. Hwang, "Queue response to input correlation functions: continuous spectral analysis," *IEEE/ACM Trans. Networking* , vol. 1, no. 6, pp. 678-692, Dec. 1993.

[9] ———, "Queue response to input correlation functions: discrete spectral analysis," *IEEE/ACM Trans. Networking* , vol. 1, no. 5, pp. 522-533. Oct. 1993.

[10] C. L. Hwang and S. Q. Li, "On input state space reduction and buffer noneffective region," *IEEE INFOCOM '94* , pp. 1018-1028, June 1994.

[11] S. Q. Li and C. L. Hwang, "Input modeling and link capacity allocation in high speed networks with monotone input power spectral functions," *IEEE/ACM Trans. Networking* , pp.1018-1028, Jan. 1993.

[12] C. J. Chang, H. M. Chi, and R. G. Cheng, "A power-spectrum based connection admission control for ATM networks," *IEEE ICC '96*, pp. 637-641, June 1996.

[13] A. Hiramatsu, "ATM communications network control by neural networks," *IEEE Trans. Neural Networks*, vol. 1, no. 1, pp. 122–130, Mar. 1990.

[14] P. Tran-Gia and O. Gropp, "Performance of a neural net used as admission controller in ATM systems," *IEEE GLOBECOM '92,* pp. 1303-1309, 1992.

[15] S. Y. Youssef, I. W. Habib, and T. N. Saadwi, "A neural network control for effective admission control in ATM networks," *IEEE ICC '96,* pp. 434–438, June 1996.

[16] R. G. Cheng, and C. J. Chang, "A neural-net based fuzzy admission controller for an ATM network," *IEEE INFOCOM '96* , pp. 777-784, Mar. 1996.

[17] R. G. Cheng, and C. J. Chang, "Neural network connection admission control for ATM networks," to be appeared in *IEE Proc. Commun.*

[18] ———, "Design of a fuzzy traffic controller for ATM networks," *IEEE/ACM Trans. Networking*, vol. 4, no. 3, pp. 1–11, June 1996.

[19] S. Chong, S. Q. Li, and J. Ghosh, "Predictive dynamic bandwidth allocation for efficient transport of real-time VBR video over ATM," *IEEE J. Select. Areas Commun.,* vol. 13, no. 1, pp. 12-23, Jan. 1995.

[20] M. E. Cotter, "The Stone-Weierstrass theorem and its application to neural nets," *IEEE Trans. Neural Networks,* vol. 1, pp. 290–295, 1990.

[21] D. E. Rumelhart, G. E. Hinton, and R. J. Williams, "Learning internal representation by error propagation," *Parallel Distributed Processing: Explorations in the Microstructure of Cognition,* Cambridge, MA: MIT Press, vol. 1, ch. 8, 1986.

Multi-class Connection Admission Control Policy for High Speed ATM Switches

G. Ramamurthy and Qiang Ren

NEC USA, Inc.
C&C Research Laboratories
4 Independence Way
Princeton, NJ 08540, USA

Abstract

Broadband networks based on ATM have to support multiple classes of services with widely different traffic characteristics and quality of services. In this paper, we propose and develop a multi-class connection admission control (CAC) policy that supports cell loss and delay requirements. In this model-based CAC, the source traffic is described in terms of the usage parameter control (UPC) parameters. Through careful analysis and approximations, we derive simple closed-form formulas to calculate the bandwidth required to meet guarantees on quality of service (QoS). While being robust, the CAC achieves a high level of resource utilization and can be easily implemented for real-time admission control.

1 Introduction

Broadband networks based on the asynchronous transfer mode (ATM) have to support multiple classes of services with widely different traffic characteristics and quality of service (QoS) requirements. To ensure the promised QoS can be met, users have to declare their traffic characteristics in terms of usage parameter control (UPC) parameters. The users must also declare their QoS expectations, which can be mapped to appropriate generic traffic classes supported by the switch. With the information provided by the users at connection setup time, the network uses the connection admission controller (CAC) to determine whether the new request for a connection should be accepted or rejected. The decision made by the CAC to accept a new connection is based on the availability of resources (bandwidth and buffers) to ensure the QoS requested by the new connection can be guaranteed, without degrading the the QoS of connections that have already been admitted. The resource requirements are computed by the CAC based on the declared UPC parameters and their QoS expectations.

The current ATM service architecture consists of the following five service classes: constant bit rate (CBR), real-time variable bit rate (rt-VBR), non-real-time variable bit rate (nrt-VBR), available bit rate (ABR) and unspecified bit rate (UBR). The QoS parameters of interest are

1) Peak-to-peak cell delay variation (CDV) and maximum cell transfer delay (CTD).

2) Cell loss ratio (CLR).

Generally, the above QoS requirements are guaranteed in a probabilistic sense.

The source traffic is characterized by the UPC descriptors $(\lambda_p, \lambda_s, B_s)$, i.e., peak cell rate (PCR) λ_p, sustainable cell rate (SCR) λ_s and the maximum burst size (MBS) B_s. The conformance of the source traffic to these UPC parameters can be achieved through shaping, using a dual leaky bucket at the source and a policing function at the network access [1].

The goal of the call admission control is to simultaneously achieve the twin objectives of

1) Maximizing the resource utilization.

2) Guaranteeing the promised QoS for all accepted connections.

Further, the CAC has to operate in real time and the computational burden must be consistent with the available processing capacity on the switch. Given the statistical nature of the offered traffic, the vague description of the traffic provided by the UPC parameters, the stringent requirements on QoS, and the need to maintain a reasonable level of resource utilization, it poses a significant challenge to the development of an efficient and yet robust CAC.

A number of connection admission control schemes using the UPC parameters have been proposed in the literature. The most trivial CAC is the one that admits new connections based on peak rate allocation alone. For bursty traffic this simple method can lead to significant under-utilization. On the other hand, due to

0-8186-7780-5/97 $10.00 © 1997 IEEE

bunching at the cell level, the peak cell rate allocation may not be sufficient for some CBR connections with stringent QoS requirements such as small cell delay variations [3]. A second approach uses a two-state Markovian model, and computes the probability of the instantaneous aggregate rate exceeding the available capacity [8]. If this probability is less than a target value, the connection is admitted. While this method is more efficient than the first one, it fails to take advantage of the buffers, leading to under-utilization. A number of algorithms have been developed that also include the buffers. They generally use the concept of effective bandwidth [6, 8]. The effective bandwidth method is reasonably accurate and efficient when the number of sources being multiplexed is small. However, when the number of multiplexed sources become large, it fails to take advantage of the benefits of statistical multiplexing. Further, in the UPC descriptors $(\lambda_p, \lambda_s, B_s)$, B_s represents the maximum burst size that can be transmitted at the peak rate λ_p. However, many of the models based on equivalent bandwidth take B_s as the average burst size as in [8]. These two factors lead to conservative estimates of the equivalent bandwidth, resulting in reduced efficiency. Recently, Elwalid, Mitra and Wentworth [7] developed new models to calculate effective bandwidth for UPC-based traffic sources and obtained some simple solutions. However, to take statistical multiplexing gain into these models, one still has to deal with a root-finding problem.

In this paper, we develop a multi-class connection admission control scheme for high-speed ATM switches. The source traffic is characterized by the UPC parameters $(\lambda_p, \lambda_s, B_s)$. This traffic descriptor along with its QoS requirement is provided by the sources to the CAC in the switch when connection or disconnection requests are made. The CAC supports the traffic classes and their QoS guarantees in the following table:

Class	QoS
CBR	Cell Delay Variation (CDV) Cell Loss Ratio (CLR)
Real time VBR (rt-VBR)	Cell Delay Variation (CDV) Cell Loss Ratio (CLR)
Non-real time VBR (nrt-VBR)	Cell Loss Ratio (CLR)
ABR	Guaranteed MCR

We emphasize that the main advantages of the CAC developed here are its high link efficiency and low computational overhead that makes it practical for real-time admission control. Through careful analysis and approximations, we derive closed form solutions with simple formulas to calculate the required bandwidth. The information needed by the CAC is minimal and is updated incrementally when a call connection or disconnection is made. These attributes greatly reduce the processing and memory burdens imposed on the switch, and therefore make it easy to be implemented. In this paper we also address the practical aspects of implementing a multi-class CAC on high speed ATM switches.

The paper is organized as follows. In section 2, we introduce the basic principle behind the CAC. We also present the basic switch architecture for which this CAC is applicable. In section 3, we present the modeling, analysis and computation procedures of our CAC for CBR, VBR and ABR classes. In section 4, simulation results are presented to evaluate the performance of the CAC. Finally we summarize and conclude our work in section 5.

2 Basic Principle of CAC

We assume that the resources to be managed are bandwidth and buffers. For purposes of illustration we assume an $M \times M$ input/output buffered switch as depicted in figure 1. The theory developed in this paper can be easily extended to other switch architectures.

The CAC developed in this paper uses a model-based approach to admit new calls. Based on the UPC parameters declared by a new connection request, the declared UPC parameters are mapped to an appropriate source traffic model. Calls that have already been accepted are also mapped into appropriate source traffic models, based on their declared UPC parameters. Using queueing theoretic approach, the CAC then determines the required capacity or bandwidth to ensure the QoS objectives are met for the class.

We assume that C_k $(k = 1, 2, \cdots, K)$ is the bandwidth logically allocated to existing connections of class k. There is a free pool of bandwidth C_f $(0 \leq C_f \leq C_{link})$, where C_{link} is the link bandwidth and

$$C_f = C_{link} - \sum_{k=1}^{K} C_k.$$

Each time a new class k connection request arrives, the CAC identifies the class of service, and determines the amount of additional bandwidth that must be allocated to the class in question (i.e., class k) if this new connection is to be accepted with guaranteed QoS. The connection is accepted if this additional bandwidth is available in the free pool, and the total bandwidth allocated to the given class k does not exceed the limit C_k^{max} set by the network management system (NMS). Otherwise, the connection is rejected. If the connection is accepted, the bandwidth available in the free pool is reduced accordingly. When a connection is disconnected, the bandwidth allocated to the the class to which the connection in question is associated, is decremented by an appropriate amount, and the bandwidth is returned to the free pool. Figure 2 shows a flow diagram of the CAC for admission and tearing down of calls. Note that the CAC only performs a logical allocation of bandwidth, and there is no strict partitioning or reservation of bandwidth. Thus, at the cell level, at any given instant, if a certain class of traffic does not make use of its allocated bandwidth, the unused bandwidth can be used by other classes.

3 Multi-class CAC: Modeling, Analysis and Computation

Since the CAC is executed for each class at each port of the switch, the multi-class connection admission control can be formulated as the following queueing problem:

As depicted in figure 3, there are n existing class k (say, VBR) connections, feeding to a single server queue with an allocated bandwidth or service rate of C_k^{old} (Mbps) and a buffer space of B_k (cells). The specified QoS guarantees (i.e., cell delay and loss) of these n connections are currently met by the system. When a new class k connection request arrives, the CAC has to determine the amount of new bandwidth C_k^{new} that is needed to ensure the same QoS guarantees for all the $n+1$ connections (including the new arrival) are met. The amount ΔC_k ($= C_k^{new} - C_k^{old}$) is the additional bandwidth required for class k if this new connection is to be admitted.

The proposed CAC scheme is designed to meet the following goals:

1) Robustness
By allocating the additional ΔC_k, the specified QoS guarantee for the new and existing connections should be satisfied. This requires us to take into account the worst source traffic scenario.

2) Link efficiency
Under the condition that the specified QoS guarantees are satisfied, the allocation of additional bandwidth ΔC_k to the class in question should be just sufficient to satisfy the QoS guarantees of the class. This requires us to take into account the statistical multiplexing gain from the $n+1$ connections. That is, as each new connection is added, the amount of additional bandwidth must progressively decrease.

3) Computational load
In order for the CAC to be used in practice, the computation to determine ΔC_k needs to be performed in real time, say in a few milli-seconds or hundreds of micro-seconds. Hence, simple closed form solutions have to be found to calculate the additional bandwidth.

The QoS requirement that the CAC shall guarantee for cell loss is

$$CLR < \epsilon_1, \tag{1}$$

where the CLR (cell loss ratio) is defined as the ratio of the total number of lost cells to the total number of cells that arrive. The QoS requirement for cell delay variation is

$$Prob[CDV > t_{max}] < \epsilon_2, \tag{2}$$

where the CDV (cell delay variation) is defined as the difference between the inter-arrival time and the inter-departure time of consecutive cells from the same virtual connection. The CDV is also called delay jitter in the literatures. t_{max} is the maximum CDV the connection can tolerate.

3.1 CAC for CBR Connections

CBR connections are characterized by their peak cell rate, i.e., their UPC parameters can be described as $\lambda_s = \lambda_p$ and $B_s = 1$. It is common to assume that the required CBR bandwidth is equal to the sum of their peak rates. However, if the CDV and CLR constraints are tight, the cell level congestion will require an allocation greater than the overall peak rate [3].

The waiting time distribution for a superposition of CBR connections can be analyzed via the $\sum D_i/D/1$ queue. In [14], Roberts and Virtamo studied the queue length distribution of a $\sum D_i/D/1$ queue and derived the upper and lower bounds. But the computation of these bounds involves complex root-finding solutions of polynomials. In [15], they derived the upper and lower bounds with a different approximation, which avoids the above root-finding problem. However, it still involves substantial computational overhead, especially when admitting and tearing down connections. In [13], Ramamurthy and Sengupta derived an exact equation for the waiting time distribution when N homogeneous CBR sources with peak rate λ_p are multiplexed. In [5], Dron, Ramamurthy and Sengupta developed an efficient approximation for the waiting time distribution. This approximation, while being very accurate, can significantly reduce the computation time. In the following, we outline the main equations of this approximation, which serve as the key for the CBR CAC.

Consider the case when n CBR traffic streams, each with peak rate R (bits/sec), are multiplexed by a multiplexer with service rate C_{cbr} (bits/sec) and infinite buffer space. From [5], we have

$$\begin{aligned} &Prob[\text{Waiting time of an arriving cell} > t] \\ &= exp\left[-2\left(\frac{t^2C_{cbr}^2}{nb^2} + \frac{(1-\frac{nR}{C_{cbr}})tC_{cbr}}{b}\right)\right] \end{aligned} \tag{3}$$

where b is the number of bits in an ATM cell.

Since the minimum waiting time of a cell is zero, the constraint on CDV can be upper-bounded by cells' waiting time distribution. That is, in order to guarantee $Prob[CDV > t_{max}] < \epsilon_2$, it is sufficient to ensure

$$Prob[\text{Waiting time of an arriving cell} > t_{max}] < \epsilon_2. \tag{4}$$

This probability can be computed from equation (3).

To compute the cell loss ratio we use the relation between the queue length Q seen on arrival, the waiting time W and the service rate C_{cbr}, i.e.,

$$Q \approx W * C_{cbr}.$$

Thus we can approximate the cell loss ratio by the overflow probability:

$$\begin{aligned} CLR &\approx Prob[\text{A cell is blocked}] \\ &\approx Prob[\text{Queue length on arrival} > B_{cbr}] \\ &= Prob[\text{Waiting time seen by arriving cell} > \frac{B_{cbr}}{C_{cbr}}] \end{aligned}$$

$$= e^{-2\left(\frac{B_{cbr}^2}{n}+(1-\frac{nR}{C_{cbr}})B_{cbr}\right)} \quad (5)$$

where B_{cbr} is the buffer capacity for the CBR queue.

Note that the above analysis only applies to the case when all n sources have the same peak rate R. As we have discussed earlier, exact solution and approximation for the case when CBR sources with different rates are multiplexed is still computationally intensive and not practical for real-time operations. However, we use a simple heuristic to address this problem. When heterogeneous CBR streams are multiplexed, the dominant parameters that affect the performance are the multiplexed load, the number of multiplexed streams, and the period of the lowest rate stream. Suppose that R_b is the lowest rate among all CBR connections. If a CBR connection with a rate $m * R_b$ is replaced by m CBR streams of rate R_b, a larger cell waiting time will result, because the superposition of m CBR streams can lead to bunched arrivals. In fact, we can show that the squared coefficient of variation of arrival process for the m multiplexed CBR streams is $\frac{m-1}{m+1}$.

Motivated by the above observations, for heterogeneous CBR connections, we first choose a basic rate as the lowest connection rate R_b (e.g., 64 kbps). We then replace any given CBR connection of rate R by $j = R/R_b$ equivalent CBR sources of rate R_b. Therefore we may use (3) as an upper-bound for cell waiting time distribution when heterogeneous CBR traffic streams are multiplexed. This approximation, while being robust, is only marginally conservative.

Given ϵ_2 and t_{max}, we can solve for the required bandwidth C_{cbr}^{delay} from (3), to meet the delay constraint on CDV in (4) as

$$C_{cbr}^{delay} = \frac{2 * K * (\alpha + K * R_b \frac{t_{max}}{b})}{K + \sqrt{K^2(1 + 4 * R_b \frac{t_{max}}{b}) + 4\alpha * K}} \frac{b}{t_{max}}, \quad (6)$$

where $\alpha = -1.15 * log_{10}(\epsilon_2)$ and K is the total number of equivalent sources with rate R_b. The amount of bandwidth required to meet the cell loss constraint from (5), given ϵ_1 and the buffer size B_{cbr}, is:

$$C_{cbr}^{loss} = \frac{K * R_b}{1 + \frac{B_{cbr}}{K} - \frac{\beta}{B_{cbr}}} \quad (7)$$

where $\beta = -1.15 * log_{10}(\epsilon_1)$.

From the above analysis, the CAC procedure for admitting a new CBR connection with peak rate λ_p^*, when n CBR connections are already in progress, is as follows:

We calculate the bandwidth required to support the K equivalent CBR connections (including the new connection request) with the QoS defined by (1) and (2) as

$$C_{cbr}^{new} = \max\left(K * R_b,\ C_{cbr}^{delay},\ C_{cbr}^{loss}\right). \quad (8)$$

where

$$K = \frac{\lambda_p^*}{R_b} + \frac{\sum_{i=1}^{n} \lambda_p^i}{R_b},$$

is the total number of equivalent basic rate CBR sources, including the contribution from the new connection request, and λ_p^i is the peak rate of CBR connection i ($i = 1, 2, \cdots, n$). Note that K is not necessarily an integer. The additional capacity Δ_{cbr} that must be added to the current capacity of the CBR class to ensure the QoS requirements of all CBR connections (including the new connection) are met, is given by

$$\Delta_{cbr} = C_{cbr}^{new} - C_{cbr}^{old},$$

The procedure for a tear-down can be carried out in a similar way.

The complexity of implementation is very low for the CBR CAC. The only information we need to keep is the sum of peak rates of all existing connections, i.e., $\sum_{i=1}^{n} \lambda_p^i$, and this quantity is updated every time when a CBR connection is admitted or disconnected.

3.2 CAC for VBR Connections

Sources whose short term average rates vary with time can be classified as variable bit rate (VBR) sources. Sources subscribing to the VBR class will specify their UPC descriptors $(\lambda_p, \lambda_s, B_s)$, where $\lambda_p \geq \lambda_s$ and $B_s \geq 1$. The QoS requirements are cell loss ratio (CLR) and cell delay variation (CDV):

$$CLR < \epsilon_1,$$
$$Prob[\text{CDV} > t_{max}] < \epsilon_2.$$

As in the case of CBR traffic, CDV can be determined via the waiting time distribution, which in turn can be related to the queue length distribution. The VBR CAC developed here can be applied to both real time and non-real time VBR classes. The values of ϵ_1, ϵ_2 and t_{max} will be different for these two classes.

The proposed VBR CAC uses two multiplexer models based on the UPC descriptors $(\lambda_p, \lambda_s, B_s)$. One is a lossless multiplexing model that performs best when the number of multiplexed sources are small; the second is a statistical multiplexing model that performs best when the number of multiplexed sources are large. In both models, we use fluid flow processes. We combine these two models when the CAC has to make decision on VBR sources.

3.2.1 Equivalent Source Traffic Model

When a new VBR connection arrives, we assume that the traffic offered to the network is regulated at the source in accordance with the declared UPC parameters $(\lambda_p^*, \lambda_s^*, B_s^*)$ through a dual leaky bucket. The departure process of such a regulator is an "on/off" process with varying rates. Doshi [4] and Worster [17] have shown that a periodic "on/off" rate process with "on" and "off" periods given by

$$T_{on}^* = \frac{B_s^*}{\lambda_p^*} \quad \text{and} \quad T_{off}^* = \frac{B_s^*}{\lambda_p^*} \frac{(\lambda_p^* - \lambda_s^*)}{\lambda_s^*} \quad (9)$$

in many cases can be considered as the *worst case* source model in the sense of having the maximum steady-state cell loss probability. The probability such a source is in the "on" state is given by

$$P_{on}^* = \frac{T_{on}^*}{T_{on}^* + T_{off}^*} = \frac{\lambda_s^*}{\lambda_p^*}. \quad (10)$$

3.2.2 Lossless Multiplexing Model

We first develop a lossless multiplexing model based on the deterministic behavior of the "on/off" sources. Assume that n VBR connections have been admitted, where the i-th connection has UPC parameters $(\lambda_p^i, \lambda_s^i, B_s^i)$, $i = 1, 2, \cdots, n$. Let C_{vbr}^{old} be the bandwidth currently allocated to the VBR class, supporting the n VBR connections.

Assume that c^i is the equivalent bandwidth allocated to the i-th connection with UPC parameters $(\lambda_p^i, \lambda_s^i, B_s^i)$, and the "on" period T_{on}^i as obtained from (9). The maximum queue accumulation Q_i for the connection i during an "on/off" cycle is

$$Q_i = (\lambda_p^i - c^i)T_{on}^i = (\lambda_p^i - c^i)\frac{B_s^i}{\lambda_p^i}, \quad (11)$$

We make the simplifying assumption that the ratio between Q_i and the overall buffer allocated for VBR traffic B_{vbr}, is same as the ratio between its burst size B_s^i and the sum of the burst sizes of all n connections. That is

$$\frac{Q_i}{B_{vbr}} = \frac{B_s^i}{\sum_{j=1}^n B_s^j}, \quad i = 1, 2, \cdots, n. \quad (12)$$

To avoid any cell loss, it is sufficient that

$$\sum_{i=1}^n Q_i \le B_{vbr}. \quad (13)$$

Solving (11), (12), and (13) for c^i and also noting that the bandwidth allocated to each connection should be at least equal to its sustainable rate λ_s^i in order to keep queue stable, we have

$$c^i = \max\left(\lambda_p^i(1 - \frac{B_{vbr}}{\sum_{j=1}^n B_s^j}),\ \lambda_s^i\right). \quad (14)$$

Therefore, the overall bandwidth required by the n connections for this lossless multiplexer model is $\sum_{i=1}^n c^i$.

If a new connection with UPC parameters $(\lambda_p^*, \lambda_s^*, B_s^*)$ wants to be admitted, we can calculate the new overall bandwidth to be assigned to the VBR class with QoS guarantee on CLR, is given by C_{vbr}^{new}:

$$C_{vbr}^{new} = \max\left((\lambda_p^* + \sum_{i=1}^n \lambda_p^i)(1 - \frac{B_{vbr}}{B_s^* + \sum_{i=1}^n B_s^i})^+,\right.$$
$$\left.\lambda_s^* + \sum_{i=1}^n \lambda_s^i\right). \quad (15)$$

Now, the maximum waiting time t for cells from all connections is $t = B_{vbr}/C_{vbr}^{new}$. If $t \le t_{max}$, then the constraint on the CDV is satisfied as well, if C_{vbr}^{new} can be allocated to VBR traffic class. If $t > t_{max}$, we have to re-calculate C_{vbr}^{new} by substituting B_{vbr} in (15) with $\hat{B}_{vbr}$, where $\hat{B}_{vbr} = C_{vbr}^{new} * t_{max}$.

Therefore the additional bandwidth required to support this new connection is given by

$$\delta_1 = C_{vbr}^{new} - C_{vbr}^{old}.$$

Notice that by allocating C_{vbr}^{new} to the VBR class, the system incurs no cell loss under the "on/off" model assumption. To implement this CAC, we only need to store one set of information for all existing VBR connections, i.e., the sum of peak rates $\sum_{i=1}^n \lambda_p^i$, the sum of sustainable rates $\sum_{i=1}^n \lambda_s^i$ and the sum of burst sizes $\sum_{i=1}^n B_s^i$. All these quantities are updated when a VBR connection is admitted or disconnected.

3.2.3 Modified Source Model

The above mechanism does not take into account the statistical multiplexing gain, but still results in efficient bandwidth allocation when the number of connections are relatively small. However, when the number of connections are relatively large, the model is overly conservative. We thus use an alternative approach to achieve better statistical multiplexing gain.

It is well-known that the cell loss performance of a multiplexer depends on the maximum burst length generated by the source, with respect to the amount of buffering. In order to take into account the buffer space B_{vbr} as well as the effects of burst length, we modify the "on/off" source model defined by (9) and (10) as follows. We define a basic time interval:

$$T_N = \frac{B_{vbr}}{2 * C_{vbr}^{max}}, \quad (16)$$

which can be viewed as the time to drain the buffers that are half-full [16]. We then construct a new two-state model for the source. The two states are a *high* rate state with rate λ_H^* and a *low* rate state with rate λ_L^* (see figure 4). These states occur with probability P_{on}^* and $(1 - P_{on}^*)$, respectively. The high and the low rates are given by:

$$\lambda_H^* = \min\left(1, \frac{T_{on}^*}{T_N}\right)\lambda_p^* + \max\left(0, 1 - \frac{T_{on}^*}{T_N}\right)\lambda_s^*$$
$$\lambda_L^* = \max\left(0, 1 - \frac{T_{on}^*}{T_N}\right)\lambda_s^* \quad (17)$$

Thus, sources with burst sizes that are small compared to the buffer size, are modeled by their average characteristics while sources whose T_{on} are larger than T_N are modeled closer to the worst case model and not significantly altered by this model. This step will reduce the bandwidth requirement for source with small burst size. Note that in the two models (9) and (17) the sources have the same average rate of λ_s^*.

3.2.4 Statistical Multiplexing Model

Based on the modified "on/off" source model in (16) and (17), we approximate the rate of the aggregate traffic stream $R(t)$ of all VBR connections by a Gaussian process. We calculate the cell loss ratio defined by

$$CLR \stackrel{def}{=} \frac{E[R(t)-C]^+}{E[R(t)]},$$

using integral approximations [12], where C is the bandwidth allocated to VBR connections.

Let $\bar{M}_{old}$ and σ^2_{old} be the mean and variance of the aggregate arrival process due to all existing VBR connections (i.e., before admitting the new connection). Let $\bar{M}_{new}$ and σ^2_{new} be the mean and variance of the aggregate arrival process due to all admitted VBR connections after the new VBR connection is admitted. Then

$$\begin{aligned}\bar{M}_{new} &= \bar{M}_{old} + \lambda^*_s \\ \sigma^2_{new} &= \sigma^2_{old} + (\lambda^*_H - \lambda^*_L)^2 P^*_{on}(1-P^*_{on}).\end{aligned} \quad (18)$$

Let

$$\eta = \frac{\bar{M}_{new}\sqrt{2\pi}}{\sigma_{new}}\epsilon \text{ and } \zeta = \frac{C-\bar{M}_{new}}{\sigma_{new}}, \quad (19)$$

where $\epsilon = \min(\epsilon_1, \epsilon_2)$.

We can show that, if $R(t)$ is approximated by a Gaussian process with mean $\bar{M}_{new}$ and variance σ^2_{new}, solving the inequality

$$CLR \stackrel{def}{=} \frac{E[R(t)-C]}{E[R(t)]} < \epsilon$$

for C is equivalent to solving the following inequality for ζ

$$\left(1-\frac{2\zeta}{\zeta+\sqrt{\zeta^2+4}}\right)e^{-\frac{\zeta^2}{2}} < \eta. \quad (20)$$

This approximation in (20) is more accurate than the one proposed in [8], which is in fact $Prob[R(t) > C]$ rather than CLR.

Solving (20) for ζ, we have

$$\begin{aligned}\zeta &= \sqrt{2\left(-log(-2\eta log(\eta)) - log(1-\frac{log(-2log(\eta))}{1-log(\eta)})\right)} \\ &\approx 1.8 - 0.46 log_{10}(\eta).\end{aligned} \quad (21)$$

From (19), the new overall VBR bandwidth required to support all VBR connections (including the new request) with QoS guarantee of CLR and CDV is given by

$$C^{new}_{vbr} = \bar{M}_{new} + \zeta * \sigma_{new}. \quad (22)$$

Therefore, the required additional bandwidth based on the statistical multiplexing model is given by

$$\delta_2 = C^{new}_{vbr} - C^{old}_{vbr}.$$

Thus, combining the lossless multiplexer and the statistical multiplexer models, the additional bandwidth Δ_{vbr} is then given by

$$\Delta_{vbr} = \min[\delta_1, \delta_2].$$

The new VBR connection is admitted if a capacity Δ_{vbr} is available in the free pool of bandwidth (i.e., $\Delta_{vbr} \le C_f$) and $C^{new}_{vbr} \le C^{max}_{vbr}$.

The complexity of using this statistical multiplexer model is low. We only need to store the mean and the variance of aggregate arrival rate, i.e., $\bar{M}_{old}$ and σ^2_{old}, and update them whenever a VBR connection is admitted or disconnected.

Note that the buffering effects in the statistical multiplexing model is taken into account by the modification of the source in (16) and (17). After this modification, we analyze a statistical multiplexer model without buffers. In this paper, we have omitted the justification of source modification in (16) and (17) as well as the derivations for Eqs. (20) and (21). The readers are referred to [12] for more details.

3.3 CAC for ABR connections

The ATM switches may explicitly compute the rate for each ABR virtual channel (VC). The key parameters of interest for the ABR connection [2] that have to be negotiated with the source are: peak cell rate (PCR), minimum cell rate (MCR), initial cell rate (ICR), rate increase factor (RIF) and rate decrease factor (RDF). The ABR CAC proposed here only guarantees MCR. The CAC for ABR service is based on the analysis in [2, 10, 11].

Let C^{max}_{mcr} be the maximum capacity that can be reserved for the ABR class to support $MCR > 0$. The capacity available in the free pool for ABR service is:

$$C_f = C_{link} - C_{cbr} - C_{vbr} - C_{mcr},$$

where C_{mcr} is service rate currently allocated to existing ABR connections.

3.3.1 MCR and RM Cell Bandwidth

When a request from a new ABR connection with $MCR = \lambda^*_{mcr}$ arrives, the call is accepted if an amount of bandwidth equal to λ^*_{mcr} is available in the free pool (i.e., $\lambda^*_{mcr} \le C_f$), and the total capacity reserved for ABR including the new request is less than C^{max}_{mcr}. In the event that the required MCR cannot be supported, the switch can either offer a lower value for MCR or set MCR=0.

An additional consideration or requirement for the ABR CAC is to reserve bandwidth for resource management (RM) cell transmission in the reverse direction. The RM cells carry congestion control information and thus have higher priority. Let C^{max}_{abr} be the maximum capacity available to ABR class in the forward direction and K be the number of active ABR connections (including the new request). Given λ^i_{mcr} and n^i_{rm}, $i = 1, 2, \cdots, K$, where n^i_{rm} is the number of data cells between successive RM cells, we can compute the required RM cell bandwidth in the reverse direction as

$$C_{rm} = \left(\frac{C^{max}_{abr} - \sum_{i=1}^{K} \lambda^i_{mcr}}{K} \right) * \sum_{i=1}^{K} \frac{1}{n^i_{rm}} + \sum_{i=1}^{K} \frac{\lambda^i_{mcr}}{n^i_{rm}}.$$

Therefore, upon receiving a new request, we also have to check if there is enough bandwidth available in the free pool for RM cells in the reverse direction.

3.3.2 Choices of PCR, ICR, RIF and RDF

When an ABR connection is being established, the parameters *PCR*, *ICR*, *RIF* and *RDF* need to be negotiated and set up.

The peak cell rate for a new ABR connection can be set equal to either the line rate C_{link} or the average available capacity for ABR connections:

$$C_{link} - \sum_{CBR} \lambda^{cbr}_p - \sum_{VBR} \lambda^{vbr}_s.$$

Let B_{abr} be the total buffer capacity available for ABR service and let the average number of sources that are likely to become active in one round-trip delay be N_{nom}. Assume that when N_{nom} users become active with a nominal initial rate ICR_{nom} during a nominal round-trip delay RTT_{nom}, the resulting increase in queue length has to be restricted to B_1, where $B_0 + B_1 < B_{abr}$, and B_0 is the steady state queue length. Thus

$$N_{nom} * ICR_{nom} * RTT_{nom} \leq B_1,$$

or equivalently

$$ICR_{nom} = \frac{B_1}{N_{nom} * RTT_{nom}}. \quad (23)$$

The fixed round-trip delays can vary between

$$RTT_{min} \leq RTT_{nom} \leq RTT_{max}.$$

The switch will inform each user the amount of buffers (TBE, i.e., transient buffer exposure) it can use:

$$TBE = \frac{B_1}{N_{nom}}.$$

If the round-trip delay of source i is RTT_i ($RTT_{min} \leq RTT_i \leq RTT_{max}$), source i will use an initial cell rate

$$ICR_i = \frac{TBE}{RTT_i}.$$

After one round-trip delay, the source can increase its rate from ICR to the advertised explicit rate (ER). Now the advertised ER carried by the first returning RM cell, may not yet reflect the activity of the new user and hence may be larger than what the network can support.

Let T_{det} be the delay in detecting an overload (due to the presence of the new source) that causes a new ER to be computed. During this time period since the N_{nom} active users would be ramping their rates from their ICR to the advertised ER, the resulting increase in queue length, assuming a nominal initial cell rate of ICR_{nom}, must be limited to

$$N_{nom} * ICR_{nom} * \int_0^{T_{det}+RTT_{nom}} e^{\frac{RIF*PCR}{N_{rm}} t} dt < B_2, \quad (24)$$

such that $B_0 + B_2 < B_{abr}$. If we can make the approximation $e^x \approx 1 + x$, the solution of Eq.(24) gives the RIF that an ABR source can use:

$$RIF \approx \frac{2 * N_{rm}(\frac{B_2}{N_{nom}*ICR_{nom}} - T_{det} - RTT_{nom})}{(T_{det} + RTT_{nom})^2 * PCR}.$$

with 1/16 being the default and maximum value. The RDF (with default value 1/16) can be taken in such a way that the ratio of RIF/RDF is compatible with other ABR connections using the given switch.

4 Examples and Simulation Results

In this section, we provide some examples with analytical and simulation results. These examples help to illustrate the performance of the CACs we have developed in section 3.

The examples in figures 5 and 6 are to evaluate the CAC for CBR connections. In figure 5, we show the complementary waiting time distributions when 1000 connections of 64 kbps CBR streams are multiplexed with one 64 Mbps CBR stream, with the constraint that the 10^{-6} quantile of the peak to peak CDV be less than 300 micro-seconds. Note that allocation based on peak rates will require 128 Mbps. From figure 5, we observe the following:

1. If the high speed 64 Mbps CBR stream is replaced by 1000 equivalent 64 kbps streams, the resulting complementary waiting time distribution for 2000 connections of 64 kbps streams as obtained from simulation is very close to the waiting time distribution computed from analysis in (3).
2. The actual complementary waiting time distribution seen by the 64 kbps CBR streams and the 64 Mbps CBR stream (from simulation), has a smaller tail probability compared to the analytic approximation used for the multiplexing of heterogeneous CBR streams.

3. The CAC allocates a capacity of 131.633 Mbps to ensure the required CDV constraint of 300 micro-seconds at the 10^{-6} quantile is met. From simulation, the actual capacity required to meet this QoS constraint is 129.3 Mbps. Thus the CAC over allocates by about 2%. The system has a utilization of 97.24%. Peak rate allocation would have required 128 Mbps, which is not sufficient to guarantee the 300 micro-seconds CDV requirement.

In figure 6, we show the complementary waiting time distributions of 40 connections of 3.5 Mbps CBR streams, with the constraint that the 10^{-6} quantile of the peak to peak CDV is less than 300 micro-seconds. The multiplexed stream is equivalent to 2188 CBR connections of 64 kbps (i.e., we treat these 40 connections as general heterogeneous traffic although in this case they happen to be homogeneous). From the CAC, we find out that the required bandwidth is 143.2 Mbps to support the required QoS, leading to a utilization of 97.8%. With this amount of bandwidth, the actual complementary waiting time distribution obtained from simulation (plotted as the circles) is smaller than the one obtained by the CAC (plotted as the solid line). However, the over-allocation of bandwidth by the CAC is less than 3%. The plot also shows the complementary waiting time distribution for traffic streams with cell delay variation tolerance (CDVT) > 0. The complementary waiting time distributions become worse when the CDVT of the arriving traffic stream increases. Nevertheless, the CAC only marginally over-allocates bandwidth, and yet meets the CDV constraint for all CBR connections with reasonable values of CDVT (up to 500 micro-seconds in this case).

The two examples in figures 7 and 8 show the performance of the CAC for VBR connections. In the example in figure 7, the VBR source is an MPEG-1 coded sequence for a mobile, called MOBI sequence. This empirical data sequence has a peak cell rate of 17.38 Mbps and an average cell rate of 8.58 Mbps. Using the method developed in [9], we can choose UPC parameters (λ_p = 17.38 Mbps, λ_s = 11.87 Mbps, B_s = 83 cells) to characterize the MOBI sequence. We consider a single server queue with a buffer space of 500 cells and a QoS constraint: $CLR < 10^{-5}$. In figure 7, given the above UPC parameters for the MOBI sequence and the different capacities for the server (i.e., C_{vbr} = 45 Mbps, 100 Mbps, 150 Mbps and 300 Mbps), we show the maximum number of MOBI sequences that can be admitted without violating the CLR requirements. We compare the results of our CAC to the results from other connection admission control policies in the literature as well as the results from simulations. The effective bandwidth is based on [8]. The PNNI CAC is the generic CAC proposed by the ATM Forum. The figure shows that the CAC developed in section 3.2 is more efficient than CACs in the literature, while being robust at the same time.

In the example in figure 8, we have a more bursty MPEG-1 coded sequence called the flower garden. This sequence has a peak cell rate of 13.91 Mbps and an average cell rate of 3.1 Mbps. The UPC parameters we choose for this sequence based on [9] is (λ_p = 13.91 Mbps, λ_s = 3.6 Mbps, B_s = 1479 cells). With same QoS requirement as for the MOBI sequence, we can see from figure 8 that the CAC is again more efficient than the other three CACs. However, the CAC performs conservatively compared to the number of connections that can be actually admitted (obtained from simulations). This is an inherent problem of model-based CACs. If one has to ensure the CAC to be robust, then the penalty is the reduced utilization of network bandwidth. This is one compelling reason for combining the model-based CAC with the measurement-based CAC to improve system utilization.

5 Conclusion and Discussion

In this paper we have proposed and developed a multi-class connection admission control policy for high speed ATM switches. The CAC is a model-based one, where the source traffic models are based on the declared UPC parameters from traffic sources. The CAC supports the QoS guarantees such as CDV and CLR. The highlights of this CAC are

1. We introduce the concept of free pool for bandwidth management in a multi-class, heterogeneous traffic environment.

2. For CBR connection admission control, we apply the approximation developed in [5] to deal with heterogeneous traffic streams. Our analysis and simulation results show that the method, while being robust, is only marginally conservative. It can also handle CBR streams with reasonable CDVTs.

3. For VBR connection admission control, we first develop a simple lossless multiplexing model for bandwidth allocation, which is efficient for small number of connections. To achieve higher statistical multiplexing gain, we modify the source model (i.e., Eqs. (16) and (17)) to take into account the effects of buffering. We then derive a more accurate approximation (i.e., Eqs. (20) and (21)) for calculating CLR.

In addition to the robustness and efficiency, the CAC can be implemented in real-time because of its computational simplicity. This is achieved by careful analysis and approximations. The formulas to calculate bandwidth (section 3) only involve simple arithmetic computations. It also requires minimal information to be stored in memory.

For more details, especially on the topics of how to deal with traffic streams with CDVTs and how to use traffic and QoS measurements to improve CAC, readers are referred to [12]. It is to be noted that the connection admission control itself cannot guarantee QoS. Appropriate traffic enforcement policies and scheduling mechanism are also necessary. Lastly, measurements can be helpful in improving the overall bandwidth utilization.

References

[1] ATM Forum, *User-Network Interface Specification*, Version 3.0, 1993.

[2] ATM Forum, *Traffic Management Specification*, Version 4.0, 95-0013R11, 1996.

[3] *Performance Evaluation and Design of Multi-service Networks*, edited by J. W. Roberts, COST 224 project, 1992.

[4] B. T. Doshi, "Deterministic Rule Based Traffic Descriptors for Broadband ISDN: Worst Case Behavior and Connection Acceptance Control", *Proc. GLOBECOM'93*, Vol.3, pp.1759-1764, Houston, November, 1993.

[5] L. Dron, G. Ramamurthy and B. Sengupta, "Delay Analysis of Continuous Bit Rate Traffic over an ATM Network", *IEEE Journal on Selected Areas in Communications*, Vol.9, No.3, April 1991.

[6] A. Elwalid and D. Mitra, "Effective Bandwidth of General Markovian Traffic Sources and Admission Control of High Speed Networks", *IEEE/ACM Trans. Networking*, Vol. 1, pp. 329-343, 1993.

[7] A. Elwalid, D. Mitra and R. Wentworth, "A New Approach for Allocating Buffers and Bandwidth to Heterogeneous Regulated Traffic in an ATM Node", *IEEE Journal on Selected Areas in Communications*, Vol.13, No.6, pp. 1115-1127, August 1995.

[8] R. Guerin, H. Ahmadi and M. Nagshineh, "Equivalent Capacity and its Application to Bandwidth Allocation in High Speed Network", *IEEE Journal on Selected Areas in Communications*, Vol. 9, pp. 968-981, 1991.

[9] B. Mark and G. Ramamurthy, "Real-time Estimation of UPC Parameters for Arbitrary Traffic Sources in ATM Networks", *Proc. INFOCOM'96*, Vol. 1, pp.384-390, 1996.

[10] H. Ohsaki, M. Murata, H. Suzuki, C. Ikeda and H. Miyahara, "Parameter Tuning of Rate-based Congestion Control Algorithms for ATM Networks", Technical Report, NEC C&C Research Laboratories, 1995.

[11] G. Ramamurthy and Q. Ren, "Analysis of the Adaptive Rate Control for ABR Service in ATM Networks", *Proc. GLOBECOM'95*, Vol.2, pp.1083-1088, Singapore, Nov. 13-17, 1995.

[12] G. Ramamurthy and Q. Ren, "Multi-class Connection Admission Control Policy for High Speed ATM Switches", Technical Report, NEC C&C Research Laboratories, 1996. Submitted for publication.

[13] G. Ramamurthy and B. Sengupta, "Delay Analysis of a Packet Voice Multiplexer by the $\sum D_i/D/1$ Queue", *IEEE Transactions on Communications*, Vol. 39, No. 7, July 1991.

[14] J. W. Roberts and J. Virtamo, "Evaluating Buffer Requirements in an ATM Multiplexer", *Proc. GLOBECOM'89*, Dallas, 1989.

[15] J. W. Roberts and J. Virtamo, "The Superposition of Periodic Cell Arrival Streams in an ATM Multiplexer", *IEEE Transactions on Communications*, Vol. 39, No. 2, pp. 298-303, February 1991.

[16] H. Saito, "Call Admission Control in an ATM Network Using Upper Bound of Cell Loss Probability", *IEEE Transactions on Communications*, Vol.40, No.9, September 1992, pp.1512-1521.

[17] T. Worster, "Modeling Deterministic Queues: the Leaky Bucket as an Arrival Process", *Proc. ITC-14*, J. Labetoulle and J. W. Roberts, Eds, New York; Elsevier, 1994, pp.581-590.

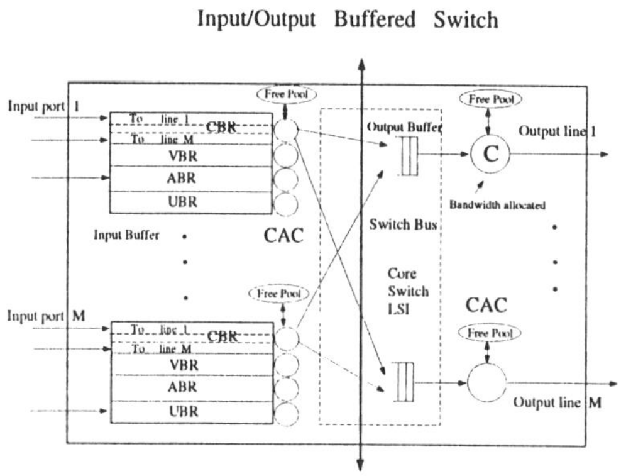

Figure 1: An input/output buffered switch architecture for which the CAC is developed.

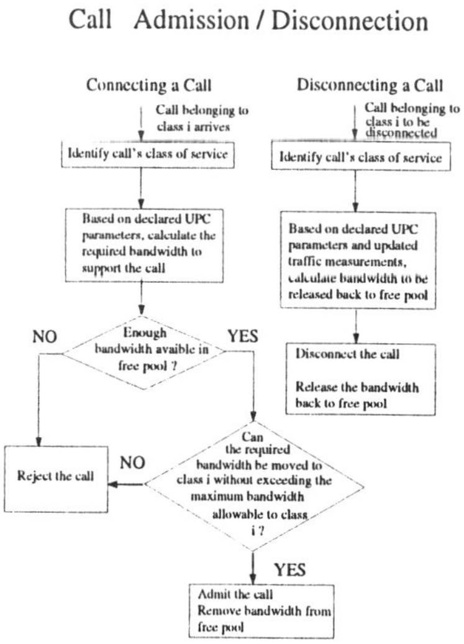

Figure 2: Schematic diagram for CAC to connect or disconnect a call.

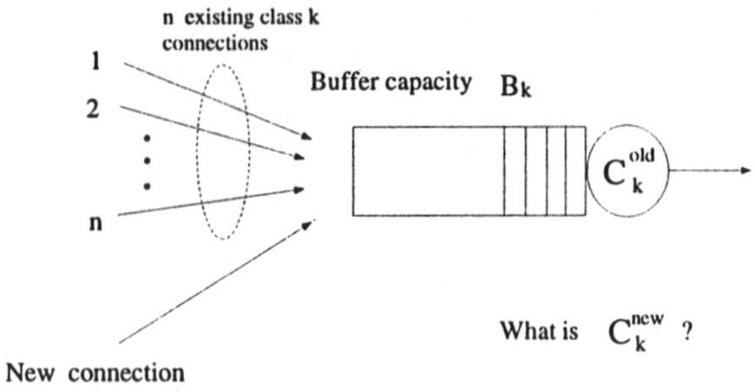

Figure 3: A single server queue model for the CAC.

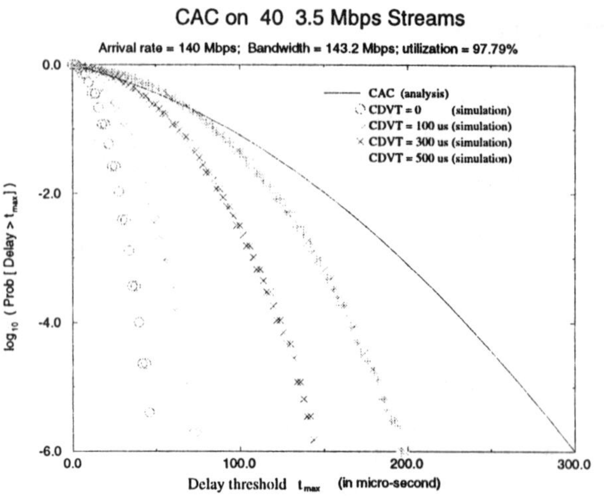

Figure 6: Complementary waiting time distribution of the superposed stream of 40 3.5 Mbps streams.

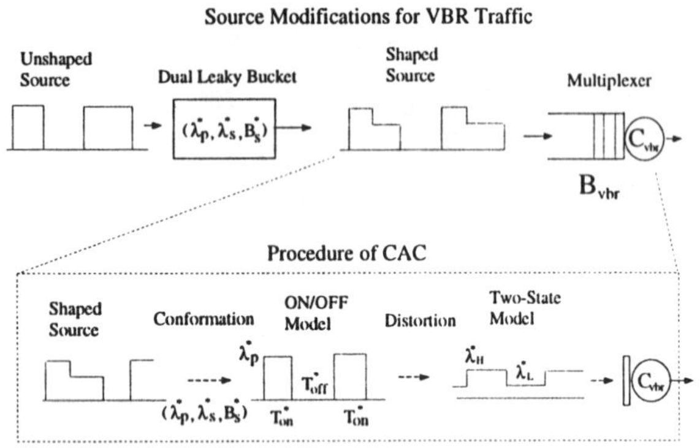

Figure 4: Source modifications for VBR connections.

VBR Source: Mobi MPEG Sequence

Link Capacity / Admission Mechnism	45 Mbps	100 Mbps	150 Mbps	300 Mbps
Simulation	4	9	14	28
CAC	3	8	12	25
Effective BW	3	7	11	22
PNNI	2	5	8	17
Peak Rate	2	5	8	17

Number of VBR streams that can be admitted

Figure 7: Number of VBR streams that can be admitted by different CAC schemes. The source streams are MPEG-1 MOBI sequences.

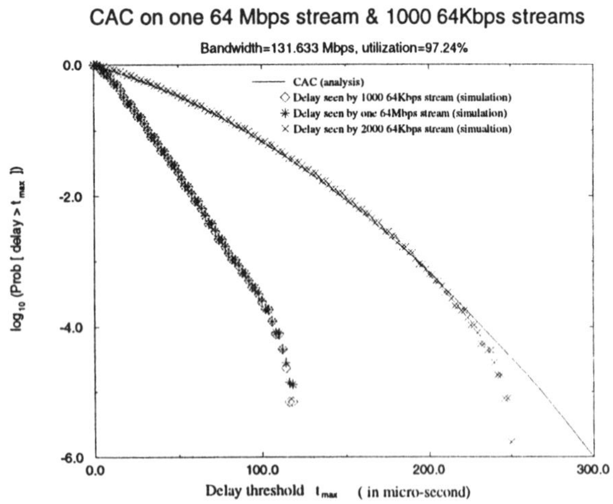

Figure 5: Complementary waiting time distribution of the superposed stream of one 64 Mbps stream and 1000 64 kbps streams.

VBR Source: Flower Garden MPEG Sequence

Link Capacity / Admission Mechnism	45 Mbps	100 Mbps	150 Mbps	300 Mbps
Simulation	8	17	30	> 64
CAC	4	9	16	43
Effective BW	3	7	11	22
PNNI	3	7	12	36
Peak Rate	3	7	10	21

Number of VBR streams that can be admitted

Figure 8: Number of VBR streams that can be admitted by different CAC schemes. The source streams are MPEG-1 flower garden sequences.

Comparison of Measurement-based Admission Control Algorithms for Controlled-Load Service

Sugih Jamin*
EECS Department
University of Michigan
Ann Arbor, MI 48109-2122
jamin@eecs.umich.edu

Scott J. Shenker
Palo Alto Research Center
Xerox Corporation
Palo Alto, CA 94304-1314
shenker@parc.xerox.com

Peter B. Danzig
Department of Computer Science
University of Southern California
Los Angeles, CA 90089-0781
danzig@usc.edu

Abstract

We compare the performance of four admission control algorithms—one parameter-based and three measurement-based—for controlled-load service. The parameter-based admission control ensures that the sum of reserved resources is bounded by capacity. The three measurement-based algorithms are based on measured bandwidth, acceptance region [9], and equivalent bandwidth [7]. We use simulation on several network scenarios to evaluate the link utilization and adherence to service commitment achieved by these four algorithms.

Keywords: Admission Control, Quality of Service (QOS), Internet.

1 Introduction

The role of any admission control algorithm is to ensure that admittance of a new flow into a resource constrained network does not violate service commitments made by the network to admitted flows. The service commitments made could be quantitative (e.g., a guaranteed rate or bounded delay), or it could be more qualitative (e.g., a "low average delay"). There are two basic approaches to admission control: the first, which we call the parameter-based approach, computes the amount of network resources required to support a set of flows given *a priori* flow characteristics; the second, the measurement-based approach, relies on measurement of actual traffic load in making admission decisions. In this paper, we report on an initial comparative study of four admission control algorithms, one parameter-based, three measurement-based. The main criterion used in evaluating any admission control algorithm must be how well it fulfills its primary role of ensuring that service commitments are not violated. The simplest way to ensure complete commitment conformance is to allocate enough resources to meet the worst-case requirements of each flow. For bursty sources, however, this scheme results in low network utilization. Hence, the second evaluation criterion is how high a level of network utilization an admission control algorithm can achieve while still meeting its service commitments.[1] The third evaluation criterion is the implementation and operational costs of an algorithm. Since admission control is a session-level, not packet-level, control mechanism, we do not expect its implementation or operational cost to be a prohibitive factor and only consider the first two criteria in this study.

Parameter-based admission control algorithms can be analyzed by formal methods. Measurement-based admission control algorithms can only be analyzed through experiments on either real networks or a simulator. We strive to make the simulation environments under which we investigate the behavior of the various algorithms as comparable as possible, but this does not mean the operating conditions would not be unfairly disadvantageous to any particular algorithm. Our intention here is not to pick a winner, but to start a dialog, not only on the evaluation criteria to be used in comparing different measurement-based admission control algorithms, but also on the definition of a meaningful comparison of measurement-based admission control algorithms given the myriad tunable parameters.

Given the reliance of measurement-based admission control algorithms on source behavior that is not static in general, service commitments made by such algorithms can never be absolute. Measurement-based approaches to admission control can only be used in the context of service models that do not make guaranteed commitments, such as the controlled-load service model. Controlled-load service is designed for adaptive real-time applications that can tolerate variance in packet delays. The *controlled-load* service model, as defined in reference [19], "tightly approx-

*Part of this work was done while Sugih Jamin was at the University of Southern California, with equipment support from the NSF small-scale infrastructure grant, award number CDA-9216321 and equipment loan from Sun Microsystems Inc.

[1] Note that in an environment where there is a large fraction of best-effort traffic, the secondary goal of the admission control algorithm may simply be to control the fraction of bandwidth allotted to realtime traffic, rather than maximizing it.

0-8186-7780-5/97 $10.00 © 1997 IEEE

imates the behavior visible to applications receiving best-effort service *under unloaded conditions*" over the same path. Furthermore, applications requesting controlled-load service may assume that its packet loss rate is on the order of the transmission medium's error rate and that its typical experienced delay should be on the order of the path's transmission and propagation delays. More specifically, average packet queueing delay should be no greater than the flow's "burst time" and there should be minimal loss rate averaged over time-scales larger than "burst time"—where the "burst time" is defined as the time required to serve a flow's maximum burst at the flow's reserved rate. For a flow described by a token bucket filter, the "burst time" is b/r, where b is the token bucket depth and r its replenishment rate (for such a flow, the total traffic during any time period of length U is bounded by $rU + b$).

The minimal commitment made by controlled-load service makes it especially well suited to the decentralized and heterogeneous Internet. This service model is in the process of being standardized by the Internet Engineering Task Force (IETF). To provide the illusion of lightly loaded network to flows receiving controlled-load service, network switches and routers must perform admission control at the call level to ensure that sufficient resources are available to serve the flows. While the specification of controlled-load service does not dictate specific target values for quality of service parameters such as delay bound or loss rate, operationally the admission control algorithms must be evaluated based on the levels of delay and loss they produce. In this paper we investigate four admission control algorithms that could support controlled-load service.

2 Four Admission Control Algorithms

Simple Sum. The first admission control algorithm simply ensures that the sum of requested resources does not exceed link capacity. Let ν be the sum of reserved rates, μ the link bandwidth, α the name of a flow requesting admission, and r^α the rate requested by flow α. This algorithm accepts the new flow if the following check succeeds:

$$\nu + r^\alpha < \mu. \quad (1)$$

We call this the "Simple Sum" algorithm in the rest of the paper. This is the simplest admission control algorithm and hence is being most widely implemented by switch and router vendors. Often, to ensure low queueing delay called for by controlled-load service, an approximation of the weighted fair queueing (WFQ) scheduling discipline is implemented with this admission control algorithm. WFQ assigns each flow its own queue served at its own reserved rate, thereby isolating flows from each other's bursts. In this paper, we always use the WFQ scheduling discipline in conjunction with the "Simple Sum" admission control—incidentally, this setup also satisfies the *committed rate* service model described in [1]. For the other, measurement-based algorithms, we assume the first-in-first-out (FIFO) scheduling discipline.

Measured Sum. Whereas the "Simple Sum" algorithm ensures that the sum of existing reservations plus a newly incoming reservation does not exceed capacity, the "Measured Sum" algorithm uses measurement to estimate the load of existing traffic. This algorithm admits the new flow if the following test succeeds:

$$\hat{\nu} + r^\alpha < \upsilon\mu, \quad (2)$$

where υ is a user-defined utilization target as explained below, and $\hat{\nu}$ the measured load of existing traffic. We will explain how load measurement is done in the next section. Upon admission of a new flow, the load estimate is increased using $\hat{\nu}' = \hat{\nu} + r^\alpha$. As we pointed out in reference [11], in a simple $M/M/1$ queue, variance in queue length diverges as the system approaches full utilization. A measurement-based approach is doomed to fail when delay variations are exceedingly large, which will occur at very high utilization. It is thus necessary to identify a *utilization target* and require that the admission control algorithm strive to keep link utilization below this level. In this paper, we let $\upsilon = 0.9$.

Acceptance Region. The second measurement-based algorithm, proposed in [9] computes an acceptance region that maximizes the reward of utilization against the penalty of packet loss. Given link bandwidth, switch buffer space, a flow's token bucket filter parameters, the flow's burstiness, and desired probability of actual load exceeding bound, one can compute an acceptance region for a specific set of flow types, beyond which no more flow of those particular types should be accepted. The computation of the acceptance region also assumes Poisson call arrival process and independent, exponentially distributed call holding times. We refer the interested readers to [9] for the computation of the acceptance region. The measurement-based version of this algorithm ensures that the measured instantaneous load plus the peak rate of a new flow is below the acceptance region. The measured load used in this scheme is not artificially adjusted upon admittance of a new flow. For flows described by a token bucket filter (r, b) but not peak rate, [7] derives their peak rates $(\hat{p})$ from the token bucket parameters using the equation:

$$\hat{p} = r + b/U, \quad (3)$$

where U is a user-defined averaging period. We have adopted the same scheme to be used with the acceptance region algorithm. If a flow is rejected, the admission control algorithm does not admit another flow until an existing one leaves the network. In the remainder of this paper, we use the terms "utilization target" and "utilization threshold" interchangeably with "acceptance region."

Equivalent Bandwidth. The third measurement-based algorithm computes the equivalent bandwidth for a set of flows using the Hoeffding bounds. The equivalent bandwidth of a set of flows is defined in references [7, 10] as the bandwidth $C(\epsilon)$ such that the stationary bandwidth requirement of the set of flows exceeds this value with probability at most ϵ. We call ϵ the "loss rate" in the remainder of the paper; however, in an environment where large portion of traffic is best-effort traffic, realtime traffic rate exceeding its equivalent bandwidth is not lost but simply encroaches upon best-effort traffic. In reference [7] the measurement-based equivalent bandwidth based on Hoeffding bounds ($\widehat{C}_H$) assuming peak rate (p) policing of n flows is given by:

$$\widehat{C}_H(\widehat{\nu}, \{p_i\}_{1 \leq i \leq n}, \epsilon) = \widehat{\nu} + \sqrt{\frac{ln(1/\epsilon) \sum_{i=1}^{n} (p_i)^2}{2}}, \quad (4)$$

where $\widehat{\nu}$ is the measured average arrival rate of existing traffic and ϵ is the probability that arrival rate exceeds the link capacity. The author of [7] indicates that the measured average arrival rate may be approximated by measured average load. We use measured arrival rate in our study, but keep the same notation ($\widehat{\nu}$) to refer to both measured arrival rate and measured load for the sake of simplicity. The admission control check when a new flow α requests admission is then:

$$\widehat{C}_H + p^\alpha \leq \mu. \quad (5)$$

Upon admission of a new flow, the load estimate is increased using $\widehat{\nu}' = \widehat{\nu} + p^\alpha$. Again, if a flow's peak rate is unknown, it is derived from its token bucket filter parameters (r, b) using Eqn. 3. Similar to the algorithm in [9], if a flow is denied admission, no other flow of similar type will be admitted until an existing one departs.

Before moving on to discuss the measurement mechanism in the next section, recall that while the admission control algorithms described here are based on meeting quality of service constraints of either loss rate or delay bound, the specific values used by the admission control algorithms are not advertised to the users of controlled-load service.

3 Three Measurement Mechanisms

We now describe the measurement mechanisms used in our study. We note that these may not be the most efficient nor the most rigorous measurement mechanisms. They are however, very simple, which help us isolate admission patterns caused by particular admission control algorithm from those caused by the measurement mechanism. We refer the interested readers to references [17, 6, 4] for alternate treatments on measurement mechanisms.

Time-window. Following [11], we use a simple time-window measurement mechanism to measure network load with the "Measured Sum" algorithm. As shown in Fig. 1, we compute an average load every S sampling period. At the end of a measurement window T, we use the highest average from the just ended T as the load estimate for the next T window. When a new flow is admitted to the network, the estimate is increased by the parameters of the new request as explained in the previous section. If a newly computed average is above the estimate, the estimate is immediately raised to the new average. At the end of every T, the estimate is adjusted to the actual load measured in the previous T. A smaller S gives us higher maximal averages, resulting in a more conservative admission control algorithm; a larger T keeps longer measurement history, again resulting in a more conservative admission control algorithm. To get a statistically meaningful number of samples, we try to keep $T/S \geq 10$.

Point Samples. The measurement mechanism used with the acceptance region algorithm takes an average load sample every S' period [12].

Exponential Averaging. Following reference [7] we use an estimate of the average arrival rate, instead of instantaneous bandwidth, to compute admission decisions with the equivalent bandwidth approach. The average arrival rate ($\widehat{\nu}^S$) is measured once every S sampling period. The average arrival rate is then computed using an infinite impulse response function with weight w, which we set to 2e-3 in this study:

$$\widehat{\nu}' = (1 - w) * \widehat{\nu} + w * \widehat{\nu}^S. \quad (6)$$

If the traffic arrival rate changes abruptly from 0 to 1 and then remains at 1, a w of 2e-3 allows the estimate to reach 75% of the new rate after 10 sampling periods. A larger w makes the averaging process more adaptive to load changes; a smaller w gives a smoother average by keeping a longer history. Recall that the equivalent bandwidth based admission control algorithm requires peak rate policing and derives a flow's peak rate from its token bucket parameters using Eqn. 3 when the peak rate is not explicitly specified. We set $U = S$ to reflect the peak rate seen by the measurement mechanism. A smaller S not only makes the measurement mechanism more sensitive to bursts, it also makes the peak rate derivation more conservative. A larger S may result in lower averages, however it also means that the measurement mechanism keeps a longer history because the averaging process (Eqn. 6) is invoked less often.

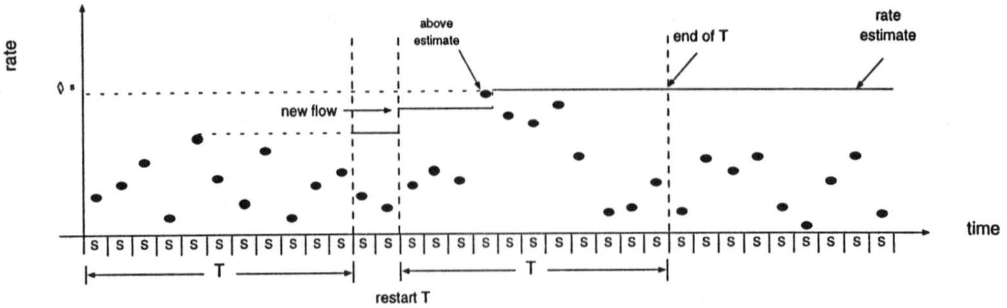

Figure 1: Time-window measurement of network load.

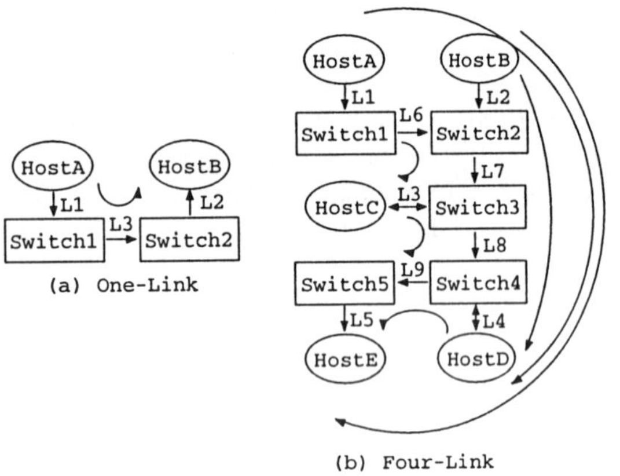

Figure 2: The ONE-LINK and FOUR-LINK topologies

4 Simulation Scenarios

For this paper, we run our simulations on two topologies: the ONE-LINK and FOUR-LINK topologies depicted in Figure 2. In both topologies, each host is connected to a switch by an infinite bandwidth link. The connection between switches are all 10 Mbps links. Buffer space at the switches are shared by all admitted flows. Buffer space of the switches connected to the bottleneck links are sized differently for each simulation, as we explain below. In the ONE-LINK topology, traffic flows from HostA to HostB. In the FOUR-LINK topologies, traffic flows between six host pairs: HostA–HostC, HostB–HostD, HostC–HostE, HostA–HostD, HostB–HostE, HostD–HostE; flow creations are distributed uniformly among the six host pairs. In Figure 2, these host pairs and the paths their packets traverse are indicated by the directed curve lines.

We use two kinds of source model in our simulations. The first is an ON/OFF model with exponentially distributed ON and OFF times. During each ON period, an exponentially distributed random number of packets, with average N, are generated at fixed rate p packet/sec. Let I milliseconds be the average of the exponentially distributed OFF times, then the average packet generation rate a is given by $1/a = I/N + 1/p$.

Recent studies ([13, 8, 2]) have shown that network traffic often exhibits long-range dependence (LRD), with the implications that congested periods can be quite long and a slight increase in the number of active connections can result in large increase in packet loss rate [16]. Reference [16, 7] further call attention to the possibly damaging effect long-range dependent traffic might have on measurement-based admission control algorithms. To investigate this and other LRD related questions, we augment our simulation study with LRD source models. Following [18], our next model is an ON/OFF process with Pareto distributed ON and OFF times (for ease of reference, we call this the *Pareto-ON/OFF* (POO) model). Pareto distribution is a heavy-tailed distribution that can be described by two parameters: its location and shape. A Pareto shape parameter less than 1 gives data with infinite mean; shape parameter less than 2 results in data with infinite variance. The Pareto location parameter can be computed from the formula: $mean * (shape - 1)/shape$. During each ON period of the Pareto-ON/OFF model, a Pareto distributed number of packets, with mean N and Pareto shape parameter β, are generated at some peak rate p packet/sec. The OFF times are also Pareto distributed with mean I milliseconds and shape parameter γ. Each Pareto-ON/OFF source by itself does not generate LRD series; the aggregation of them does.

In addition to each source's burstiness, network traffic dynamics is also effected by the arrival pattern and duration of flows. We use exponentially distributed lifetimes with the Markov-ON/OFF source model, following [14]. The duration of Pareto-ON/OFF sources, however, are taken from a lognormal distribution, following [3, 5]. The interarrival times of all flows are exponentially distributed [16].

We use six instantiations of the above source models as summarized in Table 1. In the table, $p = \infty$ means that after each OFF time, packets for the next ON period are transmitted back to back. The shape parameter of the Pareto distributed ON time (β) of the Pareto-ON/OFF sources are selected following the observations in [18]. According to the same reference, the shape parameter of the Pareto dis-

Table 1: Six Instantiations of the Two Source Models

	Model Parameters				TB Filter			Switch Parameters				
Model Name	p pkt/ sec	I msec	N pkts	p/a	r tkn/ sec	b tkns	max qlen	D^* msec	D msec	Υ (%)	S ptime	$\widehat{p}$ pkt/ sec
EXP1	64	325	20	2	64	1	0	16	16	98	5e3	–
EXP2	1024	90	10	10	320	50	17	160	160	40	1e3	832
EXP3	∞	684	9	∞	512	80	1	160	160	–	5e2	2150
				β								
POO1	64	325	20	1.2	64	1	0	16	16	98	5e3	–
POO2	64	2925	20	1.2	64	1	0	16	16	98	5e3	–
POO3	256	360	10	1.9	240	60	220	256	160	44	5e3	363

tributed OFF time (γ) stays mostly below 1.5; in this paper we use $\gamma = 1.1$ for all Pareto-ON/OFF sources. For the POO1 and POO2 models, we use a token bucket rate equal to the source's peak rate so that the token bucket filter does not reshape the traffic. For the POO3 model, some of the generated packets were queued; this means during some of the source's alleged "OFF" times, it may actually still be draining its data queue onto the network.

In the same table, we also list the settings of the token bucket parameters assigned to each source. In this study, we assign each flow a data queue with infinite length (i.e. packets that arrive at an empty token bucket are queued, and the queue never overflows). Column 7 of the table, labeled *max qlen*, shows the maximum data queue length a flow can expect to see. Our packets are of fixed size (1 Kbits) and each of our token is worth 1 packet of data.

When a flow with token bucket parameters (r, b) is served with WFQ, the maximal queueing delay (ignoring terms proportional to a single packet time) is given by b/r [15]. Column 8 of the table, labeled D^*, lists the maximal delay for each source given its assigned token bucket filter. This is also the "burst time" queueing delay acceptable under the definition of controlled-load service. Column 9, labeled D, lists the delay bound we assigned to each source. We have chosen the token bucket parameters such that, in most cases, the delay bounds given to a flow will be the same as its "burst time" queueing delay. This facilitates analyzing the performance of the algorithms under controlled-load service. In the few cases where the delays are not the same, such as in the POO3 case, the utilization comparison is less meaningful. For each simulation with measurement-based admission control algorithm, we size the buffer at the switches with enough space to accommodate the delay bound (D). For example, simulations with EXP1 source, given a link speed of 10 Mbps, use a buffer size of 160 packets. In simulations with multiple source models having different delay bound requirements, we use the maximum of the required buffer sizes; for example, in a simulation with both EXP1 and EXP2 models, we use a buffer size of 1600 packets. Simulations with the parameter-based admission control algorithm assume infinite buffer size. Column 10, labeled Υ, contains the utilization threshold used to simulate the acceptance region algorithm. This utilization threshold should not be confused with the utilization target used with the "Measured Sum" scheme, where the value is set to 90% link bandwidth. The acceptance region is computed in [9] for ϵ of 1e-12. For simulations with the equivalent bandwidth algorithm, we use ϵ of 1e-7. The next column, labeled S, gives the sampling period used with the measurement mechanisms in packet transmission time (*ptime*). For the time-window mechanism, the window size is $10 * S$. The sampling period used with the acceptance region algorithm is $S' = 5 * S$. The last column, labeled $\widehat{p}$, contains the derived peak rates computed with Eqn. 3. Note that for source POO3, the derived peak rate is larger than the actual peak rate. In this paper, we also consider using the token rate (r) as the peak rate.

For each simulation, flow interarrival times are exponentially distributed with an average of 400 milliseconds. The average holding time of all Markov-ON/OFF sources is 300 seconds. The Pareto-ON/OFF sources have lognormal distributed holding times with median of 300 seconds and shape parameter 2.5. We run simulations with Markov-ON/OFF sources for 3000 seconds simulated time, serving 1e8 packets. The data presented are obtained from the later half of each simulation. By visual inspection, we determined that 1500 simulated seconds is sufficient time for the simulations to warm up. Simulations involving Pareto-ON/OFF sources require a longer warmup period and a longer simulation time for the LRD effect to be seen, thus we run them for 5.5 hours simulation time, serving close to 1e9 packets, with reported data taken from the later 10000 seconds.

Table 2: Single-hop Homogeneous Sources Simulation Results. Entries in *italics* indicate simulations with non-zero loss rate.

Model	Simple Sum		Measured Sum		Acc. Rgn. ($\hat{p}$)		Eqv. Bw. ($\hat{p}$)		Eqv. Bw. (r)		Eqv. Bw. (r, ϵ=1e-1)	
Name	%Util	#Actv	%Util	#Actv	%Util	#Actv	%Util	#Actv	%Util	#Actv	%Util	#Actv
EXP1	46	144	*79*	*250*	*97*	*308*	71	223	–	–	–	–
EXP2	28	28	75	74	38	37	12	12	41	40	68	67
EXP3	2	18	54	406	–	–	0.3	2	5	40	23	171
POO1	39	144	86	330	*99*	*381*	70	270	–	–	–	–
POO2	7	144	78	1539	*97*	*1912*	45	885	–	–	–	–
POO3	3	38	72	965	43	582	2	27	12	159	37	505

5 Simulation Results

In the following three subsections, we present results from simulations on the ONE-LINK topology. A summary of the results is presented in Table 2. Each row of the table contains results from up to six simulations using the source model named at the leftmost column and the admission control algorithm indicated at the head of the columns. The "%Util" columns list the average utilization achieved at the bottleneck link of the ONE-LINK topology. The "#Active" columns list the average number of concurrently running flows in steady state. We have repeated some of the simulations reported in the table with up to ten different random seeds; the 99% confidence intervals are less than one of the least significant digit in most cases. We close this section by presenting results from simulations on the FOUR-LINK topology.

5.1 Single-hop Results

The first two columns of Table 2 show results from simulation using the "Simple Sum" parameter-based admission control algorithm. There are no lost packets. The second set of two columns show results from the "Measured Sum" algorithm. Except for the POO1 cases, where the "Measured Sum" algorithm gives a loss rate on the order of 1e-7, simulations with other source models using this algorithm do not result in any loss. We can achieve no loss with POO1 sources if we reduce the utilization target to 80% of link bandwidth, in which case the average link utilization achieved is 77% and the average number of concurrently served flows is 297.

The next two columns, under the heading "Acc. Rgn. ($\hat{p}$)" give the results of simulations with the acceptance region algorithm; here the peak rate of sources with token bucket greater than 1 is derived from their token bucket parameters using Eqn. 3. We do not study the performance of this algorithm for EXP3 source because the utilization threshold for this model is 0 [9]. The loss rate for sources EXP1, POO1, and POO2, from three simulations of each with different random seeds, are 6e-3, 2e-2, and 1e-2 respectively. Since EXP1 and POO1 sources have mostly the same characteristics except for the distributions of their ON and OFF times, we conjecture that by not taking these into account, the acceptance region algorithm is overly optimistic for sources having heavy-tailed ON and OFF times distributions. As the grain size of flows, i.e. the p/μ ratio, enlarges, this algorithm becomes more conservative. For the EXP2 and POO3 sources, achievable utilization is about half of the utilization under "Measured Sum." Since the acceptance region algorithm does not artificially adjust its measurement values upon admittance of a new flow, and given its point sampling measurement process, we do not see any significant difference in performance between simulations using derived peak rates and token rates as peak rates.

The two columns of Table 2 under the heading "Eqv. Bw. ($\hat{p}$)" show results from simulations using the equivalent bandwidth based admission control algorithm. In the case of simulations with EXP2, EXP3 and POO3 sources, the flows' peak rates are derived from their token bucket parameters using Eqn. 3. We showed the derived peak rates for the three sources in Table 1 and pointed out that in the POO3 case the derived peak rate is higher than the actual peak rate. To see how a less conservative peak rate effects the performance of the algorithm on the EXP2, EXP3, and POO3 sources, we simulate them with their token bucket rates as their peak rates, ignoring the token bucket depths. The two columns of Table 2 under the "Eqv. Bw. (r)" heading show results from these simulations. The performance of the algorithm improves significantly, but still lags behind the other measurement-based algorithms. Next we experiment with ϵ = 1e-1, using the token rate as peak rate, for sources EXP2, EXP3, and POO3. The results are presented under the "Eqv. Bw. (r, ϵ=1e-1)" heading. Note that these numbers are still lower than those achieved with the "Measured Sum" algorithm. Due to its conservativeness, none of the simulations with the equivalent bandwidth algorithm results in packet loss.

5.2 Multiple-hop Results

Table 3 contains the average link utilization and average number of connections of the four links in the FOUR-LINK

Table 3: Multiple-hop All Sources Simulation Results. Entries in *italics* indicate simulations with non-zero loss rate.

Link	Measured Sum		Acceptance Rgn. 1		Acceptance Rgn. 2		Equivalent Bw.	
	%Util	#Actv	%Util	#Actv	%Util	#Actv	%Util	#Actv
L6	47	282	23	145	54	332	9	64
L7	79	485	38	242	*94*	*563*	16	104
L8	77	469	36	228	*93*	*547*	18	116
L9	77	469	38	234	*93*	*532*	25	158

Table 4: Percentage Composition of Type of Admitted Flows

Algorithm	EXP1	EXP2	EXP3	POO1	POO2	POO3
Measured Sum	21%	9	12	21	22	15
Acceptance Rgn. 1	21	9	13	21	21	16
Acceptance Rgn. 2	19	13	15	19	19	16
Equivalent Bw.	26	3	7	26	27	12

topology from simulations where we run all six sources, with the choice of sources uniformly distributed. Simulations with the "Measured Sum" and equivalent bandwidth algorithms use a sampling period of 1e3 packet transmission times while that of acceptance region use a sampling period five times as large. The switches have buffer space for 1600 packets in all these simulations. The table shows that the equivalent bandwidth algorithm is, again, rather conservative in this scenario. The "Acceptance Rgn. 1" scenario uses a utilization threshold of 40%, whereas the "Acceptance Rgn. 2" scenario uses 98%. With a 98% utilization threshold, the acceptance region algorithm results in 5e-5, 6e-5, and 8e-7 loss rate at links L7, L8, and L9 respectively. Under both the acceptance region and equivalent bandwidth algorithms, sources that do not declare their peak rates are admitted based on their derived peak rates per Eqn. 3.

Note that link L6 consistently achieves lower utilization than the other links. We call this the *under-representation* phenomenon in reference [11], and attribute its cause to unconsummated reservations when multi-hop flows admitted by the switch attached to L6 are rejected by one of the downstream switches. Table 4 shows the composition of the type of admitted flows, in percentages. It confirms our earlier observation in [11] that more resource demanding sources, namely EXP2, EXP3, and POO3, can suffer from another form of *under-representation*, where they are discriminated against by the network.

While the utilization achieved under the acceptance region algorithm is high when the utilization threshold is 98%, the choice of the utilization threshold is not from computation in [9], rather it is a "best case," but *ad-hoc*, choice for this scenario—hence does not allow the load estimation error to be quantified and assessed any more more rigorously than under the "Measured Sum" method. To compute the acceptance region, one must know the source characteristics *a priori*. On environments such as the Internet, where new applications are introduced at a high rate, and source characteristics depend not only on the applications but also their use, one cannot make *a priori* characterization of sources with any degree of certainty.

6 Conclusion

We have presented some preliminary results from the comparison of four admission control algorithms for controlled-load service. We hope that this paper will start a dialog with others in the field on a suitable method to conduct such study. We ourselves plan to do further, more systematic, comparative analysis of the various algorithms presented here.

Acknowledgments

We have benefited from various discussions with Lixia Zhang on measurement-based admission control, probability and statistics, running simulations, and writing papers. We thank Sally Floyd for many fruitful discussions on long-range dependent traffic and equivalent bandwidth. Frank Kelly and Richard Gibbens assisted us in understanding their scheme. This paper has also been improved by comments from Lee Breslau, Sally Floyd, and Lixia Zhang. We also thank the anonymous referees for their comments.

References

[1] F. Baker, R. Guérin, and D. Kandlur. *Specification of the Committed Rate Quality of Service*. Internet-Draft, Jun. 1996.

[2] J. Beran, R. Sherman, M.S. Taqqu, and W. Willinger. "Long-range Dependence in Variable-Bit-Rate Video Traffic". *IEEE Transactions on Communications*, 43:1566–1579, 1995.

[3] V.A. Bolotin. "Modeling Call Holding Time Distributions for CCS Network Design and Performance Analysis". *IEEE*

Journal of Selected Areas in Communication, 12(3):433–438, Apr. 1994.

[4] C. Casetti, J. Kurose, and D. Towsley. "A New Algorithm for Measurement-based Admission Control in Integrated Services Packet Networks". *Proc. of the Protocols for High Speed Networks Workshop*, Oct. 1996.

[5] D.E. Duffy, A.A. McIntosh, M. Rosenstein, and W. Willinger. "Statistical Analysis of CCSN/SS7 Traffic Data from Working CCS Subnetworks". *IEEE Journal of Selected Areas in Communication*, 12(3):544–551, Apr. 1994.

[6] Z. Dziong, M. Juda, and L.G. Mason. "A Framework for Bandwidth Management in ATM Networks — Aggregate Equivalent Bandwidth Estimation Approach". *Submitted for publication*, 1996.

[7] S. Floyd. "Comments on Measurement-based Admissions Control for Controlled-Load Service". Submitted to *Computer Communication Review*, 1996. **URL** ftp://ftp.ee.lbl.gov/papers/admit.ps.Z.

[8] M. Garrett and W. Willinger. "Analysis, Modeling and Generation of Self-Similar VBR Video Traffic". *Proc. of ACM SIGCOMM '94*, pages 269–279, Sept. 1994.

[9] R.J. Gibbens, F.P. Kelly, and P.B. Key. "A Decision-Theoretic Approach to Call Admission Control in ATM Networks.". *IEEE Journal of Selected Areas in Communication*, 13(6):1101–1114, Aug. 1995.

[10] R. Guérin, H. Ahmadi, and M. Naghshineh. "Equivalent Capacity and Its Application to Bandwidth Allocation in High-Speed Networks". *IEEE Journal of Selected Areas in Communication*, 9(7):968–981, Sept. 1991.

[11] S. Jamin, P. B. Danzig, S. J. Shenker, and L. Zhang. "A Measurement-based Admission Control Algorithm for Integrated Services Packet Networks (Extended Version)". *ACM/IEEE Transactions on Networking*, Dec. 1996. **URL** http://netweb.usc.edu/jamin/admctl/ton96.ps.Z.

[12] F. Kelly. Personal communication. Workshop on System and Control Issues in Communication Networks, Airlie, VA, Aug. 10, 1996.

[13] W.E. Leland, M.S. Taqqu, W. Willinger, and D.V. Wilson. "On the Self-Similar Nature of Ethernet Traffic (Extended Version)". *ACM/IEEE Transactions on Networking*, 2(1):1–15, Feb. 1994.

[14] E.C Molina. "Application of the Theory of Probability to Telephone Trunking Problems". *The Bell System Technical Journal*, 6:461–494, 1927.

[15] A.K. Parekh. *A Generalized Processor Sharing Approach to Flow Control in Integrated Services Networks*. PhD thesis, MIT, Lab. for Information and Decision Systems, Tech. Report LIDS-TR-2089 1992. Parts of this thesis were also published with R.G. Gallager in the *ACM/IEEE Transactions on Networking*, 1(3):344-357 and 2(2):137-150.

[16] V. Paxson and S. Floyd. "Wide-Area Traffic: The Failure of Poisson Modeling". *Proc. of ACM SIGCOMM '94*, pages 257–268, Aug, 1994. An extended version of this paper is available as **URL** ftp://ftp.ee.lbl.gov/papers/poisson.ps.Z.

[17] R. Warfield, S. Chan, A. Konheim, and A. Guillaume. "Real-Time Traffic Esitmation in ATM Networks". *International Teletraffic Congress*, June 1994.

[18] W. Willinger, M.S. Taqqu, R. Sherman, and D.V. Wilson. "Self-Similarity Through High-Variability: Statistical Analysis of Ethernet LAN Traffic at the Source Level". *Proc. of ACM SIGCOMM '95*, pages 100–113, Aug. 1995.

[19] J. Wroclawski. *Specification of the Controlled-Load Network Element Service*. Internet-Draft, Nov. 1995.

Measurement-based Call Admission Control: Analysis and Simulation

David Tse*

Dept. EECS
University of California
Berkeley, CA 94720, USA
dtse@eecs.berkeley.edu

Matthias Grossglauser†

INRIA
Sophia Antipolis
France
matthias.grossglauser@inria.fr

Abstract

We consider the problem of admission control for variable-rate traffic sources sharing a bufferless link, in order to provide a quality-of-service in terms of overload probability. Through analysis and simulations, we study the performance of a scheme which has no prior knowledge of the traffic statistics and makes admission decision based on the current network state only. We analyze the dynamics of the system under this control, and show that in the regime of large link capacity and separation of call and burst time-scales, this scheme performs as well as the optimal scheme which has full knowledge of the statistics. We evaluate the performance of the scheme on real traffic sources.

1 Introduction

Integrated-services networks are expected to carry a class of traffic that requires Quality of Service (QoS) guarantees. One of the main challenges consists in providing QoS to users while efficiently sharing network resources through statistical multiplexing. The role of Call Admission Control (CAC) is to limit the number of flows admitted into the network such that each individual flow obtains the desired QoS.

Traditional approaches to call admission control require an *a priori* traffic specification in terms of the parameters of a deterministic or stochastic model. The admission decision is then based on the specifications of the existing and the new flow. This approach suffers from several drawbacks. First, it is usually difficult for the user to tightly characterize his traffic in advance [1]. This is true even for stored media such as video-on-demand, as the user is expected to be able to exercise interactive control (such as pause, fast-forward etc.) As a result, traffic specifications can be expected to be quite loose. Second, there exists a modeling tradeoff between the ability to police and the statistical multiplexing gain. Deterministic models such as leaky buckets are easy to police, as they specify the *worst-case* behavior of traffic on a single time-scale, but they fail to provide a sufficient characterization to extract a large fraction of the potential statistical multiplexing gain. While a sequence of leaky buckets can approach such a multiple time-scale characterization, the number of model parameters grows accordingly [2]. Stochastic models such as those based on effective bandwidth are better suited to achieve good statistical multiplexing gain, but at the expense of policing [3]. It is not clear how to ensure that a traffic flow correspond to the specified parameters, without which call admission control can easily be "fooled".

In this paper, we focus on a different approach, in which admission control decisions are made based on network measurements alone. Instead of assuming a statistical or worst-case model for the traffic, the behavior of the current calls are monitored, and this information is used to make admission decisions. This measurement-based approach alleviates the burden on the users to provide accurate traffic models, and thus is a more practical approach for achieving statistical multiplexing gain with variable-rate traffic.

In this paper, we concentrate on a single-link bufferless model for the network. The QOS measure is the probability of network overload when the aggregate bandwidth requirements of the calls currently in the system exceeds the link capacity. The goal of admission control is to keep this overload probability below a desired threshold while minimizing the call blocking probability, or equivalently, maximizing the utilization of the network. We restrict ourselves to the homogeneous case, in which the statistical behavior of calls are similar.

The specific admission control scheme we are investigating is of the *certainty equivalent* type. The admission controller assumes that the measured statistics

*This author was supported by AFOSR F49620-96-1-0199 and a grant from Pacific Bell.

†This author was supported in part by a grant from France Telecom/CNET.

0-8186-7780-5/97 $10.00 © 1997 IEEE

are the true statistics of the calls, and uses the information to make decisions in the same way as a controller which has perfect *a priori* knowledge of the call statistics. Certainty-equivalent controllers are generally sub-optimal, as they do not take the *measurement errors* into account. We shall examine the impact of such measurement errors on the performance of the schemes via both theoretical analysis and simulations with synthetic and real traffic.

Our main theoretical result is that in the regime of large link capacities and separation of call and burst time-scale, a memoryless certainty-equivalent control can achieve the performance of an optimal scheme with knowledge of the traffic statistics. The proof of this result yields the important insight that it is essential to consider the *dynamics* of the controlled system to gain a full understanding of its performance. Thus, even though the controller is prone to measurement errors at any single admission decision, it turns out that in the above parameter regime, overload occurs only after a *succession* of admission mistakes, which is an unlikely event.

Past work on measurement-based admission control [4], [5], [6] have either ignored measurement errors or assumed a static situation where calls do not arrive or depart the system and there is arbitrarily long time to make accurate measurements. Recent work by Gibbens et. al. [7] advocates the explicit incorporation of call-level dynamics into the model and provides much inspiration to the present work. However, there are several major differences. First, the separation of time-scale assumption is already built into their model, whereas we deal directly with the interplay between call and burst dynamics. Given that a lot of traffic sources have long-range structure, such a separation of time-scale assumption should not be taken for granted *a priori*. However, due to this complexity in our model, we have to resort to a combination of asymptotic large deviations analysis and simulations. Second, the focus of their work is on the use of prior knowledge about the sources, whereas our scheme uses no such information. Lastly, the performance of their schemes are evaluated on on-off sources, whereas we test on real multi-level traffic sources.

We conclude this section by outlining two reasons for focusing on a bufferless model. First, the dynamics leading to the overload event in a bufferless system is much simpler than that of overflowing in a buffered system, as the event occurs whenever the instantaneous aggregate traffic load exceeds the link capacity. This simplification allows us to focus on the measurement problem that is of central interest in this paper. Second, recent work on multiple time-scale traffic [8] such as compressed VBR video has indicated that a significant bulk of the statistical multiplexing gain can be obtained by a Renegotiated Constant Bit Rate (RCBR) service. In this service model, buffering only occurs at the network edge. Bandwidth renegotiations fail when the current aggregate bandwidth demand exceeds the link capacity, and the renegotiation failure probability is the QOS measure of this service. Thus, our bufferless model is directly applicable to this problem.

2 Analysis

2.1 Basic Model

The network resource is a single bufferless link with capacity C. Calls arrive according to a Poisson process at rate λ and stay for an exponential distributed time with mean T if admitted. The calls have identical bandwidth requirement statistics, described by a continuous-time ergodic Markov fluid process. There are K states in the Markov process, and a call generates fluid at rate of μ_k in state k. The transition rate from state k to state l is r_{kl}. Let π_k be the steady-state probability that the source is at state k. Also, assume that when a call begins to transmit data, the Markov process is at steady state. The fluid processes of different calls are assumed to be independent.

A measurement-based admission control scheme decides whether to accept a new call based on the observed past history of calls that are currently in the system and possibly those that have already departed the system. Note that given any admission control scheme, the entire system is a stationary process. We are interested in two performance measures of a scheme: the steady-state probability of the event that the system overloads, i.e. the instantaneous aggregate fluid rate of calls in the system exceeds C, and the expected fraction of the total bandwidth utilized. For a given arrival rate, maximizing the latter is equivalent to minimizing the blocking probability. The success of the admission control scheme is evaluated by how well it meets the QOS-requirement (in terms of overload probability) and how close its bandwidth utilization is to that of the optimal scheme which knows the bandwidth requirements statistics *a priori*.

Suppose the statistics of each call is known a priori. Then one can estimate the overload probability given the number of calls in the system. For large number of calls, an accurate approximation is the Chernoff's estimate: the probability of overload when there are m calls in the system is approximately

$$\exp(-mL^*(\frac{C}{m})) \tag{1}$$

where

$$L^*(\mu) = \sup_{r>0}[\mu r - L(\mu)], \qquad L(r) = \log(\sum_{i=1}^{K} \pi_k \exp(\mu_k r))$$

assuming that the average rate $\bar{\mu}$ of each call is less than $\frac{C}{m}$ so that overloading is indeed a rare event. This is the well known approximation for the tail of the distribution of the sum of n i.i.d. random variables having the stationary bandwidth requirement distribution of a call. To satisfy a desired overload probability p_{qos}, one can *a priori* compute the maximum number of calls m^* such that the above approximation is less than p_{qos}. The admission control is simply to accept a new call if there are less than m^* calls in the system, and reject it otherwise. The notion of *effective bandwidth* for bufferless system is developed using this approximation [3]; in this homogeneous case, the effective bandwidth of a call is simply $\frac{C}{m^*}$.

Now we should focus on the problem of interest, when no prior information about the statistics of the calls is available. The idea now is to estimate the statistics of the calls from observing their past empirical behavior. We will study a very simple scheme to focus on the essential issues. Motivated by the recent work of Gibbens et al. [7] on measurement-based admission control, we consider a scheme which is *memoryless*, i.e. every time a new call arrives, the scheme uses only information about the *current* state of the network in making the decision of accepting or rejecting the call. More specifically, the scheme determines the number of calls $n_k(t)$ that is currently generating data at rate c_k, for each k ($k = 1, \ldots, K$). This yields an empirical distribution $\{\hat{\pi}_k\}$ of bandwidth requirements for a typical call, where $\pi_k = \frac{n_k(t)}{x(t)}$ and $x(t)$ is the number of calls currently in the system at time t. The idea is to use $\{\hat{\pi}_k\}$ to estimate the distribution $\{\pi_k\}$ of the bandwidth requirements throughout the entire lifetime of a call. The admission criterion for the new call for a given threshold p_{qos} on the renegotiation failure probability is taken to be:

$$\exp\left(-\hat{L}^*\left(\frac{C}{x(t)+1}\right)\cdot(x(t)+1)\right) \le p_{qos} \qquad (2)$$

and

$$\sum_{k=1}^{K} \hat{\pi}_k \mu_k < C \qquad (3)$$

where

$$\hat{L}(r) = \log \sum_{k=1}^{K} \hat{\pi}_k \exp(\mu_k r) \qquad \hat{L}^*(\mu) = \max_{r>0}[\mu r - \hat{L}(r)]$$

Note that the left hand side of inequality (2) is the Chernoff approximation of the failure probability for a system with $n+1$ calls each with bandwidth requirements distributed as $\{\hat{\pi}_k\}$. Thus, this admission control scheme is of the certainty-equivalent type: the controller assumes that the measured values are the true parameters and acts like the optimal controller which has perfect knowledge of the values of those parameters.

2.2 Asymptotic Analysis

To get some insights into the dynamics of this scheme and to compare its performance to the scheme with perfect knowledge, we will consider a fluid approximation as well as a large deviations analysis for the above model. Such an analysis is relevant in the asymptotic regime of large link capacity and small loss probabilities.

Let the total capacity be scaled as $C \equiv n$, and the call arrival rate as $\frac{\lambda n}{T}$, where n is a large parameter. Thus, $n\lambda\bar{\mu}$ is the offered load, and $\lambda\bar{\mu}$ is the offered utilization, i.e. offered load normalized by the the link capacity. Keeping the ratio of offered load to system capacity fixed in this scaling means that we are assuming that the link capacity is sized so that it is of the same order of magnitude as the demand. Also, note that the offered load is *independent* of the average call holding time. We also set the quality-of-service requirement $p_{qos} = \exp(-n\delta_{qos})$, for a parameter δ_{qos} which specifies the exponential decay rate. Thus, the larger the system, the more stringent is the QOS requirement.

To explain ideas in the simplest terms, let us focus on two-state on-off sources. When it is on, the source transmits fluid at the peak rate of 1; when it is off, rate 0. Let p be the steady-state probability that a source is on, i.e. its mean rate is p. By an appropriate normalization of the time unit, we can assume that the on-to-off transition rate is $1-p$ and the off-to-on transition rate is p.

2.2.1 Known Statistics

Consider first the case when admission control is done using the Chernoff's estimate eqn. (1) of the overload probability based on perfect prior knowledge of the source statistics. For the n th system, let $G_n^*(t)$ and $H_n^*(t)$ be the total number of calls in the system and the number that are on at time t respectively. (The superscript '*' denotes quantities associated with scheme with perfect prior knowledge.) Define the scaled processes:

$$X_n^*(t) \equiv \frac{G_n^*(t)}{n}, \qquad Z_n^*(t) \equiv \frac{H_n^*(t)}{n}$$

and let $u^*(n,T) \equiv \mathbb{E}[Z_n^*(t)]$ be the average utilization.(We indicate explicitly the dependence on the mean call holding time T.). Also, let $p^*(n,T)$ be the overload probability.

For the nth system, the maximum number of calls $m^*(n)$ admitted under the admission control is the largest m such that

$$mL^*(\frac{n}{m};p) \geq n\delta_{qos} \quad \text{and} \quad \frac{n}{m} \geq p$$

where L^* is large deviations rate function for on-off sources with mean rate p. It can be explicitly calculated as:

$$L^*(\mu;p) = \mu\log(\frac{\mu}{p}) + (1-\mu)\log(\frac{1-\mu}{1-p}) \qquad (4)$$

for $\mu \in [0,1]$ and equals ∞ otherwise. Note that $L^*(1;p) = -\log p$, correspond to the exponent of the probability that all sources are on.

As $n \to \infty$, it can be seen that $\frac{m^*(n)}{n}$ converges to $x^*(\delta_{qos})$ which is the largest $x \in [1, \frac{1}{p}]$ satisfying:

$$xL^*(\frac{1}{x};p) \geq \delta_{qos}$$

or equivalently,

$$-\log(xp) + (x-1)\log\frac{x-1}{x-xp} \geq \delta_{qos}$$

If $\delta_{qos} \leq -\log p$, then $x^*(\delta_{qos})$ is the unique solution to the equation

$$-\log(xp) + (x-1)\log\frac{x-1}{x-xp} = \delta_{qos}$$

On the other hand, if $\delta_{qos} > -\log p$, then $x^*(\delta_{qos}) = 1$. In this case, the QOS requirement is too stringent (relative to the burstiness of the traffic) such that peak-rate admission control has to be done. The system will never overload but also no statistical multiplexing gain is possible.

We now examine the behavior of the system as $n \to \infty$. It can be seen that typical behavior of the scaled system is well approximated by a *fluid limit* in which calls arrive at a deterministic rate of $\frac{\lambda}{T}$ and they transmit data at the mean rate of p once they are admitted into the system. The expected utilization of the system in this fluid limit depends on the offered rate λ:

$$\lim_{n\to\infty} u^*(n,T) \equiv u^*_\infty = \begin{cases} \lambda p & \text{if } \lambda < x^*(\delta_{qos}) \\ x^*(\delta_{qos})p & \text{if } \lambda > x^*(\delta_{qos}) \end{cases}$$

where $x^*(\delta_{qos})$ is computed as above. In the first case, the offered load is sufficiently low such that almost all calls are admitted. In the second case, the offered load is too high so that to maintain the desired QOS, a fraction of the offered calls has to be rejected. In this case, the number of calls in the system most of the time is close to the maximum possible for a given QOS. Moreover, since the number of calls in the system is no greater than $x^*(\delta_{qos})$ at all times, it is clear that by definition of $x^*(\delta_{qos})$, that the QOS is satisfied, i.e. for all T,

$$\lim_{n\to\infty}\frac{1}{n}\log p^*(n,T) \leq -\delta_{qos}.$$

In particular, in the case when $x^*(\delta_{qos}) = 1$, $p^*(n,T) = 0$ for all n and T. In the case when $x^*(\delta_{qos}) > 1$ and $\lambda > x^*(\delta_{qos})$, the QOS is satisfied exactly (in an exponential sense) for large call holding time T, i.e.

$$\lim_{T\to\infty}\lim_{n\to\infty}\frac{1}{n}\log p^*(n,T) = -\delta_{qos}.$$

2.2.2 Unknown Statistics

We now turn to an asymptotic analysis of the memoryless admission control scheme. In analogous to the previous analysis, for the nth system, let $G_n(t)$ and $H_n(t)$ be the total number of calls in the system and the number that are on at time t respectively, under the memoryless admission control scheme. Note that $(G_n(t), H_n(t))$ is the state of the system at time t. Define the scaled processes:

$$X_n(t) \equiv \frac{G_n(t)}{n}, \qquad Z_n(t) \equiv \frac{H_n(t)}{n}$$

and let $u(n,T) \equiv \mathbb{E}[Z_n(t)]$ be the average utilization. Also, let $p(n,T)$ be the overload probability. Our goal is to compare the average utilization and the overload probability to the corresponding quantities under the scheme with perfect prior knowledge, for n grows large.

The measurement-based scheme estimates the statistics of the sources under their current bandwidth requirements. In the case of on-off sources, the only parameter to estimate is p, the mean bandwidth requirement. The estimate $\hat{p}(t)$ of p at time t is $\hat{p}(t) = \frac{H_n(t)}{G_n(t)}$. Using the certainty-equivalent admission criterion (2), a call is admitted at time t if and only if

$$L^*(\frac{n}{G_n(t)+1};\hat{p}(t)) \geq n\delta_{qos} \quad \text{and} \quad H_n(t) < n \qquad (5)$$

where L^* is given by eqn. (4).

The scaled process $(X_n(t), Z_n(t))$ is a jump Markov process on the state space $\mathcal{S}^{(n)} \equiv \{(\frac{i}{n},\frac{j}{n}) : 0 \leq j \leq i\}$. Define the sets

$$\mathcal{S}_a^{(n)} \equiv \left\{\left(\frac{i}{n},\frac{j}{n}\right) \in \mathcal{S}^{(n)} : L^*\left(\frac{n}{i+1};\frac{j}{i}\right) \geq n\delta_{qos} \quad \text{and} \quad \frac{j}{n} < 1\right\}$$

$$\mathcal{S}_r^{(n)} \equiv \mathcal{S}^{(n)} - \mathcal{S}_a^{(n)}$$

New calls are admitted if the state of the system is in $\mathcal{S}_a^{(n)}$ and rejected if in $\mathcal{S}_r^{(n)}$. For large n, the scaled processes $(X_n(t), Z_n(t))$ converge to a fluid limit which take values in a two dimensional continuous state space $\mathcal{S} \equiv \{(x,z) : 0 \leq z \leq x\}$. The regions $\mathcal{S}_a^{(n)}$ and $\mathcal{S}_r^{(n)}$ converge into two regions in $\mathcal{S}$ divided by a boundary. Define f on $\mathcal{S}$ as

$$f(x,z) = \begin{cases} -\log z + (x-1)\log\frac{x-1}{x-z} & \text{if } x \geq 1 \\ \infty & \text{else} \end{cases}$$

Then in the region $\mathcal{S}_a \equiv \{(x,z) \in \mathcal{S} : f(x,z) \geq \delta_{qos}, z < 1\}$, calls are accepted where in the complement $\mathcal{S}_r$, calls are rejected. We shall call $\mathcal{S}_a$ the *acceptance region* and $\mathcal{S}_r$ the *rejection region*. It should be noted that this partitioning depends both on the number of sources x in the system and the number z which are on, whereas in the case with known source statistics, it depends only on the number of sources x which are on (i.e. whether $x \geq x^*(\delta_{qos})$). This is the essence of the difference between a measurement-based scheme and one with known statistics.

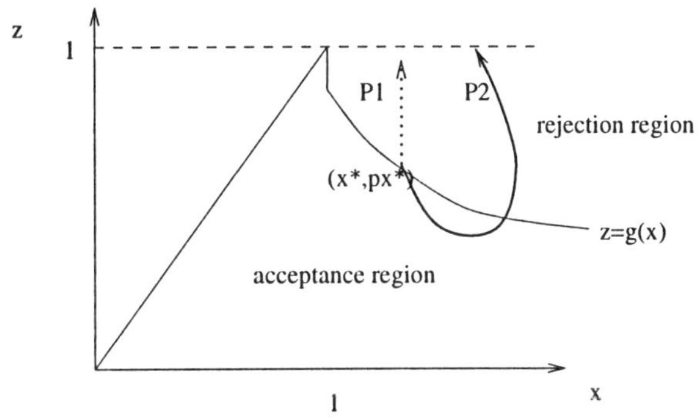

Figure 1: State space of fluid limit.

We shall now gather more information about the boundary. Clearly, $(x,z) \in \mathcal{S}_a$ if $x \leq 1$. (No possibility of overload even if all sources in the system transmit at peak rate.) For $x \geq 1$, $(x,z) \in \mathcal{S}_a$ if $f(x,z) \geq \delta_{qos}$ and $z < 1$. Further analysis reveals that one can find a function g such that this condition is equivalent to $z \leq g(x)$, where g satisfies $f(x, g(x)) = \delta_{qos}$ and has the properties that:1) $\lim_{x\to 1+} g(x) = \exp(-\delta_{qos})$; 2) $g(x)$ decreases monotonically with x; and 3) $\lim_{x\to\infty} g(x) = z^*$ where $z^* > 0$ satisfies

$$z^* - \log z^* - 1 = \delta_{qos}$$

Note that when there are x sources, $\frac{g(x)}{x}$ is the mean rate of each source such that the overload probability requirement is just satisfied. For the number of sources x close to 1 (link capacity), the only way to have an overload event is for all sources to transmit at peak rate. To satisfy the desired QOS, the mean rate of each source should then be $\exp(-\delta_{qos})$. Properties (2) and (3) imply that as there are more sources in the system, the maximum number of them that can be on and still permits new admissions decrease, and moreover approaches a non-zero limit as x goes to infinity. The situation is depicted in Figure 1. Note that the boundary consists of two segments: $z = g(x)$ for $x \in (1,\infty)$ and $x = 1$ for $z \in (\exp(-\delta_{qos}), 1)$. Also, the boundary partitions the state space into two connected regions.

In the fluid limit, the process follows a deterministic vector field starting from any initial point. In region $\mathcal{S}_a$, calls are accepted into the system at deterministic rate $\frac{\lambda}{T}$, while in region $\mathcal{S}_b$, the acceptance rate is zero. We now find the stable equilibrium points of the vector field and thus compute the average utilization in the fluid limit. First, one can easily see that the stable equilibrium points must lie on the line $z = px$, since p is the (true) mean rate of each source. As a consequence of the law of large numbers, the typical fraction of sources in the system that are on must be p. Moreover, there are no stable equilibrium points strictly inside the rejection region $\mathcal{S}_r$, since in this region, sources leave the system and no new sources enter. Thus, the stable equilibrium points must be strictly inside $\mathcal{S}_a$ or on the intersection of the boundary and the line $z = px$.

Suppose the line $z = px$ intersects the boundary at the point $(x^*(\delta_{qos}), px^*(\delta_{qos}))$. If $\delta_{qos} \leq -\log p$, the intersection is with the segment $z = g(x)$, and $x^*(\delta_{qos}) \geq 1$ satisfies the equation:

$$-\log(xp) + (x-1)\log\frac{x-1}{x-xp} = \delta_{qos}$$

If $\delta_{qos} > -\log p$, the intersection is with the segment $x = 1$, and $x^*(\delta_{qos}) = 1$. Note that $x^*(\delta_{qos})$ is precisely the maximum (scaled) number of calls that the scheme with perfect knowledge of the source statistics would admit. If $\lambda < x^*(\delta_{qos})$, the (unique) stable point $(\bar{x}, \bar{z})$ is $(\lambda, \lambda p)$, which lies strictly inside $\mathcal{S}_a$. In this case, almost all calls are accepted. If $\lambda \geq x^*(\delta_{qos})$, the stable equilibrium point $(\bar{x}, \bar{z})$ is on the boundary: $(x^*(\delta_{qos}), px^*(\delta_{qos}))$. In this case, a fraction of the calls are rejected. Thus, the stable equilibrium for the fluid limit under the measurement-based admission control is *exactly* the same as that under the scheme with perfect knowledge. This implies that the average utilization under the two schemes are asymptotically the same as $n \to \infty$, i.e.

$$\lim_{n\to\infty} \frac{u(n,T)}{u^*(n,T)} = 1 \qquad (6)$$

We now turn to an analysis of the overload probability $p(n,T)$ under the memoryless admission control scheme. This corresponds to the event $\mathcal{O} = \{(x,z) : z > 1\}$. Since this set does not contain the stable equilibrium, it is a rare event for n large, with probability decaying exponentially with n. We have:

$$p(n,T) \approx \exp[-nI^*(T)] \tag{7}$$

where

$$I^*(T) = \inf_{(\vec{r}(\cdot),\tau)\in F} \int_0^{\tau} l(\vec{r}(t), \dot{\vec{r}}(t))dt \tag{8}$$

and

$$F = \{(\vec{r}(\cdot),\tau) : \vec{r}(0) = (\bar{x},\bar{z}), \vec{r}(\tau) \in \mathcal{O}\} \tag{9}$$

Thus, the exponent is given by the cost of the cheapest path starting from the equilibrium point and leading to an overload. This is in accordance with *Laplace's* principle: the probability of the most likely way for a rare event to happen is approximately the same as the probability of the rare event. Here, $l(x,z,\vec{v})$ is the *local rate function*, which gives the cost of traveling with velocity $\vec{v}$ at the state (x,z).

At present, we do not have a rigorous large deviations limit theorem justifying the approximation (7); thus, it is only a heuristic. To have such a theorem, we need to prove a large deviations principle for the scaled processes $(X_n(\cdot), Z_n(\cdot))$, which have discontinuous jump rates across a *curved* boundary. Dupuis and Ellis [9] have proved a large deviations principle for discrete-time processes with jump rates across a *straight* boundary, and Alanyali and Hajek [10] has proved one for continuos-time processes. The local rate function we use is a natural generalization of theirs.

Our main result about the overload probability performance is the following.

Theorem 2.1 *If $x^*(\delta_{qos}) > 1$ and $\lambda \geq x^*(\delta_{qos})$ then*

$$\lim_{T\to\infty} I^*(T) = \delta_{qos}$$

If $x^*(\delta_{qos}) = 1$ or $\lambda < x^*(\delta_{qos})$ then

$$\lim_{T\to\infty} I^*(T) \geq \delta_{qos}$$

The first case corresponds to the situation when the stable equilibrium is on the segment $z = g(x)$ of the boundary, whereas the second is when the equilibrium is on the segment $x = 1$ or in the interior of $\mathcal{S}_a$.

A large T means that the average call holding time is much longer than the time-scale of the fluctuation of the bit-rate of the sources, and thus implies a regime of separation of call and burst time-scales. Thus, for large T, the memoryless scheme satisfies the QOS requirement in terms of the exponential decay rate of the overload probability, and also performs asymptotically as well as the scheme which have perfect prior knowledge in terms of average utilization (from (6)). We can conclude that for large capacities and a separation of time-scales, the memoryless scheme is *asymptotically optimal.* This is somewhat surprising since the measurement-based scheme has no *a priori* knowledge about the sources and only uses information about the current state of the network to make admission decisions. Due to space limitation, we shall only outline the intuition behind the proof of this result.

If the statistics of the bandwidth requirements of the call were known, then the maximum number of calls allowed in the system, approximately $nx^*(\delta_{qos})$, can be determined, such that the overload probability when there are that many calls in the system satisfy the QOS requirements. The measurement-based scheme essentially tries to estimate $nx^*(\delta_{qos})$ based on observing the current state of the network. Due to statistical fluctuations in the bandwidth requirements of the calls, the estimate may be too high due to atypically large number of calls being off. This may result in the control scheme making a mistake in accepting a new call which it should have rejected. However, the key point is that for a large system, the overload probability will deteriorate significantly only if the number of calls in the system is considerably larger than $nx^*(\delta_{qos})$; thus, making an occasional mistake in admitting a call is not fatal. Rather, making a succession of mistakes in accepting calls will lead to serious degradation in performance. However, because of the separation of the time-scales of call arrivals and fluctuations of bandwidth requirements, it is very unlikely for the state of the network to remain atypical over the period of time for the arrivals of a succession of calls. In fact, it can be shown that the probability of making a succession of mistakes is much smaller than that of overload due to having a typical number $nx^*(\delta_{qos})$ of calls in the system but atypically large number of calls being on.

This intuition can be translated into a proof of Theorem 2.1 via an analysis of the costs of the paths in F (the set of paths leading to overload, as defined in (8)) as T grows large. Two candidate paths are depicted in Fig. 1. Suppose the stable equilibrium is $(x^*(\delta_{qos}), px^*(\delta_{qos}))$ on the segment $z = g(x)$ of the boundary. Consider the straight-line path $P_1 = \{(x^*(\delta_{qos}), z) : z \in [px^*, 1]\}$. This corresponds to the event that the measurement-based scheme estimates the maximum admissible number of calls $nx^*(\delta_{qos})$ correctly, and overload occurs during call rejection phase with $nx^*(\delta_{qos})$ calls in the system but an atypical fraction of them turning on. Also, no call departs the system during this phase. We observe that as the average call holding time increases, the cost of this path approaches δ_{qos}, since the probability of overload when there are $nx^*(\delta_{qos})$ calls *permanently* in the system is approximately $\exp(-n\delta_{qos})$.

Now let us consider alternate paths of which an example is P_2, shown in Fig. 1. These paths consists of two phases. In the first phase, calls are admitted by mistake due to an atypically large fraction of the existing calls in the system turning off. This phase ends at time τ_1, resulting in nx_1 calls in the system, where $x_1 > x^*(\delta_{qos})$. In the second phase, new calls are rejected, but many of the existing calls turn back on, resulting in overload. Let us consider the costs of these paths in the regime of large holding time T. First, observe that the call arrival rate is $\frac{\lambda}{T} \cdot n$; hence, for those paths with $\tau_1 << T$, the cost is high because it is unlikely to have $n(x_1 - x^*(\delta_{qos}))$ arrivals in duration τ_1. On the other hand, for those paths with long duration τ_1, the cost is also high because it is unlikely for the calls in the system to be in an atypical state for so long. Using similar logic, it can be shown that the costs of all paths bounded away from P_1 go to infinity uniformly as average holding time $T \to \infty$. This implies that the cost of the cheapest path approaches δ_{qos} as $T \to \infty$.

We have only considered the case when the equilibria is on the segment $z = g(x)$. For the cases when the stable equilibrium point is on the segment $x = 1$ or in the interior of $\mathcal{S}_a$, one can show that the cost of the cheapest path must in fact be greater than δ_{qos}.

So far, we have focused on only on-off sources for ease and concreteness of exposition. The analysis and the Theorem 2.1 carry over to the general case of Markov fluid sources with general state space.

3 Experiments

In the previous section, we obtained some analytical insights into the performance of a memoryless measurement-based admission control scheme using fluid and large deviations analysis. Such results are valid in the asymptotic regime of large link capacities and for Markov sources. In this section, we will complement the theoretical investigations with simulation results for finite-size systems and on both real and synthetic traffic sources. In particular, we study the following issues: 1) the impact of parameters such as link capacity and offered load on the performance of the memoryless scheme; 2) the appropriateness of using Markov models in studying the performance of measurement-based schemes on real traffic sources.

3.1 Basic Simulation Set-up

Our simulation set-up is based on the Renegotiated CBR (RCBR) service [8]. Each call is represented as an RCBR schedule, i.e., as a sequence of intervals over which the bandwidth consumed by the call is assumed constant. This schedule represents the slow time-scale dynamics of the traffic source. Times at which the bandwidth changes correspond to instants when the source renegotiates for a new CBR rate. In this service, renegotiation fails when there is insufficient capacity in the link to cater for a requested bandwidth. Thus, this corresponds to the overload event in our bufferless model. For a real traffic source, we use a two-hour long MPEG-1 Star Wars trace [11], from which the RCBR schedule is computed by the off-line optimization algorithm presented in [8]. This schedule has a peak-to-mean bandwidth ratio of about 5. One important advantage of using the RCBR set-up is efficiency: we do not simulate on a per video frame basis but rather per renegotiation event. Since the particular schedule we use has about one renegotiation every 20 seconds on the average, this leads to an increased efficiency of 2 to 3 orders of magnitude.

In the simulations, calls arrive according to a Poisson process. We measure both the average network utilization and the renegotiation overload probability. We consider that the system state between time instants separated by more than twice the average call length is independent. Therefore, each interval of that size provides us with one sample for these metrics. We collect samples until the 95%-confidence interval for both metrics is sufficiently small with respect to the estimated value (within ± 30% of the estimated value.) For the overload probability, we also stop if the target overload probability of 10^{-5} lies to the right of the confidence interval, i.e., if we are confident that the actual failure probability is lower than the target. This is necessary in order to terminate simulations within reasonable time when the observed overload probability is very low (e.g. 10^{-8}).

3.2 Performance of Memoryless Scheme

The first set of experiments evaluates the impact of the link capacity and of the offered load on the performance of the memoryless scheme as defined by (2), where the desired overload probability p_{qos} is chosen to be 10^{-5}.

Arriving calls are randomly phase-shifted versions of the *entire* RCBR schedule for the two-hour Star Wars trace. Fig. 2 and 3 show the overload probability and the average network utilization respectively, plotted as a function of link capacity, expressed as a multiple of the call average rate, and the offered utilization, which is the offered load normalized by the link capacity. The network utilization is normalized to the utilization that is achieved with the same parameter values when call admission is performed based on the Chernoff approximation (1) and perfect knowledge of the call's marginal distribution. Thus, for example, a value of 1 means that the memoryless scheme does equally well as the scheme with perfect knowledge.

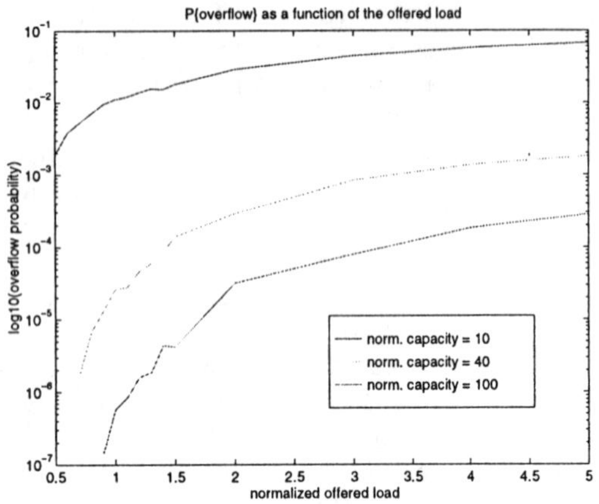

Figure 2: Overload probability for call duration equals length of entire trace

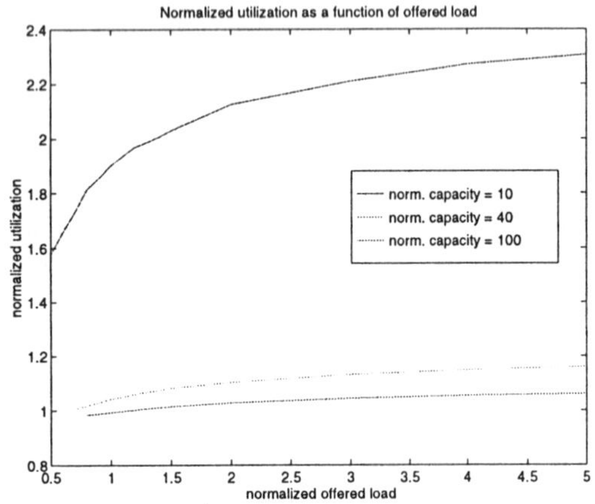

Figure 3: Utilization for call duration equals length of entire trace

It can be seen from Fig. 2 that the memoryless scheme performs poorly for small link capacities, say less than 60. The overload probability is much larger than the target of 10^{-5}.

3.3 Equivalent Markov Model

Our analysis in the previous section is based on a Markov model of the traffic source. It is therefore of interest to see how well a Markov model of a real traffic source can predict the performance of a measurement-based admission control scheme on the actual traffic source. In particular, we would like to investigate if the *long-range dependence* in the correlation structure, postulated recently to be present in many types of traffic, has any impact on the performance.

For a real traffic source, such as the Star Wars RCBR schedule, we obtain an *Equivalent Markov* model in the following way. We match both the marginal distribution π_i of the bandwidth, as well as the average residence time per bandwidth level τ_i. The bandwidth is described by a random process that stays at one of the bandwidth levels μ_i for an exponentially distributed time with mean τ_i. It then jumps to a new bandwidth level μ_j with probability f_j. The lengths of the intervals and the bandwidth levels within intervals are individually and mutually independent. To match the marginal distribution, we want

$$\pi_i = \frac{f_i \tau_i}{\sum_{j=1}^{M} f_j \tau_j}. \tag{10}$$

Thus,

$$f_i = \left(\sum_{j=1}^{M} \frac{\pi_j}{\tau_j} \right) \frac{\pi_i}{\tau_i}. \tag{11}$$

Note that the actual expected residence time per bandwidth level is slightly higher than τ_i, as with probability f_i, the model selects the same bandwidth in two consecutive intervals[1]. We thus have a traffic model that allows us to match the first-order characteristics of an RCBR trace, namely the marginal distribution of the bandwidth, and the mean residence time per bandwidth level, but which exhibits an exponentially decreasing correlation function, and therefore no long-range dependence (LRD).

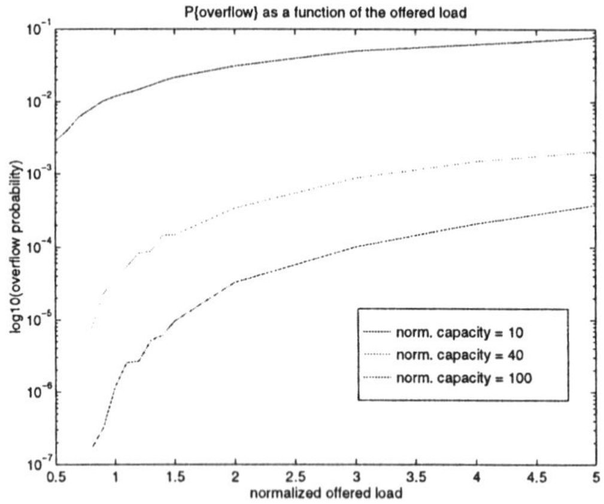

Figure 4: Overload probability for equivalent Markov model

We now evaluate the performance of the memoryless scheme when the Equivalent Markov model of the Star Wars RCBR scheme is used. Figs. 4 and 5 show

[1] The actual expected residence time is $\tau_i/(1 - f_i)$.

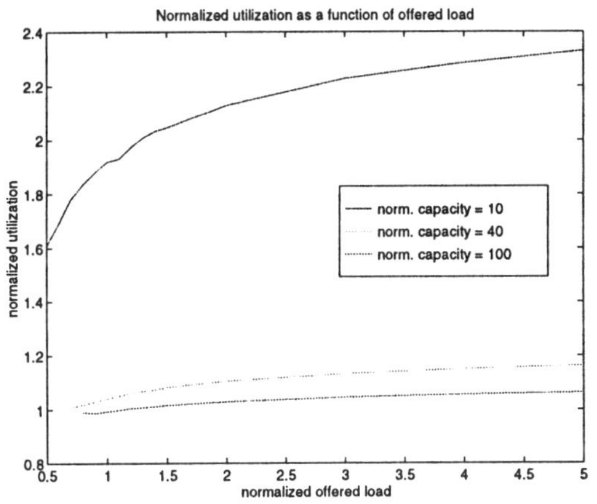

Figure 5: Utilization for equivalent Markov model

the overload probability and utilization respectively in the scenario when the bandwidth processes of calls are generated independently and according to the Equivalent Markov model of the Star-Wars schedule, and the calls stay for the same duration as the entire trace (approx. 2 hours). Comparing them to the corresponding Figs. 2 and 3 when the actual RCBR schedule is used, we see that the performance is quite similar in the two scenarios.

It is interesting that [11] concluded that this traffic exhibits long-range dependence, based on a statistical analysis of the Star Wars video trace. Our results indicate that such long-range dependence has little impact on the performance of the measurement-based admission control scheme considered here.

4 Conclusions

To obtain insights on the problem of measurement-based admission control, we have focused on a simple scheme, which has the main characteristics of being memoryless (admission decision based only on the current network state) and certainty-equivalent (measured statistics taken to be true values of the unknown parameters). We have studied this scheme through a combination of asymptotic analysis and simulations on real and synthetic traffic sources. The main theoretical result is that the scheme is asymptotically optimal in the regime of large link capacity and a separation of call and burst time-scales, in the sense of attaining the performance of the optimal scheme which has perfect knowledge of the traffic statistics. The performance is measured in terms of the ability to maximize the utilization of the network while maintaining the overload probability below a desired threshold. Our simulation results on the Star Wars trace indicate that the scheme only works well for large link capacities ($>$ 100 times the mean rate of a call) and not too high offered load (no more than 2 to 3 times the link capacity.) For small link capacities, it makes too many admission mistakes due to measurement errors. Wars trace serves as a good predictor of the performance of the admission control scheme on the actual traffic, despite the claimed presence of long-range dependence in the latter. Our current work focuses on finding schemes which have better performance under high offered load.

References

[1] E. P. Rathgeb, "Policing of Realistic VBR Video Traffic in an ATM Network," *International Journal of Digital and Analog Communications Systems*, vol. 6, pp. 213–226, 1993.

[2] E. Knightly and H. Zhang, "Traffic Characterization and Switch Utilization using a Deterministic Bounding Interval Dependent Traffic Model," in *Proc. IEEE INFOCOM '95*, (Boston, Mass.), April 1995.

[3] J. Hui, "Resource allocation for broadband networks," *IEEE Journal on Selected Areas of Communications*, Dec. 1988.

[4] C. Courcoubetis, G. Kesidis, A. Ridder, J. Walrand, and R. Weber, "Admission control and routing in ATM networks using inferences from measured buffer occupancy," *to be published.*

[5] H. Saito and K. Shiomoto, "Dynamic call admission control in ATM networks," *IEEE Journal on Selected Areas of Communications*, vol. 9, pp. 982–989, 1991.

[6] I. Hsu and J. Walrand, "Dynamic bandwidth allocation for ATM switches," *submitted to J. of Applied Probability.*

[7] R. Gibbens, F. Kelly, and P. Key, "A decision-theoretic approach to call admission control in ATM networks," *IEEE Journal on Selected Areas of Communications*, pp. 1101–1114, Aug. 1995.

[8] M. Grossglauser, S. Keshav, and D. Tse, "RCBR: A Simple and Efficient Service for Multiple Time-Scale Traffic," in *Proc. ACM Sigcomm '95*, (Boston, Mass.), pp. 219–230, August 1995.

[9] P. Depuis and R. Ellis, *A Weak Convergence Approach to the Theory of Large Deviations.* to be published.

[10] M. Alanyali and B. Hajek, "On large deviations of Markov processes with discontinuous statistics," *submitted to* Annals of Applied Probability, 1996.

[11] M. W. Garrett and W. Willinger, "Analysis, Modeling and Generation of Self-Similar VBR Video Traffic," in *ACM Sigcomm '94*, (London, UK), pp. 269–280, August 1994.

Earthworm: A Network Memory Management Technique for Large-Scale Distributed Multimedia Applications
(Extended Abstract)

Kien A. Hua   Simon Sheu   James Z. Wang
Department of Computer Science, University of Central Florida
Orlando, FL 32816-2362, U. S. A.

Abstract

The two main operating constraints of today's multimedia servers are the I/O bandwidth and communication bandwidth limitations. Both of these problems are addressed in this paper using a novel technique called Earthworm. *In this scheme, the network memory is used as a huge cache for buffering multimedia data. Dramatic reduction in the demand on the I/O bandwidth, therefore, can be achieved. This scheme also chains display stations to allow them to forward video streams. This strategy eliminates the congestion at the communication port of the server. Removing this bottleneck allows our technique to operate on the vast aggregate bandwidth of the WAN, rather than being constrained by the very limited local bandwidth available to the server. A unique feature of the Earthworm approach is that every display station using the server attempts to make some contribution to the caching space and communication bandwidth. The arrival of a new request, therefore, can be seen as a contributor, rather than just a burden to the server. This characteristic ensures the scalability of our design to support very large multimedia applications.*

1 Introduction

While the CPU gets most of the attention in providing high performance, it is not always realized that the mass storage medium plays an equally important role. In a *video-on-demand* (VOD) system, the bandwidth of the storage subsystem limits the number of customers who can be served simultaneously [20, 17]. Due to the large volume of video files and the strictly sequential access pattern [15], traditional LRU buffer management technique will not work well in this environment. To address this problem, a modified LRU scheme [19] presented in [8] uses two LRU chains: one for prefetched pages and one for referenced pages. The goal of this scheme is to ensure that the prefetched data to be used before replaced. Another LRU variant, L/MRP (Least/Most Relevant for Presentation), in [14] extends LRU by also considering potential future references in its replacement policy. By looking ahead to retain aging but soon needed data in the buffer, L/MRP is able to provide some advantage over the standard LRU technique. The ability to look ahead, however, comes at a cost. As described in [14], whenever a playback advances to the next data block in a video file, the degree of preference of each data block in the buffer must be re-evaluated. A method [18] trying to maximize the reusability of cached data partitions the buffer into several, say n, sections, where n is derived from the underlying disks. Each section corresponds to a group of viewers to ensure that a video block retrieved from the storage subsystem will be reused by all members of the group before being cast out. This interesting scheme, however, is limited to a single video being displayed at a time.

Although these techniques can provide noticeable improvement, it is still impossible for them to cache enough data in memory for reused. The fundamental problem in caching video objects is that these objects are too large compared to traditional data. This brings up the hard fact that affordable cache sizes are too small for large-scale multimedia applications. To address this problem, one needs to explore techniques for managing network memory, rather than relying solely on the limited size of the server memory. *Earthworm*, presented in this paper, is one such scheme which treats the aggregate memory space of the server and all the display stations as a unified space for caching video objects. In our scheme, display stations who request the same video file can be "chained" together. These playback stations are said to form a *video chain*. Display stations belonging to the same video chain are ordered by their relative starting time of the video object. As the playbacks of the video progress, the server sends a video stream to the display station that "leads" this video chain, while each display station in the chain is responsible

 0-8186-7780-5/97 $10.00 © 1997 IEEE

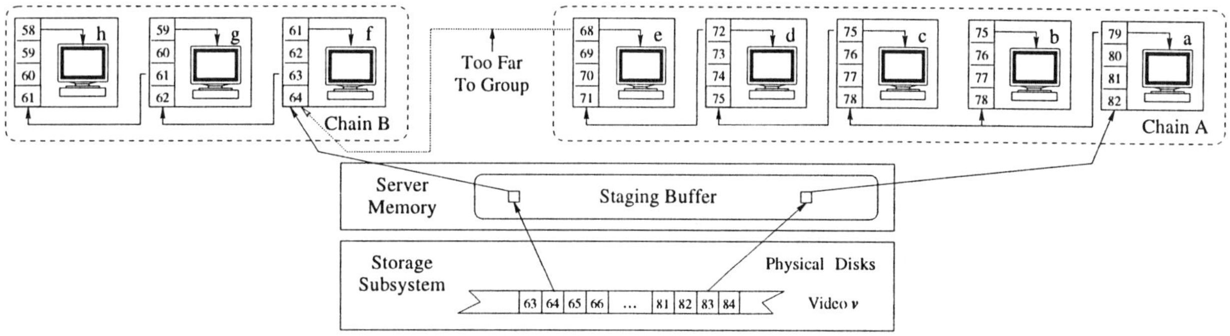

Figure 1: Chaining strategy.

for forwarding this video stream to the display station next in the chaining order. By chaining a number of display stations to a single video stream, we conserve the I/O bandwidth and the buffer space in the server.

The Earthworm technique gets its name from the fact that the video chains behave like earthworms crawling along the video frames of various video files. They can be multiplied by cutting the video chains (earthworms) into smaller chains (earthworms). As we will discuss later, the number of these chains and their lengths are dynamically controlled to maximize the system performance. The remainder of this paper is organized as follows. Three earthworm features are described in Section 2. A cache design based on these features are also introduced therein. In Section 3, we present our simulation study. An analytical model is used in Section 4 to make sense of the performance characteristics of the Earthworm features. Finally, we give our conclusions in Section 5.

2 The Earthworm Buffer Management Technique

Currently, the most common standard to represent video objects is MPEG. In this scheme, a set of frames can be defined to form a *group of frames* (GOF) consisting of one or more of the following three types of frames: I-, P-, and B-frame, In this research, we group every k consecutive GOFs into a data unit called *retrieval block* (R-block); and an R-block is the minimum unit of data we refer to in terms of buffer refreshes. This approach is commonly used today [8, 13, 14, 18]. In the following subsections, we first introduce three Earthworm features: *Chaining, Connection without Returning, Connection with Returning.* These features are then used to design an Earthworm scheme for network memory management.

2.1 Chaining

We assume that R-blocks of a video are numbered from 1 to the length of the video file according to their temporal positions in the video. Let D_m and D_n be two display stations which are currently playing back the i-th and j-th R-blocks, respectively. $d(m,n)$ denotes the *playback distance* of D_m and D_n, and is computed as $j-i$, assuming $j > i$. In this case, D_m and D_n can be served by the same *video chain* if D_n has at least $d(m,n)$ units of memory space to momentarily cache data for D_m. Fig. 1 illustrates this strategy. It shows that each station has four units of buffer space (denoted as $b_d = 4$). Each unit can store an R-block. A number i in a buffer indicates that it currently has a copy of the i-th R-block. A shaded block indicates that it is being refreshed. We note in this example that stations D_a, D_b, D_c, D_d, and D_e are served by video chain A, while another video chain B is serving stations D_f, D_g, and D_h. The relevant playback distances are $d(b,a) = 4$, $d(c,b) = 0$, $d(d,c) = 3$ and $d(e,d) = 4$ in Chain A; $d(g,f) = 2$ and $d(h,g) = 1$ in Chain B. Since all of them are less than or equal to b_d $(= 4)$, these stations can share the corresponding video stream. The two video chains, however, cannot be combined because $d(f,e) = 7 > b_d$.

To illustrate the data flow in Chaining, let us consider *Chain A* shown in Fig. 1. The video server needs only to retrieve the R-blocks for the station D_a which is called the *head* of this video chain. D_a is responsible for forwarding the R-blocks to D_b and D_c which were admitted to the video chain as a batch [5, 1]. We note, however, that the data is now delivered from a client, instead of the server. Eventually, each R-block traversing the chain will arrive at D_e. As the *tail* of the chain, D_e discards the R-blocks after they are played out. In this approach, a receiving station sees the forwarding station as a "server".

A major advantage of Chaining is that it can significantly reduce the demand on I/O bandwidth. If the average length of the video chains is l, this scheme requires a video bandwidth which is nearly l times less than that of a conventional system. We note that a technique similar to Chaining in concept was proposed by Franklin, Carey and Livny [7] for conventional client-server computing. In this scheme, a client workstation is allowed to retrieve data cached in other workstations which have the latest version of the data items. The similar studies on the operating systems design were discussed in [3, 6]. Their works, however, are primarily concerned with cache consistency and transaction processing issues. Handling continuous media requires Chaining to address entirely different matters. We note that if the requests momentarily sparsely arrive, the playback distances become too large (*i.e.*, $> b_d$) rendering chaining impossible. To address this problem, the server can "loan" its buffer space to fill the gaps of the otherwise broken chains. Two ways to mend these broken chains are described in the next two subsections.

2.2 Connection without Returning (CWOR)

As we have discussed, Chaining allows several stations to share I/O streams; thus, combining video chains will save I/O bandwidth for additional users. This is achievable if sufficient buffer space is available to cache the R-blocks for these video chains. Let D_{ha} and D_{hb} be the heads of two arbitrary video chains A and B playing the same video. At the time of combining, let us assume that D_{ha} and D_{hb} are playing back the ha-th and hb-th R-blocks, where $ha > hb$. To combine these two video chains, we allocate $(ha - hb)$ units of the server memory. This strategy is illustrated in Fig. 2, where three initial chains are shown. Chains

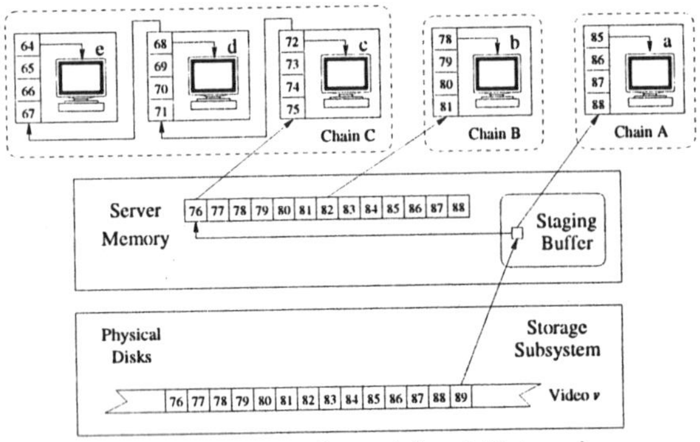

Figure 2: Connection without Returning.

A and B were created to serve stations D_a and D_b. Chain C is more efficient. It has three stations D_c, D_d, and D_e. These three chains can be combined using $(85 - 78) + (78 - 72) = 13$ units of buffer space. This buffer space can be seen as a window into the corresponding video file. The buffer blocks are continuously refreshed by an I/O stream in a round-robin fashion. At any time, it buffers the appropriate fragment of the video file to support the three simultaneous entries to the same video. We note that station D_a could get its data from this buffer. However, bypassing is possible [2]. As the data are loaded to refresh the caching buffer, we can forward a copy to station D_a. The heads D_b and D_c must get their data from the caching buffer. Stations D_d and D_e can receive their data through the video chain headed by D_c.

We observe in Fig. 2 that every R-block initially loaded for station D_a will be cached and reused exactly four times. By combining video chains, we have improved the hit ratio of the buffer. The application of this technique is limited only by the capacity of the server memory. When the buffer space is full, one can perform some optimization by breaking a video chain with a high connection cost to make room for less expensive connections which are not currently connected. We discuss this mechanism in more detail in the following. Given two arbitrary video chains, their *connection cost* is defined as the amount of server buffer space used to connect them. For instance, the connection cost of the two video chains A and B, as shown in Fig. 2, is 7. When an additional I/O stream is needed and the I/O bandwidth has been exhausted, the buffer can attempt to disconnect the most expensive connection. By disconnecting a connection of cost c, we make c units of free buffer space available to the less expensive connections. Although disconnecting the expensive connection requires one additional I/O stream for the breakaway video chain, being able to use the freed buffer space to make several less expensive connections will create a number of I/O streams available for the pending requests.

2.3 Connection with Returning (CWR)

As in CWOR, the trade-off between buffer space and I/O bandwidth is feasible. Trading between communication bandwidth and buffer space is also possible, which is discussed as follows. In Fig. 2, 13 units of buffer space are needed to connect chains A, B, and C. We observe that some R-blocks are redundantly stored on both the server and stations. For instance, R-block 80 is stored on both the server and station D_b. We can remove this redundancy by storing on the server only the R-blocks not cached by any involved stations. This is illustrated in Fig. 3, where only five units are necessary. In this strategy, after chain A finishes an R-block, it is returned to the server. These returned R-blocks will be used by chain B which, in turn, will return its R-blocks after being played. Finally, chain C will use the R-blocks returned by chain B; and it discards the blocks after playing them. Obviously, we are trading communication bandwidth for more free buffer space. The additional communication costs are due to the return of the R-blocks.

We discuss the general case in the following. Let D_{ta} and D_{hb} be the tail and the head of two video chains A and B playing the same video. Assume D_{ta} is currently playing the t-th R-block, and D_{hb} has

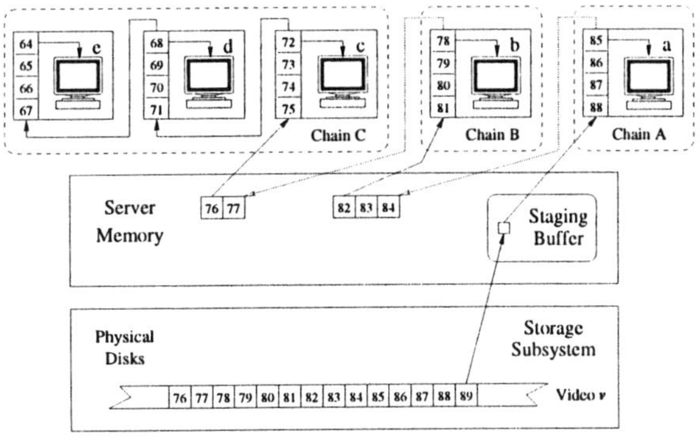

Figure 3: Connection with Returning.

buffered in its local memory up to the h-th R-block. To combine these two video chains, we need to allocate $(t - h - 1)$ units of buffer space on the server. In this strategy, we can view the video chain A as forwarding data to the video chain B through the server buffer. Alternatively, we can see the two combined video chains as a longer chain with the server being a dummy member of the combined group. Since the buffer space on the server is very large, it can be used as dummy members in many chain connections. Nevertheless, the buffer space is finite. When it is used up, disconnections as discussed previously are necessary to return some of the free space to the buffer pool.

2.4 An Earthworm Design

The above three buffer management techniques should be used as features to design more general Earthworm techniques. Our implementation that uses all three features is described as follows. We maintains an *I/O pool* and a *communication pool* as counters to model the amount of I/O and communication bandwidths currently available. Initially, the I/O pool is initialized to the total number of concurrent I/O streams sustainable by the server. Similarly, the communication pool is initialized according to the network capacity. At runtime, communication and I/O resources are checked out from these pools to serve a new request, and then they are returned to the pools when the service is completed. Given a new arrival, our scheme performs the following tasks:

1. It first tries Chaining since this is the simplest and least expensive Earthworm feature. (The criterion for using Chaining has been discussed in Section 2.1.)
2. If chaining is not possible, it allocates an I/O stream and a communication stream for the request if they are available.
3. On the other hand, if the I/O pool has been exhausted, the server tries to apply CWR or CWOR to connect a pair of existing chains in order to return an I/O stream to the pool. This I/O stream can then be given to the requester. (The criteria for applying CWOR and CWR have been discussed in Sections 2.2 and 2.3, respectively.)
4. If none of the above steps work, it tries to replace the most costly connection (*i.e.*, using a large buffer space) by n least expensive connections which have not been connected yet. If this is successful, $n - 1$ I/O streams become available; and one of them can be allocated to the requester.
5. When the server has exhausted the above strategies, but still cannot come up with enough resources to schedule the request, the requester must wait until some station returns its I/O stream to the pool.

We note that Step 4 is a chain optimization step. It is more beneficial to connect chains with less expensive connections [10, 4, 12, 16]. However, in this step, the buffer space is not enough to make the connections. To generate some buffer space, it disconnects the most expensive chain and uses its buffer space for the new and less expensive connections. Although breaking the expensive chain requires one additional I/O stream, the n new connections will return n I/O streams to the I/O pool resulting in a gain of $n - 1$ free I/O streams.

A connection can be built over time by gradually accumulating the R-blocks in the server buffer until they fill the "gap" between the two video chains. If this approach is used, the I/O stream cannot be returned until the connection is completely built. Alternatively, some I/O bandwidth can be reserved for this purpose. When the system needs to make a connection, this bandwidth is used to fill the "gap" instantly. We note that in our implementation, all other pending requests for the same video are also grouped with the one at the head of the queue, and the same resource is used to serve this batch of requests [5].

3 Simulation Study

In our simulation study, we implemented a detailed simulator for the earthworm scheme. To assess its benefits, we also implemented a simulator for *Love Prefetch* [8] which was used in our study as a representative of conventional methods. Our simulation model is similar to the one used in [21]. The servers and display stations are interconnected in the ATM network, where they may deliver data to others via attached ATM hubs. Each user request is characterized by an interarrival time and choice of video. User request interarrivals were modeled using a Poisson process. The

Parameter	Value	Unit
Memory capacity of each client	4 (1, 2, 4, 8, 16)	R-block
Memory capacity of the server	8000 (1000, 2000, 4000, 8000, 16000, 32000)	R-block
Server IO bandwidth	20,000	R-blocks/second
Effective aggregate bandwidth of the network	140,000	R-blocks/second
Request rate	30 (10, 15, 20, 25, 30, 35, 40)	request/second
Skew factor	0.7 (0.0 0.2, 0.4, 0.6, 0.8, 1.0)	N/A
Wait Tolerance Level	3 (1, 2, 3, 4, 5)	minute
Total number of video objects	128 (128, 256, 384, 512, 640, 768, 896, 1024)	video
Size of each video	4000	R-block

Table 1: Simulation parameters.

selection of videos follows a Zipf-like distribution [9]. That is, the probability of choosing the i-th video is $\frac{1}{i^z \cdot \sum_{j=1}^{N} 1/j^z}$, where N is the number of videos in the system, and z is the *skew factor*. It is defaulted at 0.7, a typical value for VOD applications [5]. Each

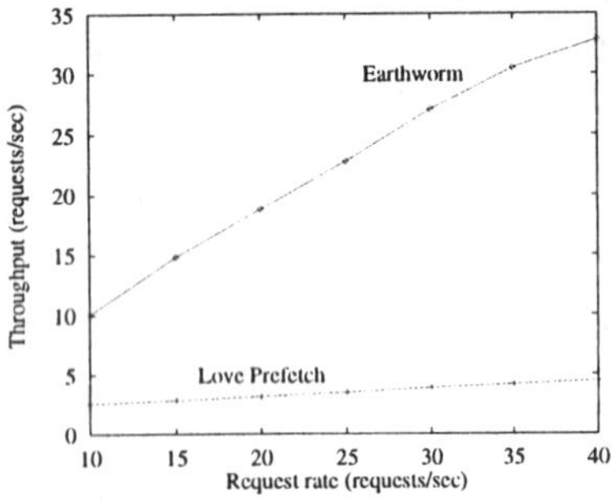

(a) Throughput

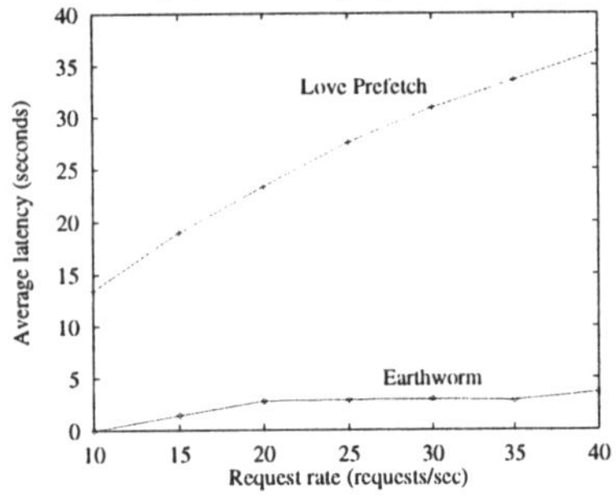

(b) Latency

Figure 4: Performance under various request rates.

simulation run consists of 120,000 to 480,000 requests depending on the request rates. In terms of hardware, we conservatively set the effective bandwidth of the ATM network to be seven times that of the server I/O bandwidth. Furthermore, we assume that Love Prefetch does not have the communication-congestion problem and can also take advantage of the aggregate bandwidth of the network. If we simulate the network-I/O bottleneck, the performance of Love Prefetch will be worse than the results presented in this paper. The default values for the system and workload parameters are given in Table 1. The values in the parentheses were used to do various sensitivity analyses with respect to the corresponding parameter.

In our performance study, *system throughput* and *average access latency* were used as the metrics. The former is calculated by dividing the number of requests finished by the total simulated time. The latter is computed as the mean of the individual latencies experienced by the requesters during a simulation run. In our study, we also simulate the human factor, *Wait Tolerance Level* (WTL) which is defined as the maximum wait time any user is willing to wait before he cancels his request. Due to space limitation, we only present some of the results in the following.

3.1 Effect of Request Rate

The performance under various request rates is plotted in Fig. 4. We observe that the improvement due to Earthworm increases with the increases in the request rate. When the request rate is 40 requests/second, the system throughput is improved more than fivefold. The improvement in terms of average latency is even more significant.

3.2 Effect of Memory Size

The effect of the buffer sizes are plotted in Fig. 5. When the buffer size of each client station is varied from 1 to 16 R-blocks, the improvement in the system throughput due to Earthworm increases from 375% to 750% (Fig. 5(a)). We note that the throughput curve for Earthworm is flat after eight R-blocks. This is due to the fact that when each client station is equipped with eight or more R-blocks, the services are completed at the same rate as new requests are arriving at the server. Adding more buffer space to the clients beyond this capacity does not help the performance unless we also increase the request rate. As in the last subsection, we again observe that Earthworm enjoys much better access latencies. Similar performance comparison can be said about the case of varying the server buffer size (Fig. 5(b)).

4 Analytical Analyses

In order to gain insight on the performance characteristics of the Earthworm approach, we also devel-

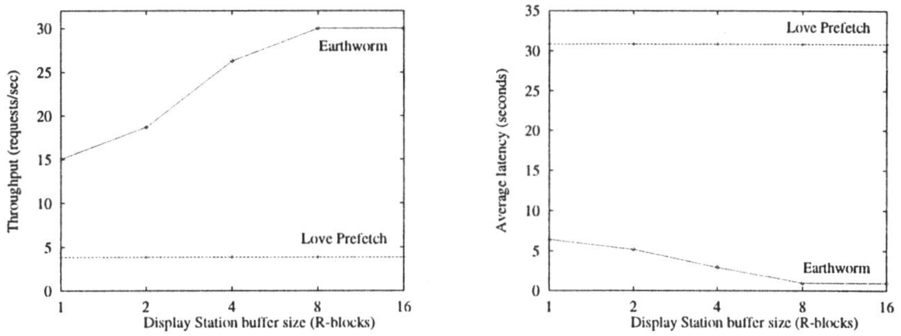

(a) Effect of client memory size

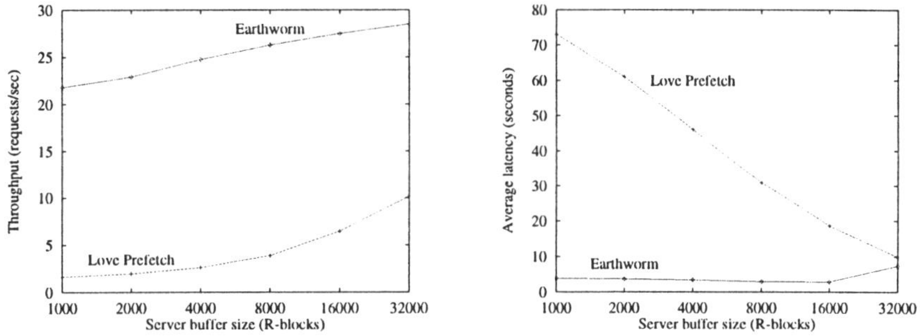

(b) Effect of server memory size

Figure 5: Performance under different memory sizes.

oped an analytical model to analyze each of the three features discussed in Section 2. We investigated their performance as compared to *No-Caching* (NC) and LRU techniques. The baseline scheme, NC, does not cache data in the server buffer. Instead, only dedicated I/O streams are used to serve the requests. Since LRU has been widely studied and its behavior is well understood, we use it as a reference in this study. Due to space limitation, only analytical results are presented in the following. Interested readers are referred to [11] for the detailed discussion of the analytical analyses.

4.1 Effect of Request Rate

Fig. 6 shows the I/O bandwidth required by each scheme in order to support a certain request rate without glitches. For comparison purposes, we define the *relative performance* of a scheme with respect to the other scheme is the inverse of the ratio of their required I/O bandwidths. For instance, when the arrival rate is 90 requests/sec, the relative performance of Chaining, CWOR, and CWR with respect to LRU approximate 608%, 658%, and 929%, respectively. Obviously, these new schemes are overwhelmingly better than LRU. They can support a much larger number of concurrent users given an I/O bandwidth. This observation is consistent with our simulation results presented in the last section.

We note that all of the performance curves shown in Fig. 6 slope down after reaching a pinnacle. At first glance, this seems counterintuitive. This phenomenon can be explained as follows. When the arrival rate of the requests is too slow, the buffer space is too small to keep the R-blocks long enough in the memory for data sharing. Therefore, the demand on the I/O bandwidth increases as we gradually increase the request rate. However, when the request rate is large enough, many requests for the same video files arrive closer together allowing them to share the R-blocks in the buffer space. Consequently, the demand on the I/O bandwidth drops. Further increases in the arrival rate beyond this point will continue to lower the requirement on the I/O bandwidth.

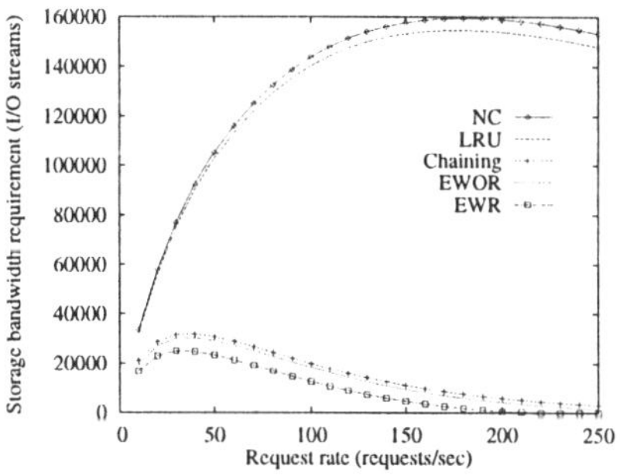

Figure 6: Effect of request rate.

This finding is quite remarkable. It says that if we

continue to increase the request rate, the demand on the I/O bandwidth will eventually decrease. Many researchers focusing their study on the low arrival rates might miss the opportunity for a much better performance at the same low I/O costs. This is particularly true for the proposed technique which can benefit from the huge aggregate bandwidth of the WAN. Since communication bandwidth is reserved for each active display station, the bandwidth capacity of the communication network ultimately determines the maximum number of concurrent users can be supported. Being able to benefit from the aggregate bandwidth of the WAN is a big asset that allows the new techniques to operate in the range of request rates to the right-hand side of their plateau shown in Fig. 6. Techniques which are constrained by the very limited local bandwidth available to the server will most likely have to operate in the left-hand side of their maximum. In the subsequent performance comparisons, we conservatively set the request rate at 30 requests/second. The reader, however, should keep in mind that the new techniques have the potential to achieve much better performance as evident in Fig. 6.

4.2 Effect of Server Buffer Size

The performance results under various server buffer size are plotted in Fig. 7. Since NC does not use the server buffer, its performance is not affected by the size of this buffer. LRU uses the server buffer. However, it benefits little from this buffer space. Even when the buffer size is as large as 32,000 R-blocks, its performance still lags far behind that of Chaining which requires no server buffer at all. Their relative performance is a whopping 216%. Comparing LRU to CWR, we observe that their relative performance increases as the server buffer size grows. This indicates that the Earthworm approach can utilize the server buffer space more effectively than LRU.

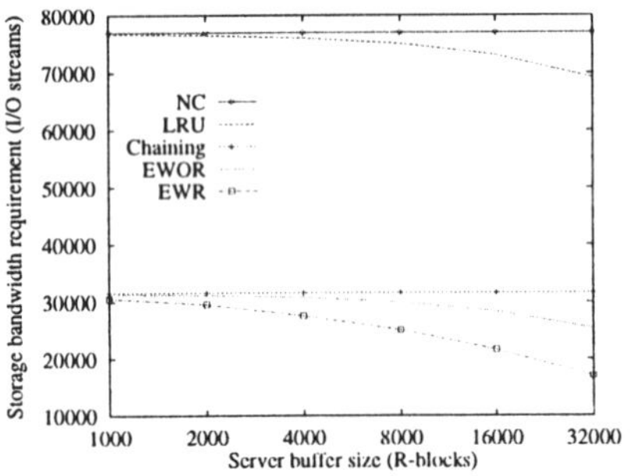

Figure 7: Effect of Server Buffer Size.

4.3 Effect of Display Station Buffer Size

The sensitivity analyses of the display stations' buffer size are shown in Fig. 8. The curves for NC and LRU are flat because they do not benefit from the buffers on the display stations. On the contrary, the savings in I/O bandwidth due to the new techniques increase with the increases in the size of the display station buffer. When the size of these buffers is 16 R-blocks, Fig. 8(b) shows that Chaining, CWOR and CWR provide an impressive relative performance with respect to LRU of 1,314%, 1,432% and 2,528%.

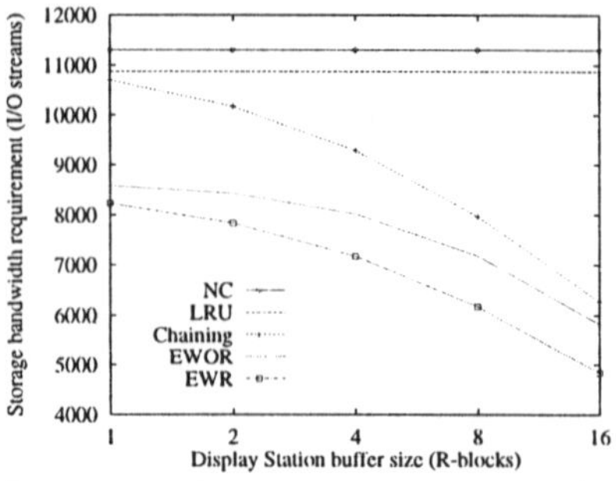

(a) Request Rate equals 3 requests/sec

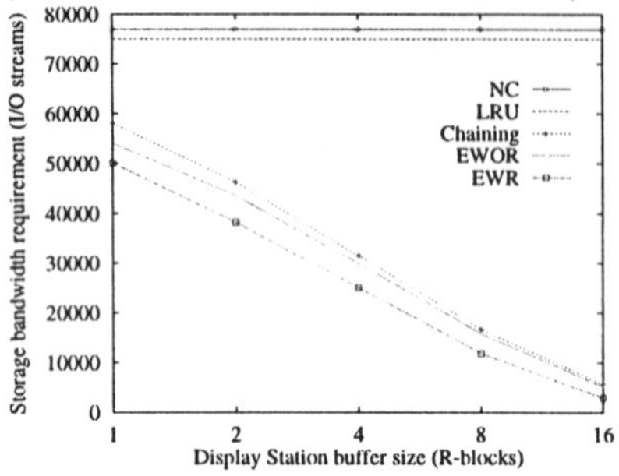

(b) Request Rate equals 30 requests/sec

Figure 8: Effect of display station buffer size.

Interestingly, only one R-block of buffer space on each display station is sufficient for CWR and CWOR to outperform LRU by a significant margin. The same can be said about Chaining if the request rate is sufficiently large. It is suggested in Fig. 8(a) that when the request rate is very slow, the performance of Chaining can suffer. This is due to the fact that Chaining does not use the buffer on the server to cache data. If the arrival rate of the requests momentarily drops to a very low level, arrivals become very sparse making chaining impossible. In this case, most playbacks will require a dedicated I/O stream. This explains why the CWR and CWOR features are necessary to ensure the robustness of the overall Earthworm technique in adapting to wobbly workloads.

5 Concluding Remarks

In this paper, we presented a network memory management technique for multimedia applications called *Earthworm*. This scheme allows its caching space to encompass the local memory of the client stations currently using the service. As a result, this approach can dramatically reduce the demand on the I/O bandwidth of the multimedia server. We note that we assumed very dump display stations that have a small amount of memory in this paper. In the near future, clients will likely to have significant memory and even local disks (this is already the case for clients that are workstations.) The benefit of Earthworm will be even greater in such an environment.

While conventional caching designs focus solely on reducing the I/O costs, *Earthworm* also addresses another equally crucial issue, namely the network-I/O bottleneck. The chaining concept allows the stations to forward video streams. This new communication strategy eliminates the congestion at the communication port of the server. Removing this bottleneck allows the new technique to operate on the vast aggregate bandwidth of the WAN (*i.e.*, maximizing the network throughput), rather than being constrained by the very limited local bandwidth available to the server. As multicast is very important to many types of applications, in this paper we proposed *chaining* as a new communication strategy for a new class of applications which involve multimedia data. In summary, multimedia storage servers differ from conventional storage servers to an extent that requires drastically new design approaches rather than relying on adapting existing solutions for conventional computing systems. We hope that this work will inspire other novel ideas to catapult the multimedia information technology into the twenty-first century.

References

[1] C. C. Aggarwal, J. L. Wolf, and P. S. Yu. On optimal batching policies for video-on-demand storage servers. In *Proc. of IEEE Multimedia Systems*, Hiroshima, Japan, June 1996.

[2] S. Berson, R. Muntz, S. Ghandeharizadeh, and X. Ju. Staggered stripping in multimedia information systems. In *Proc. of ACM SIGMOD*, pp. 79–90, Minneapolis, Minnesota, May 1994.

[3] M. Dahlin, R. Wang, T. Anderson, and D. Patterson. Cooperative caching: Using remote client memory to improve file system performance. In *Proc. of USENIX Symposium on OSDI*, pp. 267–280, Nov. 1994.

[4] A. Dan, Y. Heights, and D. Sitaram. Generalized interval caching policy for mixed interactive and long video workloads. In *Proc. of SPIE's conf. on Multimedia Computing and Networking*, pp. 344–351, San Jose, California, Jan. 1996.

[5] A. Dan, D. Sitaram, and P. Shahabuddin. Dynamic batching policies for an on-demand video server. *Multimedia Systems*, 4(3):112–121, June 1996.

[6] M. Feeley, W. Morgan, F. Pighin, A. Karlin, H. Levy, and C. Thekkath. Implementing global memory management in a workstation cluster. In *Proc. of ACM SOSP*, Dec. 1995.

[7] M. Franklin, M. Carey, and M. Livny. Global memory management in client-server DBMS architectures. In *Proc. of VLDB Conf.*, pp. 596–609, Aug. 1992.

[8] C. S. Freedman and D. J. DeWitt. The SPIFFI scalable video-on-demand system. In *Proc. of ACM SIGMOD*, pp. 352–363, San Jose, California, May 1995.

[9] K. A. Hua, C. Lee, and C. M. Hua. Dynamic load balancing in multicomputer database systems using partition tuning. *IEEE Trans. on Knowledge and Data Engineering*, 7(6):968–983, Dec. 1995.

[10] K. A. Hua. SOBE: A Scalable Technology for Designing Very Large Multimedia Server. CS-TR-96-01, UCF, Orlando, Florida, Jan. 1996.

[11] K. A. Hua, S. Sheu, and J. Z. Wang. *Earthworm*: A network memory management technique for large-scale distributed multimedia applications. CS-TR-96-05, UCF, Orlando, Florida, Nov. 1996.

[12] K. A. Hua, S. Sheu, and J. Z. Wang. HOPE: A scalable technology for very large networked video-on-demand systems. In *Proc. of CASAF '96*, St. Petersburg, Florida, June 1996.

[13] K. Keeton and R. H. Katz. Evaluating video layout strategies for a high-performance storage server. *Multimedia Systems*, 3:43–52, 1995.

[14] F. Moser, A. Kraiβ, and W. Klas. L/MRP: A buffer management strategy for interactive continuous data flows in a multimedia DBMS. In *Proc. of VLDB Conf.*, pp. 275–286, Zurich, Switzerland, Sep. 1995.

[15] B. Özden, A. Biliris, R. Rastogi, and A. Silberschatz. A low-cost storage server for movie on demand databases. In *Proc. of VLDB Conf.*, pp. 594–605, Santiago, Chile, Sep. 1994.

[16] B. Özden, R. Rastogi, A. Silberschatz, and C. Martin. Demand paging for video-on-demand servers. In *Proc. of IEEE ICMCS*, pp. 264-272, May 1995.

[17] A. Reddy and J. Wyllie. I/O issues in a multimedia systems. *IEEE Computer*, 27(3):69–74, March 1994.

[18] D. Rotem and J. L. Zhao. Buffer management for video database systems. In *Proc. of IEEE Data Engineering*, pp. 439–448, Taipei, Taiwan, March 1995.

[19] J. Z. Teng and R. A. Gumaer. Managing IBM database 2 buffers to maximize performance. *IBM Systems Journal*, 23(2):211–218, 1984.

[20] H. M. Vin and P. V. Rangan. Designing a multiuser HDTV storage server. *IEEE Journal on Selected Areas in Communications*, 11(1):152–164, Jan. 1993.

[21] J. Wang, K. A. Hua, and H. Young. SEP: A space efficient pipelining technique for managing disk buffers in multimedia servers. In *Proc. of IEEE Multimedia Systems*, Hiroshima, Japan, June 1996.

Checkpoint and Rollback in Asynchronous Distributed Systems

Hiroaki Higaki Kenji Shima Takayuki Tachikawa Makoto Takizawa

Department of Computers and Systems Engineering
Tokyo Denki University
{hig,sima,tachi,taki}@takilab.k.dendai.ac.jp

Abstract

This paper proposes a novel algorithm for taking checkpoints and rolling back the processes for recovery in asynchronous distributed systems. The algorithm has the following properties: (1) Multiple processes can simultaneously initiate the checkpointing. (2) No additional message is transmitted for taking checkpoints. (3) A set of local checkpoints taken by multiple processes denotes a consistent global state. (4) Multiple processes can initiate simultaneously the rollback recovery. (5) The minimum number of processes are rolled back. (6) Each process is rolled back asynchronously. The number of messages for rolling back the processes is $O(l)$ where l is the number of channels. Therefore, the system is kept highly available by the algorithm presented in this paper.

1 Introduction

Information systems become distributed and are getting larger by including various kinds of component systems and interconnecting with various systems, e.g., by the Internet, in the world. The distributed systems are designed and developed by using widely available products including free softwares rather than specially designed hardwares and softwares. Distributed applications are realized by cooperation of multiple processes executed in multiple computers. These components are not always guaranteed to support enough reliability and availability for the applications. It is critical to discuss how to make and keep the systems so reliable and available that even fault-tolerant applications could be computed in the systems.

Checkpointing and rollback recovery are well-known time-redundant techniques to allow processes to make progress even if some processes fail. The processes take checkpoints by saving their state information in the local logs while executing the applications. If the processes fail in the system, the processes are rolled back to the checkpoints by restoring the saved state information and then the applications are restarted to be executed from the checkpoints. In this paper, we assume that every failure is *transient*, e.g., hardware errors, process crashes, transaction aborts, and communication deadlocks. The failures are unlikely to recur after the processes are restarted.

We have to consider how to keep the system consistent when taking checkpoints and rolling back the processes. The consistency of the global state is formalized by Chandy and Lamport [3]. Many papers [2, 3, 5, 6, 7, 9, 10, 11, 12, 13, 14] have discussed so far how to take the consistent checkpoints among multiple processes. In addition, we have to discuss how to roll back the processes for recovery if some process fails. If each process is rolled back independently of the other processes, the system state may be inconsistent. One idea [7] is to synchronize all the processes to be rolled back by using the protocols similar to the two-phase commitment protocol [1]. However, it takes time to exchange messages among the processes. In this paper, we would like to discuss a new method where the processes are allowed to be asynchronously rolled back and restarted.

In section 2, the conventional checkpointing and rollback recovery methods are reviewed. In section 3, we show a basic algorithm for taking checkpoints and rolling back processes. In section 4, we make clear how livelocks occur in the rollback recovery. A livelock-free algorithm is proposed in section 5. The evaluation of the algorithm is presented in section 6.

2 Checkpoint and Rollback

2.1 Consistent state

A distributed system is composed of multiple processes interconnected by channels, i.e., $\langle V, L\rangle$ where $V = \{p_1, \dots, p_n\}$ is a set of processes and $L \subseteq V^2$ is a set of channels. $\langle p_i, p_j\rangle \in L$ indicates a channel from p_i to p_j. In the distributed system, three kinds of events occur: message-sending, message-receiving and local events. A state of the process is changed when an event occurs. An event e_s *happens before* e_t ($e_s \rightarrow e_t$) iff one of the following conditions is satisfied [8]:

- e_s occurs before e_t in the same process.
- e_s is a message-sending event for a message m and e_t is a message-receiving event for m.

0-8186-7780-5/97 $10.00 © 1997 IEEE

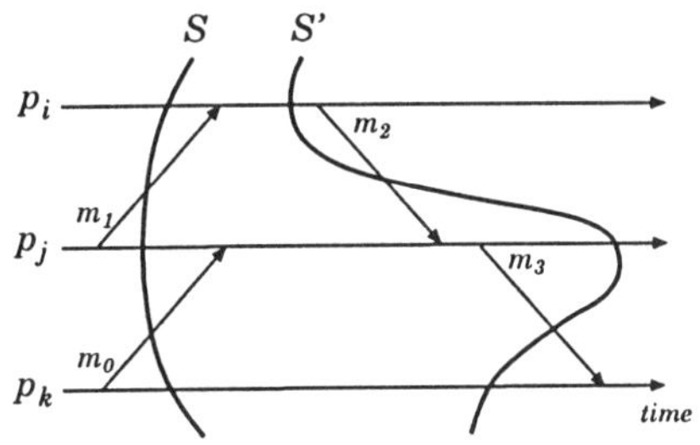

Figure 1: Consistent global state

- There is an event e_u such that e_s happens before e_u and e_u happens before e_t.

A local state of p_i is determined by the initial state and the sequence of events occurring in p_i. Messages are transmitted from p_i to p_j via a channel $\langle p_i, p_j \rangle$. Here, $\langle p_i, p_j \rangle$ is named a *channel of* p_i. If there is a channel $\langle p_i, p_j \rangle$, p_j is referred to as a *neighbor* process of p_i. A state of $\langle p_i, p_j \rangle$ is defined as a sequence of messages sent by p_i but not yet received by p_j, i.e., messages in transmission from p_i to p_j. A global state of $\langle V, L \rangle$ is a collection of states of the processes in V and of the channels in L.

A local checkpoint c^i of p_i is taken by recording the state information of p_i in the local log. A global checkpoint is a set of local checkpoints taken by all the processes in V, i.e., $\{c^1, \ldots, c^n\}$. If the processes take the local checkpoints and are rolled back to the local checkpoints independently of the other processes, there may exist two kinds of inconsistent messages: *lost messages* and *orphan messages*. Here, suppose that p_i sends a message m to p_j. m is lost iff a message-sending event of m occurs before p_i takes a checkpoint and a message-receiving event of m occurs after p_j takes a checkpoint. m is an orphan iff a message-sending event of m occurs after p_i takes a checkpoint and a message-receiving event of m occurs before p_j takes a checkpoint. By recording the received messages in the log after p_j takes a local checkpoint, lost messages can be received by taking them out of the log after p_j is rolled back. However, if there exist orphan messages, the system becomes inconsistent after the rollback recovery. Even if the processes record messages in the log each time message-sending events occur, the non-deterministic processes may send messages different from the messages in the log after the rollback recovery. Therefore, the global state of the system can be defined to be *consistent* iff there is no orphan message. Figure 1 shows three processes p_i, p_j and p_k. A global state S is consistent because there is no orphan message while m_0 is lost. However, another global state S' is inconsistent because m_2 is an orphan message.

2.2 Checkpointing

There are two approaches to taking checkpoints among multiple processes: *asynchronous* and *synchronous* checkpointing. In the asynchronous checkpointing [2, 5, 13, 14], the processes take the checkpoints without cooperating with the other processes. This approach implies less overhead because it requires no communication among the processes. However, *domino effects* may occur [11]. On the other hand, in the synchronous checkpointing [3, 6, 7, 11, 12], multiple processes are coordinated to take the checkpoints by using the protocols similar to the two-phase commitment protocol [1]. Here, the overhead for taking checkpoints is higher than the asynchronous checkpointing while no domino effect occurs. This paper discusses the synchronous checkpointing.

In the conventional checkpointing [3, 5, 7, 11, 12, 13, 14], if some process takes a local checkpoint, all the processes in the system are required to take local checkpoints. Moreover, in the conventional synchronous checkpointing, additional messages to take the checkpoints are transmitted and the processes are suspended during the checkpointing procedure. However, all the processes are not always needed to take local checkpoints to keep the system consistent after the rollback recovery. We would like to discuss which processes have to take the local checkpoints. We define a *semi-consistent* global state.

Definition (semi-consistent) For a distributed system $\langle V, L \rangle$, let P be a subset of V. A global state S is *semi-consistent* for P iff there is no orphan message for every channel of each process in P. □

The system is kept consistent after the rollback recovery iff a global state S is semi-consistent for a subset P of processes and only and all the processes in P are rolled back. Here, suppose that a process p_i takes a checkpoint c^i. If p_i sends a message m to p_j after taking c^i, m is referred to as a *checkpoint message* of c^i to p_j. In our checkpointing algorithm, m contains the information on whether p_i takes c^i before sending m or not. In order that a global checkpoint denotes a semi-consistent global state, p_j takes a checkpoint c^j if the following condition is satisfied:

Checkpoint If a message-receiving event e for a checkpoint message m occurs in a process p_j and p_j does not take a local checkpoint c^j, p_j takes c^j just before e. □

This means that p_j can newly take a local checkpoint after p_j is rolled back but cannot if p_j had taken a local checkpoint. By using this checkpointing algorithm, the minimum number of processes take checkpoints and no additional message is transmitted to take the checkpoints.

2.3 Rollback

In the conventional rollback algorithms [3, 5, 7, 11, 12, 13, 14], the processes have to be synchronized to be restarted by the following procedure:

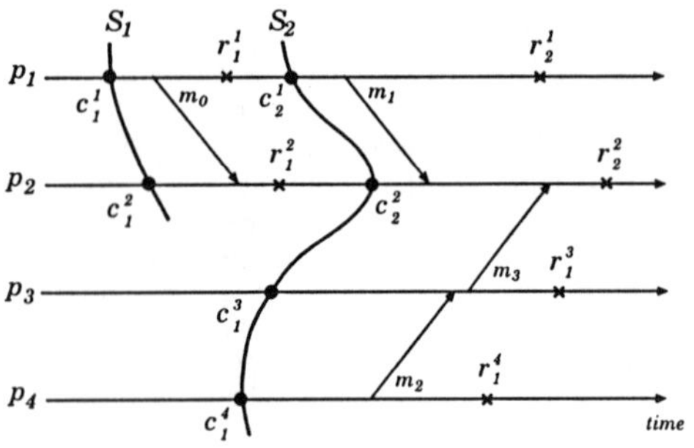

Figure 2: Semi-consistent global state.

1) Request messages are transmitted from the *coordinator process* to all the other processes called *cohort processes.*
2) Each cohort is rolled back to the checkpoint and a reply message is transmitted from each cohort to the coordinator.
3) The coordinator transmits restart messages to all the cohorts. Each cohort is restarted from the checkpoint.

One of the disadvantages of the algorithms is that all the processes are suspended and additional messages are transmitted to synchronize all the processes. The larger the system becomes, the longer the processes are suspended. Thus, the system becomes less available. In order to keep the system highly available with the rollback recovery, we would like to discuss a method where the processes are asynchronously restarted from the checkpoints.

3 Basic Algorithm

In this section, we would like to show a basic algorithm for taking checkpoints and rolling back processes by using an example shown in Figure 2. The system consists of four processes $\{p_1, p_2, p_3, p_4\}$ fully connected by bidirectional channels. Each process p_i takes a checkpoint c_s^i. If some process fails, p_i is rolled back to c_s^i and restarted from c_s^i. c_s^i represents the sth checkpoint taken by p_i. r_s^i represents a possible rollback event where p_i is rolled back to c_s^i. c_s^i is *active* if p_i takes c_s^i and r_s^i does not occur. For example, c_2^1 is active when p_1 sends m_1. After r_2^1 occurs and p_1 is restarted from c_2^1, c_2^1 is not active.

If p_i fails, it is not sufficient to restart p_i from an active checkpoint c_s^i because there may be orphan messages. For example, if r_1^1 occurs in p_1 and p_1 is restarted from c_1^1, m_0 is an orphan message. In order to obtain a semi-consistent global state after the rollback recovery, p_2 has to be restarted from c_1^2. That is, if p_i is restarted from c_s^i, an event e_t^j in p_j where $c_s^i \to e_t^j$ has to be canceled by a rollback recovery in p_j. Even if p_1 and p_2 are rolled back and restarted from c_1^1 and c_1^2, respectively, p_3 and p_4 are not required to be rolled back. That is, if no event e_t^j where $c_s^i \to e_t^j$ occurs in p_j, p_j is not required to be rolled back. Thus, if p_i is rolled back, we have to identify which processes are required to be rolled back in the system.

First, we would like to define the precedence relation among the active checkpoints.

Definition (checkpoint precedence) Let c_s^i and c_t^j be active checkpoints taken by processes p_i and p_j, respectively. Let e^i and e^j be events such that $c_s^i \to e^i$ and $c_t^j \to e^j$. c_s^i *precedes* c_t^j ($c_s^i \Rightarrow c_t^j$) if $e^i \to e^j$. □

In Figure 2, when p_2 receives m_3, $c_2^1 \Rightarrow c_2^2$, $c_1^4 \Rightarrow c_1^3$, $c_1^3 \Rightarrow c_2^2$ and $c_1^4 \Rightarrow c_2^2$. Next, we define a *rollback domain* $D(p_i)$ for determining a set of processes to be rolled back if p_i is rolled back.

Definition (rollback domain) A *rollback domain* $D(p_i)$ of a process p_i is defined to be a following subset of processes in the system:

1) $p_i \in D(p_i)$ if there is an active checkpoint c_s^i in p_i. Otherwise, $D(p_i) = \emptyset$.
2) $p_j \in D(p_i)$ if c_t^j is active in p_j and $c_t^j \Rightarrow c_u^k$ or $c_u^k \Rightarrow c_t^j$ where c_u^k is active in $p_k \in D(p_i)$.
3) Only the processes satisfying 1) and 2) are included in $D(p_i)$. □

In Figure 2, m_0 is transmitted from p_1 to p_2, p_2 takes c_1^2 before accepting m_0. Here, $D(p_1) = D(p_2) = \{p_1, p_2\}$.

For each $p_j \in D(p_i)$, it is clear that $p_i \in D(p_j)$ and $D(p_i) = D(p_j)$. $D(p_i) \cap D(p_j) = \emptyset$ if $p_j \notin D(p_i)$. A set $C = D(p_i)$ of processes is referred to as a *rollback class*. According to the definition, two different rollback classes are disjoint. Each time a message-sending or message-receiving event occurs in a process p_i, a rollback class C^i of p_i is changed as follows.

Change of rollback class If p_i in a rollback class C_s^i is changed to be in C_{s+1}^i on sending a message m and p_j in C_t^j is changed to be in C_{t+1}^j on receiving m from p_i, $C_{s+1}^i = C_{t+1}^j = C_s^i \cup C_t^j$. □

In Figure 2, before m_3 is transmitted, $D(p_1) = D(p_2) = C = \{p_1, p_2\}$ and $D(p_3) = D(p_4) = C' = \{p_3, p_4\}$. When m_3 is transmitted from p_3 to p_2, C and C' are changed to $C'' = C \cup C' = \{p_1, p_2, p_3, p_4\}$.

For every state S of a system $\langle V, L \rangle$ and a subset $V' \subseteq V$, let $S_{V'}$ denote a projection of S into V', i.e., a collection of the local states of the processes in V' and the states of the channels of the processes in V'. Let $A_{V'}$ be a set of the local states denoted by the active checkpoints taken by the processes in V'. If some process $p_i \in V'$ has no active checkpoint, the local state of p_i in S is included in $A_{V'}$.

Theorem 1 For every rollback class C at every system state S, $S_{V-V'} \cup A_{V'}$ is semi-consistent for V' iff 1) $C \subseteq V'$ and 2) $V' \cap C' = \emptyset$ or C' for every rollback class $C' \neq C$. □

That is, if a process p_i in a rollback class C fails, the system state is semi-consistent for C if all the pro-

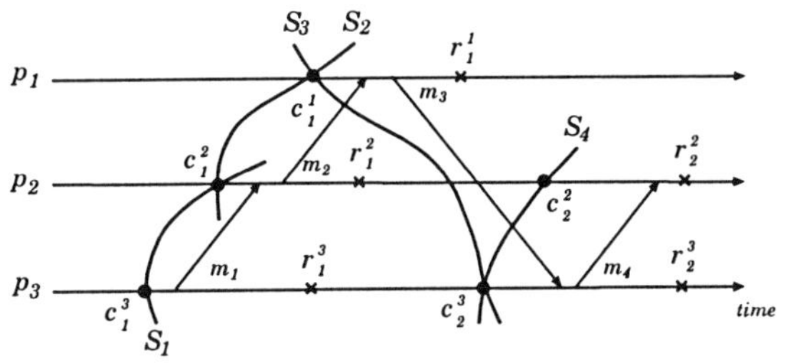

Figure 3: Livelock in rollback recovery.

cesses in C are rolled back to the active checkpoints. This also means that C is the minimum set of processes to be rolled back for keeping the system semi-consistent after the recovery.

Suppose that p_1, p_2, p_3, and p_4 in Figure 2 are at r_2^1, r_2^2, r_1^3 and r_1^4, respectively. p_1 does not know that p_3 and p_4 are in $D(p_1)$ while knowing that p_2 is in $D(p_1)$. Thus, p_i does not have the complete information on which processes are included in C.

Definition (rollback view) A process p_j is included in a p_i's *rollback view* $W(p_i)$ of $D(p_i)$ if p_i knows $p_j \in D(p_i)$. □

Thus, $W(p_i) \subseteq D(p_i)$.

Based on the view $W(p_i)$ of p_i, p_i can be rolled back and restarted from the active checkpoint c_s^i by using the message diffusion protocol [4]:

1) If p_i fails, p_i sends a rollback request m_r to all the processes in $W(p_i)$.
2) On receipt of m_r, p_i also sends m_r to all the processes in $W(p_i)$.
3) If p_i receives m_r from all the processes in $W(p_i)$, p_i is rolled back and restarted from c_s^i.

4 Livelock in Rollback Recovery

Let us consider the following scenario shown in Figure 3.

1) p_3 takes c_1^3 and sends m_1 to p_2. m_1 is a checkpoint message. Here, c_1^3 is active and $D(p_3) = \{p_2, p_3\}$.
2) p_2 receives m_1 and takes c_1^2 where the local state of p_2 just before receiving m_1 is recorded in the log. Here, c_1^2 is active and $D(p_2) = D(p_3) = \{p_2, p_3\}$. A set of local checkpoints $S_1 = \{c_1^2, c_1^3\}$ is semi-consistent for $C_1 = \{p_2, p_3\}$ because there is no orphan message in the channels of p_2 and p_3.
3) p_2 sends m_2 to p_1. p_1 receives m_2 and takes c_1^1. Here, c_1^1 is active. $D(p_1) = D(p_2) = D(p_3) = \{p_1, p_2, p_3\}$. p_1 does not know that p_3 is in the same rollback class, i.e., $W(p_1) = \{p_1, p_2\} \subset D(p_1)$.
4) p_3 fails and is rolled back from r_1^3 to c_1^3. Now, since c_1^3 becomes inactive, p_3 is not in the rollback class. Here, $D(p_1) = D(p_2) = \{p_1, p_2\}$ and $D(p_3) = \emptyset$. $S_2 = \{c_1^1, c_1^2\}$ is semi-consistent for $C_2 = \{p_1, p_2\}$.
5) p_1 sends m_3 to p_3. p_3 receives m_3 and takes a new checkpoint c_2^3. Here, c_2^3 is active. $D(p_1) = D(p_2) = D(p_3) = \{p_1, p_2, p_3\}$. $W(p_1) = D(p_1) = \{p_1, p_2, p_3\}$, $W(p_2) = \{p_1, p_2\}$ and $W(p_3) = \{p_1, p_3\}$.
6) p_2 is rolled back from r_1^2 to c_1^2 because p_3 is rolled back at step 4). Here, $D(p_1) = D(p_3) = \{p_1, p_3\}$ and $D(p_2) = \emptyset$. $S_3 = \{c_1^1, c_2^3\}$ is semi-consistent for $C_3 = \{p_1, p_3\}$.
7) p_3 sends m_4 to p_2. p_2 receives m_4 and takes c_2^2. $D(p_1) = D(p_2) = D(p_3) = \{p_1, p_2, p_3\}$, $W(p_3) = D(p_3) = \{p_1, p_2, p_3\}$, $W(p_1) = \{p_1, p_2\}$ and $W(p_2) = \{p_2, p_3\}$.
8) p_1 is rolled back from r_1^1 to c_1^1 because p_2 is rolled back at step 6). Here, $D(p_1) = \emptyset$ and $D(p_2) = D(p_3) = \{p_2, p_3\}$. $S_4 = \{c_2^2, c_2^3\}$ is semi-consistent for $C_4 = \{p_2, p_3\}$.

Thus, the rollback class C_s does not become empty and the rollback recovery may be continued forever, i.e. livelock occurs.

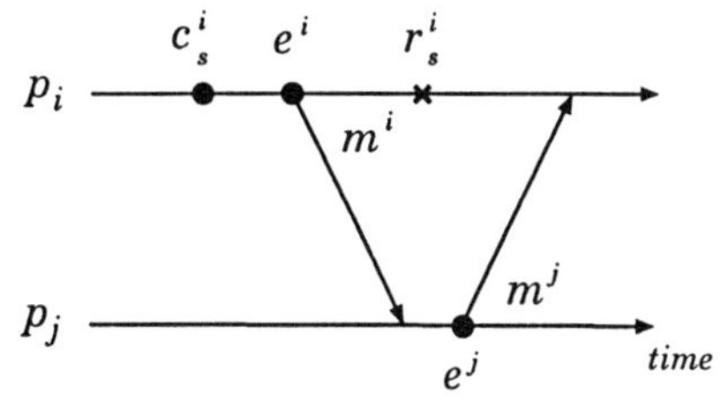

Figure 4: Cause of livelock.

One way to resolve the livelock is to synchronize all the processes to be restarted, e.g., by using two-phase commitment protocol. However, it takes time and the control messages have to be transmitted to synchronize the processes. In this paper, we would like to discuss a new method where the processes can be restarted asynchronously. Suppose that a process p_i sends a checkpoint message m^i at an event e^i after taking a local checkpoint c_s^i and p_j sends m^j at e^j after receiving m^i as shown in Figure 4. Here suppose that a rollback r_s^i occurs in p_i. Since $e^i \rightarrow e^j$ and $c_s^i \rightarrow e^i \rightarrow r_s^i$, p_i cannot receive m^j after p_i is rolled back from r_s^i, i.e. e^i is canceled. This is because p_i is sure that p_j would be rolled back owing to the rollback of p_i and the message-receiving event for m^j has to be canceled. If p_i receives m^j, p_i is required to be rolled back again due to the rollback recovery in p_j. Thus, the livelock may occur. Hence, in Figure 3, p_3 is not allowed to receive m_3, i.e., discards m_3 to realize the livelock-free rollback recovery.

In order to identify the messages to be discarded, we introduce *generation* concept as follows:

Definition (generation of a process) A generation $g(p_i)$ of a process p_i is given as follows:

1) $g(p_i) = 0$ before r_1^i occurs in p_i.
2) $g(p_i) = s$ between r_s^i and r_{s+1}^i. □

Definition (generation of an event) A generation $g(e)$ of an event e in a process p_i is given when e occurs as follows:

1) $g(e) = s$ if p_i has an active checkpoint c_s^i.
2) $g(e) = \perp$ (unknown) if p_i has no active checkpoint.□

Each time p_i is rolled back, the generation of p_i is incremented. $g(e)$ of an event e occurring in p_i is set to $g(p_i)$ if the checkpoint taken most recently by p_i is active. If an event e^i precedes a message-sending event of a message m^j in p_j, $g(e^i)$ is piggied back with m^j. On receipt of m^j, p_i knows of $g(e^i)$. If $g(e^i) < g(p_i)$, p_i knows that the message-sending event of m^j would be canceled by the rollback recovery in p_j.

In Figure 4, $g(p_i) = s - 1$ when e^i occurs. Thus, $g(e^i) = s - 1$ is piggied back with m^i and m^j. When r_s^i occurs in p_i, $g(p_i)$ is changed to s. When p_i receives m_j, p_i obtains $g(e_i) = s-1$ piggied back with m_j while $g(p_i) = s$. Thus, p_i discards m^j because p_i detects $g(e^i) < g(p_i)$.

In the succeeding section, we would like to present the detailed algorithm using vectors of the generations for preventing the livelock.

5 Algorithms

5.1 Assumptions and definitions

A distributed system $S = \langle V, L\rangle$ consists of a finite set $V = \{p_1, \ldots, p_n\}$ of processes and a set $L \subseteq V^2$ of channels. We make the following assumptions on S.

A1 Every channel in L is bidirectional.
A2 Every channel in L is reliable.
A3 In each channel $\langle p_i, p_j\rangle \in L$, messages are transmitted in the first-in-first-out order from p_i to p_j.
A4 S is asynchronous, i.e. a maximum message transmission delay is unbounded.

The following events occur in p_i:

- Message-receiving: p_i takes out a message m from a channel $\langle p_j, p_i\rangle$ and accepts m from p_j.
- Message-sending: p_i puts a message m to a channel $\langle p_i, p_j\rangle$ to send m to p_j.
- Checkpoint: p_i records the local state information in the log. The sth checkpoint taken by p_i is denoted by c_s^i. Initially, every p_i takes c_0^i.
- Rollback: If p_i fails at r between c_s^i and c_{s+1}^i, p_i is restarted from c_s^i. The rollback to occur at r is denoted by r_s^i. r_s^i exists only if p_i is rolled back to c_s^i.

c_s^i is *active* since c_s^i is taken until r_s^i occurs. c_s^i is discarded if c_{s+1}^i is taken.

A message m contains the data $m.data$ and the following information in the header:

- A flag $m.flag$.
- A vector clock $m.clock = \langle m.cl_1, \ldots, m.cl_n\rangle$.

A process p_i manipulates the following variables. Here, let N^i be a set of neighbor processes of p_i.

- A vector clock $c.CL^i = \langle c.cl_1^i, \ldots, c.cl_n^i\rangle$ named a *checkpoint clock*: Each $c.cl_j^i$ shows the generation of the active checkpoint in p_j that p_i knows. That is, when an event e^i occurs in p_i, $c^j_{c.cl_j^i} \rightarrow e^i$ if $c.cl_j^i \neq \perp$. $c.cl_i^i$ is incremented by one each time p_i takes a local checkpoint. Initially, $c.cl_i^i = 0$ and $c.cl_j^i = \perp$ for $j \neq i$.
- A vector clock $r.CL^i = \langle r.cl_1^i, \ldots, r.cl_n^i\rangle$ named a *rollback clock*: Each $r.cl_j^i$ shows the generation of the rollback most recently occurring in p_j that p_i knows. That is, on receipt of a message m, if p_i has no active checkpoint and $m.cl_j \leq r.cl_j^i$, p_i detects that m is canceled by the rollback recovery. $r.cl_j^i$ is updated to be $c.cl_j^i$ each time a rollback occurs in p_i. Initially, $r.cl_i^i = 0$ and $r.cl_j^i = \perp$ for $j \neq i$.
- A flag $flag^i$: If c_s^i is active, $flag^i = True$. Otherwise, $flag^i = False$.
- A set $W^i \subseteq N^i$ of the neighbor processes of p_i included in the rollback domain $D(p_i)$ of, i.e., $W(p_i)$: Initially, $W^i = \emptyset$.
- A sequence M^i of messages received after taking the active checkpoint in p_i: Initially, $M^i = \emptyset$.

For a pair of vector clocks $v^i = \langle v_1^i, \ldots, v_n^i\rangle$ and $v^j = \langle v_1^j, \ldots, v_n^j\rangle$, $max(v^i, v^j)$ is defined to be $\langle v_1, \ldots, v_n\rangle$ where each $v_k = v_k^j$ if $v_k^i = \perp$, $v_k = v_k^i$ if $v_k^j = \perp$, $v_k = max(v_k^i, v_k^j)$ otherwise.

5.2 Checkpointing

The checkpointing algorithm has to satisfy the following requirements:

R1 A process which has an active checkpoint is included in exactly one rollback class.
R2 The global state is semi-consistent for a set of checkpoints taken by the processes in each rollback class. That is, there is no orphan message.
R3 Every process p_i has the rollback view W^i on which neighbor processes are included in the same rollback class.
R4 There is no lost message.

A process p_i takes a local checkpoint c_s^i if one of the following conditions is satisfied:

C1 If p_i decides to take a local checkpoint by such a trigger as user request or timeout, p_i takes c_s^i.
C2 If a message-receiving event e occurs in p_i where p_i has no active checkpoint and p_i receives a checkpoint message m transmitted from a neighbor process p_j of p_i, p_i takes c_s^i just before e.

C1 means that the checkpointing can be initiated independently by multiple processes. By taking the checkpoints as presented in C2, there is no orphan message in the channel $\langle p_i, p_j\rangle$. Thus, R2 is satisfied.

Suppose that p_i and p_j have active checkpoints c_s^i and c_t^j, respectively. If p_i sends a message m to p_j, m is a checkpoint message, i.e., $m.flag = True$ because $flag^i = True$. When p_j receives m, p_j does not take another checkpoint even if $m.flag = True$. As presented in the preceding section, if p_i in a rollback class C_u^i sends a checkpoint message to p_j in a rollback class C_v^j where $C_u^i \cap C_v^j = \emptyset$, C_u^i and C_v^j are changed to C_{u+1}^i and C_{v+1}^j, respectively, where $C_{u+1}^i = C_{v+1}^j = C_u^i \cup C_v^j$. Thus, R1 is satisfied.

The system has to prevent from the livelock caused by the rollback recovery as discussed in the previous section. Here, we would like to present the checkpointing algorithm for the livelock-free rollback recovery. Suppose that p_i and p_j are in the same rollback class C where p_i and p_j have active checkpoints c_s^i and c_t^j, respectively, and p_i receives a checkpoint message m from p_j. Let $e^i(m)$ denote the message-receiving event of m in p_i and $e^j(m)$ denote the message-sending event of m in p_j. If r_s^i occurs before $e^i(m)$, p_i discards m because p_i knows that $e_j(m)$ is canceled eventually. In order to discard m, p_i uses $c.CL^i$, $r.CL^i$ and $m.clock$. Each time p_j sends m, $m.clock = \langle m.cl_1, \dots, m.cl_n \rangle$ where $m.cl_k = c.cl_k^j (k = 1, \dots, n)$.

Livelock-free message reception On receipt of a checkpoint message m from p_j, p_i discards m if $m.cl_k \neq \perp$ and $m.cl_k \leq r.cl_k^i$ for some k. □

Suppose that processes p_i, p_j and p_k are in a rollback class C and a checkpoint message is transmitted from p_k to p_j. Suppose that p_k is rolled back and a rollback request m_r is transmitted and that p_j sends a checkpoint message m to p_i before receiving m_r and p_i receives m_r before m. Here, $r.cl_k^i$ is incremented by one if the rollback recovery occurs in p_i. $m.cl_k$ is the same as one given before the rollback recovery. Hence, $m.cl_k \leq r.cl_k^i$ and m is discarded in p_i.

An identifier of a neighbor process $p_j \in N^i$ is included in the rollback view W^i of p_i if p_i has an active checkpoint c_s^i and one of the following events occurs in p_i:

- A message-receiving event of a checkpoint message m from p_j and $m.cl_j \neq \perp$.
- A message-sending event of a checkpoint message m to p_j.

Hence, p_i knows that p_i and p_j are in the same rollback class even if no checkpoint message is transmitted between p_i and p_j. Therefore, R3 holds.

Moreover, in order to assure that no message is lost after the rollback recovery, if p_i receives a message m from p_j where p_i has an active checkpoint c_s^i and p_j has no active checkpoint, p_i records m in M^i. If p_i is rolled back to c_s^i and is restarted, p_i takes m out of M^i before receiving a message from the channels of p_i. By this algorithm, R4 is satisfied.

The following procedures Send(m) and Receive(m) is executed when a message-sending event of a message m to a process $m.receiver$ and a message-receiving event of a message m from a process $m.sender$ occur in p_i, respectively:

```
Send(m)
  m.flag ← flag^i;
  m.clock ← c.CL^i;
  send m to m.receiver;
Receive(m)
  if m.flag = True
    if m.cl_k ≠⊥ and m.cl_k ≤ r.cl^i_k for some k
      discard m;
    else
      foreach p_j ∈ N^i do
        if m.cl_j ≠⊥
          add p_j to W^i
        fi
      od
      c.CL^i ← max(c.CL^i, m.clock);
      if flag^i = False
        c.cl^i_i ← c.cl^i_i + 1;
        flag^i ← True;
        checkpoint;
      fi
      accept m;
    fi
  else
    if flag^i = True
      add m to M^i;
    fi
    accept m;
  fi
```

5.3 Rollback recovery

If a process p_i fails, a rollback recovery procedure is initiated. The procedure is finished if the rollback class C of p_i becomes empty. The rollback recovery is realized by using the message diffusion protocol [4]. If p_i receives the rollback request m_r from p_j, p_i sends m_r to all the processes in W^i except p_j. Then, p_i restores the state information recorded at the active checkpoint c_s^i taken by p_i and is restarted from c_s^i. Thus, on being rolled back to the checkpoint, p_i can be restarted independently of the other processes while p_i has to be suspended to be synchronized with the other processes in the other algorithms [5, 7, 11, 12, 13, 14]. When p_i is restarted, $r.CL^i$ is updated to be $c.CL^i$.

The following procedure Rollback() is executed when p_i is recovered or p_i receives a rollback request message m_r:

```
Rollback()
  foreach p ∈ W^i do
    send a rollback request m_r to p;
  od
  flag^i ← False;
  r.CL^i ← c.CL^i;
  foreach j ≠ i do
    c.cl^i_j ←⊥;
  od
  restart from the active checkpoint of p_i;
```

6 Evaluation

First, we would like to show the logical properties of the algorithm presented in this paper.

Theorem 2 The rollback algorithm is terminated in finite time.

Proof Suppose that a process p_i is included in a rollback class C. Let $|C|$ be the number of processes included in C. Consider a case that p_i receives a checkpoint message from a process $p_j \in C$ and then p_i is rolled back and restarted from the active checkpoint. If p_i receives a checkpoint message m from p_j where $p_j \in C$, p_i discards m because $m.cl_i < r.cl^i_j$. Thus, p_i can be included in C at most $|N^i|$ times where $|N^i|$ is the number of the neighbor processes of p_i. Therefore, $|C|$ is incremented by one at most $I = \sum_i |N^i|$ times. Since the number of processes in the system is finite, I is also finite. On the other hand, $|C|$ is decremented by one if a process $p_k \in C$ receives a rollback request message. In our algorithm, once the rollback recovery is invoked by a process in C, rollback request messages are transmitted among the processes in C while $C \neq \emptyset$. Therefore, eventually $|C| = 0$ and the rollback algorithm is terminated. □

Thus, there occurs no livelock in the rollback recovery algorithm.

Theorem 3 The number of rollback request messages transmitted in a rollback class consisting of l channels is $O(l)$.

Proof As shown in the proof of the theorem 1, each process p_i does not receive a checkpoint message more than once from the same neighbor process p_j included in a rollback class C. Thus, since the rollback is initiated in C until C becomes empty, the rollback request is transmitted only once through each channel in the system. Therefore, the number of request messages transmitted in the rollback algorithm is $O(l)$. □

Next, we would like to evaluate the algorithm by comparing with the conventional one [7]. Table 1 represents the overhead for checkpointing and rollback recovery. The number of additional messages in [7] is $O(N)$ where N is the number of processes in the system and the required time is $O(D)$ where D is the diameter of the system because the two-phase commitment protocol is used. In our algorithm, no additional message is transmitted for checkpointing and $O(n)$ additional messages are transmitted and $O(d)$ time overhead is required for rollback recovery where n is the number of processes in a rollback class and d is the diameter of the rollback class. Therefore, our algorithm reduces the number of messages especially in a large-scale distributed system because $n \ll N$ and $d \ll D$ are satisfied.

Here, we would like to evaluate the availability of the system $\langle V, L\rangle$ executing a distributed application. The application is characterized by a communication pattern $\langle V, H\rangle$ where $V = \{p_1, \ldots, p_n\}$ is the set of processes and the subset $H \subseteq L$ of channels. $\langle p_i, p_j\rangle \in H$ if messages are transmitted from p_i to p_j in the application. Here, each channel in H is assumed to be bidirectional. The following types of communication patterns in applications are considered:

1) Linear type: $H = \{\langle p_i, p_{i+1}\rangle | i = 1, \ldots, n-1\}$, i.e., each p_i communicates only with p_{i-1} and p_{i+1}.
2) Star type: $H = \{\langle p_1, p_i\rangle | i = 2, \ldots, n\}$, i.e., each p_i only communicates with p_1.
3) Binary-tree type: $H = \{\langle p_i, p_{2i}\rangle, \langle p_i, p_{2i+1}\rangle | i = 1, \ldots, (n-1)/2\}$, i.e., p_1 is the root and each p_i communicates with p_{2i} and p_{21+1}.

Let t be the time when p_1 fails and t^i be the time when p_i is restarted from the checkpoint. It takes $t^i - t$ to roll back p_i. Figures 5, 6 and 7 show the total recovery time $T = \sum_i (t^i - t)$ for the types 1), 2) and 3), respectively. The shorter T is, the more highly available the system is. Following the figures, these systems are made more highly available by using the proposed algorithm than the conventional algorithms.

Table 1: Overhead.

	Checkpointing		Rollback	
	Message	Time	Message	Time
Koo & Toueg	$O(N)$	$O(D)$	$O(N)$	$O(D)$
Ours	0	0	$O(n)$	$O(d)$

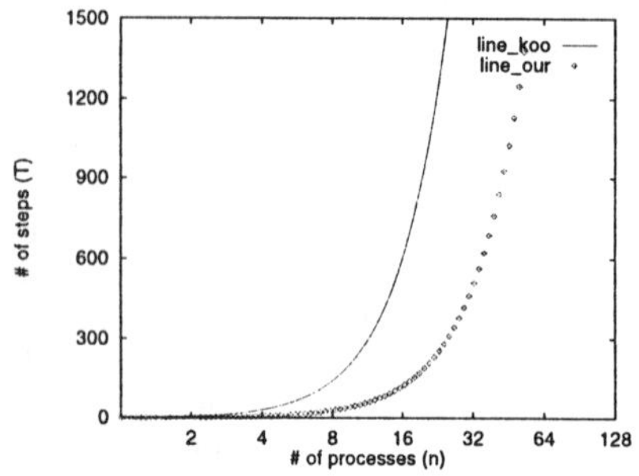

Figure 5: Overhead in linear-type application.

In a large-scale distributed system, most of the elements in $m.clock$ are unknown, i.e., $m.cl_k = \perp$ for most of k. Thus, when the algorithm is implemented in a real system, each message m had better contain only pairs $\langle k, m.cl_k\rangle$ where $m.cl_k \neq \perp$ than the n-dimensional vector.

7 Concluding Remarks

This paper has proposed the new algorithm for taking checkpoints and rolling back processes in asynchronous distributed systems. The minimum number of processes take checkpoints. The processes are rolled back asynchronously. Each process manipulates $O(n)$ information and each message contains $O(n)$ information for the algorithm. The rollback algorithm is terminated with $O(l)$ message transmissions where l is

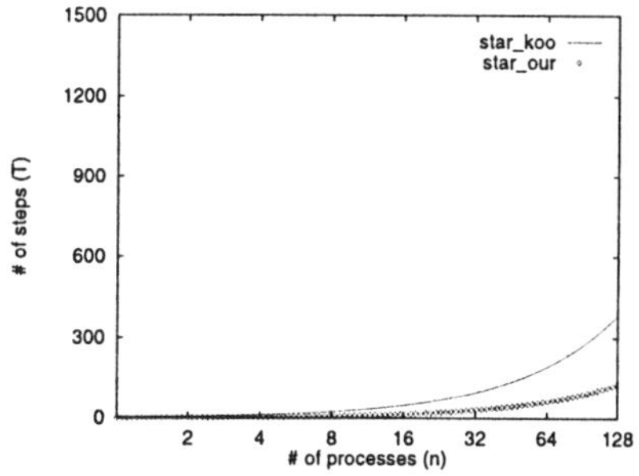

Figure 6: Overhead in star-type application.

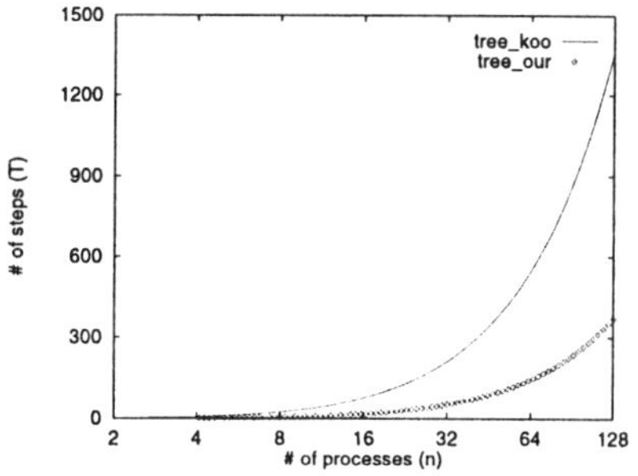

Figure 7: Overhead in binary-tree-type application.

the number of channels. The algorithm realizes the more highly available system than the conventional one because the processes in the system can take the checkpoints without transmitting additional messages and and can be asynchronously rolled back without stopping the data transmission. Therefore, the algorithm will play an important role to develop the reliable and available large-scale distributed systems.

References

[1] Bernstein, P. A., Hadzilacos, V., and Goodman, N., "Concurrency Control and Recovery in Database Systems," *Addison-Wesley*, pp. 222–261 (1987).

[2] Bhargava, B. and Lian, S.R., "Independent Checkpointing and Concurrent Rollback for Recovery in Distributed Systems," *Proc. of the 7th International Symposium on Reliable Distributed Systems*, pp. 3–12 (1988).

[3] Chandy, K. M. and Lamport L., "Distributed Snapshots: Determining Global States of Distributed Systems," *ACM Trans. on Computer Systems*, Vol. 3, No. 1, pp. 63–75 (1985).

[4] Dijkstra, E. W. and Scholten, C. S., "Termination Detection for Diffusing Computation," *Information Processing Letters*, Vol. 11, No. 1, pp. 1–4 (1980).

[5] Juang, T. T. Y. and Venkatesan, S., "Efficient Algorithms for Crash Recovery in Distributed Systems," *Proc. of the 10th Conference on Foundations of Software Technology and Theoretical Computer Science (LNCS)*, pp. 349–361 (1990).

[6] Kim, J.L. and Park, T., "An Efficient Protocol for Checkpointing Recovery in Distributed Systems," *IEEE Trans. on Parallel and Distributed Systems*, Vol. 4, No. 8, pp. 955-960 (1993).

[7] Koo, R. and Toueg, S., "Checkpointing and Rollback-Recovery for Distributed Systems," *IEEE Trans. on Software Engineering*, Vol. SE–13, No. 1, pp. 23–31 (1987).

[8] Lamport, L., "Time, Clocks, and the Ordering of Events in a Distributed System," *Communications of the ACM*, Vol. 21, No. 7, pp. 558–565 (1978).

[9] Manivannan, D. and Singhal, M., "A Low-Overhead Recovery Technique Using Quasi-Synchronous Checkpointing," *Proc. of the 16th International Conference on Distributed Computing Systems*, pp. 100–107 (1996).

[10] Perterson, S.L. and Kearns, P., "Rollback Based on Vector Time," *Proc. of the 12th International Symposium on Reliable Distributed Systems*, pp. 68–77 (1996).

[11] Randell, B., "System Structure for Software Fault Tolerance," *IEEE Trans. on Software Engineering*, Vol. SE–1, No. 2, pp. 220–232 (1975).

[12] Tong, Z., Kain, R. Y., and Tsai, W. T., "Rollback Recovery in Distributed Systems Using Loosely Synchronized Clocks," *IEEE Trans. on Parallel and Distributed Systems*, Vol. 3, No. 2, pp. 246–251 (1992).

[13] Venkatesh, K., Radhakrishnan, T., and Li, H. F., "Optimal Checkpointing and Local Recording for Domino-Free Rollback Recovery," *Information Processing Letters*, Vol. 25, pp. 295–303 (1987).

[14] Wood, W. G., "A Decentralized Recovery Protocol," *Proc. of the 11th International Symposium on Fault Tolerant Computing Systems*, pp. 159–164 (1981).

Atomic Resource Sharing in Noncooperative Networks*

Lavy Libman and Ariel Orda
Department of Electrical Engineering
Technion - Israel Institute of Technology
Haifa 32000, Israel
{libman@tx, ariel@ee}.technion.ac.il

Abstract

In noncooperative networks, resources are shared among selfish users, which optimize their individual performance measure. We consider the generic and practically important case of atomic *resource sharing, in which traffic bifurcation is not implemented, hence each user allocates its whole traffic to one of the network resources. We analyze topologies of parallel resources within a game-theoretic framework and establish several fundamental properties.*

We prove the existence of and convergence to a Nash equilibrium. For a broad class of residual capacity performance functions, an upper bound on the number of iterations till convergence is derived. An algorithm is presented for testing the uniqueness of the equilibrium. Sufficient conditions for achieving a feasible equilibrium are obtained. We consider extensions to general network topologies. In particular, we show that, for a class of throughput-oriented cost functions, existence of and convergence to a Nash equilibrium is guaranteed in all topologies. With these structural results at hand, we establish the foundations of a design and management methodology, that enables to operate such networks efficiently, in spite of the lack of cooperation among users and the restrictions imposed by atomic resource sharing.

1. Introduction

Traditional computer networks were designed and operated with systemwide optimization in mind. Accordingly, the actions of the network users were determined so as to optimize the overall network performance. Consequently, users would often find themselves sacrificing some of their own performance for the sake of the entire network. In recent years it has been recognized that systemwide optimization may be an impractical paradigm for the control of modern networking configurations [1, 2, 3, 4, 5]. Indeed, control decisions in large-scale networks are often made by each user independently, according to its own individual performance objectives. Such networks are henceforth called *noncooperative*, and game theory [6] provides the systematic framework to study and understand their behavior. Under the noncooperative paradigm, the network is considered as a site of competition for the network resources among selfish users.

Game theoretic models have been employed in the context of flow control [1, 2, 4], routing [7, 3], and virtual path bandwidth allocation [8]. These studies investigate the structure of networking games and provide valuable insight into the nature of networking under decentralized, noncooperative control. Their results provide the foundations for new design methodologies, e.g. pricing schemes, that attempt to operate noncooperative networks efficiently [9, 5].

In this paper we study the fundamental problem of noncooperative *resource sharing* among multiple network users. This problem generically deals with typical network scenarios, in which a decision maker has to decide how to use a given set of network resources in order to satisfy a certain demand. A typical resource sharing problem is that of routing, in which each decision maker has to assign each connection (or packet) to one of several paths or links. Noncooperative resource sharing can be observed at higher network layers as well, such as the use of mirror database sites (FTP sites on the Internet providing a good example), World-Wide Web servers, and similar systems. In fact, the problem extends beyond the realm of networking. Multiprocessor systems that are shared by noncooperative tasks provide yet another field for the potential application of the present study.

Since routing is a particular case of the general resource sharing problem, our study is related to the area of noncooperative network routing. All previous works in that area, e.g. [7, 3], exclusively deal with *bifurcated routing*, where each user splits its flow among the various possible paths, according to its optimization rule. However, it is often impractical to implement flow bifurcation [10], due to constraints imposed by the network or the switch architecture. For example, in ATM networks all the flow associated with a connection has to traverse through the same route. Even when not imposed by the architecture, lack of bifurcation is typical of various resource sharing scenarios. For instance, a client typically connects to only one mirror FTP site at a time; another example is that of a processor sharing system, where a task may be run in only one processor at once. In such cases, we say that resource sharing is *atomic*, in the sense

* This work was supported by the Ministry of Science in Israel.

0-8186-7780-5/97 $10.00 © 1997 IEEE

that each demand cannot be split among two or more resources. Noncooperative networks with atomic resource sharing are henceforth referred to as *atomic noncooperative networks (ANNs).*

The practical importance of the atomic resource sharing problem in noncooperative networks motivated the study presented in this paper. We establish several fundamental properties of ANNs and characterize the behavior of their users. Most notably, we establish the existence of an operating (equilibrium) point, prove dynamic convergence to the equilibrium, and derive the conditions for its uniqueness. It will be shown that atomic resource sharing systems possess substantially different properties than when bifurcation is possible. With these structural results at hand, we establish a framework for the proper design and management of ANNs, which results in their efficient use in spite of the inherent lack of cooperation.

The text is organized as follows. Following the introduction, Section 2 defines the model and outlines several game-theoretic concepts. Section 3 deals with networks of parallel resources. General topologies of resources are analyzed in Section 4. Based on the above analysis, Section 5 sets up the framework for a proper design and management methodology of atomic noncooperative networks. Conclusions and possible directions for future research are presented in Section 6. Due to space limits, proofs are omitted from this version; they can be found in [14].

2. Model Formulation

For the sake of concreteness, we present the analysis in terms of a routing problem. Nevertheless, as mentioned in the Introduction, the study applies to a variety of atomic resource sharing problems in communication networks. Therefore, the following terms should be understood generically.

We consider a set $\boldsymbol{I}=\{1,\ldots,I\}$ of users, sharing a set of parallel links $\boldsymbol{L}=\{1,\ldots,L\}$ connecting a common source to a common destination. Each user $i\in\boldsymbol{I}$ has a flow rate demand $r^i>0$, which is assumed to be constant though in fact it may be an ergodic process for which r^i is the average rate. It is assumed, without loss of generality, that $r^1\geq\ldots\geq r^I$. Each user is allowed to select one link to attend its flow demand; the link selected by user *i* is denoted l^i. The selection of a user will also be referred to as its *strategy*. The set of users selecting link *l* is denoted by $U_l=\{i|l^i=l\}$. The *total flow* of link *l* is $f_l=\sum_{i\in U_l}r^i$. A *flow configuration* is the vector of strategies $\mathbf{f}=\langle l^1,\ldots,l^I\rangle$.

Each link $l\in\boldsymbol{L}$ has a cost function $\mathrm{J}_l(f_l)$. We do not make any assumptions about the cost function except that it is defined for any possible value of the total flow (i.e. for any $U_l\subseteq\boldsymbol{I}$), and that it is increasing at these values. (An obvious interpretation of the cost may be, for instance, the link delay.) Each user selfishly attempts to optimize its performance by selecting a link in which its incurred cost is smallest. This setting gives rise to a *noncooperative game* [6]. A flow configuration **f** is said to be a *Nash Equilibrium Point (NEP)* if each user considers its chosen link to be the best under the given choices of other users. More formally, user *i* that currently utilises link l^i may decide to switch to link m^i if and only if

$$\mathrm{J}_{l^i}\left(f_{l^i}\right)>\mathrm{J}_{m^i}\left(f_{m^i}+r^i\right). \quad (1)$$

A flow configuration is an NEP if and only if, for no user *i* and the corresponding link l^i, there exists another link m^i which satisfies (1).

At this point, some important questions may be raised regarding the existence of an NEP and convergence to one, as well as the ability to detect efficiently whether it is unique. In the next section we shall give affirmative answers to these questions.

3. Parallel-link networks

In this section we derive several fundamental properties of parallel-link ANNs, defined above. Section 3.1 defines and studies the class of *residual-capacity* link cost functions. Section 3.2 extends the results for general link cost functions.

3.1. Residual capacity costs

In the model presented in Section 2, the only requirement on the link cost functions $\mathrm{J}_l(f_l)$ was that they increase in their argument. In particular, there need be no relation among the cost functions of different links. We now define an important class of link cost functions, namely *residual capacity* functions, that encompasses many practical ANN scenarios. We assume that with each link $l\in\boldsymbol{L}$ is associated a parameter $C_l>0$, called its *capacity*, and that, without loss of generality, $C_1\geq\ldots\geq C_L$. The difference $C_l-f_l=C_l-\sum_{i\in U_l}r^i$ is termed the *residual capacity* of the link, and is denoted by RC_l. An ANN is called a *Residual Capacity ANN (RC-ANN)* if the link costs depend only on their residual capacities, i.e. if there exists a single function $\mathrm{J}(\bullet)$, decreasing in its argument, so that $\mathrm{J}_l(f_l)=\mathrm{J}(\mathrm{RC}_l)$ for every $l\in\boldsymbol{L}$.

Before proceeding, we point out the practical importance of the residual capacity model. For instance, if the cost of a link is its end-to-end delay, then the widely used M/M/1 queue model, in which the expected delay is $\mathrm{J}_l(f_l)=\frac{1}{C_l-f_l}$, provides a good example of an RC-ANN. Note that the cost functions in the examples at the end of the previous section were of this type. Cost functions can be encapsulated in terms of residual capacity in problems other than routing as well. For example, in a processor sharing system with processors of different computing strength, a processor's capacity can be associated with its IPS (instructions per second) rating. This way, the more tasks run on a processor, the less residual capacity (number of instructions per second remaining for other tasks) remains there, and each task's average running rate is reduced.

In an RC-ANN, a user's strategy of selecting a link with the least cost is equivalent to selecting a link with the largest residual capacity (excluding that user's own flow). More formally, user i that currently utilises link l^i will want to switch to link n^i if and only if

$$C_{l^i} - f_{l^i} + r^i < C_{n^i} - f_{n^i}, \text{ i.e. } \left(C_{n^i} - f_{n^i}\right) - \left(C_{l^i} - f_{l^i}\right) > r^i . \quad (2)$$

Thus, a flow configuration is an NEP if and only if for no user i and its corresponding link l^i there exists another link n^i which satisfies the above condition. Notice that the exact nature of the cost function $J(\bullet)$ is irrelevant, as long as it is decreasing.

3.1.1. Convergence to an NEP

Consider the game defined by an RC-ANN. Assume the users update their strategies in iterations, such that in one iteration a single user updates its choice of link, namely moves its flow to the link that has the largest residual capacity excluding that user's own flow (as per (2)). There is no special requirement on the order by which the users make their choices, as long as the number of iterations before any particular user gets a chance to make a move is bounded.

Theorem 1: *The dynamic scheme described above converges to an NEP after a finite number of steps.*

Corollary: *At least one NEP always exists in an RC-ANN.*

We proceed to estimate the number of iterations that elapse before the NEP is reached. Obviously, the number of iterations may depend on the order by which users make their moves. It is shown, however, that no order of the users can result in a number of moves that is larger than a quadratic bound on the number of users. Furthermore, there is a scheme that guarantees reaching the NEP after each user makes no more than one move. To prove these claims, the following lemma is needed.

Lemma 1: *Suppose user i is in its best link and thus does not want to move, and then a different user j makes a move. Then, after j's move, either user i is still in its best link, or* $r^i < r^j$ *and user j has just moved to i's link.*

It follows from the lemma that once a user chooses a link, no moves made by users with lesser flow demands can change its choice. Consequently, from any initial flow configuration, if the moves are made by users in the order of decreasing flow demand, then each user has to make just one move to reach its equilibrium link. Therefore, the total number of iterations until the NEP is reached in that case is at most I.

We proceed to derive the bound on the number of moves for any order. If user i moves to link l at any time and later moves away from there, then inevitably there exists a user j, with $r^i < r^j$, that made a move into link l between these two moves of user i and caused it to cease to be i's best link. The moment of j's move into l is called a *pushout event*, and user i is said to be *pushed out* of link l by user j. We emphasize that it is not necessarily the case that i moves immediately after the pushout; it may be that after j pushes i out, other users make several moves before i leaves link l. Furthermore, after those moves of other users, link l may regain the status of i's best link, thus canceling the effect of the pushout. Nevertheless, in any sequence of moves, if user i makes k moves, it must have been pushed out at least $k-1$ times (the first move of any user may be made without having been pushed out, simply because the user may have wanted to make the move ever since the initial configuration). For example, the largest user can only make at most one move in any sequence, because it cannot be pushed out by any other user. The second-largest user can make at most two moves in any sequence, because it can only be pushed out by the largest user, which can happen only once. To extend this notion formally, the following definition is introduced.

Definition: *The* pushout potential *of a subset of users is the maximum number of times that an outside user, with a smaller flow that any member of the subset, can be pushed out by members of that subset.*

For example, the pushout potential of a single user is simply the number of moves it makes, because, conceivably, each move could constitute a pushout event for a smaller user. It may seem at first glance that the pushout potential of several users is the total number of moves they make, but in fact it is less than that. The next lemma states the potential explicitly.

Lemma 2: *For any* $i \le I$, *if the pushout potential of users* $\{1,\ldots,i-1\}$ *is P, then:*

- *a) User i can make at most P+1 moves.*
- *b) The pushout potential of the subset* $\{1,\ldots,i\}$ *is at most P+1.*

As stated before, the pushout potential of user number 1 is at most 1. According to Lemma 2, for any $1 \le i \le I$ user i can make at most i moves before an NEP is reached (after having been pushed out at most $i-1$ times itself). Hence, the following theorem is proved.

Theorem 2: *The total number of moves before an RC-ANN reaches an NEP is at most* $\dfrac{I(I+1)}{2}$.

It can be shown [14] that the bound proved above is tight: for any I, an ANN of two links (and any larger number of links as well) can be constructed that may make $\frac{I(I+1)}{2}$ moves before converging to an equilibrium.

3.1.2. NEP uniqueness conditions

Possessing a unique NEP is usually considered a desirable property. In fact, noncooperative networks which do not possess unique operating points are generally more difficult to design and manage [5]. This section derives the conditions for the uniqueness of the NEP in an ANN.

Recall that Lemma 1 implied that after a user switches to its best link, no moves made by other users with lesser flow demands can alter its decision. Therefore, an NEP can always be found in an ANN in the following manner: take the users in the order of decreasing flow, and put each one in turn in the link with the largest residual capacity so far. Application of the lemma for each user in turn shows that the resulting configuration is an NEP. This NEP is henceforth termed the *natural NEP* of the ANN.

For a network to have a unique NEP, then, it is required that no other NEP than the natural one exists. This requirement can be replaced by the following set of recursive requirements:

1. After the user with the largest flow demand (initially user 1) enters the link with the largest capacity (initially link 1), the other users are left with a unique NEP to reach.
2. No NEP exists in which the user with the largest flow demand occupies any other link.

The following lemma states the necessary and sufficient condition for the satisfaction of the second requirement.

Lemma 3: *For no NEP to exist with user 1 in any link other than link 1, a necessary and sufficient condition is*

$$\sum_{i=2}^{I} r^i < C_1 - C_2 . \quad (3)$$

The next algorithm puts all the above considerations together.

Algorithm RC-ANN NEP Uniqueness (RNU):

(1) If $\sum_{i=2}^{I} r^i \geq C_1 - C_2$, go to step 6.
(2) Assign $C_1 \leftarrow C_1 - r^1$, and reorder the indexes to maintain the capacities in decreasing order.
(3) Assign $r^1 \leftarrow r^2, \ldots, r^{I-1} \leftarrow r^I$ and $I \leftarrow I - 1$.
(4) If $I > 1$, return to step 1.
(5) Stop: there is a unique NEP in the network.
(6) Stop: the NEP in the network is not unique.

The correctness of the algorithm follows from the fact that it implements the recursive check of the necessary and sufficient condition stated in Lemma 3. This is stated in the following theorem.

Theorem 3: *Algorithm RNU provides the correct answer about the uniqueness of the NEP in an RC-ANN.*

3.1.3. Feasibility considerations

So far, the capacity of a link has been treated as a parameter introduced solely for the purpose of defining residual capacity cost functions. In many RC-ANNs, however, the capacity imposes an upper bound on the flow that can be attained in the link. Such a bound is equivalent to assigning an infinite cost for any value of the total flow that exceeds the capacity, i.e. $J(RC) = \infty$ for any $RC < 0$. A flow configuration **f** is considered *feasible* if $RC_l \geq 0$ for every $l \in \boldsymbol{L}$; otherwise, it is termed *virtual*.

It has been shown in Section 3.1.1 that at least one NEP always exists in an RC-ANN. This result, however, does not take the issue of feasibility into consideration. In fact, a network may not have any feasible configuration at all. For example, there is no way two users with $r^1 = r^2 = 6$ can use a pair of links with $C_1 = 10$, $C_2 = 5$, even though the total capacity of the network exceeds the total flow. Another problem is that even if a feasible flow configuration exists, users that enter the network one by one may not find it. For example, consider an RC-ANN with $C_1 = 20$, $C_2 = 15$, $r^1 = 13$, $r^2 = 9$, $r^3 = 8$. Assigning user 1 to link 1 and user 2 to link 2 leaves the third user with no link to join without violating the feasibility condition (and the network reaches the virtual NEP $\langle 1,2,1 \rangle$; note that this is the natural NEP). Yet, another configuration would result in a feasible NEP (namely, $\langle 2,1,1 \rangle$).

On the other hand, if a network has at least one feasible flow configuration, then it has a feasible NEP. The reason is that no sequence of moves made from an initially feasible configuration can lead to a virtual configuration, because no user ever switches to a link with infinite cost. Therefore, the equilibrium to which the network converges is feasible as well.

Unfortunately, the problem of deciding whether a given network has at least one feasible flow configuration and/or finding it is NP-complete [11]; the proof can be found in [14]. The remainder of this section presents sufficient conditions for a network to have a feasible flow configuration, and therefore a feasible NEP. Proposition 1 states that a feasible configuration exists if the total flow demand is small enough. Proposition 2 presents a sufficient condition in terms of an upper bound on the flow demand of each individual user, i.e. it assures the existence of a feasible configuration in RC-ANNs shared by small users.

Proposition 1: *If* $\sum_i r^i \le 0.5 \cdot \sum_{l=1}^{L-1} C_l + C_L$, *and for every* $1 \le i \le \min(I, L)$, $r^i \le C_i$, *then a feasible configuration exists.*

Proposition 2: *If* $r^1 \le \frac{K}{L-1}$, *where* $K = \sum_l C_l - \sum_i r^i$, *then a feasible configuration exists.*

The limits presented in propositions 1 and 2 are sufficient conditions for a feasible flow configuration to exist in an RC-ANN. It is not known whether a weaker limit exists for either of the two values that guarantees, if not the existence of a feasible configuration *per se*, at least the decidability of the issue in polynomial time.

Before concluding the discussion on feasibility, we note that the question of whether an RC-ANN possesses a unique feasible NEP is also intractable. Algorithm **RNU**, presented in Section 3.1.2, may report that there exist several equilibria, when actually all of them but one are virtual. It can be shown that the problem is NP-hard even if restricted to networks that are known to have a feasible flow configuration (and, hence, a feasible NEP). However, the sufficient conditions presented above for the existence of a feasible configuration are also sufficient for the feasible NEP uniqueness problem to be equivalent to the simple NEP uniqueness problem. This means that if a network satisfies one of these conditions, then an algorithm similar to **RNU** gives an affirmative answer if and only if the network has a unique feasible NEP. The details and proof are presented in [14].

3.2. General cost functions

In this section we extend the results derived so far to ANNs with link cost functions that do not belong to the residual capacity class. In other words, nothing is assumed about the link cost functions except that they increase in the link flows.

First, we extend Theorem 1 for the general case. Recall that the theorem considers a dynamic scheme in which users update their strategies in iterations, so that in each iteration one user gets the opportunity to switch to the best link.

Theorem 4: *For general link cost functions, the dynamic scheme described in Section 3.1.1 converges to an NEP after a finite number of steps.*

The results concerning the rate of convergence (more precisely, a bound on the number of iterations required to reach an NEP) and the NEP uniqueness in residual capacity ANNs were based on Lemma 1. The lemma, however, does not hold for general cost functions. As a counterexample, consider an ANN with three links whose cost functions are: $J_1(f_1) = 3.5 + 0.1 f_1$, $J_2(f_2) = f_2$, $J_3(f_3) = 0.5 (f_3)^2$. The ANN is shared by two users, $r^1 = 3$ and $r^2 = 1$, initially at the configuration $\langle 1,2 \rangle$. In this configuration, user 1 is in its best link. User 2, however, decides to switch from link 2 to link 3, where its cost drops from 1 to 0.5. Now, link 1 is no longer the best link for user 1, since by switching to link 2 it can reduce its cost from 3.8 to 3.

It turns out, however, that the lemma still holds for general cost functions in networks of two links [14]. Hence, so does the upper bound on the number of iterations ($\frac{I(I+1)}{2}$). Also, the algorithm for checking the NEP uniqueness is still correct, though it needs to be rephrased for general cost functions.

Algorithm General-Costs NEP Uniqueness (GNU):

(1) Assign $f_1 \leftarrow 0$, $f_2 \leftarrow 0$, $i \leftarrow 1$.

(2) If $J_1(f_1 + r^i) \le J_2(f_2 + r^i)$, proceed to step 3; otherwise, go to step 5.

(3) If $J_1\left(f_1 + \sum_{j=i}^{I} r^j\right) < J_2(f_2 + r^i)$, proceed to step 4; otherwise, go to step 8.

(4) If $i = I$, proceed to step 7; otherwise, assign $f_1 \leftarrow f_1 + r^i$, $i \leftarrow i+1$ and return to step 2.

(5) If $J_2\left(f_2 + \sum_{j=i}^{I} r^j\right) < J_1(f_1 + r^i)$, proceed to step 6; otherwise, go to step 8.

(6) If $i = I$, proceed to step 7; otherwise, assign $f_2 \leftarrow f_2 + r^i$, $i \leftarrow i+1$ and return to step 2.

(7) Stop: there is a unique NEP in the network.

(8) Stop: the NEP in the network is not unique.

Proposition 3: *In an ANN of two links with general cost functions:*

a) The number of moves made by users before an NEP is reached is bounded by $\frac{I(I+1)}{2}$.

b) Algorithm ***GNU*** *provides a correct answer about the NEP uniqueness.*

4. General topologies

This section extends the results obtained above for parallel-link ANNs to general topology networks. We begin by extending the model and notations of Section 2. The network is now described by a graph, $\boldsymbol{G} = (\boldsymbol{V}, \boldsymbol{L})$, where $\boldsymbol{V}$ is the set of nodes and $\boldsymbol{L} = \{1, \ldots, L\}$ is the set of links. Two special nodes $\{s, d\} \subseteq \boldsymbol{V}$ are the common source node and the common destination node. We denote by $\boldsymbol{P}$ the (non-empty) set of paths connecting the source with the destination; each path $p \in \boldsymbol{P}$ is a sequence of links. Each user is allowed to select one path to attend its flow demand; the path selected by user i is denoted p^i, and a user is said to be using all the links on that path. As before, the set of users in link l is denoted as $U_l = \{i | l \in p^i\}$ and the total flow of link l as $f_l = \sum_{i \in U_l} r^i$. A flow configuration is the vector of selections $\mathbf{f} = \langle p^1, \ldots, p^I \rangle$.

The definition of a link cost function remains unaltered from the original model; in particular, we continue to assume that it is increasing in the total flow of the link. The cost of a path can be defined in several ways. Naturally, the path cost should depend on its link costs, and be at least non-decreasing in them. In the sequel, we concentrate on two of the possible definitions for the path cost:

Cost-Sum: The sum of its links' costs, $J_p = \sum_{l \in p} J_l(f_l)$;

Max-Cost: The maximum of its links' costs, $J_p = \max_{l \in p}[J_l(f_l)]$.

Both definitions have their uses in typical interpretations of the cost function. The cost-sum definition is appropriate when users are primarily concerned with end-to-end delays, which is the sum of link delays. The max-cost definition is appropriate when the user performance is mostly affected by the connection bandwidth; the link cost then inversely reflects its available bandwidth. In that case, the bottleneck link determines the cost over the entire path.

We note in passing that a network may have the property that no two distinct paths have a common link. In such a network, the total flow in all the links of a path is the same, enabling the path to be replaced by a single link with a cost function that equals the cost of the path. Hence, the network is essentially equivalent to a network of parallel links, and can thus be analyzed with the tools of Section 3. In this section we focus on the case that paths are allowed to overlap.

If the path cost is defined as the cost of its most expensive link, any set of users always converges.

Theorem 5: *For a general topology as defined above, if* $J_p = \max_{l \in p}[J_l(f_l)]$, *the dynamic scheme described in Section 3.1.1 converges after a finite number of steps.*

Matters become substantially more complex when the path cost is defined as the sum of its link costs. In [14] we present an example of a network which does not possess an NEP under this definition, and therefore does not converge.

5. Design and management issues

In this section we indicate how the analysis of ANNs, carried out in the previous sections, is used to establish a proper design and management methodology. Henceforth, methods employed during the provisioning phase of a network, such as topology design and capacity allocation, are referred to as *design* methods, while those used during run-time, e.g. admission control and pricing, are *management* methods.

As mentioned in the Introduction, traditional design and management methods in computer networks assumed that users cooperate in order to reach network optimality. Problems such as capacity allocation, for example, were solved assuming that the routing of the users would be optimal [12]. In noncooperative networks, however, routing is performed at a Nash equilibrium point rather than an optimal point. Nash equilibria are inherently inefficient due to the noncooperative nature of the users, and they are even more so in our setting because of the further constraint imposed by the atomicity of resource sharing. Any network design and management methodology must take this fact into consideration. The importance of this proposition will become apparent later in this section, where we shall see an example in which traditional design methods lead to network performance substantially worse than what is achieved when the noncooperative and atomic behavior of the users is accounted for.

The formulation of design and management problems includes the definition of a criterion that assesses the quality of the solution, in terms of network performance at the operating point. The following are typical criteria for our setting:

- The average user cost, $\sum_i r^i J_{p^i}$.
- The worst user cost, $\max_i J_{p^i}$.
- The worst weighted user cost, $\max_i \{r^i J_{p^i}\}$.

The worst user cost criterion is especially valuable in RC-ANNs, where it can be translated in terms of $\min_l RC_l$ (minimizing the worst user cost is equivalent to maximizing the least residual capacity), regardless of the exact nature of the cost function. The other criteria depend on the cost function itself.

Note that, unless an ANN has only a single NEP, one has to make an assumption as about which of the NEPs will be the operating point of the network, because the performance of the network may differ among them. It is tempting to simply take the NEP that gives the best performance, but it can be shown (see [14]) that not only is the problem of identifying that NEP NP-complete, but that even if it were known, the separate problem of finding the sequence of moves that would lead the users to it (a management problem) would be NP-complete as well. If the number of users is large, a more practical approach is to assume that the network is always operated at its natural NEP (defined in Section 3.1.2).

Consider the following capacity allocation problem. Given an RC-ANN and an additional amount of capacity ΔC, the question is how to distribute ΔC among the links so that the resulting ANN exhibits the best performance possible. The capacity allocation problem has been analyzed in the past for bifurcated routing (as opposed to atomic). In [12] it is shown that, if the users' routing is optimal for the average cost, the optimal solution is to put the entire amount ΔC in the link with the largest capacity. The problem was treated in a noncooperative (non-atomic) setting in [13], where it was shown that adding any amount of capacity to the link with the originally largest capacity improves the performance of each individual user in the resulting (unique) NEP. The following simple example demonstrates that with atomic routing, careless addition of capacity (and, in particular, according to the above rule) may degrade the performance of the network.

Example: Let an ANN have M/M/1 links with $C_1 = 12$ (i.e. $J_1(f_1) = \frac{1}{12 - f_1}$), $C_2 = 5$ (i.e. $J_2(f_2) = \frac{1}{5 - f_2}$), $r^1 = 8$, $r^2 = 3$. It can be easily verified that there exists a unique NEP, namely $\langle 1,2 \rangle$. The average cost is $\frac{8}{4} + \frac{3}{2} = 3.5$.

Let $\Delta C = 2$ be added to link 1 (the link with the originally largest capacity). In the resulting network, $C_1 = 14$ and $C_2 = 5$, and the only NEP is $\langle 1,1 \rangle$, with an average cost of $\frac{8}{3} + \frac{3}{3} = 3.667$ - worse than the original average cost. On the other hand, investing ΔC in link 2 would result in a network with $C_1 = 12$, $C_2 = 7$, and the cost in the (still unique) NEP $\langle 1,2 \rangle$ would be $\frac{8}{4} + \frac{3}{4} = 2.75$.

However, this is still not the best solution. It turns out that the best average cost is achieved if $\Delta C_1 = \frac{44 - 16\sqrt{6}}{5} \approx 0.962$ is added to link 1, and $\Delta C_2 = \frac{16\sqrt{6} - 34}{5} \approx 1.038$ is invested in link 2. The only NEP in the resulting network is $\langle 1,2 \rangle$, and the average cost then becomes $\frac{8}{4.962} + \frac{3}{3.038} \approx 2.6$.

Consider a similar network with the same original capacities, but with user flow demands of $r^1 = 6$, $r^2 = 3$. The only NEP is then $\langle 1,1 \rangle$ with an average cost of $\frac{6}{3} + \frac{3}{3} = 3.0$. It is obvious that if $\Delta C = 1.001$, it is better to put it in the empty link 2, so that the NEP becomes $\langle 1,2 \rangle$ with a cost of $\frac{6}{6} + \frac{3}{3.001} \approx 2.0$, rather than to link 1, for which the cost is $\frac{6}{4.001} + \frac{3}{4.001} \approx 2.25$. On the other hand, if $\Delta C = 0.999$, then the only NEP remains $\langle 1,1 \rangle$ no matter how ΔC is split, so it is best to add it entirely to link 1.■

The above example demonstrates the startling phenomena that can occur in atomic noncooperative networks and emphasizes the importance of a proper design methodology, in particular for capacity allocation. In [14] we tackle the capacity allocation problem when the performance criterion is taken to be the worst user cost. It is shown that under that criterion, adding a capacity to any link never degrades the network performance (i.e. the worst user cost never increases). Additionally, the optimum solution is stated explicity for most of the possible values of ΔC.

Our study of ANNs also provides the foundations for a management methodology. This is depicted by the following management problem. Given the capacities and the total flow demand, what is the division of the total flow among individual users so that the performance of the resulting ANN (at its NEP) is the best possible? The optimum division could be enforced through an admission control or pricing scheme, that would provide incentives to users to match their flow demands accordingly. The solution for the criterion of worst cost is rather trivial, resulting in an infinite amount of infinitesimal users, which force the residual capacity to be balanced among all the links occupied in any NEP. The problem is more involved under the criterion of average cost, and is solved in [14] for M/M/1 parallel links. The solution consists of a set of flow demand values that represent the optimum division of the total flow.

6. Conclusion

In this paper we studied the behavior of atomic noncooperative networks (ANNs) within a game-theoretic framework. Other models of resource sharing in noncooperative networks have been studied in the past, but they dealt exclusively with *bifurcated sharing*. The ANN model is important in that it deals with resource sharing networks where bifurcation of the demand is impossible or impractical. This is indeed the case in many practical scenarios, such as utilisation of virtual circuits in packet-switched networks, mirror database sites and World-Wide Web servers, and also beyond the world of communication networking, e.g. in multiprocessor networks.

Several fundamental properties have been established. Parallel-link ANNs have been shown to possess at least one Nash Equilibrium Point (NEP) and to converge there from any initial configuration. For a special yet practically important class of link cost functions, namely residual capacity costs, we have established an upper bound on the number of iterations that it takes to reach an NEP. It has been shown that the question of whether an ANN has a unique NEP can be answered through an efficient algorithm. For networks where the capacity imposes an upper bound on the total flow of a link, we proposed two independently sufficient conditions that guarantee the existence of a feasible flow configuration. For ANNs with general topologies, an example showed that even the existence of an NEP depends on the definition of a path cost, and cannot be guaranteed for users whose cost reflects, for instance, the end-to-end delay. However, defining the path cost as the maximum of its link costs, which is typical of users whose main objective is throughput, brings about a network where convergence is guaranteed.

Our study clearly indicates that atomic noncooperative resource sharing networks have quite different properties than networks in which the demand may be bifurcated among the resources. The latter, under a noncooperative paradigm, have been analyzed in [3], where it has been shown that, under certain convexity conditions, a unique NEP always exists; on the other hand, convergence remains an open issue except for a few simple cases. Moreover, the unique NEP was shown to possess certain monotonicity properties, that do not hold in the atomic case. It is interesting to note that in 'hybrid' networks, in which the flow demand may be bifurcated but only to a restricted subset of the available links, existence of an NEP can be proved, but neither uniqueness (as in the full-bifurcation case) nor convergence (as in the atomic case) can be established [14].

Because the NEP is the operating point of a noncooperative system, its existence is of fundamental importance from a practical standpoint. Since an NEP has been shown to exist in a network of parallel resources but not necessarily in one based on a general topology, our study indicates that the network designer or manager should aim at presenting the users with a setting of parallel resources or its equivalent. This aim can be achieved, for instance, in broadband networks when bandwidth is separated among different virtual paths, resulting effectively in a system of parallel and non-interfering 'links'. Furthermore, if the link costs can be forced to comply with the residual capacity model, either through proper network design or by a run-time pricing scheme, then convergence to an operating point is guaranteed to be completed within a relatively small number of moves.

Maintaining a unique NEP in a network is obviously desirable, since the operating point is then independent of the initial configuration and hence stable even if the flow rates of the users experience short-term changes. The algorithm that checks the NEP uniqueness provides an efficient method for achieving that target. For example, whenever a new user wants to enter the network, an admission control scheme can use the algorithm to verify that the network continues to have a unique operating point with that user, and reject it otherwise.

The sufficient conditions for flow feasibility are valuable in both the run-time and the design phases. At run-time, a proper admission control scheme should observe them to avoid a situation in which a user finds itself unable to use any link. They are also a valuable tool in the provisioning phase, where they can be used to determine the minimum amount of capacity that guarantees a feasible configuration in an ANN for a given set of users.

Our analysis provides the foundation for a design and management methodology of atomic noncooperative networks, that enables their efficient operation. It should be realized that the distinct properties of ANNs require special design and management techniques, different from the ones for networks with central control or networks with bifurcated routing. In particular, the optimal solutions of such problems as capacity allocation and admission control have different structures than the traditional ones. Several results in that respect have been outlined in this paper.

There is much scope for further research in the analysis of ANNs. We outline several potential directions. The rate of convergence and the conditions for uniqueness of the NEP in parallel-link ANNs of more than two links are open issues. Regarding feasibility, additional sufficient conditions can be expected to exist. Another interesting subject for further research is identifying topologies, other than that of parallel links, in which existence of an NEP and convergence can be established. A topology based on a series-parallel graph can be especially interesting. The issue of design and management of ANNs also provides a fertile ground for further research.

References

[1] Z. Zhang and C. Douligeris. Convergence of Synchronous and Asynchronous Greedy Algorithms in a Multiclass Telecommunications Environment. *IEEE Transactions on Computers*, 40(8): 1277-1281, August 1992.

[2] E. Altman. Flow Control Using the Theory of Zero-Sum Markov Games. *IEEE Transactions on Automatic Control*, 39(4): 814-818, April 1994.

[3] A. Orda, R. Rom, and N. Shimkin. Competitive Routing in Multiuser Communication Networks. *IEEE/ACM Transactions on Networking*, 1(5): 510-521, October 1993.

[4] Y. A. Korilis and A. A. Lazar. On the Existence of Equilibria in Noncooperative Optimal Flow Control. *Journal of the ACM*, 42(3): 584-613, May 1995.

[5] Y. A. Korilis, A. A. Lazar, and A. Orda. Architecting Noncooperative Networks. *IEEE Journal on Selected Areas in Communications*, 13(7): 1241-1251, September 1995.

[6] R. B. Myerson. *Game Theory: Analysis of Conflict*. Harvard University Press, Cambridge, Massachusetts, 1991.

[7] A. A. Economides and J. A. Silvester. Multi-Objective Routing in Integrated Services Networks: A Game Theory Approach. *Proceedings of INFOCOM'91*, pp. 1220-1225, Bal Harbor, FL, April 1991.

[8] A. A. Lazar, A. Orda, and D. E. Pendarakis. Virtual Path Bandwidth Allocation in Multi-User Networks. *Proceedings of INFOCOM'95*, pp. 312-320, Boston, MA, April 1995.

[9] R. Cocchi, S. Shenker, D. Estrin, and L. Zhang. Pricing in Computer Networks: Motivation, Formulation and Example. *IEEE/ACM Transactions on Networking*, 1(6): 614-627, December 1993.

[10] A. Kershenbaum. *Telecommunications Network Design Algorithms*. McGraw-Hill, 1993.

[11] M. R. Garey and D. S. Johnson. *Computers and Intractability*. Freeman, San Francisco, 1979.

[12] D. Bertsekas and R. Gallager. *Data Networks*. Prentice-Hall, Englewood Cliffs, NJ, 2nd edition, 1992.

[13] Y. A. Korilis, A. A. Lazar and A. Orda. Capacity Allocation under Noncooperative Routing. To appear in the *IEEE Transactions on Automatic Control*.

[14] L. Libman and A. Orda. Atomic Resource Sharing in Noncooperative Networks. *EE Pub. No. 1034*, Department of Electrical Engineering, Technion, Haifa, Israel, 1996. May be obtained from "ftp://ftp.technion.ac.il/pub/supported/ee/Network/LO-atomic96.ps".

Server Selection Using Dynamic Path Characterization in Wide-Area Networks

Robert L. Carter and Mark E. Crovella
Computer Science Department
Boston University
Boston MA 02215

Abstract

Replication is a commonly proposed solution to problems of scale associated with distributed services. However, when a service is replicated, each client must be assigned a server. Prior work has generally assumed that assignment to be static. In contrast, we propose dynamic server selection, *and show that it enables* application-level congestion avoidance.

Using tools to measure available bandwidth and round trip latency (RTT), we demonstrate dynamic server selection and compare it to previous static approaches. We show that because of the variability of paths in the Internet, dynamic server selection consistently outperforms static policies, reducing response times by as much as 50%.

However, we also must adopt a systems perspective and consider the impact of the measurement method on the network. Therefore, we look at alternative low-cost approximations and find that the careful measurements provided by our tools can be closely approximated by much lighter-weight measurements. We propose a protocol using this method which is limited to at most a 1% increase in network traffic but which often costs much less in practice.

Keywords: Distributed Systems, Internet and Network Algorithms

1 Introduction

The increasing popularity of distributed information services like the World Wide Web has resulted in a number of problems of scale. Three scaling impediments to such distributed information services are excessive server load due to document popularity, wasted network bandwidth due to redundant document transfer, and excessive latency in delivering documents to the client due to the potential for transfers over slow paths. While caching can alleviate the problem of repeated transfer, a technique that promises to address the remaining problems is service (or document) replication. However, when a service is replicated, clients face the additional task of finding the best provider of that service.

In many cases, clients may know in advance which service providers are best for them. Such a static server selection scheme is used, *e.g.*, in the distribution of network news using NNTP. However, static server selection is inappropriate in a number of cases. For example: 1) The authors in [5] employ a dynamic protocol to find the best server for a document: the client probes a set of servers who may have a replica of the document, as well as the document's home server, and chooses the first to reply as the source of the document. 2) A mobile client using a replicated service will want to find the best server to serve the client's requests; the choice will depend on the changing location of the client. 3) Finally, our current interest is in replicating WWW documents. In this context, dynamic server selection has the potential to reduce the response time – the elapsed time between document request and document arrival. In addition, as we will show, a dynamic server selection mechanism enables a very flexible, simple policy for document replication.

In this paper we report on tools and techniques for selecting good service providers without assuming knowledge of server location or network topology. Our only assumption is that the client can obtain a list of addresses of servers that provide the required service.

In our initial experiments we consider two principal metrics for measuring distance in the Internet — hops, and round-trip latency — and study their use as the basis for a server selection decision. Surprisingly, we show that these two metrics yield very different results in practice. We then present evidence that dynamic server selection polices based on instantaneous measurements of round-trip latency provide considerable reduction in response time compared to static policies (which in this case are based on either geographical location of client and server or distance measured using network hops).

However, round-trip latency alone does not capture all the information one would want about the quality of a connection. In the context of server selection, another important characteristic of a network connection is the bandwidth available to clients of that connection. All other things being equal, higher available bandwidth implies faster document transfer time. Available bandwidth depends on two things: 1) the underlying capacity of the path between client and server which is limited by the slowest (or *bottleneck*) link, and 2) the presence of competing traffic (*congestion*).

These two useful pieces of information are not readily available to applications. In order to discover this information we developed two tools: BPROBE, which measures the uncongested bandwidth of the bottleneck link of a connection; and CPROBE, which estimates the current congestion along the bottleneck link of the path. The design and validation of these tools is described in [4]. In the remainder of this work, we use CPROBE and its available bandwidth measurements.

Armed with measurements of the current network state we can perform application-level congestion avoidance. By application-level congestion avoidance we mean that applications can use estimates of traffic volume to actively avoid paths that are currently heavily loaded. Specifically, in this paper we examine how a combination of measurements of latency and available bandwidth can be used to formulate a dynamic algorithm for server selection. We show that the combination of both measurements improves our dynamic server selection policy over any one metric alone.

The current load at the server is also an important factor when choosing a server. However, it is difficult to assess without system software modifications at servers. In [3], we do show the results of a simple experiment using a surrogate metric for server load, and show evidence of the importance of including a measure of server load in dynamic server selection. Our results suggest that a low-cost method of measuring server load would be useful and we plan to pursue this issue.

Our methods can be viewed from two standpoints: from a client-oriented standpoint, they reduce response time, which is good; from a system-oriented standpoint, they add traffic to the network, which is bad. In the first part of the paper we concentrate on showing that response time can be radically reduced using (sometimes expensive) measurements. In the latter part of the paper we show how almost all client-oriented benefits can be obtained using much less expensive, but approximate, measurements. Our final scheme obeys a strict limit of not increasing overall traffic in the network by more than 1%.

In the remainder of the paper we describe our proposed solution to the server selection problem and evaluate it in terms of both user-oriented and system-oriented costs and benefits. First, we divide the universe of documents into two classes: small and large documents. We expect the transfer time for small documents to be dominated by RTT, so we use simple, low overhead, RTT measurements as a basis for dynamic server selection. Then, for larger documents, where we expect bandwidth limitations will dominate the transfer time, we use a combination of RTT measurements and measurements of available bandwidth derived from our CPROBE tool. After considering the costs of various measurement approaches we show that simpler measures can be as effective while costing less both in terms of measurement time and network bandwidth overhead. We then present our limited overhead dynamic server selection protocol suitable for documents of any size and show its improved performance compared to static policies and minimal impact on network bandwidth. We conclude with a discussion of ongoing and future work.

2 Related Work

In [8], a replication technique (and presumed server assignment) based on geographical distance is proposed. In their design, servers are responsible for placing replicas near sources of high demand. Clients request the address of the nearest replica from the home server which calculates distances in miles to find the replica closest to the requesting client. This is essentially a static method of server selection and relies on the server maintaining a large amount of geographical information. In contrast, we show below that a dynamic server selection policy can provide high performance and a simplified placement policy.

Distance measures are also the focus of [7] where the objectives are to keep communication local and limit the use of long-haul links. The authors consider that the high variability of round-trip times renders them unattractive in practice. Conversely, we show this high variability is an essential feature that can be exploited when selecting a server. Instead of using hops or round-trip time, all of the methods explored in that work attempt to determine a subset of the network topology and build a distance metric on that topology. Hence, the result is again a static policy. In contrast, our dynamic server selection polices do not require explicit knowledge of topology. Furthermore, as we will show, the quickly changing and highly variable conditions in the Internet require a degree of dynamic assessment that static policies do not provide.

A dynamic server selection policy based on measured latency was used to choose among hierarchically organized caches in Harvest [5]. The cache's resolution protocol performs a remote procedure call to all of the siblings and parents of the cache and checks for hits. The cache then retrieves the object from the responding site with the smallest measured latency. This is similar to the policy we call Dyn 1 below. In this paper, we show that the additional time required for more complete measurement of current network conditions often results in improved performance.

3 Dynamic Server Selection

3.1 Why Dynamic Server Selection?

In any server selection scheme, a client seeking a document would like to choose the server which it has reason to expect will deliver the document in the shortest amount of time. In this section, we show that the impact of this choice is strongly affected by whether it is made based on static assignment or based on dynamic measurements of current conditions.

The difference between dynamic and static approaches to server selection is illustrated by the measurement of distance. Two obvious metrics for measuring distance in the Internet are hops, and round-trip latency. However, the static nature of the hops metric (the number of hops between any two hosts rarely changes) is considerably different from the quickly changing, widely varying RTT metric. These differences are important in solving the server selection problem.

We begin by comparing empirically measured distributions of each metric. We measured the values of both metrics between a fixed client host and 5262 servers selected randomly from a list of WWW servers [9].

Figure 1 shows on the top, the measured distribution of hops to the set of servers; and on the bottom, the distribution of round-trip latencies (in ms, measured using *ping*). These distributions are strikingly different. The distribution of hops appears to be fairly symmetric about its mean, whereas the distribution of latencies has a median (125) much less than the mean (241). The differences between the distributions suggest that hops is a poor predictor of latency.

The fact that hops is not a good predictor of latency suggests that either variation in link speed or

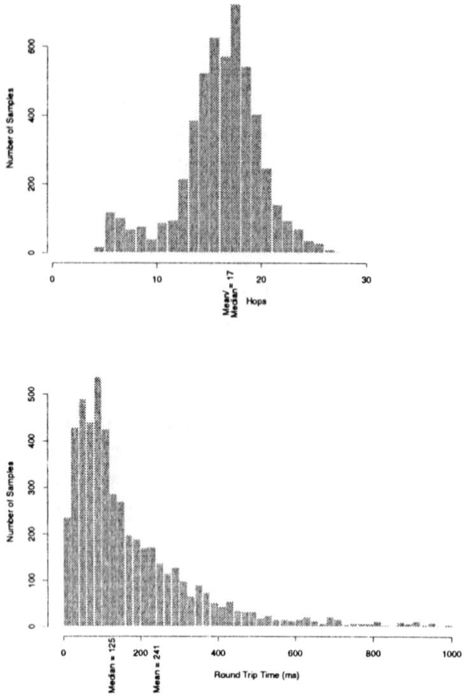

Figure 1: Empirical Distribution of Hops and RTT to 5262 Random Servers

delays due to congestion dominate the round trip time of packets. The impact of congestion is made clear by examining time series plots of round trip times to a single host. Unsurprisingly, these time series plots show extreme variance over short time periods. Consider Figure 2, which presents measurements of latency to a single host gathered over a period of two days at intervals of 30 seconds. On the top is a time-series plot; on the bottom a histogram of the same data. The variation in latency measurements reflects the underlying changes in congestion. A dynamic server selection policy can be designed to take advantage of exactly this sort of variation.

In fact, the difference between the characteristics of hops and latencies is fundamental enough to also suggest differences in algorithms for server replication. An initial replica placement policy might try to place replicas "close" to the clients that will use them (*e.g.*, [8]). This follows naturally when thinking about hops as the distance metric. Because the bulk of the hops distribution is centered about the mean, care is re-

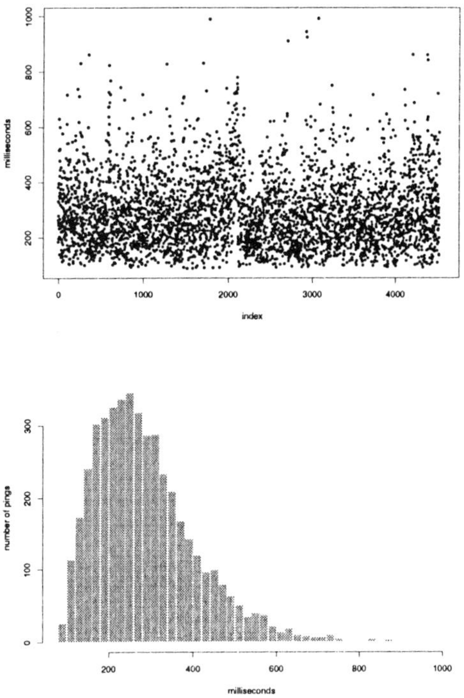

Figure 2: Round Trip Times to a Single Host

quired in placing replicas if the goal is to minimize the number of hops between client and server. In other words, a random distribution of replicas will not significantly change the mean distance in hops between clients and the servers they use. On the other hand, this is clearly not the case when the measure is round-trip latency. Because the bulk of the probability mass of the latency distribution lies below the mean, a random placement strategy should markedly reduce the mean latency between client and server.

Taken together these observations indicate that the performance of a replicated server system that uses dynamic server selection based on round-trip latency will be less sensitive to replica placement than a system that relies on the static approach where hops is the measure of distance.

3.2 Server Selection for Small Files - RTT

Having established the theoretical benefit of dynamic server selection, in this section we present experimental results to show that even very simple dynamic server selection policies can outperform static approaches in the real Internet. As previously stated, our dynamic policy operates under the assumption of widespread replication of documents (such as proposed in [1, 6]). We further assume that it is possible for a client to obtain a list of hosts serving replicas of the document of interest (perhaps by contacting the home server of a document).

In order to simulate such a system, we identified 10 hosts with approximately equal average round-trip latency as measured from our test client. Then, over a 3-day period, for each host we measured (about once per hour) the round-trip latency using *ping*, and the transfer time for documents of sizes 1KB, 5KB, 10KB and 20KB. We chose these smaller file sizes as appropriate to test the simple RTT-based server selection methods since latency should be the dominant factor for small transfers.

Using this data we then simulated several server selection policies: 1) Static, based on minimizing geographic distance; 2) Static, based on minimizing the number of network hops between client and server; 3) Dynamic, based on random selection of a server; and 4) Dynamic, based on minimizing the mean of 1,2,3,4 or 5 round-trip measurements. The results are summarized in Figure 3. For comparison, we also include Optimal and Pessimal polices which are simply the minimum and maximum transfer times observed, respectively. The graph shows the average time to fetch an object for each of the 4 file sizes. For the policies based on RTT measurements, the time plotted includes the time to make the required number of RTT measurements. Static policies are presumed to have no additional cost since the preferred server can be found by consulting a table.

All of these policies were evaluated with the objective of minimizing user response time. In this respect, as can be seen in Figure 3, the dynamic policies consistently outperformed the static policies and the benefit of a dynamic policy generally increased with document size. Even random selection is preferable to static polices for documents larger than 5KB. In this simulation, the dynamic policy based on the mean of 4 round-trip time measurements, gives the best results, minimizing the transfer time (inclusive of measurement time). Dynamic policies based on fewer (1,2 or 3) RTT measurements do a little worse. A policy using 5 RTTs does worse still, exhibiting a phenomenon of diminishing returns for extra measurement overhead.

The best dynamic policy in this simulation required an average transfer time that was only 4 times the optimal for 5KB files and this improved to less than 2 times optimal for larger files. In contrast, the static

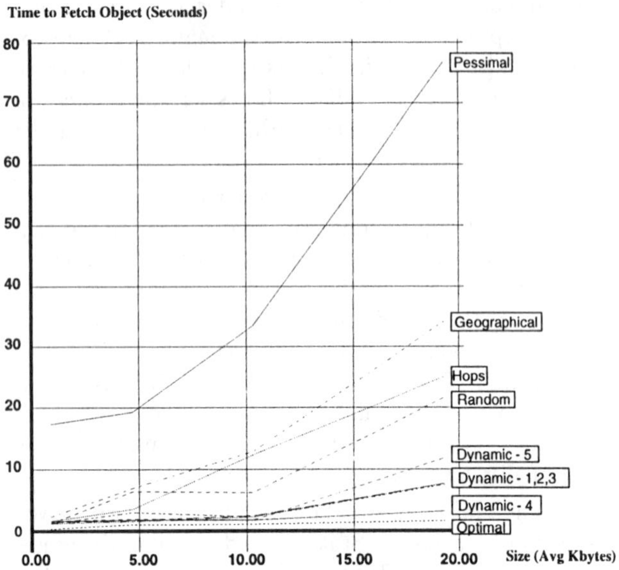

Figure 3: Fetch Times of Static and Dynamic Policies Plotted Against Document Sizes.

hops policy which was also about 4 times optimal for small files, showed increasingly worse performance as transfer size increased, up to 20 times optimal for 20KB files. These results use 7 replicas, certainly not a very large number for WWW document replication. The results would surely improve with a greater degree of replication.

However, as seen in Figure 3, the benefit of multiple measurements of round-trip time as a predictor of transfer time relative to the optimal value decreases with increasing file size. We believe that this indicates the effect of limited available bandwidth due to competing traffic, which will have a greater impact on larger document transfers, while small document transfers would have their transfer time dominated by instantaneous latency. This observation led us to formulate the techniques mentioned earlier for measuring the bottleneck link speed and available bandwidth of a path. Server load may also be a contributing factor, but as we discuss further below, the current lack of a simple way of measuring server load prevented us from studying this directly. We next discuss dynamic server selection using measurements of available bandwidth in addition to latency and its application to larger service times.

3.3 Server Selection for Large Files - PTT

The results of the previous section clearly show the benefit of dynamic policies. However, the relative benefit was observed to decrease with increasing transfer size, a portion of this effect was hypothesized to be due to bandwidth limitations. In this section we present a server selection policy, PTT, appropriate for larger files, based on dynamic bandwidth measurements. We use the term *available bandwidth* to refer to the estimated transfer rate available to an application – that is, the portion of raw bandwidth not currently used by competing traffic.

We suspected that one of the factors involved in the reduction in predictive ability of the RTT policies as document size increased was limited available bandwidth. In order to estimate available bandwidth, we developed the CPROBE tool mentioned above (and presented in detail in [4]) . In this section we study the use of bandwidth measures concentrating on documents larger than those considered in Section 3.2. In the context of server selection for WWW documents, given these measurements and the size of the document to be retrieved, it is possible to estimate the transfer time directly. If the document size is not known, then a choice could be made based on, for example, highest available bandwidth.

Given the bandwidth probing tools in addition to the RTT estimators commonly available, two questions arise: 1) can we improve the predictive capability of our dynamic server selection algorithm? and 2) what is the additional cost of the probes?

3.3.1 Evaluating Detailed Server Selection

In order to evaluate server selection policies based on available bandwidth measurements, we collected data from several WWW servers in the Internet. From earlier work [2] we have available a database of document size and location information. From this source we extracted sets of documents of sizes 100KB, 500KB, 750KB and 1MB. We chose these larger sizes because the transfer times of these large documents should be influenced by available bandwidth as well as latency. Periodically, over a several hour period we recorded the following data for each document: 5 round-trip time measurements (using *ping*), the available bandwidth (using CPROBE) and the transfer time for the document.

Before beginning simulation of the various selection policies, we used linear regression to analyze the dependence of measured transfer time on: 1) the RTT as measured by *ping*; and 2) the predicted transfer time using a combination of RTT and available bandwidth. Table 1 gives the R^2 values of the regressions. The regression analysis shows an improvement in accuracy of predicted transfer time when the measurements from the bandwidth probing tools are added to latency measurement provided by a single ping. Also the predictive value of our measure increases with larger document size, except for the very largest documents. We suspect that the long transfer times associated with the largest documents extend beyond a valid prediction window. As we have shown above, the effect of competing traffic on available bandwidth is a highly variable one. Therefore, estimates have a limited useful lifetime; we are currently exploring methods for assessing those limits.

	Document Sizes			
Regression Formula	100K	500K	750K	1MB
xfer time vs. single *ping*	0.053	0.186	0.477	0.081
xfer time vs. *ping* and CPROBE	0.291	0.280	0.638	0.145

Table 1: Regression Analysis: R^2 values for two metrics for 4 document sizes

To use *ping* and CPROBE together, we formulate the predicted transfer time metric. We use the regression coefficients k_1 and k_2 which relate the predicted transfer time to round-trip latency and a bandwidth-limited component, as follows:

$$\text{PredictedTransferTime} = k_1 \text{RTT} + k_2 \frac{\text{document size}}{\mathcal{B}_{avail}},$$

where $\mathcal{B}_{avail}$ is the available bandwidth as measured by CPROBE. In the simulation of this selection policy (PTT), the predicted transfer time is calculated for all candidate servers and the server with the minimum value is chosen.

We again simulated both static and dynamic server selection algorithms using the data collected from our survey of WWW servers. For each document size (100K, 500K, 750K and 1MB) we selected 7 data points uniformly from the recorded data and applied the dynamic algorithm based on RTT and available bandwidth to make a selection from among the 7 sites. The results are presented in Table 2. Each entry in the table represents the mean transfer time in seconds over 1000 simulated server selection decisions: that is, transfers of documents of the size given by the column heading when the server is selected according to a policy given by the row heading.

The policies simulated were: 1) Pessimal, which simply chooses the worst (largest) transfer time among the 7 servers; 2) Random, which picks a server

	Transfer Sizes			
Selection Policy	100K	500K	750K	1MB
Pessimal	21.836	21.800	18.357	696.680
Random	6.857	7.989	10.572	281.919
Hops	2.267	8.958	10.120	46.190
PTT	2.712	2.001	5.721	31.897
Optimal	0.985	1.296	4.265	17.529

Table 2: Simulation results for large transfers - mean transfer time in seconds

uniformly; 3) Hops, which chooses the server which is the fewest hops away; 4) PTT, as defined above; and 5) Optimal, which chooses the best (smallest) transfer time.

The superiority of the dynamic policy for server selection is clear from Table 2. The improvement is especially marked for large documents. For example, for 500KB documents, an improvement of over 75% is found when using PTT rather than Hops (2 seconds versus nearly 9 seconds). The transfer time chosen by the dynamic policy is less than 2 times the Optimal time for large documents, while the Hops policy results in transfers taking at least $2\frac{1}{2}$ times the Optimal time.

4 Cost Considerations

In addition to time overhead for network probing, which is reflected in the response time measurements we present, the impact on the network is also a critical issue. Probes that add many extra bytes of network load certainly will be unwelcome.

The current implementation of CPROBE uses 4 sets of 10 packets each with a maximum timeout of 1 second per set. Packet sizes of 600, 700, 800 and 900 bytes are used for a total overhead of 30,000 bytes and up to 4 seconds of measurement time. So, the probe may add up to an additional 30,000 bytes to the network load and a few extra seconds for an accurate measurement of available bandwidth. Such costs are too high for widespread use.

To address this, we explored measurement methods that can have much lower network impact and yet would approximate the more expensive CPROBE. In the next section we present such methods, and then propose a policy based on these lower-cost measurements which limits probe overhead to no more than 1% additional traffic in the network.

Selection Policy	Transfer Sizes 100K	500K	750K	1MB
Hops	2.267	8.958	10.120	46.190
Dyn 1	2.124	2.147	6.612	50.857
Dyn 5	2.301	2.028	5.762	31.175
PTT	2.712	2.001	5.721	31.897

Table 3: Simulation results for large transfers - mean transfer time in seconds

4.1 Approximate approaches to PTT

Previously we showed that, in theory, the bandwidth measurements combined with latency (RTT) measurements have greater predictive capability than latency alone. However, we suspected that a less expensive policy based the mean of more than one RTT measurement, might provide a rough approximation to a bandwidth estimation since long RTTs may be indicative of low available bandwidth. First, we compare the performance of the combined policy (PTT) with the simpler RTT-only policies. Then we address the issue of cost of the additional measurements.

In Table 3 we add two more dynamic policies: 1) Dyn 1, which performs a *ping* to each server and chooses the server with minimum RTT; and 2) Dyn 5, which computes the mean of 5 *ping* measurements and chooses the server with the minimum value. Both of which were also used in the initial study described in section 3.2. Once again, this table shows that a dynamic policy is always superior to the static policy based on distance measured using hops, confirming our earlier results. Also, for large files, the use of the probe measurements improves over the results from a single latency measurement.

The surprising result is that the Dyn 5 policy which relies solely on RTT measurements gives results very close to those of PTT which uses the additional measurement of available bandwidth. A similar though weaker correlation persists when using fewer than 5 RTT measurements. Table 4 gives values for the correlation coefficient between the reciprocal of the available bandwidth (measured using CPROBE) and the average of n RTT measurements for $n = 1, 2, 3, 4, 5$. Clearly the correlation increases with the number of RTT measurements, implying a strong link between the number of RTT measurements made and the degree to which those measurements capture the available bandwidth. As shown in the graph, more RTT measurements give an estimate with greater correlation to the available bandwidth.

Number of pings 1	2	3	4	5
0.236	0.293	0.346	0.372	0.400

Table 4: Correlation between available bandwidth measurement and RTT measurement (average of 1,2,3,4 or 5 RTT measurements).

To summarize, both Table 3 and Table 4 suggest that the policy of minimizing the mean of 5 *ping* measurements already accounts in a way for congestion effects. In other words, direct measurement of congestion as we have done with CPROBE can by simulated to some degree by using a sequence of RTT measurements. This is significant because of the (currently) high overhead of the probe measurements. These observations suggest a limited overhead dynamic server selection policy introduced in the next section.

4.2 The OnePercent Protocol

Since the performance of the lighter-weight probes closely approximates the more expensive ones, we devised the following probing protocol. Paying particular attention to impact on the network, we propose a protocol that permits at most a one percent overhead in terms of additional bytes injected into the network. We therefore refer to this policy as OnePercent. That is, for each document request, the number of additional bytes used to probe the network is limited to at most one percent of the size of the document requested. This protocol also ensures that the additional time needed to probe the network state is proportional to the document size. Thus, larger documents, which will benefit from more precise measurements of network conditions, are provided with better measurements while smaller documents for which latency is the dominant factor will not increase response time or use network bandwidth unnecessarily.

The OnePercent policy is formulated as follows: for files under 10,000 bytes, we use a single ping; under 20,000 bytes, we use the mean of two pings, etc. Because the CPROBE overhead is 30,000 bytes, all of the larger documents will use the mean of 5 pings in the OnePercent protocol. Thus, we use at most one ping per 10K bytes to be transferred.

Figure 4 presents the results of applying the OnePercent protocol. For each document size, there are 5 bars showing the response (transfer) time in seconds for the best and worst transfer times (Optimal and Pessimal, respectively); for Random selection of server; for static selection based on minimizing number of Hops; and for the OnePercent dynamic probing policy. In order to make visible the values for smaller documents, the bar chart was cut off at 100 seconds (the 1MB Pessimal time is 700 seconds, the 1MB Random time is 281 seconds). From the figure, it is clear that the OnePercent policy is in every case no worse than the static and random policies and in most cases performs close to Optimal. It is important to recall that the time for performing the measurement probes is included in the OnePercent values presented in the graph. Thus, even with the measurement overhead accounted for, the OnePercent dynamic server selection policy is superior to static policies.

Turning to network load we find that in fact substantially less than 1 percent overhead was necessary to achieve these results. In fact, using the 500 byte (5 100 byte ping packets) overhead for the larger files results in an aggregate network bandwidth overhead of about 0.1 percent.

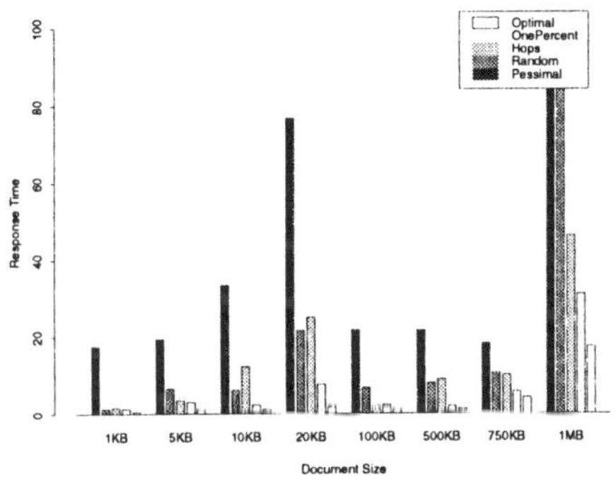

Figure 4: Performance of OnePercent dynamic server selection policy.

5 Future Directions and Conclusions

In order to deploy our dynamic server selection protocol in the current WWW environment we plan to modify a browser to support multiple URLs per link in a document. This list of alternate servers can be used as input to dynamic server selection by the browser. This represents a step along the way to integrated support for replication in which the browser would *obtain* a list of replicas.

We have also packaged the probe tools as a daemon that can be placed strategically throughout a network to allow probing of conditions in remote parts of the network. This will allow measurement of a link as a part of several paths and could be used to provide confirmation of probe estimates.

In conclusion, we have motivated the need for dynamic selection of servers by observing that the combination of random placement of replicas with dynamic server selection can result in a reduced average response time for service clients when compared with static policies. We presented simulation results that show the distinct benefit of dynamic server selection over standard static server assignment policies. We then illustrated how available bandwidth measurements (such as made by CPROBE) could be used by clients of replicated services as input to a server selection decision in the context of WWW documents, thus demonstrating the use of our tools in support of application-level congestion avoidance. In addition, we have also shown that most of the benefits of out detailed measurement approach can be achieved by a policy that adds less than 1% additional traffic to the network.

References

[1] Azer Bestavros. Demand-based resource allocation to reduce traffic and balance load in distributed information systems. In *Proceedings of SPDP'95: The 7th IEEE Symposium on Parallel and Distributed Processing*, pages 338–345, San Anotonio, Texas, October 1995.

[2] Azer Bestavros, Robert L. Carter, Mark E. Crovella, Carlos R. Cunha, Abdelsalam Heddaya, and Sulaiman A. Mirdad. Application-Level Document Caching in the Internet. In *IEEE SDNE'95: The Second International Workshop on Services in Distributed and Networked Environments*, June 1995.

[3] Robert L. Carter and Mark E. Crovella. Dynamic Server Selection using Bandwidth Probing in Wide-Area Networks. Technical Report BU-CS-96-007, Boston University, March 1996.

[4] Robert L. Carter and Mark E. Crovella. Measuring Bottleneck Link Speed in Packet-Switched Networks. In *Performance Evaluation (Proceedings of Performance '96)*, volume 27&28, pages 297–318, Lausanne, Switzerland., 1996.

[5] Anawat Chankhunthod, Peter B. Danzig, Chuck Neerdales, Michael F. Schwartz, and Kurt J. Worrell. A hierarchical internet object cache. Technical Report CU-CS-766-95, University of Colorado - Boulder, Mar 1995.

[6] Yasuhiro Endo, James Gwertzman, Margo Soltzer, Christopher Small, Keith A. Smith, and Diane Tang. VINO: The 1994 fall harvest. Technical Report TR-34-94, Harvard University Department of Computer Science, 1994.

[7] James D. Guyton and Michael F. Schwartz. Locating nearby copies of replicated internet servers. In *Proceedings of SIGCOMM '95*, pages 288–298, Boston, MA, August 1995.

[8] James Gwertzman and Margo Seltzer. The case for geographical push-caching. In *HotOS '94*, 1994.

[9] net.Genesis Corporation. Comprehensive list of sites. Available at `http://www.netgen.com/cgi/comprehensive.`, April 1995.

Performance Evaluation of Packet Data Services Over Cellular Voice Networks *

Young Yong Kim San-qi Li
Department of Electrical and Computer Engineering
University of Texas at Austin
Austin, Texas 78712
(Tel) (512)471-3513 (Fax) (512)471-5532
{young,sanqi}@globe.ece.utexas.edu

December 4, 1996

Abstract

In this paper we develop a Markov chain modeling framework for throughput/delay analysis of data services over cellular voice networks, using dynamic channel stealing method. Some effective approximation techniques are also proposed and verified for simplification of modeling analysis. Our study identifies the average voice call holding time as the dominant factor to affect data delay performance. Especially in heavy load conditions, namely when the number of free voice channels becomes momentarily less, the data users will experience large network access delay in the range of several minutes or longer on average. We also examine the data performance improvement by using priority data access scheme and speech silence detection technique.

1 Introduction

The growing demand on low-cost wireless data services gave the idea of providing packet data transmission over cellular voice networks. Since radio channels are the most precious resource in wireless communication, a natural approach is to borrow free voice channels for data services, so-called Dynamic Channel Stealing (DCS) method. On free voice channels, data packets are transmitted using contention-based medium access protocol. Two examples are cellular digital packet data (CDPD) system over advanced mobile phone system (AMPS) and general packet radio service (GPRS) over global system for mobile communications (GSM). Due to the trunking inefficiency of circuit-switched wireless voice networks, a large amount of radio frequency bandwidth would be wasted otherwise. The data base station continuously monitors the presence of voice traffic on each channel. As soon as the voice appearance is detected, it immediately transfers its traffic to other free voice channels without interrupting real time voice transmission.

A key issue in the design of DCS system is the throughput delay performance of data services. The existing analytical works [2, 3, 4] took an oversimplified model by neglecting the variation of free voice channels and the effect of uplink multiple access contention. Obviously, these two neglecting factors should have significant impact on system performance. In this paper, we propose an analytical Markov model for the analysis of DCS systems such as CDPD and GPRS. We first develop a quasi-birth-death (QBD) model for the computation of maximum data throughput based on a carrier sense multiple access contention scheme on multiple channels with high priority voice transmission. A quasi-static approximation technique is then introduced to significantly simplify the data delay analysis. The QBD modeling in our application also requires to solve a large number of boundary values, which can be a numerical bottleneck for large systems. An effective simplification technique is then proposed to eliminate the boundary evaluation problem. With the quasi-static approximation and the boundary elimination, the modeling of DCS systems are generally much simplified without losing solution accuracy.

Our study shows that the average voice call holding time has dominant impact on data delay performance. Especially when more voice calls are momentarily transmitted, data users will experience large network access delay in the range of several minutes or longer on average. We then investigate the data performance improvement by using priority data access contention scheme and speech silence detection technique.

The remainder of the paper is organized as follows. Section

*The research reported here was supported by the National Science Foundation under grant NCR-9314387, the Texas Advanced Research Program under grant TARP-33 and Southwestern Bell.

0-8186-7780-5/97 $10.00 © 1997 IEEE

2 provides the general description of DCS system. Section 3 develops the QBD modeling. Section 4 derives the maximum throughput analysis and Section 5 shows the delay performance. Section 6 examines the performance improvement by priority data access and speech silence detection. Section 7 is the conclusion.

2 Description of DCS System

The mobile data base station (MDBS) in DCS system detects free voice channels and uses their bandwidth for packet data services. The underlying circuit-switch voice services are not interfered by the data transmission. Upon detection of each free voice channel, MDBS sets up an air link for data transmission, which is composed of an uplink channel and a downlink channel. Each air link is shared by multiple mobile end stations (M-ES). The downlink channel is a contentionless broadcast channel. MDBS collects all the incoming packets in a global queue and schedules their transmission to appropriate M-ES's on downlink channels without contention. The transmission of data packets from M-ES's to MDBS on the uplink channel is based on a contention multiple access scheme, so-called slotted digital sense multiple access with collision detection (DSMA/CD). The DSMA/CD scheme is similar to the slotted carrier sense multiple access with collision detection (CSMA/CD) that Ethernet uses. The DSMA/CD scheme is used in the CDPD system, and explained extensively in [5].

Fig. 1 shows the downlink frame structure of the DSMA/CD MAC protocol. In AMPS system, one carrier frequency consists of a single voice channel. For each idle voice channel, the MDBS sets up data streams for CDPD services. Every downlink frame consists of a fixed number of microslots (MS) (7 in CDPD). Frame is unit for channel coding and decoding. The uplink frame is composed of dotting sequence preamble, reverse channel synchronization words, and Reed-Solomon coded data block. Microslot is unit for the contention. Every microslot in downlink frame is associated with a busy bit (B), indicating if the corresponding uplink voice channel is being used for voice or data transmission. When an M-ES has data to send, it will monitor the busy bit of a selected free channel on the downlink. If and only if when the busy bit is set to '0' by MDBS, the corresponding uplink channel will be contended with random access by M-ES's for transmission of new data packets. Whenever MDBS detects a successful uplink contention by a single M-ES, the corresponding busy bit on the downlink channel will be marked to '1' in the next microslot. Otherwise, the busy bit will remain at zero in the next microslot for further contention access, providing no voice transmission. The synchronization and timing indicators of microslot clock are broadcasted by MDBS on downlink channels to all M-ES's. Data packets involved in collision, which can be detected by MDBS due to the failure of channel decoding, are put in the backlog queue with random delay before the next contention access at the

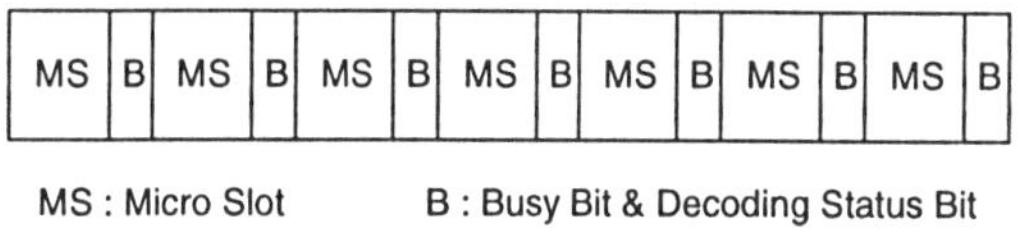

Figure 1: Downlink frame structure for the DSMA/CD MAC protocol

corresponding M-ES. In GSM system, one carrier frequency consists of several time slots, each of which represents a voice channel. In GPRS sytem, each idle voice channel can be used for the packet data service using similar MAC protocol as DSMA/CD protocol. Since the microslot size is substantially smaller than data packet size, the contention overhead of the DSMA/CD protocol should not be significant and a high data throughput can therefore be achieved.

3 Markov Chain Modeling

In this section, we build a quasi-birth-death (QBD) structure [8] to model downlink/uplink data transmission in DCS system. The uplink modeling is similar to the downlink modeling except with contention. The voice call arrival process is modeled by Poisson at rate λ_v. A voice call is accepted if and only if at least one voice channel is free. Each accepted voice call has an exponential holding time at rate μ_v. As in most circuit-switched voice network analyses, the quality of voice services is measured by the call blocking rate. The voice performance is modeled by a birth-death process and independent of the data transmission in DCS system. In contrast, since the data packets are only transmitted on free voice channels, the voice traffic characteristics are expected to have strong impact on data performance, which has been largely neglected in the previous DCS system analyses. Similar to voice, the data packet arrival process is modeled by Poisson at rate λ_d. Each packet requires an exponential transmission time on a free voice channel at rate μ_d. Whenever a free channel is taken back by voice transmission, the data packet interrupted during the transmission will be immediately directed to another free channel or wait in the queue for retransmission if no other free channels are available. In our analysis, the downlink modeling is separate from the uplink modeling.

3.1 Downlink Modeling

For the downlink transmission, the incoming packets are buffered in a global queue at MDBS and transmitted in any free voice channel. As in a typical circuit-switched voice system, the number of active voice channels in an m-channel system is modeled by a birth-death process at birth rate λ_v and death rate $i\mu_v$ when i channels are taken by voice transmission. For Poisson data arrival process, the downlink data transmission can then be described by an M/MMEP/m queueing system, which has the QBD structure as shown in Fig. 2. The M/MMEP/m queueing system is characterized

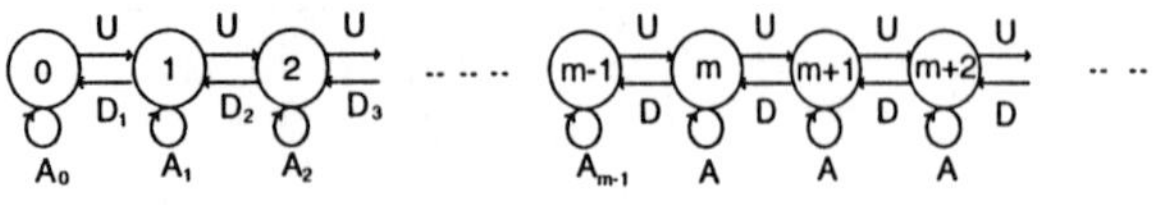

Figure 2: QBD model for the downlink channel of DCS system

by Poisson arrival process with m servers which are modeled by Markov modulated exponential process. The buffer occupancy is measured in data packet units.

The $U = [u_{ij}]$ matrix characterizes each data packet arrival at rate λ_d, which is an $(m+1)\times(m+1)$ diagonal matrix with $u_{ii} = \lambda_d, \forall i$. In our definition, i represents the number of active voice channels for $0 \le i \le m$. The $D = [d_{ij}]$ matrix describes each data packet departure when all the available free channels are used for data transmission, which is also a diagonal matrix with $d_{ii} = (m - i)\mu_d, \forall i$. The $A = [a_{ij}]$ matrix describes the change of active voice channels, which is modeled by the birth-death process,

$$a_{ij} = \begin{cases} i\mu_v & \text{if } j = i-1 \\ -\lambda_v - i\mu_v - d_{ii} - u_{ii} & \text{if } j = i \\ \lambda_v & \text{if } j = i+1 \\ 0 & \text{elsewhere} \end{cases} \qquad (1)$$

where d_{ii} and u_{ii} appeared in a_{ii} are for QBD transition rate matrix normalization. Note that the row sum of $D + U + A$ is zero. The boundary transitions of the QBD process are associated with matrices D_k and A_k for $0 \le k < m$, which represent the situation when the number of data packets can be less than the number of available free channels. In other words, some free channels at the boundary levels will remain unused while all the data packets are being transmitted. The matrix $D_k = [d_{ij,k}]$ represents the data departing rate when k data packets are in the queue, which is described by a diagonal matrix with $d_{ii,k} = \min(k\mu_d, (m-i)\mu_d)$ for $0 \le i \le m$. The matrix A_k is identical to A except to substitute d_{ii} by $d_{ii,k}$ for the definition of a_{ii} in (1) for normalization.

In the QBD analysis, we consider a finite buffer capacity model. The Folding algorithm is used for the computation of steady state queue length distribution, which is an efficient and accurate numerical method developed on the basis of Markov chain reduction theory [7]. The numerical solutions at the boundary levels are iteratively derived, which can become complicated for large m. One design issue in DCS system is the buffer size requirement at MDBS. Here we choose a substantially large buffer capacity to avoid significant packet loss.

For voice traffic, the average voice call holding time is kept at $\mu_v^{-1} = 90$ sec and the voice call blocking probability is fixed at 2% for each given m, from which the voice call arrival rate λ_v is identified. For data traffic, the average packet service time is fixed at $\mu_d^{-1} = 300$ msec; the average data arrival rate λ_d is then determined at each given data utilization ρ which is also called *offered load*. All these parameters are consistent

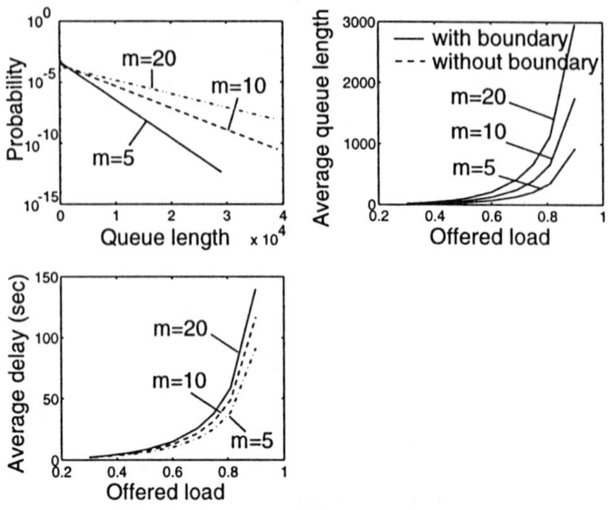

Figure 3: The performance of downlink (a) queue distribution (b) effect of ignoring boundary (c) delay performance

with the CDPD standard [5].

Fig. 3 (a) shows the queue length distribution at $\rho = 0.9$ for the system size $m = 5, 10, 20$. As one can see, a large amount of buffer capacity is required at MDBS which is in the range of several thousands of messages.

Since each data packet size contains 720 bytes on average, it amounts to the buffer capacity of several M bytes or higher to avoid significant packet loss. Such a large data buffer requirement is mainly attributed to the high correlation of voice traffic. As one can see, whenever a channel is taken back for voice transmission, its data transmission will be interrupted for 90 sec on average, during which the data queue can be built up substantially (especially when more channels are simultaneously taken for voice transmission).

Notice that the buffer capacity required is much greater than m, which implies the possibility to neglect the effect of the m boundary levels on the overall queueing solution. In other words, one may replace all the A_k's and D_k's in Fig. 2 by A and D, such that all the boundary levels are removed to simplify the numerical analysis. Such approximate solutions are also plotted in fig. 3 (b), which shows an excellent agreement with the exact solutions.

Fig. 3 (c) displays the average data packet delay on the downlink in DCS system for $m = 5, 10, 20$. As one can see, the average data packet delay can be as high as several minutes under heavy load conditions.

3.2 Uplink Modeling

On the uplink, the transmission of each new data packet arrival requires to be scheduled by MDBS through the DSMA/CD contention. Each M-ES will detect a free channel and contend each other for data access. Only when its contention has succeeded through the DSMA/CD MAC protocol, the M-ES will be able to transmit a data packet. Whenever its contention fails, the M-ES will wait for a random retransmission time before joining the next contention. Further, we assume that each M-ES has equal probability to randomly choose one of the detected free channels to contend.

The analysis of our DSMA/CD protocol is somewhat similar to that of CSMA/CD protocol which were well documented in the data local area network literature, except that here we have multiple channels with voice interruptions, which significantly complicates the analysis. One assumption commonly made in the standard analysis of CSMA/CD protocol is to let the retransmission process of all data users to the channel (or bus) be modeled by Poisson at constant rate γ. The retransmission rate γ is normally identified via the maximum throughput analysis. A similar assumption is made here. That is, the retransmission process from all the M-ES's to each free available channel is assumed to be Poisson at constant rate γ. The evaluation of γ by maximum throughput analysis is postponed to the next section.

The following analysis is based on the CSMA/CD analytical framework in [1] with extension to voice interruption and multiple channels. Starting with a single channel case at $m = 1$, one can model the system by a two-dimensional Markov chain with its state defined by $(N_d(t), C_s(t))$. $N_d(t)$ represents the total number of M-ES's who have data packets to transmit at time t. It forms a 'distributed' queueing system with a single channel as the server. $C_s(t)$ represents the channel status at time t, which can be in one of the following five states:

$$C_s(t) \in \{0, 1, s, c, v\}.$$

State 0 is for channel in the idle, i.e., no data packet transmission. State 1 is for channel in transmission of one packet. State s is for successful transmission of one packet (i.e., its transmission is detected by all other M-ES's). State c is for channel in collision of multiple packet transmissions. State v is for channel taken away by voice. A free channel is defined in one of the states 0, 1, s and c. After we make the assumption for detection time and collision resolution time to be exponential at rate ξ_d and ξ_c as in most Ethernet analyses, the transitions among the five states of the channel will be described by a Markov chain. Fig. 4 shows the state transition diagram of the channel when there are n data packets in the queue. State $(n, 0)$ takes the transition to state $(n, 1)$ at rate γ upon a packet retransmission access, to state (n, v) at rate λ_v upon a new voice call arrival, or to state $(n+1, 1)$ at rate λ_d upon a new packet arrival. State (n, v) takes the transition to state $(n, 0)$ at rate μ_v upon a voice call termination. Similarly, state $(n, 1)$ takes the transition to state (n, s) at rate ξ_d upon transmission detection, to state (n, c) at rate γ upon a packet retransmission access, or to state $(n+1, c)$ at rate λ_d upon a new packet arrival. Other transitions can be described accordingly. Since all the transitions among the states (n, x), $(n-1, x)$ and $(n+1, x)$ for $x \in \{0, 1, s, c, v\}$ are independent of n, the entire system is modeled by a QBD

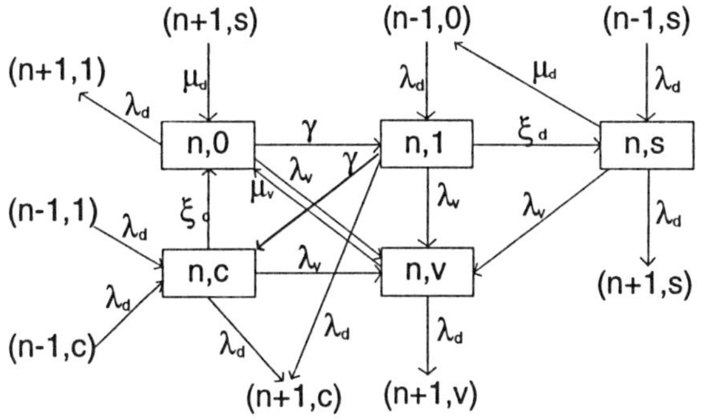

Figure 4: State transition diagram for a single channel case

process.

The analysis is complicated in the multiple channel case. One difficulty is the channel state space explosion. With five states per channel, the total number of states for m channels is 5^m. Since each packet has the equal probability to contend on every free channel in state 0 or 1, the retransmission rate γ on each individual channel should be identical. In other words, it is not necessary to distinguish the state of individual channels in our modeling. Upon grouping the identical state of different channels, the total number of states is reduced to $\binom{m+5-1}{5-1}$. The second difficulty is the evaluation of boundary values of the QBD modeling as in the downlink modeling. The boundary values are associated with the transitions when the number of data packets in the queue is less than the number of channels. By the same approximation as used in the downlink modeling, one can neglect the effect of boundary values on the queueing performance.

The assumption of identical γ on each free channel can be justified. For the GPRS system, each M-ES randomly and independently accesses any time slot in a frame at a given carrier frequency. For the CDPD system, it is the MDBS to dynamically allocate M-ES's among the presently available channels for best performance.

The state of the grouped channels is now defined by $n_c = (n_0, n_1, n_s, n_c, n_v)$, where n_x represents the number of channels in state $x \in (0, 1, s, c, v)$, providing $n_0+n_1+n_s+n_c+n_v = m$ for $n_x \geq 0$. The entire system can then be described by a two-dimensional Markov chain with state (n_d, n_c), where n_d represents the number of data packets in the queue. Since the transitions of n_c are independent of n_d except at the boundaries, the system is modeled by a QBD process.

The QBD transition matrices, $\{U, D, A\}$, are readily constructed by the following state transitions:

$(n_d, n_c) \to (n_d, n_c(n_0^-, n_1^+))$ at γn_0:
a packet retransmission on a channel in state 0,

$(n_d, n_c) \to (n_d, n_c(n_1^-, n_c^+))$ at γn_1:
collision caused by a packet retransmission,

$(n_d, n_c) \rightarrow (n_d, n_c(n_1^-, n_s^+))$ at $\xi_d n_1$:
packet transmission detection on a channel in state 1,
$(n_d, n_c) \rightarrow (n_d, n_c(n_c^-, n_0^+))$ at $\xi_c n_c$:
collision resolution on a channel in state c,
$(n_d, n_c) \rightarrow (n_d, n_c(n_0^-, n_v^+))$ at $\frac{\lambda_v n_0}{m-n_v}$:
a channel in state 0 taken away by a voice call,
$(n_d, n_c) \rightarrow (n_d, n_c(n_1^-, n_v^+))$ at $\frac{\lambda_v n_1}{m-n_v}$:
a channel in state 1 taken away by a voice call,
$(n_d, n_c) \rightarrow (n_d, n_c(n_s^-, n_v^+))$ at $\frac{\lambda_v n_s}{m-n_v}$:
a channel in state s taken away by a voice call,
$(n_d, n_c) \rightarrow (n_d, n_c(n_c^-, n_v^+))$ at $\frac{\lambda_v n_c}{m-n_v}$:
a channel in state c taken away by a voice call,
$(n_d, n_c) \rightarrow (n_d, n_c(n_v^-, n_0^+))$ at $\mu_v n_v$:
a channel released by a voice call departure,
$(n_d, n_c) \rightarrow (n_d^+, n_c(n_0^-, n_1^+))$ at $\frac{\lambda_d n_0}{m-n_v}$:
a new packet arrival on a channel in state 0
$(n_d, n_c) \rightarrow (n_d^+, n_c(n_1^-, n_c^+))$ at $\frac{\lambda_d n_1}{m-n_v}$:
a new packet arrival on a channel in state 1
$(n_d, n_c) \rightarrow (n_d^+, n_c)$ at $\frac{\lambda_d (n_c+n_s)}{m-n_v}$:
a new packet arrival on a channel in state c or s
$(n_d, n_c) \rightarrow (n_d^-, n_c(n_s^-, n_0^+))$ at $\mu_d n_s$:
a packet departure

where the notation n_x^- represents $n_x - 1$ and n_x^+ represents $n_x + 1$ for $x \in \{d, 0, 1, c, s, v\}$.

4 Maximum Throughput Analysis

This section provides the uplink maximum throughput analysis based on the QBD modeling. We use the following stability theory of QBD process in [8].

Theorem: *Let R be the minimal nonnegative solution of the equation $R^2D + RA + U = 0$. The QBD Process is recurrent nonnull, i.e., the spectral radius of R is less than unity ($sp(R) < 1$), if and only if*

$$\pi U < \pi D$$

where π is uniquely determined by $\pi A' = 0$ and $\pi e = 1$ with $A' = U + D + A$. The QBD process is null recurrent if $sp(R) = 1$ and transient if $sp(R) > 1$.
Similar to the study of CSMA-CD system in [1], one can use the above QBD stability theorem to derive the maximum throughput. The only unknown in the definition of U and D matrices is γ, which is the packet retransmission rate on each available free channel. By definition, we have πDe equal to the packet departure rate, where D is the departure rate transition matrix and e is the column unit vector. For each λ_d we can find a set $\Gamma(\lambda_d)$ such that

$$\Gamma(\lambda_d) = \{\gamma : \pi U < \pi D\}.$$

One can obtain the set $\Gamma(\lambda_d)$ at each given $\{m, \lambda_d, \mu_d, \lambda_v, \mu_v\}$. Define the maximum throughput by

$$\lambda_{dmax} = \text{Sup}\{\lambda_d : \Gamma(\lambda_d) \neq \emptyset\}.$$

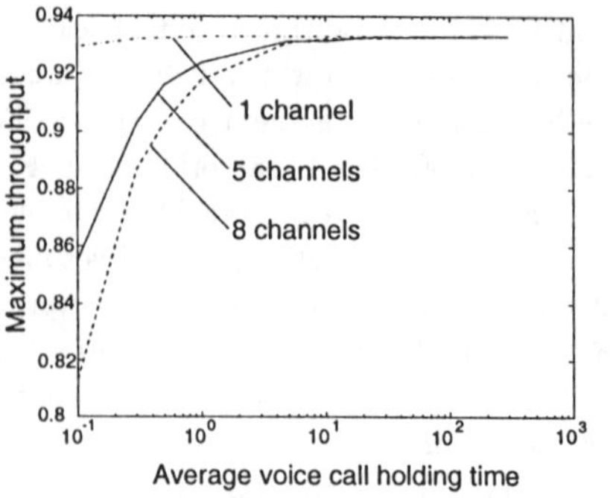

Figure 5: Maximum throughput vs. voice call holding time

which is identified by the value of λ_d at which $\Gamma(\lambda_d) = \emptyset$ when we gradually increase λ_d.

Fig. 5 shows the maximum throughput performance as a function of average voice holding time μ_v^{-1} with respect to m=1, 5, and 8. Recall that the voice call arrival rate λ_v at each given m is determined under the 2% call blocking rate constraint. The mean data packet transmission time on each channel is fixed at $\mu_d^{-1} = 300$ msec according to the standard [5]. Denote the average data link capacity by $\overline{C}_d$ which is readily obtained from the total link capacity and the voice traffic load. The maximum throughput in Fig. 5 is normalized by $\overline{C}_d$. First, we find that the maximum throughput reduces as m increases, especially for small average voice holding time μ_v^{-1}. This occurs mainly because of the trunk efficiency improved by large m for voice transmission. In other words, the idle period of a voice channel tends to be statistically shortened for large m, which degrades the data performance. Secondly, the maximum throughput is improved as the average voice holding time increases. Again, this is attributed to the extended idle period of voice channels for the increased μ_v^{-1}. More importantly, the effect of m and μ_v on the maximum throughput is found diminishing rapidly once $\mu_v^{-1} > 10$ sec. In practice we normally take $\mu_v^{-1} = 90$ sec. The same maximum throughput results can then be applied to systems with different μ_v and m. Notice that $\overline{C}_d - \lambda_{dmax}$ gives us the average contention overhead of the multiple access scheme.

5 Delay Performance Analysis

Although the grouping substantially reduces the QBD state space, the resulting state space still grows rapidly with m, which may prohibit the computation in practice for large m. Compared to the downlink modeling, the complication of the uplink modeling is due to the Markov chain characterization of multiple access contention. Nevertheless, the characteristics of maximum throughput is found to be insensitive to the system size m for practical μ_v. In other words, one can use the results of maximum throughput derived from a small m for large m's. The question then becomes how much the multiple access contention will affect the data de-

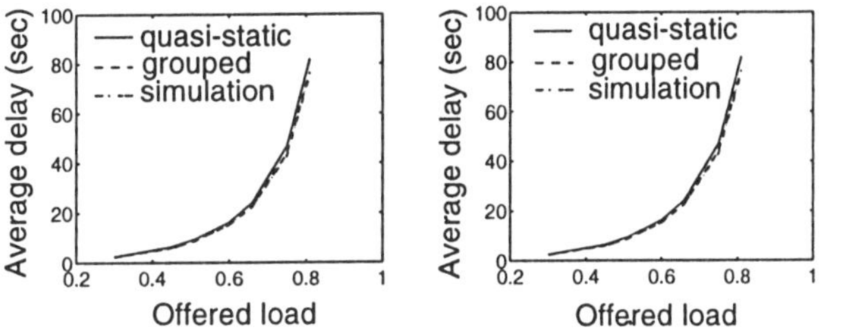

Figure 6: Validity of the assumptions for the uplink model (a) m=5 (b) m=8

lay performance. The study of the downlink modeling has already shown the dominant role of the voice holding time on the data delay performance, which suggests the possibility to neglect the effect of multiple access contention in the uplink data delay analysis except to subtract the average contention overhead from the average data link capacity. Namely, we can use the downlink modeling for the analysis of the uplink by assuming that the data channel capacity is reduced to the maximum throughput. Such approximation is called quasi-static since we ignore the dynamic effect of the multiple access contention on data delay performance. The Markovian states associated with contention can therefore be completely removed; the complexity of the uplink modeling is reduced to that of the downlink modeling.

In Fig. 6 we compare the three solutions of the average delay performance for $m = 5$ and 8 at $\mu_v^{-1} = 90$ sec, obtained from computer simulation, *grouped* analytical modeling and *quasi-static* analytical modeling. In contrast to the simulation model, the grouped analytical modeling has neglected the boundary effect; the quasi-static analytical modeling has further ignored the dynamics of the contention. All the three solutions are found to agree very well for the wide range of λ_d, which verify the proposed approximation techniques.

Fig. 7a shows the impact of average voice holding time on the data delay performance at $m = 8$ with respect to $\mu_v^{-1} =$ 60 sec, 120 sec and 180 sec. Again, the voice call blocking probability is fixed at 2%; the average packet transmission time on a channel is taken to be 300 ms. Similar to the downlink, the voice holding time has dominant impact on the uplink delay performance. In Fig. 7b we examine the delay performance for different system size m = 8, 15, 50. Because of the improved trunk efficiency for voice transmission, the data delay performance is degraded for large m. This is also consistent to what we observed in the downlink modeling.

As one can see, the average data delay in DCS system is expected to be substantially long, typically in the range of a few minutes in heavy load condition. Moreover, the delay performance experienced by M-ES's at different time can vary significantly, depending on the number of free channels presently available. Fig. 7c shows the average delay performance conditioned on the number of free voice channels available upon a data packet arrival. Two extreme conditions are examined. Under the best condition, all 8 voice channels are free for data transmission upon a data packet arrival, which will experience much less delay. Under the worst condition, none of the voice channels are free upon a data packet arrival, which will have to wait long enough before transmission. Notice that the difference in the average delay between the two extreme conditions is in the range of a few minutes, which is significant to certain applications (e.g., for stock quotation). The unconditional average delay is also displayed in Fig. 7c for comparison purposes.

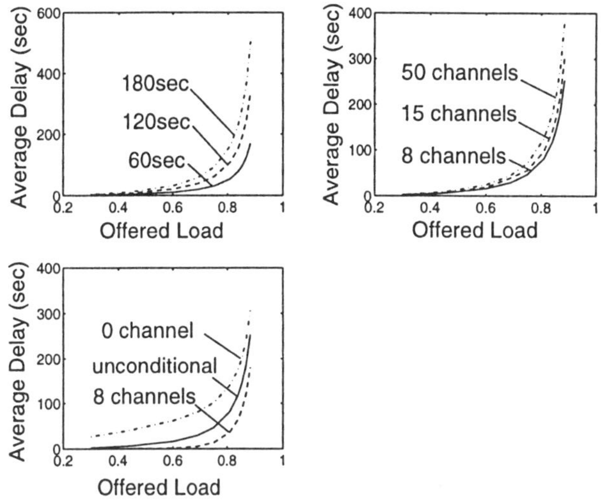

Figure 7: Average data packet delay performance (a) average voice call holding time (b) number of channels (c) conditional delay on the number of idle voice channel

6 Performance Improvement

Two techniques are possibly used to improve the data performance: *priority access* and *silence detection*. In the design of priority access, all M-ES's are classified into low-priority and high-priority to access the free channels. The low-priority M-ES's can send packets if and only if the number of presently active voice channels, n_v, is less than or equal to a given threshold T_h. That is, the MDBS will accept both high- and low-priority packet arrivals when $n_v \leq T_h$, but only accept high-priority packet arrivals when $n_v > T_h$. Notice that once a low-priority packet arrival is accepted when $n_v \leq T_h$, its successful transmission may actually take place when $n_v > T_h$. There is no difference in the multiple access contention scheme between low- and high-priority packets once they are accepted. In other words, the accepted low-priority packets will experience the same delay performance as the high-priority packets. The overall controlled delay performance can be significantly improved at the expense of blocking low-priority packet arrivals in overload periods.

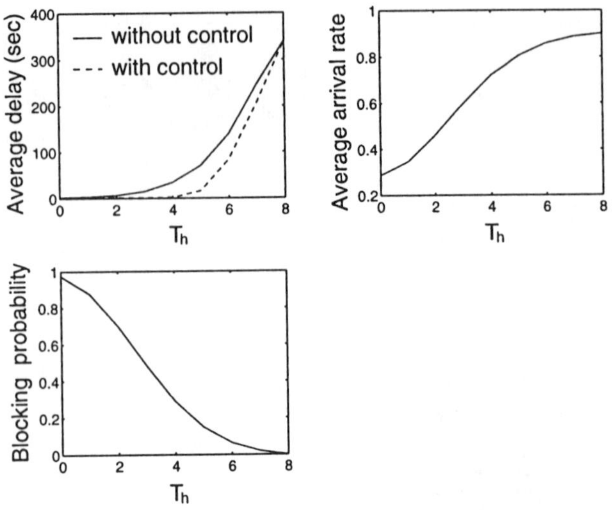

Figure 8: Performance improvement by priority control (a) delay (b) average arrival rate and (c) low-priority blocking.

Let λ_h and λ_l be the Poisson rate of high- and low-priority packet arrivals, respectively. For the QBD modeling we define

$$\lambda_d = \begin{cases} \lambda_h + \lambda_l & \text{if } n_v \leq T_h \\ \lambda_h & \text{otherwise.} \end{cases}$$

The average data arrival rate is then given by $\overline{\lambda}_d = \lambda_h + \lambda_l Pr(n_v \leq T_h)$. Assume that there are 30% high-priority M-ES's and 70% low-priority M-ES's in the controlled DCS system. The aggregate arrival rate before blocking, $\lambda_h + \lambda_l$, is kept at 90% of the available data link capacity. The QBD modeling of the controlled system is basically identical to the noncontrolled system except to make the data arrival rate λ_d dependent on the number of presently active voice channels.

Fig. 8a shows the controlled average delay performance as a function of the threshold T_h for $m = 8$. With the increase of T_h, less low-priority packets are blocked, which deteriorates the overall delay performance. Also displayed in Figs. 8b,c are the corresponding average data arrival rate $\overline{\lambda}_d$ (normalized by $\overline{C}_d$) and the low-priority blocking probability. For comparison purposes, we show in Fig. 8a the noncontrolled delay performance at each given $\overline{\lambda}_d$ (through T_h) as if no priority control is applied. Obviously, the priority control improves the overall delay performance at the expense of blocking low-priority packet arrivals in overload periods.

As we know, the large data delay in DCS system is mainly caused by the expected long voice call holding time, which is typically in the range of a few minutes. Consider that each speech process actually experiences the alternation of talkspurt and silence periods and no signals need to be transmitted on the voice channels during the silence periods. The speech silence detection is originally proposed for the statistical multiplexing of voice traffic. It can also be used as a degenerate case of circuit-switch mode in cellular voice networks to reduce the co-channel interference [9]. Similarly, the MDBS can be designed to detect and use the voice silence periods for data transmission to improve its delay performance. Depending on detection mechanisms, the average silence can be in the range of a few hundred msec to a sec. A typical example is to model the alternation of talkspurt and silent periods in a speech process by a two-state Markov chain with the average talkspurt and silent periods set at 600ms and 400ms, respectively.

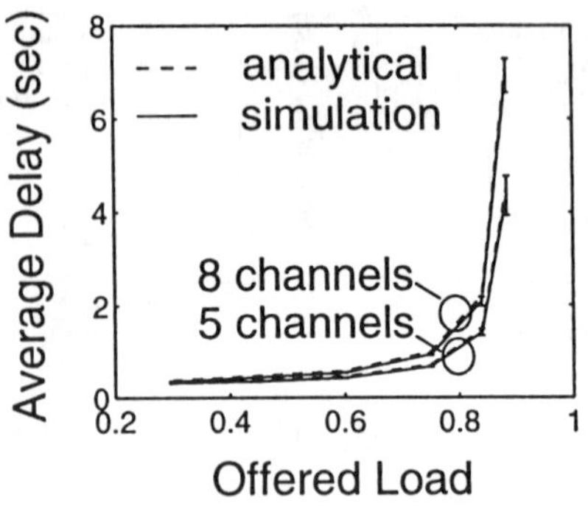

Figure 9: Performance improvement by silence detection

Let us consider the delay performance improvement by silence detection in the worst case scenario, i.e., all the m channels in the DCS system are presently used to support their voice transmission. Without silence detection, the DCS system would have zero data throughput. Fig. 9 shows the data delay performance with silence detection in this worst scenario as a function of the offered data load λ_d for $m = 5, 8$. Note that λ_d is normalized by the available average data link capacity. As one can see, although this is the worst case with silenct detection, its average data delay performance is much reduced compared to all the previous examples (reduced from a few minutes to a few seconds). In this analysis, our QBD modeling does consider the effect of boundary values since the queue length is much reduced. But, the quasi-static approximation is still applied for simplicity. To verify this approximation, the simulation results with 95% confidence interval are also plotted in Fig. 9.

7 Conclusions

The previous analyses of DCS system neglected the important effect of voice traffic statistics on data performance, which led to over optimistic solutions. In this paper we have developed a QBD modeling framework for DCS system, which characterizes not only the voice interruption on data transmission but also the random access contention of multiple data users on free voice channels. Because of the dominant influence of voice call holding time, the average data delay for DCS system in heavy load conditions is found typically in the range of a few minutes. The maximum throughput analysis also indicates that the contention overhead is relatively insensitive to the system size m and the voice call holding time, which led to the qausi-static approximation for simplified queueing analysis. The possibility of boundary value elimination in the QBD modeling has also be proposed and verified. We have further introduced and studied the data priority access scheme and voice silence detection technique to improve the data delay performance.

References

[1] E. J. Coyle and B. Liu, "A Matrix Representation of CSMA/CD Networks," *IEEE Transactions on Communications*, Vol. 33, No. 1, Jan. 1985, pp. 53-64.

[2] W.D. Grover, W.A. Krzymien, and J.C. Chin. "Background Data Service for Cellular Mobile Radio," *Proc. of IEEE VTC'93*, pp. 766-769.

[3] N. Jain. "Queueing Model of CDPD Implementation on American Cellular Systems" *ITC Mini-Seminar 1994*.

[4] K. Budka. "Cellular Digital Packet Data: Channel Availability," *Proc. of PIRMC'95*.

[5] "Cellular Digital Packet Data System Specification: Release 1.1," CDPD Forum, Inc., Jan. 1995

[6] G. Bianchi, A. Capone, L. Fratta, and L Musumeci "Packet Data Service over GSM networks with Dynamic Stealing of Voice Channels," *Proc. IEEE Globecom'95*, Nov. 1995, pp. 1152-1156.

[7] J. Ye and S. Q. Li, "Folding Algorithm: A Computational Method for Finite QBD process with Level-Dependent Transitions" *IEEE Transactions on Communications*, Vol. 42, No. 2, Feb. 1994, pp. 625-639

[8] M. F. Neuts, *Matrix-Geomtric Solutions in Stochastic Model*, MD: Johns Hopkins Univ. Press, 1981.

[9] G. Anastasi, D. Grillo, L. Lenzini, and E Mingozzi "A Bandwidth Reservation Protocol for Speech/Data Integration in TDMA-Based Advanced Mobile Systems" *Proc. IEEE Infocom'96*, Mar. 1996, pp. 722-729.

A Cellular Wireless Local Area Network with QoS Guarantees for Heterogeneous Traffic

Sunghyun Choi and Kang G. Shin
Department of Electrical Engineering and Computer Science
The University of Michigan
Ann Arbor, Michigan 48109–2122
E-mail: {shchoi,kgshin}@eecs.umich.edu

Abstract

A wireless local area network (WLAN) or a cell *with quality-of-service (QoS) guarantees for various types of traffic is considered. A centralized (i.e., star) network topology is adopted as the topology of a cell which consists of a base station and a number of mobile clients. Dynamic Time Division Duplexed (TDD) transmission is used, and hence, the same frequency channel is time-shared for downlink and uplink transmissions under the dynamic control of the base station. We divide traffic into two classes: class I (real-time) and II (non-real-time). Whenever there is no eligible class-I traffic, class-II traffic is transmitted, while uplink transmissions are controlled with a reservation scheme. Class-I traffic is handled with the framing strategy [1] combined with the admission test for adding new class-I connections. Finally, we present the performance (average delay and throughput) evaluation of the reservation scheme for class-II traffic using both analytical calculations and simulations.*

1 Introduction

Wireless LANs (WLANs) are emerging as an attractive alternative or complementary to wired LANs [2,3], because they allow us to set up and reconfigure LANs easily without incurring the cost of wiring. They are generally characterized as high-speed wireless systems which cover relatively small areas compared to other wireless systems such as cellular, PCS, and mobile data radio systems. It is expected that they will meet the growing demand that mobile clients should have access to the existing high-speed wired networks. As the interest in broadband multimedia communications involving digital audio and video grows, a number of researchers have been looking into ways of providing QoS guarantees in wired point-to-point WANs [1,4,5] and LANs [6].

In this paper, we consider how to provide QoS guarantees for heterogeneous traffic on a WLAN. The following three types of QoS are considered: (1) maximum packet delivery delay; (2) transmission throughput; and (3) packet loss tolerance. We categorize various traffic into two classes: (1) class-I real-time traffic like real-time data, video, and voice which requires bounded delay and guaranteed throughput, but is usually loss-tolerable; and (2) class-II non-real-time traffic like the conventional data traffic which requires zero loss, but requires no bounded delay nor guaranteed throughput. Class II is also divided further into two subclasses: (i) delay-sensitive class II-A like FTP and remote log-in; and (ii) delay-tolerable class II-B like paging and e-mail. Class II-A has priority over class II-B.

We adopt a reservation scheme which is similar to the reservation ALOHA [7] or PRMA [8] for uplink class-II traffic transmissions. (The reservation scheme proposed in this paper differs from the previous work, but appears similar in the sense of adopting collision-based reservation schemes.) This reservation scheme is a promising multiple access protocol for class-II traffic, as it provides higher throughput and smaller average delay than other collision-based random access protocols like ALOHA as in [9]. Basically, class-II traffic is transmitted when there is no class-I traffic to be transmitted since it has a lower priority than class I.

The framing strategy [1], which was originally proposed as a framework for congestion management in integrated service packet networks, is used with some modifications. The framing strategy is composed of a smoothness traffic model and stop-and-go queueing, and provides both packet-delay bound and guaranteed transmission throughput. Each connection of class I should follow a smoothness traffic model, and each new connection needs to pass the *a priori* admission test with a traffic model, implying that the framing strategy reserve slots for class-I connections according to their traffic model. To implement the framing strategy, it is necessary to schedule the uplink and downlink transmissions.

The paper is organized as follows. Section 2 shows the specifications and assumptions of the WLAN under consideration. Section 3 describes the proposed protocol, including the reservation scheme for class-II traffic. Section 4 considers the framing strategy with QoS guarantees for class I and defines the admission test for establishing a new connection. Section 5 presents the analysis and simulation results of the performance of the reservation scheme for class II. Finally, the paper concludes with Section 6.

*The work reported in this paper was supported in part by the US Department of Transportation under Grant No. DTFH61-93-X-00017. Any opinions, findings, and conclusions or recommendations expressed in this publication are those of the authors and do not necessarily reflect the views of the funding agency.

0-8186-7780-5/97 $10.00 © 1997 IEEE

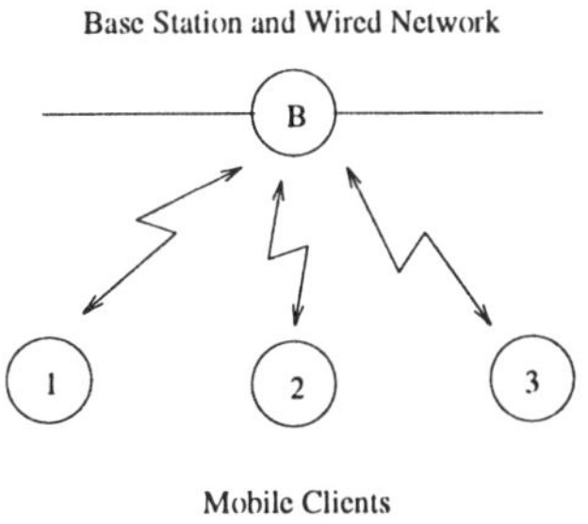

Figure 1: A centralized wireless network with a base station.

2 Specifications and Assumptions of System

As shown in Fig. 1, the WLAN under consideration consists of a base station (denoted by B) and several mobile clients (denoted by numbers) forming a star network, called a *cell.* The base station is connected to a wired high-speed network. In this topology, the uplink (mobile-to-base) is not a broadcast channel while the downlink (base-to-mobile) is. Hence, mobile clients are not able to listen directly to other mobiles using the same frequency channel. This assumed situation can occur in real world due to the existence of *hidden* terminals [3].

The entire wireless network may consist of several cells, and mobile clients may move from one cell to another. However, we will in this paper focus on the communication within a single cell, hence the uplink and downlink transmissions only. Since wireless links usually have much less bandwidth than the wired counterpart, the former might become a bottleneck. Since the base stations are connected to a wired network, the other communicating party of each mobile in a cell can be a node in the wired network, or a mobile in another cell, or another mobile in the same cell. In any case, the wireless link in the cell is considered as the end-most link (for downlink) or the front-most link (for uplink) of the entire multi-hop communication. Note that the downlink traffic comes from the wired network or mobiles in the same cell, and the uplink traffic is generated by mobiles.

Dynamic Time Division Duplexed (TDD) transmission is used in the network, and hence, the base station multiplexes the uplink and downlink packet transmissions dynamically according to the traffic load over a frequency channel. We could instead use frequency division duplexed (FDD) transmission, in which two different frequency channels are allocated for uplink and downlink transmissions, or static TDD in which a portion (usually a half) of each time frame is allocated for uplink and the other part for downlink. FDD is the common duplexing mode in cellular systems, and static TDD was adopted in the DECT system [2]. But, dynamic TDD allows for more efficient link utilization in the case of unbalanced uplink and downlink traffic, e.g., non-interactive data transmissions, as shown in [9]. We assume all packets, like ATM cells, to be of the same fixed size. Throughout the remainder of this paper, we will ignore the packet-propagation delay, because it is usually small relative to the other delay components like queuing and transmission delays in the cell.[1]

Since the wireless channel is inherently unreliable (due to noises, interferences, and multipath fadings), we need a special means to ensure the error-free delivery of packets through each wireless link. Usually, a combined channel coding and diversity scheme [2] is used to meet this need. To handle various types of traffic in our system, we can apply error-handling schemes adaptively. We adopt an ARQ (Automatic Retransmission reQuest) scheme for class II to ensure virtually error-free transmission of data. But, it is ruled out for class I because of its difficulty in making delivery-delay guarantees. We use an FEC (Forward Error Correction) scheme for class I, instead.[2] To this end, the receiver is equipped with a dual-mode channel decoder: a received packet is decoded by an error-correction decoder (if class I) or an error-detection decoder (if class II). The dual-mode receiver is expected to work well since using a channel code, the decoder can detect more errors than those correctable. We will not consider error-combating techniques any more since they are not within the primary scope of this paper, but we assume that a packet is received correctly unless that packet collides with concurrent packets.

3 Protocol Description

When a mobile wants to send a packet, regardless whether it is destined for another client in the same cell or for a remote cell, it must send the packet to its base station first, which will then forward the packet to the final destination, sometimes via other base stations. We adopt two different strategies for class I and II. First, class-I traffic is transmitted via connections, i.e., for each of class-I (downlink or uplink) connections, a finite number of slots are reserved to meet the required QoS. Each connection (between the base station and a mobile) is identified by: (1) for which client and (2) for downlink or uplink. For the QoS provision, class-I traffic has priority over class-II traffic, where the transmission is controlled by the framing strategy (to be discussed in the next section). Class-II traffic doesn't need the concept of connection, but if there is a pending message (which consists of a number of packets), it will be transmitted when there are available slots, i.e., when no class-I traffic is being transmitted over the link. For uplink class-II traffic, a request of slot reservation for transmission is made for each message.

A *slot* and a *control mini-slot* alternate continuously as shown in Fig. 2. In a slot of duration T_s, a packet is transmitted. By dynamic TDD transmission, each slot can be used for either downlink or uplink transmission under the control of the base station. A control mini-slot of duration T_{ms} is used to transmit a control packet. Control packets are used by the base station

[1] A cell in this paper refers to a *micro-cell*, which has coverage of the order of a few hundred meters, or a *pico-cell*, which covers small indoor areas [2].

[2] Although combined FEC and diversity seems to be the only way for error-protection of class I, it is extremely difficult to guarantee the virtually error-free transmission of packets of these classes over the wireless link due to the error-correcting capability limit of the underlying FEC scheme. So the proposed scheme here might not be applicable for reliability-critical real-time data traffic of class I.

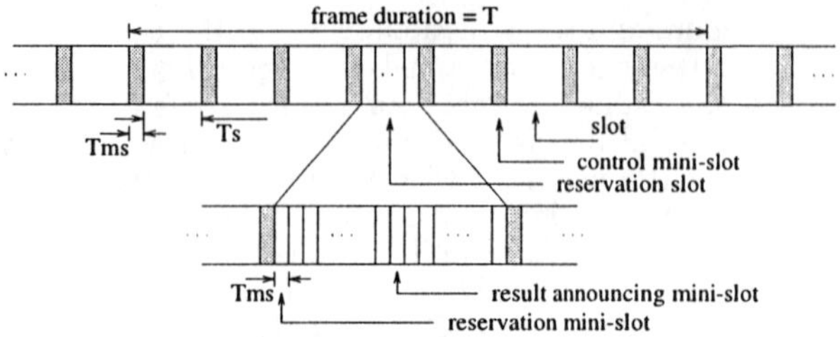

Figure 2: Dividing the time-axis into mini-slots, slots, and reservation slots. A frame includes a number of slots.

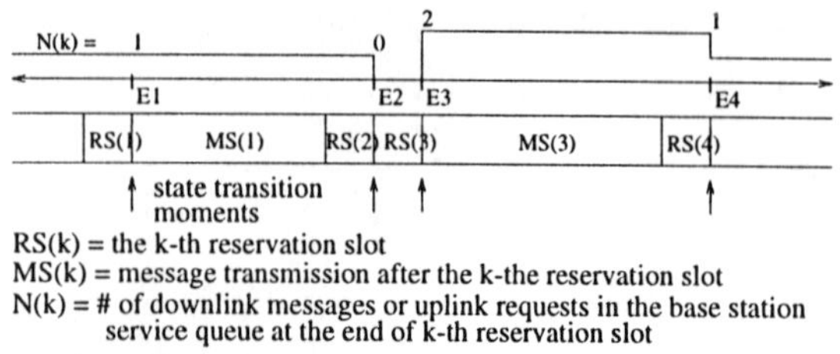

Figure 3: Timing diagram of class-II communications during the absence of class-I traffic.

to announce to the mobiles information of the next slot (1) for downlink or uplink, (2) for class I or II, and (3) for which client. These regularly alternating slots and mini-slots are expected to help each mobile synchronize to the global transmission system. We will henceforth use T_{ms} as a basic time unit. Assume that a slot duration is an even number multiple of a mini-slot duration, i.e., $K = T_s/T_{ms}$ is an even number.

There exist slots, called *reservation slots*, which are used for requesting an uplink class-I connection establishment or an uplink class-II message transmission. A reservation slot consists of K mini-slots of duration T_{ms}. It is divided into two parts: (1) the first half is a set of $K/2$ *reservation mini-slots* used by mobiles to request uplink transmissions; and (2) the second half is a set of $K/2$ *result-announcing mini-slots* for each of the corresponding previous reservation mini-slots. The reservation mini-slots are accessed by a slotted ALOHA-like random access protocol: when a reservation slot is issued by the base station, each mobile with a pending request chooses one of $K/2$ mini-slots randomly, and then sends the request in that chosen mini-slot with the traffic information. The result of each of $K/2$ mini-slots can be success (of which mobile[3]), or collision, or empty/unused. Using each of the next $K/2$ downlink mini-slots, the result of the corresponding reservation mini-slot is announced.

If a reservation slot contains only "collided" reservation mini-slots, the base station will issue reservation slots consecutively until a successful reservation mini-slot appears in a reservation slot. Using this policy, the base station will obtain at least one successful reservation request for mobiles who want to make a slot reservation. A mobile whose reservation request collided with others will retransmit the request again in the subsequent reservation slots with the probability q_r until it is successful. (The retransmission probability q_r can be determined adaptively according to the results of all of $K/2$ reservation mini-slots.) If a reservation request is successful, the base station will be informed that the mobile who made the request wants (1) to send a pending class-II message, or (2) to establish a class-I connection.

For dynamic TDD transmission, the base station needs to multiplex between downlink and uplink transmissions. The base station does not know if a mobile has a pending message without receiving a reservation request. Basically, a reservation slot is issued after completing the transmission of a (downlink or uplink) class-II message as shown in Fig. 3, where only class-II traffic (without subclasses) exists. Two first-in-first-out (FIFO) base station class-II service queues are implemented for two subclasses of class II, in which both the uplink requests (from mobiles) and the downlink messages are queued together. The contents of the queues are updated at the end of every reservation slot (marked with arrows in Fig. 3): at the end of the k-th reservation slot, E_k, all the downlink messages which arrived at the base station between E_{k-1} and E_k, and all the uplink requests which were successfully received during the k-th reservation slot are queued in a random order. By this random queueing policy, the uplink transmission achieves fairness since the uplink reservation requests might suffer excessive delays compared to the downlink transmission due to the collision-based reservation request access. The second queue for class II-B can be served whenever the first queue for class II-A is empty. When both queues are empty, the base station issues a reservation slot for each available slot.

With the scheme explained above, the maximum achievable throughput of class II might be very low depending on the average message length, i.e., the smaller the average message length, the smaller maximum achievable throughput. To solve this problem, we assign the Minimum Next Reservation Slot Length ($MNRSL$) defined as the minimum number of slots between two consecutive reservation slots. Assume that a (downlink or uplink) message transmission was completed after a reservation slot. If less than $MNRSL$ packets were transmitted since the reservation slot, the base station will serve more messages until the entire transmitted packets exceed $MNRSL$. Thus, the maximum achievable throughput is guaranteed to be $\geq (MNRSL \cdot T_s)/((MNRSL + 1)(T_s + T_{ms}))$.

4 Framing Strategy for QoS Provision

In this section, we describe the framing strategy to guarantee QoS for class-I traffic. The time axis is divided into frames, each of which is composed of a finite number of slots (and so mini-slots) as shown in Fig. 2. If there are N slots and mini-slots in a frame of time duration T, then $T = N \cdot (T_s + T_{ms})$.

4.1 Traffic Model

For each connection i of class-I traffic, we adopt the (M_i, T_i)-smooth model, i.e., during each frame of length T_i, no more than M_i packets arrive (or be generated) for connection i. If connection i is for uplink transmissions, the mobile regulates its uplink traffic to follow the (M_i, T_i)-smooth model using the packet admission

[3]Due to the *capture effects* [3], a reservation request can be transmitted successfully even in the presence of concurrent reservation requests from other mobiles.

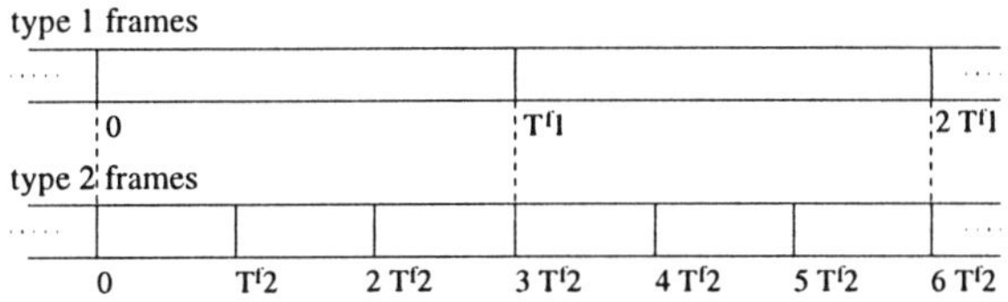

Figure 4: Two frames with duration $T_1^f = 3T_2^f$.

policy, by which any packet which violates the smoothness is assumed not to be generated until the beginning of the next frame. In the wired part of the network, we assume the existence of a traffic regulator like the (M_i, T_i)-smooth admission policy or leaky-bucket [4] in the source end nodes and a flow/congestion control or packet scheduling scheme such as the framing strategy and Weighted Fair Queueing (or PGPS) [4] in intermediate nodes. Thus, the traffic arriving at the base station from the wired network will have the smoothness property, which can then be converted to the (M_j, T_j)-smooth model. Moreover, the downlink traffic from a mobile within the cell (in case of the intra-cell communications) will also have the the smoothness property (as explained later). So, it is possible to adopt the (M_j, T_j)-smooth model for a downlink connection j as well.

Suppose there are G frame sizes, $T_1^f, T_2^f, \cdots, T_G^f$, and each frame size is a multiple of smaller frame sizes, i.e.,

$$T_g^f = I_g \cdot T_{g+1}^f, \quad g = 1, 2, \cdots, G-1, \tag{1}$$

for some integer I_g. For all g,

$$T_g^f = K_g \cdot (T_s + T_{ms}), \tag{2}$$

for some integer K_g, i.e., there are a finite number of slots in each frame. Each frame of duration T_g^f is called a *type-g frame*. For each connection i, $T_i = T_g^f$ for some g, and the connection is called the *type-g connection*. Fig. 4 shows the case of $G = 2$ and $T_1 = 3T_2$. Note that all frames are incorporated into a single frequency channel. As shown in the next subsection, the packets in a type-g connection will be guaranteed to have a delivery delay bound $2T_g^f$, implying the existence of G delivery delay bounds.

4.2 Stop-and-Go Queueing

__Downlink Transmissions:__ The transmission from the base station to mobile clients can be viewed as taking place over a single link in a wired network since it is broadcast-type communication. Stop-and-go queueing is used for downlink transmissions with the following rules.

R1. A downlink packet of a type-g connection that has arrived at the base station during a frame does not become *eligible* until the beginning of the next frame. During a frame, the set of eligible packets of the corresponding type are transmitted.

R2. Any eligible packet of a type-g connection, $g = 2, 3, \cdots, G$, has priority over eligible packets of type $g' < g$.

R3. The wireless link should not be left idle whenever there are eligible packets in the queues.

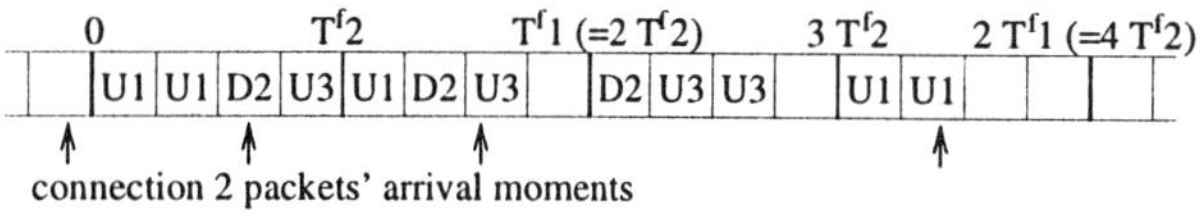

Figure 5: An example of stop-and-go queueing.

To implement the above rule, the base station is equipped with G FIFO queues.

__Uplink Transmissions:__ During each type-g frame, the base station issues (via mini-slots) up to $\sum_{\{T_i = T_g^f\}} M_i$ slots for type-g uplink connections with the same priority given in **R2**. Within the same type, uplink connections have priority over downlink connections, and so in each frame, uplink slots are issued first, and then eligible downlink packets are transmitted. For uplink connection i, the base station will issue up to M_i uplink slots or until the corresponding mobile sends a packet marked as the last packet. Then, the next connection is served. When a slot is issued for connection i in a frame, the connection i mobile transmits a packet which was generated during the previous frame via the issued slot, and marks the last packet arrived in the previous frame. Now, the traffic arrived at the base station from each mobile client also has the (M_i, T_i)-smoothness.

Using the above transmission rules, all of the connection-i packets, which conform to the smoothness, will be transmitted until the end of the next type-g frame (when $T_i = T_g^f$), and thus are guaranteed to be transmitted within a delay of $2T_i$. For each connection i, up to M_i packets can be transmitted over a frame of duration T_i, and so, it is guaranteed to have the throughput of $M_i \cdot T_s / T_i$.

Example 1 *We ignore the mini-slots assuming that $T_{ms} \ll T_s$. Suppose there are three class-I connections, where connection 1 and 3 are for the uplink and connection 2 is for the downlink with the smoothness parameters $\{(M_i, T_i)\} = \{(2, 4T_s), (1, 4T_s), (2, 8T_s)\}$. So, there are two frame sizes, i.e., $G = 2$, where $T_1^f = 8T_s$ and $T_2^f = 4T_s$. In Fig. 5, an example of stop-and-go queueing for this set of connections is shown. The slots for connection 1, 2, and 3 are marked with $U1$, $D2$, and $U3$, respectively. The packet arrivals of connection 2 are also marked by arrows. One can see that connection 1 has priority over connection 2 since connection 1 is uplink. Connection 3 has the lowest priority. Through the blank slots in the figure, class-II traffic, if any, will be transmitted by the rules presented in Section 3.* □

4.3 Admission Tests

If a new connection is to be added, it has to pass the following simple admission test depending on the frame-size constraints. Downlink connections requests come from the wired network (or from a mobile originating a connection within the same cell) with the traffic characteristics (M_i, T_i), while uplink connection requests come from mobile clients via a reservation slot. The admission test is given as

$$\sum_{g=1}^{G} M_g^f \cdot (T_s + T_{ms}) / T_g^f \le 1, \tag{3}$$

where $M_g^f = \sum_{\{T_i=T_g^f\}} M_i$ is the number of the reserved slots within a type-g frame, in which the existing connections and the newly-requested connection are included. If the results of the above test is positive, it is possible to provide the required QoS to the new connection without compromising the existing connections' guarantees, and so, the base station starts to serve the new connection beginning at the next frame. The basic idea of the admission test is the total reserved throughput for class-I connections plus the redundancy of mini-slots should be less than, or equal to, one. The readers are referred to [10] for a formal proof. Note that in Example 1, the summation in Eq. (3) is exactly one, implying that all of the slots be reserved for the three class-I connections. It might sometimes be desirable to set aside a certain portion of throughput for class-II traffic (say S). In such a case, Eq. (3) should be modified by replacing one with $1 - S(T_s + T_{ms})/T_s$.

5 Performance Analysis of Class-II Communications

This section analyzes the performance of the reservation scheme for class-II communications, where smaller average delay and larger throughput are desirable. Here, all traffic belongs to class II, where class II-A and II-B are not differentiated for simplicity, and hence, only one base station service queue is implemented. As described in Section 3, when there exists class-I traffic, the reservation scheme considered here is activated whenever there are no eligible class-I packets to be transmitted.

For uplink accesses using the reservation scheme, we use the model of K_u clients with the following assumptions.

A1. Message length has a geometric distribution with parameter p_l measured in the number of packets.

A2. Downlink messages arrive from the wired network according to a Poisson process with the overall arrival rate λ_d (messages/mini-slot).

A3. Messages are generated at each of the K_u clients according to independent Poisson processes with the generation rate λ_u/K_u (messages/mini-slot).

A4. Each collided request must be retransmitted in a later reservation mini-slot until the request is successfully received.

A5. Closed-loop behavior of clients, i.e., backlogged clients will discard newly-generated messages until the successful transmission of the request.

A client is said to be *backlogged* when it was notified by the base station to have a collided request and hence must retransmit it. Note that from **A1**, we consider the inter-cell communications only since downlink messages are assumed to arrive exclusively from the wired network. We also make the following simplifications of the scheme to facilitate the derivation.

S1. Even if a reservation slot contains only collided reservation mini-slots, the base station will not issue another reservation slot.

S2. *MNRSL* will be set to 1.

S3. The retransmission probability q_r will be assigned a fixed constant.

By **S1** and **S2**, a message transmission and a reservation slot will alternate continuously when the base station service queue is not empty.

Markov Chain Modelling: The pair $(M(k), N(k))$ is modelled by a 2-dimensional Markov chain, where $M(k)$ is the number of the backlogged clients requesting uplink message transmission and $N(k)$ is the number of the downlink messages or uplink requests in the base station service queue at the end of the k-th reservation slot. Fig. 3 shows a timing diagram of class-II communications with the state transition moments and the change of state $N(k)$. Each of the $M(k)$ backlogged clients will transmit a request in the $(k+1)$-th reservation slot, independently of each other, with probability q_r. Each of the $K_u - M(k)$ other clients will transmit a request in the $(k+1)$-th reservation slot if one (or more) such messages are generated since the last reservation slot. $T_{nr}(k)$ $(= L_{nr}(k)(T_{ms} + T_s))$ is the time period from the k-th reservation slot to the $(k+1)$-th reservation slot, and so $L_{nr}(k)$ is the number of corresponding slots including the reservation slot during $T_{nr}(k)$ with the following conditional distribution given $N(k) = n$:

$$q_l(l|n) = \begin{cases} 1, & \text{if } l = 1, n = 0, \\ 0, & \text{if } l \neq 1, n = 0, \\ 0, & \text{if } l < 2, n \neq 0, \\ p_l(1-p_l)^{l-2}, & \text{if } l \geq 2, n \neq 0. \end{cases} \tag{4}$$

The distribution of the number of the downlink message arrivals, $N_a(k)$, from the end of the $(k-1)$-th reservation slot to the end of the k-th reservation slot given $L_{nr}(k-1) = l$ is

$$q_a^l(i) = e^{-\lambda_d l(T_{ms}+T_s)} \frac{(\lambda_d l(T_{ms}+T_s))^i}{i!}. \tag{5}$$

The probability that a non-backlogged client requests in the k-th reservation slot given $L_{nr}(k-1) = l$ is

$$q_g^l = 1 - e^{-\lambda_u l(T_{ms}+T_s)/K_u}. \tag{6}$$

Let $Q_g^l(i, m)$ be the probability that i out of $K_u - m$ non-backlogged clients transmit requests in the k-th reservation slot, and let $Q_r(i, m)$ be the probability that i of m backlogged clients transmit requests given $M(k-1) = m$ and $L_{nr}(k-1) = l$, then

$$\begin{aligned} Q_g^l(i,m) &= \binom{K_u - m}{i}(1 - q_g^l)^{K_u - m - i}(q_g^l)^i, \\ Q_r(i,m) &= \binom{m}{i}(1 - q_r)^{m-i}(q_r)^i. \end{aligned} \tag{7}$$

Now, $N_r(k) + N_g(k)$ clients will transmit requests in the k-th reservation slot. Accordingly, we obtain the following state transition relationship:

$$\begin{aligned} N(k) &= N(k-1) + N_s(k) + N_a(k) - T(k-1), \\ M(k) &= M(k-1) + N_g(k) - N_s(k), \end{aligned} \tag{8}$$

where $T(k) = 0$ if $N(k) = 0$ and 1 if $N(k) \geq 1$, and $N_s(k)$ is the number of the successful requests during the k-th reservation slot.

The probability $P_u(\hat{j}, \hat{k}, \hat{l})$ that $\hat{j}$ out of $\hat{k}$ clients succeed in the k-th reservation slot (with $\hat{l}$ reservation request mini-slots) is given by

$$P_u(\hat{j}, \hat{k}, \hat{l}) = \begin{cases} 0, & \text{if } \hat{j} > \hat{l} \text{ or } (\hat{j} = \hat{l} \text{ and } \hat{k} > \hat{l}), \\ \binom{\hat{k}}{\hat{j}} \frac{\hat{l}!}{(\hat{l}-\hat{j})!} A(\hat{k} - \hat{j}, \hat{l} - \hat{j})/\hat{l}^{\hat{k}}, & \text{otherwise}, \end{cases} \tag{9}$$

where $A(k', l')$ is the number of cases such that k' clients requested during one of l' mini-slots, and all of them failed:

$$A(k', l') = \begin{cases} 1, & \text{if } k' = 0, \\ 0, & \text{if } k' = 1, \\ \sum_{g=1}^{\lfloor k'/2 \rfloor} \binom{l'}{g} \sum_{\mathbf{C(n)}} \binom{k'}{n_1 n_2 \cdots n_g} \\ \cdot \binom{g}{m_1 m_2 \cdots m_{g'}}, & \text{if } k' \geq 2, \end{cases} \tag{10}$$

where $\binom{k'}{n_1 n_2 \cdots n_g}$ $(= k'!/n_1!n_2! \cdots n_g!)$ is the g-th order multinomial coefficient, and the condition $\mathbf{C}$ of the g-th order vector $\mathbf{n} = \{n_1, n_2, \cdots, n_g\}$ is: (i) $\sum_{i=1}^{g} n_i = k'$; (ii) for all i, $n_i \geq n_{i+1}$; and (iii) for all i, $n_i \geq 2$. The g'-th order vector $\mathbf{m} = \{m_1, m_2, \cdots, m_{g'}\}$, which directly depends on the vector $\mathbf{n}$, satisfies: (i) $\sum_{i=1}^{g'} m_i = g$; (ii) $g' = \max_{i=1}^{g} n_i$; and (iii) m_i is the number of n_j's such that $n_j = i$.

Finally, we can easily derive the state transition probabilities of $M(k)$ and $N(k)$, respectively, given $(M(k), N(k), L_{nr}(k)) = (m, n, l)$:

$$P_{m,m+i}(m, n, l) = \sum_{g=0}^{K_u - m} \sum_{r=0}^{m} Q_g^l(g, m) Q_r(r, m) \cdot P_u(g - i, g + r, L_{ms}), \tag{11}$$

for $K_u - m \geq i \geq -L_{ms} + 1$ if $m > L_{ms}$ and $K_u - m \geq i \geq -m$ if $m \leq L_{ms}$, where L_{ms} is the number of the reservation mini-slots in a reservation slot, i.e., $L_{ms} = K/2 = T_s/(2T_{ms})$, and

$$P_{n,n+j}(m, n, l) = \begin{cases} \sum_{a=0}^{j} q_a^l(a) Q_s(j - a|m, l), & \text{if } n = 0, \\ \sum_{a=0}^{j+1} q_a^l(a) Q_s(j + 1 - a|m, l), & \text{if } n > 0, \end{cases} \tag{12}$$

for $j \geq 0$ if $n = 0$ and $j \geq -1$ if $n > 0$, where $Q_s(i|m, l)$ is the probability of $N_s(k) = i$ given $M(k-1) = m$ and $L_{nr}(k - 1) = l$:

$$Q_s(i|m, l) = \sum_{g=0}^{K_u - m} \sum_{r=0}^{m} P_u(i, r+g, L_{ms}) Q_g^l(g, m) Q_r(r, m). \tag{13}$$

The conditional state transition probability of the 2-dimensional Markov chain $(M(k), N(k))$ given $L_{nr}(k) = l$ is:

$$P_{(m,n),(m+i,n+j)}^l = P_{m,m+i}(m, n, l) P_{n,n+j}(m, n, l). \tag{14}$$

Averaging the effect of the condition $L_{nr}(k)$, we obtain the state transition probability:

$$P_{(m,n),(m+i,n+j)} = \sum_{l=1}^{\infty} P_{(m,n),(m+i,n+j)}^l P_{L_{nr}(k)|N(k)}(l|n). \tag{15}$$

Finally, we can obtain the steady-state probability:

$$\pi_{m,n} = \lim_{k \to \infty} P(M(k) = m, N(k) = n). \tag{16}$$

Uplink Request Success Rate: The request success rate from the $(k - 1)$-th reservation slot to the k-th reservation slot given $N_s(k) = i$ and $L_{nr}(k - 1) = l$ is:

$$R_u^s(i, l) = \frac{i}{l(T_{ms} + T_s)}. \tag{17}$$

By averaging $N_s(k)$ and $L_{nr}(k)$, we get the uplink request success rate given $M(k-1) = m$ and $N(k-1) = n$.

$$R'_s(m, n) = \sum_{i=1}^{L_{ms}} \sum_{l=1}^{\infty} R_u^s(i, l) Q_s(i|m, l) q_l(l|n). \tag{18}$$

We define two new continuous-time processes $\hat{M}(t) = M(k)$ and $\hat{N}(t) = N(k)$, if $t \in [E_k, E_{k+1})$, where E_k is the end time of the k-th reservation slot. Note that $\hat{M}(t)$ denotes the number of backlogged clients at time t. We can obtain the steady-state probability of this process as follows:

$$\hat{\pi}_{m,n} = \frac{\pi_{m,n} E[L_{nr}^n]}{\pi_0^{bsq} E[L_{nr}^0] + (1 - \pi_0^{bsq}) E[L_{nr}^1]}, \tag{19}$$

where $E[\cdot]$ is the expectation of a random variable, $\pi_n^{bsq} = \lim_{k \to \infty} P(N(k) = n) = \sum_m \pi_{m,n}$, and L_{nr}^n is the number of the slots between two consecutive reservation slots, $L_{nr}(k)$, given $N(k) = n$. It is easily shown to be $E[L_{nr}^0] = 1$ and $E[L_{nr}^1] = 1 + 1/p_l$. For a given time t, if $\hat{M}(t) = n$ and $\hat{N}(t) = m$, then the conditional request success rate is $R'_s(m, n)$. Thus, by averaging this over time, we get the average request success rate:

$$R_u^s = \sum_m \sum_n R'_s(m, n) \hat{\pi}_{m,n}. \tag{20}$$

Average Request Success Delay: We derive the delay from the generation of a message to a successful request for its transmission. The first term in the delay is the average time V from the message generation to the beginning of next reservation slot. When $N(k) = 0$, $L_{nr}(k) = 1$. Then the generation time of a message — generated in $[B_k, B_{k+1})$ for an arbitrary k — will be uniformly distributed in $[B_k, B_{k+1}]$ [11], where $B_{k+1} - B_k = T_s + T_{ms}$, since messages are generated according to a Poisson process, and so $E[V|N(k) = 0] = (T_s + T_{ms})/2$. When $N(k) > 0$, $L_{nr}(k)$ has a geometric distribution plus one. Since the geometric distribution is memoryless, when a message was generated, $E[V|N(k) > 0]$ is approximated to be

$E[L^1_{nr}-1](T_s+T_{ms})$. Consequently, we obtain the mean value of V as:

$$E[V] \approx \frac{E[L^0_{nr}]}{2}(T_s+T_{ms})\hat{\pi}_0^{bsq} + E[L^1_{nr}-1] \cdot (T_s+T_{ms})(1-\hat{\pi}_0^{bsq}). \quad (21)$$

Secondly, according to Little's theorem, the average time spent in the backlog is the ratio of the average of backlogged clients to the average message generation rate G_{new} or $E[\hat{M}]/G_{new}$, where the average of backlogged clients $E[\hat{M}] = \sum_m \sum_n m\hat{\pi}_{m,n}$. Now, the average delay measured is given as:

$$D^s_u = E[V] + T_s + \frac{E[\hat{M}]}{G_{new}} \quad \text{(mini-slots)}, \quad (22)$$

where the first term corresponds to the time to the next reservation slot, the second term to a reservation slot time, and the third term to the average backlog delay. For the whole system to be stable, the average rate of new message generation must equal the average message transmission request success rate, i.e., $G_{new} = R^s_u$. Finally, we get the desired throughput-delay relation under the stable condition:

$$D^s_u = E[V] + T_s + \frac{E[\hat{M}]}{R^s_u} \quad \text{(mini-slots)}. \quad (23)$$

Throughput Analysis: Due to the existence of control mini-slots and reservation slots, the maximum achievable throughput W^{max}_{total} is less than one, and is dependent on the message length distribution. Assuming that for all k, $N(k) > 0$, a reservation slot and a message transmission will alternate continuously, thus achieving the maximum possible throughput which is given by

$$W^{max}_{total} = \frac{T_s}{T_s+T_{ms}} \frac{E[L^1_{nr}-1]}{E[L^1_{nr}]}. \quad (24)$$

Note that the actual total incoming rate (including both uplink and downlink) to the base station service queue is $\lambda_{total} = \lambda_d + R^s_u$. Now, if $\lambda_{total} E[L^1_{nr}-1]T_s \leq W^{max}_{total}$, i.e., if the base station service queue is in the stable condition, the downlink throughput W_d and uplink throughput W_u would be

$$W_d = \lambda_d E[L^1_{nr}-1]T_s,$$
$$W_u = R^s_u E[L^1_{nr}-1]T_s. \quad (25)$$

Average Delay: First of all, we need the queueing delay in the base station service queue, i.e., the average delay from the entrance of a downlink message or an uplink request into the service queue to the start of its transmission. We first obtain the average number of the queued downlink messages or uplink requests in the base station service queue which is given by

$$E[\hat{N}-1|\hat{N}>1] = \sum_n (n-1)\hat{\pi}_n^{bsq}, \quad (26)$$

because $\hat{N}(t)-1$ corresponds to the number of downlink messages or queued requests in the base station service queue for $[E_k, E_{k+1})$. Now, the queueing delay is given using Little's theorem:

$$D_q = E[\hat{N}-1|\hat{N}>1]/G'_{new}, \quad (27)$$

where $G'_{new} = \lambda_{total} = \lambda_d + R^s_u$ for the system to be stable. Now, the downlink delay is given by

$$D_d = E[L^1_{nr}-1](T_s+T_{ms}) + E[V] + D_q, \quad (28)$$

where $E[V]$ is the average time from a downlink message arrival to the end of the next reservation slot, which is approximated to the value from Eq. (21), and the uplink delay is given by

$$D_u = E[L^1_{nr}-1](T_s+T_{ms}) + D^s_u + D_q. \quad (29)$$

In both equations, the first terms stand for the message transmission delays, the second terms for the delays from the arrival/generation of a message to the entrance into the base station service queue, and the third for the queueing delays in the service queue.

Numerical and Simulation Results: We show some analytical calculation results using the equations above, and compare them with the simulation results. For the simulations, we generated Poisson traffic, and followed the assumptions given at the beginning of this section. The results are based on $p_l = 0.1$, $q_r = 1.$, $K_u = 5$, $K = T_s/T_{ms} = 10$ (and so $L_{ms} = 5$).

Fig. 6 (a) plots the uplink delays D_u as λ_u increases for three different λ_d values, while Fig. 6 (b) plots the downlink delays D_d as λ_d increases. We observe that the numeric calculations (with mark *calc*) and the simulations (with mark *sim1*) are very close to each other for the same parameters. Note that we did rarely use approximations for our analysis except for in Eq. (21). In both cases, delays are almost constant for small rates, but monotonically increase, and then go to infinity as the actual total incoming rate λ_{total} ($= \lambda_d + R^s_u$) goes to $W^{max}_{total}/(E[L^1_{nr}-1]T_s)$ ($\approx 8.26e^{-3}$ in the results). Due to the closed-loop behavior of the clients, $R^s_u \leq \lambda_u$. Hence, in the figures, the marginal rates (at which delays become infinite) appear larger for uplink under the same parameters. Note that the uplink delays are larger than the downlink delays by as much as $T_s + E[\hat{M}]/R^s_u$ under the same condition from Eqs. (28) and (28).

Fig. 7 compares the simplified protocol with the simplifications **S1** and **S2** (marked with *sim1*) and the actual protocol without **S1** and **S2** (marked with *sim2*) using the simulation results of the delay-versus-rate relationship. For the actual protocol, $MNRSL = 10$ was used. In both graphs, we observe that delays are smaller for the actual protocol, especially for large rates, since the messages can be transmitted consecutively without the appearance of a reservation if the first message has less than $MNRSL$ packets. Consequently, the marginal rates are larger for the actual protocol, implying that the maximum achievable throughput be larger for the actual protocol.

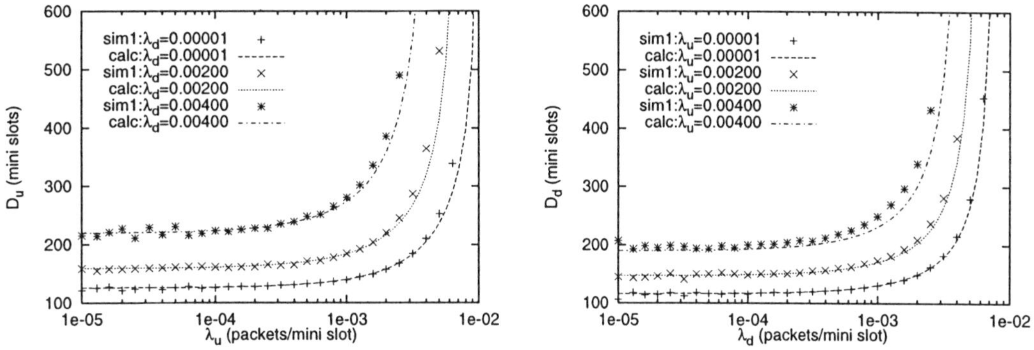

(a) Uplink; D_u vs. λ_u (b) Downlink; D_d vs. λ_d

Figure 6: Comparison between analytical calculations (marked with *calc*) and simulations (marked with *sim1*).

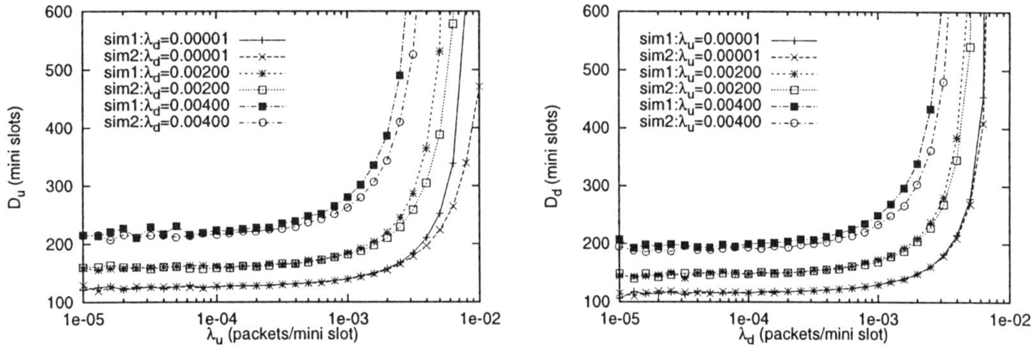

(a) Uplink; D_u vs. λ_u (b) Downlink; D_d vs. λ_d

Figure 7: Comparison between the simplified protocol (marked with *sim1*) and the actual protocol (marked with *sim2*).

6 Concluding Remarks

In this paper, we have considered a WLAN providing QoS guarantees for heterogeneous traffic in a cell. According to the required QoS, traffic is categorized into class I (real-time) and class II (non-real-time). The protocol is based on the framing strategy for class I and a reservation scheme for class II, where class I has priority over class II. When each class-I connection follows a smoothness model, it was shown to be possible to guarantee the delay bound and throughput using the stop-and-go queueing. The admission test for a new class-I connection was also defined. When there is no eligible class-I traffic, class-II traffic is transmitted. Uplink class-II transmission reservation and uplink class-I connection establishment were requested using the reservation scheme. We finally analyzed the average delay and throughput of the reservation scheme for class-II traffic, and presented the numerical calculation and simulation results.

References

[1] S. J. Golestani, "A framing strategy for congestion management," *IEEE Journal on Selected Areas in Communications*, vol. 9, no. 7, pp. 1064–1077, September 1991.

[2] K. Pahlavan and A. H. Levesque, *Wireless Information Networks*, Wiley-Interscience, New York, NY, 1995.

[3] H. Ahmadi, A. Krishna, and R. O. LaMaire, "Design issues in wireless LANs," *Journal of High-Speed Networks*, vol. 5, no. 1, pp. 87–104, 1996.

[4] A. K. Parekh and R. G. Gallager, "A generalized processor sharing approach to flow control in integrated services networks: the single-node case," *IEEE/ACM Trans. on Networking*, vol. 1, no. 3, pp. 344–357, June 1993.

[5] D. D. Kandlur, K. G. Shin, and D. Ferrari, "Real-time communication in multi-hop networks," *IEEE Trans. on Parallel and Distributed Systems*, vol. 5, no. 10, pp. 1044–1056, October 1994.

[6] J. F. Kurose, M. Schwartz, and Y. Yemini, "Multiple-access protocols and time-constrained communication," *ACM Computing Surveys*, vol. 16, no. 1, pp. 43–70, March 1984.

[7] S. Tasaka and Y. Ishibashi, "A reservation protocol for satellite packet communication a performance analysis and stability considerations," *IEEE Trans. on Communications*, vol. 32, no. 8, pp. 920–927, August 1984.

[8] D. J. Goodman, "Cellular packet communications," *IEEE Trans. on Communications*, vol. 38, no. 8, pp. 1272–1280, August 1990.

[9] S. Choi and K. G. Shin, "Centralized wireless MAC protocols using slotted ALOHA and dynamic TDD transmission," *Performance Evaluation*, vol. 27 & 28, pp. 331–346, October 1996.

[10] S. Choi and K. G. Shin, "A cellular wireless local area network with QoS guarantees for heterogeneous traffic," Technical Report CSE-TR-300-96, University of Michigan, August 1996. Available at http://www.eecs.umich.edu/~shchoi/papers.html.

[11] S. M. Ross, *Stochastic Processes*, Wiley, New York, NY, 1983.

Performance Analysis of Multicast Flow Control Algorithms over Combined Wired/Wireless Networks *

Amy Huayan Wang and Mischa Schwartz †

Department of Electrical Engineering
Columbia University, New York, NY 10027, USA

Tel: 212-939-7158, 212-854-3125; Fax: 212-316-9068.
Email: {whycu, schwartz}@ctr.columbia.edu

Abstract

*A multipoint flow control framework for data traffic traversing both a wired and wireless network is proposed. A Markov modulated fluid model is used for the receiver to capture the dynamics of the wireless links. We discover that the phase difference of the instantaneous throughput of the receivers is a distinctive feature of multicast connections. The objectives of the multicast flow control algorithms are to cope with the receiver phase difference cost-effectively in addition to the general goals such as maximizing throughput and minimizing delay. Three ad hoc algorithms have been studied: Listen to Slowest Request (**LSQ**), Source Estimation (**SE**), and Open Loop Control. A fluid analysis technique is applied to study the effect of receiver phase difference assuming zero delay. The effect of propagation delay is then discussed. Simulation results are presented to verify the analysis for the zero delay case and to compare the performance of the algorithms under non-negligible delay.*

1 Introduction

Flow control has been an important and active area of research for many years. Most of the schemes developed or investigated have been for point-to-point communications. They have generally focused on one type of traffic, and have assumed a wired, relatively high-speed communication infrastructure. Interest in the past few years has begun to shift to universal personal communication, involving both wired and wireless transmission media, to users on the move, to multimedia communication, and, as one prominent set of applications, transmission of the information to multiple users/receivers. In order to design such systems cost-effectively, one of the key issues is to develop efficient multipoint flow control algorithms [1].

There have been many multicast protocols proposed but all of them have significant problems [2, 3]. One common missing feature is an effective flow control mechanism. In fact, there is a lack of fundamental theory about multipoint flow control which possesses distinctive features but is not well understood yet. The few existing works on multipoint flow control have proposed several possible schemes such as "listening to the slowest request", "weighted sum", "voting", etc. [4, 5, 6]. But there is no performance analysis available and no deep understanding of the trade-offs of the different policies [7, 8].

Based on the above observation of the current work, we feel it is necessary to formulate the problem within a simple framework in order to discover the fundamental and distinctive features of multicast flow control. We focus on how to control the source transmission rate in this paper. We do not discuss multicast error control here which has been handled recently in a number of papers. In the next section we propose a multicast flow control framework and discuss its essential elements. We describe three *ad hoc* algorithms in section 3. A special case of zero propagation delay, which manifests the effect of the phase differences of the instantaneous throughput capability of the receivers, is studied and analyzed using a fluid flow analysis technique in section 4. In section 5, the effect of propagation delay is discussed and the performance of the two feedback control schemes is compared using simulation. It turns out that the zero delay case provides good performance bounds in the reasonable operating region for the case with non-negligible propagation delay. Section 6 concludes the paper.

2 Multicast Flow Control Framework

We propose a multipoint flow control framework for data traffic traversing both a wired and wireless network. We have focused on the simple case of two mobile receivers located at different distances from the source located within the (error-free) wired network. The service rate or throughput characteristic of the mobile receivers is modeled by a two-state Markovian fluid model representing heavy fading (no throughput) and no fading (normal throughput). This model could also be generalized to capture the dynamics of the communication links such as shared-media links and

*This material is based upon work supported by the U.S. Army Research Office under grant number DAAH04-95-1-0188.

†Corresponding author: Amy Huayan Wang

0-8186-7780-5/97 $10.00 © 1997 IEEE

flow controlled links [9]. The source makes binary decisions whether to start or stop transmission according to the feedback information received from the receivers. Different feedback schemes return different amounts of information about the receiver queue occupancy. Figure 1 illustrates a simple multicast scenario and the corresponding abstract framework is shown in figure 2. Note that our mobile receivers in figure 2 refer to the receiving systems, where the receiver buffer is located at the base station and the on-off receiver server models the noisy/fading wireless link.

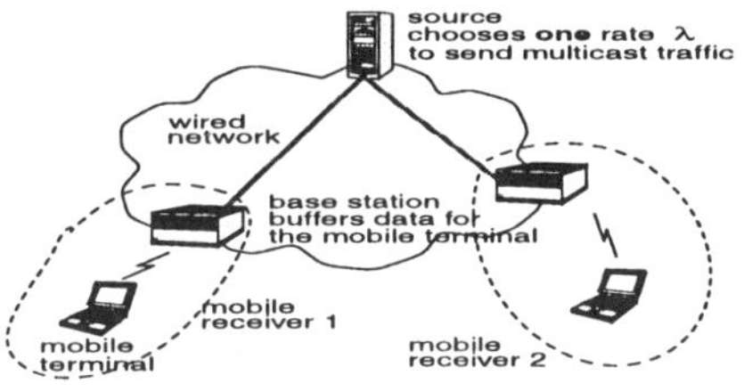

Figure 1: A Simple Scenario for Multicast.

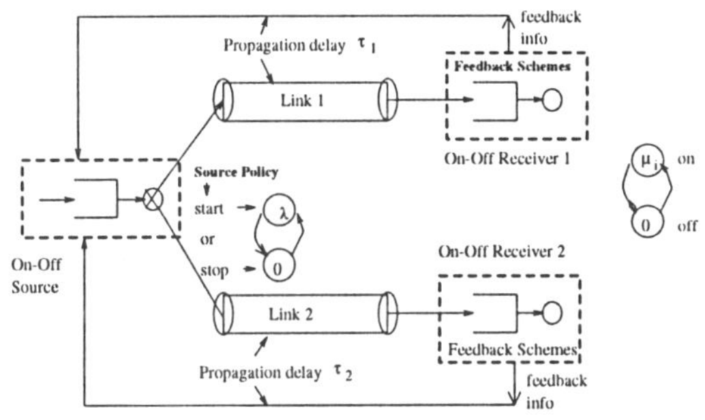

Figure 2: A framework for Multicast Flow Control.

An essential part of a multipoint flow control algorithm is that the source has to choose a proper transmission rate based on the feedback from all the receivers. We call this decision scheme a *source policy*. The challenge is how to combine and use the feedback information from different receivers which experiences different delays and could conflict with each other. Understanding the effect of different source policies is the key to the design of good multipoint flow control algorithms. We also need to specify the *feedback schemes* adopted at the receiver side.

The on-off stochastic receiver model has more significant meaning than in the unicast case because it introduces a new concept: *receiver phase difference* (**RPD**). That is, the receivers' instantaneous throughput capabilities could be significantly different even if they have the same average throughput. In a multicast session, receiver phase differences cause conflicting feedback information to the source. Obviously the pattern of RPD directly affects the performance. If the propagation delays are significant, the proper reaction of the source to the delayed feedback signals is an even more complicated issue. Buffering can be used to accommodate RPD and improve throughput. An interesting question is, what is the most cost-effective way to make use of the buffering in a multicast setting? The objectives of the multicast flow control algorithms are, therefore, to cope with RPD cost-effectively in addition to the general flow control goals such as maximizing throughput and minimizing delay.

We summarize the standard notation used in the paper for a receiver on-off model in figure 3.

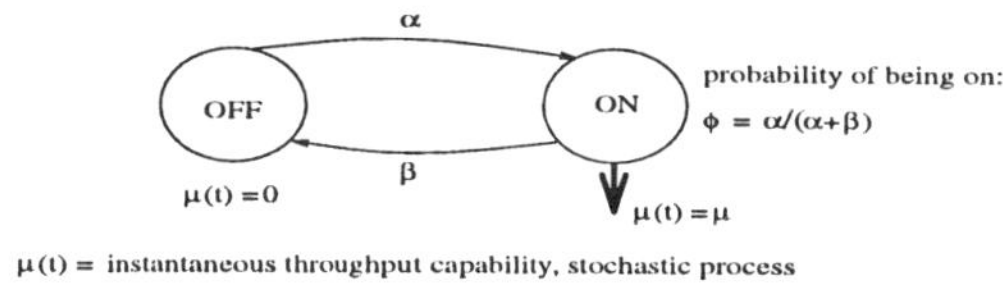

Figure 3: Notation for a receiver on-off model.

Some other notation: $q_i(t)$ is the buffer occupancy of receiver i at time t, B_i is the buffer size of receiver i, τ_i is the one-way propagation delay of receiver i, D_i is the round-trip propagation delay of receiver i. D_{max} is the maximum propagation delay among a group of receivers in one multicast session.

The receivers participating in a multicast connection are classified according to the following situations:

- **Homogeneous receivers**: the receivers have the same μ and ϕ. If they have the same α and β we call them ***absolutely homogeneous***.
- **Family receivers**: the receivers have the same μ but different ϕ.
- **Heterogeneous receivers**: the receivers have different μ.

For example, if all the active mobiles in a cellular cell are allocated one channel with the same bandwidth, we say that they have the same μ. If, furthermore, some mobiles maintain the same throughput, on the average, then they are homogeneous receivers. If they experience the same fading statistics we call them absolutely homogeneous receivers. They are family receivers if their capabilities are different although they are using channels with the same bandwidth.

3 Algorithms

3.1 Listen to Slowest Request (LSQ)

In this algorithm a single-bit "start-stop" feedback scheme is adopted. That is, each receiver sends a "stop" signal to the source when its queue length crosses a high threshold, and sends a "start" signal when the queue length drops below a low threshold. The source stops sending traffic whenever at least one receiver has sent a "stop" signal. It sends at peak rate otherwise.

To maximize throughput, we should try to have all feedback messages signal "start" as much as possible. Hence both the high and low thresholds should be as high as possible. In our simulation we choose the high threshold as $B_i - D_i$ for receiver i to avoid overflow [10], and the low threshold is chosen as $B_i - D_i - \Delta$ where Δ is used to avoid oscillation.

3.2 Source Estimation (SE)

Each receiver sends back both its queue length and the queue growth rate whenever the queue growth rate changes sign; i.e., whenever it goes from increasing to decreasing rate, or vice versa. The source estimates the future queue length of each receiver, taking the propagation delay time into account, using the feedback information. The source maintains high and low queue threshold values for each receiver. It transmits at peak rate only if at least one estimated queue length drops below its low threshold and all the other queues stay below their high thresholds. Otherwise it stops transmitting.

In our simulation we choose the high threshold as $B_i - D_i$ for receiver i to avoid overflow and the low threshold as D_i to "try" to avoid starvation [10]. The queue length estimation at the source is simply to increase or decrease the estimated queue length by 1, or no change, on a per packet basis, depending on the sign of the received queue growth rate. The source adjusts its estimates when it receives feedback information.

3.3 Open Loop Control

The source collects information from each receiver at call setup time as to its average rate of reception, its peak rate, and quality of service requirements, among other parameters. It then adjusts its own rate of transmission to satisfy those parameters, with no signal fed back.

In our simulation, we choose a constant peak rate λ for the source which ensures the blocking probability is small. The delay-throughput performance can be easily analyzed as a special case of [11] and is independent of propagation delay. The Open Loop algorithm provides the basic benchmark with which to compare all strategies.

Extensive simulations have been carried out to study the performance trade-offs of these algorithms [12]. We have focused on the case of homogeneous receivers. In this paper we show that the LSQ and SE algorithms best apply to such situations. We have studied the performance in terms of the throughput-delay characteristics, delay jitter and control overhead under various system parameters. The effect of different on-off time scales of the receivers (fading statistics), buffer size, various propagation delays and delay differences of the receivers have been studied.

[12] provides some interesting simulation results for the multicast case that analysis, if carried out, could help us interpret. It is found that the multicast with zero delay case provides some useful clues, particularly as to the role played by multicast. This case is discussed in the next section.

4 Multicast with Zero Delay

In this section we focus on a special case: multicast without delay. It is of great importance for several reasons: It provides the performance upper bounds for the cases with non-negligible delays. It is not a trivial problem as in the unicast case and reveals the complexity of the problem caused by multiple receivers. It provides helpful insight into a major distinction of multicast connections: receiver phase differences (RPD).

Consider the framework in figure 2 with zero propagation delays. We know that a buffer can be provided at the receiver side to accommodate the phase difference and to improve the throughput. Given the objectives of the source policy are to maximize throughput, minimize delay at each receiver side, and to guarrentee certain fairness, etc., what is the best way to utilize the receiver buffers? It is a complicated stochastic optimization problem, depending on the RPD pattern, fairness criterion, and other control objectives.

As in the unicast case, some *ad hoc* flow control algorithms have been selected since they are comparatively simple to analyze and work well in many situations [10]. Hence, we focus on the algorithms proposed in section 3 in the zero delay setting. The performance of the algorithms is analyzed using fluid flow analysis as a special case of [11]. The analytical results are verified by simulation. The trade-offs of the different algorithms and the effect of receiver phase difference are investigated.

The rest of this section is focused on a multicast session with two receivers with the same normalized $\mu = 1$. We also assume the source is persistent, i.e., it always has traffic to send if allowed. We discuss how to generalize the results to heterogeneous and/or larger numbers of receivers later.

4.1 LSQ with Zero Delay

The LSQ algorithm in the zero delay case can be summarized in one sentence: the source shuts off whenever one of the receivers' queues tends to overflow. It is a simple algorithm with the following **properties** to be shown later:

1. Lossless system and achieves maximum throughput for a given buffer size.
2. Simplest scheme to achieve Property 1.
3. Buffer occupancy evolves periodically with alternation of one queue staying full and the other queue staying below a full buffer until they exchange position.

A formal description of the algorithm is as follows:

$$\dot{q}_i(t) = \begin{cases} \lambda(t) - \mu_i(t) & \text{if } 0 < q_i(t) < B_i, i = 1, 2, \\ [\lambda(t) - \mu_i(t)]^+ & \text{if } q_i(t) = 0, i = 1, 2, \\ [\lambda(t) - \mu_i(t)]^- & \text{if } q_i(t) = B_i, i = 1, 2. \end{cases} \tag{1}$$

$$\lambda(t) = \begin{cases} 0 & \text{if } (q_1(t) = B_1 \text{ and } \mu_1(t) = 0) \\ & \text{or } (q_2(t) = B_2 \text{ and } \mu_2(t) = 0), \\ \mu = 1 & \text{otherwise.} \end{cases} \tag{2}$$

Here $q_i(t)$ is the queue length at time t for queue i; $\dot{q}_i(t)$ is the queue growth rate at time t; $\mu_i(t)$ is the instantaneous throughput of the on-off receiver model(see figure 3); $\lambda(t)$ is the rate with which the source sends traffic at time t; B_i is the buffer size for receiver queue i; and $[x]^+ := \max(x, 0)$, $[x]^- := \min(x, 0)$. Equation (2) follows from the LSQ algorithm described in section 3.1 by setting both the high and the low thresholds to B_i for each receiver. (For the fluid-flow analysis to follow it is valid to have $\Delta = 0$.)

The lossless property is obvious. Maximum throughput for a given buffer size for a lossless system can be achieved by maximizing the ON time of the source which in turn can be achieved by turning the source off only if it is necessary, i.e., there is one queue tending to overflow. Note this is exactly the LSQ algorithm. It is an obvious way to achieve the maximum throughput given the lossless constraint but it incurs too large a delay because it always tries to keep the receiver buffer full.

The LSQ scheme is simple because it only requires the receiver to send a single bit of feedback whenever its queue tends to overflow or drop below a full buffer, and the source makes a decision by a logical AND operation whenever there is a feedback signal coming in. These are the simplest feedback and decision making schemes.

Property 3 is not difficult to see from equations (1) and (2). Figure 4 illustrates a typical periodic evolution of the buffer occupancy of the two receiver queues. The shaded areas indicate that $q_i(t)$ could be anywhere between $[0, B_i)$ when $q_j(t) = B_j$, depending on the outcome of the random receiver models. The solid line illustrates a possible sample path.

An interesting observation from this property is that the LSQ algorithm in the zero delay case forces $\lambda(t) = \mu_i(t)$ when $q_i(t)$ stays full. Notice that it says exactly *"listen to the slowest receiver"* because while queue 1 stays full and queue 2 is below a full buffer, which means during this period receiver 1 has a lower capability than receiver 2, the source listens to receiver 1. Another benefit of this result is that during the period in which $q_1(t) = B_1$, the growth rate of queue 2 is $\mu_1(t) - \mu_2(t)$ where $\mu_1(t)$ and $\mu_2(t)$ are independent on-off Markov processes. Thus the two queues can be decoupled except at the boundary points and the stationary distribution of each queue can be studied as a special case of [11].

By applying the fluid flow analysis technique and manipulating the boundary conditions carefully, we solve the stationary buffer distributions for the homogeneous and family receivers. The results are stated in the Appendix and the derivation can be found in a complete version of this paper (URL: http://www.ctr.columbia.edu/~whycu/res.html).

4.2 SE with Zero Delay

The SE with zero delay case degenerates to the case for which the source is on **iff** one queue stays empty and the other queue is not full; the source is off otherwise. The SE algorithm tries to drive the two queues to zero as much as possible (least backlog) under the lossless constraint.

More precisely, with the same governing equation (1) for buffer occupancy as in the LSQ case, the control policy is different and specified as follows:

$$\lambda(t) = \begin{cases} \mu = 1 & \text{if } (q_1(t) = 0 \text{ and } q_2(t) < B_2) \\ & \text{or } (q_2(t) = 0 \text{ and } q_1(t) < B_1), \\ 0 & \text{otherwise.} \end{cases} \quad (3)$$

With zero delay the source knows $q_i(t)$ exactly because of the timely feedback of $\dot{q}_i(t)$ and $q_i(t)$. The corresponding low and high thresholds are chosen as 0 and B_i. As we will see later, the problem is found to be a **dual problem** of the LSQ with zero delay. We will show the following **properties** of the SE with zero delay:

1. Lossless system and achieves maximum throughput for a given buffer size.
2. Achieves minimum delay for a system with Property 1.
3. Buffer occupancy evolves periodically with alternation of one queue staying empty and the other queue non-empty until they exchange position.

The periodic evolution of buffer occupancy is pictured in figure 5. As we can see, the figure is quite symmetric to the one for the LSQ case (figure 4) with the system operating at the zero boundary in the SE algorithm and the B_i boundary in the LSQ algorithm. Note that in the SE case, $\lambda(t) = \mu_i(t)$ when $q_i(t) = 0$ except that it is forced to be zero if the other queue becomes full. As in the LSQ case, the stationary buffer distribution can be solved analytically and the results are listed in the Appendix.

Property 1 is proved by analysis which shows that the SE algorithm achieves the same throughput as the LSQ algorithm (see Appendix). Property 2 follows from the nature of the SE algorithm, i.e., keeping least backlog in the buffer. The duality refers to the phenomenon that the LSQ algorithm operates at the full buffer boundary while the SE algorithm operates at the empty buffer boundary in a symmetric way. It is evident from several aspects: The buffer occupancy evolutions are quite symmetric; the stationary buffer occupancy distributions show that $Pr(q_i = B_i)$ and $Pr(q_i = 0)$ in the LSQ case are equal to $Pr(q_i = 0)$ and $Pr(q_i = B_i)$ in the SE case, respectively. The derivations of the stationary distributions precisely reflect the duality of the two systems (refer to the complete version of this paper).

4.3 Comparison

The fluid analysis directly applies to the case of two heterogeneous receivers as well, but there is no closed form solution. In general, the analysis of a multicast connection with n receivers requires solving n correlated buffer distributions. The above feature of the LSQ and SE algorithms in the zero delay case reduces the dimension of the problem to $n - 1$ and thus the two receiver case reduces to a special case of [11]. A higher dimensional system with $n \geq 3$ is very difficult to solve to obtain useful results.

The closed-form solutions listed in the Appendix can be used to study the effect of system parameters on the throughput-delay performance. The results are verified by simulation. Some of the results we have obtained are summarized below.

In our study, we choose a receiver 1 with $\mu_1 = 1$, $\beta_1 = 1/500$, and $\phi_1 = 0.6$. All time units are in packet lengths. We compare the performance when receiver 1 participates in a multicast session with different kinds of receivers. In figures 6 and 7, the curves are computed from analysis with simulation points superimposed. (In figure 7b we only draw the simulation points corresponding to the absolutely homogeneous receiver case to keep the picture clear.) We can see that the analytical results fit the simulation results well. The slight discrepancy is due to the fluid approximation which gives larger throughput than the simulation results.

Figure 6 compares the performance of the family receivers with that of the absolutely homogeneous receivers. For the family receiver case, we picked another receiver 2 with $\mu_2 = 1, \beta_2 = 1/500$, and $\phi_2 = 0.7 > \phi_1$. The results show that for family receivers with different throughput capabilities, the faster receiver 2 is limited by the slower one and suffers from reduced throughput. More importantly, if we apply these two algorithms to the family receiver case, the slower receiver experiences too large a delay even for the SE algorithm (see figure 6b). Therefore we suggest avoiding the use of the LSQ and SE algorithms to multicasting with receivers of different capabilities. We should group the homogeneous receivers together and set up multicast connections based on such groups.

Figure 7 illustrates the effect of different on-off time scales for homogeneous receivers. Figure 7b shows that there is no significant difference in the delay performance with different on-off times. Receiver 1 achieves better throughput if it is in a session with the other receiver having faster on-off time scales; the throughput reduces otherwise. The throughput reduction is significant only if the differences of the on-off times are huge and it vanishes as the buffer size increases. Therefore we conclude that the case of absolutely homogeneous receivers is of the greatest interest to study because the LSQ and SE algorithms are best applied to the homogeneous receiver case and small variations of on-off time scales among homogeneous receivers do not cause too much difference in the throughput-delay performance.

Comparing the LSQ with the SE algorithm, they achieve the same throughput in this zero-delay case, but the SE algorithm has a better delay performance. We have drawn a similar conclusion based on our earlier simulation results in [12] where we observed similar throughput performance of the two algorithms and better delay performance of the SE algorithm in the presence of propagation delay. For the zero delay case with homogeneous receivers we can show from the analysis that the ratio of the two mean buffer occupancies is $\frac{E(q)^{LSQ}}{E(q)^{SE}} = \frac{3B+2b}{B+2b}$ which is roughly 3 if buffer size B is large compared to $b = (1-\phi)/\beta$ which is on the order of the average on time $1/\beta$. A ratio of 3 represents a significant reduction of the average delay in the SE algorithm.

We conclude this section by pointing out that it is the RPD phenomenon that makes multicast with zero delay of interest to study. Suppose there is no RPD, for example, if the receivers are always on with possibly different service rates $\mu_1 \neq \mu_2$. Since the source rate has to settle down to the slower one for stability requirement, we can expect that LSQ will work well in most of the situations. But the constant throughput assumption is not valid for a dynamic environment such as wireless networks or ABR traffic over wired networks. In these cases, algorithms exploring RPD are worthwhile studying.

5 Effect of Propagation Delay

The effect of propagation delay in a multicast connection can be summarized as follows:

1. The propagation delay contributes to the phase difference.
2. The propagation delay affects the control capability of the source policy.
3. The presence of the propagation delay makes the system non-Markovian and the fluid flow analysis cannot be applied directly.

With the presence of propagation delays, the feedback signals experience different delays from different receivers. Then the source acquires an inaccurate picture of the receivers' status through feedback in which the phase differences of the receivers' status could be due to either the phase differences of the receiver capability or the delay differences among the receivers. Therefore, the source faces a tougher challenge of how to react to the different requests from the receivers. Using fluid models, such a system can be formulated as a set of stochastic delay-differential equations which, at this point, appears too difficult to solve to obtain any useful results. Approximations could be used to restore the Markovian property in order to apply the fluid flow analysis. This work is proceeding.

We discuss next how the LSQ and SE algorithms cope with delay and the effect of delay on the performance degradation.

5.1 LSQ and SE with Delay

With the presence of propagation delays, the algorithms have to adjust the threshold values to avoid overflow and starvation as discussed in section 3. This results in less throughput and larger delay in general.

The effect of propagation delay on the LSQ algorithm is simple. The source shuts off more than necessary because the high threshold $B_i - D_i$ is a worse case consideration to avoid any possibility of buffer overflow.

For the SE algorithm, the presence of the propagation delay makes control more difficult. We need to estimate the future queue length in the SE algorithm. There are estimation errors and the accuracy depends on the estimation procedure and how much information the source has. The estimation procedure may require intensive processing and the estimation error may further reduce the throughput. Thus the propagation delay has more severe impact on the SE algorithm than the LSQ algorithm.

5.2 Simulation Results

Here we present some simulation results to illustrate the performance degradation due to the presence of propagation delay and also contrast the performance of different algorithms. The parameters used are for absolutely homogeneous receivers with $\beta = 1/120$, $\alpha = 1/100$, $B_1 = B_2$ varying from $2D_{max}$ to 3000, and $\Delta = 10$. The propagation delays D_1 and

D_2 are as indicated in figure 8. Note the set $\{D_1 = 100, D_2 = 500\}$ has much larger delay and larger delay difference than the set $\{D_1 = 50, D_2 = 100\}$. Note again that time units are in packet lengths. Figure 8 describes the performance of receiver 1, the one closer to the source.

As we can see from figure 8a the throughput reduces as propagation delay increases. The results are as expected. The source is shut off when one of the buffer occupancies is bigger than its $B - D$ which results in a large throughput drop. The reduction is not very significant if the buffer is reasonably large and it vanishes as the buffer size tends to infinity. The throughput also reduces more for the SE algorithm than the LSQ algorithm, as expected.

Figure 8b shows that the average buffer occupancy (and thus average delay) increases if the propagation delay is present. The large increment of mean buffer occupancy in the LSQ strategy is mainly because of the delay difference of the two receivers which makes the one further out, number 2, a "slower" one. The LSQ algorithm favors the one further out which results in larger buffer occupancy at receiver 1 as shown in the figure. If we draw the mean buffer occupancy of receiver 2, it is actually below the zero delay curve. Note also that the curve for $\{D_1 = 50$ and $D_2 = 100\}$ is actually below the one for $\{D_1 = 100$ and $D_2 = 500\}$. This is because the high threshold is chosen as $B - D_i$ which is lower for the latter case. On the other hand, for the SE algorithm, the mean buffer occupancy increases as propagation delay increases because the lower threshold is chosen as D_i.

Examining figures 8 (a) and (b) together, we can see a reasonable operating region for the LSQ algorithm is $B_1 \in (500, 1000)$. The mean buffer occupancy grows too much beyond this region. The reasonable operating region for SE is $B_1 \in (1000, 2000)$ which achieves larger throughput but with smaller average delay at the expense of more processing and more signalling load compared to the LSQ algorithm. The throughput gain is small when $B_1 > 2000$.

As we can see from the figures, the zero delay case exhibits the same trend as the cases with propagation delay present. The zero delay case provides a useful bound for the throughput-delay performance in the reasonable operating region.

6 Summary and Future Work

In summary, the performance analysis and comparison of multipoint flow control algorithms over combined wireless/wired networks is a brand-new area and represents a significant research challenge. There are three major challenges we face: multiple receivers (multicasting), stochastic receivers (combined wired/wireless networks), propagation delay and delay differences. The buffer behaviors of multiple correlated queues governed by stochastic delay-differential equations need to be studied, but this obviously presents great difficulty.

In this paper, we address the problem via a divide and conquer approach. We are able to do some performance analysis in the case where we assume zero propagation delay and select algorithms with a special property to be able to decouple the buffer evolution behavior. The effect of the propagation delay in multicast connections is then discussed. Our work shows that the multicast flow control in the simplest form is already a very difficult problem but of great interest. We are investigating a method to approximate the multicast flow control problem by a point-to-point flow control with random delayed feedback. In this manner, we can study more complicated algorithms with delay incorporated. Ultimately we hope to be able to understand multicasting better and develop good flow control algorithms to improve performance over the simplest LSQ or even SE algorithms.

References

[1] M. Schwartz, "*Network Management and Control Issues in Multimedia Wireless Networks*", IEEE Personal Communications, pp. 8–16, June 1995.

[2] S. Armstrong, A. Freier and K. Marzullo, "*Multicast Transport Protocol*", RFC 1301, Xerox, Apple, Cornell University, February 1992.

[3] R. Braudes and S. Zabele, "*Requirements for Multicast Protocols*", RFC 1458, TASC, May 1993.

[4] S. Pejhan, M. Schwartz and D. Anastassiou, "*Refinements to Rate-Based Congestion Control with Extensions to Multicast, Multimedia Applications*", Proc. of IFIP/IEEE Broadband Communications'96, pp.147-160, April, 1996, Canada.

[5] D. Cavendish, S. Mascolo and M. Gerla, "*Rate Based Congestion Control for Multicast ABR Traffic*", Proceedings of GLOBECOM'96, pp. 1114-1118, November, London, Britain.

[6] A. Acharya and B.R.Badrinath, "*A framework for delivering multicast messages in networks with mobile hosts*", to appear in ACM/Baltzer Journal of Wireless Networks, special Issue on Routing in Mobile Communication Networks.

[7] Xiaomin Chen, "*Gigabit Network Multicast Protocols. Chap 4, Flow Control Techniques*". Ph.D. Dissertation, Dept. of ECE, University of California, Santa Barbara, 1996.

[8] J. C. Lin and S. Paul, "*RMTP: A Reliable Multicast Transport Protocol*", Proceedings of INFOCOM'96, pp. 1414-1424, March, 1996, San Francisco, CA, USA.

[9] K. Lee, "*Performance Bounds In Communication Networks with Variable-rate Links*", Proc. SIGCOMM'95, Cambridge, MA, pp. 126–136.

[10] Y. T. Wang and B. Sengupta, "*Performance analysis of a feedback congestion control policy under nonnegligible propagation delay*", in Proceedings of ACM SIGCOMM, 1991, pp. 149–157.

[11] D. Mitra, "*Stochastic Theory of a Fluid Model of Producers and Consumers Coupled by a Buffer*", Adv. Appl. Prob. Vol. 20, pp. 646–676, 1988.

[12] H. Wang and M. Schwartz, "*Comparison of Multicast Flow Control Algorithms Over Combined Wireless/Wired Networks*", Proc. of 3rd International Workshop on Mobile Multimedia Comm., Princeton, NJ, Sept., 1996. URL: http://www.ctr.columbia.edu/~whycu/res.html.

Appendix

Case 1 *The LSQ algorithm, zero propagation delay, homogeneous receivers with $\mu_1 = \mu_2 = 1$ and $\phi_1 = \phi_2 := \phi$. For $i, j \in \{1, 2\}$, we have:*

$$Pr(q_i \le x) = \frac{x + b_i}{B_1 + B_2 + b_1 + b_2}, \quad 0 \le x < B_i, \tag{4}$$

$$Pr(q_i = 0) = \frac{b_i}{B_1 + B_2 + b_1 + b_2}, \tag{5}$$

$$Pr(q_i = B_i) = \frac{B_j + b_j}{B_1 + B_2 + b_1 + b_2}, \tag{6}$$

where

$$b_i = (1-\phi)(\frac{\phi}{\beta_i} + \frac{(1-\phi)}{\beta_j}), \quad j \ne i. \tag{7}$$

The throughput of the two receivers is the same and given by

$$\gamma_i = \phi - \frac{\phi(1-\phi)(b_1+b_2)}{B_1 + B_2 + b_1 + b_2}. \tag{8}$$

The average buffer occupancy is given by

$$E\{q_i\} = \frac{1}{2}B_i\left(\frac{B_i + 2(B_j + b_j)}{B_1 + B_2 + b_1 + b_2}\right). \tag{9}$$

Case 2 *The LSQ algorithm, zero propagation delay, family receivers with $\mu_1 = \mu_2 = 1$ and $\phi_1 \ne \phi_2$. For $i, j \in \{1, 2\}$, we have:*

$$Pr(q_i \le x) = \pi^{(i)}(x) = \frac{1 - \frac{(\alpha_1+\alpha_2+\beta_1+\beta_2)^2}{(\alpha_1+\alpha_2)(\beta_1+\beta_2)}(1-\phi_i)\phi_j e^{z_i x}}{1 - \frac{(1-\phi_i)\phi_j}{\phi_i(1-\phi_j)}e^{z_i(B_1+B_2)}},$$

$$0 \le x < B_i, j \ne i, \tag{10}$$

$$Pr(q_i = 0) = \pi^{(i)}(0), \quad Pr(q_i = B_i) = \pi^{(j)}(B_j), \tag{11}$$

where

$$z_i = \frac{(\alpha_j\beta_i - \alpha_i\beta_j)(\alpha_1 + \alpha_2 + \beta_1 + \beta_2)}{(\alpha_1 + \alpha_2)(\beta_1 + \beta_2)}. \tag{12}$$

The throughput of the two receivers is given by

$$\gamma_i = \phi_i - \frac{\phi_i - \phi_j}{1 - \frac{(1-\phi_i)\phi_j}{\phi_i(1-\phi_j)}e^{z_i(B_1+B_2)}}. \tag{13}$$

The average buffer occupancy is given by

$$E\{q_i\} = \frac{B_i + \frac{(\alpha_1+\alpha_2+\beta_1+\beta_2)\alpha_i\beta_j}{(\alpha_1+\beta_1)(\alpha_2+\beta_2)(\alpha_j\beta_i-\alpha_i\beta_j)}e^{-z_iB_j}(e^{-z_iB_i} - 1)}{1 - \frac{\alpha_i\beta_j}{\alpha_j\beta_i}e^{-z_i(B_1+B_2)}}. \tag{14}$$

Case 3 *The SE algorithm, zero propagation delay, homogeneous receivers, with $\mu_1 = \mu_2 = 1$ and $\phi_1 = \phi_2 := \phi$. For $i, j \in \{1, 2\}$, we have:*

$$Pr(q_i \le x) = \frac{x + B_j + b_j}{B_1 + B_2 + b_1 + b_2}, \quad 0 < x < B_i, j \ne i, \tag{15}$$

$$Pr(q_i = 0) = \frac{B_j + b_j}{B_1 + B_2 + b_1 + b_2}, \tag{16}$$

$$Pr(q_i = B_i) = \frac{b_i}{B_1 + B_2 + b_1 + b_2}, \tag{17}$$

where b_i is given by equation (7).
The throughput of the two receivers is the same. Moreover, it is the same as in the LSQ case given by equation (8).
The average buffer occupancy is given by

$$E\{q_i\} = \frac{1}{2}B_i\left(\frac{B_i + 2b_i}{B_1 + B_2 + b_1 + b_2}\right). \tag{18}$$

Case 4 *The SE algorithm, zero propagation delay, family receivers, with $\mu_1 = \mu_2 = 1$ and $\phi_1 \ne \phi_2$. For $i, j \in \{1, 2\}$, we have:*

$$Pr(q_i \le x) = \pi^{(i)}(x) = \frac{1 - \frac{(\alpha_1+\alpha_2+\beta_1+\beta_2)^2}{(\alpha_1+\alpha_2)(\beta_1+\beta_2)}\phi_j(1-\phi_i)e^{z_i(x+B_j)}}{1 - \frac{\phi_j(1-\phi_i)}{\phi_i(1-\phi_j)}e^{z_i(B_1+B_2)}},$$

$$0 \le x < B_i, j \ne i, \tag{19}$$

$$Pr(q_i = 0) = \pi^{(i)}(0), \quad Pr(q_i = B_i) = 1 - \pi^{(i)}(B_i), \tag{20}$$

where z_i is given by equation (12).
The throughput of the two receivers is the same as in the LSQ case given by equation (13).
The average buffer occupancy is given by

$$E\{q_i\} = \frac{B_i + \frac{(\alpha_1+\alpha_2+\beta_1+\beta_2)\alpha_i\beta_j}{(\alpha_1+\beta_1)(\alpha_2+\beta_2)(\alpha_j\beta_i-\alpha_i\beta_j)}(e^{-z_iB_i} - 1)}{1 - \frac{\alpha_i\beta_j}{\alpha_j\beta_i}e^{-z_i(B_1+B_2)}}. \tag{21}$$

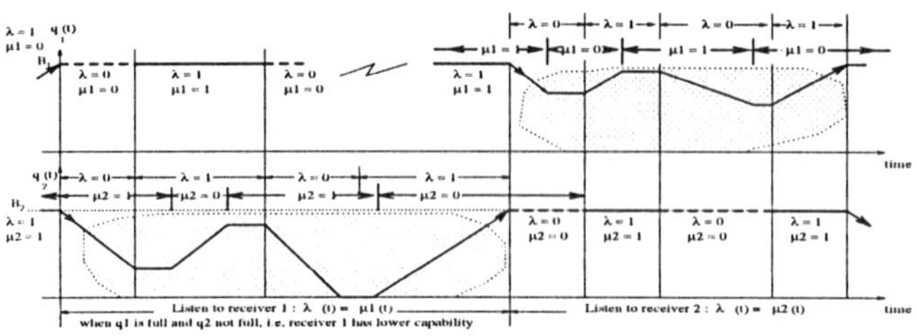

Figure 4: Periodic Evolution of the Buffer Occupancy for LSQ with Zero Delay.

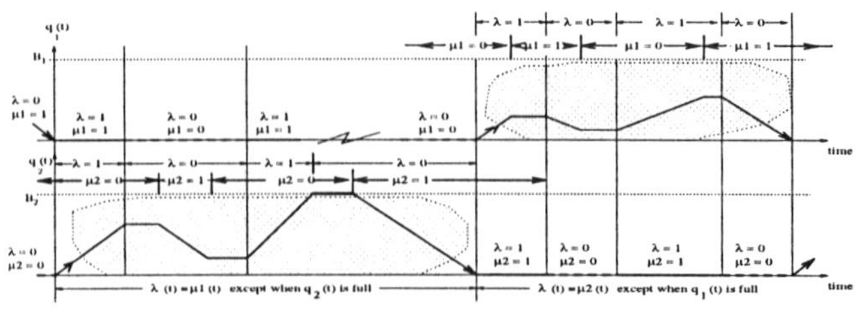

Figure 5: Periodic Evolution of the Buffer Occupancy for SE with Zero Delay.

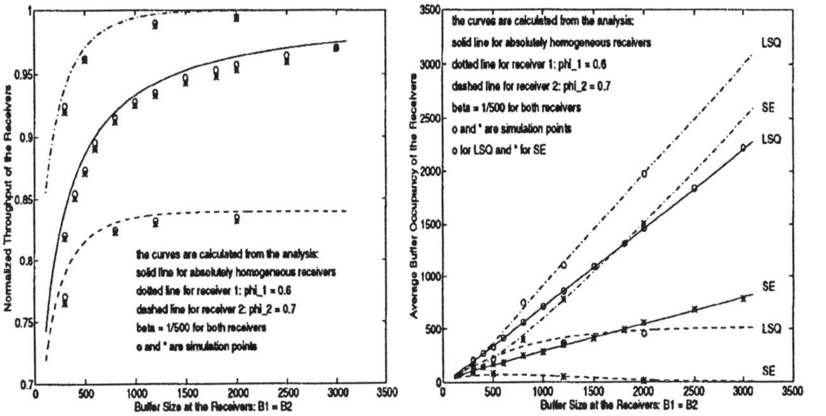

(a). throughput (b). average buffer occupancy

Figure 6: Performance Comparison: Homogeneous vs Family Receivers.

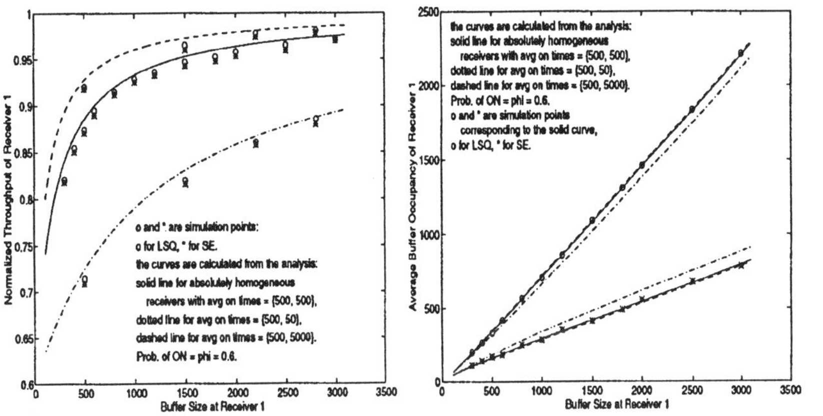

(a). throughput (b). average buffer occupancy

Figure 7: Performance Comparison: Homogeneous Receivers.

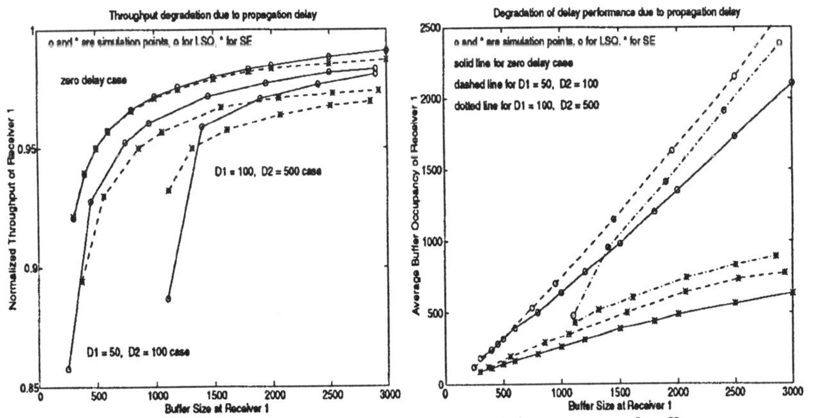

(a). throughput (b). average buffer occupancy

Figure 8: Performance Degradation due to Propagation Delay

On Accommodating Mobile Hosts in an Integrated Services Packet Network

Anup K. Talukdar, B. R. Badrinath*

Department of Computer Science
Rutgers University
New Brunswick, NJ 08903

Arup Acharya

C&C Research Labs
NEC USA
Princeton, NJ 08540

Abstract

This paper considers the support of real-time applications to mobile hosts in an Integrated Services Packet Network. We have proposed a service model for mobile hosts that can support adaptive applications which can withstand wide range of available bandwidth, as well as applications which require mobility independent service guarantees. We describe an admission control scheme and a reservation protocol for implementing this service model. Our admission control scheme achieves high utilization of network resources.

1 Introduction

Recent progress in computing technology and wireless digital communication has made portable computers easily available. This has led to an intensive research in the area of *Mobile Computing* to provide mobile users access to an inter network. The research, so far, has focussed on the problem of maintaining connectivity at the network and transport layer inspite of the mobility of the mobile hosts[11, 3, 2].

Also, there have been several proposals for supporting real-time applications in an Integrated Services Packet Network (ISPN). Typical applications that require real-time services include audio library, image browsing, video conferencing and video-on-demand. These multimedia applications require a bound, which may be absolute or statistical, on the delivery delay of each packet. Clark et al.[4] have described an architecture for an ISPN that supports real-time traffic. In this architecture they have described a service model for real-time traffic with two service classes, *guaranteed and predictive*. Jamin et al.[6] have described a scheme to implement the service model described in [4].

*This research work was supported in part by DARPA under contract number DAAH04-95-1-0596, NSF grant numbers CCR 95-09620, IRIS 95-09816

As portable computers become more powerful and the accessibility of a fixed network from a mobile host becomes easier, the number of mobile users will grow and additionally the mobile users will demand the same real-time services available to fixed hosts. In this paper, we investigate the problems of providing real-time services to mobile hosts in an ISPN. As described in [4], to handle real-time services an enhanced architecture is required for a network. This architecture has five key components. The first component is the nature of *service commitments* the network can provide. The second component is the *service interface parameters* passed between the network and the flow endpoints; this includes both the characterization of the quality of service the network can provide and the characterization of the behavior of the endpoints of the flow. The third component is the functionality of the network elements, namely *scheduling algorithms*, required to meet the service commitments. The fourth component is the *admission control* mechanism by which the service commitments are established at each network element. The last component is the *reservation protocol* to setup the required states in the network elements for providing the required service. In this paper, we discuss how mobile users can be accommodated within this architecture.

This paper is organized as follows. In Section 2 we discuss the problems of providing real-time services to mobile users in an ISPN. In Section 3 we outline the related works in this area and describe our approach to the problem. In Section 4 we describe the service interfaces and propose the service models required for the ISPN with mobile users and describe the scheduling algorithms used for the service classes; Section 5 describes the admission control mechanisms for our proposed service models and mobile handoff techniques; in Section 6 we describe reservation protocols; we conclude in Section 7 with some future directions

0-8186-7780-5/97 $10.00 © 1997 IEEE

of this work.

2 Real-time services to mobile users : Problems

In an ISPN, the main Quality of Service (QoS) parameter is the delay experienced by a packet traveling from a sender to a receiver. The packet delay has three components. The first component, *propagation delay*, is the propagation time of the packet at the speed of light; this is fixed once the data path is chosen. The data path, usually, consists of multiple hops, connected by switches or routers. The second component is the delay in transmission at each switch waiting for the entire packet to arrive before it can be transmitted onto the next link; this delay depends on the packet size. The third component, *congestion delay*, arises due to the statistical sharing of the finite link bandwidth by packets belonging to multiple flows: packets arriving at a switch are buffered in a service queue until the outgoing link is available. *Congestion delay* of a packet is the time spent by it in the service queue; this delay depends on the number of flows using a link, the link capacity and the traffic generation rate of different sources. To provide real-time services, this congestion delay must be bounded or minimized.

In [4], real-time applications have been classified into two classes, *tolerant* applications which can adapt to packet delays and thus can tolerate occasional delay bound violations, and *intolerant* applications which cannot tolerate any delay bound violations. Correspondingly, they have defined two service models: *guaranteed* service for intolerant applications and *predictive* service for tolerant applications. In an ISPN consisting of static hosts QoS guarantee is provided by reserving sufficient bandwidth at each link along the path from the sender to the receiver for the duration of the session, so that the congestion delay at each switch is bounded. In a mobile computing network, a geograhic area is divided into several cells. Each cell is served by a *base station* (also called *mobility agent*) connected to the fixed network. A mobile host maintains connectivity with the fixed network through the base station of the cell in which it is currently located. When a mobile host moves from one location to another, the delivery delay of a packet is affected in two ways. The first factor is that the propagation delay may change due to the change in the length of the path from the sender to the receiver. Secondly, the congestion delay at the switches along the new path may be different. Therefore, when a mobile host initiates a session with a certain QoS guarantee by reserving link bandwidth along the path from the sender to its current location, the QoS guarantee is valid only in that location; when the mobile host moves to a new location, the QoS guarantee is not valid in the new location.

There are two broad ways to provide service guarantees to mobile hosts. The first approach is location dependent: the QoS is guaranteed specific to a location, i.e., QoS guarantee is maintained as long as the mobile host stays at the location from where it initiated the session. To obtain such a service the mobile host makes a reservation for a certain QoS from its current location. As soon as it moves to a new location, the QoS guarantee is no longer valid. The application has to renegotiate its desired QoS at the new location. If sufficient resources are not available along the new data flow path, the mobile host may suffer service degradation, which we call *handoff failure*. The second approach is location independent: the mobile host receives the same QoS guarantee at all locations (given by a mobility profile[1]) where it may move during the lifetime of the session. For example, suppose at time t_1, the mobile host is at cell C_1 where it initiates a session with a certain QoS guarantee, and at time t_2 it is located in cell C_2 where $t_1 < t_2$. It will receive the same QoS guarantee at time t_2 as long as C_2 is within its mobility profile. To obtain mobility independent QoS, a mobile host must make reservations along the data flow path from the sender to each location it may visit. However this leads to very low utilization of resources because, although data is physically flowing to all locations, data is being used only at the current location of the mobile. The utilization of the network resources can be significantly improved if the reserved resources of unused data flows could be used by other flows. However, the users who are utilizing these unused resources may suffer service degradation when the original reservers start using these resources. For example, suppose a mobile host M_1 has made reservation at the two cells, C_1 and C_2, and it is currently located at C_1 and hence using the reserved resources at C_1. In this situation, another host M_2 which is located in C_2 can use the resource reserved by M_1 in C_2. But when M_1 moves into C_2, M_2 must release the resources reserved for M_1 at C_2.

3 Related works and our approach

Recently there has been some work addressing the problem of providing QoS to mobile hosts. In [1] an architecture for a high-speed mobile ATM network using a new concept known as the *virtual connection tree* is proposed and an analytical method of admission control for mobile hosts is described. In [12], Singh has

[1]mobility profile of a mobile host is the set of locations the mobile host is expected to visit

introduced two new QoS parameters, *loss profile* and *probability of seamless communication*, arising due to the mobility of the mobile host and described a network architecture and a suite of transport level services to satisfy these QoS parameters. Lee, in [7], has presented an "adaptive reserved service" framework for use in integrated services networks to support mobile connections carrying multimedia traffic. They have proposed an adaptive link partitioning scheme to reserve a fraction of the link bandwidth to enhance handoff success for mobile hosts. In [8], Levine et al. have proposed resource allocation and admission control schemes based on a new concept, called *Shadow Cluster*, to improve the QoS of mobile calls by reducing the number of dropped calls in an wireless-ATM network. In [9], an adaptive resource management algorithm is described for indoor mobile environments.

These research have focussed on providing QoS guarantees to adaptive applications which can withstand wide range of available bandwidth. In these works, the main objective of the admission control and resource allocation schemes is to reduce the rate of handoff failures of the mobile hosts without significant degradation in the utilization level of the network bandwidth. Mobile applications subscribing to those services may suffer variable degrees of QoS degradation as they move from one location to another. Therefore these schemes are not suitable for more rigid applications which require QoS guarantees that are not affected by mobility of hosts.

In this paper we propose an architecture that accommodates those applications which are adaptive to variable degradation in QoS and also those applications which require mobility independent QoS guarantees in the same network. A salient feature of this architecture is that, a mobile host is required to negotiate its desired QoS only at the start of a data flow session and eliminates the need of fresh reservation every time it moves to a new location during the lifetime of the session. The admission control scheme, we propose, attempts to increase utilization of network bandwidth by statistical multiplexing of link bandwidth among flows of different classes of applications.

4 Service Interfaces and Service Models

To obtain a certain QoS in an ISPN, the endpoints of a data flow is required to provide characterization of the data traffic they will generate, so that the network can reserve sufficient resources for the flow. This characterization is done with a *token bucket filter*. A token bucket filter has two parameters: its token generation rate, r, and the depth of its bucket, b. Tokens are generated at the fixed rate r and accumulate into the bucket. When the bucket becomes full, i.e. contains b tokens, newly generated tokens are discarded. When a packet of size p is generated, it can be released into the network only after removing p tokens from the bucket. In addition to securing the required number of tokens from the bucket the traffic is constrained to enter the network at a maximum rate of $C > r$, called *peak rate*. A traffic flow conforms to a token bucket filter (r, b) if there are enough tokens in the bucket whenever a packet is generated.

In a fixed network the required resources are reserved at the switches along the data flow path. In a mobile environment the data flow path changes as a mobile host moves from one cell to another. To provide real-time services to a mobile host, it is necessary to reserve resources along all possible data paths which may be used during the lifetime of a connection. Therefore, in addition to the traffic characterization, the mobile host is also required to provide its mobility characterization to the network. In this paper we assume that, the mobility of an user is predictable so that mobility can be characterized precisely by *mobility specification* which consists of the set of cells the mobile host is expected to visit during the lifetime of the flow. In the rest of this section we describe the service models for the mobile multimedia applications and the scheduling algorithms used for these service models.

4.1 Service Models

The service models, we propose, are derived from the two service models, *guaranteed* and *predictive* services, described in [4] by Clark et al. We define three service classes to which mobile users may subscribe. These are:

1. Mobility Independent Guaranteed service (MIG class): A mobile user admitted to this service class will receive *guaranteed* service with respect to packet delay bounds as long as its moves are limited to its *mobility specification* and it is conforming to its traffic characterization. This class is appropriate for the intolerant applications which require absolute bound on packet delay.

2. Mobility Independent Predictive service (MIP class): A mobile user admitted to this class will receive *predictive* service with respect to packet delay bound as long as its moves are limited to its *mobility specification* and it is conforming to its traffic characterization. This class is appropriate for those tolerant applications which require fairly reliable delay bounds in all cells it might

visit and does not want to be affected by mobility of the hosts.

3. Mobility Dependent Predictive service (MDP class): A mobile user admitted to this service class will receive *predictive* service with high probability in all cells it may visit during the lifetime of its connection as long as its moves are limited to its *mobility specification* and it is conforming to its traffic characterization. However it may occasionally fail to get *predictive* service and experience severe degradation of QoS. This class is appropriate for tolerant applications, which can tolerate the effects of delay violations due to mobility of hosts.

The *predictive* flows (both in MIP and MDP classes) are categorized into a number of levels with widely separated delay bounds. The delay bounds of the corresponding levels of MIP and MDP flows are same, i.e. MIP level j and MDP level j have the same delay bounds.

To implement the above service models for mobile hosts in ISPN, it is not enough to reserve resources along the path from the sender to the current location of the mobile host; it is necessary to make reservation along the paths to other locations where the mobile host may visit. However, it is not necessary to initiate the data flow along each of those paths; data flow is initiated only along the path from the sender to the current location of the mobile host. Thus we define two types of flows:

1. *Active* : A flow is active at a switch along a data path if resources are reserved for the flow at the switches along the data path and data is being transmitted to a receiver along that path. The corresponding reservation is called an active reservation.

2. *Passive* : A flow is passive at a switch along a data path if resources are reserved for the flow at the switches along the data path but the data is not passing through the switch. The corresponding reservation is called a passive reservation.

One approach to reservation in an ISPN is to use the *a priori* worst-case traffic characterization of each reserving flows to compute the resource requirements to provide the requested services. However,if the flow traffic is bursty, the average flow rate is significantly less than their *a priori* worst-case characterization and as a result the network utilization will be very low. To achieve higher utilization, Jamin et al.[6] have proposed a measurement-based admission control scheme for predictive services. This scheme uses *a priori* characterization of new flows, but uses measurement to characterize existing flow. They have shown significant gain in utilization when there is a high degree of multiplexing.

In our proposed reservation scheme, we use the above measurement-based admission control algorithm. For a flow of MIG or MIP class, the required amount of bandwidth is reserved along the paths from the sender to all locations in the *mobility specification* of the receiving mobile host. However the flow is active only along the path to the current location. To increase the utilization of the network bandwidth, we allow the flows of the MDP class to use the reserved but unused resources of the passive reservation of MIG and MIP classes. When a passive flow becomes active at a switch (i.e. the mobile who made the passive reservation moves into the cell), some MDP flow may suffer QoS degradation if the MDP flows were using the unused resources of the passive flow.

4.2 Scheduling Algorithm

From a scheduling point of view, the flows at a switch are divided into two classes: *guaranteed and predictive.* The MIG flows belong to the guaranteed service class; the MIP and MDP flows belong to the predictive class. There are multiple levels of predictive service with widely separated delay bounds. The scheduling algorithm considers only the active flows at a switch. The unified scheduling algorithm of [4] is used, i.e., guaranteed service is provided by the Weighted Fair Queuing scheduling discipline described in [10, 5] and the predictive service is provided by the priority queuing algorithm using the bandwidth leftover from serving guaranteed service. The flows within each predictive level are scheduled by FIFO algorithm.

5 Admission Control Scheme

The goal of the admission control algorithm should be to admit as many mobile users as possible with the requested QoS and achieve a very high utilization of the resources. However, when a new mobile user is admitted, the system should ensure that it meets its prior commitments to previously admitted users. To admit a new flow it is necessary to perform admission control at all switches and base stations along the paths from the sender to the cells where the mobile host may visit. The admission control criteria at a switch for a flow will depend on the following two factors: *service class* and whether the flow is *active* or *passive* at that switch when the flow starts. A flow is admitted to the network only if it passes the admission control criteria at each switch or base station where the flow requires reservation.

Our admission control algorithm is derived from the measurement-based admission control scheme for ISPN proposed by Jamin et al. in [6]. In Reference [6], Jamin et al. have described a technique to measure the queuing delays, usage rates of the guaranteed service class and each predictive class. These quantities have been used to compute, for each predictive class, the *equivalent token bucket filter* that characterizes the currently existing aggregate traffic pattern of the active flows of that class. In their scheme, the maximal delay bounds of predictive flows are approximated by replacing the worst-case parameters in the analytical models with *equivalent token bucket filter.* A new flow is admitted only if it can get the requested service and the delay bounds of the existing flows are not violated after admitting this new flow. The admission control criteria in our service models will use the same *equivalent token bucket filter* parameters whenever possible. In addition, we augment the measurement process of [6] to measure the parameter, *token generation rate* of the equivalent token bucket filter for each individual active flow. Before describing the admission control criteria for the different service classes in our model, we first describe how the worst-case delays of predictive services are computed.

5.1 Worst-case delay computation

We assume that there are N levels of predictive services. The delay bound of level i is smaller than the delay bound of level j for $i < j$. The aggregate *token bucket filter* parameter of predictive class j is (r_j, b_j) and μ is the link capacity such that $\sum_{j=1}^{N} r_j \leq \mu$. Parekh, in [10], has shown that in a network with arbitrary topology, under WFQ scheduling discipline the delay bounds of a guaranteed flow depends only on its reserved flow rate and its bucket depth. This implies that, WFQ isolates the guaranteed flows from each other and in addition it isolates all the guaranteed flows from all predictive traffic.

When the packet size is small, i.e. the transmission time of each packet is sufficiently small compared to other delays and hence can be ignored, the worst-case delay, D_j, of priority queue level j is given by the following theorem in [10]:

Theorem 1 *Parekh [10]: The worst-case class j delay, with FIFO discipline within the class and assuming infinite peak rates for the sources, is*

$$D_j^* = \frac{\sum_{i=1}^{j} b_i}{\mu - \sum_{i=1}^{j-1} r_i}$$

for each class j. Further, this delay is achieved for a strict priority service discipline under which class j has the least priority.

When a mobile host h requests to initiate a flow α, it specifies its traffic characteristics with a token bucket filter (r_α, b_α) and mobility specification with a set of cells C_h. In addition it specifies the class of service and if it requests MIP or MDP service, it also specifies the desired delay bound. Depending on the requested service class, the switches and the base stations along the paths from the sender to each of the cell in C_h checks appropriate admission control conditions. The new flow will be admitted only if the admission control criteria are satisfied at all of those switches and base stations. Before describing the admission control criteria for each service class, we describe the notations used in those conditions:

- μ = total link bandwidth, v = utilization target of the link bandwidth
- $MIP_i^a(MIP_i^p)$ = set of active(passive) flows in MIP class i at a switch
- $MIP_i = MIP_i^a \cup MIP_i^p$
- $MIG^a(MIG^p)$ = set of active(passive) flows in MIG class at a switch
- $MIG = MIG^a \cup MIG^p$
- $MDP_i^a(MDP_i^p)$ = set of active(passive) flows in MDP class i at a switch
- $MDP_i = MDP_i^a \cup MDP_i^p$
- $P_i^a = MIP_i^a \cup MDP_i^a$ = set of active flows of predictive class i
- $\nu_C, \hat{\nu}_C, b_C, \hat{b}_C$ = total aggregate bandwidth, measured aggregate bandwidth, aggregate bucket depth, measured aggregate bucket depth of all flows in class C respectively
- $b_\beta, \hat{b}_\beta, r_\beta, \hat{r}_\beta$ = bucket depth, measured bucket depth, requested traffic rate, measured traffic rate of flow β respectively

The parameter v, utilization target, is used to keep some portion of the link bandwidth unreserved. This unreserved bandwidth can be used by the best-effort traffic.

5.2 Admission Control Criteria for MIG service

The flow α, active or passive, is admitted to the MIG service class, if all of the following conditions are satisfied at the switch or base station:

1. The total reserved bandwidth of all flows of MIG class, both active and passive, including r_α does not exceed the targeted utilization of the link bandwidth : $v\mu > r_\alpha + \nu_{MIG}$
2. The sum of the requested flow rate r_α and the current usage should not exceed the targeted link utilization: $v\mu > r_\alpha + \hat{\nu}_{MIG} + \sum_{i=1}^{N} \hat{\nu}_{P_i^a}$
3. After the flow α is admitted, the delay bound of MIP level j, $D^*_{MIP_j}(1 \le j \le N)$, should not be violated when all flows of MIG and MIP class which have made reservation at this switch are in active state. The new delay of MIP level j, D'_{MIP_j}, after α is admitted, is given by:

$$D'_{MIP_j} = \frac{\sum_{i=1}^{j} \hat{b}_{MIP_i}}{\mu - \hat{\nu}_{MIG} - \sum_{i=1}^{j-1} \hat{\nu}_{MIP_i} - r_\alpha} = \frac{\sum_{i=1}^{j}(\sum_{\beta\in MIP_i^a} \hat{b}_\beta + \sum_{\beta \in MIP_i^p} \hat{b}_\beta)}{\mu - \hat{\nu}_{MIG} - \sum_{i=1}^{j-1}(\sum_{\beta\in MIP_i^a} \hat{r}_\beta + \sum_{\beta\in MIP_i^p} \hat{r}_\beta) - r_\alpha}$$

Although we can estimate the bucket depth in the equivalent token bucket filter of the aggregate traffic of each predictive class from the observed packet delay for that class, it is difficult to estimate the bucket depth in the equivalent token bucket filter of each individual flow in that class. Therefore in the above equation we make the following substitutions :

(a) $\sum_{\beta\in MIP_i^a} \hat{b}_\beta$ is replaced by $MIN(\sum_{\beta\in MIP_i^a} b_\beta, \sum_{\beta\in P_i^a} \hat{b}_\beta)$

(b) $\sum_{\beta\in MIP_i^p} \hat{b}_\beta$ is replaced by $\sum_{\beta\in MIP_i^p} b_\beta$

All other quantities in the above equation can be estimated by measurement. Therefore, the condition to be satisfied is: $D^*_{MIP_j} > D'_{MIP_j}$ for $1 \le j \le N$.

4. The delay bound $D^*_{MDP_j}$ of the MDP level j, $(1 \le j \le N)$, should not be violated when this new flow is admitted. The new delay of MDP level j, $D'_{MDP_j^a}$, after admitting α is computed by taking into account only the active flows of all classes and is given by the following equation:

$$D'_{MDP_j^a} = \frac{\sum_{i-1}^{j} \hat{b}_{P_i^a}}{\mu - \hat{\nu}_{MIG} - \sum_{i=1}^{j-1} \hat{\nu}_{P_i^a} - r_\alpha}$$

The quantity $\sum_{i-1}^{j} \hat{b}_{P_i}$ can be computed from the observed delays of the predictive class traffic. Therefore the condition to be satisfied is $D^*_{MDP_j} > D'_{MDP_j^a}$ for $1 \le j \le N$.

5.3 Admission Control Criteria for MIP service

The flow α, active or passive, will be admitted to the MIP class k at a switch or base station if all of the following conditions are satisfied:

1. The sum of the flow's requested rate r_α and the current usage should not exceed the targeted link utilization:
$$v\mu > r_\alpha + \hat{\nu}_{MIG} + \sum_{i=1}^{N} \hat{\nu}_{P_i^a}$$
2. After α is admitted, the delay bound $D^*_{MIP_j}$ of the MIP level j, $j \ge k$ should not be violated when all flows of MIG and MIP class who have made reservation at this switch are in active state. The delay bound of the MIP class k, D'_{MIP_k}, is estimated by the following equation after α is admitted:

$$D'_{MIP_k} = \frac{\sum_{i=1}^{k} \hat{b}_{MIP_i} + b_\alpha}{\mu - \hat{\nu}_{MIG} - \sum_{i=1}^{k-1} \hat{\nu}_{MIP_i}} = \frac{\sum_{i=1}^{k}(\sum_{\beta\in MIP_i^a} \hat{b}_\beta + \sum_{\beta\in MIP_i^p} \hat{b}_\beta) + b_\alpha}{\mu - \hat{\nu}_{MIG} - \sum_{i=1}^{k-1} \sum_{\beta\in MIP_i^a} \hat{r}_\beta}$$

For $k < j \le N$, the estimated delay, after α is admitted, is given by :

$$D'_{MIP_j} = \frac{\sum_{i=1}^{j} \hat{b}_{MIP_i} + b_\alpha}{\mu - \hat{\nu}_{MIG} - \sum_{i=1}^{j-1} \hat{\nu}_{MIP_i} - r_\alpha} =$$

$$\frac{\sum_{i=1}^{j} (\sum_{\beta \in MIP_i^a} \hat{b}_\beta + \sum_{\beta \in MIP_i^p} \hat{b}_\beta) + b_\alpha}{\mu - \hat{\nu}_{MIG} - \sum_{i=1}^{j-1} \sum_{\beta \in MIP_i^a} \hat{r}_\beta - r_\alpha}$$

In the above equations we make the following substitutions:

(a) $\sum_{\beta \in MIP_i^a} \hat{b}_\beta$ is replaced by $MIN(\sum_{\beta \in MIP_i^a} b_\beta, \sum_{\beta \in P_i^a} \hat{b}_\beta)$

(b) $\sum_{\beta \in MIP_i^p} \hat{b}_\beta$ is replaced by $\sum_{\beta \in MIP_i^p} b_\beta$

Therefore the condition to be satisfied is: $D^*_{MIP_j} > D'_{MIP_j}$, for $k \leq j \leq N$.

3. The delay bound $D^*_{MDP_j}$ of the MDP level j, $j \geq k$ which are active at this switch should not be violated when the new flow α is admitted. The new delay of the MDP class k after admitting α is estimated by the following equation (considering only active flows):

$$D'_{MDP_k^a} = \frac{\sum_{i=1}^{k} \hat{b}_{P_i^a} + b_\alpha}{\mu - \hat{\nu}_{MIG} - \sum_{i=1}^{k-1} \hat{\nu}_{P_i^a}} =$$

$$D_{MDP_k^a} + \frac{b_\alpha}{\mu - \hat{\nu}_{MIG} - \sum_{i=1}^{k-1} \hat{\nu}_{P_i^a}}$$

The new delay of the MDP class j, $k < j \leq N$, after admitting α is estimated by the following equation (considering only active flows):

$$D'_{MDP_j^a} = \frac{\sum_{i=1}^{j} \hat{b}_{P_i^a} + b_\alpha}{\mu - \hat{\nu}_{MIG} - \sum_{i=1}^{j-1} \hat{\nu}_{P_i^a} - r_\alpha}$$

Therefore the condition to be satisfied is: $D^*_{MDP_j} > D'_{MDP_j^a}$, for $k \leq j \leq N$.

5.4 Admission Control Criteria for MDP service

The flow α will be admitted to the MDP class k at a switch in an active state, if all of the following conditions are satisfied:

1. The sum of the flows requested rate r_α and the current usage of the link bandwidth does not exceed the targeted link utilization:

$$v\mu > r_\alpha + \hat{\nu}_{MIG} + \sum_{i=1}^{N} \hat{\nu}_{P_i^a}$$

2. The delay bounds of the MDP levels k and above should not be violated after admitting this flow; i.e. this condition is same as the condition 3 in the previous subsection.

The flow α will be admitted to the MDP class k at a switch in a passive state without any admission control; it will only be entered into the set of MDP flows who have made passive reservation.

5.5 Handling Handoffs

When a mobile host with an existing flow in a particular service class moves into a new cell within its mobility specification, the delay bounds of the already existing flows in the new cell may be violated or the utilization target may be exceeded. Since the flows of MIG and MIP service classes cannot tolerate the consequences of mobility, we move flows of MDP classes to service classes with higher delay or convert them to best-effort traffic. Whenever a mobile host leaves a cell or a flow is terminated, the existing flows are given preferences to upgrade to their requested class rather than admitting new flows. When a mobile host with an MDP class flow enters a new cell within its mobility specification which cannot provide its existing QoS, the QoS of the mobile host degrades.

6 Reservation Protocol

In ISPN, a reservation protocol, *RSVP* [14], has been proposed that sets up reservation state at each router along the path from a sender to a receiver. It uses two types of messages to setup the reservation states in the routers, *PATH* message to setup the data flow path, and *RESV* message to make the bandwidth reservation. To accommodate mobile hosts, we propose a reservation protocol, *MRSVP*, which is an extension of *RSVP*. It has the following characteristics :

1) It makes an active reservation from the current base station of the mobile host to the sender along which data flow will start immediately.

2) It also makes passive reservations along the data

paths from all other base stations in the *mobility specification* of the mobile host to the sender.

We briefly outline the protocol *MRSVP*. The details of *MRSVP* can be found in [13]. Let S be the *mobility specification* of a mobile host m. We assume that the underlying routing protocol is the IETF Mobile-IP routing protocol[11], in which data packets are routed to a mobile hosts via mobility agents, *home agent* and *foreign agent*. The protocol works as follows:

1. The sender sends a *PATH* message to m or the multicast group address.
2. On receiving a *PATH* message for the first time, m will send the flow specification to all mobility agents in S. If the reservation is for a unicast flow, m will send S to its home agent. If the reservation is for a multicast flow, m will ask the mobility agents of S to join the multicast group. Then it will send a *RESV* message to the sender to make an active reservation. On receiving subsequent *PATH* messages, it will only send the *RESV* message to the sender.
3. On receiving S, the home agent will tunnel all *PATH* messages for m to all mobility agents in S.
4. On receiving a *PATH* message for a non-local mobile host, a mobility agent will send a *RESV* message to the sender to make a passive reservation.
5. When m detects a significant change in the data flow rate, it will send the new flow specification to all mobility agents in S.

7 Conclusion and Future Work

In this paper we have investigated the problems of providing real-time service guarantees to the mobile hosts in an Integrated Services Packet Network. We presented a service model for real-time services to mobile hosts that can accommodate highly adaptive applications as well as applications which requires mobility independent QoS guarantees. We proposed an admission control scheme for this model that can achieve very high utilization of network bandwidth.

We are currently running simulation experiments to check the validity of our service model and its implementation scheme. Some of the issues we are currently looking at are, handoff techniques for reducing QoS degradation rate, the different ways to reduce handoff failure and the relationships among network utilization, handoff failure rate, QoS degradation rate and the degree of multiplexing.

References

[1] Acampora, A. S. and Naghshineh, M., An Architecture and methodology for Mobile-Executed Handoff in Cellular ATM Networks., IEEE JSAC, Vol 12, No. 8, October 1994.

[2] Bakre, A. and Badrinath, B. R., Handoff and system support for indirect TCP/IP, In Proc. of the 2nd Usenix symposium on mobile and location independent computing, pp. 11-24, April 1995.

[3] Balakrishnan, Hari, et.al., A comparison of mechanisms for improving TCP performance over wireless links, In Proc. SIGCOMM'96, August 1996.

[4] Clark. D.D., Shenker. S. and Zhang. L., Supporting Real-Time Applications In An Integrated Services Packet Network : Architecture and Mechanism., Proc. SIGCOMM '92, 1992.

[5] Demers. A., Keshav. S. and Shenker. S., Analysis and simulation of a Fair Queuing Algorithm, Proc. SIGCOMM '89, Sept. 1989

[6] Jamin. S., Danzig. P.B., Shenker. S and Zhang. L., A Measurement-based Admission Control Algorithm for Integrated Services Packet Networks., Proc. SIGCOMM '95, 1995.

[7] Lee, K., Adaptive Network Support for Mobile Multimedia, In Proc. of the 1st Annual International Conference on Mobile Computing and Networking, pp. 62-74, November 1995.

[8] Levine, D. A., Akyldiz, I. F. and Naghshineh, M., The Shadow Cluster Concept for Resource Allocation and Call Admission in ATM-Based Wireless Networks, In Proc. of the 1st Annual International Conference on Mobile Computing and Networking, pp. 62-74, November 1995.

[9] Lu, S. and Bharghavan, V., Adaptive Resource Management Algorithms for Indoor Mobile Computing Environments, Proc. SIGCOMM'96, August 1996.

[10] Parekh. A. K., A Generalized Processor Sharing Approach to Flow Control in Integrated Services Networks., PhD Theses, MIT, LIDS, Tech. Report LIDS-TR-2089 1992.

[11] Perkins, Charlie, IP Mobility Support, IETF Draft, May 1996.

[12] Singh, S., Quality of Service guarantees in Mobile Computing, To appear in Journal of Computer Communications.

[13] Talukdar, A. K., Badrinath, B. R. and Acharya, A., Admission Control Algorithms and Reservation Protocol for Supporting Mobile Hosts in an Integrated Services Packet Network, Dept. of Computer Science Technical Report, Rutgers University.

[14] Zhang, L., Deering. S., Estrin. D., Shenker. S. and Zappala. D., RSVP: A New Resource ReSerVation Protocol. IEEE Network Sept. 1993.

A Scalable Architecture for Fair Leaky-Bucket Shaping

Jennifer Rexford
AT&T Labs Research
Murray Hill, NJ
jrex@research.att.com

Flavio Bonomi
ZeitNet, Cabletron
Santa Clara, CA
flavio@zeitnet.com

Albert Greenberg
AT&T Labs Research
Murray Hill, NJ
albert@research.att.com

Albert Wong
Lucent Technologies
Red Bank, NJ
akwong@lucent.com

Abstract

This paper presents a shaper architecture that scales to a large number of connections with diverse burstiness and bandwidth parameters. The architecture arbitrates fairly between connections with conforming cells by carefully integrating leaky-bucket traffic shaping with rate-based scheduling algorithms. Through a careful combination of per-connection queueing and approximate sorting, the shaper performs a small, bounded number of operations in response to each arrival and departure, independent of the number of connections and cells. To handle a wider range of rate parameters, a hierarchical arbitration scheme can reduce the implementation overheads and the interference between competing connections. Simulation experiments demonstrate that the architecture limits shaping delay and traffic distortions, even under heavy congestion.

1 Introduction

The advent of integrated networks for voice, data, and video applications introduces new challenges in supporting performance guarantees. With high-speed links and small cell sizes, modern ATM (asynchronous transfer mode) switches must process cell arrivals and departures every few microseconds, if not faster; in addition, these architectures should scale to a large number of connections with diverse traffic parameters and quality-of-service requirements. End-to-end guarantees for delay, throughput, and loss depend on the successful provisioning of buffer and bandwidth resources in the network, based on traffic contracts established during admission control. To regulate connections and avoid buffer overflow, broadband networks can employ traffic *shaping* to delay incoming cells until they conform to connection burst and bandwidth descriptors.

Many new networking applications, such as large-scale web or video servers, require traffic shaping for hundreds or even thousands of connections with different burst and bandwidth descriptors. ATM switches can also amortize implementation costs across multiple end systems by providing traffic shaping as a service at the network edge. In addition to shaping at the network end points, ATM available-bit-rate connections require traffic enforcement in the *interior* of the network at each virtual source node, where a connection's bandwidth allocation may change over time in response to feedback from the network [1]. Other connections may also be reshaped in the interior of the network to limit delay variation and buffer requirements at the downstream switches [2–5].

Most existing traffic shapers [6–11] employ some version of *leaky-bucket* control to enforce burstiness and bandwidth restrictions on each connection. Conceptually, a leaky-bucket controller generates tokens at rate ρ, where the token bucket holds at most σ credits [12]; an arriving cell must claim a token before receiving service. Given the status of the token bucket, the shaper can determine the conformance time of each arriving cell [13]. Conflicts arise when multiple cells, from different connections, become eligible for transmission during the same time slot. As a result, the shaper can develop a *backlog* of conforming cells, particularly when traffic arrives from multiple input links or a single high-speed link. Depending on how the switch arbitrates amongst conforming cells, collisions can distort connection leaky-bucket parameters and increase cell shaping delays, even for cells that are conforming on arrival. As a result, the outgoing cells may violate the traffic descriptors expected by downstream switches, possibly increasing delay and loss.

In contrast to first-in first-out scheduling, fair arbitration schemes [14–19] can limit these traffic distortions by guaranteeing that each connection receives its share of the link bandwidth on a small time scale. If the incoming traffic were *already* leaky-bucket compliant, weighted fair scheduling could ensure that multiplexing the connection with other traffic would never inflate σ by more than one cell [15]. However, a traffic shaper must handle a *mixture* of conforming and non-conforming cells, as shown in Figure 1. In fact, a spike in the non-conforming backlog can rapidly become a spike in the conforming backlog, if multiple cells reach

0-8186-7780-5/97 $10.00 © 1997 IEEE

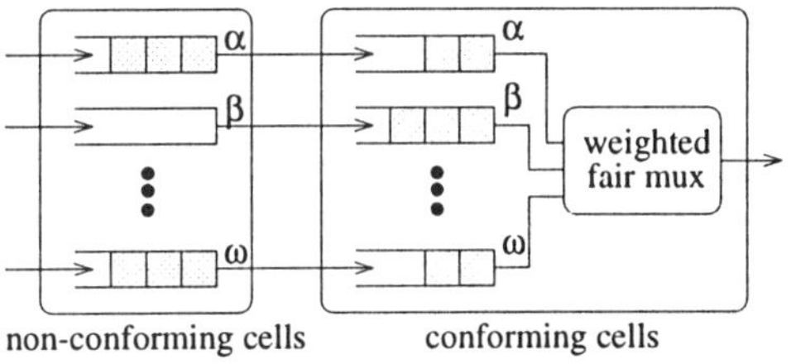

Figure 1: **Idealized Fair Traffic Shaping**

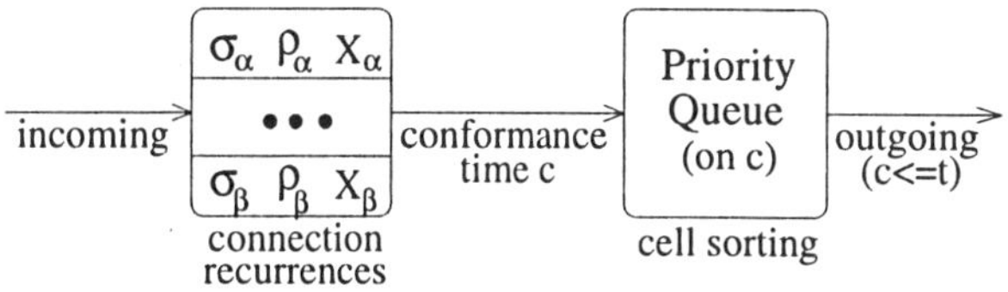

Figure 2: **Leaky-Bucket Traffic Shaper**

conformance in a small interval of time.

Instead of *concatenating* the traffic shaping and fair multiplexing operations, as in Figure 1, this paper presents an efficient architecture that *integrates* rate-based scheduling into the shaping logic. After a review of existing shaper designs in Section 2, Section 3 describes how the proposed architecture combines per-connection queueing, approximate sorting algorithms, and hierarchical arbitration to reduce implementation complexity. Section 4 extends the architecture to minimize traffic distortions through weighted fair link scheduling. The simulation experiments in Section 5 demonstrate that the shaper scales to a large number of connections with diverse traffic descriptors, even under heavy congestion. Section 6 concludes the paper with a discussion of future research directions.

This paper complements existing work on traffic shaper architectures [6–11] by emphasizing implementation and performance scalability. Ongoing research on rate-based link scheduling [14, 15, 17–19] motivates the use of weighted fair arbitration to improve the shaper's performance. Recent work in this area considers schemes that improve fairness by temporarily "stalling" connections that have received link bandwidth ahead of schedule [20–22]. In contrast to our traffic shaper, these link-scheduling schemes define cell eligibility in terms of the underlying fair queueing discipline, without necessarily enforcing burst and bandwidth parameters for each connection. The hierarchical arbitration scheme extends our earlier work on efficient link-scheduling algorithms [23].

2 Review of Shaper Architectures

High-speed shaper designs typically employ per-connection recurrences to assign a conformance time to each arriving cell, followed by a sorting unit that schedules cells for departure, as shown in Figure 2.

2.1 Connection Recurrences

Instead of dropping or marking non-conforming cells, a traffic *shaper* delays incoming cells until they conform to the connection's burst and bandwidth descriptors. Although a traffic shaper could conceivably have a separate leaky-bucket controller and cell buffer for each connection, a more scalable solution maintains a table that stores the leaky-bucket status of each connection [6]. The shaper uses this information to compute the time that an arriving cell first conforms to the connection traffic descriptors. To limit the amount of non-conforming traffic, the shaper can discard cells with conformance times far in the future.

Figure 3 shows a leaky-bucket shaping scheme based on the *virtual scheduling algorithm* [13]. The shaper assigns a conformance time c to each incoming cell, using a state variable X that represents the cell's *estimated* arrival time, based on the connection's shaping rate ρ. A cell arriving at most σ/ρ time units ahead of X can still claim a token; otherwise, the cell must wait until the controller generates an additional token at time $X - \sigma/\rho$. For a connection with no burst tolerance (i.e., $\sigma = 0$), the algorithm reduces to $c = X = \max\{X + 1/\rho_{peak}, t\}$. The shaper can enforce both peak and sustainable cell rates by using a dual leaky-bucket algorithm to compute c, resulting in a $(\sigma, \rho, \rho_{peak})$ specification for each connection.

2.2 Cell Sorting

The shaper uses the cell conformance times c to schedule traffic for transmission. One approach employs a priority queue to rank cells in order of increasing c values; during each time slot, the link transmits the queue's head cell if its conformance time has been reached (i.e., $t \geq c$). High-speed operation typically requires hardware support for cell scheduling [7]. To avoid the complexity of an exact priority queue implementation, a shaper could dynamically construct a link transmission schedule as each cell arrives. In this approach, the schedule consists of a large collection of bins, where each bin corresponds to a single transmission slot [8], as shown in Figure 4(a).

The shaper sequences through the bins at the link rate, transmitting a cell in each time slot unless the current bin is empty. An arriving cell enters the first empty location at or after c, modulo the number of bins; this requires complex logic for locating empty slots in the schedule. The shaper drops the incoming cell if $c - t$ exceeds the range of the bins. When

```
X = X + 1/ρ;               // Estimated time
if (X ≤ t)                 // Full bucket
  c = X = t;
else if (X ≤ t + σ/ρ)      // Partially full
  c = t;
else                       // Empty bucket
  c = X − σ/ρ;
```

Figure 3: **Computing Cell Conformance Times**

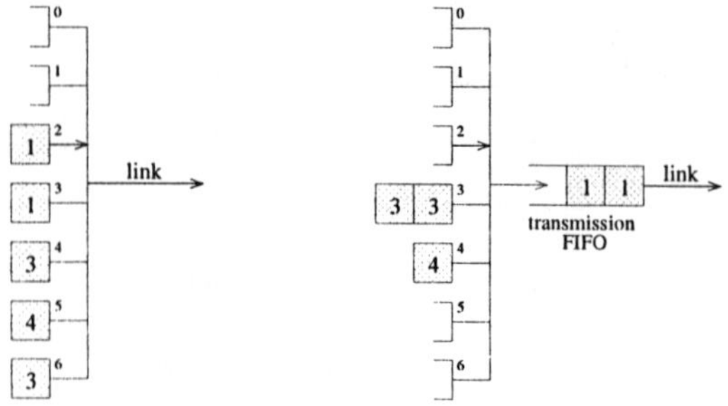

(a) One cell per bin (b) Linked list per bin

Figure 4: **Ranking Cells in Sorting Bins**

the scheduler services a large number of connections, under heavy load, the shaper may have to schedule a cell for transmission much later than its conformance time c. The insertion mechanism favors earlier arrivals, possibly delaying a well-behaved connection to serve other cells with larger conformance times.

To transmit cells in order of increasing conformance times, the shaper can employ a *calendar queue* [24], as shown in Figure 4(b). Instead of storing a single cell in each bin, this architecture maintains a logical *linked list* of cells at each conformance time [9]. Although this requires additional memory to store a pointer field with each cell, an arriving cell can join the linked list that corresponds to its c value without searching for an empty slot in the schedule. Since the link cannot transmit more than one cell in each time slot, the shaper maintains a separate FIFO for holding any cells that have reached their conformance times; in each time slot, the shaper appends this transmission FIFO with the contents of the current sorting bin. Hence, under a backlog of conforming traffic, the shaper transmits cells in order of increasing c values.

Although the sorting bins obviate the need for a complex priority queue, cells may have c values ranging far into the future, particularly when a low-bandwidth connection has a backlog of non-conforming traffic. To reduce the size of the shaper, each bin can represent a range of g consecutive conformance times. However, shaping with a large bin granularity can introduce excessive jitter that distorts the leaky-bucket parameters of the outgoing traffic, particularly for high-bandwidth connections. In addition, existing shaper architectures do not control the interference between competing connections when multiple conforming cells await service.

3 Scalable Traffic Shaper

This section introduces a new shaper architecture that limits implementation complexity by combining per-connection queueing, approximate sorting, and hierarchical arbitration.

3.1 Approximate Sorting

Although a connection α may have a large backlog of cells, with a wide range of conformance times, the connection's ***head-of-line*** cell has a c value at most $1/\rho_\alpha$ time slots into the future; otherwise, the shaper would not have already transmitted the connection's previous cell. To reduce the number of sorting bins, a shaper can consider just the head cell from each backlogged connection, while holding the connection's remaining cells in a FIFO list. In addition to limiting shaper complexity, per-connection queueing enhances architectural flexibility by facilitating effective buffer-management and link-scheduling policies, as well as rapid responses to changes in connection rate parameters. Although per-connection queueing can complicate the implementation of exact sorting, approximate schemes can significantly reduce complexity.

To illustrate the difficulty of implementing exact sorting, consider the situation when a cell enters the sorting unit upon the departure of the connection's previous cell. If the shaper has accumulated a backlog of conforming traffic, this new head cell may have *already* reached its conformance time (i.e., $c < t$). To transmit cells in order of their c values, the shaper would have to insert this cell ***in between*** other conforming cells awaiting service. To handle these cells, the sorting unit could include extra data structures to hold conforming traffic, in addition to the bins for the non-conforming head-of-line cells [11]. However, this requires a large number of extra sorting bins, as well as more complicated sequencing logic.

Approximate sorting algorithms may be necessary to avoid these overheads in high-speed implementations. Instead of exact sorting, a shaper can reduce complexity by placing all conforming head-of-line cells in a single transmission FIFO, as shown in Figure 5. Since the sorting bins hold only *non-conforming* head-of-line cells, the shaper requires at most $b = 1/(g\rho_{\min})$

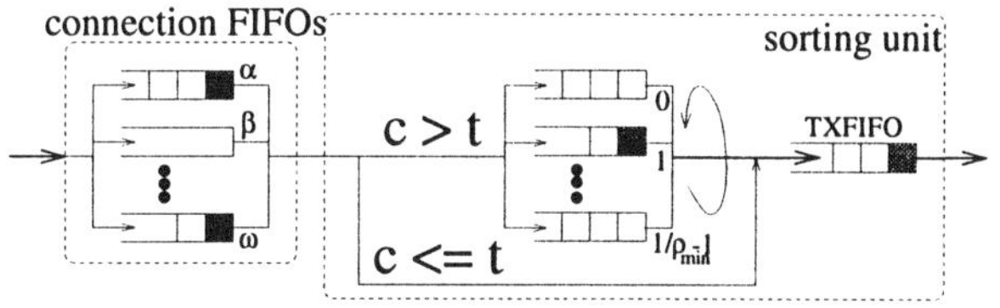

Figure 5: **Scalable Shaper Architecture**

bins, independent of the number of connections or the amount of backlogged traffic, where g is the bin granularity. Every g time slots, the shaper concatenates a single sorting bin with the transmission FIFO, as in Figure 4(b). After transmitting a cell, the connection's next cell proceeds to a sorting bin (if $c > t$) or directly to the transmission FIFO (if $c \leq t$), as shown in Figure 6. If the new head-of-line cell has already reached its conformance time, this policy sacrifices accuracy in order to reduce implementation complexity.

To quantify these overheads, consider a shaper with s cells, v connections, and b sorting bins. The shaper consists of $v + b + 1$ logical linked lists that represent the connection FIFOs, the sorting bins, and the transmission FIFO, where each list consists of a head pointer, a tail pointer, and an empty flag; each connection includes an additional flag to indicate whether or not the connection has a head-of-line cell in the sorting unit. To connect cells in the various linked lists, each buffered cell includes a small pointer field that consists of $\lceil \log_2 s \rceil$ bits to denote a location in the cell memory. As shown in Figure 6, each cell arrival or departure introduces a small, bounded number of pointer manipulations on these linked lists, independent of s and v. The shaper also includes a free list for assigning unused memory locations to arriving cells; initially, this list includes every element in the memory. Upon cell departure, the shaper returns the free memory location to the head of the free list.

3.2 Bandwidth Groups

Although the algorithm in Figure 6 has $\Theta(1)$ enqueue and dequeue complexity, handling a wide range of rate parameters would require a large number of sorting bins. For a low-rate connection, even the head-of-line cell could have a conformance time far into the future. Although low-bandwidth traffic requires the sorting unit to handle a wide *range* of c values, these connections can tolerate some inaccuracy in cell scheduling, permitting coarse-grain sorting bins. On the other hand, a large bin granularity g can introduce significant shaping delay and jitter to high-rate connections. To reconcile these conflicting requirements, the shaper can group connections based on their bandwidth requirements, allowing each sorting unit to select a different grain (g) and range (bg) for its bins. This results in a two-level architecture, where each group consists of a sorting unit that handles a large number of connections with similar rates.

With this hierarchical approach, the shaper can select a small sorting granularity for high-rate connections to reduce delay and jitter, relative to the existing architectures in Section 2. To formalize these trade-offs, consider a shaper with bandwidth parameters that can vary from $\rho_{\min}$ to $\rho_{\max}$, where each group handles rates within a factor $m > 1$ of each other. As a result, group i includes any connections α_i with $\rho_{\alpha_i} \in [m^i \rho_{\min}, m^{i+1}\rho_{\min})$, where $i = 0, 1, \ldots, n-1$ and the shaper consists of $n = \log_m\{\rho_{\max}/\rho_{\min}\}$ groups; for example, if $m = 16$, the shaper can support rates ranging from 1 kilobit/second to 1 gigabit/second with just *five* groups (since $\log_{16}\{2^{30}/2^{10}\} = 5$). In each group, the *low*-bandwidth connections dictate the range of the sorting bins; for group i, a head-of-line cell can have a c value at most $1/(m^i\rho_{\min})$ time units into the future. To prevent delay and traffic distortions for the *high*-bandwidth connections, each group should select a bin granularity g_i based on the requirements of its largest possible rate; i.e., $g_i = 1/u(m^{i+1}\rho_{\min})$, where a larger value of u corresponds to more precise sorting.

As a result, each group i requires at least

$$b = \frac{\text{range of the bins}}{\text{grain of each bin}} = \frac{1/(m^i\rho_{\min})}{1/u(m^{i+1}\rho_{\min})} = mu$$

sorting bins, for a total of mnu bins in the shaper. The number of bins increases under more precise scheduling (larger u) or a wider range of connection rates (larger n or m). However, if the shaper did *not* divide connections into groups, a single sorting unit would have to handle the maximum range of $1/\rho_{\min}$ and the minimum granularity of $1/(u\rho_{\max})$, for a total of $m^n u$ bins. With rates ranging from 1 kilobit/second to 1 gigabit/second, this shaper would require over 13,000 times more sorting bins than a hierarchical architecture with $m = 16$, for the same value of u. Alternatively, for the same number of sorting bins, the hierarchical architecture can support much more precise scheduling (with u over 13,000 times larger).

4 Integrating Fair Link Scheduling

The hierarchical architecture in Section 3 scales well with the number of connections, the number of cells, and the range of connection rate parameters. However, good performance depends on how well the switch arbitrates between connections when multiple conforming cells await service. By carefully multiplexing cells from different connections, the shaper can en-

Cell Arrival

```
compute c for the new cell;
if (connection is currently idle) {
   // New head-of-line cell
   if (c == t) // Conforming cell
      enqueue cell onto transmission FIFO;
   else // Non-conforming cell
      enqueue cell onto bin ⌊(c mod bg)/g⌋;
}
else // backlogged connection
   enqueue cell onto connection FIFO;
```

Cell Departure

```
if (connection is still backlogged) {
   dequeue cell from connection FIFO;
   // New head-of-line cell
   if (c ≤ t) // Conforming cell
      enqueue cell onto transmission FIFO;
   else // Non-conforming cell
      enqueue cell onto bin ⌊(c mod bg)/g⌋;
}
else
   // No action for idle connection
```

Conforming Bin

```
if (t mod g == g − 1)
   append bin ⌊(t mod bg)/g⌋ onto transmission FIFO;
```

Figure 6: **Shaping Algorithm with Per-Connection Queueing**

sure that each connection receives a fair share of the link bandwidth on a small time scale.

4.1 Fair Arbitration Within a Group

Ideally, a traffic shaper schedules an arriving cell for transmission at its conformance time c, forwarding conforming cells directly to the outgoing link. However, since the link carries traffic for multiple connections, several cells may become eligible for transmission at the same time; as a result, the shaper can develop a backlog of conforming traffic, especially during periods of heavy congestion; this is particularly likely in switches with a large number of input ports and connections. As discussed in Section 2, most existing traffic shapers transmit conforming cells in order of increasing conformance times. Under a backlog of conforming cells, this "exact sorting" favors connections with larger σ values since these connections can have multiple cells in a small range of c values. These bursts restrict link access for connections with smaller σ values; by the time this transient congestion begins to dissipate, a low-σ connection can have a large backlog of conforming traffic, which may generate an unexpected burst on the output link.

The shaper can mitigate these collision effects by *interleaving* the conforming cells from competing connections based on their rate parameters. The approximate architecture in Figure 5 suggests an efficient mechanism for fair link scheduling when the shaper consists of a single group. In this architecture, when connections have a backlog of conforming traffic, each cell transmission triggers the insertion of the connection's next cell into the transmission FIFO, behind the head-of-line cells from each of the other conforming connections. As a result, the shaper implicitly sequences through these connections in a *round-robin* fashion, guaranteeing a minimum bandwidth to each connection on a relatively small time scale.

However, round-robin arbitration does not provide truly "fair" service when connections have different ρ values, since low-rate and high-rate connections receive the same fraction of the bandwidth. Instead, the shaper should employ *weighted* round-robin scheduling. With a small extension, the architecture in Figure 5 can allow connections to insert *multiple* cells into the sorting unit, in proportion to their rates. In particular, the shaper should allow connection α to have up to $\lfloor \rho_\alpha / \rho_{\min} \rfloor$ consecutive cells in the sorting unit. This allows a high-bandwidth connection to have several conforming cells in the transmission FIFO, ahead of conforming traffic from low-bandwidth connections, even if the low-bandwidth connections have cells with *smaller* c values. When the shaper has a backlog of conforming traffic, this ensures that connections are served in proportion to their rates.

Even though some connections have multiple cells in the sorting unit, the weighted fair arbitration does not require additional sorting bins, since these cells have conformance times at most $1/\rho_\alpha \cdot \lfloor \rho_\alpha / \rho_{\min} \rfloor$ time units into the future, which is within the range $(1/\rho_{\min})$ of sorting bins. Relative to the architecture in Section 3, the weighted fair shaper includes a count of the number of cells in the sorting unit for each connection. The shaper increments (decrements) this *counting semaphore* as the connection's cells enter (leave) the sorting unit; when the count reaches $\lfloor \rho_\alpha / \rho_{\min} \rfloor$, the connection cannot insert another cell into the sorting unit until a cell departs. This results in a very efficient architecture, with $\Theta(1)$ enqueue and dequeue complexity, that gives fair service to conforming connections on a small time scale.

4.2 Fair Arbitration Between Groups

The weighted round-robin arbitration can provide fair service to connections in a single group, but the hierarchical shaper architecture requires an effective mechanism for interleaving conforming cells from *different* groups. For an efficient implementation, the shaper can also apply weighted fair scheduling algorithms to divide link bandwidth between groups. To coordinate bandwidth sharing, the weights ϕ_i represent the *aggregate* rate requirements of each group i; in the simplest case, $\phi_i = \sum \rho_{\alpha_i}$. A variety of rate-based link-scheduling algorithms [14–17, 25–27] can guarantee that group i receives a fair portion $\phi_i / \sum_{j=0}^{n-1} \phi_j$ of the link bandwidth on a small time scale.

With these static weights ϕ_i, an idle connection divides its bandwidth amongst the busy connections in the same group, instead of sharing with other connections in different groups. This type of hierarchical link sharing is particularly useful when groups correspond to different institutions, traffic classes, or protocol families [20, 28, 29], and can ensure that the link guarantees a minimum bandwidth to each connection. As a heuristic extension [23], the shaper could share excess bandwidth between individual connections by dynamically adjusting the ϕ_i values to reflect the aggregate throughput requirements of the *backlogged* connections in each group. That is, a group could assign

$$\phi_i(t) = \sum_{\alpha_i \in B_i(t)} \rho_{\alpha_i}$$

where $B_i(t)$ is the set of backlogged connections in group i at time t.

Changes to $B_i(t)$ occur upon cell arrivals and departures, facilitating efficient updates to ϕ_i by adding (subtracting) ρ_{α_i} when connection α_i becomes backlogged (idle). To demonstrate the use of dynamic weights, Section 5.4 evaluates an extension to the *self-clocked fair queueing* [25–27] algorithm that adjusts to changes in the ϕ_i values. Although the dynamic arbitration scheme can sometimes deviate from connection-level fairness [23], the shaping function in each group ensures that each connection makes forward progress based on the leaky-bucket conformance times of its incoming cells; a group continues to compete for link access until it clears its temporary backlog of conforming cells. Ultimately, static weights provide a minimum rate to each connection on a small time scale, while dynamic weights provide a fairer division of excess link bandwidth. Both approaches provide an efficient, event-driven way to multiplex a large number of connections with diverse bandwidth requirements.

5 Performance Evaluation

This section focuses on how the various shaper architectures affect the burstiness of the outgoing cell streams. Inherently, the architectures have similar performance under low traffic loads, since the shaper does not develop a significant backlog of conforming traffic. Hence, most of the experiments consider the effects of congestion, particularly when the shaper mixes connections with different traffic parameters.

5.1 Simulation Environment

The simulation experiments evaluate connections sharing access to a single link that can transmit one cell in each time slot; for stability, the link bandwidth must exceed the sum of the connections' sustainable cell rates. Each connection generates periodic bursts of cells according to an on/off model with leaky-bucket parameters (σ_{in}, ρ_{in}), with the peak rate equal to the link bandwidth; the burst length σ_{in} could correspond to the packet or message size in a data transmission. The simulation experiments generate temporary backlogs of non-conforming cells by allowing σ_{in} to exceed the burstiness parameter σ enforced by the shaper.

To control the interaction between cell streams, each connection has an independent starting time, uniformly distributed in an interval $[0, x]$; the length of this interval can vary from 0 to the connection's on/off period. Smaller values of x generate periods of heavier congestion and can capture the effects of multiple input links (or one high-speed input link) entering the switch. With this parameterized model of incoming traffic, the simulation experiments can evaluate the performance scalability of the shaper architectures under different arrival patterns (σ_{in}, ρ_{in}), shaping parameters (σ, ρ), and degrees of congestion x.

When the shaper accumulates a backlog of conforming cells, link arbitration policies can affect the leaky-bucket parameters of the outgoing streams. Multiplexing a connection with other network traffic results in an outgoing stream that is (σ_{out}, ρ)-compliant, where σ_{out} may exceed the shaping parameter σ. To evaluate the burstiness of the output stream, the simulator feeds a connection's outgoing cells to a hypothetical link of rate ρ; σ_{out} ($\overline{\sigma}_{out}$) represents the worst-case (average) queue length encountered by the connection's cells. Ideally, the switch produces a well-shaped, (σ, ρ)-compliant stream, resulting in $\sigma_{out} \leq \sigma$. The experiments compare the proposed shaper architecture against a traditional shaper that transmits conforming traffic in order of increasing conformance times.

5.2 Different Burst Parameters

The architecture in Figure 5 reduces implementation complexity through per-connection queueing and

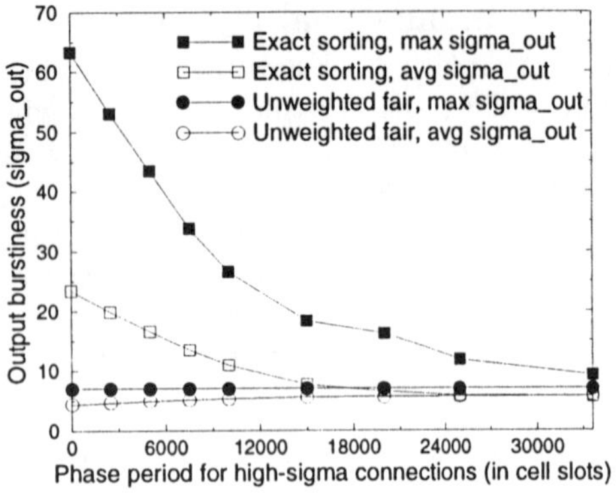

Figure 7: **Mixing Different Burst Parameters**

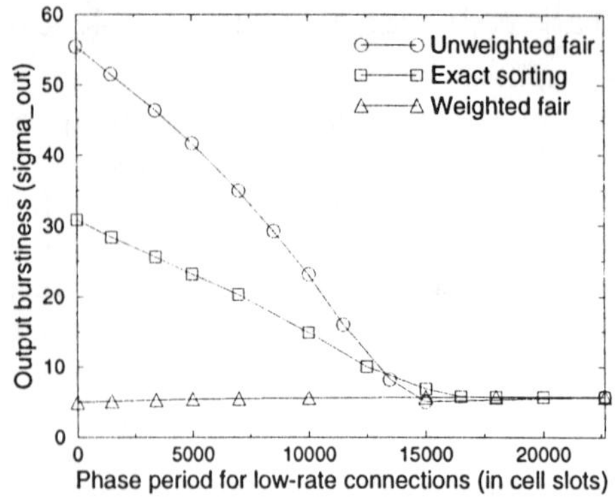

Figure 8: **Mixing Different Rate Parameters**

approximate sorting of backlogged conforming cells. Figure 7 compares the architecture to a shaper that always transmits cells in order of their conformance times. In this experiment, the input traffic consists of 80 connections with high burstiness ($\sigma_{in} = 300$ and $\sigma = 100$) and 10 connections with lower burstiness ($\sigma_{in} = 50$ and $\sigma = 5$); all connections have $\rho_{in} = 0.009$ and $\rho = 0.010$ for a total link utilization of 81%. To generate periods of congestion in the shaper, the experiment varies the phase of the 80 high-σ connections from 0 to their on/off period, while the low-σ connections have uniform random start times during their on/off period. With an on period of length $\sigma_{in}/(1 - \rho_{in})$ and an off period of length σ_{in}/ρ_{in}, the high-σ connections have an on/off period of 33636 time slots, as shown by the x-axis in Figure 7.

Under exact sorting, this congestion has an adverse effect on the leaky-bucket parameters of the low-σ connections; the high-σ connections do not experience significant traffic distortion under either shaper architecture. Exact sorting favors connections with larger σ values, which can inject a burst of cells with a small range of conformance times. In times of congestion, these bursts can restrict link access for connections with smaller σ values; by the time this transient congestion begins to dissipate, a low-σ connection can have a large backlog of conforming traffic, which can then generate an unexpected burst on the output link. This can introduce significant traffic distortions in the outgoing cell streams, particularly when multiple high-σ connections are active simultaneously. In contrast, the fair arbitration scheme effectively interleaves backlogged connections in a round-robin fashion, resulting in virtually no inflation in σ_{out}, even under heavy load. Since this experiment assigns the same ρ value to all connections, the weighted and unweighted fair architectures have identical performance.

5.3 Different Bandwidth Parameters

Although the unweighted fair architecture guarantees a minimum bandwidth to each backlogged connection, on a small time scale, round-robin arbitration does not provide fair service when connections have different bandwidth parameters. To demonstrate this effect, Figure 8 shows the performance of 10 high-rate connections ($\rho_{in} = 0.0090$ and $\rho = 0.0100$) in the presence of 320 low-rate connections ($\rho_{in} = 0.0022$ and $\rho = 0.0025$), for a total link utilization of 79%. The high-rate traffic has $\sigma = 5$ and the low-rate traffic has $\sigma = 25$, with $\sigma_{in} = 50$ for all connections. The experiment varies the phase of the 320 low-rate connections from 0 to their on/off period (22644), while the high-rate connections have uniform random start times during their on/off period.

Although all three shaper architectures perform well under low levels of congestion, unweighted fair arbitration significantly inflates the burstiness of the high-rate connections during periods of heavy load, as shown in Figure 8; the low-rate connections have $\sigma_{out} \approx \sigma$ throughout the experiment. Exact sorting also introduces traffic distortions, since the shaper services connections with different burstiness parameters. The high-rate connections also experience high cell shaping delays (not shown) under these two architectures. In contrast, weighted fair arbitration successfully preserves the leaky-bucket descriptors and limits cell shaping delay, even under extremely heavy congestion, by guaranteeing sufficient bandwidth to each connection on a small time scale.

5.4 Hierarchical Arbitration

Although the weighted fair architecture performs well under diverse leaky-bucket parameters, handling a wide range of connection rates requires a large number of sorting bins. To quantify this cost-performance trade-off, Figure 9 compares four different configurations of the proposed shaper, serving a mixture of connections that employ weighted fair arbitration, with a total link utilization of nearly 90%. The experiment mixes five high-rate, low-burstiness connections ($\sigma_{in} = 10$, $\rho_{in} = 0.0909$, $\sigma = 0$, $\rho = 0.1000$) with ten medium-rate connections ($\sigma_{in} = 50$, $\rho_{in} = 0.0094$, $\sigma = 25$, $\rho = 0.0100$) and seventy low-rate connections ($\sigma_{in} = 40$, $\rho_{in} = 0.0048$, $\sigma = 20$, $\rho = 0.0050$). The experiment varies the phase period of the 70 low-rate connections from 0 to their on/off period (8528) to study the effects of congestion in the shaper; the other 15 connections have uniform random start times.

The low-rate connections dictate the range of the sorting bins, since a head-of-line cell can have a c value up to 200 time slots into the future. With coarse-grain sorting, the shaper can limit the number of bins:

Key	Configuration
○	Single group with 201 bins of grain 1
□	Single group with 10 bins of grain 21
◇	High-rate group with 11 bins of grain 1; low-rate group with 201 bins of grain 1
×	High-rate group with 5 bins of grain 3; low-rate group with 5 bins of grain 41

at the expense of the burstiness parameters for the high-bandwidth traffic, as shown by comparing the top two curves in Figure 9. To highlight the differences in the four configurations, the graph omits the "exact sorting" configuration, which performs dramatically worse, particularly for small values of x. For example, when $x = 4000$, exact sorting has an output burstiness of $\overline{\sigma}_{out} = 60$, in contrast to values of less than 8 for each of the configurations in Figure 9. The low-rate connections do not experience significant traffic distortions under any of the shaper architectures. By dividing connections into two groups, the hierarchical architecture can reduce the number of sorting bins without distorting the high-bandwidth traffic, even under heavy congestion. In this configuration, one group services the five high-rate connections, while the second group handles the remaining traffic. Even with just ten sorting bins, the coarse-grain hierarchical architecture has small $\overline{\sigma}_{out}$ values, since each group tailors its bin granularity to the connection rate parameters.

Interestingly, the two hierarchical architectures even outperform the more expensive, fine-grain sorting scheme. This occurs because, even with weighted fair arbitration, a group can have multiple cells, from different connections, within a small range of sorting bins. Hence, when all connections share a single group, a high-rate connection may wait behind a long FIFO of low-bandwidth traffic before receiving service. In contrast, hierarchical arbitration limits the number of low-rate connections that can receive service between visits to the high-rate group, providing a minimum bandwidth to the high-rate connections on a smaller time scale.

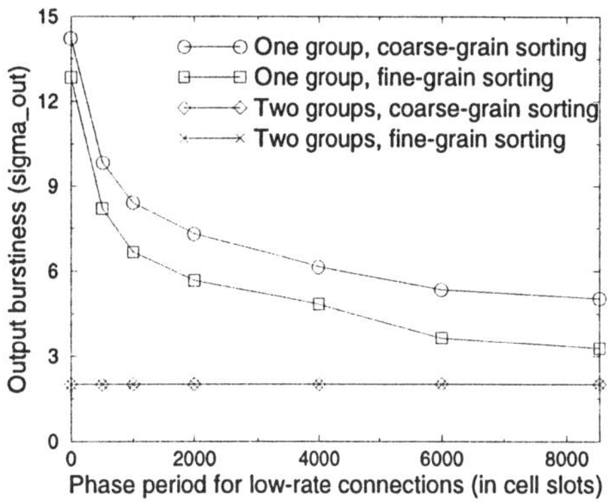

Figure 9: **Hierarchical Fair Arbitration**

6 Conclusion

Modern high-speed networks require efficient traffic shapers that can service a large number of connections with a wide range of bandwidth and burstiness parameters. To reduce complexity, traffic shaper designs can incorporate per-connection queueing, approximate sorting algorithms, and hierarchical arbitration policies. With a careful selection of sorting and arbitration schemes, these designs can also limit the traffic distortions that arise when multiple conforming cells await service. This is particularly important for shaping at the egress of a network, where the incoming traffic rate may temporarily exceed the outgoing link capacity, and in switches with multiple input links.

Ultimately, traffic shaping and link scheduling require a careful balance between implementation complexity and accuracy in approximating an idealized scheme. In contrast to the model in Figure 1, the proposed architecture avoids both the replication of complex sorting logic and the expensive movement of cells between two separate priority queues. As future work, we are further analyzing the properties of the integrated architecture, through additional simulation experiments with more realistic traffic patterns. Finally, we are considering extensions to the hierarchical traffic-shaping and link-scheduling framework, including arbitration schemes that differentiate between ATM traffic classes, as well as support for connections that do not require reshaping at every switch.

References

[1] F. Bonomi and K. W. Fendick, "The rate-based flow control framework for the available bit rate ATM service," *IEEE Network Magazine*, pp. 25–39, March/April 1995.

[2] H. Zhang and D. Ferrari, "Rate-controlled service disciplines," *Journal of High Speed Networks*, vol. 3, no. 4, pp. 389–412, 1994.

[3] H. Zhang, "Providing end-to-end performance guarantees using non-work-conserving disciplines," *Computer Communications*, vol. 18, pp. 769–781, October 1995.

[4] L. Georgiadis, R. Guerin, V. Peris, and K. N. Sivarajan, "Efficient network QoS provisioning based on per node traffic shaping," *IEEE/ACM Trans. Networking*, vol. 4, pp. 482–501, August 1996.

[5] J. Rexford, J. Hall, and K. G. Shin, "A router architecture for real-time point-to-point networks," in *Proc. Inter. Symposium on Computer Architecture*, pp. 237–246, May 1996.

[6] H. J. Chao, "Design of leaky bucket access control schemes in ATM networks," in *Proc. Inter. Conference on Communications*, pp. 180–187, June 1991.

[7] H. J. Chao and N. Uzun, "A VLSI sequencer chip for ATM traffic shaper and queue manager," *IEEE J. of Solid-State Circuits*, vol. 27, pp. 1634–1643, November 1992.

[8] P. E. Boyer, F. M. Guillemin, M. J. Servel, and J.-P. Coudreuse, "Spacing cells protects and enhances utilization of ATM network links," *IEEE Network Magazine*, pp. 38–49, September 1992.

[9] E. Wallmeier and T. Worster, "The Spacing Policer, an algorithm for efficient peak bit rate control in ATM networks," in *Proc. Inter. Switching Symposium*, pp. 22–26, October 1992.

[10] T. Moors, N. Clarke, and G. Mercankosk, "Implementing traffic shaping," in *Proc. Conf. on Local Computer Networks*, pp. 307–314, October 1994.

[11] G. Mercankosk, T. Moors, and A. Cantoni, "Multiplexing spacer outputs on cell emissions," in *Proc. IEEE INFOCOM*, pp. 49–55, April 1995.

[12] J. Turner, "New directions in communications, or which way to the information age?," *IEEE Communication Magazine*, vol. 24, pp. 8–15, October 1986.

[13] ATM Forum, "Traffic management specification, version 4.0." ATM Forum/95-0013R10, February 1996.

[14] A. Demers, S. Keshav, and S. Shenker, "Analysis and simulation of a fair queueing algorithm," *J. Internetworking: Research and Experience*, pp. 3–26, September 1990.

[15] A. K. Parekh and R. G. Gallager, "A generalized processor sharing approach to flow control in integrated services networks: The single node case," *IEEE/ACM Trans. Networking*, vol. 1, pp. 344–357, June 1993.

[16] A. K. Parekh and R. G. Gallager, "A generalized processor sharing approach to flow control in integrated services networks: The multiple node case," *IEEE/ACM Trans. Networking*, vol. 2, pp. 137–150, April 1994.

[17] H. Zhang and S. Keshav, "Comparison of rate-based service disciplines," in *Proc. ACM SIGCOMM*, pp. 113–121, September 1991.

[18] H. Zhang, "Service disciplines for guaranteed performance service in packet-switching networks," *Proc. of the IEEE*, vol. 83, pp. 1374–1396, October 1995.

[19] C. M. Aras, J. F. Kurose, D. S. Reeves, and H. Schulzrinne, "Real-time communication in packet-switched networks," *Proc. of the IEEE*, vol. 82, pp. 122–139, January 1994.

[20] J. C. R. Bennett and H. Zhang, "Hierarchical packet fair queueing algorithms," in *Proc. ACM SIGCOMM*, pp. 143–156, August 1996.

[21] D. Stiliadis and A. Varma, "A general methodology for designing efficient traffic scheduling and shaping algorithms." To appear in *Proc. IEEE INFOCOM*, April 1997.

[22] S. Suri, G. Varghese, and G. Chandranmenon, "Leap forward virtual clock: A new fair queuing scheme with guaranteed delays and throughput fairness." To appear in *Proc. IEEE INFOCOM*, April 1997.

[23] J. Rexford, A. Greenberg, and F. Bonomi, "Hardware-efficient fair queueing architectures for high-speed networks," in *Proc. IEEE INFOCOM*, pp. 638–646, March 1996.

[24] R. Brown, "Calendar queues: A fast O(1) priority queue implementation for the simulation event set problem," *Communications of the ACM*, vol. 31, pp. 1220–1227, October 1988.

[25] J. R. Davin and A. T. Heybey, "A simulation study of fair queueing and policy enforcement," *Computer Communication Review*, pp. 23–29, October 1990.

[26] J. W. Roberts, "Virtual spacing for flexible traffic control," *Inter. J. on Communication Systems*, vol. 7, pp. 307–318, October–December 1994.

[27] S. J. Golestani, "A self-clocked fair queueing scheme for broadband applications," in *Proc. IEEE INFOCOM*, pp. 636–646, 1994.

[28] S. Shenker, D. D. Clark, and L. Zhang, "A scheduling service model and a scheduling architecture for an integrated services packet network." Working paper, Xerox PARC, August 1993.

[29] S. Floyd and V. Jacobson, "Link-sharing and resource management models for packet networks," *IEEE/ACM Trans. Networking*, vol. 3, pp. 365–386, August 1995.

Rate-Function Scheduling

Norival R. Figueira and Joseph Pasquale

Computer Systems Laboratory
Department of Computer Science and Engineering
University of California, San Diego
La Jolla, CA 92093-0114

Abstract

Rate-Function Scheduling (RFS) is a new deadline-based packet-scheduling service discipline that supports quality-of-service guarantees for applications with real-time communication requirements. RFS is distinguished from other service disciplines in that it achieves all of the following goals: analytically-derived performance bounds, performance isolation among sessions, flexible and efficient allocation of bandwidth, implementation simplicity, work-conserving operation, and bandwidth-fair operation (defined in the paper). Through the specification of rate functions, sessions can control their bandwidth usage and their upper bounds on delay. For a class of rate functions, which we show is sufficient for providing sessions with delay bounds, RFS is as simple to implement and to calculate service bounds such as Zhang's VirtualClock service discipline. We also show that the Non-Preemptive Earliest Deadline First Policy is a simple degeneration of RFS.

1 Introduction

Real-time distributed applications often require a certain quality of service (QoS) from the underlying network in terms of performance guarantees such as throughput, end-to-end delay, and packet loss rate. By controlling the amount of bandwidth allocated to a session, one can control a session's throughput, and to some degree, end-to-end delay (via the queueing components). In fact, this is the basis for how most service disciplines that support analytic performance bounds work, including Delay-EDD (Earliest Due Deadline) [3], HRR (Hierarchical Round Robin) [11], Jitter-EDD [16], Leave-in-Time [6], PGPS (Packet-by-Packet Generalized Processor Sharing) [14], RCSP (Rate-Controlled Static-Priority) Queueing [17], Stop-and-Go [10], and VirtualClock [19].

This research was supported in part by NASA grant NASA-NAGW-4260. The opinions and conclusions contained in this document are those of the authors and should not be interpreted as representing official views or policies of the U.S. Government.

Among them, Delay-EDD [3] has the distinction of being "delay-optimal" [8] in a single server, i.e., if packets can be transmitted with a maximum specified delay using any single server scheduling policy, they can also be transmitted using a single Delay-EDD server. Delay-EDD is based on a Non-Preemptive Earliest Deadline First (NPEDF) scheduling discipline.

Service disciplines based on an NPEDF scheduler suffer from the following drawbacks. NPEDF schedulers are *bandwidth-unfair* (or cost-unfair) because bandwidth reservation is not taken into account in the calculation of transmission deadlines. In an NPEDF scheduler, the *reserved bandwidth* of a session is determined by its declared traffic characterization (or traffic envelope) and the required delay bound of the session. Thus, the burstier the declared traffic of a session is and the shorter its required delay bound is, the more bandwidth is reserved for the session in an NPEDF scheduler, resulting in a higher cost connection. If two sessions have the same required delay bound, but one session reserves (and pays for) more bandwidth than the other, then the former should receive a better service (i.e., smaller average delay). However, this is not the case with an NPEDF scheduler when these two sessions generate similar traffic over an interval of time. These sessions will receive similar treatment from the server because the server accounts only for the assigned delay bounds and not for the reserved bandwidth of these sessions, which is unfair to the session that reserved (and payed for) more bandwidth.

The sessions sharing an NPEDF scheduler must be *rate controlled* since, if a session violates its declared traffic characterization, the NPEDF scheduler may not be able to honor the service guarantees given to any of the sessions sharing the scheduler. A drawback of rate-controlled NPEDF service disciplines is that rate control makes them *non-work-conserving* (i.e., the server may become idle when there are packets being delayed in rate controllers), which increases the average delay of packets.

0-8186-7780-5/97 $10.00

Alternative service disciplines have been developed to provide performance isolation among sessions, i.e., no need for separate rate control, which is generally referred to as the *firewall property* [19]. Most of the alternative service disciplines, including HRR [11], Leave-in-Time [6], PGPS [14], Stop-and-Go [10], and VirtualClock [19], provide the firewall property but lack flexibility in the allocation of bandwidth since they allocate a *fixed* bandwidth to a session. This may lead to a waste of bandwidth because the worst-case behavior of a session dictates its reserved (fixed) bandwidth.

In this paper, we describe a new deadline-based service discipline called *Rate-Function Scheduling* (RFS). RFS is unique in that it achieves *all* of the following goals, whereas all the service disciplines we are aware of achieve only a proper subset: analytically-derived performance bounds, performance isolation among sessions, flexible and efficient allocation of bandwidth, implementation simplicity, work-conserving operation, and bandwidth-fair operation.

The RFS service discipline allows sessions to define service parameters such as long-term bandwidth and short-term bandwidth. Intuitively, long-term bandwidth means the long-term average of the amount of bandwidth a session is provided. Short-term bandwidth means the amount of bandwidth available to service a burst of packets. Once the entire short-term bandwidth is used up, a certain amount of idle time must pass before it can be used again.

A session specifies these service parameters through a *rate function* whose rate of change describes the bandwidth needs of the session, i.e., the slope of this function expresses rate. The key advantage of RFS' rate-function specification is that it can satisfy the needs of sessions with diverse delay and throughput requirements. For example, RFS can satisfy the needs of a session that requires a relatively low long-term bandwidth and a short delay by simply providing that session with a larger short-term bandwidth.

A rate function can be almost any non-decreasing function. However, the calculation of transmission deadlines is simplified for an important class of rate functions: *delayed-concave functions* composed solely of straight line segments (delayed-concave functions are defined later in this paper). For this class of rate functions, we show that the calculation of transmission deadlines is as simple as it is in VirtualClock. Besides, we show that this class is sufficient to provide sessions with delay bounds.

The RFS service discipline provides service guarantees such as an upper bound on end-to-end delay and an upper bound on buffer space requirements. For the special case of delayed-concave functions as described above, the calculation of service guarantees is also as simple as it is in VirtualClock [5].

We develop a necessary and sufficient schedulability condition for RFS and show that the NPEDF policy is a simple degeneration of RFS.

The remainder of this paper is organized as follows. Section 2 presents a motivation for the way RFS works. Section 3 presents the RFS service discipline. Section 4 presents the service guarantees of RFS. Section 5 presents the simplified transmission deadline calculation of RFS for delayed-concave rate functions composed solely of straight line segments. Section 6 discusses the advantages of RFS over other service disciplines. Section 7 is a summary of the paper contributions. Space considerations have forced us to omit the proofs of our results. The interested reader is referred to [7].

2 Motivation and Preliminary Definitions

The RFS service discipline was inspired by the simplicity of VirtualClock [19]. The VirtualClock service discipline works as follows: It calculates transmission deadlines for all arriving packets of all sessions and serves packets in increasing order of transmission deadlines. The equation used to calculate transmission deadlines is very simple:

$$F_{i,s} = \max\{F_{i-1,s}, t_{i,s}\} + \frac{L_{i,s}}{r_s}, i \geq 1, F_{0,s} = t_{1,s}, \quad (1)$$

where the packets of session s are numbered according to the order of their arrival at a server, $t_{i,s}$ is the arrival time of the ith packet of session s (a packet has arrived only after its last bit has arrived), $L_{i,s}$ is the length of the ith packet of session s, r_s is the reserved rate of session s, and $F_{i,s}$ is the transmission deadline of the ith packet of session s.

VirtualClock provides sessions with a *fixed* reserved rate. Its admission control insures that the reserved rates of all sessions sharing a server are constrained by

$$\sum_{s \in \varphi} r_s \leq C,$$

where C is the capacity of the outgoing link of the server and φ is the set of sessions sharing the outgoing link of the server.

The following result provides for an alternative way to calculate transmission deadlines in VirtualClock.

Theorem 1: In VirtualClock,

$$F_{i,s} = \max\left\{\sum_{k=j}^{i} \frac{L_{k,s}}{r_s} + t_{j,s} : 1 \leq j \leq i\right\}. \quad (2)$$

We can rewrite (2) as

$$F_{i,s} = \max\left\{Y_s\left(\sum_{k=j}^{i} L_{k,s}\right) + t_{j,s} : 1 \leq j \leq i\right\}, \quad (3)$$

where $Y_s(l) = l/r_s$. Note that $Y_s(l)$ is the inverse of the function $R_s(t) = r_s t$ that calculates how many bits the session wants the server to transmit in t seconds. For VirtualClock, this function is a straight line whose slope is equal to the reserved rate of the session (see Figure 1).

But what would happen if $R_s(t)$ were not a straight line? In fact, (3) forms the basis of our proposed RFS discipline's transmission deadline calculation, allowing sessions to reserve a *rate function*, $R_s(t)$, which does not need to be a straight line. VirtualClock may then be considered to be a special case where all sessions reserve a straight line as rate function. Most importantly, one can define more general rate functions that allow sessions to reduce their end-to-end delay without reserving more long-term bandwidth.

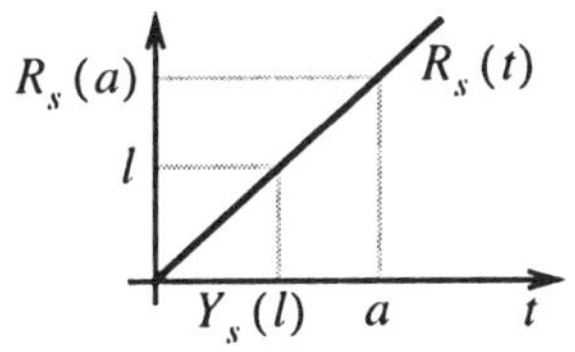

Figure 1: $R_s(t)$ and $Y_s(l)$ for VirtualClock.

A rate function $R_s(.)$ can be interpreted as the description of the service capabilities of an *ideal* server. In this interpretation, (3) calculates the end of transmission times that packets of a session would have if the session were served alone by the ideal server that is defined by the session's reserved rate function. Roughly speaking, the rate function measures how many bits the ideal server is able to transmit since the beginning of a server busy period if a certain amount of idle time occurs before the server busy period. A *server busy period* is a maximum period of time in which a server always has packets to serve.

We now formalize some of the terms we introduced previously.

Definition 1: The *rate function* $R_s(t)$ of session s is a *non-decreasing* piecewise continuous function for which $R_s(t) = 0$ for $t < 0$ and $R_s(t_0) > 0$ for some $t_0 > 0$.

Definition 2: The *delay function* $Y_s(l)$ of session s is defined as (see Figure 2)

$$Y_s(l) = \min\{t_0\colon R_s(t_0) \geq l\},\ l > 0. \tag{4}$$

If $R_s(t)$ is continuous and monotonic, then $Y_s(l)$ is the inverse of $R_s(t)$ for all t such that $R_s(t) > 0$.

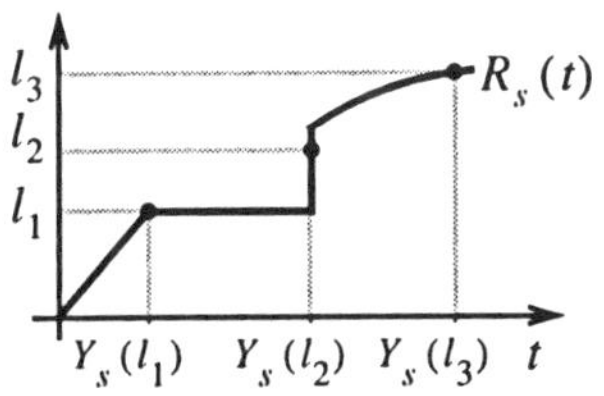

Figure 2: $R_s(t)$ and $Y_s(l)$.

3 Rate-Function Scheduling

RFS is a work-conserving non-preemptive service discipline where packets are served in increasing order of transmission deadlines and the transmission deadline of the ith packet of a real-time session s is

$$F_{i,s} = \max\left\{Y_s\left(\sum_{k=j}^{i} L_{k,s}\right) + t_{j,s}\colon 1 \leq j \leq i\right\}. \tag{5}$$

Non real-time sessions (i.e., sessions that do not require QoS guarantees) have transmission deadlines set to infinity.

Theorem 2 provides a sufficient and necessary schedulability condition for RFS.

Theorem 2: Consider an RFS server that allows the presence of non real-time sessions. We have that

$$\sum_{s \in \Omega} R_s(t) \leq Ct - \theta,\ t \geq \frac{\theta}{C} \text{ and } t \geq 0, \tag{6}$$

if and only if

$$\hat{F}_{i,s} < F_{i,s} + \upsilon_s,\ i \geq 1, \tag{7}$$

for all sessions s in Ω, where Ω is the set of all real-time sessions sharing the server, $\hat{F}_{i,s}$ is the actual finishing transmission time of the ith packet of session s,

$$\upsilon_s = \frac{L_{\max,\bar{s}}}{C} - \frac{\theta}{C},$$

$L_{\max,\bar{s}}$ is the maximum length of packets *not* from session s sharing the outgoing link of the server (i.e., $L_{\max,\bar{s}} = \max\{L_{\max,s'}\colon s' \neq s$ and s' shares the server$\}$, and θ is an amount in bits (θ can assume any real value).

The parameter θ allows the service discipline to customize υ_s. For example, if $\theta = L_{MAX}$ the term $L_{\max,\bar{s}}/C$ in υ_s is cancelled out, where L_{MAX} is the maximum packet length allowed in the server (or network). Note that (6) has a simple graphical interpretation; the sum of the rate functions of all sessions cannot be above the curve $Ct - \theta$ (see Figure 3). See [4] for more details on the use of θ.

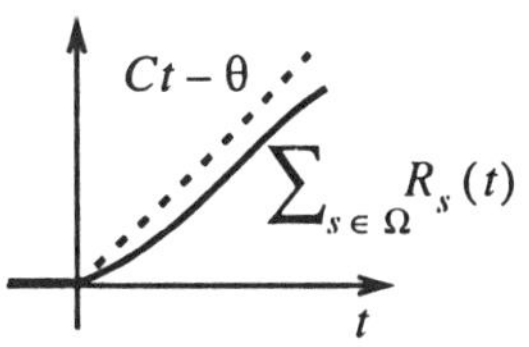

Figure 3: Graphical interpretation of (6) for $\theta = 0$.

4 Service Guarantees of RFS

RFS provides sessions with an upper bound on end-to-end delay and an upper bound on buffer space requirements. The end-to-end delay refers to the delay experienced by a session in a connection composed of servers in tandem. Since some measures vary with the server node, we need to extend our notation. Thus, $F_{i,s}$, $t_{i,s}$, $\hat{F}_{i,s}$, υ_s, $L_{\max,\bar{s}}$, C, $R_s(t)$, and $Y_s(t)$, will now be written as $F^n_{i,s}$, $t^n_{i,s}$, $\hat{F}^n_{i,s}$, υ^n_s, $L^n_{\max,\bar{s}}$, C_n, $R^n_s(t)$, and $Y^n_s(t)$, respectively, where n is the index of the server node. This notation allows sessions to reserve different rate functions at different server nodes.

In order to present some of the results of this section, we need the following definitions:

Definition 3: Given a non-decreasing piecewise continuous function $A_s(.)$, called an *arrival function*, for which $A_s(t) = 0$ for $t < 0$, we say that the input traffic of session s satisfies the arrival constraint defined by $A_s(.)$ if

$$A_s(t-s) \geq T^{\text{in}}_s[s,t], \; s \leq t, \tag{8}$$

where

$$T^{\text{in}}_s[a,b] = \sum_{j=\min\{i:\, t_{i,s} \geq a\}}^{\max\{i:\, t_{i,s} \leq b\}} L_{j,s} \tag{9}$$

is the sum of the lengths of all the packets of session s that arrived in the interval of time $[a, b]$ (recall that a packet is considered to have arrived only when its last bit arrives).

Note that $A_s(0) \geq L_{\max,s}$ because $A_s(0) \geq T^{\text{in}}_s[t_{i,s}, t_{i,s}]$, $i \geq 1$.

A common model of incoming traffic is the arrival function $A_s(t) = \sigma_s + \rho_s t$, which is similar to the one proposed by Cruz [1]. This arrival function is used in some examples in this paper, but note that RFS is *not* restricted to any specific model of incoming traffic.

Definition 4: A rate function $R_s(t)$ is called *delayed-concave* (see Figure 4) if

1. $R_s(t) = 0, \; t < \tau_s, \; \tau_s \geq 0$;
2. $R_s(\tau_s) = \sigma_s, \; \sigma_s \geq 0$;
3. $R_s(t)$ has at most one discontinuity point, and it must occur for $t = \tau_s$; and
4. $R_s(t)$ is *concave*[1] and *increasing* on $[\tau_s, \infty)$.

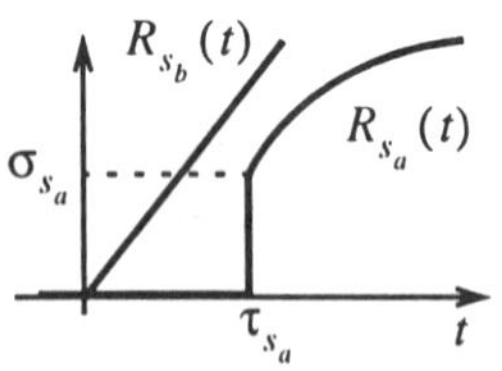

Figure 4: Two delayed-concave rate functions.

The following defines a parameter that is used in the specification of some of the service guarantees of RFS.

[1] A function $f(.)$ is called *concave* [13] on a segment $[a, b]$ if and only if $f(\lambda x + (1-\lambda)y) \geq \lambda f(x) + (1-\lambda) f(y)$ holds for all $x, y \in [a, b]$ and all real numbers $\lambda \in [0, 1]$.

Definition 5:

$$\chi_s(l_c) = \max\{Y_s(l_a + l_c) + Y_s(l_b + l_c) - Y_s(l_a + l_b + l_c) : l_a \geq 0, l_b \geq 0\}, l_c > 0. \tag{10}$$

Lemma 1: If $R_s(t)$ is delayed-concave, then $\chi_s(l_c) = Y_s(l_c)$.

In the service guarantees we present for RFS, we use $\chi^n_{\text{MAX},s} = \max\{\chi^n_s(L_{j,s}) : j \geq 1\}$, where $\chi^n_s(L_{j,s})$ is the value of $\chi_s(L_{j,s})$ at server node n. Hence, $\chi^n_{\text{MAX},s} = Y^n_s(L_{\max,s})$ for delayed-concave rate functions.

In the results of this section, we assume that the delay functions that are assigned to session s in server nodes 1 to N of its connection satisfy

$$Y^{n+1}_s(l) \leq Y^n_s(l) + \delta^{n+1}_s, \; 1 \leq n \leq N-1, \tag{11}$$

where δ^{n+1}_s is a constant that defines a bound for the delay function of server node $n+1$ relative to the delay function of server node n. We assume that $\delta^1_s = 0$.

The simplest use of δ^{n+1}_s is to allow a session to reserve in one server node the rate function that is reserved in the previous server node shifted to the right (or left) by a constant displacement. Thus, δ^{n+1}_s may be positive, negative, or zero (it may be zero if the rate functions are identical).

4.1 Upper Bound on End-to-End Delay

Theorem 3: If $R^n_s(t)$ is the reserved rate function of session s in server node n of its connection and $\chi^n_{\text{MAX},s}$ exists for $1 \leq n \leq N-1$, then

$$D^{1,N}_{\max,s} < D^{\text{ideal}}_{\max,s}(R^1_s) + \Upsilon^{1,N}_s, \; N \geq 1, \tag{12}$$

where $\Upsilon^{1,N}_s$ is a constant for the session with value

$$\Upsilon^{1,N}_s = \sum_{n=1}^{N-1} \chi^n_{\text{MAX},s} + \sum_{n=1}^{N} (\delta^n_s + \upsilon^n_s + \Gamma_n), \tag{13}$$

N is the number of server nodes of the connection, $D^{1,N}_{\max,s}$ is the maximum delay that packets of session s experience in the connection, $D^{\text{ideal}}_{\max,s}(R^1_s)$ is the maximum delay packets of the session would experience if the session were served alone by the ideal server defined by the rate function $R^1_s(t)$, and Γ_n is an upper bound on the propagation delay of the outgoing link of server node n.

If $R^n_s(t) = r_s t$, $n \geq 1$, (12) reduces to the well-known upper bound on the delay of VirtualClock [5] since, in this case, $\delta^n_s = 0$, $\chi^n_{\text{MAX},s} = L_{\max,s}/r_s$ and $D^{\text{ideal}}_{\max,s}(R^1_s)$ is just an upper bound on delay of the session in a fixed-rate server of rate r_s.

We now develop a graphical interpretation for the term $D^{\text{ideal}}_{\max,s}(R^1_s)$ as a function of the reserved rate function and the arrival function of the session. We will show later that $D^{\text{ideal}}_{\text{max},s}(R^1_s)$ is very simple to calculate for the case of delayed-concave rate functions composed of straight line segments.

Theorem 4: If session s with arrival function $A_s(t)$ is being served alone by the ideal server defined by the rate function $R_s(t)$, then

$$D^{\text{ideal}}_{\text{max},s}(R_s) \le \max\{\min\{d\colon A_s(k) \le R_s(k+d) \text{ and } d \ge 0\} \colon k \ge 0\}, \tag{14}$$

where

$$D^{\text{ideal}}_{\text{max},s}(R_s) = \max\{D^{\text{ideal}}_{i,s}(R_s) : i \ge 1\}, \tag{15}$$

$D^{\text{ideal}}_{i,s}(R_s) = F_{i,s} - t_{i,s}$, and F_{is} is the end of transmission time of the ith packet of the session in the ideal server, which is calculated by (3).

We use the same notation (i.e., F_{is}) for the transmission deadlines of packets in an RFS server and for the end of transmission time of packets in an ideal server, since the former assumes the same values as the latter.

The graphical interpretation for inequality (14) is that the maximum delay of a session in an ideal server is less than or equal to the maximum horizontal distance between the arrival and the rate functions (see Figure 5). Inequality (14) and its graphical interpretation are similar to a result developed by Cruz to calculate the delay of a session as a function of its *service* and *arrival curves* [2].

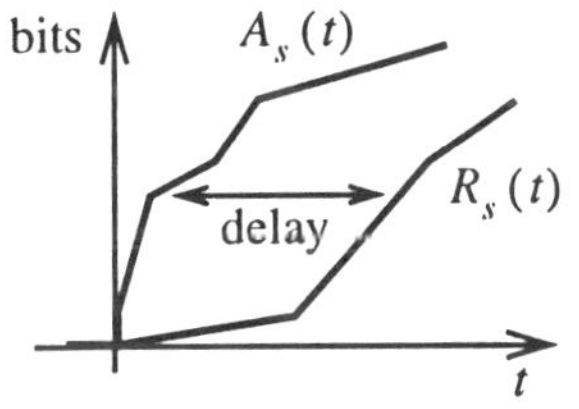

Figure 5: Delay in the ideal server defined by $R_s(t)$.

According to (12) and (13), the delay bound of a session s in the first server node of its connection is $D^{\text{ideal}}_{\text{max},s}(R^1_s) + \upsilon^1_s + \Gamma_1$. From (14), if session s reserves a rate function equal to the session's arrival function shifted to the right by a positive displacement, say d_s, then $D^{\text{ideal}}_{\text{max},s}(R^1_s) \le d_s$. Thus, the rate function $R_s(t) = A_s(t - d_s)$ is sufficient to provide an upper bound on delay for the session. Note that other rate functions are possible that provide the same upper bound on delay (i.e., $d_s + \upsilon^1_s + \Gamma_1$) for a session with arrival function $A_s(t)$. Figures 6 and 7 show examples of rate functions that provide the same upper bound on delay in the first server node for a session s with arrival function $A_s(t) = \sigma_s + \rho_s t$. It is important to note that RFS is able to provide delay bounds for other types of arrival functions. For example, in Figure 6-a, the session with arrival function $A'_s(t)$ will have the same upper bound on delay as the session with arrival function $A_s(t) = \sigma_s + \rho_s t$ if both sessions have the same reserved rate function $R_s(t) = A_s(t - d_s)$.

Now, suppose that a session s with arrival function $A_s(t) = \sigma_s + \rho_s t$ reserves the same rate function in all the server nodes in its route, i.e., $\delta^n_s = 0$, $1 \le n \le N$. We consider three cases, which are represented in Figures 6 and 7.

Case 1: If $R_s(t) = A_s(t - d_s)$ (this is Figure 6-a and Figure 7-a), the upper bound on delay in a connection composed of N server nodes in tandem is $Nd_s + \sum_{n=1}^{N}(\upsilon^n_s + \Gamma_n)$, since $\chi^n_{\text{MAX},s} = Y^n_s(L_{\text{max},s}) = d_s$ and $D^{\text{ideal}}_{\text{max},s}(R^1_s) \le d_s$.

Case 2: If $d_s < \sigma_s/\rho_s$ and the session reserves the rate function (this is Figure 6-b)

$$R'_s(t) = \begin{cases} \sigma_s t/d_s, & \text{if } 0 \le t < d_s \\ \rho_s(t - d_s) + \sigma_s, & \text{if } t \ge d_s, \end{cases} \tag{16}$$

the upper bound on delay in a connection composed of N server nodes in tandem is $d_s + (N-1)(d_s L_{\text{max},s}/\sigma_s) + \sum_{n=1}^{N}(\upsilon^n_s + \Gamma_n)$, since $\chi^n_{\text{MAX},s} = Y^n_s(L_{\text{max},s}) = d_s L_{\text{max},s}/\sigma_s$ and $D^{\text{ideal}}_{\text{max},s}(R^1_s) \le d_s$. This upper bound on delay is smaller than or equal to the upper bound on delay obtained in Case 1 above, since $\sigma_s \ge L_{\text{max},s}$ (it is strictly smaller if $\sigma_s > L_{\text{max},s}$).

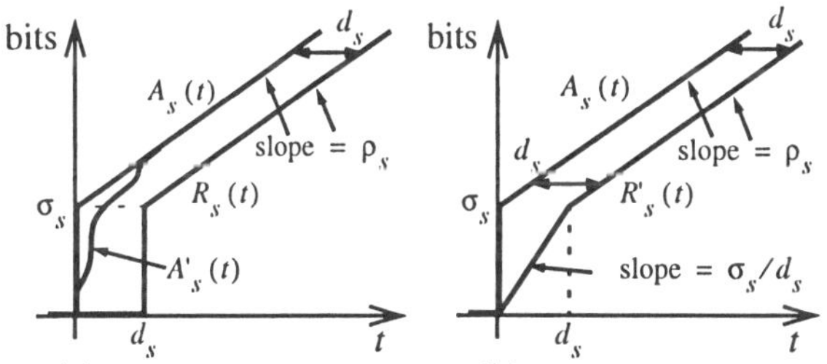

(a) $R_s(t) = A_s(t - d_s)$ (b) $R'_s(t)$ (see text)

Figure 6: Two rate functions that provide the same upper bound on delay in the first server node for a session with $A_s(t) = \sigma_s + \rho_s t$ and for $d_s < \sigma_s/\rho_s$.

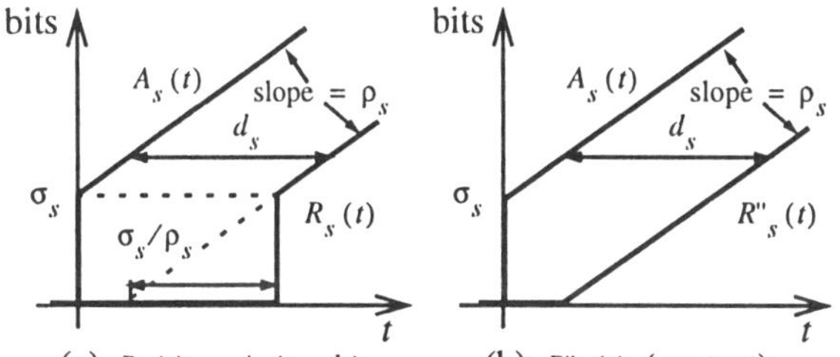

(a) $R_s(t) = A_s(t - d_s)$ (b) $R''_s(t)$ (see text)

Figure 7: Two rate functions that provide the same upper bound on delay in the first server node for a session with $A_s(t) = \sigma_s + \rho_s t$ and for $d_s \ge \sigma_s/\rho_s$.

Case 3: If $d_s \geq \sigma_s / \rho_s$ and the session reserves the rate function (this is Figure 7-b)

$$R''_s(t) = \begin{cases} 0, \text{ if } t < d_s - \sigma_s / \rho_s \\ \rho_s (t - d_s) + \sigma_s, \text{ if } t \geq d_s - \sigma_s / \rho_s, \end{cases} \quad (17)$$

the upper bound on delay in a connection composed of N server nodes in tandem is $Nd_s - (N-1)(\sigma_s - L_{\max,s}) / \rho_s + \sum_{n=1}^{N} (\upsilon_s^n + \Gamma_n)$, since $\chi_{\mathrm{MAX},s}^n = Y_s^n(L_{\max,s}) = d_s - \sigma_s/\rho_s + L_{\max,s}/\rho_s$ and $D_{\max,s}^{\text{ideal}}(R_s^1) \leq d_s$. This upper bound on delay is smaller than or equal to the upper bound on delay obtained in Case 1 above, since $\sigma_s \geq L_{\max,s}$ (it is strictly smaller if $\sigma_s > L_{\max,s}$).

Besides a possibly smaller upper bound on delay, Cases 2 and 3 also provide a smaller average delay for the session because those rate functions provide (on average) earlier transmission deadlines than the rate function used in Case 1.

4.2 Upper Bound on Buffer Space Requirements

Definition 6: The buffer space used by session s in a server at time t is defined as

$$Q_s(t) = T_s^{\text{in}}[0, t] - T_s^{\text{out}}[0, t), \quad (18)$$

where

$$T_s^{\text{out}}[a, b) = \sum_{j = \min\{i : \hat{F}_{i,s} \geq a\}}^{\max\{i : \hat{F}_{i,s} < b\}} L_{j,s} \quad (19)$$

is the sum of the lengths of all the packets of session s that ended transmission in the interval of time $[a, b)$ ($T_s^{\text{in}}[a, b]$ is defined by (9)).

Theorem 5: If $R_s^n(t)$ is the reserved rate function of session s in server node n of its connection and $\chi_{\mathrm{MAX},s}^j$ exists for $1 \leq j \leq n$, then

$$Q_{\max,s}^n \leq R_s^n\Big(D_{\max,s}^{\text{ideal}}(R_s^1) + \sum_{j=1}^{n} (\delta_s^j + \chi_{\mathrm{MAX},s}^j + \upsilon_s^j) - \sum_{j=1}^{n-1}\Big(\frac{L_{\min,s}}{C_j} + \gamma_j - \Gamma_j\Big)\Big), \; n \geq 1, \quad (20)$$

where $Q_{\max,s}^n = \max\{Q_s^n(t) : t \geq 0\}$, $Q_s^n(t)$ is the buffer space session s uses at server node n at time t, and γ_j is a lower bound on the propagation delay of the outgoing link of server node j.

Theorem 6: For a single RFS server and a session s with arrival function $A_s(.)$ and reserved rate function $R_s(.)$,

$$Q_{\max,s} \leq \max\{A_s(k) - R_s(k - \upsilon_s) : k \geq 0\} + L_{\max,s}, \quad (21)$$

where $Q_{\max,s} = \max\{Q_s(t) : t \geq 0\}$ is an upper bound on buffer space in this RFS server.

The graphical interpretation for (21) is that the maximum backlog of a session in a single server node is a function of the maximum vertical distance between the arrival function and the reserved rate function shifted to the right by the constant υ_s (see Figure 8). Inequality (21) and its graphical interpretation are similar to a result developed by Cruz [2] to calculate the backlog of a session as a function of its service and arrival curves.

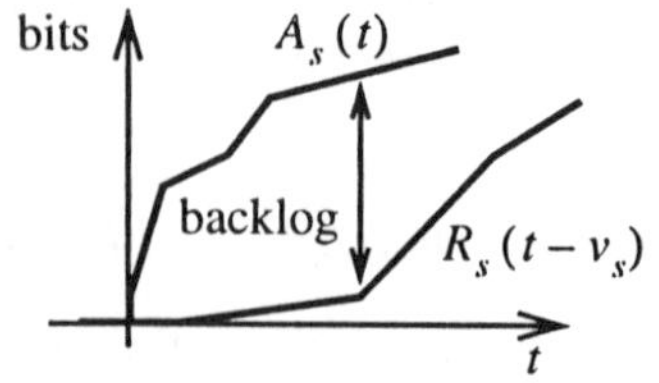

Figure 8: Backlog in a single RFS server.

5 Simplified Deadline Calculation

We now show that (5) can be simplified for a class of rate functions that provides the following properties: (a) it provides delay bounds; and (b) the calculation of transmission deadlines is as simple as it is in the VirtualClock service discipline.

This class is composed of delayed-concave rate functions that are composed solely of straight line segments (as in Figure 9). These functions can be described by a few parameters: the number of inclined straight line segments, n, the slope of each inclined straight line segment, $r_s^1 > r_s^2 > \ldots > r_s^{n-1} > r_s^n > 0$, and the "knees" of the curve, $\tau_s = v_s^1 < v_s^2 < \ldots < v_s^{n-1} < v_s^n$. For these rate functions,

$$R_s(t) = \begin{cases} 0, & \text{if } t < \tau_s = v_s^1 \\ r_s^j(t - V_s^j), & \text{if } v_s^j \leq t < v_s^{j+1}, \; 1 \leq j \leq n-1 \\ r_s^n(t - V_s^n), & \text{if } t \geq v_s^n, \end{cases} \quad (22)$$

where

$$V_s^j = v_s^j - \frac{\sigma_s}{r_s^j} - \sum_{m=2}^{j} \frac{(v_s^m - v_s^{m-1}) r_s^{m-1}}{r_s^j}, \; 1 \leq j \leq n. \quad (23)$$

V_s^j is the horizontal coordinate of the point where a prolongation of the line segment j intersects with the horizontal axis (see Figure 9).

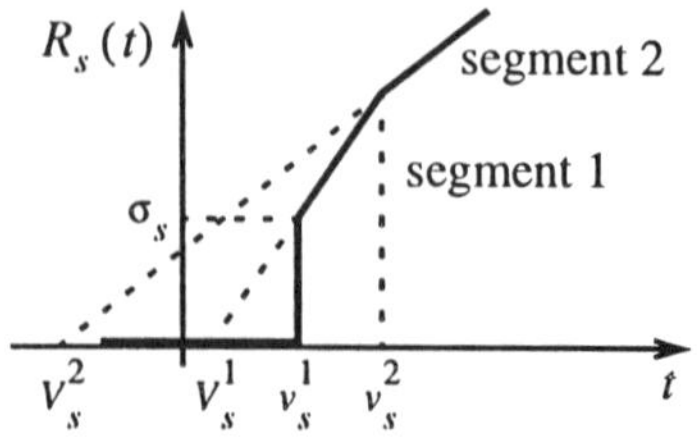

Figure 9: A delayed-concave rate function composed of two inclined straight line segments.

In [5], it was proven that only *leaky bucket constrained* sessions have an upper bound on delay in finite capacity servers. Leaky bucket constrained sessions can be modeled by an arrival function $A_s(t) = \sigma_s + \rho_s t$. The rate function $R_s(t) = \sigma_s + \rho_s(t - d_s)$, which belongs to the class of rate functions described by (22), provides an upper bound on delay for a session with arrival function $A_s(t) = \sigma_s + \rho_s t$ (see Figures 6 and 7). Therefore, the class of rate functions described by (22) suffices to provide delay bounds.

Theorem 7: For rate functions as defined by (22),

$$F_{i,s} = \max\{\ t_{i,s} + \tau_s, K^j_{i,s} + V^j_s : 1 \le j \le n\}\ , \qquad (24)$$

where

$$K^j_{i,s} = \max\{K^j_{i-1,s}, t_{i,s}\} + \frac{L_{i,s}}{r^j_s}, \quad i \ge 1, \qquad (25)$$
$$K^j_{0,s} = t_{1,s}, \quad 1 \le j \le n.$$

The previous result has two important consequences. First, (24) is simpler to calculate than (5). Second, $D^{\mathrm{ideal}}_{\max,s}(R^1_s)$ is very simple to calculate. If we define $D^{r^j_s}_{i,s} = K^j_{i,s} - t_{i,s}$, where $D^{r^j_s}_{i,s}$ is the delay of the session in a fixed-rate server of rate r^j_s (where r^j_s is the slope of the straight line segment j), then

$$D^{\mathrm{ideal}}_{i,s}(R^1_s) = \max\{\tau_s, D^{r^j_s}_{i,s} + V^j_s : 1 \le j \le n\}\ , \qquad (26)$$

which implies that

$$D^{\mathrm{ideal}}_{\max,s}(R^1_s) = \max\{\tau_s, D^{r^j_s}_{\max,s} + V^j_s : 1 \le j \le n\}\ , \qquad (27)$$

i.e., the maximum delay of the packets of the session in the ideal server defined by $R^1_s(t)$ is a simple function of the maximum delay of the session in a set of fixed-rate servers. Note, however, that this computation is rarely necessary, since (14) provides a graphical way to determine the delay bound in the ideal server.

6 Comparing RFS to Others Schemes

RFS shares many common characteristics with VirtualClock (especially for the class of rate functions described in Section 5), which has already been compared in detail with many other service disciplines [18]. Because of this, we compare RFS only with NPEDF service disciplines [3,8,9,20] and SCED [15].

6.1 Comparison to NPEDF Scheduling

In an NPEDF scheduler, the transmission deadline of the ith packet of a real-time session s is $F_{i,s} = t_{i,s} + d_s$, where $d_s \ge 0$ is the required delay bound of session s.

The following result establishes a necessary and sufficient schedulability condition for NPEDF schedulers. This result is more general than related results found by others [12, 20].

Theorem 8: Consider an NPEDF server that allows the presence of non real-time sessions. We have that

$$\sum_{s \in \Omega} A_s(t - d_s) \le Ct - \theta\ , \ t \ge \frac{\theta}{C} \text{ and } t \ge 0\ , \qquad (28)$$

if and only if

$$\hat{F}_{i,s} < F_{i,s} + \upsilon_s\ , i \ge 1, \qquad (29)$$

for all sessions s in Ω, where $A_s(t)$ is the arrival function of session s, Ω is the set of all real-time sessions sharing the server, and θ is an amount in bits. See Theorem 2 for an interpretation for the constant θ.

A comparison of Theorems 8 and 2 (see also Theorem 4) shows that RFS is more general than rate-controlled NPEDF service disciplines since, in RFS, it is *sufficient but not necessary* for a session s to reserve a rate function equal to $A_s(t - d_s)$ in order to obtain a delay bound equal to $d_s + \upsilon_s$ in a single RFS server. The propagation delay of links, which we omit, is irrelevant in the discussions of this section.

To further demonstrate RFS' generality, we show how one can degenerate RFS into a rate-controlled NPEDF service discipline. Suppose that a session s reserves a rate function equal to $A_s(t - d_s)$ in an RFS server. If we assume that session s conforms to its arrival function $A_s(t)$, we have from Theorems 3 and 4 that the delay bound of session s is $d_s + \upsilon_s$ and that $F_{i,s} \le t_{i,s} + d_s$. If RFS calculates the transmission deadlines of the packets of session s as $F_{i,s} = t_{i,s} + d_s$ (Theorem 9 below shows that one can loosen up the transmission deadlines in RFS), then RFS will still provide a delay bound equal to $d_s + \upsilon_s$ for this session. Note, however, that we have assumed that session s voluntarily conforms to its arrival function $A_s(t)$, which may not necessarily be the case. Thus, as in an NPEDF scheduler, session s must be forced to conform to its arrival function $A_s(t)$; otherwise, service guarantees cannot be provided to this session and, more importantly, to any other session sharing the server, since *the bandwidth utilization of session s is now unrestricted.* Hence, RFS would loose its firewall property and need a rate controller for this session (and only for this session) to be able to provide service guarantees. In summary, the transmission deadline calculation in RFS has built-in rate control which, if disabled as in this example, degenerates RFS into an NPEDF scheduler that needs separate rate control.

Theorem 9: In the RFS service discipline, if the transmission deadline constraints of packets are loosened such that

$$F_{i,s} \ge \max\left\{Y_s\left(\sum_{k=j}^{i} L_{k,s}\right) + t_{j,s}: t_{j,s} \le t_{i,s}\right\},$$

$F_{m,s} \ge F_{n,s}$, $m \ge n$, and

$$\sum_{s \in \Omega} R_s(t) \le Ct - \theta,\ t \ge \frac{\theta}{C} \text{ and } t \ge 0,$$

where Ω is the set of all real-time sessions sharing the server, then $\hat{F}_{i,s} < F_{i,s} + \upsilon_s$, $i \ge 1$, for all sessions s in Ω.

In a "naive" [9] rate-controlled NPEDF service discipline, rate-controllers force sessions to conform to their pre-specified traffic characterizations, i.e., the ones that are declared at connection establishment time. RFS has a wider *schedulability region* [8] than the naive rate-controlled NPEDF service discipline for connections with more than one server node. We illustrate this result with an example. Consider two sessions, say s_a and s_b, that traverse a connection composed of two servers of capacity C. Suppose that $A_{s_a}(t) = A_{s_b}(t) = \sigma + (C/2)t$, where $\sigma > L_{\max, s_a}$. We first calculate the delay bound of these sessions for the case of RFS servers. Suppose that sessions s_a and s_b reserve the rate function $R_{s_a}(t) = R_{s_b}(t) = (C/2)t$ in both server nodes of the connection. Note that these rate functions satisfy Theorem 2 (θ is irrelevant in the discussions of this section since RFS can match any value used by an NPEDF service discipline). The end-to-end delay bound of sessions s_a and s_b in this connection is $2\sigma/C + 2L_{\max,s}/C$ (since $D^{\text{ideal}}_{\max,s}(R^1_s) \le 2\sigma/C$ and $\chi^1_{\text{MAX},s} = 2L_{\max,s}/C$) where, to simplify our discussions, we assume that the additional constants (i.e., υ^n_s and Γ_n) that compose the end-to-end delay bound of both sessions are identical for both sessions, which we then omit. Since $\sigma > L_{\max, s_a}$, this end-to-end delay bound is smaller than $4\sigma/C$ for both sessions.

We now observe that at least one of these sessions cannot obtain the above end-to-end delay bound if the connection is composed of naive rate-controlled NPEDF servers since, for these sessions, Theorem 8 implies that $d^1_{s_a} + d^1_{s_b} \ge 4\sigma/C$ and $d^2_{s_a} + 4d^2_{s_b} \ge \sigma/C$, which imply that $d^1_{s_a} + d^2_{s_a} \ge 4\sigma/C$ or $d^1_{s_b} + 4d^2_{s_b} \ge \sigma/C$, where $d^1_{s_a}$ and $d^2_{s_a}$ are the assigned delay bounds of session s_a in server nodes 1 and 2, respectively ($d^1_{s_b}$ and $d^2_{s_b}$ are defined in the same manner)

In [9], a more involved scheme is proposed for rate-controlled NPEDF service disciplines in which rate controllers enforce a "proper" reshaping of the traffic of sessions. Proper reshaping means that the rate controllers reshape the sessions' traffic to conform to traffic patterns that provide a lower upper bound on delay than the one obtained with the naive rate-controlled NPEDF service discipline. We now show that one gains no more in this scheme than what is already provided by RFS.

Theorem 10: For a rate controller that enforces a traffic pattern to session s such that $A'_s(t)$ is the (new) arrival function of session s after the rate controller,

$$e_{i,s} \ge \max\left\{Y'_s\left(\sum_{k=j}^{i} L_{k,s}\right) + t_{j,s}: 1 \le j \le i\right\}, \tag{30}$$

where $e_{i,s}$ is the eligibility time of the ith packet of session s (i.e., $e_{i,s}$ is the earliest time the ith packet of session s may exit the rate controller) and $Y'_s(l)$ is the delay function that corresponds to the rate function that is equal to $A'_s(t)$.

With proper reshaping, the transmission deadline of the ith packet of session s in the NPEDF scheduler is then $e_{i,s} + d'_s$, where d'_s is the delay bound that is assigned to the packets of the session after they leave the rate controller. In this case, bandwidth reservation in the NPEDF scheduler is governed by $A'_s(t - d'_s)$. RFS can provide a transmission deadline to the ith packet of session s that is *no later* than $e_{i,s} + d'_s$ by simply assigning the rate function $A'_s(t - d'_s)$ to session s since, in this case,

$$F_{i,s} = \max\left\{Y'_s\left(\sum_{k=j}^{i} L_{k,s}\right) + t_{j,s}: 1 \le j \le i\right\} + d'_s,$$

i.e., $F_{i,s} \le e_{i,s} + d'_s$. Thus, RFS provides the same upper bound on delay as in the previously proposed scheme by using the same bandwidth reservation in the server, i.e., $A'_s(t - d'_s)$. Hence, the schedulability region of RFS is *at least the same as* that for the rate-controlled NPEDF service discipline with proper reshaping. Note, however, that RFS provides a smaller average delay for sessions than the rate-controlled NPEDF service discipline because RFS is work conserving.

6.2 Comparison to Service Curves

The rate function concept is similar in purpose to Cruz's service curve [2] concept, but they are not the same. As explained in Section 2, the rate function of a session defines an ideal server for the session, which RFS emulates. Based on RFS' operation, a "service curve" is induced (using Cruz's terminology); *this induced service curve is not the same as the rate function.* This is because RFS incurs an *emulation error* (the emulation error is clear from the service guarantees of RFS). Accepting the emulation error, which is small and bounded, results in the simplicity of RFS' analysis and implementation.

SCED [15] is based on the "allocation approach" (according to Cruz's terminology in [2]) in which a session explicitly defines the service curve it expects to receive from the server. On the other hand, RFS is based on the "induction approach" (again, Cruz's terminology). In spite of this distinction, the rate function of RFS provides the same functionality of the service curve of SCED. However, RFS and SCED differ significantly in other key aspects. RFS is defined for feed-forward servers and is analyzed in a continuous-time model. SCED is defined for cut-through servers and is analyzed in a discrete-time model, i.e., time assumes only integer values. Thus, we believe that RFS may be more applicable than SCED, since cut-through servers are not as common as feed-forward servers, and a discrete-time analysis is restricted to ATM (asynchronous transfer mode) servers.

7 Conclusions

We have presented the Rate-Function Scheduling (RFS) service discipline and its necessary and sufficient schedulability condition. One basic requirement is that a session must declare its required rate function at each link along a path carrying the session. The rate function allows for more flexible allocation of bandwidth, since a session can define service parameters such as long-term bandwidth and short-term bandwidth, which are not selectable with most other service disciplines. For a class of rate functions, which we show is sufficient for providing sessions with service bounds, RFS is as simple to implement and calculate service bounds as VirtualClock. We showed that RFS provides sessions with upper bounds on end-to-end delay and buffer space requirements.

We also showed that the NPEDF policy is a simple degeneration of RFS and that it lacks some of RFS' important properties, including performance isolation among sessions, bandwidth-fair operation, and work-conserving operation (which reduces average delay). We showed that RFS has a larger schedulability region than the "naive" rate-controlled NPEDF service discipline for connections with more than one server node and that RFS has at least the same schedulability region of the rate-controlled NPEDF service discipline that employs proper reshaping. Based on the above results, we believe that RFS is a feasible service discipline for networks that carry real-time traffic.

References

[1] R. L. Cruz, "A Calculus of Delay, Part I: Network Elements in Isolation," *In IEEE Transactions on Information Theory*, Vol. 37, No. 1, pp. 114-131, January 1991.

[2] R. L. Cruz, "Quality of Service Guarantees in Virtual Circuit Switched Networks," *In IEEE Journal on Selected Areas in Communications*, Vol. 13, No. 6, pp. 1048-56, August 1995.

[3] D. Ferrari and D. Verma, "A Scheme for Real-Time Channel Establishment in Wide-Area Networks," *In IEEE Journal on Selected Areas in Communications*, Vol. 8, No. 4, pp. 368-379, April 1990.

[4] N. R. Figueira and J. Pasquale, "A Schedulability Condition for Deadline-Based Service Disciplines," *To appear in IEEE/ACM Transactions on Networking*.

[5] N. R. Figueira and J. Pasquale, "An Upper Bound on Delay for the VirtualClock Service Discipline," *In IEEE/ACM Transactions on Networking*, Vol. 3, No. 4, pp. 399-408, August 1995.

[6] N. R. Figueira and J. Pasquale, "Leave-in-Time: A New Service Discipline for Control of Real-Time Communications in a Packet-Switching Network," *In Proceedings of ACM SIGCOMM '95*, pp. 207-218, August 1995.

[7] N. R. Figueira and J. Pasquale, "Rate-Function Scheduling," Technical Report CS96-488, Department of Computer Science and Engineering, University of California at San Diego, July 1996.

[8] L. Georgiadis, R. Guérin, and A. Parekh, "Optimal Multiplexing on a Single Link: Delay and Buffer Requirements," *In Proceedings of IEEE INFOCOM '94*, Vol. 2, pp. 524-532, June 1994.

[9] L. Georgiadis, R. Guérin, V. Peris, and K. N. Sivarajan, "Efficient Network QoS Provisioning Based on per Node Traffic Shaping," *In Proceedings of IEEE INFOCOM '96*, Vol. 1, pp. 102-110, March 1996.

[10] S. J. Golestani, "A Stop-and-Go Queueing Framework for Congestion Management," *In Proceedings of ACM SIGCOMM '90*, pp. 8-18, September 1990.

[11] C. Kalmanek, H. Kanakia, and S. Keshav, "Rate Controlled Servers for Very High-Speed Networks," *In Proceedings of IEEE GlobeCom '90*, pp. 300.3.1-300.3.9, December 1990.

[12] J. Liebeherr, D. E. Wrege, and D. Ferrari, "Exact Admission Control for Networks with Bounded Delay Services," Technical Report CS-94-29, University of Virginia, Department of Computer Science, July 1994.

[13] D. S. Mitrinovic, "Analytic Inequalities," Springer-Verlag, New York-Heidelberg-Berlin, 1970.

[14] A. K. Parekh, and G. Gallager, "A Generalized Processor Sharing Approach to Flow Control in Integrated Services Networks: The Single-Node Case," *In IEEE/ACM Transactions on Networking*, Vol. 1, No. 3, pp. 344-357, June 1993.

[15] H. Sariowan, R. L. Cruz, and G. C. Polyzos, "Scheduling for Quality of Service Guarantees via Service Curves," *International Conference on Computer Communications Networks*, September 1995.

[16] D. Verma, H. Zhang, and D. Ferrari, "Delay Jitter Control for Real-Time Communication in a Packet Switching Network," *In Proceedings of IEEE TriCom '91*, pp. 35-43, April 1991.

[17] H. Zhang and D. Ferrari, "Rate-Controlled Static-Priority Queueing," *In Proceedings of IEEE INFOCOM '93*, pp. 227-236, March 1993.

[18] H. Zhang and S. Keshav, "Comparison of Rate-Based Service Disciplines," *In Proceedings of ACM SIGCOMM '91*, pp. 113-121, August 1991.

[19] L. Zhang, "VirtualClock: A New Traffic Control Algorithm for Packet Switching Networks," *In ACM Transactions on Computer Systems*, Vol. 9, No. 2, pp. 101-124, May 1991.

[20] Q. Zheng and K. G. Shin, "On the Ability of Establishing Real-Time Channels in Point-to-Point Packet-Switched Networks," *In IEEE Transactions on Communications*, Vol. 42, No. 2/3/4, pp. 1096-1105, February/March/April 1994.

Real-time Cell Loss Ratio Estimation and Its Applications to ATM Traffic Controls

Shigeo SHIODA and Hiroshi SAITO

NTT Multimedia Networks Laboratories
3-9-11 Midori-cho, Musashino-shi, Tokyo, 180 Japan
s-sioda@hashi.tnl.ntt.jp

Abstract

The asymptotics of cell-loss ratio (CLR) in the regime of large buffers are characterized by two parameters, the asymptotic constant and asymptotic decay rate. Both parameters can be expanded in powers of one minus the link utilization (heavy traffic expansion). Thus, once the coefficients in this expansion are obtained, the CLR can be very easily estimated from the measured link utilization by using CLR asymptotics. This paper proposes an algorithm for estimating these coefficients in real time. For this purpose, the notion of state-space representation for a single-server queue is introduced: the elements of the state vector are the coefficients in the expansion of the asymptotic constant and asymptotic decay rate. Bayesian regression analysis is applied to estimate the state vector based on the buffer measurement. Our approach does not require any models describing the statistics of the traffic other than the asymptotic behavior of the CLR in the regime of large buffers. In addition, it allows us to estimate the effective bandwidth of the aggregated process easily, so it is applicable to a wide range of ATM traffic control methods, such as connection admission control and VP bandwidth control. We describe how this method of CLR estimation will be applied to connection admission control and VP bandwidth control by using results from simulation experiments.

Key words: *ATM, traffic control, VP bandwidth control, connection admission control, effective bandwidth, Bayesian estimation*

1 Introduction

In asynchronous transfer mode (ATM) networks, cell-loss ratio (CLR) and cell delay (variation) are considered to be the major quality-of-service (QoS) factors. Cell loss and cell delay mainly occur in the output buffers of the network nodes, on which the correlation of cell-interarrival time has a major impact. The bursty traffic models, such as the Markov modulated Poisson process (MMPP)[13], have been widely used as reference traffic models for ATM because these models can describe the correlation of cell-interarrival time. However, they involve a large number of parameters that describe the correlation of traffic input; this often makes analytical computation based on these models intractable. Application of these models to real-time traffic control, such as connection admission control (CAC), is almost impossible.

The cell-interarrival-time correlation is unlikely to be accurately estimated from measurements. No traffic descriptor has been proposed that provides relevant correlation information and is still easy to monitor. This has triggered a search for alternatives to performance evaluation in ATM; we do not need to know everything about the correlation from the measurement; rather we should make reasonable assumptions about the correlation *a priori*. Some evaluation formulas for the CLR, e.g. the "burst overflow rate" [15] and the "cell-loss-ratio upper bound" [16, 17, 21], were proposed in this context. These evaluate the performance in the limit of long-range correlation; in other words, the burst duration time is infinite. Performance evaluation in the long-range-correlation limit is attractive for conservative traffic management in the sense that it usually gives the worst case performance. Furthermore, much less computation is required than in the bursty traffic models. In some cases, however, the worst case performance is very different from the actual performance, which might lead to overallocation of network resources.

Other alternatives, mainly for application to connection admission control, have been proposed. These methods use real-time measurements, compensating for the above long-range-correlation assumption [9, 11, 17, 18]. There is, however, still controversy about which parameters should be measured and a unified framework has not yet been developed.

Recent progress in queueing analysis based on the large deviation principle theoretically reveals that, for a wide-ranging traffic input, the CLR exponentially decays as the buffer size increases [4, 7]. The CLR in the regime of large buffers is thus characterized by two parameters, the asymptotic constant β, and the asymptotic decay rate η, such that

$$CLR = \beta e^{-K\eta}, \qquad (1)$$

where K is the buffer size. This asymptotic naturally interpolates between the CLR in the long-range-correlation limit and the actual CLR: the asymptotic

0-8186-7780-5/97 $10.00 © 1997 IEEE

constant gives the CLR in the long-range-correlation limit, and the asymptotic decay rate determines how the actual CLR becomes smaller than the long-range-correlation-limit CLR due to the effect of cell buffering. It has been reported that these two parameters can be expanded in powers of one minus the link utilization ρ (traffic intensity) [5]. Therefore, if we knew the coefficients in this expansion *a priori*, we could guess the CLR simply from the measurement of link utilization.

The aim of this paper is to design an algorithm for estimating these coefficients on an on-line basis from the buffer measurement. For this purpose, the notion of the state-space representation for a single-server queue is introduced: the elements of the state vector are the coefficients in the expansion of the asymptotic constant and asymptotic decay rate. The state vector can be estimated by Bayesian regression analysis based on the buffer measurement. As explained in the above paragraph, once we have obtained the coefficients in the expansions of β and η, we can easily estimate the CLR under various link utilizations. Our approach does not require any models describing the statistics of the traffic besides the asymptotic behavior of the CLR in the regime of large buffers. This will have a large advantage over traditional queueing analyses based on parametric models because, in ATM, the traffic statistics may be quite complex and the appropriate statistical model seems to be difficult to identify. In addition, our proposal allows us to estimate the *effective bandwidth* of the aggregated process easily, so it might be applicable to a wide range of traffic control in ATM, as shown in this paper.

This paper is organized as follows. In Section 2, we show recent results regarding asymptotic behavior of the CLR in the regime of large buffers. In Section 3, the notion of state-space representation of the single-server queue is introduced. The state vector estimation of the single-server queue based on the buffer measurement is also described in this section. Once the state vector has been obtained, we can easily estimate the effective bandwidth of aggregated sources. In Sections 4 and 5, we describe how our proposal can be applied to connection admission control and VP bandwidth control, respectively. Finally, in Section 6, several simulation results are presented to demonstrate the effectiveness of our proposal.

2 Cell-loss-ratio asymptotics

2.1 Cell-loss-ratio asymptotics and effective bandwidth

In this section, we overview recent results concerning CLR asymptotics in the regime of large buffers [3, 4, 7, 10].

Consider a single server queue that has an infinite buffer with stationary and ergodic cell arrivals from a single source. Let A_t denote the number of arrivals during $(0,t]$, and let Q be the number of customers in the queue in the stationary state. The rate function of the arrival process is defined by

$$I(x) \stackrel{\text{def}}{=} \lim_{t\to\infty} \log P(A_t > xt), \quad (2)$$

whenever this limit exists. The large deviation principle tells us that the logarithm of the queue length distribution has the following asymptotics:

$$\lim_{k\to\infty} \frac{1}{k} \log P(Q \geq k) = -\eta. \quad (3)$$

Moreover,

$$\eta = \inf_{x>0} \frac{I(x)}{x-C}, \quad (4)$$

where C is the number of cells that can be served in unit time. This implies the following asymptotic tail distribution of queue length:

$$p_k \stackrel{\text{def}}{=} P(Q \geq k) \approx \beta e^{-\eta k}. \quad (5)$$

It is known that the CLR of a single-server queue with a finite buffer size, K, is less than p_K [7]. Hence, we have

$$CLR \leq \beta e^{-\eta K}. \quad (6)$$

Equation (4) is not convenient for obtaining the asymptotic decay rate η. Let $M(\theta)$ be the cumulant generating function

$$M(\theta) \stackrel{\text{def}}{=} \lim_{t\to\infty} \frac{1}{t} \log E\exp[\theta A_t]. \quad (7)$$

It is obtained from the Legendre transform of the rate-function, that is

$$M(\theta) = \sup_x \{x\theta - I(x)\}. \quad (8)$$

Combining Eqs. (4) and (8) yields the following simple relation [4, 7]:

$$\eta = \sup\{\theta : \frac{M(\theta)}{\theta} \leq C\}. \quad (9)$$

Equation (9) is a key for deriving the notion of *effective bandwidth* [4]. From Eq. (6), the QoS objective of the CLR, CLR_{objec}, is satisfied if

$$\eta \geq \eta_{objec} \stackrel{\text{def}}{=} \frac{\log\beta - \log CLR_{objec}}{K}. \quad (10)$$

According to Chang [4], $M(\theta)/\theta$ is an increasing function of θ. Substituting Eq. (10) into Eq. (9) thus yields the following necessary and sufficient condition for meeting the QoS objective of the CLR:

$$\alpha(\eta_{objec}) \stackrel{\text{def}}{=} \frac{M(\eta_{objec})}{\eta_{objec}} \leq C. \quad (11)$$

The function $\alpha(\eta)$ is called the effective bandwidth function of the source subjective to the condition that the tail distribution of the queue length has the decay rate η. In particular, we simply call $\alpha(\eta_{objec})$ "effective bandwidth", given the decay rate objective η_{objec}. In general, the effective bandwidth satisfies the *additive* property [4]; that is, the effective bandwidth of the aggregation of independent sources is equal to the sum of the effective bandwidths of aggregated sources. Thus, when the single server queue is shared by N independent sources, Eq. (11) is written as

$$\sum_{n=1}^{N} \alpha_n(\eta_{objec}) \leq C, \tag{12}$$

where $\alpha_n(\cdot)$ is the *effective bandwidth* function of the n-th source. Equation (10) implies that if the sum of effective bandwidths of the multiplexed sources is less than the link capacity, the QoS objective is satisfied.

Elwalid *et al.* made an intuitive and quite clear argument about the asymptotic constant [10]: they show that, when N on-off sources are multiplexed, the asymptotic constant is (approximately) given by

$$\begin{aligned} \beta &= \sum_{n:n\cdot M \geq C}^{N} \binom{N}{n} \left(\frac{A}{M}\right)^n \left(1 - \frac{A}{M}\right)^{N-n} \\ &\sim \exp\{-N(c\log\frac{c}{p} + (1-c)\log\frac{1-c}{1-p})\}, \end{aligned} \tag{13}$$

where

$$c \stackrel{\text{def}}{=} \frac{C}{NM}, \qquad p \stackrel{\text{def}}{=} \frac{A}{M}, \tag{14}$$

and "A" is the average rate and "M" is the peak rate of each on-off source. The right side of Eq. (13) is same as the CLR given by the buffer-less model [14, 15, 16], which has been used as the approximate estimate of the CLR in the extreme-correlation case.

2.2 Heavy traffic expansion

Provided that the input process satisfies some mild technical conditions, effective bandwidth function $\alpha(\theta)$ strictly increases for θ [4]. Hence, η is given by the unique solution of the following equation:

$$\alpha(\eta) = C. \tag{15}$$

The effective bandwidth function $\alpha(\eta)$ can be expanded by η (Cumulant Expansion) as follows:

$$\begin{aligned} \alpha(\eta) &= \lim_{t\to\infty} \frac{1}{t\eta} \log E[e^{A_t\eta}], \\ &= \lim_{t\to\infty} \frac{1}{t\eta} \sum_{k=1}^{\infty} \frac{\langle A_t^k \rangle_c}{k!} \eta^k, \end{aligned} \tag{16}$$

where $\langle A_t^k \rangle_c$ is called the k-th cumulant. It is easy to see the following:

$$\begin{aligned} \langle A_t^1 \rangle_c &= E[A_t], \\ \langle A_t^2 \rangle_c &= Var[A_t], \end{aligned} \tag{17}$$

where $Var[\cdot]$ denotes the variance. Equation (16) is further simplified as follows:

$$\alpha(\eta) = A \sum_{k=0}^{\infty} d_k^{(2)} \eta^k, \tag{18}$$

where

$$d_k^{(2)} = \lim_{t\to\infty} \frac{\langle A_t^{k+1} \rangle_c}{(k+1)!\langle A_t^1 \rangle_c}, \tag{19}$$

and A is the average cell rate. Substituting Eq. (18) into Eq. (15) yields the following simple relation:

$$\frac{1-\rho}{\rho} = \sum_{k=1}^{\infty} d_k^{(2)} \eta^k, \tag{20}$$

where ρ is VP utilization. Regarding the asymptotic constant, we also have the following similar expansion by η [3, 23]:

$$\begin{aligned} \log\beta &= \sum_{k=1}^{\infty} d_k^{(1)} \eta^k, \\ d_k^{(1)} &= -\lim_{t\to\infty} \{\langle A_t^k \rangle_c - (\lim_{t\to\infty} \frac{\langle A_t^k \rangle_c}{t})t\}. \end{aligned} \tag{21}$$

Once we know the coefficients, $\{d_i^{(1)}\}$ and $\{d_i^{(2)}\}$, the effective bandwidth of the source can be estimated simply. For example, by taking only the first term in the expansion of η in Eq. (21), we have

$$\begin{aligned} \eta_{objec} &= \frac{\log\beta - \log CLR_{objec}}{K} \\ &\approx \frac{d_1^{(1)}\eta_{objec} - \log CLR_{objec}}{K}, \end{aligned} \tag{22}$$

or

$$\eta_{objec} = \frac{\log CLR_{objec}}{d_1^{(1)} - K}. \tag{23}$$

We therefore have

$$\begin{aligned} \alpha(\eta_{objec}) &= A\{1 + d_1^{(2)} \frac{\log CLR_{objec}}{d_1^{(1)} - K} \\ &\quad + d_2^{(2)} (\frac{\log CLR_{objec}}{d_1^{(1)} - K})^2 + \cdots\}. \end{aligned} \tag{24}$$

The reversion of the series of Eq. (20) yields the following (Heavy Traffic Expansion) [5]:

$$\eta = \sum_{k=1}^{\infty} c_k^{(2)} (\frac{1-\rho}{\rho})^k, \tag{25}$$

and similarly,

$$\log\beta = \sum_{k=1}^{\infty} c_k^{(1)} (\frac{1-\rho}{\rho})^k, \tag{26}$$

where $\{c_i^{(1)}\}$ and $\{c_i^{(2)}\}$ are given in terms of $\{d_i^{(1)}\}$ and $\{d_i^{(2)}\}$ [5]: for example

$$\begin{aligned} c_1^{(1)} &= \frac{d_1^{(1)}}{d_1^{(2)}}, \quad c_2^{(1)} = \frac{d_1^{(2)} d_2^{(1)} - d_1^{(1)} d_2^{(2)}}{(d_1^{(2)})^3}, \\ c_1^{(2)} &= \frac{1}{d_1^{(2)}}, \quad c_2^{(2)} = -\frac{d_2^{(2)}}{(d_1^{(2)})^3}. \end{aligned} \tag{27}$$

These expansions enable us to estimate the CLR under different utilizations.

3 Bayesian regression analysis for the cell-loss ratio

In this section, we propose a method for estimating these coefficients, $\{d_i^{(1)}\}$ and $\{d_i^{(2)}\}$, in real time from the buffer measurement. Suppose that, at two different thresholds, k_1 and k_2, the buffer occupancy levels $\{p_{k_j} : j = 1,2\}$ and the link utilization are periodically observed. Let $\{p_{k_j}(n)\}$ and $\{\rho(n)\}$ be the buffer occupancy levels and the link utilization of the n-th measurement, respectively.

The asymptotics of the queue length distribution (Eq. (5)) yield

$$\begin{aligned} \eta(n) &= \frac{\log p_{k_1}(n) - \log p_{k_2}(n)}{k_2 - k_1}, \\ \log\beta(n) &= \frac{k_2}{k_2 - k_1}\log p_{k_1}(n) \\ &\quad - \frac{k_1}{k_2 - k_1}\log p_{k_2}(n). \end{aligned} \quad (28)$$

Furthermore, assume the following relations:

$$\begin{aligned} \log\beta(n) &= \sum_{i=1}^{I_1} d_i^{(1)}(n)\eta(n)^i + \sigma_1(n), \\ \frac{1-\rho(n)}{\rho(n)} &= \sum_{i=1}^{I_2} d_i^{(2)}(n)\eta(n)^i + \sigma_2(n), \end{aligned} \quad (29)$$

where $\sigma_j(n)$ is Gaussian white noise, representing the measurement error. To take into account traffic pattern variation, suppose that the coefficients $\{d_i^{(1)}\}, \{d_i^{(2)}\}$ (system characteristics) can change with time according to the following equations:

$$\begin{aligned} d_i^{(1)}(n) &= d_i^{(1)}(n-1) + \omega_i^{(1)}(n), \\ &\qquad i = 1,\cdots,I_1, \\ d_i^{(2)}(n) &= d_i^{(2)}(n-1) + \omega_i^{(2)}(n), \\ &\qquad i = 1,\cdots,I_2, \end{aligned} \quad (30)$$

where $\omega_i^{(1)}(n)$ and $\omega_i^{(2)}(n)$ are also Gaussian white noise with mean 0. Equations (29) and (30) are written in vector form as

$$\begin{aligned} \boldsymbol{x}(n) &= \boldsymbol{x}(n-1) + \boldsymbol{\omega}(n), \\ \boldsymbol{p}(n) &= H\boldsymbol{x}(n) + \boldsymbol{\sigma}(n), \end{aligned} \quad (31)$$

where

$$\begin{aligned} \boldsymbol{x}(n) &= (d_1^{(1)}(n), \cdots d_{I_1}^{(1)}(n), \\ &\qquad d_1^{(2)}(n), \cdots, d_{I_2}^{(2)}(n))^T, \\ \boldsymbol{p}(n) &= (\log\beta(n), (1-\rho(n))/\rho(n))^T, \\ \boldsymbol{\omega}(n) &= (\omega_1^{(1)}(n), \cdots, \omega_{I_1}^{(1)}(n), \\ &\qquad \omega_1^{(2)}(n), \cdots, \omega_{I_2}^{(2)}(n))^T, \\ \boldsymbol{\sigma}(n) &= (\sigma_1(n), \sigma_2(n))^T, \end{aligned} \quad (32)$$

and

$$H = \begin{bmatrix} \eta & \cdots & \eta^{I_1} & 0 & \cdots & 0 \\ 0 & \cdots & 0 & \eta & \cdots & \eta^{I_2} \end{bmatrix}. \quad (33)$$

In the terminology of the control system, Eq. (31) is called the "state-space representation" of a single server queue, and the vector $\boldsymbol{x}$ is the state vector of the system. Bayesian regression analysis can be applied to estimate the state vector $\boldsymbol{x}$. The state vector can be recursively estimated at the end of every measurement epoch by the following Kalman Filter formulation:

[State Renewal]

$$\begin{aligned} \hat{\boldsymbol{x}}(n) &= \hat{\boldsymbol{x}}(n \mid n-1) \\ &\quad + K_n(\boldsymbol{p}(n) - H\hat{\boldsymbol{x}}(n \mid n-1)), \\ K_n &= X(n|n-1)H^T(HX(n \mid n-1)H^T \\ &\qquad + \Sigma(n))^{-1}, \\ X(n) &= (I - K_nH^T)X(n|n-1), \\ \Sigma &\stackrel{\text{def}}{=} E\{\boldsymbol{\sigma}(n)\boldsymbol{\sigma}^T(n)\}. \end{aligned} \quad (34)$$

[Projection]

$$\begin{aligned} &\hat{\boldsymbol{x}}(n \mid n-1) = \hat{\boldsymbol{x}}(n-1), \\ &X(n \mid n-1) = X(n-1) + \Omega(n), \\ &\Omega(n) \stackrel{\text{def}}{=} E\{\boldsymbol{\omega}(n)\boldsymbol{\omega}^T(n)\}. \end{aligned} \quad (35)$$

Here $\hat{\boldsymbol{x}}(n)$ and $\hat{\boldsymbol{x}}(n|n-1)$ are respectively estimates of the state vector $\boldsymbol{x}(n)$ at the n-th and $n-1$-th measurement epochs, and $X(n)$ and $X(n|n-1)$ are respectively the covariant matrices of $\hat{\boldsymbol{x}}(n)$ and $\hat{\boldsymbol{x}}(n|n-1)$. Initial values (and variances) of the state vector can, for example, be given under the assumption that A_t is a stationary Gaussian process, and we have

$$\begin{aligned} &d_1^{(1)} = 0, \\ &d_1^{(2)} = IDC \stackrel{\text{def}}{=} \lim_{t\to\infty} \frac{Var[A_t]}{E[A_t]}, \\ &d_i^{(2)} = 0 \qquad \text{for all } i \geq 2. \end{aligned} \quad (36)$$

(The first two are valid even for the case where A_t is not Gaussian.)

4 Application to connection admission control

The notion of effective bandwidth is very attractive for CAC because the connection acceptance can be judged simply by comparing the link capacity and the sum of effective bandwidths of individual virtual channel (VC) connections. The drawback to the effective bandwidth approach is that it might be quite conservative due to its essential neglect of statistical multiplexing gains [6]. This problem could be overcome by estimating the effective bandwidth of the aggregated connections based on real-time measurement. Several proposals for estimating the effective bandwidth of aggregated connections have been made [8, 12, 24, 25]: for example, Duffield et al. [8] proposed using Eq. (9) directly for effective bandwidth estimation based on the measured number of cells arriving during a very short time period. Gün et al. [12, 24] proposed estimating the effective bandwidth of the source policed by the leaky bucket scheme based on the negotiated peak cell rate, monitored average cell rate, and the probability that the token pool is empty. Veciana et al. [25] proposed measuring the asymptotic constant of aggregated sources to obtain grater accuracy for effective bandwidth estimation. Our proposal for effective bandwidth estimation in Sections 2.2 and 3 differs from these proposals in the following points: unlike [8], our proposed method dose not need to measure the number of cells in very short periods; unlike [12, 24], it does not need to know the peak cell rate; and unlike [25] it takes into account the utilization dependency of the asymptotic constant.

Consider the adaptive CAC implementation by combining the effective bandwidth estimation of Eq. (24) and the Bayesian regression analysis of Section 3. First, by using the technique in Section 3, one estimates the coefficients in the heavy traffic expansion of the queue length distribution periodically. At the connection-setup phase, one evaluates the effective bandwidth required for the multiplexed VC connections by Eq. (24). The residual capacity of the VP is therefore given by the link capacity minus the estimated effective bandwidth of the multiplexed VCs. The connection admission can be judged by comparing the residual capacity of the VP and the effective bandwidth required for a newly requested VC connection.

The effective bandwidth of a newly requested VC connection must be evaluated from a source traffic descriptor. The following theorem [22] shows that its effective bandwidth should be given by its peak cell rate even if its sustainable cell rate is notified.

Theorem 4.1 *The largest effective bandwidth of the VC connection whose traffic parameters are peak and sustainable cell rates is given by the peak cell rate regardless of the sustainable-cell-rate value.*

In the following, we show the simplest realization of CAC by setting $I_1 = I_2 = 1$, where only two parameters, $d_1^{(1)}$ and $d_2^{(1)}$, should be identified. Suppose that an output buffer is dedicated to each VP at the virtual channel handler (VCH) (Fig. 1). The CAC based on the real-time estimate of the effective bandwidth can be implemented as follows (Fig. 2):

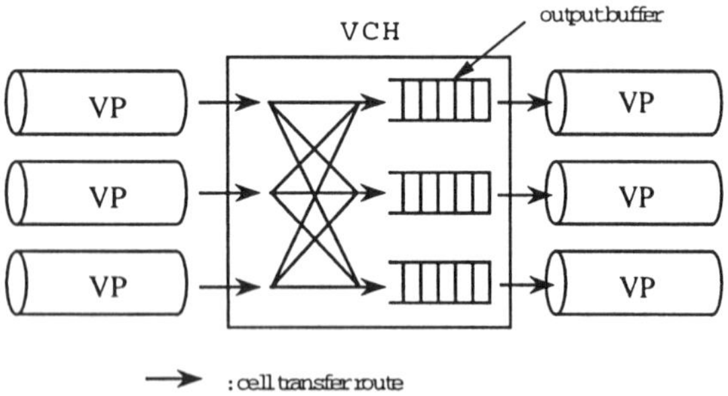

Fig. 1. Virtual channel handler.

1. At two different thresholds, k_1 and k_2, the frequencies by which the number of cells in the output buffer exceeds the thresholds, p_{k_1} and p_{k_2}, are periodically measured.

2. At the end of every measurement period, the coefficients, $d_1^{(1)}$ and $d_1^{(2)}$, are updated in the manner explained in Section 3.

3. Let Ω_n be the set of VC connections established during the n-th period, and $\hat{\Omega}_n$ be the set of VC connections that are multiplexed at the beginning of the n-th period. When a connection-set-up request arrives, the effective bandwidth required for the aggregation of VC connections in $\hat{\Omega}_n$, α_{agg}, is evaluated by the following:
$$\alpha_{agg} = \sum_{l \in \hat{\Omega}_n} A_l^*(1 + d_1^{(2)} \frac{\log CLR_{objec}}{d_1^{(1)} - K}), \quad (37)$$
where A_l^* is the negotiated sustainable cell rate of the l-th connection. On the other hand, the effective bandwidth of the l-th connection in Ω_n is assumed to be given by its negotiated peak cell rate, M_l^*.

4. Let M_{new}^* be the negotiated peak cell rate of a newly requested connection. If
$$\alpha_{agg} + \sum_{l \in \Omega_n} M_l^* + M_{new}^* \leq C, \quad (38)$$
the newly requested connection is established and the established connection is added to the set Ω_n; otherwise, the connection-setup request is rejected.

5. If a connection in Ω_n or $\hat{\Omega}_n$ is released during the n-th period, it is removed from Ω_n or $\hat{\Omega}_n$, respectively.

5 Application to VP bandwidth control

The VP bandwidth control that dynamically allocates VP bandwidth according to variations in traffic demand is very important [1, 2, 19, 20]. Most previous studies (e.g. [19]) on VP bandwidth control consider the case where the switched bandwidth-guaranteed VCs are multiplexed in the VP. In such a case, the cell-level QoS is always guaranteed by the combination of CAC and UPC; therefore a shortage of VP bandwidth leads to an increase in call blocking probability without affecting the cell-level QoS. The VP bandwidth control should therefore be triggered based on the measurement of the call blockings.

Regarding the VPs where best-effort VCs are multiplexed, however, the call blocking does not give enough information on VP congestion because ATM provides insufficient functions for guaranteeing cell-level QoS for these VCs. (The network might accept the VC-connection-set-up request even if the cell-level QoS deteriorates.) As for the VPs that multiplex the permanent VCs, call blocking cannot be observed. Therefore, the cell-level QOS must be measured to apply VP bandwidth control to such VPs.

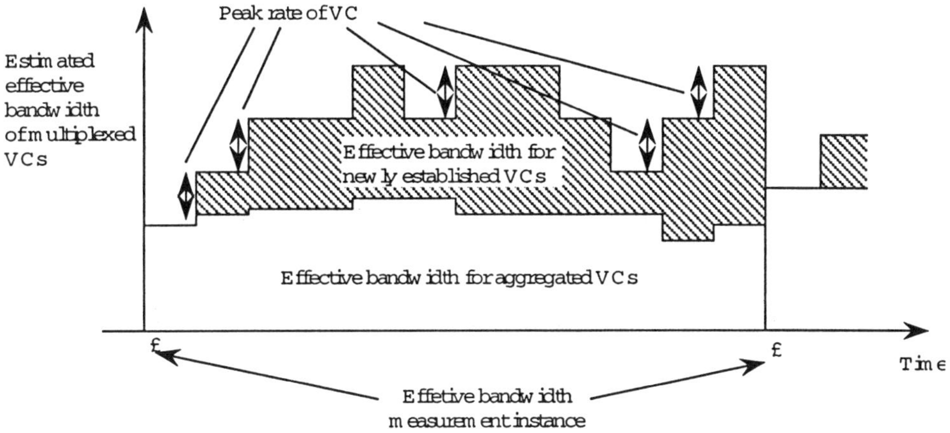

Fig. 2. Effective bandwidth estimation.

The simplest realization of VP bandwidth control is to replace the VP bandwidth by the estimated effective bandwidth of the cell stream transferred in VP. The estimated effective bandwidth is, for example, given by

$$\alpha = A(1 + d_1^{(2)} \frac{\log CLR_{objec}}{d_1^{(1)} - K}), \tag{39}$$

where A is the observed average cell rate of the cell stream transferred in the VP. Thus, VP bandwidth control based on the buffer measurement can be implemented as follows:

1. At two different thresholds, k_1 and k_2, the frequencies by which the number of cells in the buffer exceeds the thresholds, p_{k_1} and p_{k_2}, are measured at the output buffers dedicated to the VP to be controlled.
2. The unknown parameters, $d_1^{(1)}, d_1^{(2)}$, are periodically estimated and updated in the manner explained in Section 3.
3. At every updating, the bandwidth of the VP is replaced by the effective bandwidth estimated by Eq. (39).

6 Simulation

6.1 Connection admission control

Here we describe simulation experiments when the CAC proposed in Section 4 was applied. The simulation conditions were as follows:

1. The VP bandwidth was 90 Mbps, and the buffer size was 128 cells.
2. At two different thresholds, the frequencies in which the number of cells in the buffer was greater than or equal to the thresholds were measured every 5 seconds. The thresholds were set at 7 and 20.
3. The unknown parameters, $d_1^{(1)}$ and $d_1^{(2)}$, in Eq. (37) were estimated by the Bayesian regression analysis of Section 3 every 5 seconds.
4. The connection-establishing requests arrived according to the Poisson process and the mean holding time of each VC connection was 100 s. When the requests arrived, the CAC proposed in Section 4 was performed. The CLR objective was 10^{-8}.
5. Each VC had on and off states. In the off-states, no cells were offered from the VC. In the on-states, cells were offered from each VC at a rate of 10 Mbps. The average rate of each VC was 2 Mbps. The durations of each on-state and each off-state were exponentially distributed, and the mean duration of the on-state was 1 ms.

Figure 3 shows the sample path of the number of multiplexed VC connections under the proposed CAC when the offered traffic of connections was 40 erlang. The multiplexable limits under the worst-case CAC proposed by Saito [16] and the theoretically multiplexable limit, given complete statistical information about cell arrivals, are also shown. (Note that complete statistical information is not available in actual situations.) Greater statistical multiplexing gain was obtained under the proposed CAC compared to the worst-case CAC. The worst-case CAC determines the connection acceptance assuming the long-range-correlation limit; instead, the proposed CAC can take into account the correlation of cell-interarrival-time indirectly measured by the buffer-occupancy level. No cell loss was found in simulation, so the CLR objective was certainly satisfied in the simulation.

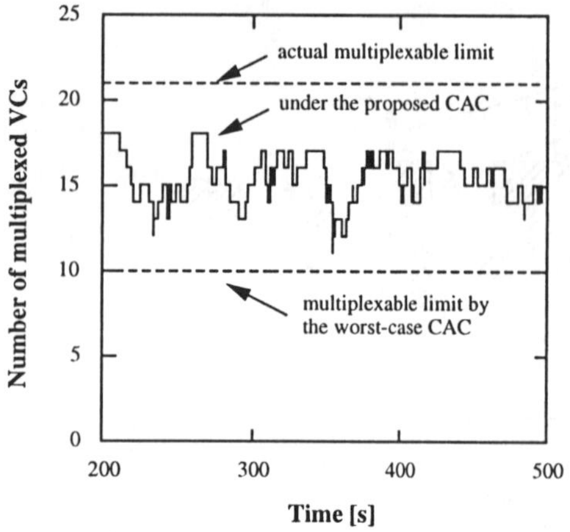

Fig. 3. Number of multiplexed connections under the proposed CAC (Average bit rate = 2 Mbps).

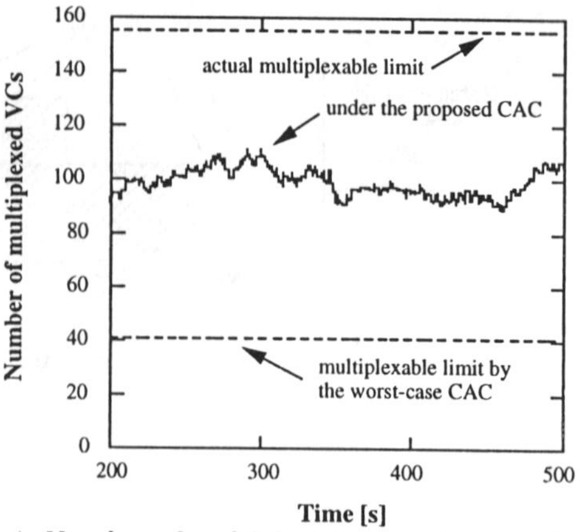

Fig. 4. Number of multiplexed connections under the proposed CAC (Average bit rate = 0.2 Mbps).

Figure 4 also shows the sample path of the number of multiplexed VC connections when the average cell rate of each VC connection is 0.2 Mbps, and the offered traffic of connections is 200 erlang. In this case, the burstiness factor (peak cell rate / average cell rate) of the connection is much higher than in the previous case, but the proposed CAC still works well and no cell loss was observed during the simulation. Greater statistical multiplexing gain was also obtained compared with the worst-case CAC.

6.2 VP bandwidth control

Figures 5 and 6 show the dynamic behavior of the VP bandwidth under the VP bandwidth control proposed in Section 5. The simulation conditions were as follows:

1. The VP bandwidth was initially 3 Mbps, and the buffer size was 128 cells.

2. The cells from 10 on-off sources arrived at the output buffer dedicated to the VP. In the on-states, cells were offered from each VC at a rate of 1 Mbps (Figure 5) or 10 Mbps (Figure 6). The average rate of each VC was 0.1 Mbps. The durations of each on-state and each off-state were exponentially distributed, and the mean duration of the on-state was 1 ms.

3. At two different thresholds, the frequencies in which the number of cells in the buffer was greater than or equal to the thresholds were measured every 20 minutes. The thresholds were set at 5 and 20.

4. Every 20 minutes, the unknown parameters, $d_1^{(1)}$ and $d_1^{(2)}$, in Eq. (39) were estimated, and the VP bandwidth was adjusted by the proposed formula. The CLR objective was 10^{-8}.

The actually required VP bandwidth was calculated through an analytical method [3, 7], given complete information about the stochastic cell arrival process. Monitoring the queueing behavior and updating the estimate caused the VP bandwidth to converge to a value slightly larger than the actually required VP bandwidth in Fig. 5. In Fig. 6, the VP bandwidth control based on buffer measurement also shows good performance, although it gives a slightly smaller VP bandwidth than the analytical method.

These figures show the measured CLR and the measured frequencies in which the number of cells in the buffer is greater than or equal to the given threshold. The measured CLR is too small except when the VP bandwidth is too small. However, the measured frequencies in which the number of cells exceeds the threshold give us stable congestion information, which enables us to control the VP bandwidth smoothly.

7 Conclusion

We proposed estimating the CLR based on its asymptotics, and discussed its application to CAC and VP bandwidth control. Simulation experiments using on/off sources showed this proposal to be quite promising, but further experiments with real traffic data will be required. There are other proposals for estimating the effective bandwidth [8, 11, 12, 25], which could possibly be applied to CAC and VP bandwidth control. Quantitative comparison of our proposal with these alternatives still remains for further study.

References

[1] N. G. Anerousis and A. A. Lazar, "Managing virtual paths on Xunet III: architecture, experimental platform and performance", *Fourth International Symposium on Integrated Network Management,* 1995.

[2] A. Ardvisson, "Management of reconfigurable virtual path networks," *ITC 14,* pp. 931-940, 1994.

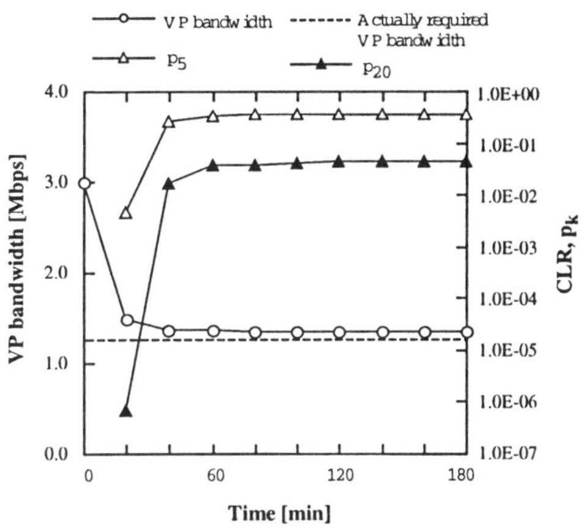

Fig. 5. Sample path of VP bandwidth under the proposed control (Peak bit rate = 1 Mbps).

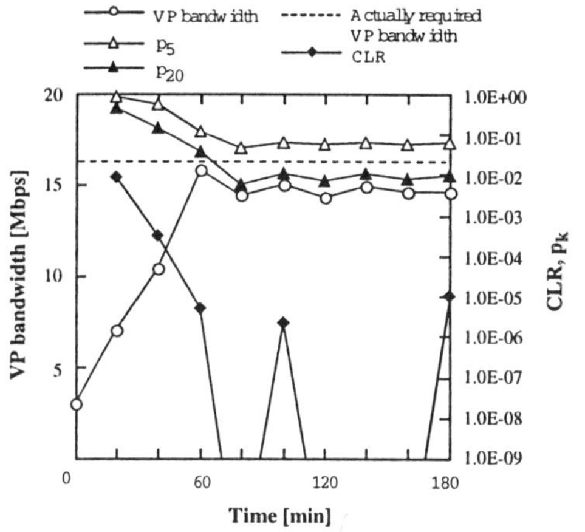

Fig. 6. Sample path of VP bandwidth under the proposed control (Peak bit rate = 10 Mbps).

[3] D. Botvich, and N. Duffield, "Large deviations, the shape of the loss curve, and economics of scale in large multiplexers," *Queueing Systems*, vol. 20, pp. 293-320, 1995.

[4] C. S. Chang, "Stability, queue length, and delay of deterministic and stochastic queueing networks," *IEEE Trans. Auto. Cont.*, vol. 39, no. 5, pp. 913-931, 1994.

[5] G. L. Choudhury, and W. Whitt, "Heavy-traffic asymptotic expansions for the asymptotic decay rates in the BMAP/G/1 queue," *Commun. Statist. – Stochastic Models*, vol. 10, no. 2, pp. 453-498, 1995.

[6] G. L. Choudhury, D. M. Lucantoni, and W. Whitt, "On the effectiveness of effective bandwidths for admission control in ATM networks," *ITC 14*, pp. 411-420, 1994.

[7] N. G. Duffield, "Exponential bounds for queues with Markovian arrivals," *Queueing Systems*, vol. 17, pp. 413-430, 1994.

[8] N. G. Duffield, J. T. Lewis, N. O'Connell, R. Russel, and F. Toomey, "Entropy of ATM traffic streams: A tool for estimating QoS parameters," *IEEE J. S. A. C.*, vol. 13, no. 6, pp. 981-990, 1995.

[9] Z. Dziong, O. Montauny, and L. G. Mason, "Adaptive traffic admission in ATM networks - optimal estimation framework," *ITC 14*, pp. 1065-1076, 1994.

[10] A. Elwalid, D. Heyman, T. V. Lakshman, D. Mitra, and A. Weiss, "Fundamental bounds and approximations for ATM multiplexers with applications to video teleconferencing," *IEEE J. S. A. C.*, vol. 13, no. 6, pp. 1004-1016, 1995.

[11] R. J. Gibbens, F. P. Kelly, and P. B. Key, "A decision-theoretic approach to call admission control in ATM networks," *IEEE J. S. A. C.*, vol. 13, no. 6, pp. 1101-1114, 1995.

[12] L. Gün, "An approximation method for capturing complex traffic behavior in high speed networks," *Performance Evaluation*, vol. 19, pp. 5-23, 1994.

[13] H. Heffes, and D. M. Lucantoni, "A Markov modulated characterization of packetized voice and data traffic and related statistical multiplexer performance," *IEEE J. S. A. C.*, vol. 4, pp. 856-868, 1986.

[14] F. P. Kelly, "Effective bandwidths at multi-class queues." *Queueing Systems*, vol. 9, pp. 5-16, 1991.

[15] T. Murase, H. Suzuki, and T. Takeuchi, "A call admission control for ATM networks based on individual multiplexed traffic characteristics," *ICC '91*, pp. 391-396, 1991.

[16] H. Saito, "Call admission control in ATM networks using upper bound of cell loss probability," *IEEE Trans. Commun.*, vol. 40, no. 9, pp. 1512-1521, 1992.

[17] H. Saito and K. Shiomoto, "Dynamic call admission control in ATM networks," *IEEE J. S. A. C.*, vol. 9, No. 7, pp. 982-989, 1991.

[18] H. Saito, "Adaptive CACs using bayesian performance estimation," *ICCCN '95*, 1995.

[19] S. Shioda, "Evaluating the performance of virtual path bandwidth control in ATM networks," *IEICE Trans. Commun.*, vol. E77-B, No. 10, pp. 1175-1187, 1994.

[20] S. Shioda et al., "Sizing and provisioning for physical and virtual path networks using self-sizing capability," *IEICE Trans. Commun.*, vol. E80-B, No. 2, 1997.

[21] S. Shioda and H. Saito, "Cell-loss-ratio analysis with insufficient knowledge of traffic characteristics," *Journal of Operation Research Society of Japan* (to appear).

[22] S. Shioda, and H. Saito, "Real-time cell loss ratio estimation and its applications to ATM traffic controls," *IEEE/ACM Trans. Networking* (submitted).

[23] S. Shioda, H. Toyoizumi, H. Yokoi, T. Tsuchiya, and H. Saito, "Self-sizing network: a new network concept based on autonomous VP bandwidth adjustment," *ITC 15* (submitted).

[24] T. E. Tedijanto, and L. Gün, "Effectiveness of dynamic bandwidth management mechanisms in ATM netwroks," *INFOCOM '93*, pp. 358-367, 1993.

[25] G. Veciana, G. Kesidis, and J. Walrand, "Resource management in wide-area ATM networks using effective bandwidth," *IEEE J. S. A. C.*, vol. 13, no. 6, pp. 1081-1090, 1995.

Switch-Aided Flooding Operations in ATM Networks

*Yih Huang and Philip K. McKinley**

Department of Computer Science
Michigan State University
East Lansing, Michigan 48824
{huangyih, mckinley}@cps.msu.edu

Abstract

In this paper, we propose a flooding method, called Switch-Aided Flooding (SAF), for use in ATM networks. SAF-based protocols take advantage of hardware-supported cell relay and cell duplication, characteristic of such networks, in order to reduce the time needed to disseminate changes in network topology and resource availability. SAF protocols use a spanning multipoint connection (SMC), which is a hardware-switched network spanning tree, but revert to conventional link-by-link flooding when the spanning MC is unavailable or under construction. The results of a simulation study reveal that the proposed flooding protocols deliver network updates several times faster than conventional approaches, while using significantly less bandwidth.

1 Introduction

ATM is a connection-oriented network switching protocol that uses small fixed-size transmission units, called *cells*, to facilitate hardware switching. An ATM cell comprises a 5-byte header and 48 bytes of data payload. An ATM switch comprises a switching fabric (the hardware component that performs hardware cell relaying), a set of input and output ports connected to incident transmission links, and a set of signaling modules that execute on a control processor. Prior to transmission, end hosts use a signaling protocol to establish a *virtual circuit* (VC), which defines a route from source to destination. During transmission, each cell is tagged with a *virtual circuit identifier* (VCI); each switching fabric receiving the cell uses the VCI to determine the output port(s) on which to place the cell.[1] In addition to cell relaying, many ATM switches are equipped with switching fabrics that support hardware cell duplication, such that an incoming cell can be forwarded to multiple output ports. In this manner, such switches implement hardware *multicast*, a communication operation whereby a traffic stream is routed to more than one destination.

The multicast capability of ATM switches enables the construction of many-to-many VCs, or *multipoint connections* (MCs). An example of an MC is depicted in Figure 1, where a set of eight switches is interconnected with a tree topology. As illustrated, the responsibility of each member switch is to forward cells arriving on one link of the tree to all the other tree links that are incident to that switch. A special type of MC, whose use is discussed later, is the *spanning* MC (SMC), which includes all switches in a network as its members. An SMC of a network can be considered as a virtual broadcast medium of the network.

Although hardware switching and cell duplication may greatly improve the communication performance observed by end hosts and their applications, the signaling activities within ATM networks proceed in a connectionless manner: VC-setup request messages are forwarded and processed hop by hop [1]. Switches along the route of the VC under construction invoke signaling modules to perform tasks such as routing,

* This work was supported in part by DOE grant DE-FG02-93ER25167, and by NSF grants CCR-9503838 and CDA-9529488.

[1] At this point, we use the term VCI to represent the VPI/VCI pair. The virtual path identifier and its use in the proposed methods are discussed later.

0-8186-7780-5/97 $10.00 © 1997 IEEE

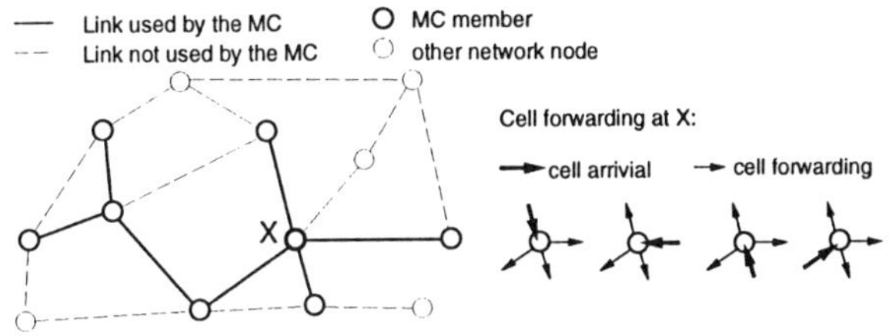

Figure 1. Examples of multipoint connections.

call admission control, and resource allocation. In general, these tasks require the knowledge of the present network status, including the topology of the network and the availability of resources.

Such information is made available to the signaling modules by the routing protocol, a critical component of ATM networks. ATM networks use *link-state routing* (LSR) [2], which periodically disseminates status information throughout the network. The local status of each switch, including the status of its incident links, is learned by the rest of the network switches via these link-state advertisements (LSAs). Based on received LSAs, each switch maintains a complete local image of the network. LSAs are distributed by means of a *flooding protocol*, a highly robust network protocol used for network-wide broadcast of messages. The flooding protocol typically used in ATM networks was originally designed for the ARPANET, a connectionless point-to-point network, and does not take advantage of the hardware capabilities of ATM.

In this paper, we propose a novel approach to flooding for use in ATM signaling protocols. The proposed method, called Switch-Aided Flooding (SAF), takes advantage of both hardware cell relaying and cell duplication to improve the performance of flooding operations. Specifically, an SAF-based protocol maintains a spanning MC, which it uses as a "broadcast medium" for distributing LSAs. The main contribution of this work is to develop and evaluate two SAF-based flooding protocols. In addition, an efficient protocol for the construction and maintenance of spanning MCs is presented. The results of a simulation study reveal that the SAF-based flooding protocols can distribute messages to network switches several times faster than the conventional algorithm.

The remainder of this paper is organized as follows. Section 2 reviews the concept of link-state routing and the conventional flooding protocol. A protocol that constructs and maintains a network-wide spanning MC is presented in Section 3. In Section 4, the two SAF protocols are presented. The first, called the basic SAF protocol, extends a conventional flooding algorithm to incorporate the use of an SMC. The second SAF protocol further addresses the issue of bandwidth consumption in flooding operations, and is called the bandwidth-efficient (BE) SAF protocol. The performance of the proposed protocols is investigated through a simulation study, the results of which are presented in Section 5. Related work is surveyed in Section 6, and conclusions are presented in Section 7.

2 Link-State Routing

A routing protocol is a set of conventions and algorithms, whereby network entities learn information about the rest of the network for use in the selection of paths traversed by traffic streams. Link-state routing [2] is a type of routing protocol that makes complete knowledge of the network available to all switches by means of the flooding of LSAs. LSR was first developed for the use in the ARPANET [2], and it was later accepted by the Internet community in the form of the Open Shortest Path First (OSPF) protocol [3]. As related to this paper, LSR is also included in the ATM PNNI (Private Network-to-Network Interface) standard [1].

The flooding protocol in LSR networks is a highly robust network-wide broadcast protocol that makes use of all network links to disseminate LSAs. In order to flood an LSA, the source switch sends the LSA to all its neighboring switches. For identification, LSAs typically contain the source address and a sequence number. When an LSA is received by another switch for the first time, it is forwarded on all incident links, except the one from which it arrived. Copies of LSAs that have already been seen by a switch are silently ignored. In this manner, every LSA is forwarded by every switch exactly once. An example of the conventional flooding protocol is depicted in Figure 2; the flooding operation requires four steps to complete.

LSAs can be either periodic or event-driven. Switches invoke flooding operations periodically so that changes in the availability of local resources are quickly learned by the network. An LSA for periodic flooding contains descriptions of all links incident to the source switch. An event-driven LSA, or simply *event LSA*, contains exactly one link description and advertises a sudden change in status, such as the failure of that link.

3 The Spanning MC Protocol

The SMC protocol constructs a tree spanning all network nodes. The SMC protocol is a variation of the

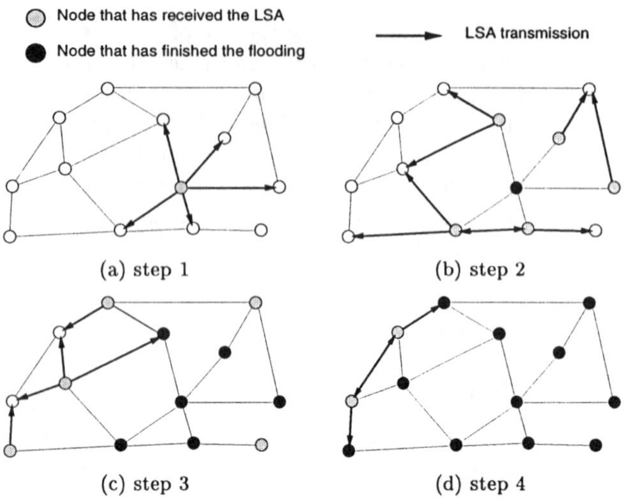

Figure 2. Example of the conventional flooding.

CBT protocol [4], a general MC protocol in which the topology of the MC is the union of shortest paths from the members to a specific node, called the *core*. The SMC protocol differs from the CBT protocol in the way that the core node is determined. In the CBT protocol, the core node is static and is determined by an "outside" mechanism (for example, by network management procedures). In the SMC protocol, the core node is dynamic in order to survive extensive network changes, including failure of the core node itself.

In the SMC protocol, every switch x selects from its local network image the least numbered, reachable switch as its selection of core node, referred to as c_x. Although core selections by switches may differ for short periods of time, it can be shown that, if the network is not permanently partitioned, the switches will reach consensus [5]. Next, each switch tries to establish a connection to its choice of core node. For a switch x to reach its core selection c_x, the switch sends a `reach_core` request one hop towards the core, according to an x-to-c_x shortest path computed locally. The receiving switch grants the request after it has successfully reached the core itself.

The process of SMC construction is illustrated in Figure 3. In the example, we assume that all nodes initially select, as the core, the darkened node in Figure 3(a); this figure also shows the direction of sending `reach_core` requests. The core node immediately grants the `reach_core` requests from its neighboring switches, which subsequently approve `reach_core` requests from downstream switches. In this way, SMC links are granted and established in a "radiating" manner; see Figures 3(b) to 3(f). Due to space limitations, details about SMC construction, the handling of inconsistent core selections, and the detection and repair of broken SMCs, are omitted here. Interested readers please refer to [5].

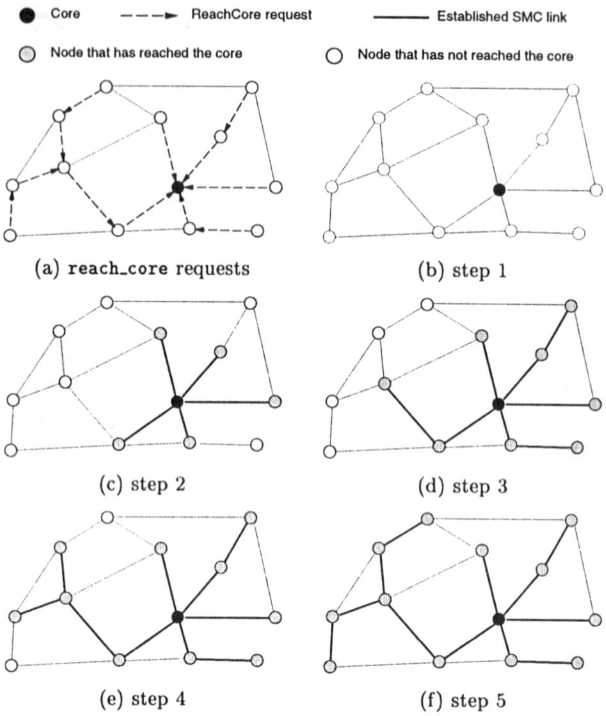

Figure 3. An example of the SMC protocol.

Because a spanning MC is effectively a broadcast medium that allows interleaving of messages, every switch in the network can broadcast messages to and receive messages from all other switches. However, cells belonging to simultaneous broadcast messages can be interleaved with one another at intermediate switches. Receiving switches must be able to demultiplex these messages according to their sources. Various methods can be used to solve this problem. For example, part of the cell payload can be used to label the sources of cells. Alternatively, spanning MCs can be switched by the *virtual path identifier* (VPI). In ATM networks, every cell is tagged with a pair of identifiers, VPI and VCI. When the VPI of a VC is used in switching, the VCI of the cells belonging to the VC is ignored (but remains intact during transmission). In this approach, the SMC used by the SAF protocol must be constructed in such a way that the VPI is in effect throughout the MC, and as such, the VCI field can be used to identify the source switch of cells. We recognize that the use of VPI-switched MCs in a general context is open to debate, due to its difficulty in allocating VPIs to MCs and in assigning VCIs to members. However, it is our opinion that these problems are minimal when restricted to the very special situation of supporting the underlying network routing algorithm.

4 The SAF Protocols

An SAF protocol is an extension to the conventional flooding protocol. In addition to a set of point-to-point links in a network, SAF protocols presume the existence of an SMC to which all the switches in the network have access. In this section, we present two protocols designed in this manner, a basic SAF protocol and a bandwidth-efficient version.

4.1 Basic SAF Protocol

This protocol works as follows. The source of an LSA broadcasts the LSA on the SMC, and subsequently sends the LSA via all its incident links. If a switch receives the LSA for the first time via the SMC, then it forwards the LSA on all its incident links. On the other hand, if the switch receives the LSA via a point-to-point link, then it forwards the LSA on all incident links except the one on which the LSA arrived. As in the case of the conventional flooding, switches silently drop LSAs that have been seen previously. To illustrate, the flooding example of Figure 2 is repeated in Figure 4, but this time using the basic SAF protocol. As we can see in the figure, the operation now requires only two communication steps. In the first step, the source switch broadcasts the LSA, which is switched and duplicated in hardware on the SMC. Provided that other switches receive the LSA in the first step, they exchange this LSA via point-to-point links in the second step.

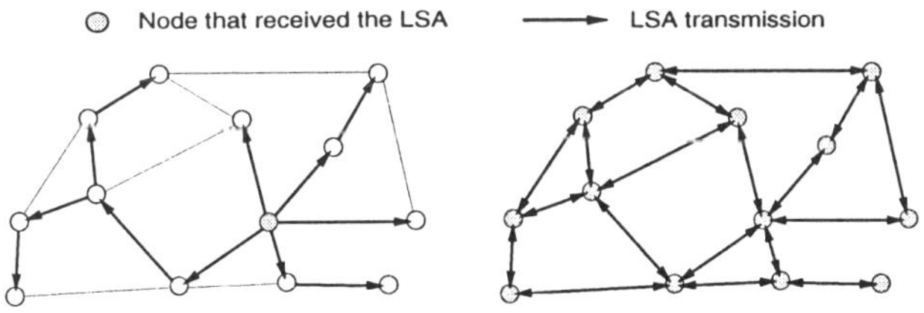

(a) step 1: hardware switched broadcast

(b) step 2: point-to-point forwarding

Figure 4. An example of the basic SAF protocol.

Shown in Figure 5 is another example of how the basic SAF protocol operates when the SMC is faulty. In this example, a link that is used in the SMC fails during a flooding operation and the broadcast of the LSA cannot reach all switches (Figures 5(b) and 5(b)). As shown in Figures 5(c) and 5(d), the remaining switches are reached via link-by-link forwarding. In extreme cases where the SMC does not exist at all (for example, when the network is re-initialized), the basic SAF protocol degenerates to the conventional flooding protocol. As illustrated in this example, SAF protocols only use the SMC as a best-effort broadcast, rather than entirely relying on it. In this manner, the construction and maintenance of the SMC could proceed in concurrent with flooding operations.

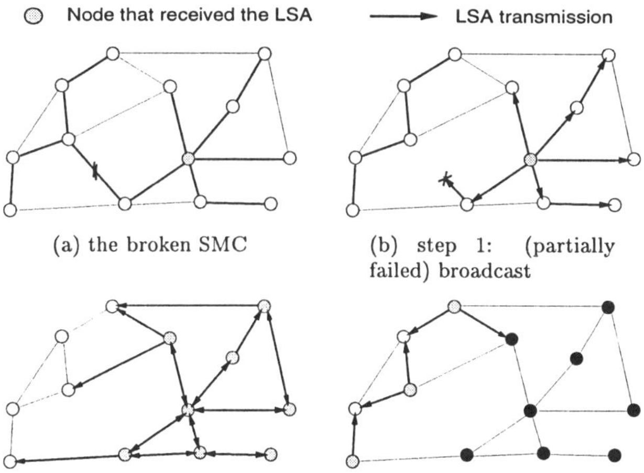

(a) the broken SMC

(b) step 1: (partially failed) broadcast

(c) step 2: link-by-link forwarding

(d) step 3: link-by-link forwarding

Figure 5. The basic SAF protocol with a broken SMC.

The basic SAF achieves its efficiency at the price of additional bandwidth consumption. Consider a network $G = (V, E)$, where V is the set of switches and E the set of point-to-point links. It is shown in [5] that

$$\frac{B_{basic}}{B_c} = \frac{AvgD + 1}{AvgD - 1},$$

where B_{basic} is the bandwidth consumption of the basic SAF protocol, B_c is that of the conventional flooding method, and $AvgD$ stands for the average node degree in the network. If the network has a small $AvgD$ value, then the basic SAF protocol may consume significantly more bandwidth than the conventional flooding protocol. However, due to the simplicity of this protocol and its advantage in flooding time, the basic SAF protocol may be attractive under a variety of conditions (see Section 5).

4.2 Bandwidth-Efficient SAF Protocol

The basic SAF protocol can be modified to reduce bandwidth consumption by introducing the concept of *dummy forwarding.* In this approach, switches receiving an LSA via the SMC forward "dummies" of the LSA to neighboring switches. A dummy of an LSA contains only the source address and sequence number of the LSA, but not its content. Switches that have finished the task of dummy forwarding also expect to see responses (either the real LSA or its dummy) from all neighboring switches. After waiting for a predetermined period of time, such switches forward the real LSA to neighboring switches that fail to respond. Switches receiving the LSA via point-to-point links forward the real LSA on all incident links except that of arrival, and expect nothing from neighbors.

Again we use examples to illustrate; protocol details are omitted due to space limitations, but can be found in the corresponding technical report [5]. The operation of the BE SAF protocol with a fully operational SMC is depicted in Figure 6. Similar to the basic SAF protocol, the BE SAF protocol in this setting requires only two communication steps. In the first step, the source switch broadcasts the LSA, which is switched and duplicated in hardware on the SMC. In the second step, however, switches exchange with neighboring switches dummies of the LSA, rather than the real one.

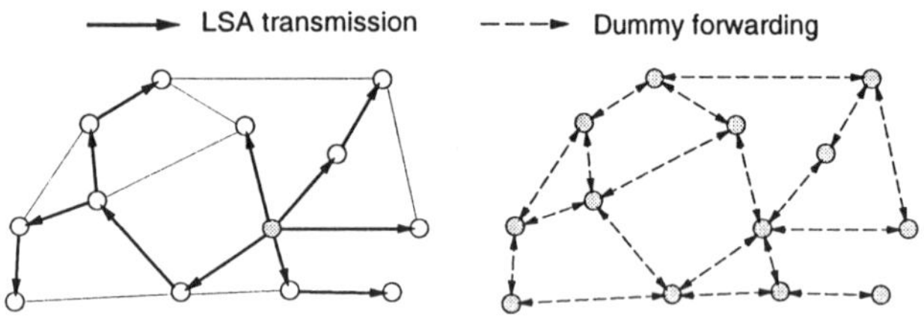

(a) step 1: hardware switched broadcast

(b) step 2: point-to-point "dummy" forwarding

Figure 6. An example of the BE SAF protocol.

Figure 7 illustrates the operation of the BE SAF protocol with a broken SMC. After the BE SAF protocol uses the SMC to reach as many nodes as possible (Figure 7(b)), switches that received the LSA via the SMC forward dummies and expect their neighboring switches to do the same. In this example, three nodes, namely X, Y, and Z, do not see all the expected dummies from neighboring switches, as depicted in Figure 7(c). The three nodes, after a predetermined timeout period, start forwarding the real LSA to their "silent" neighbors, as depicted in Figure 7(d). Switches that receive the LSA via link-by-link forwarding further forward the LSA to all incident links except the incoming one, as shown in Figure 7(e).

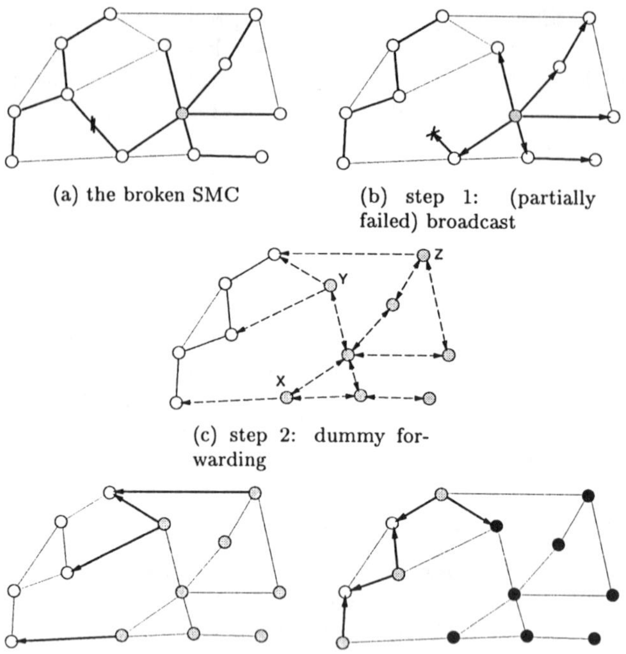

(a) the broken SMC

(b) step 1: (partially failed) broadcast

(c) step 2: dummy forwarding

(d) step 3: real forwarding after timeout

(e) step 4: link-by-link forwarding triggered by real forwarding

Figure 7. The BE SAF protocol with a broken SMC.

5 Performance Evaluation

The performance of the three alternative flooding methods (conventional flooding, basic SAF, and BE-SAF) is studied through simulation. The simulator is based on the CSIM package [6]. We are interested in both temporal and bandwidth metrics. Given a flooding operation and a switch x, the temporal metrics of the flooding operation include the time to receive an LSA, called the receipt time of x, and the time for a flooding operation to complete at x, called the completion time of x. (Completion time includes handling of duplicate LSAs and responses.)

The bandwidth consumption of a flooding operation can be measured by the number of links traversed by the LSA and, in the case of the BE-SAF protocol, that of its dummy. The former number is denoted by B^a and the latter by B^d. Given length ℓ_a of an LSA and length ℓ_d of its dummy, the bandwidth consumed by a flooding operation is $B_f^a \times \ell_a + B_f^b \times \ell_b$, where $f \in$ {conventional, basic SAF, and BE-SAF} is the method of the flooding. In this study, we obtained the B^a and B^d values through simulation runs, and we used the Fore SPANS NNI specification, where an n link-description LSA comprises $4 + 28 * n$ bytes [7], to determine the ℓ_a value; ℓ_d is assumed to be one cell.

Networks comprising up to 256 switches were simulated; 20 graphs were generated randomly for each network size. For each communication operation, such as message forwarding, we used software overheads measured on the ATM testbed in our laboratory. The testbed comprises Sun SPARC-10 workstations equipped with Fore SBA-200 adapters and connected by three Fore ASX-100 switches. From these measurements, we obtained the figure 600 μsec, which includes the overhead at both the sending and receiving switches. We set the length of the interval that the BE-SAF protocol uses in awaiting responses from neighboring switches, according to the average degree of the given network graph G. Specifically, we set the timer to be of length $AvgD(G) \times \alpha$, where α is the time to forward an LSA via a point-to-point link.

Experiment 1: Ideal cases. By ideal, we refer to situations in which the SMC is completely operational during flooding operations. Such is the case for periodic flooding during "normal" periods, when all network components function properly. The simulation results pertaining to this setting are plotted in Figure 8. As shown in Figures 8(a) and (b), the two SAF protocols offer significant advantage in both LSA receipt time and flooding completion time, due to their use of the SMC as a "short cut" broadcast medium.

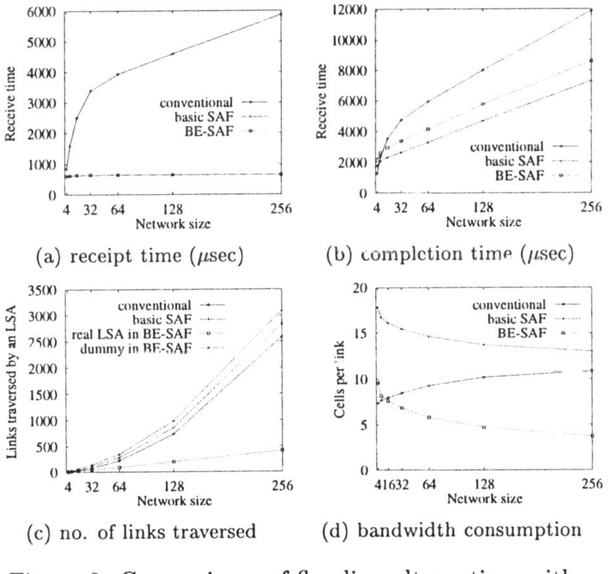

(a) receipt time (μsec) (b) completion time (μsec)

(c) no. of links traversed (d) bandwidth consumption

Figure 8. Comparisons of flooding alternatives with a correctly functioning SMC.

Figure 8(c) plots the number of links traversed by a real LSA or its dummy for the three protocols. As predicted by earlier analysis, the basic SAF protocol consumes more bandwidth than does the conventional flooding algorithm; both methods do not use dummies, but the latter has smaller B^a values. With the use of dummy forwarding, the B^a values of the BE-SAF protocol are significantly less than that of the conventional protocol, especially when the network is large. Figure 8(d) plots the number of cells per link incurred by the three alternatives, assuming the use of Fore SPANS NNI and the inclusion of 10 link-state descriptions in the LSA. In most cases, the bandwidth savings of the BE-SAF protocol are substantial.

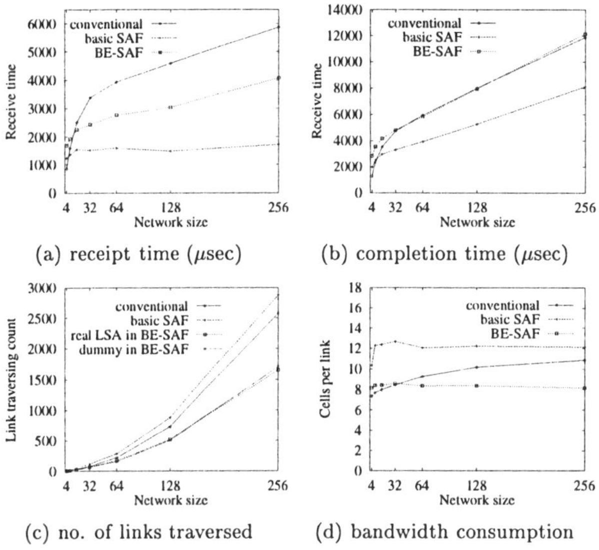

(a) receipt time (μsec) (b) completion time (μsec)

(c) no. of links traversed (d) bandwidth consumption

Figure 9. Comparisons of flooding alternatives with partitioned SMC.

Experiment 2: Partitioned SMC. Next, we investigate the performance of the flooding algorithms when a (random) link used in the SMC fails, partitioning the MC into two segments. In this case, the two SAF protocols still use the MC to reach as many nodes as possible, and resort to link-by-link forwarding to reach the remaining nodes. The results are presented in Figure 9. As expected, the average receipt times for the two SAF protocols are larger than those of the previous experiment. However, they are still significantly smaller than those of the conventional flooding protocol. Provided that the component failure rate of the network is low, the occurrences of simultaneous failures should be rare. We suspect that the results of this experiment, which represent single-failure situations, combined with those of the previous experiment, which represent zero-failure situations, cover a very large fraction of network flooding situations.

Interestingly, the bandwidth consumption problem

with the basic SAF protocol diminishes with a partitioned SMC, as shown in Figure 9(d). This is because LSA broadcasts do not traverse all links of the partitioned SMC. On the other hand, the BE-SAF protocol in this situation must forward real LSAs, rather than dummies, in order to reach switches that are not covered by the SMC. Hence, the protocol consumes more bandwidth than it does in the previous experiment. However, its bandwidth consumption is still lower than that of the other alternatives.

Experiment 3: Non-existent SMC. Let us now consider the worst-case setting for the SAF protocols: when the SMC does not exist at all. This situation may happen after network re-initialization and prior to reconstruction of the SMC, and can also be considered as a worst-case situation with respect to multiple link failures that partition the SMC. As we can see in Figure 10, the conventional flooding protocol outperforms the two SAF protocols in receipt time and completion time. The time differences between the conventional flooding protocol and the basic SAF protocol are marginal, but those between the conventional flooding protocol and the BE-SAF protocol are much more significant. The BE-SAF protocol suffers in this experiment because each switch has to perform two rounds of forwarding to neighbors, one for dummies and one of real LSAs. In this experiment, the three flooding alternatives consume essentially the same amount of network bandwidth, because the two SAF protocols, like the conventional flooding protocol, use only link-by-link forwarding when the SMC does not exist. Corresponding plots are omitted due to space limitations.

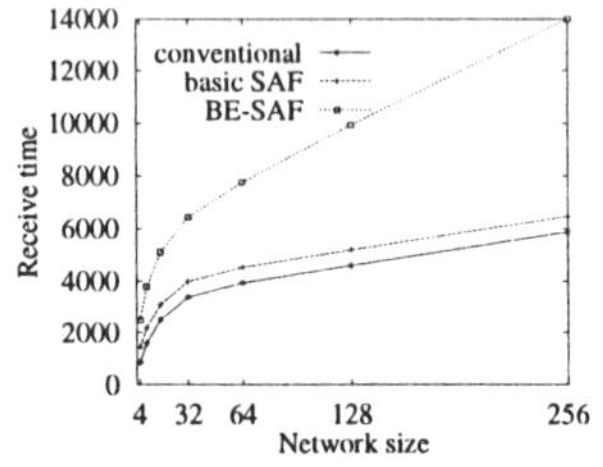

(a) receipt time (μsec)

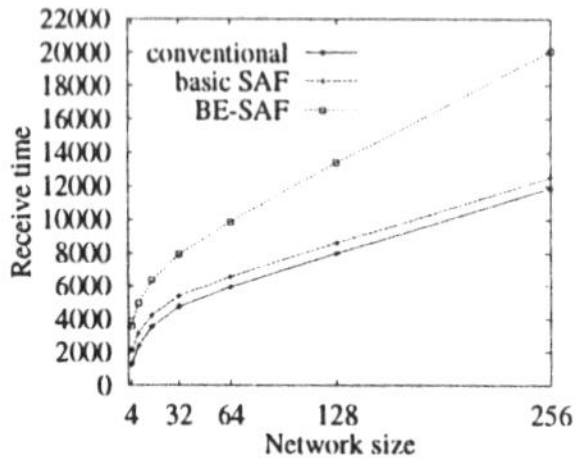

(b) completion time (μsec)

Figure 10. Comparisons of flooding alternatives when SMC does not exist.

Experiment 4: Performance of the SMC protocol. We also studied the performance of the SMC protocol under two scenarios: reorganization of an existing SMC when an SMC link fails, and construction of a new SMC. Due to space limitations, we summarize the results as follows: a partitioned SMC requires less than 2.5 milliseconds to reorganize, while constructing an SMC from scratch (a relatively rare event) requires less than 12 ms. Details can be found in [5].

6 Related Work

The conventional flooding protocol described in this work was first used in ARPANET [2]. If network status values comprise simple ON/OFF states, it is possible to design LSR protocols that do not rely on periodic flooding [8, 9]. However, ATM networks must disseminate the availability of network resources at a high rate for the purpose of accurate call admission control. This requirement forces the use of periodic flooding and emphasizes the importance of efficient flooding protocols.

Extensions to LSR have been proposed to support multicast communication [10], generic MC protocols [11], group address management [10, 7], and so forth. These extensions introduce new types of advertisements, such as group membership advertisements [10, 7], and MC topology advertisements [11]. Efficient flooding protocols can further improve the performance of these LSR extensions; investigation of these issues constitutes one aspect of our ongoing work.

We re-emphasize that the SAF protocols are independent of the particular SMC protocol used. Although we presented a specific SMC protocol in this paper, general-purpose MC protocols can also be used/adapted to construct spanning MCs. Examples include the CBT protocol [12], the PIM protocol [13], and the GMC protocol [11]. The SMC protocol, a variation to the CBT protocol, has an advantage in automatic and dynamic core selection. Moreover, all of the above alternatives invoke some form of MC membership management, a task that is unnecessary for spanning MCs. In addition to applications in SAF, spanning MCs and attendant protocols may be important to ATM applications that require a virtual network-wide broadcast medium. One such application is LAN emulation [14].

7 Conclusions

In this paper, we have proposed two switch-aided flooding protocols and an accompanying protocol to construct spanning MCs. The protocols are designed to exploit ATM hardware cell switching and cell duplication. SAF protocols use the SMC as a broadcast medium to reduce flooding time. However, the protocols do not rely entirely on the SMC, but rather revert to point-to-point message forwarding if the SMC is damaged or under construction.

Two SAF protocols were described: the basic SAF protocol and the bandwidth-efficient SAF protocol. Under normal operating conditions, both protocols deliver network updates several times faster than the conventional flooding algorithm. Our simulation study shows that the difference in the bandwidth consumed by the basic SAF protocol and the conventional flooding is significant for small networks, but is only marginal for large networks. The advantage of the basic SAF protocol over the BE-SAF protocol is its stability in performance under adverse circumstances, for example, when the SMC is partitioned or under construction. We also note that the bandwidth consumption of this protocol may be even smaller when flooding event LSAs, due to their short lengths.

The BE-SAF protocol addresses the bandwidth consumption issue by introducing dummy LSA forwarding. The bandwidth savings of this method is particularly significant when the network size is large or when the LSAs are long. The performance of the BE-SAF protocol is more sensitive to adverse network circumstances, however. As a simple heuristic, an "adaptive" network management system could use the BE-SAF protocol for periodic flooding operations (whose corresponding LSAs are typically sufficiently long to benefit from the use of dummy forwarding), but switch to the basic SAF protocol in the presence of emergency events, such as link failures. The investigation of this hybrid approach is one of our ongoing research activities.

Further Information

A number of related papers and technical reports, including the technical report version of this paper [5], of the Communications Research Group at Michigan State University are available via anonymous ftp and world-wide web. The respective addresses are `ftp://ftp.cps.msu.edu/pub/crg` and `http://www.cps.msu.edu/~mckinley/crgweb`.

References

[1] ATM Forum, "Private network-network interface specification version 1.0." ATM Forum technical specification af-pnni-0055.0000, March 1996.

[2] J. M. McQuillan, I. Richer, and E. C. Rosen, "The new routing algorithm for the ARPANET," *IEEE Transactions on Communications*, pp. 711–719, MAY 1980.

[3] J. Moy, "OSPF version 2." Internet RFC 1583, March 1994.

[4] T. Ballardie, "Core Based Tree (CBT) multicast – architectural overview and specification." Internet Draft, October 1995.

[5] Y. Huang and P. K. McKinley, "Switch-aided flooding operations in ATM networks," Tech. Rep. MSU-CPS-96-27, Department of Computer Science, Michigan State University, East Lansing, Michigan, June 1996.

[6] H. D. Schwetman, "CSIM: A C-based, process-oriented simulation language," Tech. Rep. PP-080-85, Microelectronics and Computer Technology Corporation, 1985.

[7] FORE Systems, Inc., *SPANS NNI: Simple Protocol for ATM Network Signaling (Network-to-Network Interface) Release 3.0*, 1993.

[8] P. A. Humblet and S. Soloway, "Topology broadcast algorithms," *Computer Networks and ISDN Systems*, vol. 16, pp. 179–186, 1988.

[9] J. M. Spinelli and R. G. Gallager, "Event driven topology broadcast without sequence numbers," *IEEE Transactions on Communications*, vol. 37, pp. 468–474, 1989.

[10] J. Moy, "Multicast extensions to OSPF." Internet RFC 1584, March 1994.

[11] Y. Huang and P. K. McKinley, "A lightweight protocol for multipoint connections under link-state routing," in *Proceedings of the 16th IEEE International Conference on Distributed Computing Systems*, (Hong Kong), May 1996.

[12] A. J. Ballardie, *A New Approach to Multicast Communication in a Datagram Internetwork.* Ph.D. thesis, Department of Computer Science, University College London, May 1995.

[13] S. Deering, D. L. Estrin, D. Farinacci, V. Jacobson, C.-G. Liu, and L. Wei, "The PIM architecture for wide-area multicast routing," *IEEE/ACM Trans. on Networking*, vol. 4, pp. 153–162, April 1996.

[14] ATM Forum, "LAN emulation over ATM version 1.0." ATM Forum Technical Specification, January 1995.

Bounds for the Tail Distribution in a Queue with the Superposition of General Periodic Markov Sources

Fumio Ishizaki
Department of Information Science
and Intelligent Systems,
The University of Tokushima
2-1 Minamijosanjima, Tokushima 770, Japan

Tetsuya Takine
Department of Information
Systems Engineering,
Osaka University
2-1 Yamadaoka, Suita, Osaka 565, Japan

Abstract

In this paper, we derive the bounds formulas for the asymptotic tail distribution in a queue whose arrival process is a superposition of general periodic Markov sources. Note that we make no assumption for the structure of the general periodic Markov sources except that the underlying Markov chains are irreducible. The periodic source model in this paper is thus rather general. Taking initial state conditions of the periodic sources into account, we construct a superposed arrival process. Contrary to the previous works, this implies that the periodic sources are not independent. We also provide examples to investigate the efficiency and the accuracy of our bound formulas.

1 Introduction

Estimating the cell loss probability or the tail distribution of the queue length in ATM networks has been considered as one of the most important issues in congestion control which is indispensable to the success of ATM. There are two important issues concerning a technique for estimating the cell loss probability. One is its *efficiency* (in terms of computation time) of the technique and the other is its *accuracy*. Unfortunately, efficiency and accuracy often conflict with each other. In ATM networks, the arrival process is essentially a superposition of sources which are typically bursty and periodic either due to their origin (e.g., periodic sampling of voice traffic) or their occupation of periodic slots allocated for transmission. When we treat such an arrival process, simple exact treatments must be unsatisfactory in terms of efficiency, though they are probably satisfactory in terms of accuracy. Thus, it is desired to develop a method which has a proper tradeoff between efficiency and accuracy.

The most powerful analytical tools which can be somewhat satisfactory in terms of both efficiency and accuracy are large deviation technique (see, e.g., [3, 5, 9] and references therein) and asymptotic analysis (see, e.g., [1, 6, 15] and references therein). Sohraby [15] has considered BMS's (binary Markov sources) and GBMS's (generalized binary Markov sources) as source models. He has considered a discrete-time queueing model with an infinite buffer where the arrival process is a superposition of independent BMS's or GBMS's. Using an asymptotic analysis and a spectral decomposition method, he has derived the asymptotic expressions for the tail distribution of the queue length. Using large deviation technique and maximal inequalities to exponential martingales, Duffield [5] has found exponential bounds for the tail distribution of the queue length where increments of the workload process are described by Markov Additive Processes. He has applied the results to the queue where the arrival process is a superposition of independent Markov sources. In both approaches, asymptotic expressions of the tail distribution only in queues where the arrival process is a superposition of *independent* sources have been discussed. However, when we consider an arrival process which is a superposition of *periodic* sources, the previous analysis does not works well because the periodic sources are synchronized. Namely, in every realization, the sources are *dependent* through their periodicity, while an straightforward application of these approaches to periodic sources implies that all the combinations of the initial phases are realizable with equal probabilities in this model.

There has been a number of previous studies on queues with periodic arrivals (see, e.g., [2, 12, 13] and references therein). However, most of the source models which have been studied, such as $\sum D_i/D/1$ queues, do not have the ability to model burst-level correlations [13]. Therefore it is not suitable for the source model in ATM networks. It is thus desired to study a queue where the arrival process is a superposition of periodic sources which have the ability to model multi-level correlations.

In this paper, we consider queues with general periodic Markov sources and derive the bounds formulas for the asymptotic tail distribution. We do not assume any particular structure of the general periodic Markov sources except that the underlying Markov chains are irreducible. The periodic source model in this paper is thus rather general and includes GBMS, $\sum D_i/D/1$ and so on. Moreover, our periodic sources have the ability to model multi-level correlations. We construct a superposed arrival process, taking account of initial state conditions of the periodic sources. Therefore, contrary to the previous works, the periodic sources are *dependent* in our construction of the arrival process.

The remainder of the paper is organized as follows.

0-8186-7780-5/97 $10.00

In Section 2, we describe the general periodic Markov source and our queueing model. In Section 3, we provide the background material for the tail distribution of the queue length. We also show the asymptotic expression of the tail distribution. In Section 4, we consider the superposition of general periodic Markov sources, and apply the results in Section 3 to our queueing model. We then obtain the bound formulas for the asymptotic tail distribution of the queue length. In Section 5, we apply the results in Section 4 to the queueing models where the arrival process is a superposition of the GBMS's. We also provide numerical examples to investigate the efficiency and the accuracy of our bound formulas.

2 Queueing model

We consider a discrete-time queueing model with an infinite buffer. We assume that customers arrive in a batch. The arrival process to the system is a superposition of K periodic sources. The kth ($k = 1, \ldots, K$) source is governed by an underlying $M^{(k)}$-state Markov chain with periodicity $R^{(k)}$. This Markov chain changes its state on slot boundaries. We assume that the number of customers from each source arriving in a slot depends on the state of the underlying Markov chain in the slot. Furthermore, we assume that all the underlying Markov chains are irreducible and stationary. Hereafter we call a source having the above features a general periodic Markov source. The service times of customers are assumed to be constant and equal to one slot.

The most common approach to deal with a superposition of sources governed by a Markov chain is using so-called Kronecker product expression. In the approach, we use the property that the probability matrix generating function for the superposed arrival process is simply Kronecker product of those of the individual sources. Note here that the underlying Markov chain for a superposed arrival process constructed by such a way is *not* irreducible when two or more underlying Markov chains are periodic. The underlying Markov chain for the superposed arrival process is then decomposed into a number of irreducible sub-Markov chain. Even in such a case, we can construct a stationary and ergodic Markov chain for the superposed arrival process by assigning realization probabilities the state vectors properly. In this paper, we construct the underlying Markov chain for the superposed arrival process in such a way. Intuitively, that is equivalent to considering the steady state associated with a particular initial state vector of the original reducible Markov chain.

We now consider our model in more detail. To do so, we first introduce some notations for each source. Let $(\Omega^{(k)}, \mathcal{F}^{(k)}, P^{(k)})$ denote a probability space for the kth source. Let $S_n^{(k)}$ denote a random variable representing the state of the underlying Markov chain of the kth source with periodicity $R^{(k)}$ in the nth slot. The state transition matrix for the underlying Markov chain of the kth source ($k = 1, \ldots, K$) defined on the probability space is denoted by $\boldsymbol{U}^{(k)} = \{U_{ij}^{(k)}\}$ ($i, j = 1, \ldots, M^{(k)}$). We assume that all the underlying Markov chains are irreducible and stationary. We denote the stationary state vector of the underlying Markov chain for the kth source by $\boldsymbol{\pi}^{(k)} = (\pi_1^{(k)}, \ldots, \pi_{M^{(k)}}^{(k)})$. $\boldsymbol{\pi}^{(k)}$ then satisfies $\boldsymbol{\pi}^{(k)} = \boldsymbol{\pi}^{(k)}\boldsymbol{U}^{(k)}$ and $\boldsymbol{\pi}^{(k)}\boldsymbol{e}_{M^{(k)}} = 1$, where $\boldsymbol{e}_{M^{(k)}}$ is an $M^{(k)} \times 1$ vector whose elements are all equal to one. Let $D_r^{(k)}$ denote the rth moving class of the kth source, i.e., if $i \in D_r^{(k)}$ ($i = 1, \ldots, M^{(k)}, r = 1, \ldots, R^{(k)}$), then $P^{(k)}\{S_{n+1}^{(k)} = j | S_n^{(k)} = i\} = 0$ for all $j \notin D_{r\oplus 1}^{(k)}$, where $\oplus$ is defined as

$$r \oplus l = (r + l - 1)\bmod R^{(k)} + 1. \tag{1}$$

Note that $D_r^{(k)}$ ($r = 1, \ldots, R^{(k)}$) is a partition on the state space of the underlying Markov chain. Let $A_n^{(k)}$ denote a random variable representing the number of customers arriving from the kth source in the nth slot. We assume that $A_{n+1}^{(k)}$ depends only on $S_n^{(k)}$. Let $\hat{a}_{ij}^{(k)}(l)$ denote the conditional joint probability of the following events: l customers arrive from the kth source and the underlying Markov chain is in state j in the next slot given that the underlying Markov chain is in state i in the current slot. Namely,

$$\hat{a}_{ij}^{(k)}(l) = P^{(k)}\{A_{n+1}^{(k)} = l, S_{n+1}^{(k)} = j \mid S_n^{(k)} = i\}. \tag{2}$$

Let $\boldsymbol{A}_n^{(k)}$ denote an $M^{(k)} \times M^{(k)}$ matrix whose (i, j)th element is given by $\hat{a}_{ij}^{(k)}(n)$ ($n \geq 0$). Note that $\boldsymbol{A}_n^{(k)}$ represents the transition matrix of the underlying Markov chain when n customers arrive to the system. Let $\rho^{(k)}$ denote the traffic intensity of the kth source which is given by

$$\rho^{(k)} = \boldsymbol{\pi}^{(k)} \sum_{n=1}^{\infty} n \boldsymbol{A}_n^{(k)} \boldsymbol{e}_{M^{(k)}}. \tag{3}$$

Next we consider a superposition of K general periodic Markov sources. Note that, because of the periodicity of the sources, the tail distribution of the queue length in our model depends on the initial state vector associated with the sources. Taking the initial state condition into account, we consider the tail distribution of the queue length in the queueing model. We define a product measurable space $(\Omega, \mathcal{F}) = (\prod_{k=1}^{K} \Omega^{(k)}, \otimes_{k=1}^{K} \mathcal{F}^{(k)})$. Let $\boldsymbol{S}_n = (S_n^{(1)}, \ldots, S_n^{(K)})$ denote a random vector representing the state of the superposed arrival process. We define an initial phase $r_0^{(k)}$ ($r_0^{(k)} = 1, \ldots, R^{(k)}$) for the kth source as $S_0^{(k)} \in D_{r_0^{(k)}}^{(k)}$. Let denote the initial phase vector by $\boldsymbol{r}_0 = (r_0^{(1)}, \ldots, r_0^{(K)})$. We then define the probability P on the measurable space $(\Omega, \mathcal{F})$ as the extension of $\tilde{P}$:

$$\tilde{P}\{B\} = \frac{1}{R} \sum_{l=0}^{R-1} \prod_{k=1}^{K} P^{(k)}\{B^{(k)} \mid S_0^{(k)} \in D_{r_0^{(k)} \oplus l}^{(k)}\}, \tag{4}$$

where $B^{(k)} \in \mathcal{F}^{(k)}$, $B = \prod_{k=1}^{K} B^{(k)}$ and $R = \mathrm{LCM}\{R^{(1)}, \ldots, R^{(k)}\}$. Note that $P\{B\} = \tilde{P}\{B\}$ for every $B \in \mathcal{F}$ such that $B = \prod_{k=1}^{K} B^{(k)}$. Further, note that $S_n^{(k)}$ and $S_n^{(l)}$ are P-dependent in our setting, and hence $A_n^{(k)}$ and $A_n^{(l)}$ are also P-dependent. The sequence $\{S_n\}_{n=-\infty}^{+\infty}$ forms a Markov chain, which we call the underlying Markov chain for the superposed arrival process. Its state transition matrix U is expressed as $U = U^{(1)} \otimes U^{(2)} \otimes \cdots \otimes U^{(K)}$, where $\otimes$ denotes Kronecker product [7]. From (4), we can confirm that, since the underlying Markov chain for the kth source ($k = 1, \ldots, K$) is $P^{(k)}$-stationary, the underlying Markov chain for the superposed arrival process becomes P-stationary. Let A_n denote a random variable representing the number of customers arriving in the nth slot. We then have

$$A_n = \sum_{k=1}^{K} A_n^{(k)}. \tag{5}$$

The overall traffic intensity for the superposed arrival process is then given by

$$\rho = \sum_{k=1}^{K} \rho^{(k)}. \tag{6}$$

Let X_n denote a random variable representing the queue length at the beginning of the nth slot. Its evolution is then described by

$$X_{n+1} = (X_n - 1)^+ + A_{n+1}. \tag{7}$$

Note that, under the stability condition $\rho < 1$, there exists a unique stationary process $\{X_n\}$ satisfying (7) [10]. Hereafter we assume that $\rho < 1$ and we consider the stationary process $\{X_n\}$.

3 Asymptotic tail distribution

In this section, we provide a background material for the asymptotic analysis of the tail distribution. We first review the distribution of the queue length in a queue where the arrival process is governed by an M-state underlying Markov chain. We define a $1 \times M$ vector $\boldsymbol{x}_n$ and an $M \times M$ matrix $\boldsymbol{A}_n$ as

$$[\boldsymbol{x}_n]_j = P\{X_0 = n, S_0 = j\}, \tag{8}$$

$$[\boldsymbol{A}_n]_{ij} = P\{A_1 = n, S_1 = j \mid S_0 = i\}. \tag{9}$$

The tail distribution T_n ($n \geq 0$) is then given by

$$T_n = \sum_{m=n+1}^{\infty} \boldsymbol{x}_m \boldsymbol{e}_M. \tag{10}$$

Further,we define $\boldsymbol{X}(z)$ and $\boldsymbol{A}(z)$:

$$\boldsymbol{X}(z) = \sum_{n=0}^{\infty} \boldsymbol{x}_n z^n, \quad \boldsymbol{A}(z) = \sum_{n=0}^{\infty} \boldsymbol{A}_n z^n. \tag{11}$$

PROPOSITION 3.1: *We assume that the underlying Markov chain is stationary. Let $\boldsymbol{\pi}$ denote the stationary state probability vector of the underlying Markov chain. If $\rho = \boldsymbol{\pi} \boldsymbol{A}'(1)\boldsymbol{e}_M < 1$, we then have*

$$\boldsymbol{X}(z)[z\boldsymbol{I} - \boldsymbol{A}(z)] = (1-\rho)(z-1)\boldsymbol{g}\boldsymbol{A}(z), \tag{12}$$

where $\boldsymbol{g}$ denotes a $1 \times M$ boundary vector, which is given by

$$\boldsymbol{x}_0 = (1-\rho)\boldsymbol{g}. \tag{13}$$

Further, $\boldsymbol{x}_n$ satisfies

$$\boldsymbol{x}_n = \boldsymbol{x}_0 \boldsymbol{A}_n + \sum_{i=1}^{n+1} \boldsymbol{x}_i \boldsymbol{A}_{n+1-i} \qquad (n \geq 0), \tag{14}$$

with the normalizing equation $\sum_{n=0}^{\infty} \boldsymbol{x}_n \boldsymbol{e}_M = 1$.

PROOF: See [16]. ∎

Remark 3.1: If we can compute $\boldsymbol{g}$, we can also compute the exact tail distribution by using the equations (10), (13) and (14). However, it is not an easy task because computing $\boldsymbol{g}$ is difficult, especially, when the size of $\boldsymbol{g}$ is large.

Remark 3.2: If the underlying Markov chain is not irreducible and the initial state probability vector is not given, we can not determine $\boldsymbol{g}$ uniquely. Thus, we can not determine the tail distribution uniquely in such a case.

Now we consider the asymptotic expression of the tail distribution. We first rewrite (12) to be

$$\boldsymbol{X}(z) = (1-\rho)(z-1)\boldsymbol{g}\boldsymbol{A}(z)\frac{\mathrm{adj}[z\boldsymbol{I} - \boldsymbol{A}(z)]}{\prod_{i=1}^{M}(z - \delta_i(z))}, \tag{15}$$

where for $z \geq 0$, $z \in \boldsymbol{R}$ such that $\boldsymbol{A}(z) > \boldsymbol{O}$, $\delta_1(z)$ is real, $\delta_1(z) > Re(\delta_i(z))$ ($2 \leq i \leq M$) and $|\delta_i(z)| \geq |\delta_{i+1}(z)|$ ($2 \leq i \leq M-1$). Namely we choose $\delta(z) = \delta_1(z)$ as the Perron-Frobenius eigenvalue of matrix $\boldsymbol{A}(z)$ (see Theorem 2.4 in Appendix of [8]). Note that $\delta(1) = 1$ and $\delta'(1) = \rho$ [11].

Note that we can easily construct an arrival process in such a way that the queue length is bounded and has no tail. To ensure that the queue length has a simple asymptotic form, we need the following assumptions:

ASSUMPTION 3.1:

1. *There exists at least one zero of $\det[z\boldsymbol{I} - \boldsymbol{A}(z)]$ outside the unit disk.*
2. *Among those, there exists a real and positive zero z^*, and the absolute values of z^* is strictly smaller than those of other zeros.*
3. $\boldsymbol{O} < \boldsymbol{A}(z) \ll +\infty, \quad 1 \leq z \leq z^*, \quad z \in \boldsymbol{R}$.
4. *The traffic intensity $\rho < 1$.*

It has been shown that the following holds on Assumption 3.

PROPOSITION 3.2: *On Assumption 3.1, for a sufficient large n, $\boldsymbol{x}_n$ is asymptotically expressed as*

$$\boldsymbol{x}_n = \frac{(1-\rho)(z^*-1)}{\delta'(z^*) - 1}\boldsymbol{g}\boldsymbol{v}(z^*)(z^*)^{-n}\boldsymbol{u}(z^*), \tag{16}$$

where $\delta(z)$ denotes the Perron-Frobenius eigenvalue of matrix $\boldsymbol{A}(z)$, and $\boldsymbol{u}(z)$ and $\boldsymbol{v}(z)$ denote the left and the right eigenvectors associated with $\delta(z)$, which satisfy the normalizing conditions: $\boldsymbol{u}(z)\boldsymbol{v}(z) = 1$ and $\boldsymbol{u}(z)\boldsymbol{e}_M = 1$. Furthermore, z^* satisfies

$$z^* - \delta(z^*) = 0. \tag{17}$$

PROOF: See, for example, [1, 6]. ■

The following theorem is the direct conclusion of Proposition 3.2.

THEOREM 3.1: *On Assumption 3.1, for a sufficient large n, the tail distribution T_n is approximately given by*

$$T_n = \frac{1-\rho}{\delta'(z^*)-1} \boldsymbol{g}\boldsymbol{v}(z^*)(z^*)^{-n}. \tag{18}$$

Note that computing the asymptotic tail distribution by using (18) may not be much easier than computing the exact tail distribution by using (10), (13) and (14), because we still have to compute $\boldsymbol{g}$ in (18). Thus, we should develop a more efficient technique to estimate the tail distribution.

4 Bounds for asymptotic tail distribution

In this section, we again consider a queueing model where the arrival process is the superposition of general periodic Markov sources. We apply the results in the previous section to our queueing model. Recall that computing $\boldsymbol{g}$ is difficult in general even if $\boldsymbol{g}$ can be determined uniquely. We therefore develop a technique to obtain the bounds for the asymptotic tail distribution which does not need to compute $\boldsymbol{g}$.

We denote by $\hat{\boldsymbol{A}}^{(k)}(z)$ the probability matrix generating function for the kth source, by $\hat{\delta}^{(k)}(z)$ the Perron-Frobenius eigenvalue for the kth source, and by $\hat{\boldsymbol{u}}^{(k)}(z)$ and $\hat{\boldsymbol{v}}^{(k)}(z)$ its associated left and right eigenvector, respectively, with normalizing conditions $\hat{\boldsymbol{u}}^{(k)}(z)\hat{\boldsymbol{v}}^{(k)}(z) = \hat{\boldsymbol{u}}^{(k)}(z)\boldsymbol{e}_{M^{(k)}} = 1$. The probability matrix generating function $\boldsymbol{A}(z)$ for the superposed arrival process is then given by

$$\boldsymbol{A}(z) = \hat{\boldsymbol{A}}^{(1)}(z) \otimes \cdots \otimes \hat{\boldsymbol{A}}^{(K)}(z). \tag{19}$$

The Perron-Frobenius eigenvalue $\delta(z)$ for the superposed arrival process is then given by

$$\delta(z) = \prod_{k=1}^{K} \hat{\delta}^{(k)}(z), \tag{20}$$

and its associated left and right eigenvectors $\boldsymbol{u}(z)$ and $\boldsymbol{v}(z)$ are given by

$$\boldsymbol{u}(z) = \hat{\boldsymbol{u}}^{(1)}(z) \otimes \cdots \otimes \hat{\boldsymbol{u}}^{(K)}(z), \tag{21}$$

$$\boldsymbol{v}(z) = \hat{\boldsymbol{v}}^{(1)}(z) \otimes \cdots \otimes \hat{\boldsymbol{v}}^{(K)}(z). \tag{22}$$

We shall show the upper and the lower bounds formulas for the asymptotic tail distribution, which are our main results. To do so, we need the following lemma.

LEMMA 4.1: *If the overall traffic intensity $\rho < 1$, then we have, for $1 \le z \le z^*$ and $z \in \boldsymbol{R}$,*

$$\min_l \prod_{k=1}^{K} \tilde{\theta}_l^{(k)}(z) \le \boldsymbol{g}\boldsymbol{v}(z) \le \frac{1}{R(1-\rho)} \sum_{l=0}^{R-1} \prod_{k=1}^{K} \theta_l^{(k)}(z), \tag{23}$$

where

$$\theta_l^{(k)}(z) = \sum_{j^{(k)} \in D^{(k)}_{r_0^{(k)} \oplus l}} q^{(k)}_{j^{(k)},l} s^{(k)}_{j^{(k)},l} \hat{v}^{(k)}_{j^{(k)}}(z), \tag{24}$$

$$\tilde{\theta}_l^{(k)}(z) = \min_{j^{(k)} \in D^{(k)}_{r_0^{(k)} \oplus l} \cap E^{(k)}} \hat{v}^{(k)}_{j^{(k)}}(z), \tag{25}$$

$$q^{(k)}_{j^{(k)},l} = P^{(k)}\{S_0^{(k)} = j^{(k)} \mid S_0^{(k)} \in D^{(k)}_{r_0^{(k)} \oplus l}\}, \tag{26}$$

$$s^{(k)}_{j^{(k)},l} = P^{(k)}\{A_0^{(k)} = 0 \mid S_0^{(k)} = j^{(k)}\}, \tag{27}$$

$$E^{(k)} = \{j^{(k)} \mid P^{(k)}\{A_0^{(k)} = 0 \mid S_0^{(k)} = j^{(k)}\} > 0\}, \tag{28}$$

$$R = LCM\{R^{(1)}, \ldots, R^{(K)}\}, \tag{29}$$

z^* satisfies (17) and $\hat{v}^{(k)}_{j^{(k)}}(z)$ denotes the $j^{(k)}$th element of $\hat{\boldsymbol{v}}^{(k)}(z)$.

PROOF: See Appendix A. ■

Now we are ready to show our main results for the asymptotic tail distribution in a queue where the arrival process is the superposition of K general periodic Markov sources. The following theorem is the direct conclusion of Theorem 3.1 and Lemma 4.1.

THEOREM 4.1: *On Assumption 3.1, in the queue with the superposition of K general periodic Markov sources, the tail distribution T_n is bounded for a sufficient large n as*

$$\frac{(1-\rho)c_L(z^*)}{\delta'(z^*)-1}(z^*)^{-n} \le T_n \le \frac{(1-\rho)c_U(z^*)}{\delta'(z^*)-1}(z^*)^{-n} \tag{30}$$

where

$$c_L(z) = \min_l \prod_{k=1}^{K} \tilde{\theta}_l^{(k)}(z), \tag{31}$$

$$c_U(z) = \frac{1}{R(1-\rho)} \sum_{l=0}^{R-1} \prod_{k=1}^{K} \theta_l^{(k)}(z), \tag{32}$$

$\tilde{\theta}_l^{(k)}(z)$, $\theta_l^{(k)}(z)$ and R are given in (24), (25) and (29), respectively.

To obtain the upper and the lower bounds for the tail distribution from Theorem 4.1, we need to compute z^*, $\delta^{(k)}(z^*)$, $\delta^{(k)'}(z^*)$, $\hat{\boldsymbol{v}}^{(k)}(z^*)$ and $q^{(k)}_{j^{(k)},l}$ for all k

and l. It is expected that we can easily obtain $\delta^{(k)}(z)$, $\delta^{(k)'}(z)$ and $\hat{v}^{(k)}(z)$ explicitly as a function of z, and also derive $q^{(k)}_{j^{(k)},l}$ explicitly, if the underling Markov chain for the kth source is not so complicated. If, for all k and l, we can obtain $\delta^{(k)}(z^*)$, $\delta^{(k)'}(z^*)$, $\hat{v}^{(k)}(z^*)$ and $q^{(k)}_{j^{(k)},l}$ explicitly, the only quantity which we have to determine *numerically* is z^*. Thus, our bound formulas are efficient in such a case. In the next section, we will show an example of queueing models with the superposition of sources in which our bound formulas become efficient.

5 Example

In this section, we apply Theorem 4.1 to a queueing model where the arrival process is a superposition of GBMS's. It will be seen that our bound formulas become efficient in the queueing model. To examine the tightness of our bounds, we also provide numerical examples. In the numerical examples, we will observe that our upper bound is more accurate than the approximation proposed in [15].

We first consider a binary Markov source (BMS), where in any slot the BMS is in one of two different states. In the off-state, it does not generate a cell, and in the on-state, it generates only one cell. The transition probability from the on-state (resp. off-state) to the off-state (resp. on-state) is denoted by $1-\alpha$ (resp. $1-\beta$), where $0 < \alpha, \beta < 1$. The matrix generating function $\hat{A}^*(z)$ for the BMS is then given by

$$\hat{A}^*(z) = \begin{pmatrix} \alpha z & 1-\alpha \\ (1-\beta)z & \beta \end{pmatrix}. \qquad (33)$$

Note that the BMS is characterized by two parameters, ρ and B, which represents the traffic intensity and the mean burst length of a single BMS, respectively. It has been shown that [15]

$$\alpha = 1 - \frac{1}{B}, \qquad \beta = 1 - \frac{\rho}{(1-\rho)B}. \qquad (34)$$

For this BMS, the Perron-Frobenius eigenvalue $\hat{\delta}^*(z)$ and its associated left and right eigenvectors $\hat{u}^*(z)$ and $\hat{v}^*(z)$ are found to be

$$\hat{\delta}^*(z) = \frac{\alpha z + \beta}{2} + \sqrt{\left(\frac{\alpha z+\beta}{2}\right)^2 - \kappa z}, \qquad (35)$$

$$\hat{u}^*(z) = \frac{1}{\hat{\delta}^*(z) - \kappa}\left(\hat{\delta}^*(z) - \beta, 1-\alpha\right), \qquad (36)$$

$$\hat{v}^*(z) = \frac{1}{2\hat{\delta}^*(z) - \alpha z - \beta}\left(\hat{\delta}^*(z) - \kappa, \hat{\delta}^*(z) - \kappa z\right)^T, \qquad (37)$$

where $\kappa = \alpha + \beta - 1$.

Note that the peak rate of the BMS is restricted to one. To overcome this difficulty, Sohraby has proposed the following source traffic model [15]. The source is constrained to generate a maximum of one cell every R slots. And in every R slots, it behaves exactly the same as the BMS. We call this source model a GBMS (generalized BMS). The matrix generating function $\hat{A}(z)$ for a GBMS with parameter R is given by

$$\hat{A}(z) = \begin{pmatrix} O_{2(R-1),2} & E_{2(R-1),2(R-1)} \\ \hat{A}^*(z) & O_{2,2(R-1)} \end{pmatrix}, \qquad (38)$$

where $O_{i,j}$ and $E_{i,i}$ denote $i \times j$ zero matrix and $i \times i$ identity matrix, respectively, and $\hat{A}^*(z)$ is given in (33). The GBMS is characterized by three parameters, ρ, B and R, where they satisfy

$$\alpha = 1 - \frac{1}{B}, \qquad \beta = 1 - \frac{R\rho}{(1-R\rho)B}. \qquad (39)$$

For the GBMS with parameter R, the Perron-Frobenius eigenvalue $\hat{\delta}(z)$ and its associated left and right eigenvectors $\hat{u}(z)$ and $\hat{v}(z)$ are given in terms of $\hat{\delta}^*(z)$, $\hat{u}^*(z)$ and $\hat{v}^*(z)$:

$$\hat{\delta}(z) = \left(\hat{\delta}^*(z)\right)^{R^{-1}}, \qquad (40)$$

$$\hat{u}(z) = \hat{\zeta}(z) \otimes \hat{u}^*(z), \qquad \hat{v}(z) = \hat{\eta}(z) \otimes \hat{v}^*(z), \qquad (41)$$

where

$$\hat{\zeta}(z) = \frac{\hat{\delta}(z) - 1}{\hat{\delta}(z)^R - 1}\left(\hat{\delta}(z)^{R-1}, \ldots, \hat{\delta}(z), 1\right), \qquad (42)$$

$$\hat{\eta}(z) = \frac{\hat{\delta}(z)^R - 1}{R\hat{\delta}(z)^{R-1}(\hat{\delta}(z) - 1)}\left(1, \hat{\delta}(z), \ldots, \hat{\delta}(z)^{R-1}\right)^T. \qquad (43)$$

Taking the first derivative of $\hat{\delta}(z)$, we have

$$\hat{\delta}'(z) = \frac{\alpha\hat{\delta}^*(z) - (\alpha+\beta-1)}{R\hat{\delta}(z)^{R-1}(2\hat{\delta}^*(z) - \alpha z - \beta)}. \qquad (44)$$

We now consider a superposition of K GBMS's. We assume that the kth source is characterized by $\alpha^{(k)}$, $\beta^{(k)}$ and $R^{(k)}$. In what follows, we assume $\rho = \sum_{k=1}^{K} \rho^{(k)} < 1$ and $\sum_{k=1}^{K} 1/R^{(k)} > 1$ so that the queue length tail exists [15]. We denote by $\hat{\delta}^{(k)}(z)$ the Perron-Frobenius eigenvalue for the kth source, and by $\hat{u}^{(k)}(z)$ and $\hat{v}^{(k)}(z) = (\hat{v}^{(k)}_1(z), \ldots, \hat{v}^{(k)}_{2R^{(k)}}(z))$, its associated left and right eigenvector with normalizing conditions $\hat{u}^{(k)}(z)\hat{v}^{(k)}(z) = \hat{u}^{(k)}(z)e_{M^{(k)}} = 1$. Then the Perron-Frobenius eigenvalue $\delta(z)$ and its associated left and right eigenvectors $u(z)$ and $v(z)$ for the superposed arrival process are given in (20), (21) and (22), respectively. Using Theorem 4.1, we have the upper and the lower bounds for the asymptotic tail distribution associated with an initial phase vector.

COROLLARY 5.1: *If $\rho = \sum_{k=1}^{K} \rho^{(k)} < 1$ and $\sum_{k=1}^{K} 1/R^{(k)} > 1$, in the queue with the superposition of K GBMS's with an initial phase vector $r_0 =$*

$(r_0^{(1)},\ldots,r_0^{(K)})$ $(1 \le r_0^{(i)} \le 2R^{(i)})$, *the tail distribution* T_n *is bounded for a sufficient large* n *as (30). In (30),* $c_L(z)$ *and* $c_U(z)$ *are given by (31) and (32), respectively, and* $\delta'(z^*)$ *is computed by*

$$\delta'(z^*) = z^* \sum_{k=1}^{K} \hat{\delta}^{(k)\prime}(z^*)/\hat{\delta}^{(k)}(z^*). \qquad (45)$$

In (31) and (32), $\tilde{\theta}_l^{(k)}(z)$ *and* $\theta_l^{(k)}(z)$ *are given by*

$$\tilde{\theta}_l^{(k)}(z) = \min\left[\tilde{v}_{2j(k,l)-1}^{(k)}(z), \tilde{v}_{2j(k,l)}^{(k)}(z)\right], \qquad (46)$$

$$\theta_l^{(k)}(z) = (1-\eta^{(k)})\bar{v}_{2j(k,l)-1}^{(k)}(z) + \eta^{(k)}\bar{v}_{2j(k,l)}^{(k)}(z), \qquad (47)$$

where

$$\eta^{(k)} = \frac{1-\alpha^{(k)}}{2-\alpha^{(k)}-\beta^{(k)}}, \qquad (48)$$

$$j(k,l) = r_0^{(k)} \oplus l, \qquad (49)$$

$$\tilde{v}_i^{(k)}(z) = \begin{cases} \hat{v}_i^{(k)}(z) & (i \neq 1), \\ +\infty & (i = 1), \end{cases} \qquad (50)$$

$$\bar{v}_i^{(k)}(z) = \begin{cases} \hat{v}_i^{(k)}(z) & (i \neq 1), \\ 0 & (i = 1). \end{cases} \qquad (51)$$

In (32), R *is given by (29).*

PROOF: See Appendix B. ■

Before we show our numerical examples, we glance over the accuracy of approximations of the tail distribution. In the past, several researchers have discussed the tail distribution and call admission control using

$$\tilde{T}_n \approx (z^*)^{-n}, \qquad (52)$$

which is the basis of the effective bandwidths technique (see [17] and references therein). On the other hand, Sohraby has proposed an approximation $\tilde{T}_n^S$ of the tail distribution T_n [15]:

$$\tilde{T}_n^S \approx \rho(z^*)^{-n}. \qquad (53)$$

It is known, however, that the coefficient of $(z^*)^{-n}$ can be much smaller than the aboves, especially when the number of multiplexed sources is large [4]. Therefore the above approximations overestimate the tail distribution when the number of sources is large.

Now we show some numerical examples. In Figs. 1–2, we assume that the number of GBMS's is equal to 20, all sources are homogeneous, i.e., $R^{(k)} = 10$, $B^{(k)} = 50.0$, $\rho^{(k)} = 0.035$ for all k $(k = 1,\ldots,20)$. The total traffic intensity ρ is then given by 0.7. For the initial phases, we consider two extreme cases. In Fig. 1, we set the initial phase of the kth source to $(k-1)\mathrm{mod}R^{(k)} + 1$. In Fig. 2, we set all the initial phases to 1. To compare the results, we also show the tail distributions obtained from the simulation results and the approximation $\tilde{T}_n^S$ from (53). In Figs. 1–2, we see that our upper bound becomes closer to the simulation result than the approximation $\tilde{T}_n^S$ from (53) for both types, although the upper bound seems to overestimate the dependency of the tail distribution on the initial phase vector. On the other hand, our lower bound seems to be meaningless in these cases. Next we show a numerical example in heterogeneous case. In Fig. 3, we assume that $R^{(k)} = 2$, $B^{(k)} = 10.0$, $\rho^{(k)} = 0.04$ for $k = 1,\ldots,10$ and $R^{(k)} = 4$, $B^{(k)} = 50.0$, $\rho^{(k)} = 0.02$ for $k = 11,\ldots,20$. The total traffic intensity ρ is then given by 0.6. We set the initial phase of the kth source to $(k-1)\mathrm{mod}R^{(k)}+1$ for $k = 1,\ldots,10$ and to $(k-11)\mathrm{mod}R^{(k)} + 1$ for $k = 11,\ldots,20$. To compare the results, we also show the tail distributions obtained from the simulation results and the approximation $\tilde{T}_n^S$ from (53). Also, in Fig. 3, we see that our upper bound becomes closer to the simulation result than the approximation $\tilde{T}_n^S$ from (53).

A Proof of Lemma 4.1

Since P is the extension of $\tilde{P}$, $P\{B\} = \tilde{P}\{B\}$, where $B = \prod_{k=1}^{K} B^{(k)}$ and $B^{(k)} = \{S_0^{(k)} = j^{(k)}, A_0^{(k)} = 0\}$. Thus, from (4), for all $\boldsymbol{j} = (j^{(1)},\ldots,j^{(K)})$, we have

$$P\{\boldsymbol{S}_0 = \boldsymbol{j}, A_0 = 0\} = \frac{1}{R}\sum_{l=0}^{R-1}\prod_{i=1}^{K} q_{j^{(i)},l}^{(i)} s_{j^{(i)},l}^{(i)}, \qquad (54)$$

where

$$q_{j^{(k)},l}^{(k)} = P^{(k)}\{S_0^{(k)} = j^{(k)} \mid S_0^{(k)} \in D_{r_0^{(k)}\oplus l}^{(k)}\}, \qquad (55)$$

$$s_{j^{(k)},l}^{(k)} = P^{(k)}\{A_0^{(k)} = 0 \mid S_0^{(k)} = j^{(k)}, S_0^{(k)} \in D_{r_0^{(k)}\oplus l}^{(k)}\}. \qquad (56)$$

We now consider the upper bound for $\boldsymbol{gv}(z)$. We define the function $f(\cdot)$ on $\boldsymbol{j}$ as

$$f(\boldsymbol{j}) = \sum_{i=1}^{K}(j^{(i)}-1)\prod_{k=i+1}^{K} M^{(k)}, \qquad (57)$$

where $\boldsymbol{j} = (j^{(1)},\ldots,j^{(K)})$ $(1 \le j^{(k)} \le M^{(k)})$. If $\rho < 1$, from (8) and (13), we then have

$$[\boldsymbol{g}]_{f(\boldsymbol{j})} = P\{X_0 = 0, \boldsymbol{S}_0 = \boldsymbol{j}\}/(1-\rho) \qquad (58)$$

From (7), $X_0 = 0$ implies $A_0 = 0$. Thus, from (58), we obtain

$$[\boldsymbol{g}]_{f(\boldsymbol{j})} \le P\{A_0 = 0, \boldsymbol{S}_0 = \boldsymbol{j}\}/(1-\rho). \qquad (59)$$

From (54) and (59), we obtain

$$[\boldsymbol{g}]_{f(\boldsymbol{j})} \le \frac{1}{R(1-\rho)}\sum_{l=0}^{R-1}\prod_{i=1}^{K} q_{j^{(i)},l}^{(i)} s_{j^{(i)},l}^{(i)}. \qquad (60)$$

On the other hand, we have

$$[\boldsymbol{v}(z)]_{f(\boldsymbol{j})} = \hat{v}^{(1)}_{j^{(1)}}(z)\hat{v}^{(2)}_{j^{(2)}}(z)\cdots\hat{v}^{(K)}_{j^{(K)}}(z). \qquad (61)$$

Therefore, from (60) and (61), we obtain

$$[\boldsymbol{g}]_{f(\boldsymbol{j})}[\boldsymbol{v}(z)]_{f(\boldsymbol{j})} \le \frac{1}{R(1-\rho)}\sum_{l=0}^{R-1}\prod_{i=1}^{K} q^{(i)}_{j^{(i)},l} s^{(i)}_{j^{(i)},l} v^{(i)}_{j^{(i)}}(z). \qquad (62)$$

From the above equations, noting $q^{(k)}_{j^{(k)},l} = 0$ if $j^{(k)} \notin D^{(k)}_{r_0^{(k)}\oplus l}$, we finally obtain

$$\boldsymbol{g}\boldsymbol{v}(z) \le \frac{1}{R(1-\rho)}\sum_{l=0}^{R-1}\left[\sum_{j^{(1)}\in D^{(1)}_{r_0^{(1)}\oplus l}} \cdots \sum_{j^{(K)}\in D^{(K)}_{r_0^{(K)}\oplus l}} \prod_{i=1}^{K} q^{(i)}_{j^{(i)},l} s^{(i)}_{j^{(i)},l} v^{(i)}_{j^{(i)}}(z)\right]$$

$$= \frac{1}{R(1-\rho)}\sum_{l=0}^{R-1}\prod_{i=1}^{K}\theta^{(i)}_l(z), \qquad (63)$$

where

$$\theta^{(i)}_l(z) = \sum_{j^{(i)}\in D^{(i)}_{r_0^{(i)}\oplus l}} q^{(i)}_{j^{(i)},l} s^{(i)}_{j^{(i)},l} v^{(i)}_{j^{(i)}}(z). \qquad (64)$$

Next we consider the lower bound for $\boldsymbol{g}\boldsymbol{v}(z)$. Recall that $\boldsymbol{v}(z)$ $(1 \le z \le z^*, z \in \boldsymbol{R})$ is strictly positive [14]. Further, all elements of $\boldsymbol{g}$ are non-negative with $\boldsymbol{g}\boldsymbol{e}_M = 1$. Note that if $P\{\boldsymbol{S}_0 = \boldsymbol{j}\} = 0$ or $P\{A_0 = 0 \mid \boldsymbol{S}_0 = \boldsymbol{j}\} = 0$, then $[\boldsymbol{g}]_{f(\boldsymbol{j})} = 0$. Thus we have

$$\min_l \left[\prod_{k=1}^{K} \min_{j^{(k)}\in D^{(k)}_{r_0^{(k)}\oplus l}\cap E^{(k)}} \hat{v}^{(k)}_{j^{(k)}}(z)\right] \le \boldsymbol{g}\boldsymbol{v}(z), \qquad (65)$$

where $E^{(k)} = \{j^{(k)} \mid P^{(k)}\{A^{(k)}_0 = 0 \mid S^{(k)}_0 = j^{(k)}\} > 0\}$.

B Proof of Corollary 5.1

In this case, we have

$$q^{(k)}_{j^{(k)},l} = \begin{cases} 1-\eta^{(k)} & \left(j^{(k)}\text{is odd}, j^{(k)} \in D^{(k)}_{r_0^{(k)}\oplus l}\right), \\ \eta^{(k)} & \left(j^{(k)}\text{is even}, j^{(k)} \in D^{(k)}_{r_0^{(k)}\oplus l}\right), \\ 0 & \text{(otherwise)}, \end{cases} \qquad (66)$$

where $\eta^{(k)} = (1-\alpha^{(k)})/(2-\alpha^{(k)}-\beta^{(k)})$. $s^{(k)}_{j^{(k)},l}$ is given by

$$s^{(k)}_{j^{(k)},l} = \begin{cases} 1 & (j^{(k)} \ne 1), \\ 0 & \text{(otherwise)}. \end{cases} \qquad (67)$$

Note that $D^{(k)}_r$ has only two elements, i.e., $D^{(k)}_r = \{2r-1, 2r\}$, and $E^{(k)} = \{2, \ldots, 2R^{(k)}\}$. From the above observation, Corollary 5.1 immediately follows.

References

[1] J.Abate, G.L.Choudhury and W.Whitt, "Asymptotics for steady-state tail probabilities in structured Markov chains of $M/G/1$-type," *Stoch. Mod.*, Vol.10, pp.99–144, 1994.

[2] I.Cidon, R.Guérin, I.Kessler and A.Khamisy, "Analysis of a statistical multiplexer with generalized periodic sources," *Queueing Systems*, Vol.20, pp.139–169, 1995.

[3] C.-S.Chang, "Sample path large deviations and intree networks," *Queueing Systems*, Vol.20, pp.7–36, 1995.

[4] G.L.Choudhury, D.M.Lucantoni and W.Whitt, "Squeezing the most out of ATM," *IEEE Trans. Commun.*, Vol.44, pp.203–217, 1996.

[5] N.G.Duffield, "Exponential bounds for queues with Markovian arrivals, " *Queueing Systems*, Vol.17, pp.413–430, 1994.

[6] E.Falkenberg, "On the asymptotic behavior of the stationary distribution of Markov chains of $M/G/1$-type," *Stoch. Mod.*, Vol.10, pp.75–98, 1994.

[7] A.Graham, *Kronecker products and matrix calculus with applications.* Ellis Horwood, Chichester, 1981.

[8] S.Karlin and H.M.Taylor, *A first course in stochastic processes, second edition*, Academic Press, London, 1975.

[9] G.Kesidis, J.Walrand and C.-S.Chang, "Effective bandwidths for multiclass Markov fluids and other ATM sources," *IEEE/ACM Trans. Networking*, Vol.1, pp.424–428, 1993.

[10] R.M.Loynes, "The stability of a queue with non-independent interarrival and service times," *Proc. Cambridge Phil. Soc.*, Vol.58, pp.497–520, 1962.

[11] M.F.Neuts, *Structured stochastic matrices of $M/G/1$ type and their applications*, Marcel Dekker, New York, 1989.

[12] G.Ramamurthy and B.Sengupta, "Delay analysis of a packet voice multiplexer by the $\sum D_i/D/1$ queue," *IEEE Trans. Commun.*, Vol.39, pp.1107–1114, 1991.

[13] J.W.Roberts and J.T.Virtamo, "The superposition of periodic cell arrival streams in an ATM multiplexer," *IEEE Trans. Commun.*, Vol.39, pp.298–303, 1991.

[14] E.Seneta, *Non-negative matrices and Markov chains, second edition*, Springer-Verlag, New York, 1981.

[15] K.Sohraby, "On the asymptotic behavior of heterogeneous statistical multiplexer with applications," *Proceedings of INFOCOM '92*, pp.839–847, 1992.

[16] T.Takine, B.Sengupta and T.Hasegawa, "An analysis of a discrete-time queue for broadband ISDN with priorities among traffic classes," *IEEE Trans. Commun.*, Vol.42, pp.1837–1845, 1994.

[17] W.Whitt, "Tail probabilities with statistical multiplexing and effective bandwidths in multiclass queues," *Telecommunication Systems*, Vol.2, pp.71–107, 1993.

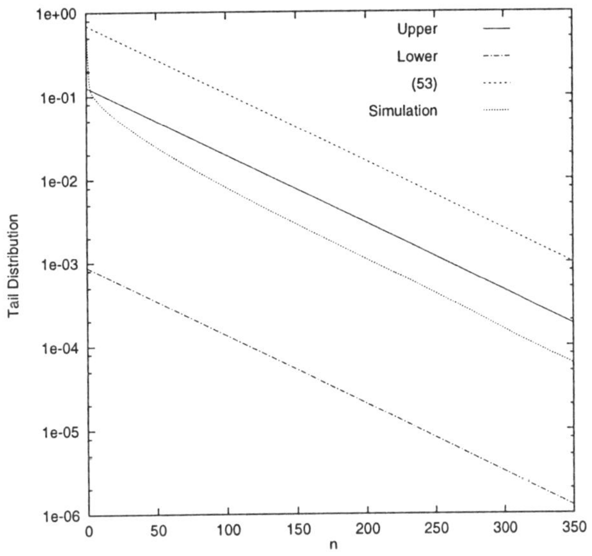

Figure 1: Tail distribution (homogeneous case)

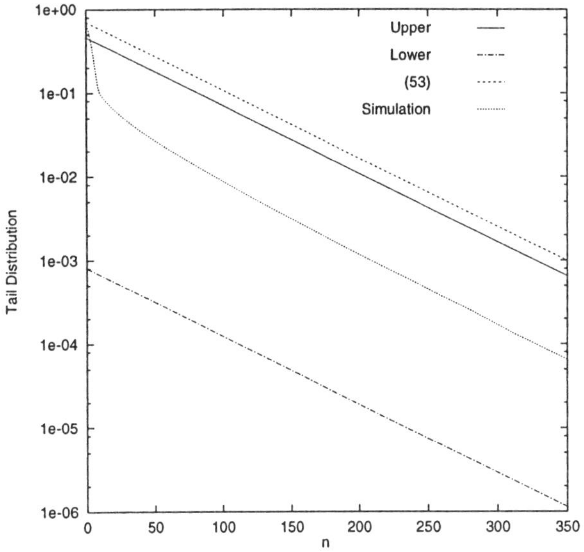

Figure 2: Tail distribution (homogeneous case)

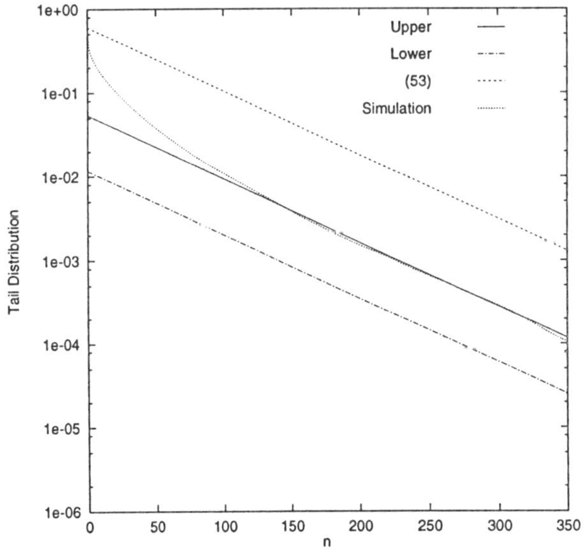

Figure 3: Tail distribution (heterogeneous case)

Fitting Mixtures of Exponentials to Long-Tail Distributions to Analyze Network Performance Models

Anja Feldmann Ward Whitt
AT&T Laboratories – Research
Murray Hill, NJ 07974-0636, USA
{anja,wow}@research.att.com

Abstract

Traffic measurements from communication networks have shown that many quantities characterizing network performance have long-tail probability distributions, i.e., with tails that decays more slowly than exponentially. Long-tail distributions can have a dramatic effect upon performance, but it is often difficult to describe this effect in detail, because performance models with component long-tail distributions tend to be difficult to analyze. We address this problem by developing an algorithm for approximating a long-tail distribution by a finite mixture of exponentials. The fitting algorithm is recursive over time scales. At each stage, an exponential component is fit in the largest remaining time scale and then the fitted exponential component is subtracted from the distribution. Even though a mixture of exponentials has an exponential tail, it can match a long-tail distribution in the regions of primary interest when there are enough exponential components.

1 Introduction

A major challenge for engineering the emerging high-speed integrated-services communication networks is to develop models that can realistically capture the performance effects of the complex traffic that will be offered to and carried by these networks. Evidence of traffic complexity appears in many forms, such as in the long-range dependence and self-similarity found in the statistical analysis of traffic measurements [11]. There is also strong evidence of important phenomena at several different time scales [13].

In this paper we focus on one phenomenon that seems to underlie much of the observed traffic complexity: long-tail probability distributions. Let F be a *cumulative distribution function* (cdf) and let the associated *complementary cdf* (ccdf) be $F^c(t) = 1 - F(t)$. We say that a cdf F (or its associated ccdf F^c) has a *long tail* (also known as fat tail or heavy tail) if the ccdf F^c decays more slowly than exponentially, i.e., if

$$e^{\gamma t} F^c(t) \to \infty \quad \text{as } t \to \infty \text{ for all } \gamma > 0 . \tag{1.1}$$

In contrast, we say that a cdf F has a *short tail* if its ccdf F^c decays exponentially, i.e., if there exists some $\gamma > 0$ such that

$$e^{\gamma t} F^c(t) \to 0 \quad \text{as } t \to \infty . \tag{1.2}$$

Neither (1.1) nor (1.2) describes the actual decay rates of the ccdf's well; they are intended for general classification. A typical long-tail cdf might have a *power tail*, i.e.,

$$F^c(t) \sim \alpha t^{-\beta} \quad \text{as } t \to \infty , \tag{1.3}$$

where α and β are positive constants and $f(t) \sim g(t)$ as $t \to \infty$ means that $f(t)/g(t) \to 1$ as $t \to \infty$, whereas a typical short-tail cdf might have *bounded support* ($F^c(t) = 0$ for some t) or an *exponential tail*, i.e.,

$$F^c(t) \sim \alpha e^{-\eta t} \quad \text{as } t \to \infty \tag{1.4}$$

for positive constants α and η.

Two familiar long-tail distributions are the Pareto distribution and the Weibull distribution. One form of the *Pareto distribution*, which we refer to as Pareto(a,b), has ccdf

$$F^c(t) = (1 + bt)^{-a} \tag{1.5}$$

for positive parameters a and b (p. 233 [10]). One form of the *Weibull distribution*, which we refer to as Weibull(c, a), has ccdf

$$F^c(t) = e^{-(t/a)^c} \tag{1.6}$$

for positive parameters a and c (Ch. 20 [10]). From (1.5) it is easy to see that the Pareto ccdf in (1.5) has a power tail and so always has a long tail. The Weibull ccdf in (1.6) has a long tail but not a power tail if $c < 1$.

In recent years, many traffic measurement studies have found long-tail distributions. For example, the analysis of a large dataset of local area Internet IP traffic collected at Bellcore showed that traffic is highly variable over several time scales. Measurements of source on and off times (high and low activity times) of individual network sources within the Bellcore dataset have indicated long-tail distributions [11], and it has been proven that such long-tailed on and off times for individual sources can explain the self-similarity in the aggregate traffic [19].

Long-tail distributions yield statistically better models for the tail behavior of durations, number of bytes, and burst bytes of ftp connections on the Internet [15]. Intervals

0-8186-7780-5/97 $10.00 © 1997 IEEE

between connection requests in Internet traffic have long-tail distributions [7]. Recent analysis of the durations of world wide web transfers have led to scrutinizing the file length distribution on file servers [6]. Both distributions have been found to be long-tailed.

The accumulated evidence is clear: many important probability distributions associated with network traffic have long tails. Moreover, it is known that long-tail distributions can have a dramatic impact upon network performance. For example the steady-state waiting-time distribution in an infinite-capacity single-server queue inherits the long-tail property of a service-time distribution. However, the impact of a long-tail distribution depends on the context and requires careful analysis. For example, in the single-server queue, large delays are caused by large service times and short interarrival times.

Not only are long-tail distributions prevalent and important, but they are difficult to analyze. For example, even the relatively simple $M/G/1$ queue is difficult to analyze when the service-time distribution is Pareto. Abate et al. [1] calculate performance measures for the $GI/G/1$ queue when the general interarrival-time and service-time distributions are long-tailed using numerical transform inversion, but it is necessary to have the Laplace transforms of these distributions, and there evidently is no convenient expression for the Laplace transforms of the Pareto and Weibull distributions.

Our main contribution in this paper is to point out that it is possible to approximate long-tail probability distributions by convenient short-tail probability distributions, so that available performance models can be effectively analyzed and so that the effect of the long-tail distribution upon performance can be determined. (We do *not* claim that the long-tail distribution has no effect.) Moreover, we develop a remarkably simple algorithm for constructing suitable approximating distributions for a large class of long-tail distributions. The class of long-tail distributions that can be approximated by the method developed here includes the Pareto and Weibull distributions in (1.5) and (1.6) as special cases.

Although at first it may be surprising that long-tail distributions can be approximated by short-tail distributions, there is a simple explanation in the notion of time scale. In almost all network performance settings, the distribution of interest only matters through its values in some finite interval $[t_1, t_2]$. For t_1 sufficiently small and t_2 sufficiently large, the precise form of the distribution outside the interval $[t_1, t_2]$ should not matter. (Because of the nature of time scales, it is usually appropriate to measure time logarithmically. Thus, we might have $t_1 = 10^{-a}$ and $t_2 = 10^b$ for appropriate constants a and b.) The main point is that, in principle, it should be possible to approximate any long-tail distribution by a short-tail distribution. A simple way to do this is to truncate the distribution at the points t_1 and t_2 and assign the negligible probabilities of the intervals $[0, t_1)$ and (t_2, ∞) to the points t_1 and t_2, respectively. Although this produces a short-tail distribution that captures the essential behavior of the original long-tail distribution, it may not be a convenient approximation.

Here we consider hyperexponential distributions as approximating distributions. A *hyperexponential* (H_k) distribution is a mixture of k exponentials for some k, i.e., the ccdf has the form

$$H^c(t) = \sum_{i=1}^{k} p_i e^{-\lambda_i t} \qquad (1.7)$$

where $p_i \geq 0$ for all i and $p_1 + \ldots + p_k = 1$. Our fitting algorithm fits a hyperexponential distribution to a given long-tail distribution, aiming to be accurate over a finite interval $[t_1, t_2]$ for suitably small t_1 and suitably large t_2.

Given data that might be well described by either a Pareto distribution or a hyperexponential distribution, we would usually prefer the Pareto distribution for a simple description because it provides a more parsimonious description. The H_k distribution in (1.7) has $2k-1$ parameters, whereas the Pareto distribution has only 2. Statistical estimation also tends to work better when there are fewer parameters. We primarily suggest replacing long-tail distributions such as the Pareto distribution by hyperexponential distributions, because performance models tend to be easier to analyze when component distributions in the model are hyperexponential. One reason is that hyperexponential distributions are special phase-type distributions, which have been found to make performance models more tractable [14]. Another reason that we might choose hyperexponential distributions is because they have simple Laplace transforms. the Laplace transform of the density h of the ccdf H^c in (1.7) and the Laplace-Stietjes Transform of the cdf H is

$$\hat{h}(s) = \int_0^\infty e^{-st} dH(t) = \sum_{i=1}^{k} \frac{p_i \lambda_i}{\lambda_i + s}. \qquad (1.8)$$

The explicit Laplace transform (1.8) makes it possible to analyze many performance models by numerical transform inversion, e.g., see [1, 5]. For these numerical transform inversion algorithms, having a relatively large number of phases (e.g., 10 or 100) presents no serious difficulty. We will illustrate this advantage by considering the $M/G/1$ queue with a long-tail service-time distribution. We have no difficulty calculating the steady-state waiting-time distribution in the $M/G/1$ queue by numerical transform inversion after making the hyperexponential approximation.

Hyperexponential distributions also make it easier to obtain Markov stochastic processes, which tend to be far easier to analyze than non-Markov stochastic processes. In particular, hyperexponential approximations can help analyze superpositions of independent on-off sources, where each source sends input at a constant rate (fluid) or as a Poisson process when it is on. If the on or off periods have long-tail distributions, then the aggregate input model tends to be intractable, but if the on and off periods of each source have hyperexponential distributions, then the aggregate input becomes a Markov-modulated fluid or Poisson process (see the longer version of this paper for details), for which there are effective algorithms. Unfortunately, however, this representation is not totally satisfactory, because the Markovian state space becomes larger when the number of exponential components in a mixture increases. Hence, if there are many sources, the state space of the approximating aggregate input model may be so large that analysis remains difficult. Nevertheless, the approximation is a step towards tractable models. If there are only a few source, then the model can now be solved, whereas it could not be solved before.

Once a hyperexponential fit is contemplated, there are many ways to proceed, such as a least squares fit using a mathematical program. A natural alternative is the expectation-maximization (EM) algorithm, which is an iterative procedure that minimizes the Kullback-Leibler "distance"; see Asmussen, Nerman and Olsson [2], Turin [17] and references therein. A difficulty with the EM algorithm is that the iteration can be slow when there are many parameters. The EM algorithm can be enhanced significantly if a good starting point can be provided. In preliminary experiments we have found that our algorithm is also useful to quickly provide a good starting point for the EM algorithm, but we do not discuss those experiments here.

We intend to compare various fitting schemes in a future paper. In this paper we present a simple recursive scheme, based on the notion of time scales. We recursively fit starting in the largest time scale that matters and successively reduce the time scale. We start by fitting a weighted exponential $p_1 e^{-\lambda_1 t}$ to the tail of the given ccdf. Since we focus on the tail, λ_1^{-1} should be suitably large. Then we subtract this weighted exponential from the original ccdf and fit a second weighted exponential $p_2 e^{-\lambda_2 t}$ to the new tail where $\lambda_2^{-1} < \lambda_1^{-1}$. Since the exponential ccdf's are short tailed, it should be possible to choose the second exponential component so that it is negligible further out in the region where the first exponential $p_1 e^{-\lambda_1 t}$ was fit. We describe the algorithm in more detail and discuss previous related work in Section 4.

To illustrate right away, we consider an example. More examples are given in an expanded version of this paper to appear in *Performance Evaluation.*

Example 1. Suppose that we consider a Weibull distribution as in (1.6) with exponent $c = 0.3$ and a chosen so that the distribution has mean 1. (That makes $a = 9.26053$.) Since c is close to 0, this Weibull distribution is strongly long-tailed. This is partly reflected by its next two moments, which are $m_2 = 29.2$ and $m_3 = 4481$. However, the first three moments do not nearly capture the full long-tail effect. To illustrate, we first consider fitting an H_2 distribution (a mixture of two exponentials, which has three parameters) to the Weibull distribution by matching the first three moments (p. 136 [18]). The resulting H_2 parameters are $p_1 = 0.00501$, $\lambda_1 = 0.019$, and $\lambda_2 = 1.355$. The approximating H_2 density and ccdf are compared to their Weibull counterparts in Figure 1 (a), (b). It is obvious that the fit is quite poor, even though the H_2 distribution has the same first three moments.

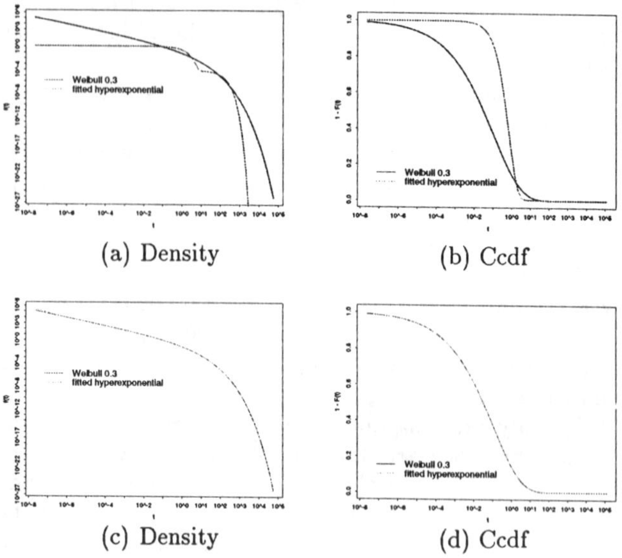

Figure 1: A comparison between the Weibull(0.3, 9.261) density and ccdf with hyperexponential approximations. This example shows the difference in the quality of fit between matching three moments (a), (b) and applying our algorithm (c), (d).

In contrast, the density and ccdf of an H_k fit obtained by our algorithm in Section 4 is shown in (c) and (d) of Figure 1. The fit is so good that it is hard to see two curves in (c) and (d). This H_k fit has $k = 20$ exponentials. The three moments of the approximating H_{20} distribution are $m_1 = 1.0060$, $m_2 = 30.6$, and $m_3 = 4640$.

By this example, we do not mean to imply that 20 exponentials are necessarily required to produce a satisfactory approximation of this Weibull distribution, but this number certainly seems to be sufficient for almost all network performance applications.

An attractive feature of our algorithm is that it does not depend on the moments. Therefore, it can be used even if the moments do not exist or are not known. However, it is useful to calculate the first few moments of the original and the approximating distributions to help judge the quality of the fit.

Here is how the rest of this paper is organized. In Section 2 we discuss robustness of performance models. We refer to some of the evidence indicating that if a component probability distribution in a performance model is well approximated by another, then the performance measures of interest will be suitably close. We also give a precise meaning for "close." In Section 3 we rigorously prove that it is possible to approximate many long-tail distributions by hyperexponential distributions. We identify a class of distributions containing many long-tail distributions, including Pareto and Weibull, for which arbitrarily close hyperexponential approximations can be made.

We present our recursive algorithm for constructing approximating hyperexponential distributions in Section 4. In Section 5 we explain when the algorithm should be effective.

In Section 6 we investigate how our fitting algorithm is related to fitting probability distributions to data. We show through simulation experiments that, consistent with intuition, it is usually much better to fit a long-tail distribution with only a few parameters to the data and then afterwards apply our algorithm to the long-tail distribution in order to obtain a high-order hyperexponential approximation than it is to apply our algorithm directly to the empirical distribution generated from the data. Finally, we state our conclusions in Section 7.

2 The Robustness of Performance Models

Since we intend to approximate component distributions in performance models by other distributions, it is important that the performance models be robust to such changes. As a specific example, we will consider approximating long-tail service-time distributions by hyperexponential distributions in the $GI/G/1$ queue. (The $GI/G/1$ queue is just one example; There are many possible applications of hyperexponential approximations besides the $GI/G/1$ queue). The $GI/G/1$ queue has a single server, unlimited waiting room and interarrival times and service times coming from independent sequences of independent and identically distributed random variables with general distributions. If we approximate the given general interarrival-time and service-time distributions by other distributions, then we want descriptive performance measures such as the steady-state waiting-time distribution also to be approximately what it would be with the original interarrival-time and service-time distributions. Fortunately, such robustness, stability or continuity properties have been established for performance models.

Even though robustness results have been established, care is needed because the robustness results do not hold unconditionally. The robustness depends upon what we mean by "close" and upon regularity conditions. We say that a sequence of random variables $\{X_n : n \geq 1\}$ converges in distribution to a random variable X, and write $X_n \Rightarrow X$, if $Ef(X_n) \to Ef(X)$ as $n \to \infty$ for all bounded continuous real-valued functions f. If F_n and F are the cdf's of X_n and X, i.e., $F_n(t) = P(X_n \leq t)$, then $X_n \Rightarrow X$ is equivalent to convergence of cdf's in the form $F_n(t) \to F(t)$ as $n \to \infty$ for all points t that are continuity points of the limiting cdf F, which we denote by $F_n \Rightarrow F$.

With this background, we can state a robustness theorem for the $GI/G/1$ queue due to Borovkov [4] p. 118. A random variable is said to be proper if it is finite with probability one.

Theorem 2.1. (Borovkov). *Consider a sequence of $GI/G/1$ queueing models indexed by n with interarrival times, service times and steady-state waiting-time distributed as $U^{(n)}$, $V^{(n)}$ and $W^{(n)}$, respectively. Consider a prospective limiting $GI/G/1$ model with corresponding random variables U, V and W. If $EV^{(n)} < EU^{(n)}$ for all n, $EV < EU$, $U_n \Rightarrow U$, $V_n \Rightarrow V$ and $EV_n \to EV$ as $n \to \infty$, then $W^{(n)}, n \geq 1$, and W are proper random variables and $W_n \Rightarrow W$ as $n \to \infty$.*

The condition $EV^{(n)} < EU^{(n)}$ in Theorem 2.1 is needed in order to ensure that the nth model is stable, i.e., that a proper steady-state waiting-time $W^{(n)}$ exists. An important point in Theorem 2.1 is that we also need to assume that the limiting system is stable ($EV < EU$), that the mean service times converge ($EV_n \to EV$), and that the limiting mean is necessarily finite ($EV < \infty$ since $EV < EU$). We need to assume that $EV_n \to EV$ as $n \to \infty$, because convergence in distribution does not imply convergence of moments. As a secondary point, note that there is no requirement that the mean interarrival times $EU^{(n)}$ and EU be finite or that $EU^{(n)} \to EU$ as $n \to \infty$.

To illustrate how we can apply Theorem 2.1, suppose that a $GI/G/1$ queueing system of interest has a generic service time V with a Pareto distribution as in (1.5). In the next section we will show that, without imposing any moment conditions, we can approximate the Pareto distribution of V arbitrarily closely by a hyperexponential distribution as in (1.7); i.e., for each n we can let $V^{(n)}$ have a hyperexponential distribution (where the number of component exponentials depends on n) and have $V^{(n)} \Rightarrow V$ as $n \to \infty$.

We would like to deduce that $W^{(n)} \Rightarrow W$ for the waiting-times in the associated $GI/G/1$ models. (Assume that the interarrival-time distribution is fixed.) However, we cannot draw this conclusion without the extra conditions in Theorem 2.1. The crucial extra condition is that $EV < \infty$; for the $GI/G/1$ application we must require that the Pareto distribution have a finite mean. If $EV = \infty$, then the approximation procedure will fail, but if $EV < \infty$, then it will work. It turns out that we can choose the approximating distributions so that $EV^{(n)} \to EV$ as $n \to \infty$, and we need to do so, but we also need to require that $EV < \infty$ and $EV < EU$ as well. However, with such extra conditions, approximating component distributions can achieve the desired result. The remaining questions are only the practical ones: How many exponentials are needed before the distribution of $V^{(n)}$ is suitably close to the distribution of V? And how do we actually find a good approximating distribution?

Example 2. To illustrate the robustness of the queueing model, we consider the Weibull distribution in Example 1 as a service-time distribution in the $M/G/1$ queue (having an exponential interarrival-time distribution). We let the arrival rate (and thus the traffic intensity) be 0.75. We focus on the steady-state waiting-time ccdf $P(W > t)$. In addition to the three-moment H_2 fit and the H_{20} fit by our algorithm in Section 4, we consider a simple exponential fit obtained by matching only the mean.

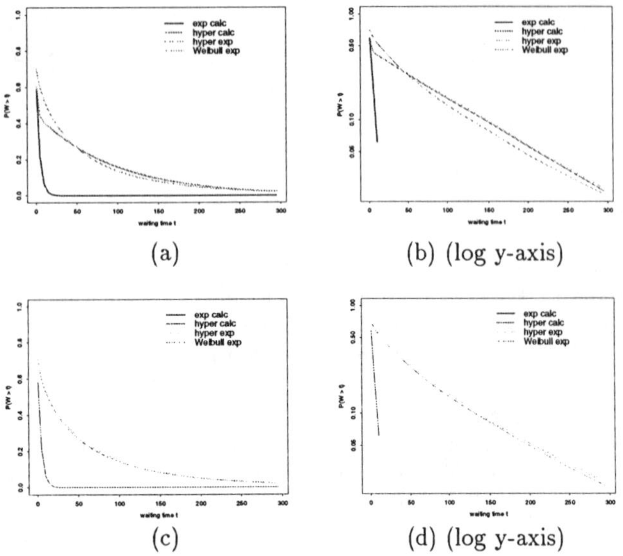

Figure 2: The steady-state $M/G/1$ waiting-time ccdf $P(W > t)$ with a Weibull(.3, 9.261) service-time distribution having mean = 1. the numerical results (calc) are for the model with the approximating hyperexponential and exponential service-time distributions. The simulations (exp) are for the model with the Weibull and the approximating hyperexponential distribution. Parts (a) and (b) contain the H_2 fit by matching the first three moments, while parts (c) and (d) contain the H_{20} fit by the algorithm in Section 4. Parts (b) and (d) are the same as parts (a) and (c), respectively, but with the y-axis in log scale.

We compare numerical results (calc) for the $M/H_2/1$ and $M/M/1$ models to simulations (exp) of the $M/H_2/1$ and $M/W/1$ models in (a) and (b) of Figure 2 (W stands for Weibull). In contrast, we compare numerical results for the $M/H_{20}/1$ and $M/M/1$ models to simulations of the $M/H_{20}/1$ and $M/W/1$ models in (c) and (d) of Figure 2. In all cases, the steady-state waiting-time ccdf is displayed, with the y-axis being in log scale in (b) and (d).

The $M/M/1$ model is appealing, because the steady-state waiting-time cdf for it is available in closed form (a simple exponential plus an atom at the origin), but it yields a remarkably poor approximation. Clearly the service-time distribution beyond its mean matters greatly. The $M/H_2/1$ numerical results could be obtained in several ways; we used numerical transform inversion [1]. The simulations were based on a time interval of 5.3×10^6, which corresponds to about 4×10^6 arrivals.

From (a) and (b) of Figure 2, we see that the $M/H_2/1$ approximation for the waiting-time ccdf is much better than the H_2 approximation for the W service-time distribution directly. This reflects the extensive experience showing that approximations based on two moments of the interarrival-time and service-time distributions can be quite effective. However, even though the $M/H_2/1$ approximation might be good enough for some engineering applications, the $M/H_{20}/1$ approximation in (c) and (d) is far better.

3 Complete Monotonicity

To have a good theoretical basis for approximating one distribution by another, it is appropriate to consider what is possible. From this perspective, it is important to note that every hyperexponential distribution has a decreasing probability density functions (pdf) and possibly an atom at 0. Thus, hyperexponential distributions cannot capture departures from this structure, such as atoms away from 0 or a non-monotone pdf.

On the other hand, there is a large class of distributions (necessarily with monotone pdf's) which can be approximately arbitrarily closely by hyperexponentials. The nice class of probability distributions are those with completely monotone pdf's. A probability density function (pdf) f is said to be *completely monotone* if all derivatives of f exist and

$$(-1)^n f^{(n)}(t) \geq 0 \quad \text{for all } t > 0 \text{ and } n \geq 1 \; ; \tag{3.1}$$

see p. 439 of [8]. the link between completely monotone pdf's and mixtures of exponential pdf's is provided by Bernstein's theorem [8].

Theorem 3.1. (Bernstein) *Every completely monotone pdf f is a mixture of exponential pdf's, i.e.,*

$$f(t) = \int_0^\infty \lambda e^{-\lambda t} dG(\lambda) \; , \quad t \geq 0 \; , \tag{3.2}$$

for some proper cdf G.

We call G in (3.2) the *spectral* cdf. (Then the support of G is called the *spectrum*. The *support* of G is the set of all t for which $G(t+\epsilon) - G(t-\epsilon) > 0$ for all $\epsilon > 0$.) Of course, the spectral cdf G appearing in (3.2) is a general cdf; it need not have finite support. (A cdf G has finite support if it has a probability mass function attaching probabilities p_i to n points t_i with $p_1 + \ldots + p_n = 1$ for some n.) However, cdf's with finite support are dense in the family of all cdf's. Hence, Theorem 3.1 implies the following result.

Theorem 3.2. *If F is a cdf with a completely monotone pdf, then there are hyperexponential cdf's $F^{(n)}$, $n \geq 1$, i.e., cdf's of the form*

$$F^{(n)}(t) = \sum_{i=1}^{k_n} p_{ni}(1 - e^{-\lambda_{ni} t}) \; , \quad t \geq 0 \; , \tag{3.3}$$

with $\lambda_{ni} \leq \infty$ and $p_{n1} + \ldots p_{nk_n} = 1$, such that $F^{(n)} \Rightarrow F$ as $n \to \infty$.

Theorems 3.1 and 3.2 are important for approximating long-tail distributions because many long-tail pdf's are completely monotone. For example, by differentiating (and using mathematical induction), it is easy to see that the pdf's of the Pareto distribution in (1.5) and the Weibull distribution with $a < 1$ in (1.6) are completely monotone. The gamma pdf with shape parameter less than 1 is also completely monotone. The Pareto mixture of exponentials (PME) distribution considered in [1] is also completely monotone, because it directly satisfies (3.2). The PME distribution is convenient because its Laplace transform is available.

4 The Recursive Fitting Procedure

In this section we specify the recursive procedure for fitting a hyperexponential (H_k) cdf H to a given cdf F on the nonnegative real line. We think of the original cdf as being a long-tail distribution such as Pareto or Weibull with exponent less than one. We think of the cdf F as having a monotone probability density function (pdf) f, but we do not require it. We discuss conditions under which the procedure should be effective in Section 5.

The H_k distribution has ccdf (1.7). Without loss of generality, let the exponential parameters λ_i be labeled so that $\lambda_1 < \ldots < \lambda_k$. Then the higher indexed components have tails which decay more rapidly. Our idea is to fit the H_k components recursively, starting with the pair (λ_1, p_1) and then proceeding to (λ_2, p_2) and so forth. If λ_2 is sufficiently greater than λ_1, then $\sum_{i=2}^{k} e^{-\lambda_i t}$ should be negligible compared to $p_1 e^{-\lambda_1 t}$ for t sufficiently large (in the tail). This should enable us to choose the pair (p_1, λ_1) without being concerned about the other H_k parameter values. We then subtract the component $p_1 e^{-\lambda_1 t}$ from both $H^c(t)$ and $F^c(t)$ and fit the second component to the remaining tail. If again λ_3 is sufficiently greater than λ_2, then $\sum_{i=3}^{k} e^{-\lambda_i t}$ should be negligible compared to $p_2 e^{-\lambda_2 t}$ for t sufficiently large, and we can fit the pair (λ_2, p_2) without being concerned about the other H_k parameters.

After deriving this recursive fitting procedure, we learned that the general recursive estimation procedure actually has a long history, being known as Prony's method (p. 114 [16]). In that context, we contribute by showing when the recursive fitting procedure should be effective (Sections 3 and 5 here) and by applying it to approximate long-tail distributions.

Here is the procedure: we first choose the number k of exponential components and k arguments where we will match quantiles: $0 < c_k < c_{k-1} < \ldots < c_1$. We assume that the ratios c_i/c_{i+1} are sufficiently large; e.g., we could have $c_i = c_1 10^{-(i-1)}$ for $2 \leq i \leq k$. Let b be such that $1 < b < c_i/c_{i+1}$ for all i; e.g., with $c_i = c_1 10^{-(i-1)}$ we could have $b = 2$.

We choose λ_1 and p_1 to match the ccdf $F^c(t)$ at the arguments c_1 and bc_1; i.e., we solve the two equations

$$p_1 e^{-\lambda_1 x c_1} = F^c(xc_1) \text{ for } x = 1 \text{ and } b$$

for p_1 and λ_1, assuming that $c_1, b, F^c(c_1)$ and $F^c(bc_1)$ are known, obtaining

$$\lambda_1 = \frac{1}{(b-1)c_1} \ln\left(\frac{F^c(c_1)}{F^c(bc_1)}\right) \text{ and } p_1 = F^c(c_1) e^{\lambda_1 c_1} .$$

With this procedure, we are assuming that λ_i will be sufficiently larger than λ_1 for all $i \geq 2$ that the final approximation will satisfy

$$\sum_{i=1}^{k} p_i e^{-\lambda_i t} \approx p_1 e^{-\lambda_1 t} \quad \text{for } t \geq c_1 .$$

We have no guarantee that this property will hold, but the accuracy can be checked when the fit is complete. (See Section 5 for further discussion.)

Next, for $2 \leq i \leq k$, let

$$F_i^c(xc_i) = F_{i-1}^c(xc_i) - \sum_{j=1}^{i-1} p_j e^{-\lambda_j x c_i} \text{ for } x = 1 \text{ and } b$$

where $F_1^c(t) = F^c(t)$. Then proceed as above, letting

$$p_i e^{-\lambda_i x c_i} = F_i^c(xc_i) \text{ for } x = 1 \text{ and } b$$

to obtain

$$\lambda_i = \frac{1}{(b-1)c_i} \ln\left(\frac{F_i^c(c_i)}{F_i^c(bc_i)}\right) \text{ and } p_i = F_i^c(c_i) e^{\lambda_i c_i}$$

for $2 \leq i \leq k-1$. Finally, for the last parameter pair (λ_k, p_k), we require that

$$p_k = 1 - \sum_{j=1}^{k-1} p_j \text{ and } p_k e^{-\lambda_k c_k} = F_k^c(c_k),$$

where $F_k^c(c_k)$ is defined, so that

$$\lambda_k = \frac{1}{c_k} \ln(p_k / F_k^c(c_k)) .$$

Assuming that we obtain probability weights ($p_i > 0$ for all i), and that the parameters λ_i are well separated, we should obtain a good fit. Assuming that we obtain probability weights, the procedure produces an H_k ccdf H^c that is larger than the original ccdf F^c at the matching points, i.e.,

$$H^c(xc_i) > F^c(xc_i), \ 1 \leq i < k, \text{ for } x = 1 \text{ and } b.$$

However, if F^c is a long-tail distribution, then there will be a t_0 such that

$$F^c(t) \geq H^c(t) \quad \text{for all } t \geq t_0 .$$

Hence, it is important to choose c_1 sufficiently large that t_0 is beyond the region of interest.

Our implementation of the algorithm in software allows the user to proceed interactively, choosing new parameter settings as desired, after looking at tables and graphs of the results. The standard approach is to specify k, c_1, c_k, and b. Then the algorithm chooses the remaining c_i such that the ratio of c_i/c_{i+1} is constant and proceeds with the fitting procedure. An available alternative is to specify one point at a time, start with the pair (c_i, b_i), inspect the preliminary result, and continue by choosing the next pair (c_{i+1}, b_{i+1}).

When we are done, we calculate several moments of the H_k distribution and compare them to the moments of F if they are available. As numerical measures of achieved fitting accuracy, we compute the absolute and relative errors of the ccdf and cdf. For both, the cdf and the ccdf, the absolute error is

$$AE(F,t) = |H^c(t) - F^c(t)| = |H(t) - F(t)|\,.$$

A relative error for both the cdf and ccdf is

$$RE(F,t) = \frac{|H^c(t) - F^c(t)|}{\min\{F(t), F^c(t)\}}.$$

We graphically display these errors as functions of t over any requested interval (l, u). We calculate the curves by considering points whose logarithms are evenly spaced over (l, u).

To illustrate, we display the absolute and relative errors of the H_2 and the H_{20} fits to the Weibull distribution in Example 1 in Figure 3. It turns out that the H_{20} fit was done with $c_k = 10^{-7}$ and $c_1 = 9 \times 10^4$. Since c_1 is not large, there are somewhat large relative errors for the H_{20} cdf in the region $10^2 - 10^5$. However, the ccdf values in this region are very small, e.g., $F^c(10^2) = 4.25e-4$, $F^c(10^3) = 1.88e-7$, $F^c(10^4) = 3.79e-14$, and $F^c(10^5) = 1.67e-27$.

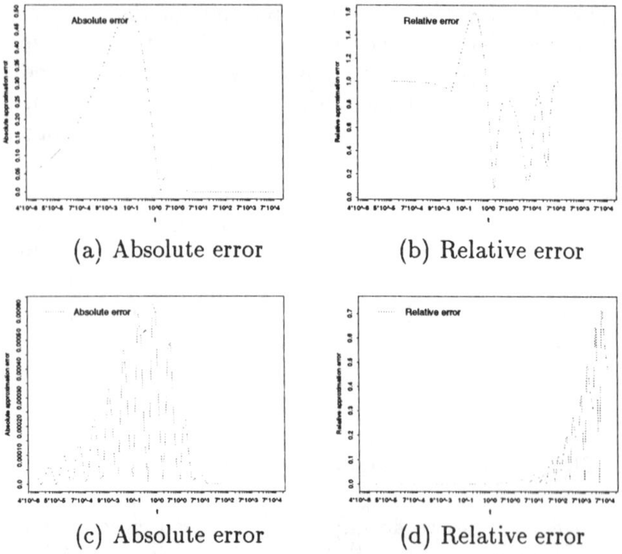

(a) Absolute error (b) Relative error

(c) Absolute error (d) Relative error

Figure 3: The relative and absolute errors of the H_2 and the H_{20} fits to the Weibull(0.3, 9.261) distribution from Example 1.

5 When Should the Procedure Work?

In this section we discuss conditions under which the fitting procedure in Section 4 should be effective. In particular, we point out that the procedure is natural for distributions with *decreasing failure rate* (DFR). to see this, note that the fitting formula for λ_i can be rewritten as

$$\lambda_i = -\frac{\ln(F_i^c(bc_i) - \ln(F_i^c(c_i)}{bc_i - c_i}\,. \qquad (5.1)$$

As $b \to 1$, formula (5.1) approaches

$$\lambda_i = -\frac{d}{dt}\ln(F^c(t)|_{t=c_i} = \frac{f(c_i)}{F^c(c_i)} = r(c_i)\,, \qquad (5.2)$$

which is the *hazard rate function* (or failure rate function) associated with the ccdf F^c evaluated at c_i [3].

The idea in the procedure of Section 4 is to have λ_i be significantly less than λ_{i+1} for all i. In order to have λ_i be less than λ_{i+1} for all i, it is natural to require that the ccdf $F^c(t)$ be DFR. This is equivalent to having $F^c(t)$ be *log-convex*. A sufficient condition for the ccdf $F^c(t)$ to be log-convex is for the pdf $f(t)$ to be log-convex (p. 73 [9]). Since mixtures of log-convex pdf's are log-convex (Theorem 5.4c, p. 66 [9]), all completely monotone pdf's are log-convex. Hence all completely monotone pdf's are DFR.

In summary, our algorithm is natural for completely monotone pdf's such as the Pareto and Weibull distributions (see Section 3) and, more generally, for DFR pdf's. However, by the same reasoning, our algorithm is inappropriate for increasing failure rate (IFR) distributions. For example, our algorithm does not work for the uniform distribution, i.e., when $F(t) = t/b, 0 \leq t \leq b$, and $F(t) = 1, t \geq b$, which clearly has a very short tail. Since many long-tail distributions are DFR, our algorithm has substantial applicability.

Even though many long-tail distributions are DFR, many others are not. Indeed, the long-tail property (1.1) is unaltered by changing the probability distribution on any initial interval $[0, t]$. Thus, the long-tail property does not nearly guarantee the DFR property.

6 Fitting to Data

Besides using the fitting algorithm to fit a hyperexponential distribution to another distribution, we can also use the fitting algorithm to fit a hyperexponential distribution to data. In this case the empirical ccdf obtained from the data replaces the ccdf of the initial probability distribution in the algorithm.

However, we would suggest caution when applying our algorithm directly to data. Our experience is that it is usually much better to first fit a suitable long-tail probability distribution with only a few parameters to the data, and then afterwards apply our algorithm to fit a multi-parameter hyperexponential distribution to the long-tail distribution. By this two-step procedure, we usually are able to obtain a good multi-parameter hyperexponential fit to data.

We considered a simulation experiment in which we try to fit a probability distribution to a sample of 1000 points drawn from the Weibull(.3, 9.261) distribution considered in Example 1 having unit mean. Even though the sample size is not very large, it is large enough to obtain a good fit to the two-parameter Weibull distribution using the maximum likelihood estimator (p. 255 [10]). The Weibull parameters achieved from one sample were $c = 0.3016$ and $a = 9.369$ (yielding a mean of 0.96532). Since the estimated values of c and a are close to the original parameters, our algorithm applied to the fitted Weibull distribution can produce an excellent H_{20} approximation to the original Weibull distribution. For this experiment, the original Weibull distribution, the fitted Weibull distribution and the H_{20} fit to the fitted Weibull distribution are all very close, just as in Figure 1.

We also considered what happens when we apply our hyperexponential fitting algorithm directly to the data. Since the sample is not large, the range of the empirical ccdf is limited. Thus, it is not possible to directly apply our algorithm with many exponential terms. We show what happens with 4 exponentials. Figure 4 (a), (b) show how the fitted hyperexponential distribution matches the experimental cdf and ccdf. Figure 4 (c), (d) compare the fitted hyperexponential distribution to two Weibull distributions: the original Weibull distribution and the fitted Weibull distribution. Although the fits in Figure 4 look quite good, the pictures are deceptive, because the small and large values are not matched well. To illustrate, the moments are not matched well. For example, the third moments of the original Weibull cdf, the data, the H_4 fit and the Weibull fit were 4481, 1592, 145, and 3820, respectively. The poor moments match can be explained in part by the fact that the sample moments of the data are not very close to the moments of the sampled distribution.

The experiment we have considered is somewhat biased, because we considered a hyperexponential fit to Weibull data. If we know in advance that the data is generated from the Weibull distribution, then using a statistical estimation procedure tailored to the Weibull distribution evidently should be good. It is less clear with an unknown data source. However, regardless of the data source, our fitting procedure is not designed to treat data. It does not address the statistical problems of the estimation. However, our procedure might well be applied effectively after some initial smoothing of the data, but that approach remains to be explored.

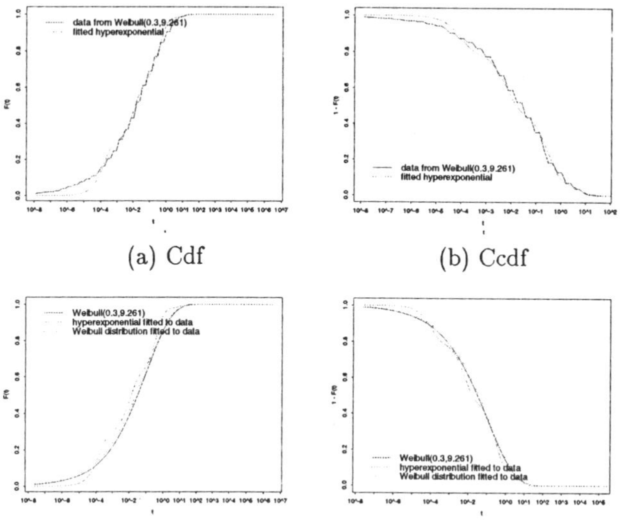

(a) Cdf (b) Ccdf

(c) Cdf (d) Ccdf

Figure 4: H_4 fit to the empirical cdf from a sample of size 1000 from a Weibull(.3, 9.261) distribution using $c_k = 0.0001$ and $c_1 = 5$.

7 Conclusions

In this paper we have developed an effective simple algorithm for approximating a large class of probability distributions with monotone densities by hyperexponential distributions (Section 4). We have found that the algorithm is effective for approximating Pareto and Weibull distributions (Sections 1, 2). We have shown that the algorithm should be effective for distributions with decreasing failure rate, and should not be used for distributions with increasing failure rate (Section 5). We have proved that, in principle, completely monotone pdf's (all of which have decreasing failure rate) can be approximated arbitrarily closely by hyperexponential pdf's, and that as a result (under extra regularity conditions) the associated waiting-time distribution in a $GI/G/1$ queue with a completely monotone service-time distribution can be approximated arbitrarily closely by the waiting-time distribution in the associated $GI/G/1$ queue with the approximating hyperexponential service-time distribution (Sections 2 and 3). Since many long-tail distributions are completely monotone, these results serve as a theoretical foundation for approximating long-tail distributions by hyperexponential distributions. Since phase-type probability distributions are dense in the family of all probability distributions, by the same reasoning, they are rich enough to approximate any distribution, if enough phases are allowed. We have pointed out that the EM algorithm is a candidate fitting algorithm for general phase-type distribution.

We believe that hyperexponential approximations of long-tail distributions can be useful, but they do not remove all difficulties. If a good fit is done, then the high variability of the long-tail distribution will be inherited by the approximating hyperexponential distribution. This high variability can make precise estimation by computer simulation difficult. Hyperexponential approximations also can make models of the superpositions of on-off sources more tractable, but since the state space of the Markovian environment process may be large, the approximating aggregate input process can still be difficult to analyze. However, we did see that the hyperexponential approximation makes it possible to calculate steady-state performance distributions in the $M/G/1$ queue with a long-tail service-time distribution by numerical transform inversion. The same technique applies to the more general $BMAP/G/1$ queue and other performance models.

We have emphasized that our fitting algorithm is intended to approximate one probability distribution by another, and not to fit a probability distribution directly to data (Section 6). In some circumstances our algorithm could be used to fit a hyperexponential distribution to an empirical distribution (histogram) obtained from data, but our algorithm is not designed for that purpose. Indeed, in simulation experiments with long-tail data, we found that much better fits are obtained by first fitting a long-tail distribution with very few parameters (e.g., 2) to the data and then applying our algorithm to obtain a hyperexponential distribution.

Finally, the algorithm presented here is only one of many possible fitting algorithms. We intend to compare alternative fitting algorithms in a future paper.

Acknowledgment

We thank our colleague William Turin for helpful discussions about the EM algorithm and the history of recursive estimation.

References

[1] J. Abate, G. L. Choudhury and W. Whitt, Waiting-time tail probabilities in queues with long-tail service-time distributions, *Queueing Systems* 16 (1994) 311–338.

[2] S. Asmussen, O. Nerman and M. Olsson, Fitting phase type distributions via the EM algorithm, *Scand. J. Statist.* (1996), to appear.

[3] R. E. Barlow and F. Proschan, *Statistical Theory of Reliability and Life Testing*, Holt, Rinehart and Winston, New York, 1975.

[4] A. A. Borovkov, *Stochastic Processes in Queueing Theory*, Springer-Verlag, New York, 1976.

[5] G. L. Choudhury, D. M. Lucantoni and W. Whitt, Squeezing the most out of ATM, *IEEE Trans. Commun.* 44 (1996) 203–217.

[6] M. E. Crovella and A. Bestavros. Self-similarity in World Wide Web traffic - evidence and possible causes. *Proceedings of Sigmetrics'96* (1996) 160-169.

[7] A. Feldmann. *On-line Call Admission for High-Speed Networks.* PhD thesis, School of Computer Science, Carnegie Mellon University, Pittsburgh, PA, 1995.

[8] W. Feller, *An Introduction to Probability Theory and Its Applications*, Wiley, New York, 1971.

[9] J. Keilson, *Markov Chain Models — Rarity and Exponentiality*, Springer-Verlag, New York, 1979.

[10] N. L. Johnson and S. Kotz, *Distributions in Statistics, Continuous Univariate Distributions*, Wiley, New York, 1970.

[11] W. E. Leland, M. S. Taqqu, W. Willinger, and D. V. Wilson. On the self-similar nature of Ethernet traffic. *IEEE/ACM Transactions on Networking* 2 (1994) 1–15.

[12] D. M. Lucantoni, The $BMAP/G/1$ queue: a tutorial, in *Models and Techniques for Performance Evaluation of Computer and Communication Systems*, L. Doniatiello and R. Nelson eds., Springer-Verlag, New York (1993) 330-358.

[13] M. Montgomery and G. de Veciana. On the relevance of time scales in performance oriented traffic characterizations. *IEEE INFOCOM'96* 513–520.

[14] M. F. Neuts, *Matrix-Geometric Solutions in Stochastic Models*, The Johns Hopkins University Press, Baltimore, 1981.

[15] V. Paxson and S. Floyd. Wide-area traffic: the failure of Poisson modeling. *IEEE/ACM Transactions on Networking* 3 (1995) 226–244.

[16] W. Turin, *Performance Analysis of Digital Transmission Systems*, Computer Science Press, New York, 1990.

[17] W. Turin, Fitting probabilistic automata via the EM algorithm, *Stochastic Models* 12 (1996) 405–424.

[18] W. Whitt, Approximating a point process by a renewal process, I: two basic methods, *Opns. Res.* 30 (1982) 125–147.

[19] W. Willinger, M. S. Taqqu, R. Sherman and D. V. Wilson, Self similarity through high variability: statistical analysis of Ethernet LAN traffic at the source level. *SIGCOMM'95* 100–113.

Finite and Infinite QBD Chains: A Simple and Unifying Algorithmic Approach

Nail Akar and Khosrow Sohraby
Computer Science Telecommunications
University of Missouri-Kansas City
Kansas City, MO, 64110

Abstract

In this paper, we present a novel algorithmic approach, the hybrid matrix geometric/invariant subspace method, for finding the stationary probability distribution of the finite QBD process which arises in performance analysis of computer and communication systems. Assuming that the QBD state space is defined in two dimensions with m phases and $K+1$ levels, the solution vector for level k, $\pi_k, 0 \le k \le K$ is shown to be in a modified matrix geometric form $\pi_k = v_1 R_1^k + v_2 R_2^{K-k}$ where R_1 and R_2 are certain solutions to two nonlinear matrix equations and v_1 and v_2 are vectors to be determined using the boundary conditions. We show that the matrix geometric factors R_1 and R_2 can simultaneously be obtained independently of K via finding the sign function of a real matrix by an iterative algorithm with quadratic convergence rates. The time complexity of obtaining the coefficient vectors v_1 and v_2 is shown to be $O(m^3 \log_2 K)$ which indicates that the contribution of the number of levels on the overall algorithm is minimal. Besides the numerical efficiency, the proposed method is numerically stable and in the limiting case of $K \to \infty$, it is shown to yield the well-known matrix geometric solution $\pi_k = \pi_0 R_1^k$ for infinite QBD chain.

1 Introduction

In this paper, we examine a finite quasi-birth-death (QBD) process which is a Markov chain with state space $\{(i,j);\ 0 \le i \le K, 1 \le j \le m\}$ and which in discrete time has a probability transition matrix of block tridiagonal form:

$$P = \begin{bmatrix} B_0 & A_0 & & & & \\ B_1 & A_1 & A_0 & & & \\ & A_2 & A_1 & \cdots & & \\ & & A_2 & \cdots & A_0 & \\ & & & \cdots & A_1 & C_0 \\ & & & & A_2 & C_1 \end{bmatrix}, \quad (1)$$

where $B_0, B_1, A_0, A_1, A_2, C_0$, and C_1 are all $m \times m$ non-negative matrices, P is finite, irreducible and of size $m(K+1) \times m(K+1)$. We define $A(z) = A_0 + A_1 z + A_2 z^2$, and we assume that the matrix $A(1)$ is irreducible, stochastic and has an invariant vector x,

$$xA(1) = x, \quad xe_1 = 1 \quad (2)$$

where the notation e_k, $k \ge 0$ is used to denote a column vector of ones of length mk. In our mathematical formulation, we assume without loss of generality that the traffic parameter

$$\gamma = xA_0e_1 - xA_2e_1 < 0, \quad (3)$$

which makes the variant of (1) with infinite number of levels positive recurrent [14]. However, this assumption is not needed for the finite QBD process and the necessary adjustments in the solution procedure for the case $\gamma > 0$ will also be provided in the sequel.

Our aim is to find the stationary probability vector π of the finite QBD process, which is the unique solution to the equations

$$\pi = \pi P, \quad \pi e_{(K+1)} = 1. \quad (4)$$

For convenience, we partition the stationary vector π as

$$\pi = \begin{bmatrix} \pi_0 & \pi_1 & \cdots & \pi_K \end{bmatrix}, \quad (5)$$

where π_k, of size $1 \times m$, will be called the solution vector of level k, $0 \le k \le K$ as in [17].

The infinite QBD process with the transition matrix of the form

$$P = \begin{bmatrix} B_0 & A_0 & & \\ B_1 & A_1 & A_0 & \\ & A_2 & A_1 & \cdots \\ & & A_2 & \cdots \\ & & & \cdots \end{bmatrix}, \quad (6)$$

has been used in numerous applications in infinite queues [16],[14]. In this case, the steady-state solution has a matrix geometric form [14], i.e.,

$$\pi_k = \pi_0 R_1^k, \ k \ge 0 \quad (7)$$

0-8186-7780-5/97 $10.00 © 1997 IEEE

where the matrix geometric rate matrix R_1 is the unique minimal non-negative solution of the following quadratic matrix equation

$$R = A_0 + RA_1 + R^2 A_2. \tag{8}$$

Once R_1 is obtained, the boundary vector π_0 in equation (7) can be computed via solving [14]

$$\pi_0 = \pi_0 B[R_1], \ \pi_0(I - R_1)^{-1}e_1 = 1, \tag{9}$$

where

$$B[R_1] = B_0 + R_1 B_1, \tag{10}$$

and I will denote the identity matrix of suitable size. The matrix-geometric rate matrix R_1 can be obtained by using the logarithmic reduction procedure of Latouche and Ramaswami [12] or the invariant subspace approach of Akar and Sohraby [3] employing in particular the matrix sign iterations, both of which have quadratic convergence rates and are shown through numerical examples to have similar performances in terms of execution time requirements [3].

In the case of finite QBD processes with transition matrices of the form given in (1), the solutions are known to be in a more complicated modified matrix geometric form [10]. However, the method proposed in [10] does not lend itself to an efficient numerical algorithm for finding the stationary distribution of the QBD process since time and space complexity of obtaining certain matrices in the modified matrix geometric form of [10] are linear on the number of levels (i.e., $K + 1$) of the process. The algorithm of Ye and Li [17] does not use the matrix-geometric approach but instead employs Markov chain reduction techniques to reduce the time complexity of solving the steady-state equations to $O(m^3 \log_2 K)$, however obtaining certain performance measures of interest from those probabilities may still require substantial computation especially in the case of large K due to the lack of simple and explicit expressions for the stationary probabilities.

In this paper we make use of the matrix-geometric approach and show that the stationary probabilities are expressible in the following modified matrix-geometric form:

$$\pi_k = v_1 R_1^k + v_2 R_2^{K-k}, \ 0 \le k \le K \tag{11}$$

where R_1 is defined as before and R_2 is the unique power-bounded solution to the following matrix quadratic equation which is the dual of equation (8):

$$R = A_2 + RA_1 + R^2 A_0. \tag{12}$$

In expression (11), v_1 and v_2 are row vectors of length m and can easily be obtained by solving a linear matrix equation of size $2m$, once R_1 and R_2 are obtained. Using the methodology developed in [3] for general M/G/1 and G/M/1 paradigms, we further show that the two matrix-geometric factors R_1 and R_2 in the expression (11) are related to the left and right invariant subspaces of *one* square real matrix of size $2m$, respectively. We also provide a particular *matrix sign iteration* [6] with quadratic convergence rates to compute a basis for these two subspaces, which in turn gives the two matrix geometric factors. The core of the algorithm lies in the matrix sign iterations for finding the associated subspaces, each iteration of which has a time complexity of $O(m^3)$ and which involves only simple block matrix operations.

In what follows, we outline the advantages of using the hybrid matrix-geometric/invariant subspace approach:

i) The number of levels do not have impact on the performance of the algorithms both in terms of accuracy and numerical stability; in the limiting case of $K \to \infty$, the solution is shown to yield the matrix-geometric form for infinite QBD processes.

ii) The simple form for the stationary probabilities makes it easy to find certain performance measures of interest, like the blocking probabilities and moments of level distribution.

iii) Central to the algorithm is the two matrix geometric factors, computation of which does not depend on the number of levels. Once these two matrices are obtained, very little additional computational effort is needed for finding the stationary probabilities.

iv) The extension to the case of piecewise homogeneous level-dependent transitions (encountered in queueing systems with multi-level overload control) is easy, see [2] for a detailed study.

The paper is organized as follows. In Section 2, we give the mathematical formulation of our approach in solving for the finite/infinite QBD process. Section 3 addresses the invariant subspace approach to find the matrix-geometric factors and the implementation via the matrix sign iterations. In Section 4, a step-by-step presentation of the numerical algorithm to solve for the finite QBD chain is presented. The extension to the case $\gamma > 0$ is addressed in Section 5. Finally, we provide a numerical example for a discrete-time PH/PH/1/K queue to demonstrate stability, accuracy, and efficiency of the algorithm.

2 Mathematical Formulation

In this section, we will show that the solution vector for level k, π_k is expressible of the form (11) for the finite QBD process described by (1). We first introduce the assumption as in [7]:

$$[zI - A(z)] \text{ is nonsingular for } |z| = 1,\ z \neq 1. \quad (13)$$

This assumption is shown to introduce no loss of generality, see [7]. We now have the following definitions based on [7]. A matrix R is power-bounded if the set of powers $R^k, k \geq 0$ is bounded, i.e., $\sup_k ||R^k|| < +\infty$. Similarly, a matrix R is power-summable if the set of powers $R^k, k \geq 0$ is summable, i.e., $\sum_k ||R^k|| < +\infty$. The eigenvalues of a power-bounded (power-summable) matrix therefore lie in the closed unit disk (open unit disk). Under the assumptions (3) and (13), it can be shown by following the approaches of [14] and [7] that, there is a unique power-summable solution R_1 of the equation (8) and the eigenvalues of R_1 are exactly the m roots of $\Delta_1(z) = [zI - A(z)]$ in the open unit disk. Similarly, there is a unique power-bounded solution R_2 of equation (12) and the eigenvalues of R_2 are exactly the m roots of the dual determinant

$$\Delta_2(z) = \det[zI - (A_2 + A_1 z + A_0 z^2)],$$

in the closed unit disk, one of which is at $z = 1$, all others lying in the open unit disk. For an extensive study on the spectra of solutions to nonlinear matrix equations of the form (8) and (12) and their generalizations, we refer the reader to [7].

Before stating the main result of the paper, we need to show that the matrix $B[R_1, R_2] \triangleq$

$$\begin{bmatrix} B_0 + R_1 B_1 & R_1^{K-1}(C_0 + R_1 C_1 - R_1) \\ R_2^{K-1}(R_2 B_0 + B_1 - R_2) & C_1 + R_2 C_0 \end{bmatrix}, \quad (14)$$

satisfies

$$B[R_1, R_2] e_2 = e_2, \quad (15)$$

i.e., e_2 is a right invariant eigenvector of $B[R_1, R_2]$. The proof is based on direct substitution using

$$P e_{(K+1)} = e_{(K+1)}, \quad (16)$$

the quadratic equations (8) and (12) that the matrices R_1 and R_2 satisfy, and the fact that $(I - R_1)$ is nonsingular since R_1 is power-summable, see [2] for a detailed proof.

Before we proceed, we will need two matrices S_1 and S_2 defined as

$$S_i = \sum_{k=0}^{K} R_i^k, \quad i = 1, 2,$$

for obtaining the normalizing equation of the QBD chain. Our aim is now to obtain closed-form expressions for S_i, $i = 1, 2$. Since, R_1 is power-summable, we have

$$S_1 = (I - R_1^{K+1})(I - R_1)^{-1}. \quad (17)$$

However, R_2 has an eigenvalue at unity and a simplification of the form (17) for S_2 is not possible. Let

$$y = (A_2 - R_2 A_0) e_1, \quad (18)$$

which can be shown to yield $R_2 y = y$, i.e., y is a right invariant eigenvector of R_2. It is not difficult to show that the invariant vector x of $A(1)$ is also a left invariant eigenvector of R_2, i.e., $x R_2 = x$. We now define the following matrix

$$M = \frac{yx}{xy}, \quad (19)$$

which is of rank one. Note that the matrix $(I - \hat{R}_2)$ is invertible where $\hat{R}_2 = R_2 - M$, since the single eigenvalue at unity of R_2 has been moved to the origin by this transformation. One can then show by induction that the following holds:

$$R_2^k = \begin{cases} \hat{R}_2^k + M, & k \geq 1 \\ I. & k = 0 \end{cases} \quad (20)$$

We then have the following explicit expression for S_2:

$$\begin{aligned} S_2 &= I + \sum_{k=1}^{K} \hat{R}_2^k + K M, \\ &= (I - \hat{R}_2^{K+1})(I - \hat{R}_2)^{-1} + K M. \quad (21) \end{aligned}$$

Besides obtaining a closed-form expression, the decomposition (20) helps in devising a numerically stable way of obtaining powers of R_2, which will be used in the algorithm. This is because eigenvalues on the unit circle lead to error-prone computation of high powers of a matrix, however $\hat{R}_2$ is free of eigenvalues on the unit circle and high powers of R_2 can be computed in a numerically stable way using the decomposition (20).

We are now ready to state the main result of this paper.

Theorem 1 *Let $v = [\, v_1 \ v_2 \,]$, v_i, $i = 1, 2$, being a row vector of length m, be the left invariant eigenvector of $B[R_1, R_2]$, i.e.,*

$$v = v\, B[R_1, R_2], \quad (22)$$

normalized so that

$$(v_1 S_1 + v_2 S_2)\, e_1 = 1. \quad (23)$$

The solution vector π_k, $0 \leq k \leq K$ for level k of the QBD process (1) is then given by

$$\pi_k = v_1 R_1^k + v_2 R_2^{K-k}, \quad 0 \leq k \leq K \quad (24)$$

Proof. The proof is by direct substitution. First, we observe that $\pi_0 B_0 + \pi_1 B_1 =$

$$\begin{aligned} &= (v_1 + v_2 R_2^K) B_0 + (v_1 R_1 + v_2 R_2^{K-1}) B_1, \\ &= v_1 + v_2 R_2^K, \text{ by (22)} \\ &= \pi_0. \end{aligned} \qquad (25)$$

In the same way, one can show that

$$\pi_{K-1} C_0 + \pi_K C_1 = \pi_K. \qquad (26)$$

For $1 \le k \le K-1$, we write $\pi_{k-1} A_0 + \pi_k A_1 + \pi_{k+1} A_2$

$$\begin{aligned} &= v_1 R_1^{k-1}(A_0 + R_1 A_1 + R_1^2 A_2), \\ &\quad + v_2 R_2^{K-k-1}(A_2 + R_2 A_1 + R_2^2 A_0), \\ &= v_1 R_1^k + v_2 R_2^{K-k}, \text{ by (8) and (12)} \\ &= \pi_k. \end{aligned} \qquad (27)$$

Finally,

$$\begin{aligned} (\sum_{k=0}^{K} \pi_k) e_1 &= v_1 (\sum_{k=0}^{K} R_1^k) e_1 + v_2 (\sum_{k=0}^{K} R_2^{K-k}) e_1, \\ &= v_1 S_1 e_1 + v_2 S_2 e_1, \\ &= 1, \text{ by (23).} \end{aligned} \qquad (28)$$

Using the equalities (25),(26),(27), and (28), it is easy to see that

$$\pi = \pi P, \ \pi e_{(K+1)} = 1$$

holds, which concludes the proof. Also note that, one cannot find two linearly independent vectors satisfying (22) and (23), since otherwise it would contradict the uniqueness of the stationary solution to the QBD process (1). □

The method presented here unifies the finite/infinite QBD process in a single framework. In order to see this, let us take a look at the coefficient vectors v_1 and v_2 in the solution (24) when the number of levels is infinite. That is, as $K \to \infty$,

$$B[R1, R2] \to \begin{bmatrix} B_0 + R_1 B_1 & 0 \\ M(R_2 B_0 + B_1 - R_2) & C_1 + R_2 C_0 \end{bmatrix},$$

since R_1 is power-summable and $\lim_{K\to\infty} R_1^{K-1} = 0$. Similarly, $\hat{R}_2^{K-1} \to 0$ as $K \to \infty$ which yields $\lim_{K\to\infty} R_2^{K-1} = M$. Then, the vector defined by

$$v = \begin{bmatrix} \pi_0 & 0 \end{bmatrix},$$

where π_0 is defined as in (9), can be shown to be a left invariant eigenvector of $B[R_1, R_2]$ satisfying the equation (23). This shows that, the solution vectors obtained by the method described in Theorem 1 yields the well-known matrix-geometric solution (7) for the limiting case of the infinite QBD process. Besides unification, this convergence ensures numerical stability of the proposed method with respect to the number of levels.

The next section addresses the invariant subspace approach to find the matrix geometric factors R_1 and R_2.

3 Invariant Subspace Approach

We divide the section into two, the first part focusing on the theory which relates invariant subspaces to matrix geometric factors R_1 and R_2. The second part addresses the use of the matrix sign function in finding left and right invariant subspaces of real matrices.

3.1 Theory

We first need definitions and notation concerning the invariant subspaces based on [8]. More details on invariant subspaces can be found in the references [8]. Let us begin with some notation on linear spaces, subspaces, and matrices. By $\mathbf{R}^m$ we mean the real linear space of column vectors of m real numbers. Then $\mathbf{R}^{m\times n}$ is the linear space of $m \times n$ matrices with real entries. A *subspace* is a subset of $\mathbf{R}^m$ that is also closed under the operations of addition and scalar multiplication. For arbitrary subspaces $\mathcal{S}_1$ and $\mathcal{S}_2$, $\mathcal{S}_1 \subset \mathcal{S}_2$ denotes either inclusion or equality. If $A \in \mathbf{R}^{m\times n}$, we define the image of A by

$$\text{Im } A = \{x \in \mathbf{R}^m | x = Ay \text{ for some } y \in \mathbf{R}^n\}.$$

If Im A = Im B, for two matrices with the same number of columns then there exists a nonsingular matrix U such that $B = AU$.

The set of all eigenvalues of a matrix $A \in \mathbf{R}^{m\times m}$ is called the *spectrum* of A and written $\sigma(A)$. Let C be a region in the complex plane. Then the matrix A is called *C-stable* if $\sigma(A) \subset C$. Let C^l, C^0, and C^r denote the left-half plane, the imaginary axis, and the right half-plane of the complex plane, respectively. We also use the notation C^{cr} to denote closed right-half plane, i.e., $C^{cr} = C^r \cup C^0$. A subspace $\mathcal{S}$ of $\mathbf{R}^m$ is said to be A ***invariant*** where $A \in \mathbf{R}^{m\times m}$, if $A\mathcal{S} \subset \mathcal{S}$. Here, $A\mathcal{S} = \{x \in \mathbf{R}^m \, |x = Ay \text{ for some } y \in \mathcal{S}\}$. If a k-dimensional subspace $\mathcal{S}$ is A invariant, then $A\mathcal{S} = \mathcal{S}A_1$ holds for a $k\times k$ matrix A_1 and an $m\times k$ matrix S whose columns form a basis for $\mathcal{S}$, i.e., $\mathcal{S} = \text{Im } S$. We call the A invariant subspace $\mathcal{S}$ the C-invariant subspace of A if $\sigma(A_1) \subset C$ and there is no larger A invariant subspace for which this inclusion holds. The dimension of $\mathcal{S}$ is the number of eigenvalues of A lying in C, counting multiplicities. We call the C^l-invariant subspace (C^r-invariant subspace) as *left* (*right*) invariant subspace for convenience of notation.

We now give an explicit characterization of the matrix geometric factors R_1 and R_2 in terms of certain invariant subspaces of a real matrix. The methodology described below is mainly based on [3] and [1]. We first need the following definitions to state our first result. Let

$$\begin{aligned} H_0 &= A_0 + A_1 + A_2 - I, \\ H_1 &= 2(A_2 - A_0), \\ H_2 &= A_0 - A_1 + A_2 + I. \quad (29) \\ Y_1 &= (R_1 + I)^{-1}(R_1 - I). \quad (30) \end{aligned}$$

We now observe that the following identity holds: $(I+R_1)^2(H_0+Y_1H_1+Y_1^2H_2) = 4(A_0+R_1A_1+R_1^2A_2-R_1)$. Since $(I+R_1)$ is nonsingular, Y_1 satisfies the matrix equation

$$H_0 + YH_1 + Y^2H_2 = 0. \quad (31)$$

Note that the transformation $z \rightarrow \frac{z-1}{z+1}$ is one-to-one and it maps the open unit disk to the the open left-half plane. Therefore Y_1 is the unique C^l-stable solution to (31) and uniqueness follows from the fact that R_1 is the unique solution to the matrix equation (8) all eigenvalues of which lie in the open unit disk.

Now defining

$$Y_2 = (I + R_2)^{-1}(I - R_2),$$

one can similarly show that Y_2 is the unique C^{cr}-stable solution to the matrix equation

$$H_0 + YH_1 + Y^2H_2 = 0. \quad (32)$$

We now define the following matrix of size $2m \times 2m$:

$$E = \begin{bmatrix} 0 & -\hat{H}_0 \\ I & -\hat{H}_1 \end{bmatrix}, \quad (33)$$

where

$$\hat{H}_i = H_iH_2^{-1}, \ \ i = 0, 1. \quad (34)$$

and the invertibility of H_2 follows directly from assumption (13), since

$$H_2 = A(-1) + I = -[zI - A(z)]|_{z=-1}.$$

Next, we present our result concerning the relationship between the matrices Y_1 and Y_2 and certain invariant subspaces of the matrix E. First, it is easy see that the following holds.

$$Y_i \begin{bmatrix} I & Y_i \end{bmatrix} = \begin{bmatrix} I & Y_i \end{bmatrix} E, \ \ i = 1, 2. \quad (35)$$

Using (35) and the definition for left and right invariant subspaces, it is easy to show that the columns of the matrix

$$\begin{bmatrix} I \\ Y_1^T \end{bmatrix}$$

form a basis for the C^l-invariant subspace of E^T. Similarly, the columns of the matrix

$$\begin{bmatrix} I \\ Y_2^T \end{bmatrix}$$

form a basis for the C^{cr}-invariant subspace of E^T.

We note that the spectrum of the matrix E satisfies $\sigma(E) = \sigma(Y_1) \cup \sigma(Y_2)$ by (35). By definition of matrices Y_1 and Y_2, the matrix E has m eigenvalues in the open left half plane, one simple eigenvalue at $\lambda = 0$ and $m-1$ eigenvalues in the open right half plane.

Recall that x is the invariant vector of $A(1)$. Let us define the two vectors α and β of size $2m$ in the following way:

$$\alpha = \begin{bmatrix} x & 0 \end{bmatrix}, \ \ \beta = \begin{bmatrix} H_1e_1 \\ H_2e_1 \end{bmatrix}. \quad (36)$$

It is easy to show that

$$\alpha E = 0, \ \ E\beta = 0,$$

i.e., α and β are the left and right eigenvectors of E associated with the simple eigenvalue at $\lambda = 0$. Therefore, the matrix E_m defined by

$$E_m = E + \frac{\beta\alpha}{\alpha\beta} \quad (37)$$

is free of eigenvalues on the imaginary axis since the simple eigenvalue of E at $\lambda = 0$ is now moved to $\lambda = 1$ (to the right half plane) by this transformation. E_m has m eigenvalues in each open left and right half planes. The following theorem is based on [3, pages 25–26] and is stated here without proof.

Theorem 2 *The columns of the matrix*

$$\begin{bmatrix} I \\ Y_1^T \end{bmatrix} \left(\begin{bmatrix} I \\ Y_2^T \end{bmatrix} \right)$$

form a basis for the left (right) invariant subspace of E_m^T.

Once the left and right invariant subspaces of the matrix E_m^T are obtained, is easy to compute the matrix geometric factors R_1 and R_2. To see this, let

$$T = \begin{bmatrix} T_1 \\ T_2 \end{bmatrix} \quad (38)$$

be an arbitrary basis for the left invariant subspace of E_m^T. But, since

$$\text{Im}\, T = \text{Im} \begin{bmatrix} I \\ Y_1^T \end{bmatrix}$$

Y_1 equals $Y_1 = (T_2 T_1^{-1})^T$. By definition of Y_1 in (30), the matrix geometric factor R_1 can be calculated as follows:

$$\begin{aligned} R_1 &= (I+Y_1)(I-Y_1)^{-1} \\ &= (T_1 - T_2)^{-T}(T_1+T_2)^T \end{aligned} \tag{39}$$

Now let

$$U = \begin{bmatrix} U_1 \\ U_2 \end{bmatrix} \tag{40}$$

be an arbitrary basis for the right invariant subspace of E_m^T. Similarly, one can show that the matrix geometric factor R_2 is given by

$$R_2 = (U_1 + U_2)^{-T}(U_1 - U_2)^T \tag{41}$$

3.2 Matrix Sign Function

We now address the computation of a basis for the left and right invariant subspaces of a real matrix. Although there are different approaches to find those subspaces we will focus on the *matrix sign function approach* of [15] which, in the past, has successfully been used to solve important equations in control theory, such as matrix Riccati and Lyapunov equations [15]. The use of matrix sign function for solving the nonlinear matrix equations arising in M/G/1 and G/M/1 paradigms has recently been proposed in [3] due to its numerical efficiency. Here, we make use of the same approach to find simultaneously the matrix geometric factors R_1 and R_2 through finding the matrix sign function of the matrix E_m^T.

We first provide some introductory material regarding the definition and simple properties of the matrix sign function based on the references [15]. Let $M \in \mathbf{R}^{m\times m}$ with no pure imaginary eigenvalues, i.e., $\sigma(M) \cap C^0 = \emptyset$. Let M have a Jordan decomposition $M = T(D+N)T^{-1}$ where $D = \text{diag}\{\lambda_1, \ldots, \lambda_m\}$ and N is nilpotent and commutes with D. Then the matrix sign of M is given by

$$Z = sgn(M) := T \text{ diag}\{sgn(\lambda_1), \ldots, sgn(\lambda_m)\}\, T^{-1}, \tag{42}$$

where for a complex scalar z with $\text{Re } z \neq 0$, the sign of z is defined by

$$sgn(z) = \begin{cases} 1 & \text{if Re } z > 0 \\ -1 & \text{if Re } z < 0 \end{cases}$$

The matrix sign function defined as above, it is known that [15] Im $(Z-I)$ (Im $(Z+I)$) gives the left (right) invariant subspace of M. Various approaches are available for finding bases for the left and right invariant subspace of a matrix [9]. We now outline a numerically stable and efficient algorithm for finding an orthogonal basis for the left invariant subspace of a matrix from its matrix sign. Let us assume r eigenvalues of M lie in the open left half plane, counting multiplicities. Now let the rank revealing QR decomposition [9] of the matrix $Z_l = sgn(M) - I = Q_l R_l \Pi_l$ be given, where R_l is upper triangular, Q_l is orthogonal, and Π_l is a permutation matrix chosen so that the leading r columns of Q_l span Im $(Z-I)$. Similarly, the *rank revealing QR decomposition* of the matrix $Z_r = sgn(M) + I = Q_r R_r \Pi_r$, where Π_r is a permutation matrix chosen so that the leading $n-r$ columns of Q_r form a basis for the right invariant subspace of M. For a pseudo-code of a particular algorithm (QR with column pivoting) on rank-revealing QR decompositions, see [9, pages 233–236]. We also note that these decompositions are readily available in linear algebra software packages like MATLAB [13] ($qr(\cdot)$ function) or LAPACK [4].

The above definition for the matrix sign does not lend itself to an efficient computation but there are several ways of evaluating the matrix sign function. A numerically efficient iteration scheme is an extension of Newton's method applied to $sgn(M)^2 = I$ with scaling given in [6]: Set $Z_0 = M$ and

$$Z_{k+1} = \frac{1}{2}(\gamma_k Z_k + \gamma_k^{-1} Z_k^{-1}), \quad \gamma_k = |\det Z_k|^{-1/m}. \tag{43}$$

Then $lim_{k\to\infty} Z_k = Z = sgn(M)$ and the convergence is *quadratic* [6]. A comparison of different scaling schemes for matrix sign function iterations is beyond the scope of this paper. Furthermore, iterations with higher convergence rates (e.g., cubic convergence) have also been proposed in [11] at the expense of more computational load at each iteration, compared with the iteration given in (43). We propose the following stopping criterion based on [5]:

$$\| Z_{k+1} - Z_k \|_1 < \varepsilon \| Z_k \|_1, \tag{44}$$

where ε is a small, user specified error bound.

4 Numerical Algorithm

We now summarize all the steps for finding the steady-state distribution for the finite QBD process with the probability transition matrix P given as in (1) when the traffic parameter γ defined in (3) is less than zero. The adjustments for the case $\gamma > 0$ will then be provided.

1. Define H_i, $i = 0, 1, 2$ as in (29), $\hat{H}_i$, $i = 0, 1$ as in (34), E as in (33), x as in (2), α, β as in (36) and E_m as in (37).

2. Find $Z = sgn(E_m^T)$ (Note that matrix sign of E_m^T is well-defined since E_m does not have any eigenvalues on the imaginary axis).

3. Find matrices T and U partitioned as in (38) and (40), whose columns form a basis for Im $(Z-I)$ and Im $(Z+I)$, respectively (one may use rank revealing QR decompositions).

4. Write the matrix geometric factors R_1 and R_2 as in (39) and (41), respectively.

5. Define y, and M as in (18) and (19), respectively, and define $\hat{R}_2 = R_2 - M$, form the matrix $B[R_1, R_2]$ as in (14) and write S_1 and S_2 as in (17) and (21).

6. Find the left invariant eigenvector $v = [\, v_1 \;\; v_2 \,]$ of $B[R_1, R_2]$ normalized as in (23).

7. Write

$$\pi_k = v_1 R_1^k + v_2 R_2^{K-k}, \; 0 \le k \le K.$$

which is the solution for level k of the QBD process.

The algorithm is mainly based on simple block matrix operations including addition, multiplication, and solving systems of linear equations. Most of the computation is devoted to the second step where $sgn(E_m^T)$ is obtained, for which time-efficient algorithms (e.g., the popular iteration (43)) with quadratic (or higher) convergence rates are available in the linear algebra literature [11]. Different matrix sign iterations or other invariant subspace computation methods (e.g., Schur decomposition methods) can also be employed [5].

5 Extension to $\gamma > 0$

When the traffic parameter γ in (3) is greater than zero, the form of stationary probabilities is still the same as in (11) but the properties of the matrix geometric factors R_1 and R_2 are a little different. Based on [7], $\Delta_1(z)$ now has exactly $m-1$ roots in the open unit disk and a simple root at $z=1$. Furthermore, R_1 turns out to be the unique power-bounded solution to the equation (8) and has a simple eigenvalue at $z=1$. Similarly, R_2 is the unique power-summable solution to the equation (12) in case $\gamma > 0$ and therefore it has all its eigenvalues inside the unit disk. Essentially, the eigenvalue at $z=1$ moves from R_2 to R_1 as γ moves from 0^- to 0^+ on the real line which makes it necessary to make some adjustments in the numerical algorithm. The modifications are simple and involve only the definition of E_m and the normalization equations.

Instead of obtaining E_m as in (37) in step 1, this time we define

$$E_m = E - \frac{\beta\alpha}{\alpha\beta}, \tag{45}$$

where the eigenvalue at $\lambda = 0$ is now moved to $\lambda = -1$ (to the left half plane). The matrix geometric factors are then obtained in the same way as in step 3 from $sgn(E_m^T)$.

For the normalization equations, first note that the expression (17) is not valid any more since R_1 is not invertible. We now define y as

$$y = (A_0 - R_1 A_2)e_1$$

and

$$N = \frac{yx}{xy},$$

one can show that x and y are the left and right invariant eigenvectors of R_1, respectively, and the following holds:

$$R_1^k = \begin{cases} \hat{R}_1^k + N, & k \ge 1 \\ I. & k = 0 \end{cases}$$

Based on above,

$$S_1 = \sum_{k=0}^{K} R_1^k = (I - \hat{R}_1^{K+1})(I - \hat{R}_1)^{-1} + K\,N,$$

where $\hat{R}_1 = R_1 - N$. On the other hand, since R_2 is now invertible S_2 is easier to write:

$$S_2 = \sum_{k=0}^{K} R_2^k = (I - R_2^{K+1})(I - R_2)^{-1}.$$

Except for the modifications involving E_m, S_1, and S_2 everything else in the numerical algorithm remains the same and we still have a modified matrix-geometric expression (11) for the stationary probabilities.

6 Numerical Example

We consider a discrete-time finite buffer single server queue in which interarrival times have a discrete time phase type distribution characterized by the pair (α_1, S_1) of dimension m_1 with mean λ^{-1}. Similarly, service times have the discrete-time phase distribution represented by (α_2, S_2) of dimension m_2 with mean μ^{-1}. In the representation of a phase-type distribution, the first variable is a row vector and the second is a square matrix, see [14] for details on phase-type distributions. The state-space describing the Markov chain for the PH/PH/1/K queue is given as $\mathcal{S} = \{(0,j) \cup (k,i,j), 1 \le k \le K,\ 1 \le i \le m_1,\ 1 \le j \le m_2\}$, where $(0,j)$ represents the states when the system is empty and the arrival is phase i and (k,i,j) represents when there are k in the system, the arrival is in phase i and service is in phase j. The transition matrix P representing this Markov chain is has the form [14]

$$P = \begin{bmatrix} B_0 & D_0 & & & & \\ B_1 & D_1 & A_0 & & & \\ & D_2 & A_1 & \cdots & & \\ & & A_2 & \cdots & A_0 & \\ & & & \cdots & A_1 & C_0 \\ & & & & A_2 & C_1 \end{bmatrix}. \tag{46}$$

Note B_0 is of size $m_1 \times m_1$, B_1 is $m \times m_1$, D_0 is $m \times m_1$, where $m = m_1 m_2$. The PH/PH/1/K model falls into the QBD paradigm and can be analyzed with the hybrid matrix geometric/invariant subspace approach presented in this paper although the transition matrix (46) in not in canonical form (1). Partitioning the stationary probability vector π as

$$\pi = \begin{bmatrix} \pi_0 & \pi_1 & \cdots & \pi_K \end{bmatrix},$$

where π_0 is of size $1 \times m_1$ and π_k, $1 \le k \le K$ being $1 \times m$, we first write

$$\pi_k = v_1 R_1^{k-1} + v_2 R_2^{K-k}, \quad 1 \le k \le K, \tag{47}$$

where R_1 and R_2 are the desired solutions to the matrix equations (8) and (12), respectively. Following the lines of Section 2, it is easy to show all block equations of (4) except the ones corresponding to levels 0, 1, and K are satisfied irrespective of v_1 and v_2. We therefore substitute the expression (47) in the three equations corresponding to levels 0, 1, and K, respectively, of $\pi = \pi P$, to obtain

$$v = v\, B[R1, R2], \tag{48}$$

where this time

$$v = \begin{bmatrix} \pi_0 & v_1 & v_2 \end{bmatrix}$$

and $B[R_1, R_2] =$

$$\begin{bmatrix} B_0 & D_0 & 0 \\ B_1 & D_1 + R_1 D_2 & R_1^{K-2}(C_0 + R_1 C_1 - R_1) \\ R_2^{K-1} B_1 & R_2^{K-2}(D_2 + R_2 D_1 - R_2) & R_2 C_0 + C_1 \end{bmatrix}.$$

Solving for the left invariant eigenvector of $B[R_1, R_2]$ normalized so that the probabilities sum up to unity, we obtain a closed form expression (47) for the PH/PH/1/K queue.

Remark. The approach described above for the PH/PH/1/K queue can be extended to solve for QBD chains with general boundaries or with level-dependent transitions, see [2] for details.

In our numerical example, we take a bursty arrival process represented by

$$\alpha_1 = [\ \kappa \quad (1-\kappa)\ ], \quad S_1 = \begin{bmatrix} .001 & 0 \\ 0 & .999 \end{bmatrix}.$$

That is, interarrival times are either very small or very large, resulting in huge variances. The parameter κ is chosen so that a desired arrival rate of the queue is attained. On the other hand, the service process is assumed to have a probability generating function of the form $b(z) = \left(\frac{(1-p)z}{1-pz}\right)^{m_2}$ where the parameter p is chosen to achieve a desired service rate. We use the matrix sign iteration (43) with the stopping criterion (44) with $\varepsilon = 10^{-7}$ for finding the matrix geometric factors. The algorithms are implemented in MATLAB version 4.2c on a DECAlphaServer 2100 4/200 supporting DEC OSF/1 V3.0 using IEEE standard double precision arithmetic with machine precision $\varepsilon \approx 2.2\ 10^{-16}$.

We first set $m_2 = 16$, $\mu^{-1} = 20$, $K = 258$, and we investigate the performance of the proposed algorithm in terms of i) the number of iterations I required in finding the matrix sign of E_m^T in step 2 of the numerical algorithm, ii) the norm of the error $||\pi - \pi P||_\infty$, with respect to the load $\rho = \lambda/\mu$ of the system, where we allow ρ to be greater than unity. We also provide two queue statistics, the expected value of the queue length ($E[queue]$) and the probability that the queue is full ($P[full]$). $P[full]$ is easy to calculate:

$$P[full] = \pi_K e_1 = v_2 + v_1 R_1^{K-1},$$

whereas $E[queue]$ can be calculated using the identity $\sum_{k=0}^{K} k B^k =$

$$(I - B^{K+1})(I-B)^{-2} - (I + K B^{K+1})(I-B)^{-1} \tag{49}$$

which holds for an arbitrary matrix B when $(I - B)$ is invertible. We now present our results in Table 1. Precision in results degrades only when the load is very close to unity (the parameter γ being very close to zero), i.e., the problem is very ill-conditioned and such observations are also reported for infinite QBD processes with available stable algorithms [12]. Otherwise, the algorithm typically gives an error very close to machine precision. We recommend to use the Schur decomposition based procedures for finding the left and right invariant subspaces of E_m^T when we seek for high precision for ill-conditioned problems, which is known

ρ	I	$\|\|\pi - \pi P\|\|$	$E[queue]$	$P[full]$
0.4	10	$3.5\ 10^{-16}$	$1.25353\ 10^{1}$	$4.51097\ 10^{-6}$
0.8	12	$3.1\ 10^{-16}$	$7.59244\ 10^{1}$	$3.33157\ 10^{-3}$
0.9	13	$1.4\ 10^{-16}$	$9.43241\ 10^{1}$	$6.14265\ 10^{-3}$
0.99	16	$3.5\ 10^{-16}$	$1.08997\ 10^{2}$	$9.33247\ 10^{-3}$
0.999	19	$1.4\ 10^{-14}$	$1.10353\ 10^{2}$	$9.68003\ 10^{-3}$
0.9999	22	$1.0\ 10^{-11}$	$1.10474\ 10^{2}$	$9.66433\ 10^{-3}$
1.0001	22	$1.1\ 10^{-11}$	$1.10517\ 10^{2}$	$9.72274\ 10^{-3}$
1.001	19	$5.5\ 10^{-13}$	$1.10651\ 10^{2}$	$9.75790\ 10^{-3}$
1.01	16	$2.1\ 10^{-14}$	$1.11982\ 10^{2}$	$1.01111\ 10^{-2}$
1.1	14	$1.2\ 10^{-16}$	$1.24178\ 10^{2}$	$1.38656\ 10^{-2}$
10.0	11	$4.1\ 10^{-17}$	$2.30577\ 10^{2}$	$4.79363\ 10^{-1}$

Table 1: Number of iterations required, norm of the error, expected queue length and the probability of queue being full for the PH/PH/1/K queue vs. load on the system

to improve the performance at the expense of larger execution time requirements. The number of iterations required are slightly affected by ρ, similar to the performance of the logarithmic reduction procedure of [12] for infinite QBD chains.

Next we fix $\mu^{-1} = 100$, $\rho = 0.99$, $K = 2050$, and vary m_2, the number of phases of the service time distribution. The performance results are given in Table 2. The accuracy is not affected by the number of phases although slightly more iterations are required when m_2 (dimension of the service time distribution) increases. Through the numerical examples, it has been observed

m_2	I	$\|\|\pi - \pi P\|\|$	$E[queue]$	$P[full]$
2	10	$4.3\ 10^{-18}$	$6.76373\ 10^{2}$	$1.15019\ 10^{-4}$
4	11	$8.9\ 10^{-18}$	$6.72554\ 10^{2}$	$9.60752\ 10^{-5}$
6	12	$5.0\ 10^{-18}$	$6.71262\ 10^{2}$	$8.95975\ 10^{-5}$
8	13	$5.4\ 10^{-18}$	$6.70613\ 10^{2}$	$8.68346\ 10^{-5}$
10	13	$1.8\ 10^{-17}$	$6.70223\ 10^{2}$	$8.50051\ 10^{-5}$
20	14	$8.2\ 10^{-17}$	$6.69440\ 10^{2}$	$8.13649\ 10^{-5}$
40	14	$1.6\ 10^{-16}$	$6.69047\ 10^{2}$	$7.95541\ 10^{-5}$
80	15	$2.6\ 10^{-16}$	$6.68850\ 10^{2}$	$7.86511\ 10^{-5}$

Table 2: Number of iterations required, norm of the error, expected queue length and probability of queue being full for the PH/PH/1/K queue vs. dimension of the service time

that the number of levels in the QBD process does not play a role in the performance of the algorithm. First, fixing everything but K results in almost unchanged accuracy in terms of the norm of the error. Second, the core of the overall algorithm dedicated to finding the left and right invariant subspaces of E_m^T is independent on K. Finally, the only step where K comes into picture is step 5, when we construct the matrix $B[R_1, R_2]$ using the matrix powers R_1^{K-1} and R_2^{K-1}. These computations can be done with a complexity of $O(m^3 \log_2 K)$ and their execution time requirements are typically far less than those of the matrix sign iterations. We therefore conclude that solution of a finite QBD process does not require a significant additional computational effort compared to that of an infinite QBD process and approximating finite QBD processes by infinite QBD processes (to facilitate solutions) are generally unnecessary.

Acknowledgments

This research was supported in part by University of Missouri Research Board (UMRB) grant K-3-40531 and by NSF under grants NCR-950814, ASC-9625748 and CDA-9422092.

References

[1] N. Akar and K. Sohraby. A new paradigm in teletraffic analysis of communication networks. In *Proc. INFOCOM 96*, pages 1318-1326, 1996.

[2] N. Akar and K. Sohraby. On the hybrid matrix geometric/invariant subspace method for the finite QBD process. submitted to Advances in Applied Probability, 1996.

[3] N. Akar and K. Sohraby. An invariant subspace approach in M/G/1 and G/M/1 type Markov chains. *Commun. Stat.-Stochastic Models*, 1997. to appear.

[4] E. Anderson, Z. Bai, C. Bischof, J. Demmel, J. Dongarra, J. Du Croz, A. Greenbaum, S. Hammarling, A. McKenney, S. Ostrouchov, and D. Sorensen. *LAPACK Users's Guide*, 1994. Second edition, also available from Web as http://www.netlib.org/lapack.

[5] Z. Bai and J. Demmel. Design of a parallel nonsymmetric eigenroutine toolbox: part I. Computer Science Division Report CSD-92-718, University of California at Berkeley, Dec. 1992.

[6] R. Byers. Solving the algebraic Riccati equation with the matrix sign function. *Lin. Alg. Appl.*, 85:267-279, 1987.

[7] H. R. Gail, S. L. Hantler, and B. A. Taylor. Solutions of the basic matrix equation for M/G/1 and G/M/1 type Markov chains. *Commun. Statist.-Stochastic Models*, 10(1):1-43, 1994.

[8] I. C. Gohberg, P. Lancaster, and L. Rodman. *Invariant Subspaces of Matrices with Applications.* John Wiley and Sons, New York, 1986.

[9] G. H. Golub and C. F. Van Loan. *Matrix Computations.* The Johns Hopkins University Press, Baltimore, 1989.

[10] B. Hajek. Birth-and-death processes on the integers with phases and general boundaries. *J. Appl. Prob.*, 19:488-499, 1982.

[11] C. Kenney and A. J. Laub. Rational iterative methods for the matrix sign function. *SIAM Matrix. Anal. Appl.*, 12(2):273-291, 1991.

[12] G. Latouche and V. Ramaswami. A logarithmic reduction algorithm for quasi-birth-death processes. *J. Appl. Prob.*, 30:650-674, 1993.

[13] The MATH WORKS Inc. *MATLAB Users's Guide for UNIX Workstations*, 1991.

[14] M. F. Neuts. *Matrix-geometric Solutions in Stochastic Models.* Johns Hopkins University Press, Baltimore, MD, 1981.

[15] J. D. Roberts. Linear model reduction and solution of the algebraic Riccati equation by the use of the sign function. *Int. Jour. Control*, 32:677-687, 1980.

[16] V. Wallace. *The solution of quasi birth and death processes arising from multiple access computer systems.* PhD thesis, Systems Engineering Laboratory, University of Michigan, 1969.

[17] J. Ye and S. Q. Li. A computational method for finite QBD processes with level-dependent transitions. *IEEE Trans. Commun.*, 42(2):625-639, 1994.

Sensitivity Analysis of the Loss Probability in a Stationary Gradual Queue for High-Speed Networks

Yoshihiro Yamada† Naoto Miyoshi‡ Toshiharu Hasegawa‡

†Sumitomo Bank, Senba Branch
Kyutarocho 1-8-7, Chuoku
Osaka 541, Japan

‡Dept. of Applied Systems Science
Graduate School of Engineering
Kyoto University
Kyoto 606-01, Japan

Abstract

In ATM networks, each node has its own buffer to store some cells. The buffer size represents a trade-off between cell loss and transmission delay, and therefore, it is a significant concern to evaluate the performance with respect to the buffer size. In this paper, we investigate the sensitivity of the loss probability with respect to the buffer size by considering a gradual input queue with a finite buffer. Gradual inputs are considered as those representing a bursty traffic of cells. Applying the perturbation analysis technique to this model, we derive the strongly consistent sensitivity estimates, and combining with the likelihood ratio method, we confirm that our estimates lead to the reasonable simulation results.
Keywords: *High-speed networks, ATM networks, gradual input queues, loss probability, sensitivity analysis, simulation.*

1 Introduction

In ATM networks, all information is divided into some *cells* with a fixed length, and the divided cells are transmitted into an ATM node. Each node transmits the cells to the next node at a very high speed. While multiplexing of such cells can gain the bandwidth efficiency, a node becomes congested when a number of sources are active. Therefore, each node has its own buffer in order to store some cells. If the buffer size is large, transmission delay tends to be large, and its constructing costs would be high. In particular, large transmission delay results in a critical problem in sending cells from the delay-sensitive sources such as video and voice. On the other hand, decreasing the buffer size makes the loss frequency higher, that is undesirable in transmitting the loss-sensitive information such as text data. Namely, the buffer size represents a trade-off between the transmission delay and the cell loss, and it is a significant concern to evaluate the performance of networks with respect to the buffer size.

Also, in such networks, a lot of cells are likely to arrive at a node consecutively, that is, the input process in the networks has a bursty property. Queueing models with such bursty inputs have been intensively studied, and a *gradual input* queue is one of such models. In a gradual input queue, the nth customer initiates its input at a random epoch T_n and the work of the customer arrives at a node gradually at some rate during $[T_n, T_n + \sigma_n)$. The work in the queue is worked off also gradually at a constant rate. This model represents the bursty behavior of traffic in high-speed networks such as ATM networks.

Related models have been so far analyzed by supposing and exploiting some Markovian frameworks: Hashida and Fujiki [5] dealt with the loss probability in a queueing model with finite exponential on-off sources and a limited buffer. Miyazawa and Yamazaki [8] reported on the loss probability of a burst arrival with synchronized service. Our main objective in this paper is to consider a general gradual input queue and to investigate the sensitivity of the loss probability with respect to the buffer size. However, it seems difficult to obtain a closed form expression of the loss probability in such models without any Markovian framework. In simulation, on the other hand, it is expected that simulation results have considerably small values because the loss probability is so small ($< 10^{-8}$) in ATM networks, and then, the variance of estimates tends to make simulation results worthless. In this paper, we adopt the *perturbation analysis* (PA) approach, which is considered as an efficient sensitivity estimation technique with less variance. And combining with likelihood ratio method, we show that our estimates lead to the reasonable values of sensitivity of the loss probability.

0-8186-7780-5/97 $10.00 © 1997 IEEE

PA is an efficient method for sensitivity estimation from a single simulation. Let $\mathrm{E}[L(\theta)]$ be a performance measure, where $L(\theta)$ is a sampled performance function with parameter θ. Before the advent of PA, at least two simulation runs have to be implemented in order to estimate the sensitivity, that is, $\mathrm{dE}[L(\theta)]/\mathrm{d}\theta$ is approximated by $(\mathrm{E}[L(\theta + \Delta\theta)] - \mathrm{E}[L(\theta)])/\Delta\theta$, where $\mathrm{E}[L(\theta + \Delta\theta)]$ and $\mathrm{E}[L(\theta)]$ are obtained from the individual simulations. This method is called *finite difference* (FD) or *brute force* (BF) estimation. On the other hand, under the *unbiasedness* condition of the stochastic sensitivity, that is, $\mathrm{dE}[L(\theta)]/\mathrm{d}\theta = \mathrm{E}[\mathrm{d}L(\theta)/\mathrm{d}\theta]$, so-called *infinitesimal* PA (IPA) gives the sensitivity estimates through a single simulation by computing $\mathrm{d}L(\theta)/\mathrm{d}\theta$. Intuitively, IPA should be preferred to the FD method because IPA responds to exactly same inputs without the finite difference $\Delta\theta$. In fact, it is well-known that IPA provides lower variance than the other [3, 10]. Besides the unbiasedness problem, another significant subject on the PA estimates is *strong consistency*, that is, the convergence problem to the steady-state performance as the time horizon goes to infinity. Accordingly, in order to estimate the steady-state sensitivity through the PA approach, we have to derive a strongly consistent estimator. In this paper, by considering the stationary and ergodic model, we derive the strongly consistent estimates. More details of IPA techniques would be found in Glasserman [4], and Zazanis and Suri [11]. For IPA in the stationary and ergodic queue, see Konstantopoulos and Zazanis [6, 7]. In relation to the sensitivity estimation for a finite buffer queueing model, Wardi *et al.* [9] derived a strongly consistent estimator for the derivative of the lost amount with respect to a buffer size.

This paper is organized as follows. In the next section, we explain our model in more details and specify some notations. In Section 3, we obtain strongly consistent estimators for the sensitivity of the steady-state loss probability. In Section 4, we present some simulation results to illustrate the validity of our estimator. Some concluding remarks are made in Section 5.

2 Model and notations

Consider a gradual input queue with a finite buffer as follows: In this paper, the terminology *burst* is used instead of *customer* in order to emphasize that each *burst* represents an arrival of a cluster of bursty cells. That is, the nth burst initiates its arrival at time T_n ($\in \mathbb{R}$), and its work arrives at a node gradually at a constant rate r_n (> 0) during the time interval $[T_n, T_n + \sigma_n)$, where $\sigma_n > 0$. Work in the queue is worked off also gradually at a constant rate c (> 0) if any. Note that $r_n \sigma_n$ indicates the amount of the work brought by the nth burst.

We regard this input process as a *marked point process* with mark space $(0, \infty)^2$ and define the probability space $(\Omega, \mathcal{F}, \mathrm{P})$ as canonical form such that a sample element $\omega = \{(T_n, \sigma_n, r_n)\}_{n\in\mathbb{Z}}$. Further we assume that point process $\{T_n\}_{n\in\mathbb{Z}}$ satisfies

$$\cdots < T_{-1} < T_0 \le 0 < T_1 < T_2 < \cdots; \quad \lim_{n\to\pm\infty} T_n = \pm\infty,$$

and $\{(T_n, \sigma_n, r_n)\}_{n\in\mathbb{Z}}$ is stationary and ergodic. Let N be a counting measure on $\mathbb{R}$ with respect to the arrival sequence $\{T_n\}_{n\in\mathbb{Z}}$, that is, $N(C) = \sum_{n\in\mathbb{Z}} 1_C(T_n)$, for $C \in \mathcal{B}(\mathbb{R})$, and suppose that the intensity $\lambda = \mathrm{E}\big[N\big((0, 1]\big)\big]$ is positive and finite. We let P^0 and E^0 denote the Palm probability measure with respect to (N, P) and the corresponding expectation, and assume that $\mathrm{E}^0[r_0 \sigma_0] < \infty$. Let $A\big((s, t]\big)$ denote the total amount of work arriving in $(s, t]$ for $s, t \in \mathbb{R}$ $(s < t)$. Then, summing up the work of arriving bursts during $(s, t]$, we have

$$\begin{aligned} A\big((s, t]\big) = \sum_{n\in\mathbb{Z}} r_n \Big\{&\sigma_n 1_{(s,t]}(T_n) \\ &+ (T_n + \sigma_n - s)\, 1_{[T_n, T_n+\sigma_n)}(s) \\ &- (T_n + \sigma_n - t)\, 1_{[T_n, T_n+\sigma_n)}(t)\Big\}, \end{aligned}$$

and from the stationarity of $\{(T_n, \sigma_n, r_n)\}_{n\in\mathbb{Z}}$, we have immediately,

$$\mathrm{E}\big[A\big((s, t]\big)\big] = \lambda\,(t - s)\,\mathrm{E}^0[r_0 \sigma_0]. \tag{1}$$

Let θ (> 0) be the buffer size in time units. When the amount of work in the buffer is θ and when the total arriving rate is larger than c, work of some bursts are discarded and the total injecting rate is c. We assume neither service discipline nor discarding one. Figure 1 shows the behavior of the amount of work in the buffer, where the solid line shows our finite buffer model, compared with the corresponding infinite buffer model depicted with the broken line. Let $L_\theta\big((s, t]\big)$ denote the amount of lost work during $(s, t]$. Then, the loss probability is defined by

$$\mathrm{P}_{\mathrm{loss}}(\theta) = \frac{\mathrm{E}\big[L_\theta\big((0, t]\big)\big]}{\mathrm{E}\big[A\big((0, t]\big)\big]}. \tag{2}$$

3 Sensitivity estimators for loss probability

In this section, we derive the strongly consistent estimators for the sensitivity of the loss probability with respect to the buffer size. This section consists of the following three subsections: In Section 3.1, we transform the loss probability expression (2) into more tractable one, and formulate the problem based on the obtained form. In Section 3.2, we derive the expressions for the right- and left-hand side derivatives of

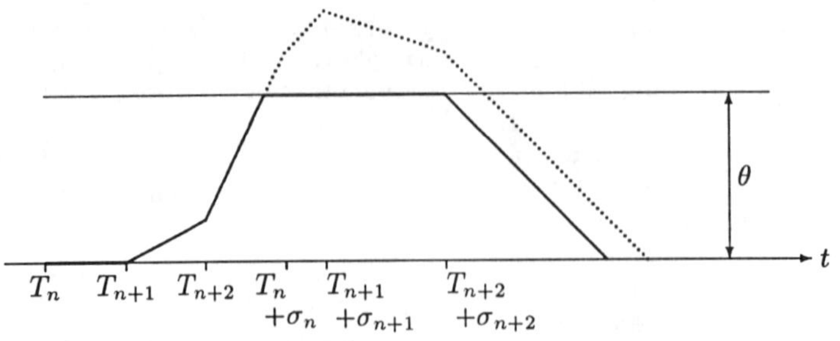

Figure 1: A sample path of gradual input queueing model

the loss probability which are reasonable to estimation, and we consider the condition in which the loss probability is differentiable. Finally in Section 3.3, we derive the strongly consistent estimators using the ergodic theorem.

3.1 The derivative of the loss probability

Consider the sequence $\{U_n\}_{n\in\mathbf{Z}}$ which is defined as $\{T_n\}_{n\in\mathbf{Z}}\cup\{T_n+\sigma_n\}_{n\in\mathbf{Z}}$ satisfying $U_0 \le 0 < U_1$. Since $\{(T_n,\, \sigma_n)\}_{n\in\mathbf{Z}}$ is stationary and ergodic, $\{U_n\}_{n\in\mathbf{Z}}$ is so and its intensity is $2\,\lambda$. We note by P_U^0 and E_U^0 the Palm probability measure and the corresponding expectation for $\{U_n\}_{n\in\mathbf{Z}}$. Let $W_\theta(t)$ denote the amount of work in the system at time t. Then, $W_\theta(t)$ is either non-decreasing or non-increasing during $[U_n,\, U_{n+1})$ for each n because the total arriving rate is constant during such a period. Therefore, noting that $0 \le W_\theta(t) \le \theta$, we have for $U_n \le s < t \le U_{n+1}$,

$$W_\theta(t) = \Big[W_\theta(s) + A\big((s,\, t]\big) - c\,(t-s)\Big]^+ \wedge \theta, \tag{3a}$$

$$L_\theta\big((s,\, t]\big) = \Big[W_\theta(s) + A\big((s,\, t]\big) - c\,(t-s) - \theta\Big]^+, \tag{3b}$$

where $x^+ = \max(0,\, x)$ and $x \wedge y = \min(x,\, y)$. Now, we transform equation (2) into more tractable one. Clearly, we have

$$L_\theta\big((0,\, t]\big) = \sum_{n\in\mathbf{Z}} L_\theta\big((U_n,\, U_{n+1}]\big)\, 1_{(0,t]}(U_n) + L_\theta\big((0,\, U_1]\big) - L_\theta\big((t,\, U_+(t)]\big),$$

where $U_+(t) = \inf(U_n > t)$. Then, from the stationarity,

$$\mathrm{E}\big[L_\theta\big((0,\, t]\big)\big] = \mathrm{E}\Bigg[\sum_{n\in\mathbf{Z}} L_\theta\big((U_n,\, U_{n+1}]\big)\, 1_{(0,t]}(U_n)\Bigg].$$

According to the definition formula of the Palm probability (cf. (3.1.10) of Baccelli and Brémaud [2, Chap. 1]), and noting that the intensity of $\{U_n\}_{n\in\mathbf{Z}}$ is $2\,\lambda$, it holds that

$$\mathrm{E}\big[L_\theta\big((0,\, t]\big)\big] = 2\,\lambda\, t\, \mathrm{E}_U^0\big[L_\theta\big((0,\, U_1]\big)\big].$$

Since we have $\mathrm{E}\big[A\big((0,\, t]\big)\big] = \lambda\, t\, \mathrm{E}^0[r_0\, \sigma_0]$ from (1), the loss probability (2) is rewritten as

$$\mathrm{P}_{\mathrm{loss}}(\theta) = \frac{2\, \mathrm{E}_U^0\big[L_\theta\big((0,\, U_1]\big)\big]}{\mathrm{E}^0[r_0\, \sigma_0]}.$$

Hence, if $\mathrm{E}_U^0\big[L_\theta\big((0,\, U_1]\big)\big]$ is continuous in θ, we have

$$\frac{\mathrm{d}^\pm \mathrm{P}_{\mathrm{loss}}(\theta)}{\mathrm{d}\theta} = \frac{2}{\mathrm{E}^0[r_0\, \sigma_0]}\, \frac{\mathrm{d}^\pm \mathrm{E}_U^0\big[L_\theta\big((0,\, U_1]\big)\big]}{\mathrm{d}\theta}. \tag{4}$$

This equation says that we can obtain the sensitivity estimator of the loss probability by acquiring an estimator for $\mathrm{d}^\pm \mathrm{E}_U^0\big[L_\theta\big((0,\, U_1]\big)\big]/\mathrm{d}\theta$ because $\mathrm{E}^0[r_0\, \sigma_0]$ is not affected by buffer size θ.

3.2 Unbiased estimators

In this subsection, we derive the unbiased forms of the derivatives of loss probability (4). To achieve this, we first obtain the unbiased expressions for $\mathrm{d}^\pm \mathrm{E}_U^0\big[L_\theta\big((0,\, U_1]\big)\big]/\mathrm{d}\theta$.

First, we present the following proposition which is concerned with the left-hand side derivative of $\mathrm{E}_U^0\big[L_\theta\big((0,\, U_1]\big)\big]$:

Proposition 1:

$$\frac{\mathrm{d}^- \mathrm{E}_U^0\big[L_\theta\big((0,\, U_1]\big)\big]}{\mathrm{d}\theta} = -\mathrm{P}_U^0\Big(\{\mathrm{d}^- W_\theta(0)/\mathrm{d}\theta = 0\} \cap \{W_\theta(U_1) = \theta\}\Big).$$

In preparation for the proof of the proposition, we prove the following lemma:

Lemma 1: *Let $\Delta\theta > 0$. Then, we have P^0_U-a.s.,*

$$0 \le W_\theta(0) - W_{\theta-\Delta\theta}(0) \le \Delta\theta, \tag{5}$$

and

$$\frac{\mathrm{d}^- W_\theta(U_1)}{\mathrm{d}\theta} = \frac{\mathrm{d}^- W_\theta(0)}{\mathrm{d}\theta} 1_{\{0<W_\theta(0)+A_0<\theta\}} + 1_{\{W_\theta(0)+A_0\ge\theta\}},$$

where $A_n = A\big((U_n, U_{n+1}]\big) - c(U_{n+1} - U_n)$ (we use this notation hereafter without any annotation).

Proof: First, consider the situation where $W_\theta(0) = W_{\theta-\Delta\theta}(0)$ on $\{U_0 = 0\}$. Indeed, such a case is observed, for instance, at the beginning of a busy period. From (3a), we have

$$\begin{aligned} &W_\theta(U_1) - W_{\theta-\Delta\theta}(U_1) \\ &= [W_\theta(0) + A_0]^+ \wedge \theta - [W_\theta(0) + A_0]^+ \wedge (\theta - \Delta\theta) \\ &= [W_\theta(0) + A_0 - (\theta - \Delta\theta)]\, 1_{\{\theta-\Delta\theta<W_\theta(0)+A_0<\theta\}} \\ &\quad + \Delta\theta\, 1_{\{W_\theta(0)+A_0\ge\theta\}}, \end{aligned}$$

and therefore, it is clear that in this case,

$$0 \le W_\theta(U_1) - W_{\theta-\Delta\theta}(U_1) \le \Delta\theta.$$

Next, we assume on $\{U_0 = 0\}$

$$0 \le W_\theta(0) - W_{\theta-\Delta\theta}(0) \le \Delta\theta. \tag{6}$$

Then, we have

$$\begin{aligned} &W_\theta(U_1) - W_{\theta-\Delta\theta}(U_1) \\ &= [W_\theta(0) + A_0]^+ \wedge \theta - [W_{\theta-\Delta\theta}(0) + A_0]^+ \wedge (\theta - \Delta\theta) \\ &= \Delta\theta\, 1_{\{W_\theta(0)+A_0\ge\theta\}} \\ &\quad + 1_{\{0<W_\theta(0)+A_0<\theta\}} \times \\ &\qquad \Big\{[W_\theta(0) + A_0 - (\theta - \Delta\theta)]\, 1_{\{W_{\theta-\Delta\theta}(0)+A_0\ge\theta-\Delta\theta\}} \\ &\qquad + [W_\theta(0) - W_{\theta-\Delta\theta}(0)]\, 1_{\{0<W_{\theta-\Delta\theta}(0)+A_0<\theta-\Delta\theta\}} \\ &\qquad + [W_\theta(0) + A_0]\, 1_{\{W_{\theta-\Delta\theta}(0)+A_0\le 0\}}\Big\}. \end{aligned} \tag{7}$$

For the last term above, we have $0 < W_\theta(0) + A_0 \le W_{\theta-\Delta\theta}(0) + \Delta\theta + A_0 \le \Delta\theta$ from (6). Other terms are clearly less than or equal to $\Delta\theta$. Hence, from the stationarity, we have (5) inductively.

In the last expression of (7), note that for a sufficiently small $\Delta\theta > 0$,

$$\begin{aligned} &\{0 < W_\theta(0) + A_0 < \theta\} \cap \{W_{\theta-\Delta\theta}(0) + A_0 \ge \theta - \Delta\theta\} \\ &\quad = \emptyset; \\ &\{0 < W_\theta(0) + A_0 < \theta\} \cap \{W_{\theta-\Delta\theta}(0) + A_0 \le 0\} \\ &\quad = \emptyset. \end{aligned}$$

Thus, we have from (7),

$$\begin{aligned} &\lim_{\Delta\theta\downarrow 0} \frac{W_\theta(U_1) - W_{\theta-\Delta\theta}(U_1)}{\Delta\theta} \\ &\quad = \lim_{\Delta\theta\downarrow 0} \frac{W_\theta(0) - W_{\theta-\Delta\theta}(0)}{\Delta\theta} 1_{\{0<W_\theta(0)+A_0<\theta\}} \\ &\qquad + 1_{\{W_\theta(0)+A_0\ge\theta\}}, \end{aligned}$$

which completes the proof. □

This lemma says that either $\mathrm{d}^- W_\theta(0)/\mathrm{d}\theta = 0$ or 1, P^0_U-a.s. Now, we prove Proposition 1:

Proof of Proposition 1: From (3b), we have

$$L_\theta\big((0, U_1]\big) = \Big[W_\theta(0) + A\big((0, U_1]\big) - cU_1 - \theta\Big]^+. \tag{8}$$

Then, using Lemma 1, we have P^0_U-a.s.,

$$\begin{aligned} &\Delta^- L_\theta((0, U_1]) \\ &= L_\theta((0, U_1]) - L_{\theta-\Delta\theta}((0, U_1]) \\ &= [W_\theta(0) + A_0 - \theta]^+ - [W_{\theta-\Delta\theta}(0) + A_0 - (\theta - \Delta\theta)]^+ \\ &= [W_\theta(0) - W_{\theta-\Delta\theta}(0) - \Delta\theta]\, 1_{\{W_\theta(0)+A_0\ge\theta\}} \\ &\quad - [W_{\theta-\Delta\theta}(0) + A_0 - (\theta - \Delta\theta)] \times \\ &\quad 1_{\{W_\theta(0)+A_0<\theta\}\cap\{W_{\theta-\Delta\theta}(0)+A_0\ge\theta-\Delta\theta\}}. \end{aligned} \tag{9}$$

This equation indicates that $\big|\Delta^- L_\theta\big((0, U_1]\big)/\Delta\theta\big| \le 1$, and applying the dominated convergence theorem,

$$\lim_{\Delta\theta\downarrow 0} \mathrm{E}^0_U\left[\frac{\Delta^- L_\theta\big((0, U_1]\big)}{\Delta\theta}\right] = \mathrm{E}^0_U\left[\lim_{\Delta\theta\downarrow 0} \frac{\Delta^- L_\theta\big((0, U_1]\big)}{\Delta\theta}\right]. \tag{10}$$

Noting that, for a sufficiently small $\Delta\theta > 0$,

$$\{W_\theta(0) + A_0 < \theta\} \cap \{W_{\theta-\Delta\theta}(0) + A_0 \ge \theta - \Delta\theta\} = \emptyset,$$

we have from (9)

$$\begin{aligned} &\lim_{\Delta\theta\downarrow 0} \frac{\Delta^- L_\theta\big((0, U_1]\big)}{\Delta\theta} \\ &\quad = \lim_{\Delta\theta\downarrow 0} \left(\frac{W_\theta(0) - W_{\theta-\Delta\theta}(0)}{\Delta\theta} - 1\right) 1_{\{W_\theta(0)+A_0\ge\theta\}}. \end{aligned}$$

Since, from Lemma 1, $\mathrm{d}^- W_\theta(0)/\mathrm{d}\theta$ is either 0 or 1 on $\{U_0 = 0\}$, we have P^0_U-a.s.

$$\frac{\mathrm{d}^- L_\theta\big((0, U_1]\big)}{\mathrm{d}\theta} = -1_{\{\mathrm{d}^- W_\theta(0)/\mathrm{d}\theta=0\}\cap\{W_\theta(U_0)+A_0\ge\theta\}}.$$

Now, substituting this into (10), we complete the proof. □

Next, we give the right-hand side derivative expression without proofs since they are similar to those of Lemma 1 and Proposition 1:

Lemma 2: *Let $\Delta\theta > 0$. Then, we have* P_U^0*-a.s.,*

$$0 \le W_{\theta+\Delta\theta}(0) - W_\theta(0) \le \Delta\theta, \tag{11}$$

and

$$\frac{d^+ W_\theta(U_1)}{d\theta} = \frac{d^+ W_\theta(0)}{d\theta} 1_{\{0 \le W_\theta(0)+A_0 \le \theta\}} + 1_{\{W_\theta(0)+A_0 > \theta\}}.$$

□

Proposition 2:

$$\frac{d^+ E_U^0 [L_\theta((0, U_1])]}{d\theta} = -P_U^0\Big(\{d^+ W_\theta(0)/d\theta = 0\} \cap \{L_\theta((0, U_1]) > 0\}\Big).$$

□

Let $R_\theta^-(t) = \max\{U_n \le t \mid W_\theta(U_n-) = 0,\ W_\theta(U_n+) > 0\}$, that is, $R_\theta^-(t)$ represents the last instance when the amount of work in the buffer starts to increase from zero before t. Then, both $\{d^- W_\theta(0)/d\theta = 0\}$ and $\{d^+ W_\theta(0)/d\theta = 0\}$ are almost equivalent to $\{L((R_\theta^-(0), 0]) = 0\}$. Hence, Proposition 1 and 2 mean that the absolute value of the derivative of expected loss amount during $(0, U_1]$ equals the probability that no work is discarded during $(R_\theta^-(0), 0]$ and some work is discarded in $(0, U_1]$ on $\{U_0 = 0\}$.

Substituting Proposition 1 and 2 into (4), we have the unbiased forms of both left- and right-hand side derivatives of the loss probability:

Proposition 3:

$$\frac{d^- P_{loss}(\theta)}{d\theta} = \frac{-2 P_U^0\Big(\{d^- W_\theta(0)/d\theta = 0\} \cap \{W_\theta(U_1) = \theta\}\Big)}{E^0[r_0 \sigma_0]},$$

$$\frac{d^+ P_{loss}(\theta)}{d\theta} = \frac{-2 P_U^0\Big(\{d^+ W_\theta(0)/d\theta = 0\} \cap \{L_\theta((0, U_1]) > 0\}\Big)}{E^0[r_0 \sigma_0]}.$$

□

Two formulae in Proposition 3 are similar but different. Now, consider the condition that both are identical. We first immediately observe that $\{W_\theta(U_1) = \theta\} \setminus \{L_\theta((0, U_1]) > 0\} = \{W_\theta(0) + A_0 = \theta\}$. Next, we consider the difference between $\{d^- W_\theta(0)/d\theta = 0\}$ and $\{d^+ W_\theta(0)/d\theta = 0\}$. From Lemmas 1 and 2, two are different in the case that $W_\theta(U_n) + A_n$ is exactly 0 or θ for some U_n satisfying $R_\theta^-(0) \le U_n < 0$. Then, we have the following:

Corollary 1: *If* $P_U^0\big(W_\theta(0) + A_0 \notin \{0, \theta\}\big) = 1$,

$$\frac{dP_{loss}(\theta)}{d\theta} = \frac{-2 P_U^0\Big(\{dW_\theta(0)/d\theta = 0\} \cap \{W_\theta(U_1) = \theta\}\Big)}{E^0[r_0 \sigma_0]}. \tag{12}$$

□

Remark 1: In an application to ATM networks, we could expect the condition of Corollary 1, and the derivative of the loss probability exists and is expressed as (12). However, on a special probability space, the left- and right-hand side derivatives may be different, for example, in sample space $(\tau_n, \sigma_n, r_n) = (2\theta, \theta, 2)$ for all n, where $\tau_n = T_{n+1} - T_n$, loss probability is not differentiable at θ because $P_U^0\big(W_\theta(U_0) + A_0 \in \{0, \theta\}\big) > 0$.

3.3 Strongly consistent estimators

In this section, we present the strongly consistent estimators for the left- and right-hand side derivatives of the loss probability with respect to the buffer size. We have, from the ergodic property, the following proposition:

Proposition 4: *We have* P*-a.s.*

$$\frac{d^- P_{loss}(\theta)}{d\theta} = -\lim_{m\to\infty} \frac{\sum_{n=1}^{m} 1_{\{d^- W_\theta(U_n)/d\theta = 0\} \cap \{W_\theta(U_{n+1}) = \theta\}}}{\sum_{n\ge 1} r_n \sigma_n 1_{\{T_n \le U_m\}}}; \tag{13}$$

$$\frac{d^+ P_{loss}(\theta)}{d\theta} = -\lim_{m\to\infty} \frac{\sum_{n=1}^{m} 1_{\{d^+ W_\theta(U_n)/d\theta = 0\} \cap \{L_\theta\left((U_n, U_{n+1}]\right) > 0\}}}{\sum_{n\ge 1} r_n \sigma_n 1_{\{T_n \le U_m\}}}. \tag{14}$$

Proof: Because $\{r_n \sigma_n\}_{n\in\mathbb{Z}}$ is ergodic, using the ergodic theorem, we have P-a.s.

$$E^0[r_0 \sigma_0] = \lim_{m\to\infty} \frac{1}{m} \sum_{n=1}^{m} r_n \sigma_n = \lim_{m\to\infty} \frac{\sum_{n\ge 1} r_n \sigma_n 1_{\{T_n \le U_m\}}}{\sum_{n\ge 1} 1_{\{T_n \le U_m\}}}.$$

Also, since $\{U_n\}_{n\in\mathbb{Z}}$ is ergodic, we have from Proposition 1, P-a.s.

$$\frac{\mathrm{d}^- \mathrm{E}_U^0 \left[L_\theta((0,\, U_1]) \right]}{\mathrm{d}\theta} = - \lim_{m\to\infty} \frac{1}{m} \sum_{n=1}^{m} 1_{\{\mathrm{d}^- W_\theta(U_n)/\mathrm{d}\theta=0\}\cap\{W_\theta(U_{n+1})=\theta\}}.$$

Thus, substituting these equations into (4), we have P-a.s.,

$$\frac{\mathrm{d}^- \mathrm{P}_{\mathrm{loss}}(\theta)}{\mathrm{d}\theta} = -2 \lim_{m\to\infty} \frac{1}{m} \sum_{n\ge 1} 1_{\{T_n \le U_m\}} \times \frac{\sum_{n=1}^{m} 1_{\{\mathrm{d}^- W_\theta(U_n)/\mathrm{d}\theta=0\}\cap\{W_\theta(U_{n+1})=\theta\}}}{\sum_{n\ge 1} r_n\, \sigma_n\, 1_{\{T_n\le U_m\}}}. \qquad (15)$$

Now, recall that both $\{T_n\}_{n\in\mathbb{Z}}$ and $\{U_n\}_{n\in\mathbb{Z}}$ are stationary and the intensities are λ and 2λ, respectively. Then, we have

$$\lim_{m\to\infty} \frac{1}{m} \sum_{n\ge 1} 1_{\{T_n\le U_m\}} = \frac{1}{2}, \quad \text{P-a.s.} \qquad (16)$$

Therefore, we have (13) from (15) and (16). In the same way, we can obtain (14) using Proposition 2, and the proof is completed. □

This proposition says that the sensitivity of the loss probability can be estimated by computing the following estimates through simulation:

$$-\frac{\sum_{n=1}^{m} 1_{\{\mathrm{d}^- W_\theta(U_n)/\mathrm{d}\theta=0\}\cap\{W_\theta(U_n)=\theta\}}}{\sum_{n\ge 1} r_n\, \sigma_n\, 1_{\{T_n\le U_m\}}}, \qquad (17a)$$

or

$$-\frac{\sum_{n=1}^{m} 1_{\{\mathrm{d}^+ W_\theta(U_n)/\mathrm{d}\theta=0\}\cap\{L_\theta((U_n,\, U_{n+1}])>0\}}}{\sum_{n\ge 1} r_n\, \sigma_n\, 1_{\{T_n\le U_m\}}}. \qquad (17b)$$

We have the following from Corollary 1:

Corollary 2: *If* $\mathrm{P}_U^0(W_\theta(0) + A_0 \notin \{0,\, \theta\}) = 1$, *we have* P*-a.s.*

$$\frac{\mathrm{d}\mathrm{P}_{\mathrm{loss}}(\theta)}{\mathrm{d}\theta} = - \lim_{m\to\infty} \frac{\sum_{n=1}^{m} 1_{\{\mathrm{d}W_\theta(U_n)/\mathrm{d}\theta=0\}\cap\{W_\theta(U_{n+1})=\theta\}}}{\sum_{n\ge 1} r_n\, \sigma_n\, 1_{\{T_n\le U_m\}}}. \qquad (18)$$

□

Remark 2: Let $\{R_n\}_{n\in\mathbb{Z}} = \{U_n \mid W_\theta(U_n-) = 0,\ W_\theta(U_n+) > 0\}_{n\in\mathbb{Z}}$. Then, if there exist only a finite number of R_n on $\mathbb{R}$, $\mathrm{dP}_{\mathrm{loss}}(\theta)/\mathrm{d}\theta = 0$ because the numerator of the right-hand side of (18) goes to some finite value although the denominator goes to infinity. Such a case occurs with a positive probability if $\rho = \mathrm{E}^0[r_0\, \sigma_0]/\mathrm{E}^0[\tau_0] > c$.

4 Simulation results

In this section, we present some simulation results in order to show the validity of our sensitivity estimators. We here use (18) and assume that $r_n = c = 1$ for any n. We consider gradual input queues with regenerative structures, where distributions of interarrival times and burst lengths are both *i.i.d.* When the analytical results of the loss probability are available, they are used for comparison. But not available, we compare the values from our estimator with the symmetric *finite difference* (FD) estimates, which are calculated by

$$\left(\frac{\mathrm{dP}_{\mathrm{loss}}(\theta)}{\mathrm{d}\theta}\right)_{\mathrm{fd}} = \frac{\left(\mathrm{P}_{\mathrm{loss}}(\theta+\Delta\theta)\right)_{\mathrm{est}} - \left(\mathrm{P}_{\mathrm{loss}}(\theta-\Delta\theta)\right)_{\mathrm{est}}}{2\,\Delta\theta}, \qquad (19)$$

where

$$\left(\mathrm{P}_{\mathrm{loss}}(\theta)\right)_{\mathrm{est}} = \frac{\sum_{n=0}^{m-1} \left[W_\theta(U_n) + A_n - \theta\right]^+}{\sum_{n\ge 0} \sigma_n\, 1_{\{T_n < U_m\}}}. \qquad (20)$$

It is, in general, difficult to estimate the sensitivity of the loss probability in ATM networks because the cell loss is a rare event and therefore the desired derivative also should be absolutely small. The rarer the event is, the larger error the crude Monte Carlo method holds in simulation. Moreover, if the probability of an event is less than 10^{-4}, in most cases, the estimates result in zero and the crude Monte Carlo method is useless. To get rid of this problem, we use the *likelihood ratio.* To apply the likelihood ratio is known as an efficient way to a regenerative rare event simulation (Asmussen et al. [1]). The main idea is to perform experiments with a different governing probability distribution instead of the original one. To apply this technique, we change a burst length distribution B to B^* under the assumption that B is absolutely continuous with respect to B^*.

We define the beginning of a busy period as an epoch when a burst finds the system idle, as in the conventional queueing models (note, however, that the amount of work in the buffer may be empty even in a busy period). Then, the beginnings of busy periods construct regenerative points of the regenerative process. We further assume that the first busy period starts at T_0 $(= U_0)$. So, if a busy period starts at time T_n, then $T_n = U_{2n}$. Under the assumption that B and B^* have densities b and b^* respectively, the likelihood ratio L_k is defined by

$$L_k = \prod_{n=M_k}^{M_{k+1}-1} \frac{b(\sigma_n)}{b^*(\sigma_n)},$$

where M_k denotes the index of the burst which initiates the kth busy period. Applying this into (18) and (20), we have

$$\left(\frac{\mathrm{dP}_{\mathrm{loss}}(\theta)}{\mathrm{d}\theta}\right)_{\mathrm{pa}} = \frac{\sum_{k=0}^{m-1}\left(\sum_{n=2M_k}^{2M_{k+1}-1} 1_{\{\mathrm{d}W_\theta(U_n)/\mathrm{d}\theta=0\}\cap\{W_\theta(U_{n+1})=\theta\}}\right) L_k}{\sum_{k=0}^{m-1}\left(\sum_{n=M_k}^{M_{k+1}-1} \sigma_n\right) L_k};$$

$$\left(\mathrm{P}_{\mathrm{loss}}(\theta)\right)_{\mathrm{est}} = \frac{\sum_{k=0}^{m-1}\left(\sum_{n=2M_k}^{2M_{k+1}-1} \left[W_\theta(U_n) + A_n - \theta\right]^+\right) L_k}{\sum_{k=0}^{m-1}\left(\sum_{n=M_k}^{M_{k+1}-1} \sigma_n\right) L_k}.$$

Noting that $r_n = c = 1$ for any n, we let $\rho = \lambda\,\mathrm{E}^0[\sigma_0]$ for burst length distribution B. The experiments were performed for three different values of ρ corresponding to the light ($\rho = 0.2$), medium ($\rho = 0.5$) and heavy ($\rho = 0.8$) traffics, respectively. In the following tables, each element without analytical results is presented with 95% confidence interval taken from 30 independent replications, where each sample path consists of 100,000 busy periods. Moreover, in applying the likelihood ratio, we let ρ^*/ρ be 2, 1.5 and 1.1 for $\rho = 0.2$, 0.5 and 0.8, respectively, where ρ^* is defined under distribution B^* as ρ.

Example 1 (Gradual M/M/1 Queue): In this example, a gradual M/M/1 queue was simulated. We take λ and θ as 0.05 and 60. We also take $\Delta\theta$ in (19) as 2, 1 and 0.5 for $\rho = 0.2$, 0.5 and 0.8, respectively. The experimental results are shown in Table 1. The results indicate that our estimator is valid with smaller variances than FD estimates.

Example 2 (Gradual M/E$_3$/1 Queue): In this example, the case of a gradual M/E$_3$/1 queue was experimented as a representative of gradual M/GI/1 queueing models. Its burst length distribution is third-order Erlang. We take λ and θ as 0.02 and 70, and $\Delta\theta$ in (19) as 5, 1 and 0.5 for $\rho = 0.2$, 0.5 and 0.8, respectively. The simulation results are shown in Table 2. We also find good agreement and find that our PA estimates have smaller variances than FD estimates.

Example 3 (Gradual Queue with Two Markov On-Off Sources): We here experimented the queueing model in Hashida and Fujiki [5] in order to compare the results from our estimator with the analytical results. The queueing model in this example is as follows. Work of bursts arrives gradually from two independent on-off sources. From each source, work of a burst arrives at rate 1 during an 'on' period whose length is exponentially distributed with mean $1/\mu$, and inter-burst time, which is 'off' period, is also exponentially distributed with mean $1/\lambda$. From [5], we have, for $\mu \neq \lambda$,

$$\mathrm{P}_{\mathrm{loss}}(\theta) = \frac{\lambda\,(\mu-\lambda)\,\exp\{-2\,(\mu-\lambda)\,\theta/\mu\}}{2\,(\mu^2 - \lambda^2\,\exp\{-2\,(\mu-\lambda)\,\theta/\mu\})};$$

$$\frac{\mathrm{dP}_{\mathrm{loss}}(\theta)}{\mathrm{d}\theta} = \frac{-\lambda\,\mu\,(\mu-\lambda)^2\,\exp\{-2\,(\mu-\lambda)\,\theta/\mu\}}{(\mu^2 - \lambda^2\,\exp\{-2\,(\mu-\lambda)\,\theta/\mu\})^2}.$$

We take λ and θ as 0.01 and 40, respectively. The sensitivity estimation results are presented in the third column of Table 3 and the fourth column shows the corresponding analytical values. We here confirm that our estimates are valid with reasonable accuracy.

5 Conclusion

In this paper, we considered a stationary gradual input queueing system, where a burst arrives gradually at a constant rate during some period. This model represents bursty arrivals of cells in high-speed networks such as ATM networks. Using this model, we investigated the sensitivity of the loss probability with respect to the buffer size. Estimating the loss probability is a critical problem because the desired values should be considerably small. We here applied the perturbation analysis (PA) method combined with the likelihood ratio (LR). We derived the strongly consistent estimators for the left- and right-hand derivatives by using the continuous property of the loss probability with respect to the buffer size and using the ergodic theorem. Furthermore, we recognized that both the left- and right-hand derivatives are identical in most cases. In order to show the validity of our estimator, we carried out simulation experiments for some kinds of models. Consequently, we confirmed that we could reduce the variance by using the PA/LR technique, and could estimate the sensitivity more accurately.

Table 1: Estimates for a Gradual $M/M/1$ queue

ρ	$(\mathrm{P_{loss}}(\theta))_{est}$	$(\mathrm{dP_{loss}}(\theta)/\mathrm{d}\theta)_{pa}$	$(\mathrm{dP_{loss}}(\theta)/\mathrm{d}\theta)_{fd}$
0.2	$6.598 \times 10^{-8} \pm 1.012 \times 10^{-8}$	$-1.381 \times 10^{-8} \pm 3.430 \times 10^{-9}$	$-1.586 \times 10^{-8} \pm 4.185 \times 10^{-9}$
0.5	$5.966 \times 10^{-3} \pm 5.981 \times 10^{-5}$	$-3.066 \times 10^{-4} \pm 3.619 \times 10^{-6}$	$-3.275 \times 10^{-4} \pm 4.312 \times 10^{-5}$
0.8	$8.021 \times 10^{-2} \pm 2.057 \times 10^{-4}$	$-1.353 \times 10^{-3} \pm 3.241 \times 10^{-6}$	$-1.335 \times 10^{-3} \pm 2.971 \times 10^{-4}$

Table 2: Estimates for a Gradual $M/E_3/1$ queue

ρ	$(\mathrm{P_{loss}}(\theta))_{est}$	$(\mathrm{dP_{loss}}(\theta)/\mathrm{d}\theta)_{pa}$	$(\mathrm{dP_{loss}}(\theta)/\mathrm{d}\theta)_{fd}$
0.2	$5.887 \times 10^{-7} \pm 1.113 \times 10^{-7}$	$-1.247 \times 10^{-7} \pm 4.956 \times 10^{-8}$	$-1.986 \times 10^{-7} \pm 1.371 \times 10^{-7}$
0.5	$1.451 \times 10^{-2} \pm 2.566 \times 10^{-4}$	$-4.993 \times 10^{-4} \pm 6.794 \times 10^{-6}$	$-4.112 \times 10^{-4} \pm 2.180 \times 10^{-4}$
0.8	$1.137 \times 10^{-1} \pm 2.342 \times 10^{-4}$	$-1.307 \times 10^{-3} \pm 2.234 \times 10^{-6}$	$-1.127 \times 10^{-3} \pm 4.052 \times 10^{-4}$

Table 3: Estimates for a Gradual $G/M/1$ queue

ρ	$\mathrm{P_{loss}}(\theta)$	$(\mathrm{dP_{loss}}(\theta)/\mathrm{d}\theta)_{pa}$	$\mathrm{dP_{loss}}(\theta)/\mathrm{d}\theta$
0.2	8.205×10^{-5}	$-1.307 \times 10^{-5} \pm 5.516 \times 10^{-7}$	-1.312×10^{-5}
0.5	2.294×10^{-2}	$-9.404 \times 10^{-4} \pm 4.649 \times 10^{-6}$	-9.389×10^{-4}
0.8	1.060×10^{-1}	$-1.510 \times 10^{-3} \pm 2.039 \times 10^{-6}$	-1.511×10^{-3}

References

[1] S. Asmussen, R.Y. Rubinstein, and C.-L. Wang, "Regenerative rare events simulation via likelihood ratios," *J. Appl. Prob.*, vol. 31, pp. 797–815, 1994.

[2] F. Baccelli and P. Brémaud, *Elements of Queueing Theory: Palm-Martingale Calculus and Stochastic Recurrences.* Springer-Verlag, Berlin, 1994.

[3] X.-R. Cao, "Convergence of parameter sensitivity estimates in a stochastic experiment," *IEEE Trans. Autom. Contr.*, vol. 30, pp. 845–853, 1985.

[4] P. Glasserman, *Gradient Estimation via Perturbation Analysis.* Kluwer Academic Publishers, Boston, 1991.

[5] O. Hashida and M. Fujiki, "Queueing models for buffer memory in store-and-forward systems," in *Proc. of ITC 7*, pp. 323/1–7, 1973.

[6] P. Konstantopoulos and M.A. Zazanis, "Sensitivity analysis for stationary and ergodic queues," *Adv. Appl. Prob.*, vol. 24, pp. 738–750, 1992.

[7] P. Konstantopoulos and M.A. Zazanis, "Sensitivity analysis for stationary and ergodic queues: Additional results," *Adv. Appl. Prob.*, vol. 26, pp. 556–560, 1994.

[8] M. Miyazawa and G. Yamazaki, "Loss probability of a burst arrival finite queue with synchronized service," *Prob. Engr. and Informat. Sci.*, vol. 6, pp. 201–216, 1992.

[9] Y. Wardi, M.A. Zazanis, and M. Luo, "Consistency of perturbation analysis for a queue with finite buffer space and loss policy," *jota*, vol. 68, pp. 181–202, 1991.

[10] M.A. Zazanis and R. Suri, "Convergence rates of finite-difference sensitivity estimates for stochastic systems," *Operat. Res.*, vol. 41, pp. 694–703, 1993.

[11] M.A. Zazanis and R. Suri, "Perturbation analysis of the $GI/GI/1$ queue," *Queueing Sys.: Theory and Applicat.*, vol. 18, pp. 199–248, 1994.

Copy Emulation in Checksummed, Multiple-Packet Communication

José Carlos Brustoloni and Peter Steenkiste
School of Computer Science
Carnegie Mellon University
Pittsburgh, PA 15213
jcb@cs.cmu.edu, prs@cs.cmu.edu

Abstract

Data copying can be a bottleneck in end-to-end communication over high-speed networks. Emulated copy is an alternative I/O data passing scheme that preserves the API and integrity guarantees of copying but avoids the latter using VM manipulations – transient output copy-on-write (TCOW), input alignment, *and* page swapping. *We characterize and evaluate the support necessary in network adapters for emulated copy in checksummed, multiple-packet communication. Our experiments on an ATM network show that: (1) Emulated copy gives performance better than that of copying even without hardware checksumming support; (2) TCOW improves multiple-packet output performance without any hardware support or changes in applications; (3) Page swapping provides additional similar improvements on multiple-packet input if there is input alignment, which requires either hardware support* (early-demultiplexed/system-aligned buffering) *or changes in applications* (pooled/application-aligned buffering)*; and (4) The performance of application-aligned buffering is largely unaffected by* header/data splitting, *a common optimization. We propose a new optimization,* buffer snap-off, *that extends system-aligned buffering to the general case of arbitrary, unmatched data transfer and application input buffer lengths.*

1 Introduction

Workstation operating systems, such as Unix [13], typically perform physical input/output (I/O) only on system buffers. The system copies data from application buffers to system buffers before output and conversely from system buffers to application buffers after input. Copying decouples applications from physical I/O and gives applications total control over the layout, allocation, and deallocation of their I/O buffers.

Despite the flexibility that it affords, copying has the drawback of burdening host memory with read and write accesses for each I/O data word. Unfortunately, workstation main memory bandwidth has been and is expected to continue increasing more slowly than the point-to-point bandwidth of communication networks [10]. This has made copying between system and application buffers a bottleneck [16] in end-to-end communication over high-speed networks. ATM, for example, is commercially available at transmission rates of 622 Mbps, capable of challenging the memory system of even top-of-the-line workstations.

We recently proposed a novel I/O data passing scheme, *emulated copy*, that uses virtual memory (VM) manipulations rather than copying to pass data between applications and operating system [3]. Because VM manipulations do not actually touch data, they are relatively insensitive to low main memory bandwidth. Emulated copy uses *transient output copy-on-write* (TCOW) to avoid copying in the common output case, where the application does not overwrite its output buffers while output is taking place. On input, *input alignment* and *page swapping* pass data without copying and without corrupting application buffers with incomplete or erroneous data. Contrary to previous copy avoidance schemes, emulated copy preserves the application programming interface (API) and integrity guarantees of copying and does not restrict application buffer location, alignment, or length.

This paper investigates whether emulated copy gives performance better than that of copying in networking applications where data needs to be checksummed and fragmented into packets. Both checksumming and fragmentation may reduce the performance advantage of emulated copy. Checksumming can be integrated with copying at very little cost [6], whereas a similar integration is not possible with emulated copy. Fragmentation may make input alignment difficult because data is in general received in packets of arbitrary length, each containing header and trailer that do not contain application data and that therefore need to be stripped.

The impact of checksumming can be eliminated if the network adapter itself checksums packets. We verify experimentally, however, that emulated copy gives performance better than that of copying even without such hardware support. Because our VM manipulations are very cheap, the additional cost of reading the data for checksumming gives a total cost that is still much less than that of copying, which requires reading and writing the data.

Likewise, fragmentation hurdles can be re-

This research is sponsored in part by the Advanced Research Projects Agency under contract number DABT63-93-C-0054 and in part by the Advanced Research Projects Agency under contract number F19628-92-C-0116.

 0-8186-7780-5/97 $10.00 © 1997 IEEE

duced by hardware support in the network adapter. *Header/data splitting*, a feature found in several current adapters, enables page swapping if packet header lengths are fixed, application input buffers are page-aligned, and both application input buffers and packet data have lengths that are multiples of the page size. We generalize these conditions in what we call *application-aligned* buffering, where applications lay out their input buffers according to the *preferred alignment and length* informed by the system. We show experimentally that emulated copy with application-aligned buffering gives performance that is much better than that of copying and is largely unaffected by hardware support (header/data splitting).

Moreover, we demonstrate experimentally that *early demultiplexing*, a feature in some form present in most ATM adapters, can be exploited in *system-aligned* buffering to input data into system buffers with the same alignment and length as the corresponding application buffers. This enables page swapping even if application input buffers have arbitrary lay-out, provided that their lengths match those of the corresponding (single or multiple-packet) data transfers.

We contribute a novel optimization, *buffer snap-off*, that extends system-aligned buffering to the general case of arbitrary, unmatched data transfer and application input buffer lengths.

The rest of this paper is organized as follows. The next section describes in greater detail the emulated copy VM manipulations. Section 3 discusses network adapter support for input alignment and checksumming. Section 4 highlights desirable characteristics of the application programming interface. Section 5 presents our experimental results. Section 6 discusses related work, and Section 7 gives our conclusions.

2 Emulated copy

Applications that use I/O interfaces such as BSD Unix *sockets* [13], which copy data between application and system buffers, expect the system to maintain a certain *buffering semantics*. For a copy avoidance scheme to be compatible with these applications, it must implement the same semantics precisely [3]. In this section, we describe how our scheme, *emulated copy*, avoids data copying while fully preserving copy semantics.

Copying from application to system buffers when an application triggers an output operation guarantees that the application cannot affect output data by overwriting its output buffers during output. Overwriting may happen because the application reuses its buffers for subsequent computation.

Emulated copy more efficiently achieves the same output behavior by using a novel VM manipulation, TCOW, instead of copying, when data is longer than a configurable threshold (between 0 and the page size). TCOW keeps counts of how many times each physical page is referenced in pending output operations. If the output count of a physical page is zero before a given output operation, TCOW removes write permissions from the page table entries of all VM mappings of that page. Consequently, VM hardware will cause any application that attempts to overwrite that page to receive a page fault. TCOW recovers from that exception, if the output count is still non-zero, by copying the contents of the output page to a new page and replacing the output page by this new page in the application buffer VM mapping; or if the output count is zero, by simply reinstating write permissions in the respective page table entry. Because copy-on-write only happens while output is taking place, we call this scheme *transient*. In the common case of applications that do not overwrite output buffers during output, no copying happens at all.

TCOW relies on *I/O-deferred page deallocation* to guarantee that output pages cannot be freed during output. Pages can normally be freed by explicit deallocation by the application, application termination, or pageout; reuse of a page with outstanding output following one of these events might corrupt output data. I/O-deferred page deallocation prevents such corruption by modifying the system's page deallocation routine to refrain from placing pages with non-zero I/O reference count in the list of free pages, whence they might be reused. The I/O subsystem frees each such page when the last I/O operation referencing the page completes.

On input, copying from system buffers to application buffers only after successful completion of the operation guarantees that application buffers will not be corrupted by incomplete or erroneous input data. To be fully compatible, a copy avoidance scheme must make the same integrity guarantees.

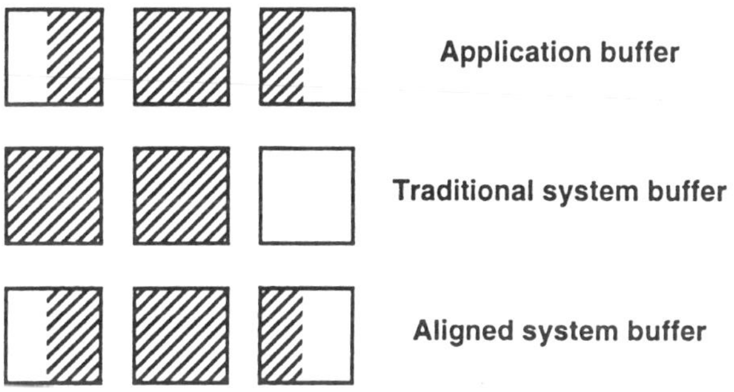

Figure 1: Input alignment makes it possible to swap pages.

Emulated copy uses *input alignment* to minimize copying on input without loss of application buffer integrity. Emulated copy inputs data into system buffers with the same page offsets and lengths as the corresponding application buffers, as shown in Figure 1. When the input completes, emulated copy transfers data to the application by *swapping pages* between application and system buffers (that is, it replaces physical pages previously mapped to the application buffer with the pages from the system buffer). Page swapping is a VM manipulation that typically can be implemented at a fraction of the cost of the equivalent copy.

Emulated copy handles partially filled pages in aligned system buffers as follows. If the data to be transferred is sufficiently short, it is more efficient to simply copy it out to the application buffer. If it is long, however, it costs less to complete the page with corresponding data from the application buffer, by what we call *reverse copy-out*, and swap pages. Assuming that the cost of swapping is s, the cost of copying is cl, where l is the length of the data copied, the data lengths in the pages in the application and system buffers are u and k, respectively, $m = \min(u, k)$, and p is the page size, copying to the application buffer costs less than swapping pages if:

$$cm < s + c(p - m) + c(k - m)$$

where $(p - m)$ is the length of data that needs to be copied from the application to the system page before swapping, and $(k - m)$ is the length of system data, beyond the end of application data, that needs to be saved for subsequent input. If $u = k$, this relation reduces to:

$$u < t = \frac{\frac{s}{c} + p}{2}$$

where t is a configurable threshold in the system, usually only slightly greater than $p/2$.

Applications can achieve input alignment by using *application-aligned buffering*. We define an interface through which applications can inquire the *preferred buffer alignment and length* for input from any given I/O module (e.g., a protocol stack). Using this interface, applications can lay out their input buffers accordingly and thereby avoid input copying whether or not there is hardware support for input alignment.

Application-aligned buffering is similar to the optimizations of IRIX, HP-UX, and Solaris [5], which replace copying by page swapping when application input buffers are page-aligned and of length multiple of the page size. Unlike those optimizations, however, application-aligned buffering does not require hardware support, as explained in Sections 3.1 and 3.2.

Unfortunately, application-aligned buffering cannot support application input buffers of arbitrary alignment and length, such as those of many existing applications written for I/O interfaces with copy semantics. To support this general case, emulated copy uses an alternate technique, *system-aligned buffering*. This optimization presupposes that applications inform the alignment and length of their input buffers to the system *before* physical input, using, for example, the API described in Section 4. The system uses that information to input data into system buffers with the same alignment and length. This customization requires hardware support, as discussed in Sections 3.3 and 3.4.

3 Network adapter support

This section describes network adapter features relevant to input alignment and checksumming, and highlights software techniques that compensate the eventual lack of hardware support.

3.1 Pooled in-host input buffering

Network adapters with *pooled* in-host input buffering receive packets into buffers allocated from a list of *buffer segments* shared among multiple *reception ports*. Buffer segments reside in host memory and are specified by (pointer, length) pairs (scatter/gather). The host enqueues segments at the tail of the buffer segment list when preparing for reception, and the adapter dequeues segments from the head of the list when receiving packets. Reception ports are the objects from which applications receive data; they are identified in packet headers and can be, for example, ATM virtual connections or TCP ports.

In hosts with physically addressed DMA, the length of each segment is such that the segment does not cross page boundaries; commonly, each segment is a page. In hosts with virtually addressed DMA, the length of each segment is normally equal to the network maximum transmission unit (MTU); to simplify emulated copy, all segments are page-aligned. In either case, at the end of a packet the adapter drops the remainder of the current segment, so that storage of the next packet starts at the next segment.

Pooled input buffering does not support input alignment. The latter is possible, however, if applications use application-aligned buffering. If: (1) Packet headers and trailers have fixed lengths; (2) Data lengths of all packets in a data transfer have a known length L ($\leq$ MTU minus header and trailer lengths), except possibly for the last packet, which may have data length of at most L; and (3) Either: (a) For each data transfer, the length of application input buffering matches that of the data transfer; or (b) All data transfers and application input buffers have lengths that are integral multiples of L, although not necessarily equal; then copying can be avoided by setting the preferred alignment equal to the header length and the preferred length equal to L.

3.2 Header/data splitting

A refinement of pooled input buffering is to have the adapter use separate *header* and *data/trailer* buffer segment lists, shared among multiple reception ports, as depicted in Figure 2. The initial portion of a packet is stored in a segment allocated from the header list, while the remainder of the packet is stored in segments allocated from the data/trailer list [12]. If segments in the header list have length equal to that of packet headers, this scheme normalizes the preferred buffer alignment to page boundaries.

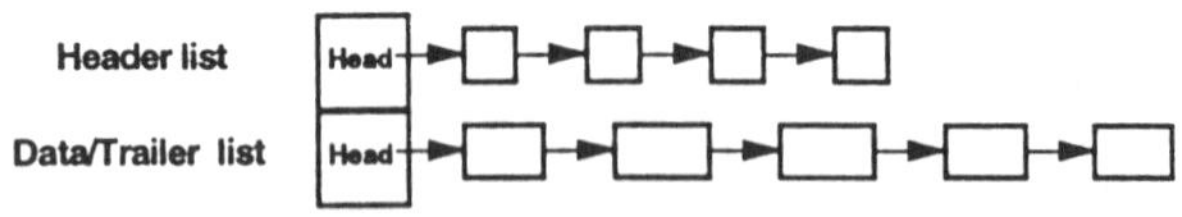

Figure 2: Separate header and data/trailer buffer lists

Solaris zero-copy TCP [5] uses this technique with L set to the largest integral multiple of the page size not greater than the MTU minus TCP/IP header length. Input copying is thereby avoided if packet headers do not contain options (so that TCP/IP headers have fixed length), application input buffers are page-aligned, and both application input buffers and data transfers have lengths that are integral multiples of the page size.

3.3 Early demultiplexing

Network adapters with *early demultiplexed* input buffering maintain *separate* buffer segment lists per reception port. When receiving the beginning of a new packet, the adapter demultiplexes the packet header to determine which input buffer list to use for reception of the packet [1], as shown in Figure 3. [1]

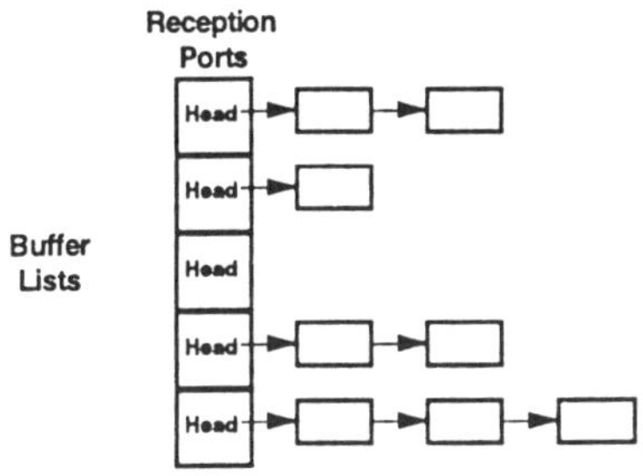

Figure 3: Early demultiplexing

Early demultiplexing supports system-aligned buffering: The system can enqueue, at the buffer segment list of each reception port, segments with alignment and length matching those of the respective application buffers. Each segment may have different alignment or length, and consequently, it must be possible for the host to *reclaim* (dequeue) specific buffer segments in case of exceptions such as timeout of the corresponding input request.

If packet header, data, and trailer lengths are predictable by the receiving system (not necessarily fixed), proper alignment of input data can be maintained by interspersing header and trailer segments at the appropriate points in the buffer list of the respective reception port. Header and trailer segments allow the remaining data segments to end up concatenated in virtual memory in spite of data packetization.

The length of data transfers may be known by previous arrangement between the end applications. Packet header, data, and trailer lengths are then predictable if the header and trailer lengths are fixed or easily computable and the protocol used follows some simple deterministic rule, such as sending all packets except possibly the last one with length equal to the MTU. The MTU may be known because it is fixed (for example, in a LAN serving a cluster of workstations) or configurable (for example, using the TCP MSS option [13]). In general, the MTU can be estimated by what we call *MTU tracking*, that is, monitoring the maximum length of packets received at the given reception port. Knowledge of the total data transfer length is necessary to avoid enqueueing more segments than necessary to hold the data.

[1] ATM adapters that reassemble packets from ATM cells must implement at least a primitive form of early demultiplexing, keeping track of the different segments being reassembled per reception port, but possibly allocating segments from a pooled (rather than per-port) buffer segment list.

3.4 Buffer snap-off

Early demultiplexing does not by itself support buffer boundaries. Consequently, it enables system-aligned buffering only if data transfers and application input buffering have matching lengths. We propose a novel technique, *buffer snap-off*, that removes this restriction.

Buffer snap-off assumes that headers and trailers have lengths h and t that are either fixed or computable on-the-fly by the adapter. The adapter maintains separate header/trailer and data buffer lists. The header/trailer list can be shared among multiple reception ports and can be further split into separate header and trailer lists. Segments in the header/trailer list have length greater than or equal to the largest allowed h and t. The first h bytes of a packet are stored in a segment allocated from the header/trailer list, the last t bytes are stored in another segment from the header/trailer list, and the remaining data is stored in segments allocated from the data buffer list (*header/data/trailer splitting*). The adapter maintains separate data buffer lists per reception port. Data buffer lists can be represented by hierarchical lists of buffer segments, or more simply by lists of buffer segments, where each segment contains an end-of-buffer (EOB) bit set only at the last segment of the respective buffer. These alternatives are shown in Figure 4.

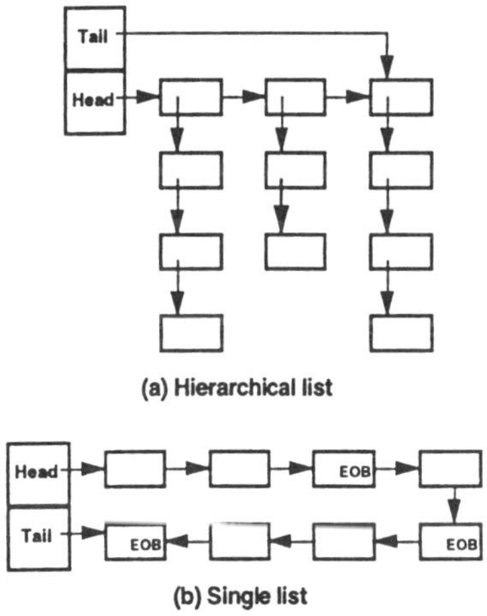

Figure 4: Data buffer representation alternatives

We define two snap-off modes, selectable per reception port: *single-packet*, suitable for datagram service, and *multiple-packet*, especially suitable for byte-stream service, as shown in Figure 5.

In single-packet mode, on end-of-packet, the adapter should dequeue and deallocate the remaining segments of the current data buffer and signal completion of the input operation. Conversely, if the packet data is longer than the current data buffer, the adapter should drop the packet.

In multiple-packet mode, on the contrary, on end-of-packet, the adapter should *snap off* the remainder of the current data buffer segment and place it at

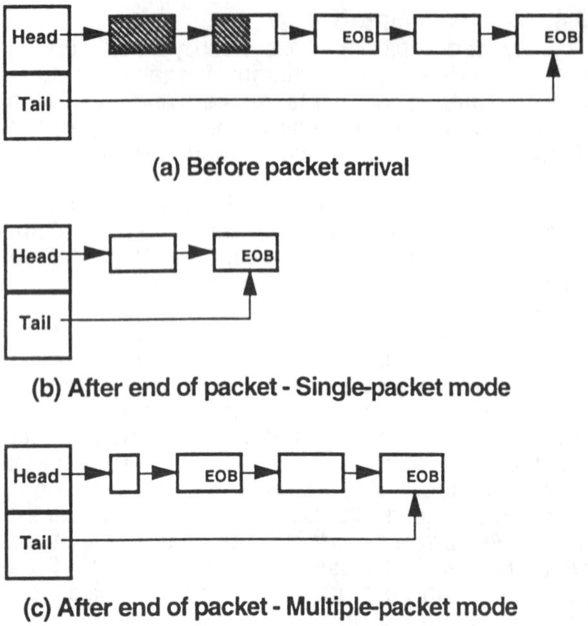

Figure 5: Buffer snap-off. Data from an incoming packet occupies the shaded area in (a). The rest of the buffer is then dequeued (b) or snapped off (c).

the head of the data buffer list of the current reception port. This way, the data of successive packets for the same reception port will be concatenated in the system input buffer, as required, even if packet data lengths are not integral multiples of the page size (as, for example, in maximally-sized Ethernet, FDDI, or ATM AAL5 packets). Input requests in this mode remain pending until the corresponding input data buffering is completely filled. Packets may span multiple buffers; end of the data buffering of an input request simply marks the completion of the request, deferred until successful end of the last packet using it. Out-of-order reception (not possible in ATM) is dealt with as an exception, in software, by copying.

Existing adapters in general do not implement buffer snap-off and instead simply drop the remainder of the current buffer segment at the end of a packet. This behavior jeopardizes copy avoidance, because: (1) In single-packet mode, if the current segment at the end-of-packet is not the last segment in the current buffer, storage for the next packet will start with the alignment of the next segment, which is not the first segment of the next buffer; and (2) In multiple-packet mode, the unfilled remainder of the current segment creates a gap in system buffers with respect to application buffers, causing data in subsequent segments to become misaligned and therefore require copying.

If the adapter supports early demultiplexing with header/data splitting per reception port, headers have fixed length, and there are no trailers (as in TCP/IP), host software may be able to approximate snap-off by dequeuing remaining segments of the current buffer (single-packet mode) or enqueuing the remainder segment at the head of the buffer list (multiple-packet mode). This software approximation does not work, however, if packets are received back-to-back, which doesn't give the host opportunity to fix the buffer list before arrival of the next packet.

3.5 Checksumming

Network adapter hardware may checksum data while it is transferred (by DMA or other block move mechanism) into or out of host memory, thereby relieving the host processor (and memory) of this task. Note that in emulated copy the adapter inputs data not into application buffers but rather into aligned system buffers. Consequently, if the checksum is incorrect, the previous contents of application buffers can be left intact, thus fully preserving copy semantics.

If checksums are transmitted in packet headers, as is the case in TCP/IP, hardware output checksumming requires packets to be staged in outboard buffers. Such staging allows the checksum field in the header to be corrected after data transfer from host memory and before transmission to the network. Given that output data is copied to outboard buffers, TCOW is unnecessary. On the other hand, outboard buffering may require a non-trivial amount of memory in network adapters. A low-cost alternative may be to use hardware checksumming only for *input*, which does not require outboard memory, and for output use TCOW and checksumming by the host processor.

4 Application programming interface

Emulated copy can be applied to any I/O interface with copy semantics. Certain features of the API can, however, expand the number of cases where copy avoidance occurs. This section highlights such features, as implemented in Genie, a new, optimized I/O framework [3].

To enable system-aligned buffering, the application must inform the alignment and length of its input buffers to the system *before* physical input of the data. Genie allows applications to invoke I/O operations synchronously or asynchronously. The latter case can be used to *pre-post* buffers that are eventually going to be needed for input. The API includes calls to poll or abort asynchronous operations.

In I/O interfaces such as sockets, input operations complete when any non-null amount of data is available, not necessarily filling the application buffer. If the application expects to receive data in the remainder of an input buffer, it can submit a new input operation. This does not generate a race condition with respect to the arrival of a new packet because reception occurs asynchronously in system buffers, without any alignment constraints. This decoupling is made possible by copying.

The same approach may not be appropriate for emulated copy. When an application invokes an input operation, Genie *prepares* system buffers with the correct alignment. When the input operation completes and control is transferred back to the application, Genie *disposes* the system buffers by page swapping and loses any further alignment or length information.

If the application had to submit a new input operation for the remainder of an input buffer, there would be a time interval during which system-aligned buffering would not be prepared for newly arrived packets.

The solution used in Genie is to allow *partial delivery* of data to the application. When the application polls the status of a pending multiple-packet input operation, Genie swaps pages filled with previously received packets, but keeps the remainder of the input buffering prepared for further input. In multiple-packet mode, an input operation completes only when the corresponding input buffering is completely full, unless the application or a timeout aborts the operation before then.

5 Evaluation on an ATM network

This section compares experimental latencies for checksummed or multiple-packet communication between applications running on different hosts connected by the CreditNet ATM network at 155 Mbps using copying or emulated copy I/O data passing at the end hosts. Applications accessed the network via an implementation of Genie on the NetBSD 1.1 operating system. We used Micron P166 (166 MHz Pentium) computers with 32 MB of main memory. All measurements presented here are the averages of five runs (except where noted) on otherwise idle hosts and network; variances were small. Immediately before the measurements, the benchmark application zero-filled all buffers and communicated 4 KB in each direction so as to warm the instruction and data caches. The benchmark application then measured round-trip times, using the Pentium on-chip cycle counter, for data lengths equal to increasing multiples of the page size (4 KB). Reported latencies are equal to the round-trip times divided by two. In this section, all graphs have legends listed in the same order as the corresponding curves.

The CreditNet network adapter supports pooled and early demultiplexed input buffering and header/-data splitting [12]. It has only limited support for data/-trailer splitting (it automatically removes ATM AAL5 trailers (depadding) only if the PDU length modulo 48 is not greater than 40) and does not support buffer snap-off or checksumming.

Figure 6 shows the single-packet latency for early demultiplexed communication using copying or emulated copy and with or without IP checksumming by the host processor. Application buffers were page-aligned. The throughput for single 60 KB datagrams with or without checksumming was, using copying, 71 or 78 Mbps, and using emulated copy, 95 or 119 Mbps, respectively. The penalty of checksumming is lower when using copying because copying brings data into the cache, which emulated copy doesn't. The penalty of checksumming with copying can be further reduced on output by integrating the checksum and copy in a single step [6], so that each data word is read and written only once (in Figure 6, copying and checksumming were performed separately, so that each data word was read twice and written once). The same optimization would be incorrect for input because the application buffer would be over-

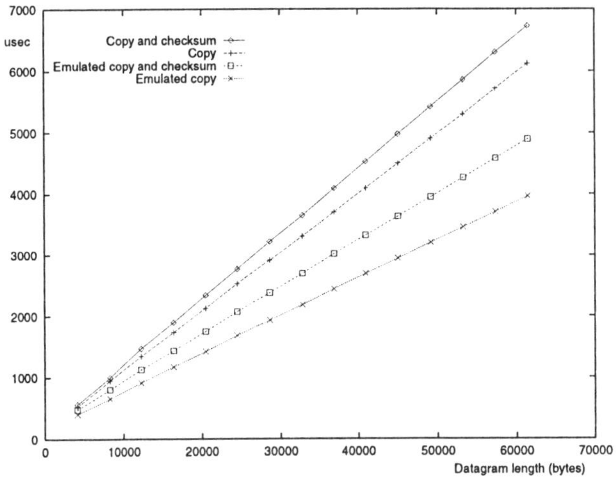

Figure 6: End-to-end latency for single packets. Emulated copy is cheaper than copying even if the host processor also has to read the data for checksumming.

written with erroneous data when the checksum fails, violating the integrity guarantees of copy semantics. The curves for "copy" and "copy and checksum" in the figure can be taken, respectively, as the lower and upper bound of the latency using integrated copy and checksum. The figure shows that the cost of emulated copy plus checksumming is substantially less than that lower bound. This is because VM manipulations are very cheap and checksumming only requires one memory access, to read data, while copying requires two memory accesses, to read and write data.

Figure 7 shows multiple-packet latencies with pooled input buffering, eight-byte packet headers (SNAP), and no transport-level flow control. All curves other than the top two use emulated copy. The bottom two curves indicate that, if the application input buffer is aligned according to the preferred offset and the MTU is equal to 8 KB (two pages), the throughput for 60 KB with or without header/data splitting is 122 or 119 Mbps, respectively. Performance is slightly worse without header/data splitting because of the overhead of reverse copy-out at the beginning and copy-out at the end of each packet. The throughput for 60 KB decreases to 93 Mbps if the MTU used is 9180 bytes (the default MTU for IP over ATM [17]) and the application input buffer starts with the preferred offset but is contiguous. Only the data in the first two pages ends up aligned, and the rest must be copied. (Note that the first two pages of *each* packet could be aligned and swapped if the application used non-contiguous input buffers, with each segment conforming to the preferred offset and length.) The throughput for 60 KB decreases further to 90 Mbps if the application input buffer already starts misaligned, so that all data needs to be copied, even if the MTU is a multiple of the page size (8 KB). Note that even in this last case, emulated copy still gives much better performance than does copying. This advantage is due to TCOW's

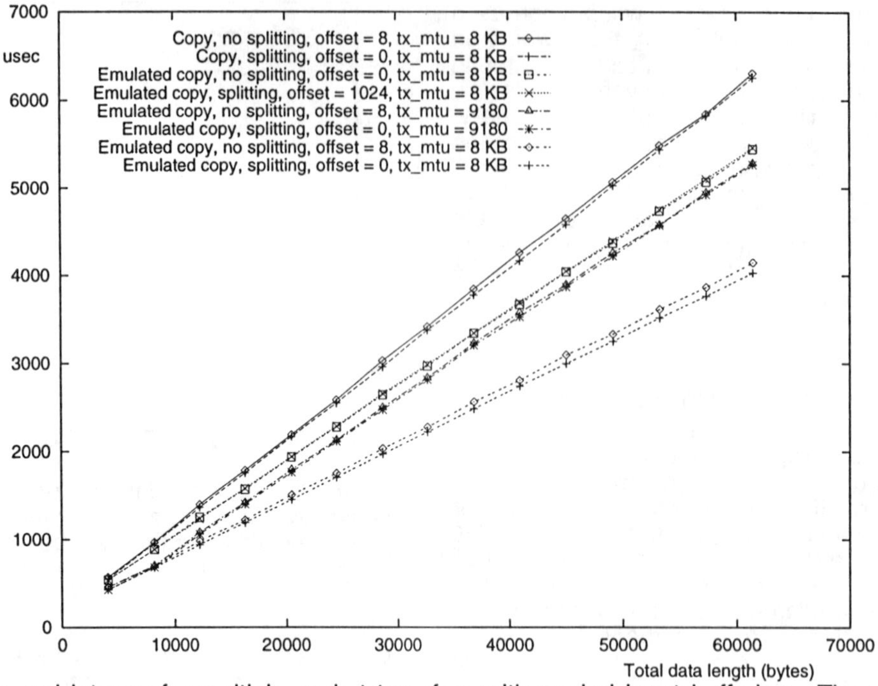

Figure 7: End-to-end latency for multiple-packet transfers with pooled input buffering. The performance of application-aligned buffering is not substantially affected by the presence or absence of header/data splitting.

copy avoidance on output. The top two curves indicate that the throughput for 60 KB using copying is 78 Mbps. We found that this value is relatively insensitive to header/data splitting, application input buffer alignment, and MTU.

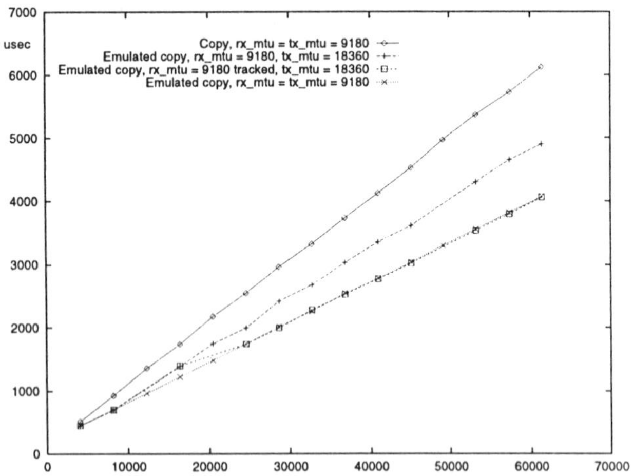

Figure 8: End-to-end latency for multiple-packet transfers with early demultiplexing. Copying is avoided regardless of application input buffer alignment and MTU. The MTU can be quickly estimated by MTU tracking.

Figure 8 shows multiple-packet latencies with early demultiplexing, eight-byte packet headers, and no transport-level flow control. Application input buffers were offset from a page boundary by 1 KB. The throughput for 60 KB with copying was 80 Mbps and is relatively insensitive to the MTU. The throughput for 60 KB with emulated copy was 121 Mbps if the actual MTU (tx_mtu) was the same as that expected by the receiver (rx_mtu), 9180 bytes. The actual MTU can vary widely without affecting performance, as long as it is the same as that expected by the receiver. If the actual MTU is 18360, twice as long as that expected by the receiver, the throughput for 60 KB falls to 100 Mbps, because data beyond the first two pages ends up not aligned in system buffers and needs to be copied to the application buffer for delivery. The figure also shows latencies for the first run using MTU tracking. After data longer than the actual MTU has been received, MTU estimation converges to the actual value, and performance becomes the same as when the MTU is fixed and known.

Buffer snap-off extends the conditions under which system-aligned buffering occurs, but does not improve the performance in situations where system-aligned buffering already occurs. Consequently, we can estimate the performance with buffer snap-off to be roughly equal to the bottom line in Figure 8.

6 Related work

TCOW differs from the Mach copy-on-write (COW) scheme [18] by being transient (Mach COW is long-term) and page-level (Mach COW operates on whole regions and requires more VM data structures to be updated). Another page-level COW scheme is that of Solaris, but it differs in important aspects from TCOW. According to the description in [5], the Solaris scheme eagerly reinstates write permissions on output completion. Eager reinstatement can be incorrect if the status of the region containing the page changes after output start. The application may, for example, change region protection to read-only, deallocate the region, or fork another process that inherits the region by copy-on-write. Additionally, if more than one output operation references the same page, output operations other than the first one either require data copying or may output corrupted data after the first operation completes, as the application may then overwrite the page. Finally, [5] does not describe whether or how the Solaris scheme prevents the page from being freed during output if the application explicitly deallocates the page or terminates.

System-allocated semantics such as *move* [3] eliminate copying without any special hardware support. The *system* then determines the location and layout of application input buffers; system buffers can be simply mapped to application address spaces, without alignment constraints. On output, the system automatically deallocates application output buffers. Unfortunately, system-allocated semantics require an API different from that of copy and other *application-allocated* semantics [3]. The API makes system-allocated semantics incompatible with many existing applications, for example those written for the socket interface. New applications that require a particular data layout, e.g. those that use arrays, or that need to retain access to output buffers after output, may not be able to use system-allocated semantics without user-level copying, which negates any performance improvements. We have experimentally demonstrated that system-allocated semantics have performance that is similar to that of application-aligned buffering [3]. The latter option will be preferable in many cases, because it is compatible with the usual application-allocated API and imposes less restrictions on applications (which can't choose data layout, but at least retain access to output buffers after output).

Outboard buffering can eliminate copying while preserving copy semantics. Data in outboard buffers can be transferred from the adapter to application buffers, rather than to system buffers, eliminating copying on input without early demultiplexing or buffer snap-off and regardless of application buffer alignment and length and packet lengths. However, outboard buffering may also add latency, complexity, and cost to the adapter. Moreover, depending on when data is checksummed, outboard buffering may result in semantics other than copy and introduce considerable jitter in transport-level acknowledgements. The Medusa [2] and Afterburner [8] adapters, for example, checksum while transferring data from outboard buffers to application buffers. Consequently, the latter may be corrupted with incorrect data, making the semantics *share* (weak integrity) rather than copy (strong integrity) [3]. Additionally, those adapters require packet acknowledgements to be delayed until the receiving process is scheduled to run *and* the application decides to receive the data. This can introduce considerable variability in round-trip times (RTT), which may interfere with transport-level algorithms that depend on precise RTT estimates. By checksumming while receiving data from the network into outboard buffers, the Gigabit Nectar WCAB [11] adapter is able to both guarantee copy semantics and maintain the usual decoupling between transport-level acknowledgements and application processing.

The Nectar protocol processor [7] and, more recently, the Charisma [15] adapter allow applications to directly map outboard buffers, in a truly zero-copy arrangement that may be beneficial if the host processor can access outboard memory as efficiently as it can access host memory. Unfortunately, adapters normally connect to the host via an I/O bus. In most current architectures, this makes outboard memory uncacheable and imposes relatively high arbitration overheads for word-sized accesses by the host. Consequently, applications that actually access the I/O data (not the case in [15]) may very well run more slowly with the data outboard than in a more conventional arrangement, where I/O data is transferred to and from host memory. Compatibility may also be a problem because the zero-copy arrangement does not provide copy semantics. Additionally, outboard memory is normally not pageable, making the scheme particularly susceptible to resource management problems when confronted with malicious or buggy applications that hog outboard buffers.

Application device channels [9] allow applications to safely enqueue I/O requests directly in the adapter, bypassing the operating system. Such bypassing may reduce latency, but also requires application buffers to be located in unpageable host memory and to have share or weak move [3] rather than copy semantics.

Carter and Zwaenepoel [4] show how driver software can approximate early demultiplexing for *blast* protocols on adapters with pooled input buffering. Blast protocols transmit long data in *blasts*, that is, multiple back-to-back packets, the last of which is acknowledged by the receiver. In [4], the driver, on receiving the first packet in a blast of more than two packets, replaces data segments at the head of the buffer segment list by segments that point directly to the receiving application's memory beyond the data of the first two packets in the blast. Data of the first two packets is copied, while the rest of the data is input directly from the network into the corresponding application memory, if the blast is not interrupted by packets destined to other reception ports. Interruptions by an unrelated packet require copying the data of that and the remaining blast packets to their correct destinations. [4] gives experimental evidence that such interruptions are very rare in practice; however, they constitute a potential security leak. Additionally, the semantics implemented is share rather than copy. The security leak could be eliminated and the semantics could be made fully compatible with copying by making replacement segments point to aligned system buffers, and swapping pages as in our scheme.

O'Malley et al. [14] modify Carter and Zwaenepoel's scheme so that each blast is preceded by a *control packet* describing the blast, and a 150 μsec delay. The delay allows the receiving host to insert, at the head of the buffer segment list, appropriate header and data segments for all packets in the blast, so that blast data ends up concatenated in a system buffer. After receiving the last packet of the blast, the system buffer is mapped to a new region in the application address space. This scheme eliminates the security leak, as in our proposed modification, but implements move rather than copy semantics.

7 Conclusions

We described a set of VM manipulations – TCOW, input alignment, and page swapping – that make it possible to fully emulate copy semantics on output or input without actually copying data. We characterized network adapter features needed for copy emulation in checksummed, multiple-packet communication, and reported the performance on an adapter with partial support.

Our results show that emulated copy gives performance better than that of copying even if the adapter does not provide checksumming and the host processor must read the data to perform that task.

Our measurements indicate that TCOW eliminates output copying and substantially reduces end-to-end latency without any special hardware support or changes in applications.

Our experiments demonstrate that page swapping provides similar additional performance gains when there is input alignment. Input alignment requires either hardware support (early-demultiplexed/system-aligned buffering) or changes in applications (pooled/application-aligned buffering). We found that header/data splitting, an optimization found in several current adapters, does not provide an attractive cost/benefit ratio: Its generalization, application-aligned buffering, achieves essentially the same performance without hardware support. In contrast, early demultiplexing, a feature that is present at least in primitive form in most ATM cards, enables input alignment under substantially more general conditions. Buffer snap-off, a novel hardware optimization, extends system-aligned buffering to the general case of arbitrary, unmatched byte stream or datagram lengths and application input buffering alignment and length.

References

[1] M. Bailey, B. Gopal, M. Pagels and L. Peterson. "PATHFINDER: A Pattern-Based Packet Classifier", in *Proc. OSDI'94*, USENIX, Nov. 1994, pp. 115-124.

[2] D. Banks and M. Prudence. "A High-Performance Architecture for a PA-RISC Workstation", in *J. Selected Areas in Communications*, IEEE, vol. 11, no. 2, Feb. 1993, pp. 191-202.

[3] J. Brustoloni and P. Steenkiste. "Effects of Buffering Semantics on I/O performance", in *Proc. OSDI'96*, USENIX, Oct. 1996, pp. 277-291.

[4] J. Carter and W. Zwaenepoel. "Optimistic Implementation of Bulk Data Transfer Protocols", in *Proc. SIGMETRICS'89*, ACM, May 1989, pp. 61-69.

[5] H. J. Chu. "Zero-Copy TCP in Solaris", in *Proc. Winter Tech. Conf.*, USENIX, Jan. 1996.

[6] D. Clark and D. Tennenhouse. "Architectural considerations for a new generation of protocols", in *Proc. SIGCOMM'90*, ACM, Sept. 1990, pp. 200-208.

[7] E. Cooper, P. Steenkiste, R. Sansom, B. Zill. "Protocol Implementation on the Nectar Communication Processor", in *Proc. SIGCOMM'90*, ACM, Sept. 1990, pp. 135-144.

[8] C. Dalton, G. Watson, D. Banks, C. Calamvokis, A. Edwards and J. Lumley. "Afterburner", in *IEEE Network*, July 1993, pp. 36-43.

[9] P. Druschel, L. Peterson and B. Davie. "Experiences with a High-Speed Network Adaptor: A Software Perspective", in *Proc. SIGCOMM'94*, ACM, Aug. 1994, pp. 2-13.

[10] J. Hennessy and D. Patterson. "Computer Architecture: A Quantitative Approach", 2nd. ed., Morgan Kaufmann Pub., San Francisco, CA, 1996.

[11] K. Kleinpaste, P. Steenkiste and B. Zill. "Software Support for Outboard Buffering and Checksumming", in *Proc. SIGCOMM'95*, ACM, Aug. 1995, pp. 87-98.

[12] C. Kosak, D. Eckhardt, T. Mummert, P. Steenkiste and Allan Fischer. "Buffer Management and Flow Control in the Credit Net ATM Host Interface", in *Proc. 20th Conf. Local Computer Networks*, IEEE, Oct. 1995, pp. 370-378.

[13] S. Leffler, M. McKusick, M. Karels and J. Quaterman. "The Design and Implementation of the 4.3BSD UNIX Operating System", Addison-Wesley Pub. Co., Reading, MA, 1989.

[14] S. O'Malley, M. Abbot, N. Hutchinson and L. Peterson. "A Transparent Blast Facility", in *Internetworking: Research and Experience*, vol. 1, 1990, pp. 57-75.

[15] B. Murphy, S. Zeadally and C. Adams. "An Analysis of Process and Memory Models to Support High-Speed Networking in a UNIX Environment", in *Proc. Winter Tech. Conf.*, USENIX, Jan. 1996.

[16] John K. Ousterhout. "Why aren't operating systems getting faster as fast as hardware?", in *Proc. Summer Tech. Conf.*, USENIX, June 1990, pp. 247-256.

[17] R. Atkinson. "Default IP MTU for use over ATM AAL5". RFC 1626, Naval Research Laboratory, May 1994.

[18] R. Rashid, A. Tevanian, M. Young, D. Golub, R. Baron, D. Black, W. Bolosky and J. Chew. "Machine-Independent Virtual Memory Management for Paged Uniprocessor and Multiprocessor Architectures", in *Proc. ASPLOS-II*, ACM, Oct. 1987, pp. 31-39.

SMART Retransmission: Performance with Overload and Random Losses

S. Keshav†

Department of Computer Science
Cornell University
Ithaca, New York 14853

S. P. Morgan

Bell Labs, Lucent Technologies
700 Mountain Avenue
Murray Hill, New Jersey 07974

Abstract

Feedback flow control, in conjunction with limited buffering in the network, inevitably leads to packet loss. Effective congestion control requires not only effective flow control but also a good retransmission strategy. We present a new retransmission strategy called SMART that combines the best features of the traditional go-back-n and selective-retransmit strategies.

We show, first, that go-back-n retransmission with static window flow control leads to congestion collapse when the nominal load exceeds the link capacity. Second, we can avert congestion collapse by replacing go-back-n with SMART retransmission, even with static window flow control. Third, SMART retransmission, when combined with Packet-Pair rate-based flow control, performs extremely well, both when losses are due to buffer overflows and when losses are random.

1 Introduction

Most current approaches to congestion control focus on the problem of flow control, that is, techniques that enable an end-system to match the currently available service rate in the network. While flow control is an important problem, it often overshadows the equally important choice of retransmission strategy. If losses due to line errors (as in wireless networks) or due to buffer overflows (as with network congestion) are common, a poor retransmission strategy can lead to congestion collapse, that is, to the catastrophic decrease of useful throughput as the offered load increases. It is important, therefore, to develop robust and efficient retransmission strategies. In this paper, we present SMART (Simple Method to Aid ReTransmissions), and use extensive simulations to show that it satisfies both the robustness and efficiency criteria. While SMART was developed in the context of a rate-based flow control protocol, it is equally applicable to window-based protocols. We will show that SMART retransmission, in conjunction with careful flow control, not only performs extremely well with congestive losses, but also performs nearly ideally in the presence of random losses. In contrast, TCP's performance grows rapidly worse in the presence of frequent random losses.

The rest of the paper is organized as follows. Section 2 describes the SMART retransmission policy. Section 3 studies the baseline case with go-back-*n* retransmission and static window flow control. Section 4 shows that adding SMART to the baseline case avoids congestion collapse. In Section 5 we describe how a combination of SMART and Packet-Pair flow control allows a source to not only avoid congestion collapse, but also obtain nearly optimal performance. Section 6 confirms that TCP will behave poorly when the loss rate is high or the bandwidth-delay product is large. Section 7 shows that SMART + Packet-Pair flow control continues to behave nearly optimally in the presence of heavy random losses. Finally, Section 8 presents our conclusions.

2 SMART strategy

SMART is a novel retransmission strategy that combines aspects of the traditional techniques go-back-*n* and selective-retransmit. To motivate our design, we first outline the traditional schemes and their drawbacks.

2.1 Go-back-n (GBN)

In GBN, a source keeps track of an *error control window*, which is the set of sequence numbers that it has transmitted, but the receiver has not acknowledged. Typically, the receiver writes the cumulative acknowledgment (ack) number in the ack header: this is the last in-sequence packet it has received, and is the one smaller than the left edge of the error control window. In strict GBN, on a timeout, the source retransmits the entire outstanding window. This is conservative, because the source treats every loss as a burst loss, but it uses bandwidth inefficiently. Moreover, loss recovery depends on a timer, which is usually hard to set [10]. If the timer is set too low, the source retransmits packets unnecessarily; if set too high, it wastes time, waiting for a timeout.

† This work was performed while S. Keshav was at Bell Laboratories.

0-8186-7780-5/97 $10.00 © 1997 IEEE

Some of this inefficiency is avoided by modified versions of GBN, as in TCP [9]. In these schemes, on a timeout, the source marks the entire window eligible for retransmission, but flow control ensures that the source retransmits only the first packet in the window. If incoming acks move the left end of the error control window, the source unmarks packets formerly marked eligible for retransmission. Thus, it is unlikely that the source would retransmit the entire error-control window. For example, suppose the error control window is 6-10, and the actual packet lost is 6. On a timeout, the source retransmits the packet with sequence number 6, and flow control ensures that the source sends no other packet for the next round trip time. If the ack moves the left edge of the error control window to 10, then the source does not retransmit packets 7-10. This scheme is clearly more efficient in its use of bandwidth. However, this comes at the expense of reduced throughput during the first round-trip-time after a loss. Besides, the source still depends on a timer to initiate retransmission.

2.2 Selective retransmit (SR)

Several SR schemes have been proposed in the literature [3]. In these schemes, every acknowledgment carries a bit-mask of the packets seen so far. Since the sender knows which packets have been received, only packets that are actually lost are retransmitted. Thus, SR allows a source to use bandwidth efficiently. Besides, there is no need for a timer to decide that a retransmission is necessary. However, every ack header must carry the bit-mask, which can be a significant overhead if the window size is large.

2.3 SMART retransmission

SMART seeks to be as efficient as SR in its choice of packets to retransmit, and as conservative as GBN in the presence of burst losses. We would like to avoid using timers where possible. Finally, we would like to decouple flow and error control.

The key idea in SMART is to build the bit-mask of correctly received packets at the sender, instead of carrying it in the ack header. Each ack therefore carries two pieces of information: the cumulative ack, as in standard GBN, and the sequence number of the packet that caused the ack to be initiated. As shown below, the second piece of information not only allows the sender to know which packets have been correctly received, but also allows the sender to correctly infer which packets have been lost, and to take corrective action, that, for the most part, does not require the intervention of a timer. This relative independence from timers is the key to its success.

Detailed description. For simplicity, assume that every correctly received packet is acked. When a source receives an ack, it compares the cumulative acknowledgment with the sequence number of the packet that caused the acknowledgment. If the two are not the same, the ack must be a duplicate ack, and the source guesses that all the packets in the sequence space between the cumulative ack and the packet being acked are lost, and places them in the transmission queue for subsequent retransmission. For example: if the source receives an ack that has a header (2,7), where 2 is the cumulative ack, and the ack was caused by the receipt of a packet with sequence number 7, then the source guesses that packets with sequence numbers 3, 4, 5, and 6 are lost. SMART is aggressive about retransmission, and so when it is uncertain whether a packet is misordered or lost, it always guesses that the packet is lost, and retransmits it. This is similar to the *fast retransmission* policy in TCP Reno, except that in TCP Reno, three duplicate acks have to be received before the source initiates a fast retransmission (this protects against reordering) [9]. A similar idea is also used in recent work by Brakmo and Peterson [2]. Here, a source saves the transmission time of each packet. On receiving a duplicate ack, it checks to see if the timeout value of any packet has been exceeded. If so, it retransmits that packet. Thus, all three schemes use a duplicate to infer that something is wrong and take corrective action.

There is one exception to this retransmission rule. If a source has already done a fast retransmission of a packet, then it will not be retransmitted by the receipt of a subsequent ack. For example, if acks (2,7), and (2,9) arrive to a source, on receiving the first ack, the source retransmits 3, 4, 5, and 6. However, on receiving the second ack, the source only retransmits 8, because packets 3-6 have been retransmitted earlier. This rule fails only when the fast retransmission itself is lost. In order to detect this, we use a different heuristic, described next.

Lost fast retransmissions. The intuition behind the scheme is that if a fast retransmission succeeds, then the cumulative ack should increase one round trip time after the fast retransmission was sent. Otherwise, the fast retransmission must have been lost. Suppose that the source sends a packet with sequence number P at time t that is lost in the network. If the source sends packet $P+1$ at time $t + \varepsilon$, and the round-trip-time is T_{RT}, then at time $t + \varepsilon + T_{RT}$, the source can discover that P is lost (because the cumulative ack and sequence number for this ack differ). Thus, the source retransmits P at time $t + \varepsilon + T_{RT}$. In the interval between $t + \varepsilon + T_{RT}$ and $t + \varepsilon + 2T_{RT}$ the cumulative acks received by the source cannot increase, since the lost packet causes a hole in the sequence space at the receiver, that is filled only when the retransmission is received. However, after time $t + \varepsilon + 2T_{RT}$, if the fast-retransmission indeed reached the receiver, the cumulative acknowledgment received by the source should have increased. In fact, if the cumulative ack received after time $t + \varepsilon + 2T_{RT}$ is not larger than the cumulative ack received at time $t + \varepsilon + T_{RT}$, then the fast-retransmission must surely have been lost. Of course, we need to allow for some variation in the round-trip-times, to allow for variable queueing delays. However, this logic underlies two algorithms to correct for most lost fast-retransmissions that we discuss next.

In the first algorithm, every time the source sends a fast retransmission, it sets a timer to expire one round-trip-time from the current time. If the cumulative acknowledgment does not increase by the time the timer expires, the packet with sequence number one larger than the cumulative-ack is retransmitted. This scheme requires frequent setting and resetting of timers, and depends on accurate measurement of round-trip-times for its success.

We can avoid these problems at the expense of another field in the packet header. In the second algorithm, the source maintains an *id* state variable that is guaranteed to be monotonically increasing with time (unlike the sequence number field, which can decrease because of retransmissions). We also add an id field to the transport-layer packet header. Every time the source sends a packet, it writes the current id value in the packet header, and increments the state variable. The id field is copied into the acknowledgment by the receiver. This field allows the source to measure round trip times without timers. For example, if the source sends a packet with id 5 at time t, then it should receive an ack with id 5 one round trip time later.

When the source sends a fast-retransmission, it stores the current cumulative-ack and the id of the fast-retransmission packet in two state variables. On receiving an ack, if the id of the packet is larger than the stored id, but the cumulative ack is the same as the stored value, then the fast retransmission must have been lost.

If a source loses a fast retransmission, the line is probably quite lossy, because the source has lost the same packet twice. To avoid losing the packet three times, the source thus places *two* copies of the same packet in the retransmission queue. This ensures that the sender will make progress (since the cumulative ack is very likely to increase — it won't increase only if *both* of the retransmissions are lost) even on very lossy lines.

Thus far, we have discussed how to recover from lost packets, and lost retransmissions, without using timers. However, timers are always needed, if only to deal with the worst case, where all packets and all acks are lost. Thus, SMART uses timers as a recovery mechanism of last resort. The source measures round trip times and exponentially averages them as in TCP. On packet transmission, a per-connection timer is set to twice the smoothed round-trip-time estimate (this is as good a value as any). On a timeout, the entire window, other than packets that are known to have been correctly received, is retransmitted. The timeout thus correctly retransmits lost packets even when the heuristics described above fail.

Error-control window size. We distinguish between the *error-control* window and the *flow-control* window at a source. The error-control window W_{EC} is the largest number of out-of-sequence packets that can be buffered at the receiver. For a window-controlled source, the flow-control window W_{FC} is the largest number of packets that the source may send without an acknowledgment. Limiting the flow-control window allows us to implicitly control the transmission rate of a connection, since the connection's rate is restricted to one flow-control window worth of packets per round-trip-time.

There are two requirements on the flow-control window: 1) It must be at least as large as the round-trip window W_{RT}, defined as the bandwidth-delay product of the connection. Otherwise the source cannot utilize the full speed of the circuit when there is no congestion. 2) It must not be larger than the error-control window, otherwise the receiver can't hold all the out-of-sequence arrivals that it might need to rearrange. If the round-trip window is less than the error-control window, as is almost always the case in practice, then the flow-control window can have any value in between.

For window-controlled circuits, where the source may transmit at full speed until the flow-control window is exhausted, too large a flow-control window runs the risk of overflowing the buffer space at bottleneck nodes. On the other hand, for rate-controlled circuits a sufficiently large error-control window permits the source to continue sending at the rate determined by the rate-control algorithm while the system recovers from losses.

Call the time between transmitting a packet and receiving its eventual acknowledgement, perhaps after multiple losses and retransmission, the *recovery time.* If the bottleneck has a rate μ, and the recovery time is T, then in order to keep the bottleneck busy, the source should be able to send $T\mu$ packets without waiting for a packet to be acked. In other words, the error-control window should be at least as large as $T\mu$.

For the SMART retransmission strategy, as long as losses are isolated, if the same packet is lost x times, then the recovery time is just greater than $(x+1)\,T_{RT}$, and the error-control window needs to be at least $(x+1)\,W_{RT}$. If losses can occur while the source is recovering from an earlier loss, then the analysis is substantially more complicated, since the recovery time depends in detail on which

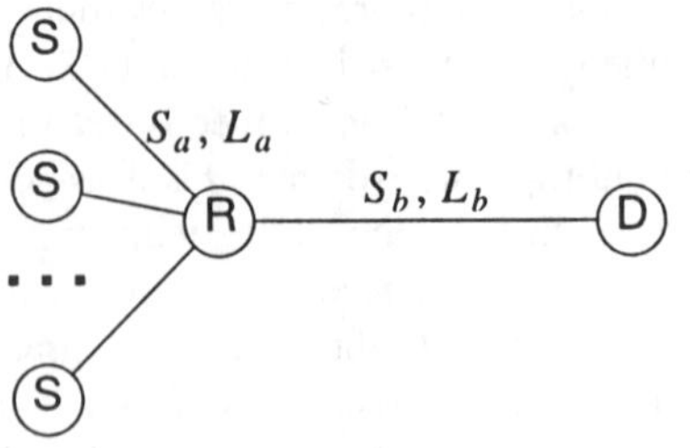

Figure 1: Simulation scenario.

packets are lost, and on the order in which the losses happen. In principle, we cannot bound the number of times a retransmitted packet is lost. However, increasing the error-control window beyond a certain size provides rapidly diminishing returns, since the events that require very large error-control window sizes are very unlikely. Instead of trying to analyze the recovery times for various combinations of losses and their relative probability of occurrence, we have studied the effect of window size on throughput through simulations (Section 7). We recommend that for normal operation, the error-control window be set to as large a value as possible, at least $2W_{RT}$, and preferably close to $4W_{RT}$.

3 Baseline case

In order to measure the effectiveness of SMART, we first study the performance of a *baseline* scenario shown in Fig. 1. In this scenario, packets from sources on access lines of speed S_a and latency L_a are multiplexed at a Fair Queueing router, which puts them onto a backbone link of speed S_b and latency L_b. The router has a fixed total buffer size and maintains a separate logical queue for each source. When a packet arrives that would cause the total buffer space to overflow, the arriving packet is discarded. The destination acknowledges every received packet with an acknowledgment of length A. Sources measure round-trip-times from the acknowledgments, smoothing them with an exponential averaging filter, as in TCP [9]. The timeout value is set to twice the smoothed round-trip-time. The sources do GBN retransmission of the entire outstanding window on a timeout, simultaneously doubling the timeout value.

After a source has generated a message containing some integral number of packets, it waits until all the packets have been correctly acknowledged. It then goes OFF for an additional, randomly chosen ''think time'', after which it again goes ON and repeats the cycle. In the simulation model, ON times are geometrically distributed with mean T_{ON}, and OFF times are exponentially distributed with mean T_{OFF}. For simplicity we assume that the link between the router and the destination is the bottleneck, that is, $S_b \le S_a$, and we assume that during an ON period, a source generates bits at a rate equal to the rate of the bottleneck link, that is, $R_{ON} = S_b$. For the average length of an ON period, we take $T_{ON} = 2T_{RT}$, where T_{RT} is the round-trip time when only one source is active, i.e., there is no contention. Thus the average message length is $2S_bT_{RT} = 2W_{RT}$.

The nominal offered load r_1 due to a single source is equal to the average utilization of the bottleneck link when only one source is present. Thus,

$$r_1 = T_{ON}/(T_{ON} + T_{RT} + T_{OFF}) .$$

The nominal offered load due to N statistically identical sources is Nr_1, and this can made as large as desired by suitable choice of N. The *goodput,* defined as the ratio of the average rate of transmission of good packets to the speed of the bottleneck link, is less than 100% if any packets have to be retransmitted.

For the simulations, we chose:

$$P = 500 \text{ bytes}, \quad A = 40 \text{ bytes}, \quad T_{RT} = 0.05 \text{ s},$$

and for the number of packets in a round-trip window,

$$S_bT_{RT}/P = 100 \text{ packets} .$$

We have considered three values of router buffer size, namely one round-trip window, 0.5 round-trip window, and 0.25 round-trip window. Each plot includes three curves, one for each value of the ratio B of buffer size to W_{RT}.

In the simulations of congestion loss, we set the error-control window equal to 600 packets. Such an window is essentially infinite for this scenario. The effects of error-control window size in a random-loss scenario are considered in Section 7.

We ran all the overload simulations with 10 statistically identical sources, that is, $N = 10$. Each simulation run lasted for 400 simulated seconds after an initial ''transient'' period of 20 seconds. Since one round-trip time is 0.05 seconds, each 20-second interval corresponds to 400 round-trip times. We varied the nominal offered load of a single source from 0.05 to 0.5, so that the total nominal offered load on the bottleneck link varied from 0.50 to 5.00. The ''fair share'' of a single source varied from 0.05 to 0.10, inasmuch as under congestion no source would be expected to get more than 1/10 of the available bandwidth on average.

To estimate the reliability of the simulator output, we went through the usual procedure of taking a sample of n values of goodput corresponding to $n = 20$ simulation intervals. We computed a sample mean $\overline{X}$ and vari-

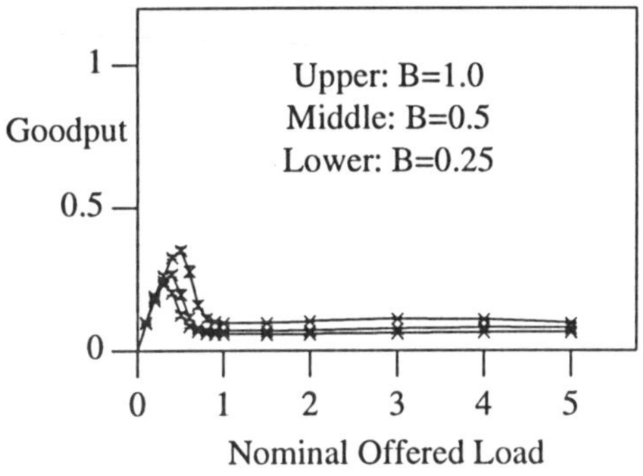

Figure 2: Goodput vs. offered load for 10 GBN sources.

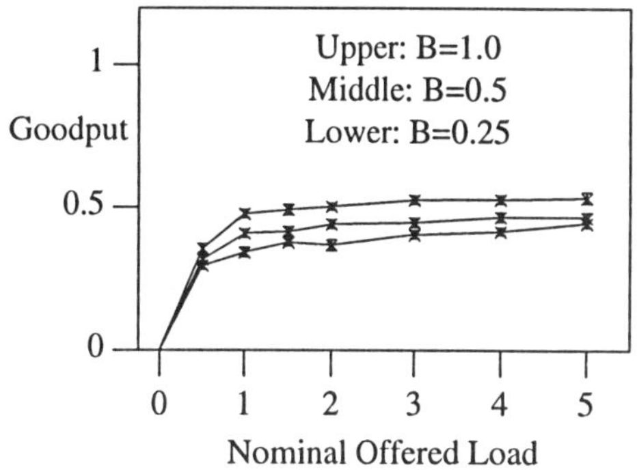

Figure 3: Goodput vs. offered load for 10 static-window + SMART sources.

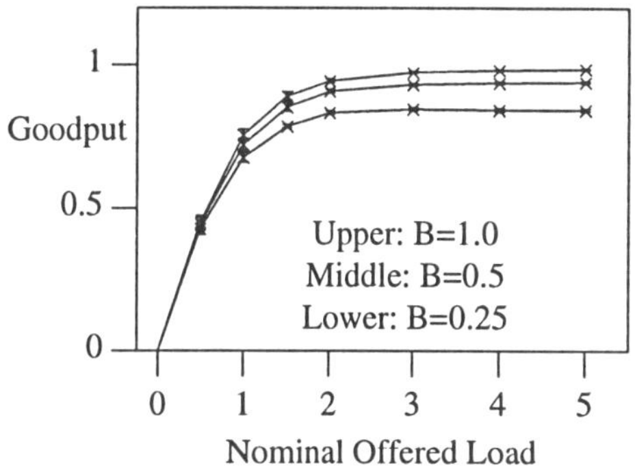

Figure 4: Goodput vs. offered load for 10 Packet-Pair + SMART sources.

ance $\hat{\sigma}^2$, and plotted the "95% confidence intervals" $(\bar{X} - 1.96\hat{\sigma}, \bar{X} + 1.96\hat{\sigma})$ on each figure (sometimes the intervals are too small to see).

Figure 2 shows the goodput as a function of the nominal offered load. The maximum goodput is between 25 and 35%, at an offered load of about 50%. As the load approaches 1, the goodput decreases dramatically, displaying classic congestion collapse. This is because GBN retransmits an entire window on a single packet loss. As the load increases, the probability of a buffer loss increases, decreasing the goodput. Note that both the peak goodput and the load at which this peak is achieved decrease with a decrease in the buffer size.

4 Baseline case with SMART retransmission

We saw that static window flow control, in conjunction with GBN retransmission, leads to congestion collapse. One way to deal with this problem, as in TCP, is to shut down the flow control window on a loss, thus reducing the load. However, *without* changing the flow control algorithm, if we simply replace GBN with SMART, we find that the congestion collapse disappears. Figure 3 shows the goodput as a function of the nominal load for a simulation scenario identical to the one above. It is clear that SMART prevents congestion collapse as the nominal load increases beyond 1.0. The achievable goodput is smaller with decreasing buffer sizes, but even with a nominal load of 500%, there is no decrease in the achievable throughput. This is a clear indication of SMART's effectiveness in dealing with buffer losses.

5 Baseline case with SMART retransmission and Packet-Pair flow control

SMART prevents congestion collapse, but does not prevent packets from being lost in the first place. This is why, in Fig. 3, the achievable goodput is around 50%, instead of around 100%. In order to achieve better goodput, we not only need smarter retransmission, but also better flow control. In this section, we study sources that implement both SMART, and Packet-Pair flow control [4, 5]. Packet-Pair (PP) is a rate-based flow control scheme designed for networks of round-robin servers. It measures the bottleneck service rate by sending all data in the form of back-to-back pairs, and measuring their inter-ack spacing. A filtered version of the measured rate is used in conjunction with a control law to ensure that the bottleneck's buffers are neither too full, nor too empty. If the network does not provide round-robin queueing but does give explicit rate feedback through the use of RM cells, a Packet-Pair source would use this rate instead of making its own rate estimates.

Figure 4 shows the goodput achievable with Packet-Pair + SMART, in the same scenario as before. Comparing this figure with Figs. 2 and 3, it is clear that sources implementing both PP and SMART not only avoid congestion collapse, but also get close to 100% goodput even when the buffer size is only a fourth of the bandwidth-delay product. For a fixed offered load, the

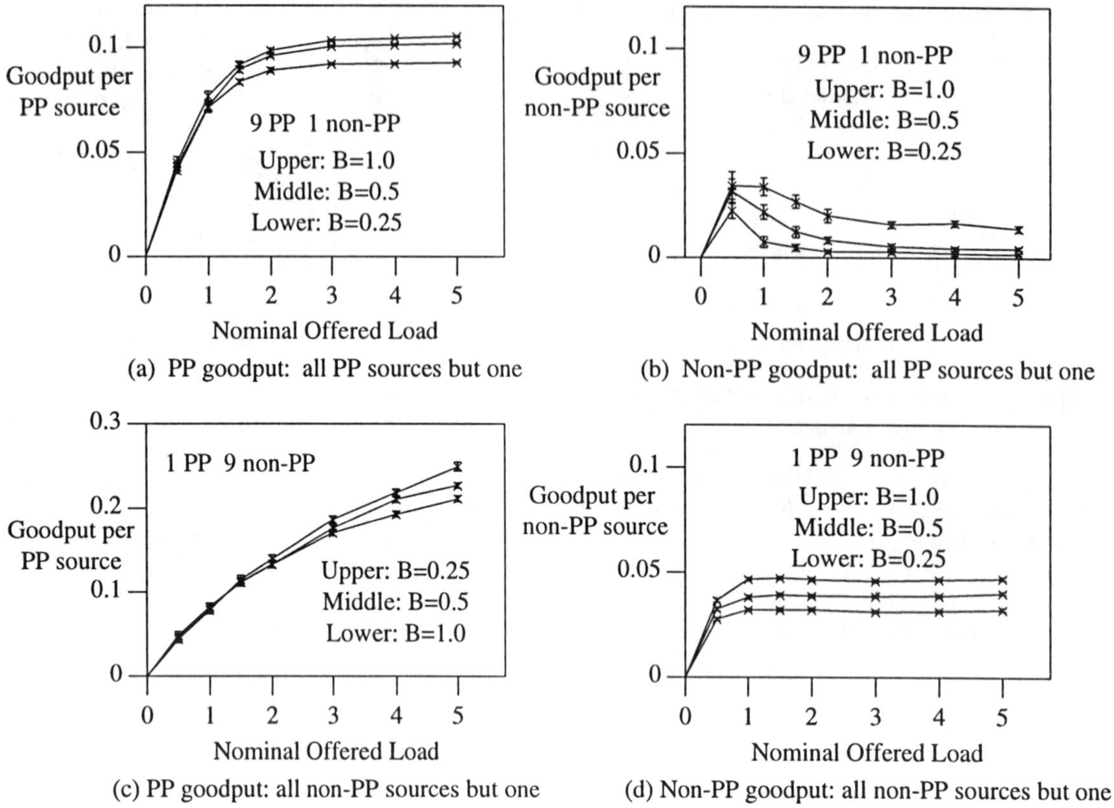

Figure 5: Goodput vs. offered load for PP and non-PP sources + SMART.

goodput decreases, but not very fast, as the buffer size B decreases. With PP, the buffer size needs to be at least $2N$ packets for N connections. In the present simulations, $2N$ packets would correspond to $B = 0.20$. Using smaller packets, SMART + Packet-Pair would undoubtedly function with still lower values of B.

We conclude this section by studying the behavior of mixtures of PP and non-PP sources when both are using SMART. The non-PP sources are ON-OFF with static window flow control, that is, they are identical to the sources in Section 4. The simulation scenario is the same as in Section 3.

The results of the simulations are plotted in Fig. 5. We have considered two combinations, namely 9 PP and 1 non-PP source, and 1 PP and 9 non-PP sources. Each plot shows per-source goodput, for each type of source, vs. nominal offered load.

Figure 5 shows that in general, when PP and non-PP sources are mixed, the PP sources capture more bandwidth per source than the non-PP sources, both when the PP sources are in the majority and when they are in the minority. This is because they gain goodput at the expense of the non-PP source (to see this, compare panel 5(a) with Fig 3). Under heavy load, several PP sources can essentially drive out a non-PP source.

When a single Packet-Pair source shares a link with many non-Packet-Pair sources, Figs. 5(c) and 5(d) show that the Packet-Pair source gets substantially more than its share, which would have been 10% of the congested link under the present scenario. Furthermore, the single Packet-Pair source actually does better with a smaller total buffer (Fig. 5(c)), because it knows how to behave while the non-Packet-Pair sources do not.

6 TCP performance with random losses

So far, we have considered losses that occur when many sources contend for a shared buffer (we call this *buffer loss*). Another interesting error model, which is common in wireless networks, is *random loss*. In the baseline simulation, we saw that sources using static window flow control and GBN do not behave well in the presence of buffer loss. The sources do equally poorly in the presence of heavy random losses, because GBN retransmits the entire window on a single loss. Next, we look briefly at how well TCP does with random losses.

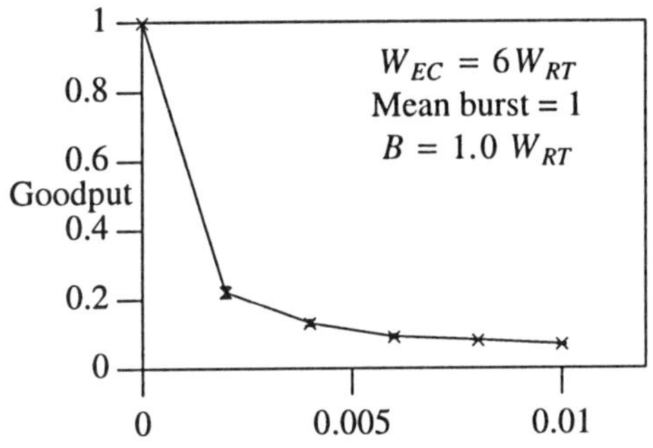

(a) Isolated packet losses

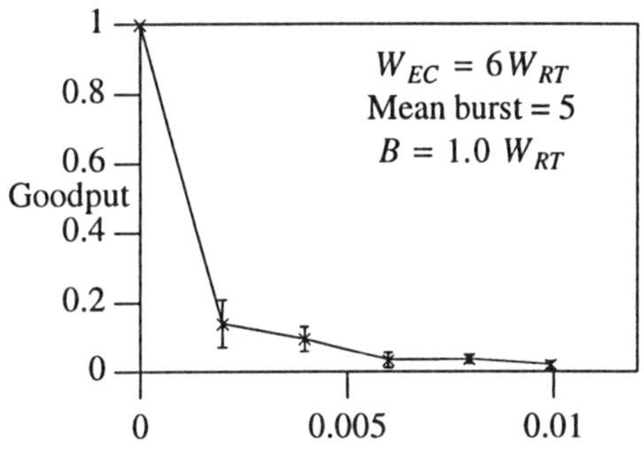

(b) Bursty packet losses

Figure 6: Reno goodput for two random-error scenarios.

The behavior of TCP, both Tahoe and Reno versions, under random losses has been extensively studied by Lakshman and Madhow [7]. They show that the performance of TCP with random packet drops is poor if the parameter $rW_{RT}^2/4$ is greater than unity, where r is the one-way packet loss rate. It's easy to discover this parameter if one notes that after a single packet loss the effective rate of the TCP circuit drops to $S/2$, and then increases linearly to S during an interval $(W_{RT}/2)T_{RT}$, where S is the backbone speed. If $W_{RT} = 100$ packets and $r = 1\%$, then $rW_{RT}^2/4 = 25$.

We confirm the predicted behavior of TCP by simulations. We consider a single virtual circuit which has no specific congestion point, but randomly drops packets at some average one-way rate r. Assuming independent losses in each direction, the failure rate for successful acknowledgments is approximately $2r$, if r is small. We can generalize this model by assuming that packet drops may occur in bursts. Then there are two parameters, namely the average loss rate r and the mean burst length.

Figure 6 shows simulated goodputs for TCP Reno with one-way loss rates from 0 to 1% and mean loss bursts of 1 and 5 packets (geometrically distributed burst lengths). In these examples, the goodput is down to a few percent when $r = 1\%$. Results for Tahoe are similar.

Current proposals to add selective acknowledgments [4] and forward acknowledgments [8] to TCP Reno do not change its performance for isolated losses, because the effective rate still drops to $S/2$ after each loss. These proposals may improve the performance for bursty losses, but they have apparently not yet been studied in scenarios comparable to those of the present paper.

In the next section, we show that, unlike TCP, sources implementing PP+SMART behave nearly optimally in the presence of random losses.

7 Packet-Pair with SMART: Performance with random losses

We assume that SMART is incorporated into a transport layer protocol that separates error control and flow control (unlike TCP). By this, we mean specifically that the flow control does not slow down when the error control detects a dropped packet, so long as the effective speed of the bottleneck node does not decrease. Only the packets that are actually lost, or whose acknowledgments are lost, have to be retransmitted. Therefore, with such a transport layer, we expect the potential goodput to be as high as $(1 - r)^2 \approx 1 - 2r$, if r is the one-way loss rate.

However, to achieve this goodput, the error-control window may have to be large enough to accommodate several round-trip windows of out-of-sequence packets while lost packets are being retransmitted. We argued in Section 2 that $W_{EC} = 4W_{RT}$ would be sufficient under normal conditions, but larger windows may be required in the presence of heavy losses, or of consecutive-loss bursts. The argument suggests that the limiting goodput $1 - 2r$ can be achieved only as W_{EC} tends to infinity.

To verify our analysis, we simulated SMART on a single lossy link. We used the Packet-Pair flow control protocol as the flow control component of the simulated transport layer. We did not test SMART in TCP because TCP's flow and error control are inextricably linked, and there is no clear way to study the effectiveness of SMART without simultaneously modifying TCP's flow control protocol. Because Packet-Pair has a clean separation of error and flow control, it is a better environment to test retransmission strategies in isolation. This separation is likely to become more common for transport layers layered over ABR service in ATM networks, where the flow control is explicitly managed at the ATM level, and the error control is relegated to the transport level [1].

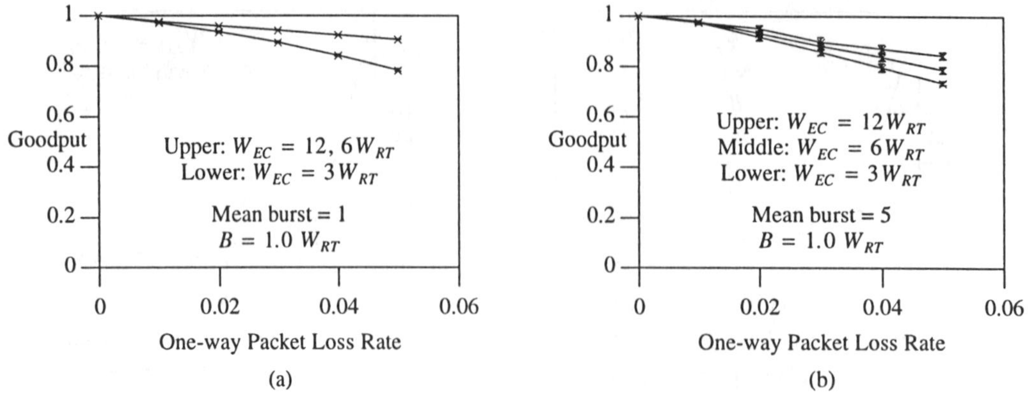

Figure 7: Packet-Pair goodput for isolated and clustered random errors.

In the simulations, the offered load is 100%; the source attempts to send continuously at the speed of the bottleneck link. The one-way loss rate varies from 0 to 5%. The mean loss burst size is 1 packet or 5 packets, geometrically distributed.

The router buffer size $B = 1$ round-trip window (100 packets). The results with $B = 0.25$ and $B = 0.50$ are statistically indistinguishable. In the absence of congestion, a single Packet-Pair circuit requires only a very small buffer. The error-control window is equal to 3, 6. and 12 round-trip windows.

Figure 7 shows the results of simulations of Packet-Pair with SMART for losses high enough so that the small-loss approximations do not necessarily hold. It is clear that SMART + Packet-Pair is much better than TCP; it can achieve nearly the maximum possible goodput under either isolated or bursty losses, provided that the error-control window is several times the round-trip window, in order to allow space for sorting out the retransmissions. Figure 7 shows that the transport layer's goodput tends toward its limiting value as W_{EC} increases, although the approach is quicker for isolated packet losses than for burst losses.

8 Discussion

We have presented a new retransmission strategy, SMART, and studied its performance with random line losses as well as buffer losses. The results of our simulation study show that SMART, in conjunction with a rate-based flow control scheme such as Packet-Pair is stable (for all engineering purposes) under congestion, that it can live with a fraction of a round-trip window of buffer space at each queueing point, and that the asymptotic goodput is in the 80-95% range, depending on buffer size. Even if used with naive flow control schemes, SMART can still avert congestion collapse. Our simulations make another important point: a good retransmission strategy alone is not sufficient to deal with packet losses. It must be combined with a good flow control policy. In particular, when Packet-Pair and non-Packet-Pair sources share a congested transmission path, the Packet-Pair sources have an advantage. This suggests that if a vendor advertises per-virtual-circuit queueing and round robin service, self-interest will lead users to use Packet-Pair rate control.

References

[1] R. Ahuja, S. Keshav, and H. Saran, "Design, Implementation, and Performance of a Native-Mode ATM Transport Layer," Proc. IEEE INFOCOM '96, March 1996, pp. 206-214.

[2] L.S. Brakmo and L.L. Peterson, "TCP Vegas: End to End Congestion Avoidance on a Global Internet," IEEE Journal on Selected Areas in Communication, Vol. 13, No. 8, October 1995, pp. 1465-1480.

[3] B.T. Doshi, P.K. Johri, A.N. Netravali, and K.K. Sabnani, "Error and Flow Control Performance of a High Speed Protocol," IEEE Transactions on Communications, Vol. 41, May 1993, pp. 707-720.

[4] K. Fall and S. Floyd, "Simulation-Based Comparisons of Tahoe, Reno, and SACK TCP," Computer Communication Review, Vol. 26, No. 3, July 1996, pp. 5-21.

[5] S. Keshav, "A Control-Theoretic Approach to Flow Control," Computer Communication Review, Vol. 21, No. 4, September 1991, pp. 3-15.

[6] S. Keshav, "Packet-Pair Flow Control," to appear, IEEE/ACM Transactions on Networking.

[7] T. V. Lakshman and U. Madhow, "Performance Analysis of Window-Based Flow Control using TCP/IP: The Effect of High Bandwidth-Delay Products and Random Loss," IFIP Transactions C-26, *High Performance Networking V*, North-Holland (1994), pp. 135-150.

[8] M. Mathis and J. Mahdavi, "Forward Acknowledgment: Refining TCP Congestion Control," Computer Communication Review, Vol. 26, No. 4, October 1996, pp. 281-291.

[9] G. R. Wright and W. R. Stevens, *TCP/IP Illustrated*, Vol. 2, Addison-Wesley, Reading, MA (1995).

[10] L. Zhang, "Why TCP Timers Don't Work Well," Proc. ACM SIGCOMM '86, August 1986.

Performance Characteristics of the D Channel Access Control Scheme

Shimpei Yagyu

Doc. Prog. in Policy and Planning Sciences
University of Tsukuba
Tsukuba-shi, Ibaraki 305, Japan

Hideaki Takagi

Institute of Policy and Planning Sciences
University of Tsukuba
Tsukuba-shi, Ibaraki 305, Japan

Abstract

In the basic user/network interface of N-ISDN (ITU-T Recommendation I.430), the D-channel is shared by up to 8 terminals for signal and data packets. An analytical model is proposed to reveal the performance characteristics of the access control scheme for the D-channel. Numerical and simulation results are shown to demonstrate the performance differentiation of the terminals with different priorities. It is observed that the mean signal delay at low load may become large because of long service time for packets, and that the priority mechanism may not work properly when the loads at terminals are very asymmetric.

1 Introduction

According to the ITU-T Recommendation I.430, the basic user/network interface of Integrated Services Digital Network (ISDN) provides 2B + D channels on a single line shared by up to 8 terminal equipments (TEs)[1]. While there is no contention for the B channel traffic and for the D channel traffic from the network termination (NT) to TEs, the D channel in the reverse direction is used by multiple TEs on the contention basis. Therefore the access must be controled so that only one TE at a time uses the channel. At the same time, a certain priority-based channel assignment algorithm is enforced for different TEs and for different kind of traffic (control/response signal or packets for user data). In the light of rapid proliferation of ISDN terminals in the recent years, it is very important to clarify the performance characteristics of this access control scheme and identify problems, if any, for possible enhancement in the future.

The purpose of this paper is to study the performance characteristics of the current D channel access control scheme using an analytic model as well as simulation. To do so, we propose a single-server queueing model with a group of single-buffer queues (each representing a terminal with signal traffic) and an infinite-buffer queue (representing all packet traffic). We analyze a Markov chain for the state space constructed so as to incorporate the essential features of the D channel access control algorithm. Our performance measures include the channel utilization by signals from each terminal, the mean time from generation to transmission completion (called delay hereafter) for signals, the channel utilization by packets, and the mean delay for packets. Comparison of the numerical results based on the analysis with those by simulation shows the correctness of our analysis and high accuracy of approximation. We make two noteworthy observations on the mean signal delay in relation with the existence of packet traffic and priority-based operation.

There seem to be few past studies on the performance aspects of the D channel access control scheme. Among them, Ozawa [2] evaluated the mean access delay for control signals, user-user signals, and packets by an approximate model.

2 Operation of the D channel Access Control

Let us begin with describing the operation of the D channel access control and the contention resolution algorithm. With the basic interface (Figure 1), it is possible to have more than one terminal, up to 8 terminals, in a passive-bus configuration. Since multiple terminals share a single physical line (2B + D), the contention resolution algorithm is required. There are three types of traffic to consider:

- B-channel traffic

  No additional functionality is needed to control access to the two B channels, since each channel is dedicated to a selected terminal by the D channel signaling.

- Incoming (from NT to TE) D channel traffic

  The D channel is available for both control signaling and packet transmission. Since each LAPD frame includes the explicit address of the destination TE, all TEs can read this address and determine whether the frame of data is for them.

- Outgoing (from TE to NT) D channel traffic

  Access must be regulated so that only one terminal at a time transmits. This is the purpose of the contention resolution algorithm.

0-8186-7780-5/97 $10.00 © 1997 IEEE

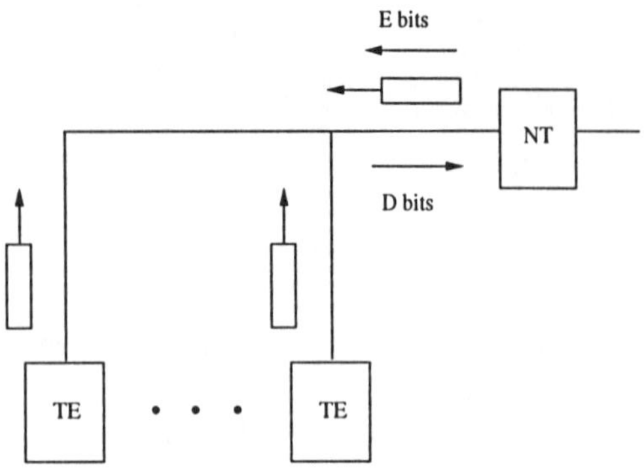

Figure 1: Basic interface [1, p.183].

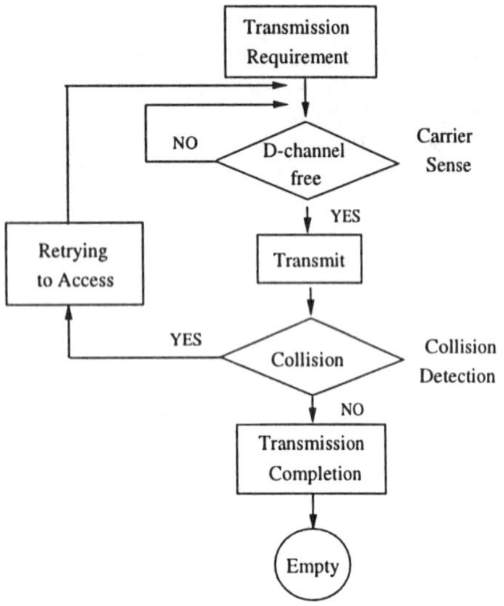

Figure 2: Contention resolution algorithm.

The contention resolution algorithm regulates transmission over the D channel so that signaling information is given priority over packets. The D channel contention resolution algorithm is carried out as follows (Figure 2).

1. When a terminal is ready to transmit a LAPD frame, it listens to the stream of incoming D channel echo (E) bits, and judges whether the D channel is now being used (Carrier Sense).
2. It may happen that several terminals are monitoring the echo stream and begin to transmit at the same time, causing a collision. To overcome this condition, a transmitting TE monitors the echo bits and compares them with its transmitted bits (Collision Detection).
3. If a discrepancy between the echo bits and the transmitted bits is detected, the terminal ceases to transmit and returns to a listen state, and tries to access again (Retrying to Access).

If "0" and "1" collide, then "0" always remains by AMI coding. Therefore, the fact that the value of SAPI field of signals is 000000 and that of packets is 010000 leads to higher priority of signals over packets. Moreover, each terminal is supposed to have each priority according to its TEI value in a LAPD frame for the same reason as above. Thus, in order to realize a fair access to the D channel among terminals, the following priority mechanism is prepared: a terminal begins at normal priority and then is reduced to lower priority after a transmission. It remains at the lower priority until all other terminals have had an opportunity to transmit [1, pp.181–185].

3 Performance Evaluation Model

For evaluating the performance of the D channel access control described in Section 2, we propose the following queueing model (Figure 3). We assume that N terminals are connected to a bus (basic interface). Our model consists of two sets of queues: one is an infinite buffer queue that represents a buffer for the packets generated at all terminals, and the other is a group of N single buffer queues for signals, one for each terminal. In order to disallow some terminals to be served temporarily, we introduce a mechanism called *inhibitors* as done by Ishigaki et al. [3]. Namely, we assume that an inhibitor is set at a terminal immediately after its signal service is completed and that the signal at that terminal may not be served before the inhibitor is reset. The server in Figure 3 models the D channel, and serves signals as well as packets in the following way:

i. In the beginning there are no signals or packets in the system and there is no inhibitor set at each terminal.

ii. After a signal from a terminal is served, an inhibitor is immediately set at the terminal.

iii. All inhibitors are reset immediately after serving all outstanding signals.

iv. Signals have nonpreemptive priority of service over packets. After serving a signal or a packet, if there is at least one signal in the system, then the server serves the signal. If there are no signals in the system and there is at least one packet, then it serves the packet. Otherwise, the system is empty until the next signal or packet arrival.

v. The service discipline at the packet queue is first-in first-out (FIFO).

vi. We assume that all signals are commands in order to make the analysis simple. Under this assumption, the value of the C/R bit for each signal in the layer 2 frame is "0". The SAPI value of all signals is equal to 0, hence the service order among signals is determined by the TEI value of its terminal. We assume that this order is the same as the order of increasing terminal numbers, i.e., terminals 1, 2, ..., up to N.

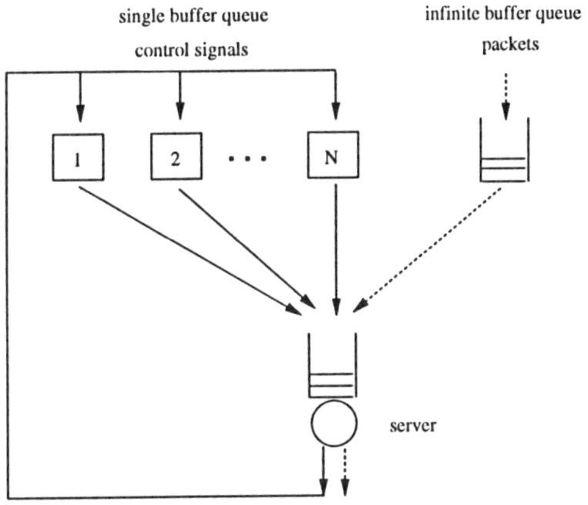

Figure 3: D channel performance evaluation model.

4 Analysis of Signal Queues

In this section, we derive performance measures for signals in N single buffer queues shown in Figure 3, following the method by Ishigaki et al. [3]. We assume that the time interval from the completion of the previous D channel usage by terminal n to the generation (arrival) of a new signal at the same terminal n is exponentially distributed with mean $1/\lambda_n$ and that its service time (D channel usage time) is a constant b_n, where $n = 1, 2, \ldots, N$. A terminal that has a signal is said to be *active*. The state (u_n, i_n) of terminal n is defined as follows:

$$u_n = \begin{cases} 1: & \text{terminal } n \text{ is active} \\ 0: & \text{otherwise} \end{cases}$$

$$i_n = \begin{cases} 1: & \text{service of terminal } n \text{ is inhibited (inhibitor is set)} \\ 0: & \text{otherwise} \end{cases}$$

According to the system state (U, I), where $U = (u_1, u_2, \ldots, u_N)$ and $I = (i_1, i_2, \ldots, i_N)$, some sets of terminal indices are defined by

$$u \equiv \{n | u_n = 1, 1 \le n \le N\}$$
$$\bar{u} \equiv \{n | u_n = 0, 1 \le n \le N\}$$
$$i \equiv \{n | i_n = 1, 1 \le n \le N\}$$
$$\bar{i} \equiv \{n | i_n = 0, 1 \le n \le N\}$$

A set of rules to select a signal at terminal n or a packet to serve next is given as follows.

1. If there are several active terminals that are not inhibited ($u \cap \bar{i} \neq \emptyset$, where $\emptyset$ denotes an empty set), the terminal, say terminal n, with the lowest index among them is selected:

$$n = \min\{j | j \in u \cap \bar{i} (\neq \emptyset)\} \quad (1)$$

2. If all active terminals are inhibited ($u \cap \bar{i} = \emptyset, u \neq \emptyset$), all inhibitors are reset to 0, and then rule 1 is applied.

3. If there are no active terminals at the end of a signal service ($u = \emptyset$), all inhibitors are reset to 0. At this moment, if there are any packets, rule 4 is applied, and if there are no packets, the D channel becomes idle and then rule 5 is applied.

4. After serving a packet, if there is at least one active terminal, then rule 1 is applied. If there are no active terminals and no packets, then the D channel becomes idle and rule 5 is applied. Otherwise, namely if there are no active terminals and there is at least one packet, this rule is applied again.

5. When the D channel is idle, if a packet arrives before a signal, then rule 4 is applied. If a signal arrives before a packet, then the terminal at which the signal has arrived is served.

After the signal service completion at terminal n, inhibitor i_n is set to 1. Note that setting an inhibitor to a terminal corresponds to the degradation of the priority at its signal service completion time. We assume that the time needed for this inhibitor setting and resetting is negligible.

The system state in which there are no active terminals is called the *idle state*. The length of the idle state is exponentially distributed with mean $1/\Lambda$, where $\Lambda = \sum_{n=1}^{N} \lambda_n$.

Having defined the system state and described the conditions for changing the states, we proceed to give the transition probability from state (U, I) to state (U', I') denoted by $Prob[(U', I')|(U, I)]$. The system state (U, I) in our queueing model changes only (i) at the time at which all inhibitors are reset to 0, and (ii) at the signal service completion time. During a signal service time at terminal n, only those terminals that are not active can generate new signals. If b_n is the service time, one of inactive terminals, say terminal i, generates a signal with probability $1 - e^{-\lambda_i b_n}$, or does not with probability $e^{-\lambda_i b_n}$. Terminals that have generated signals become active, while terminal n becomes inactive at the end of the service. From these considerations, we can write down the state transition probabilities as follows:

$$Prob[(U', I')|(U, I)] = \begin{cases} 1 & \text{the time at which all inhibitors are reset to 0} \\ \prod_{j \in u' \cap \bar{u}} (1 - e^{-\lambda_j b_n}) \prod_{j \in \bar{u}' \cap \bar{u}} e^{-\lambda_j b_n} & \text{the signal service completion time} \\ 0 & \text{otherwise} \end{cases} \quad (2)$$

where n is determined by (1). Note that $u \cap \bar{i} \neq \emptyset$, $u - \{n\} \subseteq u'$, and $i + \{n\} = i'$ at the signal service completion time.

For the numerical calculation, it is convenient to map the system state space (U, I) onto a linear space, where $U = (u_1, \ldots, u_N)$, $I = (i_1, \ldots, i_N)$; $u_n = \{0, 1\}$,

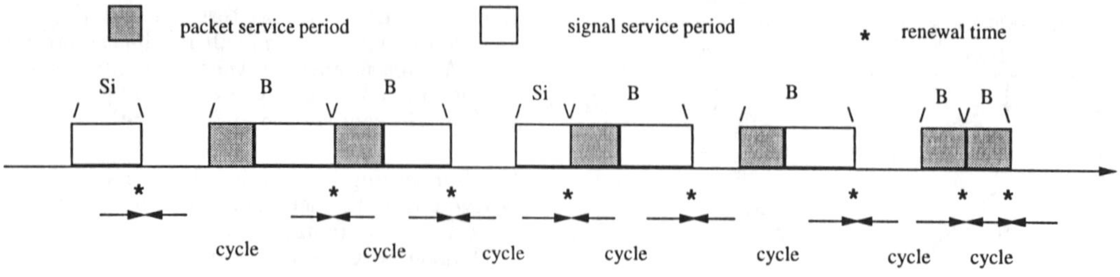

Figure 4: State transitions in the D channel.

$i_n = \{0,1\}$ for $1 \le n \le N$, namely, map (U, I) to

$$p = \sum_{n=1}^{N} \left(2^{N+n-1} u_n + 2^{n-1} i_n\right) \in \{0,1,2,\ldots,4^N - 1\}$$

We may consider the following performance measures related to the signal traffic. The *throughput* γ_n of terminal n is defined as the mean number of signals served per unit time at terminal n, where $n = 1,2,\ldots,N$. The *D channel utilization* U_n of terminal n is the fraction of time that terminal n uses the D channel. This is given by

$$U_n = \gamma_n b_n \tag{3}$$

where b_n is the D channel usage (service) time of a signal generated by terminal n. The *mean delay* T_n of terminal n is the mean time from the instant at which a new signal is generated at terminal n to the instant at which the D channel usage of that signal has been completed. In other words, T_n is the mean duration of an active state at terminal n. Since the state of terminal n alternates between the active state of mean duration T_n and the inactive state of mean duration $1/\lambda_n$, we have the relationship

$$\gamma_n = \frac{1}{T_n + 1/\lambda_n} \tag{4}$$

We show the D channel state transitions in Figure 4. We call those points in time when there are no signals after one signal or one packet service completion (indicated by asterisks $*$ in Figure 4) *renewal times*. The period between two successive renewal times is called a *cycle*; let C denote the mean cycle length. The mean number of signals of terminal n served during a cycle is denoted by N_n. The throughput γ_n of terminal n is then given by

$$\gamma_n = \frac{N_n}{C} \tag{5}$$

We call the period in which there is at least one active terminal in the system a *busy period*. Let $\Theta(U, I)$, where $\Theta(0,0) = 0$, denote the mean time from the instant at which the system enters state (U, I) to the end of the current busy period. The set $\{\Theta(U, I)\}$ is given as a solution to the equations

$$\Theta(U,I) = b_n I(u \cap \bar{i} \neq \emptyset) + \sum_{(U',I') \neq (0,0)} Prob\left[(U',I')|(U,I)\right] \Theta(U',I') \tag{6}$$

where n is determined by (1), and $I(\cdot)$ is the indicator function.

Let $E[B]$ denote the mean length of a period from the instant at which a packet service is started to the first renewal time, and let $E[S_i]$ denote the mean length of a busy period started by a signal arrival at terminal i. Then we get

$$E[B] = \sum_{U} \prod_{i=1}^{N} \left\{u_i \left(1 - e^{-\lambda_i x}\right) + (1 - u_i) e^{-\lambda_i x}\right\} \Theta(U, 0) + x \tag{7}$$

$$E[S_i] = \Theta(e_i, 0) \tag{8}$$

where x is a packet service time (assumed to be constant) and e_i is a vector whose ith element is 1 and all others are 0. Letting π_0 be the probability that there are no packets at a renewal time (we will derive π_0 in Section 5; see (15)), the mean cycle length C is given by

$$C = \pi_0 \left(\frac{1}{\Lambda + \lambda} + \frac{1}{\Lambda + \lambda} \sum_{i=1}^{N} \lambda_i E[S_i] + \frac{\lambda}{\Lambda + \lambda} E[B] \right) + (1 - \pi_0) E[B] \tag{9}$$

where λ is the packet arrival rate.

Let $N_k(U, I)$, where $(U, I) \neq (0,0)$, denote the mean number of signals of terminal k that are served during a busy period started with state (U, I), where $k = 1,2,\ldots,N$. The set $\{N_k(U,I)\}$ is given as a solution to the equations

$$N_k(U,I) = \delta_{kn} + \sum_{(U',I') \neq (0,0)} Prob\left[(U',I')|(U,I)\right] N_k(U',I') \tag{10}$$

where δ_{kn} is Kronecker's delta defined by

$$\delta_{kn} = \begin{cases} 1 & \text{if } k = n \\ 0 & \text{otherwise} \end{cases}$$

We then obtain N_n, the mean number of signals of terminal n served during a cycle as

$$N_n = \pi_0 \left[\frac{1}{\Lambda+\lambda} \sum_{i=1}^{N} \lambda_i N_n(e_i, 0) + \frac{\lambda}{\Lambda+\lambda} \left\{ \sum_{U\neq 0} \prod_{i=1}^{N} \left[u_i \left(1 - e^{-\lambda_i x}\right) + (1-u_i) e^{-\lambda_i x} \right] N_n(U,0) \right\} \right] + (1-\pi_0) \left\{ \sum_{U\neq 0} \prod_{i=1}^{N} \left[u_i \left(1 - e^{-\lambda_i x}\right) + (1-u_i) e^{-\lambda_i x} \right] N_n(U,0) \right\} \quad (11)$$

The numerical procedure is as follows. Given the values of $N, \{\lambda_n; 1 \leq n \leq N\}, \lambda, \{b_n; 1 \leq n \leq N\}$, and x, we first compute the state transition probabilities $Prob[(U', I')|(U, I)]$ by (2). From the solution to (6) we can calculate C by (7)–(9). From the solution to (10), we can calculate N_n in (11). Substituting C and N_n into (5), we obtain the throughput γ_n. The D channel utilization U_n and the mean delay T_n are then calculated from (3) and (4), respectively. Since the D channel utilization by packets is λx in a steady state, the utilization by both packets and signals is given by

$$\lambda x + \sum_{n=1}^{N} U_n \quad (12)$$

We note that if all load conditions are identical for all terminals ($\lambda_n = \Lambda/N \equiv \lambda_1, b_n \equiv b$ for $n = 1, 2, \ldots, N$), the mean busy period started with the state that there are k signals is equivalent to that of a finite population queueing system M/D/1//N, which is given by [4, pp.71–76].

$$E[\Theta_k] = b \sum_{n=1}^{N} \left[\binom{N}{n} - \binom{N-k}{n} \right] \prod_{j=1}^{n-1} \left(e^{j\lambda_1 b} - 1 \right) \qquad 1 \leq k \leq N$$

The mean number $E[\Gamma_k]$ of signals served during $E[\Theta_k]$ is then given by

$$E[\Gamma_k] = \frac{E[\Theta_k]}{b} \qquad 1 \leq k \leq N$$

We have confirmed by numerical calculation that the numerical values for $E[\Theta_k]$ and $E[\Gamma_k]$ given by these expressions agree with the results computed by (6) and (11).

5 Analysis of a Packet Queue

In this section, we analyze the infinite buffer queue for packets shown in Figure 3. To do so, we consider the renewal times (the times marked with $*$ in Figure 4). Let π_k be the stationary probability that there are k packets in the system at a renewal time. And, let α_k be the probability that k packets arrive during B which is the period from the instant at which a packet service is started to the first renewal time, and $\alpha_k^{(S_i)}$ be the probability that k packets arrive during S_i which is the busy period started by a signal arrival at terminal i. We assume that packets arrive according to a Poisson process at rate λ. From these assumptions, we can write the balance equations in a Markov chain of the queue length seen at renewal times as follows.

$$\pi_k = \sum_{j=0}^{k} \pi_{j+1} \alpha_{k-j} + \frac{\pi_0}{\Lambda+\lambda} \sum_{i=1}^{N} \lambda_i \alpha_k^{(S_i)} + \frac{\pi_0 \lambda}{\Lambda+\lambda} \alpha_k \qquad k = 0, 1, 2, \ldots \quad (13)$$

We define the probability generating functions for π_k, α_k, and $\alpha_k^{(S_i)}$ respectively, as follows.

$$\Pi(z) = \sum_{k=0}^{\infty} \pi_k z^k, \quad G(z) = \sum_{k=0}^{\infty} \alpha_k z^k = B^*(\lambda - \lambda z)$$

$$H_i(z) = \sum_{k=0}^{\infty} \alpha_k^{(S_i)} z^k = S_i^*(\lambda - \lambda z)$$

where $B^*(s)$ and $S_i^*(s)$ are the Laplace-Stieltjes transforms of the distribution function for B and S_i, respectively. In terms of these generating functions, (13) leads to

$$\Pi(z) = \frac{\Pi(z) - \pi_0}{z} G(z) + \frac{\pi_0}{\Lambda+\lambda} \sum_{i=1}^{N} \lambda_i H_i(z) + \frac{\pi_0 \lambda}{\Lambda+\lambda} G(z)$$

Solving for $\Pi(z)$, we obtain

$$\Pi(z) = \frac{\pi_0 \left\{ z \sum_{i=1}^{N} \lambda_i H_i(z) + \lambda z G(z) - (\Lambda+\lambda) G(z) \right\}}{(\Lambda+\lambda)(z - G(z))} \quad (14)$$

From the normalizing condition $\Pi(1) = 1$ and l'Hôpital's rule, we get

$$\pi_0 = \frac{(\Lambda+\lambda)(1 - \lambda E[B])}{\Lambda(1 - \lambda E[B]) + \lambda \left(1 + \sum_{i=1}^{N} \lambda_i E[S_i]\right)} \quad (15)$$

Note that this probability π_0 is used in (9).

Since the arrival process of the present queue is Poisson and the departure occurs by unit jumps only, the equilibrium probability that the queue length is k at an arbitrary moment is equal to that immediately after a departure (consider B as an expanded service period of packets). Thus by using the conditional probability to remove the renewal times that are not packet service completion times, the probability generating function $P(z)$ of the packet queue length at an arbitrary moment is given by

$$P(z) = \frac{\Pi(z) - \frac{\pi_0}{\Lambda+\lambda}\sum_{i=1}^{N}\lambda_i H_i(z)}{1 - \frac{\pi_0}{\Lambda+\lambda}\sum_{i=1}^{N}\lambda_i}$$

$$= \frac{(1-\lambda E[B])\,G(z)\left\{\sum_{i=1}^{N}\lambda_i H_i(z) + \lambda z - (\Lambda+\lambda)\right\}}{\lambda\left(1+\sum_{i=1}^{N}\lambda_i E[S_i]\right)(z - G(z))} \quad (16)$$

Since the mean queue length L_p for packets is obtained by differentiating $P(z)$ and then setting $z = 1$, it follows from Little's result that the mean packet delay time W_p is given by

$$W_p = \frac{1}{\lambda}L_p - E[B] + x$$

$$= \frac{\sum_{i=1}^{N}\lambda_i E[S_i^2]}{2\left(1+\sum_{i=1}^{N}\lambda_i E[S_i]\right)} + \frac{\lambda E[B^2]}{2(1-\lambda E[B])} + x \quad (17)$$

Since $E[B^2]$ and $E[S_i^2]$ cannot be obtained in Section 4, whereas $E[B]$ and $E[S_i]$ can, we replace $E[B^2]$ and $E[S_i^2]$ by $(E[B])^2$ and $(E[S_i])^2$, respectively, for the purpose of approximate calculation of W_p. This would result in smaller values of W_p.

6 Simulation Model

In this section, we describe a simulation model developed for checking the accuracy of numerical values obtained in the analysis. We simulate our queueing model using RESQME (The RESearch Queueing Modeling Environment) [5], a discrete-event simulation software package from IBM Research Division.

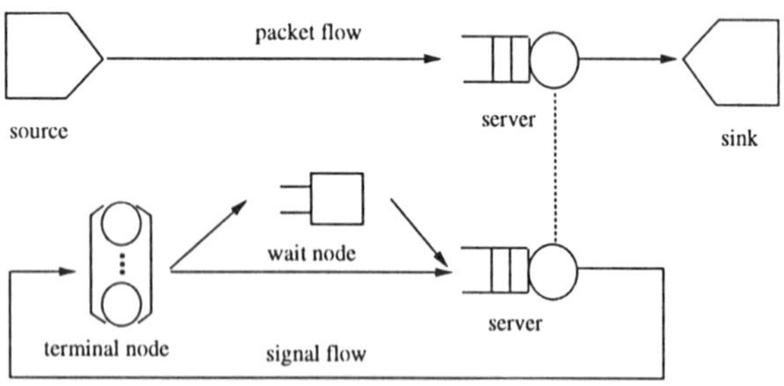

Figure 5: Simulation model.

The simulation model is shown in Figure 5 using RESQ symbols. On a signal flow, one signal per terminal continues to circulate along the closed network. A signal is generated at terminal n in the terminal node with an exponentially distributed time with mean $1/\lambda_n$. It then goes to the wait node if an inhibitor is set to that terminal, and waits until the inhibitor is reset. If an inhibitor is not set to that terminal, the signal goes to the server and is served for a constant period b_n. After service completion, it goes back to the terminal node. On a packet flow, a packet generated at a source according to a Poisson process at rate λ is served for a constant period x at the server and goes to the sink.

There are as many signal flows as terminals, and each signal flow is given a priority level equal to the associated terminal number. There is only one packet flow, to which is given the lowest priority. The two servers connected with a broken line in Figure 5 actually work as one server, serving both signals and packets according to their priorities.

7 Numerical Examples

In this section, we investigate the performance characteristics of the D channel access control scheme by numerical examples. We consider a system in which 4 terminals are connected to the channel ($N = 4$). The following set of parameters is assumed: packet arrival rate $\lambda = 0.1/sec$, its service time $x = 0.5$ *sec*, and the signal service time $b = 10$ *msec* (1/50 of x). The two cases are examined in which the signal arrival process (signal traffic) is symmetric and asymmetric among the terminals. Under this situation, we observe the values of several performance measures by changing the signal arrival rate. Our performance measures are the channel utilization by signals from each terminal, the mean signal delay, and the mean packet delay. By comparing the results of analysis with those by simulation, we demonstrate the accuracy of approximation of the mean packet delay.

7.1 Symmetric case

Under the symmetric condition that signals arrive at all terminals with the same rate, each signal arrival rate (ArrivalRate) is changed. In Figures 6a and 6b, we only show the results from analysis because they are supposed to be exact. In Figure 6c the deviation of analysis values from simulation increases as the arrival rate. The reason is that the second moment $E[B^2]$ and $E[S_i^2]$ are replaced by the $(E[B])^2$ and $(E[S_i])^2$, respectively, in (17).

From the display of channel utilization by each terminal in Figure 6a, it is observed that the difference in the channel utilization among terminals, which appears at medium load, decreases as the arrival rate increases and all utilizations approach to $1/N$. The effects of priority disappear by the inhibitor mechanism as the arrival rate increases. At high load each arriving signal is served irrespective of its priority only after all other $N-1$ signals have been served. This is consistent with the observation that the mean signal delay at each terminal in Figure 6b approaches to bN uniformly as the arrival rate increases. A notable tendency that the signal delay is rather long when the load is low in Figure 6b can be interpreted as follows. Since signals hardly arrive at low arrival rate, a packet can easily receive the service which is 50 times longer than the signal service time. Thus, the signals that arrive during a packet service time have to wait for a time longer than those signals that arrive during a signal service period.

The more signals arrive, the more the packet delay increases as shown in Figure 6c. This is because the channel is used mostly by signals and it is difficult for packets to use it at high load.

In Ozawa's study [2], it is reported that both high traffic of user–user signals and their large batch sizes cause very long control signals delay. This is another kind of traffic that prevents signal traffic and incurs a large signal delay as in the present case.

7.2 Asymmetric cases

The asymmetric condition that there is one special terminal at which signals arrive at a rate different from the rates at others is considered. Especially, two asymmetric conditions that the special terminal has the signal arrival rate 10 times as large as those of other terminals and that it has the signal arrival rate 10 times as small as those of other terminals have been examined. The two asymmetric conditions and four different locations at which the special terminal is placed result in 8 distinct cases. Among them we present the numerical results based on the analysis only in selected cases; see [6] for the results in all cases. In case 1 (terminal 1 is special) and case 2 (terminal 4 is special), the special terminal has the signal arrival rate 10 times as large as those of other terminals. Under this condition, the signal arrival rate (ArrivalRate) is changed.

In Figures 7 and 8 for cases 1 and 2, respectively, the special terminal shows high utilization at low load, irrespective of what priority it has. As the signal arrival rate increases, the utilization by the special terminal approaches to the same utilization as others because the inhibitor mechanism works. This also explains the observation that while the signal delay at the special terminal is short at low load, it is long at high load.

It should be noted in cases 1 and 2 that the special terminal which has the signal arrival rate 10 times as large as those of other terminals shows the same behavior in terms of channel utilization and mean signal delay, irrespective of its priority. We may conclude from this observation that the priority mechanism does not work effectively in extremely asymmetric cases. In asymmetric cases as well as in the symmetric case, the signal delay is extended because of packets service time at low load.

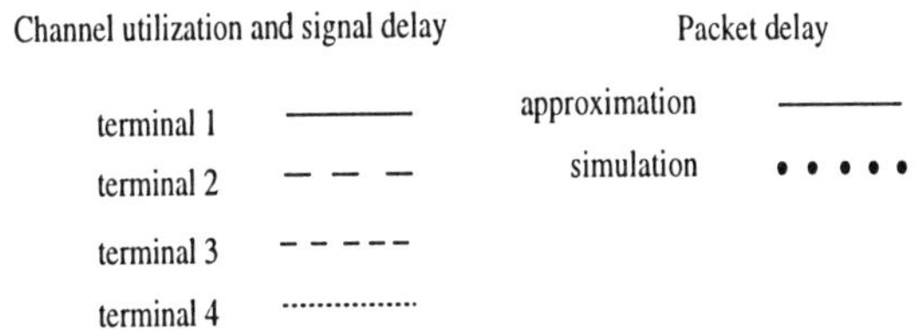

Legend for Figures 6–8.

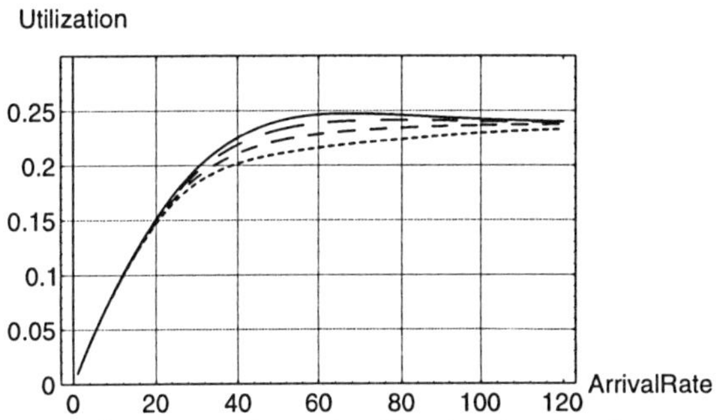

Figure 6a: Channel utilization by signals.

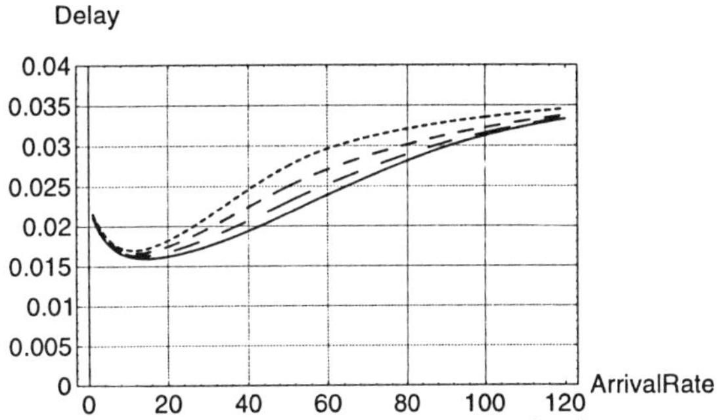

Figure 6b: Mean signal delay [sec].

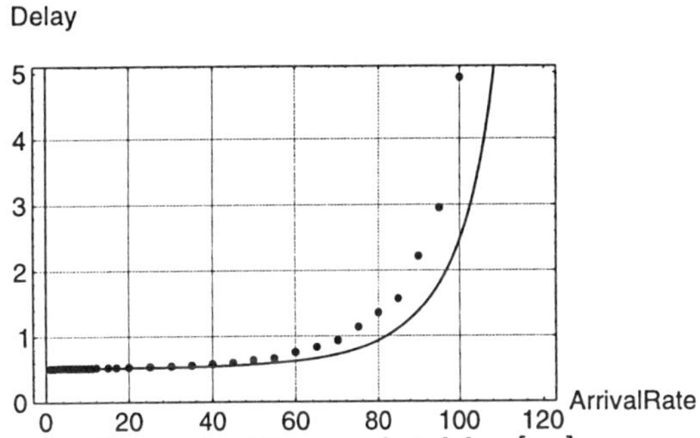

Figure 6c: Mean packet delay [sec].

Case 1: terminal 1 is special ($\lambda_1 = 10\lambda_2 = 10\lambda_3 = 10\lambda_4$).

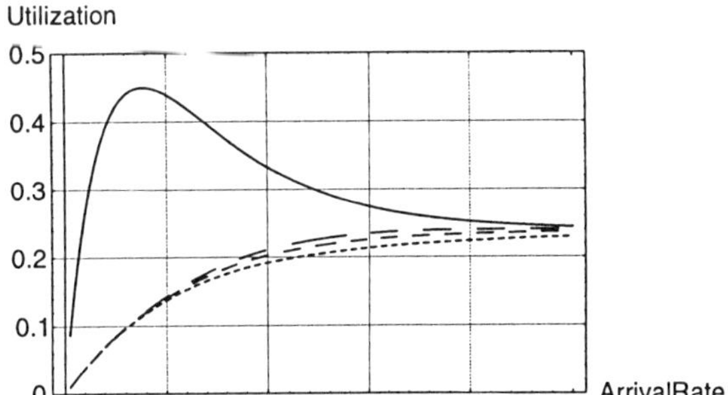

Figure 7a: Channel utilization by signals.

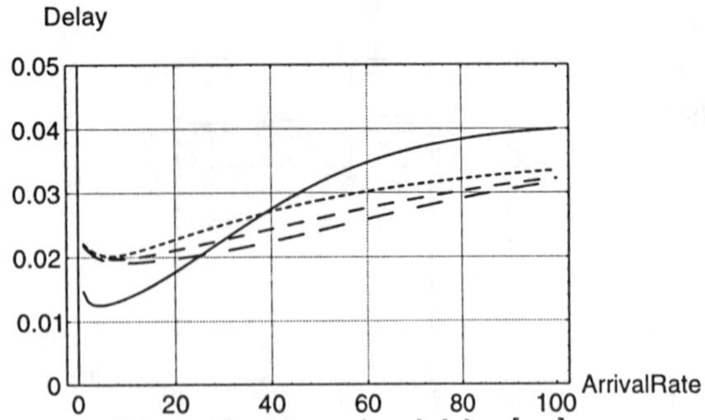

Figure 7b: Mean signal delay [sec].

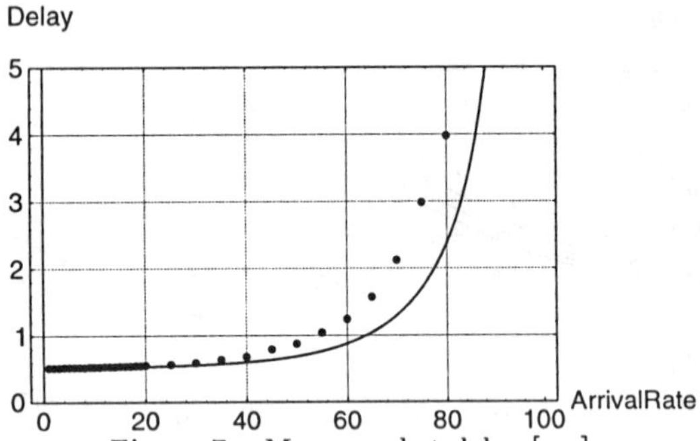

Figure 7c: Mean packet delay [sec].

Case 2: terminal 4 is special
($\lambda_4 = 10\lambda_1 = 10\lambda_2 = 10\lambda_3$).

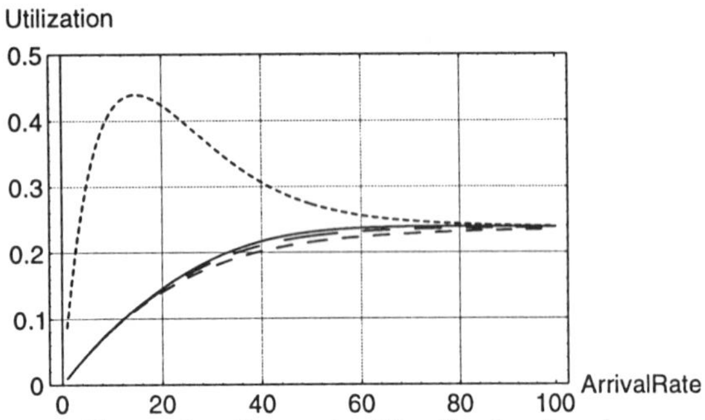

Figure 8a: Channel utilization by signals.

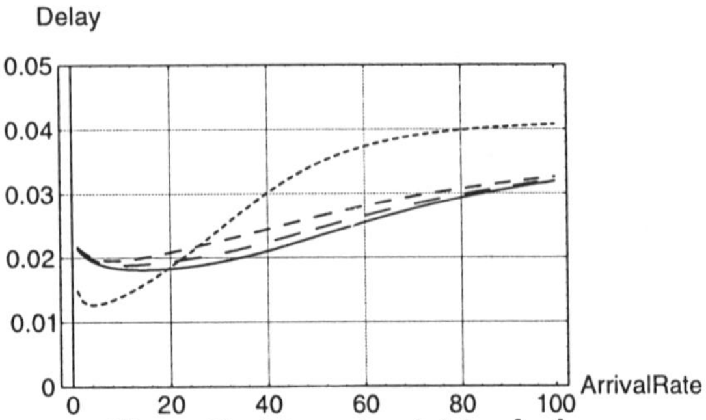

Figure 8b: Mean signal delay [sec].

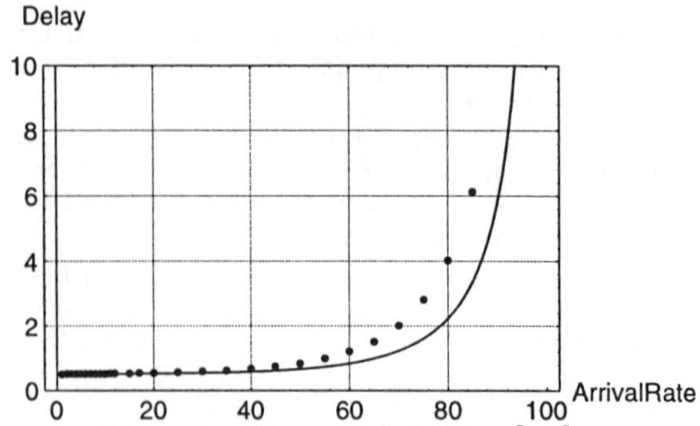

Figure 8c: Mean packet delay [sec].

8 Concluding Remarks

The study in this paper has revealed two potential problems in the current D channel access control scheme of ISDN. First, control signals may suffer large delay at low load when the channel is used by low-priority (long) packet traffic in a nonpreemptive manner. Second, the priority-based service mechanism intended to differentiate terminals may not work properly when the signal loads are extremely asymmetric among the terminals. It is hoped that some modification of the algorithm is made in the future implementation.

Acknowledgments

This work is supported by the Telecommunication Advancement Foundation. The authors are grateful to Mr. Toshihisa Ozawa of NTT Telecommunication Laboratories for indicating references.

References

[1] W. Stallings, *ISDN and Broadband ISDN with Frame Relay and ATM*, Prentice-Hall, 1995.

[2] T. Ozawa, Analysis of a multiqueue model for an ISDN access interface, *Performance Evaluation* 15 (1992) pp.65–76.

[3] M. Ishigaki, H. Takagi, Y. Takahashi, and T. Hasegawa, Throughput and fairness analysis of prioritized multiprocessor bus arbitration protocols, *Proceedings of the International Symposium on Shared Memory Multiprocessing*, pp.166–174, Tokyo, April 2–4, 1991.

[4] H. Takagi, *Queueing Analysis: A Foundation of Performance Evaluation, Volume 2: Finite Systems*, Elsevier, 1991.

[5] C. H. Sauer and E. A. MacNair, *Simulation of Computer Communication Systems*, Prentice-Hall, 1983.

[6] S. Yagyu, Performance Evaluation of the D channel Access Control Scheme in N-ISDN, Bachelor Thesis, College in Socio-Economic Planning, University of Tsukuba, March 1996 (in Japanese).

Proactive Network Fault Detection

Cynthia S. Hood and Chuanyi Ji†

Department of Computer Science and Applied Mathematics
Illinois Institute of Technology, Chicago, IL 60616

†Department of Electrical, Computer, and Systems Engineering
Rensselaer Polytechnic Institute, Troy, NY 12180

ABSTRACT

The increasing role of communication networks in today's society results in a demand for higher levels of network availability and reliability. At the same time, fault management is becoming more difficult due to the dynamic nature and heterogeneity of networks. We propose an intelligent monitoring system using adaptive statistical techniques. The system continually learns the normal behavior of the network and detects deviations from the norm. Within the monitoring system, the measurements are segmented, and features extracted from the segments are used to describe the normal behavior of the measurement variables. This information is combined in the structure of a Bayesian network. The proposed system is thereby able to detect unknown or unseen faults. Experimental results on real network data demonstrate that the proposed system can detect abnormal behavior before a fault actually occurs.

1. Introduction

High-speed communication networks play an increasingly important role in today's society. A key challenge in fulfilling this role, maintaining network availability and reliability, is the responsibility of network management. To meet this challenge, network management tools and methodologies must evolve to meet the needs of current and future communication environments [18].

Fault management is the part of network management responsible for detecting and identifying faults in the network. Interest in fault management has increased over the past decade due to the growing number of networks that have become a critical component of the infrastructure of many organizations, making faults and downtime very costly. In addition, as computer networks evolve from providing only "best effort" service to providing a range of service guarantees to accommodate real-time applications (e.g. video), higher levels of reliability are required. By preserving network reliability, fault management lays the foundation for the stringent Quality of Service (QoS) requirements placed on networks by real-time applications.

As the fault management problem becomes more important, it has also become more difficult. This can be traced primarily to the dynamic nature and heterogeneity of current networks. Fundamental changes to the network occur much more frequently due to the growing demands on the network and the availability of new, improved components and applications. With network components and applications developed in an open environment, a network can be configured by mixing and matching several vendors' hardware and software. While this allows the network to utilize the latest technologies and be customized to the needs of the users, it also increases the risk of faults or problems [18].

Current implementations of the fault management part of network management systems generally rely on a human network manager to transfer his or her network expertise into a set of rules. These rules are eventually translated into threshold levels on the measurement variables being collected. When some prescribed set of one or more thresholds is exceeded, an alarm is sent to the network manager. The fault management system must correlate the alarms to identify the problem and take corrective action. Alarm correlation is difficult, due largely to the lack of accurate temporal information available to the fault management system [11]. Additionally, as the rate of change in networks increases, it becomes more difficult for a human network manager to maintain a sufficient level of expertise on the behavior of the network.

Previous research in fault management has covered approaches such as expert systems [7], Finite State Machines (FSMs) [13], advanced database techniques [17], and probabilistic approaches [3]. A review of communication network fault detection and identification can be found in [8]. The approaches mentioned above require specification of the faults to be detected. This limits the performance of these approaches since it is not feasible to specify all possible faults. In addition, changes in network configuration, applications and traffic can change the types and nature of faults that may

0-8186-7780-5/97 $10.00

occur, making modeling faults more difficult and in many cases impractical. Research using learning machines to detect anomalies [11] addresses the issue of fault modeling, but does not provide a method for correlating the information collected in space or time.

The problem we will tackle is automated fault detection without specific models of faults. We propose an adaptive learning system for network monitoring. The system learns the normal behavior of each measurement variable. Deviations from the norm are detected and the information gathered is combined in the probabilistic framework of a Bayesian network. Benefits from this approach include the ability to detect unknown faults, the ability to correlate information in space and time, and the ability to detect subtle changes occurring before the actual failure. This allows faults to be detected when they are developing so the network manager has time to take corrective action to prevent outages or downtime. In addition, this approach requires minimal amounts of network specific information, so it can be generalized across network nodes and types of networks. Our approach is tested on a computer network. We monitor the Management Information Base (MIB) variables collected within the Simple Network Management Protocol (SNMP) framework. No specialized hardware is required for monitoring.

The paper is organized as follows. Section 2 provides background material on Bayesian networks. Our intelligent monitoring approach is described in Section 3. Detailed information about the data we collected is given in Section 4, and Section 5 contains results and comparisons. Conclusions and areas for further investigation are discussed in Section 6.

2. Bayesian network background

A Bayesian network, also called a belief network or a causal network, is a graphical representation of relationships within a problem domain. More formally, a Bayesian network is a directed acyclic graph (DAG), where certain conditional independence assumptions hold [7]. The nodes of the DAG represent random variables. The conditional independence assumptions are as follows: Given a DAG $G = (N,E)$, where $n \in N$ is a node in the network and $e \in E$ is a directed arc. For each $n \in N$, let $p(n) \subseteq N$ be the set of all parents of n, and $d(n) \subseteq N$ be the set of all descendents of n. For every subset $W \subseteq N - (d(n) \cup \{n\})$, W and n are conditionally independent given $p(n)$. In other words, for any node in the DAG, given that node's parents, that node is independent of any other node that is not its descendent. Figure 1 illustrates the independence assumptions for a Bayesian network similar to the one we will use in our monitoring system.

These assumptions allow us to estimate the conditional probabilities of any of the nodes (or random variables) in the Bayesian network given the observed information or evidence. The strength of Bayesian networks is that they provide a theoretical framework for combining statistical data with prior knowledge about the problem domain. Therefore, they are particularly useful in practical applications.

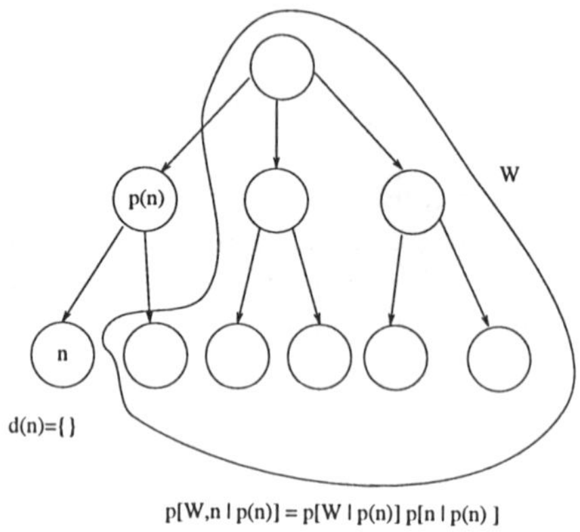

Figure 1 Example of independence assumptions

Bayesian networks have been widely used for medical diagnosis [15] [4], troubleshooting [5], and in the communication network field, they have been proposed to diagnose faults in Linear Lightwave Networks [6]. In [6] other methods have been used for detection and the Bayesian networks are used for diagnosis only. In this work, we propose using a Bayesian network as a mechanism to combine information from different variables for the purpose of detecting anomalies.

3. Monitoring system

We propose an automated monitoring system that is able to detect anomalies without specific models of the behavior to be detected. The premise of this approach is that anomalous or unusual network behavior is an indication of a fault within the network. The monitoring system components are shown in Figure 2.

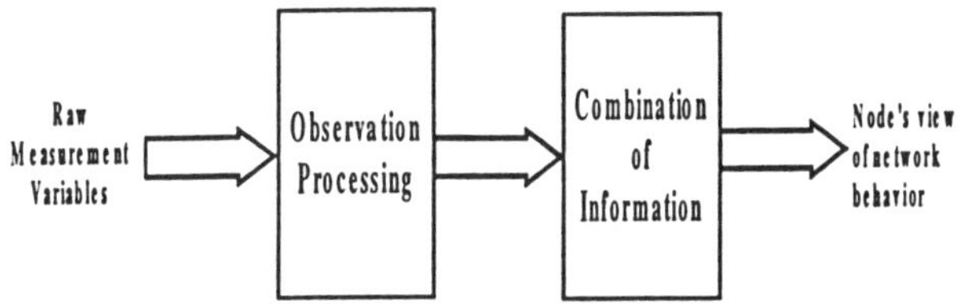

Figure 2 Monitoring system

The system resides locally, allowing each node in the network to compose a picture of the network's health. To get this picture, measurement information must be combined with prior knowledge about the network. To accomplish this, the monitoring system has two main components; observation processing and combination of information. The raw measurement variables are processed to estimate the probability of each measured variable at a given time. The probabilities are then combined using a Bayesian network to provide a broader picture of the network's behavior. By doing this locally, we can correlate this information in time and space. This allows the central network manager to receive a more complete, less noisy picture of each node's view of network health. This can ease the alarm correlation problem. It also allows the node to take corrective actions if necessary.

3.1. Observation processing

The goal of the observation processing part of the monitoring system is to take the raw measurement variables and transform them into a set of measures indicating the behavior of each variable. Each measurement variable is a time series. Many of the measurement variables are representative of network traffic. To date, the characterization of network traffic signals is an active research area [9]. Therefore, the signals (i.e. measurement variables) to be processed are not considered to be well understood and as such there is not an optimal, or even standard method to characterize the behavior of these signals.

In processing the information we use a change detection methodology. Since the behavior of the network is dynamic, the behavior of the measurement variables change frequently. As most changes are related to network traffic, simply detecting that a change has occurred is not enough. The goal is to try to recognize the changes that are important in terms of fault detection. We do this by characterizing the behavior of the measurement variables.

3.1.1 Segmentation. One of the challenges presented by the network dynamics is the non-stationarity of the observations. Since our goal is to extract pertinent information, we need to group the time series data in some way so that features can be calculated. To do this we segment the data into variable length pieces. Each piece contains a portion of the time series that is statistically similar.

There are two primary benefits realized from segmentation: (1) the statistics calculated from each segment are more representative of the signal, and (2) signal processing techniques requiring a stationary signal can be used within each segment. In terms of monitoring, the segmentation provides the benefit of temporally correlating the observations. Since many of the network signals are bursty, the temporal correlation can help distinguish between a burst and a change in the nature of the signal. The sequential segmentation algorithm described in [1] is used. Once the observations have been grouped into segments, the pertinent information must be captured from each segment.

3.1.2 Feature extraction. Before our approach to feature extraction is discussed, we first need to examine the shortcomings of commonly used methods. Thresholds are the primary method currently used in both practice [10] and research [3] for detecting abnormal behavior. The feature is not the value of the threshold itself, but the information on whether or not the threshold has been exceeded by a particular measurement variable. There can be both upper and lower thresholds, in which case the feature would be the information on whether the variable is within the thresholds. One of the difficulties with thresholds is properly setting the threshold level, since they are highly dependent on the traffic level. Improperly set, the thresholds may never be exceeded, thereby letting problems go undetected, or they may be exceeded too often, flooding the network manager with false alarms.

While properly set thresholds do a good job of detecting large rises and falls in a measurement variable, more subtle behavior changes are missed. For example, a change in the variance of a signal, or a subtle change in the mean will not be detected using thresholds. These types of changes may be symptoms of something problematic in the network - this behavior is unusual for the variable. Detection of the more subtle signs of problems may allow corrective action to be taken to avoid a bigger problem. Identification of the problem also becomes easier with a more complete description of the symptoms rather than just the extreme cases.

Our goal is to extract information that will help determine whether the behavior of the measurement variable is normal or abnormal. Ideally we want to capture information in the signal that will change or become abnormal only when a problem is occurring. To do this we would need a feature that is invariant to the network traffic patterns and other influences that cause the non-stationarities. This is an open problem, so we choose a feature that changes along with the network and continually adapt the model of normal behavior.

To detect the more subtle changes in the nature of the measured variables, we use the parameters of an AR(2) or second-order autoregressive process as features. The AR(2) process is defined as

$$y(t) = a_1 y(t-1) + a_2 y(t-2) + \epsilon(t),$$

where $y(t)$ is the value of the signal at time t, a_1 and a_2 are the AR parameters that we use as features, and $\epsilon(t)$ is white noise. Additional features have been investigated in [6].

3.1.3 Learning the behavior. The features provide the ability to detect subtle changes, but they must first be used to establish a description of normal behavior. The description of the behavior is in the form of a probability distribution. Changes can then be detected relative to the distribution.

Ideally, for each sample we would like to estimate its likelihood given that, (1) the network is operating normally, and (2) there is a fault. To do this, we need to know exactly when the network as a whole, and each of its functions is operating normally. This type of information is not typically available. We are able to get some information about the health of the network from the tools currently used to report problems (i.e., log files). The information available contains reports on certain types of serious network problems that have occurred. From a learning perspective, we can use these reports as labels.

One way of using the labels is to learn the probability distribution of each measurement variable, given that its related network function is abnormal. This sounds promising, but in fact is extremely difficult due to the sparse nature of abnormal data. With so few examples of problems, we do not have the variety (i.e., many examples of different problems) or the depth (i.e., several examples of the same type of problem) to effectively learn the distribution [2].

Instead we learn only the likelihood of the sample given the network function is normal. We define normal behavior to be the behavior of the variable during the time period when the distribution is learned. This time period will be referred to as the learning window. Since what we are learning is the usual behavior of the variable during the learning window, there is no guarantee that this always corresponds to the network or network functions being healthy. If there is a problem in the network that impacts the behavior of the network for a significant portion of the learning window, the problematic behavior will be learned as the usual behavior. We assume that this is rarely the case.

We still need to estimate the likelihood of the sample given the network function is abnormal. Since we are unable to estimate this from the data, we treat this distribution as unknown as in [14], and assume a uniform distribution over the range of the AR(2) parameters. If the AR(2) process is stationary

$$a_1 + a_2 < 1,$$
$$a_2 - a_1 < 1,$$
$$-1 < a_2 < 1.$$

Any sample falling outside the range is assumed to be abnormal.

3.2 Combination of Information

The goal of this part of the monitoring system is to combine the processed measurement variable information into higher-level measures of network behavior. These higher-level measures provide the monitored node's view of the network behavior. These measures can be used to trigger local control actions or a message to a centralized network manager.

Each measurement variable measure is combined in the probabilistic framework of a Bayesian network. The Bayesian network is used because it provides a method for estimating probabilities and it allows observed information to be combined with prior knowledge.

We begin by defining the random variables or nodes in the Bayesian network. There are two types of variables, those that are observed and those that are not observed and thus need to be estimated. We will call the variables that are not observed the internal variables. The observed variables directly correspond to the MIB variables. The internal variables are defined to be *Network Interface (IF), IP,* and *UDP*. The IF, IP, and UDP variables correspond to the MIB groups. Logically they represent different types of network functionality. The MIB variables within a group are the measurement variables for that network function (nf).

The Network variable is defined to correspond to all of the network functionality. In this work, we assume that the network is comprised only of the IF, IP, and UDP functions since these were the functions being used at the router where we were monitoring. Other network functions can easily be added. The structure of the Bayesian network is shown in Figure 3. The arrows between the nodes in Figure 3 go from cause to effect.

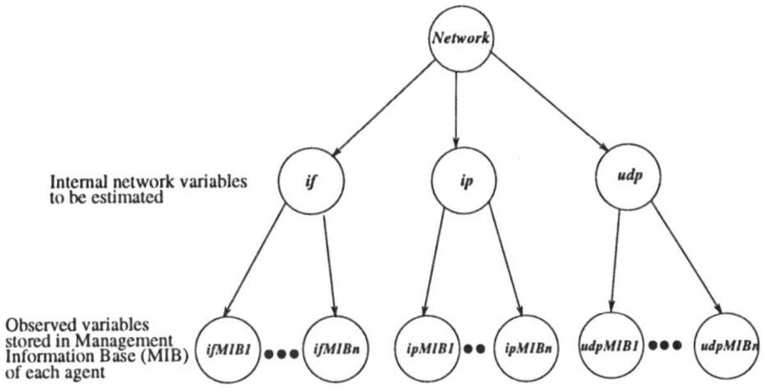

Figure 3 Bayesian network for fault detection

In our model, the health of the network is the most general information estimated and can be considered to be an underlying influence on the rest of the nodes in the Bayesian network. The overall health of the network directly influences the health of the three functions of the network (i.e., IF, IP, and UDP). This is indicated in our model by the arrows from the network random variable to the IF, IP, and UDP random variables. Likewise, for each network function, the health of that function directly influences the values of the individual measurement or MIB variables for that function. One way of interpreting this is that a problem in the network will cause symptoms to occur within the network functions, and likewise, problems within a network function will cause symptoms to show up in the MIB variables for that function.

The model has been designed based on these intuitive relationships from the structure of the MIB. The Bayesian network model requires the conditional independence assumptions described in Section 2. These assumptions are reasonable since each of the network functions represent independent functional components of the network. These components may fail independently, although there is a relationship between the functions, and serious problems in one component can eventually impact the other components. Since propagation of a fault through the functional components depends on the type and location of the fault (i.e., faults may propagate from low-level functions to high-level functions, or vice versa) [16], it is difficult to incorporate a propagation structure into the model that will accommodate all types of propagation.

In addition, the relationships between the nodes of the Bayesian network (network functions and MIB variables) are complex and not well understood. Therefore, as a starting point, we have proposed a simple model where no a priori relationship between the network functions is assumed, given the overall health of the network is known. Therefore we have not assumed a fault propagation structure in our model. Alternative Bayesian network structures that assume fault propagation structures have been investigated in [6].

Each of the internal variables is defined to be discrete with two states, *normal* and *abnormal*. Each of the observable variables is defined to be continuous. We are interested in estimating the following posterior probabilities:

$$p(network = normal / abnormal \mid MIBs) \quad (1)$$

and

$$p(nf = normal / abnormal \mid MIBs). \quad (2)$$

Due to the tree or singly connected structure of the Bayesian network, these probabilities can be calculated efficiently either using Pearl's algorithm [12] or directly. The equations for the direct calculation can easily be derived using the conditional independence assumption stated above.

The following quantities are necessary to calculate the probabilities in (1) and (2):

$$p(network = normal / abnormal), \quad (3)$$

$$p(nf = normal / abn \mid network = normal / abn), \quad (4)$$

and

$$p(MIB\ variable \mid nf = normal / abnormal). \quad (5)$$

The prior probabilities in (3) and the conditional probabilities in (4) are estimated using prior knowledge of the network behavior gained from observations and conversations with the network managers. These probabilities remain constant throughout the monitoring process. The conditional probabilities in (5) are estimated using the observed MIB variables. Section 3.1 contains the details of how these are obtained.

Since we are monitoring locally, all of the evidence or probabilities estimated from the observed MIB variables is available to the system. This enables the system to calculate the desired posterior probabilities using a complete and current set of observations.

4. Data Collection

Data for this work was collected from the RPI Computer Science Department network. The network as shown in Figure 4 is comprised of 7 subnetworks, or subnets, and two routers. The individual nodes (e.g., workstations, printers, etc.) on the subnets are not shown. Router 1 is the gateway between this network and the campus network, with all the traffic to and from the campus and the outside world flowing through this router. Router 2 mainly routes the local traffic flowing between the subnetworks. A large portion of this traffic is access from workstations to the fileservers. Data was collected from Router 2, the internal router.

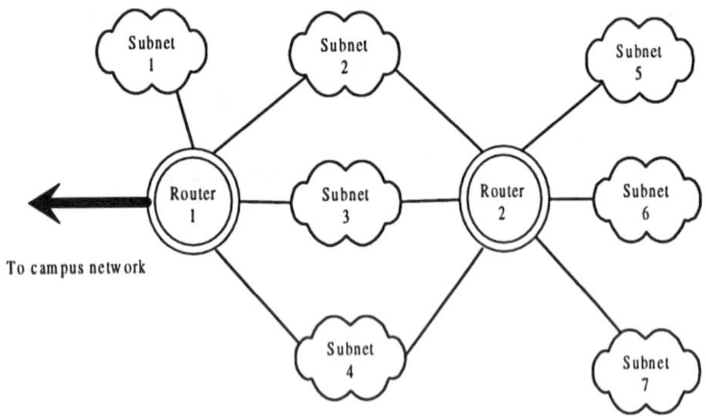

Figure 4 Configuration of the monitored network

The data was collected by polling the router using SNMP queries. The router was polled every 15 seconds. All of the available router MIB variables were collected. Of these variables, we studied the 14 that were active. The other variables changed infrequently and during the times of recorded faults, they rarely provided information that was not provided already by the active variables.

We monitored the router for approximately seven months. The monitoring was continuous for most of the time. During this time the log files generated by the *syslog* function were also saved to label the faults within the data. As *syslog* is not targeted specifically for network errors, only a subset of all network problems will be reported by *syslog*. The network related problems reported by *syslog* are usually severe. In fact, the type of network problem we found to be most commonly reported by *syslog* was server not responding. This type of message indicates a severe problem that may be occurring for a number of reasons (e.g. server down, path unavailable). The *syslog* messages do not provide any information about the cause of the problem.

5. Experimental Results

The system proposed for anomaly detection was tested on a set of 10 faults observed on the network in Figure 4 between October 1995 and March 1996. Most of the faults (9 out of 10) have been recorded as server not responding. The remaining fault is a report of excess Ethernet collisions on one of the subnets. Due to the mechanism currently used to log faults on this network (*syslog*), we could only observe types of faults where a service provided by the network is not operational. This mechanism provided accurate reports of severe faults, but no account of less severe network faults.

Although nine of the faults studied were the same, we did not observe the same types of changes in the data from fault to fault. This can possibly be traced to the fact that the faults were caused by different sets of circumstances or root causes. Even if the root causes were similar, the problems could have manifested themselves differently due to the network environment at the time they occurred. Specific root cause information may not be available without knowledge of the implementation details of the nodes comprising the network.

The results along with comparisons with threshold methods are shown for one of the faults. The results for the remaining faults are summarized.

5.1. Our Results

One of the faults the system was tested on was a fault that was reported as *server not responding* between 6:33 am and 6:36 am on December 23, 1996. The fileserver that was not responding was on Subnet 2. A total of 13 machines reported this problem (7 on Subnet 2, 4 on Subnet 3, and 2 on Subnet 4).

The results for the posterior probabilities estimated:

$$p(network = abnormal \mid MIBs),$$
$$p(IF = abnormal \mid MIBs),$$
$$p(IP = abnormal \mid MIBs),$$
$$\text{and } p(UDP = abnormal \mid MIBs)$$

are shown in Figure 5.

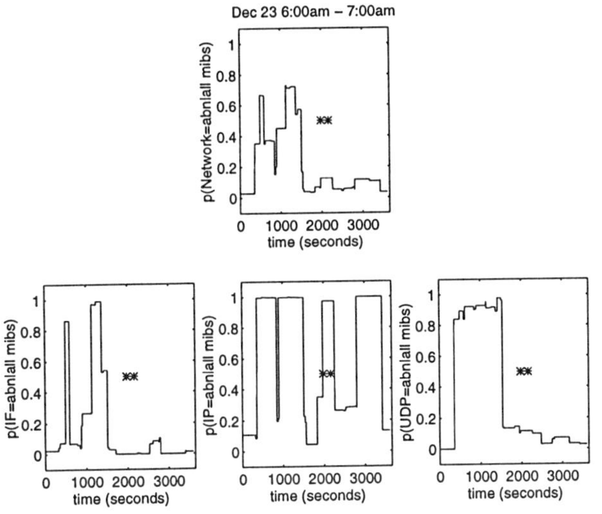

Figure 5 Results using 1 hour learning window

The asterisks denote the fileserver downtime period. Abnormal behavior is detected in the Network approximately 12 minutes before the server is reported unreachable. Anomalies are present before the problem in all three network functions, but only IP detects an anomaly during the crash. Similar results were obtained when a 4 hour learning window was used.

It is important to keep in mind the structure of the network in Figure 4. The router that we are monitoring continues to route all other traffic normally. The fileserver being down is not problematic to the router, but still we are able to detect the problem by monitoring the router. The router is able to detect that there is an anomaly in the network through changes to its MIB variables. Therefore, the results that we have are from the routers view of the network.

5.2. Comparisons

Since thresholds are commonly used to detect faults, we compared our results to those obtained using a feature set of an upper and lower threshold. The feature is whether the particular variable is within the thresholds or not. To combine the information from each MIB variable, we counted the total number of variables exceeding their thresholds at each time instance. The thresholds were calculated using learning windows of 1 hour, 4 hours and 1 week. The first two correspond to the windows used by the monitoring system. The third corresponds to the common practice of determining threshold levels using a large amount of data.

The results from all of these methods are shown in Figure 6. The asterisks denote the period where the fileserver was down. The results for 1 and 4 hour learning windows are identical. Both have small peaks where thresholds have been exceeded by 3 of the 14 MIB variables. The results using a 1 week learning window are essentially the same for the entire hour, thereby providing no useful information.

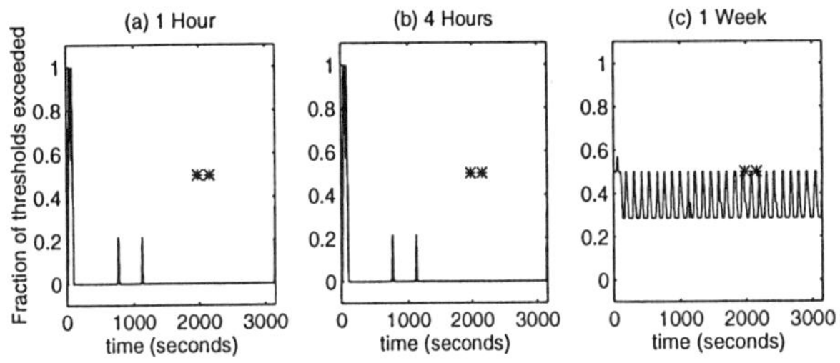

Figure 6 Results using thresholds

5.3 Composite results

More generally, 7 out of the 10 faults studied were detected using a 1 hour learning window and 5 out of 10 were detected using a 4 hour learning window. We considered a fault to be detected if the posterior probability that Network is abnormal is greater than 0.5.

These results need to be put into perspective. Ideally, we could calculate the number of times that a fault is detected when there is no fault (false alarms). Since we only have labels from the log file for the severe faults, it is not clear where other faults should or should not be detected. Therefore, to get some measure of the sensitivity we calculated the percentage of time that the posterior probability of the Network, IF, IP, and UDP is abnormal. The following figures indicate the percentage of abnormal time.

Network abnormal
- 6.29% of time using 1 hr learning window
- 3.85% of time using 4 hr learning window

IF abnormal
- 35.97% of time using 1 hr learning window
- 24.85% of time using 4 hr learning window

IP abnormal
- 42.03% of time using 1 hr learning window
- 33.32% of time using 4 hr learning window

UDP abnormal
- 42.24% of time using 1 hr learning window
- 30.29% of time using 4 hr learning window

Abnormalities at the highest level of our monitoring system (Network) are being detected a small percentage of the time. Therefore the detection of the test faults is significant. On the other hand, the faults that were not detected may not have had symptoms present at the router, or the features we used may not have captured adequate information to detect symptoms that were present.

6. Conclusion

We have shown that it is possible to use an adaptive learning machine to detect network faults without using models of specific faults. The Bayesian network provided a theoretical framework within which we were able to use prior knowledge to determine a structure and learn the normal behavior of the measurement variables. The system was tested on real data involving a fileserver crash on a computer network. It was able to successfully detect something abnormal approximately 12 minutes before the fileserver crashed. The detection was done from a router on the network which was operating properly. The router detected that something was wrong in the network from changes to its measurement variables.

With early detection, the network manager can be warned of impending failure, take corrective action and avoid the failure and costly downtime. Our approach is able to accomplish early detection by recognizing deviations from normal behavior in each of the measurement variables, correlating this information in time and then combining the information in a probabilistic framework.

This work is viewed as a first step in the direction of an automated fault management system that can generalize from network to network with minimal network specific information required a priori. The fault management problem is very complex and the nature of the problem evolves as networks evolve. Future work involves expanding the scope of the experiment, as well as further investigation of the methods.

The Bayesian formulation of this detection problem can be extended to incorporate more types of information or MIB groups. It can also be extended to combine the observations of several nodes in the network at the central network manager. With this extension, the Bayesian network's ability to estimate probabilities with incomplete information could be utilized. In addition, the use of learning to identify other possible structures for the Bayesian network is also an area for further investigation. Another area to investigate is better usage of the fault information that is available. This information can be used to help detect and diagnose known faults and to improve the feature extraction.

Acknowledgments

The authors would like to thank Dave Hollinger, Roddy Collins, and Nathan Schimke for helping us with the data collection. We would also like to thank John Miller, Ken Vastola, and George Nagy for helpful discussions and suggesting related references. The support of the National Science Foundation (ECS-9312594 and (CAREER) IRI-9502518) is gratefully acknowledged.

References

[1] U. Appel, A.V. Brandt, "Adaptive Sequential Segmentation of Piecewise Stationary Time Series," *Information Sciences,* vol. 29, 1983, pp. 27-56.

[2] C. Cortes, L.D. Jackel, W-P Chiang, "Predicting Failures of Telecommunication paths: Limits on Learning Machine Accuracy Imposed by Data Quality," *Proceeding of the International Workshop on Applications of Neural Networks to Telecommunications 2,* Stockholm, 1995.

[3] R.H. Deng, A.A. Lazar, W. Wang, "A Probabilistic Approach to Fault Diagnosis in Linear Lightwave Networks," *IEEE JSAC,* vol. 11, no. 9, Dec. 1993, pp. 1438-1448.

[4] D. Heckerman, "A tractable algorithm for diagnosing multiple diseases," *Proceedings of the Fifth Workshop on Uncertainty in Artificial Intelligence,* Windsor, ON, 1989, pp. 174-181.

[5] D. Heckerman, J.S. Breese, K. Rommelse, "Decision-Theoretic Troubleshooting," *Communications of the ACM,* vol. 38, March 1995, pp. 49-57.

[6] C. Hood, "Intelligent Detection For Fault Management of Communication Networks," Ph.D. Dissertation, Rensselaer Polytechnic Institute, 1997.

[7] G. Jakobson, M.D. Weissman, "Alarm Correlation," *IEEE Network,* Nov. 1993, pp. 52-59.

[8] A.A. Lazar, W. Wang, R. Deng, "Models and Algorithms for Network Fault Detection and Identification: A Review," *ICC,* Singapore, Nov. 1992.

[9] W. Leland, M. Taqqu, W. Willinger and D. Wilson, "On The Self Similar Nature of Ethernet Traffic (extended version)," *IEEE/ACM Trans. Networking,* vol. 2, pp. 1-15, Feb., 1994.

[10] E.L. Madruga, L.M.R. Tarouco, "Fault Management tools for a Cooperative and Decentralized Network Operations Environment," *IEEE JSAC,* vol. 12, no. 6, Aug. 1994, pp. 1121-1130.

[11] R. Maxion, F. Feather, "A Case Study of Ethernet anomalies in a Distributed Computing Environment," *IEEE Trans. on Reliability,* vol. 39, Oct. 1990, pp. 433-443.

[12] J. Pearl, *Probabilistic Reasoning in Intelligent systems: Networks of Plausible Inference.* San Mateo, CA: Morgan Kaufman, 1988.

[13] I. Rouvellou, "Graph Identification Techniques Applied to Network Management Problems," Ph.D dissertation, Columbia University, 1993.

[14] P. Smyth, "Markov Monitoring with Unknown States," *IEEE JSAC,* vol. 12, 1994, pp. 1600-1612.

[15] D.J. Spiegelhalter, A.P. Dawid, S.L. Lauritzen, R.G. Cowell, "Bayesian Analysis in Expert Systems," *Statistical Science,* vol. 8, no. 3, 1993, pp. 219-288.

[16] Z. Wang, "Model of network faults," Integrated Network Management I, B. Meandzija and J. Westcott (eds.), New York, NY, Elsevier Science Publishing Company, 1989.

[17] O. Wolfson, S. Sengupta, Y. Yemini, "Managing Communication Networks by Monitoring Databases," *IEEE Transactions on Software Engineering,* vol. 17, no. 9, 1991.

[18] Y. Yemini, "A Critical Survey of Network Management Protocol Standards," Telecommunications Network Management Into the 21st Century, S. Aidarous and T. Plevyak (eds.), New York, NY, IEEE press, 1994.

Panel 3

Microcellular Personal Communication Systems — PHS, DECT and PACS

Moderator

Takeshi Hattori, *NTT Telecommunications Network Group*

Panelists

Giovanni Colombo, *CSELT*
Andy Gent, *PHS International Corporation*
Robert J. Hayes, *PCS Strategy, Motorola Corporation*
Nicolas Huery, *C.G.R.P.*
Y. Nakamura, *NTT Personal Communications Network Corporation*

Architecture for Two-way Data Services Over Residential Area CATV Networks[1]

Chiung-Shien Wu, Gin-Kou Ma
Computer and Communication Research Labs.
Industrial Technology Research Institute
E000, Chutung, Hsinchu, Taiwan 310, R.O.C.
E-mail : cwu@e0sun3.ccl.itri.org.tw

Po-Ning Chen
Department of Communication Engineering
National Chiao Tung University
Hsinchu, Taiwan 300, R.O.C.
E-mail: poning@cc.nctu.edu.tw

ABSTRACT – *An architectural design for high speed residential data access using the traditional IEEE 802.3 medium access protocol over the existing CATV network is proposed. The described architecture is attractive in using the existing infrastructure combined with the exisiting access scheme in the residential area and thus it is cost effective and well suited for home internet access. However, the traditional CSMA/CD protocol is not suitable for the cable TV network due to its long propagation delay. Thus, we propose to combine the existing IEEE 802.3 CSMA/CD MAC with the segmented cable subnetworks so that a home user can get access to the internet as if he is using the Ethernet at* $10 Mbps$*, or Fast-Ethernet at* $100 Mbps$*. Only three subcarriers in the passband cable is used and therefore it will not interfere with the traditional broadcasting channels and the future digital video channels. The segmented cable are interconnected by the defined Cable Bridge (CB) and a simple flow control mechanism is proposed among the CBs. Functional components and operations of each CB will also be described. For a fair performance among the subnetworks, a prioritized queueing scheme is also proposed on each CB.*

1 Introduction

CATV (Community Antenna TV) networks are traditionally one-way, broadcasting, analog infrastructure for residential area TV distribution. However, two-way data access demands arise since more and more people at home want to make connections to the internet for WWW services. Internet services are becoming more and more popular not only to those special researchers, engineers, or students but also to all kinds of people who might want to make connections to the internet at home. Telephone modems have been used to provide this service to home but the access rate is limited to only several tens of $Kbps$. Another solution using cable modem over the existing CATV networks is receiving much attention in the industry. CATV network is the most important candidate for delivering integrated services to the subscribers as it is already installed at most of the families with a very high bandwidth available [1]. It can provide multiple channels in a single cable to carry analog or digital signals. Hence, it serves as a good infrastructure to connect the large number of home users who may be using the multimedia service, video broadcasting service, voice service, and the internet service [2], [3]. Many venders have been devoted to the design and manufacture of the cable modem which is intended for the data access over the cable.

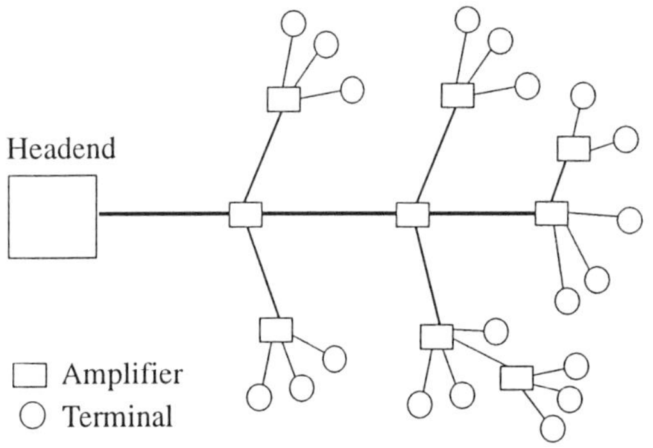

Figure 1: The tree-and-branch CATV networks.

The CATV network uses a tree-and-branch topology such that the number of users on the network is growable, as shown in Figure 1. Some amplifiers and splitters are required to extend the tree to each home user in the residential area. A head end is located at the end of the cable and it serves as a gateway between the cable and other signal sources such as ATM (Asynchronous Transfer Mode) backbone or the satellite channels. The cable is configured as a multi-channel bus using the frequency division multiplexing (FDM) technology [4], [5]. Each channel is referred to as a subcarrier which uses a passband of the frequency offset in the frequency spectrum of the cable. Digital data transmission can be achieved on each subcarrier by some modulation methods such as QPSK (Quadrature Phase Shift Keying) or Quadrature Amplitude Modulation (QAM). For two-way data services, some subcarriers are defined as the upstream channels for cable modems transmitting their data up to the head end and some other subcarriers are defined as the downstream channels for head end transmitting data down to each cable modem.

[1]This work is currently supported by the *R.O.C. Ministry of Economic Affairs* under the project No. 37H3100 conducted by ITRI.

0-8186-7780-5/97 $10.00 © 1997 IEEE

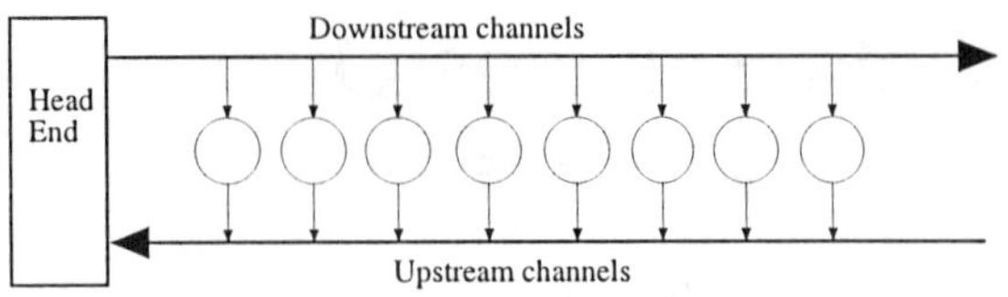

Figure 2: The logical structure of the CATV networks.

For simplicity, a CATV network is usually represented by a logical dual bus structure as shown in Figure 2. Since each subcarrier is a broadcast medium, there are contention problems in the upstream channel when multiple cable modems wish to transmit on the channel simultaneously. Several medium access methods have been proposed for the two-way services over the CATV networks [6], [7], [8]. Most of the proposed methods use contention resolution schemes such as ALOHA to resolve the collision among multiple cable modems. However, the schemes could be more complicated if one wants to obtain high throughput in broadcasting channels with long propagation delay, i.e., using the tree resolution algorithm [9]. Meanwhile, standardization activity has been undertaken by IEEE 802.14 project [10] and DAVIC (Digital Audio Visual Council) [11]. It usually takes a long time for the standard process to be formally finalized. And even the standard having been released, it is quite uncertain whether the standard protocol will be widely used or not. Besides, the development of a new protocol is costly and time-consuming.

In this paper, we propose to use the traditional IEEE 802.3 CSMA/CD protocol over the existing cable networks while maintaining the transmission rate at $10Mbps$ or higher. Since the geographical size of a residential area is quite larger than the maximum segment size of the Ethernet, the cable is configured by dividing the cable into segments which we refer to as the *Segmented CAble (SCA) Architecture* . The proposed architecture is attractive in its advantages of using the existing infrastructure in the residential area and thus it is cost effective and well suited for home internet access. The proposed scenario is achieved by using only three subcarriers in the passband cable without interfering with the traditional broadcasting channels and the future digital video channels. The segmented cable are interconnected by the defined Cable Bridge (CB). Flow control mechanism is required between two CBs. Functional components and operations of each CB will also be described in this paper.

2 The Segmented Cable Architecture

The Segmented Cable Architecture (SCA) is shown in Figure 3. The cable tree is divided into several subtrees which we call the *Cable Segment (CS)*. In addition to the amplifiers, between adjacent CSs there are *Cable Bridges (CB)* for connecting two subtrees. Within each CS, the CSMA/CD

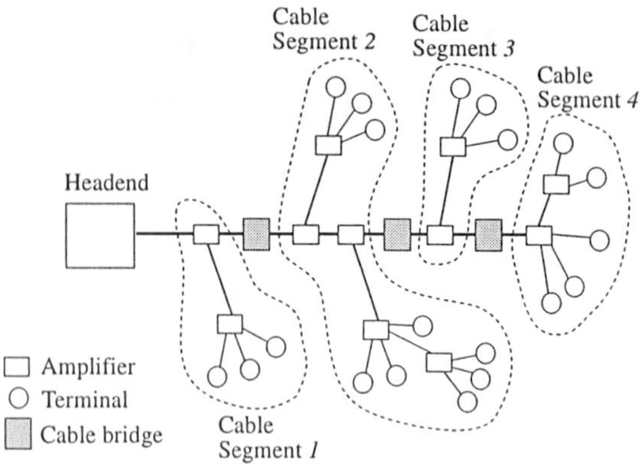

Figure 3: The segmented cable architecture for CATV networks.

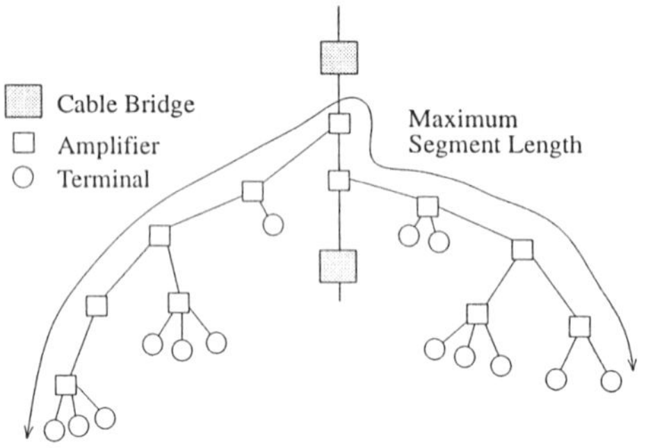

Figure 4: The maximum segment length of each CS.

protocol can be used to resolve the collision on the cable as defined by IEEE 802.3B - the broadband version of the IEEE 802.3 [13]. Each CS has a *Maximum Segment Length (MSL)* to model the maximum propagation delay within this CS. Each CS is a tree as shown in Figure 4. The MSL is defined as the cable length of the deepest branch plus the second deepest branch. By limiting each CS's MSL, a higher throughput for data transmission can be guaranteed. For example, we can achieve $10Mbps$ in each CS if we set the MSL to 2.5 kilometer, or $50Mbps$ within 1 kilometer.

Within each CS, all terminals are using the same subcarrier for upstream access. Therefore, CSMA/CD protocol is necessary for contention resolution in the upstream channel. We define the upstream subcarrier as *Channels A*, as shown in Figure 5 which explains the subcarrier configuration in a SCA network. In each CS, all terminals can communicate with each other in Channel A. For communications across two or more CSs, the packets are collected in each cable bridge and will be forwarded to the head end. Another subcarrier called *Channel B* is used to forward the inter-CS packets to the head end. And the head end will finally broadcast these packets to each CS using another downstream subcarrier called *Channel C*. To realize the architecture we may think Channels B and C as the superhighway along the cable and Channel A as the

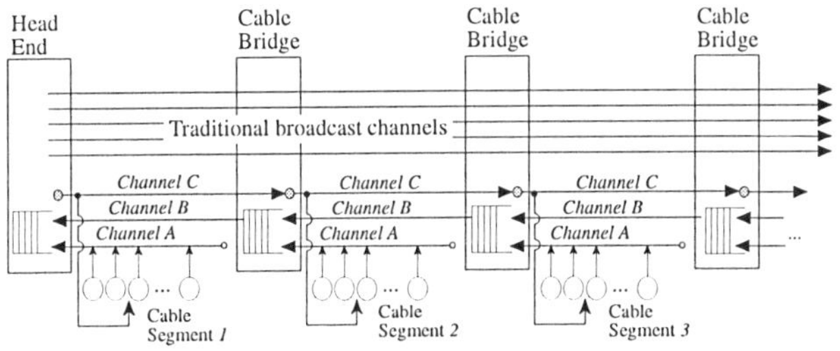

Figure 5: Subcarrier configuration in a SCA network.

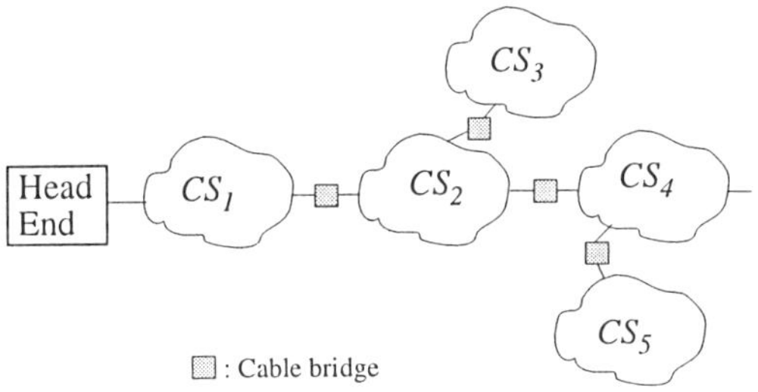

Figure 6: The logical tree structure of a SCA network.

branch which connects the local towns to the highway. To ensure the fairness along the superhighway, some gateway control mechanism is necessary. Since the packets are forwarded, some temporary buffers in the cable bridge is also necessary.

The proposed SCA network shown in Figures 3 and 5 is logically a cascaded bus network. A bus-type network is more simple to design, manage, and maintain. Several metropolitan area networks have been designed using a bus structure, i.e., IEEE 802.6 DQDB (Distributed Queue Dual Bus) [14], or the CRMA (Cycle Reservation Multiple Access) [15]. While these metropolitan area networks are also physically bus networks, they are hard to be installed and wired. However, the proposed SCA network is a logically bus-type and a physically tree-type networks. A physically tree-type network is very easy to install especially in the residential or metropolitan area.

Some designers would like also to have a logically tree-type network for reliability or management purpose. The proposed SCA network can be designed as a logically tree-type network, as shown in Figure 6. Here the Channel B is still used for inter-CS communications. For both tree-type and bus-type SCA networks, Channel C is used for downstream packet broadcast. Therefore, the bandwidth of Channel C may be several times greater than that of the Channel A or B, for example, using QAM (Quadrature Amplitude Modulation), or alternatively, using multiple channels for Channel C.

One problem arises in the bus-type SCA network, namely the reliability problem. Since these CBs are linearly cascaded, a fault in one of the CBs would cause the segments following that CB out of order. Thus, a bypass mechanism in the CB is

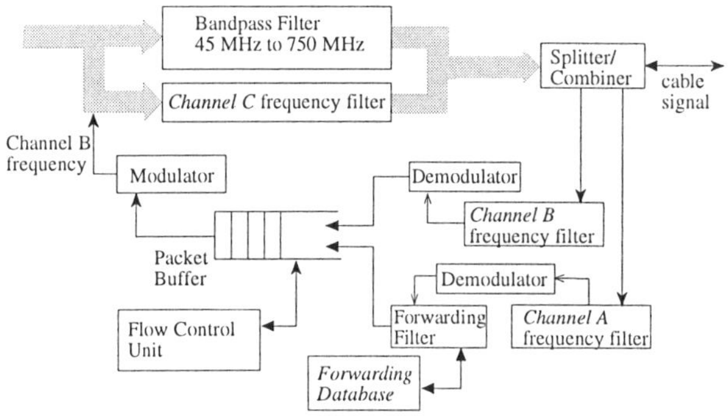

Figure 7: Functional block diagram of a cable bridge.

very essential when there is a fault or power failure occurred within the CB. This will be discussed in the next section.

3 Cable Bridge Architecture

Each cable bridge has a territorial CS. For simplicity, we call the cable bridges which are closer to the head end as the upper cable bridges or the upstream cable bridges, and those in the opposite side as the lower or the downstream cable bridges. Each cable bridge has the following functionalities:

1. Storing and forwarding the packets to upper cable bridge from its territorial CS in Channel A.
2. Storing and forwarding the packets to upper cable bridge from lower cable bridge in Channel B.
3. Broadcasting the packets from upper cable bridge to its territorial CS in the downstream Channel C.
4. Propagating the traditional TV signal to the lower cable bridges.

A functional block diagram of the cable bridge is shown in Figure 7, where several frequency filters are used for extracting the passband signals in which the Channels A, B, and C are modulated and transmitted. Another bandpass filter is used for bypassing the frequencies ranging from $45MHz$ to $750MHz$ which are used for traditional analog TV or future digital interactive TV. Modulation in Channels A, B, and C should be more reliable as the upstream signal can be very noisy. QPSK (Quadrature Phase Shift Keying) is a robust modulation scheme which is suitable for the upstream channel [11].

After recognizing a packet from Channel A or Channel B, the packet is forwarded to the packet buffer. Packets from Channel B are directly shifted into the buffer, while packets from Channel A are fed into the forwarding filter first. The forwarding filter is a mechanism used for distinguishing the packets to be forwarded from those packets which are only transmitted within the CS. A forwarding database is a lookup

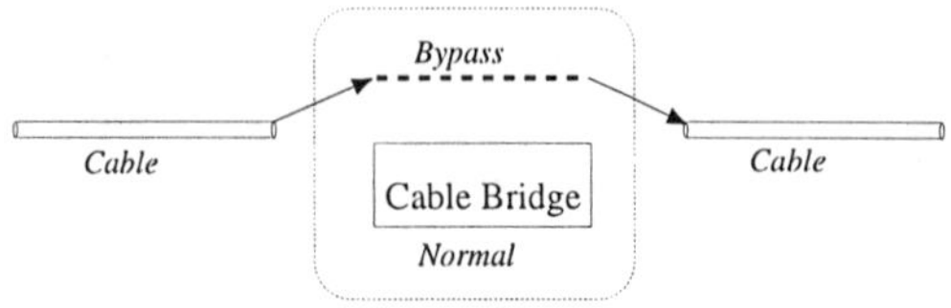

Figure 8: The bypass function of a cable bridge during a power failure condition.

table associated with each forwarding filter for the decision of whether forwarding the packet or not. Although there are proposed and standard methods for transparent bridge routing, we can still use a simpler method in the SCA network since the network topology is linearly cascaded . The learning of forwarding on each cable bridge depends upon the destination address it receives in each packet. There are three types of destination address sent on the cable, as follows.

1. **CASE 1:** Packets from CS or lower cable bridge destined for the head end to go outside of the cable. Usually in this case, the cable serves as a router.
2. **CASE 2:** Packets from this CS destined for another CS. In this case, the packets should be forwarded to the head end via Channel C.
3. **CASE 3:** Packets are transmitted only within the CS.

Packets should be forwarded in cases 1 and 2 and should not be forwarded in case 3. Each CS should maintain a forwarding database to control the packet filtering. The bridge learning scheme defined by IEEE 802.1d spanning tree algorithm can be used here. According to the scheme, the cable bridge can collect the source address located in its CS whenever there is a packet sent out by the users located in this CS. Furthermore, we don't need to establish the spanning tree since it is already there, the linear cascaded structure.

The flow control unit is responsible for resolving the congestion in the packet buffer since there are two input sources to the buffer. Also we should guarantee a fair access to the upstream channel in such a linear cascaded queueing system. The system can be modeled by a famous tandem queueing system which will be introduced in the next section. A simple flow control scheme will also be proposed after the next section.

To provide a more robust solution for the proposed SCA networks, a bypass mechanism may be designed as shown in Figure 8. During a power failure or a system fault condition in a CB, an automatic bypass system will be triggerred to pass the signal to or from its territorial CS. As a result, two adjacent CSs are combined into one CS and the speed of the related CS should be decreased by half.

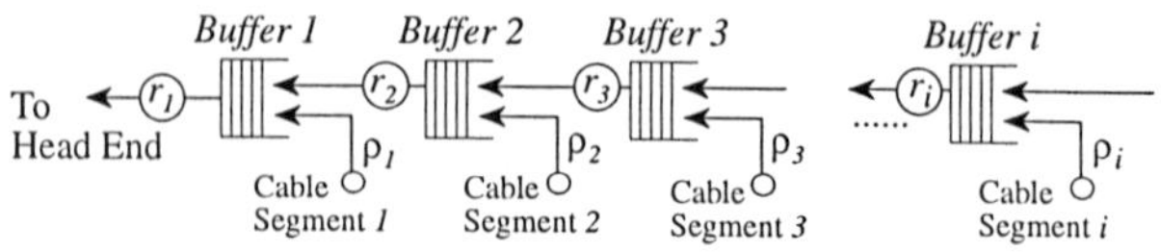

Figure 9: Tandem queueing in the SCA networks.

4 Tandem Queueing System

The tandem queueing system was encountered in most of the wide area packet switching network. It has been analyzed and the result is shown to be very complicated in terms of the end-to-end packet delay and the mean queue length [16], [17]. Here we use a very simplified approach to model the system. A tandem queueing system is represented in Figure 9, where *Buffer i* denotes the packet buffer in the ith cable bridge. Let the cable bridges be numbered from upstream to downstream, i.e, CB_1 to CB_i and so is each CS associated with each cable bridge, i.e., CS_1 to CS_i. Each *Buffer i* is associated with a server for sending the packets in *Buffer i* to *Buffer (i-1)* at a service rate r_i. Also let CS_i have an offer load ρ_i of sending packets to be forwarded. Suppose that there are all together n cable bridges, then *Buffer i* is loaded by an input rate of $\rho_i + r_{i+1}$. When $\rho_i + r_{i+1} > r_i$, an infinite queue length will occur. A discussion on performance consideration will be given based on M/D/1 queueing system in the next section. A flow control mechanism for preventing the congestion will be given following the next section.

5 Performance Consideration

If the transmission rate on Channel B is fixed, then we may think the server for outputting packets in *Buffer i* is a deterministic server. Let the service rate $r_i = 1$ for all i. Also let $\rho_i = \rho$, for all i. Then, the queueing system in each cable bridge is a standard $M/D/1$. Refer to [18], an $M/D/1$ queuing system with a deterministic service rate of 1 and an input utilization factor of ρ would have a mean queue length $\overline{q}$ equal to

$$\overline{q} = \frac{\rho}{1-\rho} - \frac{\rho^2}{2(1-\rho)} \quad (1)$$

CB_i is loaded by $(n-i+1)\cdot\rho$. Assume that the server in the $M/D/1$ queuing system is fairly shared by these $(n-i+1)$ traffic sources. Hence, the queuing system becomes a single server queuing system with a deterministic service rate of $1/(n-i+1)$. Let $\overline{q}_i$ represent the mean queue length of the *Buffer i*. The system can be approximated by the queue length of the $M/D/1$ system with a service rate of 1 and an input utilization factor of $\rho\cdot(n-i+1)$. That is

$$\overline{q}_i = \frac{\rho\cdot(n-i+1)}{1-\rho\cdot(n-i+1)} - \frac{\rho^2\cdot(n-i+1)^2}{2(1-\rho\cdot(n-i+1))} \quad (2)$$

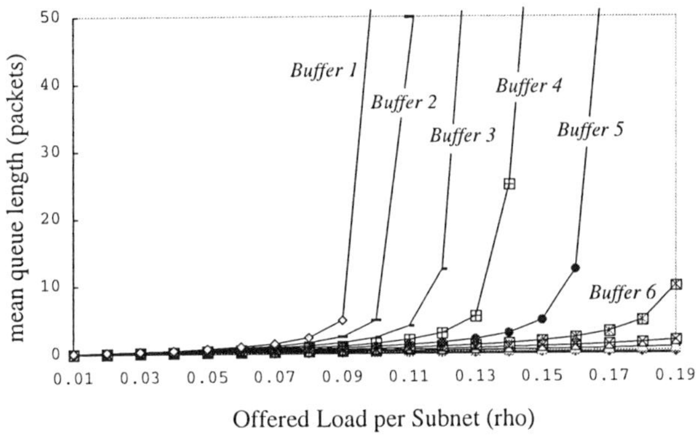

Figure 10: Mean queue length on each cable bridge.

In Figure 10, we plot the mean queue length of each cable bridge. We assume there are totally 10 CSs and each CS is producing a traffic load from 0.01 to 0.2. When the offered load is only 0.1, the mean queue length grows to infinite.

6 Flow Control

The proposed flow control scheme includes two parts, the prioritized queueing and the feedback policy. Let's assume a condition that $\rho_i = 1$ and $r_i = 1$ for all $i = 1, 2, ..., n$. In this case we have $\rho_i + r_{i+1} = 2 > r_i = 1$. If CB_i serves the packets from Channel A and Channel B with equal probability, then packets from CS_i will be served in an output rate of 0.5 in *Buffer i* and in an output rate of 0.25 in *Buffer (i-1)*. As a result, the equivalent service rate of the packets from CS_i in the first cable bridge is $1/2^{(i-1)}$. However, packets from the first CS has an equivalent service rate of $1/2$. This is an unfair condition to all of the terminals in each CS and it is the reason to propose a prioritized queueing scheme. Also we need a feedback scheme when the buffer space is insufficient to store the packet. The proposed feedback scheme prevents packet loss very simply and efficiently as described in the following text.

6.1 Prioritized Queueing

To prevent the unfairness as described above, the service rate for packets from Channel B and Channel A needs to be controlled. We refer to the packets coming from Channel B as the cross traffic and the packets from Channel A as the local traffic. *Buffer i* is reconfigured into two queues, *A-Buffer* for local traffic and *B-Buffer* for cross traffic, as shown in Figure 11. A scheduler is inserted before the server for controlling the service rate of each buffer. Let s_i denote the equivalent service rate for *A-Buffer* in CB_i, $s_i < 1$ for all i. Then the equivalent service rate for *B-Buffer* is $r_i - s_i$. For simplicity, we let $r_i = 1$ for all i. Also let u_i represent the equivalent service rate for packets from CS_i in the first cable bridge. Thus, we have

$$u_1 = s_1 \quad (3)$$
$$u_2 = s_2(1 - s_1) \quad (4)$$
$$u_3 = s_3(1 - s_2)(1 - s_1) \quad (5)$$
$$u_4 = s_4(1 - s_3)(1 - s_2)(1 - s_1) \quad (6)$$
$$\cdots \quad (7)$$
$$\cdots \quad (8)$$
$$u_n = s_n(1 - s_{(n-1)}) \cdots (1 - s_2)(1 - s_1) \quad (9)$$

For fairness, we must let

$$u_i = u_{(i+1)}, 1 \le i \le n-1, \forall i \quad (10)$$

As a result, we have

$$s_{(i+1)} = \frac{s_i}{1 - s_i}, 1 \le i \le n-1, \forall i \quad (11)$$

And

$$s_i = \frac{1}{n - i + 1}, 1 \le i \le n, \forall i \quad (12)$$

That is,

$$s_1 = \frac{1}{n} \quad (13)$$
$$s_2 = \frac{1}{n-1} \quad (14)$$
$$s_3 = \frac{1}{n-2} \quad (15)$$
$$s_4 = \frac{1}{n-3} \quad (16)$$
$$\cdots \quad (17)$$
$$s_{n-1} = \frac{1}{2} \quad (18)$$
$$s_n = 1 \quad (19)$$

6.2 Feedback Control

The feedback mechanism is needed for *Buffer i* to send the congestion notification back to the traffic sources (both cross and local traffic) which are producing too many packets, for example, to make feedback on both CS_i and the $(i+1)$th cable bridge. When *A-Buffer* is running out, the feedback is sent on Channel A on which CS_i is transmitting, as shown in Figure 11. Since the CSMA/CD protocol is used on Channel A, the feedback signal can be sent by simply producing continuous redundant packets on the Channel. This can easily prevent terminals on the Channel from sending out packets since each terminal will sense a busy carrier. For *B-Buffer*, the same scheme can be applied and each cable bridge senses the carrier before it sending out the packets on Channel B. We refer to this kind of flow control as the *Implicit Feedback Flow Control (IFFC)*. The rule of IFFC method is as follows.

- Whenever the buffer is full, send the redundant packets (busy signals) on the input channel.

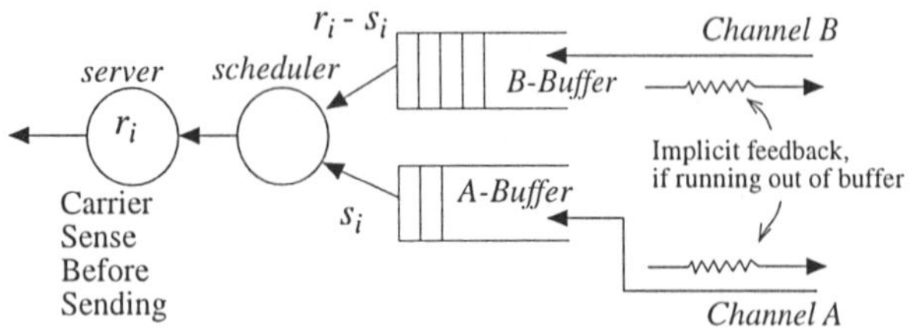

Figure 11: Prioritized queueing and implicit feedback flow control.

Therefore, each terminal on the input channel cannot send any packet out if the buffer is full, which means that no packet will be lost during the transmission to the headend. With this reliable flow control, the SCA system becomes a very robust interconnected network.

6.3 The Scheduler

There are two buffers in each CB and we have defined the equivalent service rate for each buffer, i.e., s_i for *A-Buffer* and $r_i - s_i$ for *B-Buffer*. However, the packets in these two buffers are to be sent on the same output channel. We need a scheduler to arrange the packets, as shown in Figure 11. A very useful scheduler can be used for our system, namely the *Generalized Processor Sharing (GPS)* server proposed in [19]. A Generalized Processor Sharing (GPS) server is work-conserving and operates at fixed rate r. It is characterized by positive real numbers ϕ_1, ϕ_2, ..., ϕ_N. Let $S_i(\tau, t)$ be the amount of session i traffic served in an interval $(\tau, t]$. A session is backlogged at time t if a positive amount of that session's traffic is queued at time t. Then, a GPS server is defined as one for which

$$\frac{S_i(\tau,t)}{S_j(\tau,t)} \geq \frac{\phi_i}{\phi_j}, j = 1, 2, \ldots, N \tag{20}$$

for any session i that is continuously backlogged in the interval $(\tau, t]$. Thus, session i is guaranteed a rate of

$$g_i = \frac{\phi_i}{\sum_j \phi_j} r \tag{21}$$

GPS is an attractive multiplexing scheme. However, analysis of a GPS system is quite complicated especially when it is combined with Tandem queueing system.

For simplicity, we still use an M/D/1 queueing system to approximate the SCA network. For any buffer with equivalent service rate $r < 1$, the mean queue length under input load ρ is approximated by the mean queue length of the buffer with a service rate of 1 under input load $\frac{\rho}{r}$. According to Equation (12), the equivalent service rate for *A-Buffer* of the ith CB is $\frac{1}{n-i+1}$. Let $\overline{qa_i}$ denote the corresponding mean queue length and $\overline{wa_i}$ denote the corresponding mean waiting time. By M/D/1 queue, we have

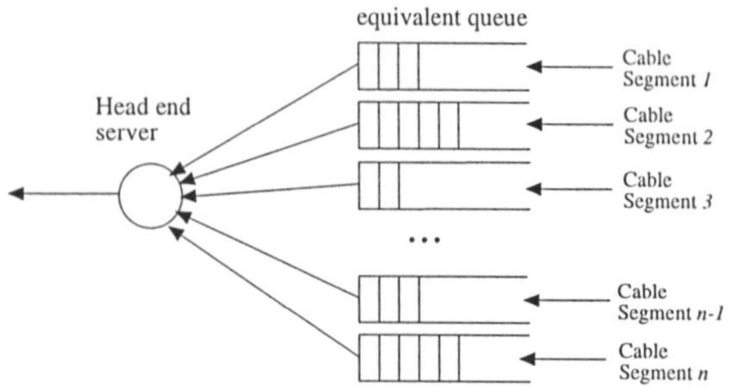

Figure 12: Equivalent queueing system for approximating the SCA networks.

$$\overline{qa_i} = \frac{\rho \cdot \beta_i}{1 - \rho \cdot \beta_i} - \frac{(\rho \cdot \beta_i)^2}{2(1 - \rho \cdot \beta_i)} \tag{22}$$

$$\overline{wa_i} = \frac{\rho \cdot \beta_i}{2(1 - \rho \cdot \beta_i)} \cdot t \tag{23}$$

where $\beta_i = n - i + 1$ and t represents the mean service time of the packets. For example, the service time of a $512 - Byte$ packet at $10Mbps$ transmission rate is $\frac{512 \cdot 8}{10^7} = 0.4096msec$.

Since it is an upstream access, packets are required to be transmitted to the head end. Packets from CS_i are stored and forwarded in between the $(i-1)$th CB and the first CB (the head end itself) as well as queued in the ith CB. To calculate the end-to-end performance from the ith CB to the head end, we define an equivalent queue for each CS, as shown in Figure 12. Packets from each CS are imaged as if they are queued in one equivalent queue and then transmitted directly to the head end server. Therefore, each CS_i has an equivalent mean queue length, denoted by Q_i, and an equivalent mean waiting time, denoted by W_i. Assume that CS_i has an offer load ρ, we approximate Q_i by the summation of the following two terms:

1. $\overline{qa_i}$
2. $\overline{qb_j}, j = 1, \ldots, i-1$

where $\overline{qb_j}$ is defined as the mean queue length of the *B-Buffer* of the jth CB with service rate $r_j - s_j$ under input load ρ on each CS_i. When $r_j - s_j < \rho$, $\overline{qb_j}$ grows to infinity. This means $Q_i \rightarrow \infty$. When $r_j - s_j > \rho$, we add the queueing effect that each *B-Buffer* of the jth CB is imaged as if it is loaded by ρ. Then, Q_i can be approximated by

$$Q_i = \overline{qa_i} + \sum_{j=1}^{j=i-1} \overline{qb_j}, \tag{24}$$

where

$$\overline{qb_j} = \frac{\rho \cdot \alpha_j}{1 - \rho \cdot \alpha_j} - \frac{(\rho \cdot \alpha_j)^2}{2(1 - \rho \cdot \alpha_j)} \tag{25}$$

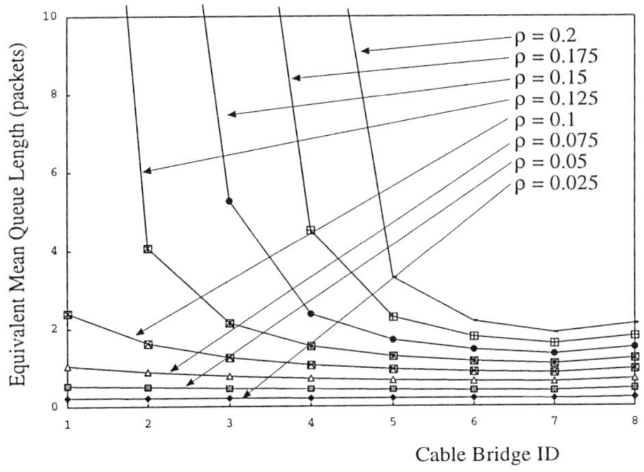

Figure 13: Equivalent mean queue length of each cable bridge.

$$\alpha_j = \frac{n-j+1}{n-j} \tag{26}$$

The same approach can be applied to the approximation of the equivalent mean waiting time W_i. We have

$$W_i = \overline{wa_i} + \sum_{j=1}^{j=i-1} \overline{wb_j}, \tag{27}$$

where

$$\overline{wb_j} = \frac{\rho \cdot \alpha_j}{2(1-\rho \cdot \alpha_j)} \cdot t \tag{28}$$

Where $\overline{wb_j}$ is the waiting effect that each CB contribute to the total waiting time W_i.

In Figure 13, we plot the equivalent mean queue length under offer load ρ for *CSs 1 to 8*. The offer load ρ is in between the range of 0.025 to 0.2. When $\rho = 0.1$, the equivalent mean queue length of each CB is under 3 packets. Since there are 8 CBs sharing the single upstream channel B, the total utilization is 80% and each CS fairly shares the upstream bandwidth. When ρ grows higher, the equivalent mean queue length of some CBs becomes infinite large. In this case, the IFFC will be effective to prevent the packet loss.

In Figures 14 and 15, we plot the equivalent mean waiting time under offer load ρ for *CSs 1 to 8*. The offer load ρ is again in between the range of 0.025 to 0.2. In Figure 14, we show the result by assuming a fixed packet size of 512 bytes. Each CS is operated at $10Mbps$. When $\rho = 0.1$, the equivalent mean waiting time of each CB is under $4msec$. In Figure 15, the packet size is set equal to 1024 bytes. The result is similar. The equivalent mean waiting time of each CB is under $8msec$.

7 Conclusion

In this paper, The segmented cable architecture for high speed internet access in the residential area is described in

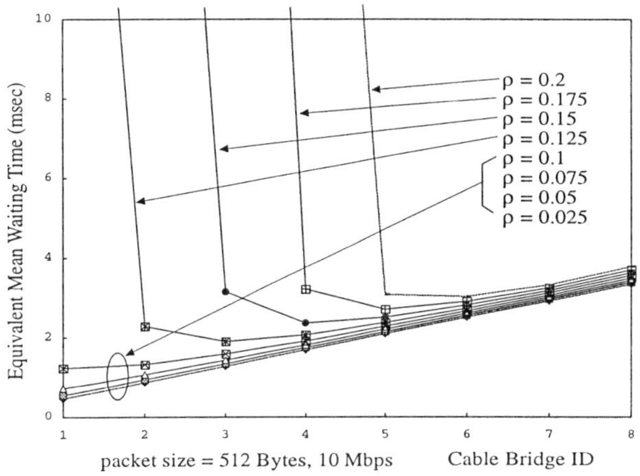

Figure 14: Equivalent mean waiting time of each cable bridge (packet size = 512 bytes).

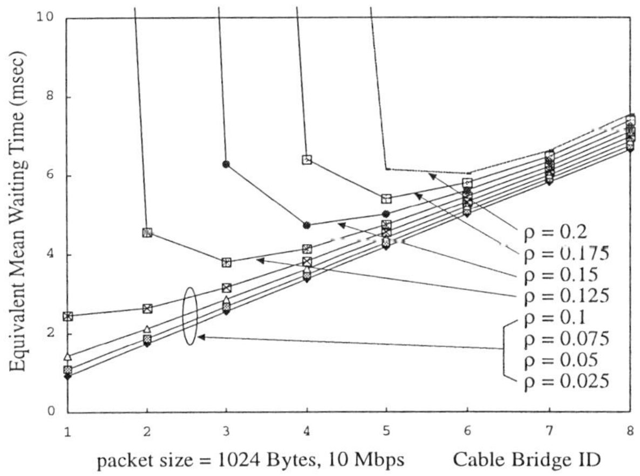

Figure 15: Equivalent mean waiting time of each cable bridge (packet size = 1024 bytes).

this paper. The proposed architecture is attractive and very cost-effective in its advantages of using the existing CATV infrastructure and the traditional IEEE 802.3 CSMA/CD MAC protocol. We use very simple flow control scheme and prioritized queueing to prevent the congestion of the tandem queueing effect in the proposed system. This makes the proposed system a reliable and robust network for home internet users.

The proposed SCA network has the following attractive characteristics:

1. *The proposed SCA network is a physically tree-type network and can be logically configured into bus-type or tree-type network.*

2. *The cost of the network is low as the CATV networks have been already installed in most of the residential areas.*

3. *Since the cable is segmented, bandwidth can be reused.*

4. *The user population on each CS is not big because the geographical area of each CS has been controlled. Besides, each CS operates at a higher bit rate, then each terminal gets more bandwidth from the shared channel.*

5. *The speed is adjustable. For example, we may limit the size of each CS in* $500m$*, so that each CS can operate at* $50Mbps$ *using CSMA/CD.*

6. *The noise problem on the upstream channel can be eliminated because cable bridge regenerates the signals on the channel. This implies that the channel modulation scheme which results in a higher transmission rate can be used, e.g., QAM.*

References

[1] B. Furht, D. Kalra, F. Kitson, A.A. Rodriguez and W.E. Wall, "Design Issues for Interactive Television Systems", *IEEE Computer,* Vol. 28, No. 5, May 1995, pp. 25–39.

[2] Digital Audio-Visual Council, "DAVIC 1.0 Specifications, Part 1: Description of DAVIC Functionalities", *Revision 3.1*, 1995.

[3] C.N. Judice *et. al.,* "Video on Demand: A Wideband Service or Myth?", *IEEE ICC'86 Conference Record,* Vol. 3 of 3, 1986, pp. 1735–1739.

[4] S.B. Weinstein, "Getting the Picture, A Guide to CATV and the New Electronic Media", *IEEE Press,* 1986.

[5] T.F. Baldwin, and D.S. McVoy, "Cable Communication", *Prentice Hall,* Second Edition, 1988.

[6] J.E. Dail, M.A. Dajer, C.C. Li, P.D. Magill, C.A. Siller Jr., K. Sriram, and N.A. Whitaker, "Adaptive Digital Access Protocol: A MAC Protocol for Multiservice Broadband Access Networks", *IEEE Communications,* Vol. 34, No. 3, March 1996, pp. 104-112.

[7] C. Bisdikian, B. McNeil, R. Norman, and R. Zeisz, "MLAP: A MAC Level Access Protocol for the HFC 802.14 Network", *IEEE Communications,* Vol. 34, No. 3, March 1996, pp. 114-121.

[8] W. Xu, and C. Graham, "A Distributed Queueing Random Access Protocol for a Broadcast Channel", *ACM SIGCOMM'93,* pp. 270-278.

[9] T. Capetanakis, "Tree Algorithm for a Packet Broadcasting Channel", *IEEE Transactions on Information Theory,* Vol. IT-25, Sept. 1979, pp. 505-515.

[10] IEEE 802.14, "Cable TV MAC/PHY Protocol Working Group: Functional Requirements", Oct. 1994.

[11] Digital Audio-Visual Council, "DAVIC 1.0 Specifications, Part 8: Lower Layer Protocols and Physical Interfaces", *Revision 3.1*, 1995.

[12] N. Maxemchuk, and A. N. Netravali, "Voice and Data on a CATV Network", *IEEE Journal on Selected Areas in Communications,* Vol. SAC-3, No. 2, March 1985, pp. 300-311.

[13] IEEE 802.3, "Carrier Sense Multiple Access with Collision Detection", *New York, IEEE,* 1985a.

[14] "IEEE Standards for Local and Metropolitan Area Networks: Distributed Queue Dual Bus (DQDB) Subnetwork of a Metropolitan Area Network (MAN)", *IEEE 802.6,* July, 1991.

[15] M. M. Nassehi, "CRMA: An Access Scheme for High Speed LANs and MANs", *Proceedings of SUPERCOMM/ICC'90,* April, 1990.

[16] F. Kamoun and M. M. Ali, "Queueing Analysis of ATM Tandem Queues with Correlated Arrivals", *IEEE Infocom'95,* Boston USA, 1995, pp. 709-716.

[17] J. Ren, J.W. Mark and J.W. Wong, "End-to-End Performance In ATM Networks", *IEEE ICC'94,* New Orleans USA, 1994, pp. 996-1002.

[18] L. Kleinrock, "Queueing Systems Volume I: Theory", *John Wiley & Sons, Inc.,* 1975.

[19] A.K. Parekh and R.G. Gallager, "A Generalized Processor Sharing Approach to Flow Control in Integrated Services Networks: The Single Node Case", *IEEE/ACM Transactions on Networking,* Vol. 1, No. 3, June 1993, pp. 344-357.

PCUP : Pipelined Cyclic Upstream Protocol over Hybrid Fiber Coax

Ying-Dar Lin Chia-Jen Wu Wei-Ming Yin
Department of Computer and Information Science
National Chiao Tung University, Hsinchu, Taiwan
E-mail : ydlin@cis.nctu.edu.tw

Abstract *In order to span NII (National Information Infrastructure) into the homes, the community cable TV networks have to be re-engineered to support two-way interactive services. In this work, we propose PCUP (Pipelined Cyclic Upstream Protocol) as the upstream MAC (Medium Access Control) protocol for HFC (Hybrid Fiber Coax) community access network. PCUP is designed with the intention of pipelining the upstream channel. This is achieved by proper station positioning, which measures the station propagation offset from the headend, and transmission scheduling, which assigns each station the transmission starting time and duration in a cycle. By taking into account the propagation offsets and the transmission times, transmitted cells can appear back-to-back, i.e. pipelined, at the headend. Since only the active stations are scheduled to transmit in a cycle, a membership control mechanism, which runs a contention-based tree walk algorithm, is executed periodically to allow the stations to join or leave. We also compare PCUP with various schemes proposed to IEEE 802.14 committee.*

1. Introduction

Cable companies have become the leading players in the search for ways to expand the ATM-based NII backbone network into the homes [1,4,5]. However, the community networks must support two-way asymmetric traffic patterns and arbitrate multiple accesses for available bandwidth. HFC [6,7] is gradually becoming the standard for many cable companies. We address the challenge of data communication over HFC and propose a suitable MAC-layer protocol in upstream for HFC.

Fig. 1-1 represents a piece of a HFC system. Clusters of homes, 500 to 2000 subscribers, are served by a fiber that comes from the headend. The signal is distributed to homes within the serving area of a fiber node via an amplified tree-and-branch feeder cable, perhaps as short as 3 miles in total length. Each branch serves 125 to 500 subscribers. One of the limitations here is that the station can not listen directly to the upstream transmissions from other stations; hence, they are incapable of detecting collisions and coordinating their transmissions all by themselves. A multiple access technology other than carrier sensing is required so that all subscribers within a branch can share the available reverse bandwidth.

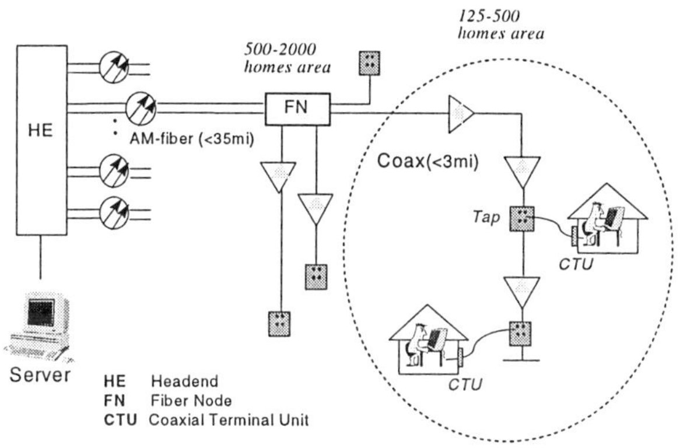

Figure 1-1 *The architecture of HFC. Subscribers in the feeder cable can only listen to the downstream from the headend and transmit in the allocated upstream.*

In practice, the analog band from a station to its headend is relatively narrow and of poor quality. In downstream, channel bandwidth is more abundant with less noise. A typical frequency spectrum for the subscribers to use is given in Fig. 1-2. Assume that a total bandwidth of at least 800 MHz is available on all the coaxial cable links. A 400 MHz band, from 150 MHz to 550 MHz, may be used to carry conventional analog broadcast programs, while digital downstream services such as VoD programs are transmitted in the range from 550 MHz to 750 MHz. A 18.5 MHz band from 8 to 26.5 MHz can be divided into multiple upstream digital channels. These upstream channels are called "*multi-access channels*" and used to carry signaling and data. A larger bandwidth in downstream, 70 to 130 MHz, is used as the downstream counterpart for those upstream *multi-access channels*. Other constant bit rate services, such as voice and video telephony, use 27 MHz to 54 MHz in upstream and 750 MHz to 800 MHz in downstream.

It is the upstream multi-access channel that this articles is addressing. The rest of the article is organized as

This work was supported in part by National Science Council, Taiwan, and Mentor Data System Inc., Hsinchu Science-based Industrial Park, Taiwan, under a joint project, NSC85-2622-E-009-006R.

0-8186-7780-5/97 $10.00 © 1997 IEEE

follows. In section 2, we survey and compare the proposed MAC schemes. Our PCUP is presented in section 3 where protocol mechanisms and messages are defined. Section 4 evaluates PCUP and compares it with one distributed protocol, R-ALOHA, and, one centralized protocol, UniLINK. Finally, section 5 concludes the article.

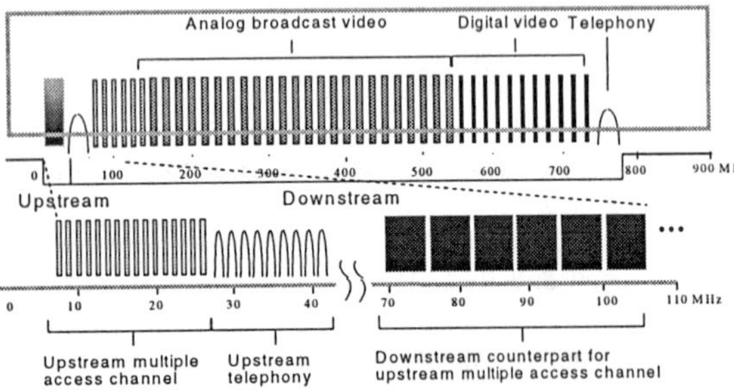

Figure 1-2 *Spectrum allocation of HFC.*

2. MAC Alternatives

The main goal of IEEE 802.14 Cable TV LAN MAC/PHY committee is to provide interactive multi-media services over HFC networks. To meet this target, the MAC protocol should satisfy the following requirements:

- Dynamic bandwidth allocation to CBR(Constant Bit rate), VBR(Variable Bit Rate) and ABR(Available Bit Rate) traffic types
- High channel throughput
- Low access delay
- Support for a large number of stations
- Metropolitan area coverage

Many MAC protocols have been proposed and studied. They can be classified into two categories : distributed protocols and centralized protocols. There is no central controller in distributed protocols, like CSMA/CD and R-ALOHA[14] protocols. The centralized protocols provide better timing mechanisms in avoiding collisions. This kind of protocols, proposed by many organizations, include MLAP(MAC Level Access Protocol) of IBM Corp.[22], XDQRAP(Extended Distributed Queuing Random Access Protocol) of Scientific-Atlanta, Inc.[23], ADAPt (Adaptive Digital Access Protocol) of AT&T Bell Lab.[21], UniLINK protocol of LANcity corp.[17], FPP(Framed Pipeline Polling) protocol of NEC corp.[19], CPR (Centralized Priority Reservation) protocol of Georgia Institute of Technology[20], traditional TDMA (Time Division Multiple Access), etc. We also present our CATV MAC protocol, PCUP, which will be detailed in the next section.

Both PCUP and MLAP support integrated services, and flexible contention and reservation modes of operation, where newly activated stations contend to establish themselves and then transmit on reserved time slots until they empty their queues.[22] FPP works similarly to them besides that the station transmits its data immediately after the headend polls it.[19] In CPR protocol, a station sends a request to the headend using a contention channel. The headend acknowledges the request and then schedules the request in a FCFS fashion, informing the station by the means of a grant message about when to transmit.[20] XDQRAP works similarly to CPR. It also provides an immediate transmission mode allowing a single cell message to be transmitted without requests.[23] ADAPt and UniLINK all support a mixture of isochronous, reservation and contention bandwidth. The isochronous bandwidth is established by a setup process and exists before being released. The reservation bandwidth means that slots are on a per-request basis granted according to requests. And the contention bandwidth is randomly accessed.[17,21]

In order to characterize these protocols, we make a comparison summarized in table 2-1. The entry of scheduling discipline means how connections' bandwidth requests are processed. These requests are either granted in a FCFS fashion or fairly allocated at the end of a cycle. From table 2-1, we see that conventional MAC protocols can not meet the multi-media requirements. For example, the R-ALOHA protocol can not support isochronous due to its random access control. Although R-ALOHA can handle bursty traffic, it has the problem of unfairness and no QoS.

In order to satisfy QoS requirements, centralized protocols with hybrid bandwidth allocation mechanism are more feasible. Although ADAPt and UniLINK protocols are centralized and hybrid, contention-based bandwidth will be the bottleneck of throughput under heavy best-effort traffic. We also see that PCUP, FPP and MLAP protocols behave in a similar way. They gather all bandwidth requests and schedule them together. Among these three, something different can be observed. In MLAP protocol, the headend uses the n-ary STAck ResolutTion (START-n) algorithm to ensure that a station can transmit in a chain of contention-free transmissions for a long message. In FPP protocol, the headend may poll every station three times for CBR, VBR and ABR traffic types in a frame. This intensive polling increases the headend processing load. Another difference between FPP and PCUP is that in a FPP frame, a station transmit its CBR, VBR and ABR traffic in three different regions, while in a PCUP frame, a station transmit these three consecutively. Furthermore, delay adjustment, which is also called positioning or ranging, is done by stations both in MLAP and FPP protocols. This adds up the station complexity. In CPR protocol, there are two factors that limits the performance. First, all bandwidth requests are contention-based. This scheme will lead to unfairness between stations and throughput degradation under heavy traffic. Second, an individual station must wait one round-trip delay before sending each message[20]. Given these observations, our PCUP stands out well in various aspects.

	R-ALOHA	MLAP	XDQRAP	ADAPt
Distributed	X			
Centralized		X	X	X
Isochronous bandwidth				X
Reservation bandwidth	X	X	X	X
Contention bandwidth	X		X	X
Scheduling discipline	none	fair scheduling	FCFS	FCFS
QoS		X	X	X
Timing implemented by	H/E	H/E & STU	H/E	H/E
Headend complexity	..	....	....	....
Station complexity	.	..	..	.

	UniLINK	CPR	FPP	PCUP
Distributed				
Centralized	X	X	X	X
Isochronous bandwidth	X			
Reservation bandwidth	X	X	X	X
Contention bandwidth	X			
Scheduling discipline	FCFS	FCFS	fair scheduling	fair scheduling
QoS	X	X	X	X
Timing implemented by	H/E & STU	H/E	H/E & STU	H/E
Headend complexity	....	...	....	...
Station complexity	..	..	..	.

H/E = Headend STU = Set Top Unit (station)

Table 2-1 *Features comparison of proposed MAC protocols*

3. Pipelined Cyclic Upstream Protocol

3.1 System overall description

Stations, each with a propagation delay from the headend, are scattered randomly over the HFC network. We can neutralize stations' propagation offsets by synchronizing them. The synchronization process, sorting the on-line stations according to their propagation offsets from the headend, is called *station positioning*. A *membership control* is done periodically to update the set of on-line stations and the channel usage status. An efficient transmission scheduling algorithm is then applied, in each cycle, to schedule the transmission starting time and duration of each station so that cells appear to be pipelined, i.e. back-to-back, at the headend. These three mechanisms, namely, station positioning, membership control, and transmission scheduling, constitute PCUP.

We divide the PCUP operations into two modes: cyclic transmission mode and negotiation mode as shown in Fig. 3-1. In Fig. 3-1, the condition to switch between the modes is triggered by a timer. PCUP runs a tree walk contention-based algorithm of the membership control in the negotiation mode so that stations may join, to be on-line, or leave, to be off-line, the PCUP operations. This process is essential in keeping the system status updated.

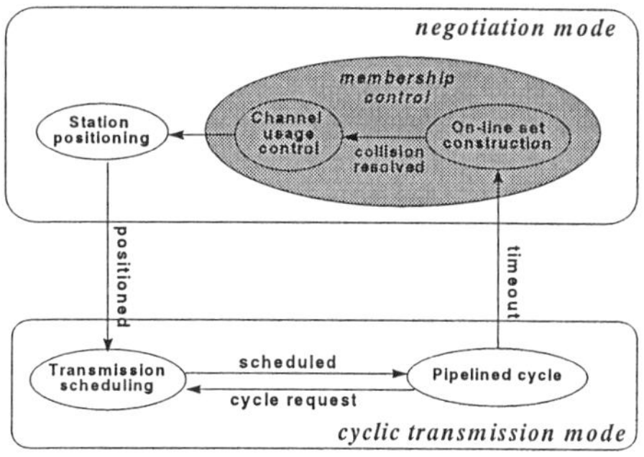

Figure 3-1 *State transition diagram of headend in the PCUP operations.*

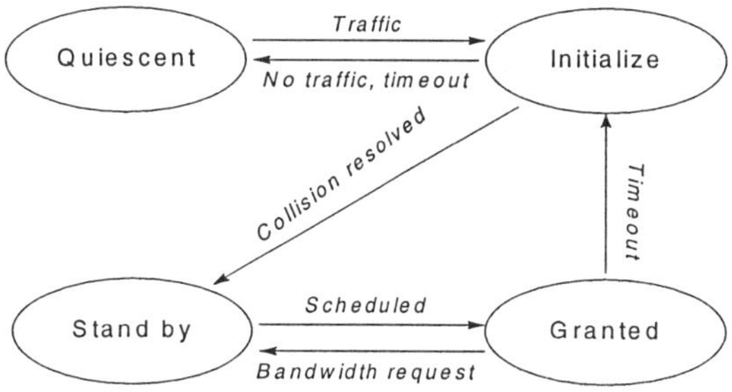

Figure 3-2 *State transition diagram of station in the PCUP operations. The initialize state includes station positioning and cycle membership control. Note that stand by is corresponding to transmission scheduling and granted is corresponding to pipelined cycle in the headend state transition diagram.*

After the tree walk algorithm, stations that are in the PCUP operations are arranged, by the station positioning algorithm, as a sequence sorted by their propagation offsets from the headend. Stations are aligned by the headend in order to schedule their precise transmission starting times. The alignment can neutralize station's propagation offset so that cells arrive at the headend as though they were sent with zero propagation delay.

While in the cyclic transmission mode, the PCUP runs a contention-free slotted mechanism within the upstream. After scheduling the transmission starting times, the headend assigns transmission slots for each station by an allocation frame according to the station's buffer queue size reported in the previous cycle. A slot time is sufficient for transmitting an ATM cell. All stations, upon receiving the allocation frame, can transmit its data in its assigned slots within the cycle, as illustrated in Fig. 3-2.

3.2 Membership control

3.2.1 On-line set construction

The set of on-line stations is established by membership control in the negotiation mode, which is triggered by a timer, *Group_Reset_Timer*. The timer is set periodically to 0.3 second or more. The headend issues a *HE.invitation* frame to the stations that do not belong to the set, i.e. not in *Request_Table*[1] and starts a tree walk algorithm [9] to update the set of on-line stations. On-line stations which have not transmitted anything after the last membership control operation are considered off-line and will not receive the *HE.invitation frame.* The other on-line stations, which have transmitted something, will be still on-line with no need to send them the *HE.invitation* frame.

3.2.2 Channel usage control

There may be about 500 subscribers contending for 17 upstream channels. It is believed that fixed allocation, say assigning 30 subscribers to each channel, is a poor solution. If an upstream channel has more stations on-line, the allocated slots per station will be fewer and the time spent in negotiate mode may be longer. Thus, dynamic channel assignment in upstream is necessary in order to balance the channel utilization.

We have a field, *assigned_channel,* in *Request_Table* which records the assigned channel for each on-line station. The number of cells transmitted in a channel can be calculated by summing up the *num_cells* of the entries having the same *assigned_channel* in *Request_Table.* The headend can rearrange the assignments of stations channels to balance the load according to the number of transmitted cells in the channel. The headend sends a control frame, *HE.balance*, to the re-arranged stations to notify them which channels to switch to.

3.3 Station positioning

One uniqueness of HFC is that stations can not listen directly to the upstream transmissions from the other stations; hence, they are incapable of detecting collisions and coordinating their transmissions all by themselves. What they can do is to listen and transmit on the downstream and allocated upstream, respectively.

Our station positioning is the key to coordinate the stations' transmissions. It aims to neutralize station's propagation offset so that cells arrive at the headend as though they were sent with zero propagation delay. With the back-to-back transmission at the headend, the upstream channel will performs more efficiency without wasting.

[1] As the complete run of tree walk algorithm is time-consuming, invitation procedure only invites those that are not the current on-line stations.

We explain the scheme by Fig. 3-3. In Fig. 3-3, X is the branching point of STU_i, and the difference of propagation delays between X to STU_i and X to STU_j is τ_{ij} ($\tau_{ij} = \tau_{jx} - \tau_{ix}$, where τ represents propagation delay). We can find out that the ideal situation at X can be modeled as

$$s_i+t_i+G = s_j+\tau_{ij}, \qquad (3\text{-}1)$$

where, s_i, $i = 1,2,.....N$, is the transmission starting time of STU_i, t_i is the allowed transmission duration for STU_i, G is the guard-band time between the consecutive data cells from different STUs. Scenario of this ideal situation is described in a clearer way by the timeline in Fig. 3-4. It is obvious that the headend needs to position the stations correctly in order to schedule transmissions in this way.

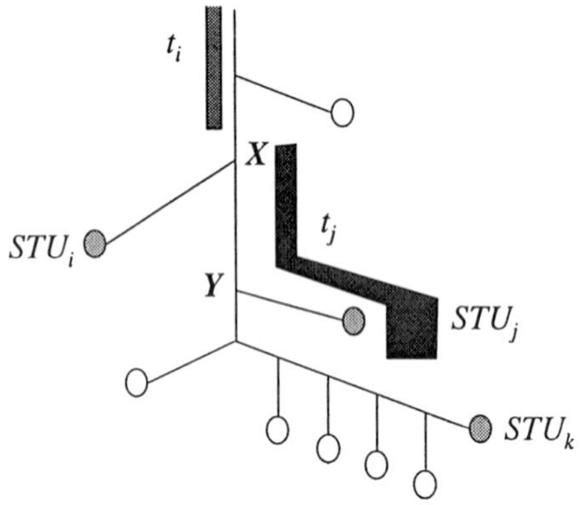

Figure 3-3 *The tree-and-branch topology with data transmission where STU_i has transmitted, and the STU_j is transmitting. STU_j is the predecessor of STU_k and the successor of STU_i.*

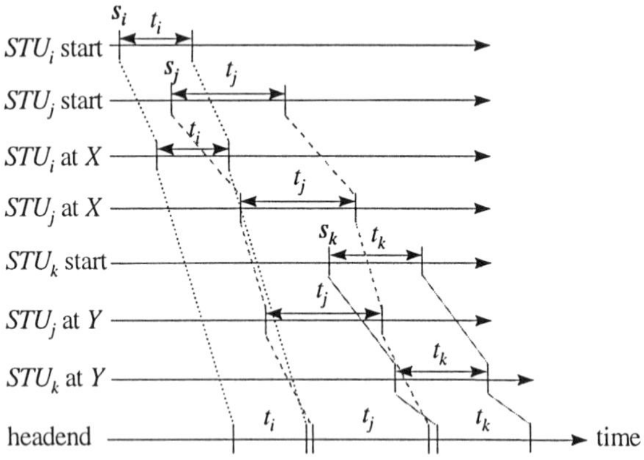

Figure 3-4 *The example timeline of pipelined data transmission. The convergence point of STU_i and STU_j is X; the convergence point of STU_j and STU_k is Y. We find that the successor starts its transmission before the end of its predecessor's transmission.*

The station positioning algorithm starts at headend.

Headend sends a *HE.position* frame to each station that has been included by the tree walk algorithm as on-line. It starts a timer for each transmitted *HE.position*. Upon receiving *HE.position,* the station modifies a special field, *check bit,* and throws back the *HE.position* frame immediately, either by hardware or firmware. Headend computes the *distance,* from the headend to the station, as

$$\text{distance} = \lfloor (t_{rec} - t_{tx} - t_{overhead}) \div 2 \rfloor \times c \qquad (3\text{-}2)$$

where t_{rec} is the time headend receives the returned *HE.position,* t_{tx} is the time headend transmits *HE.position*, $t_{overhead}$ is the transmission delay and possible processing delay, and c is the signal propagation speed. A 16-bits timing counter with units of 61 *ns* is sufficient for the CATV length specified by [10]. Headend sorts these stations in the increasing order of the distance.

3.4 Transmission scheduling

We are now ready to schedule the transmission starting time and duration of each station in this section. In order to help the headend to schedule the next cycle for the set of on-line stations, each station appends its buffer status, as requests shown in Table 3-1, at the end of its transmission duration.

Fields	Descriptions	Size (bytes)
b_i	number of best-effort cells at *STUi*	2
g_i/G_i	minimum/requested number of guaranteed cells at *STUi*	2/2
α_i/β_i	urgency of guaranteed/best-effort cells at STU_i	1/1

Table 3-1 *Station slot requests, appended in the final slot of its transmission.*

Requests have two priority levels in PCUP: best-effort and guaranteed. Slots are allocated according to the reported requests. Even if empty buffer is reported, headend allocates one slot to the station so that it can report its status in the coming cycle. If the required transmission time for the summation of the reported buffer queue lengths exceeds the *Cycle_Time*, it would allocate a proper number of slots according to the traffic urgency parameters (α_i and β_i). The headend allocates transmission quota, t_i, for station *i*, as described in equation 3-3. where *CBT* is the *Cycle_Time* and W_i is the guard-band time overhead. The situations for these six cases are:

- ***Case (1)***
  There is only best-effort traffic. Summation of all best-effort requests does not exceed the link capacity; thus, all of them can be served.
- ***Case (2)***
  There is only best-effort traffic. Summation of all best-effort requests exceeds the link capacity; thus, these best-effort cells are served partially and proportionally according to their urgency parameters, β_i.
- ***Case (3)***
  Summation of all best-effort and guaranteed services does not exceed the link capacity; thus, all of them can be served.
- ***Case (4)***
  Summation of all best-effort cells and minimum guaranteed cells can be served. The left-over capacity is used to serve as many, up to G_i-g_i for station *i,* guaranteed cells as possible.
- ***Case (5)***
  Summation of all minimum guaranteed services is less than the link capacity, but the remaining capacity is not enough for all the best-effort cells. Thus, these best-efforts cells are served partially according to their urgency parameters, β_i. β_i is used as the weight of station *i* in distributing the left-over capacity.
- ***Case (6)***
  The case is the worst situation where the link capacity is less than the summation of minimum guaranteed services. Thus, the guaranteed cells are served partially by their urgency parameters, α_i. α_i, again, is used as the weight to distribute the capacity.

$$t_i = \begin{cases} (1)\ if\ \Sigma(b_i + W_i) < CBT \\ \quad max(b_i, 1) + W_i, \\ (2)\ if\ \Sigma(b_i + W_i) > CBT \\ \quad max(CBT \times \beta_i / \Sigma\beta_i, 1) + W_i, \\ (3)\ if\ \Sigma(G_i + b_i + W_i) < CBT \\ \quad max(G_i + b_i, 1) + W_i, \\ (4)\ if\ \Sigma(g_i + b_i + W_i) < CBT < \Sigma(G_i + b_i + W_i) \\ \quad max(g_i + b_i, 1) + W_i + ((CBT - \Sigma(g_i + b_i)) \times (G_i - g_i) / \Sigma(G_i - g_i)) \\ (5)\ if\ (CBT - \Sigma b_i) < \Sigma(g_i + W_i) < CBT \\ \quad max((CBT - \Sigma(W_i + g_i)) \times \beta_i / \Sigma\beta_i, 1) + W_i + g_i, \\ (6)\ if\ \Sigma(g_i + W_i) > CBT \\ \quad max((CBT - \Sigma W_i) \times \alpha_i / \Sigma\alpha_i, 1) + W_i, \end{cases} \qquad (3\text{-}3)$$

After that, the headend then computes the transmission starting time, s_i, precisely as follows:

$$s_i = \sum_{j=1}^{i-1} t_j - \tau_i \qquad (3\text{-}4)$$

Then, headend can assign a proper starting time and transmission duration time by the allocation frame, *HE.schedule.*

Note that with the possible long propagation delay, the headend may need to pre-allocate the *HE.schedule* frame several cycles ahead, as illustrated in Fig. 3-5. The amount of this look-ahead has to be larger than the longest propagation delay. Since the propagation delay is usually small compared to the cycle time, 323 μs vs. 50 *ms* in some of our simulations, we need to look ahead only one cycle in most cases.

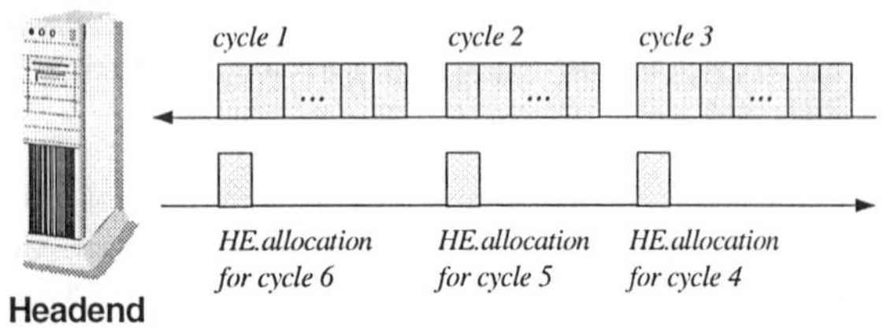

Figure 3-5 *Look-ahead allocation.*

3.5 Summary of PCUP

We now summarize the PCUP operations in Fig. 3-6 and Fig. 3-7. The pseudo code includes: station operations and headend operations.

CASE (*HE.schedule* received)
transmit cells in allocated time slots
request the buffer status of its own at the end of transmission
CASE (*HE.invitation* received)
run tree walk algorithm (if it is necessary to become on-line)
CASE (*HE.balance* received)
tune the receiver and transmitter frequency
CASE (*HE.position* received)
throw back the frame immediately

Figure 3-6 *Pseudo code of station operations.*

IF (time up of *Group_Reset_Timer*)
cycle membership control
station positioning
ELSE
seize a cell from input buffer
process the cell, upgrade *Request_Table,* ack to station
issue *HE.schedule* frame if all the on-line stations requesting are collected

Figure 3-7 *Pseudo code of headend operations.*

4. Simulation study

We show the numerical results in this section regarding loss ratio, throughput, access delay, cell delay variance and fairness. We first examine the HFC network configuration and traffic models in section 4.1 and section 4.2., followed by the simulation results of R-ALOHA, UniLINK and PCUP .

4.1 Network configuration

We assume the values of some configuration parameters based on the existing proposals [6, 7, 10, 15]:

- A 40 MHz band can be divided into multiple upstream channels. Each of them can be 1 MHz to 6 MHz wide and 1.6 Mbps to 10 Mbps in capacity. According to [7], we assume the upstream frequency range to be 8-26.5 MHz and 1.544, 2.048, 6 and 10 Mbps transmission rate per channel. By this assumption, 17, 14, 5 and 3 upstream channels can be used simultaneously. Since each branch serves 125 to 500 homes. That means each upstream channel is shared by about 30, 35, 100 and 167 subscribers respectively. The scale of network is assumed to be 80 km.
- Length of an upstream cell is assumed to be 424 bits (53 bytes), which is equal to 275 μs transmission time with the 1.544 Mbps transmission rate. Moreover, stations have a limited buffer size of 500 cells. Each station's hardware addresses is 48 bits.

4.2 Traffic models

Three types of traffic models, recommended by IEEE 802.14 cable TV protocols working group[24], are applied in the simulations. Traffic model A contains only ABR service. In traffic model B, the CBR applications contribute 50% traffic load, the rest 50% remains to be ABR. And in traffic model C, the VBR applications present 30% traffic, CBRs pump 30%, and the rest is for ABR service. Under these three traffic models, we examine the performance behavior of R_ALOHA, UniLINK and PCUP protocols.

4.3 Numerical results

4.3.1 System throughput

In Fig. 4-1 and Fig. 4-2, we can find that the throughput of R-ALOHA and UniLINK are not ideal under heavy traffic. This scenario is due to their contention bandwidth. In traffic model A, UniLINK behaves similarly to S-ALOHA. Since a UniLINK with ABR traffic has to contend the slots each time, it performs even worse than R-ALOHA. Because of PCUP's perfect centralized bandwidth scheduling, it achieves excellent channel throughput under various traffic types.

In Fig. 4-3, PCUP obtains higher throughput than the R-ALOHA and UniLINK no matter what the channel capacity is. At 1.544 Mbps channel bandwidth and 90% traffic load, PCUP has throughput 15% higher than UniLINK's, while at 10 Mbps channel bandwidth and the same traffic load, PCUP has throughput 37.6% higher than UniLINK's. UniLINK performs worse than PCUP due to the effect of contention bandwidth. But it works better than R-ALOHA since it provides isochronous bandwidth assignment and reservation scheme to support CBR and VBR traffic, respectively.

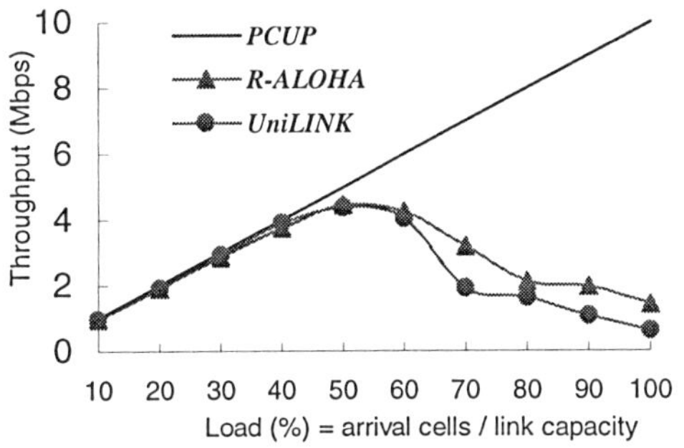

Figure 4-1 *Throughput of PCUP, R-ALOHA and UniLINK under traffic model A. The channel capacity is 10 Mbps.*

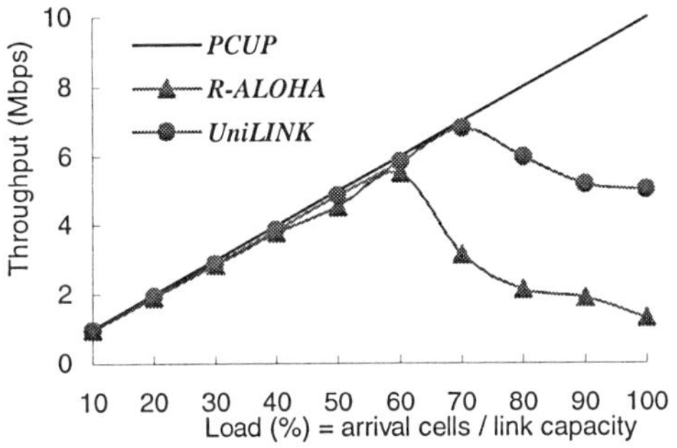

Figure 4-2 *Throughput of PCUP, R-ALOHA and UniLINK under traffic model B. The channel capacity is 10 Mbps.*

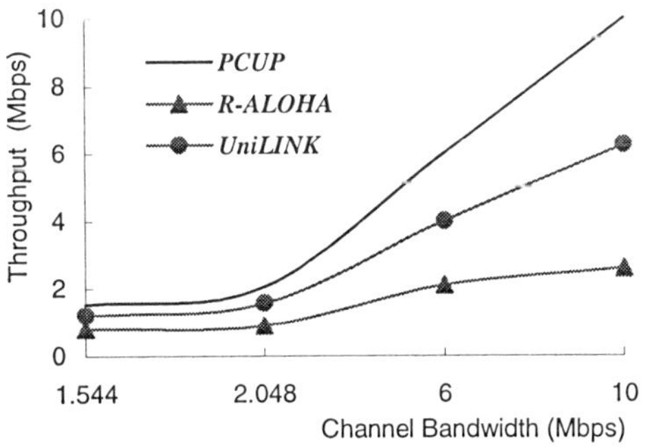

Figure 4-3 *Throughput of PCUP, R-ALOHA and UniLINK under different channel capacities. The traffic model is C and traffic load is 90%.*

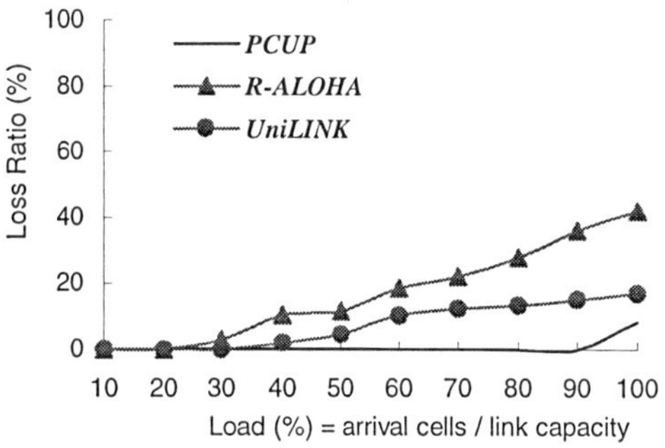

Figure 4-4 *ABR traffic lost ratio of PCUP, R-ALOHA and UniLINK under traffic model C.*

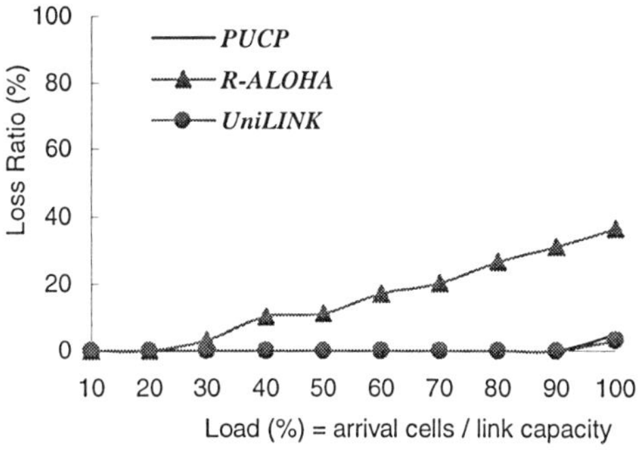

Figure 4-5 *CBR traffic lost ratio of PCUP, R-ALOHA and UniLINK under traffic model C.*

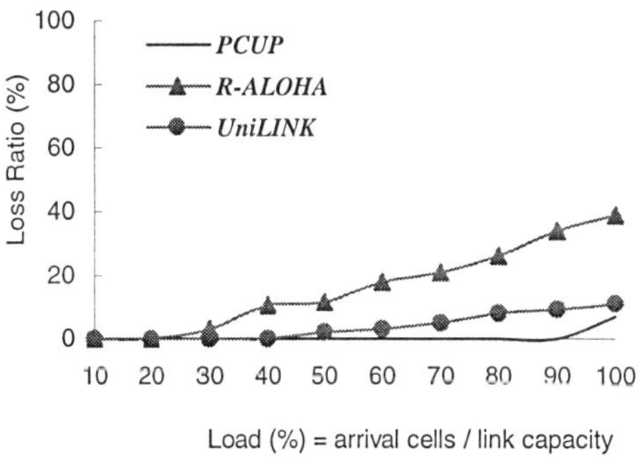

Figure 4-6 *VBR traffic lost ratio of PCUP, R-ALOHA and UniLINK under traffic model C.*

4.3.2 Loss ratio

After examining the numerical result of throughput, we investigate the channel performance in another aspect. Now we focus on the loss ratio, which is defined to be lost cells over arrival cells. From Fig. 4-4, it is obvious that PCUP does well than R-ALOHA and UniLINK over ABR traffic since R-ALOHA and UniLINK are contention-based in processing ABR traffic requests. In Fig. 4-5, we find that UniLINK has better performance than PCUP. UniLINK has only 3.1% loss ratio when the system is fully loaded, while PCUP has 5.1% loss ratio. This result is expected since UniLINK provides isochronous bandwidth over CBR traffic, while PCUP satisfies minimum CBR and VBR requests first. PCUP is still remarkable in dealing with CBR traffic. Comparing Fig. 4-6 with Fig. 4-4, the curves are similar, but UniLINK achieves lower loss ratio of VBR traffic. This scenario is due to applying reservation scheme over VBR traffic.

4.3.3 Access delay

In Fig. 4-7, R-ALOHA has larger access delay when traffic load is high. Because of higher collision ratio under heavy traffic, collided cells may be retransmitted many times. Thus access delay grows up accordingly. UniLINK performs well on access delay since CBR and ABR cells, which are generated in a frame interval, can access time slots in the same frame. In order to fully utilize channel bandwidth, PCUP gathers all bandwidth requests and schedules them together. So cells, which are generated in a frame interval, may not be transmitted in the same frame.

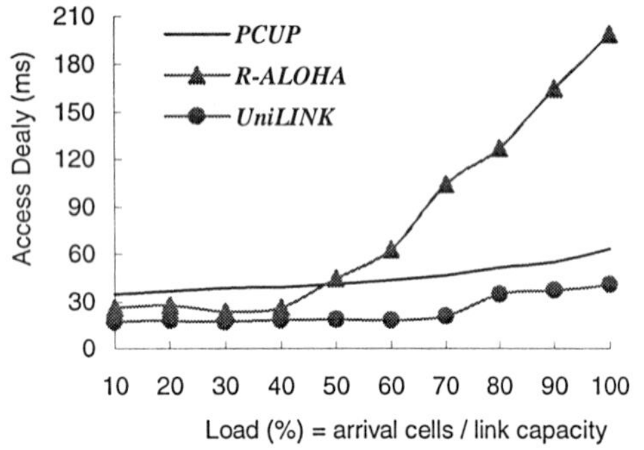

Figure 4-7 *Access delay of PCUP, R-ALOHA and UniLINK under traffic model A.*

4.3.4 Cell delay variance (CDV)

From Fig. 4-8 and Fig. 4-9, R-ALOHA can not achieve the QoS requirement. This result is due to its random access control and single-priority treatment to all traffic types. Because of providing isochronous bandwidth, UniLINK gets excellent CDV performance of CBR traffic. It also performs well over VBR traffic since they are transmitted on the specified regions. PCUP is still remarkable in CDV performance under high throughput.

4.3.5 Fairness

Fairness is another issue while considering performance of an interactive CATV MAC protocol. In Fig. 4-10, we randomly select 15 stations from 167 stations sharing the 10 Mbps channel to compare their access delay and throughput. These 15 stations are sorted by their propagation delays with station 1 being the nearest to the headend. It is obvious that R-ALOHA is unfair. The reason is that a station can monopolize a slot in every consecutive frame once it successfully captures a slot. Thus, other stations may starve and have higher access delay, when most slots are reserved. In contrast, if a time slot is successfully reserved for some station, the station receives a lower access delay. For example, station 12 has an average access delay of 80.8 ms, but station 8 has 229.8 ms. PCUP and UniLINK are fair and latency guaranteed. Since the bandwidth scheduling of PCUP takes the stations' offset into consideration, it results in larger access delay for farther stations and lower access delay for nearer stations.

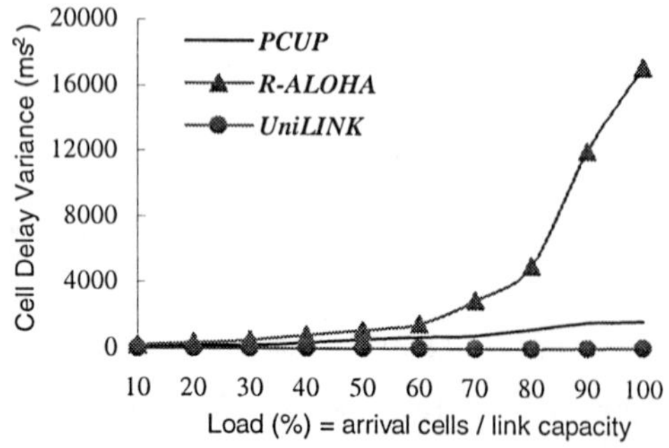

Figure 4-8 *CBR traffic cell delay variance(CDV) of PCUP, R-ALOHA and UniLINK under traffic model C.*

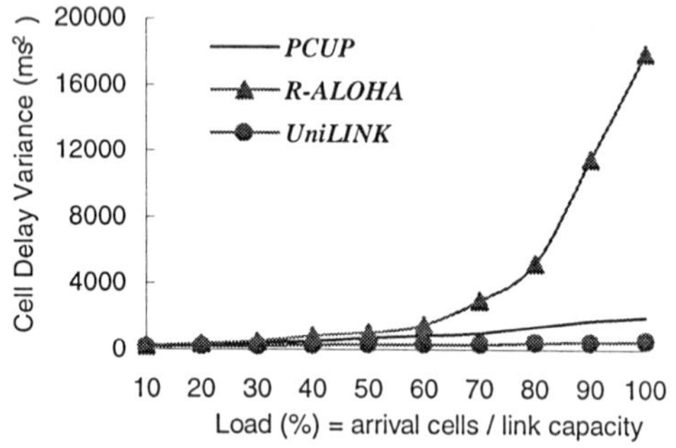

Figure 4-9 *VBR traffic cell delay variance(CDV) of PCUP, R-ALOHA and UniLINK under traffic model C.*

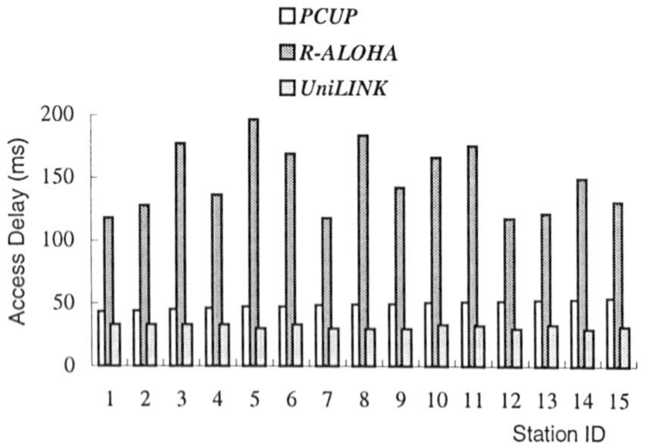

Figure 4-10 *Access delay of PCUP, R-ALOHA and UniLINK under traffic model C. The channel bandwidth is 10 Mbps and traffic load is 90%.*

5. Conclusions

To achieve interactive broadband multimedia services requirements over the HFC network, a MAC protocol with centralized and hybrid bandwidth allocation features is essential. A centralized protocol can fairly schedule the bandwidth and easily synchronize the stations. A hybrid bandwidth allocation MAC protocol can satisfy QoS requirements according for various traffic types. We have proposed a centralized and hybrid MAC protocol, PCUP, for IEEE 802.14 network. It provides integrated broadband services to the home and supports QoS for various types of traffic. PCUP's performance is contributed by several features: 1) a membership control which periodically updates the set of on-line stations and the channel usage status, 2) a synchronization process which neutralizes stations' propagation offsets, and 3) an efficient transmission scheduling algorithm to schedule, in each cycle, the transmission starting time and duration of each station so that cells appear to be pipelined, i.e. back-to-back, at the headend.

With station positioning and cyclic scheduling, PCUP achieves a pipelined perfect transmission scheduling, which results in throughput over 98%. When the load is below 95%, the throughput for PCUP is close to the theoretical bounds and no loss occurs. Concerning the random access protocols under medium to heavy load, re-transmitted traffic dominates and results in serious loss, which is not suitable for reliable and delay-sensitive transmission. Starvation in R-ALOHA raises the fairness problem. Although the UniLINK protocol achieves better latency and CDV performance, it obtains lower throughput due to the contention-based transmission of ABR traffic. The higher station complexity also raises STU cost.

Acknowledgments

The authors would like to express their thanks to Dr. Chein-Hsun Wang at Mentor Data System Inc. (Hsinchu Science-based Industrial Park, Taiwan) and Prof. Ying-Shih Way at Dept. of Communication Engineering, National Chiao Tung University (Hsinchu, Taiwan) for their thought-provoking discussion and suggestion during the course of this work.

6. References

[1] Ying-Dar Lin and Chia-Jen Wu, *"NII Community Network: Interactive CATV"*, International Conference on Computer Systems Technology for Industrial Applications (CSIA's), Hsinchu, Taiwan, Apr. 1996.

[2] Sam Churchill, *"Telecommunications Alliances"*, http://www.teleport.com/-~comc/cable8.html.

[3] Christine Blank, *"The FSN challenge: Large-scale interactive television"*, IEEE computer, pp. 9-13, May 1995.

[4] Chuck Carroll, *"Development of Integrated Cable/Telephony in the United Kingdom"*, IEEE communication magazine, pp. 48-60, August 1995.

[5] Bronwyn Fryer, *"Consumers Take Control"*, http://www.sgi.com/ion/Spring_95-/Orlando.html.

[6] William Pugh and Gerald Boyer, *"Broadband Access: Comparing Alternatives"*, IEEE communication magazine, pp. 34-46, Aug 1995.

[7] Digital Audio Visual Council, *"DAVIC 1.0 Specifications Revision 4.0"*, Sep 1995.

[8] Andre E. Bigras, *"Listen up! Digital audio is Canada cable's next step"*, International cable, pp. 28-34, Feb 1993.

[9] William Stallings, *"Handbook of Computer Communications Standards vol. 2 2nd. edition"*, Howard W. Sams & Company, 1990.

[10] IEEE 802.14, *"Cable TV MAC/PHY Protocol Working Group Functional Requirements"*, Oct 19, 1994.

[11] Fouad A. Tobagi, *"Multiaccess Protocol in Packet Communication Systems"*, IEEE transactions on communications, vol. com-28, no. 4, pp. 468-488, Apr 1980.

[12] Andrew S. Tanenbaum, *"Computer Networks 3rd. edition"*, Prentice Hall, 1996.

[13] W.R. Crowther, R. Rettbert, D. Walgen, S. Ornstein, and F. Heart, *"A System for Broadcast Communication: Reservation-ALOHA"*, in Proc. 6th HICSS, Univ. Hawaii, Honolulu, Jan 1973.

[14] Simon S. Lam, MEMBER, IEEE, *"Packet Broadcast Networks - A Performance Analysis of the R-ALOHA Protocol"*, IEEE transactions on computers, vol. c-29, no. 7, pp. 596-603, Jul 1980.

[15] Jon W. Eng and James F. Mollenauer, *"IEEE Project 802.14: Standard for Digital Convergence"*, IEEE communication magazine, pp. 20-23, May 1995.

[16] ATM Forum, *"ATM User-Network Interface Specfication Version 4.0"*, Nov 1995.

[17] John M. Ulm, LANcity Corp. *"A MAC proposal for 802.14"*, IEEE 802.14/95-134, draft proposal.

[18] William Stallings, *"Data and Computer Communications, 3rd edition"*, Macmillan, pp. 363-365, 1991.

[19] Morihisa momona, Shuntaro yamazaki, *"Framed Pipeline Polling for Cable TV Networks"*, March 1995, IEEE 802.14-96/076, draft proposal.

[20] Dolors Sala, John O. Limb, *"A Protocol for Efficient Transfer of Data over Fiber/Cable Systems"*, pp. 904-911, IEEE INFOCOM'96.

[21] James E. Dail, Miguel A. Dajer, Chia-Chang Li, Peter D. Magill, Curtis A. Siller, Jr., Kotikalapudi Sriram, and Norman A. Whitaker, *"Adaptive Digital Access Protocol : A MAC Protocol for Multiservice Broadband Access Networks"*, IEEE Communication Magazine, pp. 104-113, March 1996.

[22] Chatschik Bisdikian, Bill McNeil, Rob Norman and Ray Zeisz, *"MLAP : A MAC Level Access Protocol for the HFC 802.14 Network"*, IEEE Communication Magazine, pp. 114-121, March 1996.

[23] Frank Koperda, Bouchung Lin, *"First Phase Simulation for XDQRAP"*, IEEE 802.14-96/062, draft proposal.

[24] John Limb, David H. Su, *"Performance Evaluation Process for MAC Protocols"*, IEEE 802.14/96-083R2 document.

Multiple Priority CSMA-type Multichannel Local Area Network

Jia-Wei Liao[1], Jun-Yao Wang[1], Wei-Tsong Lee[2] and Ling-Yang Kung[1]

[1] Computer Lab., Department of Electrical Engineering,
National Cheng Kung University, 701, Tainan, Taiwan, R.O.C.
[2] Department of Electronic Engineering,
Nantai Institute of Technology, Tainan, Taiwan, R.O.C.

Abstract

In this paper, we will introduce a new network access protocol for CSMA-type multichannel local area network (MLAN). This new protocol has the capability of providing different network access priority among the various applications. From the earlier research, it has been shown that the CSMA-type MLAN is superior to a single channel on the equal network bandwidth. On the basis of the developed MLAN architecture, we construct a new network access protocol to provide multiple transmission priorities for various applications, e.q., text, voice, video, image, etc. This protocol is called Multiple-Priority Multichannel Local Area Network (MP-MLAN). The data transmission of MP-MLAN is collision-free, and we can find the throughput characteristics of MP-MLAN are higher and more stable than the conventional CSMA/CD or Multichannel CSMA/CD network from the analysis results. A queueing analysis model for representing the MP-MLAN protocol is established, and simulation results are also provided to evaluate the performance of this network.

1. Introduction

As the progress of network technologies and services, people can easily get a lot of useful information from computer network. One impact of this phenomenon is that there are more and more users willing to join the computer network, and this will quickly result in the insufficiency of current network bandwidth. At the same time, the data transmitted on the network is not only text-type. Currently, the most attractive service is to provide the users with friendly user interfaces of a network environment. In other words, These newly developed network services not only provide text-type information to the users, but also offer them with the information about image, voice, video, etc., and this becomes another challenge to conventional computer network.

In order to accommodate the evolution of computer network, there are two important issues in the modern network design: one is to increase the availability of network bandwidth, and the other is to support a multimedia transmission environment. One way to provide more available bandwidth is to increase the transmission speed of network, namely, it relates to high speed network technique. However, high speed circuit is more complex to design and more costly to implement. Another alternative to increase available bandwidth is to adopt multichannel technique. Multichannel network consists of many low speed subchannels, and the total bandwidth from the summation of each subchannel can be enough for the need of future bandwidth requirement. These subchannel circuits are easier to design and cost less than the high speed network.

In addition, CSMA-type multichannel Local Area Networks have recently attracted much attention in a way that it achieves higher throughput and transmission speed than corresponding single channel LANs with the same total bandwidth. The major benefit of using multichannel architecture is that the propagation delay-transmission time ratio of each subchannel in MLANs is lower than that of corresponding single channel LANs with the same aggregate bandwidth. Further advantage of MLANs is their expandability, such as, the possibility of modular growth following users' need, for example.

As for multimedia applications, each data type has different transmission requirements and problems in time constraint, bandwidth and synchronization, etc. However, all these requirements cannot be achieved in one single layer protocol. It is to believe that in order to deal with the various multimedia applications, we can provide a

This work was supported by National Science Council, Taiwan, ROC.

0-8186-7780-5/97 $10.00

transmission protocol with a priority mechanism and a global information about the network traffic distribution. The upper layer protocols can easily use this to establish a network environment suitable for multimedia transmission.

There are two common method to resolve priority transmission problem. One is to control retransmission back-off time. Another method suitable for multichannel network is proposed by Ko[5]. It simply uses the number of idle subchannels to provide a priority transmission. However, both solutions can only deal with the different transmission order among different type of data, such as the voice has the higher transmission priority than video, and video is superior than image and text. As for the transmissions with equal priority, they cannot prevent the occurrence of collisions.

In this paper, we propose a new CSMA-type multichannel protocol with multiple transmission priorities. This protocol is named Multiple-Priority Multichannel Local Area Network, MP-MLAN. This new protocol not only provides a priority transmission between the services of different data, but also has a strictly FIFO strategy to the transmissions with equal priority. Furthermore, MP-MLAN protocol has the ability to collect traffic distribution information for all network terminals. Each terminal can easily choose a subchannel with less load to transmit the data. Therefore, MP-MLAN can provide a collision-free and low latency transmission network environment.

Another interesting topic of multichannel study is about the number of transceivers to be used on a network terminal. In recent studies, only one fixed transceiver on a common channel and one tunable transceiver for the other subchannels are utilized[6][7]. Although these methods can probably achieve some economic benefits, the availability of bandwidth to a terminal is limited in just one subchannel even there are other idle subchannels. In MP-MLAN protocol, we assume that each terminal has a fixed transceiver on every subchannel, and the terminals can fully use the total bandwidth of the network.

A simplified queueing mode of MP-MLAN protocol has been constructed. Both the programming simulation and numerical analysis are also provided to evaluate the performance of this protocol. From the simulation and analysis results, we can find that MP-LAN not only supports the priority transmission but also has a high and stable throughput characteristic under heavy network load. The MP-LAN protocol actuarially overcomes the insufficiency of the traditional CSMA-type LANs and MLANs.

This paper is organized as follows. Section 2 describes the MP-LAN architecture and protocols. In section 3 we present a simplified queueing model for MP-LAN protocol. The analysis of MP-MLAN queueing model is shown in section 4. The analytical and simulation results are made in section 5. Finally, we conclude this paper in section 6.

2. MP-MLAN protocol

In order to understand the operation of the protocol, we first have to examine the structure of it. This network protocol is assumed to be able to support *P* priorities. We suppose that it consists of *N* terminals attached to a single channel. The channel is logically divided into *M* subchannels. Physically, however, it needs not be separated. The subchannels are obtained by equally dividing the bandwidth of the channel. Since all terminals are attached to the channel, all the terminals, therefore, are attached to each subchannel. A simple illustration of the logical structure of MP-MLAN is shown in Figure 2-1.

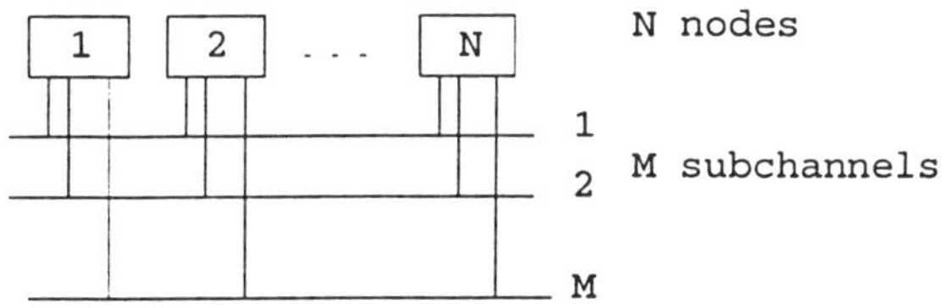

Fig. 2-1. Logical Architecture of MP-MLAN

There are 2 types of subchannels -- scheduling subchannel and data subchannel. The scheduling subchannel is used only for delivering data transmission information such as the selected data subchannel and the data priority. The data subchannel is simply for data transmission. By default, *Subchannel M* is assigned to be the scheduling subchannel.

A data subchannel status table is obtained by each terminal. It shows the current load of each subchannel with different priorities. This table, shown in Table 2-1, is updated every time data gets transmitted. The status tables of all terminals have to be identical and concurrently updated. The first column of the table labels different data subchannels from *1* to *M-1*. The buffer status of each subchannel is recorded in the second column. Suppose that each transmission buffer can only hold one data packet at a time. "*B*" denotes busy, indicating that there is already a packet in the transmission buffer. "*I*" denotes idle, indicating that the buffer is empty and is available for new transmission request. The rest of the column headings are simply different priorities labeled from *1* to *P*. We assume that the packet with *Priority 1* has the highest priority to access the network. The numbers in the table matrix indicates the number of waiting packets with associated priority having announced the access request to the particular data subchannel. For example, there are one *Priority 2* and two *Priority 1* packets waiting to access *Subchannel 1*.

Subchanne Lable	Transmit Buffer Status	Priority P	Priority P-1	....	Priority 2	Priority 1
1	B	0	0	....	1	2
2	B	1	0	....	2	1
3	I	0	0	....	1	2
⋮		⋮	⋮	....	⋮	
M-1	I	0	1	....	2	1

Table 2-1. Subchannel Status Table

Each terminal is also equipped with a transmission counter and a transceiver at each data subchannel. The transmitting and receiving buffers are located in the transceiver. The counter is implemented to differentiate the order of packets with equal priority in the same subchannel. This operation will be explained later in this section.

The operation of this protocol is simply to select a data subchannel with the least traffic load to transmit packets with higher priority. This is to avoid contention and delay of packet transmission. The operation starts with the selection of data subchannel.

When the packet with *Priority n* comes to request an access to the other terminal, the transmitting terminal will first assign a subchannel with the least load for transmission. This assignment is determined by using the subchannel selection algorithm to search the status table. The subchannel selection algorithm is as follows.

Subchannel selection algorithm

{
For i = 1 to M-1
    Find the subchannel with the empty transmit buffer and the minimum $U_i(n)$
    If there are multiple subchannels with the same minimum $U_i(n)$
        Find the subchannel with the minimum $L_i(n)$
        If there are several subchannels with the same minimum $L_i(n)$
            Random select a subchannel with the minimum $U_i(n)$ ***and the minimum*** $L_i(n)$
            Select subchannel i
        Else
            Select subchannel i
        End if
    Else
        Select subchannel i
    End if
End for
}

From the algorithm, "*i*" denotes the subchannel being selected. The first step is to find the subchannel with highest efficiency for transmission. To do this, the terminal has to go through the status table from *Subchannel 1* to *Subchannel M-1*. $U_i(n)$ denotes the sum of the numbers of waiting packets with the priorities greater than or equal to *n* on *Subchannel i*. Theoretically, it is more efficient to assign a subchannel not only with empty buffer but also with the least waiting packets of higher priorities. As shown in the algorithm, if there are multiple subchannels with such characteristics, the terminal then finds the subchannel with the minimum $L_i(n)$ which denotes the sum of the numbers of waiting packets with the priorities less than or equal to *n* on *Subchannel i*. This is to insure that the selected subchannel has the least traffic load.

After the *Subchannel i* is selected, the terminal then is ready to broadcast the scheduling packet onto the scheduling subchannel. The scheduling packet contains the information of the selected *Subchannel i* and the *Priority n* of the data packet. The size of it is much smaller than the data packet. Since the scheduling subchannel only uses the regular protocol for transmission, it is very likely for collision to happen. Once the collision occurs and the scheduling packet is lost, the terminal has to repeat the subchannel selection procedure because the status table might already be updated during the loss of its original announcement.

Once the scheduling packet has been transmitted successfully, every terminal is informed that there is a request of a data packet with *Priority n* waiting to access the selected *Subchannel i*. Every terminal then adds *1* to the number correlated to *Priority n* and *Subchannel i* on the status table. Following this modification of the table, the terminal that successfully broadcast the scheduling packet would put the data packet onto the transmission buffer in the transceiver of the selected *Subchannel i*.

As mentioned earlier, the transmission counter is located in the transceiver of each data subchannel. The counter value determines the order of packet transmission with the same priority on the same data subchannel. The value, $C(i)$, must be either 0 or a positive integer. When $C(i)$ equals to 0, it means that the terminal has no transmission request on this data *Subchannel i*. When a terminal has a packet with *Priority n* to transmit in *Subchannel i*, the counter value is set to equal to 1 plus the number of the waiting packet correlated to the status table of the terminal labeled *Priority n* and the *Subchannel i*. The packet can only be transmitted when $C(i)$ equals to 1, meaning there is no any higher priority packets requesting to use the same subchannel. However, if the value is $C(i)$ which greater than 1, then the terminal cannot use this subchannel to transmit this packet even the subchannel is idle. This counter value $C(i)$ is subtracted by 1 every time when the terminal receives a broadcast information that a packet with the same priority is received by other terminals. After receiving $C(i)-1$ broadcasting information, the value is counted down from $C(i)$ to 1, and this terminal finally gains its permission to transmit the packet in its buffer.

It is possible, however, that there are requests with higher priorities waiting to access this *Subchannel i*. In order to achieve the transmission priority, the packets with higher priorities still should be transmitted first. To differentiate the priority orders, we let $V_i(n)$ equals to the summation of all the numbers of waiting packets with priorities higher than n requesting to use *Subchannel i*. The packets with *Priority n* cannot be transmitted if $V_i(n)$ is greater than 0. Even though $C(i)$ is 1 and the terminal is ready to transmit the packet with *Priority n*, it is necessary to wait for a period of time called idle detection time. It is to see if there is any arriving request of higher priorities. If there is, then the packet with *Priority n* has to wait until the transmission of higher priority has completed. The algorithm of this counter operation is as follows.

Transmission algorithm

```
{
If C(i) > 0 and channel i is sensed idle
        Wait for a idle detection time
        If Vi(n)=0 and C(i)=1
                Transmit buffer send the packet on the
                        channel i
        Else
                Wait for receiving a data packet
                If R(i) = n
                        Let C(i) = C(i) - 1
                End if
        End if
End if
}
```

3. Queueing model for MP-MLAN protocol

A simplified queueing model for MP-MLAN protocol is presented in Fig. 3-1. This queueing model consists of three sections: generation section, contention section and transmission section.

1) The generation section has infinite numbers of user terminals. We assume that the packets of each priority are generated by a single packet generator with total packet arrival rate equal to G.
2) The contention section can be seen as a single server queue where all the packets from the generation section are contended on scheduling subchannel for broadcasting their scheduling packets.
3) The transmission section is composed of $M-1$ single server priority queueing models. We assume that the length of each priority queue is limited.

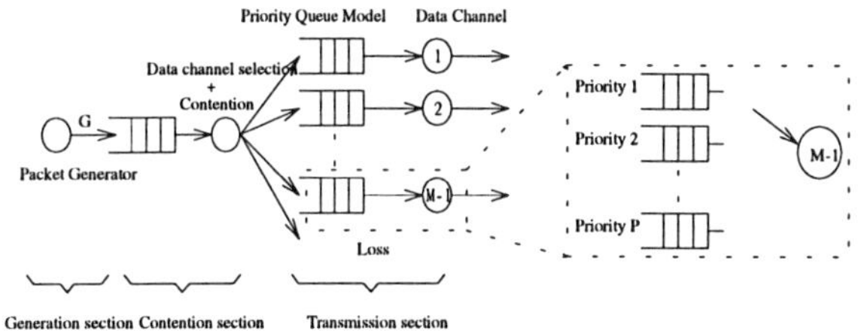

Fig. 3-1. The Queueing Model for MP-MLAN Protocol

We consider that the MP-MLAN has infinite population, where the number of terminals, N, is infinitely large. We assume the total traffic forms a Poission process with the packet arrival rate G. It is possible that the packet arrival rate G may be very large, and the traffic load may exceed the total network bandwidth. In order to prevent the number of waiting packets on data subchannel to become infinite, we assume that for each data subchannel, it can only accommodate a finite number of waiting packets. If all the data subchannels have the maximum waiting packets, then the newly arrival packet will be lost. After contention section, the packets will be uniformly distributed into data subchannels. These packets on all data subchannel are transmitted in sequence according to the packet priority and the counter value. Then we consider that the transmission section is composed of $M-1$ single server priority queueing model.

4. Analysis

We assume T_0 is the time needed to transmit a packet on a single channel with channel bandwidth W. As for the MP-MLAN with the equal bandwidth W. Let T_i be the packet transmission time on the ith subchannel, and W_i be bandwidth of the ith subchannel bandwidth, where $T_i=M \times T_0$, $W_i=W/M$. Let A be the channel end-to-end propagation delay time. Let the normalized propagation for the entire channel be a_0, and the normalized propagation delay for subchannel be a_i, where $a_0=A/T_0$ and $a_i=A/T_i$. Finally we assume that, the size of scheduling packet is $1/L$ to a data packet, and the maximum waiting packets in each data subchannel is K.

4.1 Contention section analysis

The throughput expressions, 4.1, 4.2, 4.3, of a single CSMA/CD channel is obtained from [8]. In this expression, the packet transmission time T_0 is chosen as 1. This is equivalent to expressing time in units of $T0$. Let a denote the normalized propagation delay; b denotes the normalized jamming period. $E[I]$ is the expected value of channel idle time. $E[B]$ denotes the expected value of channel busy time, and $E[Y]$ is defined as Expected value of vulnerable time period.

$$E[I]=\frac{1}{G} \tag{4.1}$$

$$E[B]=e^{-aG}(1+a)+(1-e^{-aG})(2a+b+E[Y]) \tag{4.2}$$

$$E[Y]=\frac{1}{G}-\frac{ae^{-aG}}{1-e^{-aG}} \tag{4.3}$$

The scheduling subchannel as mentioned, uses CSMA/CD protocol to broadcast the scheduling packet. We can use the previous equations, substituting the channel variables for the scheduling subchannel variable with subscript *i*. Please notice that the normalized scheduling packet transmission time, *M/L*, is used to substitute the 1 in equation 4.2. The equations are as follows:

$$E_i[I]=\frac{1}{G} \tag{4.4}$$

$$E_i[B]=e^{-a_iG}(\frac{M}{L}+a_i)+(1-e^{-a_iG})(2a_i+b_i+E_i[Y]) \tag{4.5}$$

$$E_i[Y]=\frac{1}{G}-\frac{a_ie^{-a_iG}}{1-e^{-a_iG}} \tag{4.6}$$

The probability of scheduling subchannel sensed to be idle, P_{si}, can be obtained as shown below.

$$P_{si}=\frac{E_i[I]+E_i[Y]}{E_i[I]+E_i[B]} \tag{4.7}$$

The probability of a successful broadcasting on scheduling subchannel, $P_0(a_i)$, represents the probability of no having scheduling packet being transmitted during the vulnerable period.

$$P_0(a_i)=e^{-a_iG} \tag{4.8}$$

After obtaining the equations above, the traffic for the contention section, ρ, can be calculated as below:

$$\rho=G\times P_0(a_i)\times P_{si} \tag{4.9}$$

4.2 Transmission section analysis

After the contention section, the traffic will be uniformly distributed among each data subchannel. The traffic load to every data subchannel, ρ', is

$$\rho'=\rho\times\frac{1}{M-1} \tag{4.10}$$

It is possible that each priority queue will be blocked when the subchannel is heavily loaded. Let P_B denote the blocking probability of priority queue, which is obtained from[9]. In equation 4.12, π_0 denotes the probability of having no packet in priority queue during the steady state. The actual load, ρ'', offered to each data subchannel can be obtained as below:

$$\rho''=\rho'\times(1-P_B) \tag{4.11}$$

$$P_B=1-\frac{1}{\pi_0+\rho'} \tag{4.12}$$

4.3 Throughput analysis

After we know the actual load of each data subchannel, ρ'', we can calculate the total system throughput easily. Moreover, it is necessary to take the scheduling subchannel bandwidth into consideration. The network throughput, *S*, is as follows:

$$S=\frac{\rho''\times(M-1)}{M} \tag{4.13}$$

4.4 Delay analysis

Packet transmission delay on MP-MLAN can be broken down into four parts: scheduling time, queueing waiting time, propagation delay and packet transmission time.

1) The scheduling delay

Let T_r be the normalized retransmission delay time. The normalized scheduling delay, T_s, can be calculated as:

$$T_s=(\frac{1}{P_{si}\times P_0(a_i)\times(1-P_B)}-1)\times T_r+a_i+\frac{M}{L} \tag{4.14}$$

2) Queueing delay

For every data subchannel, all the waiting packets are transmitted in sequence according to the packet priority and the transmission counter value. Then the packet transmission on the data subchannel forms a M/D/1//K priority queueing model. Here we assume that the traffic from contention section consists of all different priority packets. Let θ_n be the ratio of packet with *Priority n*. Then the actual load of *Priority n* offered to each subchannel,

ρ_n , can be defined as

$$\rho_n'' = \theta_n \times \rho'' \tag{4.15}$$

$$\sum_{n=1}^{P} \theta_n = 1 \tag{4.16}$$

Let λ_n be the arrival rate of the packet with *Priority n* , and $\overline{X^2}$ be the second moment of service time. The formula for the queueing waiting time of the packet with *Priority n* can be found in [10]:

$$W_n = \frac{R}{(1-\rho_P-\rho_{P-1}-\ldots-\rho_{n+1})(1-\rho_P-\rho_{P-1}-\ldots-\rho_n)} \tag{4.17}$$

$$R = \frac{1}{2}\sum_{n=1}^{P} \lambda_n \overline{X^2} \tag{4.18}$$

3) Propagation delay

The normalized propagation delay is defined as a_i

4) Packet transmission delay

The normalized packet transmission delay is defined as M

Finally, the total transmission delay, D_n, of the packet with *Priority n* can be obtained as:

$$D_n = T_s + W_n + a_i + M$$

5. Analysis and simulation results

The throughput comparison of analytical and simulation results for MP-MLAN is shown in Fig. 5-1. We select different numbers of subchannels *M=5,10,15* receptively. Assume that the normalized propagation delay a_0 is 0.05, and the size of data packet equals it of 50 scheduling packets. The maximum number of waiting packets on each subchannel is assumed to be 20.

In Fig. 5-1, we can find that the analytical results are very close to the simulation results, and the error is below 1%. Moreover, the maximum throughput archived in MP-MLAN by two subchannels is 0.5. It is due to one of the two subchannels being selected as scheduling subchannel. Therefore, the available bandwidth for data transmission is only half of total network bandwidth.

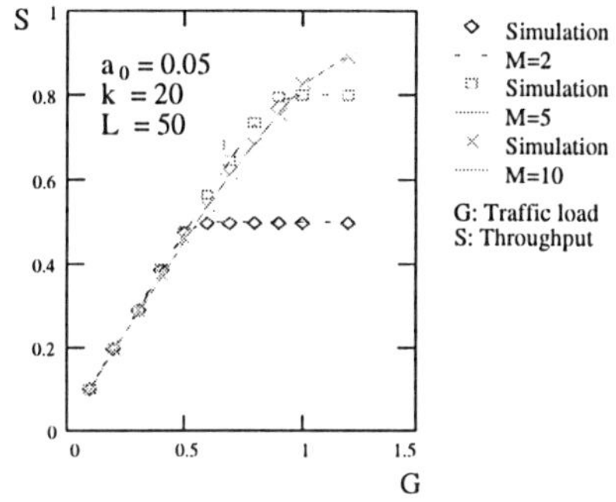

Fig. 5-1. Simulation and Analytical Results Comparison of MP-MLAN

Throughput characteristics of various traffic load ***G*** in MP-MLAN is presented in Fig. 5-2. From this figure, we can find that MP-MLAN remains a very stable throughput characteristic under a heavy network load. Additionally, we observe that dividing the total bandwidth into more subchannels not only can achieve much higher network throughput but also enhances the tolerance of heavier traffic overload.

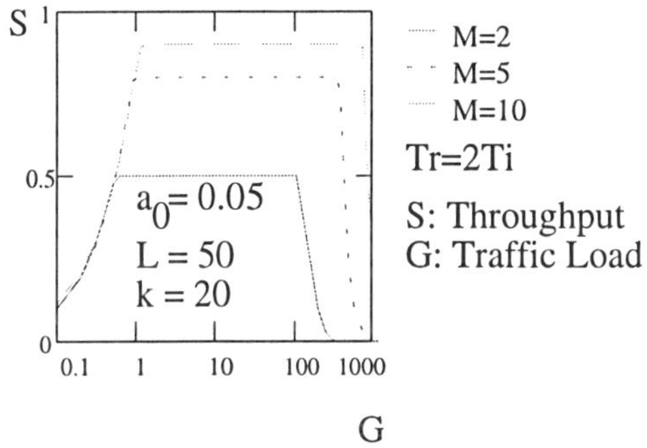

Fig. 5-2. MP-MLAN Throughput Characteristics

Fig 5-3 is the delay-throughput characteristics of MP-MLAN. We assume that it supports four different priority transmissions, and the ratios of each priority, θ_1, θ_2, θ_3, θ_4 are 10%, 10 %, 40%, and 40% respectively. We also assume that the number of total subchannels ***M*** is 10.

From Fig. 5-3 we observe that when the traffic load is little, all the packets can be transmitted with little delay which is very close to the packet transmission time. As the network load gets heavier, the packets with higher transmission priority also have a lower transmission delay than other packets with lower priorities. This phenomenon is being illustrated in the graph. When S equals to 0.3, for example, the delay time of all four priorities are similar and low. On the other hand, when S equals to 0.8, although the delay time increases, the packets with higher priority have lower delay time than the ones with lower priority.

Therefore, we know that MP-MLAN indeed supports priority transmission.

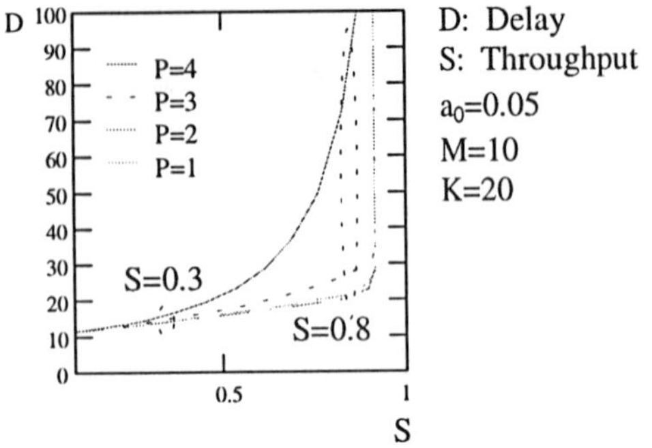

Fig. 5-3. Delay-Throughput Characteristic of MP-MLAN for Four Priority Packets

The throughput of five different network access protocols is compared in Fig. 5-4. These five protocols are : MP-MLAN, CSMA, CSMA/CD, M-CSMA-IC, M-CSMA/CD-IC.

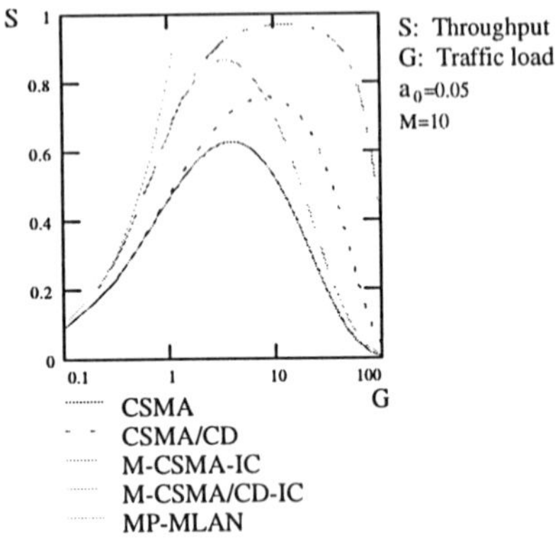

Fig. 5-4. Throughput Comparison for Five Different Network Access Protocols

In Fig. 5-4 we can find that MP-MLAN has higher throughput when the traffic load is as small as *G=0.5*, for example. As the network being heavily overloaded, MP-MLAN stabilizes its throughput at a high constant level. Even when *G* equals to 100, MP-MLAN still demonstrates the highest and the most stable throughput close to 0.9, unlike the other protocols having poor throughput.

In order to see how MP-MLAN can support video and audio transmission, we use Simscript II.5 to simulate the network transmission. Fig. 5-5 and Fig. 5-6 show the delay-load characteristic of the MP-MLAN with ten subchannels, *M=10*, and four priority transmission, *P=4*. Here we assume that the total network bandwidth is *100 Mbit/s*, and each subchannel has *10 Mbit/s* transmission bandwidth. We define *Priority 1* to be for audio applications with *16 bits, 44.1 KHz* sampling rate. So it requires the bandwidth of $44.1K \times 16 = 705.6$ *Kbit/s*. We also define *Priority 2* to be for video applications with *24 bits*, 640×480 resolution and 30 picture/sec. In addition, we suppose that the video picture has 1:30 compression ratio by using MPEG, then it consumes the bandwidth of *7.4 Mbit/s*. As for *Priority 3* and *Priority 4* packets, we assume that they are related to the general type of data with Poission arrival. Here we assume each data packet is 1000 bits, and the packet transmission time on data subchannel will be 100 μs.

In Fig. 5-5, we assume that there are one video and one audio applications being transmitted, and the applications would consume about 8% of total network bandwidth. Comparatively, in Fig. 5-6, the network supports five video and five audio applications, and 40% of total network bandwidth would be consumed. The other traffic load in network is assumed to be general type of data equally divided into *Priority 3* and *Priority 4*. The traffic load, *G*, consists of packets of each priority.

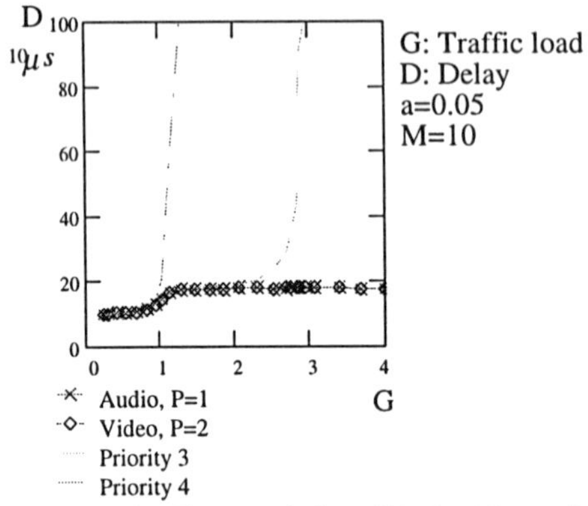

Fig. 5-5. The Characteristics of Delay Time with One Audio and one Video Applications

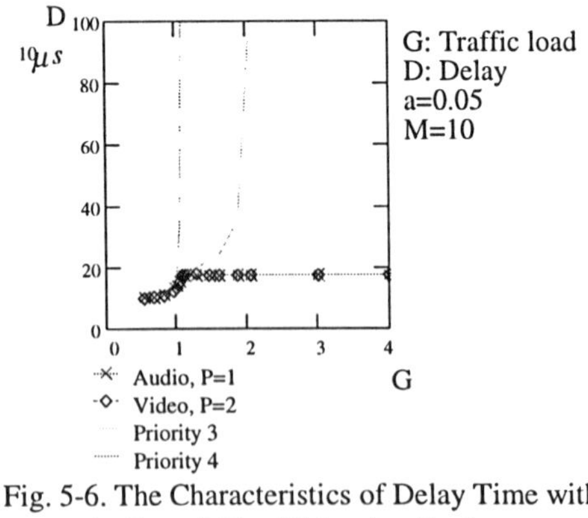

Fig. 5-6. The Characteristics of Delay Time with Five Audio and Five Video Applications

The difference of these two graphs focuses on the

relationship of the delay time with different priorities and different channel bandwidth consumption. From both Fig. 5-5 and Fig. 5-6 we can find that as the traffic load increase, the video and audio applications will not be affected by the low priority traffics. .These high priority packets can be transmitted with a bounded delay about 200 μs when the network is heavily loaded.

Due to the different numbers of high priority applications supported by the simulations with two different assumptions, the channel bandwidth consumption varies. As the number grows from one to five, more bandwidth is occupied by the higher priority applications. Therefore, the availability of remaining bandwidth for *Priority 3* and *Priority 4* reduces. The subchannel would reach the state of saturation with less traffic load of *Priority 3* packets. The infinite delay of *Priority 4* packets is similar in both situations because there is not much bandwidth available for low priority when the network is overloaded.

6. Conclusion

In this paper, a multichannel network protocol with multiple transmission priority, MP-MLAN, is presented. A queueing model is also constructed evaluate this protocol. After analyzing the proposed model, this new protocol is shown to have the following benefits:

1) The subchannel selection algorithm and transmission algorithm is fully decentralized, MP-MLAN can be used in a distribution network system.
2) MP-MLAN provide a collision-free transmission environment which prevents the unnecessary waste of channel bandwidth causing by collision.
3) MP-MLAN supports a priority transmission scheme for different media transmission.
4) MP-MLAN provides a FIFO transmission strategy among packets with the same priority.
5) From the analysis results we can find that MP-MLAN has a low delay characteristics under slight load, and a high and stable throughput characteristics under heavy load.
6) MP-MLAN provides a global traffic information, for the upper layer protocols to implement a more suitable transmission environment for multimedia or real-time transmission.

Moreover, we use a simulation program to see how the MP-MLAN can support voice and video packet transmissions. From the simulation results we can find that the transmission delay of these applications is bounded at a low value while the network is overloaded.

MP-MLAN uses multiple low-speed and easy design subchannels to archive a high bandwidth network environment. It also provides a priority transmission for different media applications, and a FIFO transmission strategy for the equal priority packets. In summary, MP-MLAN equips a high and stable throughput characteristics under heavy network load, and this indeed overcomes the insufficiency of other CSMA-type network protocols.

Reference

[1] R. M. Metcalfe and D.R. Boggs, "Ethernet: Distributed Packet Switching for Local Computer Network," Commun. ACM, Vol. 19, pp. 642-647, July 1976.

[2] "Local area network standards: Carrier Sense Multiple Access with Collision Detection (CSMA/CD) and Physical Layer Specifications," ANSI/IEEE Standard 802.3, 1985.

[3] M. Ajmone Marsan and D. Roffinella, "Multichannel Local Area Network Protocols," IEEE Journal on Selected Areas in Communications, pp. 885-897, Nov. 1983.

[4] D. H. C. DU, S. P. Chang, and G. Subbaro, "Multiple Packet Multiple Channel CSMA/CD Protocols for Local Area Networks," IEEE INFOCOM '89, Ottawa, pp.163-172, 1989.

[5] C. C. Ko, K. M. Lye and W. C. Wong, "Simple Priority Scheme for Multichannel CSMA/CD Local Area Network," IEE Proceedings, Vol. 137, Pt. I, No. 6, pp. 365-370, Dec. 1990.

[6] I. M. I. Habbab, M. Kavehard and C. E. W. Sundberg, "Protocols for Very High-Speed Optical Fiber Local Area Networks Using A Passive Star Topology," Journal of Lightwave Technology, Vol. LT-5, No.12, pp. 1782, Dec. 1987.

[7] N. Mehravari, "Performance and Protocol Improvements for Very High Speed Optical Fiber Local Area Networks," Journal of Lightwave Technology, Vol. 8, No. 4, pp.520-530, Apr. 1990.

[8] F. A. Tobagi and V. B. Hunt, "Performance Analysis of Carrier Sense Multiple Access with Collision Detection," Computer Networks, Vol. 4, Nov. 1980.

[9] T. Hideaki, "Queueing Analysis: a foundation of performance evaluation," Vol. 2, pp.198-203, Elsevier Science Pub. Co., 1991.

[10] Wolff, R. W, "Possion arrivals see time averages," Operations Research, Vol. 30, No. 2, pp.223-231, 1982.

Group Allocation Multiple Access with Collision Detection

Andrew Muir J.J. Garcia-Luna-Aceves
Computer Engineering Department
University of California
Santa Cruz, CA 95064

Abstract

The Group Allocation Multiple Access with Collision Detection (GAMA/CD) protocol for scheduling variable-length packet transmissions in a local area network is specified and analyzed. GAMA/CD provides the advantages of both TDMA and CSMA/CD by maintaining a dynamically-sized cycle that varies in length depending on the network load; each cycle is composed of a contention period and a group-transmission period. During the contention period, a station with one or more packets to send competes for membership in the transmission group. Once a member of the transmission group, a station is able to send data without collision during each cycle; as long as a station has data to send, it maintains its position in the group. This can be viewed as either allowing stations to "share the floor" in an organized manner, or as establishing frames that are not synchronized on a slot-basis and vary their length dynamically based on demand. Both the throughput and the delay of GAMA/CD are presented and analyzed. To validate our analysis, the results of both models are compared to the throughput and delay produced by a simulation of GAMA/CD.

1 Introduction

Such medium access control (MAC) protocols as CSMA/CD [10] that require a station to contend for the ability to send each data packet of a message cannot provide performance guarantees. This is a significant problem for real-time multimedia applications requiring long-term connections and bounded jitter. Many strategies have been proposed that can provide some form of performance guarantees in the MAC protocols of LANs; these include: fixed assignment (e.g., TDMA, FDMA), polling, token passing, and dynamic reservation protocols. However, each of these strategies can be improved in terms of its performance or implementation complexity.

This work was supported in part by DARPA under Grant DAAB07-95-C-D157.

In TDMA, the average delay experienced by a station that has been assigned a data slot is constant, regardless of the channel load; this is good if the load is high, but if the load is low the delay is longer than necessary, unless data slots can be quickly reallocated to the active stations. Polling requires a central station to direct the transmission of the other stations, and wastes polling time when the majority of stations are idle. A token passing network does not require a central station, but must deal with cases in which the token is lost or duplicated, which increases the complexity of the protocol. Dynamic reservation protocols are based on the premise that "control frames" can be defined in which stations can reserve the right to use slots in "data frames," the length of the control frames may be fixed or variable, but it is a function of the number of stations in the system. A control frame whose size is defined by the number of stations complicates the addition and deletion of stations and does not scale very well.

We describe and analyze a new MAC protocol for LANs, which we call Group Allocation Multiple Access with Collision Detection (GAMA/CD). GAMA/CD provides a trade off between the complexity and overhead needed to provide some levels of performance guarantees to certain users, and the performance perceived by bursty users. GAMA/CD provides dynamic reservations of the channel and its implementation complexity is comparable with that of CSMA/CD protocols.

GAMA/CD builds a dynamically-sized "cycle" that grows and shrinks depending upon traffic demand. Each cycle consists of a contention period of up to a maximum duration that is independent of the number of user stations, and a group-transmission period during which one or more stations transmit data packets without collisions. A position in the transmission group is allocated to an individual station, and a station can continue to transmit in this position as long

0-8186-7780-5/97 $10.00 © 1997 IEEE

as it has data to send.

We believe that GAMA/CD combines the best features of CSMA/CD and contention-free protocols like TDMA. On the one hand, like CSMA/CD, GAMA/CD is very efficient under light load. On the other hand, GAMA/CD is much more stable under heavy loads than CSMA/CD, because it permits stations in the transmission group to send packets independently of new requests for additions to the transmission group. GAMA/CD ensures that, once a station has reserved a position in the group-transmission period, it will be able to transmit at or better than a guaranteed rate. The guaranteed rate is given by the maximum length of any given cycle, which is the sum of a maximum contention period and a maximum transmission period. A maximum contention period is directly proportional to the maximum propagation delay over the LAN, is independent of the number of stations, and is very short in high-speed LANs. Therefore, just like in other schemes (e.g., token ring schemes) the time between two transmissions by the same station is bounded.

Much work has been done in the area of real-time data transmission across a multi-access LAN. In [7] and [13] window protocols are decribed which require that stations are synchronized in order to support time slotting. In [4] a protocol similar to GAMA/CD is described; however, this protocol requires time synchronization, and the frame size does not vary with the level of network traffic. In [1] a protocol that transmits voice packets over virtual circuits is described; voice traffic is given a higher priority than data traffic, and therefore, the performance of data traffic degrades as the amount of voice traffic increases. Other schemes which use a token passing scheme are described in [11], [12] and [14].

Section 2 describes GAMA/CD in detail; section 3 analyzes the throughput of GAMA/CD. Section 4 studies its average delay using an approximate model. Section 5 compares the results of our analytical models to simulated results. Finally, section 6 offers some concluding remarks.

2 Protocol Description

GAMA/CD divides the channel into a series of cycles; each cycle consists of a contention period and a group-transmission period. The group-transmission period is further divided into a set of individual transmission periods; the number of individual transmission periods per cycle varies with the amount of network traffic. An individual transmission period corresponds to a slot in a synchronized network; however, GAMA/CD does not require that network stations be synchronized by time. During the contention period stations contend for membership in the "transmission group"; each group member is able to transmit data without collision during the tranmission period allocated to the station when it joined the transmission group. GAMA/CD uses a form of "limited sensing" as in [3] to allow a newly activated station to contend for group membership without knowing the entire state of the transmission group.

When a station receives a message to transmit, it listens to the channel for 2τ seconds, where τ is the maximum end-to-end propagation delay. As will be explained later in this section, the value 2τ is chosen in order to ensure that no data transmitted by a group member is involved in a collision. If the listening station does not detect a signal on the channel within the 2τ second interval, it transmits the *initial packet* of the message. As the station transmits the *initial packet*, it also senses the channel for a possible collision. If a collision is detected (fig. 2), the station stops transmitting; since the propagation delay is at most τ, any collision which occurs will be detected within 2τ seconds of the start of transmission. After sensing the collision the transmitting station sends a jamming packet; the purpose of this packet is to ensure that every station is aware of the collision. If the transmission of the *initial packet* is succesfully completed (fig. 1), and the transmission group is not full, a transmission period is created and allocated to the new member.

The header of each transmission period contains the number of group members; thus, a new member is able to determine this value by reading the header of a transmission period. While a station is a group member, it is required to listen to each contention period, to determine whether or not a station has been added to the group. Each member is also required to listen to every transmission period; an idle transmission period means that a group member has either failed, or voluntarily left the group; in either case, the transmission period is removed. Because a group member listens to every contention and transmission period, it knows the number of group members, and its own position within the group.

The contention period begins with up to 3τ seconds of idle time; therefore, any message which arrives in the first τ seconds of the contention period will generate an *initial packet*. If the first station in the transmission group does not detect a signal 5τ seconds after the start of the contention period, the contention period must be idle, and the first station begins its transmission period; otherwise, the first station waits until the channel is clear before beginning its transmission. The first station must wait for up to 5τ seconds because it is possible that another station τ seconds away from the first station begins the contention period τ seconds after the first station; if a message arrives at this other station τ seconds into the contention period, an *initial packet* is transmitted 2τ seconds later, and arrive at the first station after another τ seconds.

An *initial packet* sent during the last τ seconds of a contention period, will collide with the first transmission period. To avoid this collision, the first station sends a 2τ second long jamming packet before it transmits its data packet; this packet will collide with any *initial packet* in the channel, and force the transmitting station to stop sending its *initial packet.* It is possible that an *initial packet* might be sent τ seconds after the first transmission period has begun; this *initial packet* will arrive up to τ seconds later. Therefore, the jamming packet must be at least 2τ seconds long to ensure that no data is involved in a collision. The jamming packet ensures that the length of the contention period is no greater than $3\tau + \delta$ (when an *initial packet* is successfully transmitted) where δ is the maximum length of the *initial packet.*

A group member begins transmitting data as soon as it senses the channel is clear following the reception of the previous transmission period. As the maximum propagation delay is τ seconds, the delay between successive transmission periods will be no longer than 2τ seconds. If a group member does not receive a signal within 2τ seconds, the transmission period must be idle (fig. 3); when this happens, each group member transmits a τ second long jamming packet. The jamming packet ensures that any *initial packet* transmitted during the idle transmission period will not be successful. If a station does not detect a signal on the channel within 3τ seconds after succesfully transmitting an *initial packet*, the transmission group must be empty; therefore, the station becomes the first member.

In order for member stations to provide quality of service guarantees, GAMA/CD ensures that the length of the group-transmission period is not larger than some value G; therefore, the interval between successive occurrences of a transmission period is bounded. When a station receives a message to transmit, it determines the portion of each cycle it requires in order to achieve its quality of service guarantees. A station assumes that the cycle length is maximized (equal to $3\tau + \delta + G$) when it calculates this value. When the the length of the cycle is small, the interval between the transmission period is also small; consequently, as the length of the cycle increases, so does the interval between successive occurrences of the transmission period. As this interval increases, a station is required to transmit more data during each cycle, in order to meet its quality of service guarantees. Therefore, the maximum cycle length is used to ensure that member stations have the required bandwidth.

The allocated length of each transmission period is contained within the transmission period's header. Each group member knows the length of the entire group-transmission period by reading each header; if the *initial packet* is transmitted without collision, the transmitting station must first read the cycle length from the header of a transmission period. If there is enough available bandwidth, the station is admitted; otherwise, it backs-off. Once the station is added to the group, it is able to send the remaining packets without contention in subsequent cycles; after a station has been added, it maintains its position until it has no has data to transmit. Once a station does not send data in its transmission period, the other stations recognize the idle period, and remove the station from the group.

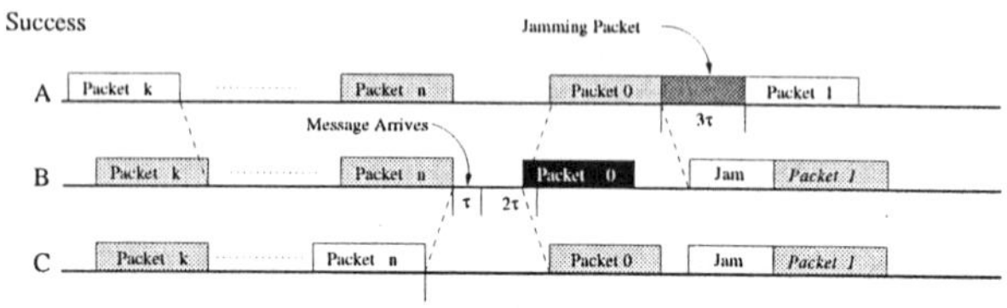

Figure 1: GAMA/CD: A successfully transmitted *initial packet.*

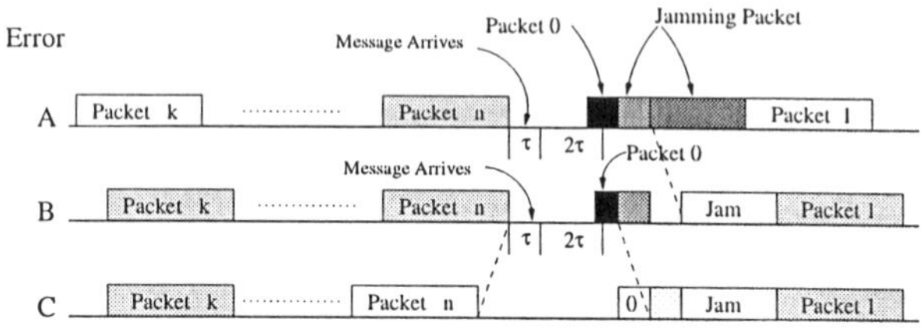

Figure 2: GAMA/CD: Two *initial packets* involved in a collision.

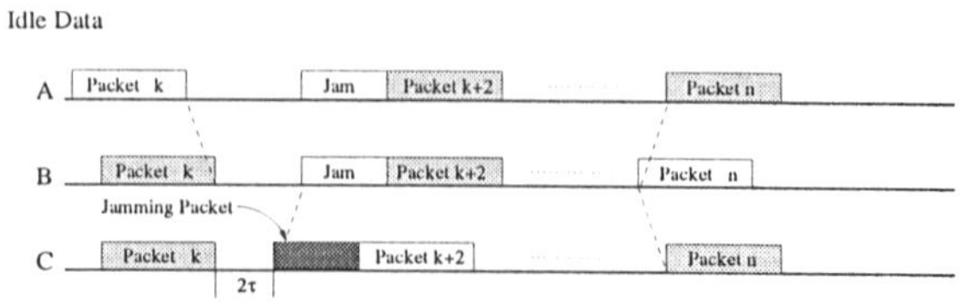

Figure 3: GAMA/CD: An idle transmission period.

3 Approximate Throughput Analysis

In the following analysis we develop a non-persistent model for the throughput of GAMA/CD. The model assumes that there are an infinite number of stations; the stations form a Poisson source which generates messages (both new and retransmitted) at a mean arrival rate of λ, and each station is assumed to have at most one message to transmit at any time. The time to transmit a single data packet is δ, the number of packets in a message is a random variable, and the probability that a message will complete its transmission (in a given cycle) is given by $\mu = \frac{1}{N}$ where N is the average number of packets in a message. The transmission channel does not introduce errors, any errors observed in received packets are the result of collisions, and collisions are detected by all stations. We assume that there are no station failures, the propagation delay is τ between all stations, and that the members in the group are ordered by the number of packets (in the message) remaining to be transmitted.

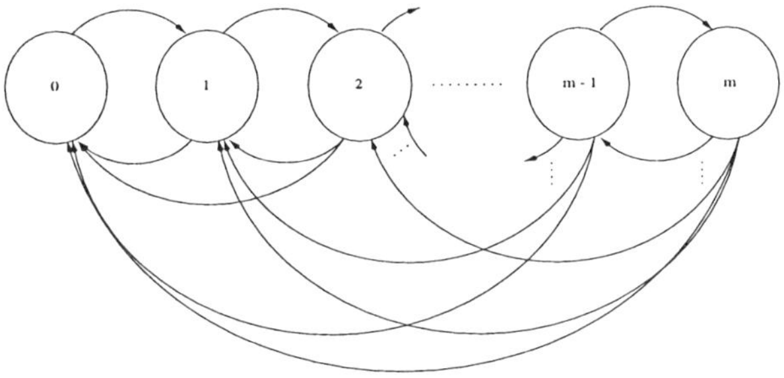

Figure 4: Markov Chain defining the average number of members in the group.

The state of the Markov chain in Fig. 4 represents the number of members in the group, where the value m is equal to the maximum number of group members. The probability that a station is added to the group $P_a(n)$ where n is the current number of group members, is equal to the probability that an *initial packet* is successfully transmitted within a contention period, which is the same as the probability that only one message arrives during the first τ seconds of the contention period. If there are m group members, no new members can be added because the transmission group is full. The value of $P_a(n)$ can be expressed as

$$P_{a(n)} = \begin{cases} \lambda\tau e^{-\lambda\tau} & \text{if } n < m \\ 0 & \text{if } n = m \end{cases} \tag{1}$$

The probability P_i that a contention period is idle is equal to the probability that no packets arrive during the first τ seconds of the contention period; Therefore,

$$P_i = e^{-\lambda\tau} \tag{2}$$

The probability P_e that a contention period results in an error is the same as the probability that more than one message is transmitted during the contention period. This value can be expressed as:

$$P_e = 1 - \lambda\tau e^{-\lambda\tau} - e^{-\lambda\tau} \tag{3}$$

If a line is drawn between any two states of the Markov chain, then the flow in one direction across the line has to equal the flow in the other direction. For an arbitrary state n where $0 \leq n < m$ the probability that the number of group members changes from n to *n+1* is equal to the probability that the state of the Markov chain transitions from a state N (where $N > n$) to a state L (where $L \leq$ n). This can be represented by the following equation.

$$\begin{aligned} &P_n P_{a(n)}(1-\mu)^n \\ &= \sum_{i=1}^{m-n} (1 - P_{a(n+i)}) P_{n+i} \sum_{j=i}^{n+i} \mu^j (1-\mu)^{n+i-j} \\ &+ \sum_{i=1}^{m-n} P_{a(n+i)} P_{n+i} \sum_{j=i+1}^{n+i} \mu^j (1-\mu)^{n+i-j} \end{aligned} \tag{4}$$

$$\begin{aligned} &P_n P_{a(n)}(1-\mu)^n \\ &= \sum_{i=1}^{m-n} P_{n+i} \sum_{j=i}^{n+i} \mu^j (1-\mu)^{n+i-j} \\ &- \sum_{i=1}^{m-n} P_{a(n+i)} P_{n+i} \mu^i (1-\mu)^n \end{aligned} \tag{5}$$

Dividing both sides of Eq. 5 by $(1 - \mu)^n P_{a(n)}$ leads to

$$\begin{aligned} P_n &= \frac{1}{P_{a(n)}} \\ &* \sum_{i=1}^{m-n} P_{n+i}[\sum_{j=i}^{n+i} \mu^j (1-\mu)^{i-j} \\ &- P_{a(n+i)} \mu^i] \end{aligned} \tag{6}$$

Successively substituting the values of P_{n+i} in Eq. 6 results in the following equation for P_n which is dependent only upon the value of P_m:

$$P_n = P_m F(n) \tag{7}$$

Where $F(n)$ is a recursive function which can be defined as follows:

$$F(n) = \sum_{i=1}^{m-n} F(n+i) \quad [\quad \frac{1}{P_{a(n)}} \sum_{j=i}^{n+i} \mu^j (1-\mu)^{i-j} - P_{a(n+i)} \mu^i] \tag{8}$$

The sum of all of the values of P_n where $0 \leq n \leq m$ is equal to 1. Therefore P_m can be expressed as,

$$P_m = \frac{1}{\sum_{i=0}^{m-1} F(i) + 1} \tag{9}$$

The average number of group members ρ is

$$\rho = \sum_{j=1}^{m} j P_j \tag{10}$$

An idle period separates successive cycles; this is either the period of time in which the transmission group is empty, or the idle period at the start of a contention period. When the transmission group is empty, i.e., no stations have packets to send, the idle period lasts $(\frac{1}{\lambda} + 2\tau)$ seconds (on average). The first term $(\frac{1}{\lambda})$ represents the time between Poisson message arrivals; the second term $(2\tau)$is the time a station must listen for a clear channel. If the number of group members is greater than 0, then the length of the idle period depends upon the result of the contention period. If the contention period is idle, the length is equal to 3τ; the first τ seconds are the period of time in which arriving messages can be successfully transmitted and, the following 2τ seconds represent the time a station must wait to sense for a clear channel. If the contention period is not idle, the channel is idle for a period of $\frac{5\tau}{2}$ seconds (on average). For an *initial packet* to be transmitted it must arrive within the first τ seconds of the contention period; on average a packet will arrive after $\frac{\tau}{2}$ seconds, and wait for 2τ seconds before the *initial packet* is transmitted. Therefore, the average length $\overline{I}$ of the idle period can be expressed as:

$$\overline{I} = P_0 \left(\frac{1}{\lambda} + 2\tau \right) + (1 - P_0) \left[P_i 3\tau + (1 - P_i) \frac{5\tau}{2} \right] \tag{11}$$

The probability that an *initial packet* (once sent) is successful P_r is equal to the probability that no other messages arrive within τ seconds of the start of transmission, i.e.,

$$P_r = e^{-\lambda\tau} \tag{12}$$

The average length $\overline{B}$ of a busy period is the length of a busy contention period plus the length of the group-transmission period. If there are no group members a busy period does not start until a message arrives at a station; therefore, when the number of group members is 0, a contention period will result in either a successful *initial packet* or in the collision of multiple *initial packets*. The probability that an *initial packet* is successful is equal to the probability that no other messages arrive within τ seconds of the arrival of the first message; this is equal to P_r, and the length of a successful contention period is $(\delta + \tau)$. Consequently, the probability that a collision occurs is equal to $(1 - P_r)$. When a contention period produces an error, the length of the contention period is equal to $\overline{Y} + 3\tau$. Where $\overline{Y}$ represents the length of the overlap between colliding *initial packets*. This value as shown in [6] can be represented as:

$$\overline{Y} = \tau - \frac{1 - e^{-\lambda\tau}}{\lambda} \tag{13}$$

The 3τ seconds represents the time before colliding stations realize a collision has occured plus the length of the jamming packet and the propagation delay for the jamming packet to reach the other stations. If the transmission group is not empty, the length of the busy period depends upon the outcome of the contention period; the length of the contention period is: $\delta + \tau$ if an initial packet is successfully transmitted, $\overline{Y} + 3\tau$ if multiple initial packets collide, and 0 if the contention period is idle. Regardless of this outcome, the length of the group-transmission period is $\rho(\delta + \tau)$. Therefore, the value of $\overline{B}$ can be expresses by the following equation:

$$\begin{aligned} \overline{B} &= P_0[P_r\tau + (1 - P_r)(\overline{Y} + 3\tau)] \\ &\quad + (1 - P_0)[P_a(\rho)(\rho + 1)(\delta + \tau) + P_i\rho(\delta + \tau) \\ &\quad + P_e[\overline{Y} + 3\tau + \rho(\delta + \tau)] + 3\tau] \end{aligned} \tag{14}$$

The average time spent transmitting data in a cycle $(\overline{U})$ is equal to the average number of group members plus the possibility that an *initial packet* is successful multiplied by the data packet length:

$$\overline{U} = (\rho + P_a(\rho))\delta \tag{15}$$

The throughput S is equal to the average time spent transmitting data in a cycle $(\overline{U})$ divided by the duration of an average cycle, i.e.,

$$S = \frac{\overline{U}}{\overline{I} + \overline{B}} \tag{16}$$

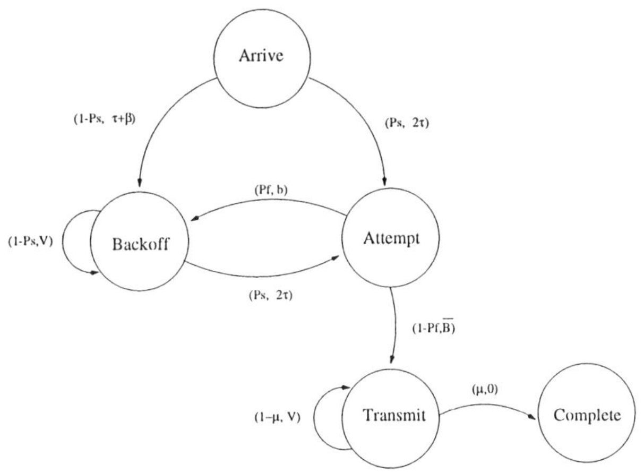

Figure 5: Process defining GAMA/CD delay characteristics.

4 Average Delay Analysis

In this section the average delay of GAMA/CD is analyzed; the delay of a message is defined as the elapsed time from the instant the message is ready to be transmitted to the time the entire message is received at the destination. The average delay is modeled by the process shown in Fig. 5.

In order to determine the average delay, one must consider the steps a station takes in transmitting a message. When a station receives a message, it is in the **Arrive** state. If the station senses the channel clear for 2τ seconds after the arrival of a message, it sends an *initial packet* (**Attempt**) otherwise it backs off. If the *initial packet* is successful the station enters the **Transmit** state, where it remains until the message is complete. If the *initial packet* is not successful the station enters the **Backoff** state.

These five states (Arrive, Backoff, Attempt, Transmit and Complete) along with the associated delay values and the transition probabilities define the process used to obtain an expression for the average delay. In Fig. 5, each link represents a transition from one state to another; for every link there is a label which consists of the probability the link is used, and the length of time spent in the state.

The transition from the **Arrive** state to the **Attempt** state is made with probability P_s, where P_s can be expressed as:

$$P_s = \frac{\overline{I}}{\overline{I}+\overline{B}}(1-P_m) \tag{17}$$

P_s is the probability that a message arrives during an idle period and that the group is not full. Because a station must sense that the channel is clear for 2τ seconds before it sends the *initial packet*, the delay caused by the transition from **Arrive** to **Attempt** is 2τ. If a station is forced to back-off, it will have spent (on average) τ seconds listening to the channel before it detects a signal. The length of time a station backs-off is a random variable with an average value of b.

After waiting in the **Backoff** state, a station will enter the **Attempt** state with probability P_s; while in the **Attempt** state, a station sends an *initial packet* which has a probability of failure equal to P_f, where $P_f = 1 - e^{\tau\lambda}$. If the *initial packet* is successful, the station transitions to the **Transmit** state; the delay accrued by this transition is equal to $\overline{B}$. If the *initial packet* fails, the **Backoff** state is entered; in this case, the additional delay is equal to b. While in the **Transmit** state, a station sends a packet each cycle; the probability that a station completes its message transmission (in a given cycle) is equal to μ. Each time a station returns to the **Transmit** state, the additional delay is equal to the time required to transmit a complete cycle.

From Fig. 5 one can obtain an expression for the average delay D:

$$D = (1-P_s)(\tau + b + E(B)) + P_s(2\tau + E(A)) \tag{18}$$

Where E(A) is the additional delay accumulated each time the **Attempt** state is entered, and E(B) is the delay caused by each stay in the **Backoff** state. The value for E(A) can be expressed as follows:

$$E(A) = (1-P_f)(\overline{B} + E(T)) + P_f(b + E(B)) \tag{19}$$

where E(T) is equal to the time spent in the **Transmit** state. The expression for E(B) is

$$E(B) = P_s(2\tau + E(A)) + (1-P_s)(b + E(B)) \tag{20}$$

solving for E(A) leads to:

$$E(A) = E(B) - \frac{1-P_s}{P_s}b - 2\tau \tag{21}$$

and the equation for E(T) is as follows:

$$E(T) = (1-\mu)(V + E(T)) \tag{22}$$

which simplifies to

$$E(T) = \frac{(1-\mu)V}{\mu} \tag{23}$$

$$E(T) = \sigma V \qquad (24)$$

Where $\sigma = \frac{(1-\mu)}{\mu}$, and V is the length of the entire cycle which can be expressed as follows:

$$V = \overline{I} + \overline{B} \qquad (25)$$

Substituting Eq. 21 into Eq. 19 leads to:

$$E(B) - \frac{1-P_s}{P_s} b - 2\tau = (1-P_f)(\overline{B} + E(T)) + P_f(b + E(B)) \qquad (26)$$

$$E(B) = \overline{B} + \sigma V + \frac{P_f}{1-P_f} b + \frac{1-P_s}{P_s(1-P_f)} b + 2\tau \qquad (27)$$

Using Eq. 21 leads to the following expression for E(A):

$$E(A) = \overline{B} + \sigma V + \frac{P_f}{1-P_f} b + \frac{1-P_s}{P_s(1-P_f)} b + 2\tau - \frac{1-P_s}{Ps} b \qquad (28)$$

Substituting the previous two equations into Eq. 18 leads to:

$$D = \overline{B} + \sigma V + \frac{P_f}{1-P_f} b + \frac{1-P_s}{P_s(1-P_f)} b + 2\tau + (1-Ps)b \qquad (29)$$

5 Performance Results

The graphs presented in this section compare the throughput as modeled by Eq. 16, and the delay (Eq. 29) to the results produced by a simulation of GAMA/CD. The comparisons are based on networks with speeds of 100 Mb/s and 10 Mb/s, packet sizes of 200 and 500 bytes, and a distance between stations of 200 meters. For all graphs the unit of time is equal to the transmission period of a single data packet. The simulation of GAMA/CD models a network of 50 stations.

Figure 6 shows the throughput for a 100 Mb/s network. In both graphs a message is broken up into 20 packets (on average); for the top graph, the average message size is 4 kb, and GAMA/CD has split the message into 200 byte packets. The average message size of the bottom graph is 10 kb; GAMA/CD has divided each message into 500 byte packets. As the message size increases, the throughput of GAMA/CD approaches the throughput of TDMA; this would be the case if stations engaged in long-term sessions. Obviously, the overhead of the contention period and the spacing required between data packets prevents GAMA/CD from reaching a throughput of 1.0; however, it is clear that the channel is used for transmitting data a large percentage of the time.

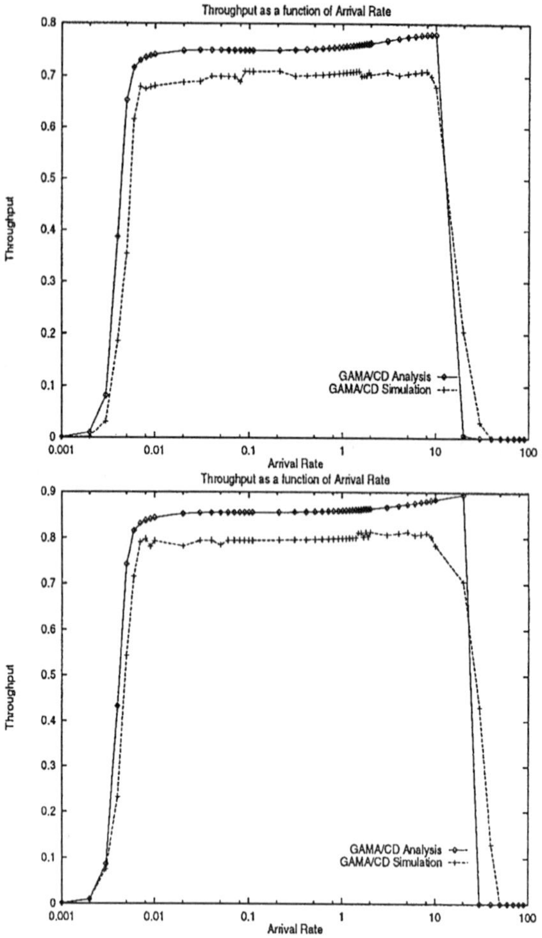

Figure 6: A comparison of the approximate throughput of GAMA/CD when the arrival rate is allowed to vary. The analysis is run on a 100 Mb/s network, and the packet sizes are 200 and 500 bytes.

The throughput for a 10 Mb/s network is modeled in, Figure 7. As in the previous figure, both graphs are divided into 20 packets (on average); the average message size of the first graph is 4 kb which has been divided into 200 byte packets. The average message size of the second graph is 10 kb; which has been split into 500 byte packets. Because the network speed has decreased by a factor of 10, the impact of the propagation delay has been lessened; this is reflected in higher maximum throughput values.

Figures 8 and 9 display the average delay of GAMA/CD for both 100 Mb/s and 10 Mb/s networks

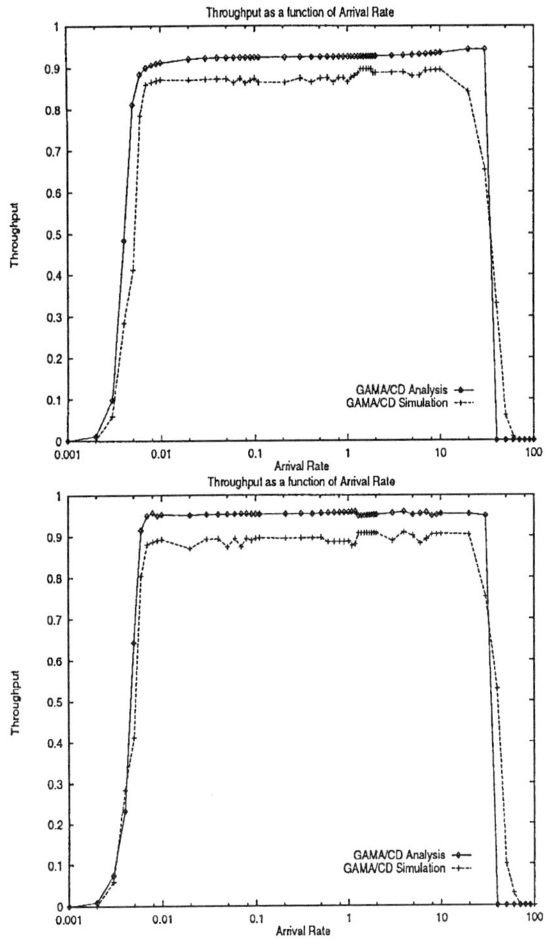

Figure 7: A comparison of the approximate throughput of GAMA/CD when the arrival rate is allowed to vary. The analysis is run on a 10 Mb/s network, and the packet sizes are 200 and 500 bytes.

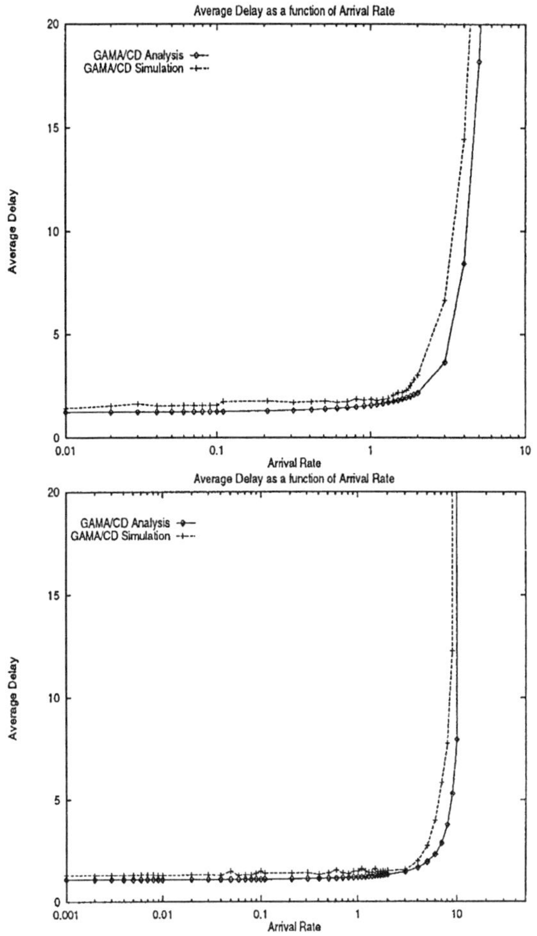

Figure 8: A comparison of the average delay of GAMA/CD when the arrival rate is allowed to vary. The analysis is run on a 100 Mb/s network, and the packet sizes are 200 and 500 bytes.

as the load varies.

6 Conclusion

GAMA/CD is able to support quality of service guarantees by organizing the channel into dynamically sized cycles, each of which is composed of a contention period, and a group-transmission period. A station is allowed to contend for membership in the transmission group during the contention period; a member of the transmission group can transmit data collision free during each cycle. When the network load is light, GAMA/CD behaves much like CSMA/CD. As the network load rises, the number of group members increases to a pre-defined maximum, after which GAMA becomes in effect TDMA, giving every station that is part of the transmission group a "slot" in which to transmit. GAMA/CD can adapt to changing network conditions, even in the presence of sudden bursts of activity, and offers performance guarantees to stations that have been successfully added to the transmission group.

Our analytical results provide an approximation of the performance of GAMA/CD for the case in which stations have variable length messages to transmit; they also provide good insight into the effect various parameters (e.g. average packet size or network load) have on the performance of the protocol. Simulation results were used to validate the simplifying assumptions used in our derivation of the approximate throughput and average delay. Our work continues to analyze the behavior of GAMA/CD after failures in the transmission group, and to introduce more so-

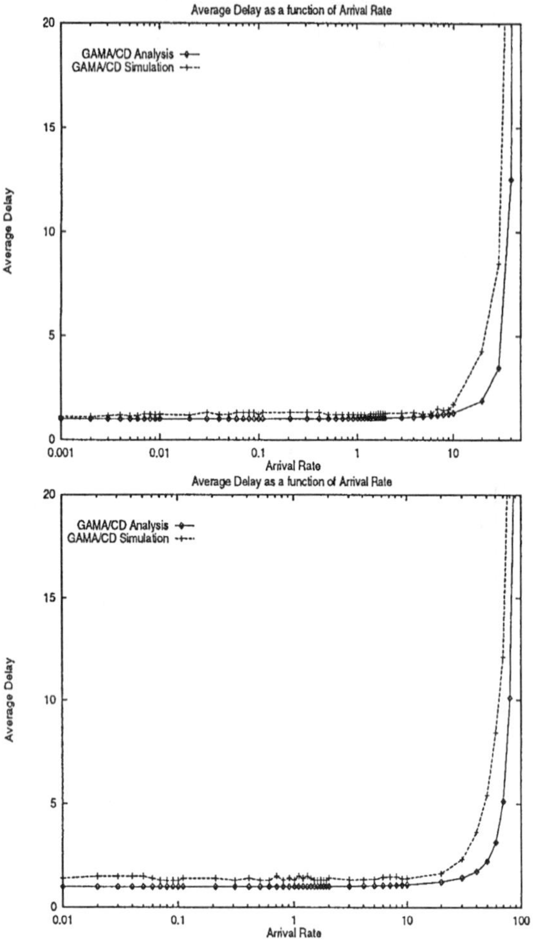

Figure 9: A comparison of the average delay of GAMA/CD when the arrival rate is allowed to vary. The analysis is run on a 10 Mb/s network, and the packet sizes are 200 and 500 bytes.

phisticated collision resolution mechanisms for *initial packets* within GAMA/CD to ensure that every cycle has a successful contention period.

References

[1] I. Chlamtac "An Ethernet Compatible Protocol for Real-Time Voice/Data Integration", *Computer Networks and ISDN Systems*, January 1985

[2] J. Hammond and P. O'Reilly "Performance Analysis of Local Computer Networks", Adison-Wesley 1986.

[3] P. Humblet "On the Throughput of Channel Access Algorithms with Limited Sensing", *Transactions on Communications*, April 1986.

[4] F. Jia and B. Mukherjee "The Superchannel Scheme for Integrated Services on Multiple Broadcast Networks", *Computer Networks and ISDN Systems*, October 1995.

[5] L. Kleinrock "Queuing Systems Volume 1: Theory", Wiley-Interscience 1975.

[6] L. Kleinrock and F. Tobagi "Packet Switching in Radio Channels: Part I-Carrier Sense Multiple-Access Modes and Their Throughput-Delay Characteristics", *IEEE Transactions on Communications*, December 1975.

[7] J. Kurose, M. Schwartz and T. Yemini "Controlling Window Protocols for Time-Constrained Communication in Multiple Access Environments", *Proc. IEEE Intl. Data Comm. Symposium*, 1993.

[8] R. Metcalf and D. Boggs "Ethernet: Distributed Packet Switching for Local Computer Networks", *Communications of the ACM*, July 1976.

[9] R. Rom and M. Sidi, Multiple Access Protocols Performance and Analysis, Springer-Verlag, 1990.

[10] F. Tobagi and V. Hunt "Performance Analysis of Carrier Sense Multiple Access with Collision Detection", *Computer Networks*, vol. 4, October-November 1980.

[11] A. Valenzano, P. Montuschi and L. Ciminiera "Some Properties of Timed Token Medium Access Protocols", *IEEE Trans. on Software Engineering*, August 1987.

[12] C. Venkatramani and T. Chiueh "Design, Implementation, and Evaluation of a Software-Based Real-Time Ethernet Protocol", *Proc. SIGCOMM '95*, 1995.

[13] W. Zhao, J. Stankovoc and K. Ramamritham "Virtual Time CSMA Protocols for Hard Real-Time Communications", *IEEE Trans. on Software Engineering*, August 1987.

[14] W. Zhao, J. Stankovoc and K. Ramamritham "A Window Protocol for Transmission of Time Constrained Messages", *IEEE Trans. on Computers*, September 1990.

Analysis of Packet Discarding Policies in High-Speed Networks*

Yael Lapid†, Rapahel Rom‡ and Moshe Sidi§
Department of Electrical Engineering
Technion - Israel Institute of Technology
Haifa 32000, Israel

Abstract

In this work, selective discarding policies, as a means for congestion avoidance, are studied and compared to non-discarding policies. The Partial Message Discard policy discards packets of tails of corrupted messages. An improvement to this policy is the Early Message Discard that drops entire messages and not just message-tails.

A common performance measure of network elements is the effective throughput which measures the utilization of the network links but which neglects the application altogether. We adopt a new performance measure, goodput, which reflects the utilization of the network from the application's point of view and thus better describes network behavior.

We develop and analyze a model for systems which employ discarding policies. The analysis shows a remarkable performance improvement when any message-based discarding policy is applied, and that the Early Message Discard policy performs better, especially under high loads. We compute the optimal parameter setting for maximum goodput at different input loads and investigate the performance sensitivity to these parameters.

1 Introduction

Many high speed networks applications generate messages which must be transported to a similar application at the other end of the network. These messages are segmented into smaller fixed or variable size packets which are then conveyed by the network. To be useful, all packets comprising a message must arrive successfully at the destination and be reconstructed into the original message. Packet-by-packet acknowledgments and retransmissions are clearly impractical, and thus, acknowledgments and retransmissions must be applied by the applications, at the message level.

The problem is therefore to deliver complete messages by a network that handles and delivers packets. Packet misdelivery happens mainly due to congestion at network elements which causes buffer overflows and packets drops. In case of congestion the network can and will discard packets that belong to best-effort type of service. The user cannot be charged for any message which is partially delivered and thus it behooves the network to deliver complete messages. The user is therefore required to designate message boundaries and the problem is which packets to discard so that as many complete messages are delivered and that congestion is alleviated or avoided altogether.

*This work was supported by the consortium for broadband communication administered by the Chief Scientist of the Israeli Ministry of Commerce and Industry.

†Also with the Department of Video Networking, ECI Telecom Ltd.; yael@ecitele.com

‡Also with SUN Microsystems Labs, 2550 Garcia Avenue, Mountain View, CA 94043, U.S.A.; rom@ee.technion.ac.il

§moshe@ee.technion.ac.il

Selective Discarding Policies

Selective discarding policies, as a means for congestion avoidance were presented in [FR94],[FJ93]. These methods are implemented at network elements and are not dependent on the cooperation of users, or the behavior of other network elements.

One discarding policy is the Partial Message Discard (PMD). According to this policy the network element discards (drops) packets that belong to messages that were already damaged, that is, experienced a packet drop in the network element. In other words, if the buffer is full when a packet arrives to the network element, this packet, and all consecutive packets that belong to the same message are discarded.

An improvement of this policy, is the Early Message Discard (EMD) in which , in addition to the forced discard executed when the buffer overflows (as in PMD), a threshold is defined at a certain buffer occupancy level. If a message *begins* to arrive when the buffer occupancy is above this threshold, the message is not accepted to the network (i.e., all its packets are dropped). In this method entire messages are discarded, while in PMD, only "tails" of messages are discarded where the beginnings are transmitted wastefully.

In [Tur96] PMD and EMD are studied. It is shown that the need for high queue capacity in order to achieve high efficiency, grows with the number of virtual circuits. The buffer fill level over time is analyzed, and an EMD with hysteresis algorithm is suggested, to achieve high efficiency with smaller queue capacities. The fair EMD with hysteresis algorithm is introduced in attempt to achieve a level of fairness among the competing virtual circuits, when their rates differ significantly.

0-8186-7780-5/97 $10.00

Performance objectives

In [FR94] and in [Tur96] the objective was to compare between discarding policies and non-controlled systems based on the *effective throughput.* Effective throughput is the ratio of good packets on the outgoing link to the total outgoing flow. Good packets are those that belong to messages that were successfully transmitted in their entirety. The yardstick of effective throughput only shows how much of the transmitted traffic is not a waste, but it gives no notion of the quality of service the user gets, i.e., the percentage of its traffic that is transmitted successfully. Messages that were completely discarded by the network do not affect the throughput, yet make a big difference to the application. In other words, a high effective throughput (near 1) can be achieved even for situations where a very small percentage of the user's data is successfully transmitted by the network element.

In our work we define another performance yardstick, *Goodput.* Goodput is the ratio of good packets out of the total number of packets that arrive at the network element's input. This performance measure represents the percentage of user's data that is successfully transmitted by the network element, and that the network can charge for. This objective better represents both the quality of service the user gets, and the utilization of the network element.

In this paper we develop and analyze a model for systems which employ PMD and EMD policies. From an analytic point of view, the main contribution of this paper is the introduction of a novel recursion for the computation of the goodput. The analysis shows a remarkable goodput improvement when any message-based discarding policy is applied, and that the EMD policy performs better, especially under high loads. We also compute an optimal EMD threshold for maximum goodput, at different input loads. We then extend the basic model to include fixed-size cells, multi-stage models and on-off sources.

2 The model

The model we use to study the behavior of various discarding policies is based on the dispersed message model introduced in [CKS93]. According to this model a message consists of a block of consecutive packets, which corresponds to a higher layer protocol data unit. The arrival epochs of the packets are dispersed over time, i.e., the packets that compose the message arrive to the system at different time slots. TCP/IP based systems are examples in which message is segmented into packets which are then transmitted through the network. At the receiving end, the transport protocol reassembles these packets back into a message before the delivery to higher layers.

We consider systems with variable length *messages*, that is, the packets that arrive to the system belong to messages whose length is geometrically distributed with parameter q (independent from message to message). Thus, the mean length of a message is $1/q$ packets. Variable message size is typical in data applications where the message can be a document, an e-mail message, or an arbitrary file. This model also assumes a variable size packet which may correspond to some natural partition of the message. We assume that packets that belong to a specific session arrive according to a Poisson process with rate λ and the transmission time of a packet is exponentially distributed with rate μ. In Section 5.1 we will consider the case of fixed length packets that is typical to ATM networks. In Section 5.3 we will consider on-off sources.

The network element in our model has a single finite input queue that can contain at most N packets (either buffered or being transmitted). When a packet arrives at the network element, it enters the input queue, if space is available. Otherwise, the packet is discarded (dropped). A packet leaves the queue when the server is available, i.e., after the service time of the previous packet expires. Hence, in terms of packets, the network element can be viewed as an $M/M/1/N$ model, with arrival rate λ and service rate μ. The *load* on the network element is defined as $\rho = \lambda/\mu$.

In terms of messages, the behavior of the network element is more complicated. Naturally, all packets that belong to a specific message have to be transferred successfully in order for the message to be useful at the receiving end. Therefore, in most applications, even if a single packet of a message is discarded, the whole message has to be retransmitted. This implies that it is wasteful to forward packets that belong to a corrupted message (a message with at least one discarded packet). In order to reduce the waste of network resources we use the PMD and the EMD discarding policies that were described in the introduction. The threshold for the EMD policy is denoted by K.

3 Analysis

3.1 Discarding policies analysis

A network element that employs no discarding policy (other than discarding packets that arrive when the buffer is full) is modeled as an $M/M/1/N$ queue with arrival rate λ and service rate μ ($\rho = \lambda/\mu$). A packet that arrives at the system that has N queued packets, is discarded (not admitted to the queue). Let P_j ($0 \leq j \leq N$) be the steady-state probability of having j packets in the system. Then it is well known that $P_j = \rho^j / \sum_{i=0}^{N} \rho_i \quad 0 \leq j \leq N$. With these probabilities, the Goodput of the network element can be derived, as is described in the next subsection.

For the PMD policy we recall that if a packet arrives when the queue is full, it is discarded and all subsequent packets that belong to the same message are also discarded until a head-of-message packet (a new message) arrives. To model this we must distinguish between two modes: the *normal mode* in which packets are admitted and *discarding mode* in which arriving packets are discarded. Let $P_{j,l}$ ($0 \leq j \leq N,\ l = 0, 1$) be the steady-state probability of having j packets in the system and the system is in mode l ($l = 0$ normal; $l = 1$ discarding). Then the following is a set of equations whose solution yields the steady state probabilities (with $\sum_{i=0}^{N}(P_{i,0} + P_{i,1}) = 1$),

$$\lambda P_{0,0} = \mu P_{1,0} \ ; \quad q\lambda P_{0,1} = \mu P_{1,1}$$

$$
\begin{aligned}
(\lambda+\mu)P_{i,0} &= \lambda P_{i-1,0}+\mu P_{i+1,0}+q\lambda P_{i-1,1} \\
&\qquad 1\le i\le N-1 \\
(q\lambda+\mu)P_{i,1} &= \mu P_{i+1,1} \quad 0\le i\le N-1 \\
(\lambda+\mu)P_{N,0} &= \lambda P_{N-1,0}+q\lambda P_{N-1,1} \\
\mu P_{N,1} &= \lambda P_{N,0} \qquad (1)
\end{aligned}
$$

The EMD policy, as mentioned before, is similar to the PMD, except that an additional threshold level is defined, say K. If a message starts to arrive when the system contains more than K packets, then all the packets of that message are discarded. With the same notation as above, the following is a set of equations whose solution yields the steady state probabilities (with $\sum_{i=0}^{N}(P_{i,0}+P_{i,1})=1$),

$$
\begin{aligned}
\lambda P_{0,0} &= \mu P_{1,0} \;;\quad q\lambda P_{0,1}=\mu P_{1,1} \\
(\lambda+\mu)P_{i,0} &= \lambda P_{i-1,0}+\mu P_{i+1,0}+q\lambda P_{i-1,1} \\
&\qquad 1\le i\le K \\
(\lambda+\mu)P_{i,0} &= p\lambda P_{i-1,0}+\mu P_{i+1,0} \\
&\qquad K+1\le i\le N-1 \\
(\lambda+\mu)P_{N,0} &= p\lambda P_{N-1,0} \;;\quad \mu P_{N,1}=\lambda P_{N,0} \\
(q\lambda+\mu)P_{i,1} &= \mu P_{i+1,1} \quad 0\le i\le K-1 \\
\mu P_{i,1} &= \mu P_{i+1,1}+q\lambda P_{i,0} \\
&\qquad K\le i\le N-1 \quad (2)
\end{aligned}
$$

3.2 Goodput Analysis

The goodput $\mathcal{G}$ is the ratio between total packets comprising good messages exiting the system and the total arriving packets at its input. Let $\mathcal{W}$ be the random variable that represents the length (number of packets) of an arriving message. Let $\mathcal{V}$ be the random variable that represents the success of a message, $\mathcal{V}=1$ for a good message, and $\mathcal{V}=0$ for a message which has one or more dropped packets. Then,

$$
\mathcal{G}=\frac{\sum_{n=1}^{\infty} n\cdot P(\mathcal{W}=n,\mathcal{V}=1)}{\sum_{n=1}^{\infty} n\cdot P(\mathcal{W}=n)} \qquad (3)
$$

We clearly have $P(\mathcal{W}=n,\mathcal{V}=1)=P(\mathcal{V}=1|\mathcal{W}=n)P(\mathcal{W}=n)$, and $P(\mathcal{W}=n)=q(1-q)^{n-1}$. Let $\mathcal{Q}$ be the random variable representing the queue occupancy at the arrival of a head-of-message packet. Then,

$$
P(\mathcal{V}=1|\mathcal{W}=n) = \sum_{i=0}^{N} P(\mathcal{V}=1|\mathcal{W}=n,\mathcal{Q}=i) \cdot P(\mathcal{Q}=i) \qquad (4)
$$

where $P(\mathcal{Q}=i)=P_{i,0}+P_{i,1}$ and $P_{i,j}$ are taken from the solution of (1) for PMD and of (2) for EMD. This is true since the head-of-message packet is an arbitrary packet (that sees the stationary probabilities upon arrival), and since the length of an arriving message is independent of the queue state. From the above we get

$$
\mathcal{G} = q\sum_{n=1}^{\infty} n\cdot q(1-q)^{n-1} \cdot\sum_{i=0}^{N} P(\mathcal{V}=1|\mathcal{W}=n,\mathcal{Q}=i)P(\mathcal{Q}=i)
$$

To complete the calculation of the goodput we therefore have to evaluate the conditional probabilities $S_{n,i}\stackrel{\triangle}{=}P(\mathcal{V}=1|\mathcal{W}=n,\mathcal{Q}=i)$. These probabilities are computed recursively as follows.

Consider first a system that employs the PMD policy. Assume that the head-of-message packet arrives at a system at state $Q=i$ and the message is of length $n\le N$. Then, if $i\le N-n$ there is enough space in the buffer to accommodate the whole message and the message is guaranteed to be good. Thus, $S_{n,i}=1$ for $0\le i\le N-n$, $1\le n\le N$. If $i=N$, i.e., the system is full, then the head-of-message packet is not admitted and the message is not a good one. Hence $S_{n,N}=0$, $1\le n\le N$. The above two equation establish the initial condition for the recursion. For $N-n+1\le i\le N-1$ and $1\le n\le N$ $S_{n,i}=(1-r)S_{n-1,i+1}+rS_{n,i-1}$, where $r\stackrel{\triangle}{=}\mu/(\mu+\lambda)$ is the probability that a departure occurs before an arrival. The latter relation holds since if the next event following the arrival of the head-of-message packet is an arrival of a packet (which happens with probability $1-r$), the probability that the message is successful is $S_{n-1,i+1}$, since this packet can be viewed as the head-of-message packet of a message of length $n-1$ that arrives at a system with $Q=i+1$ packets. If the event following the arrival of the head-of-message packet is a departure of a packet (which happens with probability r), the probability that the message is successful is $S_{n,i-1}$, since the situation is as if the head-of-message packet had arrived at a system with $Q=i-1$ packets. For messages of length $n>N$, there is no situation where success is guaranteed from the outset and success depends more heavily on the evolution of the system after the arrival of the head-of-message. From the same reason as explained above, the latter relation holds for $1\le i\le N-1$. A slightly different relation holds when the head-of-message packet arrives at an empty system ($i=0$). If the head-of-message arrived at an empty system and the next event is a departure (which happens with probability r), the system is empty again and no further departures are possible; thus the probability that the message is successful is $S_{n-1,0}$ since the arrival of the next packet can be viewed as an arrival of the head-of-message packet of a message of length $n-1$ to an empty system. Thus, for $n>N$ we have the following recursion: $S_{n,0}=(1-r)S_{n-1,1}+rS_{n-1,0}$, $S_{n,i}=(1-r)S_{n-1,i+1}+rS_{n,i-1}$ for $1\le i\le N-1$ and $S_{n,N}=0$.

It is easy to see that for the EMD policy we have the following probabilities:

$$
\hat{S}_{n,i}=\begin{cases} S_{n,i} & i<K \\ 0 & K\le i\le N \end{cases}
$$

4 Numerical Results

The parameters we use in our examples were set to correspond to realistic ratios between queue size and

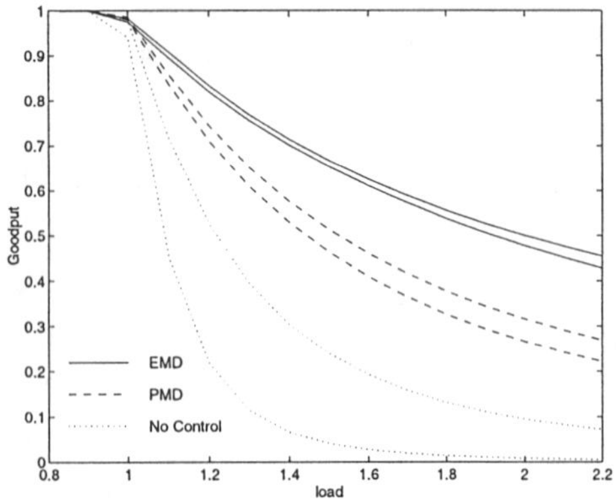

Figure 1: Goodput vs. Load for EMD / PMD / No control [$N = 120$; $K = 60$; $1/q = 6, 30$]

mean message length. Ratios of $1 \div 20$ (i.e., queue size of 20 times the mean message length) to $1 \div 2$, were checked. From the geometric message length distribution it follows that the mean message length is $1/q$ packets. In our examples we set the queue size to $N = 120$, and calculated the goodput for messages of mean length of 6, 15, 30 and 60. The traffic loads on the network element (ρ) are in the range of 0.6 to 2.2 where loads of $\rho < 1$ are referred to as moderate loads, while higher loads correspond to congestion build-ups or noncooperative users.

Figure 1 shows the goodput of the network element for mean message lengths of 6 and 30 packets, as a function of the offered load and for different policies: without any discarding policy (the dotted curves), when PMD policy is introduced in the network element (the dashed curves) and when EMD policy is applied with a fixed threshold at half the queue size (the solid curves). In all cases, systems with shorter mean message length yield better goodput. Figure 2 is a zoom of Fig. 1 for average message size of 30 packets, at moderate loads with PMD or EMD applied.

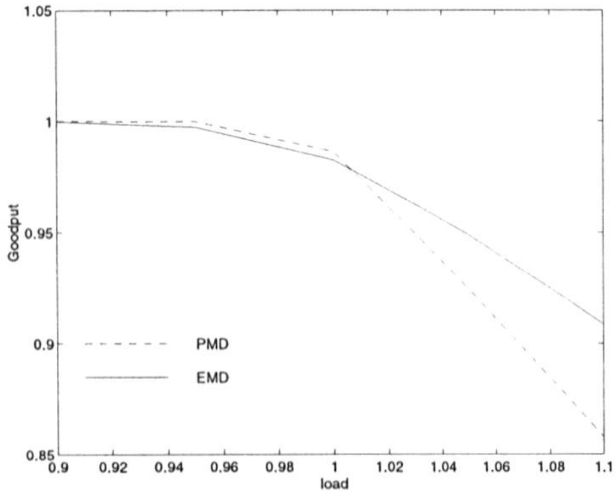

Figure 2: Goodput vs. Load for EMD and PMD policies (zoom of Fig. 1) [$N = 120$; $K = 60$; $1/q = 30$]

It is evident that when high loads are introduced both discarding policies perform much better than a system with no discarding policy. At moderate loads, the PMD policy and the EMD policies perform similarly, with a slight advantage to the PMD policy. For heavy traffic loads, the EMD outperforms the PMD by up to 20% in terms of the goodput, and improves the network element's performance by a factor of up to 6 for the relatively short messages (see $1/q = 6, \rho = 2.2$) and even by a higher factor for long messages. It also appears that the behavior of the system is not sensitives to changes in average message lengths. Furthermore, a controlled system (where some discard policy is implemented) is less sensitive to the message length, and the EMD is, again, better than the PMD in that perspective.

Given the superior performance of the EMD policy, it is natural to investigate the optimal threshold K_{opt} with respect to loads, message lengths, and buffer sizes. Figure 3 depicts K_{opt} for a queue of size $N = 120$, mean message lengths of 6, 15, 30 and 60, and loads in the range of 0.6 to 2.2. This figure shows that the optimal threshold is not very sensitive to the average messages length.

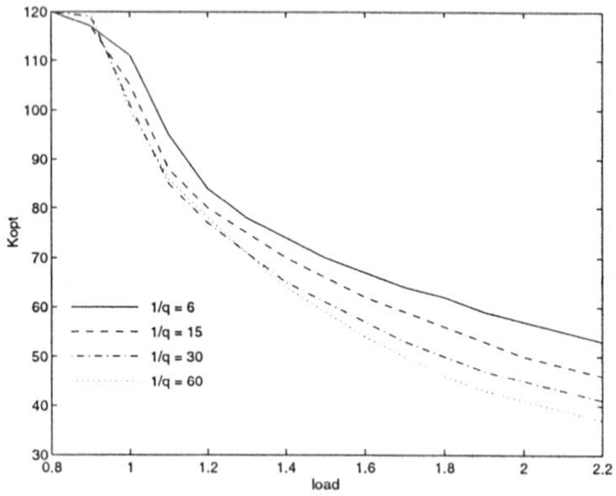

Figure 3: $Kopt$ vs. load for the EMD policy [$N = 120$; $1/q = 6, 15, 30, 60$]

Figure 4 depicts K_{opt}/N for queue sizes of $N = 30, 60, 90$, mean message length of 6, and loads in the range of 0.6 to 2.2. We consider the ratio of the optimal threshold to the queue size so that the cases could be compared. The figure demonstrates that changes in the queue size for a given average message size, hardly affect the optimal threshold. This is an encouraging result since it means that one can easily approximate the optimal threshold for a given system.

Figure 5 shows the dependence of goodput on K for a system employing the EMD policy with several loads (the value of the goodput obviously decreases as the load increases). The figure shows that the goodput is rather insensitive to the EMD threshold, in a very wide range of thresholds (not too low and not too high). This is a remarkable result as it means that the EMD policy is rather robust and the choice of the threshold is not a crucial one. An optimum threshold, as expected, does exist but is not significant at all in terms of goodput (and is therefore invisible in these graphs). The explanation of this phenomenon is as follows. Clearly, when the value of the threshold is set high, the system behaves almost as with the PMD policy and looses its relative advantage. Similarly, when the threshold is set too low, the buffer is not well utilized since many messages that could have been accepted are discarded. In a medium setting, at relatively high loads, the system will operate most of the time with a buffer occupancy around K. Lowering K means that longer messages are more likely to make it but these messages are rather rare and therefore their effect on the goodput is negligible. Thus, although an optimal threshold does exist its effect on the goodput is non-essential.

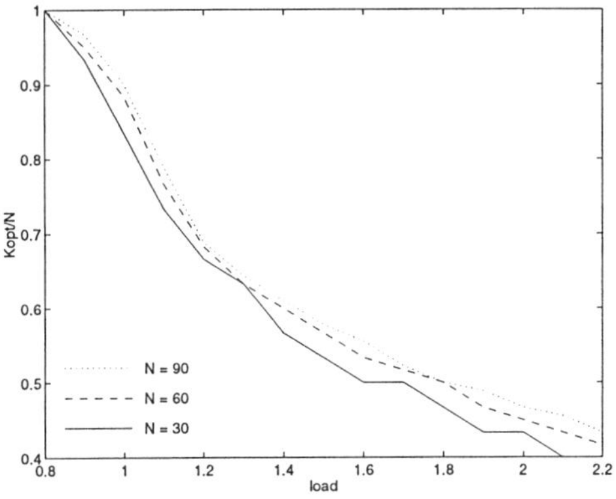

Figure 4: $Kopt/N$ vs. load for the EMD policy [$N = 30, 60, 90$; $1/q = 6$]

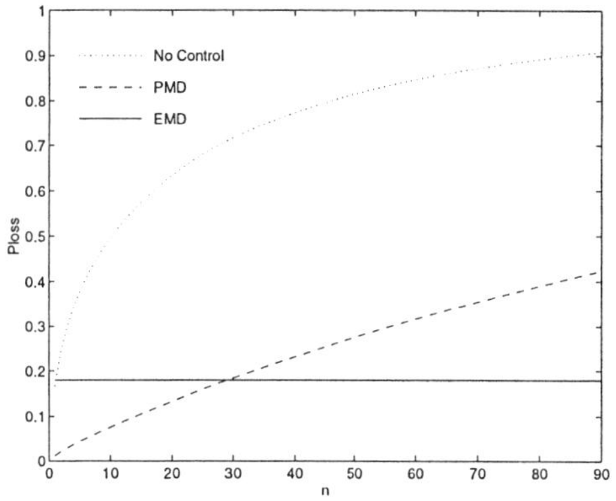

Figure 6: Prob. of message loss vs. message length for the EMD / PMD / No control [$N = 120$; $K = 60$; $\rho = 1.2$; $1/q = 30$]

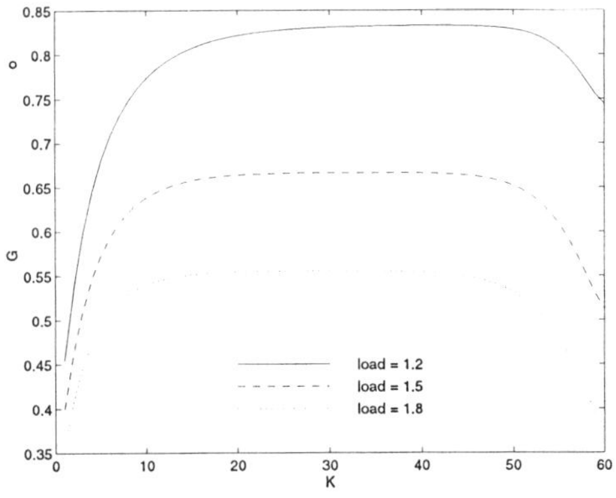

Figure 5: Goodput vs. K for the EMD policy [$N = 90$; $1/q = 6$; $\rho = 1.2, 1.5, 1.8$]

Figure 6 depicts the probabilities of a message of length n packets to be discarded by the system. (This probability does not include the probability of such a message to arrive at the queue). In this example the queue size is of length $N = 120$, $K = 60$ and messages are of average length of 30 packets, the traffic load is $\rho = 1.2$. It is evident that the system with no control (dotted) gives little chance for any message, especially the longer ones. The PMD control (dashed) performs much better and the loss probability curves rises much slower. But it is clear that EMD control (solid) is the most fair mechanism in terms of loss probability for a message of any length. In this figure we can see again that PMD, in comparison with EMD, performs better for short messages and worse for messages longer than the expected length. From this result, the distribution of good messages length can be derived, and it is clear that the EMD mechanism preserves the message length distribution of the arriving traffic.

5 Extensions to the basic model

5.1 ATM Networks

In our model we assumed that messages are segmented into exponentially sized packets, which translates into an exponential transmission (service) time.

In ATM networks, however, messages are segmented into fixed size packets, called cells. To test the applicability of our model to ATM networks we simulated an ATM network element, employing a discarding policy, and compared it with an equivalent exponential network element. The results exhibit an extremely tight match. Figure 7 shows the goodput of an ATM network element employing EMD policy (the dashed curve) resulting from simulation, and the calculated goodput of the modeled system with the same parameters and an exponential packet size with mean identical to that of the ATM cell. It is clearly evident that as far as goodput (and throughput) is concerned, the difference between the exponential and deterministic packet sizes (with the same mean service time) is negligible. Therefore, the results of our model can be used to describe ATM network elements, as a specific case of message based high-speed network elements.

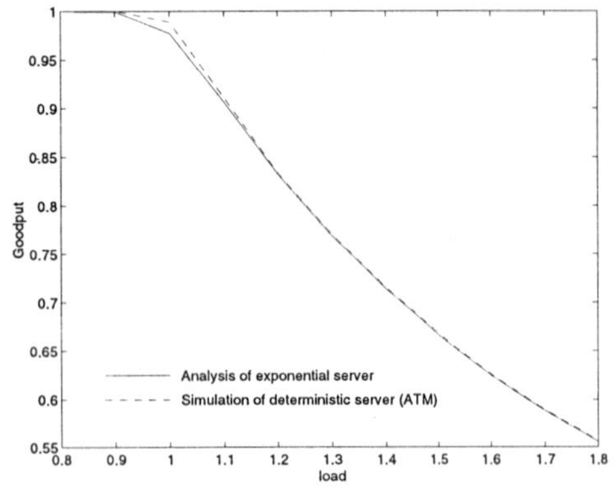

Figure 7: Goodput Vs. Load, fixed and exponential packet size [$N = 100$; $K = 50$; $1/q = 10$]

Implementation of a selective discard policy in ATM networks is suggested in [Kam95] for applications that use AAL5 as an adaptation layer to the ATM layer, using a single end-of-message bit in cell's header.

5.2 Multi-stage Model

In this section we investigate the performance of a multi-stage sub-network whose elements apply the EMD mechanism to the aggregated traffic at their inputs. We assume that each stage in the sub-network is that presented and analyzed in the previous section. The output of each stage leaves the system with probability Γ and continues to the following stage with probability $1 - \Gamma$. Thus the input into a stage is comprised of a local source and a portion of the output of the previous stage. The local source generates messages comprised of packets as described in Section 2. At every stage, the EMD mechanism is applied to every arriving message (both messages from previous stage and from the local source). The *goodput* measure we use here is for a single stage and per data source, namely the ratio between transmitted "good" packets and incoming packets, of a specific stream (this is an "application oriented" objective).

Figure 8 presents simulation results on the behavior of three stages in tandem implementing the EMD. The three stages have identical traffic sources with mean message length of 30 packets. Each of the three stages has queue of length 120 and the EMD threshold is set to 90. In this example $\Gamma = 0$. The loads of the first and second traffic sources are 0.8 (each) and the load of the third varies from almost 0 to 2.0. The dotted and dashed lines show the goodput of the local sources at stage 1 and 2 respectively, the dash-dot and solid lines show the goodput of the traffic coming form the previous stage for the above. It is seen that the third stage yields almost the same goodput for external and internal traffic.

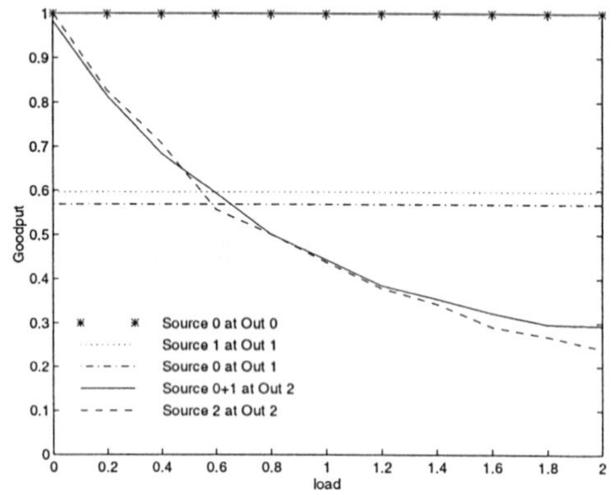

Figure 8: Three EMD stages: Goodput vs. load [$N1 = N2 = N3 = 120$; $K1 = K2 = K3 = 90$; $1/q1, 2, 3 = 30$; $\rho 0 = \rho 1 = 0.8$]

5.3 On-Off Source Model

5.3.1 Non-controlled On-Off Model

Consider an on-off source, where during "on" periods it generates messages segmented into packets as described in the basic model (Section 2). During "off" periods, the source does not generate any traffic. The number of messages generated during the "on" period is geometrically distributed with parameter α, i.e., with every head-of-message packet, the source remains in the "on" state with probability $(1 - \alpha)$ and another message is generated, or the source switches to the "off" state with probability α. The "off" period is exponentially distributed with parameter β. The state transition diagram describing the non-controlled system is given in Figure 9. In the diagram, a state

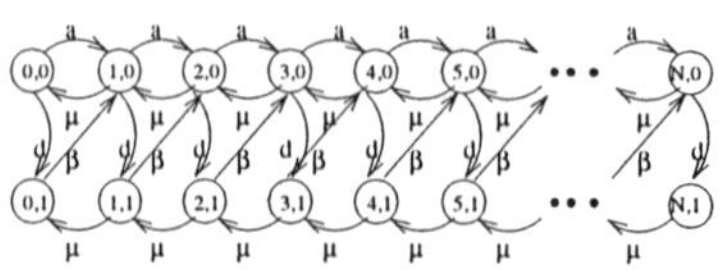

Figure 9: The model of a network element with On-Off source [$a = ((1 - \alpha)q + p)\lambda$; $d = \alpha q \lambda$]

$(j, 0)$ describes the system having j packets operating

in the "on" state, while a state $(j,\ 1)$ describes the system with j packets operating in the "off" state.

Let the vector of the above probabilities be $\mathcal{P} = [P_{0,0},\ P_{0,1},\ P_{1,0},\ P_{1,1}, \ldots,\ P_{N,0},\ P_{N,1}]$ and let $\mathcal{R}$ denote the transition rate matrix. Then,

$$\mathcal{P} \cdot \mathcal{R} = 0\ ; \quad \sum_{i=0}^{N} (P_{i,0} + P_{i,1}) = 1 \qquad (5)$$

The transition rate matrix can be easily derived from the state diagram in Figure 9 and the steady state probabilities can be calculated.

The goodput analysis for the on-off model is similar to that of the basic model, with slight changes. Here, a distinction should be made, between messages that arrive during an "on" period and messages that arrive as the first message of an "on" period, and find the system in the "off" state, i.e. one of $(j,\ 1)$ states. In the calculation of the probability of a message to be successful given it has arrived at the buffer at some state, we should consider the probability of this arrival (either within an "on" period, or as the ending of an "off" period). Let $\mathcal{M}$ be the random variable representing the state of the system, $\mathcal{M} = 0$ for an "on" state and $\mathcal{M} = 1$ for an "off" state. Let $\mathcal{N}$ be the random variable representing the number of messages during an "on" period, and $\bar{\mathcal{N}}$ its average. The probability of a message finding the system in an "on" state with i packets in the queue is

$$\hat{P}_{i,0} = (\bar{\mathcal{N}} - 1)/\bar{\mathcal{N}} P(\mathcal{Q} = i, \mathcal{M} = 0) \qquad (6)$$

where $P(\mathcal{Q} = i, \mathcal{M} = 0)$ are the steady state probabilities for $(i,\ 0)$ from above. However, the probability of a message of finding the system in an "off" period, i.e., as the first message of an "on" period with i packets in the queue is

$$\begin{aligned} \hat{P}_{i,1} &= 1/\bar{\mathcal{N}} \sum_{l=i}^{N} P(\mathcal{Q} = l, \mathcal{M} = 0) \\ &\quad \cdot \alpha q (\mu/(\mu+\beta))^{(l-i)} (\beta/(\mu+\beta)) \qquad (7) \end{aligned}$$

The goodput in this case is given by,

$$\begin{aligned} \mathcal{G} &= \frac{q}{\hat{P}_{i,0} + \hat{P}_{i,1}} \sum_{n=1}^{\infty} n \cdot q(1-q)^{n-1} \\ &\quad \sum_{i=0}^{N} P(\mathcal{V} = 1 | \mathcal{W} = n, \mathcal{Q} = i)(\hat{P}_{i,0} + \hat{P}_{i,1}) \end{aligned}$$

5.3.2 On-Off Model with EMD

When the EMD mechanism is deployed in the above system, it has two modes of operation in the "on" state: normal mode and discarding mode. In the "off" state there is only one mode of operation since no packets arrive at this state. Here a state $(j,\ 0)$ describes the system when there are j packets in the buffer, the source is in the "on" state and arriving packets enter the buffer. A state $(j,\ 1)$ describes the system when there are j packets in the buffer, the source is in the "on" state but each arriving packet is discarded. In particular, if a head-of-message arrives (with probability q) when the queue level is $j \geq K$, the packet is not admitted to the queue and the system enters state $(j,\ 1)$ in the discarding mode. As a head-of-message packet arrives during an "on" state, the system switches to the "off" state with probability α, no packet enters the queue and the system enters state $(j,\ 2)$. The "off" state ends with rate β and the system enters state $(j,\ 0)$ or $(j,\ 1)$ according to the queue level, j. The state transition diagram of this system is given in Figure 10.

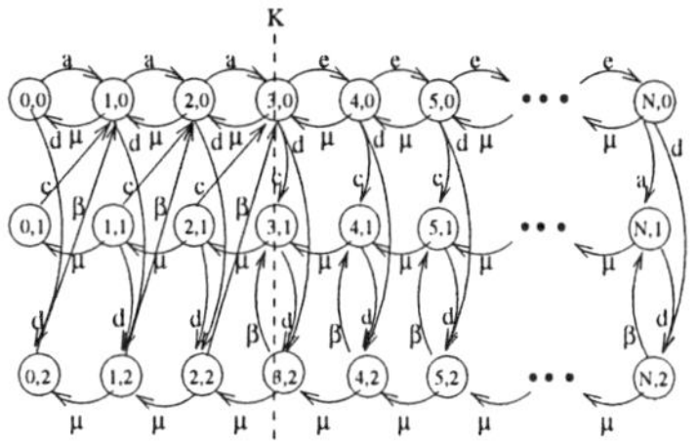

Figure 10: On-Off source – a network element under EMD policy $[a = ((1-\alpha)q+p)\lambda\ ;\ c = (1-\alpha)q\lambda\ ;\ d = \alpha q\lambda\ ;\ e = p\lambda]$

Let $\mathcal{P} = [P_{0,0},\ P_{0,1},\ P_{0,2},\ P_{1,0},\ P_{1,1},\ P_{1,2},\ \ldots,\ P_{N,0},\ P_{N,1},\ P_{N,2}]$ be the vector of the above state probabilities and let $\mathcal{R}$ denote the transition rate matrix. Then,

$$\mathcal{P} \cdot \mathcal{R} = 0\ ; \quad \sum_{i=0}^{N} (P_{i,0} + P_{i,1} + P_{i,2}) = 1 \qquad (8)$$

The transition rate matrix can be easily derived from the state diagram in Figure 10 and the steady state probabilities can be calculated.

With the state probabilities the goodput of this system is calculated, as described for the non-controlled bursty model, were in (7) and (8) $P(\mathcal{Q} = i, \mathcal{M} = 0)$ are the steady state probabilities for the "on" state, i.e. $P_{i,0} + P_{i,1}$.

5.3.3 On-Off models Results

Solving the equations for the state probabilities of the EMD and the non-controlled systems with On-Off sources, gives goodput values for different system parameters. In Figures 11 and 12, the improvements in goodput for systems with EMD versus the non-controlled system (see legends in figures) are presented. Various parameters for the "on" period or "off" period length are given. In figure 11, α ranges between 0.01 and 0.99 and since α is the probability of ending an On period - as α is increased - the goodput increases (and the positive effect of the EMD mechanism decreases). The explanation for that is that since α is the probability to end an "on" period, as it

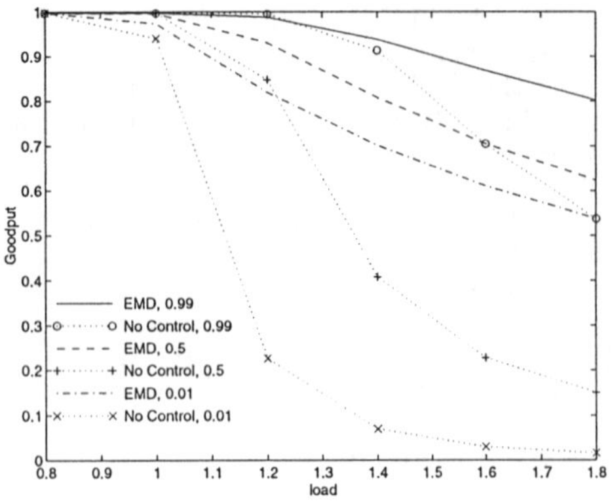

Figure 11: On-Off source: Goodput vs. load EMD / No control, different On periods [$N = 120$; $K = 60$; $1/q = 30$; $\alpha = 0.01, 0.5, 0.99$; $\beta = 0.1$]

increases - the system goes more often into an "off" state - and the queue "has more time" to free space, and the probability of messages to be successful increases (hence goodput increases). EMD improves the goodput of the described system for all cases, but by a larger scale for small α, where the goodput of the non-controlled system becomes very low for high loads (as in the basic "all-on" model). In figure 12, β ranges from 1 to 0.0001. As β is the rate at which Off periods end, the smaller it is, Off periods are longer and the goodput is higher, and, again the significance of the EMD mechanism is diminished. This is expected since for long Off periods, little or no congestion is developed and the need for a selective discarding policy is alleviated. Both figures show that EMD improves system's goodput significantly, especially for high loads (i.e., $\rho > 1$).

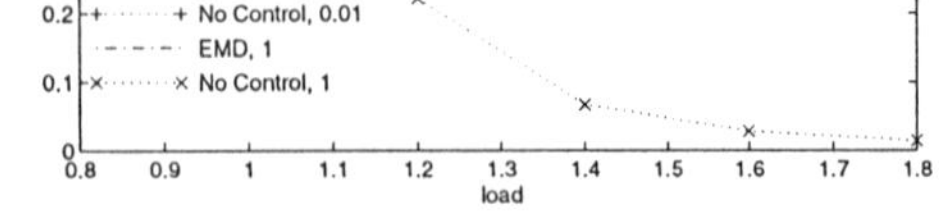

Figure 12: On-Off source: Goodput vs. load EMD / No control, different Off periods [$N = 120$; $K = 60$; $1/q = 30$; $\alpha = 0.1$; $\beta = 1, 0.01, 0.001$]

6 Conclusions

In this paper we developed an analytical model to examine the performance of systems with no discarding policies in place and systems that deploy the PMD and EMD policies. The results show that congestion is much better controlled with any message based discarding policy yielding a remarkable improvement in network performance.

The two policies examined perform differently depending on network load. For moderate traffic loads, PMD policy gives best performance of the network element's goodput. When the load increases, and congestion is more likely to develop, the EMD policy performs better than the PMD with a significant improvement in goodput performance of the system, compared to the non-controlled case.

These results can also be applied to the specific case of ATM, were selective discarding can improve the quality of service of best- effort (or UBR) services. Our analysis showed that improvement in goodput with the EMD mechanism is also achieved for the case of an on-off source, in particular when the basic system performs poorly. Finally, it may be interesting to further investigate a case of several sources subject to selective discarding, for their individual performance improvements and their mutual effects.

References

[CKS93] I. Cidon, A. Khamisy, and M. Sidi. Analysis of packet loss processes in high speed networks. *IEEE Transactions on Information Theory*, IT-39(1):98–108, January 1993.

[FJ93] S. Floyd and V. Jacobson. Random early detection gateways for congestion avoidance. *IEEE/ACM Transactions on Networking*, 1(4):25–39, August 1993.

[FR94] S. Floyd and A. Romanow. Dynamics of TCP traffic over ATM networks. In *Proc. ACM/SIGCOMM'94*, pages 79–88, September 1994.

[Kam95] A.E. Kamal. A performance study of selective cell discarding using the end-of-packet indicator in AAL type 5. In *Proc. INFOCOM'95*, pages 1264–1272, Boston, April 1995.

[Tur96] J. S. Turner. Maintaining high throughput during overload in ATM switches. In *Proc. INFOCOM'96*, pages 287–295, San-Francisco, April 1996.

Window-based error recovery and flow control with a slow acknowledgement channel: a study of TCP/IP performance

T. V. Lakshman† U. Madhow* Bernhard Suter†

† Bell Labs
Lucent Technologies
101 Crawfords Corner Road
Holmdel, NJ 07733 USA

* University of Illinois
Electrical and Computer Engineering Department
Urbana, Illinois 61801.
USA

Abstract

With the envisaged growth in Internet access services over networks with asymmetric links such as Asymmetric Digital Subscriber Line (ADSL) and Hybrid Fiber Coax (HFC), it becomes crucial to evaluate the performance of window-based protocols over systems in which the reverse link is considerably slower than the forward link. Even if the actual bandwidth asymmetry is moderate, high effective asymmetries can result because of bidirectional traffic. Our objective is to determine, whether TCP/IP performs reasonably in a setting in which the reverse link is the primary bottleneck. Our main results are:

(1) For both the prevalent Tahoe version with Fast Retransmit and the Reno version of TCP, we determine the throughput as a function of buffering, round-trip times and normalized asymmetry (taken to be the ratio of the transmission time of ACKs in the reverse path to that of data packets in the forward path). We identify three modes of operation which are dependent on the forward buffer sizes and the normalized asymmetry.

(2) Asymmetry increases TCP's already high sensitivity to random packet losses that might be caused by transient bursts in real-time traffic. Specifically, random loss leads to significant throughput deterioration when the product of the loss probability, the asymmetry *and the* square *of the bandwidth delay product is large.*

(3) Congestion in the reverse path adds considerably to TCP's unfairness when multiple connections share the reverse link. Link bandwidth sharing is unfair even for connections with identical round-trip times and hence use of per connection buffer allocation on the reverse path appears essential.

1 Introduction

It is expected that high-speed Internet access services to residential subscribers will be provided using asymmetric access networks, such as networks using ADSL and its variants, HFC (i.e., cable) networks, and combinations such as a downstream path (network to subscriber) over a cable or satellite link and a telephone upstream link (subscriber to network or service provider). These systems have an inherent bandwidth asymmetry which can be as low as 10 for some of the proposed cable modem and ADSL access services, to as high as 100 or more when a telephone return path is used. Even higher asymmetries in the bandwidths seen by downstream connections will result if the access traffic is bidirectional and hence causing the slow upstream link from the subscriber to the network to be shared by both data packets (where the destination is upstream) and ACK packets (where the destination is downstream). Moreover, asymmetric traffic can cause congestion in the acknowledgement path even when there is no bandwidth asymmetry.

Since TCP uses the arrival rate of ACKs in the reverse channel to control packet flow in the forward direction, congestion in the reverse path may lead to poor utilization of the forward path. The objective of this paper is to characterize TCP performance in such a setting. Previous studies of TCP performance [3, 5, 7] have only considered bottlenecks in the forward path.

It is to be noted that the asymmetry in raw bandwidth (in bits per second) is not the asymmetry directly affecting TCP performance; rather, it is the *normalized asymmetry*, defined as the ratio of the transmission time of ACKs on the bottleneck link on the reverse path to that of packets on the bottleneck link on the forward path, that affects TCP performance. Indeed, the raw bandwidth asymmetry is alleviated by the fact that TCP ACKs (typically 40 bytes) are much shorter than data packets, and can be shortened further using header compression. Despite this, the normalized asymmetry can be very high when there is bidirectional traffic where some connections send data packets on the reverse path while others send ACKs on the same link. This is a likely scenario on a shared reverse link as in an HFC upstream channel.

Our goal is to develop an understanding of TCP behavior as a function of the normalized asymmetry, the buffering on the forward and reverse path bottlenecks, and the bandwidth-delay product. We study both the prevalent Tahoe version of TCP with fast retransmit and the later Reno version [1, 2] (henceforth referred to as TCP-Tahoe and TCP-Reno, respectively). We gain basic insight into TCP behavior by means of an idealized model consisting of a single forward and reverse link, together with a propagation delay. Next, we consider the scenario where packets may be lost randomly in the forward path. Random loss for our purposes is not necessarily due to link errors. Rather, it includes all losses that an ideal congestion control mechanism should not react to; that is, all losses not due to sustained congestion (e.g., transient congestion caused by high priority real-time cross traffic). However, since TCP combines error recovery with congestion control, it does re-

0-8186-7780-5/97 $10.00 © 1997 IEEE

act to all such losses by scaling back its transmission rate, which results in throughput reduction. A setting of particular interest is TCP supported over an Available Bit Rate (ABR) ATM virtual circuit, where transient congestion in the ATM network may cause TCP packet loss. Random loss may also occur in heterogeneous networks which contain lossy, time-varying, wireless links. We show that TCP throughput is very sensitive to the random loss probability: the throughput deteriorates rapidly once the product of the loss probability, the *asymmetry* and the *square* of the bandwidth delay product exceeds a threshold.

For multiple connections, we present simulation studies that show that, in the absence of network level control of bandwidth or buffer allocation, asymmetry exacerbates the inherent unfairness of TCP. Also, link bandwidth sharing over the slow link becomes grossly unfair for bidirectional connections. These problems can be alleviated by using fair queueing (or weighted round robin with per connection queueing) for the slow link.

We only consider persistent sources, which could be thought of as modeling long file transfers. While it has been observed that many Internet connections are of short durations, the impact of a slow acknowledgement channel on TCP congestion avoidance behavior is best understood by considering persistent sources.

2 System Model

2.1 Forward and Reverse Path Model

Our model is similar to that considered in [5], [7], [3], with the following key difference: the path followed by acknowledgements is explicitly modeled. We consider an infinite data source which always has packets to send, so that the units of data on the forward path are maximum sized packets. We consider a forward link with capacity μ_f packets per second and a FIFO forward buffer of size B_f packets. For each packet that is received by the destination, a cumulative acknowledgement is generated which contains the next expected segment number. The fact that acknowledgements are cumulative implies that later ACKs contain all the information contained by earlier ACKs, so that ACK loss simply results in bursty traffic on the forward path. This is the key to our analysis of the impact of asymmetry on performance. It is assumed that the speed of the reverse link is μ_r ACK packets per second, and the the reverse buffer is FIFO of size B_r ACK packets. The forward and reverse buffer sizes do not include the packet in service. We assume that $\mu_f = k\mu_r$, with $k > 1$, where k is the *normalized asymmetry factor*, i.e. the effective bandwidth asymmetry nomalized by the ratio of forward to reverse packet sizes..

While the path traversed by the connection may include links other than the forward and reverse links explicitly modeled here, it is assumed that the performance is dominated by the bottleneck links in each direction. The remainder of the network is modeled via a constant "propagation" delay, which includes queueing delays on other links, propagation delays, and processing delays at nodes in the path of the connection. The propagation delay on the forward path is defined as the time between when a packet is completely transmitted on the forward link and when it arrives at the destination, and is denoted by τ_f. The delay on the reverse path is analogously defined as the time between when an ACK packet completes transmission on the reverse link and when it arrives at the source, and is denoted by τ_r. While we distinguish these two delays in our notation because of the asymmetry between the forward and reverse paths, we will see that only the net propagation delay $\tau = \tau_f + \tau_r$ affects performance. This delay can range from several milliseconds to several hundreds of milliseconds. The *round-trip time* is the time between when a packet is sent by the source and when the source receives an acknowledgement for that packet, and includes queueing at the forward and reverse links in addition to the propagation delay. The average round-trip time will be denoted by T.

We model random loss as follows: each head-of-the-line packet in the forward buffer has a probability q of being lost after transmission, and different packet losses are independent. While much of the analysis will be for the case $q = 0$, we will show that random loss can have a significant impact on performance.

The model described above is shown in Figure 1.

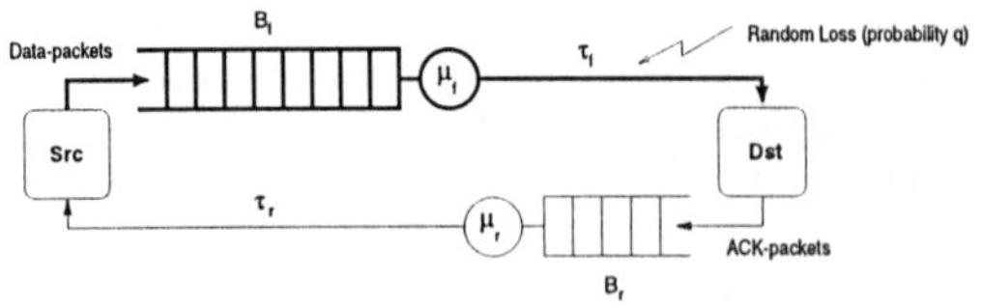

Figure 1: System model for a single connection

Throughout the paper, it is convenient to consider the following example.

Running Example:

The reverse link is of speed 320 Kbps, ACK packets are of length 40 bytes. Forward packets are of length 1000 bytes. The reverse link speed μ_r is therefore 1000 ACKs/s, so that a asymmetry factor $k = 5$ (i.e., a μ_f of 5000 packets/s) corresponds to a raw forward link speed of 40 Mb/s. [1] The propagation delay τ for the simulations shown in Section 3 to aid the analytical development is kept fixed at 2 milliseconds, although it is varied in our numerical results in Section 4 in order to illustrate several points. The forward buffer size $B_f = 8$ packets. The reverse buffer size is $B_r = 5$ ACK packets.

2.2 Background on TCP

The connection of interest uses a window flow control protocol. At time t, the window size is denoted by $W(t)$, and is equal to the maximum allowed number of unacknowledged packets (not counting retransmissions). Since we assume an infinite data source, the connection uses its allowable window to the fullest extent, i.e., at time t, there are indeed $W(t)$ unacknowledged packets. The window varies dynamically in response to acknowledgements and to detection of packet loss. Upon receiving a packet, the destination is assumed to send a cumulative acknowledgment back immediately. Even though selective ACKs or NACKs are not available, a single packet loss can be detected by consecutive acknowledgements having the same "next expected" number. Both TCP-Tahoe and TCP-Reno therefore have a *fast retransmit* option, in which a packet is

[1] In practice, both the forward and reverse link speeds might be scaled down considerably in order to support multiple connections, but normalized asymmetry factors of up to 25 could occur.

retransmitted after the number of such *duplicate acknowledgements* exceeds a threshold (typically three). If packet loss is not detected in this manner, it leads to expiry of a timer. We use coarse-grain timers with a 500 ms granularity (i.e., the time between the release of a packet and the expiry of the timer associated with it is at least 500 ms).

See [6] for a detailed description of TCP, [1] for the original version of TCP-Tahoe, [2] for a description of TCP-Reno, [5, 7] for simulation studies, and [3] for an analytical characterization of TCP with a bottlenecked forward link (the latter study ignored the reverse path).

The following description of the window evolution is sufficient for our purpose.

Description of TCP-Tahoe and TCP-Reno

The algorithm followed by each connection has two parameters, current window size W and a threshold W_t, which are updated as follows.

> **(1 Tahoe/Reno)** After every non–repeated ack:
> if $W < W_t$, set $W = W + 1$; **Slow Start Phase**
> else set $W = W + 1/[W]$. **Congestion Avoidance Phase**
> ($[x]$ denotes the integer part of x)
> **(2 Tahoe)** After a packet loss is detected (when timer expires or the number of repeated ACKs exceeds a threshold):
> set $W_t = W/2$;
> set $W = 1$.
> **(2 Reno)** When the number of repeated ACKs exceeds a threshold,
> retransmit "next expected" packet;
> set $W_t = W/2$, then set $W = W_t$ (i.e. halve the window);
> resume congestion avoidance using new window once retransmission is acknowledged .
> **(3 Reno)** Upon timer expiry, the algorithm goes into slow start as before:
> set $W_t = W/2$;
> set $W = 1$.

While TCP-Reno cuts its window by half after detection of each packet loss via duplicate ACKs, in order to prevent a burst of packets from being transmitted when the retransmission is finally acknowledged, it temporarily expands the window size to permit new packets to be transmitted with duplicate ACKs until the "next expected" number in the acknowledgement advances. The window expansion takes place after that $W/2$ ACKS have been received, in order to ensure that the number of outstanding packets has been reduced to the new window size.

3 A single TCP connection

The results of Sections 3.2 and 3.3 are summarized in Figure 2, which shows the throughput, as a function of the normalized asymmetry, of TCP-Tahoe and TCP-Reno. The system considered is the running example described in Section 2, with a propagation delay of 2 ms. The match between analysis and simulation is excellent, which implies that the analytical description of TCP behavior in Sections 3.2 and 3.3 is reasonably accurate within the considered framework. The figure shows that there are several different regimes of operation; we will show that these are determined by the relationship between the normalized asymmetry and the forward buffer size.

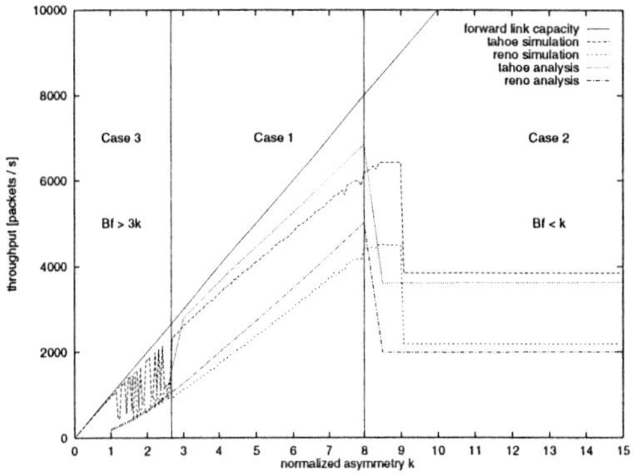

Figure 2: Analytical and simulation results of the throughput of TCP-Tahoe and TCP-Reno as a function of the normalized asymmetry k.

3.1 Analysis for Fixed Windows

Assume that the connection is using a fixed window size of W, which can be thought of as a snapshot of a TCP window at a given time. The minimum round-trip time T incurred by a packet is given by $T = \tau + \frac{1}{\mu_r} + \frac{1}{\mu_f}$. This subsection is based on applying Little's law (and a modification thereof) as a means of relating window size (or the number of outstanding packets) to the throughput (or the rate of successful transmission of forward link packets). The analysis gives optimistic throughput estimates, since it assumes that the minimum possible average delay is incurred by a packet. This assumption of traffic that is as smooth as possible is made for analytical convenience, but is a good approximation for the deterministic system model in Section 2. Refinements to the analysis will be introduced as necessary when explaining the behavior with dynamic windows.

Condition for fully utilized reverse link

Applying Little's law, we get the following condition for the reverse link to be fully utilized: $W \geq \mu_r T$. This condition is necessary but not sufficient, since the round-trip delay incurred by a packet can be larger than the minimum round-trip time T due to bursty arrivals at the forward or reverse buffer.

Condition for attaining throughput $\lambda > \mu_r$

If the rate of packet transmissions on the forward link is λ, ACKs arrive at the reverse link at the same rate. If $\lambda > \mu_r$, on average only one out of every λ/μ_r ACKs get through on the reverse link, the others have to be dropped as the reverse link buffer is overflowing. Thus, on average, each ACK in the reverse buffer and each ACK in flight in the reverse link actually represents acknowledgement information for λ/μ_r forward packets. [2] Since the reverse pipe is completely full, any ACK that does make it into the reverse buffer sees B_r ACKs ahead of it, so that the net delay it incurs in the reverse buffer (including its service time) is B_r/μ_r.

The modified Little's law that results from the preceding

[2] In turn, for each ACK arriving back at the source, an average of λ/μ_r packets are released and arrive at the forward buffer. However, we will ignore the resulting burstiness in our calculations to obtain a simpler formula.

arguments reads as follows:

$$W = \lambda(\tau_f + \frac{1}{\mu_f}) + \frac{\lambda}{\mu_r}[\mu_r(\tau_r + \frac{1}{\mu_r}) + B_r] \quad (1)$$

The first term corresponds to the number of packets in the forward pipe, while the second is the number of surviving ACKs in the reverse pipe, multiplied by λ/μ_r, the number of forward packets represented by each surviving ACK on average. This yields the following estimate of the throughput λ as a function of the window size.

$$\lambda = \frac{W}{T + \frac{B_r}{\mu_r}} \quad (2)$$

The preceding argument assumes that the forward buffer is large enough to withstand the bursty traffic resulting from ACK loss. A necessary condition for this is that the forward buffer is larger than the average burst size, i.e., that $B_f \geq \frac{\lambda}{\mu_r}$. This condition is not sufficient: loss on the forward path can occur even when this condition is satisfied, since not all bursts contain an equal number of packets.

The window size W_{full} for which the forward link can be fully utilized is obtained by setting $\lambda = \mu_f$ in (1), which yields $W_{full} = \mu_f(T + B_r/\mu_r) = \mu_f T + kB_r$. For the running example, $W_{full} = 41$ for an asymmetry factor $k = 5$.

Window size for a full pipe

The pipe is completely full when both the forward and reverse links are always busy, the forward and reverse buffers are full, and there are as many packets as possible in flight. The window size corresponding to this is denoted by W_{max}, and is given by $W_{max} = W_{full} + B_f = \mu_f T + kB_r + B_f$. When analyzing TCP evolution, we will assume that increasing the window beyond W_{max} will cause packet loss. Note that packet loss might occur at a smaller window size because the traffic is burstier than that assumed in our application of Little's law. For the running example, $W_{max} = 49$ for $k = 5$.

Forward buffer size requirement

For a fully utilized forward link, one out of k ACKs is lost, so that the average burst size into the forward buffer is k packets. Thus, $B_f \geq k$ should lead to good forward link utilization.

3.2 TCP-Tahoe evolution without random loss

The typical evolution is cyclical: the window size grows slowly during congestion avoidance to a maximum value of W_{final}, at which point there is a packet loss. This loss may or may not result in a timeout, depending on the system parameters. Subsequently, the window drops down to one, followed by rapid growth in slow start until it reaches $W_{final}/2$. At this point, the window dynamics switch to congestion avoidance until the window size reaches W_{final} again, at which point there is another loss, resulting in a new cycle. The long run throughput can therefore be computed as the number of packets successfully transmitted in a cycle, divided by the cycle duration. If a cycle ends in a timeout, the length of the timeout must be included in the cycle duration, even though no packets are transmitted during most of the timeout period.

Since the slow start phase is much shorter than the congestion avoidance phase, we will ignore it for our throughput estimates. For a detailed analysis of slow start without a reverse link constraint, see [3]. The window growth in congestion avoidance is relatively slow, and is well modeled by a continuous time approximation described by a differential equation, as in [3] and [5]. In contrast to the latter references, which ignore the reverse link, here the window growth is slowed down due to the loss of ACKs on the reverse path. We will need to consider three different cases, depending on the relative size of the forward buffer and the normalized asymmetry factor:
Case 1: $k \leq B_f \leq 3k$
Case 2: $B_f < k$
Case 3: $B_f > 3k$

Case 1 can be thought of as a regime in which TCP operates normally. Case 2 corresponds to a situation in which the forward buffer is too small to handle bursts resulting from asymmetry and ACK loss, which leads to poor performance even though the forward link is very fast. Case 3 is an anomaly, in that the performance gets worse as forward buffer size becomes large. We will see that the problem that causes this can be resolved by implementing a drop from front policy at the reverse buffer. Each case is considered in detail in what follows.

3.2.1 Case 1: $k \leq B_f \leq 3k$

In congestion avoidance, the rate $\frac{dW}{da}$ of window growth with arriving acknowledgements is given by $dW/da = 1/W$. Assuming that the window size during congestion avoidance is large enough to keep the reverse link busy (i.e., $W \geq W_r = \mu_r T$), the rate at which the acknowledgements arrive back at the source is given by $da/dt = \mu_r$. We obtain, therefore, that the rate of window growth with time is given by $dW/dt = \mu_r/W$, which is easily solved to get

$$W(t) = \sqrt{W^2(0) + 2\mu_r t} \quad (3)$$

Denoting the window size at which packet loss occurs by $W = W_{final}$, the window size W_0 at the beginning of congestion avoidance is $W_{final}/2$. For Case 1, $W_{final} = W_{max} = \mu_f T + kB_r + B_f$. The congestion avoidance period can be divided into two phases as follows.

Phase 1: $W(t) \leq W_{full}$, so that the forward link is underutilized. The instantaneous throughput $\lambda(t)$ is given by (2) and (3). From (3), the duration of this phase is

$$t_{ca1} = \frac{W_{full}^2 - W_0^2}{2\mu_r} \quad (4)$$

($t_{ca1} = 0$ if $W_{full} \leq W_0$.)

Phase 2: $W_{full} \leq W(t) \leq W_{final}$, so that the forward link is fully utilized. The throughput $\lambda(t) = \mu_f$, and the duration of this phase is

$$t_{ca2} = \frac{W_{final}^2 - W_{full}^2}{2\mu_r} \quad (5)$$

($t_{ca2} = 0$ if $W_{final} \leq W_{full}$).

The net duration of the congestion avoidance phase is

$$t_{ca} = t_{ca1} + t_{ca2} = \frac{W_{final}^2 - W_0^2}{2\mu_r} \quad (6)$$

The average throughput is equal to the throughput computed over a cycle, and is given by

$$\bar{\lambda} = \frac{1}{t_{ca}} \int_0^{t_{ca}} \lambda(t)\, dt \quad (7)$$

Using (2), (3), and (4)-(6), we obtain upon simplification that

$$\bar{\lambda} = [\frac{2(W_{full}^3 - W_0^3)}{3(T + \frac{B_r}{\mu_r})} + \mu_f(W_{final}^2 - W_{full}^2)]/(W_{final}^2 - W_0^2) \quad (8)$$

Ideally, $\bar{\lambda}$ should be close to μ_f, the forward link capacity. As Figure 2 shows, for fixed μ_r, $\bar{\lambda}$ grows almost linearly with k (and therefore with μ_f) in the regime of Case 1.

A typical window evolution for Case 1 is shown in Figure 3. For our running example, with $k = 5 < B_f = 8$, our analysis predicts that the largest window size attained for our running example is $W_{final} = W_{max} = 49$. This matches the simulated window evolution shown in Figure 3.

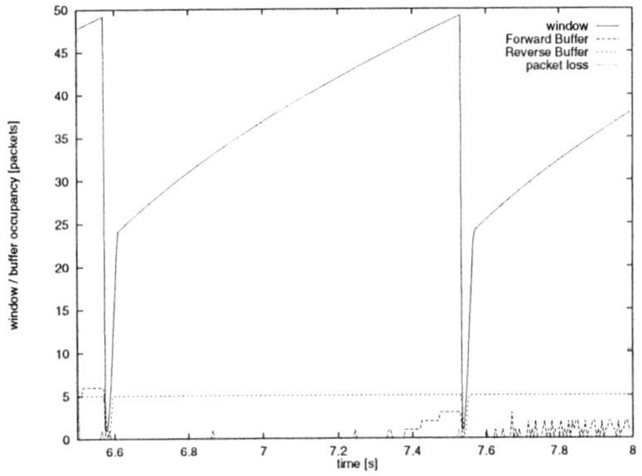

Figure 3: Simulation of the window evolution for the running example with TCP-Tahoe when $k = 5$. Similar evolutions are seen for all k satisfying the condition in Case 1.

3.2.2 Case 2: $B_f < k$

For large k, TCP performance is dominated by the ability of the forward buffer to accomodate bursts, so that the performance is relatively insensitive to k in this regime. It is therefore convenient to consider the case $k = \infty$.

Once the reverse link is fully utilized, ACKs arrive back at the source with a spacing of $1/\mu_r$. If the throughput is larger than μ_r, each ACK represents a number of successful forward packets, so that, when it is received, a burst of packets is released into the forward buffer. The maximum number of such bursts that are outstanding is simply the number of outstanding packets whose ACKs will successfully reach the source, and is equal to the maximum capacity of the reverse pipe, $W_r = \mu_r T + B_r$, which is assumed to be an integer for simplicity. Since $k = \infty$, the ACKs corresponding to all packets in the burst appear at the same instant at the reverse buffer, and at most one of these ACKs can be served. This surviving ACK leads to another burst being released, with $W_r - 1$ bursts having been released between this burst and the earlier burst being ACKed. These two bursts (and every W_rth burst before and after them) can therefore be thought of as the same burst circulating in the path of the connection. With such an identification, there are W_r circulating bursts, and we denote by X_i the current size of the ith burst, $i = 1, ..., W_r$. The current window size is therefore $W = \sum_{i=1}^{W_r} X_i$. Suppose now that the window size gets incremented from W to $W + 1$ when an ACK from burst i arrives. Then X_i is incremented to $X_i + 1$ (i.e., one more packet is added to the burst). In congestion avoidance, the next increment occurs after $W + 1$ more ACKs have been received by the source, i.e., once the ACKs for $W + 1$ further bursts have arrived. Thus, in terms of our modulo W_r indexing scheme, the next burst that gets incremented has index

$$j = (i + W + 1) \text{ modulo } W_r \quad (9)$$

The preceding can be used to deduce the deterministic evolution of the window and burst sizes. Clearly, some bursts could be incremented more often than others during this evolution. When the burst with the largest size has more than $B_f + 1$ packets, there is a buffer overflow and the cycle ends. We would now like to predict the window size W_{final} at which this happens, after which the analysis of Case 1 applies for estimating the throughput. The successive choices of indices dictated by (9) appears chaotic, but more study of this map (which in itself is an approximation to actual TCP behavior) is necessary. For our purpose here, we approximate the evolution due to (9) by the following random evolution: for each increment of the window size, the burst whose size is to be increased by one is chosen uniformly at random among the W_r bursts. Let $X_k^{(n)}$ denote the size of the kth burst after the nth window increment, where $k = 1, ..., W_r$, and where we assume that $X_k^{(0)} \equiv 1$ when the reverse link first gets fully utilized (i.e., when $W = W_r$). Let I_n denote the index of the burst that is incremented for the nth window increment. We will assume that the I_n are independent and identically distributed random variables which are uniformly distributed on $\{1, ..., W_r\}$. Then the evolution of the burst sizes is given by

$$X_k^{(n)} = \begin{cases} X_k^{(n-1)} + 1 & k = I_n \\ X_k^{(n-1)} & else \end{cases}$$

The size of the largest burst after the nth increment is denoted by $X_{max}^{(n)} = max_k X_k^{(n)}$. In order to estimate the window size reached before the largest burst exceeds $B_f + 1$, we consider the following criterion: Let n^* denote the smallest n such that

$$P[X_{max}^{(n)} > B_f + 1] \geq 0.5 \quad (10)$$

This is the median number of increments before a buffer overflow due to the maximum sized burst. The window size corresponding to this is $W^* = n^* + W_r$, and this is taken to be W_{final} in our throughput estimates.

Using a union bound for the left-hand side of (10), and using the fact that the $\{X_k^{(n)}\}$ are identically distributed (though not independent), we obtain

$$P[X_{max}^{(n)} > B_f + 1] \leq W_r P[X_1^{(n)} > B_f + 1] \quad (11)$$

Now, $X_1^{(n)} - X_1^{(0)} = X_1^{(n)} - 1$ is binomially distributed with parameters n and $1/W_r$, so that the extreme right-hand side of (11) can be computed by summing over the tail of the distribution. Actually, the first term in the tail is a good approximation to the entire tail, and the computation is further simplified by using the Poisson approximation to the binomial distribution. We finally obtain that

$$P[X_{max}^{(n)} > B_f + 1] \approx W_r e^{-n/W_r} \frac{(n/W_r)^{B_f+1}}{(B_f+1)!} \quad (12)$$

For $k > B_f$, the W_{final} predicted by the preceding computations for our running example is 54.5. As shown in the Figure 4, the actual maximum window size reached in the cycle is 45 for $k = 10$ (recall that $B_f = 8$).

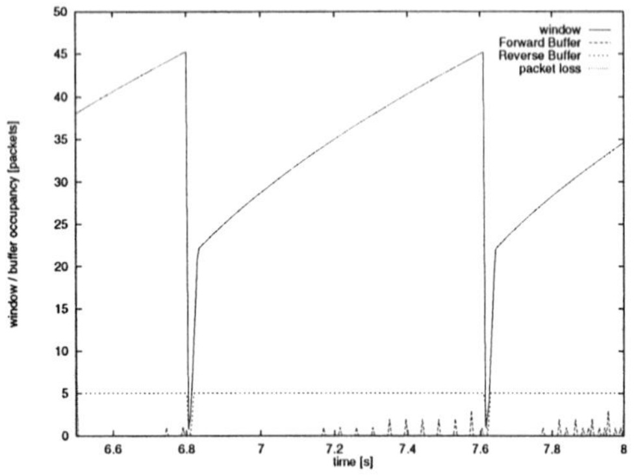

Figure 4: Simulation of the window evolution for the running example with TCP-Tahoe when $k > B_f = 8$. The evolution shown is for $k = 10$, but similar evolutions are seen for all $k > B_f$.

It is natural to ask why burstiness does not determine the performance for Case 1 ($B_f \geq k$), for which $W_{final} = W_{max}$, corresponding to a full pipe. In this case, the buffer can accomodate bursts of size upto $k + 1$ (since the buffer capacity is $k + 1$, including the packet in service). When $X_{max}^{(n)}$ first goes from k to $k + 1$, at least two ACKs from this burst are served (since at least one ACK packet is transmitted for every k packets transmitted on the forward link). This results in the large burst getting broken up into smaller bursts. This is probably what enables all bursts to maintain roughly equal sizes, so that buffer overflow occurs due to a full pipe rather than due to large burst sizes.

3.2.3 Case 3: $B_f > 3k$

The evolution here is exactly as in Case 1, except that a timeout may occur at the end of congestion avoidance because of a failure of the fast retransmit option. Consider a packet loss that occurs when

$$W_{final} = W_{max} = \mu_f T + kB_r + B_f$$

If packet n is lost, once all packets upto $n - 1$ are ACKed, the outstanding packets are $n, n+1, ..., n+W_{final}-1$. For all packets among these that are successful, the destination generates cumulative ACKs saying "next expected = n." After 3 duplicate ACKs arrive at the source, packet n is retransmitted and the window is dropped to one, so that no new transmissions are attempted. However, by the time 3 duplicate ACKs are received (spaced by $1/\mu_r$), the forward buffer is reduced by $3k$. If this does not drain the forward buffer (which will happen if $B_f > 3k$), the reverse link will remain fully utilized, and the reverse buffer will be full by the time the ACK for the retransmission arrives at the reverse buffer, so that the latter is likely to get lost. When this happens, the source keeps waiting for the ACK to arrive until there is a timeout. This can be thought of as Phase 3, and is of duration t_o, the length of the timeout period. Prior to this, Phase 1 and Phase 2 of the evolution are exactly as in Case 1, except for W_t to be one because of the two consecutive losses.

With the durations t_{ca1} and t_{ca2} as in (4)-(5), the net duration of congestion avoidance becomes

$$t_{ca} = t_{ca1} + t_{ca2} + t_o$$

and the average throughput is obtained by plugging into the formula (7), noting that $\lambda(t) = 0$ in Phase 3, since the window size is one and there is an unacknowledged packet.

A simple change that prevents the timeout from happening is to implement a drop from front policy at the receive buffer, which makes sure that the latest ACK information gets through to the source. This works because, with cumulative ACKs, the amount of information carried by later ACKs is always more than that contained by earlier ACKs. Simulations show that implementation of this policy eliminates all timeouts in Case 3, so that the throughput formula becomes similar to that in Case 1. Note that drop from front has been previously proposed for the forward path for TCP over ATM for an entirely different reason [4].

Typical window evolutions without and with drop from front are shown in Figures 5 and 6, respectively. The time over which the window is constant at one in Figure 5 corresponds to the timeout period.

3.3 TCP-Reno evolution without random loss

3.3.1 Cases 1 and 3: $B_f \geq k$

The evolution of TCP-Reno is similar to that for TCP-Tahoe, except that recovering from a packet loss is more problematic for TCP-Reno because of the slow reverse link. Suppose packet n is lost at $W = W_{final}$, and suppose that all packets sent before and after packet n get through. Thus, ACKs for packets $n+1, ..., n+W_{final} - 1$ will be generated by the destination, each saying "next expected = n." After three such duplicate ACKs are received by the source, packet n is retransmitted, and the window is cut back to $W_{final}/2$. Further, in order to avoid a burst when the ACK for the retransmitted packet gets through, after $W_{final}/2$ duplicate ACKs arrive, TCP-Reno starts transmitting a packet for each further duplicate ACK that arrives even though that is not allowed according to the window-based protocol. If the reverse link were not a bottleneck,

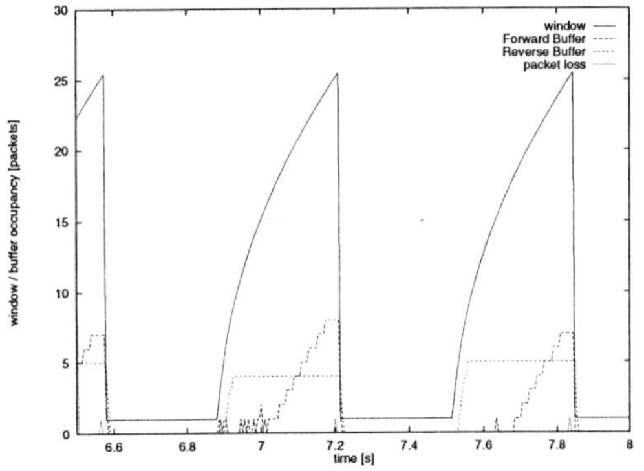

Figure 5: Simulation of the window evolution for the running example with TCP-Tahoe when $k = 2$ with a FIFO reverse buffer. The window size is constant at one for the duration of the timeout at the end of the cycle.

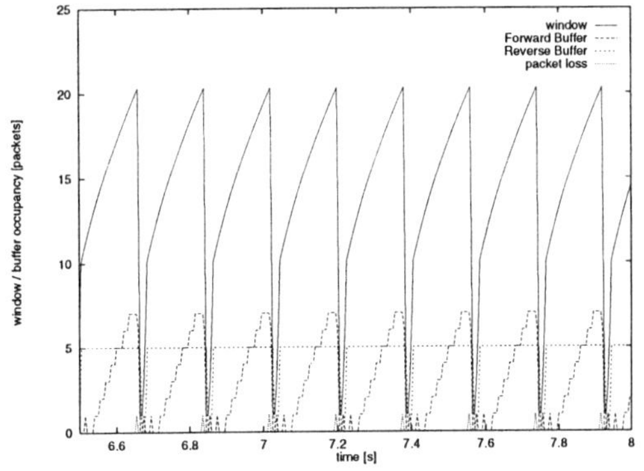

Figure 6: Simulation of the window evolution for the running example with TCP-Tahoe when $k = 2$ and drop from front is implemented at the reverse buffer. Note that the timeout is eliminated.

this would enable transmission of roughly $W_{final}/2$ new packets (which is equal to the new window size) by the time the ACK for the retransmission gets back, which means that there would be no burst of packets at that point. However, due to the slow reverse link, by the time the retransmitted ACK gets back, the number of duplicate ACKs received is roughly only $\mu_r T + 3$ (since ACKs can arrive back at a rate no faster than μ_r), even though actually $W_{final} - 1$ packets have been served. Since this is typically smaller than $W_{final}/2$, no new packets are released, so that when the ACK for the retransmitted packet is finally received, a burst of $W_{final}/2$ packets is released into the forward buffer by the source. This is larger than the forward buffer size B_f for most situations of interest, so that multiple packet losses occur. This causes a cascade of window cutbacks. Further, fast retransmit using cumulative ACKs is only able to recover from very small bursts of multiple packet loss, so that a timeout eventually occurs.

Since for the running example the timeout at the end of congestion avoidance occurs at $W = W_{final}/4$, the slow start phase in the next cycle ends at $W_{final}/8$. Thus, congestion avoidance starts at $W_0 = W_{final}/8$ and continues till W_{final}, being terminated by a timeout. The timeout occurs for both Case 1 and Case 3 (i.e., for all $B_f \geq k$), and the average throughput is computed as in Case 3 for TCP-Tahoe. Since congestion avoidance begins at a smaller window value for TCP-Reno, which causes it to have a smaller throughput than TCP-Tahoe. An illustrative window evolution is shown for $k = 5$. As for TCP-Tahoe, the analysis predicts $W_{final} = 49$. Note that there are two consecutive window cutbacks, as well as a timeout, at the end of the cycle.

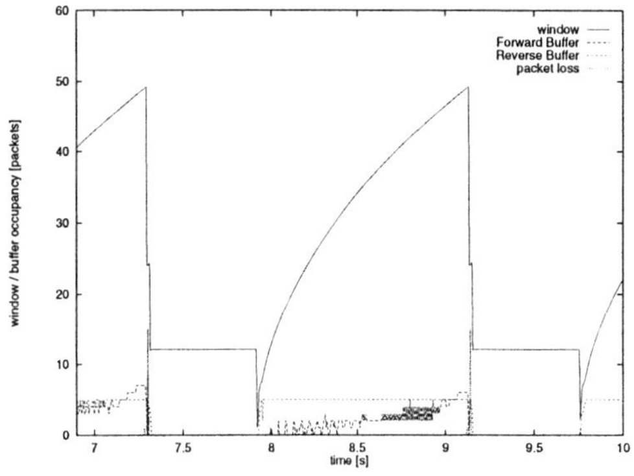

Figure 7: Simulation of the window evolution for the running example with TCP-Reno when $k = 5$. Note that there is a timeout at the end of the cycle, unlike Case 1 for TCP-Tahoe.

3.3.2 Case 2: $B_f < k$

The behavior here is similar to Case 2 for TCP-Tahoe, except for the following caveat. If W_{final} is the window size when loss occurs due to a burst, slow start ends at $W = W_{final}/8$. Since the bursts are formed at the slow start phase, if $W_{final}/8 < W_r$, then there are only $W_{final}/8$ bursts circulating and getting incremented (pseudo)randomly during congestion avoidance. Let n_b denote the number of bursts. Then, if the cycle terminates after n increments during congestion avoidance, then $W_{final} = n + n_b$, and $n_b = min(W_{final}/8, W_r$, which gives $n_b = min(n/7, W_r)$. Replacing W_r by n_b in Case 2 of TCP-Tahoe as before, we obtain n^* and thus W_{final}. We then apply Case 1 of TCP-Reno to compute the throughput. For our running example, the analysis predicts $W_{final} = 39.4$, which, while different from the window evolution simulated in Figure 8, is good enough to yield a reasonable throughput prediction (see Figure 2).

3.4 Evolution with random loss

According to our loss model, any packet served at the forward link may be lost with probability q, and such losses are independent. To focus on the effect of random loss, we consider the normal operating condition for TCP-Tahoe, which corresponds to Case 1 ($k \leq B_f \leq 3k$) in Section 3.2. The effect of random loss on TCP performance has been considered previously in [3] for a model in which the reverse path is ignored (i.e., assumed to be fast and lossless). The result derived in [3] was that TCP throughput deteriorates significantly due to random loss if $q(\mu_f T)^2$ is

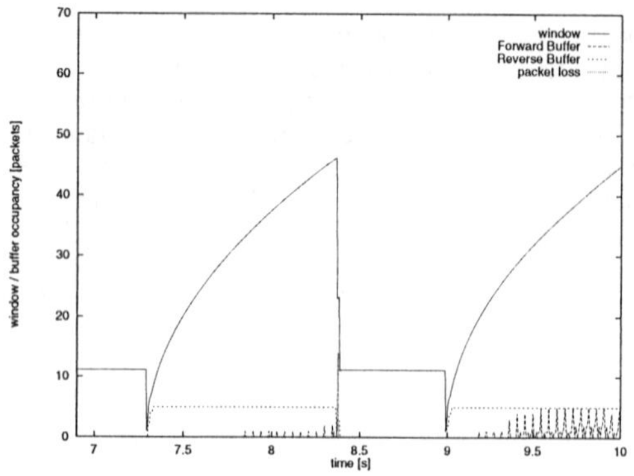

Figure 8: Simulation of the window evolution for the running example with TCP-Reno when $k > B_f = 8$. The evolution shown is for $k = 10$, but similar evolutions are seen for all $k > B_f$.

large (say 10 or more). Here, we use similar arguments to show that the performance is further affected by the slow reverse link: the throughput deteriorates if $kq(\mu_f T)^2$ is large.

The preceding threshold rule is roughly explained as follows. If the loss probability is low enough, the likelihood of a random loss rather than a buffer overflow terminating a cycle is small, so that the evolution is similar to that without loss. On the other hand, if the loss probability is high, packet losses occur relatively early in a cycle, and result in small initial values for the congestion avoidance phase that follows. This results in small window sizes (determined by random losses rather than congestion) throughout the congestion avoidance phase, and therefore causes low link utilization. Since window growth is timed by ACKs arriving at the source, a slow reverse link results in slower window growth after a loss, causing even worse utilization.

Our objective is to determine when random loss causes the congestion avoidance phase to have a significantly smaller average window size than that for a lossless evolution. Ignoring the slow start phase, we consider the following "fixed point" approximation in an attempt to characterize the "average" behavior of a TCP cycle due to random loss. Let w_q be the average window size at the beginning of congestion avoidance. In order for the congestion avoidance phase in the next cycle to also begin with w_q, the present congestion avoidance cycle should end with a loss at a window size of $2w_q$. We find w_q such that exactly $1/q$ packets (which is the average number of packets transmitted between losses for a loss probability of q) are transmitted on the forward path by the time the window evolves from w_q to $2w_q$.

As before, the differential equations in Section 3.2 model TCP evolution in congestion avoidance. Assuming that the reverse link is fully utilized throughout congestion avoidance, we obtain $W(t) = \sqrt{W^2(0) + 2\mu_r t}$, where $W(0) = w_q$ for our fixed point approximation. If t_q is the duration of the congestion avoidance phase, we have $W(t_q) = 2w_q$. The number of packets transmitted during this time is estimated by

$$n_q = \int_0^{t_q} \frac{\sqrt{w_q^2 + 2\mu_r t}}{T + \frac{B_r}{\mu_r}}\, dt = \frac{7w_q^3}{3(\mu_r T + B_r)}$$

Setting $n_q = \frac{1}{q}$, we obtain that

$$w_q^3 = \frac{3(\mu_r T + B_r)}{7q} \qquad (13)$$

In order for random loss not to affect performance significantly, we should have $2w_q$ equal or exceed the maximum window size for lossless evolution, $W_{max} = \mu_f T + B_f + kB_r$. This results in the following criterion:

$$q\frac{(\mu_f T + B_f + kB_r)^3}{\mu_r T + B_r} \leq 24/7$$

Ignoring the buffer sizes on the forward and reverse links, the left-hand side is lower bounded by $kq(\mu_f T + B_f + kB_r)^2$. If B_f and kB_r scale with the forward bandwidth-delay product $\mu_f T$, we arrive at a threshold rule in $kq(\mu_f T)^2$ as promised. When this quantity is large, throughput is expected to deteriorate as compared to lossless performance.

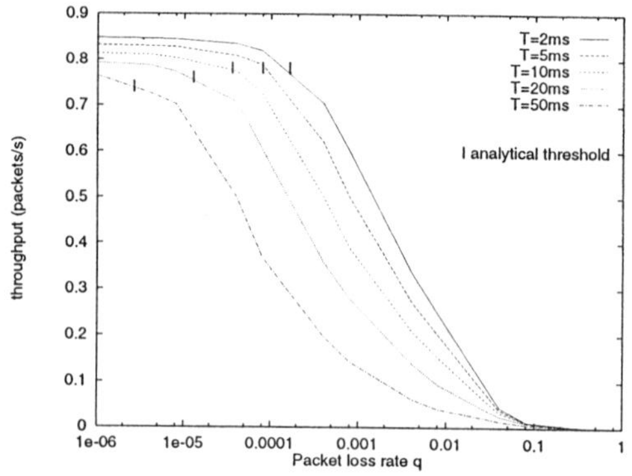

Figure 9: Throughput as a function of loss probability q for the modified running example using $B_f = 10$ when $k = 5$. The mark on the curves represents $kq(\mu_f T)^2 = 1$

Figure 9 shows the throughput as a function of random loss for different values of k and τ (note that the round-trip time T is larger than τ). Note the drastic decrease in throughput when the loss probability is an order of magnitude higher than the analytically derived threshold values marked on the curves.

4 Multiple TCP Connections

We consider multiple TCP connection which fully share the downstream bandwidth and buffers. When there is bidirectional traffic, the slow upstream channel serves as both a data path (for reverse connections where the source is at the subscriber end) and as an ack path (for forward connections). The upstream buffers are either fully shared (i.e., all connections effectively have access to a single

FIFO buffer) or are partially shared amongst the multiple connections (i.e., there are several buffers among which service could be allocated using an arbitration mechanism such as weighted round robin, but the service within each buffer is FIFO). For partial sharing, we only consider the case in which separate buffers and round robin service are provided to each forward and reverse connection on the slow upstream link.

4.1 Full sharing of Upstream Buffers

Connections fully share the upstream buffer when several hosts are connected to the same network interface (such as a cable modem). We have seen in Section 3 that ACK losses are very high (as high as $k-1$ out of k) when $k > 1$. This leads to adverse interactions when multiple TCP connections fully share the reverse buffer.

4.1.1 Sharing with Forward and Reverse Connections

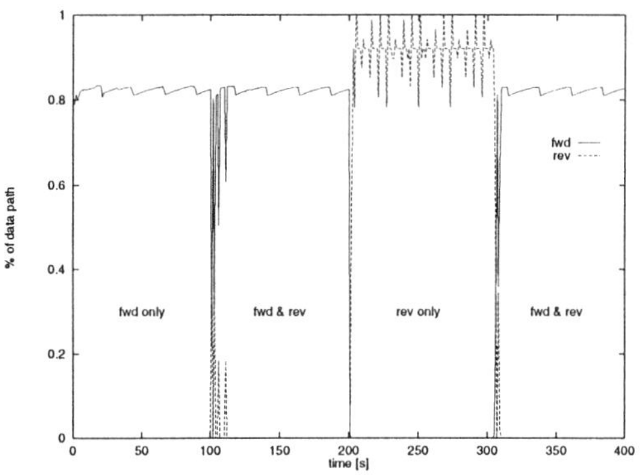

Figure 10: Forward and reverse connection. ($\mu_r = 1000$ pkt/s, $k = 5$, $\tau_f = \tau_r = 1ms$, $B_f = 10$, $B_r = 5$)

Figure 10 shows throughputs (as percentages of their maximum data path bandwidths) obtained by one forward and one reverse TCP connection. The buffer sizes indicated in the figure give the total buffering available for ACK and data packets (one buffer location is consumed irrespective of whether the packet is an ACK or a data packet).

Initially, the forward connection is the only connection. It achieves a throughput of 84% and the upstream link buffer is full with ACKs being sent by this connection. When the reverse connection starts, it experiences a high packet loss in the upstream link buffer. This forces this connection to operate using small windows and high timer backoff values, leading to poor throughput. The forward connection cuts down its rate only if there is packet loss in the forward path, of it it loses a whole window's worth of ACKs in the reverse path. Since neither event happens often enough, the reverse connection gets high throughput only after the forward connection ends at $t = 200$s. Thus, uncontrolled sharing of buffers between forward and reverse connections leads to poor performance for the latter, so that per connection queues appear to be necessary.

4.1.2 Sharing with Forward Connections Only

Figure 11 shows how four TCP-Tahoe connections with equal round-trip times share bandwidth for a system with $k = 5$. The plot shows the fraction of the forward connection utilized by the different connections as a function of connection time. Over short intervals (tens of seconds), increasing cumulative throughput for a given connection indicates larger instantaneous throughput, while decreasing cumulative throughput indicates smaller instantaneous throughput. It is seen from the figure that, while the cumulative throughputs for all connections converge slowly to equal values, the link sharing is grossly unfair (i.e., there are large variations in the instantaneous throughputs) over time scales of the order of tens of seconds. This short term unfairness is in contrast with earlier results on TCP performance without ACK path congestion [3], for which connections with equal round trip times typically see a synchronized evolution which is roughly fair in both the short and long term.

An explanation for the short-term unfairness is as follows. Assume connections start at slightly different times. The first active connection saturates the reverse path and because of the high $1 - 1/k$ ACK loss rate, a newly started connection will almost always lose the ACK corresponding to its first packet. This causes a time-out and a backoff of the timer. The retransmit faces the same situation resulting in very large timer values and large periods of idleness (of the order of tens of seconds because of the large timer backoffs) for all connections other than the one currently saturating the reverse link. This continues till a loss in the forward path for the currently active connection reduces that connection's window to one (with a timeout occurring in some cases, as seen in Section 3). One of the idle connections now becomes the dominant connection. Over the very long term connections tend to share the forward link fairly but over intervals of tens of seconds (500ms timer granularity multiplied by backoff values of 32 or 64), one of the connections gets most of the bandwidth. If connections are used for long file transfers, a connection will see virtually no progress for tens and possibly hundreds of seconds (depending on the number of competing connections) and then get a period of high bandwidth (corresponding to a few TCP cycles for the single connnection case analyzed in in Section 3). If the file transfer does not complete in one of these periods, another pause of 10 to 100s of seconds will follow.

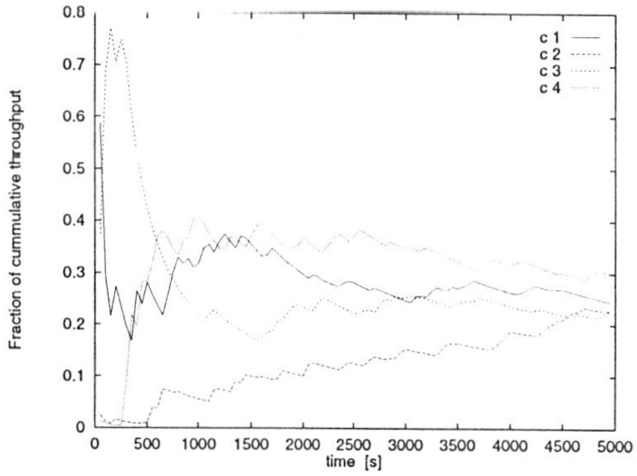

Figure 11: Temporary lockouts between 4 equivalent connections with TCP tahoe using shared reverse buffer. ($\mu_r = 1000$ pkt/s, $k = 5$, $\tau_f = \tau_r = 1ms$, $B_f = 10$, $B_r = 5$)

Unequal round trip times exacerbates the inherent unfairness. Simulations show that some connections get shut out for long periods. Also, the system evolution is highly sensitive to slight changes in packet arrival times, burst lengths and system parameters.

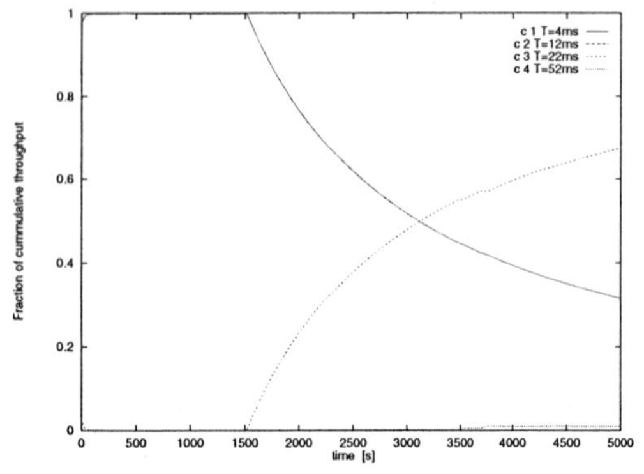

Figure 12: 4 forward connections with different round–trip time and shared reverse buffer. (μ_r = 1000 pkt/s, k = 5, B_f = 10, B_r = 5)

Figure 12 illustrates this for a system carrying 4 forward connections with different round trip times. Connection 1 with 4 ms round trip time gets most of the link bandwidth for a very long time while other connections are almost shut out. This apparently stable situation changes suddenly with connection 4 now getting increasing bandwidth share. Connections 2 and 3 still remain almost shut out.

We conclude that full sharing of upstream buffers leads to highly unfair and highly sensitive behavior and is not suitable for TCP over an an asymmetric network operating in the context outlined in Section 2.

4.2 Partial Sharing

Partial sharing of the upstream link is the natural configuration in systems where connections access the network using different network access devices but share the same reverse link (e.g. HFC upstream channel). The simulation results in this subsection use weighted round robin scheduling for the upstream link with weights being picked so that data and ACK packets have the same service time. This is not the best scheduling scheme. In order to fully utilize the forward link while using as little of the reverse link for ACK traffic as possible, one would have to pick the weights of the round robin scheduler so that forward connections have k slightly less than B_f (otherwise the forward link throughput is determined by B_f rather than the link speed). This in turn limits the link capacity seen by the data packets for reverse connections. Further study of this issue is required.

4.2.1 Sharing with Forward and Reverse Connections

Figure 13 shows results for the same configuration as that for the results in Figure 10 except that per TCP connection queueing is used at the upstream link. We see that when the reverse connection starts, it is mostly unaffected by the ACK packets produced by the forward connection. However, the forward connection's k is increased by a_{TCP}

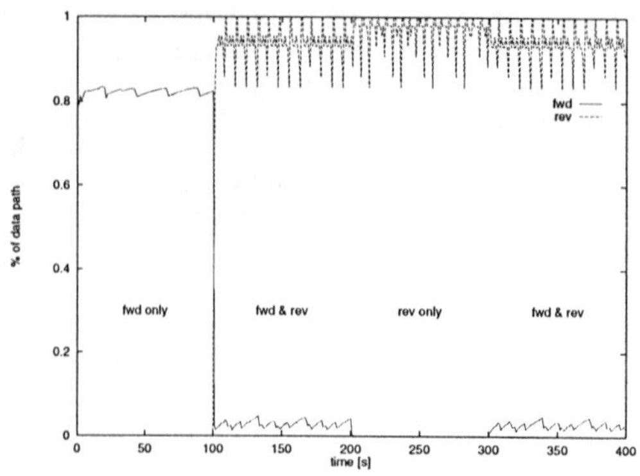

Figure 13: Forward and reverse connection with per-connection reverse buffer. (μ_r = 1000 pkt/s, k = 5, $\tau_f = \tau_r = 1ms$, B_f = 10, B_r = 5)

since the round robin scheduling has weights for the reverse and forward connections in the ratio a_{TCP}:1. Here a_{TCP} is the ratio of data packet size to the size of its associated ACK packet. For the running example in section 2, $a_{TCP} = 1000/40 = 25$. The increase in k makes the forward connection operate with throughput equal to that of the $B_f < k$ regime (Case 2) studied in Section 3, which causes the forward connection's utilization of the downstream link to decrease considerably. Even in networks with moderate or no bandwidth asymmetry, the presence of bidirectional traffic causing congestion in the reverse path can cause forward connections (or connections with uncongested data paths) to operate in the $B_f < k$ regime.

4.2.2 Sharing with Forward Connections Only

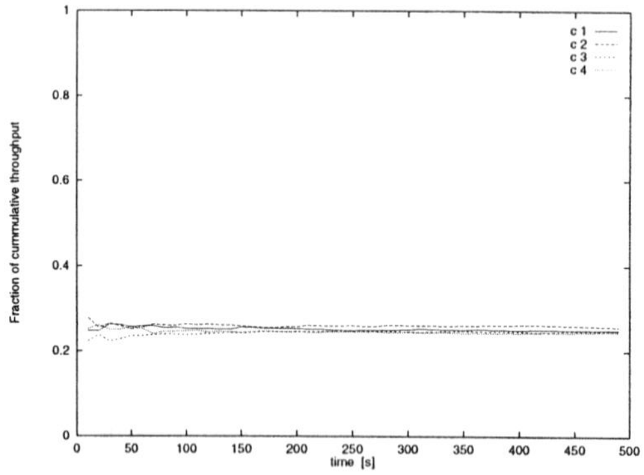

Figure 14: 4 equal forward connections and per connection reverse buffer. (μ_r = 1000 pkt/s, k = 5, B_f = 10, B_r = 5)

Figure 14 shows that per connection queueing results in a high level of fairness for the same 4 equal round trip time connection configuration whose unfair link sharing behavior when using shared buffers was shown in Figure 11. With unequal round-trip times TCP is inherently unfair (see [3] for a quantitative explanation). However, it can be seen from Figure 15 that per connection queueing eliminates

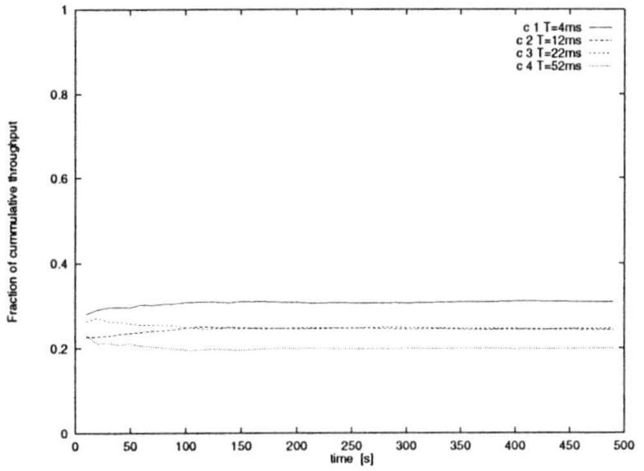

Figure 15: 4 forward connections with different round–trip time and per connection reverse buffer. ($\mu_r = 1000$ pkt/s, $k = 5$, $\tau_f = \tau_r = 1ms$, $B_f = 10$, $B_r = 5$)

the lockout of some connections shown for the case of full buffer sharing shown in Figure 12.

5 Concluding Remarks

Our study of the consequences of a slow reverse link yields the following conclusions and recommendations:

(1) For a single connection, the performance of TCP-Tahoe is superior to that of TCP-Reno. This is because the slow reverse link prevents TCP-Reno's loss recovery mechanism from functioning as designed, resulting in a timeout after every loss.

(2) In order to obtain good utilization, it is essential that the buffer size B_f on the forward link is at least equal to the normalized asymmetry factor k. Indeed, if B_f is fixed and the forward link speed is increased, the throughput is ultimately limited by B_f, so that the utilization goes to zero.

(3) For large forward buffers ($B_f > 3k$), TCP-Tahoe also may incur a timeout after every cycle, resulting in throughput loss (in general, replace 3 by the threshold for duplicate ACKs used in the TCP fast retransmit mechanism). This problem can be eliminated by implementing drop from front at the reverse buffer. Doing this restores a monotonic improvement of throughput with forward buffer size.

(4) Asymmetry increases TCP's already high sensitivity to random loss anywhere in the forward path of the TCP connection. Specifically, we show that random loss leads to significant throughput deterioration when the product of the loss probability, the *asymmetry* and the *square* of the bandwidth-delay product exceeds a threshold.

(5) For multiple connections using a fully shared upstream buffer (with FIFO service), poor performance results both for undirectional and bidirectional traffic. For multiple forward TCP connections, small changes in timing can cause a connection to be locked out for tens or even hundreds of seconds because of congestion on the reverse link, since TCP window growth is timed by ACKs. Reverse TCP connections sharing the upstream link with ACKs from forward TCP connections can get shut out: the congestion due to ACKs for the forward connection cause data packets of the reverse connection to be lost, causing the reverse connections to cut back their windows (the ACK loss for the forward connection only leads to burstiness).

6) For multiple connections with per connection upstream queues served in weighted round robin fashion, the performance is much better. In particular, for multiple forward connections, the only remaining problem is the inherent unfairness of TCP towards connections with large round-trip delays [3] (which can be remedied by per connection queueing and round robin service on the forward path, for instance). For bidirectional traffic, the performance depends on the weights used by the round robin scheduler. In particular, if ACKs are not served fast enough on the reverse link, the normalized asymmetry factor k for the forward connection can be large ($k > B_f$), leading to a throughput for forward connections limited by the forward buffer size rather than by the forward link speed. The weights on the upstream round robin scheduler therefore have to be chosen so as to provide a good tradeoff between the throughput attained by forward and reverse connections.

Problems that merit further investigation include analysis of the behavior of multiple connections and design of MAC protocols and study of their effect on TCP performance. Further thought is also required as to how well our random evolution model matches the true (possibly chaotic) TCP evolution for high asymmetries ($k > B_f$).

Acknowledgements

The second author would like to thank Bruce Hajek for useful technical discussion regarding the analysis in Section 3.2.2.

References

[1] V. Jacobson, "Congestion avoidance and control," *Proc. ACM SIGCOMM '88*, pp. 314-329.

[2] V. Jacobson, "Berkeley TCP evolution from 4.3-tahoe to 4.3-reno," *Proc. of the 18th Internet Engineering Task Force*, Vancouver, August 1990.

[3] T. V. Lakshman and U. Madhow, "Performance Analysis of Window-Based Flow Control using TCP/IP: the Effect of High Bandwidth-Delay Products and Random Loss" *IFIP Transactions C-26, High Performance Networking V*, pp. 135-150, North-Holland, 1994.

[4] T. V. Lakshman, A. Neidhardt and T. J. Ott, "The Drop from Front Strategy in TCP over ATM and its Interworking with other Control Features" *Proc. Infocom '96*, pp. 1242-1250

[5] S. Shenker, L. Zhang, and D. D. Clark, "Some observations on the dynamics of a congestion control algorithm," *Computer Communication Review*, pp. 30-39, October 1990.

[6] G. R. Wright and W. R. Stevens, "TCP/IP Illustrated, Volume 2, The Implementation", Addison Wesley, 1995.

[7] L. Zhang, S. Shenker, and D. D. Clark, "Observations on the dynamics of a congestion control algorithm: the effects of two-way traffic," *Proc. ACM SIGCOMM '91*, pp. 133-147.

TCP BOSTON

A Fragmentation-tolerant TCP Protocol for ATM Networks*

Azer Bestavros
best@cs.bu.edu
Gitae Kim
kgtjan@cs.bu.edu
Computer Science Department
Boston University
Boston, MA 02215

Abstract

We propose a new transport protocol, TCP Boston, that turns ATM's 53-byte cell-oriented switching architecture into an advantage for TCP/IP. At the core of TCP Boston is the Adaptive Information Dispersal Algorithm (AIDA), an efficient encoding technique that allows for dynamic redundancy control. AIDA makes TCP/IP's performance less sensitive to cell losses, thus ensuring a graceful degradation of TCP/IP's performance when faced with congested resources. In this paper, we introduce AIDA and overview the main features of TCP Boston. We present detailed simulation results that show the superiority of our protocol when compared to other adaptations of TCP/IP over ATMs.

1. Introduction

The flexibility and popularity of TCP/IP[20, 19] coupled with the premise of high speed communication using emerging ATM technology have prompted the network research community to propose and implement a number of techniques that adapt TCP/IP to ATM network environments, thus allowing these environments to smoothly integrate (and make use of) currently available TCP-based applications and services without much (if any) modifications [11]. However, recent studies [7, 15, 22] have shown that TCP/IP, when implemented over ATM networks, is susceptible to serious performance limitations.

The poor performance of TCP over ATMs is mainly due to *packet fragmentation*, which occurs when an IP packet flows into an ATM virtual circuit through the AAL5 (ATM Adaptation Layer 5). AAL5 acts as an interface between the IP and ATM layers. It is responsible for the task of dividing TCP/IP's large data units (*i.e.*, the TCP/IP packets) into sets of 48-byte data units called *cells*. Since the typical size of a TCP/IP packet is much larger than that of a cell, fragmentation at the AAL is inevitable. In order for a TCP/IP packet to successfully traverse an ATM switching network (or subnetwork), all the cells belonging to that packet must traverse the network *intact*. The loss even of a single cell in any of the network's ATM switches results in the corruption of the entire packet to which that cell belongs. Notice however that when a cell is dropped at a switch, the rest of the cells that belong to the same packet still proceed through the virtual circuit, despite the fact that they are destined to be discarded by the destination's AAL at the time of packet-reassembly, thus resulting in low effective throughput.

There have been a number of attempts to remedy this problem by introducing additional switch-level functionalities to preserve throughput when TCP/IP is employed over ATM. Examples include the Selective Cell Discard (SCD)[1] [2] and the Early Packet Discard (EPD) [22]. In SCD, once a cell c is dropped at a switch, all subsequent cells from the packet to which c belongs are dropped by the switch. In EPD, a more aggressive policy is used, whereby all cells from the packet to which c belongs are dropped, including earlier cells still in the switch buffer. Notice that both SCD and EPD require modifications to switch-level software to be aware of IP packet boundaries—a violation of the layering principle that was deemed unavoidable for performance purposes in [22].

The simulation results described in [22] show that both SCD and EPD improve the effective throughput of TCP/IP over a single ATM switch. For realistic, multi-hop ATM networks the cumulative wasted bandwidth may be large, and the impact of the ensuing packet losses on the performance of TCP is likely to be severe.[2] To understand these limitations, it is important to realize that while dropping cells belonging to a packet at a congested switch preserves the bandwidth of that switch, it does not preserve the ABR/UBR bandwidth at all the switches preced-

*This work has been partially funded by NSF grant CCR-9308344.

[1] Also called Partial Packet Discard (PPD) in [22].
[2] Analytical comparisons for multi-hop networks appear in [6].

ing that (congested) switch along the virtual circuit for the TCP connection. Moreover, any cells belonging to a corrupted packet which would have made it out of the congested switch will continue to waste the bandwidth at all the switches following that (congested) switch. Obviously, the more hops separating the TCP/IP source from the TCP/IP destination, the more wasted ABR/UBR bandwidth one would expect even if SCD or EPD techniques are used. This wasted bandwidth translates to low effective throughput, which in turn results in more duplicate data packets transmitted from the source.

In this paper, we present a new transport protocol, TCP Boston, that turns fragmentation into an advantage for TCP/IP, thus enhancing the performance of TCP in general and its performance in ATM environments in particular. The rationale that motivates the design of TCP Boston lies in our answer to the following simple question: *Could a partial delivery of a packet be useful?* Our answer is *yes*. In other words, the *en route* loss of one fragment (or more) from a packet does not render the rest of the fragments belonging to that packet useless. TCP Boston manages to make use of such partial information, thus preserving network bandwidth. At the core of TCP Boston is the Adaptive Information Dispersal Algorithm (AIDA), an efficient encoding technique that allows for dynamic redundancy control. AIDA makes TCP/IP's performance less sensitive to cell losses, thus ensuring a graceful degradation of TCP/IP's performance when faced with congested resources.

2. AIDA: An Introduction

AIDA is a novel technique for dynamic bandwidth allocation, which makes use of minimal, controlled redundancy to guarantee timeliness and fault-tolerance up to *any* degree of confidence. AIDA is an elaboration on the Information Dispersal Algorithm of Michael O. Rabin [21]. To understand how IDA works, consider a segment S of a data object to be transmitted. Let S consist of m fragments (hereinafter called *cells*). Using IDA's *dispersal operation*, S could be processed to obtain N distinct pieces in such a way that recombining *any* m of these pieces, $m \leq N$, using IDA's *reconstruction operation*, is sufficient to retrieve S. The dispersal and reconstruction operations are simple linear transformations using *irreducible polynomial arithmetic* and can be performed in real-time.[3] The dispersal operation amounts to a matrix multiplication that transforms the m cells of the original file into the N cells to be dispersed. The N rows of the transformation matrix $[x_{ij}]_{N\times m}$ are chosen so that any m of these rows are mutually independent, which implies that the matrix consisting of any such m rows is not singular, and thus inversible. This guarantees that reconstructing the original file from *any* m of its dispersed cells is feasible. Indeed, upon receiving any $r \geq m$ of the dispersed cells, it is possible to reconstruct the original segment through another matrix multiplication. The transformation matrix $[y_{ij}]_{m\times m}$ is the inverse of a matrix $[x'_{ij}]_{m\times m}$, which is obtained by removing $N-m$ rows from $[x_{ij}]_{N\times m}$. The removed rows correspond to the cells that were not used in the reconstruction process. To reduce the overhead of the algorithm, the inverse transformation $[y_{ij}]_{m\times m}$ could be precomputed for some or even all possible subsets of m rows.

[3]For more details, we refer the reader to [21, 4].

Several *redundancy-injecting* protocols have been suggested in the literature, whereby redundancy is injected in the form of parity, which is only used for error detection and/or correction purposes [14]. The IDA approach is radically different in that redundancy is added *uniformly*; there is *no* distinction between data and parity. It is this feature that makes it possible to scale the amount of redundancy used in IDA. Indeed, this is the basis for *Adaptive* IDA (AIDA) [5]. Using AIDA, a *bandwidth allocation* operation is inserted after the dispersal operation but *prior* to transmission as shown in figure 1. This bandwidth allocation step allows the system to *scale* the amount of redundancy used in the transmission. In particular, the number of cells to be transmitted, namely n, is allowed to vary from m (*i.e.*, no redundancy) to N (*i.e.*, maximum redundancy).

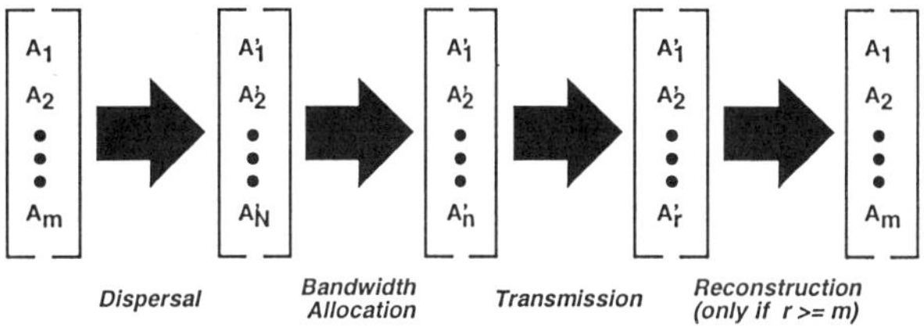

Figure 1. AIDA dispersal and reconstruction

In order to appreciate the advantages that AIDA brings to TCP Boston, we must understand the main difficulty posed by fragmentation. When a cell is lost *en route*, it becomes impossible for the receiver to reconstruct the packet to which that cell belonged unless: (1) there is enough extra (redundant) cells from the packet in question to allow for the recovery of the missing information (*e.g.*, through parity), or (2) the cell is retransmitted.

The first solution above suggests the use of spatial redundancy to mask erasures (cell losses). While feasible, such a technique may be quite wasteful of bandwidth (since the redundant information will have to be communicated whether or not erasures occur), and is not likely to help when cell losses exceed the forward erasure capacity of the encoding scheme, which is almost certainly the case since cells are typically dropped in "batches" when switches run out of buffer space. An example of the use of this approach is the study in [8], which suggests the use of *Forward Error Correction* (FEC) for real-time, unreliable video communication over ATM. In that study, FEC was shown to allow the trading of bandwidth for timeliness. FEC's performance was shown to depend on many parameters including the network load, the level of redundancy injected into FEC traffic, and the percentage of connections (traffic) using FEC. FEC was shown to be most effective when corruption is restricted to few cell erasures per data block (*e.g.*, video frame).

Similar to FEC, AIDA supports the use of spatial redundancy to mask erasures. Furthermore, when incorporated with TCP, AIDA allows this support to be fully integrated within the flow control mechanism of TCP, thus making it possible to perform forward error correction *without* necessarily overloading the network resources. For example, if network congestion is detected, one could increase AIDA's level of spatial redundancy (thus protecting against likely cell drops), while decreasing TCP's congestion window size (thus protecting against buffer overflow by reducing the number of bytes "on the wire"). This integration of redundancy control and flow control in a reliable transport protocol[4] could be quite valuable for real-time communication as reported in [5].

The second solution above suggests the use of temporal redundancy to recover from erasures. Two possibilities exist—each representing an extreme in terms of the functionality required at the sender and receiver ends. The first extreme would be for the receiver to do nothing, and simply wait for the sender to automatically retransmit all cells from the packet in question as would be dictated by TCP's packet acknowledgment protocol. This is exactly what current adaptations of TCP over ATMs do (including the SCD and EPD techniques). As we explained before such an approach is not effective in terms of its use of available bandwidth, especially in multi-hop networks. Of course it has the advantage of being quite simple to implement since it requires no additional functionality at the sender and receiver ends. The other extreme would be for the receiver to keep track of which cells are missing and then to request retransmission of only those cells. This technique, which we will revisit later in this paper, has the advantage of being effective in terms of its use of available bandwidth, but may result in considerable overhead, especially when the level of fragmentation (*i.e.* number of cells per packet) is high.

The incorporation of AIDA in a TCP protocol allows us to strike a critical balance between the above two extremes. To explain how this could be done, consider the following scenario. The sender disperses an outgoing m-cell segment (packet) into N cells, but sends a packet of only m of these cells to the receiver, where $N >> m$. Now, assume that the receiver gets r of these cells. If $r = m$, then the receiver could reconstruct the original segment, and acknowledge that it has *completely* received it by informing the sender that it needs *no* more cells from that segment. If $r < m$, then the receiver could acknowledge that it has *partially* received the packet by informing the sender that it needs $(m-r)$ more cells from the original segment. To such an acknowledgment, the sender would respond by sending

[4] FEC is *not* a reliable transport mechanism.

a packet of $(m - r)$ fresh cells (*i.e.* not sent the first time around) from the original N dispersed cells. The process continues until the receiver receives enough cells (namely m or more) to be able to reconstruct the original segment.

Two important points must be noted. First, using AIDA, *no* bandwidth is wasted as a result of packet retransmission or partial packet delivery; every cell that makes it through the network is used. Moreover, this cell-preservation behavior is achieved *without* requiring individual cell acknowledgment. Second, using AIDA, *no* modification to the switch-level protocols is necessary. This stands in sharp contrast to the SCD and EPD techniques, which necessitate such a change. The incorporation of AIDA into TCP/IP over ATMs requires only additional functionality at the interface between the IP and ATM layers (*i.e.*, the AAL), which we discuss later in the paper.

Figure 2 shows the transmission window managed by AIDA in TCP Boston. As explained before, prior to a packet transmission, AIDA encodes the original m-cell packet into N cells ($N >> m$). Based on network congestion conditions, it dynamically adjusts n the *transmission window size*, which represents the size of the packet to be actually transmitted.

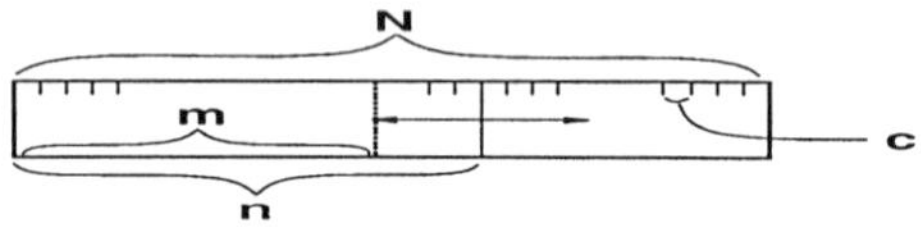

Figure 2. AIDA Transmission Window

The transmission window manager can be custom-tuned to meet the spatial redundancy requirements of particular applications or services. For example, time-critical applications may require that the level of spatial redundancy be increased to mask cell erasures (up to a certain level), and thus to avoid retransmission delays should such erasures occur. By avoiding such delays, the likelihood that tight timing constraints will be met is increased (at the expense of wasted bandwidth).

3. TCP Boston: Overview and Implementation

The purpose TCP Boston is to provide a reliable transfer of data for end-to-end applications. The protocol, when properly tuned, can be implemented over both ATM and packet-switched networks. But, since it is designed in such a way that it takes advantage of ATM's relatively small 53-byte cells, it can achieve a high performance gain when it is deployed over ATM networks. The main functions included in the protocol are: *session management*, *segment management*, and *flow control and transmission*.

Session Management: The protocol manages a TCP session in three phases: a *connection establishment* phase, a *data transfer* phase, and a *termination* phase. The purpose of these phases, as well as the functions performed therein, generally follow those of current TCP implementations, except that information specific to IDA which are required by the receiver for reconstruction purposes (such as the value of m for example), are piggy-backed onto the protocol packets during the three-way handshaking at the connection establishment phase.[5]

Segment Management: Processes for (1) segment encoding and (2) segment reconstruction are unique to TCP Boston.

At the source, segment encoding works as follows: Given a data block (segment) of size b bytes, the protocol divides the data block into m cells of size c, where $m = b/c$ bytes. Next, the m cells are processed using IDA to yield N cells for some $N >> m$. Once this encoding is done, the first m cells from the segment are transmitted as a single packet and the unused $N - m$ cells are kept in a buffer area for use when (if) more cells from that segment must be transmitted to compensate for lost cells (see below).

At the sink, segment reconstruction works as follows: When a packet of cells is received, the protocol first checks if it has accumulated m (or more) different cells from the segment that corresponds to that packet. If it did, it reconstructs the original segment using the proper IDA reconstruction matrix transformation and signals the flow control component to send an acknowledgment (hereinafter referred to as an ACK) indicating that reconstruction was successful. If not, it keeps the received cells for later reconstruction, and signals the flow control component to send an ACK, piggy-backed with the number of cells that have been accumulated so far from the segment. Such an ACK would inform the sender that reconstruction is not possible, and that the pending number of cells from that segment need to be transmitted at the time of next packet retransmission.

Flow Control and Transmission: Any feedback-based TCP flow control algorithm (*e.g.*, Tahoe, Reno, and Vegas) can be used with TCP Boston with a minor modification to handle the revised feedback mechanism of TCP Boston. When an ACK arrives, the sender checks a flag to determine if that ACK signals the successful reconstruction (at the receiver) of a segment. If it does, the sender calls the standard ACK procedure. If it doesn't, the sender extracts from the ACK the number of cells r received so far (see above) and then prepares $m - r$ additional cells from the desired segment in a single *new* packet that will be transmitted at the next retransmission time. This process continues until the receipt of an ACK from the receiver indicating that the segment has been successfully reconstructed, in which case any remaining cells from that segment are discarded from the sender's buffer.

Notice that the partial delivery of a packet does not result in updating the received-segment number for the receiver's TCP window manager.[6] Also, an ACK signaling a partial packet delivery does not cause an increase in the sender's congestion window. Rather, it acts as a hint to the sender to update the number of cells included in the next packet retransmission.

In our current implementation, the protocol is composed of three modules: a *Session Management Module*, a *Segment Management Module*, and a *Flow Control Module*. Each of these modules executes the corresponding function described in the previous section. Figure 3 depicts the configuration and interaction of the three modules for both the sender and the receiver.

The use of TCP Boston in ATM environments requires a modification to the AAL5 functionality; namely, AAL5 must allow the reassembly of partial IP packets when ATM cells are missing, instead of simply discarding such packets. To that effect, we propose two simple solutions. The first is that AAL5 could simply insert dummy cells in place of any missing cells.[7] If the assembled IP packet is to traverse other subnetworks, the insertion of these dummy cells may be deemed wasteful of bandwidth. The second solution remedies this by requiring AAL5 to simply pack the available cells into an IP packet (*i.e.* no dummy cells are inserted), and to update the IP headers to reflect among other things, the new (shorter) length of the IP packet.

For simulation purposes, we tuned the system so as to use *no* spatial redundancy. We chose to do so for three reasons: (1) We wanted to evaluate the effectiveness of TCP Boston in dealing with fragmentation. This required that our measurements be unaffected by the forward error correction capability provided by AIDA, which is enabled through spatial redundancy. (2) We wanted to compare the performance of TCP Boston with that of other TCP implementations (*e.g.*, TCP Reno [16]) with and without switch-level enhancements (*e.g.*, EPD [22]). Since these other protocols do not support forward error correction, this feature of TCP Boston had to be turned off. (3) To work properly, the dynamic redundancy control mechanism of TCP Boston requires a congestion avoidance algorithm that provides accurate forecasting of network congestion. An example of such an algorithm is the one used in TCP Vegas, which provides better congestion forecast by detecting the incipient stages of congestion before losses start to accrue (rather than using the loss of segments as a signal of congestion) [9]. TCP Reno, which was the best available option in the simulation package at the time of our experiment, is reactive (rather than proactive), and thus would not bring much performance benefits when used to forecast congestion for the dynamic redundancy control mechanism in our protocol.

[5] For efficiency, such information could be permanently *"coded"* into TCP Boston.

[6] This enables the receiver to send duplicate ACKs to signal a packet drop to the sender.

[7] Identifying missing cells in an ATM environment is quite simple since cells are transmitted over a virtual channel, and thus delivered to AAL5 in-order.

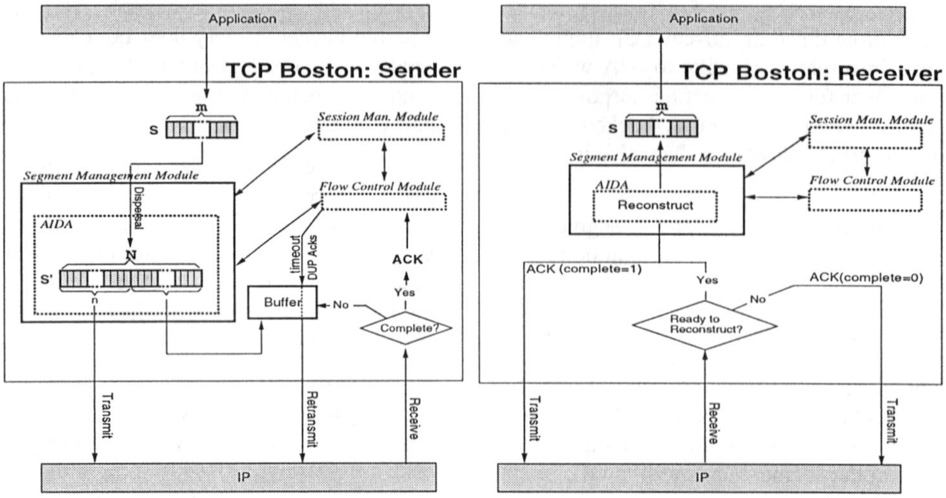

Figure 3. TCP Boston: Protocol Outline for Sender (left) and Receiver (right)

4. TCP Boston: Performance Evaluation

In this section we present the results of our experimental evaluation of TCP Boston. For a more detailed treatment, we refer the reader to [6].

4.1. Simulation Environment

As shown in Figure 4, the simulated network consists of 16 source nodes and 1 sink node, where all the nodes are connected to a single switch node. The link bandwidth is set to 1.5 Mbps with propagation delay of 10 msec. The link bandwidth does not represent any particular technology. It was chosen to simulate a relatively low bandwidth-delay product network. This configuration simulates a WAN environment with a radius of 3,000 km and a bottleneck link bandwidth of 1.5 Mbps.

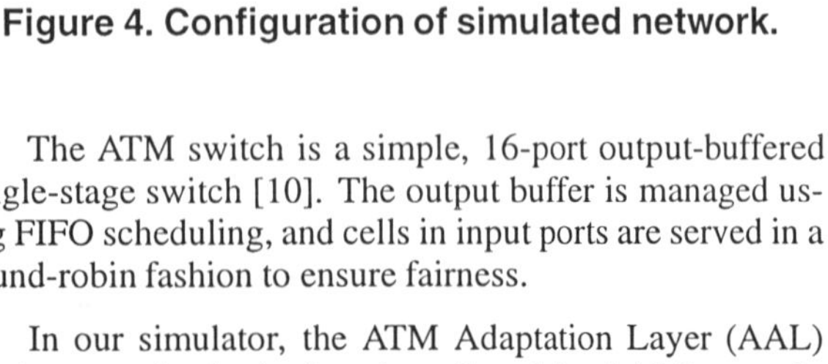

Figure 4. Configuration of simulated network.

The ATM switch is a simple, 16-port output-buffered single-stage switch [10]. The output buffer is managed using FIFO scheduling, and cells in input ports are served in a round-robin fashion to ensure fairness.

In our simulator, the ATM Adaptation Layer (AAL) implements the basic functions found in AAL5, namely fragmentation and reconstruction of IP packets [1, 13]. AAL divides IP packets into 48-byte units for transmission as ATM cells, and appends 0 to 47 bytes of padding to the end of data. A special flag in the cell header is used to mark the last cell in a packet. To support TCP Boston the destination AAL reconstructs a packet out of the received cells even when the resulting packet is incomplete. Incomplete packets are discarded by the destination AAL for Reno implementation.

Our simulations use a total of 16 TCP connections, each is established for one of the configuration's source-sink pairs. Each source generates an infinite stream of data bytes. Each simulation runs for 700 simulated seconds to transfer a total of 120 MB of data.

The parameters used in the simulation include the TCP packet size, the TCP window size, and the switch buffer size. Three different packet sizes were selected to reflect maximum transfer unit (MTU) of popular standards: 576 bytes for IP packets, 1,500 bytes for Ethernet, 4,470 bytes for FDDI link standards [17], and 9,180 bytes which is the recommended packet size for IP over ATM [3]. The values for the maximum TCP window size are 8, 16, 32, and 64 kB. Buffer sizes used for the ATM switch are 64, 256, 512, 1,000, 2,000, and 4,000 cells.

The LBNL Network Simulator (ns) [12] was used for both packet-switched and ATM network simulations. To simulate TCP Boston, we modified ns extensively to implement the three main modules described in the previous section. Since ns is originally designed to support packet-switched network environments, major modifications were necessary to allow it to support ATM-like network environments. In particular, the essential functions of AAL5 were added to simulate the handling of IP packets (*i.e.*, fragmentation and reassembly of IP packets) [1, 13]. Also, the link layer of ns has been modified to include basic functions of ATM switches and virtual circuit management. The ns package has also been enhanced to allow for the gathering of additional performance statistics, such as *effective throughput* (hereinafter interchangeably termed *goodput*), *cell loss rate*, *effective packet loss rate*, and *response time*.

4.2. Performance Characteristics of TCP Boston

We measured the performance of TCP Boston versus that of TCP Reno using four metrics: loss rate, response time, retransmission rate, and effective throughput. Unless otherwise noted, each one of the graphs presented in this section portrays one of these performance metrics (on the y-axis) as a function of the switch buffer size (on the x-axis). The function is shown as a family of curves, each corresponding to one of the four different packet sizes considered.

Figure 5(a) shows the loss rates of Reno and Boston over an ATM network. The loss rate for Reno refers to the packet loss rate caused by cell drops at the ATM switch. In both plots, as the size of the switch buffer decreases, the loss rate gradually increases until the buffer size reaches 50 kB. From this point on, the loss rate for Reno grows exponentially toward the marginal buffer size, while the the loss rate for Boston increases at a much slower pace, except for the largest packet size.

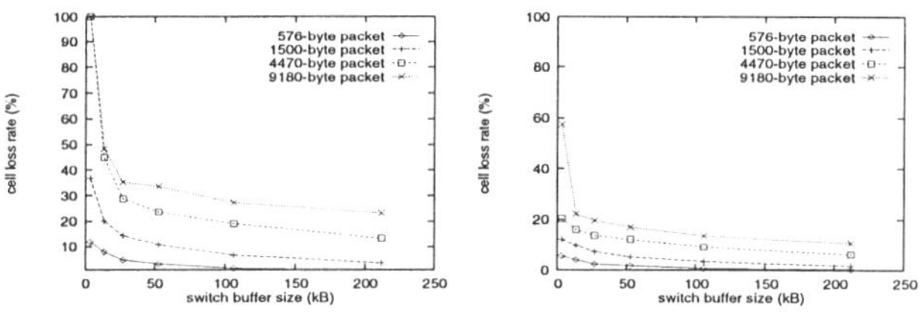

(a) Cell loss rate of Reno (left) and Boston (right)

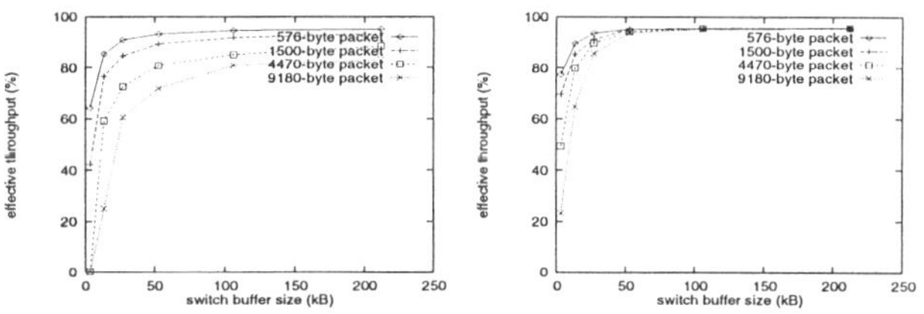

(b) Effective throughput of Reno (left) and Boston (right)

Figure 5. TCP run for an 64 kB window size

The ratio between Reno's loss rate and Boston's loss rate increases toward the marginal buffer size. This increase is more pronounced as the packet size increases. This is because, as the packet size increases, the number of cells per packet increases, and the chance of a cell in a packet being dropped at a switch increases (as a result of fragmentation), which results in a packet loss under Reno. For small buffer sizes, this phenomenon becomes more remarkable, resulting in near 100% packet loss rate for Reno when the buffer size is smallest. On the contrary, using Boston, cells that are not dropped will be accumulated for eventual packet reconstruction at the receiver end, thus reducing the chance of repeated retransmissions. This leads to a relatively lower cell loss rate.

According to our simulation results, the ratio between Reno's loss rate and Boston's loss rate ranges between 1.7 and 2.4, which means that about one half of the cells in a packet are dropped by switch buffer overflow on average. The plots for retransmission rates for both Boston and Reno are almost identical to the plots for cell loss rates shown in figure 5(a), and thus were omitted from this paper. Figure 5(b) shows the effective throughput (goodput) for Reno and Boston under a 64 kB TCP window size. The effective throughput refers to a throughput where only the bytes that are useful at application layer are considered.

The goodput of Reno stays low, especially for larger-size packets, throughout the entire range of buffer sizes, while that of Boston approaches the optimal level near 100 kB buffer sizes and stays almost optimal for larger buffer ranges. The low goodput of Boston under small buffer size is caused by the link idle time (since all the cells that pass through the link are counted as useful cells). The link idle time is the result of the interaction between the 16 source-sink pairs, each of which runs under TCP (Reno in our case) flow control algorithm. Recent studies on network traffic have shown that TCP can augment traffic self-similarity, which causes performance degradation especially when the buffer space is limited [18]. In Reno's case, the extremely low goodput at small buffer sizes turned out to be the result of the wasted bandwidth due to cells that pass through the bottleneck switch but get discarded at AAL5, as well as the link idle time that affects Boston.

Table 1 compares the average response time of the two protocols under 64 kB TCP window size. The response time in the table represents an average time taken for an application at a higher layer to receive a byte.

For buffer sizes between 3.5 kB and 13.5 kB, Reno's average response time increases hyper-exponentially for the two larger packet sizes, and the ratio between Reno's response time and Boston's response time increases sharply. As the bottleneck buffer size decreases, the cell drop rate increases, resulting in a larger number of packets being corrupted and discarded for Reno, which in turn results in the retransmission of the same packet repeatedly, and hence sharply increasing Reno's response time. For Boston, the increased cell drop rate results in a proportional amount of additional cell transmissions (but not as many as in Reno's case), which results in a gradual increase in response time. On the other hand, as the buffer size increases, less cells are lost, increasing the probability of successful packet transfer in a minimal number of rounds, which in turn results in good response times for both protocols, with Boston edging Reno by a margin of 7 μsec/byte on average. Notice

Packet Size (Byte)	Buffer Size (kB)											
	3.5		13.5		27		54		104		208	
	Bos	Ren	Bos	Ren	Bos	Ren	Bos	Ren	Bos	Ren	Bos	Ren
512	111	119	88	91	82	85	80	83	79.5	82	77.2	81
1,518	114	138	90	99	85	91	80	87	79	85	77	83
4,352	212	893	100	118	84	101	79	90	79	88.2	77	86
9,180	591	3,125	129	138	89	116	80	94	79	89.5	77	88

Table 1. Response times of Boston and Reno over ATM for 64 kB window size

that this difference is per byte. Thus, for large-size file transmissions, the impact on the response time may be non-negligible, even when the buffer size is moderately large.

So far, the results we have presented for Boston and Reno were under a TCP window size equal to 64 kB. The results for the two protocols under window sizes of 32 kB, 16 kB, and 8 kB show a gradual convergence in the performance of the two protocols as the window size decreases. Figure 6 shows the impact of a small 8 kB TCP window size.

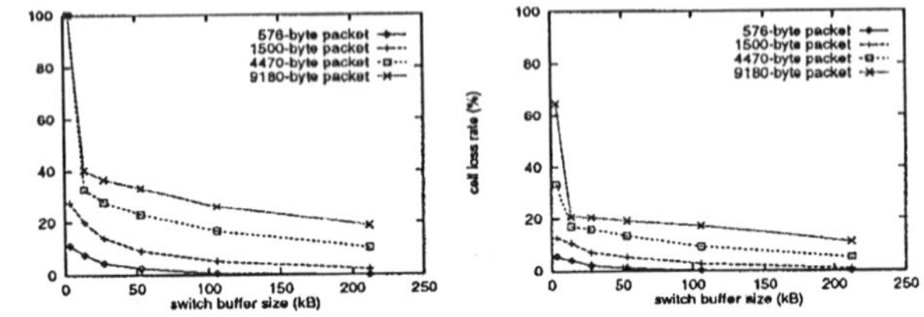

(a) Cell loss rate of Reno (left) and Boston (right)

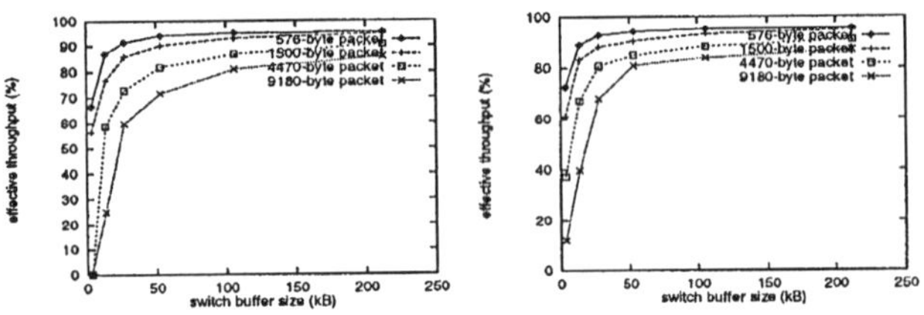

(b) Effective throughput of Reno (left) and Boston (right)

Figure 6. TCP Run for an 8 kB window size

4.3. Effect of TCP Boston on Flow Control

Boston's ability to accept incomplete packets (as opposed to counting them as lost ones) is likely to impact the flow control behavior by making it less sensitive to network congestion, and thus somewhat more aggressive in its use of network bandwidth. To understand how this could happen, it suffices to note that using Boston, retransmitted packets are smaller (containing only the pending number of cells) and thus more likely to be delivered intact. Therefore, the likelihood that a sender utilizing TCP Boston will detect a packet loss (as a result of repeated acknowledgments received for the same packet) is reduced, which in turn, increases the probability that the sender will not decrease the congestion window (not to mention the possibility that it may even increase it).

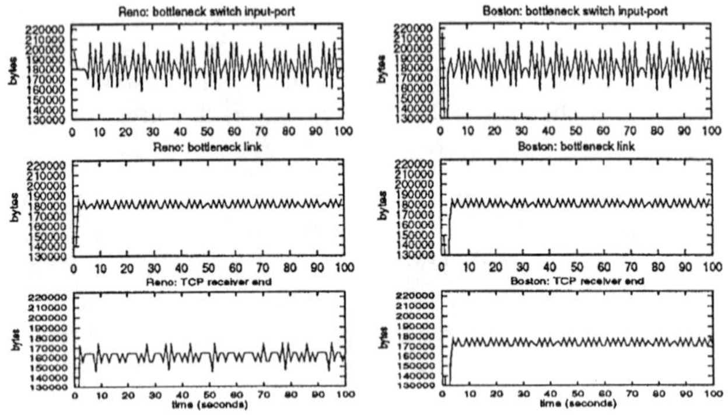

(a) Traffic generated by 1 TCP server

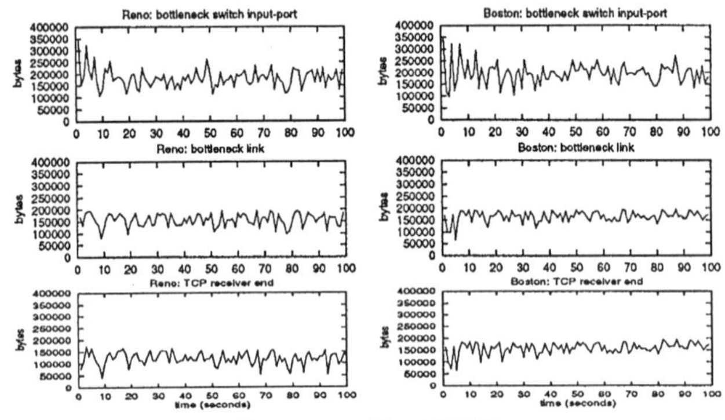

(b) Traffic generated by 16 TCP servers

Each plot depicts the first 100-second period of the 700-second simulation, where the total bytes measured per second are plotted on the y axis as a function of the elapsed time at the input-port of the bottleneck switch (top), bottleneck link (middle), and TCP receiver end (bottom) for Reno (left) and Boston (right): 64 kB window, 27 kB (512-cell) bottleneck switch buffer, 9180-byte/packet.

Figure 7. Traffic generation

Despite Boston's aggressive use of bandwidth, our experiments confirmed that it conserves the basic dynamics of the underlying TCP flow control. Figure 7(a) shows the traffic pattern of Reno (left) and Boston (right) for the first 100 seconds in 700 simulated seconds when single TCP server is active in the network (the total bytes measured per second are plotted on the y axis as a function of the elapsed time in seconds plotted on the x axis). The bottleneck switch buffer size was set to 27 kB (512 cells), which resulted in a cell drop rate of 2.3% for Boston and a packet drop rate of 4.9% for Reno. The top two graphs show the total bytes measured at the input port of the bottleneck switch (*i.e.*, total bytes generated by the source), the middle two show the total bytes passing through the bottleneck link, and the bottom two represent the total bytes accepted by the receiver-end. In the top and middle graphs, Boston (right) and Reno (left) do not show visible differences in the amount of total bytes, though Boston generated 3.2% more traffic than Reno during the entire period of the 700 simulation seconds.

The bottom two plots show the dramatic difference between the two protocols, where Boston's acceptance and Reno's discarding of incomplete packets result in a big gap between the two protocols in the plots. In particular, Boston showed 7.83% increase in the effective throughput over Reno in this scenario.[8] The low effective throughput of Reno is the result of AAL5 cell discards and the smaller average TCP window size at the Reno's TCP source[9]. The aggregated traffic when the 16 TCP sources are competing is captured in figure 7(b), where Boston achieved a 78.9% effective throughput, whereas Reno achieved 59.1%.

The above experiments as well as others (not included in this paper) show that as the number of TCP sources increase, the performance gap between Boston and Reno is more pronounced. This is because resources (such as switch buffers) become limiting factors as more TCP sources compete for them. In our experiments, we have observed that while packet size, window size, and switch buffer size play important roles that affect performance, TCP Boston was consistently able to provide a more gracefully degrading performance (compared to TCP Reno) when network resources become limited.

5. Summary

In this paper we presented TCP Boston, a novel, fragmentation-tolerant TCP protocol, especially suited for ATM network environments. TCP Boston integrates a standard TCP/IP protocol (such as Reno or Vegas) with a powerful encoding mechanism based on AIDA (an adaptive version of Rabin's IDA dispersal and reconstruction algorithms [21]). We have presented our implementation of TCP Boston and have shown its performance superiority through simulation method, when compared to TCP techniques that are more vulnerable to fragmentation, namely TCP Reno and TCP Reno with EPD switch-level enhancements.

[8]The effective throughput of Reno was 83.1%, whereas that of Boston was 89.6%.

[9]The average window size of Boston during the 700 simulation seconds was 27.7 kB (*i.e.*, 3.02 segments), and Reno maintained an average window size of 23.9 kB (*i.e.*, 2.57 segments).

References

[1] ANSI. AAL5 – A New High Speed Data Transfer AAL. In *ANSI T1S1.5 91-449*. November 1991.

[2] G. Armitage and K. Adams. Packet Reassembly During Cell Loss. *IEEE Network Mag.*, 7(5):26–34, September 1993.

[3] R. Atkinson. Default IP MTU for use over ATM AAL5. In *RFC 1626*. May 1994.

[4] A. Bestavros. SETH: A VLSI chip for the real-time information dispersal and retrieval for security and fault-tolerance. In *Proceedings of ICPP'90, The 1990 International Conference on Parallel Processing*, Chicago, Illinois, August 1990.

[5] A. Bestavros. An adaptive information dispersal algorithm for time-critical reliable communication. In Frisch, Malek, and Panwar, editors, *Network Management and Control, Volume II*. Plenum Publishing Co., NY, NY, 1994.

[6] A. Bestavros and G. Kim. TCP Boston: A Fragmentation-tolerant TCP Protocol for ATM Networks. Technical Report BUCS-TR-96-014, Boston University, Computer Science Department, July 1996.

[7] A. Bianco. Performance of the TCP Protocol over ATM Networks. In *Proceedingds of the 3rd International Conference on Computer Communications and Networks*, pages 170–177, San Francisco, CA, September 1994.

[8] E. Biersack. Performance Evaluation of Forward Error Correction in ATM Networks. *CACM*, pages 248–257, Aug 1992.

[9] L. Brakmo, S. O'Maley, and L. Peterson. TCP Vegas: New Techniques for Congestion Detection and Avoidance. Technical Report TR 94 04, The University of Arizona Computer Science Department, Tucson, AZ 85721, Febrary 1994.

[10] T. Chen and S. Liu. *ATM Switching System*. Artech House, Inc., 685 Canton St., Norwood, MA 02062, 1995.

[11] D. E. Comer. *Internetworking with TCP/IP*, volume 1. Prentice Hall Inc., Englewood Cliffs, NJ, 1995.

[12] S. Floyd. Simulator Tests. Available from `ftp://ftp.ee.lbl.gov/papers/simtests.ps.Z`. ns(v1.0b4) is available at `http://www-nrg.ee.lbl.gov/nrg`., July 1995.

[13] A. Forum. *ATM User-Network Interface Specification*. Prctice Hall, Inc, Englewood Cliffs, New Jersey 07632, 1993.

[14] G. A. Gibson and D. A. Patterson. Designing disk arrays for high data reliability. *Journal of Parallel and Distributed Computing*, 17(1-2):4–27, January/February 1992.

[15] M. Hassan. Impact of Cell Loss on the Efficiency of TCP/IP over ATM. In *Proceedings of the 3rd International Conference on Computer Communications and Networks*, pages 165–169, San Francisco, CA, September 1994.

[16] V. Jacobson. Berkeley TCP Evolution from 4.3-Tahoe to 4.3-Reno. In *Proceedings of the British Columbia Internet Engineering Task Force*, July 1990.

[17] S. Mirchandani and R. Khanna, editors. *FDDI Technology and Applications*. John Wiley & Sons, Inc., 1993.

[18] K. Park, G. Kim, and M. E. Crovella. The Effects of Traffic Self-Similarity on TCP Performance. Technical report, Boston University Computer Science Department, 1996.

[19] J. Postel. Internet Protocol. In *RFC 791*. September 1981.

[20] J. Postel. TCP. In *RFC 793*. September 1981.

[21] M. O. Rabin. Efficient dispersal of information for security, load balancing and fault tolerance. *Journal of the Association for Computing Machinery*, 36(2):335–348, April 1989.

[22] A. Romanow and S. Floyd. Dynamics of TCP Traffic over ATM Networks. *IEEE Journal on Selected Areas in Communication*, 13(4):633–641, May 1995.

Client-Server Performance on Flow-Controlled ATM Networks: A Web Database of Simulation Results

H. T. Kung and S. Y. Wang
Division of Engineering and Applied Sciences
Harvard University
Cambridge, MA 02138, USA

Abstract

*Extensive simulation has demonstrated the effectiveness of credit-based ATM flow control in supporting client-server applications. In particular, request/response protocols used in these applications allow efficient sharing of switch buffer, for the case when all the VCs sharing the same buffer are subject to the same degree of downstream congestion. The required buffer size can be as small as the minimum of bandwidth*RTT for the link and #Clients*Reply_Size. Request/response protocols generally tolerate congestion better than greedy loads. Being able to avoid synchronization, FIFO scheduling is sometimes more efficient than VC round-robin scheduling. These findings are derived from an online Web database of simulation results covering more than 10,000 network and load configurations. The Web database approach has proven to be effective in managing and navigating a large set of simulation results.*

1. Introduction

Client-server systems such as the World Wide Web represent one of the most demanding networking applications. To accommodate high load, some of these servers will need to use high-speed ATM connections of 155Mbps or higher speeds. Increasing transmission rates does not always help, as this also changes the rules of network control substantially. For example, Web transfers over these high-speed networks may now be short enough [11, 14] that existing end-to-end flow control mechanisms do not have enough time to be effective.

On the other hand, ATM offers the opportunity to deploy new techniques such as flow control at the ATM layer. ATM flow control [4, 8, 9] can be efficient because it works at a sufficiently low level in the protocol stack. It can also have fast reaction times when operating between switches within the network rather than end-to-end. It can therefore avoid shortcomings associated with traditional protocols such as TCP's slow start and NFS/UDP's lack of sophisticated flow control.

ATM flow control is new enough, however, that little is known about its behavior over the full range of possible network and load conditions. For example, the interaction between the request/response protocol employed by a client-server system and ATM flow control can be complex, and difficult to envision. Extensive simulation is therefore essential.

In the past most ATM flow control simulations used the so-called "greedy" load [7, 15], for which sources continuously attempted to pump as much data into the network as possible. Results from those relatively simple-minded simulations do not in general carry over to client-server applications using closed-loop, request/response protocols.

One of the reasons for the lack of sufficient simulation results for the client-server model is the high complexity and large scope of the required effort. That is, to derive useful and conclusive results, the simulation study would need to explore and manage a large space of network and load configurations.

This paper describes an approach for using a Web database to archive simulation results. Users over the Internet can use their own Web browsers to navigate the database. We have found this approach, which appears to be new in the network simulation area, effective in managing and using a large set of simulation results.

Currently, the Web database contains precomputed simulation results covering more than 10,000 network and load configurations. These results were generated by a simulator with approximately 6,500 lines of C++ code developed at Harvard over the past year.

This simulator has been developed for the purpose of studying the effectiveness of using ATM flow control in supporting client-server applications. The ATM flow control scheme used by the simulator is a version of credit-based ATM flow control [6, 8, 9] called Quantum Flow Control (QFC) [1], specified by an international consortium of companies. In QFC, both VC flow control and link flow control are used simultaneously. A similar scheme is under development within ITU-T Study Group 13, under the name "Controlled Dynamic Transfer."

0-8186-7780-5/97 $10.00 © 1997 IEEE

Also described in this paper are a number of findings resulting from this Web database:

- Credit-based ATM flow control, using both VC and link flow control simultaneously, can achieve high performance for client-server applications while allowing many VCs to share efficiently relatively small switch buffers, under the assumption that all the VCs sharing the same buffer are subject to the same degree of downstream congestion. (See Section 3.3 for discussions about this assumption.) The simulations have found that buffer over-subscription by a factor of 100 or more, and use of link flow control to prevent possible cell loss due to buffer over-subscription, cause no performance degradation (Sections 4 and 5). Moreover, as shown in Section 6, to achieve maximum performance in throughput and delay, the buffer shared by all the VCs arriving at an input port of a switch can be as small as:

  ```
  Min_Buffer_Size
  = Min (BW*RTT, #Clients*Reply_Size)
  ```

  where `BW` and `RTT` are the bandwidth and roundtrip time of the input link, respectively.

- Request/response protocols employed by client-server systems are more tolerant of downstream congestion than greedy loads (Section 7).

- FIFO scheduling can yield higher throughput than round-robin scheduling for request/response protocols (Section 5). This somewhat unintuitive result is due to the fact that FIFO scheduling is able to prevent synchronization among requests/replies from multiple clients and servers.

- Performance of credit-based flow control can be predicted with high confidence. In fact, essential properties of our simulation results can all be explained by analysis (see Sections 4, 5.2, 6 and 7).

In the next section we will briefly review credit-based ATM flow control. Section 3 describes the simulator responsible for generating the Web database of simulation results. Section 4 presents several representative simulation results and discusses their significance. Sections 5, 6 and 7 highlight some interesting lessons we have learned from the simulation results. Section 8 overviews how users with Web browsers can navigate the database. In the last section, we describe our ongoing and future work, and present some concluding remarks.

2. Background information on credit-based ATM flow control

Credit-based, link-by-link flow control [5, 6, 8, 13] is a method of implementing ATM flow control. The method applies to each VC (virtual circuit) over a link or the entire link itself. That is, a link under credit-based ATM flow control is subject to both VC and link flow control at the same time.

2.1. VC flow control

Credit-based VC flow control, for a VC over a link, generally works as follows. Before forwarding any data cell over the link, the sender needs to receive credits for the VC from the receiver. At various times, the receiver sends credits to the sender indicating availability of buffer space for receiving data cells of the VC. After having received credits, the sender is eligible to forward some number of data cells of the VC to the receiver according to the received credit amount. Each time the sender forwards a data cell of a VC, it decrements its current credit balance for the VC by one.

There are two phases in flow controlling a VC [9]. In the first *buffer allocation* phase, the VC is given an allocation of buffer memory in the receiver. In the second *credit control* phase, the sender maintains a non-negative credit balance to ensure no overflow of the allocated buffer in the receiver.

The *Credit Update Protocol* (CUP) [6] is an efficient and robust protocol for implementing credit control over a link. As depicted by Figure 1, for each flow-controlled VC, the sender keeps a running total `Tx` of all the data cells it has transmitted, and the receiver keeps a running total `Fwd` of all the data cells it has forwarded. The receiver will enclose the up-to-date value of `Fwd` in each credit record transmitted upstream via a credit cell. When the sender receives a credit record with value `Fwd`, it will update the credit balance, `Crd_Bal`, for the VC:

```
Crd_Bal = Buf_Alloc -(Tx - Fwd)     (1)
```

where `Buf_Alloc` is the total number of cells allocated to the VC in the receiver.

Note that the quantity computed by the sender, `Tx - Fwd`, represents the "outstanding credits" corresponding to those cells of the VC that the sender has transmitted but the receiver has not forwarded. As depicted in Figure 1, these cells are "in-flight cells to arrive" and "cells in queue" at the time when the receiver sends the credit record containing the `Fwd` value to the sender. Thus `Crd_Bal` computed by the sender using Equation (1) is the proper new credit balance in the sense that, as long as the sender transmits no

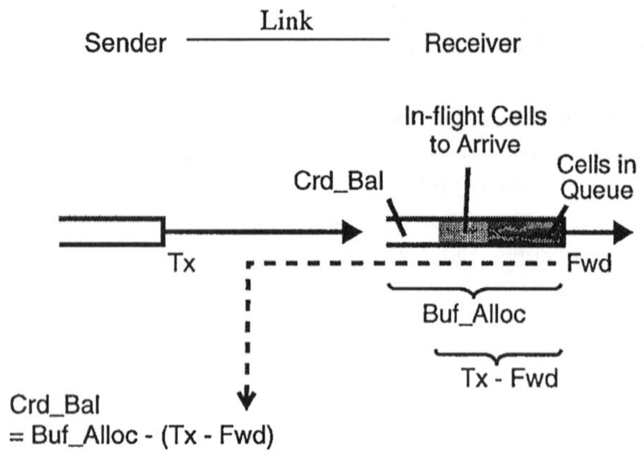

Figure 1: Credit Update Protocol (CUP). The dotted arrow indicates the transport of a credit record upstream containing the current Fwd value at receiver.

more than `Crd_Bal` cells, it will not overrun the VC's allocated buffer in the receiver.

The frequency at which the receiver sends credit records for a VC depends on the VC's progress. More precisely, each time after the receiver has forwarded a certain number of cells, "`N2`" cells [8] for some positive integer `N2`, the receiver will send a credit record upstream. The value of `N2` can be set statically or adaptively.

The `Buf_Alloc` value given to a VC determines the maximum bandwidth allowed to the VC by credit flow control. Without loss of generality, we assume that the maximal peak bandwidth of any link is 1, and represent the rate of a VC as a fraction of 1. Let `RTT` be the round-trip time, in cell transmission time, of the link between the sender and the receiver (see Figure 1) including both propagation delays over the link and credit processing time at the two end nodes. Assume that when forwarding cells out from the output link, the sender employs a fair scheduling policy among those VCs which have both cells to send and positive `Crd_Bal`. Then, if `N` such VCs compete for the same output link, the maximum average bandwidth over `RTT` that each VC can achieve is:

$$BW = Buf\_Alloc/(RTT + N2*N) \qquad (2)$$

To allow the VC to reach the peak link rate, `Buf_Alloc` must therefore be at least `RTT + N2*N`. Since the achieved aggregate bandwidths of all the competing VCs can not exceed the peak link rate, their allocated buffers need not all be used at any given time.

An important area of study in credit-based flow control is on the over-allocation, or over-subscription, of a shared buffer to multiple VCs without compromising performance. As discussed in Section 3.4, we would like to over-subscribe a shared buffer by a large factor such as 100 or more.

2.2. Link flow control

Credit-based link flow control [1, 13] works in the same way as VC flow control, except that link flow control regulates data flow over the entire link rather than individual VCs of the link. The primary purpose of link flow control is to avoid buffer overflow in the over-subscription situation. Several switches have implemented link flow control. A recent example was the experimental OC-12 ATM switch [3] jointly developed by Harvard and Nortel in 1994.

Simulation results throughout this paper assume a credit-based link flow control scheme [1] with `N2` = 10. In all the simulations, when link flow control is applied to a link, VC flow control is also applied to all the VCs over the link (see Section 3.4).

3. Configurations of the simulator

We have purposely chosen a set of simple configurations for the simulator to allow relatively easy analysis of how various settings of parameters in our system affect performance. We have also made sure that these configurations are sufficiently rich to capture the essence of usual client-server usages such as WWW.

3.1. Network configuration

Figure 2 depicts the network configuration of the simulator, where Si and Hi denote switches and hosts, respectively.

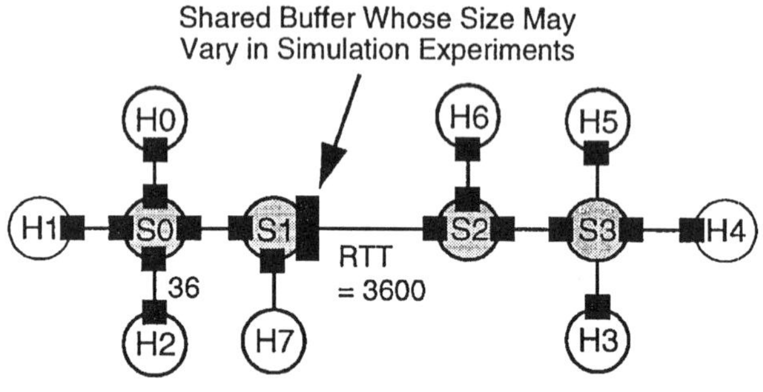

Figure 2: Network and node configurations, with input buffers shown as square and rectangular boxes.

Link between S1 and S2 is a wide-area OC-3 link with Propagation_Delay * Bandwidth = 1800 cells. This corresponds to the one-way delay for a OC-3 link of approximately 1000Km. Thus, the `RTT` of this link in OC-3 cell times is 3600. All the other links are shorter, and they have `RTT` = 36.

3.2. Node configuration

Referring to Figure 2, the simulator assumes that all switches are input-buffer switches. The input port buffer of S1 for the link connecting to S2, denoted as a rectangular box in Figure 2, has a varying size to be specified by the simulation experiment. Each of the other input port buffers, denoted as a square box, has a fixed size of 7,000 cells. These buffers each are sufficiently large so that they can accommodate the maximum number of VCs (i.e., 128 VCs) used in the simulation results reported in this paper, with each VC allocated with enough cells (i.e., 50 cells) to achieve the peak link rate. Thus, the buffer denoted by the rectangular box in Figure 2 is the only buffer that could be a performance bottleneck due to insufficient buffer size. The simulation will focus only on this buffer when studying the effect of shared buffer sizes on the overall performance of the client-server system.

3.3. Connection configuration

Figure 3 depicts the connection configuration of the simulator, where "C" stands for clients, "V" for servers, and "B" for background traffic source or destination.

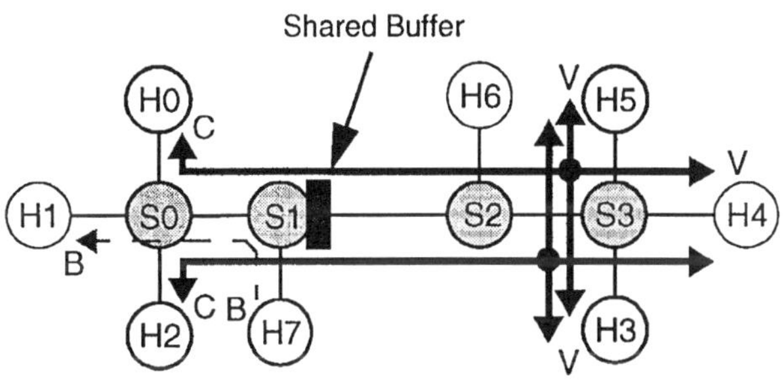

Figure 3: Configuration for connection, flow control, scheduling policy, and load. The simulator uses a maximum of 128 client (C)-server (V) VCs, and a background (B) VC.

The bidirectional VCs connecting clients and servers are evenly distributed among them. That is, if there are N bidirectional client-server connections in the network, N/2 of these will originate at H0, and the other N/2 at H2. Similarly, connections originating at H0 or H2 evenly distribute their destinations among H3, H4 and H5 in a round-robin manner. That is, if H0 has N/2 client-server connections, then H3, H4 and H5 will each have N/6 of these connections.

Requests of each client-server connection travel from left to right along the path: H0/H2 -> S0 -> S1 -> S2 -> S3 -> H3/H4/H5. Replies travel from right to left along the path: H3/H4/H5 -> S3 -> S2 -> S1 -> S0 -> H0/H2.

There is an interfering background traffic (see Section 3.6) from right to left along the path: H7 -> S1 -> S0-> H1. Switches S0 and S1 treat this background traffic with higher priority than any client-server traffic.

Since all the client-server VCs in the reply direction are interfered by the same background traffic, they are subject to the same degree of downstream congestion. It turns out that this assumption of equal downstream congestion assumption will guarantee high performance of credit-based flow control. (In Section 9 we mention a new adaptive credit control scheme by the authors, called ZQFC, which can guarantee high performance without assuming equal downstream congestion.)

3.4. Flow control configuration

As depicted in Figure 3, the simulator assumes that all the links are VC flow controlled using credit control with N2 = 10. Buffer allocation for *each* VC over the link between S1 and S2 is 4,000 cells, and for *each* VC over any other link is 50 cells. By Equation (2), these allocations are large enough to allow each VC to reach the peak link bandwidth under credit-based flow control.

Suppose that the shared buffer of S1, denoted by the rectangular box in Figure 2, has 4,000 cells, and that there are 128 VCs over the link from S2 to S1. Then, because each of these VCS is allocated to 4,000 cells, the over-subscription factor is 128. Simulation results of Sections 4 and 5 show that even with such a high over-subscription factor, client-server systems perform well in all the cases considered.

The link between S1 and S2 also employs link flow control with N2 = 10. The input port where the link enters S1 is the only place in our system where buffer over-subscription may occur. Thus, none of the other links need to employ link flow control.

3.5. Scheduling policy configuration

Referring to Figure 3, the simulator implements the following scheduling policies in scheduling cells to output from each switch output port:

- *VC round-robin scheduling*. The scheduler will round-robin among those VCs which have both credit and data.
- *Cell FIFO scheduling*. The scheduler will pick the earliest arriving cell from those VCs which have both credit and data.
- *VC FIFO scheduling*. The scheduler records the most recently scheduled VC and will first try to pick the cell from that VC again if it has both credit and data. Otherwise, another VC that has the earliest arriving cell and has credit will be scheduled.

The cell and VC scheduling policies will be discussed in more detail in Section 5.2.

3.6. Load configuration

As depicted in Figure 3, the simulator handles both client-server and background loads.

For the client-server load, a client will not issue a new request before receiving the reply of its current request. The time between the client's receiving of a reply and its issuing of the next request is called client's thinking time. This thinking time is randomly chosen from 0 to 400 cell-time with the mean equal to 200 cell-time. The time between the server's receiving the last bit of a request and its transmitting of the first bit of the reply is called server's processing time. This processing time is randomly chosen from 0 to 400 cell-time with the mean equal to 200 cell-time. The randomness in the client's thinking time and in the server's processing time makes the clients' requests not synchronized, to reflect expected usage patterns in real-world applications.

The size of each request is assumed to be 25 cells. The size of each reply can vary and is specified by the simulation experiment. It is assumed that each reply has at least N2 = 10 cells.

Having priority over the client-server traffic, the background traffic is a periodical square-wave, characterized by three parameters:

- BPR: Background Peak Rate of the periodic square-wave traffic,
- BLP: Background Load Period, which is the length of the periodic square-wave cycle in cell cycles, and
- BDR: Background Duty Ratio in each periodic square-wave cycle.

By giving appropriate values to BPR, BLP and BDR, the background traffic can model various load conditions. For example, BDR = 60% means that during 60% of the BLP, the background will operate at the BPR rate, while during the remaining 40% of the BLP, it will not consume any bandwidth.

4. Representative simulation results under VC round-robin scheduling

Figure 4 depicts the average utilization of the link from S2 to S1 in Figure 3, as a function of the shared buffer size, for various numbers of clients (NC), under the VC round-robin scheduling policy of Section 3.5. See Figure 9 for definitions of notations such as NC (Number of Clients), RS (Reply Size), and BS (Buffer Size).

Because the priority background traffic consumes 50% of the link bandwidth, the maximum-possible utilization for the client-server application is 50%. We note the following from Figure 4: Suppose that the number of clients is sufficiently large that they can generate enough load to make full use of the link. Then the average link utilization for the client-server application is at the maximum-possible level when the shared buffer size exceeds the link RTT, which is about 3,600 cells.

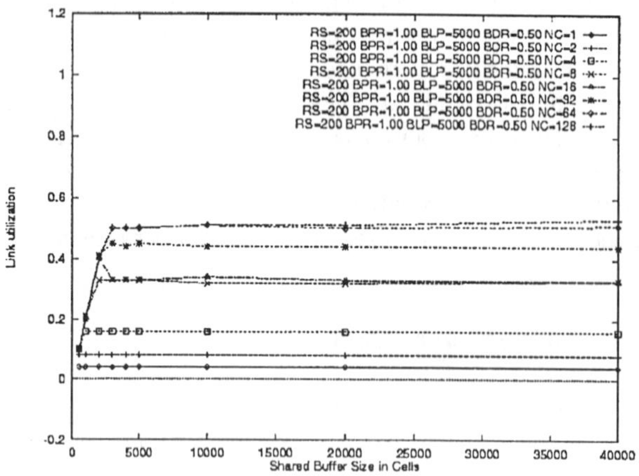

Figure 4: Average utilization of the link from S2 to S1 (in Figure 3) as a function of the shared buffer size, for various numbers of clients (NC), under the VC round-robin scheduling policy.

Figure 5 depicts a related result on the client's average request-reply throughput as a function of the shared buffer size, for several values of NC. Note that when there are NC = 64 or 128 clients, they can generate enough load to make full use of the link, i.e., 50% of the link bandwidth left by the background traffic. Because there are 366,792 OC-3 cell times in a second and the server reply size in this example is 200 cells, the maximum-possible total throughput offered by this system is limited to (366,792 * 0.5)/200 = 916 replies/second. This implies that each of the clients in the system can achieve a throughput of, at most, 916/64 = 14.32 or 916/128 = 7.16 replies/second, respectively, for NC = 64 or 128. Figure 5 shows that these maximum-possible throughputs are reached for these values of NC. The maximum-possible throughputs can be also reached for the case when NC = 16 or 32, if cell or VC FIFO scheduling is used (see Figure 7 for the case when NC = 16). In general, the maximum-possible throughputs can be reached with any value of NC.

Note the anomaly for NC=16 in Figure 5 that client's request-reply throughput decreases when the shared buffer size (BS) increases from 2,000 to 3,000. This contradicts to the expectation that performance improves as the shared buffer increases its size. (The same anomaly can also be noticed in Figure 4.) We show in Section 5 that the use of

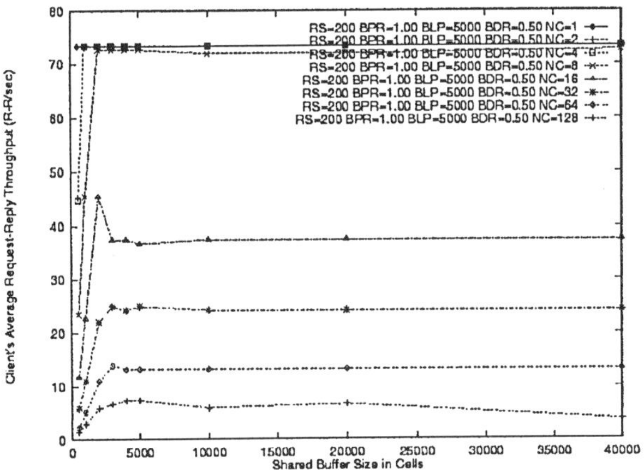

Figure 5: Client's average request-reply throughput in number of request-reply transactions per second as a function of the shared buffer size, for various numbers of clients (NC), under the VC round-robin scheduling policy. The curve for NC=16 of this figure will be compared with others in Figure 7 that use the cell FIFO and VC FIFO scheduling policies.

cell or VC FIFO scheduling, instead of VC round-robin scheduling, will remove this anomaly.

5. FIFO scheduling to improve client-server performance

By using the cell or VC FIFO policy (referring to Section 3.5) client-server performance over a flow-controlled ATM network can be improved.

5.1. Performance degradation due to request-reply synchronization

Figure 6 depicts a simple scenario showing that even under the same configuration and load conditions, different timing relationships between clients's requests can lead to different throughputs. In Case 1, over the same link, client 2 sends out its request immediately after client 1 has sent out its request. Both clients' request-reply turnaround times are 250 cell times. The link utilization is therefore (25+25)/ 250 = 1/5.

In Case 2, both client 1 and client 2 send out their requests at the same time. The two clients' requests and servers' replies are fully interleaved over the same link, and thus their transmission time gets doubled to be 50 cell times. Both clients' request-reply turnaround times are now 300 cell times. The link utilization decreases to (25+25)/300 = 1/6.

We have plotted detailed timing diagrams produced by the simulator. They have confirmed that the performance anomaly of Figure 5 for NC=16, pointed out in the end of Section 4, is indeed caused by this synchronization problem.

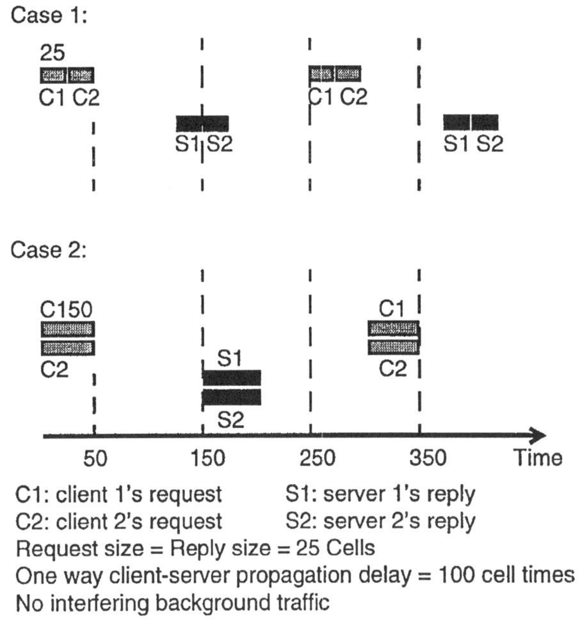

Figure 6: A simple scenario showing that due to synchronization of request-reply operations from clients 1 and 2, Case 2 has a lower throughput than Case 1, although the two cases have the same average load.

5.2. FIFO scheduling for minimizing request-reply synchronization and improving throughput

To avoid the synchronization problem described in Section 5.1, the cell or VC FIFO scheduling policy of Section 3.5 can be used, instead of the VC round-robin scheduling policy. The cell FIFO scheduling can maintain the relative timing relationships between replies, and it is easy to implement in switches. The VC FIFO scheduling attempts to use each reply as a scheduling unit rather than each cell, and thus can reduce the chance that multiple replies are interleaved in transmission.

Figure 7 compares the client's average request-reply throughputs for "VC round-robin", "cell FIFO" and "VC FIFO" scheduling policies, in the case when NC=16, RS=200, BPR=1, BLP=5,000 and BDR=.5. We see that "cell FIFO" and "VC FIFO" scheduling policies perform equally well, and both outperform the "VC Round-Robin" scheduling policy. In addition, we notice that with the FIFO scheduling policies, the abnormality seen in Figures 4 and 5 disappears, and client-server applications achieve their maximum-possible throughput with fewer VCs.

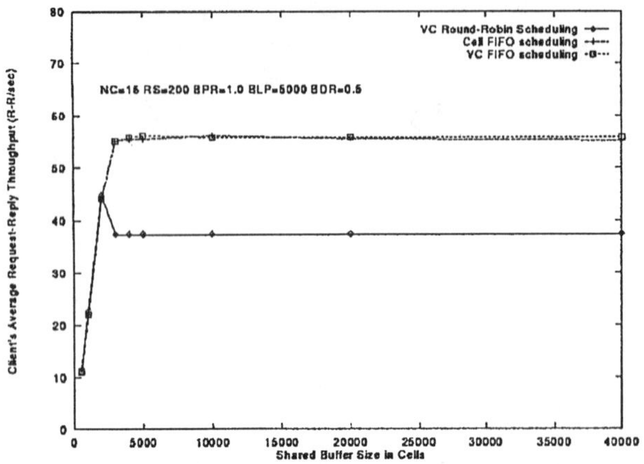

Figure 7: Client's average request-reply throughput as a function of the shared buffer size for the case NC=16, under "VC round-robin", "cell FIFO" and "VC FIFO" scheduling polices. This figure is to be compared with Figure 5 for the case NC=16, which uses the VC round-robin scheduling policy.

6. Minimizing buffer allocation for request/response protocols

Request/response protocols employed by client-server systems allow each credit-based flow-controlled VC to be allocated with a buffer of size as small as the reply size, without sacrificing performance. This is attractive for links with large RTT and bandwidth, since the allocation is independent of these quantities.

Consider any node on the VC over which a reply is carried. Suppose that the VC is allocated a buffer in the downstream node of size equal to the reply size. Soon after forwarding the reply, the VC will be left with no credit. The VC will be replenished with new credits in time before they are needed. That is, the VC will not need to send out the next reply until the client's next request arrives at the server side. But by that time, the credit level of the VC will have been raised to the reply size again because the link's one-way delay is always no greater than the end-to-end client-server connection's one-way delay.

To provide a simulation validation, we have re-run configurations in Figure 5 with buffer allocation of each VC between S1 and S2 reduced to 200 (the number of cells in the reply) from 4,000 as specified in Section 3.4. The new simulation results are exactly the same as those shown in Figure 5. This confirms that the achieved performance remains the same when the buffer allocation of each VC is reduced to the reply size.

7. Request/response protocols tolerate congestion better than greedy loads

All the simulation results reported in this paper use link credit-based flow control to protect over-subscribed buffer from overflowing. One possible drawback of this scheme is that the shared buffer may be totally or largely occupied by cells of some VCs blocked downstream, and due to link flow control this will block other "live" VCs' traffic and result in poor link utilization. It turns out that request/response protocols can tolerate congestion of this type better than greedy loads.

When a reply VC is blocked downstream, its cells will be queued in the network along the upstream path of VC. Because there will not be another reply again until the current reply arrives at the client and the next client request is issued, the total buffer space that this VC can occupy in the network is limited to the current reply size. In contrast, a blocked greedy VC would have filled all the buffers along its upstream path.

Moreover, suppose that at some time a link is totally closed by some blocked VCs and no other VCs' traffic can flow through. When this blocked VC is no longer blocked downstream and starts forwarding its cells out, we would want the shared buffer to be freed up quickly. However, if this VC has a greedy load, its buffer occupancy could remain at the nearly full level because new cells will continue arriving while old cells depart. In contrast, if this VC carries a reply for a request/response protocol used in client-server applications, the VC's buffer occupancy will go down to zero after the last cell of the current reply is sent out.

Simulation results have confirmed that request/response protocols can tolerate congestion better than greedy loads. For example, Figure 8 depicts the link utilization as a function of the reply size, for the configurations of Section 3 without the background traffic. It is assumed that each client's reply may get blocked downstream with an equal probability of 1/1000. When a reply is blocked, it will be blocked for 9,000 consecutive cell times, and the client will not be able to receive the cells of its reply during this period. Since RTT + BS = 3,600 + 5,000 is less than 9,000, a very large blocked reply can occupy the whole link buffer and thus shut down the entire link.

Under this downstream blockage assumption, the simulation results of Figure 8 show that link utilization decreases as reply size increases. Since reply loads behave like greedy loads when the reply size is large, the results of Figure 8 confirm that when there is downstream blockage, request/response protocols will work better than greedy loads.

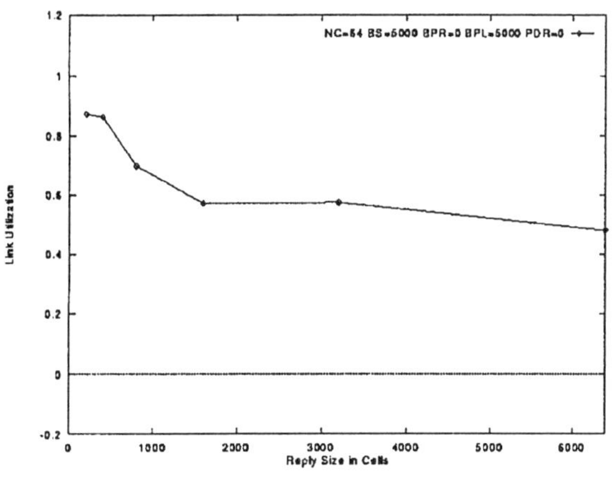

Figure 8: Link utilization as a function of the reply size under the assumption that clients' replies may get blocked downstream.

8. Web navigation of the database of simulation results

Web users on the Internet can interactively access the Web database described in this paper at http://www.eecs.harvard.edu/atm/client-server-web-database. Currently the database contains precomputed simulation results corresponding to more than 10,000 network and load configurations. Thus, the results presented in Section 4 constitute less than .1% of the total results available in the database!

As depicted in Figure 9, using a Web browser, a user first chooses simulation configuration parameters along a number of dimensions, such as NC and BS, and then selects a performance quantity to observe, such as link utilization, client's throughput or client's turnaround time. By clicking on the submit button, the user submits the selections and asks for the plotting of the requested performance curves. The requested graph, sent over the net in postscript files, will show up on the user's display using the public-domain ghostview software.

Currently, as shown in Figure 9, the user can choose values for each of the six parameters. A pull-down menu from which the user can make selection is provided for each parameter and for the performance quantity to examine. For example, the pull-down menu for NC has the following entries: X-axis, 1, 2, 4, 8, 16, 32, 64, 128 and Z-axis.

Figure 9 depicts a set of selected values. By submitting these selected values, the graph shown in Figure 4 will be plotted on the user's display.

9. Ongoing and future work

Beyond continuing to expand the Web database for additional simulation results, we plan to simulate new loads types such as TCP and self-similar loads [2, 10], and adaptive buffer allocation algorithms [6, 7, 13]. In particular, we will simulate the authors' Zero Queueing Flow Control (ZQFC) algorithm. This new algorithm, to be described in a forthcoming paper, will allow client-server applications to achieve high performance, without the present paper's assumption of equal downstream congestion among the VCs sharing the same buffer.

To provide improved flexibility of this database resource over the Web, we will consider implementing

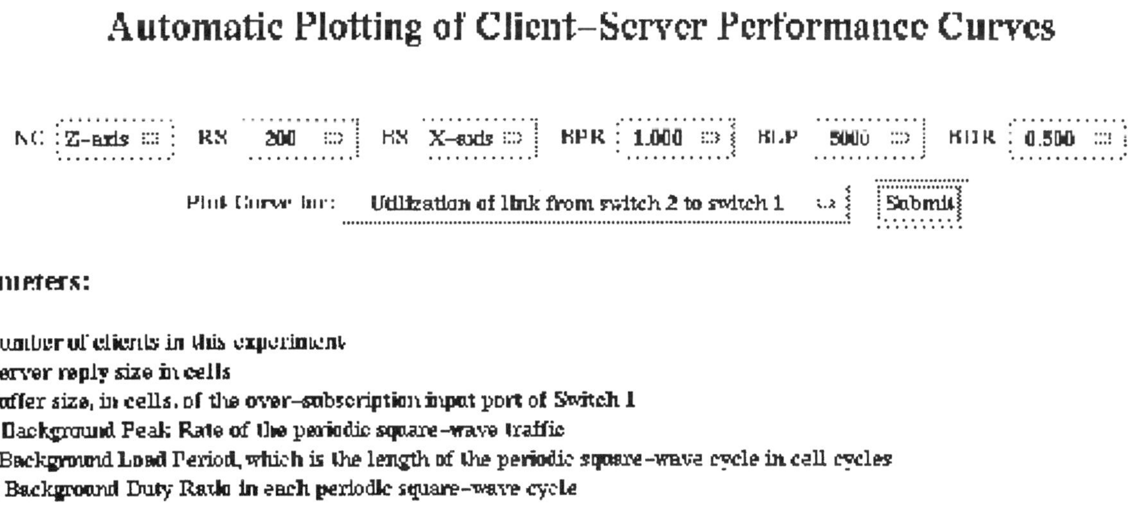

Figure 9: Web browser interface for the Web database http: //www.eecs.harvard.edu/atm/client-server-web-database. For example, by submitting the selected values shown for the six parameters, the graph of Figure 4 will be plotted on the user's display.

dynamic configuration of the simulator, and on-the-fly generation of simulation results. To minimize the network bandwidth required to browse the results, we hope to use Java to allow download of just the data points and generation of the graph in the local browser.

In addition, we have ideas that could lead to substantially improved Web-based user interface. For example, a history of recently selected parameters will facilitate user's comparing simulations and spotting trends. Longer-term bookmarks will help recollection of particularly interesting data sets for future reference or to help prepare demonstrations.

10. Concluding remarks

Under the assumption of equal downstream congestion (Section 3.3), credit-based flow-controlled ATM networks support client-server applications well. Near maximum link utilization is generally achieved, while VC fairness is maintained. Moreover, switch buffer can be efficiently shared by VCs. The buffer associated with an input port need only be of size `minimum` (`BW*RTT`, #clients*Reply_Size), where `BW` and `RTT` are bandwidth and roundtrip time of the input link, respectively.

Web databases, that support archiving and navigation of a large set of performance results, represent a powerful tool for studying complex networking problems. Any user on the Internet can dynamically form their own hypotheses and then navigate the database to determine whether or not the data support their hypotheses. Interpretation of the simulation results is therefore no longer static. In contrast, today's research papers typically present only a dozen of diagrams or fewer, and do not allow the reader to perform any substantial "if then else" type of analysis. In addition, the database can be kept online for a long period of time, say, several years, to allow reuse of the data for answering new research questions, to help formulate new theory, and to cross-check with other databases results.

Acknowledgments

This work has been supported in part by a grant from Ascom Nexion, and assisted by research support from several other companies including Digital, Intel, Nortel and Sprint. Comments from INFOCOM reviewers were helpful.

References

[1] The QFC Alliance, *Quantum Flow Control*, Version 2.0, 1995. Also available from http://www.qfc.org.

[2] J. Beran, R. Sherman, M.S. Taqqu and W. Willnger, "Long Range Dependence in Variable Bit Rate Video Traffic," *IEEEE Transactions on Communications*, Vol. 43, No. 2/3/4, Feb./March/April. 1995.

[3] T. Blackwell, et al. "An Experimental Flow Controlled Multicast ATM Switch," *Proceedings of First Annual Conference on Telecommunications R&D in Massachusetts*, Vol. 6, pp. 33-38, October 25, 1994.

[4] F. Bonomi and K. W. Fendick, "The Rate-based Flow Control Framework for the Available Bit Rate ATM Service," *IEEE Network Magazine*, March/April 1995, pp. 25-39.

[5] M. G. H. Katevenis, "Fast Switching and Fair Control of Congested Flow in Broadband Networks," *IEEE J. on Selected Areas in Commun.*, vol. SAC-5, no. 8, pp. 1315-1326, Oct. 1987.

[6] H. T. Kung, T. Blackwell and A. Chapman, "Credit-Based Flow Control for ATM Networks: Credit Update Protocol, Adaptive Credit Allocation, and Statistical Multiplexing," *Proc. ACM SIGCOMM '94 Symposium on Communications Architectures, Protocols and Applications*, August 31-September 2, 1994, pp. 101-114.

[7] H. T. Kung and K. Chang, "Receiver-Oriented Adaptive Buffer Allocation in Credit-Based Flow Control for ATM Networks," *Proc. INFOCOM '95*, April 1995, pp. 239-252.

[8] H. T. Kung and A. Chapman, "The FCVC (Flow-Controlled Virtual Channels) Proposal for ATM Networks," Version 2.0, 1993. A summary appears in *Proc. 1993 International Conf. on Network Protocols*, October 19-22, 1993, pp. 116-127. (Postscript files of this and other related papers by the authors and their colleagues are available via anonymous FTP from virtual.harvard.edu:/pub/htk/atm.)

[9] H. T. Kung and R. Morris, "Credit-Based Flow Control for ATM Networks," *IEEE Network Magazine*, March/April 1995, pp. 40-48.

[10] W. Leland, M.S Taqqu, W. Willinger and D.V. Wilson, "On the Self-Similar Nature of Ethernet Traffic (Extended Version)," *IEEE/ACM Transactions on Networking*, Vol. 2, No. 1, February 1994.

[11] J. C. Mogul, "Network Behavior of a Busy Web Server and its Clients," Digital Western Research Laboratory Research Report TN-49, May 1995.

[12] R. Morris and H. T. Kung, "Impact of ATM Flow Control on TCP Performance: Measurements on an Experimental ATM Switch", *Proc. GLOBECOM'95*, Stamford Press, Singapore, pp. 888-892.

[13] C. Ozveren, R. Simcoe, and G. Varghese, "Reliable and Efficient Hop-by-Hop Flow Control," *Proc. ACM SIGCOMM '94 Symposium on Communications Architectures, Protocols and Applications*, August 31-September 2, 1994, pp. 89-100.

[14] A. Schmidt and R. Campbell, "Internet Protocol Traffic Analysis with Applications for ATM Switch Design," ACM SIGCOMM Computer Communication Review, Vol. 23, No. 2, pp. 39-52, April, 1993.

[15] R. J. Simcoe, "Configurations for Fairness and Other Test," ATM_Forum/ 94-0557, 1994.

Two-Way TCP Traffic over ATM: Effects and Analysis

Lampros Kalampoukas and Anujan Varma
Computer Engineering Department
University of California
Santa Cruz, CA, 96064
{lampros, varma}@cse.ucsc.edu

K. K. Ramakrishnan

AT&T Research
Murray Hill, NJ 07974
kkrama@research.att.com

Abstract

We examine the performance of bidirectional TCP/IP connections over Asynchronous Transfer Mode (ATM) networks using the Available Bit Rate (ABR) service. The problem of "ack-compression" re-appears, although the queues are primarily at the end-systems. We further the understanding of the problem by quantitatively analyzing the periodic bursty behavior of the source IP queue. We are able to predict the peak values for the queue and arrive at a simple robust predictor for the degraded throughput, applicable for relatively general situations. The degradation in throughput due to bidirectional traffic can be significant. For example, even in the simple case of symmetrical connections with adequate window sizes, the throughput of each connection is only 66.67% of that under one-way traffic.

We validate our analysis using simulation, where the ATM network uses the Explicit Rate option. We show that the analysis predicts the behavior of the queue and the throughput degradation. We observe the need to separate the flow of acknowledgments and data for the bidirectional TCP connection and for inter-leaving their processing at the end-systems to overcome the problem of ack compression.

1 Introduction

The Transmission Control Protocol (TCP) has become the most widely used transport-layer protocol today, due largely to the explosive growth of the TCP/IP Internet in recent years. An important component of TCP is the collection of algorithms used to perform congestion control and recovery [1, 2]. These algorithms give rise to a variety of interesting dynamics, some of which have been studied extensively [3, 4, 5, 6]. In this paper, our interest is in analyzing the dynamics of TCP connections in an Asynchronous Transfer Mode (ATM) network in the presence of two-way traffic.

We define *two-way* or *bidirectional* traffic as the traffic pattern resulting from two or more TCP connections transferring data in opposite directions between the same pair of end nodes over a network path. The TCP segments transmitted by the connections in one direction share the same physical path with the acknowledgements (acks) of connections in the opposite direction. These packets and acknowledgements may share a common buffer in the end systems as well as network switches/routers. This sharing has been shown to result in an effect called *ack compression*, where acks of a connection arrive at the source bunched together [6, 7]. The result of ack-compression is a marked unfairness in the throughput received with competing connections, and reduced overall throughput compared to what could be expected without this effect [7]. Ack compression may occur either at the end system or in a switch/router. In either case, the smooth flow of acknowledgements to the source is disturbed, potentially resulting in reduction of throughput for the TCP connections involved.

Some of the reduced throughput in datagram networks under two-way traffic could be attributed to the bunching of acks at the bottleneck link, behind data packets. Since the acks typically take less time to process in the routers as compared to data packets, the former tend to become bunched as they travel through the network. Our interest, instead, is in TCP operating over the Available Bit Rate (ABR) service provided by an Asynchronous Transfer Mode (ATM) network, where the two-way effects introduced by the network are likely to be much less pronounced. However, we observe that undesirable interaction between connections can still occur at the end systems, leading to similar behavior. Although our analysis is focussed on TCP over ABR, the results apply equally well to TCP operating over other networks providing a steady rate, predictable delay, and in-order delivery. Several earlier studies have been reported on the behavior of TCP in ATM networks [8, 9, 10], but none of them considers the effects of two-way traffic on TCP behavior.

The use of ABR service with the explicit-rate option can facilitate a smooth flow of TCP traffic in the network, mitigating the effects due to interaction of traffic flows in the switches. However, we show that the effect of ack compression and the resulting throughput loss still persists in a rate-controlled network if the segments and acknowledgements share a common queue at the end systems. This common queue may either be at the IP layer, or at the ATM layer where the data segments of a TCP connection may share a virtual channel with the acks of a reverse connection.

This research is supported by the Advanced Research Projects Agency (ARPA) under Contract No. F19628-93-C-0175 and by the NSF Young Investigator Award No. MIP-9257103. The OPNET modeling tool used for simulations was donated to us by MIL-3, Inc.

0-8186-7780-5/97 $10.00 © 1997 IEEE

Figure 1: Model for 2-way traffic in a general network.

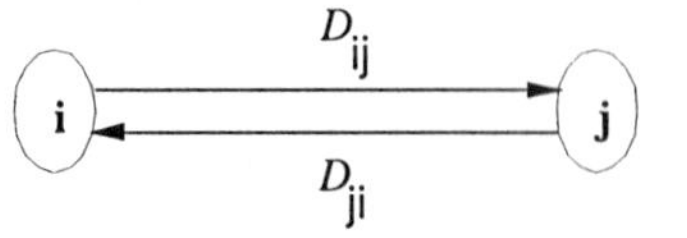

Figure 2: Simplified model for 2-way traffic.

The primary objective of this paper to analyze the dynamics of two-way TCP traffic using the ABR service in an ATM network, develop analytical models that describe the system behavior, quantify the performance degradation, and validate the models by simulation.

The remainder of the paper is organized as follows: In Section 2, we describe the models of the network and the end nodes assumed in our analysis. We illustrate the occurrence of ack compression with an example, and argue that TCP dynamics similar to those observed in datagram networks will cause performance degradation even while operating over the ABR service. In Section 3 we analyze the effects of two-way traffic in networks with symmetric link rates and derive expressions for throughput and maximum queue size. We validate our analytical results with simulations in Section 4. Finally, we provide a summary of our results and directions for future work in Section 5.

2 Dynamics of TCP in a Two-Way Traffic Environment

In this section we introduce the end-system and network models assumed in our analysis and simulations, and illustrate how ack compression occurs in a two-way TCP environment. A detailed quantitative analysis of the effect of this behavior on TCP throughput will be dealt with in Section 3. Due to space constraints we limit our analysis to the symmetric case where the link bandwidths are identical in both directions. In addition, we also ignore the effect of TCP processing time in the end systems. The case of asymmetric link rates, as well as the effect of TCP processing time, are considered in [11].

2.1 End-System and Network Models

The basic network configuration we consider has of two nodes i and j communicating over a rate-controlled network providing in-order delivery, such as the Available Bit-Rate (ABR) service offered by an ATM network (Figure 1). The simplest configuration consists of a pair of two one-way TCP connections, one transferring data from i to j and the other from j to i. Since our interest is in analyzing the end-system effects, we assume that the transmission rates of the nodes remain steady throughout the interval under observation and that the network provides a fixed-bandwidth pipe for the TCP connections between the nodes in each direction, with in-order delivery. Furthermore, in the analysis of Section 3, we assume that the network provides a constant-delay path between the end nodes. Such an assumption is realistic in the ATM ABR environment when the switches employ explicit rate allocation, since the queue sizes in the switches can be maintained small [12]. The queueing delays in network switches are taken into account in the simulation results in an expanded version of this paper [11].

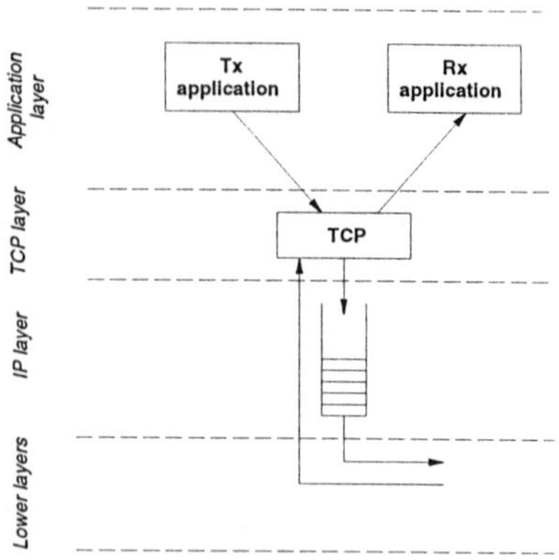

Figure 3: Model of an end node in the analysis.

The data segments transmitted by the TCP connection in one direction shares a common outgoing ATM virtual channel with the acks transmitted by the connection in the other direction. Thus, for the purpose of our analysis, the configuration in Figure 1 can be replaced by the simpler configuration of Figure 2, where the nodes are interconnected by dedicated point-to-point links, each representing a virtual channel in the actual network. Note that pairs of TCP connections between nodes that are part of a larger network can be abstracted by this model if the network maintains a constant transmission rate and delay for the connections over the interval of observation.

We refer to the TCP connection transferring data from node i to j as *connection* i and the opposite connection as *connection* j. We denote by D_{ij} the constant delay seen by TCP segments transmitted from i to j, and by D_{ji} the delay seen by segments from j to i. We also assume for simplicity that the TCP segments transmitted are of constant size, and that the transmission rate in each direction is identical, denoted by ρ in units of TCP segments/second.

The model assumed for the end nodes is shown in Figure 3. The TCP and IP protocols operate over a rate-controlled ATM layer. We assume that appropriate segmentation and reassembly, adaptation, and transmission-rate control procedures have been implemented below the IP layer. Two applications reside within each node, a sending application that acts as the source of data for the TCP connection originating at that node and a receiving application that acts as the sink for data arriving from the opposite node. The transmitting applications are assumed to be greedy and the receiving ones are assumed to absorb all received data immediately. Note that our analysis applies equally well when a single application in each node that both sends and receives data over a bidirectional TCP connection is assumed instead of the two applications communicating over separate TCP connections, as long as the applications are greedy.

A common process handles all TCP processing within the node. The TCP process receives data segments from the network and delivers them to the receiving application. In addition, an acknowledgement is generated and added to the outgoing queue for each segment received. The same TCP process also handles transmission of data to the opposite node by queueing one or more data segments from the transmitting application into the outgoing queue each time an ack is received from the opposite node. Finally, the TCP process is responsible for controlling the window growth of the sending TCP during the slow-start phase by incrementing it each time an ack is received, until the window reaches its maximum size. Since our analysis pertains to steady-state operation of the connections in a loss-free network, we can ignore other details of the congestion control function at the TCP layer, such as the congestion avoidance phase and recovery on packet losses.

Segments of the forward connection and acks to the backward connection share a common FIFO queue at the IP layer that is serviced at the transmission rate of the outgoing link. This common queue is key to the occurrence of ack compression where acks to the backward connection get bunched while waiting in the queue behind data segments of the forward connection, causing the TCP dynamics we study in this paper. However, the assumption of the IP service rate being equal to transmission rate on the link is not critical if the acks of the backward connection and data segments of the forward connection share a common ATM virtual channel. A higher service rate out of the IP queue reduces queueing at the IP layer, but the same bunching effect will now occur at the ATM or adaptation layer where the data will be queued.

The functionality assumed for the IP layer is simple. For incoming traffic the IP layer is responsible for forwarding data from the lower layer to the local TCP process. Since TCP processing time is assumed to be small, no queueing is required for incoming traffic at the IP layer. For the outgoing traffic, on the other hand, a queue may be built up at the IP layer, awaiting transmission on the link, as a result of ack bunching. Thus, in the worst case, an entire window worth of segments may be added to the outgoing queue in quick succession due to a bunch of acks received from the opposite end. Therefore, to avoid packet losses at the source node, we assume that the IP queue has a size equal to the maximum window size of the sending TCP. The interaction between TCP and IP described above is consistent with the 4.4 BSD-Lite Unix Release [13].

2.2 The Onset of Ack Compression

We will now illustrate with an example how the window-growth process during the TCP slow-start phase leads to ack compression in a two-way configuration. The result is that, on completion of the slow-start phase, each connection will always transmit an entire window of segments as a burst, followed by acknowledgements of the opposite connection.

First, we note that the sum of the window sizes of the two connections must exceed the bandwidth-delay product of the round-trip pipe for ack compression to occur. If this condition is not satisfied, it is easy to see that no persistent queueing will occur at the IP queues at both nodes in steady state. Thus, the data segments of each connection are isolated from the acks of the other connection. Hence, if W_i and W_j are the window sizes of the two connections in segments, we must have

$$W_i + W_j > \rho(D_{ij} + D_{ji}), \qquad (2.1)$$

for ack compression to occur. We will therefore assume that this condition always holds.

The example in Figure 4 illustrates how the TCP window growth process during slow-start leads to ack compression in a two-way configuration. Assume that the maximum window-size for both connections is set at 4 segments. To start with, we assume that connection i, transmitting data from node i to j, has already reached steady-state with a window size of $W_i = 4$ segments, while connection j in the opposite direction is not yet open. This initial state, say at time t, is shown in Figure 4(a). The transmission time of a segment is taken as one unit and the one-way delay in each direction as 2 units. We assume that this delay includes the processing time at the destination; thus, and ack is generated when the first bit of a segment reaches its destination. For convenience, we number the segments transmitted from node i as $1, 2, 3, \ldots$, and those transmitted in the opposite direction as $1', 2', 3', \ldots$. In Figure 4(a), segments 3 and 4 are in transit from node i to j, while the acks to the two previous segments (segments 1 and 2) are returning to i.

Now assume that node j opens its connection at time t and completes transmission of its first segment to i at time $t+1$. The network state at time $t+1$ is shown in Figure 4(b). The segment $1'$ transmitted by connection j travels immediately behind the ack to segment 3 of connection i, and reaches node i at time $t+2$. The ack to $1'$ will travel back to j behind segment 7 of connection i, and reach node j at time $t+4$. On receipt of this ack, node j increases its window by one, and adds two segments ($2'$ and $3'$) to the outgoing queue. Segment $2'$, the first of these, is transmitted at time $t+5$ behind the ack to segment 7. The network state at this time is shown in Figure 4(c). Note that the ack to segment 8 will now be queued behind segment $3'$ in node j's IP queue, and will be delayed by the transmission time of one segment, causing it to be bunched with the ack to the next segment, segment 9. Thus, segments $2'$ and $3'$ will reach node i as a bunch, followed by the bunched acks to segments 8 and 9 at time $t+8$.

Figure 4(d) shows the network state at time $t+8$ when the bunched acks to segments 8 and 9 are about to reach node i. Note that node i was unable to transmit a segment after segment 11, because the ack to segment 8 did not arrive in time. This results in loss of throughput for connection i.

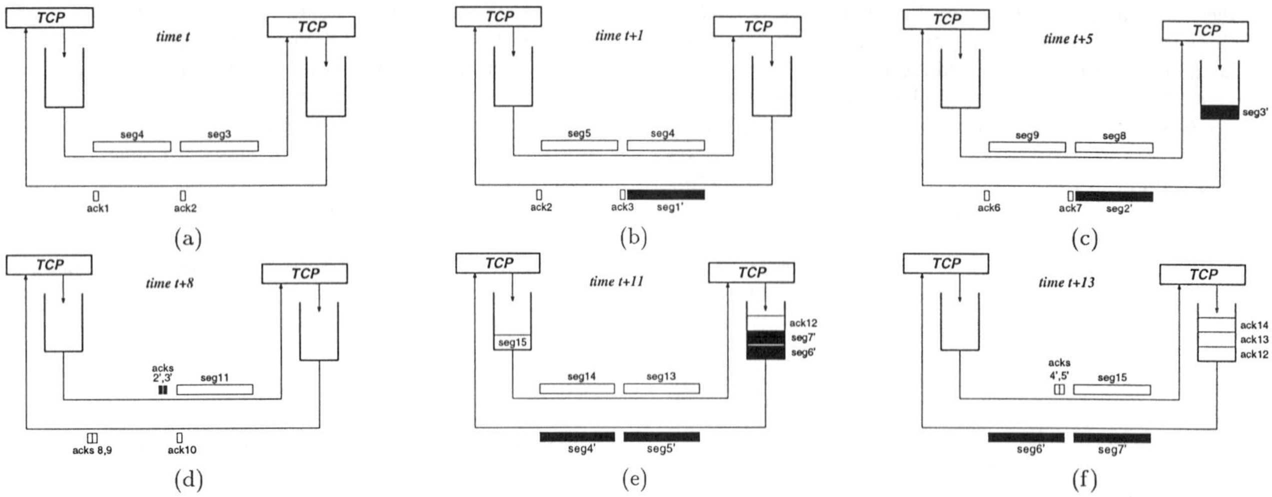

Figure 4: Illustration of the occurrence of ack compression during the slow-start phase in a two-way TCP configuration.

The acks to segments $2'$ and $3'$ arrive at node j at time $t+9$, each effecting a window increase at j. Thus, at time $t+9$, four segments ($4'$ through $7'$) are added to node j's IP queue. At this point, the slow-start phase of connection j is complete and its window size has reached 4 segments.

Figure 4(e) shows the network state at time $t+11$ when node j has completed transmission of segments $3'$ and $4'$, while $6'$ and $7'$ are still queued in node j. Note that no acks to connection i are interleaved between segments $1'$ and $4'$. Thus, acks to segments 12, 13 and 14 will be accumulated in the IP queue and transmitted as a bunch at time $t+13$, as shown in Figure 4(f).

Note that since node i receives no acks between segments $4'$ and $7'$, the acks to segments $4'$ through $7'$ will return to j with no intervening segments of connection i. The four new segments generated by connection j in response will, in turn, contain no acks of connection i, and so on. This illustrates how the bunching effect built up during the slow-start phase may persist for the entire life of the connections in a loss-free network.

It is important to realize how ack compression reduces the throughput of a TCP connection. Assume that a set of k acks returning from node i to j are bunched. Node j will generate k segments in response to these acks, which arrive back-to-back at node i. If the outgoing IP queue of node i has less than k segments at the time the segments start to arrive, node i will complete transmission of its entire IP queue before it can receive the next ack from j, causing it to be idle for a period of time, except for transmitting an ack for each segment received. This is the fundamental cause of throughput loss with two-way TCP traffic. Furthermore, if this behavior is periodic, the result is a sustained loss of throughput for one or both of the connections. In the next section we will show that such sustained loss of throughput is inevitable in a two-way configuration satisfying condition (2.1), regardless of the phase difference between the two connections at startup.

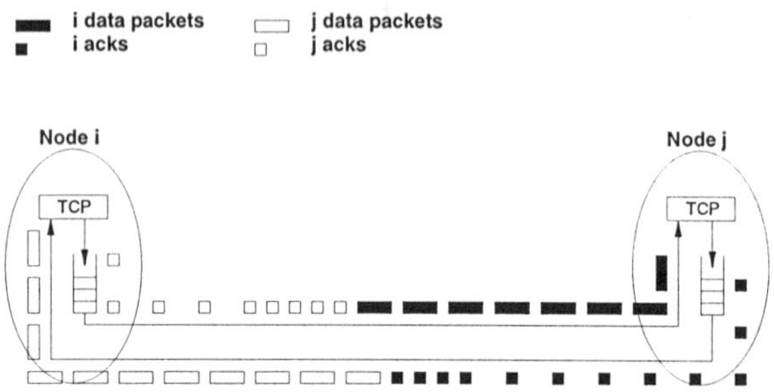

Figure 5: Traffic pattern in a two-way traffic configuration.

Figure 5 illustrates the steady-state traffic pattern in a general two-way TCP configuration. Note that there is no interleaving between the data and ack streams transmitted in each direction. The ack stream, in general, consists of a set of compressed acks followed by a set of spaced acks that are transmitted at a spacing of one segment. It is the latter that causes throughput degradation, since the spaces between acks cannot be filled with data segments.

From the preceding discussion, it is clear that the loss of throughput of a TCP connection depends on the number of bunched acks arriving at the transmitter and the number of queued segments in the IP queue at that time. In the next section, we will quantify this throughput degradation and derive analytical expressions for throughput as a function of the window sizes, link rates, and delays.

3 Analysis of Two-Way TCP Dynamics in Networks with Symmetric Links

In the previous section, we described how the TCP window growth during the slow-start process gives rise to the effect of ack compression under two-way traffic. In this section, we derive analytical expressions for the steady-state throughput of TCP connections in a simple network configuration with a pair of TCP flows in opposite directions after the windows have reached their maximum size. Later, in Section 4, we will validate the analytical results with extensive simulations.

Before proceeding further, we introduce the following definitions and notations. We observed in Section 2 that ack compression causes the segments of a TCP connection to be separated from the acks of the opposite connection. That is, each of the nodes transmits an entire window of segments as a single burst, followed by acks of the opposite connection. We will refer to an interval of time during which a node transmits its data segments as a *busy period* of the connection originating at the node. The busy periods for a given connection can easily be identified since these are separated by the acknowledgements of the opposite connection. We assume that the data segments transmitted are of the same size and that the transmission rates in each direction are identical, denoted by ρ in units of segments per second. The transmission time of an acknowledgment is considerably smaller than the transmission time of a data segment. Therefore, to make the analysis simple, we assume the former to be zero.

The window sizes of the two connections are assumed steady, denoted by W_i and W_j segments, respectively, for the connections originating at nodes i and j. We will denote the number of segments that are needed to fill the one-way link from i to j as L_{ij}, and that for the opposite link as L_{ji}. That is,

$$L_{ij} = \rho \cdot D_{ij}, \text{ and } L_{ji} = \rho \cdot D_{ji}.$$

Let $Q_i(t)$ denote the occupancy of the outgoing IP queue of node i at time t, considering only data segments and ignoring the space occupied by acks. Similarly, let $Q_j(t)$ denote the IP queue occupancy for node j. Furthermore, let $\tau_{i,k}$ denote the time at which the first segment transmitted by node i during the kth busy period of connection i reaches node j. Likewise we denote with $\tau_{j,k}$ the time at which the first segment transmitted by node j during the kth busy period of connection j reaches node i. Note that the number of acks that will be bunched together behind the busy period in progress at time $\tau_{i,k}$ of connection j is then given by $Q_j(\tau_{i,k})$, the number of segments in node j's outgoing queue when the first segment of the kth busy period reaches it.

Throughout this section we will assume condition (2.1), that the sum of the window sizes exceeds the delay-bandwidth product of the round-trip pipe, since this is a necessary condition for ack compression to occur. In our analysis of the effect of ack compression, we will consider two separate cases, a simple case followed by a more complex one. The simple case occurs when the window sizes and delays are such that

$$W_i > W_j + (L_{ij} + L_{ji}). \tag{3.1}$$

In this case, since the worst-case queueing delay of an ack of connection i in node j is W_j, node i never exhausts its window. Thus, each busy period of connection i will consist of W_i segments, accompanied by a sequence of W_j acks bunched together, and followed immediately by the next busy period. Since we assume that the acks are transmitted in zero time, connection i achieves perfect throughput in this case. However, the throughput of connection j is affected, since it experiences an effective round-trip delay that is equal to the transmission time of W_i segments. We will next prove these results formally.

Lemma 1 *If $W_i > W_j + (L_{ij} + L_{ji})$, then*

$$\begin{aligned} \tau_{i,k+1} &= \tau_{i,k} + W_i/\rho, \\ \text{and } \tau_{j,k+1} &= \tau_{j,k} + W_i/\rho. \end{aligned}$$

That is, the busy periods of the connections will be spaced apart by the window size W_i, exhibiting periodic behavior. Note that the above result is true in steady state, independent of the relative phase of the two interacting TCP connections at startup. Since each of the connections transmits a window of segments during this period, the throughput efficiencies of the connections are given by

$$F_i = 1, \text{ and } F_j = W_j/W_i. \tag{3.2}$$

Proof of Lemma 1:

When the first segment of the kth busy period of connection i reaches node j, the occupancy of the IP queue of node j is $Q_j(\tau_{i,k})$. Therefore, the ack to the first segment of the busy period will leave node j at time $\tau_{i,k} + Q_j(\tau_{i,k})/\rho$ and reach node i at time t_1, where

$$t_1 = \tau_{i,k} + Q_j(\tau_{i,k})/\rho + D_{ji}. \tag{3.3}$$

We can calculate the occupancy of the outgoing IP queue in node i at time t_1 as follows: Node i started transmitting its kth busy period at time $\tau_{i,k} - D_{ij}$. Therefore, by the time the first ack to the busy period returns to node i, it would have transmitted

$$\rho\,(t_1 - (\tau_{i,k} - D_{ij})) = Q_j(\tau_{i,k}) + (L_{ij} + L_{ji}) \tag{3.4}$$

segments. Since each busy period of node i consists of W_i segments, the outgoing queue of node i must have

$$Q_i(t_1) = W_i - (Q_j(\tau_{i,k}) + L_{ij} + L_{ji}) \tag{3.5}$$

segments when the first ack of the kth busy period returns at time t_1. Note that since $Q_j(\tau_{i,k}) \leq W_j$ and $W_i > W_j + (L_{ij} + L_{ji})$, at time t_1 when the first ack to the kth busy period returns to node i the queue size will be $Q_i(t_1) > 0$. Thus, all the acks for connection j will return to node j as a bunch and connection i will always have data available in the outgoing queue for transmission. The next busy period will start at node i at time $t_1 + Q_i(t_1)/\rho$ and reach node j at time $t_1 + Q_i(t_1)/\rho + D_{ij}$. Thus,

$$\tau_{i,k+1} = t_1 + Q_i(t_1)/\rho + D_{ij}.$$

Substituting for t_1 and $Q_i(t_1)$ from equations (3.3) and (3.5), respectively, this becomes

$$\tau_{i,k+1} = \tau_{i,k} + W_i/\rho. \tag{3.6}$$

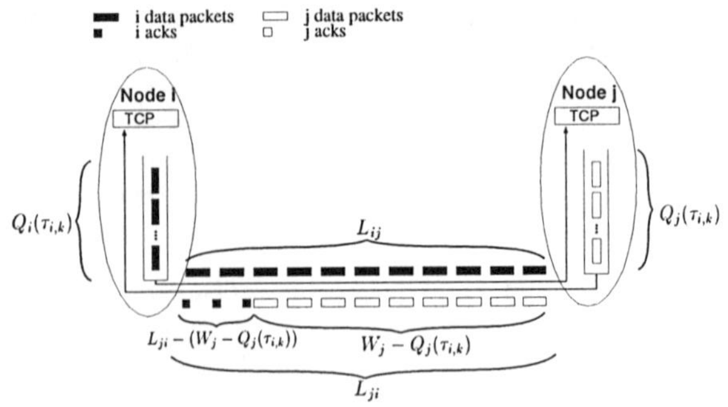

Figure 6: Illustration of network behavior for the proof of Lemma 2. the first segment of the kth busy period of connection i arrives at node j at time $\tau_{i,k}$ while the first segment of the mth busy period of connection j is still in transit.

Similarly, we can show that

$$\tau_{j,k+1} = \tau_{j,k} + W_i/\rho. \tag{3.7}$$

This concludes the proof of Lemma 1.

Lemma 1 applies to the case of $W_i > W_j + (L_{ij} + L_{ji})$. The case of $W_i < W_j - (L_{ij} + L_{ji})$ is complementary, and can be handled by the same analysis. We consider the more complex case next, where the window of each connection is not large enough to overflow a pipe consisting of a full window of the other connection and the round-trip delay. That is,

$$W_j - (L_{ij} + L_{ji}) \leq W_i \leq W_j + (L_{ij} + L_{ji}). \tag{3.8}$$

This case covers all the instances not covered by Lemma 1, assuming Eq. (2.1) holds. In this case, we will again show that the busy periods of the connections exhibit periodic behavior, but the behavior can be more complex.

Lemma 2 *Let $\tau_{i,k}$ denote the time at which the first segment of the kth busy period of connection i reaches node j, and $Q_j(\tau_{i,k})$ the queue length in node j at that time. Then,*

$$Q_j(\tau_{i,k+1}) = \min\left((W_i + W_j) - (L_{ij} + L_{ji}) - Q_j(\tau_{i,k}), W_j\right).$$

From this lemma, it is easy to observe that $Q_j(\tau_{i,k+2}) = Q_j(\tau_{i,k})$. That is, the queue behavior is periodic and the maximum queue size does not exceed $\min\left((W_i + W_j) - (L_{ij} + L_{ji}), W_j\right)$.

Proof of Lemma 2:

We need to determine $Q_j(\tau_{i,k+1})$, the queue size in node j when the $(k+1)$th busy period of connection i reaches it. Note that this queue was created by the bunched acks received by node j just before the $(k+1)$th busy period of connection i, and will be equal in number to the number of bunched acks in that ack stream. Assume that this ack stream acknowledges segments transmitted during the mth busy period of connection j.

Let $\tau_{j,m}$ denote the time at which the first segment in the mth busy period of connection j reaches node i. We can determine $\tau_{j,m}$ from $\tau_{i,k}$ as follows: At time $\tau_{i,k}$, node j had transmitted $W_j - Q_j(\tau_{i,k})$ segments of its mth busy period, as illustrated in Figure 6. Therefore, it would have started transmission of the mth busy period at time $\tau_{i,k} - (W_j - Q_j(\tau_{i,k}))/\rho$ and the first segment of this busy period would have reached node i after a delay of D_{ji}. Therefore,

$$\tau_{j,m} = \tau_{i,k} - (W_j - Q_j(\tau_{i,k}))/\rho + D_{ji}. \tag{3.9}$$

Let t_1 denote the time when node i completes transmission of its kth busy period. Then,

$$t_1 = \tau_{i,k} - D_{ij} + W_i/\rho. \tag{3.10}$$

During the interval $(\tau_{j,m}, t_1)$, node i is receiving segments from the mth busy period of connection j, but its outgoing queue remains non-empty, causing the acks generated by node i towards node j to be bunched. The number of bunched acks during the interval $(\tau_{j,m}, t_1)$ is given by $\min(\rho(t_1 - \tau_{j,m}), W_j)$. Using Eq. (3.9) and (3.10),

$$\rho(t_1 - \tau_{j,m}) = (W_i + W_j) - (D_{ij} + D_{ji})\rho - Q_j(\tau_{i,k}). \tag{3.11}$$

Therefore, the queue size seen by the first segment of the $(k+1)$th busy period of connection i is

$$\begin{aligned} Q_j(\tau_{i,k+1}) &= \min\left((W_i + W_j) - (D_{ij} + D_{ji})\rho - Q_j(\tau_{i,k}), W_j\right) \\ &= \min\left((W_i + W_j) - (L_{ij} + L_{ji}) - Q_j(\tau_{i,k}), W_j\right). \end{aligned} \tag{3.12}$$

This concludes the proof of Lemma 2.

Although Lemma 2 establishes the periodic nature of the queue behavior in the nodes, it does not provide us an expression for the period. We can now use this result to calculate the interval between busy periods transmitted by a node, and thus the throughput efficiencies of the connections. The following lemma allows us to quantify the effect of ack compression on throughput.

Lemma 3 *If the window sizes and delays are such that $W_j - (L_{ij} + L_{ji}) \leq W_i \leq W_j + (L_{ij} + L_{ji})$, then*

$$\tau_{i,k+2} - \tau_{i,k} = (W_i + W_j)/\rho + (D_{ij} + D_{ji}). \tag{3.13}$$

That is, each connection gets to transmit two consecutive busy periods within an interval of $(W_i + W_j)/\rho + (D_{ij} + D_{ji})$. Thus, the throughput efficiencies of the connections are given by

$$F_i = \frac{2W_i}{(W_i + W_j) + (L_{ij} + L_{ji})},$$

and

$$F_j = \frac{2W_j}{(W_i + W_j) + (L_{ij} + L_{ji})}.$$

Proof of Lemma 3:

Let t_1 denote the time at which the first ack to the kth busy period of connection i returns to node i. Then,

$$t_1 = \tau_{i,k} + Q_j(\tau_{i,k})/\rho + D_{ji}. \tag{3.14}$$

When this ack reaches node i, the outgoing queue of i may or may not be empty. We consider these two cases separately below:

Case 1: $Q_i(t_1) > 0$. This case occurs when node i has not completed transmission of segments in its kth busy period at time t_1. That is,

$$W_i/\rho > t_1 - (\tau_{i,k} - D_{ij}).$$

Substituting for t_1 from Eq. (3.14), this condition becomes

$$W_i > (L_{ij} + L_{ji}) + Q_j(\tau_{i,k}). \qquad (3.15)$$

In this case, node i will follow transmission of the kth busy period with compressed acks for an entire window W_j of connection j, followed by the $(k+1)$th busy period of connection i. Since we ignore the transmission time of acks, node i will begin transmission of the $(k+1)$th busy period at time $\tau_{i,k} + W_i/\rho - D_{ij}$, the first segment of this busy period will reach node j at $\tau_{i,k+1} = \tau_{i,k} + W_i/\rho$, and the last bit of the last packet transmitted in the $(k+1)$th busy period will depart from node i at time $t'_1 = \tau_{i,k} + 2(W_i/\rho) - D_{ij}$.

Since the $(k+1)$th busy period follows compressed acks for W_j segments of connection j, the first bit of this busy period will see a queue size of $Q_j(\tau_{i,k+1}) = W_j$ segments in node j. Note that the same result can be obtained by combining Eq. (3.12) and Eq. (3.15). Therefore, the first ack to the busy period will leave at time $\tau_{i,k+1} + W_j/\rho$ and will arrive at node i at time $t_2 = \tau_{i,k+1} + W_j/\rho + D_{ji}$. Since $W_i \leq W_j + (L_{ij} + L_{ji})$, we can easily conclude that $t_2 \geq t'_1$ and therefore, node i would have completed transmission of the $(k+1)$th busy period of connection i by then. Thus, the $(k+2)$th busy period will begin at time t_2 and arrive at node j after a delay of D_{ij}. Therefore,

$$\begin{aligned}\tau_{i,k+2} &= t_2 + D_{ij} \\ &= \tau_{i,k+1} + W_j/\rho + D_{ji} + D_{ij} \\ &= \tau_{i,k} + (W_i + W_j)/\rho + (D_{ij} + D_{ji}).\end{aligned}$$

Case 2: $Q_i(t_1) = 0$. This case can occur only if $W_i \leq W_j + (L_{ij} + L_{ji})$. In this case the $(k+1)$th busy period of connection i will start at node i at time t_1, and its first segment will reach node j at time $t_1 + D_{ij}$. Hence,

$$\tau_{i,k+1} = t_1 + D_{ij} = \tau_{i,k} + Q_j(\tau_{i,k})/\rho + (D_{ij} + D_{ji}). \quad (3.16)$$

The first ack to this busy period will leave node j at time $\tau_{i,k+1} + Q_j(\tau_{i,k+1})/\rho$ and will reach node i at time

$$t_3 = \tau_{i,k+1} + Q_j(\tau_{i,k+1})/\rho + D_{ji}. \qquad (3.17)$$

Substituting for $\tau_{i,k+1}$ from Eq. (3.16) and for $Q_j(\tau_{i,k+1})$ from Eq. (3.12), this becomes

$$t_3 = \tau_{i,k} + (W_i + W_j)/\rho + D_{ji}. \qquad (3.18)$$

Node i would have transmitted its entire $(k+1)$th busy period at time t_3, so the $(k+2)$th busy period begins at t_3. The first segment of this busy period reaches node j at time $t_3 + D_{ij}$. Therefore,

$$\begin{aligned}\tau_{i,k+2} &= t_3 + D_{ij} \\ &= \tau_{i,k} + (W_i + W_j)/\rho + (D_{ij} + D_{ji}). \quad (3.19)\end{aligned}$$

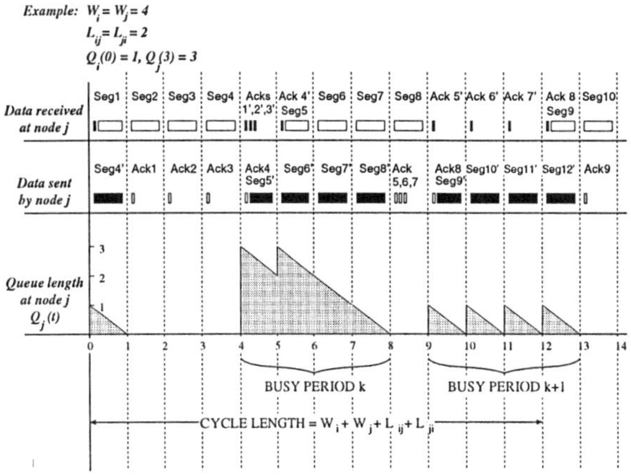

Figure 7: Example behavior of node j in a two-way TCP configuration.

This concludes the proof of Lemma 3.

The example in Figure 7 illustrates the periodic behavior of the TCP connections for the case $W_j - (L_{ij} + L_{ji}) \leq W_i \leq W_j + (L_{ij} + L_{ji})$. In this case, the window sizes are taken as $W_i = W_j = 4$ segments, and the time to transmit each segment on the link as one unit. The network delay in each direction is assumed as 2 units, that is $L_{ij} = L_{ji} = 2$. Thus, a window size of 4 segments allows each connection to achieve its maximum throughput in a one-way configuration. We will show that the throughput is substantially reduced in a two-way configuration because of the interaction between the connections.

Figure 7 illustrates the operation of node j during an interval of time. The segments transmitted by connection i are marked as $1, 2, 3, \ldots$ in the figure, and those transmitted by connection j as $1', 2', 3', \ldots$. At time 0, node j is transmitting the last of the four segments constituting the $(k-1)$th busy period of connection j. This segment is labeled as $4'$ in the figure. At the same time, node j is receiving the first segment of the mth busy period of the opposite connection. The last segment of this mth busy period is completely received by time $t = 4$. Note that each of the acks to segments of this busy period leaves node j immediately without any ack compression.

The acks to the $(k-1)$th busy period of connection j starts arriving at $t = 4$. The acks to the first three segments arrive bunched at time $t = 4$, while the ack to the last segment is received in the next time-slot. When the first three acks are received, a queue of three segments is immediately built up at node j. By time $t = 5$, the first segment of this queue is transmitted, and a new segment is added in response to ack 4', maintaining the queue size at 3 segments. The queue is completely drained by time $t = 8$. Note that the segments transmitted from $t = 4$ to $t = 8$ consists of the kth busy period of connection j.

The arrival of the $(m+1)$th busy period of connection i at node j occurs at time $t = 5$ and overlaps with the transmission of the kth busy period of connection j. Therefore, the acks to the first three segments of the former are queued behind the segments of the latter, and transmitted as a bunch at time $t = 8$ (acks 5, 6, 7 in figure).

The acks to segments of the kth busy period of connection j starts to arrive at time $t = 9$ with no bunching. As a result, node j is receiving one ack in each of the time-slots 9, 10, 11, 12 and transmitting a segment in response. These transmitted segments constitute the $(k+1)$th busy period of connection j. It is easy to observe that the state of the system at $t = 12$ is identical to that at time $t = 0$, so the behavior will repeat indefinitely.

Note that during time-slots 1, 2, 3 and 8, node j is transmitting only acks, but no segments, leaving its outgoing link virtually unused. Thus, the throughput efficiency of connection j is only $8/12 = 66.67$ percent. Similarly, it can be seen that the throughput efficiency of the opposite connection is also 66.67 percent. It is important to note that the queue lengths at node j in this example will change if the relative phase of the two connections is changed, but both the periodic behavior and the throughput efficiency will remain unchanged.

The following theorem summarizes the throughput efficiencies of TCP connections under two-way traffic for all ranges of window sizes, under the condition that $W_i + W_j > L_{ij} + L_{ji}$.

Theorem 1 *The throughput efficiency F_i of connection i in a two-way traffic configuration with symmetric link rates is given by*

$$F_i = \begin{cases} 1, & \text{if } W_i > \beta; \\ \frac{2W_i}{(W_i+W_j)+(L_{ij}+L_{ji})}, & \text{if } \alpha \le W_i \le \beta; \\ \frac{W_i}{W_j}, & \text{otherwise}; \end{cases} \tag{3.20}$$

where $\alpha = W_j - (L_{ij} + L_{ji})$ and $\beta = W_j + (L_{ij} + L_{ji})$.

The proof of this theorem follows directly from Lemmas 1, 2, and 3. Note that the third part is complementary to the first, and is covered by Lemma 1. The theorem asserts that, under two-way traffic, the throughput of one or both connections will always be degraded, as long as the sum of the window sizes is larger than the round-trip delay-bandwidth product. The connection with the larger window always receives a higher proportion of the attainable throughput. Furthermore, in the extreme case where there propagation delays are small compared to the window sizes (as may be the case in a local-area network), differences in the window-sizes of the two connections will result in throughput unfairness. Another important conclusion that can be drawn from Eq. (3.20) is that, under two-way traffic, the throughput of one connection cannot be maximized without degrading that of the other. The throughput of both connections, however, can be increased by increasing their window sizes. To make this point clear, consider a simple case where the windows of both connections are of equal size and the propagation delays in both directions are also equal, that is, $W_i = W_j = W$ and $L_{ij} = L_{ji} = L$. In this case the efficiency F for each of the connections will be $F = W/(W + L)$, as compared to $\min(W/2L, 1)$ with one-way traffic. If the window size is just large enough to fill the round-trip network pipe, that is if $W = 2L$, the efficiency for each connection will be only 66.67%. Increasing the window size of both connections beyond this point improves their throughput, but has the undesirable consequence of large queues at the end systems.

We conclude this section with an expression for the maximum size of the outgoing IP queue in each node under two-way traffic. It is easy to see that the maximum queue size in node j is seen when the first segment of a busy period of connection i reaches node j. In addition, the queue size can never exceed the window size of the connection originating at the node. Thus, we can state the following lemma.

Lemma 4 *In steady state, the maximum occupancy $Q_{i,max}$ of the IP queue of node i under two-way traffic is given by*

$$Q_{i,max} \le \begin{cases} W_i - (L_{ij} + L_{ji}), & \text{if } W_i > \beta; \\ (W_i + W_j) - (L_{ij} + L_{ji}), & \text{if } \alpha \le W_i \le \beta; \\ W_i, & \text{otherwise}; \end{cases} \tag{3.21}$$

where $\alpha = W_j - (L_{ij} + L_{ji})$ and $\beta = W_j + (L_{ij} + L_{ji})$.

Proof: The second case follows directly from Lemma 2, and the third case from the fact that the queue size can never exceed the window size of the connection originating at the node. Now consider the first case. The maximum queue size in node i is seen when the first segment of a busy period of connection j reaches it. Let $\tau_{j,m}$ denote the time at which the first segment of the mth busy period of connection j reaches node i. The queue size at this time can be found by noting that the number of queued segments in node i, plus the number of segments and acks belonging to connection i in the rest of the network, must equal its window size W_i.

The first segment of the mth busy period of connection j would have been transmitted by node j at time $t_1 = \tau_{j,m} - D_{ji}$. At time t_1, the outgoing queue of node j contained no acks of connection i. During the interval $(t_1, \tau_{j,m})$, a total of $(\tau_{j,m}, t_1)\rho = D_{ji}\rho = L_{ji}$ segments from connection i arrived at node j. In addition, L_{ij} segments of connection i are in transit on the link from i to j at time $\tau_{j,m}$. Therefore, the total number of segments and acks of connection i in the entire system at time $\tau_{j,m}$ is given by

$$Q_i(\tau_{j,m}) + L_{ij} + L_{ji}.$$

Equating this to the window size W_i, we get

$$Q_i(\tau_{j,m}) = W_i - (L_{ij} + L_{ji}).$$

This concludes the proof of Lemma 4.

4 Model Validation

In this section we validate the analytical results derived in the previous section by simulation. Due to space constraints we present simulation results for only one network configuration. Simulation results for more general network configurations, as well as a discussion of the effect of non-zero TCP processing time, can be found in [11].

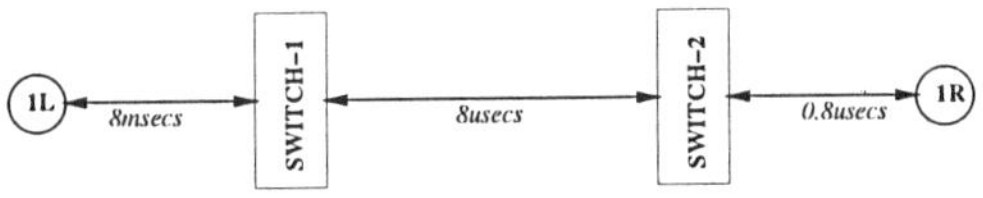

Figure 8: Two-Way traffic configuration with a single TCP connection in each direction.

The simulations were performed using the OPNET simulation tool. The links in the network are full-duplex with a capacity of 155 Mbits/second each, unless otherwise specified. The switches are nonblocking, output-buffered crossbars. There is one queue per output port for ABR traffic and its scheduling policy is FIFO, with each output queue being shared by all the virtual channels (VCs) sharing the outgoing link. The switches support the explicit rate allocation algorithm of Kalampoukas, et al. [12]. Each of the nodes implements the ABR source policy defined by ATM Forum [14].

At the source, we implemented models of ATM Adaptation Layer Type 5 (AAL 5), IP, and TCP. The AAL performs segmentation and re-assembly between IP packets and ATM cells. Each IP packet is extended by eight bytes to accommodate the AAL header. Unless stated otherwise, the service rate of the outgoing IP queue is set at the transmission rate of the connection at the ATM layer. The model for TCP used in the simulations is based on the TCP-Reno version. The TCP segment size was set at 9180 bytes in all the simulations.

We consider the configuration shown in Figure 8, consisting of two nodes and a pair of TCP connections set up between them, one in each direction. The connections originating at the left and right nodes are designated as 1L and 1R, respectively, in the figure. The link capacity in each direction is identical and equal to 155 Mbits/second. In our simulation results, the measured efficiency for a connection is normalized to this maximum throughput attainable by a TCP connection.

The one-way propagation delay in this configuration is 8 msecs. This is approximately equal to the transmission time of 14 segments. However, the fragmentation of a segment to cells at the end system causes an additional delay equivalent to the transmission time of one segment. Therefore, the effective one-way delay between end systems, expressed in number of segments, is about 15. The window size for both the connections is set to 256 Kbytes, equivalent to 28 segments.

We assume in this scenario that both the connections open at time $t = 0$. Since the behavior of the connections will be symmetric, we have plotted the simulations only for the left-to-right connection. The progress for the left-to-right TCP connection is shown in Figure 9, in terms of the increase in TCP sequence numbers transmitted by the connection. Note that these are the sequence numbers of the packets as they exit the TCP layer, not when they exit the outgoing IP transmission queue. Also shown in Figure 9 for comparison is the slope of the optimal sequence number growth that would have occurred if the two-way

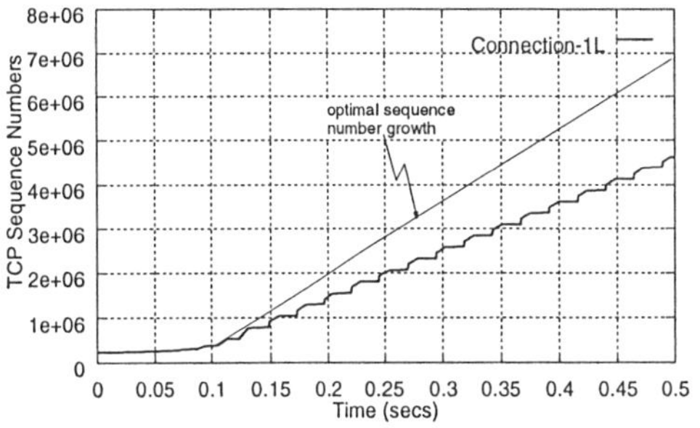

Figure 9: Sequence number growth for the left-to-right connection.

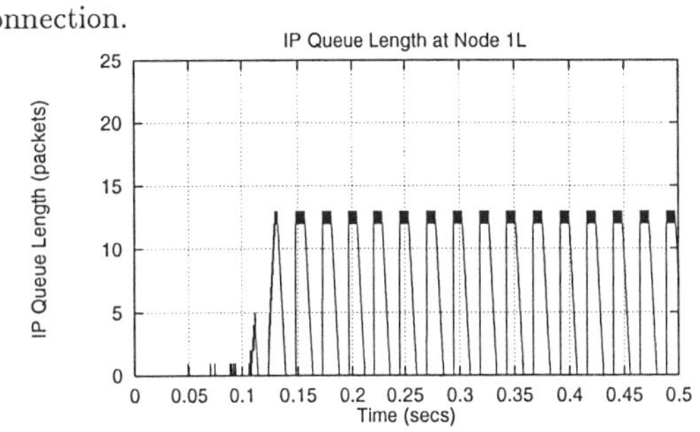

Figure 10: IP queue size at node 1L (data packets only).

traffic effects were absent. Thus, the difference in slope between the optimal and the measured sequence number growth plots is a direct measure of the performance degradation caused by two-way traffic. Except for the initial start-up period during which the transmission rate and the congestion window size are still increasing, the progress is steady. However, notice the step-like increase of the TCP sequence numbers. These jumps are caused when a cluster of bunched acknowledgments arrive at the source and cause a corresponding number of segments to be added to the outgoing queue. The queue size at the end-systems exhibits oscillatory behavior, as observed in the analysis of Section 3. Figure 10 shows the queue-size behavior observed in the simulation. Because the two connections open simultaneously, the queue size reached at the beginning of each busy period is identical, about 13 segments. The solid black areas shown at the peaks of Figure 10 signify the busy periods of the connection, and are caused by the high-frequency transitions occurring from the addition of new segments into the outgoing queue in response to the arrival of acks. The analytical result of Lemma (2) asserts that, if the queue size is 13 segments during a given busy period, the queue size during the next busy period will be be $W_i + W_j - L_{ij} - L_{ji} - 13 = 28 + 28 - 15 - 15 - 13 = 13$, which is exactly what we observe in the simulation results. Considering that in the analysis we have ignored the transmission time of acknowledgements and the fact that packet arrivals and departures may not be synchronized, we conclude that there is a very good match between the simulation results and the analysis with respect to the IP queue size at the end-systems.

Since $W_i = W_j = 28$, and $L_{ij} = L_{ji} = 15$, the expected throughput efficiency F_i for the left-to-right connection, from analysis, will be

$$F_i = \frac{28}{28 + 15} \approx 65.1\%.$$

The actual throughput observed in the simulation is in close agreement with this analytical result, as may be observed from the sequence-number plot of Figure 9.

5 Conclusion

We have examined the performance of bidirectional TCP/IP connections over the Available Bit Rate class of service in ATM networks. We find that the problem of ack compression observed in packet networks manifests itself again in ATM networks, although the queueing of acks behind data packets is now primarily at the end systems. We observe the penalty of ack compression that has been found in the past: bunching of data packets flowing in either direction, and throughput degradation as a result of the periodic behavior of the queue going through idle intervals. For example, with symmetric bandwidths in each direction and window sizes large enough to fill the round-trip pipe, the throughput of each connection is only 66.67% of that under one-way traffic.

The analysis in this paper is extended to the more general asymmetric case in [11], where the transmission rates of the connections in opposite directions are different. This is likely to be a common case with cable access or satellite links where the bandwidth in one direction can be large compared to that in the opposite direction. The throughput degradation is even more dramatic when the transmission rates allocated to connections in opposite directions are widely different, even if the window of each connection is matched to the bandwidth in its direction. For example, with a one-way delay of 5 milliseconds, window size of 128 Kbytes, and transmission rates of 155 Mbits/second and 30 Mbits/second in the two directions, the high-speed connection is able to achieve only 20% of its throughput under one-way traffic.

In an earlier paper [12] we examined the performance of TCP connections having very different round-trip times (RTT) in an ATM network. The maintenance of a current bandwidth allocation per virtual channel (VC) at the ATM switches was shown to achieve fairness in throughput superior to that in a datagram network. However, with bidirectional TCP traffic, the maintenance of a steady rate-allocation for each VC is no longer sufficient to achieve throughput fairness. The periodic behavior of the connections is now a function of the allocated rates, window sizes, and delays, causing significant disparity in throughput. Although the resources in the network are fairly allocated, and the flows may be virtually isolated from each other in the network, the efficiency of a connection with a smaller RTT in the bidirectional environment is better than that of a longer connection. This is primarily because of the excessive idle intervals imposed on the longer connection while it is awaiting acks.

Bidirectional TCP conversations are not unusual, since most TCP connections are set up in this manner: the behavior we observe is expected to occur when both ends have data to send. Therefore, we believe that the general problem deserves further research, and that the insight and results presented here will be valuable in devising solutions to the problem.

References

[1] V. Jacobson, "Congestion avoidance and control," in *Proceedings of ACM SIGCOMM'88*, pp. 314–329, 1988.

[2] V. Jacobson, "Modified TCP Congestion Avoidance Algorithm." message to end2end-interest mailing list, April 1990.

[3] S. Floyd and V. Jacobson, "On Traffic Phase Effects in Packet-Switched Gateways," *Internetworking: Research and Experience*, vol. 3, no. 3, pp. 115–156, September 1992.

[4] J. C. Mogul, "Observing TCP dynamics in real networks," in *Proceedings of ACM SIGCOMM'92*, pp. 305–317, August 1992.

[5] L. Zhang and D. D. Clark, "Oscillating Behavior of Network Traffic: A Case Study Simulation," *Intenetworking: Research and Experience*, vol. 1, no. 2, pp. 101–112, December 1990.

[6] L. Zhang, S. Shenker, and D. D. Clark, "Observations on the Dynamics of a Congestion Control Algorithm: The Effects of Two-Way Traffic," in *Proceedings of ACM SIGCOMM'91*, pp. 133–147, September 1991.

[7] R. Wilder, K. K. Ramakrishnan, and A. Mankin, "Dynamics of Congestion Control and Avoidance of Two-Way Traffic in an OSI Testbed," *ACM Computer Communication Review*, vol. 21, no. 2, pp. 43–58, April 1991.

[8] D. E. Comer and J. C. Lin, "TCP Buffering and Performance over an ATM Network," *Internetworking: Research and Experience*, vol. 6, pp. 1–13, 1995.

[9] S. Floyd and A. Romanow, "Dynamics of TCP traffic over ATM networks," in *Proceedings of ACM SIGCOMM'94*, pp. 79–88, September 1994.

[10] L. Kalampoukas and A. Varma, "Performance of TCP over Multi-Hop ATM Networks: A Comparative Study of ATM Layer Congestion Control Schemes," in *Proceedings of ICC'95*, pp. 1472–1477, June 1995.

[11] L. Kalampoukas, A. Varma, and K. K. Ramakrishnan, "Two-Way TCP Traffic over ATM: Effects and Analysis," Tech. Rep. UCSC-CRL-96-23, Univ. of California, Santa Cruz, 1996.

[12] L. Kalampoukas, A. Varma, and K. K. Ramakrishnan, "Dynamics of an Explicit Rate Allocation Algorithm for ATM Networks," in *Proceedings of International IEEE-IFIP Conference on Broadband Communications*, Montreal, Canada, pp. 111–122, April 1996.

[13] W. R. Stevens and G. R. Wright, *TCP/IP Illustrated*, vol. 2, Addison-Wesley Publishing Company, 1995.

[14] S. S. Sathaye, *Traffic Management Specification, Version 4.0, ATM-Forum/95-0013R10*, ATM Forum, Traffic Management Working Group, April 1996.

Key to the Success of Asynchronous Transfer Mode: An Application Programming Interface

Mengjou Lin, Alagu Periyannan and **David Singer**
Communications Products and Technologies
Apple Computer, Inc.
{mjlin, alagu, singer}@apple.com

Abstract

Asynchronous Transfer Mode (ATM) networks are scalable via a wide variety of physical link speeds and can be run in both local and wide area. Bandwidth reservation and quality of service guarantees make ATM attractive to deliver multimedia information in real-time. Existing protocol suites can be extended. However, they do not give access to those characteristics. Therefore, applications demand an ATM Application Programming Interface (API) to take advantage of those features. This paper covers a special syntax mapping of the ATM API services on top of X/Open Transport Interface (XTI) which is able to give applications access directly to the special quality and traffic services of an ATM network. A particular realization of the API on XTI environment is proposed and implemented on the MacOS networking platform. It provides a flexible and modular design of the ATM networking. Finally, the paper concludes with one ATM-aware application (video on demand) which requires real-time streaming data.

Keywords: Asynchronous Transfer Mode (ATM), X/Open XTI, Open Transport, Winsock.

1 Introduction

ATM networks are scalable in turn of network bandwidth (various physical link speeds) and location (local and wide area). ATM networks provide not only bandwidth reservation, but also quality of service guarantees. This special characteristic differentiates ATM from almost every other existing network technologies.

One of the most obvious ways to access these characteristics are to write "native softwares" (ATM-aware applications) which need these network characteristics on a computer with an ATM interface .

The development of such software is greatly accelerated when there is a platform-independent way to use the ATM services. Then programmers can write applications with the knowledge that they are not confined to a particular combination of network interfaces and operating systems.

The ATM Forum Service Aspects & Applications (SAA) working group was given the task to formulate an ATM API that provides access to native ATM services. This work was carried out by the SAA API subworking group (henceforth called the API group). These concerns came to a head at the Munich ATM Forum meeting in June '94. At that meeting a C API for ATM services was presented. Much useful detailed work was shown, in the mapping of signaling information to C structures and calls, for example.

The ATM Forum initially decide to do a service definition – what was called the API semantics and leave the actual syntax of an API to bodies with existing network APIs. Thus, just as TCP/IP services are well defined and can be accessed through BSD Sockets, XTI (and its predecessors), or Winsock, so we would allow ATM services to be accessed through these protocol independent network APIs, given appropriate syntax extensions.

It was recognized that the important contribution from the ATM Forum would be to ensure that a pro gram could be ported between these APIs by making the underlying service consistent. This would enable software authors to use a variant of the normal network API for the platform which they target – an API which they are presumably already familiar with.

The document produced by the API group is called "Native ATM Services: Semantic Description" [1] (henceforth called the semantics document). This was approved by the ATM Forum in December '95. We elaborate some important issues for syntax mapping in the Section 2. Drafts of the Winsock2 mapping and X/Open XTI mapping [2] were presented in February

0-8186-7780-5/97 $10.00 © 1997 IEEE

'96, and the Winsock2 (Window Socket API version 2) mapping [3] was reviewed for conformance in April '96.

Syntax mapping of the semantics document to X/Open XTI mapping was proposed and described here. Our proposal has been brought toward the XTI standard group's final approval. A realization of the proposed syntax mapping of the ATM API (adopted by Macintoshs' networking) is described. Way of using this particular implementation is also shown. Some other ATM-aware applications including video-on-demand and fast file sharing are under construction. We expect to see further deployment of various ATM applications in a near future.

This paper is organized as follows. ATM Forum's API semantics model is presented systematically in the Section 2. In the Section 3, way to map XTI to semantics model is described. A special XTI implementation on Macintosh environment is presented in the Section 4. ATM-aware applications are introduced in Section 5. Then we conclude with the future work in the Section 6.

2 ATM Service Semantic Specification

The semantic description developed by the ATM Forum API group is not limited to aiding the implementation of APIs on popular operating systems. Rather, the API model can be used internally in products as a way to access ATM services. It can also be used to implement services such as LAN emulation over ATM inside an operating system kernel protocol stack.

Some of the issues covered by the semantics document are more important than others when mapping onto a syntactic interface. The two key contributions of the semantics document are:

- Mechanics of application access to parameters supported by the UNI 3.x [1] signaling protocol [4].
- Definition of an ATM Service Access Point (SAP) and distribution of incoming calls within an endsystem.

ATM API implementations that conform to the scheme proposed in the semantics document in the above two areas will be able to support interoperable applications across different implementations.

2.1 Semantic Model

The native ATM services model recognizes the need for the use of traditional protocols over ATM networks. Hence, the model ensures that the native ATM API as well as traditional protocol APIs co-exist on an ATM end system. The native ATM services reference model (see Figure 1) illustrates this co-existence.

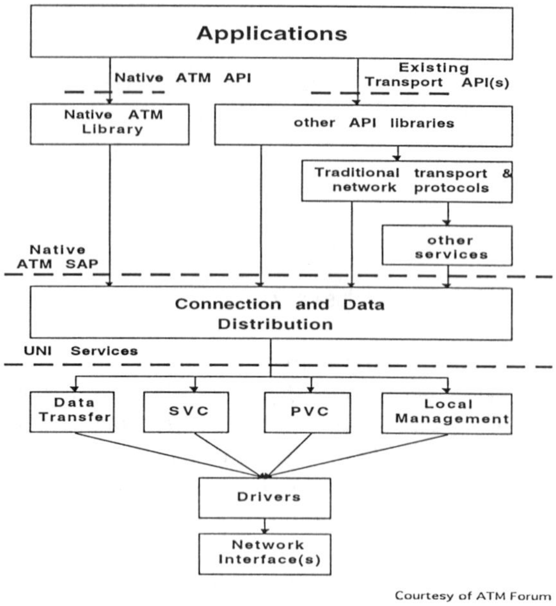

Figure 1: Reference model for native ATM services (native ATM SAP)

The connection and data distribution layer within an ATM end system acts as the arbitrator for accessing the UNI services. This layer, though shown as one entity, could be a collection of components. The exact realization of this layer is implementation dependent, as it is with almost all other functionality proposed by the semantics document.

The UNI services are broadly classified into, Data Transfer, SVC handling, PVC handling, and Local Management. The data transfer and PVC services interact with the local ATM AAL hardware on the end system. The SVC services provide UNI signaling that interacts with an ATM Switch over the signaling virtual circuit. The Local Management services provide access to the Interim Local Management Interface (ILMI) and ATM address registration functionality.

Take, for example, two entities that wish to communicate over an ATM SVC using AAL5 packets. They achieve this by accessing the connection and data distribution layer. UNI signaling will be first used to set up the circuit end-to-end. Then the AAL5 hardware will be used to transfer the data. This model is used for both applications that use the native ATM API as well as internal layers such as ATM Forum's LAN emulation.

[1] ATM UNI 3.x includes both UNI 3.0 and UNI 3.1.

The semantics used by native ATM applications to access the connection and data distribution layer are described in the form of, an API State machine, a set of API primitives, and a set of procedures

A one-to-one mapping of these primitives or states to syntax primitives and states in a given syntax specification is not achievable in many cases. It is intended that syntax specifications will merely support the functionality in the state machine, primitives and procedures, described in the semantics document. Interoperability between multiple implementations does not require identical syntax. Source code compatibility between multiple implementations would have been the ideal goal, but almost surely unachievable in today's multi-platform, multi-implementation world of communication systems.

The state machine proposed by the semantics document is not very different from currently popular API state machines such as XTI, Sockets or Winsock. The only added functionality described by the state machine is in the point-to-multipoint connections area, which is not present in most current APIs. Hence, in most cases the state machine proposed in the semantics document will be modeled by an API state machine already available in a given implementation.

The primitives proposed by the semantics document are also similar to current popular APIs, except in the area of point-to-multipoint circuits. Those primitives serve as a basis for describing the semantic model's procedures. They are divided into, control plane (functionality for setting up and tearing down ATM connections), date plane (primitives to send and receive data packets), and management plane (access to the local ILMI Management Information Base).

Among the proposed primitives, the most important ones are those doing point-to-multipoint connections. It consists of primitives such as ATM_add_party() and ATM_drop_party() that are used to add and drop leaves by the root of a point-to-multipoint ATM connection. Leaf[2] initiated joins are not support by UNI 3.x signaling and hence are not reflected in the list of point-to-multipoint primitives.

The procedures to be followed in an ATM API implementation are by far the most important aspect of the semantic model proposed in the semantics document. They describe the methods used to setup switched and permanent connections, reliable data transfer using the Service Specific Connection-Oriented Sublayer (SSCOP) [5], incoming call dispatching, ATM Service Access Points, etc. These procedures will be discussed in detail in subsequent sections.

[2]Leaf initiated joins will be supported by the UNI 4.0 signaling specification which is nearing completion.

Table 1: ATM SAP Vector Elements

SVE	UNI 3.x Signaling Information Element
ATM_address	Called Party Address (exclude the selector byte[3])
ATM_selector	Selector Byte (from the called party address)
BLLI_id2	Broadband Low Layer Information - Layer 2
BLLI_id3	Broadband Low Layer Information - Layer 3
BHLI_id	Broadband High Layer Information

2.2 ATM Service Access Point

A clear definition for an ATM Service Access Point (SAP) is essential to the co-existence of multiple ATM applications and services on a single end system. A service access point is like an ID card. It helps to differentiate multiple entities using ATM services within a system. Incoming ATM connections are matched up with the correct entity using this ID information. Similarly, outgoing calls must contain this ID information for the call to be routed through the ATM network and within the destination endsystem.

Every native ATM application or service that needs to accept incoming connections must bind to an ATM SAP using the ATM_prepare_incoming_call() primitive in the control plane. Similarly, an ATM SAP is supplied to the ATM_connect_outgoing_call() primitive when initiating a connection.

The ATM SAP is similar to a (IP address, protocol, port) triplet for those familiar with TCP/IP programs. For example, to connect to the Telnet service on a TCP/IP endsystem, one must know the system's IP address and Telnet server's protocol and port number. In the case of Telnet, the TCP protocol and the well-known port number of 25 are used on most servers (although this need not be the case.) Similarly, many of the popular TCP/IP services such as FTP, HTTP, NFS, etc. have well-known protocols and port numbers which can be combined with the destination address to form an IP SAP. Other protocols like AppleTalk do not have well known SAPs for services. Instead, the AppleTalk address and the Datagram Delivery Protocol (DDP) socket pair are advertised using the Name Binding Protocol (NBP) so that other systems on the network can find them. The ATM SAP definition proposed in the semantics document is closer to the TCP/IP model with well-known SAPs.

The ATM SAP consists of a subset of the information contained within a SETUP message in UNI 3.x signaling. This subset includes only those pieces of information required to dispatch an incoming connection within an endsystem to the correct application or service. The ATM SAP can be represented as a vector of the 5 elements shown in Table 1. Each of the elements is referred to as a SAP Vector Element (SVE).

One might argue, why the AAL type, QOS class or Called Party Subaddress[4] was not included in the SAP vector? There are both arguments for and against the inclusion of all pieces of information present in the signaling SETUP message. The API group decided on the above list as it had the minimal set of information required to dispatch an incoming call to the right application.

An SVE semantically consists of a tag, length and value . The tags have special meanings as ABSENT (information absents in the SETUP message), PRESENT (information element presents in the SETUP message, value specified), and ANY (information element matches any value in the SETUP message). The value fields correspond to the information elements in UNI 3.x signaling.

Two ATM SAPs are considered equal when all their corresponding SVEs are equal. Two SVEs are equal when either of their tags are ANY or the two SVEs are exactly the same.

2.3 Data Transfer

The data transfer primitives proposed by the semantics document are similar to those found in popular API syntax specifications such as XTI and Winsock. The semantics document lists a choice of polling, blocking and messaging implementations for these primitives. Implementations can do optimizations to attain better data throughput by avoiding intermediate copying of data between the ATM network interface and the application. Appendix A of the semantics document discusses some of the issues involved in data transfer.

- *Reliable vs. Unreliable Data Transfer:* Both reliable and unreliable packet-oriented data transfer mechanisms are available. For reliable data transfer the SSCOP [5] is supported. If end-to-end reliability is not required, then AAL5 is used. AAL5 provides a mechanism to detect errors, but recovering from an error is left to a higher layer protocol.

- *AALs Supported:* Among the AALs, only AAL5 is currently supported. Other AALs such as AAL1 or null-AAL are left as implementation dependent. The primary reason for this is that AAL1 or null-AAL would require mechanisms that provide time synchronized data transfer of a few bytes at a time. Such mechanism are usually dependent on the implementation's operating system environment. The simple block mode of AAL3/4 could also be readily supported; however, applications needing just this functionality typically use AAL5.

- *Special Features:* Some features provided by the AAL5 layer are such as tagging indication, congestion indication, user-user indication, and errored packet delivery are not support by the data transfer primitives proposed. Each of these features is available to a varying degree in current AAL5 hardware and hence dropping them was a good toward maintaining interoperability.

[3] The selector byte is the last byte in the 20-byte ATM (Private) End System Address format. This byte has no meaning in the context of the ATM (Public) E.164 address format.

[4] The called party subaddress was a key contender to get onto the ATM SAP. However, it was dropped since its exact use in UNI signaling was not well understood at the time the API document was created.

[5] SSCOP runs over AAL5 to provide reliable data transfer.

3 X/Open XTI ATM Programming Interface

The ATM Forum API semantic specifications have been taken up by two industry groups to map onto industry standard syntax API specifications, namely,

- X/Open Consortium's XTI [6],

- Winsock Group's Winsock2 Interface [6].

There may be other efforts underway that the authors are not aware of.

In this section we will try to describe the XTI interface specifications. However, at the time of the writing the specification was works-in-progress and subject to change. The information presented here is in no way a substitute for the documents published by these groups [2, 3].

The X/Open Transport Interface (XTI) network programming interface is a standard part of X/Open-compliant Unix systems from companies such as Sun, HP, SCO, IBM, Unisys and many others. The XTI interface has also been adopted by Apple Computer's latest MacOS. Most implementations of XTI-based protocol stacks are in the Unix streams environment. The MacOS XTI implementation is also based on portable streams implementation. In this section, we shall discuss a generic XTI interface to ATM. However, we shall also bring in a few MacOS specifics, in places where XTI leaves a functionality as implementation-dependent.

[6] X/Open is also working on an ATM API definition for use with XSockets, which is the X/Open version of BSD Sockets.

For the purpose of the discussion in this section, we assume that the reader is familiar with XTI programming interfaces using other traditional protocols such as TCP/IP, AppleTalk, etc. We shall only explain the following areas in each of these interfaces for use with ATM:

- Opening ATM communications endpoints,
- ATM Addressing and SAPs,
- Point-to-multipoint SVCs

3.1 Opening ATM communications endpoints

The t_open() call is used to open a native ATM endpoint. The name argument of this call is used to identify the name of the native ATM XTI service provider. Since the XTI interface is available on multiple operating systems, this name is implementation dependent.

XTI requires two service providers to support the ATM Forum API semantics. One is the AAL5 service provider and the other is the SSCOP service provider. Each of these providers will require a different name argument to t_open().

On MacOS, the AAL5 service provider's name is defined in the macro kRawATMUNI3xName and the SSCOP service provider is defined in the macro kSSCOPUNI3xName [7].

3.2 ATM Addressing and SAPs

XTI has traditionally never specified the format for addresses. As far as the XTI interface is concerned, an address is just a string of bytes. The internal structure is left implementation dependent. This is changing with the ATM XTI service provider.

The ATM service provider has defined a basic address structure. This address structure could be embedded within some other structure in an implementation dependent fashion. The following is the ATM SAP address,

```
struct  tatm_sap {
 struct {                  // ATM Address
  char  SVE_tag_addr;      // ATM_address SVE tag
  char  SVE_tag_selector;  // ATM_selector SVE tag
  char  address_format;    // E164 or AESA format
  char  address_length;
  char  address [20];
 } tatm_sap_addr;
 struct {                  // BLLI Layer 2
  char  SVE_tag;           // BLLI_id2 SVE tag
  char  ID_type;           // union field selector
  union  {
   char  simple_ID;
   char  user_defined_ID;
  }  ID;
 } tatm_sap_layer2;
 struct {                  // BLLI Layer 3
  char  SVE_tag;           // BLLI_id3 SVE tag
  char  ID_type;           // union field selector
  union  {
   char  simple_ID;
   char  IPI_ID;
   struct  {
    char  OUI [3];
    char  PID [2];
   }  SNAP_ID;
   char  user_defined_ID;
  }  ID;
 } tatm_sap_layer3;
 struct {                  // BHLI
  char  SVE_tag;           // BHLI_id SVE tag
  char  ID_type;           // union field selector
  union  {
   char  ISO_ID [8];
   struct  {
    char  OUI [3];
    char  app_ID [4];
   }  vendor_ID;
   char  user_defined_ID[8];
  }  ID;
 } tatm_sap_appl;
}
```

The SVE tags have 3 values, T_ATM_ABSENT, T_ATM_PRESENT or T_ATM_ANY. The ATM_address and the ATM_selector SVEs from the semantic specification are combined into one sub-structure without loss of functionality.

The ATM SAP structure alleviates the burden of parsing the BLLI and BHLI information. The ID_type fields are filled with one of the macro values defined in the header file. These fields point out the field in the union to be used.

The ATM SAP structure can be used in two different contexts, i.e. as a Network Address and as a Protocol Address. A network address is used to specify just the ATM address (without the BLLI and BHLI fields). Such an address is used in t_listen() to get the address of the calling user or in t_addleaf() to add another leaf to a point-to-multipoint connection. A protocol address is the entire ATM SAP structure. It is used in t_bind() by an application that needs to register an ATM SAP and listen for incoming calls.

Under MacOS, the tatm_sap structure is encapsulated into a ATMSAPAddress structure with a 2-byte address family, AF_ATM, as its first field.

```
typedef struct ATMSAPAddress {
```

```
    OTAddressType     addressType; /* AF_ATM  */
    struct tatm_sap  sap;          /* ATM SAP */
} ATMSAPAddress;
```

Each XTI implementation also provides an implementation specific API call to obtain the list of valid addresses available at the ATM UNI. This information is used when binding to an ATM SAP. In MacOS, the ATMGetInterfaceInfo() function is used for this purpose.

3.3 Point-to-multipoint SVCs

Point-to-multipoint connections are supported by 3 new primitives added to XTI. It is yet undecided whether these functions will be ATM specific additions or protocol-independent, as are the rest of the XTI primitives. The three new functions are,

- t_addleaf() - add a leaf to a point-to-multipoint connection,
- t_removeleaf() - remove a leaf from a point-to-multipoint connection,
- t_rcvleafchange() - receive an indication about a leaf change.

The first leaf of the point-to-multipoint connection should be added using the standard t_connect() primitive. When doing this the T_ATM_BEARER_CAP option must be negotiated to specify point-to-multipoint. Subsequent leaves are added using the t_addleaf() function. The leaf ID argument in t_addleaf() is generated by the user.

This leaf ID is used in the other functions to refer to a specific leaf. The first leaf is always referred to with a leaf ID of zero.

4 ATM API Implementation

In implementing an ATM API there are challenges not normally faced by network API designers. Five major issues arise:

- ATM can carry high-bandwidth traffic. Copy-avoidance, scatter/gather and other techniques may need to be used to ensure that the operating system can carry the bandwidth to the application.
- The non-packet adaptation layers (principally AAL1) will need some special handling (although the current semantics document supports only AAL5).
- For data streams where the timing is important, that timing information may need to be presented to the application as well as the data. This might include clock recovery from the line (often at 8kHz) or the SRTS recovery from AAL1.
- ATM networks go to some lengths to ensure bandwidth and jitter. Few operating systems can offer guarantees as good, or reservation of bandwidth (e.g. on the bus) or CPU time. Nonetheless, some attempt to control the introduction of delay or jitter by the operating-system may be required.
- Some of the applications running on ATM benefit from tight control of end-to-end delay. The overhead of high-level protocols and the delays caused by interactions with the host operating system can be varied by using different APIs which are available on different communication layers. Several recent papers have found that a significant portion of communication overhead occurs due to these interactions [8].

In the following subsection, we present one possible implementation of the ATM API using the XTI's mapping to the semantics model.

4.1 An XTI ATM API Implementation

XTI implementations in most operating systems go hand-in-hand with a Unix System V-style streams protocol stack. This is also the case in Apple's MacOS OpenTransport XTI implementation. However, there are XTI implementations that are not based on streams. XTI specifies the API and is neutral to the underlying implementation scheme.

In this section, we shall briefly describe one way of implementing the XTI ATM API in a streams-based environment. The ATM API on MacOS follows the design described here. Figure 2 shows the basic structure of the design.

Applications reside in user space and communicate through the XTI interface. The stream head serves as the boundary between kernel and user space. Communication across the stream head is done using messages. The ATM protocol stack is implemented as a set of streams modules that reside in kernel space. The modules are appropriately interconnected using streams queues by a stack configuration entity. These modules communicate with each other through the exchange of messages.

The lowest level module is the ATM DLPI driver. The driver is responsible for communicating with the ATM network interface card. It presents a Data Link

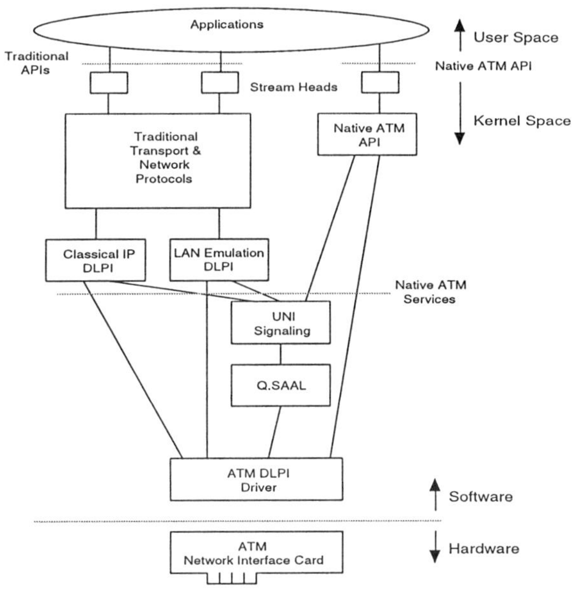

Figure 2: One possible realization of XTI ATM API

Provider Interface (DLPI) at its upper end. This DLPI interface is an extended version of the standard connection-oriented DLPI interface. The driver is only concerned with enabling/disabling virtual circuits, transmitting/receiving AAL data on VCs and a few other basic operations. The concept of UNI signaling, LAN emulation, etc. are not known to this layer.

UNI signaling and Q.SAAL (also called Q.2110 [7]/Q.2130) are implemented as separate modules that sit above the ATM driver and use the well-know signaling VCI to run the UNI signaling protocol. Other modules such as LAN emulation and Classical IP make use of the signaling module and the ATM driver to provide a MAC layer service. Their upper ends present a standard Ethernet-style DLPI interface to traditional protocol stacks such as TCP/IP and AppleTalk.

The Native ATM API module implements the messages required to support the XTI ATM API. This module makes use of the signaling module and the ATM driver to provide its service. For every new ATM API endpoint, a new stream is opened to the ATM driver. Thus, each virtual circuit is kept isolated from others. Functionality such as incoming call dispatching and ATM SAP registration is implemented by the signaling module. The connection attribute negotiation functionality is distributed between the signaling module, API module and the ATM driver.

The model presented here is flexible, both in terms of adding new ATM applications in user space as well as adding new services (as streams modules) in kernel space.

[7]SSCOP (Q.2110) is part of the Q.SAAL Specification.

5 Sample Client/Server Model and ATM-aware Applications

In time one would expect ATM services to be used by a more abstract layer which manages bandwidth and quality of service. Until that time, the driving applications are those which can afford to give up the internetworking offered by protocol systems such as IP (which run on many network layers) in favor of the unique characteristics of ATM.

Audio/video applications cover the most common examples of such applications: high-quality video-conferencing, and video-on-demand are often cited. However, applications which benefit from statistical "guarantees" of bandwidth and quality of service can be drawn from many other areas - remote telemetry is another example sometimes used.

Finally, "traditional" applications such as file sharing or remote access can benefit from such characteristics in some environments. Even though file sharing will work without bandwidth reservation, service to the end-user can be improved by using the application in selected areas for users with time-critical needs. There also efficiency gained by eliminating protocol overhead by directly using ATM rather than using a higher layer protocol such as TCP.

In this section, we first present a client/server model of using the XTI's ATM API implementation. Figure 3 shows one possible implementation of the client/server model using the XTI's format. The client configures its traffic and QoS requirement based on its particular need. The Server waits for connection after binding a local ATM address with the endpoint. Once client makes a connection request to server, the server will verify the request based on its available resources. Once the connection is granted, the client could send/receive data/requests to server before either side decide to tear down the connection.

After introducing the simple client/server model, we further utilize the XTI ATM API and implement one useful application (video on demand). In our experiment [9], Macintoshes are used as VOD clients. The client has installed one MPEG-1 hardware decoder and one OC-3 ATM interface (or 25 Mbits/sec ATM interface). The client application retrieves streaming data from ATM interface to the preallocated buffer of the QuickTime software (QuickTime is the Macintosh's video standard) and then pushes streaming data to MPEG decoder. On the server side, a PowerMac is

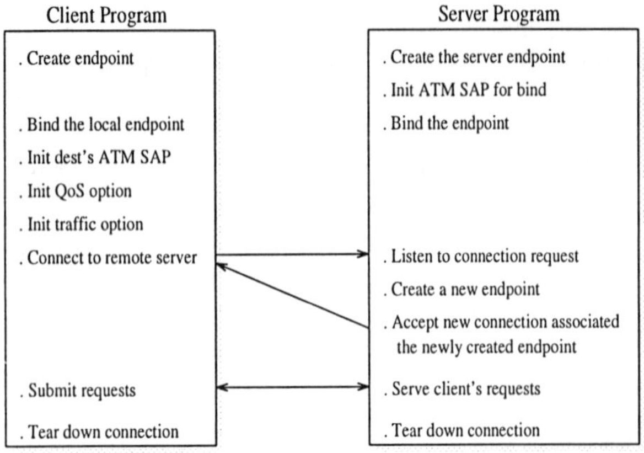

Figure 3: A sample client/server diagram using ATM API

used. The server has installed one multiple Gbyte drive and one OC-3 ATM interface. MPEG-1 movies and profiles associated with each movie are stored within the hard drive.

Control messages of VOD system (movie selection, pause and play) are delivered via reliable channel (either TCP or AppleTalk's ADSP). However, the real streaming data is delivered via native ATM service (AAL5) with reserved bandwidth at 1.5 Mbits/sec per stream. This VOD prototype serves a good example of using the native ATM service (guaranteed QoS and network traffic control).

6 Conclusion and Future Work

The native ATM API is a key technology to make ATM networks attractive. It gives access to unique features of ATM which are obscured when ATM is used to carry 'legacy' traffic. This API enables programmers to write ATM-aware applications and take advantages of bandwidth guarantees and QoS management. The API co-exists with other uses of the ATM services, such as LAN Emulation, enabling a smooth transition.

This paper provided an overview of the development of ATM APIs, their status and possible future work. It also covers some implementation issues. The ATM Forum semantic model serves as the basis for X/Open's XTI and the Winsock 2 API.

The XTI API is becoming available on a variety of platforms including the Macintosh operating system and various adapters running in UNIX systems. The Winsock 2 API is being actively supported on 32-bit Windows systems. These APIs should catalyze the creation of multimedia applications which take advantage of native ATM services.

There are quite a few issues that need to be solved by standard bodies. The existing semantic definition from the ATM Forum covers UNI 3.1. There are a considerable number of features in UNI 4.0 which will need extensions to the semantics. In addition, work on telephony on ATM is prompting the coverage of non-packet AALs (AAL1 in particular). The prospect that the AAL1 (telephony) data may not pass through the API but into the telephony sub-system directly, and the possibility of some sort of ATM "backplane", has raised the question of how to re-direct data from passing through the API to passing directly to the client hardware or software sub-system. It may be possible that a particular need (for example, real-time network streaming) for a special purpose of ATM API syntax will be identified.

The API itself may become subsumed, in time, through more general network management APIs and techniques such as the resource reservation protocol (RSVP) from the IETF, which would apply to a variety of physical networks. However, until that time, the ATM API provides a valuable route into the unique advantages of ATM networks.

References

[1] ATM Forum. Native ATM Services: Semantic Specifications. December 1995.

[2] X/Open Company. XTI ATM Transport Provider Appendix, draft. April 1996.

[3] ATM Forum. WinSock 2 ATM Annex. February 1996.

[4] ATM Forum. ATM User-Network Interface Specification, Version 3.1. 1994.

[5] ATM Forum. Signaling ATM Adaptation Layer (SAAL) Specification. April 1993.

[6] Winsock Group. Windows Sockets Application Programmers Interface Version 2.1.0. 1996.

[7] Apple Computer. ATM Applications Developer Note. May 1996.

[8] M. Lin, J. Hsieh, D.H.C. Du, J.P. Thomas, and J.A. MacDonald. Distributed Network Computing over Local ATM Networks. *IEEE Journal on Selected Areas in Communications*, pages 733–748, May 1995.

[9] M. Lin and D. Singer. An Experimental ATM-based Video-on-demand System on a Macintosh Platform. In *Proceedings of the 21st IEEE Local Computer Conference*, pages 59–68, October 1996.

Object-Oriented Network Protocols

Stefan Böcking

Siemens AG, Corporate Research and Development
81730 Munich, Otto-Hahn-Ring 6, Germany

Abstract

A wide-range of various network communication services and protocols is required to efficiently support the diverse networks and their applications. It is usual to design a protocol for each new service which is required. An attractive alternative is to use a modular and object-oriented architecture for the design and implementation of network protocols. With it, protocols for individual service provision can be created by simply combining generic protocol functions blocks.

The first part of this paper presents a new reference model which gives a foundation for the object-oriented design and implementation of modular network protocols. The second part discusses a case study of an existing object-oriented network communication system.

1: Introduction

The growing diversity of network technologies (such as Ethernet, ISDN, ATM) and networked applications (such as file transfer, WWW, multimedia conferencing) calls for a multitude of network communication services and protocols. To counter this challenge, the conventional approach, i.e. to design completely new services and protocols for each new class of application requirements and network properties, is becoming more and more unsuitable and inefficient, because common functionality will be specified and implemented redundantly. For example, the Internet Protocol Suite today comprises more than 100 network protocols and still does not satisfy all requirements of newer applications, such as the support of reliable group communications. Moreover, many of these protocols possess redundant functions, such as those for connection, error, and flow control which have been designed and implemented many times.

An attractive alternative for modern network protocols is the concept of a modular and object-oriented architecture. Object orientation is a widely accepted and used software engineering technique which has been successfully introduced for the design and implementation of networked applications and middleware software such as CORBA. But surprisingly, it is scarcely used for the development of network protocols such as TCP/IP.

The benefits of the object-orientation method can be used to design and implement modular network protocols which are composable, reusable, and extendable. Programmers are then able to implement protocols and services by composing (rather than programming) them from a set of already specified, implemented, and tested elementary protocol objects according to the application needs and the network environment. Therefore, it is expected that object orientation will generally ease and accelerate the design and implementation of new services and protocols.

As presented in [1], modular network protocols can provide improved performance compared to monolithic ones due to their ability to compose only those functions that are really required to provide the requested service. This may in some way also reassure protocol programmers, who may think that applying modular and object-oriented design or implementation methods will decrease the overall performance of their protocols.

The remainder of this paper is organized as follows: the next section briefly describes our new object-oriented reference framework for modular communication systems encompassing one or more network protocols. It provides a common terminology and modeling technique for the description, specification, and implementation of object-oriented and modular communication systems and protocols by taking other well-known reference models such as the ISO, the B-ISDN/ATM, and the Internet Reference Model into account. Section 3 finally discusses a case study of an object-oriented network communication system, which is the Transport and Internetworking Package (TIP).

2: The object-oriented reference framework

This section introduces a new object-oriented framework for modular communication systems which for short is called the MCS (Modular Communication Systems) framework. One of its novel feature compared to the ISO, the B-ISDN/ATM, and the Internet Reference Model is its object-orientation. Object-oriented modeling is a powerful and

0-8186-7780-5/97 $10.00 © 1997 IEEE

well-accepted software engineering method whose modeling properties of information hiding, encapsulation, abstraction, and inheritance eases the design of composable, extendable, and reusable systems in general, and of modular network communication systems in particular. In addition, it eases the collaboration with systems dealing with other networking aspects such as network management [2] and open distributed processing [3], which already have an object-oriented foundation.

Another novel feature is its universal communication model, which provides an abstraction of a multipoint connection. The universality of the model enables modular network communication systems to compose (combine) a variety of communication services each with differing capabilities, but all of which are based on the same communication model.

The MCS framework described below consists of 4 models: an object model, with the fundamentals for the object-oriented modeling, a system model structuring communication systems into service objects of different layers and planes, a communication model defining the application's view of a network conversation, and a composition model describing in general terms the concept of communication service composition.

2.1: Object model

Designing, specifying, and implementing a system quickly becomes cumbersome when its functionality grows. Thus, a modularization method is typically applied in order to break down the system's functionality into better manageable functional modules.

The *object-oriented* modularization method goes one step further. Functional modules (which are then called objects, and are instances of specific classes) additionally possess general modeling properties such as encapsulation, information hiding, abstraction, and inheritance. Encapsulation refers to the fact that objects encapsulate a certain functionality that is only accessible through their well-defined interface, so that objects are free of side-effects. Information hiding means that objects hide their internal data structures and the processing algorithms required for the object's functionality. The abstraction property emphasizes that an object can provide a higher-level view of the actual encapsulated functionality. Inheritance enables designers to derive new classes from existing ones by specifying or implementing only the differences.

In general, object orientation eases the design of composable, extendable, and reusable components.

Composibility. A modular system can produce communication protocols for new communication services by composing appropriate protocol functions. In monolithic systems, each new communication service typically requires a new communication protocol to be designed and implemented.

Extendability. Modular systems can add new communication service capabilities later on by introducing new protocol functions without affecting existing protocol functions. Monolithic systems typically require a re-design and implementation modification of the whole communication protocol in case new capabilities are to be incorporated.

Reusability. Modular systems can reuse protocol functions in different communication protocols at different layers. Communication protocols of monolithic systems are typically developed as separate systems, which can result in redundant designs and implementations of functions used in different protocols.

Object decomposition. Objects can be decomposable into objects. An object and its decomposition have the equivalent external behavior. A decomposition, however, provides a more detailed view of the problem domain than the composed object does. The object decomposition is repetitive. That means an object which is part of a decomposition can also be decomposed. Beginning with a system as the topmost object, more details are revealed with each level of decomposition.

Objects in networks. In a network environment and depending on the abstraction and decomposition level, we can differentiate objects of being *node-local* or *distributed*. A node-local object resides on one node at any time. It may migrate but is never located on two nodes simultaneously. A distributed object may reside on multiple nodes at the same time, and is typically composed of multiple node-local objects that perform a *protocol* to provide the distributed object's capability.

2.2: System model

Modular network communication systems are functionally decomposed into service objects (cf. Figure 1). Each *service object* represents a particular service and makes the capabilities of the service available to its users.

The system decomposition is based on a reference architecture, which categorizes service objects according to a defined set of layers and planes. Layers provide a vertical categorization of service objects, while planes provide horizontal categorization.

A *layer* represents a collection of service objects which provide a subset of the communication system's functionality, resulting from its vertical decomposition.

A *plane* represents a collection of service objects which provide a subset of the communication's functionality, resulting from its horizontal decomposition. Introducing planes into a layered system subdivides layer service objects into a set of plane service objects. It also replaces layer services by a collection of *plane services*.

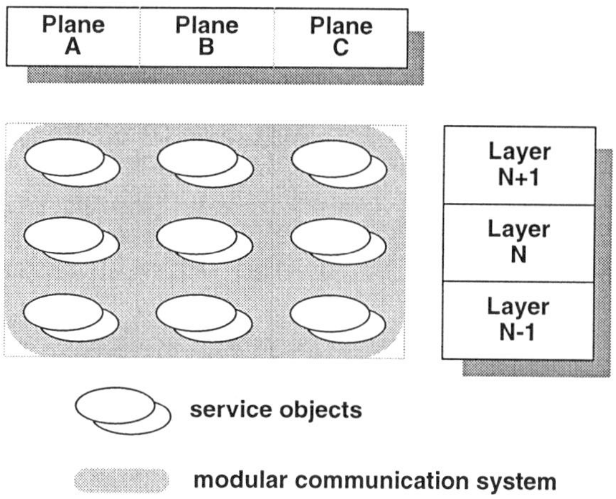

Figure 1. Decomposition of a modular communication system into service objects

Reference architecture. The proposed MCS framework does not stipulate any number, hierarchy, or functionality of layers for the definition of a modular communication system. It is thus different than the OSI and Internet architectures, for instance. On the other hand, a number of planes are predefined guiding the structuring of layer services. These planes are: management plane, composition plane, access plane, control plane, and transfer plane.

Service objects of the management plane provide the interface to and from network and systems management which is defined elsewhere. Service objects of the composition plane provide the capability to configure individual communication services, which are collectively provided by service objects of different planes: access, control, and transfer. Service objects of the access plane enable applications to establish communications possessing the *a priori* defined communication capabilities. Users can employ control plane objects to influence active communications, e.g. to introduce new communication participants or to move the local communication endpoint to another node. The service provided by objects of the transfer plane enables participants of a communication association to transfer user information.

Protocol objects. Protocol functions represent the functionality that is encapsulated by the service objects and that is required for service provision. Thus, we can also view a service object to be composed of a collection of objects providing a specific protocol function. These objects are subsequently called *protocol objects*.

For implementation or design purposes, service and protocol objects can be composed or decomposed in order to obtain a coarser or finer granularity, respectively.

2.3: Communication model

In our MCS framework, communication services of a modular communication system are based on the abstraction of a multipoint connection. A *multipoint connection* represents a communication association in which two or more users can participate. Only users affiliated to the same connection are able to communicate by exchanging information. User information is conveyed by the provider as *service data units* (*SDUs*). SDUs are transparently transferred by the provider, i.e. without any restriction as regards the information's content, format, and encoding. At any time, multiple connections with different participants can exist.

A connection itself only provides the logical binding between users. The path of information exchange is defined by using the abstraction of a *data stream*. Streams are sequences of SDUs that flow unidirectionally from one *stream source* to one or more *stream sinks*.

Principally, connections can encompass an unlimited number of streams which can be freely arranged and rearranged. Throughout a connection's lifetime, new streams can be created and existing ones can be terminated.

The streams' arrangement of a connection is defined by a *communication pattern*. A pattern contains the communication addresses of all connection participants and defines between which of them data streams exist. Pattern addressing enables applications to define various communication structures, such as point-to-point or point-to-multipoint and various symmetries such as unidirectional or bidirectional.

The communication *quality of service* (*QoS*) defines connection and stream properties as regards reliability, security, and performance. Different stream QoS may be assigned to streams of the same connection.

The multipoint communication model also enables the definition of datagram-oriented or transaction-oriented services, which we call short-lived connections.

Short-lived connection. The communication phases and their related service actions can be combined into a single phase and single service action for the provision of a so called short-lived connection. Common types of short-lived connections are as follows:

- *Datagram.* A single, self-contained SDU can be conveyed with a single short-lived connection.
- *Acknowledged datagram.* The producer receives a notification when the sent SDU has arrived at the consumer's site. Only one SDU can be sent during the lifetime of this connection type.
- *Transaction (request/response).* The consumer confirms the receipt of the SDU by returning a reply SDU. With each short-lived connection of this type, only a single request and reply SDU can be exchanged.

Basic service object classes. Following the MCS framework, modular communication systems provide two types of services: composition services and communication services. Composition services, which enable the configuration of customized communication services, are provided by service objects of class: *composer.* Communication services, which enable the addressing of corresponding users, the maintenance of connections and the exchange of SDUs, are provided by service objects of class: service access point, connection endpoint, stream source, and stream sink.

- *Composer class.* A composer object configures and controls customized communication services. Each communication service may possess different capabilities. Composers may control and maintain multiple communication services at the same time.
- *Service access point (SAP) class.* A communication service is represented by a number of corresponding SAP objects. Each SAP object provides access to its representing service, which enables users to establish and release communication connections. To each SAP object a communication address is bound, which identifies the related user within the service provider's scope.
- *Connection endpoint (CEP) class.* A connection is represented by a number of corresponding CEP objects. Each CEP object provides access to a particular connection. Users related to a CEP object may modify the communication pattern or QoS of the represented connection throughout its lifetime.
- *Stream source class, stream sink class.* A stream is represented by one stream source object and one or more stream sink objects. At a stream source object, SDUs can be sent over the representing stream, which can be received subsequently at corresponding stream sink objects.

Figure 2 illustrates basic service objects of various classes, their semantic relationships, and their position in the reference architecture of the MCS framework.

2.4: Composition model

According to the MCS framework, modular communication systems provide a composition service that enables applications to customize their individual communication service. The composition service is offered by composers, which are service objects of the composition plane. On request, an (N)-composer (i.e. composer object at layer N) configures all relevant (N)-communication service objects providing the required (N)-communication service (see also Figure 3).

The composition process performed by composers is to accept the required (N)-communication service capabilities as input and produce the appropriate (N)-communication service objects as output by considering the available node resources and protocol functions.

The required information is assumed to be stored in a *Composition Information Base* (*CIB*), which is accessible by composers of all layers. Possible information stored in a CIB are the available node resources, the available protocol functions and their profiles, and inter-layer information.

Below, we briefly look into the service capabilities that are used by the application to describe its requirements, the node resources to be considered and the composition process.

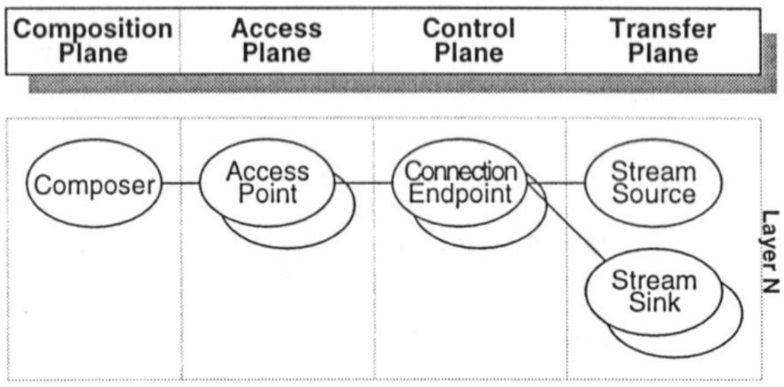

Figure 2. Service objects

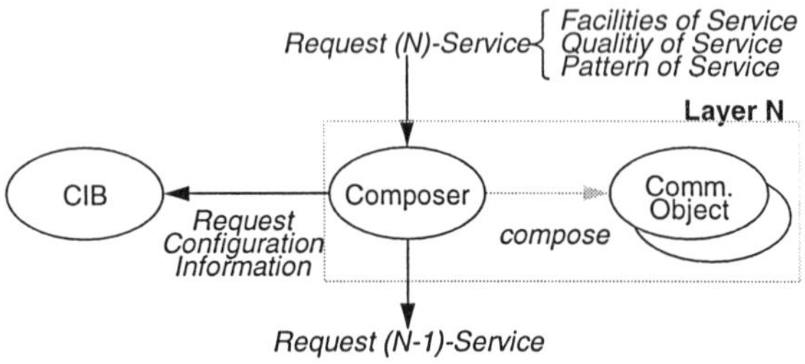

Figure 3. Communication service composition

Service capabilities. Service capabilities can be categorized as follows:

- *Facilities of Service (FoS).* With FoS, applications determine which basic and enhanced communication facilities - such as the connection establishment and the connection migration facilities - the new communication service should comprise.
- *Quality of Service (QoS).* With QoS, applications determine which properties the communication should have as regards the quality attributes of reliability, security, and performance.
- *Pattern of Service (PoS).* With PoS, applications determine which communication structure, symmetry, and addressing concept the new service should support in order to yield, for example, unidirectional point-to-point or bidirectional point-to-multipoint communications.

Node resources. Service objects are composed of protocol functions which consume buffer and CPU resources of the local node when executed. The limitation of these resources requires that the composer check whether a potential service object composition is executable. If a communication service is composed of a collection of service objects, the required resources for all objects must be considered when selecting and composing each object.

Composition of service objects. The communication model of the MCS framework defines four basic classes of service objects which commonly provide a communication service. These classes are service access point, connection endpoint, stream sink, and stream source class. This structuring eases the composition process of communication services by dividing it into smaller composition steps, where at each step only a reduced scope of capabilities and protocol functions has to be considered per service object (e.g. because not every protocol function is relevant for every service object).

To compose the actual service object, different composition strategies can be applied to find the best-suited protocol functions' composition for the requested (N)-service capabilities and a given set of available protocol functions, node resources, and (N-1)-service capabilities. Examples of basic composition strategies (which can also be combined) are as follows:

- *Selection.* Select service object from a collection of service objects pre-composed before system run-time.
- *Composition.* Compose service object on demand at run-time.
- *Configuration.* Configure service object by setting object parameters at run-time.

Composing service objects, however, can easily become a complex task considering that protocol functions may possess different variants, may oblige a specific arrangement, and may effect other service capabilities. Composition strategies may be based on a simple mapping table or a sophisticated expert system.

3: System architecture of TIP

This section studies the architecture and design principles of the Transport and Internetworking Package (TIP) [4]. TIP is an adaptive system based on a modular and object-oriented architecture and enables applications to configure their individual communication services. The current version runs over UDP/IP or directly over ATM.

TIP comprises a protocol operating system [5] and a library of basic building blocks with application programming interface, network interface, and protocol functions. Other experimental modular systems are: ADAPTIVE[6], DaCaPo[7], DyCAT[8], F-CSS[9], HOPS[10], and Micro Protocols[11].

3.1: Layers and planes

TIP's architecture consists of one layer and four planes. The planes are the ones defined in the MCS framework which are composition, access, control, and transfer plane. For each plane, a service object is defined which are composer, access point, connection endpoint and stream source and sink object.

3.2: Service and protocol objects

TIP service objects are structured into three sublayers as shown in Figure 4. The top sublayer contains local service objects which are responsible for the interfacing between the application and TIP. The bottom sublayer encompasses service objects concerned with the interfacing between TIP and the network. The middle sublayer comprises protocol objects performing the relevant protocol functions. All objects of the top sublayer constitute the TIP's application programming interface which is called Sockets++. All objects of the bottom sublayer provide the TIP's network interface component which is called Netglue. Finally, all objects of the middle layer define the transport-oriented protocol of TIP named Tempo.

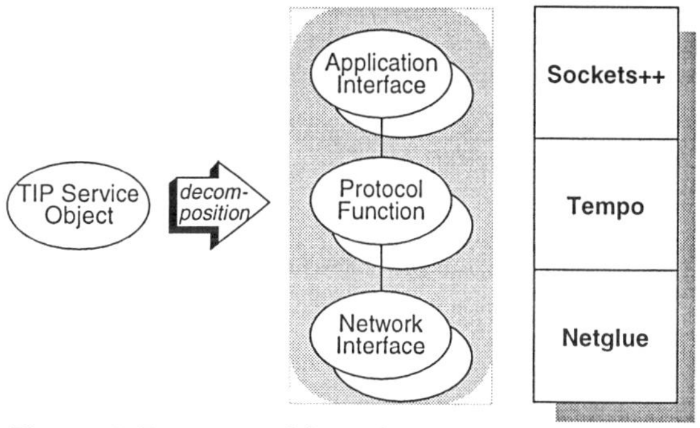

Figure 4. Decomposition of a TIP service object

Sockets++. The Application Programming Interface (API) used for TIP is Sockets++ [12]. It is a revised version of the well-known BSD Sockets paradigm. Sockets++ has an object-oriented, platform-independent and protocol-independent design and is implemented in C++. The local service objects provided by Sockets++ are as follows:

- *Composer.* An object that enables applications to configure their individual communication services. A communication service consists of four object types representing sockets, connection endpoints, stream sources and sinks.

- *Socket.* An object that enables applications to access an individual communication service for the establishment and release of connections with the configured service capabilities.
- *Connection endpoint.* An object that represents the local access to a connection and that enables applications to control the connection's configuration (e.g. the number and arrangement of the participants or the related QoS settings).
- *Stream source and sink.* Objects which represent the local access of a unidirectional data stream of which multiple may exist per connection. At a stream source, the application can issue data for transmission, at a stream sink, the application can receive transferred data.

Tempo. The protocol functions used for TIP have been derived by decomposing the Tempo protocol [13]. Tempo is actually a transport protocol providing reliable multipoint connections. Due to its functional decomposition for TIP, individual transport services can be configured to provide services ranging from unreliable services with a point-to-point communication structure to reliable services with a multipoint-to-multipoint communication structure. Tempo's protocol mechanisms have been selected and designed to be lightweight, i.e. the instruction path and the number of control PDU exchanges (e.g. acknowledgments) are minimized for error-free communication. In addition, the PDU format has been kept simple for a possible hardware implementation, such as defining header and trailer fields of constant length and positioning fields in a sensible order to allow pipeline processing.

The implementation of Tempo is based on the MCS framework. Accordingly, Tempo is decomposed into a collection of protocol objects that can be composed to form service objects such as a Tempo composer, Tempo service access point, Tempo connection endpoint, Tempo stream source, and Tempo stream sink. For service provision, some of these objects, i.e. connection endpoints, stream sources and sinks, coordinate their collaboration by a protocol, which is a defined set of rules, data formats, and functions. Between Tempo service access points a *service control protocol* is defined, and between Tempo stream sources and sinks a *stream control protocol*. Currently, Tempo's composer and connection endpoint objects perform only local actions thus no protocol is performed.

The service control protocol is responsible for establishing and releasing connections including setup and release of all related data streams. A data stream provides a service to transfer unidirectionally a sequence of SDUs (user data) between one source and multiple sinks. The semantic and syntax of the cooperation between stream sources and sinks is defined by the stream control protocol.

The Tempo protocol function classes provided are as follows:

- *Blocking*. Object maps multiple SDUs into a compound SDU. In the reverse direction, the object deblocks a compound SDU into a sequence of SDUs.
- *Checksumming*. Object builds a checksum over a given SDU. The checksum is appended to the SDU. In the reverse direction, the object verifies a checksum found at the end of an SDU.
- *Composer.* Object configures Tempo's service access point, connection endpoint, stream source and sink objects.
- *Concatenation.* Object maps multiple PDUs (Protocol Data Units) into a compound PDU. In the reverse direction, the object separates a compound PDU into a sequence of independent PDUs.
- Service Control. Object provides functions for connection establishment and release.
- *Transfer control.* Protocol function which requires two complementary co-working objects which are called sender and receiver. Both objects collaborate in order to transfer SDUs or SDU blocks with a specific level of reliability.
- *Jitter compensation.* Object that smooths interval variances between subsequent SDUs.
- *Multiplexing.* Object that merges SDUs issued by different applications into a single stream of SDUs. In the reverse direction, the object performs a demultiplexing, i.e., it forwards SDUs of a single stream to their related application.
- *Rate control.* Object that regulates the interval between subsequent data units (i.e. SDUs or PDUs).
- *Segmentation.* Object that splits SDUs into a sequence of SDU blocks. In the reverse direction, the object reassembles related SDU blocks to the original SDU.
- *Splitting.* Object that distributes data units (PDUs or SDUs) of single stream onto multiple streams. In the reverse direction, the object recombines these SDUs to single stream again.
- *Traffic control.* Object that monitors the flow of SDUs to detect traffic contract violations.

These classes are used as the base classes for the protocol function they represent. Protocol functions can be implemented by various protocol mechanisms. Thus, each protocol function class may have multiple derived classes representing the same function but using different mechanisms. A possible (maximum) configuration of a Tempo stream source is shown in Figure 5.

Netglue. The network interface of TIP is responsible for enhancing and unifying the features of the underlying network to a well defined network service for the Tempo protocol configuration. The interfacing functionality has been implemented as a set of Channels modules representing the Netglue component of TIP [14]. Typical functions of the network interface are the mapping of service capabilities (e.g. multicasting) and QoS between TIP and the underlying network.

The defined class hierarchy for Netglue comprises a TCP class that provides access to the Internet TCP service, a UDP class to access the UDP service, an ATM_SIG class to establish ATM connections, and an ATM_AAL5 class to transfer data over established ATM connections.

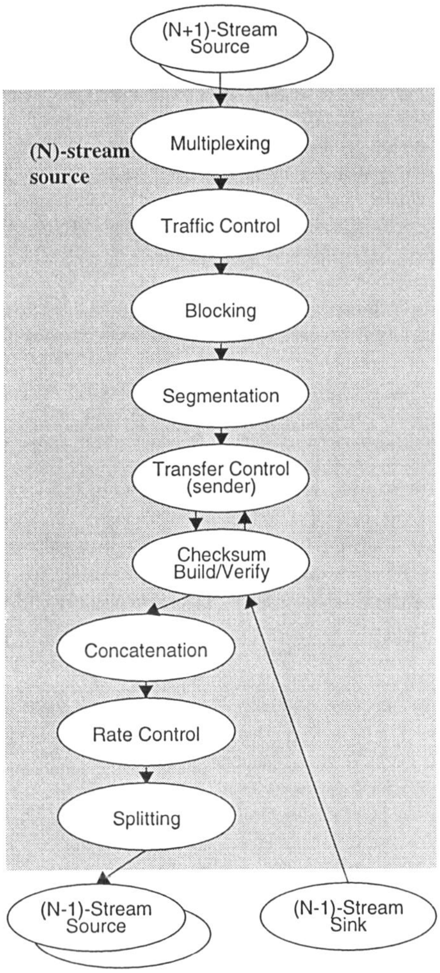

Figure 5. Possible configuration of a Tempo stream source objects

3.3: Communication model and service capabilities

TIP provides a communication service for multipoint connections [15] similar to the one defined in the MCS framework. One limitation of TIP concerns the arrangement of data streams within a connection. Currently, each participant can have multiple incoming streams but only one outgoing stream.

The service capabilities are structured similarly to the one defined in the MCS framework, which are Quality of Service (QoS), Facilities of Service (FoS), and Pattern of Service (PoS). The QoS parameters describe reliability and performance communications attributes [16]. The reliability parameters enable applications to define the required protection level against duplication, damage, loss, and reorder. The performance parameters enables the setting of throughput (SDU interval and SDU size), delay, jitter, error ratio, workahead, and playback. With the FoS parameters, an application denotes its required communication mode (e.g. unconfirmed connection establishment) and facilities (e.g. connection forwarding facility). With the PoS parameters, the addressing capabilities can be selected such as group addressing and address format.

3.4: Service composition

Application requirements are formulated by using the service capabilities parameters which are QoS, FoS, and PoS. These requirements are passed with the service composition request to the composer. The composer configures the appropriate communication service objects, which are socket (service access point), connection endpoint, stream source, and stream sink. On success, a new socket is returned to the application and can be used subsequently to establish one or more connections. Connections related to the same socket possess the same configured service capabilities.

A composer maintains a repository of communication service objects which are pre-configured by a protocol engineer. In addition, the provided service capabilities (i.e. QoS, FoS, PoS) are specified and stored for each service object. For service configuration, the composer searches its repository to find the best suited service objects by assessing the requested and the provided service capabilities.

As alternative to the manual service composition, the Configuration of Protocols in TIP (CogPiT) project has investigated concepts for an automatic configuration of Tempo protocol objects [17]. The CogPiT component is implemented as a Tempo composer object. It uses a repository of Tempo protocol objects whose interfaces and properties are specified in a specific module description language. The information specified for each protocol object are: the required resources (i.e. CPU and buffer), the expected input and produced output parameters, and the possible successor, predecessor, and alternative protocol objects.

4: Conclusion

The presented MCS framework comprises four description models providing a common terminology and modeling technique for the design and implementation of modular, object-oriented network communication systems. The main new features provided by the MCS framework compared to other reference models can be summarized as follows:

- object-oriented method applied for system modeling
- dynamic layering
- layer decomposition into five planes
- single communication model
- concept for service composition
- extendable collection of service capabilities
- extendable collection of protocol functions

First performance measurements of TIP show that it is possible to build communication systems based on a modular and object-oriented architecture with competitive performance [1]. In addition, using the service composition facility to configure the appropriate protocol functions in accordance with the required service and underlying network, modular communication systems can produce clear performance improvements.

Some of our experiences gained with the development of TIP are as follows:

- *Small software size.* The Tempo software that is required for a TCP service provision has 905 lines of code with 54 operations, the compared TCP software has 3885 lines of code and 95 functions.
- *Comprehensible complexity.* The Tempo protocol software comprises 23 classes structured into 3 hierarchy levels. A typical TCP software has about 41 lines of code per operation. A comparable Tempo software has 181 lines of code per class and 17 per operation. The largest Tempo class and operation have 324 and 61 lines of code, respectively.
- *Little implementation effort.* The specification, implementation, re-design, and re-implementation took about 12 person-months. The 13 basic Tempo protocol classes of the last version took about 2 person-months for implementation. Class variants required less implementation effort than it was required for their base classes. Most time was spent to specify an appropriate set of composable protocol objects and to verify the correctness of all sensible compositions.

Some of the open issues with modular communication systems in our view are as follows:

- *Modularization rules.* The selection of protocol object classes decisively determines the modular communication system's performance and its quality as regards reusability, extendability, and composibility. Therefore, rules are desirable guiding the modularization process to yield best possible reusability and performance.
- *Automatic verification.* With a growing number of protocol object classes, it will become cumbersome to prove the correctness of all sensible protocol compositions. Thus, an automatic verification tool is desirable.

5: References

[1] S. Böcking: **Performance and Software Evaluation of the Modular TIP Communication System**, IEEE Global Telecommunications Conference, GLOBECOM '96, Nov 1996.

[2] H.G. Hegering, S. Abeck: **Integrated Network and System Management**, Addison-Wesley, 1994.

[3] ISO/IEC 10746-1: **Reference Model of Open Distributed Processing (ODP)**, June 1995.

[4] S. Böcking: **The TIP Project: Supporting Advanced Communications on High-Speed Networks**, IEEE GLOBECOM '93, Nov 1993.

[5] S. Böcking, V.Seidel, P. Vindeby: **CHANNELS - A Run-Time System for Multimedia Protocols**, ICCCN, Sep 1995.

[6] D.F. Box, D.C. Schmidt, T. Suda: **ADAPTIVE - An Object-Oriented Framework for Flexible and Adaptive Communication Protocols**, High Performance Networking IV, A. Danthine and O. Spaniol (Eds.), North-Holland, 1993.

[7] T. Plageman, B. Plattner, M. Vogt, T. Walter: **A Model for Dynamic Configuration of Light-Weight Protocols**, 3rd Workshop on Future Trends of Distributed Computing Systems, Taipei, Taiwan, April 1992.

[8] B. Heinrichs: **DYCAT - A Flexible Transport system Architecture**, ICC '93, May 1993.

[9] M. Zitterbart, B. Stiller, A.N. Tantawy: **A Model For A Flexible Function-based Communication Subsystem**, IEEE Journal on Selected Areas in Communications, vol 11, no 4, May 1993.

[10] Z. Haas: **A Communication Architecture for High-speed Networking**, IEEE INFOCOM, June 1990.

[11] S.W. O'Malley, L.L. Peterson: **A Highly Layered Architecture for High Speed Networks**, Protocols for High Speed Networks II, North-Holland, 1991.

[12] S. Böcking: **Sockets++ - A Uniform Application Programming Interface for Communication Services**, IEEE Communications Magazine, Dec 1996.

[13] S. Böcking: **TEMPO: A Lightweight Transport Protocol**, Proc. of the Third Workshop on Future Trends of Distributed Computing Systems, April 1992.

[14] S. Böcking, P. Vindeby: **TIP: A Transport and Internetworking Package for ATM**, 2nd Int. Workshop on Advanced Teleservices and High-Speed Communication Architectures (IWACA), Sep 1994.

[15] B. Stiller: **CogPiT - Configuration of Protocols in TIP, Technical Report No 368**, University of Cambridge Computer Laboratory, June 1995.

[16] S. Böcking: **TIP's Configurable Transport Service**, IEEE Symposium on Global Data Networking, Cairo, Dec. 1993.

[17] S. Böcking: **TIP's Performance Quality of Service**, IEEE Communications Magazine, vol 33, no 8, Aug 1995.

Analyzing Non-determinism in Telecommunication Services Using P-Invariant of Petri-Net Model

Masahide Nakamura, Yoshiaki Kakuda and Tohru Kikuno
Department of Information and Computer Sciences
Faculty of Engineering Science, Osaka University
Machikaneyama 1-3, Toyonaka City, Osaka 560, Japan
E-mail: {masa-n, kakuda, kikuno}@ics.es.osaka-u.ac.jp

Abstract

The non-deterministic behaviors in telecommunication services are well-known as one of the most typical Feature Interactions, and they should be detected and eliminated from the telecommunication service specifications. The conventional analysis method of this non-determinism is based on reachability analysis. Since the method must exhaustively enumerate all reachable global states, it cannot be applied to the complex communication services which include many users.

In this paper, we propose an alternative method based on a Petri-net model. The method constructs a logically equivalent Petri-net for a given service specification, and obtains a set of states which cause the non-deterministic behaviors using rules in the service specification. Then, the method identifies states in the set which are not reachable from the initial state using P-invariant of the Petri-net, and deletes them from the set. As P-invariant is utilized as the necessary condition, we must finally apply reachability analysis to states in the resultant set. Since the number of states in the resultant set may be reduced to relatively small, the new method enables us to analyze the more complex services.

1 Introduction

The future advanced networks, such as Intelligent Networks (IN)[11], will drastically increase the requirement and development of new telecommunication services. In developing such new services, the services have to be designed so that they satisfy some fundamental and desirable properties(e.g., all of services are free from deadlocks). Moreover, designers have to check if the new services conflict with features of the existing services or not. Recently, this conflict checking becomes the essential problem for development of new telecommunication services, and the conflict is generally called feature interaction[2].

With respect to feature interaction, one of the most desirable properties in telecommunication services is that "any service must be provided deterministically in the system". Telecommunication services can be often modeled by a state transition machine, in which a state consisting of local states of service users successively moves to a next state by a trigger of user's event. If multiple transitions are allowed to be executed for a certain pair of a state and a user's event, then a non-deterministic transition occurs and this non-deterministic transition may cause an illegal state change against the user's intention. This kind of non-deterministic behavior is also well-known as one of the most typical feature interaction [3, 4, 9, 10], which should be detected and eliminated.

The conventional analysis method is based on reachability analysis. This method at first enumerates all possible reachable states by applying reachability analysis to the state transition machine, and then checks the existence of non-determinism for each reachable state[5]. However, it takes a lot of time and space, because the number of reachable states exponentially increases along with the increase of the number of users. So it may be impossible for the design process of complex services, which include many users and user's events, to apply this conventional analysis.

In this paper, we propose an alternative new analysis method which doesn't require state enumeration at the first stage. In our approach, we at first construct a logically equivalent Petri-net for a given service specification, then obtain a set of all the states which may cause the non-deterministic behavior using rules in the service specification. Then we identify all states in the set which are not reachable from the initial state using P-invariant of the Petri-net, and delete them from the set. As P-invariant is used as necessary condition, we must finally apply reachability analysis to states in the resultant set. By using the proposed method, we can reduce the number of states in the resultant set drastically. As a result, the proposed method may reduce the cost of analyzing non-determinism in a given telecommunication service specification, and enable us to design the more complex services.

2 Practical Example

Example 1 Let us consider a service which has both *Call Waiting* (CW) feature and *Call Forwarding Variable*(CFV) feature [11, 12]. CW feature provides such a capability that a CW user can receive an additional call from a third party when the CW user is talking with someone. On the other hand, CFV feature forwards the incoming call to the terminal number preset by the CFV user. Suppose that user A subscribes

0-8186-7780-5/97 $10.00 © 1997 IEEE

both features CW and CFV whose forwarding address is user D, and that A is talking with user B. In this situation, if user C makes a call to user A, then should the call from C be received by A or forwarded to D?

Many other examples of non-deterministic behaviors are presented in [3, 9, 10](e.g., combination service of CW and Three Way Calling(TWC) feature, etc.)

3 Preliminaries

3.1 Service Specification

Service specification studied in this paper is defined as a set of rules of service logic such as STR[7] and *declarative transition rules*[4]. These rule-based methods have been widely studied towards the practical use since (a) the modularity of the rule facilitates the addition or modification of the new service, and (b) a simple IF-THEN form of each rule enables non-experts to easily design the service logic[9].

Definition 1 *A service specification* S is defined by $S = \langle R, s_0 \rangle$, where R is a finite set of *rules* and s_0 is an *initial global state*(or simply *initial state*). Each rule $r \in R$ is defined as follows.

$$r: \quad A_1, ..., A_s \xrightarrow{E} B_1, ..., B_t$$

A_i or B_j is called a *predicate* and is represented by $p(x_1, ..., x_k)$, where p represents a predicate symbol and $x_1, ..., x_k$ are *variables*. E is called a *user's event* (or simply *event*) and is represented by $e(x_1, ..., x_k)$, where e represents an event symbol. Next, we interpret that $A_1, ..., A_s$ and $B_1, ..., B_t$ represent AND-conjunctions of predicates A_i's and B_j's, and we call them *pre-condition* and *post-condition* of rule r, respectively. The pre-condition is allowed to include *negation of predicate* such as $\neg p(x_1, ..., x_k)$. For convenience, let $e[r]$ denote the event of rule r in the following.

A *global state*(or simply state) is an AND-conjunction of all instances of predicates in rules, and is represented by

$$C_1, ..., C_q$$

where each C_i is an *instance* of predicate defined by $p(a_1, ..., a_k)$, where $a_1, ..., a_k$ are constants which identify the service users. For convenience, in the following we list up only the instances which take true value at the state and may refer it also as the state. In particular, the initial state s_0 is generally defined as

$$s_0 = idle(U_1), idle(U_2), ..., idle(U_n)$$

where U_i is an identifier for specifying a service user and n is the number of the users.

Definition 2 A state can be changed to the *next state* by application of a rule. Let s be a current state of the service and let $r\theta$ denote an instantiation of a rule $r \in R$ based on a substitution θ. If state s includes the pre-condition of $r\theta$, then we say rule r *is applicable to* s *for* θ and we rewrite the corresponding predicates in s into the post-condition of $r\theta$. As the result, a new state s' is generated from s, which is interpreted as "current state s moves to next state s' by a trigger of event in $r\theta$". A state s is *reachable* from an initial state s_0 iff there exists at least one sequence of states such that $s_0, s_1, ..., s_j = s$, where each s_i $(1 \le i \le j)$ is the next state of s_{i-1}.

Example 2 The following is an example of a rule which describes a fundamental function "Suppose that x receives a dial-tone and y is idle. In this situation, if x dials y, then x will be calling y" of telephone service:

$$r: \quad dialtone(x), idle(y) \xrightarrow{dial(x,y)} calling(x, y)$$

In rule r, the pre-condition of r is "*dialtone(x), idle(y)*", the post-condition of r is "$calling(x, y)$", and the event of rule r is $e[r] = dial(x, y)$. Next, we show an example of a state s which represents that users A,B and D are idle and user C receives a dialtone.

$$s = \quad idle(A), idle(B), dialtone(C), idle(D)$$

If we apply a substitution $\theta = \{x|C, y|D\}$ to rule r, then we obtain

$$r\theta: \quad dialtone(C), idle(D) \xrightarrow{dial(C,D)} calling(C, D)$$

Since state s includes the pre-condition of $r\theta$, rule r is applicable to s for θ. As a result, the event $dial(C, D)$ changes the state into a next state s' defined by

$$s' = \quad idle(A), idle(B), calling(C, D)$$

Example 3 The following shows an example of service specification of simplified Plain Ordinary Telephone Service (POTS). For simplicity, we assume that the number of users is only four (A,B,C,D).

$$
\begin{aligned}
R = \{ & \\
r_1: &\quad idle(x) \xrightarrow{offhook(x)} dialtone(x) \\
r_2: &\quad dialtone(x) \xrightarrow{onhook(x)} idle(x) \\
r_3: &\quad dialtone(x), \neg idle(y) \xrightarrow{dial(x,y)} busytone(x) \\
r_4: &\quad dialtone(x), idle(y) \xrightarrow{dial(x,y)} calling(x, y) \\
r_5: &\quad calling(x, y) \xrightarrow{onhook(x)} idle(x), idle(y) \\
r_6: &\quad calling(x, y) \xrightarrow{offhook(y)} talk(x, y) \\
r_7: &\quad talk(x, y) \xrightarrow{onhook(x)} idle(x), busytone(y) \\
r_8: &\quad talk(x, y) \xrightarrow{onhook(y)} idle(y), busytone(x) \\
r_9: &\quad busytone(x) \xrightarrow{onhook(x)} idle(x) \quad \} \\
s_0 = &\quad idle(A), idle(B), idle(C), idle(D)
\end{aligned}
$$

3.2 Non-deterministic Behaviors

Intuitively, the non-deterministic behavior occurs when two or more rules are simultaneously applicable to a global state for the identical instance of event. The non-deterministic behavior on a global state s is formally defined as follows.

Definition 3 Let $\mathcal{S} = \langle R, s_0 \rangle$ be a service specification. Then, we say that "state s causes a non-deterministic behavior" iff s satisfies both of the following conditions.
Condition P1: s is reachable from s_0.
Condition P2: There exist at least two different rules $r_i, r_j \in R$ and two substitutions θ_i, θ_j such that r_i and r_j are applicable to s for θ_i and θ_j, respectively, and that $e[r_i\theta_i] = e[r_j\theta_j]$ holds.

Now, we explain the non-deterministic behaviors using Example 1, again.

Example 4 Consider the following two rules r_1 and r_2 and state s.

$$r_1: \quad CW(x), talk(x,y), dialtone(z) \stackrel{dial(z,x)}{\rightarrow} CW(x), CWcalling(z,x), talk(x,y)$$
$$r_2: \quad CFV(y,z), idle(z), dialtone(x) \stackrel{dial(x,y)}{\rightarrow} CFV(y,z), calling(x,z)$$
$$s = \quad CW(A), CFV(A,D), talk(A,B), dialtone(C), idle(D)$$

Rule r_1 implies a CW feature such that "a CW user x can receive an additional call from a third party z while x is talking with y". And rule r_2 implies a CFV feature such that "If a CFV user y set the forwarding address to z, the call to y is forwarded to z". State s means that user A has both CW feature and CFV feature with forwarding to D, A is talking with B, C receives a dialtone, and D is idle.

Now, we suppose that s is reachable. It is clear that r_1 is applicable to state s for $\theta_1 = \{x|A, y|B, z|C\}$, and that $e[r_1\theta_1] = dial(C, A)$. Simultaneously, r_2 is also applicable to s for $\theta_2 = \{x|C, y|A, z|D\}$, and $e[r_2\theta_2] = dial(C, A)$. Thus, $e[r_1\theta_1] = e[r_2\theta_2]$, and Condition $P2$ holds. So, s causes the non-deterministic behavior. This is exactly the one explained in Example 1.

4 Previous Analysis Method

The goal of the analysis discussed in this paper is to check if there exist such states that satisfy both conditions P1 and P2 in Definition 3 for the given service specification $\mathcal{S}$. Here, let U, S_{p_1} and S_{p_2} denote a set of all global states, a set of states satisfying Condition P1 and a set of states satisfying Condition P2, respectively. The goal of the analysis is to determine the intersection of S_{p_1} and S_{p_2}.

The straight-forward and conventional analysis method[5] is based on the state enumeration, and consists of the following two phases.

Phase 1: Enumerate all reachable states from s_0 by exhaustive applications of rules.

Phase 2: Check Condition P2 for each reachable state obtained in Phase 1.

Figure 1 shows a schematic representation of the conventional approach. At first, Phase 1 identifies S_{p_1} (i.e., a set of reachable state) and then Phase 2 extracts $S_{p_1} \cap S_{p_2}$ by applying Condition P2 to each state in S_{p_1}.

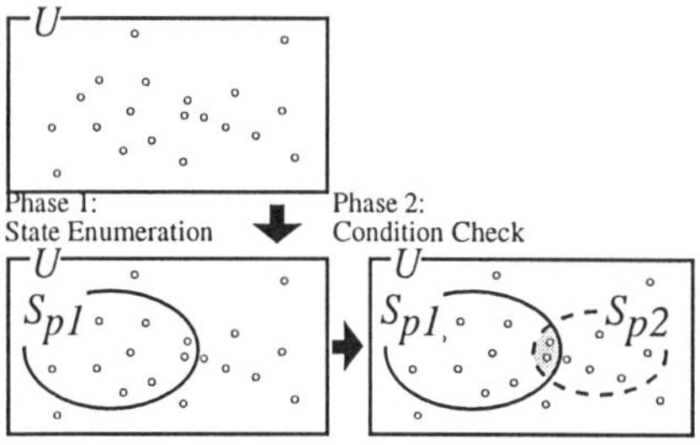

Figure 1: Concept of conventional method

Let us briefly estimate the time complexity of this approach. In the following, m and n denote the number of rules and the number of users in the service specification, respectively.
Cost of Phase1 (C_1): This depends on the number of the reachable states. As an instance, consider the service specification of the simplified POTS in Example 3. If the number of users who take part in the service is four, then the number of reachable states is 345. In the cases of 5, 6 and 7 users, the number of reachable states exponentially grows to 2043, 13029 and 88119, respectively. From this observation, it is natural to estimate C_1 to be exponential order of n.
Cost of Phase2 (C_2): To check whether a state s satisfies Condition P2 or not, we have to apply each pair of rules with the same event symbol to the state s. The number of those pairs is bounded by $m(m-1)/2$. So, C_2 is estimated as $m(m-1)/2 * C_1 \approx m^2 * C_1$.
Total Cost: Since C_1 is exponential order of n, the total cost is also exponential of n. Thus, the previous method needs a lot of time and cost (especially if we apply it to the services in which many users take part).

In this paper, we propose an alternative analysis method using a high level Petri-Net. Next section presents a kind of high level Petri-Net model onto which the service specification is mapped.

5 New Petri-Net Model

5.1 Labeled Pr/T Net

In this section, we define a kind of Petri-Net which is an extension of *predicate transition nets(Pr/T Nets)*[8].

Definition 4 A labeled Pr/T net $\mathcal{N}$ is defined by $\mathcal{N} = \langle P, T, F, H, U, V, E, L_a, L_t, M_0 \rangle$, where

(1) P is a set of *places*.
(2) T is a set of *transitions*, and $P \cap T = \phi$.
(3) $F \subseteq (P \times T) \cup (T \times P)$ is *flow relation*. Each element of F is called *arc*.
(4) $H \subseteq (P \times T)$ is a set of *inhibitor arcs*.
(5) U is a set of constants.
(6) V is a set of variables ranging over U.
(7) E is a set of predicates, and each element is represented by $e(x_1, ..., x_n)$, $x_i \in V$.

(8) L_a is the *arc labeling function* which attaches a label $\langle x_1, ..., x_k \rangle$, where each $x_i \in V$, to the arc or the inhibitor arc, and k is called arity of the arc. For any input/output arc of each place $p \in P$, its arity k is a unique constant associated with p.

(9) L_t is the *transition labeling function* which attaches the element of E to each transition.

(10) M_0 is an initial marking (Marking will be defined in Definition 5).

$In(t) = \{p | (p,t) \in H \cup (F \cap (P \times T))\}$ and $Out(t) = \{p | (t,p) \in F \cap (T \times P)\}$ are called *input places* and *output places* of transition t, respectively.

Remark 1 The differences between our labeled Pr/T net and Pr/T net are that (1) our model includes the inhibitor arcs to represent the negation of predicates(see Definition 1) and (2) the label is attached to each transition.

Definition 5 *Color set of place* p, denoted by $C(p)$, is the set of all constant k-tuples $\langle a_1, ..., a_k \rangle$, where each $a_i \in U$ and k is the arity of p. Each element of $C(p)$ is called *colored token*(or simply token) and it can be allocated to a place p. The allocation of the tokens to each place $p \in P$ is called *marking* and it is defined as a mapping function from P to the multiset over $C(p)$. A marking M can be also expressed in terms of a vector: $M = (M(p_1), ..., M(p_m))$.

Let $Q(t)$ be a set of variables that occur at the incident arcs of t and at the predicate on t. Let $x_1, ..., x_l$ be an arbitrary (but fixed) sequence of all variables in $Q(t)$. Then, *color set of transition* t, denoted by $C(t)$, is the set of all constant l-tuples $\langle a_1, ..., a_l \rangle$ obtained by substituting each x_i in the sequence by a constant in U. Thus, each color $c = \langle a_1, ..., a_l \rangle \in C(t)$ can be interpreted as a substitution such that $\{x_1 | a_1, ..., x_l | a_l\}$. We represent this substitution by $\theta(c)$.

Definition 6 Consider $t \in T$, $c \in C(t)$, and a marking M. For $L_a(p,t)$, define $L_a(p,t)\theta(c)$ be a constant tuple obtained by substituting the variables in $L_a(p,t)$ according to $\theta(c)$. Then, t is *enabled* for $\theta(c)$ under M iff

$$\forall p \in In(t) \quad \begin{array}{ll} \{L_a(p,t)\theta(c)\} \subseteq M(p) & \cdots \textbf{ if}(p,t) \in F \\ \{L_a(p,t)\theta(c)\} \not\subseteq M(p) & \cdots \textbf{ if}(p,t) \in H \end{array}$$

If $t \in T$ is enabled for $\theta(c)$ under M, then t can fire. Firing of t changes the current marking M into the *next marking* M' as follows:

$$M'(p) = \begin{cases} M(p) \\ \quad \cdots \textbf{ if } p \notin In(t) \cup Out(t) \\ M(p) -_{ms} \{L_a(p,t)\theta(c)\} \\ \quad \cdots \textbf{ if } p \in In(t) - Out(t) \\ M(p) \cup_{ms} \{L_a(t,p)\theta(c)\} \\ \quad \cdots \textbf{ if } p \in Out(t) - In(t) \\ M(p) -_{ms} \{L_a(p,t)\theta(c)\} \cup_{ms} \{L_a(t,p)\theta(c)\} \\ \quad \cdots \textbf{ if } p \in In(t) \cap Out(t) \end{cases}$$

where $\cup_{ms}$ and $-_{ms}$ are the union and difference operations defined on multisets[8].

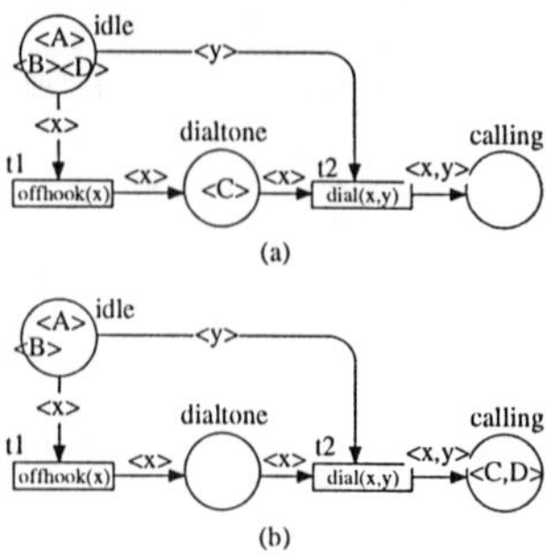

Figure 2: An explanation of firing

A marking M is called *reachable* from M_0 iff $M = M_0$ or there exists at least one sequence of marking $M_0, M_1, ..., M_n = M$ such that M_{i+1} is a next marking of M_i.

Example 5 We explain the firing of transitions using Figure 2. Consider the marking M in Figure 2(a), which is also specified by

$$M = \begin{array}{ccc} \textit{idle} & \textit{dialtone} & \textit{calling} \\ (\{\langle A \rangle, \langle B \rangle, \langle D \rangle\}, & \{\langle C \rangle\}, & \phi \ ). \end{array}$$

For example, take transition t_2 and $\theta\langle C, D \rangle = \{x|C, y|D\}$. Then $In(t_2) = \{dialtone, idle\}$, and $\{L_a(dialtone, t_2)\theta\langle C, D \rangle\} = \{\langle C \rangle\} = M(dialtone)$ and $\{L_a(idle, t_2)\theta\langle C, D \rangle\} = \{\langle D \rangle\} \subseteq M(idle)$. Thus, t_2 is enabled for $\theta\langle C, D \rangle$ under M.

Now, suppose that t_2 fires for $\theta\langle C, D \rangle$ under M. Then, tokens $\langle C \rangle$ and $\langle D \rangle$ are respectively removed from places *dialtone* and *idle*, since $\{dialtone, idle\} = In(t_2) - Out(t_2)$, $L_a(dialtone, t_2)\theta\langle C, D \rangle = \langle C \rangle$ and $L_a(idle, t_2)\theta\langle C, D \rangle = \langle D \rangle$. Moreover, a new token $\langle C, D \rangle$ is allocated to place *calling*, because $\{calling\} = Out(t_2) - In(t_2)$ and $L_a(t_2, calling)\theta\langle C, D \rangle = \langle C, D \rangle$. As the result, M is transformed into the following next marking M', which is also shown in Figure 2(b).

$$M' = \begin{array}{ccc} \textit{idle} & \textit{dialtone} & \textit{calling} \\ (\{\langle A \rangle, \langle B \rangle\}, & \phi, & \{\langle C, D \rangle\} \ ) \end{array}$$

5.2 Service Specification Net

Here, we define the particular labeled Pr/T net for a service specification $\mathcal{S}$.

Definition 7 Let $\mathcal{S} = \langle R, s_0 \rangle$ be a service specification. Then, a *service specification net* $\mathcal{N}(\mathcal{S}) = \langle P, T, F, H, U, V, E, L_a, L_t, M_0 \rangle$ for a given service specification $\mathcal{S}$ is a labeled Pr/T net which satisfies the following conditions.

(1) E is a set of all events in rules of $\mathcal{S}$.

(2) P is a set of all predicate symbols in rules of $\mathcal{S}$.

(3) U is a set of all service users in s_0.

(4) V is a set of all variables in rules of $\mathcal{S}$.

(5) For each rule $r_i \in R$, there is exactly one transition $t_i \in T$ such that $L_t(t_i) = e[r_i]$.

(6) For each predicate $p_{ij}(x_{i1}, ..., x_{im})$ in pre-condition of rule $r_i \in R$, exactly one arc with a label $\langle x_{i1}, ..., x_{im} \rangle$ exists from place p_{ij} to transition t_i.

(7) For each predicate $\neg p_{ij}(x_{i1}, ..., x_{im})$ in pre-condition of rule $r_i \in R$, exactly one inhibitor arc with a label $\langle x_{i1}, ..., x_{im} \rangle$ exists from place p_{ij} to transition t_i.

(8) For each predicate $p_{ij}(x_{i1}, ..., x_{im})$ in post-condition of rule $r_i \in R$, exactly one arc with a label $\langle x_{i1}, ..., x_{im} \rangle$ exists from transition t_i to place p_{ij}.

(9) If the initial state s_0 includes $p(c_1, ..., c_m)$, then the initial marking $M_0(p) = \langle c_1, ..., c_m \rangle$.

According to Definition 7, we can easily understand that (1) the pre(post)-condition of a rule corresponds to the input(output) places of a transition, (2) the event of a rule corresponds to the predicate attached to a transition, (3) the initial state corresponds to the initial marking.

Remark 2 A state s of $\mathcal{S}$ uniquely corresponds to a marking M on $\mathcal{N}(\mathcal{S})$. That is, if a predicate $p(a_1, ..., a_n)$ holds(that is, takes the true value) on state s, then place p has a token $\langle a_1, ..., a_n \rangle$ under M. Suppose that states s and s' correspond to markings M and M', respectively, and that rule r_i corresponds to transition t_i. Then, a state transition from s to s' by rule r_i exactly corresponds to a firing of transition t_i which transforms M into M'.

Example 6 Consider again Example 5. Then a labeled Pr/T net shown in Figure 2(a) is a service specification net for the service specification consisting of the following two rules.

$$r_1: \quad idle(x) \overset{offhook(x)}{\longrightarrow} dialtone(x)$$
$$r_2: \quad dialtone(x), idle(y) \overset{dial(x,y)}{\longrightarrow} calling(x,y)$$

Next, consider the following two states:

$$s = idle(A), idle(B), dialtone(C), idle(D)$$
$$s' = idle(A), idle(B), calling(C,D)$$

Then markings M and M' in Example 5 respectively represent these two states s and s'. The state transition from s to s' by rule r_2 is already explained in Example 2. For this state transition, we can correspond it to a firing of t_2 for $\theta\langle C, D\rangle = \{x|C, y|D\}$ which transforms M into M'.

The following lemma implies that $\mathcal{N}(\mathcal{S})$ is logically equivalent to $\mathcal{S}$ with respect to reachability analysis.

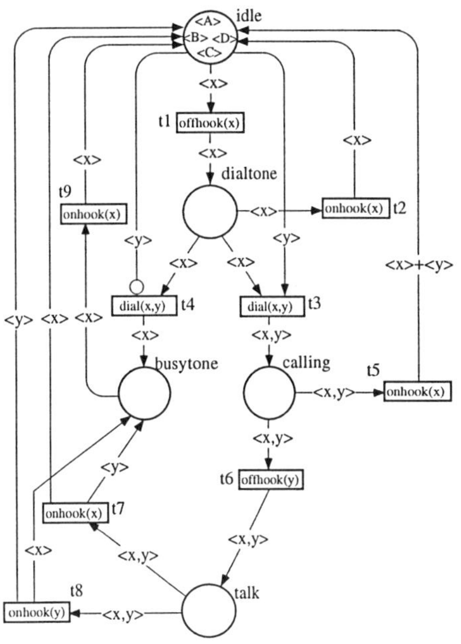

Figure 3: Service specification net for POTS

Lemma 1 *For a given service specification $\mathcal{S}$ and a service specification net $N(\mathcal{S})$ for $\mathcal{S}$, there exists one-to-one correspondence between a set of reachable markings of $\mathcal{N}(\mathcal{S})$ and a set of reachable states of $\mathcal{S}$.*

Example 7 Figure 3 shows a service specification net obtained from the service specification of POTS in Example 3. We can completely simulate the behavior of service specification on this net model.

6 Proposed Analysis Method

6.1 Outline of Our Method

An outline of the proposed analysis method is shown in Figure 4. At first, we calculate a set S_{p_2} of states which satisfy Condition $P2$(Phase 1) and then check reachability of each state in S_{p_2}(Phase 2 and Phase 3).

The set S_{p_2} can be easily calculated using the rules of service specification. Intuitively, a state in S_{p_2} can be generated by joining pre-conditions of two rules which have the same event symbol. Therefore, the essential problem to realize this new approach is how nicely we check the reachability of states in S_{p_2}. On performing this checking, we utilize extensively *P-invariant* of the service specification net.

6.2 P-Invariant

Definition 8 [6] Let $\mathcal{N}(\mathcal{S})$ be a service specification net with u places and v transitions, and let $p \in P$, $t \in T$ with $(p,t) \notin H$. Then, $W(p,t)$ (or $W(t,p)$) is a linear function $[C(t) \rightarrow C(p)]$ such that $\forall c = \langle a_1, ..., a_l \rangle \in C(t)$, $W(p,t)(c) = L_a(p,t)\theta(c)$ (or,

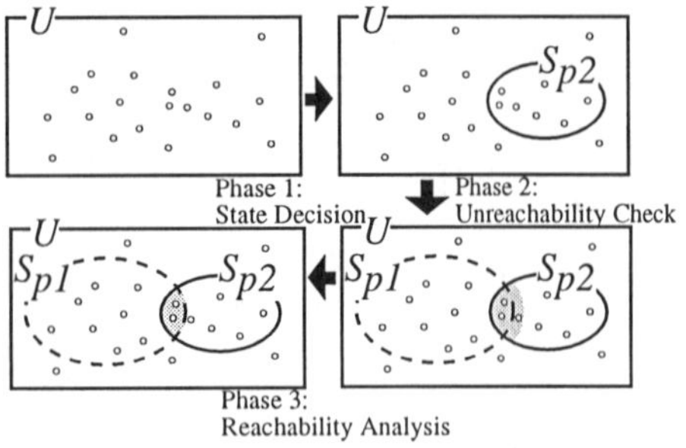

Figure 4: Outline of our method

$W(t,p)(c) = L_a(t,p)\theta(c)$, respectively). In our discussion, we consider only four kinds of linear functions defined as follows: (1) identity function id, (2) zero function o, (3) projection functions p_1 and p_2 such that $p_1\langle\alpha,\beta\rangle = \langle\alpha\rangle$, $p_2\langle\alpha,\beta\rangle = \langle\beta\rangle$.

Then the *incident matrix* A of $\mathcal{N}(\mathcal{S})$ is the $u \times v$ matrix defined as follows.

$$A[p,t] = W(t,p) - W(p,t)$$

Then u-dimensional vector Y such that $Y * A = \mathbf{0}$ is called *P-invariant* of $\mathcal{N}(\mathcal{S})$, where $*$ is a formal product operation of matrix[6, 8].

Example 8 Consider the service specification net shown in Figure 3. Then the incident matrix A of this net is

	t_1	t_2	t_3	t_4	t_5	t_6	t_7	t_8	t_9
idl	$-id$	id	$-p_2$	o	p_1+p_2	o	p_1	p_2	id
dil	id	$-id$	$-p_1$	$-p_1$	o	o	o	o	o
clg	o	o	id	o	$-id$	$-id$	o	o	o
bst	o	o	o	p_1	o	o	p_2	p_1	$-id$
tlk	o	o	o	o	o	id	$-id$	$-id$	o

The following vector Y is a P-invariant of $\mathcal{N}(\mathcal{S})$ since a relation $Y * A = \mathbf{0}$ holds.

$$Y = \begin{pmatrix} \overset{idle}{id} & \overset{dialtone}{id} & \overset{calling}{p_1+p_2} & \overset{busytone}{id} & \overset{talk}{p_1+p_2} \end{pmatrix}$$

We can apply the procedure for the calculation of the P-invariant[1, 6]. The following theorem for the P-invariant is a well-known theorem to be used for checking reachability.

Theorem 1 *Let Y be the P-invariant of the service specification net $\mathcal{N}(\mathcal{S})$. If marking M is reachable from the initial marking M_0, then $Y * M^t = Y * M_0^t$.*

Remark 3 The equation $Y * M^t = Y * M_0^t$ is only a necessary condition for any reachable marking M. Hence, even if $Y * M^t = Y * M_0^t$ holds, we cannot conclude, in general, that M is reachable.

6.3 Analysis Algorithm Ω

This subsection shows the analysis method of nondeterminism. The input of the algorithm is a service specification $\mathcal{S} = \langle R, s_0\rangle$. Figure 5 shows the proposed algorithm Ω. In the following, we briefly explain Ω.

In Phase 0, we first construct the service specification net $\mathcal{N}(\mathcal{S})$, and then calculate P-invariant Y of $\mathcal{N}(\mathcal{S})$ by applying the available method proposed in [1, 6]. MS_{p_2} is a set of markings each of which corresponds to a state in S_{p_2}(defined in Section 4).

Next, Phase 1 determines a set of states S_{p_2} satisfying Condition P2. At first, we construct a condition C to which two rules r_i and r_j are simultaneously applicable(Step1-3). Then, we make a marking corresponding to C and extend it to all marking which covers C by wild-cards(they represents an arbitrary multisets of tokens)(Step4).

Next, in Phase 2 we check for each marking $M \in MS_{p_2}$, if M is not reachable from M_0 by solving the equation $Y * M^t = Y * M_0^t$. According to Theorem 1, if the equation is not solvable (i.e., there is no assignment of U to wild-cards which satisfy $Y * M^t = Y * M_0^t$), then M is not reachable. Hence, we delete M from MS_{p_2}. If the equation is solvable, then we do not derive any decision on the reachability of M, thus we leave M in MS_{p_2}.

Finally in Phase 3 we must apply conventional reachability analysis method to the resultant MSp_2 (i.e., the size of MS_{p_2} may be reduced using P-invariant in Phase 2). To be explained in Example 9 and in subsection 6.4, the cost needed in Phase 3 depends on the size of the resultant MS_{p_2} in Phase 2.

Example 9 We apply the algorithm Ω to the POTS specification in Example 4.

Phase 0(Preliminary): We obtain $\mathcal{N}(\mathcal{S})$ shown in Figure 3. Then we calculate the following P-invariant:

$$Y = \begin{pmatrix} \overset{idle}{id} & \overset{dialtone}{id} & \overset{calling}{p_1+p_2} & \overset{busytone}{id} & \overset{talk}{p_1+p_2} \end{pmatrix}$$

Phase 1(Decision of States in S_{p_2}):
Step1: We select the following rules with the same event symbol $offhook$:

$$r_1: \ idle(x) \overset{offhook(x)}{\rightarrow} dialtone(x)$$

$$r_6: \ calling(x,y) \overset{offhook(y)}{\rightarrow} talk(x,y)$$

Step2: We can apply $\theta_1 = \{x|A\}$ and $\theta_6 = \{y|A\}$ to r_1 and r_6, respectively, since $e[r_1\theta_1] = e[r_6\theta_6] = offhook(A)$. Then we get the following instances of rules r_1 and r_6:

$$r_1\theta_1: \ idle(A) \overset{offhook(A)}{\rightarrow} dialtone(A)$$

$$r_6\theta_6: \ calling(x,A) \overset{offhook(A)}{\rightarrow} talk(x,A)$$

Step3: By combining pre-conditions of $r_1\theta_1$ and $r_6\theta_6$, we get the following condition C:

$$C = idle(A), calling(x,A)$$

Analysis algorithm Ω:

Phase 0(Preliminary): Construct the service specification net $\mathcal{N}(\mathcal{S})$ for a given service specification $\mathcal{S} = \langle R, s_0 \rangle$. Then calculate P-invariant Y of $\mathcal{N}(\mathcal{S})$. Define a set MS_{p_2} to be a set of markings, each of which corresponds to a state in S_{p_2}, and make the initial value of MS_{p_2} to be empty.

Phase 1(Decision of States in S_{p_2}):

Step1: Select two rules r_i and r_j from R whose event symbols are identical.

Step2: Apply a pair of substitutions θ_i and θ_j such that $e[r_i\theta_i] = e[r_j\theta_j]$ to r_i and r_j, respectively.

Step3: By combining two pre-conditions of $r_i\theta_i$ and $r_j\theta_j$, using AND operation, obtain a condition(say it condition C). If C forms null condition, we conclude that r_i and r_j are mutual exclusive with each other, and go to Step 5. Otherwise, go to Step 4.

Step4: At first, put tokens to places based on predicates in C. Then, to each place $p \in P$, put the *wild-card of tokens* $\Sigma\langle x_{p_1}, ..., x_{p_k}\rangle$, where x_{p_i} is a variable and k is arity of p. Construct a marking M_c which corresponds to the resulting net, and put M_c into MS_{p_2}.

Step5: If some pairs of rules to be checked still remain, then go to Step1.

Phase 2(Check of Unreachability using P-invariant): Check if for each marking $M \in MS_{p_2}$ is reachable by solving the equation $Y * M^t = Y * M_0^t$. If the equation is not solvable, then we conclude that state s corresponding to M is not reachable, and delete M from MS_{p_2}.

Phase 3(Reachability Analysis for Resultant MS_{p_2}): Apply so-called reachability analysis method to the resultant MS_{p_2} finally obtained in Phase 2.

Figure 5: Analysis algorithm Ω

Step4: At first, we obtain a marking M according to C as follows:

$$\begin{array}{rccccc} & \textit{idle} & \textit{dialtone} & \textit{calling} & \textit{busytone} & \textit{talk} \\ M = & (\{\langle A\rangle\}, & \phi, & \{\langle x, A\rangle\}, & \phi, & \phi) \end{array}$$

Next, we put five wild-cards to places, and finally get the following marking M_c:

$$\begin{array}{rccc} & \textit{idle} & \textit{dialtone} & \textit{calling} \\ M_c = & (\{\langle A\rangle, \Sigma\langle x_1\rangle\}, & \{\Sigma\langle x_2\rangle\}, & \{\langle x, A\rangle, \Sigma\langle x_3, x_4\rangle\}, \\ & \textit{busytone} & \textit{talk} & \\ & \{\Sigma\langle x_5\rangle\}, & \{\Sigma\langle x_6, x_7\rangle\}) & \end{array}$$

In this example, we can get ten other markings in Phase 1, thus get $|MS_{p_2}| = 11$.

Phase 2(Check of Unreachability using P-invariant): Consider marking M as an example. Then we get[1]

$$\begin{aligned} Y * M_0^t &= id(\{\langle A\rangle, \langle B\rangle, \langle C\rangle, \langle D\rangle\}) + id(\phi) + \\ &\quad (p_1 + p_2)(\phi) + id(\phi) + (p_1 + p_2)(\phi) \\ &= \{\langle A\rangle, \langle B\rangle, \langle C\rangle, \langle D\rangle\}, \\ Y * M^t &= id(\{\langle A\rangle, \Sigma\langle x_1\rangle\}) + id(\{\Sigma\langle x_2\rangle\}) + (p_1 + p_2) \\ &\quad (\{\langle x, A\rangle, \Sigma\langle x_3, x_4\rangle\}) + \\ &\quad id(\{\Sigma\langle x_5\rangle\}) + (p_1 + p_2)(\{\Sigma\langle x_6, x_7\rangle\}) \\ &= \{2\langle A\rangle, \langle x\rangle, \Sigma\langle x_1\rangle, \Sigma\langle x_2\rangle, \Sigma\langle x_3\rangle, \Sigma\langle x_4\rangle, \\ &\quad \Sigma\langle x_5\rangle, \Sigma\langle x_6\rangle, \Sigma\langle x_7\rangle\} \end{aligned}$$

For this, no matter how we nicely choose assignment of constant such as $\langle A\rangle, \langle B\rangle, \langle C\rangle, \langle D\rangle$ to $\langle x\rangle$ and $\Sigma\langle x_i\rangle$'s, the equation $Y * M^t = Y * M_0^t$ never holds(i.e., this equation is unsolvable). Therefore, we can conclude that M is not reachable.

Similarly, we check the reachability for other ten markings in MS_{p_2}. As the result, all markings in MS_{p_2} are deleted and finally MS_{p_2} becomes an empty set in Phase 2. Therefore, in this example, Phase 3 is not executed. (We can guarantee that the service specification of POTS is free from non-deterministic behavior without any state enumeration in Phase 3.)

6.4 Properties of Our Method

Here, we discuss the corectness, the cost and the advantages of the proposed method.

Theorem 2 *For any state s, if s causes a non-deterministic behavior, then a marking M corresponding to s exists in MS_{p_2}.*

As shown in the algorithm Ω, we must apply Phase 3 (that is, conventional reachability analysis method) to the resultant set MS_{p_2}. Thus, from Theorem 2 it is clear that algorithm Ω (Phase 0,1,2 and 3) identifies $S_{p_1} \cap S_{p_2}$.

Next, let us briefly estimate the cost of the algorithm Ω. In the following, m and n denote the number of rules and the number of users, respectively.

[1] In [6], the definition of linear functions is extended for the multi-set. For any linear function f, we define $f(\{\langle \alpha_1, \beta_1\rangle, ..., \langle \alpha_k, \beta_k\rangle\}) = \{f\langle \alpha_1, \beta_1\rangle, ..., f\langle \alpha_k, \beta_k\rangle\}$.

Cost of Phase0(C_0): The cost of transformation of a given service specification into the net model is obviously order m. The calculation of P-invariant depends only on net structure and it needs the time of exponential order of m(thus, the cost doesn't depend on n). So, $C_0 = m + c^m \approx c^m$.

Cost of Phase1(C_1): This depends on the number of the states satisfying Condition P2 and the total number is normally exponential order of n. However, by utilizing the wild-card, the execution of Step1 through Step 5(i.e., the number of loops) in Phase 1 is bounded by the number of rule's pairs with the same event symbol. So, C_1 is approximately estimated as $m * (m-1)/2 \approx m^2$.

Cost of Phase2(C_2): To check if a marking M is reachable or not, we have to evaluate $Y * M^t$ and $Y * M_0^t$. The number of total multiplications needed for these evaluations is equal to the dimension of P-invariant, i.e., the number of predicate symbols in all rules. This is generally bounded by polynomial order of m. Finally, this checking must be repeated for all M's in MS_{p_2}, thus $C_2 = m^c * C_1 = m^c * m^2 \approx m^c$.

Cost of Phase 3(C_3): C_3 deeply depends on the size of resultant MS_{p_2}, and it is generally exponential order of n. Since MS_{p_2} seems to depend on the service specification, C_3 cannot be evaluated reasonably without experimental application to many practical services(Surely if $MS_{p_2} = \phi$ then $C_3 = 0$ as shown in Example 9).

Finally, the major advantages of our method are summarized as follows:

(a) By changing orders of phases in the conventional method, we can put the application of reachability analysis at the last phase of the algorithm Ω(rather than at the first phase in the conventional method). As the result, we may reduce the number of states drastically, for which the reachability analysis should be applied.

(b) By utilizing P-invariant for the reachability checking, we can execute state reduction very efficiently without any state enumeration.

(c) Especially for a case that a given service specification doesn't include any non-determinism, we can very quickly convince it (at the end of Phase 2). The cost in this case is c^m and thus it does not depend on the number of users.

7 Concluding Remarks

In this paper, we have proposed a new analysis method based on a Petri-net for checking non-determinism in a given service specification. The proposed method consists of four phases: construction of the service specification net(Phase 0), decision of non-determinism(Phase 1), checking of unreachability(Phase 2) and reachability analysis(Phase 3). The most attractive point of our method is that the reduction of the cost in Phase 3 is realized efficiently using P-invariant in Phase 2.

As mentioned in Section 6, in order to show the usefulness of our method, we must execute the experimental evaluations using practical service specifications. Currently we are planning to apply the algorithm Ω to practical services[11, 12], and are developing a computer aided tool for the experiments.

Acknowledgement

This reasearch was partly supported by Kokusai Denshin Denwa Co.,Ltd. (KDD). The authors would like to thank Prof. T.Ohta (Souka University), Mr. Y.Ueda (OKI Electric Industry Co., Ltd.), Mr. Y.Wakahara(KDD), and research staffs in KDD R&D Laboratories for their helpful discussion.

References

[1] Alla, H., Ladet, P., Martinez and J., Silva-Suarez, M., "Modelling and validation of complex systems by coloured Petri-nets: Application to a flexible manufacturing system," *Lecture Notes in Computer Science*, Vol 188, Springer-Verlag, pp.215-233, 1985.

[2] Cameron, E.J. and Velthuijsen, H., "Feature interactions in telecommunications systems," *IEEE Communication Magazine*, Vol.31, No.8, pp.18-23, 1993.

[3] Cameron, E.J., Griffeth, N.D., Lin, Y-J., Nilson, M.E., Schnure W.K. and Velthuijsen, H., "A feature interaction benchmark for IN and Beyond," *Proc. of Second Workshop on Feature Interactions in Telecommunications Systems*, pp.1-23, 1994.

[4] Gammelgaard, A. and Kristensen E.J., "Interaction detection, a logical approach," *Proc. of Second Workshop on Feature Interactions in Telecommunications Systems*, pp.178-196, 1994.

[5] Harada, Y., Hirakawa, Y., Takenaka, T. and Terashima, N., "A conflict detection support method for telecommunication service descriptions," *IEICE Trans. Commun.*, Vol. E75-B, No.10, Oct, 1992.

[6] Jensen, K., "Coloured Petri Nets," *EATCS Monographs on Theoritical Computer Science*, Vol1-2, Springer Verlag, 1992.

[7] Hirakawa, Y. and Takenaka, T., "Telecommunication service description using state transition rules," *Proc. of IEEE Int'l Workshop on Software Specification and Design*, pp.140-147, Oct. 1991.

[8] Murata, T. and Zhang, D., "A predicate-transition net model for parallel interpretation of logic programs," *IEEE Trans. on Software Engineering*, Vol.14, No.4, pp.481-497, Apr. 1988.

[9] Ohta, T. and Harada Y., "Classification, detection and resolution of service interactions in telecommunication services," *Proc. of Second Workshop on Feature Interactions in Telecommunications Systems*, pp.60-72, 1994.

[10] Wakahara, Y., Fujioka, M., Kikuta, H., Yagi, H. and Sakai, S., "A method for detecting service interactions," *IEEE Communication Magazine*, Vol.31, No.8, pp.32-37, 1993.

[11] ITU-T Recommendations Q.1200 Series., "Intelligent Network Capability Set 1 (CS1)", Sept. 1990.

[12] Bellcore, "LSSGR Features Common to Residence and Buisiness Customers I, II, III," Issue 2, July 1987.

On Dynamically Establishing and Terminating Isochronous Message Streams in WDMA-based Local Area Lightwave Networks

Bin Wang, Chao-Ju Hou, and Ching-Chih Han

Department of Electrical Engineering
The Ohio State University
Columbus, OH 43210-1272
{bwang,jhou,cchan}@ee.eng.ohio-state.edu

Abstract

Complement to our prior work in [10], we address in this paper the problem of dynamically *establishing/terminating real-time message streams in response to call setup/clear requests in single-hop star-coupled WDMA-based optical networks. We consider a network architecture in which N stations are connected to a star coupler with W data channels ($W \leq N$) and one control channel. Each of the W data channels is slotted and shared by the N stations by means of time division multiplexing. The control channel is used for stations to coordinate the call establishment and termination operations. We propose a distributed, dynamic slot allocation scheme to allocate/de-allocate, in response to call setup/clear requests, time slots on the W data channels to message streams, with the objective of meeting message deadlines. We formally prove the properties, and the correctness of, the proposed dynamic slot allocation scheme.*

1 Introduction

Optical networks have been proposed to meet the demand of emerging applications using wavelength division multiple access(WDMA) technique. In a WDMA-based optical network, different channels correspond to different optical wavelengths which can be multiplexed onto a single fiber. Several physical network topologies have been proposed, among which the passive star topology using a broadcast-and-select star coupler has been most commonly used [1, 6]. In the passive star topology, inputs from all stations are combined in a star coupler and the mixed optical information is broadcast to all stations. Each station is equipped with tunable and/or fixed-tuned transmitter(s) and receiver(s). The transmitter of a source station, or the receiver of a destination station, or both must be appropriately tuned for data transmission/reception.

Many channel access schemes have been proposed, and can be classified into two categories [8]: in the multi-hop approach, fixed wavelength(s) are preassigned to each station and each station uses fixed wavelength transmitters and receivers. Usually, there is no full physical connectivity between stations, and packets traveling between stations must make several hops through intermediate station(s) before reaching their destination. Virtual network topologies, e.g., a perfect shuffle or a de Bruijn graph, can be imposed on the physically connected stations to provide several advantages, including simple routing and predictable mean and maximum path length. In the single-hop approach, any pair of stations is established direct communications over a channel by employing tunable transmitter(s) and/or receiver(s). Both the transmitter of the source station and the receiver of the destination station must be tuned to the same wavelength for the transmission duration. Efficient dynamic channel access is then necessary to maximize the network throughput, minimize the packet delay, or overlap transmitter/receiver tuning with transmission to hide long transceiver tuning time. A number of media access control protocols have been proposed for single hop WDMA-based optical networks [1, 6, 9], all of which can be broadly divided into *reservation based* and *preallocation based* schemes, depending on the methods used to arbitrate the demand for network resources [1].

All (perhaps except [12, 10]) the aforementioned research focuses on minimizing the average delay, reducing the call blocking probability, increasing the user accessible bandwidth, or increasing the network throughput. What is not addressed is the issue on supporting time-constrained communications for messages with delivery deadlines for embedded real-time systems or for interactive distributed services(audio/video and multimedia applications). Yan *et al.* [12] considered the problem and proposed, with the use of tokens, a reservation based protocol for single-hop lightwave networks with one control channel and multiple data channels. However, their scheme can not provide deterministic guarantees, and is mainly targeted for *soft* real-time applications.

We proposed a preallocation based scheme in [10] to statically provide deterministic timing guarantees in single-hop star-coupled networks in which data transmission operates in a time slotted mode. In this paper, we complement our work in [10] and consider the problem of *dynamically* allocating/de-allocating slots on time-slotted data channels to establish/terminate real-time message streams in response to call setup/clear requests. We consider a network architecture in which N stations are connected to a star coupler with W data channels and one control channel. Each data channel

The work reported in this paper was supported in part by NSF under Grant NCR-9625064 and by DARPA under Contract DABT63-95-C-0117.

0-8186-7780-5/97 $10.00 © 1997 IEEE

is slotted and shared by up to N stations by means of time division multiplexing (TDM). The control channel is used for stations to coordinate the call establishment and termination operations and to keep a consistent view of the channel status. The slots on each data channel are *dynamically allocated* as the call setup/clear requests arrive during system operation. We first characterize each message stream M_i with two parameters: the relative message deadline D_i and the maximum (total) message size C_i that can arrive within any time interval of length D_i. Second, to facilitate slot assignment, we decompose each message stream into a set of message sub-streams, and group the slots on each data channel into sub-channels. Then, we propose a dynamic slot allocation scheme which consists of channel establishment and termination procedures. In response to a call setup request, the channel setup procedures allocate one or more empty sub-channels available over the W data channels to a message stream, subject to the *source/destination* constraints and that the timing guarantees to existing message streams should not be violated. For a call clear request, the termination procedures release the slots (sub-channels) allocated to the terminated message stream, and merge, if appropriate, empty sub-channels to facilitate future message stream establishment. We formally prove the properties, and the correctness of, the proposed dynamic slot allocation scheme.

The rest of the paper is organized as follows. In Section 2, we briefly discuss the network architecture and the message model used to characterize message streams with timing requirements. We also define the slot assignment problem there. In Section 3, we lay a formal basis for the proposed dynamic slot allocation scheme, and discuss several component operations needed in the proposed scheme. We present the proposed *dynamic* slot allocation scheme in Section 4. In Section 5, we prove several properties of the proposed dynamic slot allocation scheme and establish the correctness of the proposed scheme. This paper concludes with Section 6.

2 System and Message Model

2.1 Network model

We consider a network of N stations interconnected through a passive star coupler that can support $W+1$ data channels, $\lambda_i, 0 \le i \le W$, where λ_0 is used as the control channel, and $\lambda_i, 1 \le i \le W$ are used as data channels. Optical information is broadcast to every station in the network through the star coupler. Each station is equipped with (i) a pair of tunable transmitter and tunable receiver, both of which are tunable over, $\lambda_i, 1 \le i \le W$; and (ii) a pair of fixed tuned transmitter and fixed tuned receiver, both of which are fixed tuned at λ_0. Since the transmitter/receiver tuning range that can be supported by current technology is limited and only a few wavelengths (e.g. a few tens) are available, we assume that $W \le N$, i.e., each data channel is shared possibly by up to N stations in the network.

Data transmission in the network operates in a slotted mode, i.e., every data channel is time slotted and slots are synchronized to slot boundaries. We assume that the transmitter/receiver tuning time can be incorporated into a data slot time, and each data slot time is set to the sum of transmitter/receiver tuning time plus packet transmission time. We call time interval $[t-1, t]$ on each data channel data slot t. The control channel λ_0 is also time slotted with each control slot equal to a data slot and divided into N mini-slots. Each mini-slot on the control channel is pre-assigned to a station, hence no collision will result. Upon arrival of a call setup/clear request, each station conveys the setup/clear information to other stations through the control channel. A distributed dynamic slot allocation algorithm runs concurrently on every station in the network, and is responsible for dynamically allocating/deallocating slots upon receipt of call setup/clear requests from the control channel. A setup request is honored if there are sufficient and well-spaced slots available on data channels to establish the message stream, subject to that all the existing guarantees to other isochronous streams in the network are not violated. Each station then tunes its tunable transmitter/receiver to appropriate data channels at appropriate time slots for data transmission/reception.

A (static or dynamic) schedule specifies, for each data channel, which slots are used for data transmission from station i to station j, for all $1 \le i \le N, 1 \le j \le N, j \ne i$. Since each station is equipped with one tunable transmitter and one tunable receiver for data transmission/reception, a schedule is valid if during slot t, the following two conditions hold:

C1. No multiple stations are scheduled to transmit to the same destination (possibly on different wavelength channels);

C2. No station is scheduled to transmit to multiple destinations (possibly on different wavelength channels);

Violation to **C1** is usually referred to as *destination conflict* and violation to **C2** as *source conflict.*

2.2 Message model

Let $\mathbf{M} = \{M_i \mid 1 \le i \le n\}$ be a set of n isochronous message streams in the network. Note that for each station, there may be zero, one, or more isochronous message streams emanating from it. We use a message model similar to the (r,T)-*smooth* traffic model [4] in which each message stream M_i is described by a 4-tuple (C_i, D_i, N_i^s, N_i^d):

- C_i is the maximum message size in M_i that can arrive in any time interval of length D_i.
- D_i is the *relative* transmission deadline (or simply, the deadline) for the messages in M_i, i.e., if a message of M_i arrives at time t, it must be transmitted by time $t + D_i$.
- $N_i^s \in [1, N]$ is the source station of M_i.
- $N_i^d \in [1, N]$ is the destination station of M_i.

This model is, in fact, a generalization of two commonly-used real-time traffic models: the *peak-rate* model and the *linear bounded* model [3]. The interested reader is referred to [5] for a detailed account, and a comparison of, the three message models. We assume that timing parameters are expressed in slots (cells), and message arrivals are aligned with the beginnings of slots.[1] Therefore, one unit of message (i.e., one cell) needs one unit of time (i.e., one slot) to transmit.

[1] We discussed in [5] how to calculate the *effective* message sizes and deadlines in slot times if either condition does not hold.

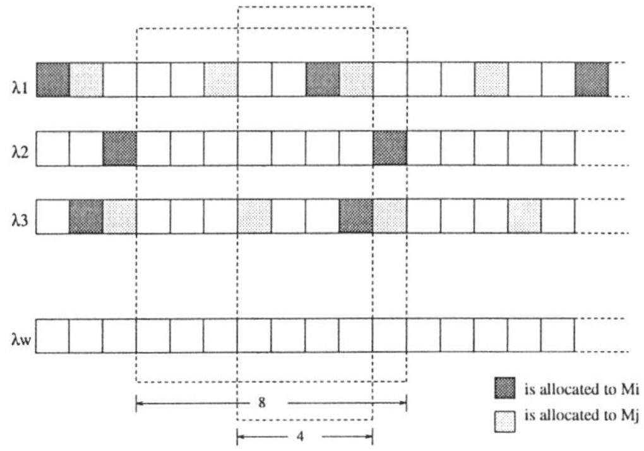

Figure 1: A valid slot schedule for two isochronous message stream $M_i = (3, 8, N_i^s, N_i^d)$ and $M_j = (2, 4, N_j^s, N_j^d)$ with $N_i^s \neq N_j^s$ and $N_i^d \neq N_j^d$ in a TT-TR system.

Message Density of Isochronous Traffic: We define the *message density* of a real-time message stream M_i as $\rho(M_i) = C_i/D_i$, and the *total message density* of a set of real-time message streams, $\mathbf{M} = \{M_i \mid 1 \le i \le n\}$, as $\rho(\mathbf{M}) = \sum_{i=1}^{n} \rho(M_i) = \sum_{i=1}^{n} \frac{C_i}{D_i}$.

2.3 Slot allocation problem

With the (C, D)-smooth message model, the notion of timing guarantee for isochronous messages can be stated as: slots available on all the data channels must be properly assigned to each isochronous message stream M_i so that every message in M_i is transmitted within a time period $\le D_i$ after its arrival as long as the maximum (total) message size in any time interval of length D_i is $\le C_i$. The problem is formally defined as follows.

Problem 1: (Slot Assignment Problem) Find a slot assignment scheme such that given a set of real-time message streams $\mathbf{M} = \{M_i = (C_i, D_i, N_i^s, N_i^d) \mid 1 \le i \le n\}$ and W data channels, the scheme allocates time slots over the W channels[2] in such a way that each message stream M_i is guaranteed to transmit each of its messages before the message deadline D_i, subject to the constraints **C1** and **C2**. □

Note that the *exact* time when a message in M_i arrives is not known *a priori* and message arrivals in different message streams do not necessarily align with one another. Hence, one way to meet the above timeliness criterion is to assign at least C_i slots to M_i for *any* time interval of length D_i subject to the constraints **C1** and **C2**. Fig. 1 depicts a valid slot schedule for two isochronous message streams $M_i = (3, 8, N_i^s, N_i^d)$ and $M_j = (2, 4, N_j^s, N_j^d)$ with $N_i^s \neq N_j^s$ and $N_i^d \neq N_j^d$.

The slot allocation problem defined above is *static* in the sense that the set of message streams is fixed and known at system initialization, and no message streams are admitted or terminated afterwards. If real-time message streams are to be dynamically set up and torn down after system initialization, the problem becomes a *dynamic* one. To solve the static slot allocation problem, we proposed a slot allocation scheme, called *binary splitting*, in [10]. In this paper, we focus on the dynamic slot allocation problem and propose a dynamic slot allocation scheme to handle call setup and teardown. In what follows, we first provide the preliminaries and present the component operations needed in the proposed dynamic scheme in Section 3, then describe the proposed scheme in Section 4.

3 Preliminaries and Component Operations

3.1 Preliminaries

We have considered a similar problem in the context of dual-bus networks [5] in which a slot allocator generates (if possible) for a message set $\mathbf{M} = \{M_i' = (C_i, D_i, N_i^s, N_i^d) \mid 1 \le i \le n\}$ a slot schedule that satisfies the criterion that for any consecutive D_i slots on *a slotted bus*, at least C_i slots are allocated to M_i, for all i. The solution scheme proposed in [5] serves as the basis for the proposed dynamic slot allocation scheme. We first consider the case in which the deadline constraint set of message set $\mathbf{M}$ consists solely of multiples, i.e., $D_i \mid D_j$ for all $i < j$. We use the *rate-monotonic* scheduling concept [7], treat C_i as the computation time and D_i as the period, and assign priorities to message streams so that the streams with tighter deadlines get higher priorities, i.e., if $D_i < D_j$ then M_i has a higher priority than M_j (ties are broken arbitrarily). We then assign C_i slots on a single bus to M_i during each time period $[(j-1) \cdot D_i, j \cdot D_i]$, for all $M_i \in \mathbf{M}$ and all $j \ge 1$. This is done by assigning the current slot, say $[t-1, t]$, to the message stream with the highest priority among all the *active* message streams, where an active stream $M_i \in \mathbf{M}$ is one to which there are less than C_i slots assigned in time interval $[(j-1) \cdot D_i, t-1]$, and $(j-1) \cdot D_i \le t-1 < j \cdot D_i$ for some integer j.

The correctness of the above slot assignment method has been established in [5] and is summarized below:

Theorem 1: For a set of isochronous message streams, $\mathbf{M} = \{M_i = (C_i, D_i, N_i^s, N_i^d) \mid 1 \le i \le n\}$, if $D_i \mid D_j$ for all $i < j$ and $\rho(\mathbf{M}) \le 1$, the above rate monotonic based slot assignment scheme will allocate C_i slots to M_i in any time window of size D_i slots, for all $M_i \in \mathbf{M}$. □

Specialization operation: The problem with the above slot assignment scheme is that the slot schedule generated may not satisfy the timeliness criterion for a message set whose deadline constraint set does not consist solely of multiples. Thus, we transform an arbitrary set of isochronous message streams $\mathbf{M'} = \{M_i' = (C_i, D_i', N_i^s, N_i^d) \mid 1 \le i \le n\}$ (without loss of generality, we assume $D_i' \le D_j'$ for all $i < j$) to another stream set $\mathbf{M} = \{M_i = (C_i, D_i, N_i^s, N_i^d) \mid 1 \le i \le n\}$ where the transformed deadline constraint set $\mathbf{D} = \{D_1, D_2, \ldots, D_n\}$ consists solely of multiples and $D_i \le D_i'$ for all i. The operation, termed *specializing* **D'** (**M'**) *with respect to* $\{x\}$ [2], finds a D_i for each D_i' such that D_i satisfies $D_i = x \cdot 2^j \le D_i' < x \cdot 2^{j+1} = 2D_i$, for some integer $j \ge 0$, where x is an integer $\in (D_1'/2, D_1']$ that results in the minimum total density increase.[3]

[2] Not necessarily all the W wavelength channels are used.

[3] Details on how to determine the value of x can be found in [2].

(Note that we also use the phrase "specializing **D'** with respect to $\{a\}$" to denote that the specialization operation is performed with the specialization factor $x = a$.) For example, given a deadline constraint set **D'** $= \{4, 7, 8, 13, 24, 28\}$, if the specialization factor $x = 4$, the set after specialization is $\{4, 4, 8, 8, 16, 16\}$. Since **D** is more restricted than **D'**, if we find a feasible slot assignment schedule for **M**, the schedule is also feasible for the original constraint set **D'**. For ease of explanation, we assume in the following discussion that the set of message streams, **M'**, is specialized with respect to $\{2\}$ into **M**. Note, however, that the proposed dynamic slot allocation scheme can be readily extended to the case in which the specialization operation is performed with respect to $\{x\}$ for $x \neq 2$.

3.2 Message Stream Decomposition

To facilitate slot assignment, we decompose each (specialized) message stream into a set of message sub-streams and will assign slots to sub-streams. Specifically, for each message stream $M_i = (C_i, D_i, N_i^s, N_i^d)$, the message density C_i/D_i can be expressed as $\frac{C_i}{D_i} = \sum_{j=1}^{m_i} \frac{C_{ij}}{D_{ij}}$, where $m_i = \log_2 D_i$, $D_{ij} = 2^j$, and $C_{ij} =$ 0 or 1, for $1 \leq j \leq m_i$. We decompose M_i into a set of sub-streams $S(M_i) \triangleq \{M_{ij} = (C_{ij}, D_{ij}, N_i^s, N_i^d) \mid 1 \leq j \leq m_i \text{ and } C_{ij} = 1\}$. It is easy to see that the decomposition is unique, and the binary representation of C_i/D_i, i.e., $.C_{i1}C_{i2}\cdots C_{im_i}$ if $C_i/D_i < 1$, or 1 otherwise, can be used to denote the set of message sub-streams of M_i.

Example 1: Suppose there are three real-time message streams, $M_1 = (1, 4)$, $M_2 = (3, 16)$, and $M_3 = (7, 16)$.[4] The sets of message sub-streams of the three message streams are $\{(1, 4)\}$, $\{(1, 8), (1, 16)\}$, and $\{(1, 4), (1, 8), (1, 16)\}$, respectively. □

If we can assign slots in such a way that for each j, at least one slot is assigned to sub-stream $M_{ij} = (1, D_{ij}, N_i^s, N_i^d)$ in any time window of size $D_{ij} = 2^j$, then the timeliness criterion is satisfied for M_i, since $\sum_{j=1}^{m_i} D_i \cdot \frac{C_{ij}}{D_{ij}} = C_i$. We denote in the following discussion the (specialized) set of sub-streams as $\mathbf{T} = \{T_i = (A_i, D_i, V_i, N_i^s, N_i^d, pos_i, \lambda_i) \mid 1 \leq i \leq n_s\}$, where C_i is deliberately dropped because it is always 1, and

- A_i is the next slot on channel λ_i to be assigned to T_i;
- D_i is the deadline constraint of T_i;
- V_i is the (unique) VCI assigned to T_i;
- N_i^s and N_i^d are the source and destination stations;
- pos_i is a sequence of $\log_2 D_i$ "L" (Left) and "R" (Right) characters if completely specified, and denotes the position of the slots assigned to T_i; pos_i is initially set to null, and will be specified by the slot allocation scheme;
- λ_i is the channel where T_i will be assigned. λ_i will also be specified by the slot allocation scheme.

3.3 Channel Decomposition

[4] We omit the source and destination stations, N_i^s and N_i^d, for each M_i since they are irrelevant in this example.

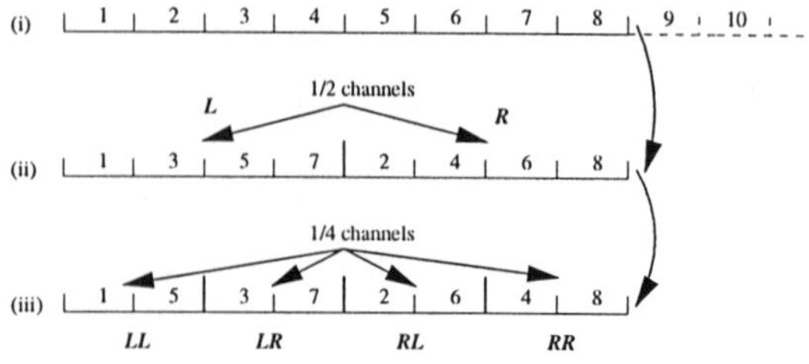

Figure 2: An example which shows how properly spaced slots can be grouped into sub-channels and how a channel can be decomposed into sub-channels.

To facilitate slot assignment in a well-spaced manner, we group the time slots on each data channel into *sub-channels* and will assign each sub-stream a sub-channel to satisfy its deadline constraint. Specifically, a $1/d$ *sub-channel* consists of evenly-spaced slots, of which any two consecutive ones are separated exactly by d slots. A $1/d$ sub-channel can be further divided into k sub-channels, each with density $1/kd$, as follows: let s denotes the start slot of the $1/d$ sub-channel ($1 \leq s \leq d$), then the ith $1/kd$ sub-channel starts at slot $s + (i - 1)d$, and two consecutive slots of the ith $1/kd$ sub-channel are separated exactly by kd slots. Fig. 2 shows how a 1/1-channel can be split into two *non-overlapping* 1/2 sub-channels, then into four non-overlapping 1/4 sub-channels. Also shown in Fig. 2 is that the slots can be conceptually shuffled such that all slots in a sub-channel are adjacent to each other. Each time a (sub-)channel is split, we tag the sub-channel to which the slots in the odd (even) numbered positions (of the split channel) are assigned with "L" ("R").

4 Description of Proposed Slot Allocation Scheme

4.1 Overview of Proposed Scheme

We configure the functions of the dynamic slot allocation scheme into two daemons: the *dynamic slot manager* daemon, DYNMGR, and the *dynamic slot allocator* daemon, DYNALO. These daemons concurrently run on all stations in the network. In addition, there are two FIFO pipes, (1) REQ, from DYNMGR to DYNALO; and (2) ACK, from DYNALO to DYNMGR.

DYNMGR gathers and processes call setup/clear requests as follows. Upon arrival of a *local* call setup/clear request, DYNMGR checks whether or not a *necessary* schedulability condition holds for the message stream to be established in the case of a call setup request. If the condition is satisfied or if the request is a call clear one, DYNMGR relays the setup/clear request to other stations by transmitting in the pre-assigned mini-slot on the control channel λ_0 a setup/clear request. Meanwhile, DYNMGR constantly monitors the control channel and processes the requests that appear on the control channel. By the fact that all control packets are broadcast by the star coupler to every station, they experience the same end-to-end propagation delay and there are no control channel collisions, the DYNMGRs on all stations process setup/clear requests in the same order. This makes all stations independently produce the same slot schedule. Upon receipt of a call setup/clear request from the control channel,

/*The daemon runs concurrently on every station in the network.*/

During System Operations:

Upon arrival of a local call setup request for a message stream $M_i' = (C_i, D_i', N_i^s, N_i^d)$ at station N_i^s:

S1. Specialize the deadline D_i' of the message stream, M_i', to be established with respect to $\{2\}$ to get D_i.

S2. if $((\sum_{j s.t.\ N_j^s = N_i^s} \frac{C_j}{D_j} + \frac{C_i}{D_i} > 1)$ or $(\sum_{j s.t.\ N_j^d = N_i^d} \frac{C_j}{D_j} + \frac{C_i}{D_i} > 1))$, reject the call setup request; else, transmit a call setup request in the pre-assigned mini-slot on the control channel λ_0.

Upon receipt of a call setup request for $M_i = (C_i, D_i, N_i^s, N_i^d)$ from the control channel λ_0:

S3. Assign a temporary unique VCI number, V_i, to M_i.

S4. Decompose M_i into a set of sub-channels $S(M_i) = .C_{i_1} C_{i_2} \cdots C_{i_{mi}}$.
Enqueue(REQ, ("setup", V_i, N_i^s, N_i^d, $S(M_i)$)).

S5. If M_i is successfully established, make the VCI assignment permanent, otherwise free the temporary VCI and reject the call setup request.

Upon arrival of a local call clear request for an existing message stream $M_j = (C_j, D_j', N_j^s, N_j^d)$ at station N_j^s or N_j^d:

S6. Transmit a call clear request in the pre-assigned mini-slot on the control channel λ_0.

Upon receipt of a call clear request for an existing message stream M_j from the control channel λ_0:

S7. Let V_j be the VCI number of the message stream M_j to be terminated.
Enqueue(REQ,("clear", V_j, N_i^s, N_i^d, $\emptyset$)).

S8. Deallocate the VCI number V_j assigned to M_j.

Figure 3: Dynamic Channel Setup and Tear-down Management Daemon.

DYNMGR inserts the request and relevant information into REQ. DYNALO gets setup/clear requests from REQ, invokes the channel establishment/termination procedures, and passes the results back to DYNMGR through the ACK pipe. In the case of a call setup request, DYNALO generates the slot allocation schedule if a message stream can be established. For a call clear request, DYNALO frees the sub-channels allocated to the message stream and merges (if appropriate) existing empty sub-channels.

Detailed description of DYNMGR: The operations of DYNMGR are outlined in Fig. 3. Upon arrival of a call setup request for a new message stream $M_i' = (C_i, D_i', N_i^s, N_i^d)$, the DYNMGR of the source station N_i^s specializes D_i' with respect to $\{2\}$ to get D_i(**S1**), then checks whether or not both

$$\rho(\{M_j = (C_j, D_j, N_j^s, N_j^d) \mid N_j^s = N_i^s\}) \leq 1 \quad \text{and}$$
$$\rho(\{M_j = (C_j, D_j, N_j^s, N_j^d) \mid N_j^d = N_i^d\}) \leq 1$$

hold. If either of the above inequalities is not satisfied, the message stream cannot be established without violating **C1** or **C2**, the call setup request is simply rejected. Otherwise, DYNMGR relays the call setup request to other stations through the control channel(**S2**). Upon receipt of a call setup request for a message stream $M_i = (C_i, D_i, N_i^s, N_i^d)$ from the control channel, DYNMGR assigns a temporary VCI number, V_i, to M_i, decomposes M_i into a set of message sub-streams $S(M_i) = .C_{i_1} C_{i_2} \ldots C_{i_{m_i}}$, then inserts the call setup request, V_i, N_i^s, N_i^d, and $S(M_i)$ into the pipe REQ (**S4**).

Dynamic Slot Allocation Scheme:

```
/* T is the set of message sub-streams, and T =
   (A, D, V, N^s, N^d, pos, λ) ∈ T is a sub-stream in the network, where*/
/* T.A is the next slot on channel λ_i to be assigned to T */
/* T.D is the deadline constraint of T, T.V is the VCI assigned to T */
/* T.N^s and T.N^d are the source and destination stations of T */
/* T.pos is the position of the slot assigned to T */
/* T.λ is the data channel where T is assigned. */
/* R = (A, V, λ) denotes that slot A on channel λ is reserved to be
   assigned to a sub-stream T with T.V = V and T.λ = λ*/

/* System initialization */
T ← {(1, 1, "E", "E", "E", "E", λ_i) | 1 ≤ i ≤ W};
T_λi ← {(1, 1, "E", "E", "E", "E", λ_i)}, 1 ≤ i ≤ W;
R ← (0, 0, null); t ← 0;
do {
   t ← t + 1;
   for i ← 1 to W do {
      foreach T ∈ T_λi do { /* T_λi ← {T_j | T_j.λ = λ_i} */
         if (T.A = t) {
            if (!((R.λ = λ_i) && (R.A = t)))
               assign current slot on wavelength channel λ_i to T;
            else {
               assign current slot on wavelength channel λ_i to the
               sub-stream T ∈ T_λi with T.λ = λ_i and T.V = R.V;
               R ← (0, 0, null);
            }
            T.A ← T.A + T.D;
         }
      }
   } /* for */
   if (R.A = 0) {
      if (there is more than one empty sub-channel in T with the
      same deadline) merge(T,R,t);
      if (R.A = 0)
         if (REQ ≠ ∅) {
            dequeue(REQ, (req, v, N^s, N^d, S));
            if (req = "setup")
               if (setup(T, v, N^s, N^d, S) = SUCCESS)
                  Enqueue(ACK,("SUCCESS", v));
               else Enqueue(ACK,("REJECT",v));
            else {
               tear_down(T, v);
               merge(T, R, t);
            }
         }
   }
} forever
```

Figure 4: Dynamic slot allocation daemon.

Whether or not M_i can be established will be determined and passed back in the ACK pipe by DYNALO. If the message stream can be established, DYNMGR marks the temporarily assigned VCI permanent. Otherwise, it frees the temporarily assigned VCI(**S5**). An existing channel $M_i = (C_i, D_i, N_i^s, N_i^d)$ can be cleared either by the source station or by the destination station. Upon arrival of a local call clear request, DYNMGR transmits a call clear request in the pre-assigned mini-slot on the control channel(**S6**). In response to a call clear request from the control channel, DYNMGR places the request and the stream's VCI number into REQ (**S7**), then deallocates the VCI number (**S8**).

Detailed description of DYNALO: The operations of DYNALO are depicted in Fig. 4. DYNALO maintains a sub-stream set, **T**. Each element $T = (A, D, V, N^s, N^d, pos, \lambda) \in \mathbf{T}$ corresponds to an existing message sub-stream. The meaning of each field is described in Fig. 4. All data channels are empty at system initialization. We artificially add to **T** W empty streams $T_i = (1, 1, \text{"}E\text{"}, \text{"}E\text{"}, \text{"}E\text{"}, \text{"}E\text{"}, \lambda_i), 1 \leq i \leq W$, one for each data channel. The set **T** will be updated during system operation. The vector R, initially set to $(A, V, \lambda) = (0, 0, null)$, is used only when two empty sub-channels are being merged and one empty subchannel is undergoing the swap operations[5].

During system operation, DYNALO (line 5-18) assigns slots to the existing message sub-streams in $\mathbf{T}$ according to the A fields of the elements in $\mathbf{T}$ and that of R. In the time interval $[t-1, t)$, there are W slots, one on each data channel. For each channel λ_i, if slot t is "reserved" in R (i.e. $R.\lambda = \lambda_i$ and $R.A = t$), DYNALO allocates the current slot to the sub-stream T with $T.\lambda = \lambda_i$ and $T.V = R.V$ and resets R to $(0, 0, null)$. (We call this slot assignment a *reservation* assignment.) Otherwise (i.e. $R.\lambda \neq \lambda_i$ or $(R.\lambda = \lambda_i)$ && $R.A \neq t$), DYNALO assigns the current slot t to the message sub-stream $T \in \mathbf{T}_{\lambda_i}$ with $T.A = t$. In either case, DYNALO resets $T.A$ to $T.A + T.D$. We prove in Section 5 that except under the case of reservation assignment, DYNALO assigns one slot to each non-empty sub-stream $T \in \mathbf{T}$ in every $T.D$ slots during its life time. Under the reservation assignment, the sub-stream T with $T.\lambda = R.\lambda$ and $T.V = R.V$ will be assigned a slot in less than $T.D$ slots after its previously assigned slot. As a result, for each real-time message stream $M_i(M_i')$, DYNALO assigns at least $\sum_{j=1}^{m_i} D_i \cdot \frac{C_{ij}}{D_{ij}} = C_i$ slots to M_i in every D_i consecutive slots on possibly W data channels. Since $D_i \leq D_i'$, the timing requirement for M_i' is satisfied.

After assigning the W current slots, DYNALO checks the FIFO pipe REQ and takes necessary actions according to the request at the head of REQ (lines 19–32) except under the following cases:

(i) $R.\lambda \neq null$ and $R.A \neq 0$, or
(ii) there exist T_1 and T_2 in $\mathbf{T}$ such that $T_1.V = T_2.V =$ "E" and $T_1.D = T_2.D$ and can be merged without violating **C1** and **C2**.

Under the above two cases, the system is said to be in a *transition period*, and the request(s) in REQ will be temporarily suspended. In case (i), the slot reserved in R ($R.A$) has not been assigned yet. DYNALO will not process any request in REQ, or merge any empty sub-channels. If $R.\lambda = null$, $R.A = 0$ and (ii) is true, DYNALO invokes procedure *merge* to merge empty sub-channels with the same deadline, subject to **C2** and **C2**. If neither (i) nor (ii) is true, DYNALO processes the request at the head of REQ. In particular, if the request is "setup," procedure *setup* is invoked, which attempts to assign each of the sub-streams a sub-channel of appropriate density, subject to **C1** and **C2**. The result (SUCCESS or REJECT) is passed back to DYNMGR through the pipe ACK. If the request is "clear," procedure *tear_down* is invoked, the sub-channels assigned to the terminated sub-streams are tagged as empty. If there exists more than one empty sub-channel with the same deadline constraint, procedure *merge* is invoked to merge (if possible) empty sub-channels with same deadline constraint. We will present the channel establishment and termination procedures in Sections 4.2 and 4.3.

4.2 Channel Establishment Procedures

The channel establishment procedures are outlined in Fig. 5. Given the set of sub-streams, $S(M_i) = .c_1c_2 \cdots c_k$, of a real-time message stream (with VCI v assigned), M_i,the *setup* procedure attempts to allocate (via the *allocate* procedure) an empty sub-channel to each of the sub-streams in $S(M_i)$, starting with the sub-stream with the largest deadline constraint. For each message sub-stream c_i, if an *conflict-free* empty sub-channel with deadline 2^i can be located,[6] it is temporarily assigned to the sub-stream. If one of the sub-streams of M_i cannot be allocated an empty sub-channel, either due to the source/destination conflict or due to the lack of empty sub-channels of equal or larger density, all the sub-channels temporarily allocated to M_i are de-allocated, all the empty sub-channels that were

```
Dynamic Channel Setup Procedures:
Procedure setup(T, v, N^s, N^d, S)
{
 let S ← .c1c2···ck;
 for i ← k downto 1 do {
    if (ci ≠ 0)
       if (allocate(T,2^i, v, N^s, N^d) = FAILURE) {
          de-allocate all the sub-channels temporarily assigned with
          VCI v in T;
          restore all the empty sub-channels that were temporarily split;
          return REJECT;
       }
}
make the sub-channels temporarily allocated in T permanently allocated;
return SUCCESS;
}

Procedure allocate(T,d, v, N^s, N^d)
{
if ((there exists an empty sub-channel T with deadline d) &&
    (conflict_free(T, N^s, N^d))) {
    temporarily relabel T = (a, d, "E", "E", "E", pos, λ) as
    (a, 2^j, v, N^s, N^d, pos, λ);
    return SUCCESS;
}
  /* consider empty sub-channels in the descending order of deadlines*/
for (t ← d/2; t ≥ 1; t ← t/2) {
    if (there exists an empty sub-channel Ti with deadline t)
       if (split_channel(T,Ti, d, v, N^s, N^d) = SUCCESS) return SUCCESS;
}
return FAILURE;
}

Procedure split_channel(T,Ti, d, v, N^s, N^d)
{
  /* split Ti into two empty sub-channels */
change Ti to Ti1 ← (a, 2di, "E", "E", "E", pos + "L", λ);
insert a new sub-channel element Ti2 ← (a + di, 2di,
  "E", "E", "E", pos + "R", λ) into T;
if (2di = d) {
    if (conflict_free(Ti1, N^s, N^d)) {
       temporarily relabel Ti1 = (a, 2di, "E", "E", "E", pos + "L", λ)
       as (a, d, v, N^s, N^d, pos + "L", λ) ;
       return SUCCESS;
    }
    else if (conflict_free(Ti2, N^s, N^d)) {
       temporarily relabel Ti2 = (a + di, 2di, "E", "E", "E", pos + "R", λ)
       as (a + d/2, d, v, N^s, N^d, pos + "R", λ) ;
       return SUCCESS;
    }
    else /* restore empty sub-channel Ti */
       change Ti1 to Ti ← (a, di, "E", "E", "E", pos, λ); delete Ti2 from T;
}
else { /* di < d/2; recursively split empty sub-channels */
    if (split_channel(T,Ti1, d, v, N^s, N^d) = SUCCESS) return SUCCESS;
    else if (split_channel(T,Ti2, d, v, N^s, N^d) = SUCCESS)
       return SUCCESS;
    else { /* restore empty sub-channel Ti */
       change Ti1 to Ti ← (a, di, "E", "E", "E", pos, λ); delete Ti2 from T;
    }
}
return FAILURE;
}
```

Figure 5: Dynamic channel setup procedures.

[5]The channel merging and swapping operations will be detailed in Section 4.3.

[6]Either such an empty sub-channel exists or it is generated by splitting an empty sub-channel of higher density.

split in the course of establishing M_i are restored, and M_i is not established (lines 6–10). Otherwise, if all the sub-streams are successfully allocated sub-channels, all the temporarily allocated sub-channels are made permanently allocated, and M_i is established (line 12).

To allocate a conflict-free empty sub-channel with deadline $d = 2^i$, the *allocate* procedure first checks if there exists an empty sub-channel T with deadline d and if assigning this empty sub-channel to M_i will violate **C1** or **C2** (via *conflict_free*). If such an empty sub-channel does exist, it is temporarily relabeled. If there does not exist any conflict-free empty sub-channel with deadline d, the *allocate* procedure attempts to (possibly recursively) split an empty sub-channel with smaller deadline $d' = 2^\ell < d = 2^i$ into a set of empty sub-channels with deadlines[7] $2^{\ell+1}$, $2^{\ell+2}$, ..., 2^i, 2^i via the *split_channel* procedure. The splitting attempt is made on all the empty sub-channels in $\mathbf{T}$, in the order of descending deadlines, until either a conflict-free empty sub-channel with deadline 2^i is generated or all empty channels are exhausted. Empty channels are ordered by data channel, i.e., $T_1.\lambda_i$ is ordered before $T_2.\lambda_j$ if $T_1.D = T_2.D$ and $i < j$, and by position field if on the same channel.

Given an empty sub-channel $T_i = (a, d_i, \text{“}E\text{”}, \text{“}E\text{”}, \text{“}E\text{”}, pos_i, \lambda)$ and the deadline d of the empty sub-channel sought for, the *split_channel* procedure first splits T_i into two empty sub-channels, $T_{i_1} = (a, 2d_i, \text{“}E\text{”}, \text{“}E\text{”}, \text{“}E\text{”}, pos_i + \text{“L”}, \lambda)$ and $T_{i_2} = (a + d_i, 2d_i, \text{“}E\text{”}, \text{“}E\text{”}, \text{“}E\text{”}, pos_i + \text{“R”}, \lambda)$ (line 29–30). If d_i equals $d/2$ and T_{i_1} or T_{i_2} can be assigned without incurring source/destination conflicts, it is temporarily relabeled, otherwise the split empty sub-channel, T_i, is restored (lines 31–41). If $d_i < d/2$, *split_channel* recursively splits T_{i_1} and T_{i_2} until either (i) a conflict-free empty sub-channel with deadline d is located or (ii) all the empty sub-channels of T_i are investigated but no conflict-free empty sub-channel with deadline d is located. In the latter case, the split empty sub-channel T_i is restored (lines 42–46).

Check on source/destination conflicts: Two sub-channels, T_1 and T_2, violate **C1** or **C2**, if (1) they contain overlapping slots (i.e., both sub-channels contain the data slot t, for some t); and if (2) $T_1.N^s = T_2.N^s$ or $T_1.N^d = T_2.N^d$. Recall that for a sub-channel T, $T.pos$ consists of a sequence of $\log_2(T.D)$ “L” (Left) and “R” (Right) characters. Whenever a sub-channel T with deadline $T.D$ is split into two sub-channels T_1 and T_2 with deadline $2D$, $T_1.pos$ and $T_2.pos$ are updated by appending “L”(“R”) to $T.pos$. It is easy to see that (1) occurs if and only if $T_1.pos$ is a proper prefix of $T_2.pos$ or $T_2.pos$ is a proper prefix of $T_1.pos$. To check whether or not the assignment of an empty sub-channel T to a message sub-stream T_i will incur source/destination conflicts, we can simply check if sub-channel T has overlapping slots with a sub-channel $T_k \in \{T_k \mid T_k \in \mathbf{T},\ T_k.N^s = T_i.N^s \text{ or } T_k.N^d = T_i.N^d\}$. If the empty sub-channel T has overlapping slots with a sub-channel T_k, then there are source/destination conflicts. This function is implemented in procedure *conflict_free* and is simple thus not listed.

[7] Note that two of the split empty sub-channels will have a deadline 2^i.

Channel Termination Procedures:

```
1. Procedure tear_down(T, v)
2. {
3. /* relabel all the sub-channels assigned to the terminated message
   stream as empty ones */
4. foreach T = (a, d, v, N^s, N^d, pos, λ) ∈ T do relabel T as
   T = (a, d, "E", "E", "E", pos, λ);
5. }

6. Procedure merge(T, R, t)
7. {
8. if (R.A = 0 and there exists more than one empty channel in T with
   the same deadline) {
9.    for (d ← D_n; d ≥ 2; d ← d/2 ){
      /* D_n is the largest deadline constraint in T */
      /* Empty channel order is maintained globally. */
10.      while (R.A = 0 and there exists some un-investigated pair of
         empty sub-channels with deadline d) {
11.         pick up a un-investigated pair of empty sub-channels, T1 and
            T2, with deadline constraint d in a predefined order;
12.         /* Without loss of generality, let T1.A + x·d < T2.A + y·d
            ≤ T1.A + x·d + d/2, for some integer x and y */
13.         if (T2.A + y·d = T1.A + x·d + d/2) {
14.            if (T1.λ = T2.λ)
               /* T1 and T2 are on the same wavelength channel */
15.               combine(T1, T2, d, T);
16.            else { /* T1 and T2 are on different wavelength channel */
17.               swap(T2, T2.A + y·d, T2.λ, T1.λ, R, t);
18.               combine(T1, T2, d, T);
19.            }
20.         }
21.         else /* T2.A + y·d < T1.A + x·d + d/2 */
22.         if (swap(T2, T1.A + x·d + d/2, T2.λ, T1.λ, R, t) = SUCCESS)
23.            combine (T1, T2, d, T);
24.         else
25.         if (swap(T1, T2.A + y·d + d/2, T1.λ, T2.λ, R, t) = SUCCESS)
26.            combine (T1, T2, d, T);
27.      } /* while */
28.   } /* for */
29.} /* if */
30. }

31. Procedure combine(T1, T2, d, T)
32. {
33.  if (T1.A < T2.A) {
34.  T1.D ← d/2; delete T2 from T;
35.  T1.pos ← T1.pos − last character of T1.pos;
36.  }
37.  else {
38.  T2.D ← d/2; delete T1 from T;
39.  T2.pos ← T2.pos − last character of T2.pos;
40.  }
41. }
```

Figure 6: Channel Termination Procedures.

4.3 Channel Termination Procedures

The channel termination procedures are outlined in Figs. 6–7. When an existing message stream, M_i, with VCI number v is to be terminated, we relabel the set of sub-channels assigned to M_i as empty ones (via Procedure *tear_down*), and merge empty sub-channels with the same deadline constraint (via Procedure *merge*). Procedure *merge* works as follows. If $R.A \neq 0$, two empty sub-channels are being merged and one of them is swapped with some other sub-channel(s) (details below). We do not invoke any further merge operation. Otherwise (i.e., $R.A = 0$), we merge two empty sub-channels with the same deadline constraint (subject to **C1** and **C2**), starting with sub-channels which have the largest deadline constraint, and progress in a *backward* manner until we finish merging empty sub-channels or until $R.A$ is set to a nonzero value, whichever occurs first. Two sub-channels of the same deadline constraint d can be combined into one with deadline constraint $d/2$. if the relative spacing of the slots assigned to the two empty sub-channels conform to the “correct” spacing of slots assigned to an empty sub-channel with deadline constraint $d/2$. By “correct” spacing, we mean that

```
Channel Termination Procedures:
1. Procedure swap(T, p, λ1, λ2, R, t)
2. {
3.   /* T is the empty sub-channel to be swapped with the sub-channel(s)
       to which slots p + j · T.D are originally assigned. */
4.   /* λ1 is the channel on which T originally resides. */
5.   /* λ2 is the channel to which T is to be swapped. */
6.   /* R is the reservation assignment vector, and t is the current slot */
7.   /* Δ is the difference between the new next_slot to be assigned to T
       and the original next_slot to be assigned to T. */
8.   Δ ← (p − T.A) mod T.D;
9.   if ( Δ = 0) {
10.    /* T is to be swapped to the channel λ2, but its slot
       positions relative to the time axis remain the same */
11.    foreach T′ ∈ T such that T′.A = p + k · T.D for some integer
       k do T′.λ ← λ1;
12.    T.λ ← λ2;
13.    return SUCCESS;
14. }

15. /* For each sub-channel T′ to which the slot T′.A = p + k · T.D
       (for some k) is assigned, check if swapping T′ with T causes
       source/destination conflicts */
16. foreach T′ ∈ T such that T′.A = p + k · T.D for some integer k do
17.    if (!conflict_free(T, T′.N^s, T′.N^d)) return FAILURE;

18. /* swapping each sub-channel T′ to which the slot T′.A =
       p + k · T.D (for some k) is assigned with T*/
19. T.λ ← λ2; T.A ← T.A + Δ;
20. T.pos ← position of slots T.A + j · T.D for integer j ≥ 0;
21. foreach T′ ∈ T such that T′.A = p + k · T.D for some integer k
    do {
22.    T′.λ ← λ1;
23.    if (T′.A − Δ > t)
24.       T′.A ← T′.A − Δ;
25.    else {
26.       R ← (T′.A, T′.V, T′.λ);
27.       T′.A ← T′.A − Δ + T′.D;
28.    }
29.    T′.pos ← position of slots T′.A + j · T′.D for integer j ≥ 0;
30. } /* foreach */
31. return SUCCESS;
32. }
```

Figure 7: Channel Termination Procedures (Cont'd).

$T_2.A+y\cdot d = T_1.A+x\cdot d+d/2$, for some integers x and y (as shown in Fig. 8(a)). Otherwise, we need to adjust, subject to **C1** and **C2**, the positions of the slots allocated to T_1 or T_2 before merging them. Specifically, given a pair of empty sub-channels, T_1 and T_2, with same deadline constraint. Without loss of generality, we assume that $T_1.A+x\cdot d < T_2.A+y\cdot d \leq T_1.A+x\cdot d+d/2$, for some integers x and y. If the relative spacing is "correct", and $T_1.\lambda = T_2.\lambda$, we merge T_1 and T_2 by invoking procedure *combine*. Depending on the relative position of $T_1.A$ and $T_2.A$ ($T_1.A < T_2.A$ or $T_2.A < T_1.A$), *combine* either (i) changes $T_1.D = d$ to $T_1.D = d/2$, sets $T_1.pos$ to $T_1.pos$ − the last character of $T_1.pos$, and deletes T_2 from **T**; or (ii) changes $T_2.D = d$ to $T_2.D = d/2$, sets $T_2.pos$ to $T_2.pos$ − the last character of $T_2.pos$, and deletes T_1 from **T**. If $T_1.\lambda \neq T_2.\lambda$, we swap T_2 to the channel on which T_1 resides by invoking procedure *swap*, then combine T_1 and T_2. Procedure *swap* simply exchanges T_2 on channel $T_2.\lambda$ with the sub-channel(s) T''s that contain $T_2.A+y\cdot T_2.D$ for all y on channel $T_1.\lambda$. In the case that the relative spacing of T_1 is not "correct", i.e., $T_1.A+x\cdot d < T_2.A+y\cdot d < T_1.A+x\cdot d+d/2$, as shown in Fig. 8 (b), we either (1) swap the empty sub-channel T_2 on $T_2.\lambda$ with the sub-channel(s) T''s that contain slots $T_1.A+j\cdot d+d/2$ for some integer j on $T_1.\lambda$, or (2) swap the empty sub-channel T_1 on $T_1.\lambda$ with the sub-channel(s) T''s that contain slots $T_2.A+j\cdot d+d/2$ for some integer j on $T_2.\lambda$, subject to **C1** and **C2**.

Procedure *swap* works as follows. Without loss of generality, we consider the swapping operation taken when T_2 is swapped with the sub-channel(s) to which

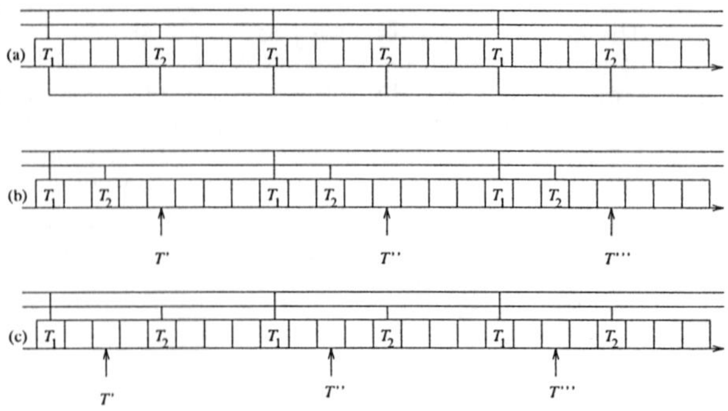

Figure 8: The relative spacing between two empty sub-channels.

slots $T_1.A+x\cdot d+d/2$, for some integer x, are assigned. Let T' be the sub-channel to which slots $(T_1.A+x\cdot d+d/2)+k\cdot d$, for some integer k, is originally assigned. (Note that there may be more than one sub-channel with which the empty sub-channel T_2 will be swapped.) The swap operation is performed such that slots $(T_2.A+y\cdot d)+j\cdot d$ will now be assigned to T' and slots $(T_1.A+x\cdot d+d/2)+j\cdot d$ will be assigned to T_2, for every j such that $(T_2.A+y\cdot d)+j\cdot d > t$, provided that no source/destination conflicts occur. (Fig. 8(c) shows the slot schedule after the swap operation is performed on Fig. 8(b).)

Specifically, procedure *swap* first sets $\Delta = (T_1.A + x\cdot d + d/2 - T_2.A) \bmod d = T_1.A + d/2 - T_2.A$, i.e., Δ is the difference between the original next slot to be assigned to T_2 and the new next slot to be assigned to T_2. If $\Delta = 0$, it implies that the relative spacing of slots assigned to T_1 and T_2 is correct in the time axis, and we need only to swap T_2 from $T_2.\lambda$ to $T_1.\lambda$. If $\Delta \neq 0$, procedure *swap* checks, for each sub-channel T' to which the slot $T'.A = T_1.A + d/2 + k\cdot d$ for some k is assigned, if swapping T' with T_2 results in source/destination conflicts. If source/destination conflicts will occur as a result of swapping, no swapping operation is performed. Otherwise, for each sub-channel T' with $T'.A = T_1.A + d/2 + k\cdot d$ for some integer k, *swap* assigns to T' the slots that are originally assigned to T_2, i.e., slots $(T'.A-\Delta)+j\cdot T'.D$ for all $j \geq 0$, and assigns to T_2 the slots that are originally assigned to other sub-channels (like T'), i.e, slots $(T_2.A+\Delta)+j\cdot d$, for all $j \geq 0$ (lines 19–30). By "moving" the next slot to be assigned to T' from slot $T'.A$ "backward" (in time axis) to slot $T'.A - \Delta$ (line 24), the timing requirement for T' will not be violated, since the distance between the most recent slot assigned to T' (i.e., slot $T'.A - T'.D$) and the next slot to be assigned to T' (i.e., slot $T'.A-\Delta$, instead of $T'.A$) is actually reduced.

Note that moving the next slot to be assigned to T' from slot $T'.A$ to slot $T'.A - \Delta$ is not possible when $T'.A - \Delta \leq t$, where t is the current slot that has been assigned. That is, we cannot assign a "past" slot $T'.A - \Delta$ to T'. In this case, we enforce that slot $T'.A$ still be assigned to T' so that the timing requirement for T' is not violated, by setting R to $(T'.A, T'.V, T'.\lambda)$ (line 26), i.e., slot $T'.A$ on wavelength $T'.\lambda$ will be reserved for channel T'. Moreover, all the slots $(T'.A - \Delta + T'.D) + j\cdot T'.D$, for $j \geq 0$, will also be assigned to T'.

That is, we reset $T'.A \leftarrow T'.A - \Delta + T'.D$ (line 27).

The function of the vector R should now be clear. $R.A \neq 0$ implies that slot $R.A$ is reserved for the sub-channel with VCI number $R.V$ on $R.\lambda$ in order to satisfy its timing requirement. The merge operation will be temporarily suspended (i.e., if $R.A \neq 0$, the while loop in the merge procedure in Fig. 6 will not be executed) and no call setup or tear-down requests in the FIFO pipe REQ will be processed in a transition period. After the reservation assignment is made, the vector R is cleared to $(0, 0, null)$ and either the temporarily suspended merge operation can be resumed or the request(s) pending in REQ can be processed.

5 Correctness Proof and Discussion

The properties used in Section 4 to devise the channel establishment and termination procedures are summarized below (See [11] for detailed proofs.).

(P1) At any time t during system operation, $T.A \geq t$ for all $T \in \mathbf{T}$ and for each channel λ_i, $1 \leq i \leq W$, either (i) $R.A = t$ and $R.\lambda = \lambda_i$, or (ii) $T.A = t$ and $T.\lambda = \lambda_i$ for exactly one $T \in \mathbf{T}$, where t is the slot to be assigned next.

(P2) In the phase of combining two empty sub-channels T_1 and T_2 with deadline $T_1.D = T_2.D = d$, if T' is a sub-channel that will be swapped with one of the empty sub-channels, then $T'.D \geq d$.

(P3) DYNALO will assign at least one slot to each sub-channel (excluding empty sub-channels) $T \in \mathbf{T}$ in every $T.D$ consecutive slots during its lifetime.

(P4) A transition period lasts no more than $4D_i$ slots, where D_i is the deadline constraint (after specialization) of the terminated message stream.

(P1) (Theorems 2) states that there exists exactly one sub-channel to which the current slot t on channel λ_i, $1 \leq i \leq W$, is assigned. **(P2)** establishes the validity of the swap operation. **(P3)** (Theorem 3) shows that the schedule produced by DYNALO satisfies the timing requirement of each established message stream, thus the schedule is correct. **(P1)**–**(P3)** establish the correctness of the DYNALO daemon. **(P4)** (Theorem 4) gives the upper bound of the time period in which no other *merge* procedure can be invoked and/or no call setup or tear-down requests in the FIFO pipe REQ can be processed.

Theorem 2: During system operation, the following properties are always true

I1. $T.A \geq t$ for all $T \in \mathbf{T}$, and

I2. for all time slots $t' \geq t$ on each channel λ_i, $1 \leq i \leq W$, either $R.A = t'$ and $R.\lambda = \lambda_i$ or there is exactly one element $T \in \mathbf{T}$ such that $T.A + j \cdot T.D = t'$ and $T.\lambda = \lambda_i$, for some $j \geq 0$. □

Theorem 3: DYNALO generates a slot allocation schedule which satisfies the timing requirement of each admitted message stream during its lifetime. □

Theorem 4: Let $M_i = (C_i, D_i, N^s, N^d)$ be a message stream to be terminated. The transition period due to combining the sub-channels assigned to M_i and other existing empty sub-channels lasts at most $4D_i - \log_2 D_i \cdot (\log_2 D_i + 1)/2 - 2\log_2 D_i$ slots. □

6 Conclusion

We complement our work in [10], address the issue of dynamically establishing and terminating message streams with timing requirements, and propose a distributed, dynamic slot allocation scheme. The proposed scheme is configured into two daemons which concurrently run on all the stations in the network so that the same slot allocation schedule is independently generated at each station. We prove the correctness of the proposed dynamic slot allocation scheme. Another notable feature of the proposed scheme is that a newly admitted message stream can be immediately set up without any delay if the corresponding call setup request does *not* arrive during a transition period. If the call setup request arrives during a transition period that results from a channel with deadline constraint D_i being terminated, we formally prove that the request will be pending in the worst case for less than $4D_i$ slots.[8]

References

[1] K. Bogineni, K.M. Sivalingam, and P. W. Dowd. Low-complexity multiple access protocols for wavelength-division multiplexed photonic networks. *IEEE J. Select. Areas Communications*, 11(4):590–603, May 1993.

[2] M. Y. Chan and F. Chin. Schedulers for larger classes of pinwheel instances. *Algorithmica*, 9, 1993.

[3] R. L. Cruz. A calculus for network delay, part I: Network elements in isolation. *IEEE Trans. on Information Theory*, 37(1):114–131, January 1991.

[4] S. Jamaloddin Golestani. A framing strategy for congestion management. *IEEE Journal on Selected Areas in Communications*, 9(7):1065–1077, September 1991.

[5] Ching-Chih Han, Chao-Ju Hou, and Kang G. Shin. On slot allocation for time-constrained messages in dual-bus networks. In *IEEE INFOCOM'96*, pages 1164–1171, 1996. An enhanced version has been accepted for publication in *IEEE Trans. on Computers.*

[6] Chung-Sheng Li, Mon-Song Chen, and Franklin Fuk-Kay Tong. POSMAC: A medium access protocol for packet-switched passive optical networks using WDMA. *Journal of Lightwave Technology*, 11(5/6):1066–1077, May/June 1993.

[7] C. L. Liu and James W. Layland. Scheduling algorithms for multiprogramming in a hard-real-time environment. *Journal of the ACM*, 20(1):46–61, 1973.

[8] Biswanath Mukherjee. WDM-based local lightwave networks — part I: Single-hop systems. *IEEE Network*, pages 12–27, May 1992.

[9] George N. Rouskas and Mostafa H. Ammar. Analysis and optimization of transmission schedules for single -hop wdm networks. *IEEE/ACM Transaction on Networking*, 3(2):211–221, April 1995.

[10] Hung-Ying Tyan, Chao-Ju Hou, Bin Wang, and Ching-Chih Han. On supporting time constrained communications in WDMA-based star-coupled optical networks. In *Proc. IEEE 17th Real-Time Systems Symposium*, Washington DC, Dec. 1996.

[11] Bin Wang, Chao-Ju Hou, and Ching-Chih Han. On dynamically establishing and terminating isochronous message streams in wdma-based local area lightwave networks. *Technical Report, EE Dept., Ohio State University*, Sept. 1996.

[12] A. Yan, A. Ganz, and C. M. Krishna. A distributed adaptive protocol providing real-time services on WDM-based LANs. *Proceedings of IEEE INFOCOM'96, San Francisco, CA*, pages 962–970, March 24-28 1996.

[8] not including the time spent on processing requests which arrived earlier but have not been processed yet.

HiPeR-ℓ: A High Performance Reservation Protocol with ℓook-ahead for Broadcast WDM Networks *

Vijay Sivaraman *George N. Rouskas*
Department of Computer Science, North Carolina State University, Raleigh, NC 27695-8206

Abstract

We consider the problem of coordinating access to the various channels of a single-hop WDM network. We present HiPeR-ℓ, a new reservation protocol specifically designed to overcome the potential inefficiencies of operating in environments with non-negligible processing, tuning, and propagation delays. HiPeR-ℓ differs from previous reservation protocols in that each control packet makes reservations for all data packets waiting in a node's queues, thus significantly reducing control overhead. Packets are scheduled for transmission using algorithms that can effectively mask the tuning times. HiPeR-ℓ also uses pipelining to mask processing times and propagation delays. We use Markov chain theory to obtain a necessary and sufficient condition for the stability of the protocol. The stability condition provides insight into the factors affecting the operation of the protocol, such as the degree of load balancing across the various channels, and the quality of the scheduling algorithms. The analysis is fairly general, as it holds for MMBP-like arrival processes with any number of states, and for non-uniform destinations.

1 Introduction

Wavelength Division Multiplexing (WDM) is the most promising technology for bridging the gap between the speed of electronics and the virtually unlimited bandwidth available within the optical medium. One of the candidate WDM architectures for implementing a new generation of high speed communication networks is the single-hop architecture [9]. In a single-hop network, both a transmitter at the source and a receiver at the destination must operate on the same wavelength for a successful packet transmission. Thus, the problem of coordinating access to the various wavelengths of the network arises. This problem is further complicated by the fact that, at high data rates, propagation delays, processing times, and transceiver tuning times all become non-negligible, and may actually be significantly larger than the packet transmission time. A number of reservation protocols for single-hop networks have appeared in the literature; we review some of these protocols in the next section.

In this paper, we present HiPeR-ℓ, a new reservation protocol for single-hop WDM local area networks. The novelty of HiPeR-ℓ lies in the fact that, by transmitting a single control packet, nodes can make reservations for multiple data packets. Thus, control overhead is significantly reduced, and nodes can use scheduling algorithms that can effectively mask tuning times [12]. HiPeR-ℓ also uses pipelining to mask processing times and propagation delays; parameter ℓ (the *look-ahead*) of the protocol controls the degree of pipelining. Drawing upon results from Markov chain theory, we obtain a necessary and sufficient condition for the stability of the protocol that provides insight in the factors affecting the protocol's operation. In the analysis, we assume arrival processes that capture the notion of burstiness and the correlation of interarrival times, two important characteristics of traffic in high speed networks [11].

In the next section, we review some of the media access protocols for single-hop WDM networks. In Section 3 we present the network and traffic model, and in Section 4 we describe HiPeR-ℓ. In Section 5 we carry out a stability analysis of HiPeR-ℓ. In Section 6 we present some numerical results, and we conclude the paper in Section 7.

2 Why A New Multiple Access Protocol?

Access to the various channels of a single-hop network is usually based on reservation schemes that require the use of control channels [4, 5, 7, 6]. Existing protocols require that control information be transmitted on the control channel for *each* packet sent on the data channels. Typically, TDMA is employed in the control channel with a control slot consisting of N mini-slots, one for each of the N nodes in the network.

In *tell-and-go* protocols [4, 6] the data packet is sent on the node's home channel immediately after the transmission of the corresponding control information. Thus, receiver collisions may arise and explicit acknowledgments are needed. Other protocols are *tell-and-wait* in nature [5, 7, 15]; in other words, nodes send the control information and wait for the control slot to reach all receivers. Then, they process the information in the control slot to determine if a data slot has been reserved for them. In the event of a successful reservation, the packet is transmitted in the corresponding slot and channel. In effect, the control slot information in tell-and-wait schemes is used by the individual nodes to build a picture of the packet queues at all other nodes in the network.

The above protocols suffer from two problems. First, the control channel represents an *electronic processing bottleneck* [6] as control information for N packets must be received and processed for *each packet transmission and reception*. Secondly, all these control channel protocols operate by schedul-

*This work was supported in part by a grant from the Center for Advanced Computing and Communication, NC State University.

0-8186-7780-5/97 $10.00 © 1997 IEEE

ing a *single* packet from each transmitter at a time (typically, the head-of-line packet is the one scheduled for transmission). This packet is scheduled *independently* of other packets waiting for transmission at the same node. Hence, depending on the protocol, one transmitter or receiver tuning time is incurred for each packet transmission/reception.

A protocol that overcomes the processing bottleneck by introducing $k > 1$ control channels was presented in [6]. The main drawback of this protocol, however, is its lack of scalability, as it requires $N + k$ wavelengths. The PROTON protocol [7] can operate with any number of wavelengths, and its design explicitly considers tuning and processing times. However, PROTON schedules one packet at a time, and the results in [7] confirm the intuition that high processing and tuning times have a significant effect on delay and throughput. The MaTPi protocol [16] also considers tuning times, and uses pipelining to mask their effect.

Distributed Queue Multiple Wavelength (DQMW) [8] is another protocol that can operate with any number of wavelengths and which considers tuning times when scheduling packets. DQMW attempts to overcome the head-of-line blocking of other media access schemes by considering multiple packets for transmission by a given node. But these packets are scheduled independently of each other, thus a tuning overhead is incurred for each. In addition, this protocol has higher processing requirements compared to other protocols, as two control packets must be sent for each data packet: one before its transmission and one after the end of its transmission. FatMAC [14] is a reservation protocol that does not require a separate control channel. Instead, all channels operate in cycles, with each cycle consisting of a control and data phase. Reservations are transmitted in the control phase, and the corresponding data packets are sent in the following data phase. As in other protocols, reservations are made only for the head-of-line packets, thus a control and tuning overhead is incurred for each data packet.

In this paper we present HiPeR-ℓ, a new reservation protocol that has the following important features: (a) t is scalable, as it can operate with any number of channels $C \leq N$; (b) it may operate without a control channel, thus all channels are available for data transmission and no extra hardware is needed to monitor and access a control channel; (c) it requires tunability only at one end; (d) it ensures that packet transmissions are free of channel and receiver collisions. (e) it schedules multiple packets for transmission by a node on a given channel to mask the tuning latency [12] and to keep the control requirements low; (f) it uses pipelining to overlap processing with packet transmissions, and to hide the effects of propagation delay.

3 System and Traffic Model

3.1 Network Model

We consider an optical broadcast WDM network with N nodes, each employing one transmitter and one receiver. There are C wavelengths in the network, $\lambda_1, \cdots, \lambda_C$, with

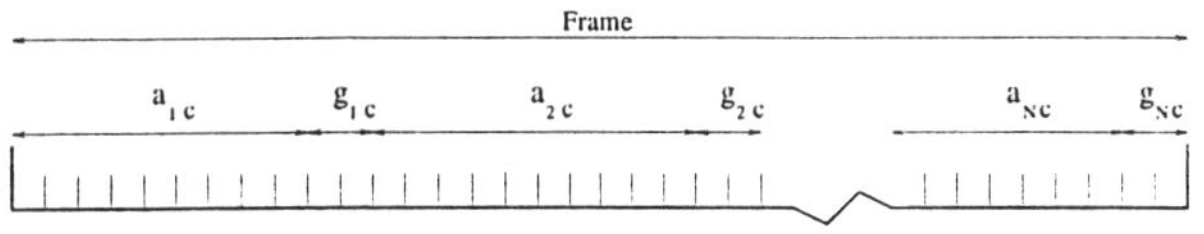

Figure 1: Part of the schedule corresponding to channel λ_c

$C \leq N$. There is no separate control channel; all channels are used for data transmission, as well as for communicating control information. Without loss of generality, we only consider tunable-transmitter, fixed-receiver (TT-FR) networks. Each tunable transmitter can tune to, and transmit on any wavelength. The fixed receiver at station j, on the other hand, is assigned a home channel $\lambda(j) \in \{\lambda_1, \cdots, \lambda_C\}$. We let $\mathcal{R}_c$ denote the set of receivers sharing wavelength λ_c: $\mathcal{R}_c = \{j \mid \lambda(j) = \lambda_c\}$.

The network is packet-switched, with fixed-size packets. The buffer space at each node is partitioned into C independent queues. Each queue contains packets destined for receivers which listen to a particular wavelength. This arrangement eliminates the head-of-line blocking problem, and permits a node to send a number of packets back-to-back when tuned to a particular channel. The network operates in a slotted mode, with a slot time equal to a packet transmission time. All nodes are synchronized at slot boundaries. Packets buffered at the c-th queue of each node are transmitted on a FIFO basis into the optical medium on wavelength λ_c.

We let integer $\Delta \geq 1$ denote the number of slots a tunable transmitter takes to tune from one wavelength to another. We also let τ denote the one way propagation delay between a pair of nodes. Without loss of generality, we take τ to be the same for all source-destination pairs in the network.

3.2 Transmission Schedules

One of the potentially difficult issues that arise in a WDM environment is that of packet scheduling in the presence of non-negligible tuning latencies. The authors have recently considered the problem of packet scheduling with tuning latencies in [12]. That work expanded upon, and generalized earlier results obtained in [1, 3]. More specifically, we have shown that careful scheduling can mask the effects of arbitrarily long tuning latencies. The key idea is to have each tunable transmitter send a *block* of packets on each wavelength before switching to the next. Doing so makes it possible to overlap the tuning latency at a node with packet transmissions from other nodes. The main result of [12] was a set of new algorithms for constructing near-optimal (and, under certain conditions, optimal) schedules for transmitting a set of traffic demands $\{a_{ic}\}$. Quantity a_{ic} represents the number of packets to be transmitted by node i onto channel λ_c. The schedules are such that no collisions ever occur. They are also easy to implement in a high speed environment, since the order in which the various nodes transmit is the same for all channels [12].

Figure 1 illustrates the part of such a schedule corresponding to channel λ_c. Each node i is assigned a_{ic} *contiguous* slots for transmitting packets on that channel. These a_{ic} slots are followed by a *gap* of $g_{ic} \geq 0$ slots during which no node may transmit on λ_c. This gap may be necessary to ensure that node $i+1$ has sufficient time to tune from wavelength λ_{c-1} before starting transmission on λ_c. However, the algorithms in [12] are such that the number of slots in most of the gaps is equal to either zero or a small integer. Thus, the length of the schedule is very close to the lower bound.

The scheduling algorithms we have developed require complete information about the traffic demands $\{a_{ic}\}$. HiPeR-ℓ is a reservation protocol that allows the network nodes to dynamically share this information.

3.3 Traffic Model

The arrival process to each node is characterized by a two-state Markov Modulated Bernoulli Process (MMBP), hereafter referred to as 2-MMBP. This is a Bernoulli process whose arrival rate varies according to a two-state Markov chain. It captures the notion of burstiness and the correlation of successive interarrival times, two important characteristics of traffic in high-speed networks. For details on the properties of the 2-MMBP, the reader is referred to [10]. We assume that the arrival process to node $i, i = 1, \cdots, N$, is given by a 2-MMBP characterized by the transition matrix $\mathbf{Q}_i$, and by $\mathbf{A}_i$ as follows:

$$\mathbf{Q}_i = \begin{bmatrix} q_i^{(00)} & q_i^{(01)} \\ q_i^{(10)} & q_i^{(11)} \end{bmatrix} \; ; \; \mathbf{A}_i = \begin{bmatrix} \alpha_i^{(0)} & 0 \\ 0 & \alpha_i^{(1)} \end{bmatrix} \quad (1)$$

In (1), $q_i^{(kl)}, k, l = 0, 1$, is the probability that the 2-MMBP will make a transition to state l, given that it is currently at state k. Obviously, $q_i^{(k0)} + q_i^{(k1)} = 1, k = 0, 1$. Also, $\alpha_i^{(0)}$ and $\alpha_i^{(1)}$ are the arrival rates of the Bernoulli process at states 0 and 1, respectively. We assume that the arrival process to each node i is given by a different 2-MMBP, independent of the arrival processes to other nodes. From [10] we obtain the average arrival rate γ_i of the i-th 2-MMBP as:

$$\gamma_i = \frac{q_i^{(10)} a_i^{(0)} + q_i^{(01)} a_i^{(1)}}{q_i^{(01)} + q_i^{(10)}} \quad (2)$$

We note that γ_i is the probability that any slot contains a packet, regardless of the state of the 2-MMBP. We will only consider 2-MMBPs for which:

$$q_i^{(kl)} > 0, \quad k, l = 0, 1, \quad i = 1, \cdots, N \quad (3)$$

Conditions (3) guarantee that the two-state Markov chain of each 2-MMBP is irreducible and aperiodic, thus it has a stationary distribution.

We let r_{ij} denote the probability that a new packet arriving to node i will have j as its destination node. We will refer to $\{r_{ij}\}$ as the *routing probabilities*. This description implies that the routing probabilities are source node dependent and non-uniformly distributed.

4 Description of the HiPeR-ℓ Protocol

We now present HiPeR-ℓ, a new reservation protocol that nodes in a single-hop WDM network can use to coordinate access to the various channels. The operation of HiPeR-ℓ is rather simple:

- Each network node periodically sends control packets informing all other nodes about its traffic demands.
- Each node has a copy of the packet scheduling algorithm developed in [12]. Upon receipt of all control packets transmitted by other nodes, each node independently runs the algorithm to determine at what time slots to transmit its own data packets. Since all nodes use the same algorithm and the same input values (obtained from the control packets), no channel or receiver collisions arise.

There are two main differences between HiPeR-ℓ and any of the protocols that have appeared in the literature. First, in HiPeR-ℓ a node does not send a reservation request for its head-of-line packet only. Instead, each control packet of a node i contains information about *all* the packets that were queued in any of i's C queues at a certain instant in time. By sending a control packet, node i is in effect making reservations for all packets it had waiting for transmission at that instant. The next time node i is scheduled to transmit on wavelength λ_c, it will send a number of data packets back-to-back equal to the number of reservations it made for this channel in the corresponding previous control packet. Secondly, control packets are not transmitted over a separate channel. Reservations are *in-band* over the same channels used for data. Furthermore, time in the channels is not divided into distinct reservation and data phases as in FatMAC [14]. Exactly when control packets are transmitted will be discussed shortly.

The next subsection describes a first version of HiPeR-ℓ. We then extend the protocol by introducing pipelining to mask the effects of long propagation delays and processing times.

4.1 The Basic Idea: HiPeR-1

The basic operation of HiPeR-ℓ is illustrated in Figure 2. For reasons that will become apparent shortly, we will refer to this version of the protocol as HiPeR-1.

Assume that, somehow, each node i has made reservations for $a_{ic}^{(k)}$ data packets on wavelength λ_c, and that these reservations are known to all nodes. Each node independently runs the scheduling algorithm in [12] to compute a packet transmission schedule. However, the input to this algorithm is not quantities $\{a_{ic}^{(k)}\}$, but rather quantities $\{a_{ic}^{(k)} + 1\}$; the extra slot is for transmitting a control packet. The algorithm will allocate $a_{ic}^{(k)} + 1$ *contiguous* slots to node i for transmission to destinations listening on wavelength λ_c. We will call this allocation of slots to source-wavelength pairs a *frame*.

Suppose now that at time t_k in Figure 2 all nodes have constructed the k-th frame from the known quantities $\{a_{ic}^{(k)} + 1\}$.

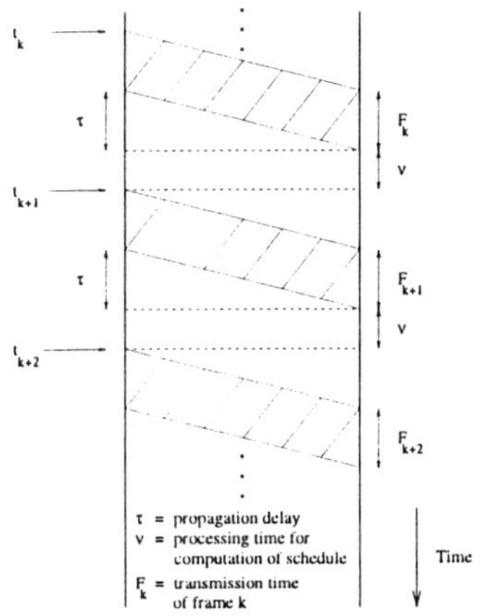

Figure 2: Operation of HiPeR-ℓ when the look-ahead $\ell = 1$

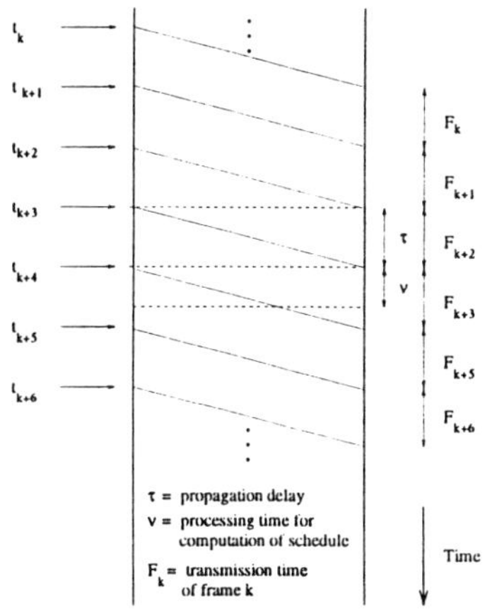

Figure 3: Operation of HiPeR-ℓ when the look-ahead $\ell = 4$

Transmission of this frame can then begin at time t_k. Consider the $a_{ic}^{(k)} + 1$ slots in the frame allocated to node i for transmissions on channel λ_c. Node i will transmit only $a_{ic}^{(k)}$ data packets in these slots (this is the number of data slots it had reserved). In the last slot node i will transmit a control packet with information about the number of data packets that were in its C queues at the beginning of the frame (i.e., at time t_k), excluding packets it transmits during this frame. In other words, a control packet from node i in frame k carries C integers, $a_{i1}^{(k+1)}, \cdots, a_{iC}^{(k+1)}$, and is used to make reservations for future transmissions on each channel. An identical copy of the control packet is transmitted by node i on each wavelength, and carries a special address recognized by all receivers in the network. As a result, by the time the last packet of the frame reaches all receivers, each node has complete information (although somewhat dated) of the queue status at all nodes. Each node can then use this information to run the scheduling algorithm anew to determine the *next* frame, as discussed above.

Let F_k be the length, in slots, of the k-th frame; F_k includes the Δ slots required for tuning the transmitters to their initial channels. Referring to Figure 2 we note that at time $t_k + F_k + \tau$ all nodes will have access to the control information transmitted in frame k (recall that τ denotes the propagation delay). Let ν denote the time it takes to run the scheduling algorithm to construct the next frame [1]. At time $t_{k+1} = t_k + F_k + \tau + \nu$, the transmission of frame $k+1$ may start. At the same time, each node i will record the number of packets in each of its C queues, and will use that information for constructing its control packets for frame $k+1$. In effect, the value of a_{ic} in a control packet transmitted in frame $k+1$ represents the number of packets that arrived to the c-th queue of node i between time t_k (the beginning of transmission of frame k) and time t_{k+1} (the beginning of transmission of frame $k+1$).

As described, the protocol is said to have a *look-ahead* $\ell = 1$, since control information transmitted during the k-th frame is used to construct the $(k+1)$-th frame; thus the name HiPeR-1. This protocol falls into the class of *gated* reservation schemes [2], since only those packets that arrived prior to the beginning of frame k will be transmitted in frame $k+1$. HiPeR-ℓ does not have a distinct reservation phase. Instead, control packets are transmitted within a frame along with data packets. This is necessary in order to minimize the tuning overhead. If there was a separate reservation phase, the transmitters would have to (a) tune to each channel during the reservation phase to transmit a single control message, and (b) tune to each channel during the data phase to transmit the data packets.

4.2 Masking Processing and Propagation Delays Through Pipelining

Observe in Figure 2 that there are no transmissions in an interval of size $\tau+\nu$ between the end of frame k (at time t_k+F_k) and the beginning of frame $k+1$ (at time t_{k+1}). If quantity $\tau + \nu$ is small compared to the average transmission time of a frame, a system running HiPeR-1 will achieve a reasonable throughput. In a high data rate environment, however, processing and propagation delays may be significantly long. As a result, the basic protocol of Figure 2 will experience long idle times with severe effects on overall throughput. We now show how pipelining can solve this problem and keep channel utilization at high levels.

Pipelining can be introduced in the protocol by using values of look-ahead greater than one. Figure 3 illustrates the operation of HiPeR-ℓ when the look-ahead $\ell = 4$. Let us consider frame $k+1$ whose transmission starts at time t_{k+1}. Control packets transmitted within this frame carry information about the number a_{ic} of data packets that arrived to the various queues in the interval $[t_k, t_{k+1})$. However, this information is not used for constructing frame $k+2$. As we see in Figure 3, the information carried by the control packets

[1] One important aspect of the scheduling algorithms in [12] is that their running time depends only on system parameters such as the number of nodes and channels, *not* on the actual frame length.

transmitted in frame $k+1$ has not been processed until after time t_{k+4} when frame $k+4$ starts. Thus, this information is used to construct frame $k+5$ whose transmission starts at time t_{k+5}. In general, we have the following rule:

> When the look-ahead is $\ell \geq 1$, the control packets of each frame k carry information about the data packets that arrived during the previous frame $k-1$. This information is used to construct frame $k+\ell$.

As Figure 3 indicates, by selecting an appropriate value for the look-ahead ℓ, we can ensure that a frame is ready for transmission immediately after the end of the previous frame, thus keeping channel utilization at high levels. Let $\bar{F}$ denote the *average* frame transmission time. Then, the value of the look-ahead should be selected as

$$\ell = \left\lceil \frac{\tau + \nu}{\bar{F}} \right\rceil \quad (4)$$

HiPeR-ℓ incurs an overhead of NC control packets for each frame transmitted (each node sends one control packet on each wavelength). In terms of efficiency, this overhead is not expected to be a problem except at very low data rates when a frame may carry a small number of data packets. On the other hand, the advantage of *in-band* reservation messages over control channel-based reservation schemes is that all available wavelengths can be used to transmit data, and no extra hardware is needed to monitor and access the control channel. However, HiPeR-ℓ can be easily adapted to use *out-of-band* reservation messages (if this is necessary). In this case, for each frame of data packets a node needs to send exactly one control packet on the control channel (as opposed to one control packet for each data packet required by existing protocols). Thus, only a small fraction of the control channel capacity is needed for reservation messages; the remaining capacity can be used for other purposes, such as network management, synchronization, etc.

5 Performance Analysis

An analysis of TDMA schemes in which a node is allocated multiple consecutive slots per frame has been carried out in [13]. There, the generating functions of the queue size and of the delay distribution are derived for fairly general arrival processes. The model in [13] assumes a fixed TDMA frame size, with each node receiving a fixed number of slots occupying the same positions in every frame. Because of the stochastic nature of our system, however, each node will make reservations for, and it will be allocated, a different number of slots from frame to frame. Consequently, the frame size will vary. Furthermore, the scheduling algorithm is run anew for each frame, therefore, the order in which the various nodes transmit may be different in consecutive frames. As a result, the techniques developed in [13] are not applicable here.

For the same reasons, an exact delay analysis of a system running HiPeR-ℓ appears to be difficult. We note, however, that packet delay is directly related to the frame size. In the following, we carry out a stability analysis of HiPeR-ℓ and obtain a necessary and sufficient condition on the total arrival rate to the network for the frame size to remain bounded. Although in our analysis we assume that the arrival process to each node is described by a 2-MMBP, it can be easily seen that the same condition applies to other MMBP-like processes with a larger number of states.

Before we proceed, we note that there are two factors that directly affect the operation of a network running HiPeR-ℓ: the degree of load balancing across the various channels, and the quality of the scheduling algorithm used. In order to quantify their effect on the performance of the protocol, we define two parameters, as follows:

- *Degree of load balancing* $\epsilon_b \geq 0$. Let A_k be the total number of data packets (traffic load) arriving to the network nodes within frame k. Each of these packets will be transmitted on one of the C channels in a future frame. If the load is perfectly balanced across the C channels, each channel will carry exactly $\frac{A_k}{C}$ of these packets. In general, the traffic load will not be perfectly balanced. Parameter ϵ_b is defined so as to provide an upper bound on the number of packets to be carried by any single channel. Specifically, for any frame k, no more than $(1+\epsilon_b)\frac{A_k}{C}$ of the packets arriving during that frame are destined for any given channel. Under perfect load balancing, $\epsilon_b = 0$. The degree of load balancing ϵ_b can be controlled if slowly tunable, rather than fixed receivers are used. Then, as the traffic pattern changes, the network can be reconfigured, i.e., nodes may be assigned new receive wavelengths, so as to keep the load evenly spread across all channels.
- *Scheduling guarantee* $\epsilon_s \geq 0$. Let $\hat{F}_k$ be the lower bound on the length of frame k, based on the data reservations made in a previous frame. Parameter ϵ_s is defined such that, the algorithm used to schedule packet transmissions will always construct a frame of length at most $(1+\epsilon_s)\hat{F}_k$. Under optimal scheduling, $\epsilon_s = 0$.

5.1 Markov Chain Model and Analysis

Consider a network running HiPeR-ℓ with a look-ahead $\ell \geq 1$. We will call a collection of $\ell+1$ consecutive frames a *superframe*. Our analysis below is based on the observation that the data packets transmitted within a superframe are exactly those packets that arrived to the various network nodes during the previous superframe.

We analyze the system by constructing its underlying Markov chain (MC) embedded at superframe boundaries. We observe the system at an instant just before the beginning of a new superframe. The state of the system is described by the tuple $(x, \underline{y})$, where x represents the length, in slots, of the superframe that is about to be transmitted ($x = 0, 1, 2, 3, \cdots$), and $\underline{y}$ is a vector $\underline{y} = (y_1, \cdots, y_N)$, with y_i indicating the state of the arrival process to node i ($y_i = 0, 1,\ i = 1, \cdots, N$).

As the state of the system evolves in time, it defines a MC $\mathcal{M}$. To see this, let $(x, \underline{y})$ be the current state of the system, and $(x', \underline{y}')$ be the state at the beginning of the next superframe. Obviously, the new state $\underline{y}'$ of the arrival processes depends only on the current state $\underline{y}$ and the number of slots x that will elapse. The length x' of the new superframe depends on (a) the number of arrivals during the current superframe and how these packets are distributed across the various channels, (b) the number of control packets to be transmitted within the superframe, and (c) the scheduling algorithm used. The number of arrivals in the current superframe depends only on the state $\underline{y}$ of the arrival processes at the beginning of the superframe, and its length x. The number of control packets transmitted within a superframe is $(\ell+1)CN$, since the superframe consists of $\ell+1$ individual frames. The scheduling algorithm used is independent of the system state. Therefore, the new length x' also depends only on the current state $(x, \underline{y})$.

Let $P[(x, \underline{y}) \rightarrow (x', \underline{y}')]$ denote the probability that the system makes a transition to state $(x', \underline{y}')$, given that it is currently in state $(x, \underline{y})$. (Given the description of the N 2-MMBPs, the value ℓ of the look-ahead, and the scheduling algorithm, the transition probabilities are completely specified. However, the exact values of these probabilities are not necessary in our analysis.) Because of conditions (3), MC $\mathcal{M}$ is irreducible and aperiodic. Thus, $\mathcal{M}$ has a stationary distribution if we can find scalars $\{\pi_{(x,\underline{y})}\}$ that satisfy:

$$\pi_{(x,\underline{y})} = \sum_{(x',\underline{y}')} \pi_{(x',\underline{y}')} P[(x', \underline{y}') \rightarrow (x, \underline{y})], \quad \forall (x, \underline{y}) \quad (5)$$

and such that $\sum_{(x,\underline{y})} \pi_{(x,\underline{y})} = 1$.

Solving the equations (5) by inspection requires writing out the actual values of the transition probabilities, a complicated task. However, we are only interested in obtaining a condition for MC $\mathcal{M}$ to have a stationary distribution. We now observe that random variable $\underline{y}$ can take exactly $K = 2^N$ values which we will denote by $\underline{y_1}, \cdots, \underline{y_K}$. Let us partition the state space of MC $\mathcal{M}$ into subsets $\underline{S_x}$ of states with the same superframe length: $S_x = \{(x, \underline{y_1}), \cdots, (x, \underline{y_K})\}$. We construct a new MC $\mathcal{M}'$ embedded at superframe boundaries, with state space $\{S_x\}$, and transition probabilities $P_{x,x'}$, where $P_{x,x'}$ is equal to equal to the transition probability in MC $\mathcal{M}$ from the states in S_x to the states in $S_{x'}$. It is now easy to prove the following lemma.

Lemma 5.1 *MC $\mathcal{M}$ has a stationary distribution if and only if MC $\mathcal{M}'$ also has a stationary distribution.*

We are now ready to prove our main result.

Lemma 5.2 *MC $\mathcal{M}'$ has a stationary distribution iff*

$$\gamma < \frac{C}{(1+\epsilon_b)(1+\epsilon_s)} \quad (6)$$

where $\gamma = \sum_{i=1}^{N} \gamma_i$ is the total arrival rate to the network.

Proof. Let D_x denote the drift at state x of $\mathcal{M}'$. Because of Pake's lemma [2, 3A.5], in order to show that $\mathcal{M}'$ has a stationary distribution, we only need to show that there exist a state $x_0 \geq 0$ and a scalar $\delta > 0$ such that:

$$D_x \leq -\delta, \quad \forall x > x_0 \quad (7)$$

The drift at state x of MC $\mathcal{M}'$ can be written as:

$$D_x = E[x' \mid x] - x \quad (8)$$

where $E[x' \mid x]$ is the expected length of the next superframe given that the length of the current superframe is x slots.

The expected number of packets that arrive in the current superframe of size x slots, independently of the state of the arrival processes at the beginning and end of the superframe, is γx, where γ is the sum of the arrival rates to the network nodes. Because of the definition of parameter ϵ_b, no more than $(1+\epsilon_b)\frac{\gamma x}{C}$ of these arriving packets are destined for any given channel. In addition, there are $(\ell+1)N$ control packets that will be transmitted on each wavelength within the next superframe. Therefore, the expected number of packets (data plus control) transmitted on any channel during the next superframe cannot be greater than $(1+\epsilon_b)\frac{\gamma x}{C}+(\ell+1)N$. Because of the definition of parameter ϵ_s, the length of this next superframe cannot be greater than $(1+\epsilon_s)$ times this last quantity. Therefore, we can bound the expected length of the next superframe by:

$$E[x' \mid x] \leq (1+\epsilon_s)\frac{(\ell+1)NC + (1+\epsilon_b)\gamma x}{C} \quad (9)$$

If we substitute this expression in (8), we obtain an upper bound on the value of the drift at state x:

$$D_x \leq (1+\epsilon_s)\frac{(\ell+1)NC + (1+\epsilon_b)\gamma x}{C} - x \quad (10)$$

After some algebraic manipulation of (10), we find that (7) is satisfied if we let

$$x_0 = \left\lceil \frac{\delta + (1+\epsilon_s)(\ell+1)N}{1 - (1+\epsilon_b)(1+\epsilon_s)\frac{\gamma}{C}} \right\rceil \quad (11)$$

This x_0 is positive if and only if (6) holds. □

Finally, by combining Lemmata 5.1 and 5.2 we obtain the desired result:

Corollary 5.1 *MC $\mathcal{M}$ has a stationary distribution if and only if the total arrival rate to the network satisfies (6).*

The stability condition (6) is simple yet powerful, as it provides insight into the two main factors that determine the performance of the network, namely, the degree of load balancing, and the quality of the scheduling algorithm. As we can see, the lower the degree of load balancing (i.e., the larger the value of ϵ_b in (6)), the lower the maximum arrival rate that the network can sustain (recall that C is the capacity of the network). Similarly with the scheduling efficiency, captured by parameter ϵ_s in (6). Although (6) was derived specifically for HiPeR-ℓ, we believe that these two factors play a similar role in any reservation protocol for single-hop networks.

Let $\bar{F}$ denote the mean frame size when the stability condition (6) is satisfied. From the definition of the look-ahead ℓ, a packet arriving during a frame k will be transmitted to its destination within frame $k+\ell+1$. We can then obtain the following expression for the mean packet delay $\bar{D}$:

$$\bar{D} = (\ell+1)\,\bar{F} \tag{12}$$

6 Numerical Results

We demonstrate the operation of the HiPeR-ℓ protocol by considering a client-server network with $N = 40$ nodes and $C = 10$ channels. There are two servers (nodes 1 and 2) and 38 clients (nodes $3, \cdots, 40$). The routing probabilities are:

$$r_{ij} = \begin{cases} 0 & i = j \\ 0.01 & i = 1, j = 2 \text{ or } i = 2,\ j = 1 \\ \frac{0.99}{38} & i = 1, 2,\ j = 3, \cdots, 40 \\ 0.114 & i = 3, \cdots, 40\ , j = 1, 2 \\ \frac{0.772}{38} & i, j = 3, \cdots, 40 \end{cases} \tag{13}$$

The arrival process to each of the nodes of the network is described by a different 2-MMBP. The total arrival rate to the network is $\gamma = 7.344$. The arrival processes were selected so that the arrival rate and squared coefficient of variation of the 2-MMBPs take a wide range of values. Based on the results of the previous section, we have assigned receive wavelengths to the various nodes so as to spread the traffic evenly across the various channels. Since there is more traffic entering the two servers, we have decided to assign one wavelength to each of the two servers, while the remaining 8 wavelengths are shared by the other 38 nodes (six of these wavelengths are each shared by 5 nodes, while the other two are each shared by 4 nodes).

We have run a number of simulations to determine the frame size and mean packet delay in these networks running HiPeR-ℓ for various values of the look-ahead ℓ. In our simulations we assume that the propagation delay $\tau = 20$ slots, the processing time $\nu = 100$ slots, and the tuning latency $\Delta = 4$ slots. Figures 4, 5, and 6 plot the actual and mean frame size when the look-ahead ℓ is 1, 2, and 3, respectively. The size of the first 3000 frames in the simulation is plotted. We can see that the mean is well-defined, and that the size of individual frames oscillates around this mean, as expected.

When ℓ is increased from 1 to 2, there is a significant decrease in the frame size. This can be explained by noting that, when $\ell = 1$, there is an idle period after the end of each frame equal to $\tau+\nu = 120$ slots (refer also to Figure 2). During this period, packets may arrive to the network nodes, but no packets are transmitted. Thus, the average frame size $\bar{F}$ has to be large enough so that, on average, the number of packets transmitted during $\bar{F}$ slots equals the number of packets arriving during $\bar{F}+120$ slots. When $\ell = 2$, the propagation delay and processing time of 120 slots are completely overlapped with the transmission of the next frame, no idling occurs, and the frame size is smaller. Since $\ell = 2$ is sufficient to completely mask the 120 slots of propagation delay and processing time, there is nothing to gain from making $\ell = 3$, and the average frame size is not affected.

In Figure 7 we show the delay versus throughput curves for this network. The mean delay values are plotted with 95% confidence intervals, which, however, are so narrow that they are not visible. A look-ahead of 1 has the worst performance, as expected. Also, at low loads, $\ell = 3$ provides for shorter delays than $\ell = 2$, while the opposite is true for higher loads. At low loads, few packets arrive during a frame, thus the average frame size when $\ell = 2$ is not large enough to completely overlap the propagation delay and processing time. Thus, idling occurs after the end of two frames, and the result is longer delays than a look-ahead $\ell = 3$. As the load increases, the average frame size for $\ell = 2$ also increases. When the load is such that the 120 slots are completely masked with $\ell = 2$, no further gain is possible by using $\ell = 3$. That is, a look-ahead $\ell = 3$ will not decrease the frame size, but will increase the delay, as seen from (12). Finally, when $\ell = 4$ or more there is no advantage compared to $\ell = 3$, resulting in a higher delay.

7 Concluding Remarks

We have considered the media access problem arising in single-hop WDM networks. We introduced HiPeR-ℓ, a new reservation protocol designed to overcome the problems posed by non-negligible processing, tuning, and propagation delays. In HiPeR-ℓ, nodes send multiple reservation requests in a single control packet. As a result, the control requirements of the protocol are low, and nodes can use algorithms that schedule multiple packet transmissions on each wavelength, effectively masking the tuning latency. The parameter ℓ controls the degree of pipelining in the operation of the protocol, and can be used to mask the propagation delay and the processing time. We have derived a condition for the protocol to reach stability that mathematically captures the effect of load balancing and of the efficiency of the scheduling algorithm on the the overall network performance.

References

[1] M. Azizoglu, R. A. Barry, and A. Mokhtar. Impact of tuning delay on the performance of banwidth-limited optical broadcast networks with uniform traffic. *IEEE JSAC*, 14(5):935–944, June 1996.

[2] D. Bertsekas and R. Gallager. *Data Networks*. Prentice Hall, Inc., 1992.

[3] M. S. Borella and B. Mukherjee. Efficient scheduling of nonuniform packet traffic in a WDM/TDM local lightwave network with arbitrary transceiver tuning latencies. *IEEE JSAC*, 14(5):923–934, June 1996.

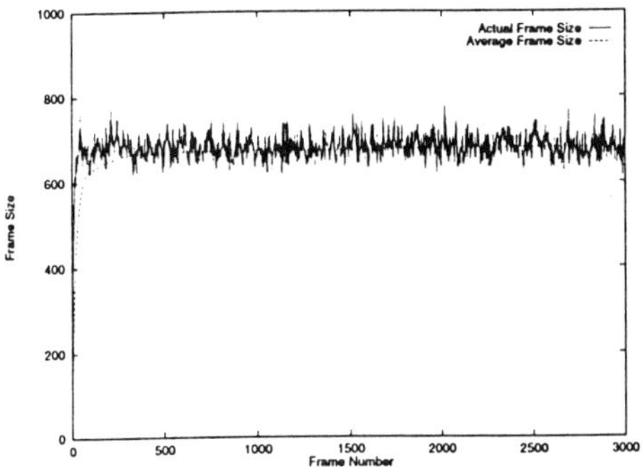

Figure 4: Frame size when the look-ahead is $\ell = 1$

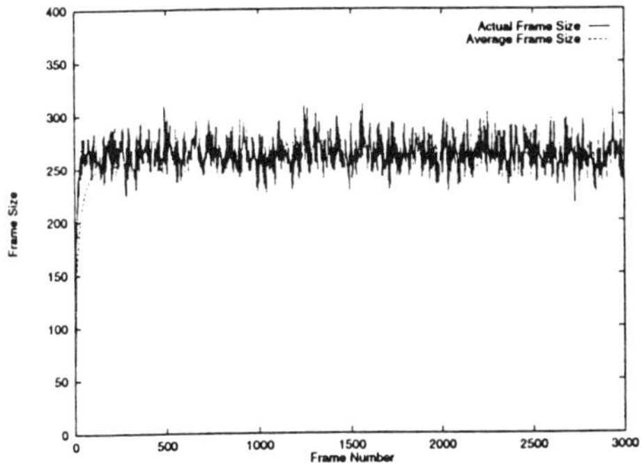

Figure 5: Frame size when the look-ahead is $\ell = 2$

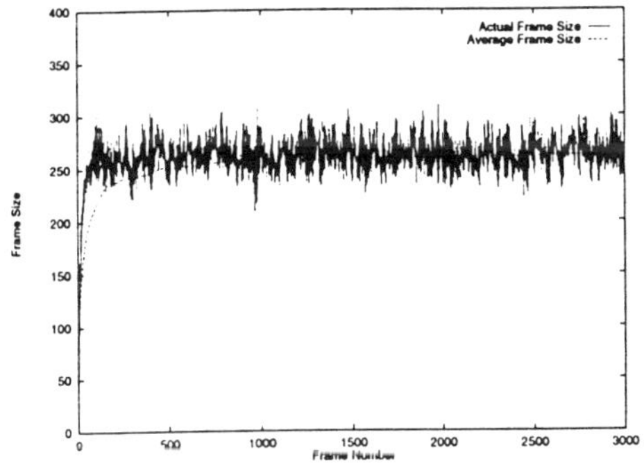

Figure 6: Frame size when the look-ahead is $\ell = 3$

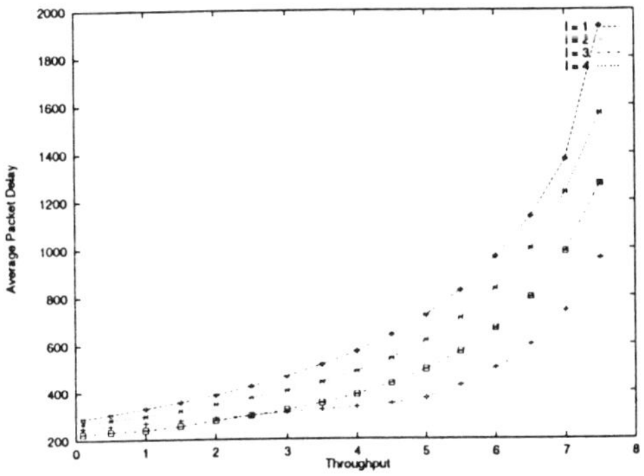

Figure 7: Delay vs. throughput for the client-server network

[4] Mon-Song Chen, N. R. Dono, and R. Ramaswami. A media-access protocol for packet-switched wavelength division multiaccess metropolitan area networks. *IEEE JSAC*, 8(6):1048–1057, August 1990.

[5] E. M. Foo and T. G. Robertazzi. A distributed global queue transmission strategy for a WDM optical fiber network. *INFOCOM '95*, pages 154–161. April 1995.

[6] P. A. Humblet, R. Ramaswami, and K. N. Sivarajan. An efficient communication protocol for high-speed packet-switched multichannel networks. *IEEE JSAC*, 11(4):568–578, May 1993.

[7] D. A. Levine and I. F. Akyildiz. PROTON: A media access control protocol for optical networks with star topology. *IEEE/ACM Trans. Networking*, 3(2):158–168, April 1995.

[8] A. Muir and J. J. Garcia-Luna-Aceves. Distributed queue packet scheduling algorithms for WDM-based networks. *INFOCOM '96*, pages 938–945. March 1996.

[9] B. Mukherjee. WDM-Based local lightwave networks Part I: Single-hop systems. *IEEE Network Magazine*, pages 12–27, May 1992.

[10] D. Park, H. G. Perros, and H. Yamashita. Approximate analysis of discrete-time tandem queueing networks with bursty and correleated input traffic and customer loss. *Operations Research Letters*, 15:95–104, 1994.

[11] G. Pujolle and H. G. Perros. Queueing systems for modelling ATM networks. In *Int'l Conf. on the Performance of Distributed Systems and Integrated Comm. Networks*, pages 10–12, Kyoto, Japan, September 1991.

[12] G. N. Rouskas and V. Sivaraman. On the design of optimal TDM schedules for broadcast WDM networks with arbitrary transceiver tuning latencies. *INFOCOM '96*, pages 1217–1224. March 1996.

[13] I. Rubin and Z. Zhang. Message delay analysis for TDMA schemes using contiguous-slot assignments. *ICC '88*, pages 418–422, 1988.

[14] K. Sivalingam and P. Dowd. A multi-level WDM access protocol for an opticall interconnected multi-processor system. *IEEE/OSA JLT*, 13(11):2152–2167, Nov. 1995.

[15] K. Sivalingam and J. Wang. Media access protocols for WDM networks with on-line scheduling. *IEEE/OSA JLT*, 14(6):1278–1286, June 1996.

[16] S. Tridandapani, J. S. Meditch, and A. K. Somani. The MaTPi protocol: Masking tuning times through pipelining in WDM optical networks. *INFOCOM '94*, pages 1528–1535. June 1994.

All-Optical LAN Interconnection with a Wavelength Selective Router *

Arun K. Somani[1,2] Murat Azizoğlu[1]
[1]Dept. of Electrical Engineering and [2]Dept. of Computer Science and Engineering
University of Washington, Seattle, WA 98195-2500

Abstract: *This paper formulates the wavelength assignment issues in interconnecting optical broadcast-star Local Area Networks (LANs) through a wavelength routing bridge. Static and dynamic approaches to partitioning of wavelengths for local and global traffic are compared using analysis and simulations. It is found that static wavelength assignment, the easiest algorithm to implement, is significantly outperformed by dynamic algorithms. Several dynamic assignment algorithms are developed, and architectural issues in interconnecting optical networks are discussed. The dependence of the call blocking performance on system parameters, such as the traffic rate, the local and global traffic statistics, and the number of available wavelengths is examined in detail. A simple, yet accurate approximation is also developed to predict the blocking performance with an arbitrary number of LANs.*

Keywords: Optical broadcast networks, wavelength routing, network interconnection, circuit switching, call blocking, static and dynamic wavelength allocation, wavelength conversion.

1 Introduction

Two architectural solutions have emerged recently for a wavelength division multiplexed (WDM) all-optical network. In a Local Area Network (LAN) with a small number of users, a broadcast-and-select architecture, where every node is connected to a passive broadcast star, provides a simple, cost-effective solution. In a Wide Area Network (WAN), power budget, scalability, and lack of wavelength reuse in a broadcast-and-select architecture make a wavelength-routing architecture more appropriate.

WDM networks have been a subject of intense research both with broadcast star and wavelength routing architectures. Surprisingly, little research has been devoted to the overall all-optical networking infrastructure in which broadcast-star LANs are interconnected via a wavelength-routed WAN, while the importance of this infrastructure has been recognized [1, 2]. The objective of the research reported in this paper is to develop viable solutions for all-optical interconnection of local area networks with high performance and low cost. In particular, we address the problem of optimal allocation of wavelengths in a multi-LAN environment for intra- and inter-LAN communication. We develop various schemes that can be used for this purpose and evaluate their performance using analytical techniques and simulations.

*This research was supported by NSF under grants NCR-9628165, NCR-9502610, and NCR-9309574 and by the University of Washington Royalty Research Fund.

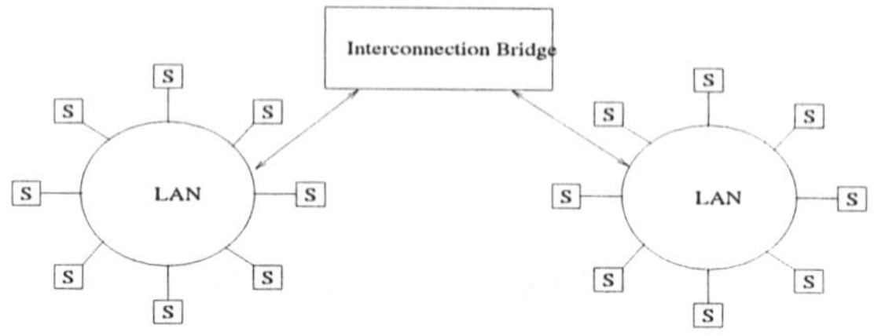

Figure 1: A two-LAN system with an interconnection bridge.

To illustrate the issues to be addressed in this paper, let us consider a two-LAN system depicted in Figure 1. The interconnection bridge is a wavelength routing device; it blocks those wavelengths carrying local traffic and routes the wavelengths carrying global traffic from the source LAN to the destination LAN. The allocation of wavelengths to local and global traffic can be accomplished in a static or dynamic fashion. Under the static scenario, the wavelength set is partitioned into fixed sets of local wavelengths and global wavelengths. The optimal fixed partitioning minimizes an appropriate cost function, which will be taken to be the overall call blocking probability in this paper. Dynamic wavelength assignment allows all traffic to use all the wavelengths and thus provides greater statistical multiplexing at the expense of increased implementation complexity.

The organization of this paper is as follows. In Section 2 we describe traffic management in an optical internetwork and establish the system model to be studied. The analysis of static and dynamic wavelength assignment schemes is given in Section 3. A Petri net model that is used to obtain numerical results from the underlying Markovian state space is described in Section 4. The results of this analysis, as well as those obtained using Monte Carlo simulations, are discussed in Section 5. The concluding remarks are presented in Section 6.

0-8186-7780-5/97 $10.00 © 1997 IEEE

2 Management of Local and Global Traffic

Consider a multi-LAN wavelength-routing optical network which consists of multiple broadcast-star LANs connected through a wavelength routing node. We refer to this wavelength routing node as the *interconnection bridge*. (See Figure 1 for a two-LAN system.) In each LAN, the traffic may originate for nodes within the LAN or for nodes in another LAN. Traffic whose source and destination nodes belong to the same LAN will be called local (or intra-LAN) traffic. Global (or inter-LAN) traffic refers to traffic whose source and destination nodes belong to different LANs.

We are interested in circuit-switched traffic in this paper. A local connection request is honored if there is a free wavelength in the particular LAN. A global connection requires a wavelength that is unused in both the source LAN and the destination LAN[1]. Since the LANs are of broadcast-and-select type, a wavelength can carry only a single connection in any given LAN.

The routing of global connections may take one of several forms. One possibility is to broadcast all traffic in each LAN to all LANs. This is very inefficient as it does not allow any wavelength reuse in the internetwork. A second option is to broadcast all the global traffic to all LANs. While this approach allows wavelength reuse with local traffic, its performance degrades rapidly with increasing global traffic rate and/or number of LANs in the system. A final option is to implement a wavelength selective switch in the bridge which routes global traffic only to the destination LAN. Since this is clearly the most efficient routing scheme, it is the one we consider in this paper.

Another important design issue is the mechanism by which wavelengths are allocated to connections. We are interested in a dynamic traffic scenario in which connections start and terminate at random time instants. In this setting, the simplest approach is to use static wavelength partitioning in which K wavelengths are allocated *a priori* to local traffic and the remaining $W - K$ wavelengths are allocated to global traffic. Here W refers to the number of available wavelengths which is assumed to be fixed in all LANs. Such a wavelength assignment can be implemented by placing, at each input link of the bridge, an optical filter that blocks the local wavelengths and passes the global wavelengths[2] [3].

An issue that arises naturally in this context is the existence of an optimal number of local wavelengths. If K is too small, many local connection requests will be blocked, while an exceedingly large K results in the starvation of global traffic. The optimal balancing of this tradeoff depends on the statistics of the arrival process and of the call durations for the two types of traffic, as well as the relative importance of blocking for these traffic types. If P_L and P_G denote the local and global call blocking probabilities respectively, one might choose K to minimize $P_L + \beta P_G$ where β is a parameter reflecting the relative "cost" of a blocked global call. The value of β may be based, for instance, on the prices of local and global calls. This optimization problem will be addressed in Section 3. In obtaining our numerical results, we shall minimize the overall call blocking probability, in effect using $\beta = (1-p)/p$ where p is the long term fraction of local calls.

Static wavelength allocation decouples the local and global traffic, and therefore sacrifices the statistical multiplexing gains that can be obtained with complete resource sharing. Dynamic wavelength allocation does not use *a priori* partitioning, but allows wavelengths to be allocated on an on-demand basis. A local connection request is honored whenever an unused wavelength exists in its LAN. A global call is established whenever there exists a wavelength which is free in both source and destination LANs.

We consider three schemes for dynamic wavelength assignment. In *Random*, one of the wavelengths that can be assigned to a call request is selected randomly. The other two schemes assign wavelengths in a more structured manner. *Packed* orders the wavelengths in a fixed order and attempts to use the wavelengths with smaller indices first. As a result, the first few wavelengths in the ordered list carry more traffic, increasing the chance of finding a free wavelength for a global call. *Coordinated* monitors the set of wavelengths that are used locally in all LANs. A local call is assigned a wavelength used in other LANs, if possible. This is done in order to leave more wavelengths free for global calls.

Certain global connection requests cannot be accommodated due to the lack of a free wavelength in both LANs. In the network of Figure 1 with two wavelengths, suppose wavelength λ_1 is being used by a local connection in LAN 1 and wavelength λ_2 is being used by a local connection in LAN 2. A global connection request that finds the system in this state will be blocked since there is no wavelength that is free in both LANs. On the other hand, if the interconnection bridge is equipped with wavelength conversion capability, this call can be established by using λ_2 in LAN 1 and λ_1 in LAN 2. In order to quantify the performance improvement with wavelength conversion, we use a fourth scheme *Convert* in which any available wavelength(s) can be assigned to any local or global call.

3 Analysis of Blocking Performance

We now describe an analytical method for evaluating the blocking performance of static and dynamic wavelength allocation schemes in interconnected optical LANs. To this end, the traffic model is introduced first.

[1] This assumes that the interconnecting bridge has no wavelength conversion capability. A wavelength converting bridge will also be discussed in this section.

[2] In a WAN with optical amplifiers, the desired wavelength isolation may be achieved by choosing the local wavelengths to lie outside the amplifier bandwidth.

3.1 Traffic Model

We assume that the call requests are generated according to a Poisson process with rate λ in each LAN. The call origination process is uniform and statistically independent across the LANs[3].

The duration of a call is assumed to be an exponentially distributed random variable with mean $1/\mu$, which is statistically independent of the arrival process and the durations of other calls. It is easy for this analysis to distinguish between the average durations of local and global calls as well as calls originating at different LANs, however this will not be considered in this paper.

The final traffic parameter is related to the rates of local and global connection requests. We assume that each connection request is for a local call with probability p, independently of all other calls. Therefore, the local call arrival process in each LAN has a Poisson distribution with rate λp. The global call requests that originate in a LAN have a Poisson distribution with rate $\lambda(1-p)$. Furthermore, the local and global arrival processes are statistically independent due to this construction. The parameter p quantifies the long-term fraction of the local calls and will be referred to as the *traffic locality* parameter.

We assume that a global connection request in a LAN is equally likely to be destined to any one of the remaining LANs. As a consequence, the global traffic that is destined to a particular LAN is also Poisson distributed with rate $\lambda(1-p)$.

3.2 Static Wavelength Allocation

Recall that under this scheme K wavelengths are allocated for local calls and $W-K$ wavelengths are reserved for global calls. The arrival processes of local and global calls are statistically independent, and there is no resource sharing between these call types. As a result, the state of local calls and that of global calls are completely decoupled. This decoupling simplifies the analysis as seen below. First consider the local call blocking. The number of local calls active at a given time in a given LAN obeys the canonical $M/M/K/K$ queueing model [4]. The resulting $K+1$ state Markov chain is a birth-death process; the birth rate in state k $(0 \le k \le K-1)$ is $\lambda_k = \lambda p$ while the death rate in state k $(1 \le k \le K)$ is $\mu_k = k\mu$. The local call blocking probability P_L is then given by

$$P_L = E(\rho p, K) \tag{1}$$

where $\rho = \lambda/\mu$ is the effective load and $E(\cdot,\cdot)$ is the Erlang-B function given by

$$E(\alpha, N) = \frac{\alpha^N/N!}{\sum_{i=0}^{N} \alpha^i/i!} \,. \tag{2}$$

Similarly, the global call blocking performance can be obtained through an $M/M/(W-K)/(W-K)$ queueing model with birth rate $\lambda_k = 2\lambda(1-p)$ and death

[3]Nonuniform traffic can be easily handled by our analytical model, uniform traffic across the LANs seems to be the practical situation.

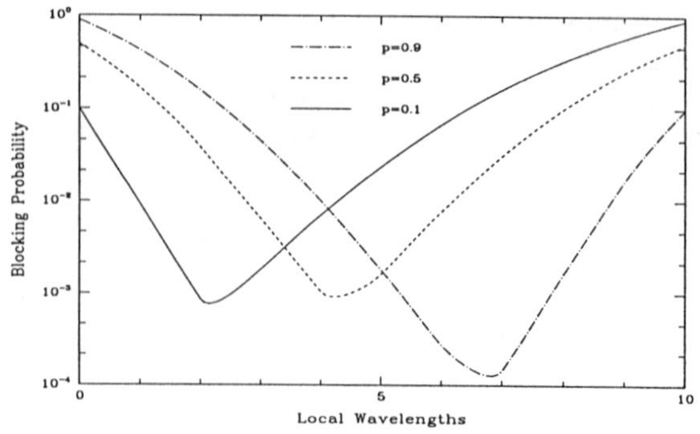

Figure 2: The dependence of the call blocking probability on the number of local wavelengths for $W = 10$ and $\rho = 1$.

rate $\mu_k = k\mu$. The extra factor 2 in the birth rate is a due to the fact that the state of the global calls in a LAN can be incremented by a call originating from or destined to that LAN. The resulting global call blocking probability P_G is

$$P_G = E(2\rho(1-p), W-K). \tag{3}$$

The overall blocking probability P_B is given by

$$P_B = pE(\rho p, K) + (1-p)E(2\rho(1-p), W-K) \,. \tag{4}$$

Figure 2 shows this blocking probability as a function of K for $W = 10$ and $\rho = 1$. The existence of a unique optimum for K is observed. It is also seen that the blocking probability is quite sensitive to the precise partitioning of the wavelength set. For instance, when $p = 0.9$, incrementing the number of local wavelengths from its optimal value of 7 to 8 results in nearly an order of magnitude increase in the blocking probability. Finally, while the optimal number of local wavelengths increases with traffic locality, the relationship between these two parameters is nonlinear. The blocking performance will be described in more detail in Section 5.

3.3 Dynamic Wavelength Allocation

Next we consider the modeling of dynamic wavelength allocation in a two-LAN system. The analysis in this case is complicated by the lack of statistical separation between local and global calls. We consider only the algorithms *Random* and *Convert* in this section as they allow a description with a compact state space, unlike *Packed* and *Coordinated*.

Define the state of the two-LAN system as the non-negative integer triplet (i, j, k) where i is the number of local calls in LAN 1, j is the number of local calls in LAN 2, and k is the number of global calls in the system. Since a wavelength can accommodate a single call in a LAN, the set of allowable states satisfies $i + k \le W$ and $j + k \le W$ defining a pyramid state space shown in Figure 3. The resulting Markov chain has $(W+1)(W+2)(2W+3)/6 \simeq W^3/3$ states and a three-dimensional birth-death structure. The rates

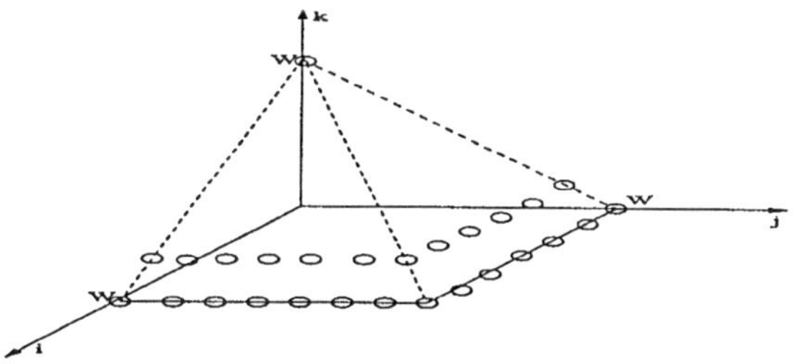

Figure 3: The state space for the two-LAN system.

of decrement from state (i, j, k) to the three states $(i-1, j, k)$, $(i, j-1, k)$ and $(i, j, k-1)$ are $i\mu$, $j\mu$ and $k\mu$ respectively.

The rates of increment in this Markov chain depend on the direction of the increment. A transition from state (i, j, k) to state $(i+1, j, k)$ corresponds to the establishment of a new local call in LAN 1. This is possible if and only if $i + k < W$. Accordingly, the rate of this transition is λp for $i + k < W$ and 0 for $i + k = W$. Similarly the rate of transition to state $(i, j+1, k)$ is λp for $j + k < W$.

The rate of increment in the k-direction depends on the wavelength allocation algorithm, as a transition in this direction indicates the establishment of a new global connection. This rate is less than the arrival rate $2\lambda(1-p)$ of global calls as blocking is possible even when the call request finds the system in a state properly within the pyramid (i.e., $i + k < W$ and $j + k < W$).

When *Random* or *Convert* is used, we assume a uniform assignment of calls to the wavelengths. More specifically, we assume that in state (i, j, k) the i local wavelengths in LAN 1 are uniformly distributed over the set of $W - k$ wavelengths not used by global calls. Similarly the j local wavelengths in LAN 2 are uniformly distributed over the same set (independently of the LAN 1 local wavelength distribution). Note that while this is a good approximation for *Random* and *Convert* which use random wavelength assignment, it cannot be used with *Packed* or *Coordinated*. A higher dimensional state space is required for the latter two schemes, making a similar analysis intractable.

Let $\alpha(i, j, k)$ be the probability that a global call request can be established when it finds the system in state (i, j, k). This is the probability that at least one of the $W - k$ wavelengths that are not currently used for global communications is free in both LANs. With the assumption above, this can be found to be

$$\alpha(i, j, k) = \begin{cases} 1 & \text{if } i + j + k < W \\ 1 - \frac{\binom{i+j}{W-k}}{\binom{i+j}{i}} & \text{if } i + j + k \geq W \end{cases}$$

using elementary counting arguments.

Note that the plane $i + j + k = W$ divides the state space into two subspaces. When $i + j + k < W$, no call blocking will occur as the existence of a free wavelength is guaranteed even if the local wavelength sets are disjoint. When $i + j + k \geq W$, global call blocking occurs with probability $1 - \alpha(i, j, k)$.

Next, we consider the algorithm *Convert*. Here a global call request is blocked if and only if there is no available wavelength in either of the two LANs. Then

$$\alpha(i, j, k) = \begin{cases} 1 & \text{if } i + k < W \text{ and } j + k < W \\ 0 & \text{otherwise.} \end{cases}$$

For both algorithms the transition rates from state (i, j, k) to state $(i, j, k+1)$ is given by $2\lambda(1-p)\alpha(i, j, k)$. Having completely characterized the Markov chains for these schemes, we need to solve for the steady state distribution $\pi(i, j, k)$. An efficient method to accomplish this using a software package based on Stochastic Petri Nets will be described in Section 4. Once the steady state distribution is obtained, the local and global call blocking probabilities can be found as

$$\begin{aligned} P_L &= \Pr(i + k = W) = \sum_{i=0}^{W} \sum_{j=0}^{W} \pi(i, j, W - i) \\ P_G &= \sum_{i=0}^{W} \sum_{j=0}^{W} \sum_{k=0}^{\min(W-i, W-j)} \pi(i, j, k)\,(1 - \alpha(i, j, k)) \end{aligned}$$

and the overall blocking probability is given by

$$P_B = pP_L + (1-p)P_G.$$

In Section 5, we describe the performance results obtained by using this analysis as well as by Monte Carlo simulations.

4 A Petri Net Model for Performance Evaluation

In this section, we describe the stochastic Petri Net model that is used to obtain the call blocking probability as explained in the previous section. We first provide a brief theoretical background on stochastic reward nets in Section 4.1, and then apply this concept to our problem in Section 4.2.

4.1 Stochastic Reward Net (SRN)

Petri nets [5] are used to specify flow of control in a system. A Petri net is a directed bipartite graph with two types of nodes: circles (called places) and bars (called transitions). *Input arcs* connect an *input place* to a transition, and *Output arcs* connect a transition to an *output place*. Each place contains a number of tokens, and has a token holding capacity. Each place represents a queue, transitions enable queue elements to move from one queue to another. A Petri net executes by firing transitions. When a transition fires, a specified number of tokens are removed from each of the input places, and are deposited in each of the output places. A vector $(m_1, m_2, \cdots, m_k)$ represents the number of tokens in k places in the Petri net such that m_i is the number of tokens in place i. This vector,

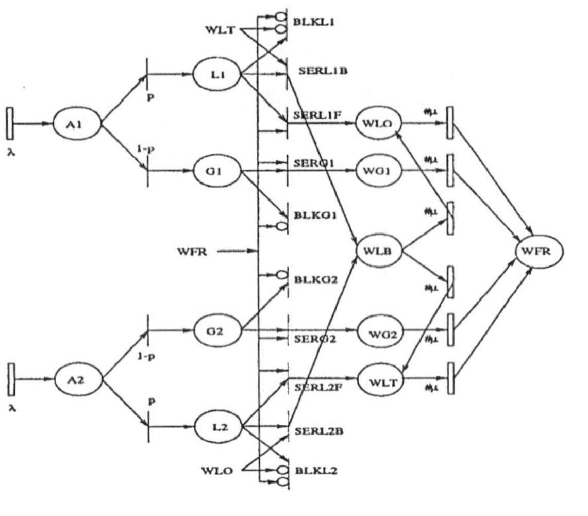

Figure 4: An SPNP model of a two-LAN system.

called a *marking*, defines a unique state of a Petri net, and therefore, that of the underlying Markov chain.

A stochastic Petri net (SPN) extends the Petri net model by assigning probability distributions to firing times for transitions. Generalized stochastic Petri net (GSPN) [6] allows two types of transitions: *immediate*, and *timed*. An immediate transition fires once it is enabled, whereas a timed transition is delayed by a random time. From a given description of a system model using SPN, a Markov chain can be automatically generated and solved using numerical methods. A stochastic reward net (SRN) extends the GSPN further by associating a reward rate with each marking. Using the steady state or transient state occupation probability distributions and rewards associated with each state and transition, appropriate measures of interest can be computed.

4.2 Application to LAN Interconnection

The queueing model specification shown in Figure 4 using a SRN framework consists of two submodels: traffic arrival and distribution model and wavelength utilization model. The model is shown for the two-LAN case, it becomes more complex if more than two LANs are involved. Traffic in each LAN arrives at a rate λ represented by the transition on the left for each LAN. In each LAN, the incoming traffic consists of two components, local and global. An incoming call is placed in a local call bin with probability p and in global call bin with probability $1-p$. This can be modeled by an immediate transition followed by the place holding a token for an incoming call. Place *Ai* (arrival), place *Li* (local), and place *Gi* (global) are the places holding a token for an incoming call, a local call, and a global call, respectively for LAN i for $i = 1, 2$. Any token in place *Ai* is immediately moved to either *Li* or *Gi*.

The second part of the model is for wavelength assignment and call service. Wavelength assignment and call service depend on the specific algorithm for wavelength allocation. For example, in *Random* the wavelength allocated to a local call can be any one of the free wavelengths in the corresponding LAN, whereas it has to be a free wavelength in both LANs for a global call. In contrast, in *Coordinated*, a local call will be assigned a wavelength that is free in both LANs only if there is no wavelength that is free in the LAN servicing the call and in use in the other LAN. Figure 4 models the system for *Random*, and can be easily modified for *Coordinated*. Although the model can be developed with fewer places, we purposely show the model in two parts, one for each LAN, for clarity.

A token in place WFR represents a free wavelength in both LANs. A global call in LAN i is blocked when there is a global call (token in place *Gi*), and there is no free wavelength (no token in WFR). This is represented by transition BLKGi. If there is a free wavelength (token in place WFR), then the call is serviced using one of the wavelengths. This is represented by firing of transition SERGi. In this case, the global call (token from Gi) and a free wavelength (token from WFR) are removed from their respective places, and the call is placed in service by depositing a token in place WGi.

A token in places WLO, WLT, and WLB represents a wavelength that is serving a local call in only LAN 1, only LAN 2, or both LANs, respectively. A local call in LAN 1 is blocked if there is no token in places WLT and WFR. This is represented by the transition BLKL1. Otherwise the call is serviced using one of the wavelengths from either set WLT or WFR. The probability of selection depends on the number of wavelengths in each set. SRN allows this probability to be computed dynamically, and exactly one of the two immediate transitions, SERL1B or SERL1F, is fired probabilistically. As a result, either a token is deposited in WLO (a free wavelength was used to serve the local call), or WLB (a wavelength in use in LAN 2 was used to serve this local call). A similar situation applies to a local call in LAN 2. In *Coordinated*, the transition SERLiB has higher priority over SERLiF.

All calls are serviced at rate μ. Whenever a call is serviced, it frees up a wavelength in that LAN. The service transition rates thus depend on the number of tokens in each place.

The above model is transformed into a Markov chain by the software tool SPNP [7]. The number of states in Markov chain clearly depends on the number of wavelengths. A state in the Markov chain will not have any tokens in places Ai, Li, and Gi. On the other hand, th number of tokens in places WLO, WG1, WLB, WG2, WLT, and WFR varies. A state can be represented by a 6-tuple, representing the number of tokens in each of the six places. The sum of all tokens in these six places will be equal to the total number of wavelengths. Initially, all the tokens are in place WFR.

This Petri net description allows for the solution of

the steady state distribution of the Markov chain with the pyramid state space without explicit enumeration of the states or the transition probability matrix by the user. The software tool enumerates all the states and transition probability matrix and solves the Markov chain. This approach is very attractive for applications which result in large Markov chains, including those in networking.

5 Results and Discussion

In this section, we present some numerical results for the blocking performance and discuss their implications. We also develop an approximate expression to predict the blocking probability with an arbitrary number of LANs. The results are obtained using the analytical framework described earlier and using Monte Carlo simulations. The simulation program was written in C on a Unix platform and allows performance evaluation with arbitrary numbers of LANs and wavelengths. For each simulation run, we generated a million arrival events in each LAN. We observed that the analytical results were always within the 95% confidence interval of the simulation results. For clarity, we do not show the confidence intervals in our graphs.

First we consider dynamic wavelength allocation using the *Random* scheme. Figures 5-8 show various performance characteristics for the two-LAN case. In all the figures, analytical results are represented by continuous curves and simulation results by symbols. Figure 5 shows the blocking probability as a function of the load ρ for a traffic locality $p = 0.5$. The agreement between the analytical and the simulation results is clearly seen. There is a significant reduction in blocking by increasing number of wavelengths. This is seen more clearly in Figure 6 which shows the blocking probability as a function of the number of wavelengths for various values of the traffic load. The performance gain with additional wavelengths is more significant when the load is lighter. For $\rho = 1/2$, the blocking probability is reduced by five orders of magnitude when W increases from 1 to 8, with $\rho = 2$ the decrease is less than two orders of magnitude. Figure 7 shows the blocking performance when the load per wavelength ρ/W is held constant as W varies. The classical statistical multiplexing gain is observed here; the performance improves as the number of channels and the total load increase proportionally.

Figure 8 shows the dependence of the blocking performance on the traffic locality parameter. It is observed that the performance improves with increasing locality of the traffic; local traffic requires less network bandwidth than global traffic. This dependence is stronger with a larger number of wavelengths and/or lighter network load.

All of the conclusions above also hold for the other dynamic wavelength allocation schemes, *Packed*, *Coordinated*, and *Convert*, as well as the static allocation scheme with optimized wavelengths partitioning. Figure 9 compares the performance of the static and dynamic schemes. The four dynamic schemes perform significantly better than optimized static allocation. This is again due to the statistical multiplexing gain afforded by dynamic resource sharing. Perhaps more surprisingly, there is very little performance difference between the four dynamic schemes. *Convert* is only slightly better than the others, while *Random* is only slightly poorer. This observation is consistent with the results of previous work on wavelength conversion [8, 9, 10]; for sparse topologies such as the one we consider here wavelength converters do not provide large performance gains. That *Packed* and *Coordinated* emulate *Random* is also consistent with the results of [11] on wavelength routing.

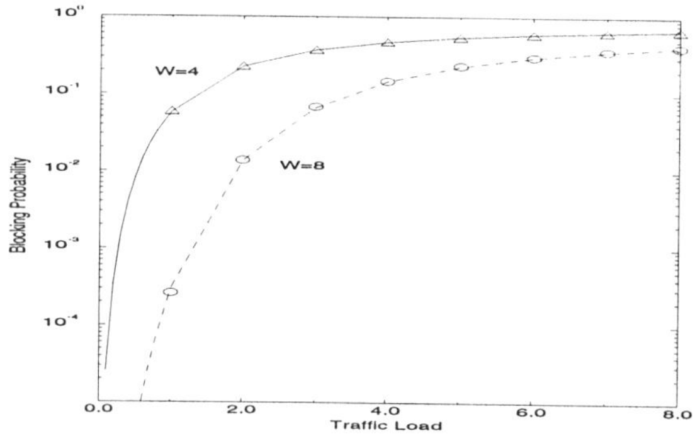

Figure 5: The dependence of the call blocking probability on the traffic load ρ for $p = 0.5$.

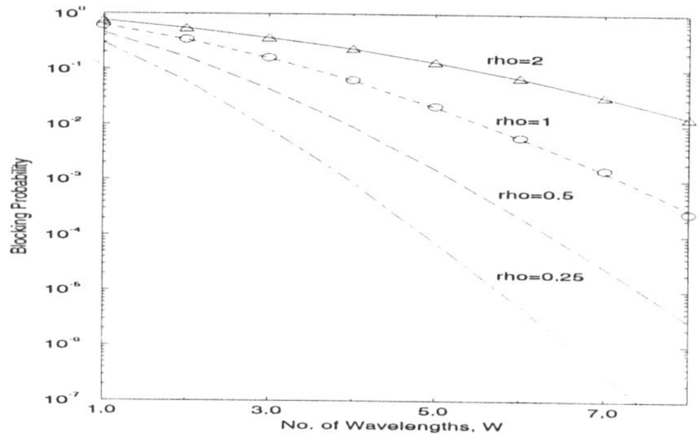

Figure 6: The dependence of the call blocking probability on the number of wavelengths for various loads ($p = 0.5$).

Given that any of the dynamic allocation schemes may be used without affecting the blocking performance, *Random* and *Packed* may be preferable due to their ease of implementation.

The results discussed so far are for a two-LAN system. In Section 5.1 we consider a system with an arbitrary number of LANs.

5.1 Multi-LAN Performance

In this section, we examine the effect of the number of interconnected LANs on the blocking performance.

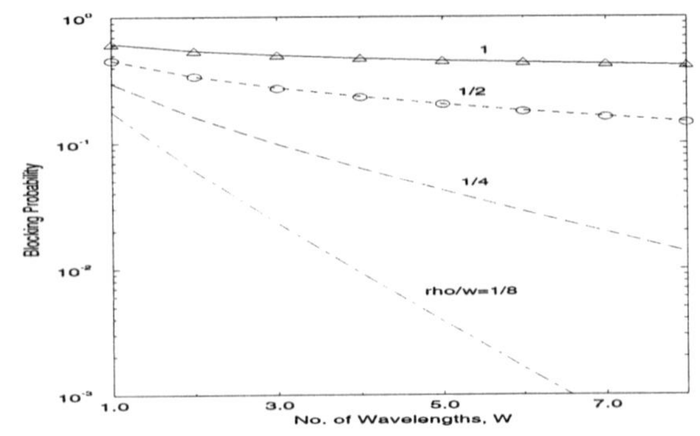

Figure 7: The dependence of the call blocking probability on the number of wavelengths for a fixed load per wavelength ($p = 0.5$).

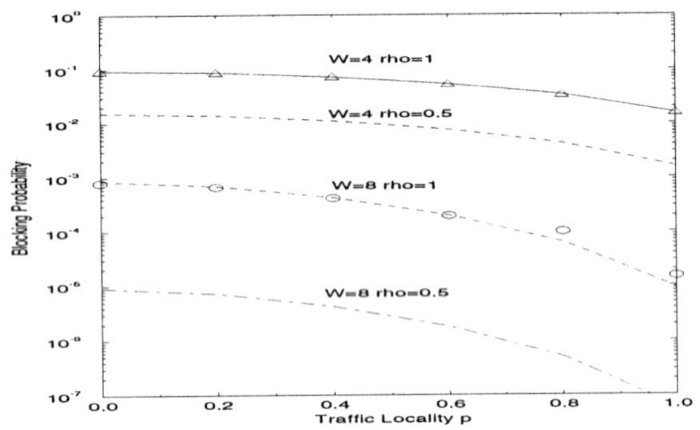

Figure 8: The dependence of the call blocking probability on the traffic locality p.

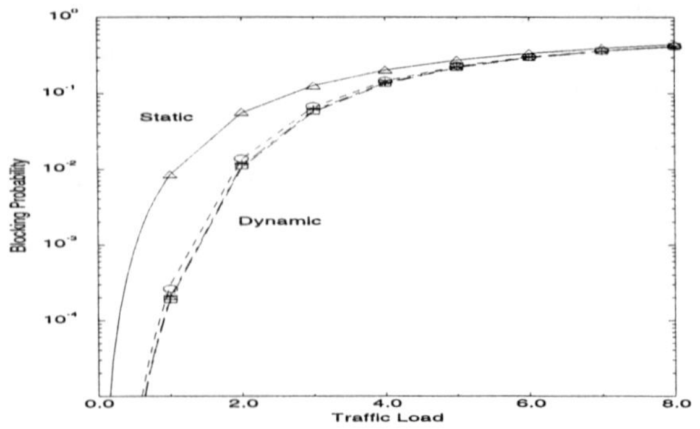

Figure 9: Comparison of static and dynamic wavelength allocation schemes ($W = 8$, $p = 0.5$).

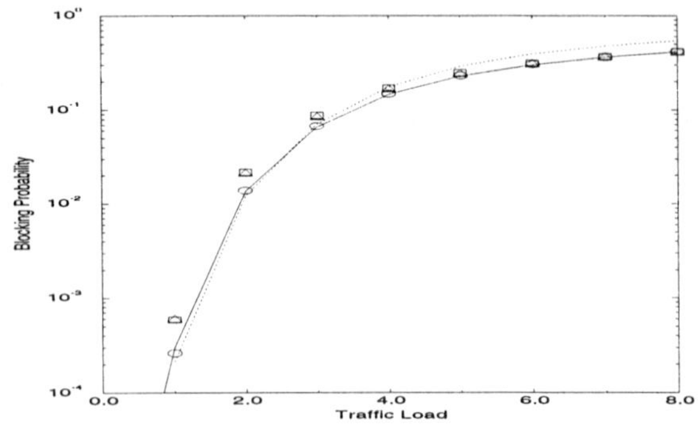

Figure 10: Call blocking probability from simulations for 2-LANs (circles), 4-LANs (triangles), and 8-LANs (squares). Also shown are the results predicted by the 2-LAN analytical model (solid curve), and the approximate model (dotted curve).

Since we do not have an exact analytical model when the number of LANs exceeds two, we first present the simulation results and then develop an approximate performance model. Figure 10 shows the simulated blocking probability as a function of the traffic per LAN for two- , four- , and eight-LAN systems with *Random*. The first observation from this figure is the relative insensitivity of the results to the number of LANs in the system. Note that the total load seen by a LAN consists of the traffic it generates (with rate λ) and the global traffic that originates in other LANs for this particular LAN (with rate $\lambda(1-p)$). Thus the total load $\rho(2-p)$ is independent of the number of LANs. The state of the source and destination LANs seen by a call request is only slightly affected by the presence of other LANs.

The empirical evidence that the blocking performance is nearly independent of the system size suggests that the analytical model for the two-LAN system developed earlier can be used as an approximation for an arbitrary number of LANs. This approximation is shown in solid lines in Figure 10. This approximation, while reasonably accurate, still requires the solution of a Markov chain whose number of states grows in a cubic fashion with the number of wavelengths. A coarser approximation with greater computational efficiency can be developed by considering a single LAN. This approach is described below.

Consider the source LAN of an arbitrary connection request. Suppose first that the request is for a local connection. Since the source LAN sees a total load which is approximately[4] $\rho(2-p)$ and has a total of W wavelengths. Therefore the local call blocking probability is approximately

$$P_L \simeq E\left(\rho(2-p), W\right) .$$

On the other hand, when the request is for a global connection, both the source and the destination LANs must not block this request for it to be honored. The probability that one of these will not block the call is approximately $1 - P_L \simeq 1 - E(\rho(2-p), W)$ as above. Assuming source and destination blocking are statistically independent events, we have the following ap-

[4] This load is approximate due to the blocking of global connection requests by the other LANs.

proximation for the global blocking probability

$$P_G \simeq 2E\left(\rho(2-p), W\right) - E^2\left(\rho(2-p), W\right) .$$

Combining the local and global blocking approximations, we obtain the approximate overall call blocking probability as

$$P_B \simeq (2-p)E\left(\rho(2-p), W\right) - (1-p)E^2\left(\rho(2-p), W\right)$$

which is shown in Figure 10 as the dotted curve. It is observed that this approximation is quite accurate for blocking probabilities below 0.1. For higher blocking probabilities, which clearly are of no practical interest, the fact that a large fraction of the calls are blocked reduces the effective load significantly below the nominal load $\rho(2-p)$. While it is possible to correct for this load adjustment through the recursive framework of an Erlang map, we do not pursue this approach due to the satisfactory accuracy of this first-order approximation in the blocking probability range of interest.

The significance of the approximation above lies in its simplicity and accuracy. It eliminates the need for solving a large Markov chain, and/or executing large simulation programs in order to estimate the approximate blocking performance for a given set of parameters. We have observed that the approximation is accurate for all ranges of W and p. In the more practical case of large p (large fraction of local calls), the agreement is even better than that shown in Figure 10. Of course, as p tends to 1, the approximation converges to the exact result.

6 Concluding Remarks

This paper has studied the issue of interconnecting optical broadcast-star LANs with a wavelength routing bridge. The problem of wavelength allocation to local and global connections was investigated with a dynamic traffic model. Static and dynamic wavelength assignment algorithms were developed and their performance was obtained using analytical and simulation techniques. It was found that the static approach which partitions the set of wavelengths into two subsets for local and global connections does not perform as well as the dynamic approaches even when the partitioning is optimized. This points out the desirability of dynamic wavelength allocation in this setting.

The dependence of the performance on the network load, the number of wavelengths, the traffic locality, and the number of interconnected LANs was studied. It was found that various dynamic allocation algorithms have similar blocking performance. In particular, the capability of wavelength conversion at the interconnection bridge was found to improve the performance only marginally. It was also observed that there is a very weak relationship between the blocking probability and the system size. Consequently, a simple, yet accurate, approximation was developed for an arbitrary number of interconnected LANs.

This initial study of all-optical LAN interconnection has considered a two-level hierarchical setting with a simple architecture. This setting needs to be extended to the case where multiple wavelength-routing nodes are connected through an arbitrary topology. A study of wavelength allocation for local and global traffic, and routing of global calls will bring the broadcast-star networks and wavelength-routing networks into a coherent, unified framework.

References

[1] S. B. Alexander *et al.*, "A precompetitive consortium on wide-band all-optical networks," *IEEE/OSA Journal of Lightwave Technology*, vol. 11, no. 5/6, pp. 714–735, May/June 1993.

[2] M. J. O' Mahony, D. Simeonidou, A. Yu, and J. Zhou, "The design of a European optical network," *IEEE/OSA Journal of Lightwave Technology*, vol. 13, no. 5, pp. 817–828, May 1995.

[3] N. F. Huang and C. S. Wu, "An efficient transmission scheduling algorithm for a wavelength-reusable local lightwave network," *IEEE/OSA Journal of Lightwave Technology*, vol. 12, no. 7, pp. 1278–1290, July 1994.

[4] D. P. Bertsekas and R. G. Gallager, *Data Networks*. Englewood Cliffs, NJ: Prentice Hall, second ed., 1992.

[5] J. L. Peterson, *Petri Net Theory and the Modeling of Systems,* Prentice Hall, 1981.

[6] M. Ajmone Marsan, G. Conte, and G. Balbo, "A class of generalized stochastic Petri nets for the performance analysis of multiprocessor systems," *ACM Trans. on Computer Systems*, vol. 2, pp. 93–122, 1984.

[7] G. Ciardo, J. Muppala, and K. Trivedi, "SPNP: Stochastic Petri net package," *Intl. Conference on Petri Nets and Performance Models*, Kyoto, Japan, pp. 142-151, December 1989.

[8] R. A. Barry and P. A. Humblet, "Models of blocking probability in all-optical networks with and without wavelength changers," *IEEE Journal on Sel. Areas in Comm.*, vol. 14, no. 5, pp. 858–867, June 1996.

[9] M. Kovacevic and A. Acampora, "Benefits of wavelength translation all-optical clear-channel networks," *IEEE Journal on Sel. Areas in Comm.*, vol. 14, no. 5, pp. 868–880, June 1996.

[10] S. Subramaniam, M. Azizoğlu, and A. K. Somani, "Connectivity and sparse wavelength conversion in wavelength-routing networks," *IEEE/ACM Trans. on Networking*, pp. 544–557, August 1996.

[11] A. Mokhtar and M. Azizoğlu, "Dynamic route selection and wavelength assignment in all-optical networks," *8th Annual LEOS Meeting*, Oct. 1995.

On the All-to-All Broadcast Problem in Optical Networks[1]

Hongsik Choi[2] Hyeong-Ah Choi[2] and Murat Azizoğlu[3]
[2]Department of Electrical Engineering and Computer Science
George Washington University, Washington, DC 20052

[3]Department of Electrical Engineering
University of Washington, Seattle, WA 98195-2500

Abstract

This paper considers the transmission of uniform deterministic traffic in an optical broadcast-star network using Wavelength Division Multiplexing. Lower bounds are established on the minimum time to exchange information between every node pair in such a network with tunable transmitters and fixed-tuned receivers. Three different scheduling algorithms are developed that are strictly optimal in three regimes of system parameters. The results are applicable to arbitrary tuning delays and arbitrary numbers of wavelength channels, and indicate the existence of a well-defined transition regime from tuning-limited operation to bandwidth-limited operation.

1 Introduction

In this paper, we consider a Wavelength Division Multiplexed (WDM) optical network with a broadcast-star architecture. This architecture has found applications in local area networks with very high speed information transfer rates. In such a network, n nodes are connected through a passive $n \times n$ broadcast star. Each node consists of a transmitter and a receiver at least one of which is tunable across the network bandwidth. The number of wavelength channels is typically limited to a small number (such as 10) due to various physical layer issues, such as interchannel crosstalk, optical amplifier bandwidth, optical filter resolution, etc. This makes it necessary to share a wavelength channel among many network nodes.

An important parameter that affects the performance of optical broadcast networks is the *tuning delay* which is the amount of time it takes an optical device (typically a laser for tunable transmitter and a filter for tunable receivers) to tune from one wavelength to another. Tuning delay limits the network throughput as nodes spend time in tuning which could otherwise be used in useful information transfer.

A simple traffic model for evaluating the effect of tuning delay on network performance was introduced in [8]. In this model, each node pair in the network is to exchange a fixed amount of information. The resulting traffic pattern is called all-to-all broadcast, although the information transfer is of point-to-point nature. We refer to the problem of designing optimum transmission policies under this traffic model as the *all-to-all broadcast problem.*

While we shall refer to the exchanged information as packets, the network may be packet-switched or circuit-switched. For an interpretation of the transmission scheduling in a circuit-switched network, see [2]. The all-to-all broadcast problem seeks minimum-time schedules to transmit n^2 packets, one between every source and every destination. This problem was first addressed in [8] and [1] which found upper and lower bounds for the schedule time. The traffic model was generalized in [2] to a stochastic model in which every node pair has a packet to exchange with some fixed probability. It was shown in [2] that a simple heuristic scheduling algorithm is nearly optimal for most traffic patterns when the tuning delay is small relative to the packet duration.

In [4], the authors studied the all-to-all broadcast problem as well as general deterministic traffic patterns. It was assumed that the number of wavelengths w is a divisor of the number of nodes n, which results in a perfectly uniform traffic load across the wavelengths with all-to-all traffic. Under this assumption, it was shown that the scheduling algorithm presented in [8] is optimal for arbitrary tuning delays. This is a somewhat surprising result since it has been recognized that there are two distinct regimes of opera-

[1]This research was supported in part by NSF under grants NCR-9309574, NCR-9502610 and MIP-9628468.

0-8186-7780-5/97 $10.00 © 1997 IEEE

tion depending on the magnitude of the tuning delay δ [2, 9]. When δ is small, the schedule time is dominated by the limited number of channels, resulting in the so-called bandwidth-limited regime. Conversely, in the case of large δ, tuning delay has an important effect on the schedule time, and this is called the tuning-limited regime. It will be shown in this paper that the strict optimality of the Pieris-Sasaki algorithm in both of these regimes is due to the uniform loading of the wavelengths, and will cease to hold when this uniformity is even slightly perturbed.

In this paper, we revisit the all-to-all broadcast problem without any assumptions on the system parameters n, w, and δ. The contribution of this paper is twofold. First, we obtain universal lower bounds on the scheduling time. The tightest one of these lower bounds depends on the location of the triplet (n, w, δ) in the three-dimensional space. It will be seen that this space is naturally partitioned into three subspaces resulting in three distinct regimes of operation. In each of these regimes, a different scheduling algorithm is optimal. The second contribution of this work is the development of three distinct algorithms which exactly meet the corresponding lower bounds. As a consequence, the all-to-all broadcast problem is resolved for almost every setting of parameters. The only exception is a small subspace of the parameter space in which the algorithms perform within a factor 13/12 of the lower bound.

The organization of the paper is as follows. Section 2 specifies the system model to be studied. The lower bounds are developed in Section 3 and the scheduling algorithms are presented in Section 4. Optimality of these schedules are established in Section 5. Concluding remarks are presented in Section 6.

2 System Model

Consider a WDM broadcast-and-select network with n users (i.e., n transmitters $t_0, \cdots, t_{n-1}$ and n receivers $r_0, \cdots, r_{n-1}$) and w_{max} wavelength channels $\lambda_0, \cdots, \lambda_{w_{max}-1}$. We assume that the transmitters are tunable and receivers are fixed-tuned. For a transmitter to tune from one wavelength channel to another, a tuning time δ (expressed in units of packet durations) is required. In [2], it was assumed that $\delta \leq 1$, while [9] considers δ to be a nonnegative integer. In this paper, we take δ to be an arbitrary, real valued parameter.

For a given w $(1 \leq w \leq w_{max})$, denote $n = \alpha w + \beta$ where $0 \leq \beta < w$; thus, $\alpha = \lfloor \frac{n}{w} \rfloor$. For any transmission schedule using w $(\leq w_{max})$ wavelength channels $\lambda_0, \cdots, \lambda_{w-1}$, let R_i, $0 \leq i \leq w-1$, denote the set of receivers tuned to wavelength λ_i. The wavelengths are loaded with receivers as uniformly as possible resulting in $|R_i| = \alpha + 1$ for $0 \leq i \leq \beta - 1$ and $|R_i| = \alpha$ for $\beta \leq i \leq w - 1$.

In the *all-to-all broadcast* problem, each of the n^2 transmitter-receiver pairs has one packet to transfer. We normalize the time such that the packets have unit-length. We also assume that each schedule requires an initial tuning phase of duration δ before packet transmissions can occur.

We consider the problem of all-to-all broadcast scheduling using w wavelength channels, where w is an arbitrary integer in $1 \leq w \leq w_{max}$. In the special case $\beta = 0$, w is a divisor of n and the problem is reduced to that considered in [8, 4]. In this case, the optimality of the scheduling algorithm suggested in [8] was established in [4] for arbitrary δ. Therefore, it is assumed that $\beta > 0$ throughout this paper and this condition implies that $|R_0| = \alpha + 1$.

We say that a transmission schedule is *continuous* if for any $0 \leq i \leq n-1$ and $0 \leq j \leq w-1$, once a transmitter t_i starts transmitting to a receiver group R_j, t_i does not transmit to any other receiver group until it completes its transmissions to all the receivers in R_j. Therefore, in any continuous schedule, each transmitter needs to tune exactly w times.

3 Lower Bounds to Optimal Schedule Lengths

In this section, we present lower bounds to optimal schedule lengths under various conditions on the system parameters. These lower bounds will be used in establishing the optimality of transmission schedules. Due to the space limit, proofs of lemmas are all omitted and they can be found in [5]

Lemma 3.1 *The length of any all-to-all transmission schedule is at least* $\delta + (\alpha+1)n$.

Lemma 3.2 *If* $\delta \geq \alpha^2 + \frac{\alpha\beta}{w}$, *the length of any continuous all-to-all transmission schedule is at least* $\alpha(\alpha+1) + n + w\delta - (\beta - 1)$.

Lemma 3.3 *If* $\delta \geq \alpha^2 + \frac{\alpha\beta}{w}$, *the length of any continuous all-to-all transmission schedule is at least* $\alpha^2 + n + w\delta$.

The lower bounds obtained in Lemmas 3.2 and 3.3 establish the following results.

Lemma 3.4 *If* $\delta > \alpha^2 + \frac{\alpha\beta}{w}$, *the length any continuous all-to-all broadcast transmission schedule is at least* $\alpha(\alpha+1) + n + w\delta - min\{\alpha,\ \beta - 1\}$.

Lemma 3.5 *If* $\alpha^2 + \frac{\alpha\beta}{w} < \delta \leq \alpha(\alpha+1)$, *the length any all-to-all broadcast transmission schedule is at least* $min\{n+(w+1)\delta,\ \alpha(\alpha+1)+n+w\delta-min\{\alpha,\ \beta-1\}\}$.

Lemma 3.6 *If $\delta \geq \alpha^2$ and $\beta > \frac{w}{2}$, the length of any continuous all-to-all transmission schedule is at least $\alpha(\alpha+1)+n+w\delta$.*

4 Construction of Transmission Schedules

In this section, we construct transmission schedules for arbitrary tuning delays and obtain upper bounds to their schedule lengths.

Time domain is represented by time slots starting with time slot 1. Transmitters and receivers, respectively, are denoted by t_i and r_k for $0 \leq i, k < n$. The set of receivers tuned to wavelength channel λ_j for $0 \leq j < w$ is denoted by R_j, where $|R_j| = \alpha+1$ for $0 \leq j < \beta$ and $|R_j| = \alpha$ for $\beta \leq j < w$. Write $R_j = \{r_k \mid j\alpha + j \leq k \leq (j+1)\alpha + j\}$ for $0 \leq j < \beta$ and $R_j = \{r_k \mid j\alpha + \beta \leq k \leq (j+1)\alpha + \beta - 1\}$ for $\beta \leq j < w$. Note that if $r_k \in R_j$, then $j = \lfloor \frac{k}{\alpha+1} \rfloor$ for $0 \leq k < \beta(\alpha+1)$ and $j = \lfloor \frac{k-\beta(\alpha+1)}{\alpha} \rfloor + \beta$ for $\beta(\alpha+1) \leq k < n$. In the subsequent discussions, each R_j is assumed to be an ordered set according to the index of $r_k \in R_j$. For example, receivers in R_0 are ordered such that $r_0 < r_1 < \cdots < r_\alpha$.

Lemma 4.1 *If $\delta \leq \alpha^2 + \frac{\alpha\beta}{w}$, then there exists an all-to-all broadcast schedule with schedule length upper bounded by $\delta + (\alpha+1)n$.*

Proof: Let $l_0 = \alpha^2 + \frac{\alpha\beta}{w}$. We will first describe an initial schedule $\mathcal{S}_0^1$ using $\delta + (n-1)(\alpha+1) + n + (w-1)l_0 \triangleq L_0^1$ time slots. Based on this, a schedule $\mathcal{S}^1$ with schedule length $\delta + (\alpha+1)n \triangleq L^1$ will be discussed.

Figure 1 shows a block diagram of our initial schedule. Transmitters are scheduled such that after the initial tuning delay δ, t_0 starts to transmit to R_0 and t_1 starts to transmit to R_0 right after the completion of t_0 to R_0, and so on. Note that as $|R_0| = \alpha+1$, each transmitter t_i starts to transmit to R_0 in time slot $\delta + i(\alpha+1) + 1$. Thus, the last transmission to R_0 is from t_{n-1}, and this transmission is done in time slot L^1. To schedule transmissions to R_1, each t_i has idle period of l_0 ($\geq \delta$) time slots (which will be used for tuning) before starting a transmission to R_1. Remaining transmissions from each t_i to R_2 through R_{w-1} are similarly scheduled. To compute the length of this initial schedule, note that t_{n-1} has the largest clearance time such that it has to wait for $\delta + (n-1)(\alpha+1)$ time slots before it starts a transmission to R_0 and still requires $n + (w-1)l_0$ time slots to complete its transmissions. Therefore, the length of $\mathcal{S}_0^1$ is $\delta + (n-1)(\alpha+1) + n + (w-1)l_0$ which is L_0^1. Based on $\mathcal{S}_0^1$, $\mathcal{S}^1$ is defined as follows.

Suppose a transmission from transmitter t_i to receiver r_k is arranged in time slot p. If $p > L^1$, rearrange this transmission to occur in time slot $p - (\alpha+1)n$. (Note that $\delta < p - (\alpha+1)n \leq L^1$ as $p \leq L_0^1$.) Otherwise, it remains in the same time slot. Figure 2 illustrates such a rearrangement.

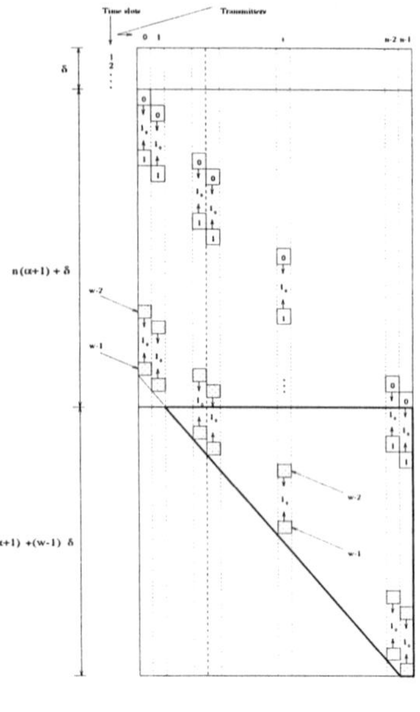

Figure 1:

Let $\mathcal{S}^1(i,k)$ denote the time slot in which t_i transmits to r_k when schedule $\mathcal{S}^1$ is used. To compute $\mathcal{S}^1(i,k)$ precisely, let $r_k \in R_j$. The time slot for the transmission from t_i to r_k using $\mathcal{S}_0^1$ is computed as $\mathcal{S}_0^1(i,k) = \delta + i(\alpha+1) + k + 1 + jl_0$. The time slot for the transmission from t_i to r_k using $\mathcal{S}^1$ is then computed as $\mathcal{S}^1(i,k) = \mathcal{S}_0^1(i,k)$ if $\mathcal{S}_0^1(i,k) \leq \delta + (\alpha+1)n$ and $\mathcal{S}^1(i,k) = \mathcal{S}_0^1(i,k) - (\alpha+1)n$ otherwise. In other words, $\mathcal{S}^1(i,k) = (\delta + i(\alpha+1) + k + 1 + jl_0) \bmod (\alpha+1)n$.

In order to prove the correctness of our schedule $\mathcal{S}^1$, we proceed to show that for any i, i', k, and k' with $r_k \in R_j$ and $r_{k'} \in R_{j'}$,

(i) if $\mathcal{S}^1(i,k) = \mathcal{S}^1(i',k')$, then $j \neq j'$ and

(ii) if $j \neq j'$, $|\mathcal{S}^1(i,k) - \mathcal{S}^1(i,k')| - 1 \geq l_0 \geq \delta$.

If both $\mathcal{S}_0^1(i,k)$ and $\mathcal{S}_0^1(i',k')$ are $\leq L^1$ or $> L^1$, then it is easy to see that $\mathcal{S}^1(i,k) = \mathcal{S}^1(i',k')$ implies $j \neq j'$. So, assume that $\mathcal{S}_0^1(i,k) \leq L^1$ and $\mathcal{S}_0^1(i',k') > L^1$, and $\mathcal{S}^1(i,k) = \mathcal{S}^1(i',k')$. Therefore, $\mathcal{S}_0^1(i',k') - \mathcal{S}_0^1(i,k) = (\alpha+1)n$, which implies $(j'-j)l_0 + (i'-i)(\alpha+1) + (k'-k) = (\alpha+1)n$. Suppose $j' = j$, which implies that $k' - k \leq \alpha$. Then, $(\alpha+1)n = (i'-i)(\alpha+1) + (k'-k) \leq (n-1)(\alpha+1) + \alpha < (\alpha+1)n$, a contradiction. Therefore, we conclude that $j' \neq j$ and this proves the claim (i).

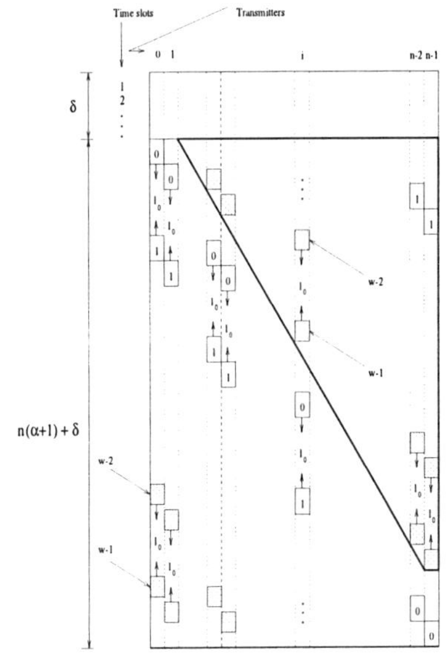

Figure 2:

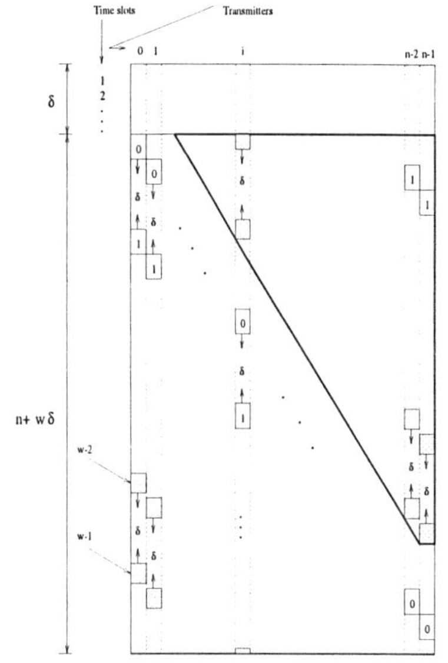

Figure 3:

To prove the claim (ii), we first note that $|\mathcal{S}_0^1(i,k) - \mathcal{S}_0^1(i,k')| - 1 \geq l_0$ for any i and $j \neq j'$. So, we only need to consider the case when $\mathcal{S}_0^1(i,k) \leq L^1$ and $\mathcal{S}_0^1(i,k') > L^1$, where $k = 0$ and $k' = n-1$ (i.e., r_k is the first receiver in R_0 and $r_{k'}$ is the last receiver in R_{w-1}). Note that $\mathcal{S}^1(i,0) = \delta + i(\alpha+1) + 1$ and $\mathcal{S}^1(i,n-1) = \delta + i(\alpha+1) + n + (w-1)l_0 - (\alpha+1)n$. Thus, we have $\mathcal{S}^1(i,0) - \mathcal{S}^1(i,n-1) = l_0 + 1$. This completes the proof of the lemma. ∎

Lemma 4.2 *If $\alpha^2 + \frac{\alpha\beta}{w} < \delta \leq \alpha(\alpha+1)$, then there exists an all-to-all broadcast schedule with schedule length bounded by $n + (w+1)\delta$.*

Proof: Let $\alpha^2 + \frac{\alpha\beta}{w} < \delta \leq \alpha(\alpha+1)$. Again, we first discuss an initial schedule $\mathcal{S}_0^2$ and a schedule $\mathcal{S}^2$ is then discussed based on $\mathcal{S}_0^2$.

The arrangements of transmissions in $\mathcal{S}_0^2$ is identical to those in $\mathcal{S}_0^1$ except that each t_i has idle period δ in $\mathcal{S}_0^2$, instead of $\alpha^2 + \frac{\alpha\beta}{w}$ in $\mathcal{S}_0^1$, between any transmissions to receiver groups R_j and R_{j+1}. Therefore, each t_i starts a transmission to R_0 in time slot $\delta + i(\alpha+1) + 1$ using $\mathcal{S}_0^2$. As t_{n-1} has the largest clearance time, the length of $\mathcal{S}_0^2$ is computed as $n + w\delta + (n-1)(\alpha+1) \triangleq L_0^2$.

To define a schedule $\mathcal{S}^2$ with schedule length $n + (w+1)\delta \triangleq L^2$, suppose t_i transmits to r_k in time slot p. If $p > L^2$, rearrange the transmission to occur in time slot $p - (n + w\delta)$. (Note that $\delta < p - (n+w\delta) \leq L^2$ since $p \leq L_0^2$ and $\delta > \alpha^2 + \frac{\alpha\beta}{w}$.) Otherwise, it remains in the same time slot. Figure 3 illustrates this rearrangement.

To compute $\mathcal{S}^2(i,k)$ precisely, let $r_k \in R_j$. We then note that the time slot for a transmission from t_i to r_k using $\mathcal{S}_0^2$ is $\mathcal{S}_0^2(i,k) = (j+1)\delta + i(\alpha+1) + k + 1$. The time slot for this transmission using $\mathcal{S}^2$ is then computed as $\mathcal{S}^2(i,k) = \mathcal{S}_0^2(i,k)$ if $\mathcal{S}_0^2(i,k) \leq n + (w+1)\delta$ and $\mathcal{S}^2(i,k) = \mathcal{S}_0^2(i,k) - (n + w\delta)$ otherwise. In other words, $\mathcal{S}^2(i,k) = ((j+1)\delta + i(\alpha+1) + k + 1) \ mod \ (n + w\delta)$.

The proof of correctness of $\mathcal{S}^2$ is similar to that of $\mathcal{S}^1$ and omitted here. ∎

In the following, we show that there exists an all-to-all broadcast schedule $\mathcal{S}^3$ with schedule length bounded by $\alpha(\alpha+1) + n + w\delta$ for any $\delta > \alpha(\alpha+1)$. Observe that the result in Lemma 4.2 also holds for any $\delta > \alpha(\alpha+1)$. However, if $\delta > \alpha(\alpha+1)$, the schedule length of $\mathcal{S}^2$ is larger than the schedule length of of $\mathcal{S}^3$.

Lemma 4.3 *If $\delta > \alpha(\alpha+1)$, then there exists an all-to-all broadcast schedule with schedule length bounded by $\alpha(\alpha+1) + n + w\delta$.*

Proof: The set of transmitters are divided into groups of an ordered set T_j for $0 \leq j < w$ such that $t_i \in T_j$ if and only if $r_i \in R_j$ for $0 \leq i < n$. The order of transmitters in each T_j are according the index of $t_i \in T_j$. We then note that $|T_j| = \alpha + 1$ for $0 \leq j < \beta$ and $|T_j| = \alpha$ for $\beta \leq j < w$, where $T_j = \{t_i \mid j\alpha + j \leq i \leq (j+1)\alpha + j\}$ for $0 \leq j < \beta$ and $T_j = \{t_i \mid j\alpha + \beta \leq i \leq (j+1)\alpha + \beta - 1\}$ for $\beta \leq j < w$. If $t_i \in T_j$, then $j = \lfloor \frac{i}{\alpha+1} \rfloor$ for $0 \leq i < \beta(\alpha+1)$ and $j = \lfloor \frac{i - \beta(\alpha+1)}{\alpha} \rfloor + \beta$ for $\beta(\alpha+1) \leq i < n$.

Let $\prec$ denote an order defined on $\{T_j \mid 0 \leq j < w\}$ such that $T_j \prec T_{j-1}$ for $2 \leq j < w$ and $T_0 \prec T_{w-1}$. Figure 4 shows a block diagram of our initial schedule $\mathcal{S}_0^3$ with schedule length $2n + (2w-1)\delta + (\alpha+1)(|T_1| - 2) \triangleq L_0^3$; transmitters are scheduled as a group by following the order $\prec$.

Transmitters in T_0 are first scheduled to transmit to R_0 such that the first transmitter in T_0 starts to transmit after the initial tuning delay δ. As soon as the wavelength channel λ_0 is available, the second transmitter in T_0 transmits to R_0, and the rest of transmitters in T_0 similarly transmit to R_0. Let $\mathcal{S}_0^3(T_j, R_0)$ denote the time slot in which the first transmitter in T_j starts to transmit to the first receiver in R_0 (i.e., r_0). We then see that $\mathcal{S}_0^3(T_0, R_0) = \delta + 1$. The remaining transmitters are scheduled to transmit to R_0 such that transmitters in group T_{w-j} are scheduled before those in group $T_{w-(j+1)}$ for $1 \leq j \leq w-2$; the first transmitter in T_{w-j} starts to transmit to r_0 in time slot

$$\mathcal{S}_0^3(T_{w-j}, R_0) = \delta + \sum_{b=1}^{j}(|T_{w-b}| + \delta) + 1 \qquad (1)$$

and continues to transmit to $r_1, \cdots, r_\alpha$, and the second through last transmitters in T_{w-j} complete transmissions to R_0 using $(|T_{w-j}| - 1)(\alpha+1)$ times slots.

Once transmissions from each transmitter t_i to R_0 are arranged, t_i has idle period of δ time slots (which will be used for tuning) before starting a transmission to R_1. Remaining transmissions from each t_i to R_2 through R_{w-1} are similarly arranged.

In this arrangement, it is remarked that transmissions from transmitters in T_0 to any receiver group are all arranged in time slots $\leq n + w\delta + \alpha(\alpha+1)$; and transmissions from transmitters in T_{w-j} $(1 \leq j \leq w-1)$ to receiver group R_p are all arranged in time slots $\leq n + w\delta + \alpha(\alpha+1)$ if $0 \leq p < w-j$ and in time slots $\geq n + (w+1)\delta + 1$ if $w - j \leq p < w$. In fact, a transmission from the first transmitter in T_{w-j} to the first receiver in R_{w-j} is scheduled in time slot $n + (w+1)\delta + 1$. The validity of this argument will follow from the subsequent discussions.

To compute the schedule length of $\mathcal{S}_0^3$, let t_{1^*} be the last transmitter in T_1. (Note that if $\beta = 1$, $|T_1| = \alpha$ which implies that $t_{2\alpha}$ is the last transmitter in T_1 and if $\beta > 1$, $|T_1| = \alpha + 1$ which implies that $t_{2\alpha+1}$ is the last transmitter in T_1.) The length of $\mathcal{S}_0^3$ is the clearance time of t_{1^*} which can be computed as

$$|\mathcal{S}_0^3| = T_{1^*}^0 + T_{1^*}^1 \qquad (2)$$

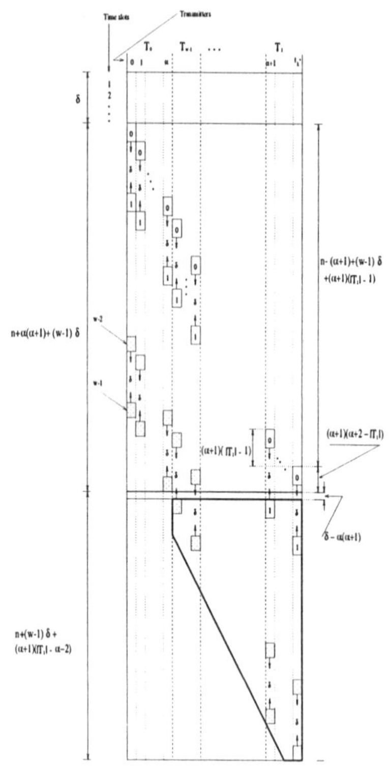

Figure 4: $\mathcal{S}_0^3$ when $\delta > \alpha(\alpha+1)$.

where $T_{1^*}^0$ is the amount of time slots for which t_{1^*} has to wait until its first transmission to r_0 occurs and $T_{1^*}^1$ is the amount of time slots to complete transmissions. We see that

$$T_{1^*}^0 = \mathcal{S}_0^3(T_1, R_0) - 1 + (|T_1| - 1)(\alpha+1) \qquad (3)$$

and

$$T_{1^*}^1 = n + (w-1)\delta. \qquad (4)$$

From Equation (1), note that $\mathcal{S}_0^3(T_1, R_0) = w\delta + n - |T_0| + 1$ which is equal to $w\delta + n - \alpha$. Putting this into Equation (3), we have

$$T_{1^*}^0 = w\delta + n + (\alpha+1)(|T_1| - 2). \qquad (5)$$

Substituting Equations (4) and (5) into Equation (2) gives that

$$|\mathcal{S}_0^3| = 2n + (2w-1)\delta + (\alpha+1)(|T_1| - 2). \qquad (6)$$

Consider an example when $n = 10$, $w = 3$, and $\delta = 13$ (note that $\alpha = 3$ and $\beta = 1$.) From Equation (6), the initial schedule for this example has length 89.

To compute the time slot in which t_i transmit to r_k, suppose $t_i \in T_p$ and $r_k \in R_q$. We then note the following.

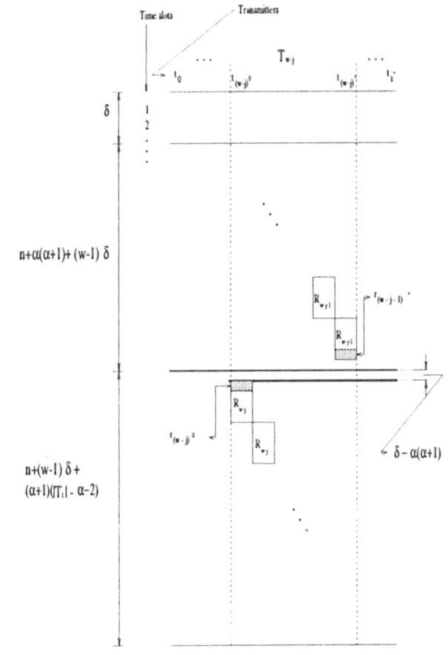

Figure 5:

($\mathcal{A}1$) If t_i is the ath transmitter in T_p, then $a = i - \lfloor \frac{i}{\alpha+1} \rfloor (\alpha+1) + 1$ for $0 \le i < \beta(\alpha+1)$ and $a = i - \beta(\alpha+1) - \lfloor \frac{i-\beta(\alpha+1)}{\alpha} \rfloor \alpha + 1$ for $\beta(\alpha+1) \le i < n$.

From ($\mathcal{A}1$), the time slot in which t_i transmits to r_0 is computed as

$$\mathcal{S}_0^3(i,0) = \mathcal{S}_0^3(T_p, R_0) + (a-1)(\alpha+1) \quad (7)$$

where $p = \lfloor \frac{i}{\alpha+1} \rfloor$ if $0 \le i < \beta(\alpha+1)$ and $p = \lfloor \frac{i-\beta(\alpha+1)}{\alpha} \rfloor + \beta$ if $\beta(\alpha+1) \le i < n$. From this, the time slot in which t_i transmits to r_k is then computed as

$$\mathcal{S}_0^3(i,k) = \mathcal{S}_0^3(T_p, R_0) + (a-1)(\alpha+1) + k + q\delta \quad (8)$$

where $q = \lfloor \frac{k}{\alpha+1} \rfloor$ if $0 \le k < \beta(\alpha+1)$ and $q = \lfloor \frac{k-\beta(\alpha+1)}{\alpha} \rfloor + \beta$ if $\beta(\alpha+1) \le i < n$. Putting Equation (1) into Equation (8), we have

($\mathcal{A}2$) $\mathcal{S}_0^3(i,k) = ((w-p) \bmod w + 1)\delta + \sum_{b=p}^{w-1} |T_b| + (a-1)(\alpha+1) + k + 1 + q\delta$, where

- (b-1) $p = \lfloor \frac{i}{\alpha+1} \rfloor$ if $0 \le i < \beta(\alpha+1)$ and $p = \lfloor \frac{i-\beta(\alpha+1)}{\alpha} \rfloor + \beta$ if $\beta(\alpha+1) \le i < n$,
- (b-2) $q = \lfloor \frac{k}{\alpha+1} \rfloor$ if $0 \le k < \beta(\alpha+1)$ and $q = \lfloor \frac{k-\beta(\alpha+1)}{\alpha} \rfloor + \beta$ if $\beta(\alpha+1) \le k < n$,
- (b-3) $a = i - \lfloor \frac{i}{\alpha+1} \rfloor (\alpha+1) + 1$ if $0 \le i < \beta(\alpha+1)$ and $a = i - \beta(\alpha+1) - \lfloor \frac{i-\beta(\alpha+1)}{\alpha} \rfloor \alpha + 1$ if $\beta(\alpha+1) \le i < n$.

Before we proceed to discuss the schedule $\mathcal{S}^3$, we will show that no transmission occurs using $\mathcal{S}_0^3$ after the time slot L^3 before the time slot $L^3 + \tau + 1$, where $L^3 = n + w\delta + \alpha(\alpha+1)$ and $\tau = \delta - \alpha(\alpha+1)$. To prove this, we show that for any $1 \le j \le w-1$, the time slot for the transmission from the last transmitter $t_{(w-j)^*} \in T_{w-j}$ to the last receiver $r_{(w-j-1)^*} \in R_{w-j-1}$ is $\le L^3$ and the time slot for the transmission from the first transmitter $t_{(w-j)^0} \in T_{w-j}$ to the first receiver $r_{(w-j)^0} \in R_{w-j}$ is equal to $L_0^3 + \tau + 1$ (see Figure 5, i.e.,

($\mathcal{A}3$) $\mathcal{S}_0^3((w-j)^*, (w-j-1)^*) \le L^3$ and $\mathcal{S}_0^3((w-j)^0, (w-j)^0) = L^3 + \tau + 1$ for $1 \le j \le w-1$.

Note that $\mathcal{S}_0^3(T_{w-j}, R_{w-j-1}) = \mathcal{S}_0^3(T_{w-j}, R_0) + (w-j-1)\delta + (|R_0| + \cdots + |R_{w-j-2}|)$. Since $\mathcal{S}_0^3(T_{w-j}, R_0) = \delta + (|R_{w-j}| + \cdots + |R_{w-1}|) + j\delta + 1$, we have

$$\mathcal{S}_0^3(T_{w-j}, R_{w-j-1}) = w\delta + (n - |R_{w-j-1}|) + 1. \quad (9)$$

The time slot when the last transmitter in T_{w-j} transmits to the last receiver in R_{w-j-1} is shown to be

$$\mathcal{S}_0^3((w-j)^*, (w-j-1)^*) = \mathcal{S}_0^3(T_{w-j}, R_{w-j-1}) - 1 + |R_{w-j-1}| \cdot |T_{w-j}|. \quad (10)$$

Substituting Equation (9) into Equation (10), we have

$$\mathcal{S}_0^3((w-j)^*, (w-j-1)^*) = w\delta + n + |R_{w-j-1}|(|T_{w-j}| - 1). \quad (11)$$

Since both $|R_{w-j-1}|$ and $|T_{w-j}|$ are bounded by $\alpha + 1$, Equation (11) proves the first part of ($\mathcal{A}3$), i.e., $\mathcal{S}_0^3((w-j)^*, (w-j-1)^*) \le w\delta + n + \alpha(\alpha+1)$.

To prove the second part of ($\mathcal{A}3$), note that $\mathcal{S}_0^3((w-j)^0, (w-j)^0) = \mathcal{S}_0^3(T_{w-j}, R_{w-j-1}) + \delta + |R_{w-j-1}|$. This, from Equation (9), implies that

$$\mathcal{S}_0^3((w-j)^0, (w-j)^0) = (w+1)\delta + n + 1 \quad (12)$$

which is equal to $w\delta + n + \alpha(\alpha+1) + \tau + 1$. This completes the proof of ($\mathcal{A}3$).

Now, we are ready to discuss our schedule $\mathcal{S}^3$ with length L^3. In $\mathcal{S}^3$, the time slot in which a transmission from t_i to r_k is defined to be

$$\mathcal{S}^3(i,k) = \begin{cases} \mathcal{S}_0^3(i,k) & \text{if } \mathcal{S}_0^3(i,k) \le L^3 \\ \mathcal{S}_0^3(i,k) - (w\delta + n) & \text{if } \mathcal{S}_0^3(i,k) > L^3 + \tau \end{cases}$$

Observe from ($\mathcal{A}3$) that $\mathcal{S}_0^3(i,k) > L^3$ implies that $\mathcal{S}_0^3(i,k) > L^3 + \tau$ $(= (w+1)\delta + n)$; thus, the schedule $\mathcal{S}_3$ considers every possible case. Figure 6 illustrates $\mathcal{S}^3$.

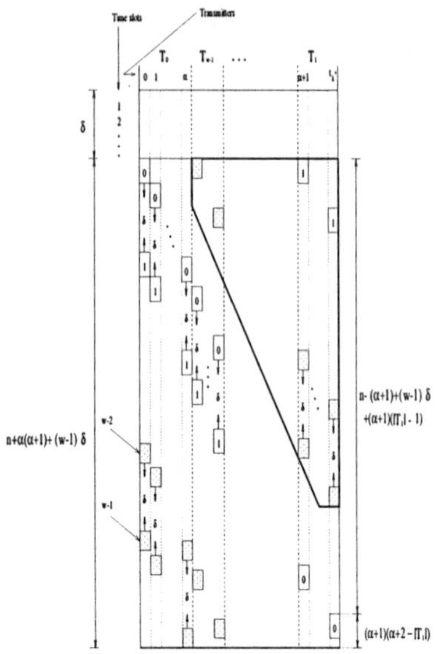

Figure 6: $\mathcal{S}^3$ when $\delta > \alpha(\alpha+1)$.

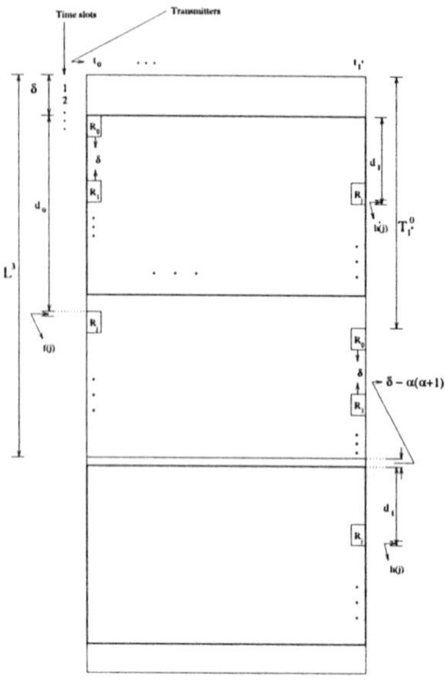

Figure 7:

In order to prove the correctness of our schedule $\mathcal{S}^3$, we proceed to show that for any i, i', k, and k' with $r_k \in R_j$ and $r_{k'} \in R_{j'}$,

(i) if $j = j'$, $\mathcal{S}^3(i,k) = \mathcal{S}^3(i',k')$ and

(ii) if $j \neq j$, $|\mathcal{S}^3(i,k) - \mathcal{S}^3(i,k')| - 1 \geq \delta$.

To prove claim (i), assume that $\mathcal{S}_0^3(i,k) \leq L^3$ and $\mathcal{S}_0^3(i',k') > L^3$ (otherwise, the proof is obvious). Suppose $\mathcal{S}^3(i,k) = \mathcal{S}^3(i',k')$. Let $f(j)$ denote the time slot in which the first transmission to the first receiver in R_j occurs using $\mathcal{S}_0^3$. Let $h(j)$ denote the time slot in which the last transmission to the last receiver in R_j occurs using $\mathcal{S}_0^3$. Let d_0 and d_1 be time periods as shown in Figure 7. We then see that $f(j) = \delta + d_0 + 1$ and $h(j) = (w+1)\delta + n + d_1$. Note that

$$d_0 = (|R_0| + \cdots + |R_{j-1}|) + j\delta \quad (13)$$

and

$$d_1 = T_0^{1^*} + (|R_0| + \cdots + |R_j|) + j\delta - ((w+1)\delta + n). \quad (14)$$

As any transmission scheduled in time slot $h(j)$ using $\mathcal{S}_0^3$ should be arranged in time slot $h'(j) = h(j) - (w\delta + n)$, we see that $h'(j) = \delta + d_1$. So, we only need to show that $f(j) > h'(j)$. Note that

$$f(j) - h'(j) = d_0 - d_1 + 1. \quad (15)$$

From Equations (5), (13) and (14), Equation (15) implies that

$$f(j) - h'(j) = \delta - (\alpha+1)(|T_1| - 2) - |R_j| + 1 \quad (16)$$

which then implies, from $|T_1| \leq \alpha+1$ and $|R_j| \leq \alpha+1$, that

$$f(j) - h'(j) \geq \delta - \alpha(\alpha+1) + 1. \quad (17)$$

Therefore, we conclude that $f(j) - h'(j) > 0$, which proves (i).

To prove the claim (ii), we first note that $|\mathcal{S}_0^3(i,k) - \mathcal{S}_0^3(i,k')| - 1 \geq \delta$ for any i and $j \neq j'$. So, we only need to consider the case when $\mathcal{S}_0^3(i,k) \leq L^3$ and $\mathcal{S}_0^3(i,k') > L^3$, where $k = 0$ and $k' = n-1$ (i.e., r_k is the first receiver in R_0 and $r_{k'}$ is the last receiver in R_{w-1}). Consider Figure 8. Let d_0 denote the idle period (after the initial tuning delay δ) before t_i starts a transmission to r_0 and d_1 denote the time period from the end of time slot $(w+1)\delta + n$ until t_i completes transmissions to R_{w-1}. We then see that $w\delta + n + d_1 = d_0 + n + (w-1)\delta$, which implies that $d_0 - d_1 = \delta$, i.e., $|\mathcal{S}^3(i,0) - \mathcal{S}^3(i,n-1)| - 1 = \delta$. This proves (ii) which in turn completes the proof of the lemma. ∎

5 Analysis of Upper and Lower bounds

In this section, we evaluate the optimality of our schedules presented in the previous section. We show that the length of our schedule achieves a lower bound for almost all cases. More precisely, (i) if $\delta > \alpha^2 + \frac{\alpha\beta}{w}$ and $1 < \beta \leq \frac{w}{2}$, the length of our schedule is no more than the optimal schedule length plus $\min\{\alpha, \beta - 1\}$

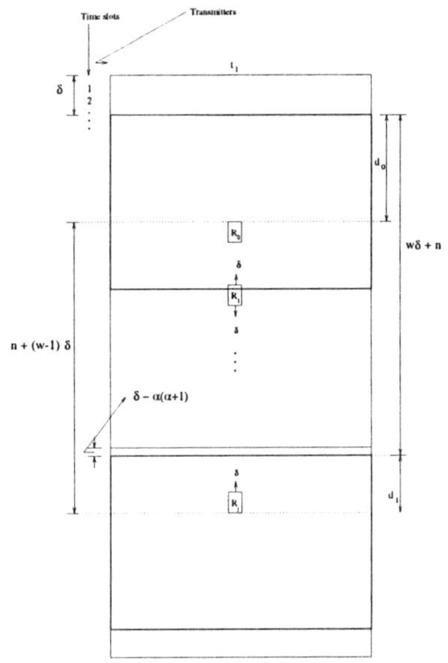

Figure 8:

and (ii) for any other case, the length of our schedule is optimal.

Theorem 5.1 *Let T_{opt} denote the length of an optimal all-to-all transmission schedule. Then, there exists an all-to-all transmission schedule with schedule length T_{sch} given by:*

(1) $\delta \leq \alpha^2 + \frac{\alpha\beta}{w}$
$T_{sch} = \delta + (\alpha+1)n \leq T_{opt}$.
(2) $\alpha^2 + \frac{\alpha\beta}{w} < \delta \leq \alpha(\alpha+1)$
(2.1) $\delta \leq \alpha(\alpha+1) - min\{\alpha,\ \beta-1\}$
$T_{sch} = n + (w+1)\delta \leq T_{opt}$.
(2.2) $\delta > \alpha(\alpha+1) - min\{\alpha,\ \beta-1\}$
(2.2.1) $\beta = 1$
$T_{sch} = n + (w+1)\delta \leq T_{opt}$.
(2.2.2) $1 < \beta \leq \frac{w}{2}$
$T_{sch} = n + (w+1)\delta \leq T_{opt} + min\{\alpha,\ \beta-1\}$.
(2.2.3) $\frac{w}{2} < \beta < w$
$T_{sch} = n + (w+1)\delta \leq T_{opt}$.
(3) $\delta > \alpha(\alpha+1)$
(3.1) $\beta = 1$
$T_{sch} = \alpha(\alpha+1) + n + w\delta \leq T_{opt}$.
(3.2) $1 < \beta \leq \frac{w}{2}$
$T_{sch} = \alpha(\alpha+1) + n + w\delta \leq T_{opt} + min\{\alpha,\ \beta-1\}$.
(3.3) $\frac{w}{2} < \beta < w$
$T_{sch} = \alpha(\alpha+1) + n + w\delta \leq T_{opt}$.

Proof: (1) The result follows from Lemmas 4.1 and 3.1.

(2) The condition of (2.1) implies that $n + (w+1)\delta \leq \alpha(\alpha+1) + n + w\delta - min\{\alpha,\ \beta-1\}$. Using this, Lemma 3.5 gives $T_{opt} \geq n + (w+1)\delta$. This lower bound and the upper bound in Lemma 4.2 prove the result of (2.1). Now, assume the condition of (2.2), i.e., $n + (w+1)\delta > \alpha(\alpha+1) + n + w\delta - min\{\alpha,\ \beta-1\}$. Then, Lemma 3.5 implies

$$T_{opt} \geq \alpha(\alpha+1) + n + w\delta - min\{\alpha,\ \beta-1\}. \quad (18)$$

Note that $n + (w+1)\delta < n + w\delta + \alpha(\alpha+1)$ from the condition of (2). Hence, from Equation (18), we have

$$T_{sch} = n + (w+1)\delta < T_{opt} + min\{\alpha,\ \beta-1\}. \quad (19)$$

This proves the results of (2.2.1) and (2.2.2). To prove the result of (2.2.3), note that $\delta \leq \alpha(\alpha+1)$ which implies $n + (w+1)\delta \leq \alpha(\alpha+1) + n + w\delta$. Hence, Lemma 3.6 proves the result.

(3) If $\delta > \alpha(\alpha+1)$, we observe that $n + (w+i)\delta > \alpha(\alpha+1) + n + w\delta$ for any $i > 0$. This means that any optimal schedule must be continuous. Therefore, the results of (3.1) - (3.3) follow from Lemmas 4.3, 3.4 and 3.6. This complete the proof of the theorem. ∎

The above theorem establishes the following result.

Theorem 5.2 *For any arbitrary δ, there exists an all-to-all transmission schedule for which the ratio of the schedule length to the optimal solution is bounded by $\frac{13}{12}$.*

Proof: From Theorem 5.1, we only to need to consider two cases (2.2.2) and (2.3). Thus, assume $\delta \geq \alpha^2 + \frac{\alpha\beta}{w}$ and $2 \leq \beta \leq \frac{w}{2}$ (i.e., $w \geq 4$). We first note that

$$T_{sch} \leq \alpha(\alpha+1) + n + w\delta. \quad (20)$$

This follows from the observation that $n + (w+1)\delta < \alpha(\alpha+1) + n + w\delta$, i.e., the schedule length of case (2.2.2) is also bounded by that of case (3.2).

Suppose $\alpha \leq \beta - 1$. From Lemma 3.4, we note

$$T_{opt} \geq \alpha(\alpha+1) + n + w\delta \quad \alpha. \quad (21)$$

From Equations (20) and (21), it is implied that

$$\frac{T_{sch}}{T_{opt}} \leq 1 + \frac{\alpha}{\alpha(\alpha+1) + n + w\delta - \alpha}. \quad (22)$$

From $\delta \geq \alpha^2 + \frac{\alpha\beta}{w}$, $n = \alpha w + \beta$, and $\beta \geq \alpha + 1$, we have $\alpha(\alpha+1) + n + w\delta - \alpha \geq \alpha(2\alpha + w + \alpha w + 2)$. Substituting this into Equation (22), we obtain

$$\frac{T_{sch}}{T_{opt}} \leq 1 + \frac{1}{2\alpha + w + \alpha w + 2}. \quad (23)$$

As $\alpha \geq 1$ and $w \geq 4$, this gives that the ratio is bounded $\frac{13}{12}$.

Next, assume that $\alpha > \beta - 1$. Lemma 3.4 then implies

$$T_{opt} \geq \alpha(\alpha+1)+n+w\delta-(\beta-1). \quad (24)$$

From Equations (20) and (24), we have

$$\frac{T_{sch}}{T_{opt}} \leq 1+\frac{\beta-1}{\alpha(\alpha+1)+n+w\delta-(\beta-1)}. \quad (25)$$

Since $n = w\alpha+\beta$, $\delta \geq \alpha^2+\frac{\alpha\beta}{w}$, $\beta \geq 2$, and $\alpha > \beta-1$, it implies that $\alpha(\alpha+1)+n+w\delta-(\beta-1) \geq (\beta-1)(\alpha+w+\alpha w+3)$. Substituting this, Equation (25) implies that

$$\frac{T_{sch}}{T_{opt}} \leq 1+\frac{1}{\alpha+w+\alpha w+3}. \quad (26)$$

As $\alpha \geq 1$ and $w \geq 4$, Equation (26) gives the desired bound. The proof of the lemma is complete. ∎

6 Concluding Remarks

We have studied the problem of all-to-all broadcast in a broadcast-star network with n nodes, w wavelengths, and a tuning delay δ. With $\alpha = \lfloor n/w \rfloor$ and $\beta = n-w\alpha$, three operation regimes emerge naturally:

1. Bandwidth-limited regime, $\delta \leq \alpha^2+\alpha\beta/w$,
2. Tuning-limited regime, $\delta > \alpha^2+\alpha$,
3. Transition regime, $\alpha^2+\alpha\beta/w < \delta \leq \alpha^2+\alpha$.

In each of these regimes, a different lower bound for the minimum schedule time and a scheduling algorithm are presented. In the bandwidth limited regime, the schedule is optimal. in the transition regime and tuning-limited regime, the corresponding schedules are optimal except for the sub-case $2 \leq \beta \leq w/2$. This sub-case, in which at least two but no more than half of the wavelengths have an extra receiver, has proved surprisingly difficult to establish exact optimality for. We have been able to show, however, that even in this case the presented schedules perform within a factor 13/12 of the lower bounds.

An interesting observation in this work is the dependence of the optimal scheduling algorithm on the value of system parameters. This is unlike the previously considered situation with perfectly uniform wavelength loading, and points out the precise role of symmetry perturbation in this problem.

References

[1] A. Aggarwal, A. Bar-Noy, D. Coppersmith, R. Ramaswami, B. Schieber, and M. Sudan, "Efficient Routing and Scheduling Algorithms for Optical Networks," Tech. Rep. RC 18967, IBM Research Report, June 1993.

[2] M. Azizoğlu, R. Barry, and A. Mokhtar, "Impact of Tuning Delay on the Performance of Bandwidth-Limited Optical Broadcast Networks with Uniform Traffic," *IEEE Journal on Selected Areas in Communications*, June 1996.

[3] M. S. Borella and B. Mukherjee, "Efficient Scheduling of Nonuniform Packet Traffic in a WDM/TDM Local Lightwave Network with Arbitrary Transceiver Tuning Latencies", *Proceedings of Infocom '95*, pp. 129–137, April 1995.

[4] H. Choi, H.-A. Choi, M. Azizoğlu, "Efficient Scheduling of Transmission in Optical Broadcast Networks",*IEEE/ACM Trans on Networking*, Dec. 1996.

[5] H. Choi, H.-A. Choi, M. Azizoğlu, "On the All-to-All Broadcast Problem in Optical Networks" *GWU IIST-95-05* (Full Version of this paper)

[6] P. E. Green, *Fiber Optic Networks,* Englewood Cliffs, New Jersey: Prentice Hall, 1993.

[7] B. Mukherjee, "WDM-Based Local Lightwave Networks– Part I: Single-Hop Systems", *IEEE Network*, vol. 6, pp. 12–27, May 1992.

[8] G. R. Pieris and G. H. Sasaki, "Scheduling Transmissions in WDM Broadcast-and-Select Networks," *IEEE/ACM Trans on Networking*, vol. 2, no. 2, pp. 105–110, April, 1994.

[9] G. N. Rouskas and V. Sivaraman, "On The Design of Optimal TDM Schedules for Broadcast WDM Networks with Arbitrary Transceiver Tuning Latencies", *Proceedings of Infocom '96*, pp. 1217–1224, March 1996.

Integrated Rate and Credit Feedback Control for ABR Service in ATM Networks

Xi Zhang and Kang G. Shin
Real-Time Computing Laboratory
Dept. of Elec. Engin. and Compt. Scie.
The University of Michigan
Ann Arbor, MI 48109–2122
{xizhang,kgshin}@eecs.umich.edu

Qin Zheng
Mitsubishi Electric Research Labs
Cambridge Research Center
201 Broadway
Cambridge, MA 02139
zheng@merl.com

Abstract

We propose a flow-control scheme that combines the merits of credit- and rate-based flow-control schemes by applying direct control over both bandwidth and buffer resources. The goal of the proposed scheme is to design an optimal rate-control policy for a given finite buffer capacity that maximizes average throughput and bounds end-to-end delay. By applying higher-order rate control, the proposed scheme not only makes the rate process converge to the neighborhood of link bandwidth, but also confines the queue-length fluctuation to a regime bounded by buffer capacity (thus guaranteeing lossless transmission). Using the fluid approximation method, we model the proposed flow-control scheme and study the system dynamic behavior for ABR (Available Bit Rate) service under the most stressful traffic condition. We derive the expressions for queue build-ups and average throughput in both transient and equilibrium states. The analytical results have shown the proposed scheme to be stable and efficient in that the source rate and bottleneck queue length rapidly converge to the designated operating region. Also, presented are examples showing that the proposed scheme outperforms the other existing schemes.

1 Introduction

An ATM network can transport a wide variety of information such as data, audio, and video. Different types of user traffic have different requirements on bandwidth, loss ratio, and delay, which are characterized by a set of traffic parameters. Based on these traffic parameters, the ATM network sets up a connection (or VC—Virtual Circuit) from the source to the destination. A connection runs through a series of intermediate switch nodes, where it shares link bandwidth and buffer space with other connections. Thus, the traffic rate flowing through a switch depends on the number of connections and the source rates of these connections. To achieve high bandwidth utilization in the face of bursty traffic, the connections sharing the same output link are statistically multiplexed at the switch. However, if all of these connections become active simultaneously, or some connections increase their rates unlimitedly, queues build up at bottle-necked switches. Eventually, the buffer capacity is exceeded and cells are dropped, resulting in low throughput, a large delay, and even network blockage. To prevent a network from falling into this kind of congestion, an efficient flow-control scheme is required.

Available Bit Rate (ABR) service, which is suitable for various data communications, can maximize network bandwidth utilization and avoid congestion. In ABR service, there is no strictly-specified contract between the network and a client that describes the traffic behavior and the expected quality of service. Rather, the network is expected to provide each client with a fair share of available bandwidth dynamically; so ABR is a best-effort service. After allocating a certain bandwidth to high-priority traffic, such as Constant Bit Rate (CBR) connections, the network divides the remaining bandwidth among ABR connections. The client should also adjust his transmission rate based on the feedback on network congestion. So, ABR service requires a closed-loop congestion-control scheme, dynamically regulating the cell-transmission rate of each source according to congestion status.

A number of flow-control schemes have been proposed for ABR service. Among these, both *credit* [1] and *rate* [2, 3] schemes have received most attention [4]. The credit scheme guarantees lossless transmission by applying direct control over buffer space for each connection in a hop-by-hop manner. However, the credit scheme cannot make a bandwidth guarantee for each connection since it is window-type flow control and does not regulate the traffic flow rate [5]. Moreover, the credit scheme attempts to keep the buffer full to achieve high utilization. This may result in unbounded end-to-end delays and large delay variations. In contrast, the rate scheme provides a bandwidth guarantee and a bounded delay to each connection by exercising direct control over the link bandwidth allocated to each connection in an end-to-end fashion. But the buffer requirement for the rate scheme is very large and increases with feedback delay, the number of active connections,

The work reported in this paper was supported in part by a grant from Mitsubishi Electric Research Center, Cambridge, MA, and by the ONR under Grant N00014-94-0291. Any opinions, findings, and conclusions or recommendations expressed in this publication are those of the authors and do not necessarily reflect the views of the funding agencies.

0-8186-7780-5/97 $10.00 © 1997 IEEE

and the initial rate [6–9]. This makes the buffer design very difficult since the exact value of each connection's feedback delay and the number of active connections over a given link are not known *a priori*.

The aforementioned problems with the credit and rate schemes stem from the fact that neither scheme exerts direct control over both link bandwidth and buffer space. In this paper, we propose an integrated flow-control scheme that applies direct control over *both* link bandwidth and buffer space, to achieve the following goals:

- Lossless transmission for given finite buffer capacity,
- Optimal rate control to maximize average throughput for given buffer capacity,
- Bounded end-to-end delay,
- Fair bandwidth share guaranteed among competing connections,
- Maximum network utilization.

Using the first-order fluid approximation method[2, 10], we model the proposed scheme and analyze the system's dynamic behavior for ABR service under the most stringent traffic condition. In previous performance analyses, the maximum queue length Q_{max} was treated as a free parameter under the unrealistic assumption of infinite buffer capacity [2, 6–11]. In contrast, we assume the buffer capacity C_{max} is *finite* and use $Q_{max} < C_{max}$ as a constraint to find the optimal rate-control function. We derive closed-form expressions to evaluate the scheme's performance and compute the evolutions of rate and queue functions for transient and equilibrium states. From the analysis, we identify the optimal control pattern/state and conclude that just exercising increase/decrease rate control cannot have the system converge to the optimal control state (specified by bandwidth and buffer allocations). A higher-order rate control is applied over the rate-increase parameter with an exponential decreasing rule. Applying a two-dimensional rate control in the transient state analysis shows that the system rapidly converges to the designated optimal operating regime.

This paper is organized as follows. In Section 2, we compare the rate and credit schemes, and identify the problems with them. Section 3 presents our proposed scheme to solve these problems. Section 4 deals with the system model and the control model for the proposed scheme. In Section 5, we derive analytical solutions for both transient and equilibrium states and evaluate the scheme's performance for the single-connection case. Section 6 analyzes the proposed scheme's performance for the multiple-connection case through examples. The paper concludes with Section 7.

2 Rate vs. Credit, and Interworking

The principles and control mechanisms of the rate and credit schemes are detailed in [1] and [3]. Here, we focus on comparing them in terms of structures and performance and arguing for the need to integrate them.

The rate scheme regulates a connection's bandwidth by directly controlling its source cell-transmission rate according to network congestion information. Using RM (Resource Management) cells and EFCI (Explicit Forward Congestion Indication) bit setting, the information feedback control loop spans the entire network in an end-to-end fashion. The rate scheme aims at providing a bandwidth guarantee to each VC, bounding end-to-end transmission delay, and achieving fair allocation of network resources. On the other hand, the credit scheme exercises direct control and feedback on the amount of space left in switch buffers, rather than the rate. Instead of exercising an end-to-end control algorithm, the credit scheme segments the control loop at each switch. The goal of credit scheme is to ensure lossless transmission with a given finite buffer capacity while maintaining high bandwidth and buffer utilization.

Depending on their different goals and structures, these two schemes each have their own advantages and disadvantages, which will be discussed below.

Lossless transmission and buffer requirement: With the rate scheme, the buffer requirement is very large and increases with feedback delay, the number of active connections, and the initial rate [6–9]. This makes buffer design very difficult, because the exact values of the network delay of each connection and the number of active connections over a given link are not known *a priori*. As a result, one is forced to compromise between buffer size and loss ratio. In contrast, the credit scheme supports lossless transmission for any given finite buffer size.

Bandwidth guarantee: By explicitly assigning a target bandwidth to each connection, the rate scheme is most suitable for bandwidth-guaranteed applications. The credit scheme, like other window-type flow-control schemes, does not provide any bandwidth guarantee to each connection since it does not directly regulate the transmission rate.

End-to-end delay and delay variation: In the credit scheme, trying to always keep the buffer full may lead to larger end-to-end delays and delay variations. On the other hand, the rate scheme guarantees bandwidth for each VC and thus, each VC can receive guaranteed throughput. So, shaping traffic for each VC allows the end-to-end delay to be bounded.

Network resource utilization: Using a hop-by-hop feedback protocol, the credit scheme tends to achieve very high network utilization even in the face of widely-varying traffic loads, because buffered data can be sent whenever such an opportunity arises. But for the rate scheme, it is difficult to achieve high utilization of bandwidth due to large end-to-end delay. Moreover, if lossless or low-loss transmission is required, a very large buffer must be provided at each switch. This large buffer may be severely underutilized when only a small portion of VCs are active. By contrast, the credit scheme can ensure lossless transmission with a much smaller buffer while keeping it highly utilized.

Flow control is basically a resource management and control problem in a shared and distributed network environment. Network resources are composed of link bandwidth and buffer space. However, neither of the two schemes exerts direct control over both of these resources. Thus, an efficient flow-control scheme should

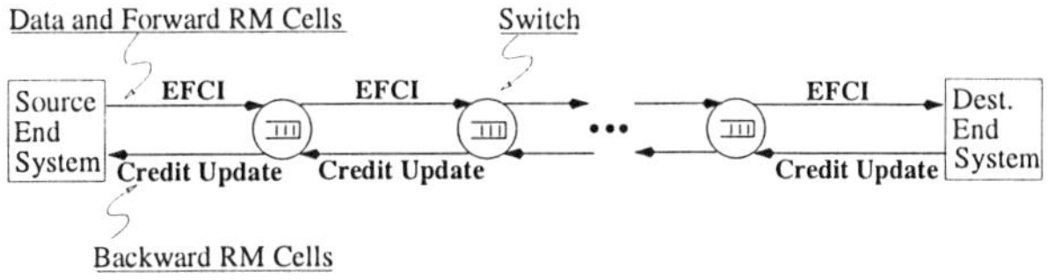

RM Cell Format:

DIR	0=Forward; 1=Backward
BN	0=Source Generated; 1= Switch Generated
CI	0=Not Congested; 1=Congested
ER	Explicit Cell Rate (two bytes)
CCR	Current Cell Rate (two bytes)
MCR	Minium Cell Rate (two bytes)
CU	Credit Update Value (two bytes)

Figure 1: Basic framework and RM cell format of the proposed scheme.

apply *direct* control over *both* bandwidth and buffer resources.

3 The Proposed Scheme

Observing the complementary features of the rate and credit schemes, we propose an *integrated* flow-control scheme which combines their merits while overcoming their drawbacks.

3.1 Key Differences from Rate or Credit Scheme

The framework and RM cell format for the proposed scheme are illustrated in Figure 1. Our scheme also uses the EFCI bit and RM cell to convey network congestion information. The EFCI bit is used for rate control and the backward RM cell is used for updating credit balance. Here the RM cell is redefined such that it contains both rate and credit control information. In particular, we added a new CU (Credit Update) field in the RM cell and use the BN (Backward Notification) bit to distinguish the RM cells generated either by the source or by intermediate switch nodes. Both rate and credit control are applied at all nodes using the redefined RM cells. Our scheme discriminates between two types of congestion: (1) *bandwidth congestion*, if queue length $Q(t) > Q_h$, a threshold; (2) *buffer congestion*, if credit balance $C_{bal} = 0$. If a buffer congestion occurs at a switch, the switch sends a backward RM cell (with BN=1) back to the source for a quick release of buffer congestion. There are two rate control modes at the source corresponding to these two types of congestion: (i) if a bandwidth congestion occurs then the source rate is reduced exponentially from its current value; (ii) if a buffer congestion occurs then the source needs to:

- cut down its current ACR (Allowed Cell Rate) to an appropriate smaller value R_c, which is less than the bottleneck bandwidth μ, but larger than its MCR (Minimum Cell Rate);
- exponentially reduce the rate-increase parameter which is the second-order rate control.

These enhanced features in structures and algorithms enable the proposed scheme to cope with the following practical problems that the other two schemes cannot handle. For given buffer capacity, our scheme adaptively adjusts rate-control parameters such that the system can quickly converge to an optimal rate-control mode, which maximizes average throughput, guarantees lossless transmission, and lowers end-to-end delay. On the other hand, when an established ABR connection specifies its MCR, ICR (Initial Cell Rate) and the corresponding rate control parameters, the proposed scheme can provide information on the optimal buffer allocation for each connection to meet its performance specifications.

3.2 The Control Algorithms

The control algorithms are involved with the Source End System (SES), the Destination End System (DES), and all Intermediate Switch Systems (ISS) between SES and DES.

The Source Node Algorithm (Table 1). SES deals mainly with two events: sending data cells (lines 03–12) and receiving RM cells (lines 13–28). When the rate-control timer expires, SES first check if credit balance C_{bal} is positive. If $C_{bal} > 0$, it sends a data cell to the downstream node and then increments the count and decrements the credit (book-keeping). SES sends an RM cell once every N_{rm} data cells. Then the rate-control timer is reset. Upon receiving an RM cell, SES first updates its local credit balance by CU contained in the RM cell and then starts rate control. SES first check if the VC is already in buffer congestion state. If

```
00. Local Variables: ACR := ICR; U_cnt := 0; C_bal := C_max;
01. Buffer_congestion := 0; Data_que_len := 0; RM_send := 0;
02. while (VC_on_line) {
03.   if (Current_time >= Next_cell_time)  ! Sending data event
04.     if (C_bal > 0 and Data_que_len > 0)
05.       send data cell with EFCI := 0;
06.       Data_que_len := Data_que_len - 1;
07.       U_cnt := U_cnt + 1;  C_bal := C_bal - 1;  ! Book-keeping
08.     if (RM_send Mod N_rm = 0)
09.       send RM(DIR := forward, CI := 0, CCR := ACR,
10.               MCR, ER := PCR, BN := 0) cell;
11.     RM_send := RM_send + 1;
12.     Next_cell_time := Next_cell_time + 1/ACR;
13.   if (receive RM(DIR = backward, CI, CCR, ER,
14.               CU = D_cnt, BN) cell)
15.     C_bal := C_max - (U_cnt - CU);
16.     if (Buffer_congestion = 0 or CI = 0)
17.       if (BN = 1)
18.         ACR := max{ER/ACR (2 * ER - ACR), MCR};
19.         AIR := 0.5AIR;      ! AIR (Additive Increase Rate)
20.         MDF := e^(-AIR/ER);
21.         Buffer_congestion := 1;
22.       else if (CI = 1)
23.               ACR := ACR * MDF;
24.               if (C_bal = 0)  ACR := MCR;
25.               else
26.               ACR := ACR + AIR;
27.               Buffer_congestion := 0;
28.     Next_cell_time := Current_time + 1/ACR;
29. }
```

Table 1: Pseudocode for SES.

no buffer congestion, then (1) if $BN = 0$ then SES *additively* increases its ACR or *multiplicatively* decreases its ACR depending on the CI bit (set ACR to MCR if C_{bal}=0); (2) If $BN = 1$ then SES turns into buffer congestion state, and exercises the buffer congetion control by setting ACR to R_c, exponentially reducing rate-increase parameter AIR and accordingly adjusting rate-decrease parameter MDF. If this VC is already in the buffer congestion state, then the source ACR stays with R_c until the first backward RM cell with CI=0 (noncongestion) is received. Finally, the rate-control timer is adjusted according to the updated ACR (for simplicity only the per-N_{rm} data cells scheme is presented. Our scheme also allows periodic rate-update control.)

The Switch Node Algorithm (Table 2). Three main events need to be handled: (1)*Receiving data* (lines 02–11): forward the data cell if the output link is ready and $C_{bal} > 0$; enqueue the data otherwise. Mark the

```
00. Local Variables: U_cnt, C_bal, Data_que, Data_que_len,
01. Local_VC_CCR; Local_VC_ER; Local_VC_CI := 0;
02. if (receive Data cell)     ! Receiving data event
03.   if (Output link is ready and C_bal > 0)
04.     forward Data cell;
05.     U_cnt := U_cnt + 1;  C_bal := C_bal - 1;  ! Book-keeping
06.   else
07.     add Data cell to Data_que;
08.     if (C_bal = 0)
09.       send RM(DIR := backward, CU := U_cnt, CI := 1,
10.                     ER := μ, BN := 1)
11.     if (Data_que_len ≥ Q_h) Local_VC_CI := 1;
12. if (receive output link ready signal and Data_que_len > 0 )
13.   schedule all active VCs {
14.   if (C_bal > 0)
15.     remove Data cell from head of Data_que;
16.     if (Data_que_len ≤ Q_l) Local_VC_CI := 0;
17.     forward Data(EFCI := EFCI ⊕ Local_VC_CI) cell;
18.     U_cnt := U_cnt + 1;   C_bal := C_bal - 1;  ! Book-keeping
19.   else
20.     send RM(DIR := backward, CU := U_cnt, CI := 1,
21.                     ER := μ, BN := 1) }
22. if ( receive RM(DIR, CI, CCR, ER, CU, BN) )
23.   if (DIR = forward)
24.     Local_VC_CCR := CCR;   Local_VC_ER := ER;
25.     send RM(DIR = forward) cell;
26.   else
27.     C_bal := C_max - (U_cnt - CU);          ! CU = D_cnt
28.     send RM(DIR = backward, CU := U_cnt,
29.                     CI := CI ⊕ Local_VC_CI) cell;
```

Table 2: Pseudocode for ISS.

local CI bit (*Local_VC_CI*) for setting EFCI bit in the data cell header if the queue length exceeds Q_h. Generate and send an RM cell directly back to the source with $BN = 1$, $CI = 1$, and $ER =$ link bandwidth if $C_{bal} = 0$ after credit book-keeping. (2)*Receiving link-ready signal* (lines 12–21): schedule the active VCs. Dequeue a data cell for the scheduled VC. If queue length drops below Q_l, the local CI bit is unmarked. Generate and send an RM cell directly back to SES with $BN{=}1$, $CI = 1$, and $ER =$ bandwidth if $C_{bal} = 0$. (3)*Receiving RM cells* (lines 22–29): for a forward RM cell, record its contents and forward it to the downstream node; for a backward RM cell, update the local credit-balance by CU contained in the RM cell, fill in the RM cell with local count and CI bit, and then send it to the upstream node.

The Destination Node Algorithm (Table 3). Two

```
00. Local Variables: Local_VC_CI, U_cnt;
01. if (receive Data cell)  ! Receiving data cell event
02.   Local_VC_CI := EFCI field of Data cell;
03.   U_cnt := U_cnt + 1;
04.   forward Data cell to user;
05. if (receive RM(DIR = forward, CI, CCR, ER, CU, BN))
06.     send RM(DIR = backward, CU := U_cnt,
07.                  CI := CI ⊕ Local_VC_CI, BN := 0 ) cell;
```

Table 3: Pseudocode for DES.

events are processed: receving data cells (lines 01–04) and receiving RM cells (lines 05–07). When a data cell is received, its EFCI bit is saved and the local count is updated. When an RM cell is received, the RM cell's CI bit is set using the EFCI bit saved from the data cell last received. Finally, return the RM cell with the updated credit and congestion information to the upstream node.

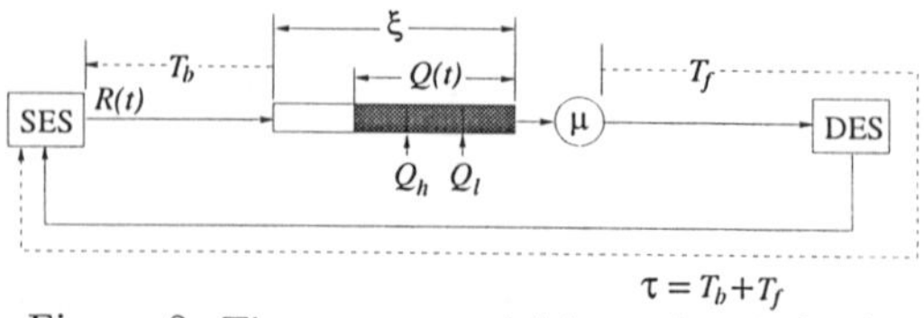

Figure 2: The system model for a virtual circuit.

4 System Model

An ATM network with ABR connections subject to the proposed flow-control scheme is a dynamic system. We model this system by using the first-order fluid approximation method [2, 10], where $R(t)$ and $Q(t)$ represent source-rate function and bottleneck queue-length function respectively (see Figure 2). Due to its simplicity, effectiveness, and approximation accuracy (particularly for heavy traffic), the fluid modeling method has been effectively applied to the analysis and evaluation of several common rate-based flow-control schemes [2, 6–11].

In all previous analyses using the fluid model, the maximum queue length Q_{max} is treated as a free parameter under the unrealistic assumption that buffer capacity is infinite [2, 6–11]. In a real network, however, this assumption does not hold, and thus, the results based on this assumption are not applicable to the case of finite buffer capacity. By contrast, our model hinges on a finite buffer capacity C_{max}, and the inequality $Q_{max} < C_{max}$ is used as a constraint in finding the optimal rate-control function. We also assume the existence of only a single bottleneck with queue length $Q(t)$ and a "persistent" source, which always has data cells to send, with ACR $= R(t)$, for each VC. Such a data source model allows us to examine the proposed scheme under the most stressful condition.

4.1 System Description

The system with the proposed flow-control scheme is characterized by the following parameters (see Figure 2):

β:	Multiplicative decrease factor for rate reduction
α:	Additive rate-increase slope
Δ:	Time interval of rate update
MCR:	Minimum cell rate for the ABR connection
Q_h:	High threshold of $Q(t)$ for traffic overload
Q_l:	Low threshold of $Q(t)$ for traffic underload
T_b:	Backward delay of the ABR connection
T_f:	Forward delay of the ABR connection
ξ:	Bottleneck maximum buffer allocation (C_{max})
μ:	Bottleneck link bandwidth (BW)

T_b is the delay experienced by *buffer congestion* signal from the bottleneck to SES. T_b also represents the delay for $R(t)$'s action to reach the bottleneck from SES. T_f is measured from the detection of *bandwidth congestion* at the bottleneck to the time when an EFCI signal reaches SES via DES. Thus, $\tau = T_b + T_f$ is the VC's round-trip delay (including processing time and propagation delay.) We use the synchronous model for rate control in which the fixed (periodic) rate-update interval Δ is usually a fraction of τ.

The additive increase and the multiplicative decrease of rate control during the n-th rate-update interval are expressed as:

$$R_n = \begin{cases} R_{n-1} + a; & \text{Add. increase, } a = AIR \\ bR_{n-1}; & \text{Multi. decrease, } b = MDF \end{cases} \quad (4.1)$$

4.2 System State Equations

The system state is specified by two state variables: $R(t)$ and $Q(t)$. According to the proposed control algorithms, the system state equations for a VC containing a single bottleneck are given by the following equations, depending on whether rate or credit control is in operation.

Rate-control: For $C_{bal} > 0$ (no-buffer congestion)

$$R(t) = \begin{cases} R(t_0) + \alpha(t - t_0); & \text{If } Q(t - T_b) < Q_h \\ R(t_0)e^{-(1-\beta)\frac{(t-t_0)}{\Delta}}; & \text{If } Q(t - T_b) \geq Q_h \end{cases} \quad (4.2)$$

$$Q(t) = \int_{t_0}^{t} [R(\alpha - T_b) - \mu]d\alpha - Q(t_0). \quad (4.3)$$

where the rate "additive increase" and rate "multiplicative decrease" are modeled by "linear increase" and "exponential decrease", respectively, in a continuous domain [2].

Credit-control: If $C_{bal} = 0$ (buffer congestion)

$$R(t) = R_c, \quad (R_c \geq MCR) \quad (4.4)$$
$$Q(t) = \xi - (\mu - R_c)(t - T_b - t_0). \quad (4.5)$$

where R_c is the cut-down rate set by SES when it receives a (BN=1) RM cell.

5 Analysis of a Single ABR Connection

The system dynamics could be in either equilibrium or transient state, which are treated below separately.

5.1 Equilibrium State Analysis

The equilibrium state is defined as the state in which the source-rate function $R(t)$ and the bottleneck queue-length function $Q(t)$ have already converged to a certain regime and oscillate with constant amplitude and frequency. The use of credit control yields three different patterns for flow-controlled rate and queue-length functions, depending on the range of the flow-control parameters.

Pattern I: $\xi > Q_{max}$. Since $\xi > Q_{max}$, no buffer congestion occurs. The rate-control mechanism governs the system dynamics (see Figure 3).

Let R_{max} be the maximum rate, then we obtain

$$R_{max} = \mu + \alpha(T_q + T_b + T_f) \quad (5.1)$$

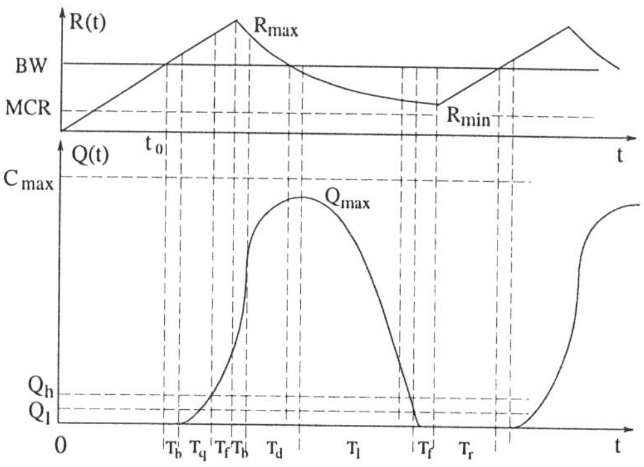

Figure 3: Dynamic Behavior of $R(t)$ and $Q(t)$ for Pattern I.

where $T_q = \sqrt{2Q_h/\alpha}$ is the time for $Q(t)$ to grow to Q_h from zero. For the convenience of presentation, we define

$$T_{max} \triangleq T_b + T_q + T_f = T_b + \sqrt{\frac{2Q_h}{\alpha}} + T_f \quad (5.2)$$

which is the time for $R(t)$ to increase from μ to R_{max}. Then, we get the maximum queue length

$$Q_{max} = \frac{\alpha}{2}T_{max}^2 + \alpha\frac{\Delta T_{max}}{(1-\beta)} + \frac{\mu\Delta}{(1-\beta)} \log \frac{\mu}{R_{max}}. \quad (5.3)$$

T_l is the duration for $Q(t)$ to decrease from Q_{max} to Q_l, and thus, is determined by the following non-linear equation:

$$e^{-(1-\beta)\frac{T_l}{\Delta}} + \frac{1-\beta}{\Delta}\left(T_l - \frac{Q_{max} - Q_l}{\mu}\right) - 1 = 0. \quad (5.4)$$

The minimum rate is given by

$$R_{min} = \mu e^{-(1-\beta)\frac{(T_l+T_b+T_f)}{\Delta}}. \quad (5.5)$$

Clearly, the rate-fluctuation cycle is $T = T_q + T_d + T_l + 2\tau + T_r$, where $T_d = -\frac{\Delta}{(1-\beta)} \log \frac{\mu}{R_{max}}$ is the time for $R(t)$ to drop from R_{max} back to μ and $T_r = (\mu - R_{min})/\alpha$ is the time for $R(t)$ to grow from R_{min} to μ.

The average throughput in equilibrium state can be calculated by averaging $R(t)$ over one cycle T as

$$\overline{R} \triangleq \frac{1}{T}\int_{t_0}^{t_0+T} R(t)dt = \frac{1}{T}\left[\mu T_{max} + \frac{\alpha}{2}T_{max}^2 + \frac{R_{max}\Delta}{1-\beta}\left(1 - e^{-(1-\beta)\frac{T_e}{\Delta}}\right) + T_r R_{min} + \frac{\alpha}{2}T_r^2\right] \quad (5.6)$$

where $T_e = T_d + T_l + \tau$ is the time for exponential-decrease rate control within a cycle.

Pattern II: $\alpha(T_{max} - 2T_b)^2/2 < \xi < Q_{max}$. In this case $Q(t)$ would grow beyond ξ without credit control, but ξ is still large enough for $R(t)$ to reach R_{max}. After $Q(t)$ reaches ξ, the source receives the buffer congestion signal and cuts down $R(t)$ to an appropriate smaller R_c to achieve a quick dissipation of the buffer congestion. Two factors affect the selection of R_c. If R_c is too large, then the queuing delay increases because the speed of draining a congested buffer is inversely proportional to R_c. On the other hand, if R_c is too small, then the average throughput decreases. To make a tradeoff between queuing delay and average throughput, we set:

$$R_c = \max\left\{\frac{\mu}{R_{max}}(2\mu - R_{max}),\ MCR\right\}. \quad (5.7)$$

Notice that if $R_{max} \geq 2\mu$ then $R_c = MCR$; and if $R_{max} = \mu$ then $R_c = \mu$.

The rate control in Pattern II is further divided into three cases because they need different analytical treatments. For convenience of presentation, we introduce a parameter T_c, the time for $Q(t)$ to increase from 0 to ξ. The system dynamics belong to one of these three cases, depending on the range T_c falls in.

Case 1: $T_{max} - 2T_b < T_c < T_{max}$. We get $T_c = \sqrt{2\xi/\alpha}$. The next key parameter is T_l, which is the time between $Q(t)$ reaching ξ and $Q(t)$ dropping to Q_l, and given by

$$T_l = 2T_b + \frac{\theta + (\xi - Q_l)}{\mu - R_c} \quad (5.8)$$

where

$$\theta = \frac{\alpha}{2}T_{max}^2 + \frac{\Delta R_{max}}{1-\beta}\left(1 - e^{-(1-\beta)\frac{T_e}{\Delta}}\right) - \mu T_e - \xi \quad (5.9)$$

is the number of "overshoot" cells the bottleneck node cannot accept due to $Q(t) = \xi$ and have been temporarily saved by the previous nodes. In Eq. (5.9) $T_e = (T_c + 2T_b) - T_{max}$. Then, we get $T = T_c + T_b + T_l + T_f + (\mu - R_c)/\alpha$.

By the definition of $\overline{R}$ given in Eq. (5.6), we get

$$\overline{R} = \frac{1}{T}\Bigg[\mu T_{max} + \frac{\alpha}{2}T_{max}^2 + \frac{\Delta R_{max}}{1-\beta}\left(1 - e^{-(1-\beta)\frac{T_e}{\Delta}}\right) + (T_l - T_b + T_f)R_c + T_r R_c + \frac{\alpha}{2}T_r^2\Bigg] \quad (5.10)$$

Case 2: $T_{max} < T_c < T_{max} + T_d - 2T_b$. Since $T_c > T_{max}$, T_c consists of two parts, $T_c = T_{max} + T_\xi$ where T_ξ is the duration for the exponential part of $R(t)$ contributing toward $Q(t) = \xi$ and is determined by a nonlinear equation:

$$e^{-(1-\beta)\frac{T_\xi}{\Delta}} + \frac{1-\beta}{\Delta}\left(\frac{\xi - \frac{\alpha}{2}T_{max}^2}{R_{max}} + \frac{\mu T_\xi}{R_{max}}\right) - 1 = 0. \quad (5.11)$$

The expressions of T_l, θ, T, and $\overline{R}$ for Case 2 are the same as Case 1 except that in Case 2, $T_c = T_{max} + T_\xi$ and $T_e = T_\xi + 2T_b$.

Case 3: $T_{max} + T_d - 2T_b < T_c < T_{max} + T_d$. Here T_l is a function of the "net" contribution of the "overshoot" cells: $\theta + \gamma$ where θ (γ) denotes the positive (negative) contribution generated in a delay interval of $2T_b$ when $R(t)$ curve intersects μ and is given by

$$\theta = \frac{\alpha}{2}T_{max}^2 + \frac{\Delta R_{max}}{1-\beta}\left(1 - e^{-(1-\beta)\frac{T_d}{\Delta}}\right) - \mu T_d - \xi \quad (5.12)$$

$$\gamma = \mu\left[\frac{\Delta}{1-\beta}\left(1 - e^{-(1-\beta)\frac{2T_b - (T_d - T_\xi)}{\Delta}}\right) - 2T_b + T_d - T_\xi\right] \quad (5.13)$$

Computing T as in Case 1, except that here

$$T_l = 2T_b + \frac{(\theta + \gamma) + (\xi - Q_l)}{\mu - R_c}, \quad (5.14)$$

we get the average throughput for Case 3 as follows:

$$\overline{R} = \frac{1}{T}\Bigg[\mu T_{max} + \frac{\alpha}{2}T_{max}^2 + \frac{\Delta R_{max}}{1-\beta}\left(1 - e^{-(1-\beta)\frac{T_d}{\Delta}}\right) + \frac{\Delta\mu}{1-\beta}\left(1 - e^{-(1-\beta)\frac{2T_b - (T_d - T_\xi)}{\Delta}}\right) + (T_l - T_b + T_f)R_c + T_r R_c + \frac{\alpha}{2}T_r^2\Bigg]. \quad (5.15)$$

Pattern III: $0 < \xi < \alpha(T_{max} - 2T_b)^2/2$. In this pattern, $T_c = \sqrt{2\xi/\alpha}$ and $R_{max} = \mu + \alpha(T_c + 2T_b)$. Using the same definitions of θ, T_l, and Eq. (5.8) as in Pattern II, we obtain

$$\theta = \frac{\alpha}{2}(T_c + 2T_b)^2 - \xi \quad (5.16)$$

$$T_l = 2T_b + \frac{\frac{\alpha}{2}(T_c + 2T_b)^2 - Q_l}{\mu - R_c}. \quad (5.17)$$

Substituting T_c and T_l into T given in Pattern II and using (5.6), we have Pattern III's $\overline{R}$ as given below:

$$\overline{R} = \frac{1}{T}\Bigg[\mu(T_c + 2T_b) + \frac{\alpha}{2}(T_c + 2T_b)^2 + (T_l - T_b + T_f)R_c + T_r R_c + \frac{\alpha}{2}T_r^2\Bigg]. \quad (5.18)$$

5.2 Numerical Evaluation of Equilibrium-State Performance

We set the bottleneck link bandwidth $\mu = 155$ Mbps and we assume $T_b = T_f = 1$ ms and hence, $\tau = T_b + T_f = 2$ ms. Also, we use $\Delta = 0.5\tau = 1$ ms, $Q_h = 50$ cells, $Q_l = 25$ cells, and the initial source rate $R_0 = \mu$. To balance the increase and decrease speeds of $R(t)$ and ensure that the average of the offered traffic load does not grow beyond the bottleneck bandwidth, we set $\alpha\Delta/(1-\beta) = \mu$ [10] throughout the rest of the paper. In the following we present some of the numerical results we obtained to evaluate system performance and the more complete and detailed results can be found in [12].

Performance Analysis for Pattern I, II, and III: As expected, Figure 4 shows Q_{max} increases monotonically with α and τ. Q_{max} also increases roughly linearly with α and Q_{max} increases faster for a larger τ. In Figure 5, $\overline{R}$ is found to decrease monotonically as α and τ increase, and to decrease faster for a larger τ. In general, a large τ has a negative effect on equilibrium-state performance, which is consistent with feedback system analysis. A small α is desired for equilibrium-state performance in terms of the maximum queue length and

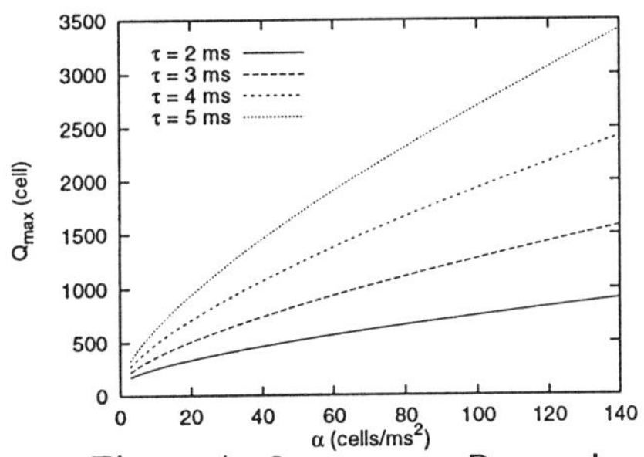

Figure 4: Q_{max} vs. α: Pattern I

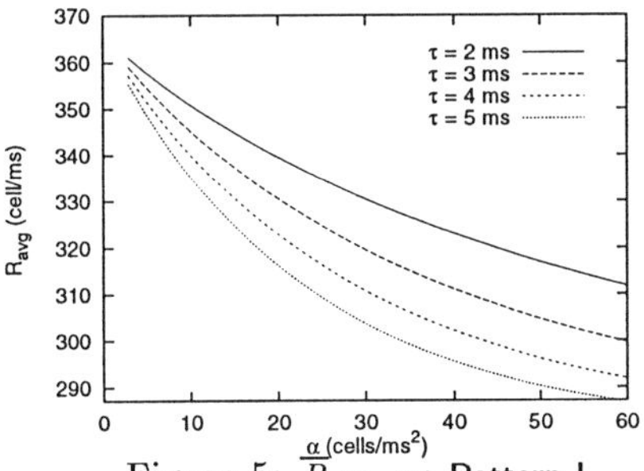

Figure 5: $\overline{R}$ vs. α: Pattern I

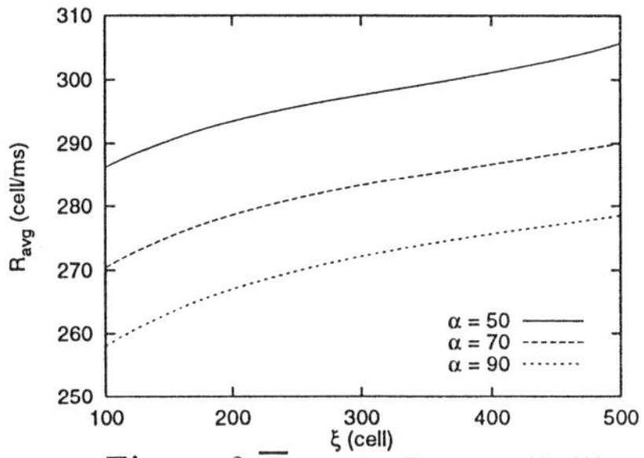

Figure 6 $\overline{R}$ vs. ξ: Pattern II, III

average throughput. In Figure 6, $\overline{R}$ is found to monotonically increase as ξ increases, but for a given ξ, $\overline{R}$ decreases as α grows.

Performance Comparison among Three Control Patterns: In Figure 7, the normalized $\overline{R}$'s are plotted against α with different values of ξ, corresponding to different control patterns. We have made the following observations. For any given α, the equilibrium state governed by Pattern I represents the optimal equilibrium state in terms of average throughput, queuing delay, and delay variation. Thus, we define control Pattern I as the optimal control pattern/state. For a given ξ, $\overline{R}$ monotonically decreases as α increases for all three patterns. $\overline{R}$ of Pattern II and III with a smaller ξ decays faster as α increases. For any given α, increasing ξ can improve $\overline{R}$, but when $\xi \geq Q_{max}$, $\overline{R}$ cannot be improved any further by increasing ξ. So, the average throughput $\overline{R}$ is upper bounded by curve $\xi \geq Q_{max}$, thus providing information on optimal buffer allocation to a VC for different α's. The larger α, the more sensitive to ξ the average throughput $\overline{R}$ is. In general, a smaller α leads to better equilibrium-state performance.

Since Q_{max} is proportional to α, we can adjust α to an appropriate smaller value such that $Q(t)$'s fluctuation is bounded by ξ and then the system operates in the optimal equilibrium state (under control Pattern I). But α should not be too small since a small α degrades transient-state performance.

5.3 Transient-State Rate Control and Performance Analysis

Transient State and Its Rate-Control Algorithm: The transient state is defined as a state between any initial state and an optimal equilibrium state. The goal of our control algorithm is to drive the system from any initial state into the optimal equilibrium state as quickly as possible while maintaining a high throughput. Since rate increase or decrease can only make $R(t)$ fluctuate around the designated bandwidth, but cannot adjust the rate-fluctuation amplitude that determines Q_{max}, we need a higher-order rate control which directly adjusts the rate parameter α (i.e., $\frac{dR(t)}{dt}$) (β is also adjusted by setting $\alpha\Delta/(1-\beta) = \mu$) to reduce the rate-oscillation amplitude. There are other reasons necessitating the dynamic adjustment of α. In a real network, the round-trip delay τ varies with time. Thus keeping Q_{max} at a given level requires α to vary with time. In this paper, however, we only consider how to reduce α to ensure Q_{max} does not grow beyond ξ while achieving a good transient-state response.

Let α_0 be the initial source rate-increase parameter. Application of the α-control rule n times will yield a sequence $\{\alpha_0, \alpha_1, \ldots, \alpha_n\}$. For a good transient response, we use an exponential control rule which is defined by

$$\alpha_n = e^{-\lambda n}\alpha_0 \quad (\lambda > 0). \tag{5.19}$$

where λ specifies the speed of reducing α.

Note that α should not be reduced further as long as $Q_{max}(\alpha_n) < \xi$, where Q_{max} is a function of α as shown in Eq. (5.3), since too small a value of α will slow down the transient system behavior, or even disable the capability of grabbing the spare bandwidth created by other idle VCs. So, the source should stop execution of the α-control rule as soon as α_n reaches its optimal value α^*:

$$\alpha^* \triangleq \max_{i \in \{1,2,3,\ldots\}} \{\alpha_i \mid Q_{max}^{(i)} < \xi\}, \tag{5.20}$$

where $Q_{max}^{(i)}$ is the maximum queue length for $\alpha_i = e^{-\lambda}\alpha_{i-1}$, $\alpha_0 > \alpha^*$.

Analytical Solutions and Performance Analysis for Transient State: We assume $\alpha_0 \geq \alpha^*$, and focus on the first-cycle dynamic behavior with initial rate $R_0 > \mu$. Transient state flow-control also divides control into three patterns, which are defined similarly to those for equilibrium state. Since for $R_0 > \mu$ the system typically operates in transient state under Patterns II and III, our analysis here will focus on these two patterns. Notice that for these two patterns, when $Q_{max} > \xi$, $R(t)$ restarts rate-increase from R_c with a smaller increase rate of $\alpha e^{-\lambda}$ instead of α.

The detailed descriptions of control patterns and derivations of their corresponding analytical expressions are available in [12]. Here we only present some numerical results on the transient-state performance. The network condition remains the same as in Section 5.2. But we use $R_0 = 4\mu$ and $\lambda = log\ 2$[1] here. In Figure 8–9, we observe that for a given ξ a larger α not only results in a higher transient-state average throughput, but also a shorter transient-cycle length. Notice that this observation is the opposite of what we observed in the equilibrium state where a small α leads to a high throughput. These observations suggest that our SES algorithm start sending data with a larger initial rate-control parameter α_0, but make α smaller as system

[1] This implies $\alpha_i = \frac{1}{2}\alpha_{i-1}$, just a left-shift operation which is easy to implement. But λ can take any other positive number.

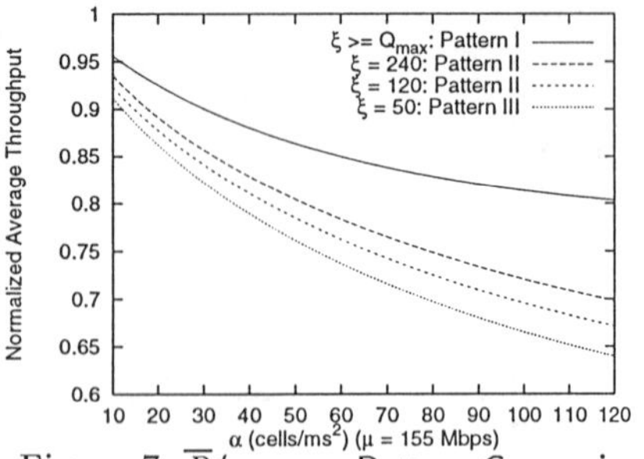

Figure 7: $\overline{R}/\mu$ vs. α: Pattern Comparison

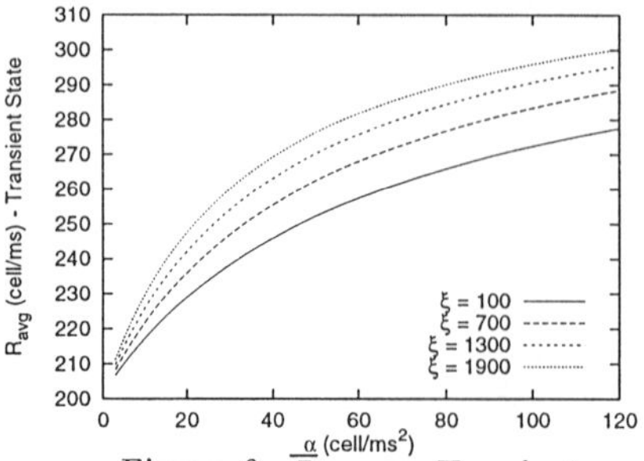

Figure 8: $\overline{R}$ vs. α: Transient

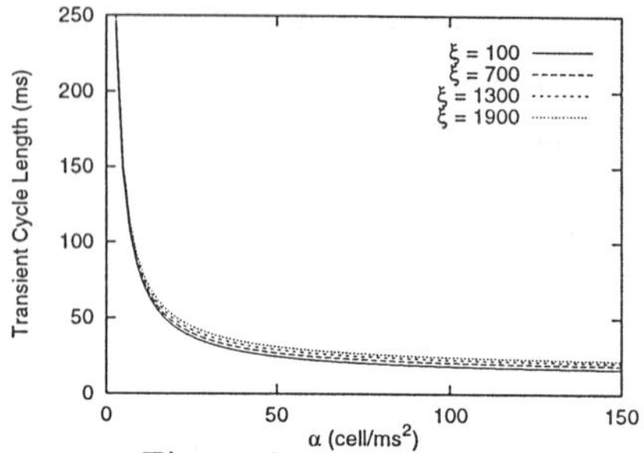

Figure 9: $\overline{T}$ vs. α: Transient

converges to the optimal equilibrium state. This observation is consistent with the conclusion: "a sharp rate reduction in the transient state and a smaller rate reduction during the equilibrium state" [2].

6 Dynamics of Multiple ABR Connections

Consider a scenario where N flow-controlled VCs share a common bottleneck. The parameters describing the VC_i in this multi-connection system are given below.

ξ_i: $\triangleq \frac{MCR_i}{\sum_{j=1}^{J} MCR_j}\xi$ is buffer share for VC_i

μ_i: $\triangleq \frac{MCR_i}{\sum_{j=1}^{N} MCR_j}\mu$ is bandwidth share for VC_i

MCR_i: MCR for VC_i; we assume $MCR_i > 0$

$Q_i(t)$: Queue length at the bottleneck node for VC_i

$R_i(t)$: Source rate for VC_i

$\alpha^{(i)}$: Rate increase parameter for VC_i

$T_b^{(i)}$: Backward feedback delay for VC_i

$T_f^{(i)}$: Forward delay for VC_i

Δ_i: Time interval of rate-update for VC_i

At the bottleneck switch, the total buffer capacity ξ is statically allocated to N existing VCs, each with a buffer share proportional to its MCR. J ($\leq N$) active VCs dynamically share the bottleneck link bandwidth μ, each VC being served in a rate proportional to its MCR. To make the analysis tractable, we ignore the scheduling time at the switch, and also consider the assigned bandwidth share as the target bandwidth share (instead of the realized bandwidth), which slightly under-estimates the throughput, but still reflects the system dynamic behavior. Then, all the expressions derived in Section 5 can be applied to the multiple-connection case with the target bandwidth and buffer capacity substituted by their shares. Next, we present two examples.

Example 1: Buffer Requirement and Average Throughput. We consider a case where there are $N = 4$ identical ABR VCs with: $R_0^{(i)} = 183.5$ cells/ms, $MCR_i = 18.35$ cells/ms, $T_b^{(i)} = T_f^{(i)} = 1$ ms, $\Delta_i = 1$ ms, $Q_h^{(i)} = 50$ cells, $Q_l^{(i)} = 25$ cells, and $\alpha_0^{(i)} = 11.45$ cells/ms^2. Assume that 4 VCs start sending cells at the same time over the bottleneck link with $\mu = 367$ cells/ms (155 Mbps).

For the rate scheme, the 4 VCs share a common FIFO output queue $Q(t)$ at the bottleneck link. Using the equations derived for Pattern I (describing rate scheme), we obtain the evolutions of $R(t) = 4R_i(t)$ and $Q(t)$, as shown in Figure 10. In transient state, a large queue build-up, $Q_{peak} = 2207.5$ cells, is observed. But in equilibrium state, Q_{max} is just 493 cells, about 1/5 of Q_{peak}. For lossless transmission, a buffer size larger than 2207 cells is required to prevent cell-loss during the short transient duration even though only 22% of buffer space will be utilized during the long equilibrium duration. The resulting equilibrium-state average throughput is 319.35 cells/ms (or $\overline{R}/\mu = 0.87$).

With the proposed scheme, we assume the bottleneck switch's $\xi = 500$ cells. Then, each VC's $\xi_i = 125$ cells and $\mu_i = 91.75$ cells/ms since all VCs are identical. The 4 VCs each have their own output queue at the bottleneck switch. Using the equations derived for Pattern I, II, and III which characterize the proposed scheme, we compute the evolutions of $R_i(t)$ and $Q_i(t)$ for both transient and equilibrium states. Since the 4 VCs are identical, we have $Q(t) = 4Q_i(t)$ and $R(t) = 4R_i(t)$. As shown in Figure 10, $R(t)$ experiences just one cycle of transient state with $\alpha_0^{(i)} = 11.45$ cells/ms^2 and then enters the equilibrium with $\alpha_1^{(i)} = 5.725$ cells/ms^2 ($\lambda = log\ 2$). In the transient state, $Q(t)$ is bounded by buffer size $\xi = 500$ without any cell-loss due to buffer overflow, and $Q_{max} = 356$ cells in equilibrium state. The resulting equilibrium-state average throughput is 336.7 cells/ms (i.e., $\overline{R}/\mu = 0.92$), which is higher than that of the rate-based scheme.

This example shows that the proposed scheme requires a much smaller (nearly 5 times less) buffer size to guarantee lossless transmissions and achieves higher average throughput than the rate-based scheme.

Example 2: Bandwidth Guarantees and Fairness. Here, we consider two ABR connections with different parameters. For connections: $MCR_1 = 12$ cells/ms, $\alpha_0^{(1)} = 22.9$ cells/ms^2, $R_0^{(1)}=0$ cells/ms; $MCR_2 = 24$ cells/ms, $\alpha_0^{(2)} = 45.8$ cells/ms^2, $R_0^{(2)}=0$ cells/ms. For networks: $\mu = 367$ cells/ms, $\xi = 450$ cells, $Q_h = 45$ cells, $Q_l = 22.5$ cells, $T_b^{(1)} = T_b^{(2)} = 1$ ms, $T_f^{(1)} = T_f^{(2)} = 1$ ms, $\Delta_1 = \Delta_2 = 1$ ms. Then, $\mu_1 = \mu/3 = 122.3$ cells/ms, $\mu_2 = 2\mu/3 = 244.7$ cells/ms, $Q_h^{(1)} = Q_h/3 = 15$ cells, $Q_h^{(2)} = 2Q_h/3 = 30$ cells, $Q_l^{(1)} = Q_l/3 = 7.5$ cells, $Q_l^{(2)} = 2Q_l/3 = 15$ cells,

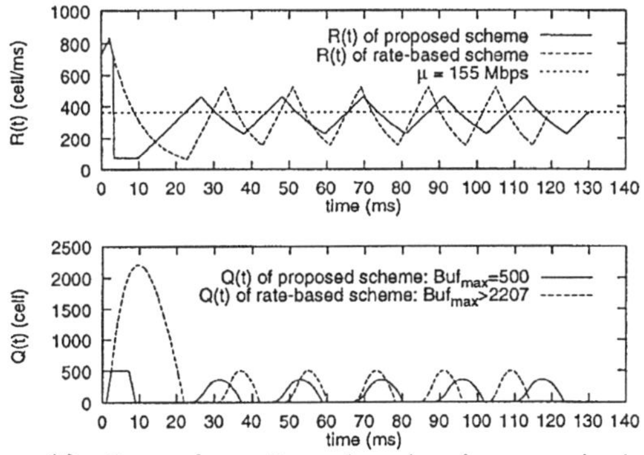

Figure 10: Comparison of rate-based and proposed schemes.

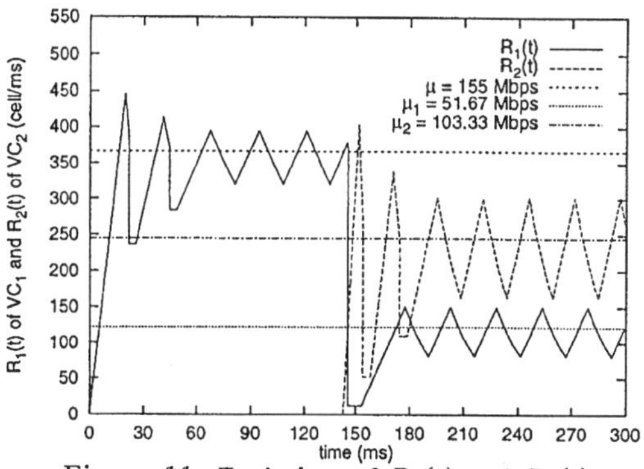

Figure 11: Evolutions of $R_1(t)$ and $R_2(t)$.

$\xi_1 = \xi/3 = 150$ cells, $\xi_2 = 2\xi/3 = 300$ cells.

We assume that VC_1 starts sending data at $t = 0$ and VC_2 starts sending data at $t = 142.78$ ms when VC_1 has already reached the optimal equilibrium state. For the proposed scheme,we compute the evolutions for $R_1(t)$ and $R_2(t)$ for transient and equilibrium states as shown in Figure 11. We observe that after 2 transient cycles (46.95 ms) $R_1(t)$ converges to μ, instead of its share μ_1. This is because there are no other VCs sharing μ with VC_1, and thus, VC_1 grabs all available bandwidth μ (ABR). At $t = 142.78$ ms, VC_2 starts sending data cells, then the scheduler at the switch assigns μ_1 to VC_1 and μ_2 to VC_2 as their target bandwidth shares. VC_2 starts competing for bandwidth in its transient cycles. In the mean time, $R_1(t)$ starts to give up the bandwidth beyond its share μ_1. Note that VC_1's α remains the same since it has reached its optimal value 5.725 cells/ms^2. After 2 transient cycles (47.52 ms), both $R_1(t)$ and $R_2(t)$ converge to their shares μ_1 and μ_2. Note that by properly reducing $\alpha^{(1)}$ and $\alpha^{(2)}$, not only do $R_1(t)$ and $R_2(t)$ converge to their shares, but also $Q_1(t)$ and $Q_2(t)$ are confined to the regimes bounded by ξ_1 and ξ_2, since the resulting $Q^{(1)}_{max} = 131$ and $Q^{(2)}_{max} = 263$, respectively.

This example shows that the proposed scheme can provide a bandwidth guarantee to each VC and achieve a fair bandwidth share among competing connections according to their MCRs. As previously discussed, a bandwidth guarantee is hard to achieve by the credit scheme, as it does not explicitly control transmission rate. These two examples also show that under the proposed scheme $R(t)$ and $Q(t)$ can rapidly converge to the optimal operating regime (within two cycles of the transient state).

7 Conclusions

In this paper, we proposed and evaluated an integrated credit- and rate-based flow-control scheme. The proposed scheme combines the merits and overcomes the weakness of the two schemes by exercising direct control over both bandwidth and buffer resources. Unlike the previous flow-control schemes and analyses, we included the buffer capacity as an important constraint in the design and analysis of the proposed scheme. From the analyses, we identified the optimal control pattern and developed a 2-dimensional rate-control scheme to drive the system to the optimal control pattern. Through examples, it is shown that our scheme outperforms the other existing schemes in terms of buffer requirement (with lossless transmission), average throughput, bandwidth guarantees, fairness, and network utilization. The simulation results have verified the analytical results for the single-connection case. We are currently extending the simulator to the multiple-connection case.

References

[1] H. T. Kung, T. Blackwell, and A. Chapman, "Credit update protocol for flow-controlled ATM networks: statistical multiplexing and adaptive credit allocation," in *Proc. of ACM SIGCOMM*, pp. 101–115, 1994.

[2] N. Yin and M. G. Hluchyj, "On closed-loop rate control for ATM cell relay networks," in *Proc. of IEEE INFOCOM*, pp. 99–109, June 1994.

[3] S. Sathaye, *ATM Forum traffic management specifications Version 4.0*, ATM Forum contribution 95-0013R7.1, August 1995.

[4] *IEEE Network Magazine-Special Issue on ATM Flow Control: Rate vs. Credit*, volume 9, March/April 1995.

[5] D. Bertsekas and R. Gallager, *Data Networks*, Prentice Hall, 2nd edition, 1992.

[6] N. Yin, "Analysis of a rate-based traffic management mechanism for ABR service," in *Proc. of GLOBECOM*, pp. 1076–1082, November 1995.

[7] H. Ohsaki, M. Murata, H. Suzuki, C. Ikeda, and H. Miyahara, "Analysis of rate-based congestion control for ATM networks," *ACM SIGCOMM Computer Communication Review*, vol. 25, pp. 60–72, April 1995.

[8] H. Ohsaki, M. Murata, H. Suzuki, C. Ikeda, and H. Miyahara, "Analysis of rate-based congestion control algorithms for ATM networks—Part 1: steady state analysis—," in *Proc. of GLOBECOM*, pp. 296–303, November 1995.

[9] M. Ritter, "Network buffer requirements of the rate-based control mechanism for ABR services," in *Proc. of IEEE INFOCOM*, pp. 1190–1197, March 1996.

[10] J. Bolot and A. Shankar, "Dynamical behavior of rate-based flow control mechanism," *ACM SIGCOMM Computer Communication Review*, vol. 20, no. 4, pp. 35–49, April 1990.

[11] F. Bonomi, D. Mitra, and J. Seery, "Adaptive algorithms for feedback-based flow control in high-speed, wide-area ATM networks," *IEEE Journal on Selected Areas in Communications*, vol. 13, no. 7, pp. 1267–1283, September 1995.

[12] X. Zhang and K. G. Shin, *Integrated Rate and Credit Feedback Control for ABR Service in ATM Networks*, Technical Report, EECS, Univ. of Michigan, July 1996.

The Rate Mismatch Problem in Heterogeneous ABR Flow Control

Nina Taft Plotkin
ninatp@erg.sri.com

Jaroslaw J. Sydir
sydir@erg.sri.com

SRI International
Menlo Park, CA 94025

Abstract

Because the ATM Forum does not standardize the ABR flow control algorithm that an ATM switch should run, some ATM networks are likely to contain switches that run different ABR flow control algorithms. Even if all the switches within a "cloud" of switches use the same algorithm, individual clouds (each with its own algorithm) will be interconnected by virtual circuits. Virtual circuits which traverse multiple clouds will therefore be controlled by two different flow control algorithms concurrently. In this paper we explore some of the ramifications of mixing different flow control algorithms in the same ATM network.

We identify the rate mismatch problem, which arises when a nonbottleneck switch (that uses one algorithm) interferes with the control of the bottleneck switch (that uses another algorithm). We formulate a hypothesis that states the conditions that lead to the rate mismatch problem. These conditions identify a specific class of problematic topologies. We validate the hypothesis formally and prove that rate mismatch causes unfairness. Using four different algorithms, in combinations of two at a time, we illustrate the interoperability of ABR flow control algorithms.

1 Introduction

The ATM Forum has standardized the behavior of Available Bit Rate (ABR) sources, and the contents of Resource Management (RM) control cells, but does not standardize the algorithm that ATM switches should use to control the rates of ABR sources. ATM switch vendors are free to choose one of the algorithms that have been suggested by the forum, or can design their own. Typically, customers do not buy all of their switches from the same vendor. Hence, two or more distinct ABR flow control algorithms can operate simultaneously within a network. A VC that traverses multiple ATM switches could therefore "pass through" a number of different congestion control algorithms. Figure 1 gives an example with two network clouds, each utilizing their own flow control scheme,

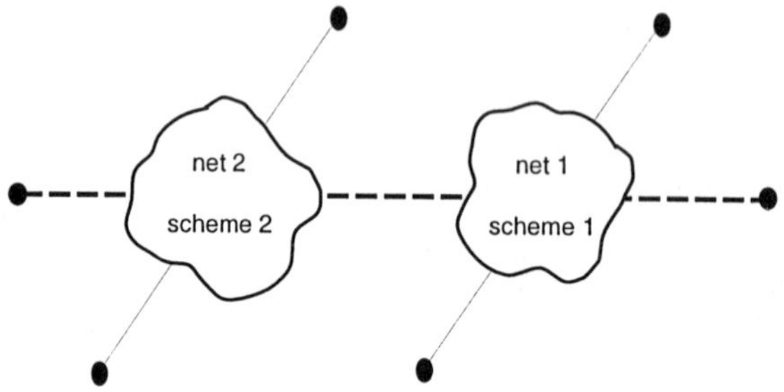

Figure 1: Network of Heterogeneous Clouds

and three virtual circuits (VC). Moreover VCs that traverse only one cloud could intersect with VCs that traverse two clouds. We use the term *heterogeneous topology* to refer to network topologies in which different ATM switches utilize different ABR flow control algorithms, and the term *homogeneous topology* to refer to topologies in which all switches utilize the same flow control algorithm. The behavior of many algorithms has been studied in homogeneous topologies [4, 12, 3, 6, 9, 10, 7, 8]. Our study focuses on heterogeneous topologies.

When two different algorithms *coexist* in a heterogeneous topology, they may try to control the same VCs simultaneously. This scenario raises the question of whether the goals of ABR flow control (max-min fairness [2], no loss, and high throughput) can be achieved when two distinct algorithms coexist in the same network. Two algorithms that coexist in a network are said to *cooperate* if the goals of ABR flow control are still achieved.

We conducted this study to address the following interoperability questions. What is the nature of the interaction of two algorithms? In which kinds of topologies can two different algorithms cooperate? In which topologies do algorithms fail to cooperate, and why? In particular, which pairs of algorithms cooperate and which pairs do not? How do these factors affect the performance of the system?

0-8186-7780-5/97 $10.00 © 1997 IEEE

We implemented four ABR flow control algorithms (presented in Section 2), in order to study heterogeneous topologies in which different combinations of two flow control schemes operate concurrently. We used our own internally developed ABR simulator tool for experimentation. First, we examined the steady-state behavior of the source rates in a homogeneous topology (in Section 3) for each of the algorithms. We found that the oscillatory behavior of these algorithms can be used to explain the performance of these algorithms in a heterogeneous topology. In our heterogeneous topologies, switches can represent either individual switches or clouds of switches.

In some of our heterogeneous topologies the two algorithms cooperated, while in others we found that unfairness could occur. In such topologies, unfairness arises because of a *rate mismatch problem*. Rate mismatch occurs if two sources bottlenecked at the same node experience the same rate decrease process but different rate increase processes. We show that rate mismatches occur when highly oscillatory and minimally oscillatory algorithms are configured in a specific topology, that we call the *rate mismatch topology*.

Section 4.1 presents some initial simulations results in heterogeneous configurations. This leads to the formulation of the hypothesis which is given in Section 4.2. We present the rate mismatch topology in Section 4.2.1 and given a detailed example of what goes wrong in this topology in Section 4.2.2. We formalize and validate the hypothesis in Section 4.2.3. Section 4.3 provides simulation results – that corroborate the hypothesis – for combinations of single bit algorithms with Explicit Rate (ER) algorithm, as well as combinations of two different ER algorithms. We discuss the consequences of the rate mismatch problem in the conclusions in Section 5.

2 ABR Flow Control

2.1 Overview

An ABR flow control algorithm controls the allowed cell rate (ACR) of each VC traffic source, by means of a feedback mechanism. Resource Management (RM) cells are sent by the source along the forward path of a VC, are turned around by the destination, and return to the source along the backward path of the same VC. Each source transmits one RM cell every *Nrm* data cells (typically, Nrm = 32), but at least once every *Trm* (Trm = 100ms) seconds. Switches in the path of a VC are allowed to set certain fields of the RM cell; thus RM cells carry feedback control information back to the source. The RM cells tell the source how it should modify its rate. In our algorithms, switches modify RM cells on their backward path. A switch is allowed to alter the RM cell bits, only if the new setting results in a lower ACR. Thus a source receives the minimum allowed rate of all the switches in its path.

2.2 The Algorithms

The behavior of the sources is the same for all of the flow control algorithms. When a source sends out an RM cell, it sets the Congestion Indication (CI) bit to zero, the No Increase (NI) bit to zero, the Current Cell Rate (CCR) field to its current Allowed Cell Rate (ACR), and the Explicit Rate (ER) field to its peak cell rate. Upon receipt of an RM cell, a source looks at the CI bit and the NI bit inside the RM cell. It adjusts its ACR as follows. Here, RDF denotes the Reduction Factor and AIF denotes the Additive Increase Factor.

if $CI = 1$	then $ACR = ACR * RDF$
if $NI = 1$	then $ACR = ACR$
if $CI = 0$ and $NI = 0$	then $ACR = ACR + AIF$

After adjusting ACR according to the CI and NI bits, the source looks at the ER field of the RM cell, and sets ACR to the minimum of ACR and ER. Finally, the source does not allow ACR to go below its minimum cell rate or above its peak cell rate.

The first three algorithms that we studied determine the feedback signal to send as a function of switch queue occupancy. All three algorithms use the same threshold level indicators. When the occupancy of a switch queue bypasses the higher threshold, denoted Q_h, the switch is considered congested, and sources are told to lower their rates (we refer to these as *decrease feedback signals*). When the occupancy of a switch queue lies below the lower threshold, denoted Q_l, the switch is considered underutilized, and sources are told to raise their rates (we refer to these as *increase feedback signals*). When the queue occupancy is between the thresholds, the sources are told to maintain their current rate (we refer to these as *do-nothing feedback signals*). In the descriptions that follow below, let Q denote the current queue occupancy, measured at the time an RM cell is marked.

Relative Rate Marking Algorithm

This algorithm (which we henceforth refer to as the RRM algorithm) is suggested by the ATM Forum [1] as a potential single bit feedback scheme. We use a version of this algorithm with two queue thresholds (rather than one). It uses the CI bit and NI bit to control a source's ACR. A switch updates the fields, in the backwards RM cells it receives, as follows.

Queue Size	CI	NI	ER
if $Q > Qh$	1	-	-
if $Qh > Q > Ql$	0	1	-
if $Ql > Q$	0	0	-

Bounded MACR Algorithm

This is an Explicit Rate (ER) algorithm and therefore uses the ER and CCR fields to control the sources' rates. The algorithm is a variation of ATM Forum suggestions I.5.2.1, "EPRCA," and I.5.2.5, "ER based on bandwidth Demand Estimate Algorithm," as they appear in the ATM Forum Traffic Management Specification Version 4.0 [1]. Each switch maintains a variable called Mean Allowed Cell Rate (MACR) which is an exponential weighted average of the ACRs of each source. (This idea was first proposed in [12].) Each time a switch receives a forward RM cell, it updates its MACR variable according to the formula $MACR = (1-\alpha)MACR + \alpha CCR$. Let ERF denote an Explicit Reduction Factor and γ denote an increase factor. A switch updates the fields, in the backwards RM cells it receives, as follows.

Queue Size	CI	NI	ER
if $Q > Qh$	-	-	$ER = ERF * MACR$
if $Qh > Q > Ql$	-	-	$ER = MACR$
if $Ql > Q$	-	-	$ER = \gamma * MACR$

We call this algorithm *Bounded MACR*, because the algorithm explicitly sets the ER field when $Ql > Q$, thus bounding the increase of the source rates.

Unbounded MACR Algorithm

As we will see below, in some environments the Bounded MACR algorithm can lead to problems because of the slow growth of the sources' rates that it allows. We designed a variation of the algorithm to allow faster growth rates. The switch still maintains the MACR variable in the same fashion as described above. The ER field is updated according to:

Queue Size	CI	NI	ER
if $Q > Qh$	-	-	$ER = ERF * MACR$
if $Qh > Q > Ql$	-	-	$ER = MACR$
if $Ql > Q$	0	0	-

This algorithm is a hybrid of the previous two algorithms in that it behaves according to the Bounded MACR algorithm in the ranges $Q > Qh$ and $Qh > Q > Ql$, but behaves according to the Relative Rate Marking algorithm in the range $Q < Ql$. We call this version of the MACR algorithm, the *Unbounded MACR* algorithm, because it can allow the source's rate to grow all the way to its peak. This algorithm is essentially equivalent to the Bounded MACR algorithm with $\gamma = \infty$.

ERICA+ Algorithm

The ERICA+ algorithm [5] is a variation of the ERICA algorithm that was originally proposed by Raj Jain et al. and appeared as the ATM Forum suggestion I.5.2.3 [1]. Both algorithms periodically measure the ABR input rate and attempt to direct this rate towards a target rate. The original ERICA algorithm performs the following computations at the end of each measurement interval.

Target_Rate = Link_Capacity * Target_Utilization
- VBR_Usage - CBR_Usage
Fairshare = Target_Rate / Num_Active_Connections
z = Input_Rate / Target_Rate

The goal of this algorithm is to drive z towards 1. The switch sets the ER in backwards RM cell according to:

VCshare = CCR/z
ER = max(Fairshare,VCshare)

The ERICA+ algorithm retains the same structure, but defines the Target_Rate as a function of the available link capacity and the queuing delay (which is a function of the queue occupancy). The Target_Rate variable from the original ERICA algorithm is calculated according to the following formulas.

Total_ABR_Capacity = Link_Capacity - VBR_Usage
- CBR_Usage
Target_Rate = $f(Tq)$ * Total_ABR_Capacity

The function $f(Tq)$ is a function of the queuing delay. The user selects a target queuing delay $T0$ and $f(Tq)$ produces a number less than one when $Tq > T0$, and a number greater than one when $Tq < T0$. The remainder of the calculations are performed in the same way as in ERICA. (See [5] for a detailed description of ERICA+, and a number of recent improvements to ERICA and ERICA+.) We implemented the following: "innovation to achieve max-min fairness", "fairshare first to avoid transient overloads", and "forward CCR used for reverse direction feedback".

In our simulations we used the following parameter settings for the above algorithms: total queue size = 2000 cells, Qh = 1200 cells, Ql = 600 cells, RDF = 15/16, $ERF = 7/8$, $\gamma = 1.1$, and $\alpha = 1/16$. We used Peak Cell Rates (PCR) of 155 Mbps, and Minimum Cell Rates (MCR) of 0.5 Mbps. In tests including the RRM algorithm we used AIF = PCR/256. In tests that included only ER algorithms, we used AIF = PCR. For ERICA+ we used the following parameter settings: $a = 1.15$, $b = 1.05$, and QDLF = 0.5 (queue drain limit factor). The authors of ERICA+ suggest $T0 = 1/8 *$ *feedback delay* (fbd) for WAN topologies and $T0 = fbd$ for LAN topologies. We used both of these values in the different tests that we performed.

3 Homogeneous Topology Behavior

In order to understand the behavior of these algorithms in heterogeneous topologies, we first present a synopsis of their behavior in a homogeneous topology. Much of this is known [4, 8], so we present only the behavior of the source rates (ACRs) in order to illustrate relative oscillatory behavior. Their oscillatory behavior is important in the analysis of heterogeneous topologies. We ran each of the algorithms in a standard parking lot topology (shown in Figure 2). Each virtual circuit, VC-i, is defined by a source-destination pair (s_i, d_i) for $i = 1, 2, \ldots, 6$. The link between switches 5 and 6 is the bottleneck link. We used greedy sources and interswitch links of 100 kilometers in length and 155 Mbps capacity. The links connecting sources to switches are 0.5 km in length.

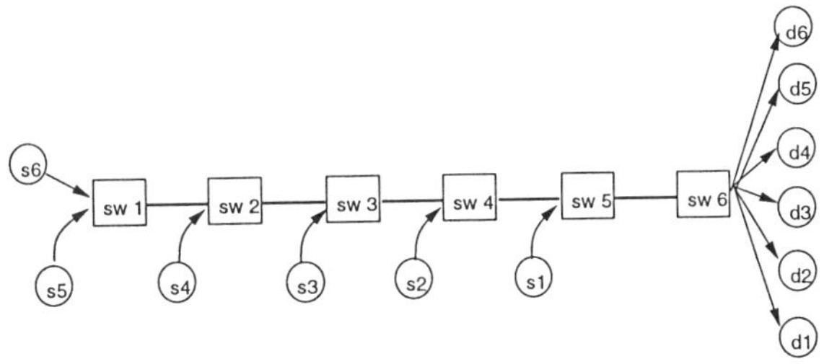

Figure 2: Parking Lot Topology

All of the source rates exhibit oscillatory behavior, although the shape of the oscillations can differ significantly from one algorithm to another. A source's ACR will oscillate around the fairshare (although not necessarily symmetrically). In this single bottleneck topology, the fairshare is simply the bottleneck link capacity (the link between switches 5 and 6) divided by six (the number of VCs), which yields approximately 60,000 cells/sec. We use the term *overshoot* (*undershoot*) to denote the difference between the largest (smallest) value ACR reaches and the source's true fairshare, respectively. The algorithm with the largest increase rate experiences the largest overshoot, because of the delay from the moment the switch detects congestion until the feedback control signal reaches the source. During this delay, an algorithm with a large increase rate will clearly increase its rate more than an algorithm with a slower increase rate. Similarly, the algorithm with the largest decrease rate will experience the largest undershoot. Thus, algorithms with large overshoots and undershoots produce large amplitudes in their oscillations. We will use the term

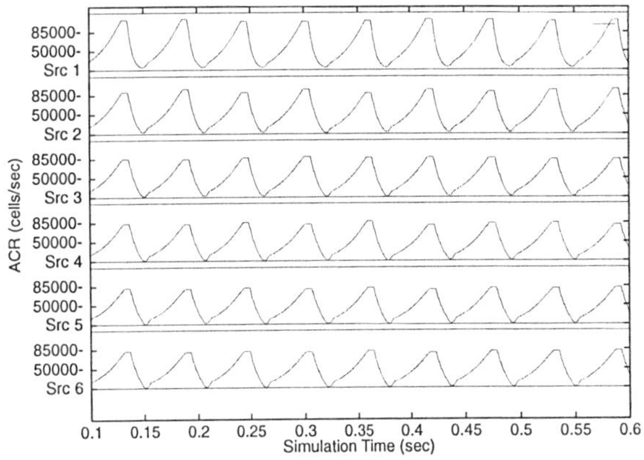

Figure 3: Relative Rate Marking Algorithm

oscillatory algorithm to denote algorithms which result in rapid increases and/or decreases in the source rates.

Figures 3, 4, 5, 6 and 7 present the instantaneous ACRs for the six VC sources, for each of the algorithms. Since ERICA+ with $T0 = 1/8fbd$ yields substantial oscillations whereas ERICA+ with $T0 = fbd$ yields insignificant oscillations, we refer to the former as osc_ERICA+ (i.e., ERICA+ in oscillatory mode), and the latter as non_osc_ERICA+ (i.e., ERICA+ in non-oscillatory mode).

The RRM, osc_ERICA+, and Unbounded MACR algorithms produce rather oscillatory source rates, whereas the Bounded MACR and non_osc_ERICA+ algorithms produce minimal oscillations in the source rates. The ordering of the algorithms (from largest to smallest) according to the size of the oscillation amplitude they produce is: RRM, osc_ERICA+, Unbounded MACR, Bounded MACR, and non_osc_ERICA+. It is not surprising that the behavior of Unbounded MACR lies in between the behavior of RRM and Bounded MACR since the algorithm is a hybrid of these two.

4 Heterogeneous Topology Results

4.1 Heterogeneous Parking Lot Topology

Before presenting the results of simulation testing, we first explain what is considered proper behavior of the system. The behavior of an ATM network supporting ABR service is considered *proper* if the bottleneck switches are the only switches that exert control over the traffic sources. If a nonbottleneck switch affects the behavior of the source, then that switch is said to *interfere* with the control of the bottleneck switches. In a heterogeneous configuration with two algorithms, if the nonbottleneck nodes do not interfere

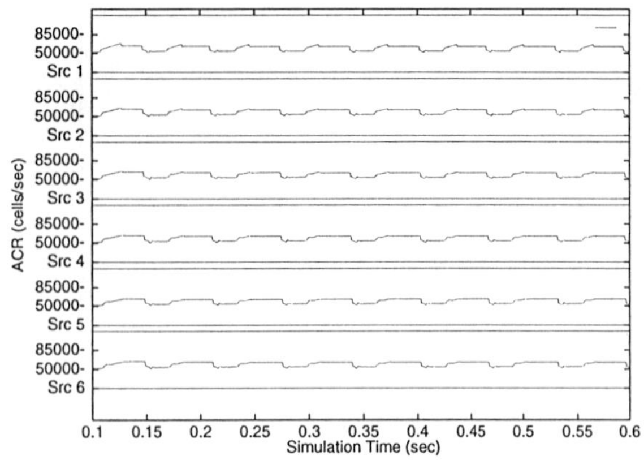

Figure 4: Bounded MACR Algorithm

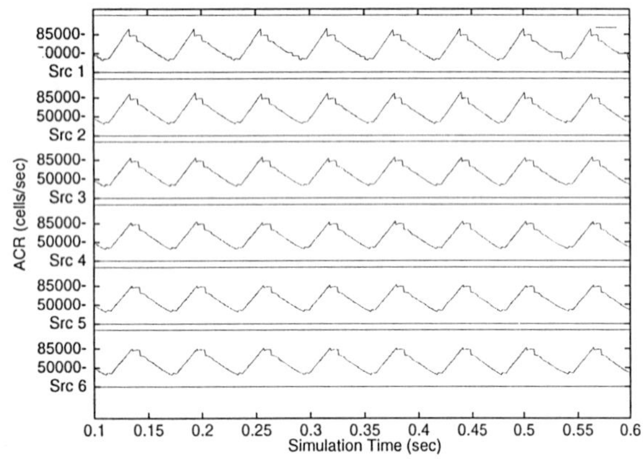

Figure 5: Unbounded MACR Algorithm

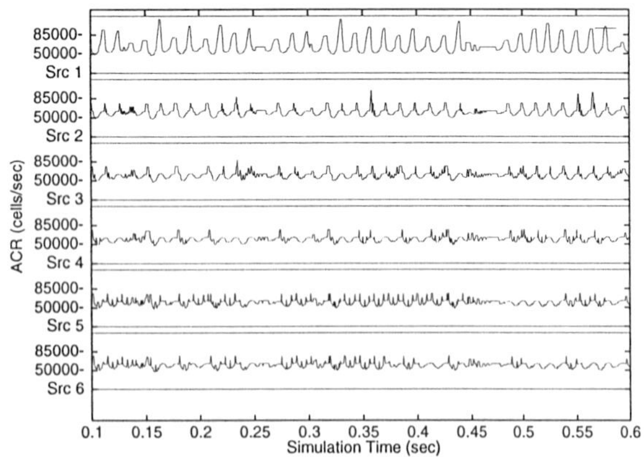

Figure 6: ERICA+ in oscillatory mode

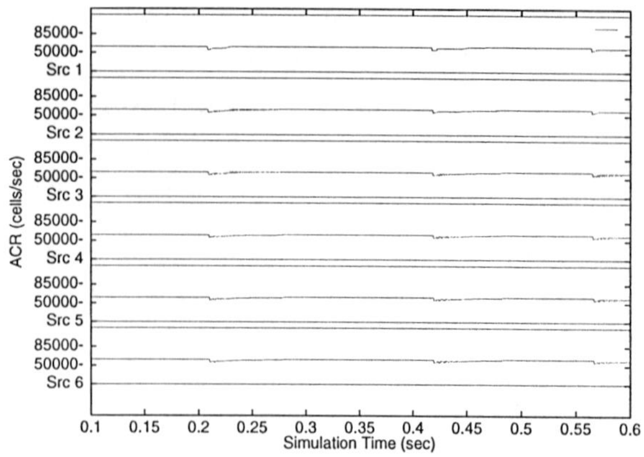

Figure 7: ERICA+ in non-oscillatory mode

	Bottleneck Switch	*Nonbottleneck Switch*	Result
Test 1	Bounded MACR	RRM	Fair
Test 2	RRM	Bounded MACR	Unfair

Table 1: Test Set 1 and Results. Heterogeneous Asynchronous Parking Lot Topology

with the control of the bottleneck nodes, then we say that the two algorithms *cooperate*.

We conducted two experiments with heterogeneous parking lot topologies. In both cases, we used one algorithm on switches 6 and 5 (the bottleneck node), and a second algorithm on switches 1 through 4. In this first set of tests, we combined the Bounded MACR and the RRM algorithms. The tests and results are given in Table 1. The results indicate whether or not the sources received their fairshare of the throughput.

In this configuration, there is one VC (VC 1) that passes through only one algorithm, whereas all the other VCs pass through two algorithms. The consequence of such a configuration is that VC 1 receives feedback from only one algorithm, whereas the other VCs receive feedback signals from both algorithms. Conceptually we can view these other VCs as receiving feedback from both algorithms, while behaving according to the minimum of these feedback signals. We use the term *VC type 1* to refer to VCs that only pass through a single algorithm, and the term *VC type 2* to refer to VCs that pass through two algorithms.

Since the ER algorithm controls the bottleneck switch in the first test, proper behavior of this configuration would require that the ER algorithm controls all the sources. Proper behavior is indeed achieved in this case, because the ACR and throughput plots of the sources are the same as in the homogeneous park-

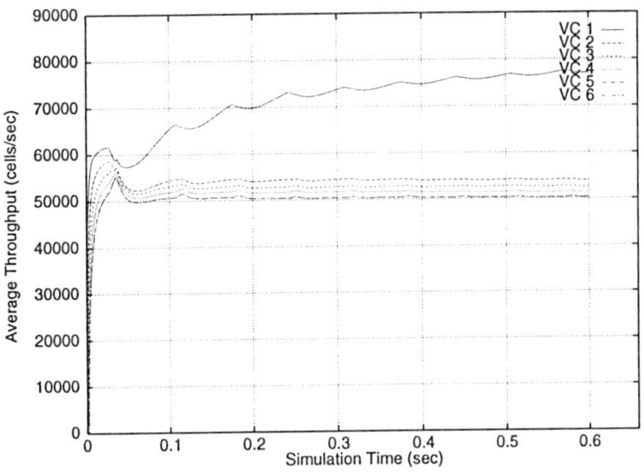

Figure 8: RRM in Bottleneck Node, and Bounded MACR in Nonbottleneck Nodes

ing lot configuration with all switches executing the ER algorithm, (plots not included). Thus, the bottleneck switch was the only controlling switch, and fairness was achieved in this case because it had been achieved in the equivalent homogeneous topology.

In our second test, we inverted the location of the algorithms, and used the RRM algorithm at the bottleneck node, and the Bounded MACR algorithm in all other nodes. Figure 8 shows the average throughput plot for this configuration. A marked lack of fairness occurs because VC 1 achieves a much higher throughput than the other VCs. The RRM algorithm at the bottleneck does *not* achieve perfect fairness in the homogeneous version of this topology. We will see below that some of the unfairness is caused by the RRM algorithm itself, and that some is caused by the interoperability of the two algorithms. In the subsections below, we will isolate the two causes of unfairness, and focus on the interoperability problem.

4.2 The Rate Mismatch Problem

We begin with two observations based on the results of the initial two tests, and then formulate a hypothesis. We demonstrate the validity of this hypothesis in the remainder of this paper.

- In the heterogeneous topology in which proper behavior *was not* achieved, the algorithm at the bottleneck was the more oscillatory of the two algorithms. Conversely, in the heterogeneous topology in which proper behavior *was* achieved, the algorithm at the bottleneck was the less oscillatory of the two algorithms.
- All of the VCs of type 2 obtained the same throughput, and the VC that obtained an unfairly large throughput was of type 1.

Hypothesis: Heterogeneous configurations with two different ABR flow control algorithms operating simultaneously will cause unfairness when the following two conditions hold: (1) the algorithm at the bottleneck switch is substantially more oscillatory than the algorithm at the nonbottleneck switch(es); and (2) there is at least one VC that only traverses the more oscillatory algorithm, and there is at least one VC that traverses both algorithms.

The reason unfairness occurs is due to a mismatch in the rate processes of the two types of VCs. We call this problem the *rate mismatch problem* because the algorithm at a nonbottleneck node interferes with the control of the algorithm at the bottleneck node, which causes different sources to experience nonidentical rate increase processes. When we say that multiple sources experience the same rate increase (decrease) process, we mean that they increase (or decrease) their rates according to the same function (that is determined by the particular algorithm). For example, an algorithm may allow a linear increase or an exponential increase.

4.2.1 Rate Mismatch Topology

In this section, we describe a general type of topology in which conditions (1) and (2) hold. This topology structure, which we call the *Rate Mismatch Topology*, is depicted in Figure 9. There can be any number of switches in network 1 running algorithm #1, and any number of switches in network 2 running algorithm #2. Algorithm #1 is more oscillatory than algorithm #2 and the bottleneck node resides in network 1. There can be any number of VCs of type 1 (such as $(s1, d1)$ in the figure), and any number of VCs of type 2 (such as $(s2, d2)$ in the figure). [1]

We will show that this configuration isolates the underlying topology substructure in which the above unfairness problem can arise. We believe it is important to identify key topologies that either isolate a particular behavior of an algorithm, or are the cause of a specific problem. This is useful if the specific problem reappears when the essential topology substructure is embedded inside larger topologies (which are then easier to analyze).

For ease of analysis, we reduce this topology to the simplest form that still exhibits the observed behavior. To capture the essential features that lead to the rate mismatch problem, it is sufficient to have one VC of each type in the reduced topology. In the rest of this

[1] The original parking lot topology we considered is a particular instance of this topology in which there is one switch in cloud 1 and 4 switches in cloud 2.

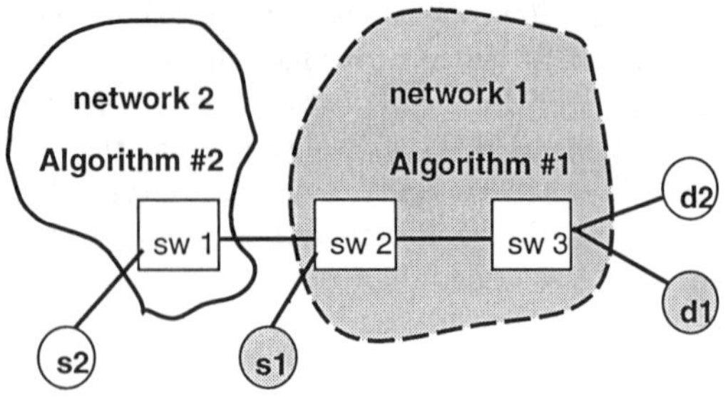

Figure 9: Rate Mismatch Topology

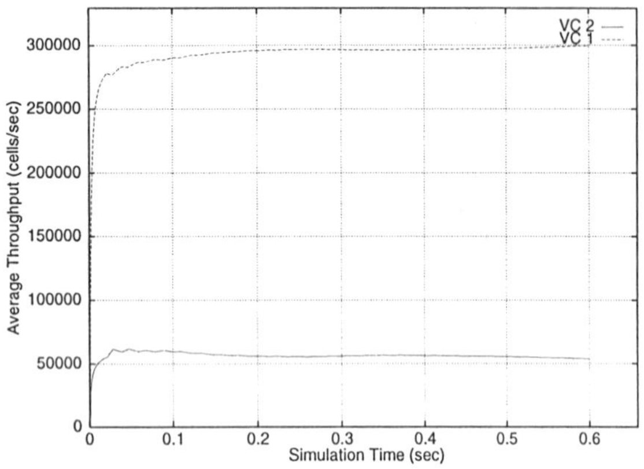

Figure 10: Throughputs for *Asynchronous* Rate Mismatch Topology with RRM at bottleneck and Bounded MACR at nonbottleneck

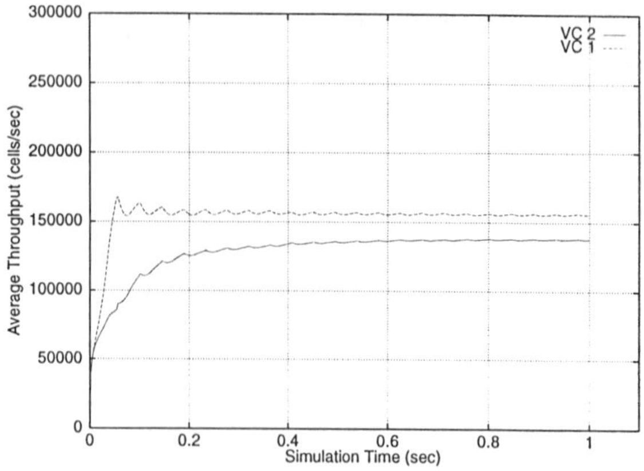

Figure 11: Throughputs for *Synchronous* Rate Mismatch Topology with RRM at bottleneck and Bounded MACR at nonbottleneck

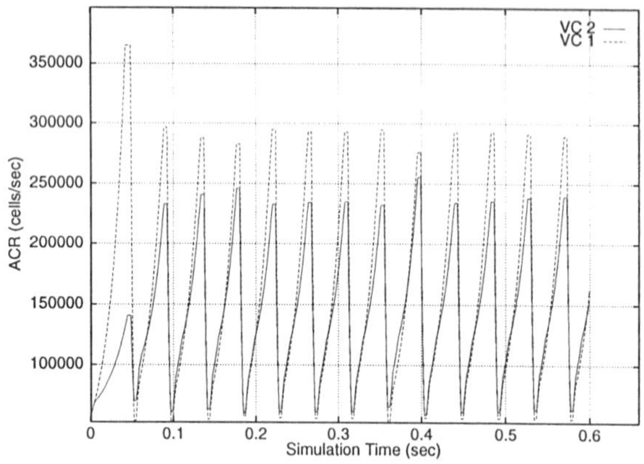

Figure 12: ACRs for Synchronous Rate Mismatch Topology with RRM at bottleneck and Bounded MACR at nonbottleneck

paper we use the specific configuration (i.e., the number of switches and VCs) as depicted in Figure 9. To demonstrate that we have retained the essential topology structure needed to regenerate the results from the tests in Table 1, we redid those tests. The results were the same. In Figure 10 we plot the average throughput of the two sources for the second test in the rate mismatch topology. The resulting throughput is dramatically unfair.

Recall that the general parking lot topology is intended to highlight the behavior of an algorithm when each of the VCs has a different feedback delay from the bottleneck node (i.e., asynchronous feedback delays). It is known that the asynchronicity of the feedback delays makes fairness harder to achieve [7, 13]. In order to remove any potential unfairness due to asynchronous feedback delays, we convert our topology into one with synchronous feedback delays by making the link between switch 2 and source 1 as long as the sum of the lengths of the link between switches 2 and 1, and the link between switch 1 and source 2. This version of the topology is called the *synchronous rate mismatch topology*. We thus isolate any unfairness which directly results from the interaction of two heterogeneous algorithms. We repeated both the tests described in Table 1, in the synchronous Rate Mismatch Topology. In Figure 11 we plot the average throughput for Test 2 of the two sources in the synchronous rate mismatch topology. The unfairness is less dramatic that in Figure 10, but still exists nevertheless. As expected, fairness is achieved for Test 1. Since condition (1) is not met in this test, we do not expect unfairness.

4.2.2 An Example Explained

We explore Test 2 in the Synchronous Rate Mismatch Topology in detail in this section. In Figure 12 we plot the ACRs of the two sources for this test. We make the following observations about the steady state behavior of the sources.

- The two sources experience the same period of oscillation.
- The lowest value reached during the cycle is roughly the same for both sources.
- The highest value reached during the cycle differs for the two sources.

The period of oscillation is primarily determined by the sum of the time it takes for the queue, starting in an uncongested state, to fill up to its congestion threshold, plus the time needed to drain the queue back down to its threshold for noncongestion. The period is the same for both sources, *not* because of synchronous feedback delays, but rather because both sources have the same bottleneck queue. This oscillation period is typically much longer than the feedback delay. In this case, the period is roughly 40 ms, whereas the feedback delays are 0.5 ms.

The behavior noted in the second observation occurs because of two effects. First, the bottleneck queue is the only queue to experience buildup and is thus the only queue to generate decrease feedback signals. Both sources experience the same rate decrease process. Second, the multiplicative backoff scheme of the RRM algorithm drives the sources towards the same value, regardless of their initial condition.

The behavior noted in the third observation occurs because the rate increase processes of the two sources are not the same. Since the throughput of each source is simply the integral of these curves, it is visibly clear that source 2 will get more throughput than source 1. What is the reason for the different rate increase processes? To examine more closely what happens within a single cycle, we enlarge the plot of the ACRs in Figure 13.

From time 0.185 until roughly 0.2, the rates of the two sources grow similarly. However, from time 0.2 until they reach their peaks, they undergo different rate growth processes. It turns out that during the time slot $0.185 - 0.2$, both sources adjust their rates according to the feedback from the RRM switch. But during the time slot $0.2 - 0.23$, source 2 grows according to the feedback from the Bounded MACR algorithm, which is now producing the minimum rate of the feedback signals. This behavior is explained as follows.

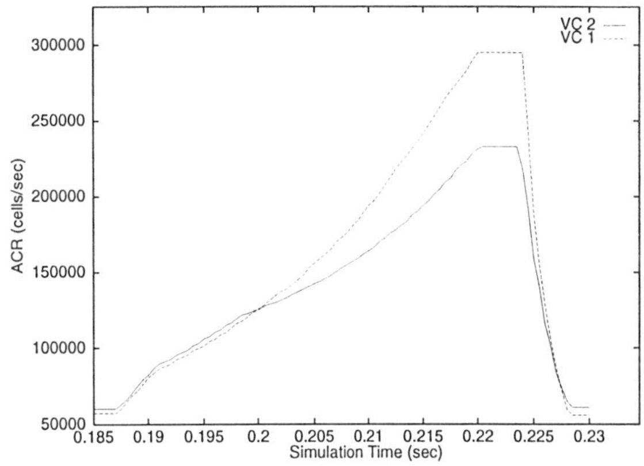

Figure 13: ACR Cycles

When switch 2 becomes congested, all the sources' rates are driven down according to the RRM algorithm. Since this algorithm is highly oscillatory, all of the rates significantly undershoot the desired rate. Since the source rates traversing the nonbottleneck switch will be very low, they will in turn drag down the value of MACR at the nonbottleneck node. After the queue drains, the source rates start to increase. MACR may not drop as low as the ACR dictated by the RRM algorithm. So for a short period both sources follow the RRM algorithm and rapidly increase their rates. However since the Bounded MACR algorithm does exponential averaging, and grows very slowly, at some point the ACRs given by the RRM algorithm will be larger than MACR. Hence, after this initial period, switch 1 produces lower ACRs than switch 2. Thus, the increase process of the VC passing through both algorithms is effectively controlled by the nonbottleneck switch. Since algorithms at nonbottleneck nodes are not supposed to control the source rates of the VCs traversing them, this constitutes an example of interference among algorithms, or improper behavior.

4.2.3 Hypothesis Validation

We define the rate mismatch problem more generally as follows. Let n be the number of sources bottlenecked at a switch. If k where $k < n$, of those sources experience a rate increase process different from that experienced by the remaining $n - k$ sources, due to interference from a nonbottleneck switch, then we say a *rate mismatch* occurs. This rate mismatch is the link between the conditions of the hypothesis and the conclusion of the hypothesis. The conditions in the hypothesis cause a rate mismatch to occur, which in turn leads to unfairness. This rate mismatch scenario leads to unfairness because the sources that are allowed larger rate increases will grab a disproportionate amount of bandwidth (more than their max-min fairshare), and thus obtain more throughput.

Since most algorithms cause the source rates to oscillate (in any environment), the behavior of a source can be described as an alternating process, one that alternates between a rate increase process and a rate decrease process. The conditions of the hypothesis, and hence the rate mismatch topology, create the following additional effects on the steady state cyclical behavior of the source rates. Figure 14 depicts one cycle of each of the two VC types. Each cycle has four phases. Let t_1 denote the beginning of a cycle, t_2 denote the time at which the behaviors of the two sources diverge, t_3 denote the time at which the sources start to receive "do-nothing" feedback signals, t_4 denote the time at which sources start to receive decrease feedback signals, and t_5 denote the end of the cycle. Let the phases be denoted by $T_i = t_{i+1} - t_i$ for $i = 1, 2, 3, 4$. The sources increase during phases T_1 and T_2, stay the same during phase T_3, and decrease during phase T_4. In some algorithms $T_3 = 0$. Let $r_1(t)$ and $r_2(t)$ denote the transmission rate of a type 1 VC and a type 2 VC, respectively.

Claim 1: *The four conditions below always hold in the rate mismatch topology.*

1. the cycle time $\sum_{i=1}^{4} T_i$ is the same for all sources
2. the sources follow the same algorithm during phases T_3 and T_4.
3. $\min_{t \in (t_1, t_5)} r_i(t)$ is roughly the same for all sources
4. $\exists$ a time t_2 after which the VCs of different types experience different growth rates.

The first condition is true for the reason given in the previous section (that the cycle time is determined by the filling and draining of the bottleneck queue). The second condition says that all the sources, of both types, will experience the same rate decrease process. This occurs because there is a single bottleneck node in this topology, because it has the more oscillatory algorithm (and thus the fastest rate reduction), and because the sources take the minimum of the feedback signals. The third condition is true because most rate reduction processes tend to drive the sources towards the same value regardless of their initial condition, $r_i(t_4)$. This occurs because the goal of ABR flow control is to drive the sources towards their max-min fairshare. The fairshares are equal in this single bottleneck environment. Note that they are driven towards the same value even if they undershoot the desired rate.

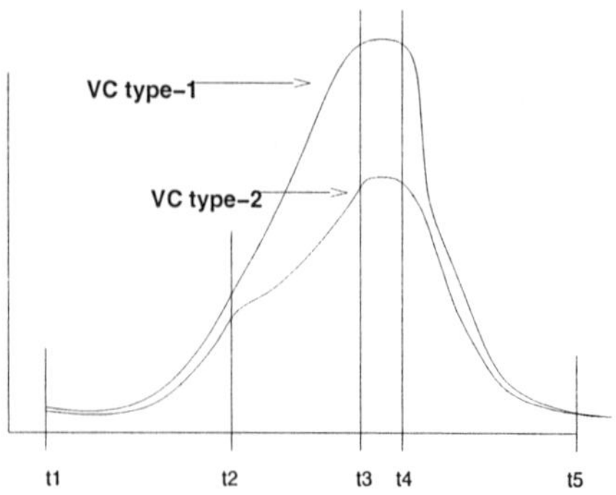

Figure 14: Rate Mismatch Cycle

The fourth condition holds due to the following. In the rate mismatch topology the more oscillatory algorithm resides at the bottleneck switch. That means, by definition, that the bottleneck switch permits a faster growth rate than the nonbottleneck switch. Clearly the sources (VC type 2) – following the minimum of the two feedback signals – will increase according to the slower growing algorithm, whereas those sources (VC type 1) that only receive feedback from the faster growing algorithm, will grow quicker (than VC type 2 sources). One algorithm can interfere with another only during the rate increase process, and not during the rate decrease process, because the sources take the minimum of all the feedback signals.

The time t_2 is a critical juncture as this denotes the moment at which the nonbottleneck switch starts to interfere with the control of the bottleneck switch. With some algorithms, the divergence of the two sources may start at the beginning of the cycle, i.e., $t_2 = t_1$ or $T_1 = 0$. However, the less oscillatory algorithm does not necessarily interfere *immediately* in the rate growth process. Although the growth rate may be slower, this algorithm could be starting from a larger initial value (as in the example in Section 4.2.2).

Claim 2: *The rate mismatch topology leads to unfairness.*

We measure (un)fairness by the total throughput received by each source type during steady state behavior. The throughput TPT_i obtained by source i in a single cycle is given by

$$\int_{t_1}^{t_2} r_i(t)dt + \int_{t_2}^{t_3} r_i(t)dt + \int_{t_3}^{t_4} r_i(t)dt + \int_{t_4}^{t_5} r_i(t)dt$$

The source rates are controlled by the bottleneck switch algorithm in phases T_1, T_3, and T_4. Because of this, and because of condition 3 in Claim 1, we have $r_1(t) \simeq r_2(t)$ during T_1. In phase T_2, the VCs of type 1 are controlled by the bottleneck switch, whereas

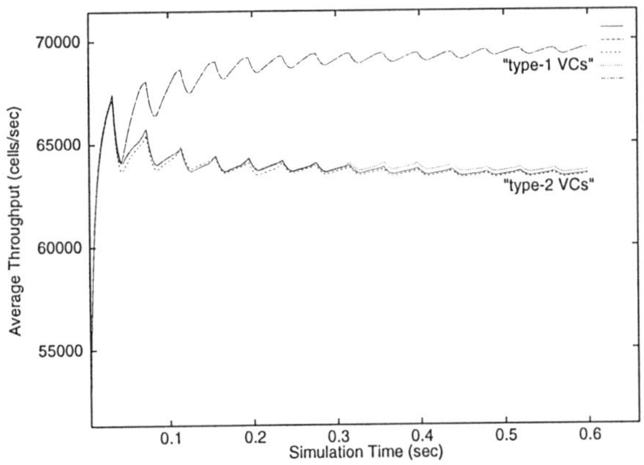

Figure 15: Multiple VCs in Synchronous Rate Mismatch Topology

the VCs of type 2 are controlled by the nonbottleneck switch. The interference of the nonbottleneck algorithm causes $r_1(t) > r_2(t)$ during phase T_2. This in turn results in $r_1(t) > r_2(t)$ during T_3 as well. During T_4 we have $r_1(t) \geq r_2(t)$. Clearly this yields $TPT_1 > TPT_2$, which is the condition for unfairness in this configuration.

Claims 1 and 2 together validate the hypothesis.

Claim 3: *The hypothesis is valid in both the synchronous and asynchronous versions of the rate mismatch topology.*

This is true because the only difference in the cyclical behavior of the two types of sources in the asynchronous version of the rate mismatch topology, is a phase shift for the sources with the longer feedback delays. Let τ denote the difference between the feedback delays of the two sources. In the calculation of TPT_2 every t_i is shifted to $t_i - \tau$. However, the value resulting from the integration remains the same.

Our discussion has centered around the case of two sources, one of each type. To show that the hypothesis holds for multiple sources of each type, we performed a test with two sources of type 1, and three sources of type 2. The results are given in Figure 15. As the hypothesis predicts, there is unfairness between the type 1 VCs and the type 2 VCs.

4.3 Rate Mismatch Experiments with Multiple Algorithms

We carried out additional experiments using other algorithms, since the hypothesis is independent of the particular algorithms used. The tests we conducted are summarized in Table 2. The notation "(o)" indicates an oscillatory algorithm, and "(n.o.)" indicates a nonoscillatory algorithm. Notice that we have

Bottleneck Switch	*Nonbottleneck Switch*	Result
RRM (o)	Bounded MACR (n.o.)	Unfair
RRM (o)	UnBounded MACR (o)	Fair
osc_ERICA+	Bounded MACR (n.o.)	Unfair
non_osc_ERICA+	Bounded MACR (n.o.)	Fair

Table 2: Test Set 2 and Results. Synchronous Rate Mismatch Topology

considered all possible combinations of oscillatory and non-oscillatory algorithms. Along with testing the interoperability of a binary algorithm (RRM) with an ER algorihm, this test set also considers the interoperability of two different ER algorithms.

The results corroborate the hypothesis. The throughput results of the first test have been given in Figure 11. The average throughput plots for the second, third and fourth tests are given in Figure 16, 17 and 18, respectively. The amount of unfairness, in a particular case of two algorithms, depends upon the amplitude of the source rate oscillations and the amount of rate mismatch. Figure 16 elucidates the fact that the algorithms interfere only in the increase process and not in the decrease process, since the the Unbounded MACR algorithm is a hybrid algorithm, which matches the rate increase process of RRM, while keeping the rate decrease process of Bounded MACR.

5 Conclusions

Our results demonstrate that some heterogeneous topologies are free from rate mismatch problems, while others are not. Therefore heterogeneous switches cannot be arbitrarily connected together to form a network. In general, guidelines should be used for network layout. Such guidelines should specify problematic configurations to avoid, or how to interconnect different vendor equipment. A sample guideline is the suggestion that rate mismatch topologies should be avoided.

Unfortunately, network configurations which contain the rate mismatch topology embedded in them, are a likely scenario, especially since WANs are frequently used to interconnect LANs. For example, a heterogeneous network would result if the WAN infrastructure is established by an operating company that buys switches from one vendor, and the LANs are setup by an individual organization that purchases switches from an alternate vendor.

Solutions in which switches need to know more information about other switches, are undesirable since they may lead to increased complexity in algorithms or protocols. Unless switch algorithms become stan-

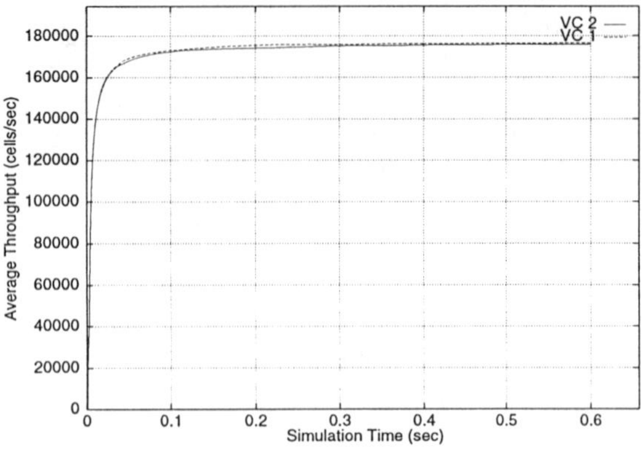

Figure 16: RRM at Bottleneck Node and Unbounded MACR at Nonbottleneck Node

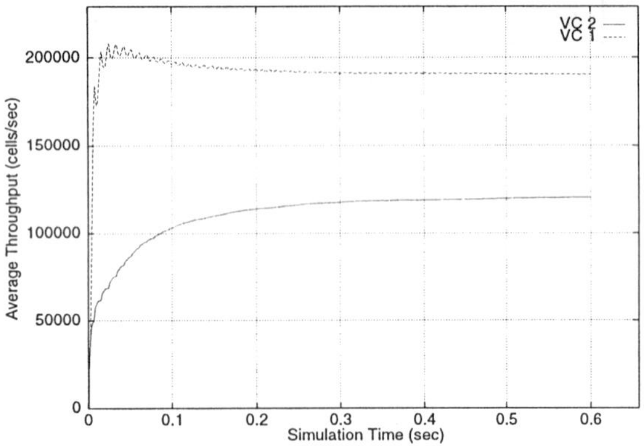

Figure 17: osc_ERICA+ at Bottleneck Node and Bounded MACR at Nonbottleneck Node

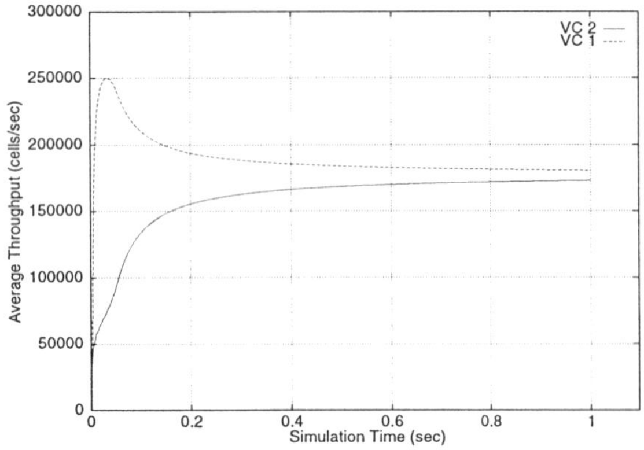

Figure 18: non_osc_ERICA+ at Bottleneck Node and Bounded MACR at Nonbottleneck Node

dardized, other approaches to handle this problem will have to be found. One possible approach is to use Virtual Source/Virtual Destination (as proposed by the ATM Forum) which artificially cuts control loops to eliminate type 2 VCs.

References

[1] ATM Forum Contribution af-tm-0056.000. *ATM Forum Traffic Management Specification*, April 1996. Version 4.0.

[2] D. Bertsekas and R. Gallager. *Data Networks*. Prentice Hall, 1993.

[3] Anna Charny, K. K. Ramakrishnan, and Anthony Lauck. Scalability Issues for Distributed Explicit Rate Allocation in ATM Networks. *IEEE Infocom Proceedings*, March 1996.

[4] H. Ohsaki and M. Murata and H. Suzuki and C. Ikeda and H. Miyahara. Rate-Based Congestion Control for ATM Networks. *Computer Communication Review*, April 1995.

[5] R. Jain, S. Kalyanaraman, R. Goyal, S. Fahmy, and R. Viswanathan. The ERICA Switch Algorithm: A Complete Description. *ATM Forum Contribution 96-1172*, August 1996.

[6] L. Kalampoukas, A. Varma, and K. K. Ramakrishnan. Dynamics of an Explicit Rate Allocation Algorithm for ATM Networks. *IFIP Broadband Communications Proceedings*, April 1996.

[7] A. Kolarov and G. Ramamurthy. Comparison of Congestion Control Schemes for ABR Service in ATM Local Area Networks. *Proceedings of IEEE Globecom*, December 1994.

[8] A. Kolarov and G. Ramamurthy. Comparison of ER and EFCI Flow Control Schemes for ABR Service in Wide Area Networks. *IFIP Broadband Communications Proceedings*, April 1995.

[9] S. Mascolo, D. Cavendish, and M. Gerla. ATM Rate Based Congestion Control Using a Smith Predictor: an EPRCA Implementation. *IEEE Infocom Proceedings*, March 1996.

[10] M. Ritter. Network Buffer Requirements of the rate-Based Control Mechanism for ABR Services. *Proceedings of IEEE Infocom*, March 1996.

[11] C. Roche and N. Plotkin. The Converging Flows Problem: An Analytical Study. *IEEE Infocom Proceedings*, April 1995.

[12] K.Y. Siu and H.Y. Tzeng. Intelligent Congestion Control for ABR Service in ATM Networks. *ACM SigComm Computer Communications Review*, September 1994.

[13] N. Taft-Plotkin and J. Sydir. Comparing the Impact of Multiple Propagation Delays on EFCI and ER Flow Control Algorithms. Technical Report ITAD-729-PA-96-187, SRI International, 1996.

Queueing Analysis of a Distributed Explicit Rate Allocation Algorithm for ABR Services *

Nasir Ghani and Jon W. Mark
Department of Electrical and Computer Engineering
University of Waterloo, Waterloo, Ontario N2L 3G1
{nghani,jwmark}@bbcr.uwaterloo.ca

Abstract

Approximate queueing analysis of a distributed explicit rate allocation algorithm for the flow control of available bit rate (ABR) service, which captures the effect of bandwidth-delay, is described. Attention is focused on bounding the worst case transient queueing behaviour in a strictly-ABR environment with persistent start-up sources. At each switch, RM cells are enqueued using a buffer separate from the data cells, and are served with a higher priority than data cells. Both single and multiple node network cases are treated for connections with differing delays. The approximate analysis shows relatively good agreement with simulation results for single node networks, but gives looser estimates for the multiple node case.

Keywords: Available Bit Rate, Explicit Rate, Feedback Flow Control, Distributed Explicit Rate Allocation

1 Introduction

The ABR (*available bit rate*) service class for data service support is designed to enhance network utilization in ATM networks. This enhancement is to be attained by having ABR traffic make efficient use of the residual link bandwidth via feedback control. However, the effectiveness of feedback control is complicated by the presence of large transmission delays. The ATM Forum has selected an overall rate-based approach for ABR services support [4]. The main concerns with this strategy are ensuring that compliant users have low cell loss rates and guaranteed *minimum cell rate* (MCR) allocations [2].

The current trend has been towards more advanced *explicit rate* (ER) algorithms [4]-[6]. Sources periodically send control information in special *resource management* (RM) cells into the data stream, which are looped back by the destination. Switches set the ER-field of backward RM cells to indicate the source's maximum *allowed cell rate* (ACR), and attempt to achieve fair and efficient rate allocation. Many schemes with differing complexities, fairness, responsiveness, etc., have been proposed [4]-[13]. In this paper we are concerned with schemes which use explicit available capacity levels to adjust sources to their fair share rates [9]-[12], generally known as *distributed explicit rate allocation* algorithms [11].

Although many algorithms have been proposed for the ABR service, to our knowledge, a comprehensive analysis is lacking. Specifically, bandwidth-delay performance needs detailed investigation. Most current analysis is limited to *proportional rate control*-type (PRCA) algorithms using differential equations to model special single node cases [5],[8],[14]-[17]. In this paper we further the scope of such analysis to investigate bandwidth-delay performance for distributed explicit rate allocation-type schemes in strictly-ABR environments. Detailed approximate fluid-flow modelling is done to bound the worst case queueing behaviour. The analysis considers both single and multiple node networks, and incorporates varying propagation delays, inter-RM cell times, and buffering delays. The results will allow service providers to properly assess buffering requirements and possibly derive gating schemes for connection admission.

The remainder of the paper is organized as follows. In Section 2 a brief overview of a distributed explicit rate allocation algorithm is given. Sections 3 and 4 derive queueing bounds for the single node and multiple node cases, respectively. Section 5 compares the derived bounds against simulation results for various test case scenarios. Conclusions are drawn in Section 6.

2 A Distributed Explicit Rate Allocation Algorithm

The distributed explicit rate allocation algorithm resides at the source-end systems and at each of the network switches. Overall details are now presented.

2.1 At the Source-End

The pseudocode for the operation of the source-end system is shown in Fig. 1. The i-th source emits an RM cell containing the values of the *minimum cell rate*, MCR^i, the *peak cell rate*, PCR^i, and the current *allowed cell*

*This work has been supported partially by the Natural Sciences and Engineering Research Council of Canada (NSERC) under Grant No. A7779 and a Postgraduate Scholarship, grants from the Canadian Institute for Telecommunications Research (CITR) under the NCE program of the Government of Canada and the Information Technology Research Centre (ITRC) under the Ontario Provincial Centres of Excellence Program, and scholarships from the Canadian Council of Professional Engineers (CCPE)/Manulife Financial and the Association of Universities and Colleges of Canada (AUCC).

0-8186-7780-5/97 $10.00 © 1997 IEEE

```
if (data cell to send)
  {
   /* check if RM cell to be sent */
   if (RM_count == Nrm)
     {
      Send RM cell (MCR^i, ACR^i, PCR^i)
      RM_count = 0 /* clear count */
     }
   else
     {
      Send data cell
      RM_count = RM_count + 1 /* increment count */
     }
  }
if (backward RM cell received)
  {
   /* update rate */
   ACR^i = max(MCR^i, min(PCR^i, ER^i_cell, ACR^i + Nrm · AIR))
  }
```

Figure 1: Source-end algorithm, connection i

rate, ACR^i, after every N_{rm} data cells. The PCR value is inserted in the ER field of the RM cell, and is adjusted downward by network switches on the *backward* pass. Before each cell transmission, the source checks to see if an RM cell needs to be emitted. This is accomplished by keeping a circular counter, *RM_count*, which ranges from 0 to N_{rm}. Upon reception of a *backward* RM cell, source i updates its ACR as

$$ACR^i = \max(MCR^i, \min(PCR^i, ER^i_{cell}, ACR^i + N_{rm} \cdot AIR)), \tag{1}$$

where ER^i_{cell} is the current value in the RM cell and AIR is the increment value. Note that this is an additive-increase mechanism which avoids fast ramp-ups [2], limiting the maximum increase to $N_{rm} \cdot AIR$ cells/sec.

2.2 At the Network Switch

The core of the algorithm lies in each of the network switches where two major operations are performed: capacity tracking and rate allocation. In the capacity tracking phase, a measurement-based approach is used to compute the available capacity levels. First, the bandwidth usage by *non*-ABR sources is measured using an interval, T_{sw}. The number of non-ABR cells departing the link buffer are counted and an approximate available bandwidth value, $\overline{C_{av}}(k)$, is derived from the last measurement interval, k (assuming output buffering). However, details are omitted since capacity tracking yields constant values in ABR-only environments (see [9],[10]).

In the rate allocation phase, network switches compute rate updates for backward RM cells, using the *MCR-plus-equal-share* bandwidth fairness criterion [2],[5]. This handles MCR guarantees and simplifies to the ubiquitous max-min criterion [1] in the zero-MCR case. The pseudocode for the rate allocation algorithm is given in Fig. 2. Each switch maintains per-connection usages, ACR^i_{sw}, which are updated by the latest ACR^i_{cell} values in *forward* RM cells (*Update_Status*(i, ACR^i_{cell}), Fig. 2). The actual rate allocation is done for *backward* RM cells, ensuring that switches use the most current fair share values and provide expedient responses (as opposed to doing both usage updates and rate allocations for only forward (backward) RM cells [9],[11],[12]). All connections are aggregated into two sets: those which are bottlenecked at the link, $\mathcal{I}$, and those which are not, $\overline{\mathcal{I}}$. Only connections in $\mathcal{I}$ require rate increases, and all start-up connections are placed in $\overline{\mathcal{I}}$ (i.e., aggressive ramp-ups). Detecting such groupings in a distributed, delayed environment is difficult, but a general rule which can be exploited is that the bottleneck link will determine a connection's maximum rate. Hence, when an RM cell is received, the scheme checks to see if the connection "deserves" to be bottlenecked at the link. This is done by simply computing its fair share allocation as if it *were* bottlenecked and comparing the result to its current usage, regardless of current grouping. Note that groupings are updated on *both* forward/backward RM cell passes, improving responsiveness.

Consider the following aggregate quantities:

$$C_{\mathcal{I}} = \sum_{i \in \mathcal{I}} ACR^i_{sw}, \tag{2}$$

$$C_{\overline{\mathcal{I}}} = \sum_{i \in \overline{\mathcal{I}}} ACR^i_{sw}, \tag{3}$$

$$C^{MCR}_{\mathcal{I}} = \sum_{i \in \mathcal{I}} MCR^i, \tag{4}$$

where $C_{\mathcal{I}}$ and $C_{\overline{\mathcal{I}}}$ are the total allocations to bottlenecked and non-bottlenecked connections, respectively, and $C^{MCR}_{\mathcal{I}}$ is the total MCR allocation to bottlenecked connections. The *elastic* bandwidth is defined as the available bandwidth *beyond* the aggregate MCR commitment to $\mathcal{I}$ and aggregate usage by $\overline{\mathcal{I}}$, i.e., $\overline{C_{av}(k)} - C_{\overline{\mathcal{I}}} - C^{MCR}_{\mathcal{I}}$. Thus the fair share, ER^i_{sw}, is given by the source MCR plus a portional share of the elastic bandwidth (i.e., divided by $|\mathcal{I}|$, where $|\cdot|$denotes set cardinality):

$$ER^i_{sw} = \begin{cases} MCR^i + \dfrac{\overline{C_{av}(k)} - C_{\overline{\mathcal{I}}} - C^{MCR}_{\mathcal{I}}}{|\mathcal{I}|} & i \in \mathcal{I} \\ MCR^i + \dfrac{\overline{C_{av}(k)} - C_{\overline{\mathcal{I}}} - C^{MCR}_{\mathcal{I}} + ACR^i_{sw} - MCR^i}{|\mathcal{I}|+1} & i \in \overline{\mathcal{I}}. \end{cases} \tag{5}$$

Using the computed ER^i_{sw} fair share, the switch appropriately adjusts a connection's grouping. A large fraction, $\rho \approx 1$, of the computed fair share is compared to the source's latest ACR value: ACR^i_{cell} on the forward pass, ACR^i_{sw} on the backward pass. If the usage is less than ρER^i_{sw}, the connection stays in or moves to the non-bottlenecked group, $\overline{\mathcal{I}}$, and vice versa. Hence bottlenecked connections must "fully" use their allocations.

Overall, the algorithm has a low parameter count and acceptable complexity ($O(1)$-computation, $O(N)$-storage). The scheme differs from those in [11],[12], the most notable differences being the added MCR handling and forward/backward RM cell processing (for improved responsiveness). In addition, *express* queueing for RM cells is performed, placing RM cells in a separate buffer at the link and giving them *non-preemptive* service priority over data cells. Results show that the queueing performance of the scheme is greatly improved via this enhancement, since data cells do not delay rate reduction RM cells in periods of congestion. More complete descriptions of similar algorithms can be found in [9],[10].

3 Single Node Case

In this section detailed approximate worst case queueing analysis at a generic node, Fig. 3, is described. The approximation uses fluid-flow modelling of data traffic in the network. Consider N *persistent* ABR connections sharing a link of capacity μ cells/second with *heterogeneous* (distinct) *source-end system* and *destination-end system* propagation delays, δ_f^i, δ_b^i, respectively. The greedy sources give maximal PCR values, μ cells/sec. Since the environment has only ABR sources, the available capacity will always equal the link rate (i.e., $\overline{C_{av}(k)} = \mu$ cells/sec.). For simplicity all connections are assumed to have zero-MCR requirements, although the analysis can be extended to incorporate non-zero MCR guarantees. The AIR increment, (Eq. (1)), is assumed to be very large, allowing direct ramp-ups to the received ER_{cell}^i values (Fig. 1). This makes the analysis tractable and also gives the worst case queueing behaviour. All connections start at time zero, transmitting at very low initial cell rates ($\ll \frac{\mu}{N}$) by first emitting an RM cell. Hence a connection must wait at least one full roundtrip delay to receive its initial ACR value from the network. Similarly, the switch will not know about a connection's ramp-up until its *second* RM cell is received. Extending the analysis to non-simultaneous starting times is also possible and will be briefly described. Since distinct connection delays significantly complicate the analysis, only express RM cell queueing (Section 2.2) is considered. This yields (roughly) bounded inter-RM cell delays which can be used for computing overload period durations.

The maximum queue buildup induced by connection i, q_{max}^i, is derived, and thus the total queue buildup is

$$q_{max} = \sum_{i=1}^{N} q_{max}^i. \qquad (6)$$

The analysis is based on the fact that when a connection ramps up, those which have ramped up before it (i.e., shorter delays) must reduce their rates to the appropriate fractions of link capacity. However, due to the reactive nature of the scheme, there are delays in source rate reduction (i.e., propagation delays, inter-RM cell times, express RM cell buffer waiting times). Therefore, by deriving the rate overloads and their durations, queue buildups can be computed. Now, in general, when the switch "knows" that k connections have ramped up (i.e., are bottlenecked), the correct rate for all connections is $\frac{\mu}{k}$. Therefore, given the delays, actual source rates can be approximated and, by subtracting their ideal values, the rate overload determined. Similarly, by using the approximated rates, the maximum overload durations can

<u>Grouping-Update Procedure</u>

procedure Update_Status(i , ACR_{latest}^i)
{
$ER_{min} = MCR^i + \frac{\overline{C_{av}(k)} - C_{\mathcal{I}}^{MCR} - C_{\overline{\mathcal{I}}}^{MCR}}{|\mathcal{I}|+|\overline{\mathcal{I}}|}$
if (connection $i \in \mathcal{I}$) /* if bottlenecked */
{
/* Compute fair share */
$ER_{sw}^i = MCR^i + \frac{\overline{C_{av}(k)} - C_{\overline{\mathcal{I}}} - C_{\mathcal{I}}^{MCR}}{|\mathcal{I}|}$
$ER_{sw}^i = max(MCR^i, ER_{sw}^i, ER_{min})$
if ($\rho ER_{sw}^i > ACR_{latest}^i$) /* check $\mathcal{I} \rightarrow \overline{\mathcal{I}}$ transition */
{
$i \rightarrow \overline{\mathcal{I}}$ /* move i to $\overline{\mathcal{I}}$, update all quantities */
$C_{\mathcal{I}} = C_{\mathcal{I}} - ACR_{sw}^i$
$C_{\overline{\mathcal{I}}} = C_{\overline{\mathcal{I}}} + ACR_{latest}^i$
$C_{\mathcal{I}}^{MCR} = C_{\mathcal{I}}^{MCR} - MCR^i$
$C_{\overline{\mathcal{I}}}^{MCR} = C_{\overline{\mathcal{I}}}^{MCR} + MCR^i$
}
else
{
/* Update bottlenecked aggregate usage */
$C_{\mathcal{I}} = C_{\mathcal{I}} - ACR_{sw}^i + ACR_{latest}^i$
}
}
else /* if not bottlenecked */
{
/* Compute fair share */
$ER_{sw}^i = MCR^i + \frac{\overline{C_{av}(k)} - C_{\overline{\mathcal{I}}} - C_{\mathcal{I}}^{MCR} + ACR_{sw}^i - MCR^i}{|\mathcal{I}|+1}$
$ER_{sw}^i = max(MCR^i, ER_{sw}^i, ER_{min})$
if ($\rho ER_{sw}^i \leq ACR_{latest}^i$) /* check $\overline{\mathcal{I}} \rightarrow \mathcal{I}$ transition */
{
$i \rightarrow \mathcal{I}$ /* move i to $\mathcal{I}$, update all quantities */
$C_{\mathcal{I}} = C_{\mathcal{I}} + ACR_{latest}^i$
$C_{\overline{\mathcal{I}}} = C_{\overline{\mathcal{I}}} - ACR_{sw}^i$
$C_{\mathcal{I}}^{MCR} = C_{\mathcal{I}}^{MCR} + MCR^i$
$C_{\overline{\mathcal{I}}}^{MCR} = C_{\overline{\mathcal{I}}}^{MCR} - MCR^i$
}
else /* if no $\overline{\mathcal{I}} \rightarrow \mathcal{I}$ transition */
{
/* Update non-bottlenecked aggregate usage */
$C_{\overline{\mathcal{I}}} = C_{\overline{\mathcal{I}}} - ACR_{sw}^i + ACR_{latest}^i$
}
}
$ACR_{sw}^i(k) = ACR_{latest}^i$ /* update local allocation */
return(ER_{sw}^i) /* return fair share */
}

<u>Backward RM Cell Algorithm</u>

/* Always allow source to ramp-up to its fair share */
ER_{sw}^i = Update_Status(i, ACR_{sw}^i) /* compute latest fair share */
$ER_{cell}^i = min(ER_{cell}^i, ER_{sw}^i)$ /* update ER-field */
Send Backward RM Cell ($MCR^i, ACR_{cell}^i, ER_{cell}^i$)

<u>Forward RM Cell Algorithm</u>

/* Update connection grouping with latest usage value */
ER_{sw}^i = Update_Status(i, ACR_{cell}^i)
Send Forward RM Cell ($MCR^i, ACR_{cell}^i, PCR^i$)

Figure 2: Network switch algorithm, connection i

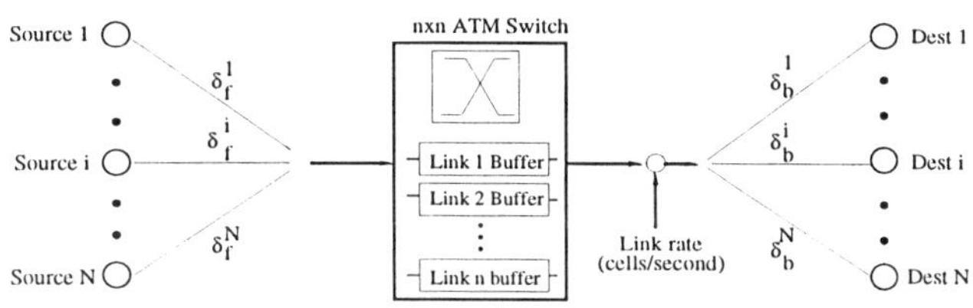

Figure 3: Single node, all connections using same link

be computed. Details are now presented. All times are in seconds, queue sizes in cells, and rates in cells/second.

Several important quantities are defined first. The roundtrip delay for the i-th connection, δ^i, is (Fig. 3)

$$\delta^i = 2\delta^i_f + 2\delta^i_b. \tag{7}$$

The *backward notification* time, T^i_b, for connection i is defined as the *minimal* time in which its first RM cell is sent by the switch to the source:

$$T^i_b = 2\delta^i_b + \delta^i_f. \tag{8}$$

Similarly, the *forward notification* time, T^i_f, is defined as the *minimal* time in which the switch is *notified* that connection i has ramped up to its initial rate, i.e., is bottlenecked. This occurs after the source receives its first backward RM cell, ramps up, and then notifies the switch δ^i_f seconds later:

$$T^i_f = \delta^i + \delta^i_f = 2\delta^i_b + 3\delta^i_f. \tag{9}$$

Eq. (9) is valid since connection groupings are also updated on *forward* RM cell passes (see Fig. 2). Note that Eq. (9) does not take into account the waiting time for the second "messenger" RM cell. Rather, this is accounted for in the subsequent analysis. Another quantity of interest is the worst case waiting time for a messenger RM cell given an input rate of r cells/second to the switch, $T_{N_{rm}}(r)$:

$$T_{N_{rm}}(r) = \frac{N_{rm}}{r}. \tag{10}$$

Although inter-RM cell times can be expressed by the right-hand-side of Eq. (10), we choose to explicitly use $T_{N_{rm}}(\cdot)$ for reasons of clarity. For large N, the waiting time in the express RM cell buffer can be significant, and this must also be approximated. For this, consider connection i's *express grouping*, $\mathcal{E}_i$, as those connections whose forward delays are within a cell transmission time:

$$\mathcal{E}_i = \left\{ j, 1 \leq j \leq N \ s.t. \ |\delta^i_f - \delta^j_f| \leq \frac{1}{\mu} \right\}. \tag{11}$$

Hence the approximate worst case RM cell waiting time in the express buffer is $\frac{|\mathcal{E}_i|}{\mu}$ seconds, and this includes the transmission time. For later analytical facility, an additional $(N+1)$-th connection with zero-MCR and infinite delay is also defined (i.e., $\delta^{N+1}_b, \delta^{N+1}_f \to \infty$).

Due to persistent sources, the rate behaviour for all connections is monotonically decreasing after the initial ramp-up (i.e., since a connection belongs to $\mathcal{I}$ after ramp-up and the number of connection ramp-ups only increases with time). As a result the rates can only decrease with time. Without loss of generality, assume that connection indices are ordered by increasing forward notification times (i.e., $T^i_f \leq T^j_f$ for $i < j$). Fig. 4 depicts the generic behaviour of connection i at the switch after ramp-up, segmenting it into three major stages. The true start-up time for connection i at the switch is always greater than T^i_f due to the inter-RM cell time for the second RM cell. However, since the major concern is bounding maximum queue increases, the ramp-up time is set to T^i_f (pessimistic). After the switch is notified that a source has ramped up, its second RM cell still has to propagate to the destination and then return to the source. Hence the source cannot be controlled for at least one roundtrip interval (Stage 1, Fig. 4). Subsequently, the RM cell stream is "established" and response times are reduced to roughly $2\delta^i_f$ (plus appropriate inter-RM cell times). This is the case for Stages 2 and 3 in Fig. 4. Worst case queue buildups are computed for each stage and summed to give the contribution by the connection:

$$q^i_{max} = q^i_1 + q^i_2 + q^i_3. \tag{12}$$

To approximate the initial start-up rate in Stage 1, *delay groupings*, $\mathcal{D}_i$, are derived. The delay grouping for a connection comprises the connection and a subset of connections with *smaller* roundtrip delays whose forward notification times are less than the reference's backward notification time, T^i_b. Specifically, connection j is bottlenecked at the switch after its first RM cell waits in the express buffer ($\frac{|\mathcal{E}_j|}{\mu}$ worst case), and propagates back to the source (T^j_b). The source then generates another RM cell ($T_{N_{rm}}(\frac{\mu}{j})$ worst case), and notifies the switch δ^j_f seconds later, i.e., approximately $T^j_f + T_{N_{rm}}(\frac{\mu}{j}) + \frac{|\mathcal{E}_j|}{\mu}$ seconds later. Therefore when connection i's first RM cell is sent, the switch "knows" that the other connections in its delay grouping have ramped up to their initial rates and are bottlenecked (i.e., $j \neq i$ and $j \in \mathcal{D}_i$ implies $j \in \mathcal{I}$ at T^i_b). Formally, this is

$$\mathcal{D}_i = \{i \cup j\} \text{ where } \left\{ j, 1 \leq j \leq N \ s.t. \ T^j_f + T_{Nrm}(\tfrac{\mu}{j}) + \tfrac{|\mathcal{E}_j|}{\mu} \leq T^i_b \right\}. \tag{13}$$

Thus the initial rate for connection i is $\frac{\mu}{|\mathcal{D}_i|}$, since all connections are initially non-bottlenecked (i.e., $i \in \overline{\mathcal{I}}$ at start-up, Section 2.2). Since delayed information is being used, $\mathcal{D}_i \neq \{1, 2, \cdots, i\}$ necessarily, and transient over-allocation can occur [9],[10]. Note that Eq. (13) is pessimistic since the $T_{N_{rm}}(\frac{\mu}{j})$-term assumes that connection j starts up at its minimum (correct) rate, yielding larger inter-RM cell times (Eq. (10)). In addition it ignores express RM buffer waiting times for connection i. Hence the computed $\mathcal{D}_i$ sets are smaller than the true $\mathcal{I}$ sets at time T^i_b, over-estimating the buildups.

Also, during Stage 1 (Fig. 4) other connections can ramp up, increasing the magnitude of the overload. The minimal index of a connection which ramps up *after* connection i's first stage is

$$m^i = \min \{ j, i < j \leq N+1 \quad s.t. \quad T^j_f > T^i_f + \delta^i + T_{N_{rm}}(\tfrac{\mu}{|\mathcal{D}_i|}) + \tfrac{|\mathcal{E}_i|}{\mu} \}. \tag{14}$$

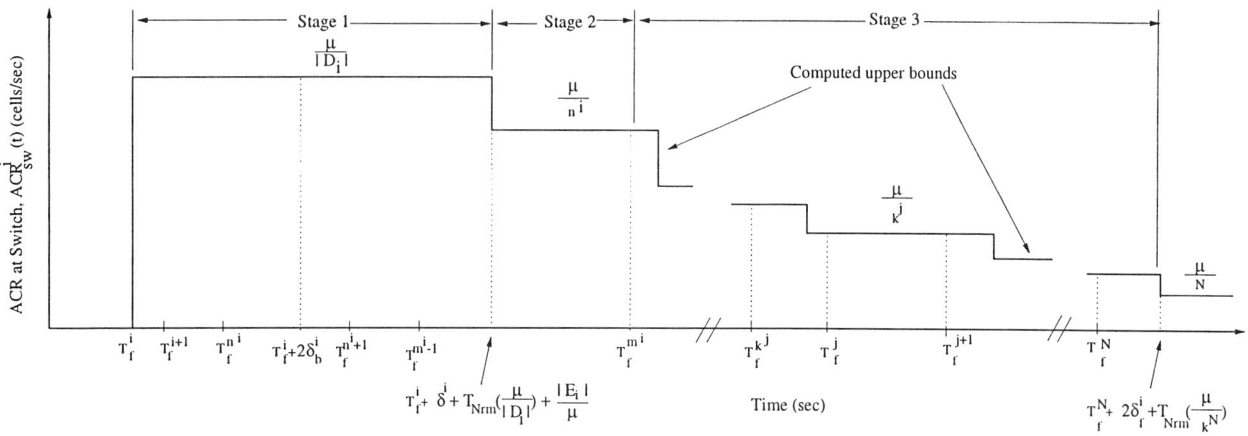

Figure 4: Generic rate behaviour of connection i at switch in Fig. 3, $ACR^i_{sw}(t)$

Therefore, by using m^i the queue buildup during Stage 1 is determined by summing the (possible) overload resulting from the connection's initial start-up rate and any connection ramp-ups (i.e., for all j, $i < j \leq m^i - 1$):

$$q_1^i = \sum_{j=i}^{m^i-1}\left(\frac{\mu}{|\mathcal{D}_i|}-\frac{\mu}{j}\right)\cdot \left(\min\left(T_f^{j+1}, T_f^i+\delta^i+T_{N_{rm}}\left(\frac{\mu}{|\mathcal{D}_i|}\right)+\frac{|\mathcal{E}_i|}{\mu}\right)-T_f^j\right). \tag{15}$$

The min-term in Eq. (15) ensures that overloads are only summed up to the end of Stage 1.

The queue buildup in Stage 2 is now considered. This stage occurs after the end of Stage 1, when the source (possibly) reduces its rate. For this we define another index, n^i, as the maximal index to which connection i will react to after its first stage:

$$n^i = \max\left\{j, 1 \leq j \leq N \quad s.t. \quad T_f^j + T_{N_{rm}}\left(\frac{\mu}{|\mathcal{D}_j|}\right) + \frac{|\mathcal{E}_j|}{\mu} < T_f^i + 2\delta_b^i\right\}, \tag{16}$$

(clearly $n^i < m^i$, Fig. 4). In the special case where n^i is undefined, it is arbitrarily set to unity. This means that at the start of Stage 2, the source rate at the switch will decline to at *least* $\frac{\mu}{n^i}$ (i.e., rate in second backward RM cell). Stage 2 ends at the first ramp-up time for a connection after the end of Stage 1, namely $T_f^{m^i}$ (see Fig. 4). Therefore the ideal rate during the second stage is $\frac{\mu}{m^i-1}$ and the queue buildup is given by

$$q_2^i = \left(\frac{\mu}{n^i}-\frac{\mu}{m^i-1}\right)\cdot\left(\min\left(2\delta_f^i + T_{N_{rm}}\left(\frac{\mu}{|\mathcal{D}_i|}\right), T_f^{m^i} - \left(T_f^i+\delta^i+T_{N_{rm}}\left(\frac{\mu}{|\mathcal{D}_i|}\right)+\frac{|\mathcal{E}_i|}{\mu}\right)\right)\right). \tag{17}$$

Again, the min-term in Eq. (17) ensures that the overload is not summed for more than $2\delta_f^i + T_{N_{rm}}(\frac{\mu}{|\mathcal{D}_i|})$ seconds after the end of the first stage, the approximate maximum time before the source will reduce its rate. In general, though, the buildups in Stage 2 are much smaller than those in the other stages.

The final stage, Stage 3, is now analyzed. Consider connection j coming on at T_f^j ($j \geq m^i$, Fig. 4). The maximum connection index to which source i has responded to by this time is approximately

$$k^j = \max\left\{k, m^i \leq k < j \quad s.t. \quad T_f^k + 2\delta_f^i + T_{N_{rm}}\left(\frac{\mu}{k-1}\right) < T_f^j\right\}. \tag{18}$$

Note that the $T_{N_{rm}}(\frac{\mu}{k-1})$-term is pessimistic, giving maximum possible inter-RM cell times. Thus the rate overload at time T_f^j is at most $(\frac{\mu}{k^j} - \frac{\mu}{j})$. Now this overload can last for either $2\delta_f^i$ (plus appropriate inter-RM cell times), or until the next connection ramp-up time at the switch, whichever occurs first. Therefore, by summing overloads for all connection indices after m^i, the queue buildup in Stage 3 is

$$q_3^i = \sum_{j=m^i}^{N}\left(\frac{\mu}{k^j}-\frac{\mu}{j}\right)\cdot\left(\min\left(2\delta_f^i + T_{N_{rm}}\left(\frac{\mu}{k^j}\right), T_f^{j+1}-T_f^j\right)\right). \tag{19}$$

Summing Eqs. (15), (17), and (19) over all connections gives the maximum buildup of Eq. (6).

In LAN environments, since the inter-RM cell times are much larger than the propagation delays, the q_1^i and q_2^i terms will dominate the queue increases. However, in WAN environments propagation delays are larger, and thus the q_3^i term will usually account for most of the queue buildup. Note that tighter approximations for q_2^i and q_3^i can also be derived by accounting for possible rate decreases between successive forward notification times (at the expense of added computations). Finally, non-simultaneous starting times can be handled by offsetting the T_b^i and T_f^i values appropriately (but not the actual propagation delays themselves, δ_b^i, δ_f^i).

The derived expressions for heterogeneous delays can be simplified for the special case of *homogeneous* delays, where all connections have equal forward, backward, and roundtrip propagation delays, i.e., δ_b, δ_f, δ, respectively.

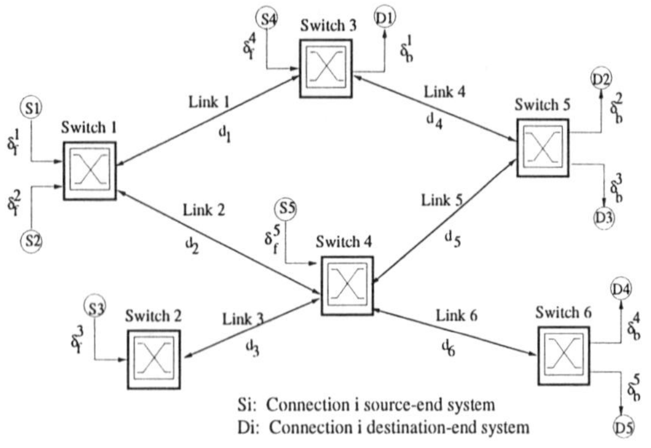

Figure 5: Sample multiple node network

Here, the delay groupings contain only one connection and sources ramp up to the link rate (i.e., $\mathcal{D}_i = \{i\}$, $|\mathcal{D}_i| = 1$). Omitting details, it can be shown that an upper-bound on the transient queue buildup is

$$q_{max} = (N-1)(\mu(\delta + 2\delta_f) + 2N_{rm} + N). \tag{20}$$

It is clear from the above expression that buildups with direct ramp-ups are significant (i.e., $O(N^2)$, $O(N\mu\delta)$).

4 Multiple Node Case

In the multiple node scenario, the rate behaviour of connections is much more complicated. Due to multiple bottlenecks, links can carry both bottlenecked and non-bottlenecked connections, and the rate behaviour in general is no longer monotonically decreasing. Nevertheless, (looser) bounds can be derived to approximate the worst case transient queue buildups for simultaneous starts. To the best of our knowledge, this has not been done for any other schemes. The required notation is first developed, and assumes express RM cell queueing.

The network is modelled as a graph, $\mathcal{G}(\mathcal{N}, \mathcal{L})$, where the sets $\mathcal{N}$ and $\mathcal{L}$ represent the network switches and *bidirectional* links, respectively. A sample six-node, five-connection network is shown in Fig. 5. Link j has capacity μ_j and propagation delay d_j. Let the set of connections traversing link j be given by $\mathcal{A}_j$, i.e., these connections all share the *output* bandwidth (i.e., $\mathcal{A}_1 = \{1, 2\}$, in Fig. 5). Each connection has an associated fixed set of links representing its traversed path, $\mathcal{P}_i = \{l_1^i, l_2^i, ..., l_{|\mathcal{P}_i|}^i\} \subseteq \mathcal{L}$ (i.e., $\mathcal{P}_2 = \{1, 3, 5\}$, Fig. 5). The end system delays, δ_f^i, δ_b^i, respectively, are defined analogous to the single node case (see Figs. 3 and 5). However, the actual forward/backward delays for a connection to the different links along its path vary and must be approximated. Consider the m-th link of $\mathcal{P}_i$, say link j (i.e., $j \in \mathcal{P}_i$, $i \in \mathcal{A}_j$, and $m \leq |\mathcal{P}_i|$). The (forward) delay between source i and link j's output buffer is

$$\delta_f^{i,j} = \delta_f^i + \sum_{k=1}^{m-1} d_{l_k^i}, \tag{21}$$

the (backward) delay between destination i and link j's output buffer is

$$\delta_b^{i,j} = \delta_b^i + \sum_{k=m}^{|\mathcal{P}_i|} d_{l_k^i}, \tag{22}$$

and the roundtrip delay for connection i for all links along its path is given by

$$\delta^i = 2\delta_f^{i,j} + 2\delta_b^{i,j} = 2\delta_f^i + 2\delta_b^i + \sum_{k=1}^{|\mathcal{P}_i|} 2d_{l_k^i}. \tag{23}$$

Note that (RM express) buffer delays are ignored, since results show that they are negligible. Moreover, delay estimates for multi-link connections are approximate at best. Using Eqs. (21)-(23), the forward/backward notification times for connection i to link j are, respectively,

$$T_f^{i,j} = \delta^i + \delta_f^{i,j} = 2\delta_b^{i,j} + 3\delta_f^{i,j}, \tag{24}$$

$$T_b^{i,j} = 2\delta_b^{i,j} + \delta_f^{i,j}. \tag{25}$$

We now define bottleneck levels/groupings for links/connections, $\mathcal{B}_k$. Since MCR guarantees are not considered, the link(s) carrying the most connections is the most bottlenecked (i.e., $\max_j |\mathcal{A}_j|$). All connections traversing this link belong to the first-level bottleneck grouping, $\mathcal{B}_1$, and have max-min fair *steady-state* rates

$$\nu_1 = \min_{j \in \mathcal{L}} \left\{ \frac{\mu_j}{|\mathcal{A}_j|} \right\}. \tag{26}$$

Let the bottleneck-level for link j be given by b^j, and j^k be the level-k bottleneck link. In other words, $b^{j^k} = k$ and $\mathcal{A}_{j^k} \subseteq (\mathcal{B}_k \cup \mathcal{B}_{k-1} \cdots \cup \mathcal{B}_1)$. As per the iterative procedure in [1], using our notation the max-min fair rate for connections in $\mathcal{B}_k$, bottleneck-level $k \geq 1$, is

$$\nu_k = \min_{j \neq j^{k-1}, \dots, j^1} \left\{ \frac{\mu_j - \sum_{l=1}^{k-1} \sum_{m \in \mathcal{A}_j} \nu_l \cdot \mathrm{I}\{m \in \mathcal{B}_l\}}{|\mathcal{A}_j| - \sum_{l=1}^{k-1} \sum_{m \in \mathcal{A}_j} \mathrm{I}\{m \in \mathcal{B}_l\}} \right\}, \tag{27}$$

where $\mathrm{I}\{\cdot\}$ is the event-indicator function. Therefore the bottleneck-level for connection i, g^i, is

$$g^i = \min_{k \in \mathcal{P}_i} \{b^k\}, \tag{28}$$

(i.e., $i \in \mathcal{B}_{g^i}$) and its steady-state max-min fair rate allocation, r^i, is

$$r^i = \min_{k \in \mathcal{P}_i} \{\nu_{b^k}\}, \tag{29}$$

(i.e., the maximum rate is limited to the minimum bottleneck rate along the connection's path). Now, in general, after the first roundtrip delay, the minimum rate guarantee for connection i is

$$r_{min}^i = \min_{j \in \mathcal{P}_i} \left\{ \frac{\mu_j}{|\mathcal{A}_j|} \right\}. \tag{30}$$

Although, the steady-state allocation, r^i, may be larger than r^i_{min}, this cannot be assumed during the initial transient period (i.e., $r^i_{min} \le r^i$).

Let $\mathcal{I}^j$ and $\overline{\mathcal{I}}^j$ be the *steady-state* bottlenecked and non-bottlenecked groupings at link j, respectively, as determined by the max-min criterion. In addition, let $C^j_{\overline{\mathcal{I}}}$ be the total steady-state bandwidth usage by non-bottlenecked connections at link j:

$$C^j_{\overline{\mathcal{I}}} = \sum_{i \in \overline{\mathcal{I}}^j} r^i = \sum_{l=1}^{b^j-1} \sum_{k \in \mathcal{A}_j} \nu_l \cdot \mathrm{I}\{k \in \mathcal{B}_l\}. \qquad (31)$$

Furthermore, let the level-k non-bottlenecked grouping at link j be given by $\overline{\mathcal{I}}^{k,j}$ ($k < b^j$) and $C^{k,j}_{\overline{\mathcal{I}}}$ be its total steady-state bandwidth usage:

$$C^{k,j}_{\overline{\mathcal{I}}} = \sum_{i \in (\overline{\mathcal{I}}^j \cap \mathcal{B}_k)} r^i = \sum_{i \in \overline{\mathcal{I}}^j} \nu_k \cdot \mathrm{I}\{i \in \mathcal{B}_k\} = |\overline{\mathcal{I}}^{k,j}| \cdot \nu_k \le C^j_{\overline{\mathcal{I}}}. \qquad (32)$$

Initially, it could be stated that the transient queue buildup at a node is bounded by that in the equivalent *isolated* single node network (i.e., Fig. 3 with modified propagation delays, Eqs. (21-22)). However, careful observation indicates otherwise. Since the single node formulation *implicitly* assumes infinite bandwidth on end systems links, connections can ramp up to any rate dictated by the switch. With multiple nodes, however, this is not the case. In fact, traversing steady-state bottlenecked connections can be *temporarily* bottlenecked elsewhere at lower rates. This technicality breaks the forward notification time ordering between connections (Section 3), and allows ramp-ups to possibly higher rates, causing larger queue buildups. A sample scenario can be derived to show this, but is excluded due to space limitations. As a result the maximum queue buildups can only be bounded by a looser formulation, which uses *bottleneck resolution* times to constrain the source rate envelope.

The bottleneck resolution time for level-k, τ_k, is defined as the maximum time in which connections in $\mathcal{B}_k$ achieve steady-state. It is not difficult to show that at the most bottlenecked link, j^1,

$$\tau_1 = \max_{i \in \mathcal{A}_{j^1}} \{T_f^{i,j^1}\} + \max_{i \in \mathcal{A}_{j^1}} \{\delta^i\} + T_{N_{rm}}(\nu_1). \qquad (33)$$

Using an iterative procedure similar to [1], a pessimistic estimate of τ_k is (i.e., link j^k)

$$\tau_k = \max(\tau_{k-1}, (\max_{i \in \mathcal{A}_{j^k}} \{T_f^{i,j^k}\} + \max_{i \in \mathcal{A}_{j^k}} \{\delta^i + T_{N_{rm}}(r^i_{min})\})) + \max_{i \in (\mathcal{A}_{j^k} \cap \mathcal{B}_k)} \{2\delta_f^{i,j^k} + T_{N_{rm}}(r^i_{min})\}. \qquad (34)$$

Note that Eq. (34) does not have any added provisions for possible inter-switch notification delays between bottleneck resolution times. Results show, however, that for all scenarios tried, the ensuing bounds hold without these enhancements. Using the above bottleneck resolution times, along with maximum rate overloads, queue buildups can be bounded. Due to space limitations, a detailed derivation is not included.

For analytical facility, we define a level-0 bottleneck grouping with $\tau_0 = 0$ and $\nu_0 = 0$. Without loss of generality, consider the link j connections ordered by their $T_f^{i,j}$ values (as in Section 3). Let k^i be the highest level bottleneck resolved by connection i's forward notification time at link j (i.e., Eq. 24):

$$k^i = \max\left\{k, 0 \le k < g^i \le b^j \;\; s.t. \;\; \tau_k < T_f^{i,j}\right\}. \qquad (35)$$

Furthermore, let the maximum connection index that has ramped up *before* the resolution of bottleneck level-k be

$$n^k = \max\left\{n, 1 \le n \le |\mathcal{A}_j| \;\; s.t. \;\; T_f^{n,j} < \tau_k\right\}, \qquad (36)$$

(and $n^k = 1$ otherwise). It can be shown that the maximum queue buildup induced by connection i at link j is upper-bounded by

$$q^{i,j}_{max} = \sum_{k=k^i}^{g^i-1} \sum_{n=max(i,n^k)}^{n^{k+1}} \Big(\mu_j - \frac{\mu_j}{n} - \sum_{l=1}^{k} (C^{l,j}_{\overline{\mathcal{I}}} - \sum_{h \in \overline{\mathcal{I}}^{l,j}} r^h_{min}) - \sum_{m=1}^{|\mathcal{A}_j|} r^m_{min} \cdot \mathrm{I}\{T_f^{m,j} + T_{N_{rm}}(r^m_{min}) + 2\delta_f^{i,j} < T_f^{n,j}\}\Big)^+ \cdot \Big(\min(\tau_{k+1}, T_f^{n+1,j}) - \max(\tau_k, T_f^{n,j})\Big), \qquad (37)$$

and thus the maximum buildup at link j is bounded by

$$q^j_{max} = \sum_{i \in \mathcal{A}_j} q^{i,j}_{max}. \qquad (38)$$

The first, large bracketed term in Eq. (37) bounds the maximum rate overload in a given $T_f^{n,j}$ or τ_k interval (i.e., by removing resolved bottleneck bandwidths and any additional, known minimum connections rates). The second bracketed term bounds the duration. Clearly the formulation is very pessimistic. First, it assumes that a connection causes maximum rate overload throughout its transient period. Secondly, it uses pessimistic bottleneck resolution estimates. The extremely complex rate behaviour in the multiple node case makes it very difficult to formulate a tighter bound on the generic source rate envelope.

5 Simulation Results

Although many different single and multiple node scenarios have been analyzed, space limitations only allow us to present a few of the results here. In order to measure real-world network performance, wherever possible, parameter settings are chosen to reflect proposed ATM system features. The link rates are fixed at 150 Mbps (353,773 cells/sec.), and the RM cell spacing, N_{rm}, is set to 32 cells. The AIR increment is set to 10 Mbps to give direct ramp-ups (i.e., $N_{rm} \cdot AIR \gg 150$ Mbps, Eq. (1)).

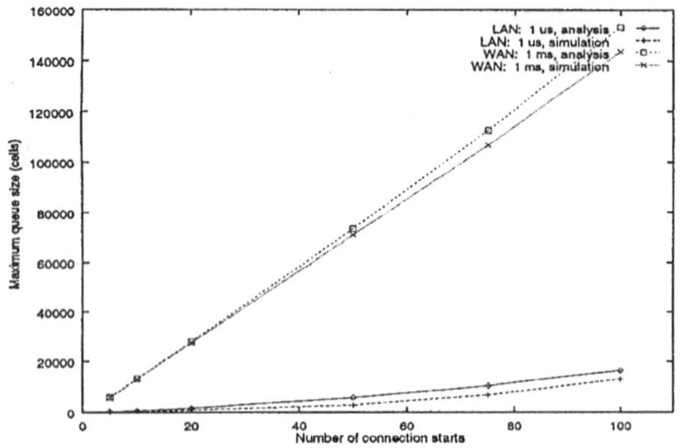

Figure 6: Single node: $\delta_f = \delta_b = 1\ \mu$s, $\delta_f = \delta_b = 1$ ms

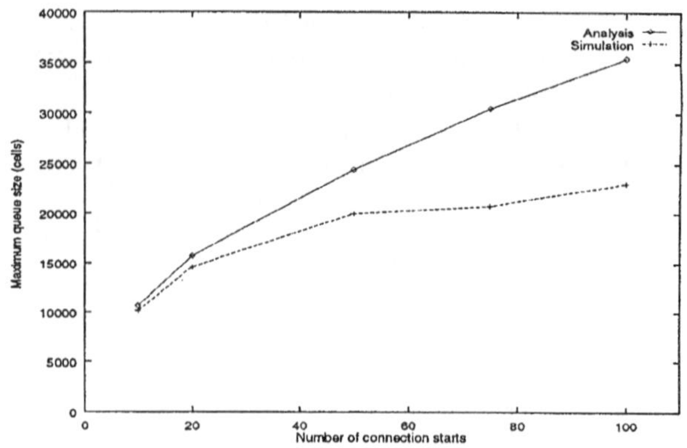

Figure 7: Single node with heterogeneous delays, δ_f, δ_b, uniform distributions: (1 μs, 10 μs) and (1 ms, 5 ms)

5.1 Single Node Scenarios

Initial tests are done for the single node scenario with homogeneous delays using express RM cell queueing. The end system propagation delays are set equal (i.e., $\delta_b = \delta_f$) and varied from LAN ranges (microseconds) to WAN ranges (milliseconds, very heavy loads). Fig. 6 shows simulation results plotted against their analytical bounds for two delay values. The analysis shows close agreement with the simulations, and results indicate that the $O(N^2)$ queueing behaviour is much more prevalent at smaller LAN delays. This occurs because the express buffer waiting times are relatively more significant at these delays. The cell transmission time at 150 Mbps is 2.82 μsec, the same order as propagation delays, making the N^2 terms in Eq. (20) dominate the queue buildups. At larger WAN delays, however, the linear terms corresponding to the propagation delays in Eq. (20) dominate the queue buildup. The results clearly show that direct ramp-ups give huge transient buildups. However, note that these are *worst case* values and simulation results with moderate AIR values show an order of magnitude reduction in the queue buildups [9],[10],[12].

To test the formulations rigourously, a heterogeneous delay scenario is used. Specifically, the forward and backward propagation delays are chosen randomly and tested for various number of connection starts. Half of the delays are chosen from a uniform distribution between 1 μs and 10 μs (i.e., LAN-range), and the other half from a uniform distribution between 1 ms and 5 ms (i.e., WAN-range). This increased delay diversity is representative of switches supporting both LAN and WAN connections. Results for this scenario are shown in Fig. 7, which indicate that the computed bounds are significantly larger than the actual buildups. This is due to the overly conservative formulation whose effect will be more pronounced for larger delay connections. For homogeneous delays, the analytical results are closer to the simulation results (see Fig. 6), since such scenarios are closer to worst case types (i.e., heterogeneous delays represent more of an average case). Nevertheless, the analytical result does bound the queue behaviours in all cases.

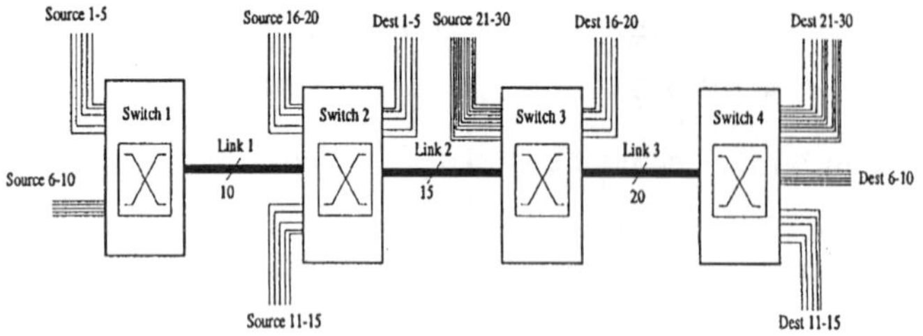

Figure 8: Parking-lot network with 30 connections

5.2 Multiple Node Scenarios

Many tests are also done with multiple node networks, but only a single heavy-load scenario is presented. Consider the *parking-lot* configuration in Fig. 8, designed to test bandwidth fairness [4],[7]. In this particular case, there are 30 connections traversing three links, with each link having a different bottleneck level (all end system-to-switch delays, δ_f^i, δ_b^i, fixed at 1 μs). The first-level bottleneck is link 3, supporting 20 connections (i.e., $b^3 = 1$, $\nu_1 = 7.5$ Mbps). Similarly, the second and third-level bottlenecks are links 2 and 1, supporting 15 and 10 connections each, respectively.

The scenario is tested for a wide range of *link* propagation delays, ranging from 10 μs (LAN) to 5 ms (WAN). In Fig. 9 the maximum queue buildups at the most and least bottlenecked links, links 3 and 1, respectively, are plotted against their computed upper-bounds (Eq. (38)). It is clear that the derived bounds significantly overestimate the true link buildups, by roughly an order of magnitude (i.e., even for direct ramp-ups). For example, the predicted values at the most congested link, link 3, are roughly three times the size of the true buildups. In general, we find that Eq. (38) is more accurate for lower-level bottleneck links (i.e., more congested), and when connection propagation delays are roughly equal. Results also indicate that the higher-level bottleneck resolution times, τ_2, τ_3, are also over-estimated by Eq. (34), worsening the bounds. Furthermore, simulation results

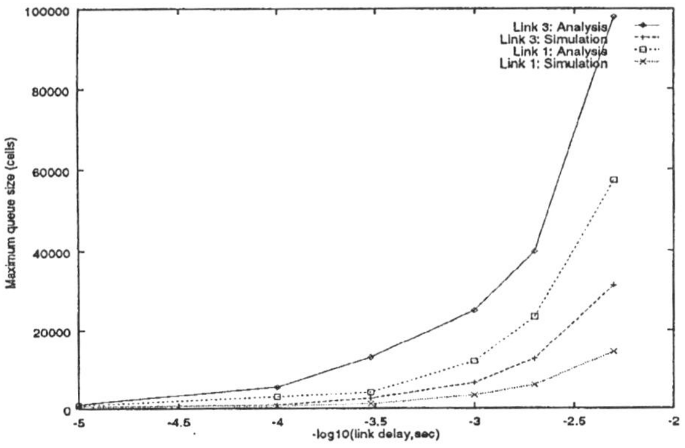

Figure 9: Queue buildups, increasing link delays, Fig. 8

with moderate AIR values (i.e., 200 kbps, [9],[10]), indicate buildups roughly an order of magnitude smaller than those observed via simulation with *direct* ramp-ups. In other words, gradual ramp-ups yield buildups about *two* orders of magnitude below the derived worst case bounds, Eq. (38). Nevertheless, we believe that by bounding the worst case behaviour, further insights and analysis can be developed.

6 Conclusions

In this paper detailed approximate transient queueing analysis of a distributed explicit rate allocation algorithm in an ABR-only environment is presented. Both the single node and multiple node network cases are modelled and the express RM cell queueing technique is used to improve performance. The formulation assumes direct ramp-ups and can be extended to handle non-simultaneous connection start times. The analysis shows good agreement with observed simulation results for the single node case. However, due to the extremely complex transient behaviour of such schemes, the derived bounds are looser for the multiple node case. Overall, the results show that queue buildups can be significant; therefore the use of moderate additive rate increments, reactive congestion indicators, and/or delayed rate updates is recommended.

References

[1] D. Bertsekas, R. Gallager, *Data Networks, Second Edition*, Prentice Hall Inc., New Jersey, 1992, Chapter 6.

[2] ATM Forum, "Traffic Management Specification Version 4.0," *ATM Forum-TM 95-0013R8*, August 1995.

[3] ITU-T, "Traffic Control and Congestion Control in B-ISDN," *Recommendation I.371 Frozen Issue*, Geneva, July 1995.

[4] F. Bonomi, K. Fendick, "The Rate-Based Flow Control Framework for the Available Bit Rate ATM Service," *IEEE Network Magazine*, Vol. 9, No. 2, March 1995, pp. 25-39.

[5] H. Ohsaki et. al., "Rate-Based Congestion Control for ATM Networks," *Computer Communication Review*, Vol. 25, No. 2, April 1995, pp. 60-72.

[6] A. Arulambalam, X. Chen, N. Ansari, "Allocating Fair Rates for Available Bit Rate Service in ATM Networks," *IEEE Communications Magazine*, Vol. 34, No. 11, November 1996, pp. 92-100.

[7] L. Roberts, "Enhanced PRCA (Proportional Rate-Control Algorithm)," *ATM Forum-TM 94-0735R1*, August 1994.

[8] K. Siu, H. Tzeng, "Intelligent Congestion Control for ABR Service in ATM Networks," *Computer Communication Review*, Vol. 24, No. 5, May 1995, pp. 81-106.

[9] N. Ghani, J. W. Mark, "Rate-Based Control Algorithm for Available Bit-Rate (ABR) Service in ATM Networks," *30th Annual Conference on Information Sciences and Systems*, Princeton, NJ, March 1996.

[10] N. Ghani, J. W. Mark, "Dynamic Rate-Based Control Algorithm for ABR Service in ATM Networks," *Proceedings of the IEEE Globecom 1996*, London, UK, Vol. 2, November 1996, pp. 1074-79.

[11] A. Charny, K. Ramakrishnan, A. Lauck, "Time-Scale Analysis and Scalability Issues for Explicit Rate Allocation in ATM Networks", *IEEE/ACM Transactions on Networking*, Vol. 4, No. 4, August 1996, pp. 569-581.

[12] L. Kalampoukas, A. Varma, K.K. Ramakrishnan, "An Efficient Rate Allocation Algorithm for ATM Networks Providing Max-Min Fairness," *Proceedings of the 6th IFIP International Conference on High Performance Networking, HPN'95*, September 1995, pp. 143-54.

[13] R. Jain, S. Kalyanaraman, R. Viswanathan, "The OSU Scheme for Congestion Avoidance Using Explicit Rate Indication," *ATM Forum-TM 94-0883*, September 1994.

[14] H. Ohsaki et. al., "Analysis of Rate-Based Congestion Control Algorithms for ATM Networks Part 1: Steady-State Analysis," *IEEE Globecom 1995*, Singapore, Vol. 1, November 1995, pp. 296-303.

[15] H. Ohsaki et. al., "Analysis of Rate-Based Congestion Control Algorithms for ATM Networks Part 2: Initial Transient State Analysis" *IEEE Globecom 1995*, Singapore, Vol. 2, November 1995, pp. 296-303.

[16] M. Ritter, "Network Buffering Requirements of the Rate-Based Control Mechanism for ABR Service," *Proceedings of the IEEE Infocom 1996*, San Francisco, CA, Vol. 3, March 1996, pp. 1190-1197.

[17] K. Siu, H. Tzeng, "Limits of Performance in Rate-Based Control Schemes," *ATM Forum-TM 94-1077*, November 1994.

...perimental Evaluation of ATM Congestion Control Mechanisms

Prashant Chandra, Allan Fisher, Corey Kosak, and Peter Steenkiste

School of Computer Science
Carnegie Mellon University
Pittsburgh, PA 15213
[prashant,alf,kosak,prs]@cs.cmu.edu

Abstract

A critical issue in the design of fast packet-switch-based networks is the avoidance of data loss due to congestion. In the context of ATM networks, many link-level congestion control mechanisms for ABR traffic have been proposed and simulated, and a few have been implemented. This paper presents, for the first time, an experimental comparison of several such mechanisms. To drive this comparison, we have developed a set of benchmarks that provide a quantitative characterization of congestion control performance. We also describe a simple but novel technique, the "virtual port card", for implementing both non-native switch behavior and long link delays in ATM networks. This technique allows us to compare a wide range of mechanisms on a single flexible hardware platform. Our measurements show that while several of the ATM flow control mechanisms can eliminate cell loss, there are still several unresolved problems. First, for some traffic scenarios we see very poor application-level performance, especially in the presence of bursty traffic. Second, performance is very sensitive to the flow control parameters and identifying an appropriate set of parameters is difficult since it depends heavily on the traffic conditions.

1 Introduction

A fundamental problem in multihop switched networks is data loss due to congestion. The problem occurs when the sum of the bandwidths of the streams crossing a link exceeds the link bandwidth for an extended time period so that switch buffers fill up and overflow. The impact of congestion on end-end performance is especially bad for ATM since the loss of even a single cell often requires the retransmission of an entire Protocol Data Unit (PDU), i.e. a single dropped cell can result in the retransmission of close to 200 cells. As a result, it is important to minimize cell loss in ATM networks.

A large number of papers have been published on the topic of congestion control for ATM networks. A number of papers observe, based on simulation or measurements, that ATM cell loss due to congestion can result in extremely poor end-to-end performance. This is especially true when using the TCP/IP protocol, since its backoff policy based on timeouts can result in very low throughput in the presence of high error rates. A number of papers proposed and evaluated "localized" mechanisms to reduce the impact of cell loss. These include early packet discard [13, 24], and the use of Cell Loss Priority to indicate what packets should be dropped in the case of congestion [22]. While these localized mechanisms can reduce the impact of cell loss, it is now widely believed that closed-loop per-VC flow control is needed for ABR traffic in ATM networks.

The many ATM flow control mechanisms that have been proposed can be divided in two classes. A first class consists of roundtrip-based rate control algorithms in which a source selects a transmit rate for each VC, based on feedback from the switches along its path [4, 7, 8, 20]. Feedback can for example consist of the EFCI bit in the ATM cell header, or of an explicit rate calculated by the switches. A second class consists of hop-by-hop, credit-based flow control algorithms in which the receiver on each link provides the sender with information on buffer status for each VC. Examples include DEC AN2 [21] and Credit Net [18]. An overview of these algorithms can be found in [12, 23]. A class of rate-based algorithms has been standardized by the ATM Forum [1], although several companies are still pursuing a credit-based alternative called Quantum Flow Control [9].

In order to evaluate the different flow control algorithms in a controlled environment, the ATM Forum traffic management group developed a test suite that specifies a set of network topologies and traffic loads [2, 25]. The suite identifies a number of performance measures, including fairness, throughput, network utilization, and buffer requirements. Fairness for ABR traffic is defined as max-min fair sharing [10]. While the suite provides a solid basis for meaningful comparison, it has some shortcomings: it is intended to be used in simulations, and evaluation is limited to static traffic patterns, i.e. the effect of bursty traffic is not considered.

Most papers evaluating ATM flow control algorithms are based on simulation. The papers typically compare throughput using a specific flow control algorithm with throughput without flow control [13, 15, 17], or they focus on a class of algorithms and analyze how throughput and buffer re-

0-8186-7780-5/97 $10.00 © 1997 IEEE

quirements change as a function of the flow control parameters [16, 27]. Several ATM Forum contributions presented simulation results based on the test suite described above [3, 6, 26, 28]. The traffic loads are usually limited to persistent generators, although a few simulations also consider dynamic effects of bursty traffic [11]. Fewer papers have reported performance measurements of actual ATM flow control implementations. Results have been reported for credit-based flow control using DEC AN2 [29] and Credit Net hardware [19]. In both cases, the performance evaluation focused on long-running TCP connections.

In this paper we present an experimental comparison of several ATM flow control mechanisms. To drive this comparison, we have developed a set of benchmarks that provides a quantitative characterization of congestion control performance for single-bottleneck networks. The benchmarks provide insight into a wide range of flow control properties including effectiveness in reducing cell loss, fairness, responsiveness and network utilization. Our evaluation uses a simple but novel technique, the "virtual port card", for implementing both non-native switch behavior and long link delays in ATM networks. This technique allows us to compare a wide range of mechanisms on a single hardware platform.

The remainder of this paper is organized as follows. We first present in Section 2 our evaluation methodology and benchmark suite. We give a brief description of our evaluation platform, including the virtual port card, and of the flow control implementations in Sections 3 and 4. We present our measurements in Section 5 and summarize in Section 6.

2 Evaluating Congestion Control Mechanisms

Our quantitative evaluation of multiple congestion control mechanisms focusses on single-congested-link scenarios, making a comprehensive evaluation possible. In this section we first outline the more general problem of evaluating flow control mechanisms before describing in detail the specific configurations that we use in our evaluation.

2.1 Properties of congestion control mechanisms

Congestion control algorithms can be evaluated by measuring network performance properties that are (in part) determined by the congestion control, and by direction measurement of flow control properties. We describe both classes of properties.

Application level performance Applications typically evaluate network performance based on the time it takes to transfer their messages. Depending on the size of the message, this will require low packet latency (small messages) or high sustained throughput (large messages). A good congestion control algorithm performs well for a number of types of traffic, so it can provide good service to, for example, both high-bandwidth and low-latency applications. This requires a flow control mechanism that is highly responsive and has low data loss.

Network utilization Network resources must be utilized efficiently. This means that, even under dynamic network conditions, the congestion control mechanism should prevent under-utilization of network links, and that efficient link utilization should be achieved with minimal resources on switches, e.g. small buffer sizes. This requires a flow control algorithm with low data loss, high responsiveness, and low overhead.

Fairness A good congestion control algorithm should allocate network resources in a fair manner amongst competing connections. The specific fairness criterium that has been defined for ATM ABR traffic is fair sharing. Fairness has both a static and dynamic component. The static fairness requirement is that, without changes in the traffic load, the network converges to a state where competing connections share bandwidth fairly. Under dynamic conditions, short term unfairness is often unavoidable, but the system should converge quickly to the new fair state. Fairness requires a congestion control algorithm that both converges correctly and is responsive.

Achieving good network performance requires a flow control mechanism with the following characteristics:

Data Loss High data losses reduce application performance (decrease sustainable throughput and increase average latency) and network utilization. Congestion control mechanisms should be designed to minimize data loss under the most severe congestion conditions and prevent congestion collapse of the network.

Responsiveness The traffic load placed on a network changes continuously and poor responsiveness to these changes reduces application performance, network utilization and fairness. A good congestion control algorithm should be responsive to dynamically changing conditions in the network: sources should quickly throttle back their data rate on the onset of congestion and should be able to quickly ramp up to any additional bandwidth that may become available in the network. The responsiveness of the congestion control algorithm depends on the delay in the feedback loop.

Overhead A good congestion control algorithm has very little overhead: the network bandwidth required for control messages is small and the processing requirements at the network nodes and end-systems are low. High overhead reduces network utilization.

The congestion control algorithm features listed above are mainly performance oriented. In addition, there are also a number of important implementation-oriented features. First, a good congestion control algorithm should be *robust* against loss of feedback information from the network. Loss of control messages should not cause congestive collapse of the network. Second, a congestion control mechanism must be ultimately *implementable.* Finally, congestion control algorithms should be *scalable*, i.e. they should perform well with varying speeds of links in the network and scale to a large number of user connections. Note that while it seems desirable to have a single algorithm for LANs, MANs and WANs, an algorithm that performs well for one category might be acceptable.

2.2 Approach

Our evaluation of congestion control methods focusses on the performance-oriented features since they are easiest to measure quantitatively. Properties such as robustness and implementation complexity are harder to characterize in a quantitative manner.

A quantitative analysis involves defining what network *configurations* are used in the measurement, and defining *traffic models* that capture the load that is placed on the network configuration during the measurements. For each combination of configurations and traffic models we also have to identify what *metrics* should be used, i.e. what quantities should be measured. A wide range of choices exists for each of these three variables:

Configurations The configurations used should be representative of actual configurations found in real networks. Some configurations that have been proposed are peer-to-peer configuration, fairness configurations (GFC 1 and GFC 2), ring configurations, and hierarchical configurations (found in telephone networks).

Traffic models The traffic models used should be representative of actual network traffic. Examples include persistent traffic (high-bandwidth), open loop bursty (various stochastic modes such as ON/OFF, Poisson etc.), and closed loop bursty (request/response or transaction-oriented traffic).

Metrics We can distinguish between *end-system-oriented metrics* such as packet loss, throughput, and response time, and *network-oriented metrics* such as buffer requirements in the switches, network utilization, (long-term and short-term) fairness, and overhead of control messages.

The evaluation of a specific set of congestion control algorithm properties requires the selection of a suite of tests, each of which is a suitable combination of configurations, traffic models and metrics.

2.3 A test suite for single-bottleneck topologies

The test suite given here combines a suitable set of metrics, traffic models and configurations, to evaluate single-congested-link scenarios in a quantitative way. The configuration used is a peer-to-peer configuration shown in Figure 1. It consists of a switch and three nodes representing end-points, S_{far}, S_{near}, and D . The link between the switch and D is the congested link.

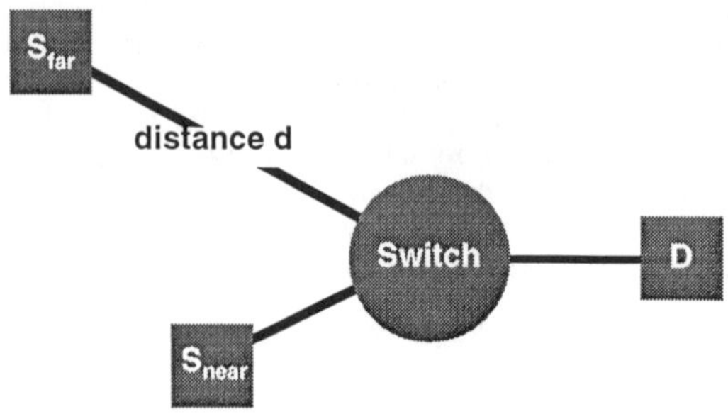

Figure 1: Test configuration

Experiment 1: Static rate matching This experiment uses only nodes S_{far} and D . S_{far} is a persistent packet source, i.e. it continuously sends packets at line rate. The output link (to node D) is run at a lower rate than the input link (from node S_{far}), and the congestion control mechanism is used to provide rate-matching. We vary switch buffer sizes and link distances, and measure data loss and throughput. This experiment provides insight into the efficiency, stability and resource requirements of the congestion control mechanisms.

Experiment 2: Burst bandwidth allocation Again, only nodes S_{far} and D are used. Node S_{far} sends packets of varying lengths, and receives short acknowledgements from D . The delay of the link is varied, and the request-response latency is measured for a variety of request sizes. This experiment shows how effectively the congestion control mechanisms can respond to bursty demands.

Experiment 3: Static congestion In this experiment, both the nodes S_{far} and S_{near} are persistent packet sources. The delay of the input link of S_{far} is varied between LAN and WAN dimensions. We measure data loss and throughput of each stream, as well as utilization of the link to node D , as switch buffer sizes are varied. This experiment sheds light on data integrity, efficiency, scalability and long-term fairness of the congestion control method under consideration.

Experiment 4: Dynamic congestion In this experiment, node S_{far} is a persistent source and node S_{near} is a ON-OFF source. S_{far} is connected via a WAN link to the switch SW. The ON-OFF duty cycle of S_{near} is varied. We measure utilization of the link to D and the throughput and loss rate of S_{far}. This provides insight into the responsiveness of the congestion control algorithm, and hence its efficiency under dynamic conditions.

Experiment 5: Dynamic fairness In this experiment, node s_{far} is again connected via a long link to SW. Both s_{far} and s_{near} are request/response sources and they query a server D. Requests have a fixed size and the inter-request times are exponentially distributed. The load generated by the sources is varied and the number of requests received at node D from both sources is measured. This experiment gives insight into throughput and fairness under dynamic conditions.

We believe that this set of experiments provides a comprehensive picture of congestion control mechanisms for single-congested-link scenarios. It does not address scalability properties with respect to number of nodes/users and fairness properties with multiple bottleneck scenarios (GFC configurations).

3 Experimental Infrastructure

Experiments were run on Credit Net, an experimental ATM local area network. Credit Net incorporates switches, host interfaces, and OC-3 and OC-12 SONET links. The Credit Net switch hardware [19] provides native support for per-VC buffering and feedback of absolute buffer credits. The Credit Net adapter [14] uses DMA to send and receive ATM data on a host's PCI I/O bus. It performs SAR and AAL5 functions on behalf of the host, and manages multiple queues of buffers for send and receive. The adapter also provides a variety of mechanisms for implementing congestion control algorithms:

- The adapter incorporates a microcode engine that can control the adapter's transmit scheduler, manipulate adapter memory, and send and receive cells on the network link.
- The adapter can be augmented with an embedded i960 microprocessor that can manipulate adapter and host memory, and coordinate with adapter microcode.
- The adapter provides the host processor with extensive access to its internal data structures, and with means to coordinate with the adapter's microcontroller.

These facilities allow implementation of a variety of endpoint behaviors with high performance. Furthermore, we can use the adapter in a "virtual port card" configuration to provide switch congestion control functionality beyond that provided in switch hardware. As is shown in Figure 2, a host with two network adapters (NA) provides the input port, output port, and scheduling capabilities of a single port of a switch.

The key difference between a virtual port and a real port is that the virtual port is downstream from the "merge" point in the switch, where we expect congestion resolution to take place. This may create the problem that cell loss occurs in the switch, away from the congestion control mechanism running on the virtual port. We avoid this condition by scheduling the virtual port's outgoing link to run at a slower rate than its incoming link, moving the point of the congestion to the virtual port. While in a completely uncontrolled situation, large congestion losses could still occur at the switch, this should not happen since we are testing mechanisms designed to control congestion, and we expect to see little or no loss of data at the switch. Monitoring of data loss at the switch during experimental runs confirms this expectation.

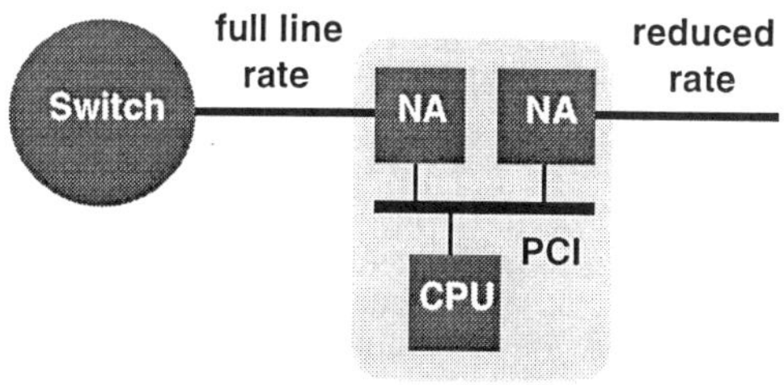

Figure 2: Virtual port card configuration

The virtual port card can also model the behavior of a long link. This is accomplished simply by feeding the scheduled output of the virtual port card into a delay FIFO of constant length, with its output rate matched to the link rate by dropping incoming cells when they arrive faster than the outgoing link can accommodate them, and inserting null cells when incoming cells arrive at less than the outgoing link rate.

4 Congestion Control Implementations

We briefly describes the congestion control implementations used in our experiments. We describe any parameter settings adopted, any simplifications or modifications of the basic algorithms, and our mapping of the mechanisms onto the Credit Net hardware.

Credit with static buffering This method uses the native flow control capabilities of the Credit Net LAN switch, which implements the FCVC N123 algorithm [18]. The N123 algorithm is implemented at the host, for these tests, on the embedded i960 processor described above. Buffer space on the switch is allocated in proportion to the propagation delay of the upstream link, in order to eliminate data loss. Because of limits on buffer space in the switch, we use the virtual port card implementation for long-latency links.

Credit with adaptive buffering This mechanism uses the same host implementation as the previous case; the only change is at the switch. Instead of making a worst-case allocation of buffer space per VC, the switch allocates space to each VC in proportion to its bandwidth, adjusting allocations periodically to track bandwidth changes. We implement adaptive buffering using the virtual port card approach; the host processor of the virtual port card runs the CUP algorithm and performs periodic buffer reallocation [15]. It is similar to the QFC algorithm [9].

Rate control with EFCI This case and the following one implement two variants of the ATM Forum ABR congestion control mechanism[1, 4]. To make implementation easier, we have simplified the format of the resource management cell, and we have not implemented timeout-related behaviors that do not arise in our test cases. The endpoint behaviors are implemented using a combination of the microcode and embedded processor cabilities of the host adapter [5]. We have implemented a rate scheduler, capable of scheduling outgoing traffic and resource management cells at OC-3 line rates, in the adapter's microcode. The embedded processor at the source is responsible for generating outgoing resource management (RM) cells, for receiving and interpreting incoming resource management cells, and for updating the transmission rates used by the scheduler.

The EFCI (explicit forward congestion indication) version of ABR algorithm calls for an additive rate increase when returning RM cells indicate no congestion, and a multiplicative decrease when returning RM cells indicate congestion. The embedded processor at the destination is responsible for receiving forward RM cells, inserting congestion indications based on the payload type congestion indications of recent incoming cells, and reflecting them back toward the source.

The switch behavior of the EFCI mechanism, implemented on the virtual port card host processor, is simply to add a congestion indication to the headers of cells that depart on a port whose buffer is filled beyond a preset threshold.

Rate control using EPRCA The Enhanced Proportional Rate Control Algorithm (EPRCA) is a variant of the ATM Forum ABR scheme in which switches provide sources with explicit rate bounds. Endpoint behavior is implemented as in the previous case, except that the source updates rates to the value provided in the explicit rate field of returning RM cells. Switch behavior is more complicated: the switch must intercept forward RM cells and periodically use their current rate information to compute a fair share rate. It must also set the explicit rate field in reverse RM cells to the minimum of the incoming rate and the fair share rate. The fair share rate is computed using the exponential averaging algorithm specified by the ATM Forum.

5 Measurements

In this section we present and analyze our performance measurements for the different congestion control implementations. All end-points and virtual ports consisted of 133 MHz and 166 MHz Pentium PCs running NetBSD.

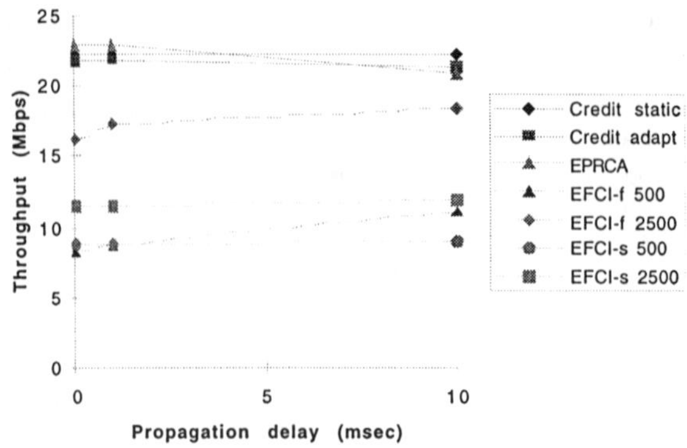

Figure 3: Throughput as a function of link delay

Static rate matching First, we consider the behavior of the congestion control mechanisms in Experiment 1, dealing with rate matching of a static stream traversing a faster link feeding into slower link. The slow link is throttled to 1/6 of OC-3 bandwidth, and the source attempts to send at 70 Mbps subject to congestion control. Figure 3 shows how the throughput of valid packet data, for IP MTU-sized packets, depends on the propagation delay of the fast link. The cases plotted include static and adaptive credit-based flow control, EFCI rate control with a variety of rate adaptation parameters, and EPRCA rate control. For EFCI, "-f" (fast) corresponds to a rate increase of 10 Mbps and a congestion slowdown of 50%; "-s" (slow) corresponds to an an increase of 100 Kbps and a decrease factor of 10%. The number following -f or -s is the congestion threshold in cells; all cases use a buffer that holds 4000 cells.

As one would expect, credit with static buffering gives the best performance, although both adaptive credit-based flow control and EPRCA give virtually identical performance. The reason is that with static traffic sources, the latter two algorithms stabilize at a point with high network utilization. Rate-based flow control using EFCI gives lower performance as a result of oscillations. For EFCI, throughput is best using an EFCI/drop threshold of 2500/4000 bytes and aggressive parameter settings. Note however that there is a cell loss of about 20% using the 2000/4000 threshold for the "fast" rate adaptation parameters, so with a reliable transport protocol added, this case is likely to give poor application level performance. In other words, for this experiment, rate control using EFCI performs best using conservative parameter settings.

Burst bandwidth allocation We now consider Experiment 2, which measures the response time of a transaction consisting of the transfer of a block of data across a link, and an acknowledgement in the reverse direction. This experiment characterizes the speed with which burst bandwidth is allocated. We measure response time for two link latencies (LAN and WAN) and, in the EFCI case, for several settings of the rate adaptation parameters. Requests are sent at 70 Mbps, and the ABR implementations are allowed to settle to their initial cell rates between requests.

Figure 4 shows response time as a function of request size in a LAN with negligible propagation delay. The EFCI curves are marked INIT+INCR, where INIT is the initial rate in Mbps and INCR is the rate increase in Mbps applied each time a resource management cell without a congestion indication is received. The EPRCA initial rate is 10 Mbps. Because this scenario does not induce congestion, rates are never lowered except when the stream is idle. Figure 5 shows the same curves on a magnified response time scale.

In this graph, the static credit algorithm provides the best response time, since its worst-case buffer allocation requires no ramp-up delay. The dynamic credit algorithm has similar performance, because our implementation of CUP uses a coarse grain buffer allocation scheme, so there is sufficient buffer space available to send one packet without waiting for credit. The EFCI response times are dominated by the initial data rate for short requests, since the entire request may be completed before any returning RM cells are received. For longer packets and lower initial rates, returning RM cells arrive before the end of transmission, so the incremental rate increase has an impact on performance. EPRCA performs slightly better than EFCI on longer requests, since its first returning RM cell permits it to ramp up to full bandwidth immediately.

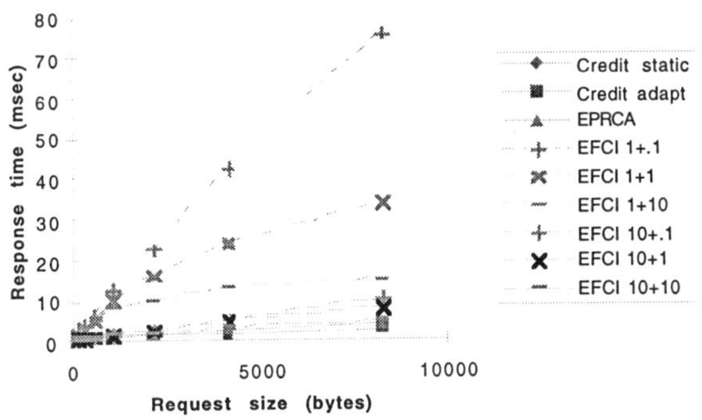

Figure 4: Response time as a function of request size (LAN)

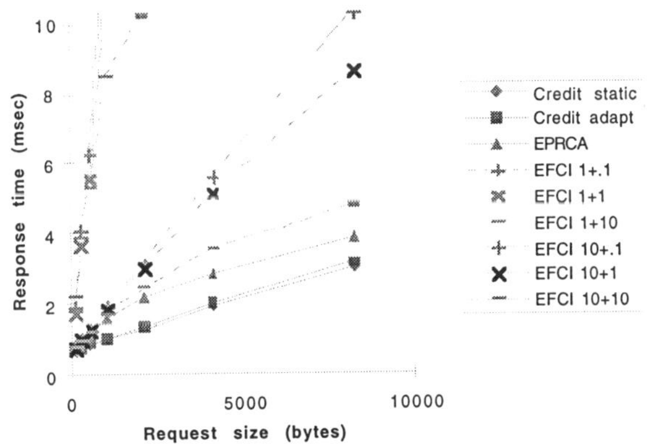

Figure 5: Response time as a function of request size (LAN)(magnified scale)

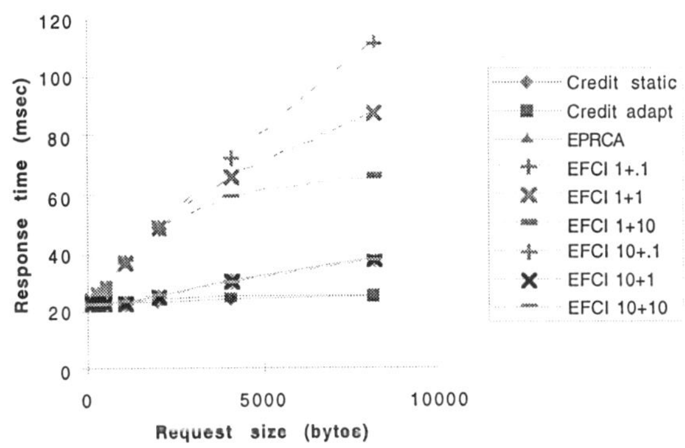

Figure 6: Response time as a function of request size (WAN)

Figure 6 shows response time using a link with a propagation delay of 10 msec. All response times in this graph have an offset of 20 msec, corresponding to the physical round-trip time of the long link. In this graph, the static and adaptive credit algorithms again provide the best response time. The reason is again the lack of ramp-up delay. Because of the long delay before RM cells return, initial rate is an even more important factor for the EFCI scheme than before. For the same reason, EPRCA performs about the same as EFCI for an initial rate of 10 Mbps.

Overall for this experiment, rate control using EFCI

performs best using the more aggressive parameter settings. The reason is that these settings allow the algorithm to adapt more quickly and oscillations, which caused problems in the static rate matching experiment, are not a concern because the data transfer is very short.

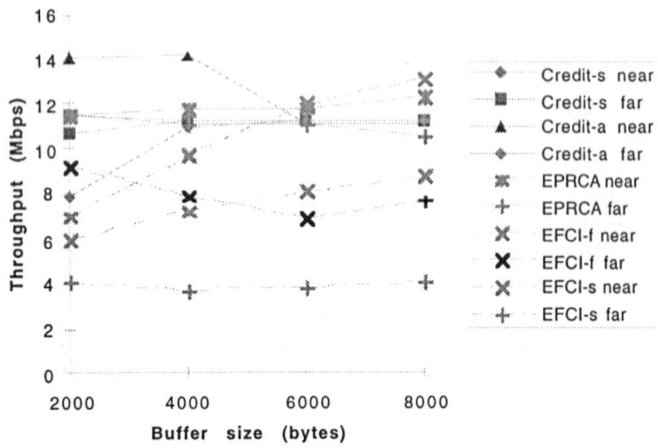

Figure 7: Throughput as a function of buffer size under static congestion

Static congestion This experiment creates congestion between a stream traversing a long link and one traversing a short link. All results are for a bottleneck link bandwidth of 25 Mbps. Figure 7 shows sender packet data throughput for this scenario as a function of switch buffer size allocated to the high-latency connection. In this case, the throughput reflects both loss of efficiency, unfairness and loss of data due to the congestion control scheme used.

The EPRCA and credit algorithms exhibit both high link utilization and fairness, although the fairness of EPRCA degrades slightly as buffer size increases. There is also negligible cell loss using these algorithms. The results using the EFCI algorithm exhibit unfairness. The more conservative parameter setting result in better fairness, since there is less oscillation. Moreover, there is a cell loss ratio of about 7% for the fast parameter settings, while there is no cell loss for the more conservative EFCI parameter settings, making the conservative settings the better choice for this experiment.

Dynamic congestion This experiment examines the behavior of a persistent stream, traversing a long link, as it encounters congestion created by a local ON-OFF source. The persistent stream crosses a link with a delay of 10 ms, and the congested link has a bandwidth of 25 Mbps. Figure 8 shows how the persistent stream's sender-side throughput of packet data, for IP MTU-sized packets, depends on the average offered bandwidth of the bursty source. The credit and EPRCA algorithms perform best, since they stabilize the rates at a fair rate, similar to what we ob-

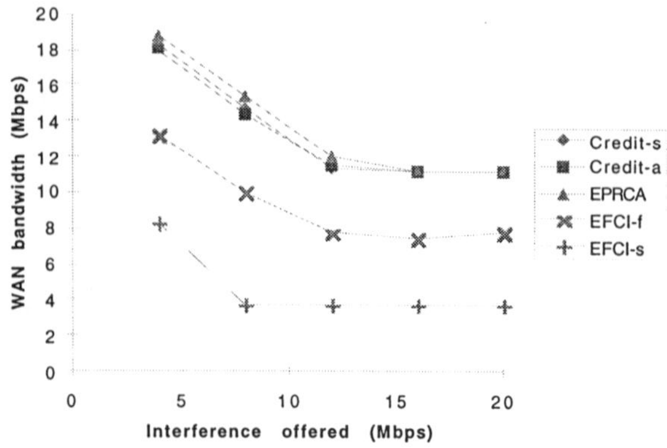

Figure 8: Throughput of a persistent WAN source with bursty interference

served in the previous experiment. Both settings of the EFCI algorithms give poor performance relative to the credit and EPRCA algorithms as a result of oscillations. While it appears that the aggressive parameter settings result in higher throughput, they also result in a cell loss rate of about 20%, while there is no cell loss with conservative settings, so we expect the conservative settings to results in better application level throughput.

Notice that for each of the algorithms, throughput initially drops as the interfering load increases, but it reaches a minimum value and remains constant, insensitive to further increases of the competing load. This is a direct result of the flow control mechanisms, which limit the bursty interference source to a certain rate. Increasing the rate of the interfering source above this rate will not have any effect on how much data will be placed on the wire by the bursty source, so the throughput of the persistent source stabilizes. Moreover, at these high rates the bursty source becomes a persistent source so we would expect rates corresponding to the flat segments in Figure 8 to be similar to the results of the previous experiments; a comparison of Figures 7 and 8 confirms this. Finally, we would expect the flow control algorithms that achieve the lowest utilization of the bottleneck link to reach this point first (i.e. for the lowest competing load), which Figure 8 confirms.

Dynamic fairness The final experimental configuration runs two request-response streams, one entering a congested link from a long-delay link (10ms) and the other from a short-delay link. The bottleneck link bandwidth is 25 Mbps and the request size is 2 KByte. Each source generates requests in a Poisson process, and the load is increased by reducing the average interpacket time. The rate configurations use a 4000-cell buffer with a congestion threshold of 2000 cells, an initial rate of 10 Mbps, an increase rate of 100 kbps, and a congestion reduction factor of 10%.

Figure 9 shows throughput for each stream as a function of the load offered. The credit and EPRCA configurations manage this situation well, up to and

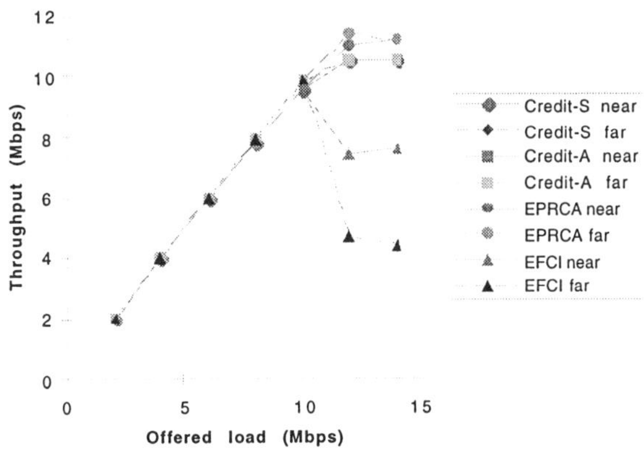

Figure 9: Requests received as a function of request size

beyond the point of link saturation. In contrast, as the EFCI implementation approaches 80% link utilization, its performance degrades substantially due to oscillations. High loads in this scenario also result in unfair allocation of bandwidth between the local and wide-area sources. Note that under high loads, the bursty sources turn into persistent sources as a result of the backpressure exercised by the flow control algorithms.

Acknowledgment

This research was sponsored by the Defense Advanced Research Projects Agency under contract number F19628-92-C-0116.

We thank our colleagues at Intel Architecture Laboratories for their vital contributions. We also thank past and present Credit Net contributors at CMU, Harvard, and BNR for many useful discussions.

6 Conclusion

This paper presents a comprehensive experimental evaluation of a variety of mechanisms for congestion control in a single-congested-link scenario. Our measurements show that several of the ATM flow control mechanisms can eliminate cell loss, but that there are a number of unresolved problems.

First, under some traffic conditions we sometimes see very poor application-level performance. Our results show that conservative credit gives the best results. This is not a surprise since it in effect reserves sufficient resources to achieve high performance. The adaptive credit and EPRCA algorithms behave in very similar ways and give good performance in all static tests. In the bursty tests they sometimes result in slow response times and unfairness as a result of slow ramp-up. The slow ramp-up is a fundamental problem: sending data at high rates without or with data loss either requires the presence of sufficient resources in the network (such as enough spare bandwidth or buffer space), or requires the sender to wait for feedback from the network, which result in slow ramp-up. Rate based flow control based on EFCI performs poorly in all tests. The poor performance is caused by oscillation which is a fundamental part of the algorithm.

The second problem area is parameter selection. Although operating parameters for adaptive control algorithms can be tuned to individual situations, no parameter setting is best under all conditions. Appropriate parameters depend heavily on traffic conditions, and defining algorithms for selecting flow control parameter settings for specific connection that will provide good application level performance, including both low cell loss and good response times, is an important open research area.

References

[1] ATM Forum Technical Committee. Traffic management specification version 4.0, April 1996.

[2] Andrew W. Barnhart. Baseline model for rate-control simulation. ATM Forum, Traffic Management Working Group submission 94-0399, Hughes Network System, May 1994.

[3] Jon C. R. Bennett, Koling Chang, H. T. Kung, and Dong Lin. A comparison of EPRCA September 1994 version and FCVC control schemes: Simulation results. ATM Forum, Traffic Management Working Group submission 94-0929, Fore Systems, Harvard University and Sandia National Laboratories, September 1994.

[4] Flavio Bonomi and Kerry Fendick. The rate-based flow control framework for the available bit rate ATM service. *IEEE Network Magazine*, 9(2):25–39, March/April 1995.

[5] Prashant Chandra, Allan Fisher, Corey Kosak, and Peter Steenkiste. Implementation of ATM endpoint congestion control protocols. In *Proceedings of the IEEE Hot Interconnect Symposium '96*, Palo Alto, CA, August 1996. IEEE.

[6] Koling Chang and H. T. Kung. Performance of credit-based flow control on challenge configuration. ATM Forum, Traffic Management Working Group submission 94-0880, Harvard University and Sandia National Laboratories, September 1994.

[7] Anna Charny and K. K. Ramakrishnan. Time scale analysis of explicit rate allocation in ATM networks. In *Proceedings of INFOCOMM 96*, March 1996.

[8] Anna Charny, K.K. Ramakrishnan, and Anthony Lauck. Scalability issues for distributed explicit rate allocation in ATM. In *Proceedings of INFOCOMM 96*, March 1996.

[9] Mike Gaddis and Walter Kelt (eds). Quantum flow control. Technical Report FCC-SPEC-95-1, Flow Control Consortium, July 1995.

[10] Ellen L. Hahne. Round-robin scheduling for max-min fairness in data networks. *IEEE Journal on Selected Areas in Communication*, 9(7), September 1991.

[11] David Hughes and Pat Daley. More ABR simulation results. ATM Forum, Traffic Management Working Group submission 94-0777, StrataCom, Inc., September 1994.

[12] Raj Jain. Congestion control and traffic management in ATM networks: Recent advances and a survey. *Computer Networks and ISDN Systems*, February 1995.

[13] Lampros Kalampoukas. Performance of TCP over multi-hop ATM networks: A comparative study of ATM-layer congestion control schemes. Technical Report 95-13, University of California, Santa Cruz, February 1995.

[14] Corey Kosak, David Eckhardt, Todd Mummert, Peter Steenkiste, and Allan Fisher. Buffer management and flow control in the credit net ATM host interface. In *Proceedings of the 20th Conference on Local Computer Networks*, pages 370–378, Minneapolis, October 1995. IEEE.

[15] H. T. Kung, T. Blackwell, and A. Chapman. Credit update protocol for flow-controlled ATM networks: Statistical multiplexing and adaptive credit allocation. In *Proceedings of the SIGCOMM '94 Symposium on Communications Architectures and Protocols*, pages 101–114. ACM, August 1994.

[16] H. T. Kung and Koling Chang. Receiver-oriented adaptive buffer allocation in credit-based flow control for ATM networks. In *IEEE INFOCOM '95*, volume 1, pages 239–252, Boston, Massachusetts, April 1995. IEEE.

[17] H. T. Kung, Robert Morris, Thomas Charuhas, and Dong Lin. Use of link-by-link flow control in maximizing ATM performance: Simulation results. In *Proceedings of the IEEE Hot Interconnect Symposium '93*, Palo Alto, CA, August 1993. IEEE.

[18] H.T. Kung and A. Chapman. The FCVC (flow controlled virtual channels) proposal for ATM networks. In *International Conference on Network Protocols*, San Francisco, CA, Oct 1993. IEEE.

[19] Robert Morris and H. T. Kung. Impact of ATM switching and flow control on TCP performance: Measurements on an experimental switch. In *GLOBECOM '95*. IEEE, November 1995.

[20] Hiroyuki Ohsaki, Masayuki Murata, Hiroshi Suzuki, Chinatsu Ikeda, and Hideo Miyahara. Rate-based congestion control for ATM networks. *Computer Communication Review*, April 1995.

[21] Cüneyt Özveren, Robert Simcoe, and George Varghese. Reliable and efficient hop-by-hop flow control. In *Proceedings of the SIGCOMM '94 Symposium on Communications Architectures and Protocols*, pages 89–100, University College, London, London, UK, October 1994. ACM.

[22] Michael Perloff and Kurt Reiss. Improvements to TCP performance in high-speed ATM networks. *CACM*, 38(2), February 1995.

[23] K. K. Ramakrishnan and Peter Neuman. Integration of rate and credit schemes for ATM flow control. *IEEE Network Magazine*, 9(2):49–56, March/April 1995.

[24] Allyn Romanow and Sally Floyd. Dynamics of TCP traffic over ATM networks. In *Proceedings of the SIGCOMM '94 Symposium on Communications Architectures and Protocols*, pages 79–88, University College, London, London, UK, October 1994. ACM.

[25] Robert J. Simcoe. Test configurations for fairness and other tests. ATM Forum, Traffic Management Working Group submission 94-0557, Digital Equipment Corporation, July 1994.

[26] Kai-Yeung Siu and Hong-Yi Tzeng. Adaptive proportional rate control (APRC) with intelligent congestion indication. ATM Forum, Traffic Management Working Group submission 94-0888, University of California, Irvine, September 1994.

[27] Kai-Yeung Siu and Hong-Yi Tzeng. Intelligent congestion control for ABR service in ATM networks. *Computer Communication Review*, 1995.

[28] Hong-Yi Tzeng and Kai-Yeung Siu. Comparison of performance among existing rate control schemes. ATM Forum, Traffic Management Working Group submission 94-1078, University of California, Irvine, November 1994.

[29] Hongbo Zhu, Luiz A. Dasilva, Joseph B. Evans, and Victor S. Frost. Performance evaluation of congestion control mechanisms in ATM networks. In *Computer Measurement Group Annual Conference (CMG '95)*, December 1995.

Long Term Resource Allocation in Video Delivery Systems

Kevin C. Almeroth

Georgia Institute of Technology
Atlanta, GA 30332-0280

Asit Dan, Dinkar Sitaram, William H. Tetzlaff

IBM T. J. Watson Research Center
Yorktown Heights, NY 10598

Abstract

In typical video delivery systems offering programs on-demand, service should be be nearly immediate and continuous. A video server can provide this type of service by reserving sufficient network and server resources for the duration of playout. Scalability and reduced cost can be achieved using a single channel to serve multiple customers waiting for the same program (referred to as batching). Batching is especially useful during high load periods typically occuring during evening prime time hours. Typical channel allocation algorithms use a greedy, allocate-as-needed policy. Variations in system load can cause these algorithms to suffer poor and unpredictable short-term performance, and non-optimal long term performance. In this paper, we develop a set of realistic workloads, identify the limitations of greedy allocation algorithms, and propose a set of rate-based allocation schemes to solve these limitations. The performance of various video delivery systems are simulated and compared. The rate-based policies are shown to be robust for the workloads examined, and are easy to implement.

1 Introduction

One paradigm for the delivery of video-based services is to stream video data on an as-needed basis from the server to one or more customers. The scheduling and delivery of video is made in response to program requests sent to the server by customers. In such systems, server and network resources (together referred to as a *logical channel*) are reserved for the duration of the program. One logical channel is sufficient to meet the real-time bandwidth demands and continuous delivery requirements of one video stream[?, ?].

Because resources in both the server and network are finite, there is a hard limit on the number of channels that can be simultaneously delivered[?, ?, ?]. However, in the presence of a multicast facility, multiple customers requesting the same program within a short interval of time can be served by the same video stream. This policy, referred to as *batching*, takes advantages of high request rates among popular programs and can result in substantial savings in server and network capacity [?, ?, ?, ?].

One of the more difficult tasks in a video delivery system is scheduling the finite number of channels in a way that optimizing some set of performance measures. One of the most important criteria is to make the most money possible which loosely translates into maximizing the number of customers serviced over the long term. One common approach to achieving this objective is make customers wait as long as possible in the hopes that additional requests for the same program will be made. However, these algorithms have several significant drawbacks: (1) they do not minimize customer waiting time, (2) they perform poorly when load conditions vary meaning they do not even achieve their goal of maximizing customers serviced, and (3) they have wild oscillations in short-term performance. As we will show, the fundamental flaw in these algorithms is that they use the greedy approach and do not control the rate of channel allocation. This is especially damaging considering that once a channel is allocated it is held for the duration of the program which can be a couple of hours long. If a large percentage of channels are allocated over a short period of time, the system will have few channels with which to satisfy additional requests. The system will be forced to reject a majority of requests until the first set of channels become available. As we will show, better performance can be achieved by using an algorithm which controls the channel allocation rate.

This paper documents our efforts in three areas. First, we develop a series of workload models that are not steady state Poisson models and more accurately reflect customer behavior over a 24-hour period. Second, using a video delivery system model, we simulate the performance and show the limitations of several greedy channel allocation algorithms. Third, we propose a set of rate-based channel allocation algorithms that solve the limitations of the greedy algorithms and show this by comparing simulation results.

The remainder of the paper is as follows. Section 2 details the architecture of a video delivery system. Section 3 describes the system and customer behavior models used in system simulation. Section 4 examines the performance of two greedy channel allocation policies. Section 5 presents our proposed set of rate-based allocation policies. Section 6 describes system capacity using various channel allocation policies. The paper is concluded in Section 7.

2 Architecture

Video delivery systems can vary in size and complexity depending on many factors including the number of simultaneous streams the system is capable of providing, and the type of service to be offered. Systems can have servers ranging from one small, cen-

0 8186 7780-5/97 $10.00 © 1997 IEEE

tralized machine to a large network of distributed file servers with several control points. The network can also varying significantly; most importantly in what transport layer functions are provided. Any number of protocols over a variety of media and topologies may be available. In order to eliminate unimportant details of any one particular system, we propose the use of a generic architecture. An overview of this system with specific emphasis on the *scheduler* is described next.

2.1 Video System Architecture

Figure 1 shows a generic architecture with three main components: video server, network, and set of clients/customers. The typical operation is based on customers making program *requests* to the video server. These requests flow over a two-way, low bandwidth channel established for the purpose of exchanging control messages. A request is received and queued by the control server until the *scheduler* is ready to allocate a logical channel for the playout of the requested program. A wide variety of policies ranging from simple on-demand strategies to more sophisticated rate-control strategies can be used. We assume that the network provides efficient multicast communication which means that if multiple requests for the same request are in the queue, they can be *batched* and serviced with one logical channel.

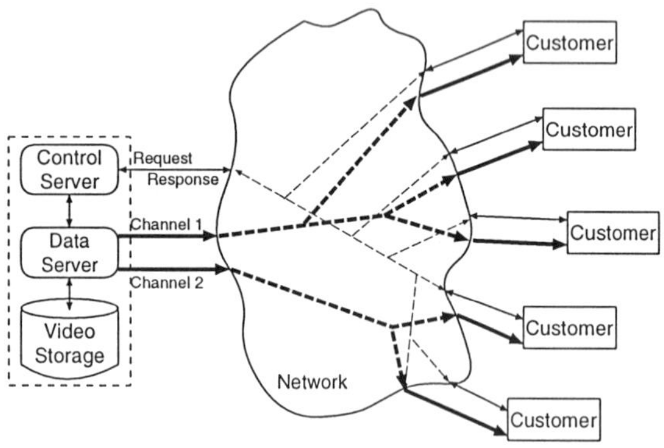

Figure 1: Overview of system architecture.

2.2 Channel Scheduling Architecture

The process of allocating a channel for the playout of a particular program is dependent on two factors: (1) which program to play, and (2) when to start playout. Choosing the order in which to satisfy requests can be a complex decision depending on fairness issues and the number of service classes. For example, one request might receive deluxe or preferred service for a higher fee and thus be served on a priority basis. However, in this paper, we assume a first come, first served (FCFS) policy because it is fair, effective, and easy to implement[?]. In accordance with FCFS, the request in the front of the queue is served first and all other requests waiting for the same program are batched and serviced together. Program playout is decided by the channel allocation policy. The analysis of different policies is the basis of this paper and they are discussed in Sections 4 and 5.

2.3 Providing VCR Control

Independent of initial channel scheduling policies, systems may need to provide means for supporting VCR control operations (e.g., pause/resume, rewind, fast forward). In general, additional resources may be needed when a VCR action moves a customer out of the original stream. Several proposals exist for efficiently providing VCR control[?, ?, ?]. These proposals are based on the reservation of *contingency* or *emergency* channels to handle VCR actions. These channels are not used to satisfy initial requests and so VCR activity after a program starts is independent of the initial channel allocation policy. Furthermore, our experience suggests VCR control and initial channel allocation policies are orthogonal video server functions.

3 Video System Model

In order to compare the performance of channel allocation policies, we must first develop a model to use as a basis for simulating the operation of various system configurations. The parameters used to describe a system can be grouped into two categories: (1) system size and operation, and (2) customer behavior. A third group of parameters are the performance measures used to compare systems. These sets of parameters are described next.

3.1 System Characteristics

Logical Channel Capacity: The number of simultaneous program streams that can be supported. The results presented in this paper are for systems with 1000 logical channels. Other numbers were tested and results suggest that as systems grow in size, additional economies of scale can be achieved. We consider 1000 channels to be a mid-sized system.

Movie Library: The number and duration of offered programs. Results are presented for systems offering 100 movies that last a uniformly random time between 105 and 135 minutes.

Batching Option: Batching, if implemented by a system, allows multiple requests to be serviced with one channel. Simulations are run for both types of systems.

Channel Allocation Policy: The policies discussed in Sections 4 and 5 are each simulated.

3.2 Customer Behavior

Request Arrival Pattern: Simulations are run for a 24-hour period from 8am of one day to 8am of the next. Customer behavior defines the request arrival pattern or *workload* at the server. Over a 24-hour simulation period the workload is expected to vary depending on the time of day[?, ?]. In Figure 2, we propose three new non-steady state workloads. The horizontal axis represents time, and the vertical axis shows the number of requests that arrive during a six minute *reporting interval.*

The first graph in Figure 2 shows a steady-state request arrival pattern computed using an exponential function. We view this as unrealistic because demand fluctuations exist especially during "prime time" viewing hours[?]. One workload based on known viewing patterns assumes the request rate between 6pm and

12am will be five times greater than the rest of the day. The second and third graphs in Figure 2 show two such workloads; one with a gradual increase to high load, and one with a jump to high load. Variations in workload are created using exponential functions with different average inter-arrival times. The fourth workload is a special case with load surges at hour intervals. This type of workload is based on the belief that broadcast programs that start and end at the start/end of each hour will still exist and impact on-demand behavior.

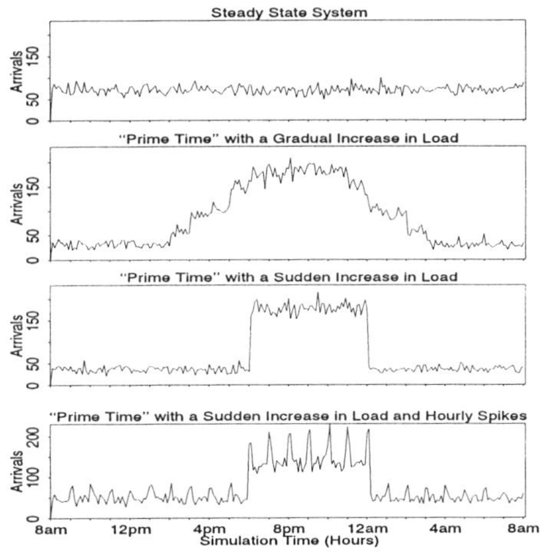

Figure 2: Various request arrival patterns.

Movie Selection: For each request, a movie is selected using a Zipf distribution[?] which states that the probability that movie i is chosen equals $\frac{c}{(i^{1+\theta})}$, where c is a normalizing constant. Empirical evidence suggests that $\theta = 0.271$ for movie rentals[?].

Reneging Behavior: Various video delivery service models have been proposed[?, ?, ?] and simulated. The model we use in this study is based on customers unwillingness to wait for service more than some finite amount of time[?]. Because servicing is first come, first served, all requests will eventually be satisfied, but with unknown and variable service time. During high-load periods waiting time may be very long (on the order of 15 or more minutes). Customers will most likely be unwilling to wait this long. Therefore, our model assumes that customers agree to wait at least 5 minutes plus up to an additional 2.5 minutes randomly chosen from an exponential distribution. If after this period of time a channel has not been allocated to satisfy the customer's request, the customer withdraws the request and *reneges*. Customer reneging is analogous to a request that cannot be satisfied and is a key performance measure.

3.3 Performance Objectives

Average Wait Time: Wait time is measured from when a customer makes a request to when program playout begins. Average wait time can be measured over short intervals (6 minutes) or over the entire simulation period.

Reneging Probability: The probability of reneging is measured by taking the number of customers who renege divided by the total number of requests made. Reneging probability is measured over the short- and long-term.

4 Greedy Allocation Policies

In this section, we describe the operation and performance of video delivery systems that implement greedy channel allocation policies. The two policies discussed are "on-demand allocation" and "forced wait". While neither policy controls the rate of allocation, both do batch requests when conditions allow. That is, when a channel is allocated, all requests in the queue waiting for the particular movie are serviced. The details of each policy and their performance are described next.

4.1 On-Demand Allocation

Allocation of channels using on-demand scheduling is the most straightforward of all the policies discussed in this paper. The algorithm is as follows:

1. When a request is received, the scheduler checks to see if there are any free channels. If a free channel exists, it is immediately allocated. Otherwise, the request is queued.

2. When a channel is freed, the scheduler checks to see if there are any requests in the queue. If requests are waiting, the freed channel is immediately allocated.

Typical operation during low-load periods is that there will be at least one free channel each time a request arrives. This means no requests will be queued, no batching will occur, and all requests are satisfied. However, during high-load periods, requests arrive faster than channels are freed so request queuing and batching are common. Because of increased queuing, wait times increase and some customers renege.

Figure 3 is the first of a series of time dependent graphs that show the performance results of simulated video system operation. The horizontal axis represents time and ranges over a 24-hour period from 8am of one day to 8am of the next. Points in the graphs represent averages over 6 minute *reporting intervals*. The dotted lines represent cumulative averages computed from the start of the simulation. Each graph has 5 parts:

1. **Arrivals**: The number of requests received during the last reporting interval.

2. **% Renege**: The percentage of requests reneged by customers who have waited too long.

3. **Channels Alloc**: The actual number of channels allocated during a reporting interval.

4. **Wait(secs)**: The average wait time of all successfully satisfied requests.

5. **In Queue**: The average number of requests waiting in the queue.

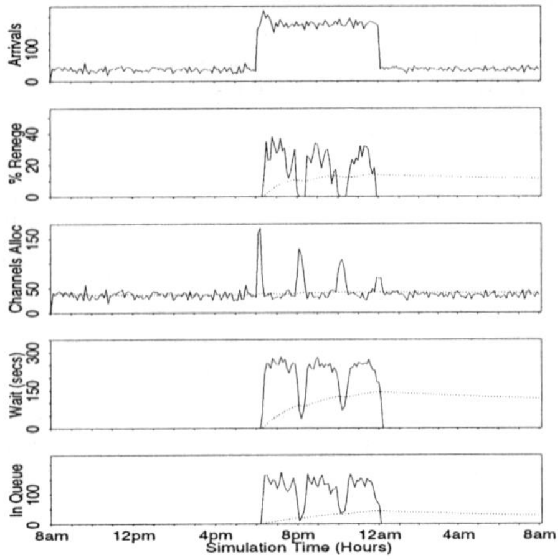

Figure 3: The on-demand channel allocation policy.

Figure 3 shows the performance of a video system that implements on-demand channel allocation[1]. This system has poor long-term reneging and very pronounced oscillations in short-term reneging (see second graph in Figure 3). Oscillations in short-term reneging occur because channels are allocated more quickly than they are being freed. When the load jumps at 6pm (see top graph in Figure 3), there are only enough channels to satisfy requests on an on-demand basis for a half hour (see third graph in Figure 3). After this time, all free channels have been allocated. Furthermore, since most of the channel pool was just allocated, these channels will not be available for the remainder of their service time (approximately two hours). Until these channels are eventually freed a majority of new requests will not be satisfied (see the second graph in Figure 3). When the group of channels does eventually becomes free they will again be completely allocated in a short period of time (see the third graph in Figure 3). These cycles eventually go away, but it takes many hours and does not occur until after the prime time period is over. The average duration of a cycle is equal to the average program duration which in our simulation is two hours. During a cycle, the system has acceptable behavior for only 25% of the time. For the other 75% of the time, average reneging is greater than 30%, and sometimes even goes above 40%.

4.2 Forced Wait

Forced wait is a scheduling policy requiring the request at the head of the queue to wait some minimum amount of time before being serviced. The goal of the *minimum wait time* parameter is to make customers wait as long as possible thereby increasing the batching factor and effective server capacity. With a forced wait algorithm, channels are allocated on an on-demand basis but only after the request at the head of the queue has waited the minimum wait time.

Forced wait suffers from several drawbacks. The first is that the minimum wait time parameter must be set by a system operator. Finding the optimal value is very difficult for three reasons: (1) customer behavior changes over time, (2) different values are appropriate for different workloads, and (3) system performance is very sensitive to the parameter. Figure 4 shows the reneging levels for the same video delivery system but with three different minimum wait times. For a system with 4, 5, and 6 minute minimum waiting time, the average reneging is 8.9%, 6.2%, and 17.6% respectively. The optimal minimum wait time is slightly more than 5 minutes and is a result of the customer behavior model used in the simulation. Other behavior models that do not assume all customers are willing to wait a least 5 minutes will actually perform worse.

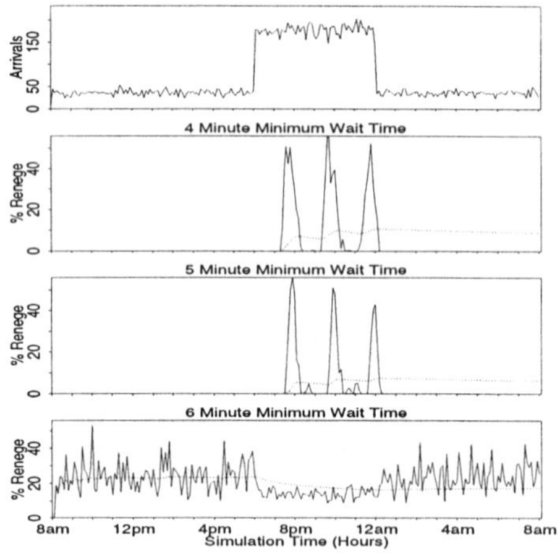

Figure 4: Forced wait with varied minimum wait.

A second major drawback of the forced wait algorithm is that it does not fix the problem of cyclical behavior even using the optimal minimum wait time. Figure 5 shows the results are similar to the on-demand policy. When the load increases, all free channels are allocated in a short period of time, starting the cyclical behavior. One difference is that the duration of high reneging periods in forced wait is not as long as with the on-demand policy.

A third major drawback of forced wait is the high waiting time experienced by each customer (see the fourth graph in Figure 5). Even during low loads, many customers are forced to wait the minimum waiting time. This policy is certainly not appropriate for systems that do not experience high load all the time. During low load periods customers should be serviced more quickly. Furthermore, for unpopular movies, the likelihood of having multiple requests in the queue at the same time is very low. Therefore, using a forced wait policy for these requests does nothing to increase capacity and only increases the average wait time.

[1]Results are shown only for the workload with a sudden increase in load during prime time. Results for the other non-steady state workloads discussed in Section 3.2 are almost identical and are not included.

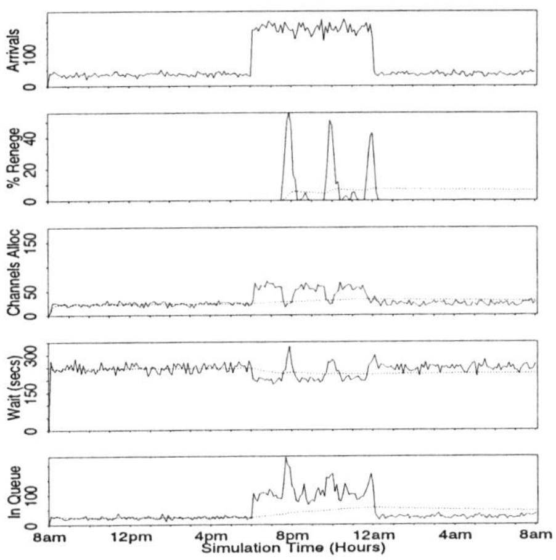

Figure 5: Forced wait with optimal minimum wait.

5 Rate-Based Allocation Policies

Greedy allocation policies suffer from poor performance in terms of short- and long-term reneging and average wait time. In this section, we propose a set of channel allocation policies which solve these problems.

5.1 Pure Rate Control

The pure rate control policy (1) puts a strict upper limit on the rate at which channels can be allocated and (2) limits the total number of channels allocated during a fixed time interval or *control interval*. The purpose of the interval is to provide a finite time period over which to accurately calculate and enforce the rate control policy. By limiting the allocation of channels to a set rate, we can ensure that some channels will be available in each control interval. This serves to eliminate the conditions leading to the development of cycles.

The pure rate control policy attempts to allocate channels at a uniform rate throughout each interval. Let T_{last} be the last time a channel was allocated, and T_{next} be the next time a channel can be allocated. T_{next} is given by $T_{next} = T_{last} + \Delta$ where Δ is the interval between successive allocations. Let T_{left} be the remaining time until the end of the control interval, C_{max} be the maximum number of channels that can be allocated during each interval, and C_{alloc} be the number of channels already allocated. Then, Δ can be computed as $\Delta = T_{left}/(C_{max} - C_{alloc})$.

The maximum number of channels that can be allocated during an interval depends on the average channel holding time (i.e., viewing time), T_{view}, and the total number of channels in the system, C_{total}. Let T_{int} be the length of the control interval. Then the maximum number of channels that can be allocated per time interval, C_{max}, is computed as $C_{max} = (T_{int} * C_{total})/T_{view}$. The video server simulated in this paper is characterized by $T_{int} = 10$ minutes, $C_{total} = 1000$ channels, and $T_{view} = 2$ hours. This yields a value of $C_{max} = 84$ channels.

This result and the allocation rate formula together

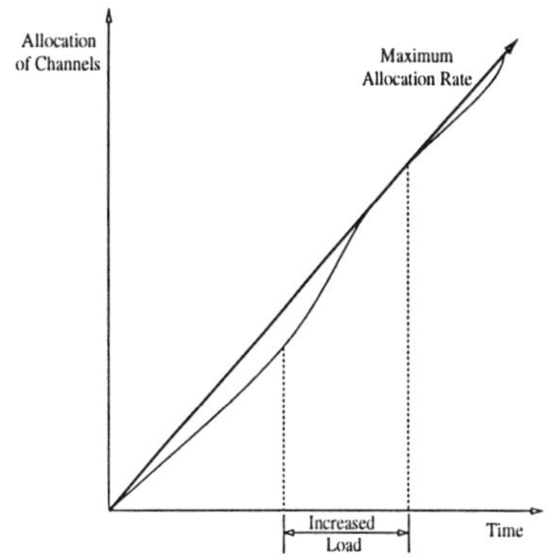

Figure 6: Max allocation for pure rate control.

establish a maximum allocation rate (see Figure 6). This limit controls the channel allocation rate within a control interval. The relationship between various request arrival patterns and these equations can be summarized as the following:

Low Load: Channels are not allocated as quickly as the allocation rate might allow. In most cases, the request inter-arrival time will exceed the delay imposed between channel allocations. During low load periods, requests will be satisfied immediately.

High Load: Requests arrive more quickly than channels can be allocated. Requests will be queued and must wait for the scheduler to allocate a channel.

Low to High Transition: During a transition, the allocation rate increases up to the maximum allocation rate. Figure 6 shows such an example. When the increased load period begins, the number of allocated channels is below the maximum. The scheduler allocates channels at an increased rate until the average equals the maximum. This mechanism allows pure rate control some flexibility in adapting to changes in workload.

Figure 7 shows the performance of a system using pure rate control. The results show that pure rate control solves the problems of the on-demand and forced wait policies. Cycles are eliminated because the number of channels allocated during the high load period does not spike, but only increases slightly. When the load is low the average wait time is almost zero, and there are few requests in the queue. During high load periods, channels are allocated at the maximum rate and some requests are queued. Multiple requests in the queue increases the likelihood that the system will be able to batch thereby increasing effective throughput. Rate control ensures reasonable channel availability and wait times even during high load periods.

5.1.1 Advantages of Rate Control

Rate-based channel allocation combines the best characteristics of the on-demand and forced wait policies. The results in Figure 8 compare the cumulative long-term average reneging and wait times for these policies. The first part of the graph shows that pure rate

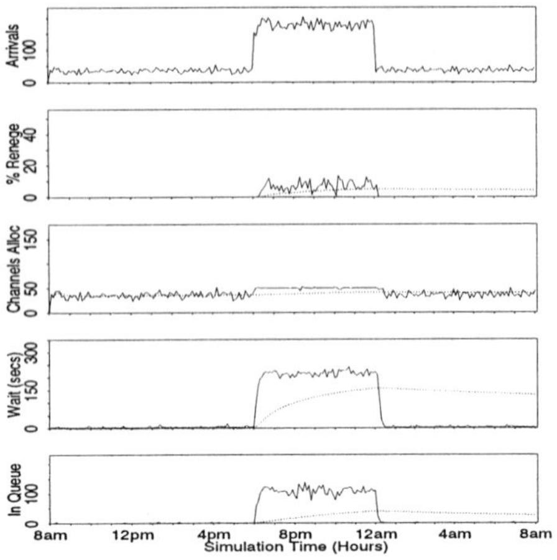

Figure 7: The pure rate control policy.

control has the best overall reneging. Furthermore, pure rate control does not require the determination of the minimum wait time parameter. The second part of the graph shows that the average wait time for pure rate control is almost optimal. Only on-demand allocation is better, but of course it suffers from both short- and long-term average reneging.

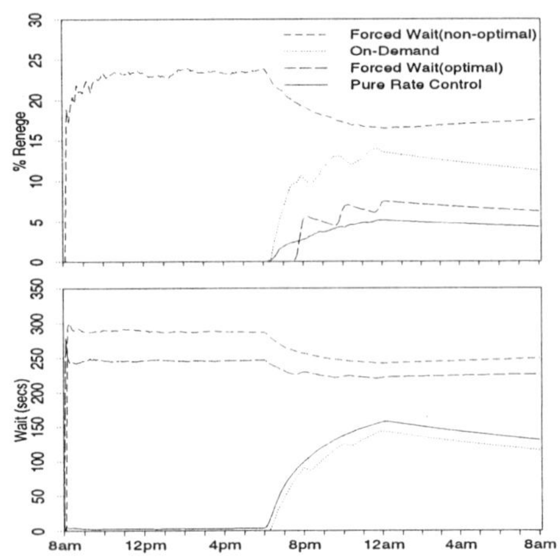

Figure 8: Comparison of channel allocation policies.

5.2 Extensions to Pure Rate Control

In this section, two extensions to pure rate control are proposed and their performance simulated.

5.2.1 Deviated Rate Control

Deviated rate control is similar to pure rate control, except that under certain conditions, deviated rate control allows the channel allocation rate to temporarily rise above the maximum allocation rate (see Figure 9). However, the maximum number of channels that can be allocated during a control interval is still the same. Additional flexibility is an important feature that can further reduce reneging during short-term load surges.

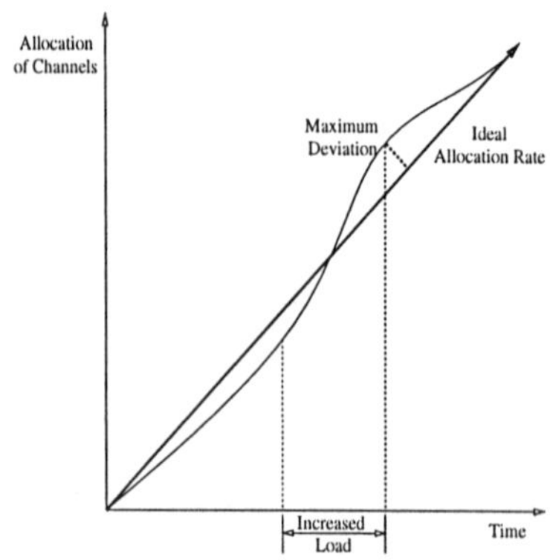

Figure 9: Max allocation for deviated rate control.

Deviated rate control requires two parameters to be defined, (1) the *maximum allowed deviation*, and (2) a *maximum tolerable wait* threshold. The maximum allowed deviation, which is defined between one and zero, shortens the delay between one channel allocation and the next. The time of the next channel allocation is still $T_{next} = T_{last} + \Delta$, but Δ becomes Δ' which is now computed as $\Delta' = \Delta * \alpha$ where α is the maximum allowed deviation.

Deviation from the ideal allocation rate should only occur when load conditions are such that either a channel be allocated quickly or customers will start reneging. This goal is achieved by allowing the allocation rate to exceed the ideal rate only when the customer at the head of the queue has exceeded the minimum wait time threshold and is believed to be close to reneging. The maximum allowed deviation parameter can be used to implement a rate-based policy with any level of control. A value of one implements the pure rate control policy while a value of zero is the same as forced wait but with a limit on the total number of channels that can be allocated per control interval.

Figure 10 compares the performance of the rate control schemes for a workload with demand spikes on each hour. This alternate type of workload demonstrates the types of scenarios in which deviated rate control performs better than pure rate control. As Figure 10 shows the long-term averaging reneging is 2.3% for pure rate control and 1.5% for deviated rate control. For the results shown, the maximum allowed deviation parameter is set to 0.45 (determined to be optimal through simulation) and the maximum tolerable wait threshold is 5 minutes. Allowing the allocation rate to deviate gives the scheduler greater ability to handle short-term surges in demand.

5.2.2 Multiple Service Classes

An allocation rate control policy using multiple service classes gives a service provider the ability to offer

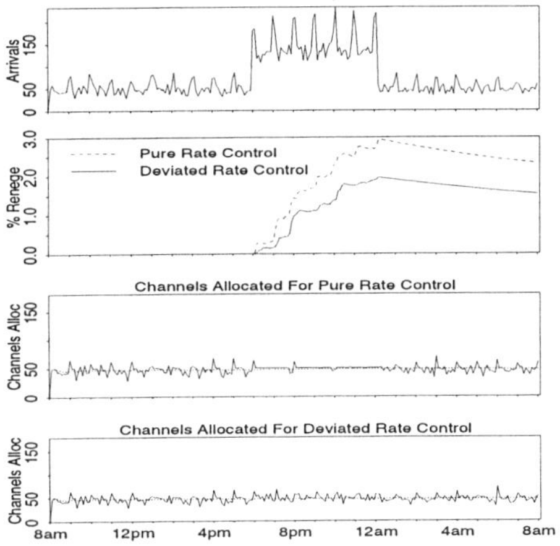

Figure 10: The deviated rate control policy.

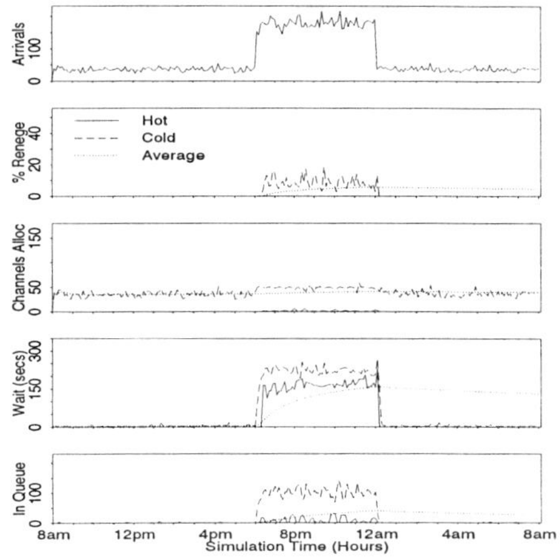

Figure 11: The multiple service class allocation policy.

a variety of service classes. One example is to give higher scheduling priority for hot movies since the likelihood of batching multiple requests is greater thereby increasing the profit potential. The determination of which movies are popular and which are not can be made many ways. Our method is to use the last control interval's request count as a heuristic. The allocation policy for each class is:

Hot Movies: The first request for a hot movie must wait the minimum wait time, similar to the forced wait policy. Hot movies have scheduling priority over cold movies, and no rate control is used.

Cold Movies: Scheduling for cold movies is done using pure rate control. However, any channels allocated for hot movies are still counted in the total number of channels that can be allocated in a control interval. Starvation is possible but unlikely since only a few movies are typically hot.

Figure 11 shows the performance of the multiple service class allocation policy. Only during the high load period were there enough requests to make any of the movies hot. During the entire simulation no request for a hot movie ever went unsatisfied (see the second graph in Figure 11). Because only a few movies were hot, only a few channels needed to be allocated for these movies (see the third graph in Figure 11). Wait time for hot movies was slightly less than for cold movies (see the fourth graph in Figure 11). Finally, only a small percentage of the queue was actually for hot movie requests (see the fifth graph in Figure 11).

6 Capacity Planning

An important aspect in the design of a video delivery system is determining the number of channels needed to provide a certain level of service. We use a simulator to determine the minimum number of channels needed to meet a long-term reneging objective of 5%, and a short-term reneging objective of 15%. Results presented in this section are generated by iteratively simulating larger and larger systems until the short- and/or long-term reneging objective are met.

6.1 Long Term Objective

The top graph in Figure 12 shows the number of channels needed to meet only the 5% long-term reneging objective. The x-axis represents the average number of requests arriving per minute. The results show that as the request arrival rate increases, the number of channels needed increases quickly in the system that cannot batch requests and more slowly for multicast-capable systems. In the system allowing batching but implementing only on-demand allocation, the number of channels needed increases rapidly but then levels off at approximately 3000. For the optimal forced wait and pure rate control policies the number of channels needed levels of about 1000 with pure rate control doing slightly better. Because the only requirement is long-term average reneging, forced wait performs nearly as well as pure rate control. Generally, in systems that allow batching, the number of channels needed levels off as economics of scale increase.

6.2 Short and Long Term Objectives

Because predictable and consistent performance is as important as overall performance, both short- and long-term reneging objectives need to be considered. The bottom graph in Figure 12 shows that for the no batching case, the slope of the line is slightly greater than the top graph indicating that some additional channels are needed to eliminate cycles. For the on-demand policy, cycles are a significant problem and 25% more channels are needed to achieve both reneging objectives. The same holds true for the forced wait policy which requires more than twice as many channels. Finally, because pure rate control was designed to smooth peaks, additional channel requirements are negligible.

6.3 Channel Utilization

A final measure of performance is the ability of a video delivery system to achieve high channel utilization during both low and high load periods. High utilization is also desirable because it means per-movie

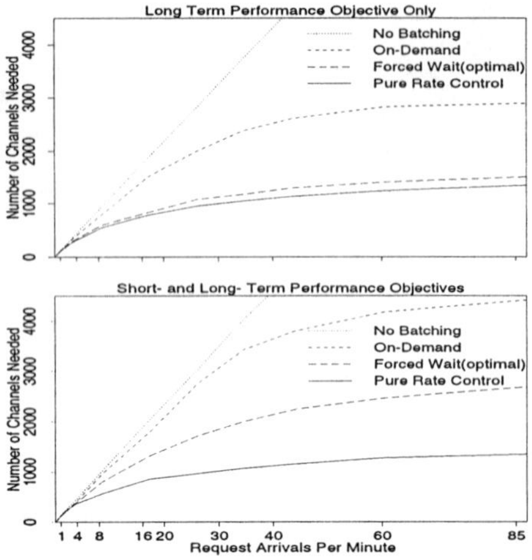

Figure 12: Server capacity for different objectives.

costs are lower. The *effective capacity* of a system is defined as the number of requests being serviced divided by the system capacity. For video systems that provide batching the effective capacity may be greater than 100%. Figure 13 shows the effective capacity for three systems. The system that does not allow batching has a high average reneging and the lowest effective capacity. The effective capacity for systems that allow batching are much higher, but implementing a rate-based allocation policy increases the effective capacity even more. Pure rate control achieves additional gains over on-demand allocation because during high load periods reneging is much lower and more requests are serviced per channel.

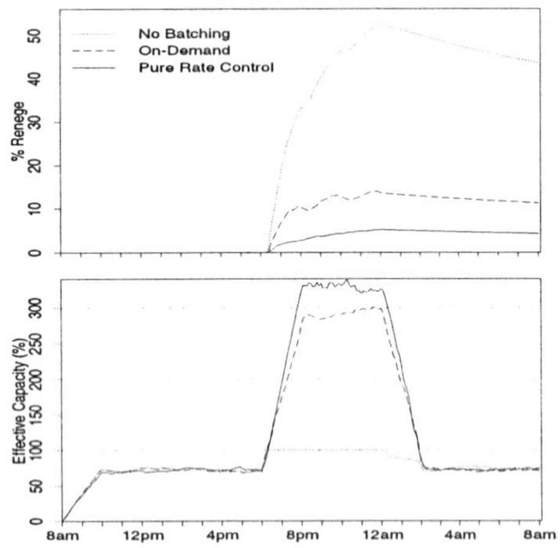

Figure 13: Effective capacity for allocation policies.

7 Summary and Conclusions

In this paper, we identify through simulation the limitations of greedy channel allocation policies, especially in the context of video delivery systems with multicast/batching capability. These algorithms are poor solutions because: (1) they do not minimize customer waiting time, (2) they perform poorly when load conditions vary meaning they do not even achieve their goal of maximizing customers serviced, and (3) they have wild oscillations in short-term performance. To solve these limitations, we propose a set of rate-based policies that work by ensuring that channels are available for allocation on a consistent basis. Not only do these policies achieve a consistent and predictable level of service in terms of customer reneging, but they also improve effective capacity and resource utilization.

A Shared Buffer Architecture for Interactive VOD Servers*

Senthil Sengodan, Victor O. K. Li

Communication Sciences Institute
Department of Electrical Engineering - Systems
University of Southern California
Los Angeles, CA 90089-2565, U.S.A.
E-mail: {sengodan,vli}@irving.usc.edu

Abstract

Video-on-demand (VOD) servers need to be efficiently designed in order to support a large number of users viewing the same or different videos at different rates. While considering a disk-array based VOD server, use of a shared buffer at the server end may be more economical than the sole use of dedicated buffers at each user's end. In this paper, we propose a simple buffer sharing architecture that may be used when disk-array based video servers are used. Our aim is to support the maximum number of users for a given number of video server disks while employing a simple scheme requiring less buffer space. The number of video segment retrievals that can occur within a certain time (the service round) is maximum when the scan disk scheduling algorithm is used. Consequently, we shall assume use of the scan algorithm for disk retrieval. The VOD server has a buffer manager that directs retrieved segments to appropriate buffer locations depending on their release and deadlines. The release and deadlines of segments are such that buffer requirement at the user's set-top box is minimized to two video segments while avoiding video starvation and buffer overflow at the user's end. We propose a novel scheme for the operation of the shared buffer that aims at increasing buffer utilization and decreasing cell loss due to buffer overflow. An ATM based broadband network is assumed and all segments are stored in buffers as fixed length ATM cells.

1 Introduction

In a Video-on-Demand (VOD) system, all videos are stored in a video server and the user (subscriber) may view any of these videos at any desired time. The user's request (to the video server) as well as the video signal (from the server back to the user) are transported by a broadband communication network such as an Asynchronous Transfer Mode (ATM) network. The user may perform several interactive operations that include pause, stop, slow/fast display and jump forward/backward to any desired location in the video sequence. We believe that reverse play does not have to be provided when a jump backward option is provided.

Since video (as well as audio) is a continuous media, it is delay sensitive. For smooth playback, video segments are needed at regular intervals at a user's end. Failure to deliver video segments when needed results in video starvation and a consequent glitch (or hiccup) in the playback. Since the start and duration of segment retrieval (from disk) as well as network delays are not deterministic, segments may need to be retrieved and transmitted in advance in order to avoid video starvation. These segments arriving at the user, then, need to be buffered until required by the user for display. In this paper, we assume the network is transparent and concern ourselves merely with the video server. The segment arrival at the user, thus, directly relates to its transmission onto the ATM network. The earlier the segment arrival at the user's end (relative to its playback), the larger is the amount of buffer required. Hence, we need to regulate the arrival of segments at a user by regulating their transmission from the server onto the ATM network. One way of achieving this is by regulating the segment retrieval from disk, and transmitting retrieved segments immediately onto the network without any buffering at the server. However, this is undesirable due to the high penalty of disk seek involved. In this paper, we relax the regulation of segment retrieval from disk by employing the scan algorithm, but store these retrieved segments in a buffer at the server and regulate their transmission onto the ATM network.

The choice of buffer location plays an important role in determining the overall cost of the system. Buffer locations affect both the total amount of buffer required as well as the number of users supported by the system. Typically, buffers may be provided at two locations - video server and user's set-top box. Buffers at the server are shared by all users while buffers at a user's set-top box are for the sole use of that user. Consequently, in most cases, use of buffers at the server results in a decrease in the buffers at each user's end and a decrease in the total amount of required buffer.

A lot of work on shared buffers for continuous media appears in the literature [4] [7]. Most of this work has been with regard to video teleconferencing where the time instant when a video frame is generated by each of the sources is

*This research is supported in part by the Pacific Bell External Technology Program.

0-8186-7780-5/97 $10.00 © 1997 IEEE

known. By shifting the time instants at which different sources generate frames, efficient use of a shared buffer can be made. In the case of a VOD system, however, the time instant when a video segment is retrieved from disk is not deterministic. For instance, when the scan scheduling or grouped sweeping scheduling (GSS) [2] algorithm is used, the order in which segments are retrieved (for the same as well as for different users) is unknown. By permitting such a variable order of segment retrieval, the total disk seek time can be greatly reduced. This is extremely desirable as it permits more number of users in the system. However, in order to regulate the transmission of segments onto the network, a simple and efficient scheme for segment buffering is needed at the server. In this paper, we propose a scheme that aims to achieve this.

The rest of the paper is organized as follows. Section 2 describes the proposed VOD architecture. Section 3 briefly mentions the scheme we adopt for grouping frames into segments. Section 4 describes the disk storage and retrieval issues, while Section 5 deals with the performance evaluation and numerical results. Finally, we conclude in Section 6.

2 VOD system architecture

The VOD system being considered is shown in Figure 1. As seen in the figure, user displays and the VOD server are interconnected by an ATM based high-speed broadband network. The interface of the user (rather, his/her remote) as well as the display to the broadband network is via a set-top box. The set-top box is assumed to have adequate buffer storage as well as circuitry for performing such functions as MPEG decoding.

The VOD server comprises a set of disk subsystems, a retrieval scheme manager, a staging buffer, a buffer manager, a main buffer (comprising several buffer modules) and a time division multiplexer (TDM). Interactive requests from a user are transported by the ATM network to the retrieval scheme manager. In order to maximize the number of supported users, the retrieval scheme used by the retrieval scheme manager is the scan disk scheduling algorithm [1][11]. These retrieved segments pass through the staging buffer prior to being directed by the buffer manager to appropriate locations in the main buffer (subject to availability of buffer space.) Both the staging buffer and the main buffer are shared by all the users and all segments are stored in them as ATM cells. Layered MPEG coding [8] may be used so that each segment comprises high priority (HP) and low priority (LP) cells. However, we will not consider this case any further here.

The storage (location) of segments in the staging buffer may be arbitrary, but that in the main buffer is based on the buffer management scheme being used by the buffer manager. The buffer manager determines the appropriate location (in the main buffer) for retrieved segments based on their release and deadlines for transmission on to the network. The release and deadline of each segment (for a given amount of dedicated buffer at the user's set-top box) depend on the latest time by which the segment is

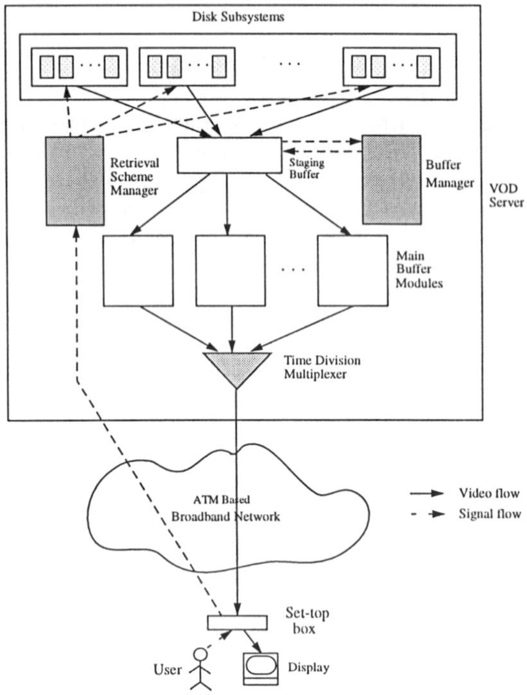

Figure 1: Architecture of VOD system

needed to avoid video starvation. In order to maximize the number of cells that may be transferred to the main buffer (and hence, minimize cell loss at the buffer), the algorithm used by the buffer manager is an Earliest Deadline First (EDF) algorithm. The TDM, then, transmits these ATM cells in a time division multiplexed fashion to the user via the broadband network.

2.1 Retrieval scheme manager

The retrieval scheme manager is responsible for determining the order in which segments required in a service round are retrieved from disk. In other words, the disk scheduling algorithm resides in the retrieval scheme manager. Several disk scheduling algorithms may be used. These include fixed order scheduling, scan scheduling, Grouped Sweeping Scheduling (GSS) [2] and Nonpreemptive Earliest Deadline First (N-EDF) [9] scheduling. The total disk seek time in a service round depends on the particular disk scheduling algorithm being used and is minimized with the scan scheduling algorithm [1]. Since a small total seek time implies that more segments may be retrieved in a round, we shall employ the scan scheduling algorithm in the retrieval scheme manager.

While the scan scheduling algorithm maximizes the number of segments that may be retrieved from disk in a service round, it has the disadvantage that no control exists over the order in which these segments are retrieved. Hence, if n segments are retrieved for a particular user in a service round, then the retrieval of these n segments from disk may be spaced uniformly apart in the service round (most desirable) or they may be retrieved consecutively (least desirable.) If a maximum of n_m segments may be retrieved for any single user in a service round, then lack of any buffer at the server implies that, in the worst case, n_m segments are transmitted onto the network (and arrive at the user) consecutively. Hence, a buffer capable of storing up to n_m segments needs to be provided at each user's set-top box in order to avoid buffer overflow. This is not an efficient way of providing buffer storage since the total buffer required becomes very large and at most times the buffer utilization is extremely low.

2.2 Buffer manager

In order to decrease the total buffer required and increase buffer utilization, the n segments retrieved for a user in a service round need to be transmitted to the user uniformly spaced within the round. If a video segment is taken to be an atomic unit, a lower bound on the buffer requirement at the user's set-top box is one segment. A buffer requirement of one segment at the user's set-top box implies that the transmission of segments for a user should take place (exactly) at required time instants in a service round. When user interactivity is permitted, the user playback rate and hence, the number of segments retrieved for a user in a service round can vary between rounds. Under such a situation, it can be shown [9] that a buffer restriction of one video segment decreases the number of possible segment transmissions in a service round.

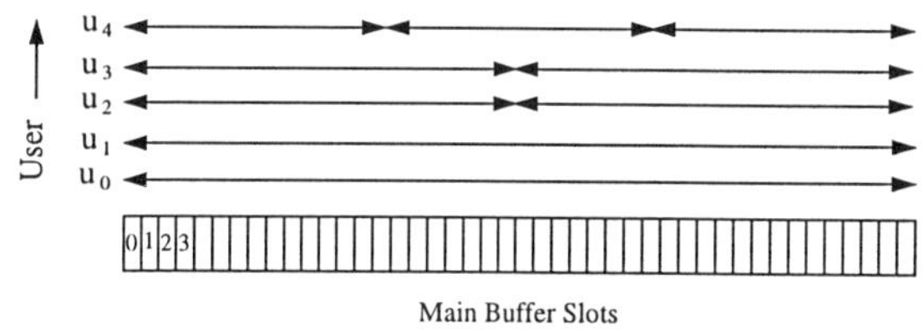

Figure 2: Illustrating user macro-slots and EDF

In order to maximize the number of segment transmissions (on to the ATM network) in a service round, we do the following. For a user requiring n segments in a round, the main buffer is divided into n equal (logical) "macro-slots" [9] and the i-th segment (where $i = 0$ to $n-1$) for the user is stored anywhere (and, possibly non-contiguously) in the i-th macro-slot. With a total of C_b slots in the main buffer, cells associated with segment i of a user requiring n segments need to be stored in slots with numbers between $\frac{i \times C_b}{n}$ and $\frac{(i+1) \times C_b}{n}$. Since different users have different playback rates, the number of macro-slots into which the main buffer is divided varies from one user to another. Macro-slots belonging to users requiring the same number of segments in a round are fully overlapping, while those belonging to users requiring different number of segments in a round may be partially overlapping. This is illustrated in Figure 2 where users u_0, u_1 have one macro-slot each; users u_2, u_3 have two macro-slots each; and user u_4 has three macro-slots. This implies that users u_0, u_1 need one segment in a service round; users u_2, u_3 need two segments; and user u_4 requires three. The numbering of cell slots comprising the buffer is according to the order in which the TDM accesses them.

Since segments belonging to different users need to be transferred from the staging buffer to contending locations in the main buffer, the order in which these segments are transferred is important. The transfer needs to take place in such a fashion that any resulting cell loss due to lack of space in the main buffer is minimized. An EDF algorithm is used for this purpose and is as follows :

1. Let **U** be the set containing all macro-slots.
2. Select the macro-slot with the earliest deadline. Transfer cells of segments which are assigned this macro-slot (in any order) to the cell slots in the buffer within this macro-slot.
3. If all cell slots comprising this macro-slot are filled, then drop any remaining cells that do not have storage space in this macro-slot. Go to step 5.
4. If all cells belonging to all segments assigned to this macro-slot have been transferred, go to step 5.
5. Delete this macro-slot from **U**.
6. Go to step 2 if **U** is non-empty. Else, stop.

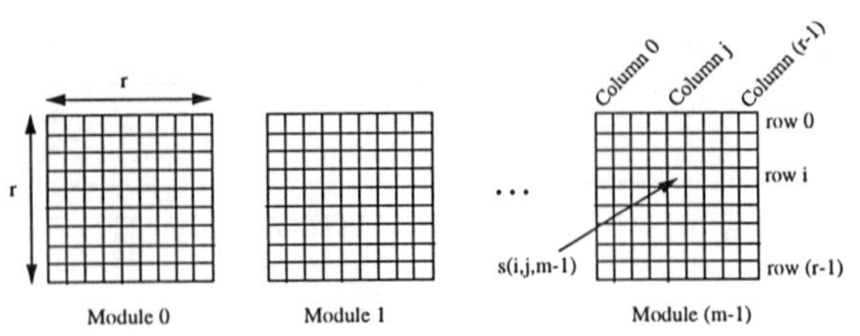

Figure 3: Main buffer

For any distribution of empty slots in the main buffer, the above algorithm minimizes cell loss during transfer. However, the distribution of empty slots greatly affects the cell loss. In the following subsection, we present a novel scheme that aims at obtaining a distribution of empty slots that minimizes cell loss.

2.3 Buffer architecture

Let C_b denote the total number of cell slots in the main buffer. As shown in Figure 3, the main buffer comprises m buffer modules. Each module comprises r^2 cell slots that are (logically) arranged as a square with r rows and r columns. We shall denote the slot corresponding to row i, column j of module k as $s(i,j,k)$, where $i,j = 0,1,2,\cdots,r-1$ and $k = 0,1,2,\cdots,m-1$. We also have : $C_b = m \times r^2$.

Associated with each cell slot $s(i,j,k)$ is a slot number, whose value depends on whether the current service round is odd-numbered or even-numbered. For even-numbered service rounds, slot $s(i,j,k)$ is assigned a number $(irm + jm + k)$. For odd-numbered service rounds, slot $s(i,j,k)$ is assigned a number $(jrm + im + k)$. Thus, cell slots in different modules with the same values of i (row number) and j (column number) are numbered consecutively. In even-numbered service rounds the slots of each module are numbered row by row, while in odd-numbered rounds they are numbered column by column. Assignment of slot numbers in this fashion results in the creation of empty slots in a desirably "uniform" manner when the TDM empties the slots (as seen later). As mentioned earlier, the macro-slots of users are based on the slot numbers and since the order of segment retrieval by the scan algorithm is random, such a "uniform" creation of empty slots is desirable for a decrease in cell loss.

At the start of any service round i, transmission of cells stored in the buffer modules onto the ATM network begins in a TDM fashion. The TDM accesses the slots in the increasing order of their slot numbers corresponding to the previous round (i.e., round $(i-1)$). This is because segments transmitted in round i are those that were retrieved (and stored in the buffer) in round $(i-1)$. Simultaneously, new segments are being retrieved from disk and need to be buffered. These new segments are stored initially in the staging buffer. When the staging buffer is full, its contents are transferred to the appropriate locations in the main buffer. Let the size of the staging buffer be denoted by C_s. For the same parameters of retrieved segments, the amount of cell loss in the main buffer decreases as the value of C_s increases. At an extreme, when C_s equals C_b and if the size of all retrieved segments does not exceed C_b, the cell loss during transfer to the main buffer (which occurs only once in a round) goes to zero. However, in order to decrease the total buffer space, C_s is usually a small fraction of C_b. Thus, even when the total size of all retrieved segments does not exceed C_b, some cell loss can result during their transfer to the main buffer.

At the end of round i, all segments retrieved from disk during round i will have been stored in the main buffer (with some loss) and all segments that had been stored in the main buffer at the end of round $(i-1)$ will have been transmitted on to the network. The staging buffer is empty at this point.

If C Mbps is the channel capacity (at the output of the TDM) and C_b the total number of cell slots in the main buffer, then the time taken by the TDM to complete one service round is $53 \times 8 \times C_b/C$ μs. As we will see later, with n_f frames per segment and r_0 fps as the slowest playback rate, the duration of the service round equals n_f/r_0 sec. Equating the two, we have $53 \times 8 \times C_b/C = (n_f/r_0) \times 10^6$. Thus, the channel capacity is determined as $C = \frac{53 \times 8 \times C_b \times r_0}{n_f \times 10^6}$ Mbps.

3 Grouping frames into segments

During video playback, the unit of video information that needs to be displayed at regular intervals is a video frame. However, the popular coding scheme for videos is MPEG coding [8] which uses interframe coding in addition to intraframe coding. Decoding of a frame, in such a case, may depend on previous as well as subsequent frames. Consequently, arrival of a frame at a user before its playback deadline is not sufficient, but all frames needed for the decoding of a particular frame need to arrive at the user prior to the deadline of that frame. Thus, it is advantageous to group frames into segments [3]. Arrival of segments at the user is such that frame decoding takes place in a causal manner. Since each segment comprises the same number of video frames, segments need to arrive at regular intervals at a user's end.

In [3], a segment is taken to comprise the set of frames from one I frame up to (and excluding) the next one. When the number of segments retrieved in a service round is proportional to the user's playback rate, decreasing the segment size decreases the duration of a service round. A decrease in the duration of the service round is extremely desirable in a quasi-static retrieval scheme such as ours (as described later) as it results in a decrease in the interactive latency. In addition, skipping segments for fast playback requires dropping (i.e., not used for playback) some frames in retrieved segments when segments are grouped as in [3]. This is because other frames necessary to decode these (dropped) frames are present in skipped segments. Due to these reasons, we introduce a different scheme for grouping frames into segments which does not suffer from the drawbacks mentioned. The scheme is described in detail in [10] but the main idea is highlighted here.

Let the number of B frames between any two consecutive I/P frames be denoted by n_B. Let the number of frames per segment be n_f. Sets of n_f consecutive I/P frames and sets of n_f consecutive B frames constitute a segment. The segment numbering is such that between any consecutive I/P segments, there exists exactly n_B B segments. With such a segment creation scheme, decoding of a frame belonging to any segment only requires frames belonging to earlier segments. When a fast playback is desired, segments have to be suitably skipped. Segment skipping needs to be such that no frames belonging to retrieved segments have to be discarded (for want of other frames needed for their decoding). Moreover, the display quality has to be within a desirable one. Techniques for segment skipping that achieve these two purposes are detailed in [10].

Hence, for our purpose, there exists a grouping scheme that can accommodate any desired number of frames per segment. During fast playback, techniques exist for selecting segments to be retrieved so that no frames belonging to retrieved segments have to be discarded (due to unavailability of other frames needed for decoding).

4 Disk storage/retrieval issues

Let the total number of disk subsystems in the VOD server be N_{ds} and the total number of disks in the system be N_d. The number of disks per subsystem is N_{ds}/N_d. We assume that a segment is striped across all disks in a subsystem. Striping segments across the disks of a subsystem results in balancing the load among disks of a subsystem. In addition, since at any given time all the disks of a subsystem are retrieving (fragments of) the same segment, the effective data transfer rate of the disk subsystem is N_{ds}/N_d times that of a single disk. While the value of N_d depends on the total number of videos to be stored, the value of N_{ds} depends on factors such as available memory and desired user QoS [9].

Each disk subsystem may be independent and hold a video in its entirety, or alternatively, different segments of the same video may be stored on different disk subsystems. Irrespective of what the case may be, the concept of service rounds exists for a disk subsystem within which a certain number of segments need to be retrieved. The service rounds associated with different disk subsystems begin and end at the same time. We will assume that the total load is balanced among the different disk subsystems for all service rounds. Hence, any performance analysis can be limited to one disk subsystem.

Let the set of playback rates that the VOD system offers the user be $\{r_0, r_1, \cdots, r_{N_r-1}\}$, where N_r is the total number of playback rates offered to the user. Without loss of generality, we assume that $r_i < r_j \ \forall \ i < j$. We will consider the duration of a service round to equal the time taken to play back a video segment at the slowest rate (r_0). If a segment contains n_f frames, then the round duration equals n_f/r_0 sec. In addition, we will also assume that all offered playback rates are integral multiples of r_0. With these requirements, each active user in the system requires at least one video segment in each service round and the number of segments needed is an integer (which are desirable features).

4.1 Number of retrieved segments

Consider a user viewing a video at a playback rate of r_{ui} fps, where $i = \{0, 1, \cdots, N_r - 1\}$. Since the number of segments retrieved for a user in any service round depends on the user's playback rate, we shall denote it by the function $f(r_{ui})$. It is desirable from a disk load and network congestion viewpoint to suitably skip segments during fast playback [3]. In such cases, the number of retrieved segments is proportional to the user's playback rate for normal and slow playback, but equals that for the normal playback during fast playback. If r_n is the normal playback rate, we have :

$$f(r_{ui}) = \begin{cases} \frac{r_n}{r_0} & \text{if } r_{ui} \geq r_n \\ \frac{r_{ui}}{r_0} & \text{otherwise} \end{cases}$$

4.2 Startup and interactive latency

Since the operation is quasi-static, startup and interactive (rate change, pause/stop, resume, jump) requests made after the start of a round are batched until the start of the next round.

We saw earlier that a macro-slot of any user in any service round encompassed a certain number of cell slots in the main buffer. These cell slots need to store one segment of that user. A segment that is retrieved in one macro-slot is played back during the next. Hence, startup and jump requests made during a round have to be batched till the end of the round, suffer from an additional delay of T_c due to the cell transfer into the main buffer and, finally, take effect at the end of the first macro-slot of the next round. Due to the continuity of video sequence for the remaining interactive requests (rate change, pause/stop, resume), requests made during a round take effect at the start of the round after the next (and not at the end of the first macro-slot of that round). Table 1 tabulates the latency due to various user requests. Here, k is the number of segments that have to be prefetched prior to start of playback. This parameter depends on the nature of grouping frames into segments. For the method of grouping frames into segments as described in [10], $k = 1$.

5 Performance analysis and results

5.1 Storage preliminaries

The data that we use is based on the MPEG encoded video "Star Wars" [6]. We will assume that this video is representative of all videos in the disk system. We assume that frames are grouped into segments as mentioned earlier. The ratio of the number of I, P and B frames for this encoding was 1 : 3 : 8. Some parameters of the frames

Interaction	Latency[1]
Start	$U[0, T_c) + T_c + kT_c(r_n/r_0)$
Jump	$U[0, T_c) + T_c + kT_c(r_n/r_0)$
Pause/stop	$U[0, T_c) + T_c$
Resume	$U[0, T_c) + T_c$
Change rate	$U[0, T_c) + T_c$

Table 1: Latency of user requests

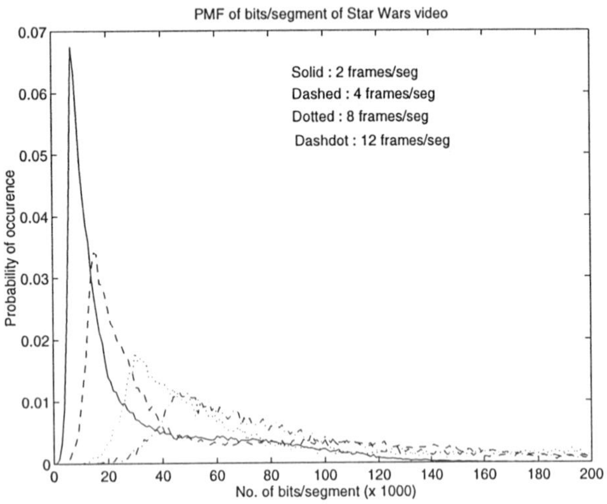

Figure 4: Probability mass function of bits/segment for the "Star Wars" video

and the resulting segments are indicated in Table 2 where n_f denotes the number of frames per segment. Figure 4 plots the probability mass function (pmf) of the number of bits/segment.

Let the system contain 1000 videos each lasting 100 minutes when played at 30 fps. The total storage required, assuming MPEG 2 compressed video, is 3 T Bytes which requires $\lceil \frac{3000}{9.1} \rceil = 330$ disks. If the number of disks per subsystem is 10, the number of disk subsystems is 33. So, each disk subsystem contains either 30 or 31 videos.

Let us assume that the possible playback rates (in fps) are:

$r_0 = 10$, $r_1 = 20$, $r_2 = 30$, $r_3 = 40$, $r_4 = 50$, $r_5 = 60$, $r_6 = 90$

For the set of playback rates indicated, the number of segments retrieved in a round for a user is given by: $x_0 = 1$, $x_1 = 2$, $x_2 = x_3 = x_4 = x_5 = x_6 = 3$

Since the duration of a service round equals the amount of time a segment would last a user at rate r_0, (for n_f frames/segment) we have :

T_c = service round duration = $100 \times n_f$ ms

Let the parameters of the main buffer be $m = 17$, $r = 100$

n_f	Max (bits)	Min (bits)	Avg (bits)	Std Dev (bits)
1	185267	476	15598.33	3.3×10^8
2	345123	1186	31197.49	31254.73
4	665058	4741	62394.98	57140.61
8	1053294	10561	124789.96	112555.24
12	1378253	16571	187196.05	167277.25

Table 2: Parameters of frame and segment distribution

resulting in a total buffer storage for 170000 cells. Let the staging buffer capacity be $\frac{1}{10} - th$ of the main buffer.

5.2 User model

Let N_r denote the total number of playback rates that the VOD system offers the user. As far as load on the disk (i.e., number of segment retrievals) is concerned, the user can be in one of $(N_r + 1)$ possible states - the N_r playback rates and the pause/stop state. In order to consider the operation during heavy load, we shall ignore the pause/stop state and only consider the case where the user changes his/her playback rate. We assume that the behaviour of each user is independent and identically distributed (i.i.d.). Let the transition probability matrix for the user states be :

$$P = \begin{pmatrix} 0 & 0.3 & 0.5 & 0.05 & 0.05 & 0.05 & 0.05 \\ 0.3 & 0 & 0.5 & 0.05 & 0.05 & 0.05 & 0.05 \\ 0.15 & 0.2 & 0 & 0.2 & 0.15 & 0.15 & 0.15 \\ 0.05 & 0.05 & 0.5 & 0 & 0.3 & 0.05 & 0.05 \\ 0.05 & 0.05 & 0.5 & 0.15 & 0 & 0.2 & 0.05 \\ 0.05 & 0.05 & 0.5 & 0.05 & 0.15 & 0 & 0.2 \\ 0.05 & 0.05 & 0.5 & 0.05 & 0.15 & 0.2 & 0 \end{pmatrix}$$

where each p_{ij} denotes the conditional probability that the next state is j given that the current state is i and that the user has just made an interactive request.

The amount of time spent by a user in a particular state is assumed to be exponentially distributed. Hence,

$T_i = \frac{1}{\mu_i}$ = mean sojourn time for user in state i; where $i = 0, 1, \cdots, m-1$

Let $[T_1\ T_2 \cdots T_7] = [5\ 5\ 600\ 10\ 10\ 10\ 10]$

In order to determine the probability that a user is in a particular state at any given time, we need to transform the user state transition chain into a markov chain. The resulting markov chain has m states where $\forall i, j = 0, 1, \cdots, m-1$:

μ_{ij} = transition rate from state i to state j = $\mu_i p_{ij}$

We can then solve the balance equations to determine the probability π_i that the user is in state i.

$\Pi = [0.0026\ 0.0029\ 0.9731\ 0.0052\ 0.0061\ 0.0054\ 0.0046]$

Associated with each user i, let us define a discrete random variable (RV) $x_i = f(r_{ui})$. Here, r_{ui} is the playback rate of user i and $f(r_{ui})$ is the number of segments retrieved in a service round for a playback rate of r_{ui}. Since

the behaviour of each user is assumed to be independent and identical, the RV's x_i are i.i.d..
We have: Mean(x_i) = 2.992; Variance(x_i) = 0.0134

5.3 Cell loss at disk system

A large load on the disk system may result in cell loss during retrieval. This loss is due to the fact that the end of a service round has been reached but some segments are yet to be retrieved. Assuming a known number of users in the system, we shall now determine the cell loss during segment retrieval from disk. In order to simplify the analysis, we will assume that the load is balanced among the various disk subsystems during all service rounds. Consequently, we only need to analyze the effect that a single disk subsystem with k users has on the cell loss probability. This value, then, equals that due to $N_{ds} \times k$ users in the entire system.

Let there be k users currently in a disk subsystem. Define an RV $X_k = \sum_{i=0}^{i=k-1} x_i$, i.e., X_k represents the total number of segments retrieved (by all k users) in a service round and is an RV that equals the sum of k i.i.d. RV's. The mean ($\eta\prime$) and variance ($\sigma\prime^2$) of the distribution of X_k is thus $k\eta$ and $k\sigma^2$ respectively. Since k is a large number, the central limit theorem states that the distribution of X_k approximates a Gaussian distribution with mean $\eta\prime$ and variance $\sigma\prime^2$.

Let y_i be an RV denoting the size of the i-th retrieved segment in a service round. Let $n = X_k$ segments be retrieved totally (for all k users) in a service round. Define an RV $Y = \sum_{i=0}^{i=n-1} y_i$, i.e., Y denotes the total size (in bits) of all retrieved segments in a service round. There exists a correlation between the segment size (RV's y_i) associated with the same user, but that associated with different users are independent and identically distributed. Since the total number of users in the system (k) is much larger than the maximum number of segments retrieved for any single user, we may again use the central limit theorem to approximate the distribution of Y by a Gaussian distribution. If η_1 and ${\sigma_1}^2$ denote the mean and variance of the segment size distribution, then the (Gaussian) distribution of Y has a mean of $\eta\prime \times \eta_1$ and a variance of $\eta\prime \times {\sigma_1}^2 + (\eta_1)^2 \times \sigma\prime^2$ [5].

Figure 5 depicts the cumulative distribution of X_k for two values of k. With $k = 650$, the average number of cells generated in a service round is nearly 159000. (The total number of available cell slots in the main buffer is 170000.) For illustration, we also consider an extreme case of $k = 1000$ users, where the average number of cells that need to be retrieved in a round is much larger than that which can be retrieved. The latter case would only affect the cell loss during disk retrieval but not that due to transfer to the main buffer. Figure 5(a) depicts the case with $k = 650$, while Figure 5(b) depicts the case with $k = 1000$. For the case with $k = 650$, the total number of required segment retrievals in a cycle varies between 650 (when all users have the slowest playback rate) and 5800 (when all users have the fastest playback rate); for the case with $k = 1000$, this value varies between 1000 and 9000.

Figure 6 depicts the cumulative distribution of Y for the two values of k. Figure 6(a) depicts the case with $k = 650$, while Figure 6(b) depicts the case with $k = 1000$. Using these figures, we can determine the probability that the total number of bits to be retrieved in a round exceeds a certain value. In other words, we can obtain statistical results for the probability of cell loss during disk retrieval.

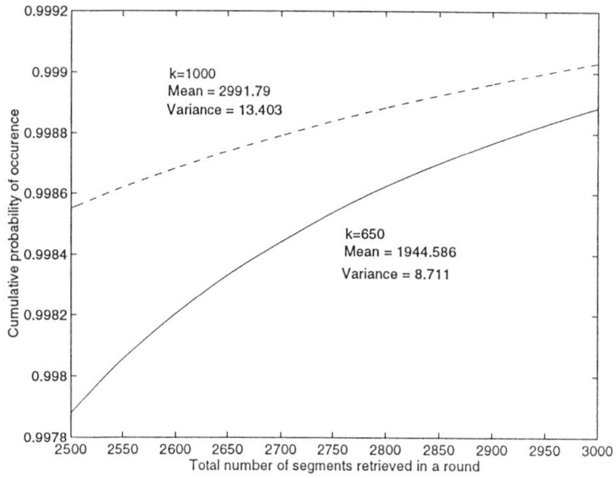

Figure 5: Distribution of total number of retrieved segments in a round for 650 (solid) and 1000 (dashed) users

5.4 Cell loss at buffer

Video segments stored in the staging buffer are transferred to the main buffer periodically. We consider the case where this transfer occurs ten times during a service round. Hence, the transfer occurs at times $i \times (T_c/10)$ from the start of the service round, where $i = \{1, 2, \cdots, 10\}$. This implies that the number of video segments that the staging buffer needs to store equals that retrieved within a time duration of $T_c/10$. As seen earlier, the value of T_c chosen was $100 \times n_f$ ms since $r_0 = 10$ fps. With 650 users using the disk subsystem and $n_f = 2$, simulations were carried out to determine the cell loss due to unavailability of storage space in the main buffer.

Simulations carried out with the parameters described resulted in a cell loss of 9003 cells among 902121 cells that passed through the staging buffer in six rounds. The maximum number of cells that can be stored in the main buffer in six rounds equals 6 × 170000 = 1020000. Thus, the utilization of the main buffer was 88.44%, for which the cells dropped due to lack of space at the main buffer was 1%.

6 Conclusion

In this paper, we proposed a new buffer sharing architecture that may be used for an interactive VOD system. Early simulations carried out resulted in a cell loss during transfer to the main buffer of 1% when the buffer was 88.44% utilized. The operation of the main buffer results in an efficient use of the buffer and in a low cell loss. Sta-

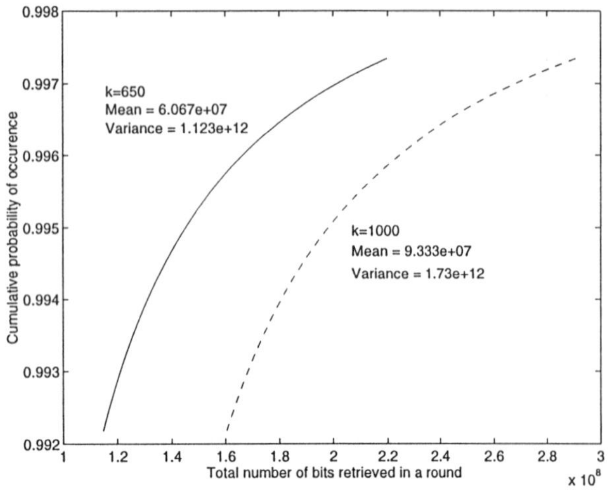

Figure 6: Distribution of total number of retrieved bits in a round for 650 (solid) and 1000 (dashed) users

tistical results for the cell loss during disk retrieval were presented. Since the interactive latency depends on the duration of the service round which depends on the size of retrieved segments, a new scheme for grouping frames into segments was used.

We are currently working on several issues that affect the system performance, some of which are :

1. For the same main buffer space (mr^2), the choice of the number of modules (m) and the dimension of each module (r) affects the nature in which empty slots are created in the buffer. The effect of a variation of these parameters on the cell loss needs to be modelled.
2. The option of not channeling some retrieved segments through the staging buffer could result in a smaller cell loss. For instance, at the start of the round, retrieved segments can be directed to the staging buffer until it is full. Any segments retrieved from this point onwards can be sent directly to the appropriate locations in the main buffer. At the end of the round, the contents of the staging buffer can be transferred to the main buffer using the N-EDF algorithm.
3. The retrieval scheme used in this paper was a quasi-static one where all user interactions take effect only at the start of service rounds. A dynamic retrieval scheme where the effect of a user interaction takes effect earlier may be desirable as it would decrease startup/interactive latencies.

We shall provide comprehensive results on these issues shortly.

References

[1] A.L.N.Reddy and James C. Wyllie. "I/O Issues in a Multimedia System". *IEEE Computer*, pages 69–74, March 1994.

[2] Ming-Syan Chen, Dilip D. Kandlur, and Philip S. Yu. "Optimization of the grouped sweeping scheduling (GSS) with heterogeneous multimedia streams". *Proceedings of the ACM International Conference on Multimedia*, pages 235–242, 1993.

[3] Ming-Syan Chen, Dilip D. Kandlur, and Philip S. Yu. "Storage and Retrieval Methods to support fully interactive playout in a disk-array-based video server". *Multimedia Systems*, 3:126–135, 1995.

[4] Shyamala Chowdhury and Kazem Sohraby. "Alternative Bandwidth Allocation Algorithms for Packet Video in ATM Networks". *IEEE INFOCOM*, pages 1061–1068, 1992.

[5] Alvin W. Drake. "Fundamentals of Applied Probability Theory". *McGraw Hill Book Company*, pages 109–112, 1967.

[6] Mark W. Garrett and Walter Willinger. "Analysis, Modeling and Generation of Self-Similar VBR Video Traffic". *SIGCOMM*, pages 269–280, 1994.

[7] Dwight J. Makaroff and Raymond T. Ng. "Schemes for Implementing Buffer Sharing in Continuous-Media Systems". *Information Systems*, 20(6):445–464, 1995.

[8] Pramod Pancha and Magda El Zarki. "MPEG Coding for Variable Bit Rate Video Transmission". *IEEE Communications Magazine*, pages 54–66, May 1994.

[9] Senthil Sengodan and Victor O.K. Li. "A Quasi-static Retrieval Scheme for Interactive Disk-Array Based Video Servers". *ICCCN*, pages 3–8, October 1996.

[10] Senthil Sengodan and Victor O.K. Li. "A Discard-Free Grouping and Retrieval Scheme for Stored MPEG Video". *IEEE ICC*, 1997. Submitted.

[11] T.L.Kunii, Y.Shinagawa, R.M.Paul, M.F.Khan, and A.A.Khokar. "Issues in Storage and Retrieval of Multimedia Data". *Multimedia Systems*, 3:298–304, 1995.

The Split and Merge (SAM) Protocol for Interactive Video-on-Demand Systems*

Wanjiun Liao and Victor O. K. Li†

Communication Sciences Institute
Department of Electrical Engineering
University of Southern California
Los Angeles, CA 90089-2565, USA

Abstract

A true Video-on-Demand (VOD) system provides the ultimate flexibility in video services by allowing users to select any video programs, at any time, and to perform any VCR-like user interactions. To allow true VOD, one approach is to have a dedicated video stream for each customer. This is expensive, especially when multiple identical video streams are sent to multiple customers accessing the same video. To be commercially viable, VOD service must be priced competitively with existing video rental services. Batching may be used to reduce this cost. It allows multiple users accessing the same video to share the same video stream. The batching approach, however, complicates the provision of user interactions. Existing batching schemes only allow near VOD services. This paper describes a new protocol, called Split and Merge (SAM), which offers true VOD services while allowing multiple users to share the same video stream. This sharing is transparent to the users and it appears as if each has a dedicated video stream. Our approach is to split an interactive user from the batch and to serve him with a dedicated video stream. We develop an innovative way to merge these individuals back to the batching streams when they resume normal play mode. The SAM protocol therefore significantly improves the system resource utilization and the number of simultaneous users, and more importantly, allows true VOD services.

1 Introduction

Video-on-Demand (VOD) combines the TV with information retrieval technology to provide electronic video rental services over the broadband network [7]. A VOD system contains many components, including the video server, the transport network, and the set-top box. Fig. 1 shows the typical architecture of a VOD system. For a more detailed description of the individual components, the reader is referred to [7].

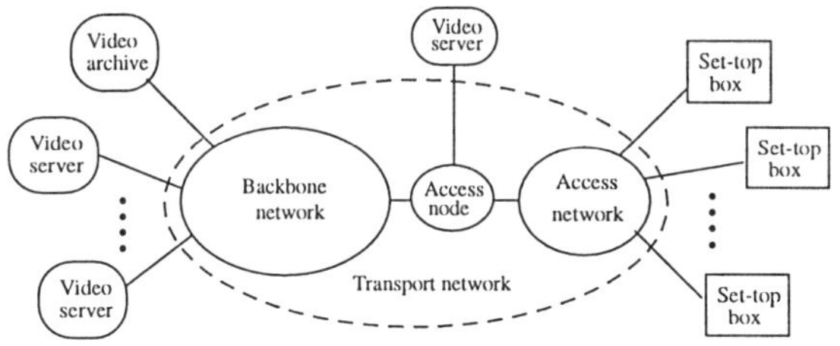

Figure 1: VOD system architecture.

In true VOD, customers are allowed to select the programs they wish, view at the time they wish, and interact with the programs via VCR-like functions, such as fast-forward, rewind, etc. [3, 4, 8, 10, 11]. A VOD system which does not satisfy all of the above requirements is called quasi-VOD or near VOD. To be competitive with existing video rental services, true VOD is desired. In fact, most existing VOD field trials [9] do provide true VOD. To allow true VOD, one solution is to have a dedicated video stream [1] for each customer. This is expensive since each stream requires high-speed [2] data transport, especially when multiple identical video streams are sent to multiple customers accessing the same video. To be commercially viable, VOD service must be priced competitively with existing video rental services. To reduce the per-user video

*This research is supported in part by the Pacific Bell External Technology Program.

†Corresponding author: vli@usc.edu, phone: (+1) 213-740-4665, and fax: (+1) 213-740-8729.

[1] A video stream will typically consist of video segments, retrieved by a read-write head from the video server, transported over a high speed network, and delivered to the set-top boxes at the customer premises.

[2] For example, existing VOD field trials typically deliver MPEG-1 or MPEG-2 compressed video, requiring 1.5 Mbps and 3 Mbps, respectively.

0-8186-7780-5/97 $10.00 © 1997 IEEE

delivery cost, batching may be used. In a batching operation, the same video stream will be multicasted to, and shared by, multiple users accessing the same video. The goal is to make this sharing transparent to the users, while allowing true user interactivity. Existing solutions fail to achieve this goal. In staggered VOD [2], for example, multiple copies (streams) of the same video program will be broadcasted, staggered in times. A user will be served by one of the streams, and user interactions are simulated by jumping to a different stream. However, not all user interactions can be simulated in this fashion, and even for those that can be simulated, the effect is limited by the staggering interval. Yu et al.[12] developed a look ahead scheduling with set-aside buffer which attempts to take advantage of batching, but only supports the interactive operation of pause and resume. Almeroth and Ammar [1] used the set-top box buffer to provide limited interactive functions, utilizing staggered streams. We would like to allow the full spectrum of user interactions. In [6], user interactions are handled by creating a new stream for each interactive user, who will hold on to this stream until disconnection. This will work only if very few users are expected to issue interactive operations. Otherwise, the system may start in a batch mode, but will degrade to a non-sharing mode as more and more users split off into their own streams. In this paper, we describe a new protocol, called Split and Merge (SAM) which allows the sharing of a video stream to be transparent to the users, while allowing true user interactivity. While user interactions are initially handled by splitting off the interactive user to a new stream in our protocol, we develop an innovative way in SAM to merge these individuals back to the batching streams. The SAM protocol therefore significantly improves the system resource utilization and the number of simultaneous users, and more importantly, allows true VOD services.

SAM may be implemented in various network infrastructures, including telephone, cable TV, direct broadcast satellite, wireless cable, local area networks, and on the Internet. For this paper, it suffices to say that we assume a generic network protocol running on a generic network infrastructure. The network protocol must support multicasting operations. In addition, some buffering, typically located at the access node, is available to be shared by all users for synchronization purposes. The rest of this paper is organized as follows. Section 2 presents the basic SAM protocol in detail. Variations of the basic scheme are presented in Section 3. Numerical results are shown in Section 4. Finally, we conclude in Section 5.

2 The Split and Merge (SAM) protocol

The goal of SAM is to reduce the per-user video delivery cost, or, alternatively, increase the number of users who can be served with given system resources, while providing true VOD services.

Since user interactions typically last a short time compared to normal play, we divide the video streams in the system into:

1. Service stream (**S** stream): such streams are used to serve the users during normal playback. It is typically a multicast stream and will serve multiple users simultaneously.

2. Interaction stream (**I** stream): such streams are used to satisfy some of the users' requests for VCR-like user interactions. An **I** stream is used by one user.

The fundamental principles of our proposed SAM protocol are as follows:

1. SAM fulfills true VOD services, while taking full advantage of batching. Originally, a number of users are batched and served by an **S** stream. Each of the batched users may initiate user interactions. As soon as a user interaction is admitted, this user will be split out of the original **S** stream, and temporarily allocated to an **I** stream to perform interaction. Once the user interaction is done, the user will be merged back to an on-going **S** stream[3]. Such split-and-merge operations are repeated, whenever a user interaction is initiated, until the original **S** stream terminates.

2. A user request for VOD service may be blocked if all **S** streams are occupied. Once the request has been admitted, however, any further user interactions will not be blocked, even if all system resources are busy, but will be allowed to wait until the resource is available. During the wait, a user continues normal playback, and switches to the user interaction mode as soon as resources are available.

3. SAM is an adaptive protocol. As demand for a particular video increases, more **S** streams will be generated in the system for that video. As demand wanes, less **S** streams will be generated. Although SAM works in any scenario, it works most efficiently for popular video.

[3]For the pause operation, no **I** stream is required and the user will be merged to an **S** stream as soon as the user resumes.

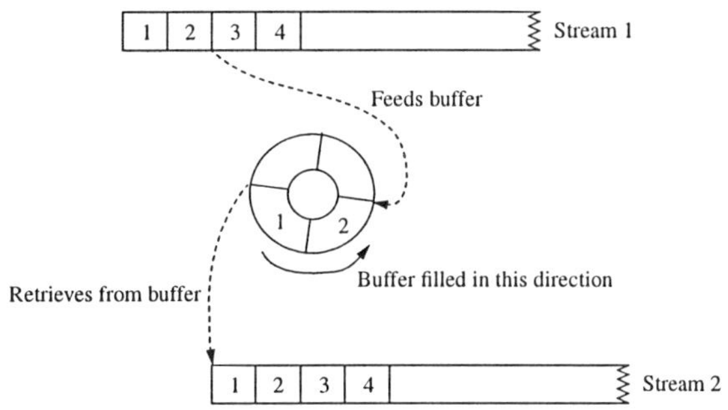

Figure 2: Illustration of how the synch buffer synchronizes two streams.

The *synch buffer*, located at the access nodes, and shared by all the users, is an important component of SAM. Each time a user resumes normal play after a user interaction, he requires a video stream (of the same video) which may be offset in time from his original **S** stream. For example, if he jumps forward by seven minutes, he needs a video stream which starts seven minutes before his original **S** stream. Since no such real stream may exist, SAM attempts to create a virtual one by utilizing one of the on-going **S** streams and the synch buffer. First we identify the closest on-going **S** stream, i.e., that with the smallest offset in time from the virtual stream. This real **S** stream feeds the synch buffer, and the virtual stream retrieves from the synch buffer, after the required time offset. Each user is dynamically allocated a synch buffer of size up to $SB \times R_p$, where SB is the maximum duration of video which can be stored for a user, and R_p is the playback rate of the stream. It is a circular buffer. Each circular buffer has two operation ends: one for putting in video contents and the other for taking them out. Fig. 2 illustrates how the synch buffer synchronizes two streams. Stream 1 (the real stream) is ahead of stream 2 (the virtual stream created). To help explain the operation, we have broken down the streams into segments[4], and labeled them 1, 2, ... Thus, stream 1 is 2 segments ahead of stream 2. Stream 1 will feed the synch buffer at one end, and stream 2 will retrieve buffer contents from the other end. Here, we show the contents of the buffer as stream 2 starts to retrieve the first segment from the buffer.

There are a number of videos available in the system. Suppose a request for a video, say video i, arrives. If there is already a batch being formed for video

[4]Note that these segments are artificial and are used to help us explain the concept. They are just equal sized pieces of the video

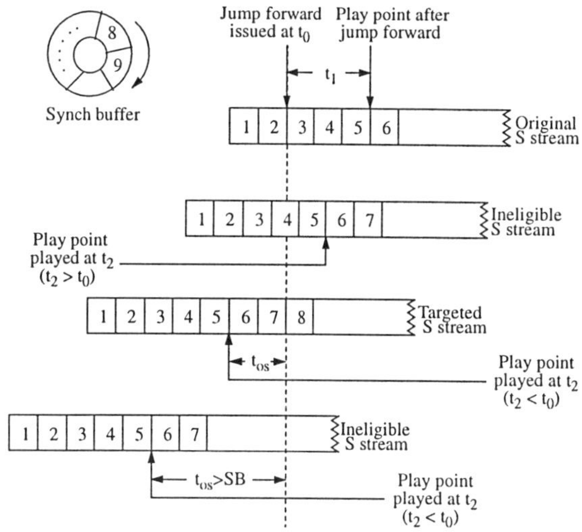

Figure 3: Illustration of the operation of jump forward.

i, this request will join the batch and wait for the end of the batching interval, at which time an **S** stream will be initiated to serve the batch; otherwise, the new request has to form a new batch. It will request an **S** stream from the pool of available **S** streams, and start a timer of duration W_i, the batching interval. If no **S** stream is available, the request will be blocked. The user may then try again later, or may just decide not to watch the video. If an **S** stream is available, it will be reserved, and after the batching interval W_i, an **S** stream will be initiated to serve this user, plus all other requests for video i which have arrived during the batching interval. Thus, after a user request is accepted, the maximum waiting time is W_i. The actual value of W_i is a system design parameter, corresponding to the maximum tolerable waiting time before a user reneges from the system. Note that each batch is initiated on-demand, rather than by periodical broadcasting, as in staggered VOD.

SAM allows users to interact with video programs via VCR-like functions including play, stop, pause, resume, fast-forward (FF), rewind (REW), jump-forward, and jump-backward. The jump operations allows the user to jump directly to a particular video location. Although not supported in current VCR machines, such random access operations, together with FF and REW, are expected to provide the most desirable search mechanism for digital video services. We will now describe how SAM supports these interactive operations.

2.1 Jump forward and jump backward

In the following, we focus on jump forward. Jump backward is handled in a similar fashion. First we determine if there is an *eligible* **S** *stream*. The concept of an eligible **S** stream is best explained by a figure. In Fig. 3, the user accessing video i is being served by the stream labeled original **S** stream. At time t_o, he issues a jump forward operation. Suppose the user jumps to a point in the video which is t_1 s in the future[5]. In Fig. 3, this corresponds to the beginning of segment 6. This is known as the *play point*, which is the location of the video at which the user will resume normal play after the user interaction. We look at all on-going **S** streams for video i and see if there is an eligible one for this user to merge into. An **S** stream is eligible if its corresponding play point (the beginning of segment 6 in this example) is before t_o, but not more than SB before, where SB is the maximum duration of video which may be stored in the synch buffer. SB is assumed to be four segments in this example. Thus in Fig. 3, the second **S** stream is ineligible because it has not reached the play point yet, while the last **S** stream is ineligible because it is more than SB segments offset in time from the virtual stream created by the jump, and the synch buffer is not large enough to synchronize to it. The stream labeled targeted **S** stream is eligible. If there are multiple eligible **S** streams, the user will merge with the one whose offset t_{os} with the virtual stream is the smallest. (This minimizes synch buffer usage.) Denote the time instant the play point in the targeted **S** stream is played by t_2. The offset t_{os} is defined as $t_{os} = t_o - t_2$.

Once a targeted **S** stream has been identified, we will find an **I** stream, and split the user from the existing batch. If no **I** stream is available, the request will join a FCFS queue. In the meantime, normal play continues from the original **S** stream. During the wait, the targeted eligible **S** stream may become ineligible, in which case we need to search for another eligible one. The **I** stream will be used for normal play for a duration equal to the time offset t_{os}. In the meantime, a connection will be made to the targeted **S** stream, which will feed the synch buffer. After the synch buffer has been fed for a period equal to t_{os}, corresponding to segments 8 and 9 in our example, the user will start to retrieve the video from the synch buffer, and release the **I** stream. In other words, the user has successfully merged with the **S** stream. If there is no eligible **S** stream to merge into, a new **S** stream will be initiated to serve this user. If there is no available **S** stream, the request will join a FCFS queue to wait for the first available **S** stream. In the meantime, normal play continues from the original **S** stream.

[5] If t_1 is too large, and carries the user beyond the end of the video, we will jump the user to the end of the video.

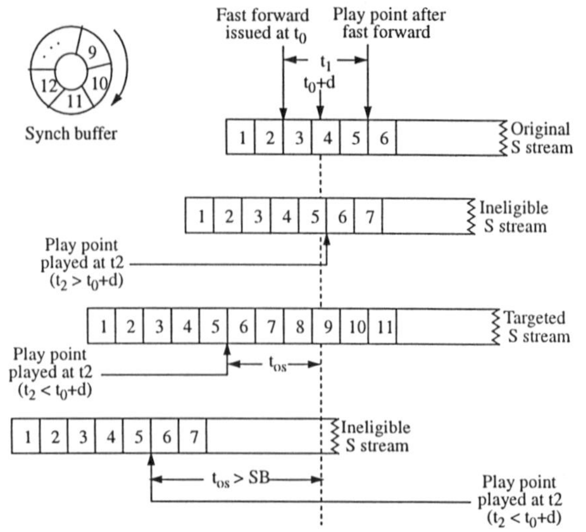

Figure 4: Illustration of the operation of fast forward.

The above assumes that the user was fed by an **S** stream directly. Suppose the user is being served by the synch buffer fed by an **S** stream, i.e., the user has issued an interactive operation earlier, how does the operation of jump forward change? Fortunately, it does not. Again, we need to identify the play point after the jump forward operation (beginning of segment 6 in this example), and the time the jump forward is issued (t_o in this example). We then try to merge with an existing **S** stream. The criteria for selecting this targeted **S** stream is the same as before. The only differences are that when we are waiting for an I or **S** stream, we will continue normal play from the buffer, fed by the original **S** stream, and when we have successfully merged with the targeted **S** stream, the connection to the original **S** stream is torn down, and everything in the buffer corresponding to the old **S** stream is discarded. In addition, if the jump forward is to a point in the video already in the buffer, we can avoid the split and merge operation altogether.

The operation of jump backward is similar, except the eligible **S** streams will have negative offsets.

2.2 Fast forward and rewind

Again each user is allocated a synch buffer of maximum size SB, assumed to be four in this example. Suppose the user accessing video i is being served by the stream labeled original **S** stream in the figure. At time t_o, he issued a fast forward operation.

An **I** stream is requested to serve the user. If one is available, video will be delivered in fast forward mode; otherwise, the request for an **I** stream joins a FCFS queue. In the meantime, normal play continues. After a duration d, the user terminates the fast forward operation, and resumes normal play. SAM will attempt to merge him back to one of the on-going **S** streams. Suppose the fast forward operation takes the user to a point t_1 beyond the initialization of the fast forward, i.e , the beginning of segment 6 in our example. We look at all on-going **S** streams for video i and see if there is an eligible one for this user to merge into. An **S** stream is eligible if its corresponding play point (the beginning of segment 6 in this example) is before $t_o + d$, but not more than SB before. Thus in Fig. 4, the second and the last **S** streams are ineligible. If there is no eligible **S** stream to merge into, a new **S** stream will be initiated to serve the user. If there is no available **S** stream in the system, the request will join a FCFS queue to wait for the first available **S** stream. In the meantime, normal play continues on the **I** stream. If there is at least one eligible **S** stream, the user will merge with the eligible **S** stream whose offset $t_{os} = t_o + d - t_2$ is the smallest. The **I** stream held by the user will continue to serve the user starting at the play point in normal play mode. In the meantime, the targeted **S** stream will feed the synch buffer. After the synch buffer has been fed for a period equal to t_{os}, corresponding to the segments 9 (last half), 10, 11, and 12 (first half) in our example, the user will start to retrieve the video from the synch buffer, and release the **I** stream. In other words, the user has successfully merged with the **S** stream.

As in jump forward, if the user is originally served by the synch buffer fed by an **S** stream, the operation of SAM remains pretty much the same.

The operation of rewind is similar, except the eligible **S** streams will have negative offsets.

2.3 Pause and resume

Again, each user is allocated a synch buffer of maximum size SB, assumed to be four in our discussion. Suppose the user accessing video i is being served the original **S** stream in Fig. 5. As soon as the pause is issued, the synch buffer is fed by the original **S** stream. After the pause operation, the only eligible **S** streams that the user may merge into must have started later than the original stream. Suppose the earliest of these eligible streams, labeled targeted **S** stream in the figure, starts a duration t later. This is the **S** stream that the user will try to merge into. We distinguish between two major cases. Case 1 occurs when $t \leq SB$, and case 2 occurs when $t > SB$. Case 1 (shown in Fig.

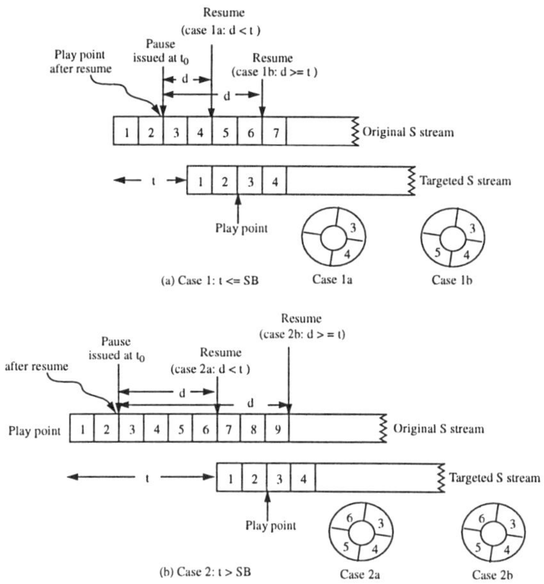

Figure 5: Illustration of the operation of pause.

5(a)) can be further divided into subcases 1a and 1b. In case 1a, the pause period $d < t$. Since $d < t \leq SB$, the synch buffer is not yet full when the user resumes (in fact, it will contain segments 3 and 4 in this example), and he can just retrieve the video from the synch buffer. In case 1b, $d \geq t$, that is, the corresponding play point (the start of segment 3 in this example) of the closest eligible stream (the targeted **S** stream) will be played before the pause operation terminates. In the figure, since t corresponds to 3 segments, the corresponding play point will arrive after 3 segments of the original **S** stream, namely, segments 3, 4, and 5, have been stored. The user is merged (switched) to the new stream, i.e., the synch buffer will be fed by the targeted **S** stream starting at the play point. Case 2 (shown in Fig. 5(b)) can be further divided into subcases 2a and 2b. If the buffer is filled before the pause terminates, we have Case 2. A new **S** stream may have to be initiated, depending on whether the pause terminates before or after an ongoing **S** stream has reached the play point. As soon as the buffer is filled, a reservation request is made for a new **S** stream, the contents are purged from the synch buffer, and the user is split from the original **S** stream. In case 2a, the pause terminates before an ongoing **S** stream has reached the play point, a new **S** stream (the one we have reserved earlier) will be initiated to serve the user; otherwise, we have case 2b. It is possible that no **S** streams are available in the system, and the user will then join a FCFS queue to wait for the

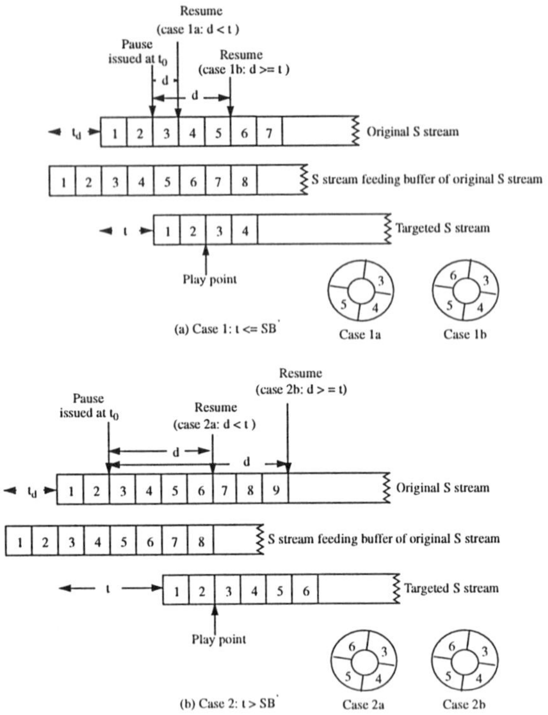

Figure 6: Illustration of the operation of pause when the user is operating from the synch buffer.

next available **S** stream, or to wait until an ongoing **S** stream has reached the play point, at which time he can merge with this ongoing stream. In case 2b, the corresponding play point (the start of segment 3 in this example) of the closest eligible stream will be played before the pause operation terminates. In the figure, since t corresponds to 6 segments, the corresponding play point will arrive after 6 segments of the original stream have arrived. Since the buffer is of size 4, it can only store four of them, namely, segments 3, 4, 5, and 6. The reserved **S** stream is released, the user is merged (switched) to the new stream as soon as the synch buffer is full, and the synch buffer is now fed by the new stream, starting at the play point.

In cases 1b and 2b, since the user is still in the pause mode after he is switched to the targeted ongoing **S** stream, the above procedure has to be repeated, perhaps multiple times, until he terminates the pause operation.

The above assumes that the user is fed by an **S** stream directly. We now study the situation in which the user is being served by the synch buffer fed by an **S** stream, i.e., the user has issued an interactive operation earlier. Fig. 6 illustrates how SAM handles pause and resume in this situation. Again, each user is assumed to be allocated a synch buffer of size four in this example. Suppose the user accessing video i is being served by the original **S** stream in Fig. 5. Note that this is a virtual **S** stream, and is fed by an ongoing **S** stream which has started two segments earlier. In other words, two segments of the synch buffer have already been taken up in order to synch to this feeding **S** stream, leaving only two segments available. This is the only difference between how SAM handles the pause operation when the user is fed directly, or via a synch buffer. Note that the synch buffer size is now $SB' = SB - t_d$, where t_d is the lead time of the feeding **S** stream compared to the original **S** stream. In addition, t, the time until the nearest eligible ongoing **S** stream, is calculated from the original **S** stream, not the feeding **S** stream. Since t_d is 2 in our example, $SB' = 2$. t is 2. The operation is the same as when the user is fed by a real **S** stream. The only difference is the size of the synch buffer shall be SB' instead of SB. In addition, once a user switched to a new stream (case 1b and case 2b), he can discard the existing contents in the synch buffer, effectively augmenting his synch buffer to the maximum value of SB again.

3 Variations of the basic scheme

The following describes variations of the basic SAM protocol:

1. No initial batching delay – As soon as a video request is received, determine if there are eligible **S** streams. If there is, serve this request with an **I** stream while feeding synch buffer with the ongoing **S** stream for an interval equal to the offset. After the offset, merge into the on-going stream for this video. Otherwise, initiate a new **S** stream to serve this request.

2. Adjustable batching intervals – Batching interval may be different for different videos, due to differences in popularity. More popular ones should have shorter batching interval. In addition, since popularity may change over time, we can periodically change the batching interval, based on observed video request rate in the previous period.

3. A variation of basic batching idea – Instead of initiating a timer when the first request in a batch arrives, we divide time into fixed length intervals, say every five minutes. If at least one request for video i arrives during an interval, initiate an **S** stream. This has the advantage that, for popular videos, average wait is equal to half of the

batching interval, instead of the batching interval. These will be not much difference for popular ones.

4. A synch buffer may have one input stream, but multiple output streams, serving different users with different time offsets. This saves buffering.

5. We can use a pricing mechanism to control the amount of user interactivity. The more the user is willing to pay, the closer he gets to true VOD service. At the high end, no initial batching delay, and full user interactivity is allowed; then, initial batching delay, full interactivity. Finally, for the least cost, initial batching delay, limited interactivity.

4 Numerical Results

In this section, we present some simulation results. The results are generated by a C program running on a HP C160. 24 hours of real time are simulated, requiring on the average 30 minutes of CPU time for each arrival rate. The following system parameters are used. There are 30 available videos, each lasting 120 minutes. The probability a particular movie is accessed, p_i, $i = 1, 2, \ldots, 30$, is assumed to follow the Zipf distribution [5]. Therefore, video 1 is the most popular, followed by video 2, etc. We also assume the following user activity model. A user starts in the normal play mode, and will stay there for an exponential amount of time with mean 30 minutes, then he goes to the interaction mode with probability 0.75, and he quits with probability 0.25. In the interaction mode, he is equally likely to issue a jump forward, jump backward, fast forward, rewind, or pause operation. Each pause is exponentially distributed with a mean of 5 minutes. Each fast forward/rewind is exponentially distributed with a mean of 0.5 minutes, i.e., the user will be holding down the fast forward or rewind button for an average of 0.5 minutes. Fast forward and rewind will take the user to a point in the video which is offset from the original point by an interval uniformly distributed between 1 and 90 seconds. Each jump operation lasts one second, and will take the user to a point in the video which is offset from the original point by an interval uniformly distributed between 1 and 1000 seconds. After a user interaction, the user resumes normal play mode. This is repeated until the user quits.

The total number of video streams is 515. The batching interval used is 10 minutes, and the maximum synch buffer allocated per user varies from one to ten minutes. Fig. 7 shows how the blocking probability changes as the video request rate increases for the

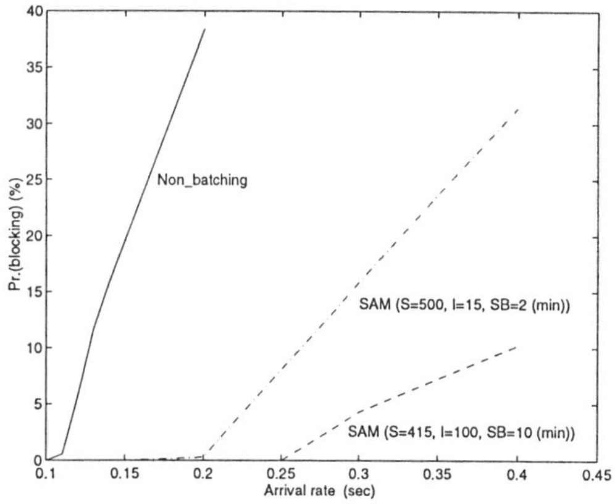

Figure 7: Blocking probability for the cases of batching and no batching.

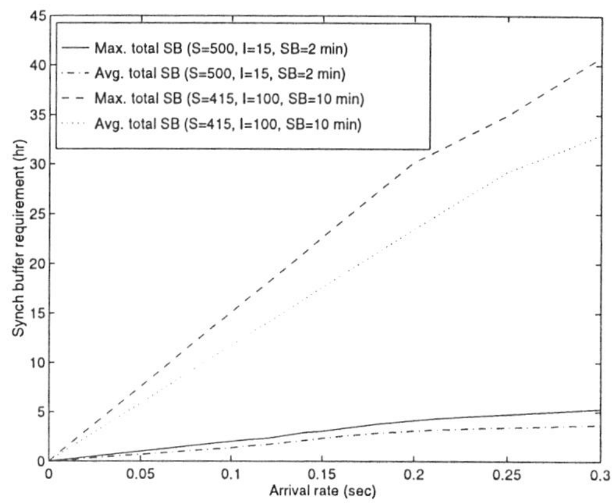

Figure 8: The average amount of synch buffer required as a function of arrival rates.

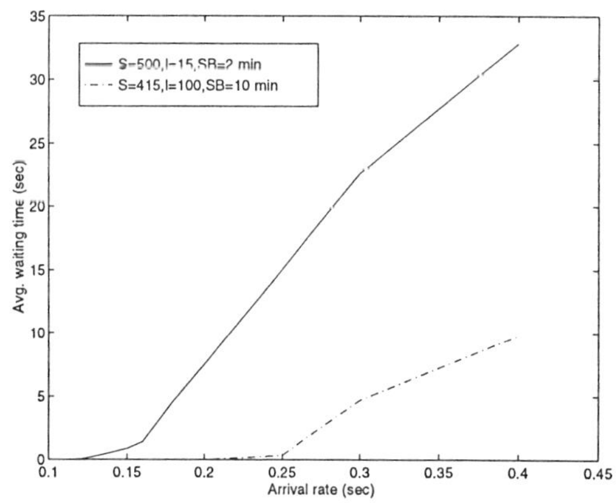

Figure 9: Average interaction delay as a function of arrival rates.

cases of batching (SAM) and non-batching (point-to-point connection for each user). As expected, there is a large reduction in the blocking probability with SAM[6]. The price we pay is the initial batching delay, which is bounded by 10 minutes, and averages 5 minutes. In addition, we require a synch buffer and the user may experience some interaction delay. Fig. 8 shows the average total synch buffer required in the system as a function of arrival rate. Note that this translates into very small per-user synch buffer requirements. For example, the buffer required is 13.2 seconds per user when the arrival rate is 0.3 requests per second, for $S=500$, $I=15$, and $SB=2$ minutes. Fig. 9 shows the average interaction delay, which is acceptable except for a highly loaded situation. (To ensure that the blocking probability is small, we will not operate the system at such high load anyway.) This leads us to conclude that our proposed SAM protocol is an excellent candidate to be used in VOD systems.

5 Conclusions

VOD is expected to be the most important commercial application of distributed multimedia systems. It provides an electronic video rental service, which gives the users the ultimate flexibility in selecting any video programs, at any time, and in performing any VCR-like user interactions. However, to be commercially successful, VOD must be priced competitively compared with existing video rental services. It is estimated that approximately half of the video rental revenues go to the program providers. That means the other half will go towards the cost of delivering the video, and for the profits of the service provider. In existing video rental stores, the major cost of the delivery is borne by the users, and the only costs incurred by the service provider is shelf space. For VOD, the costs of video delivery include the costs of the high capacity video server, and the high speed network, both of which are substantial. Our proposed protocol allows multiple users to share the same video stream, thereby dramatically increasing the capacity of the system, and greatly reducing the costs per user. At the same time, the price to be paid, i.e., batching delay, interaction delay, etc. are tolerable. This leads us to conclude that our proposed SAM protocol is an excellent candidate to be deployed in interactive VOD systems.

[6] Actually, the improvement for popular videos is much more dramatic than that indicated in the figure, which shows the reduction in blocking probabilities averaged over all videos, including both popular and unpopular ones.

References

[1] K. C. Almeroth and M. H. Ammar. The use of multicast delivery to provide a scalable and interactive video-on-demand service. *IEEE Journal On Selected Areas in Communications*, 14(6):1110–1122, August 1996.

[2] Robert O. Banker et al. Method of providing video on demand with VCR like functions. In *U.S. Patent 5,357,276*, 1994.

[3] Y. H. Chang et al. An open-systems approach to video on demand. *IEEE Communications Magazine*, 32(5):68–80, May 1994.

[4] D. Deloddere, W. Verbiest, and H. Verhille. Interactive video on demand. *IEEE Communications Magazine*, 32(5):82–88, May 1994.

[5] D. Knuth. *The art of computer programming, Vol 3: Sorting and searching.* Addison-Wesley, 1973.

[6] V. O. K. Li et al. Performance model of interactive video-on-demand systems. *IEEE Journal On Selected Areas in Communications*, 14(6):1099–1109, August 1996.

[7] V. O. K. Li and W. J. Liao. Distributed multimedia systems. *Report No. CSI-96-05-01, Communication Sciences Institute, University of Southern California*, May 1996. (Submitted for publication).

[8] T. D. C. Little and D. Venkatesh. Prospects for interactive video-on-demand. *IEEE Multimedia*, pages 14–24, Spring 1994.

[9] T. S. Perry. The trials and travails of interactive TV. *IEEE Spectrum*, pages 22–28, April 1996.

[10] W. D. Sincoskie. System architecture for a large scale video on demand service. *Computer Networks and ISDN Systems*, 22:155–162, 1991.

[11] J. Sutherland and L. Litteral. Residential video services. *IEEE Communications Magazine*, pages 36–41, 1992.

[12] P. S. Yu, J. L. Wolf, and H. Shachnai. Design and analysis of a look-ahead scheduling scheme to support pause-resume for video-on-demand application. *Multimedia Systems*, 3(4):137–150, 1995.

BiHOP: A *Bi*directional *H*ighly *O*ptimized *P*ipelining Technique for Large-Scale Multimedia Servers

Kien A. Hua *James Z. Wang* *Simon Sheu*

Department of Computer Science
University of Central Florida
Orlando, FL 32816-0362, U. S. A.
{kienhua, zwang, sheu}@cs.ucf.edu

Abstract

We present a technique, called Bidirectional Highly Optimized Pipelining *(BiHOP), for managing disks as a buffer for the tertiary storage of a multimedia server. We implement a simulator to compare its performance to that of a recently proposed scheme called SEP. The results show that BiHOP performs significantly better. Its superior performance is attributed to a novel caching approach which caches every other data fragment of the multimedia file, rather than caches consecutive fragments as in traditional practice. This new approach allows us to use tiny staging buffers for pipelining, which can be implemented in the memory to conserve disk bandwidth. Furthermore, the whole disk space can be dedicated for caching purposes to improve hit ratio. Another important advantage of BiHOP is its ability to pipeline in either forward or reverse direction with the same efficiency. This unique feature, not possible with existing schemes, makes it natural for implementing VCR functions.*

1. Introduction

The high storage cost of video files is a major concern for many potential multimedia applications. Even with the most sophisticated compression, video has a voracious appetite for storage. For example, to compress a 30-second ad with MPEG-2 running at 4 megabits per second. we would need 15 MBytes, and a 100-minute movie would take 3 GByte. One way to reduce the storage costs is to organize the storage subsystem as a hierarchy, in which the magnetic disks are used as a cache for the tertiary storage devices (e.g., optical disk arrays).

When a cache miss occurs in a hierarchical storage subsystem, the simplest way to deal with this is to materialize the whole object onto the disk before sending it to the display station. This approach, however, will result in unacceptable latencies. A pipelining technique, called PIRATE, was proposed in [4] by Ghandeharizadeh and Shahabi to address this problem. In their scheme, a video file X is divided into a sequence of slices $(X_0, X_1, \cdots, X_{n-1}, X_n)$ such that the display time of X_{i-1} eclipses the time required to *materialize* X_i (i.e., loading X_i into disk), where $1 \leq i \leq n$. This strategy ensures a continuous display while reducing the latency time because the system can initiate the display of an object as soon as a fraction of the object (i.e., X_0) is disk resident. In this paper, X_0 is referred to as the *HEAD*, and the following slices (i.e., $X_1, \cdots, X_{n-1}, X_n$) are collectively referred to as the *TAIL* of the object. A drawback of this scheme is that sufficient disk space large enough to contain the entire video file must be reserved before the pipelining mechanism can take place. Waiting for the availability of such a large disk space can lengthen the access latency. The demand for the large buffer space will also flush out many potentially useful data.

To address the afordmentioned issues, SEP (*Space Efficient Pipelining*), proposed by Wang, Hua and Young in [8], pipelines the slices in the TAIL through a staging buffer equal the size of X_1. As soon as the pipelining is completed, the space occupied by this buffer is immediately returned to the buffer pool. To further improve the performance, three additional features were used in SEP [8]: *buffer shrinking*, *space stealing* and *object pinning*. Although we showed in [8] that SEP significantly improved the long latency times of PIRATE, its space requirement is still very significant. Another disadvantage of this scheme is that pipelining can only be done in the forward direction. This drawback makes it unsuitable for implementing VCR functions.

In this paper, we propose a different pipelining approach, called BiHOP (*Bidirectional Highly Optimized Pipelining*). Our design is motivated by the following two factors:

0-8186-7780-5/97 $10.00 © 1997 IEEE

1. Reducing Pipelining Cost: The admission cost for a request under SEP is still quite expensive. Even when the HEAD of an object is already disk resident, it needs to reserve a staging buffer about the size of the second slice of the object before pipelining can take place. We should be able to reduce this size to only a few disk blocks. If this goal is achieved, we will be able to free up a lot of disk space to support a larger number of concurrent users; the lower admission costs will also help to reduce the access latencies.

2. Supporting VCR functions: It is highly desirable to provide common VCR functions such as *fast-forward* and *fast-reverse*. These features are not well supported by PIRATE or SEP. We need to design a bidirectional pipelining strategy. Such a symmetric approach will allow the user to scan in either direction with the same efficiency. Preferably, the caching strategy can effectively support fast-forward and fast-reverse without having to involve the tertiary devices because their bandwidths are very limited.

Thus our ambition is to address both the performance and functionality issues. Both of these objectives were achieved in BiHOP which is bidirectional in functionality and optimal in space utilization.

The remainder of this paper is organized as follows. BiHOP and its benefits are discussed in Section 2. In Section 3, we describe our simulation model. The results of the performance study are examined in Section 4. In Section 5, we focus on the implementation of VCR functions. Finally, we give the conclusions and discuss our future research in Section 6.

2. BiHOP Approach

We describe the pipelining strategy and data replacement policy used by BiHOP in the following subsections. Discussions on the VCR functions are deferred until Section 5.

2.1. Intelligent Pipelining

In BiHOP, we divide the whole object into two categories of fragments. One category is called *disk-resident fragment* (or D-fragment) and the other is called *tertiary-device-resident fragment* (or T-fragment). The D and T-fragments interleave the data file as illustrated in Figure 1. With this file organization, the pipelining is performed as follows. As the system displays the first D-fragment D_0, it materializes the next T-fragment T_1 from tertiary devices. For $i > 0$, it materializes T_{i+1} while displaying T_i and D_i. Obviously, to maintain the continuous display, The elapsed time of displaying D_0 should be equal to the elapsed time of materializing T_1; and the elapsed time of displaying T_i

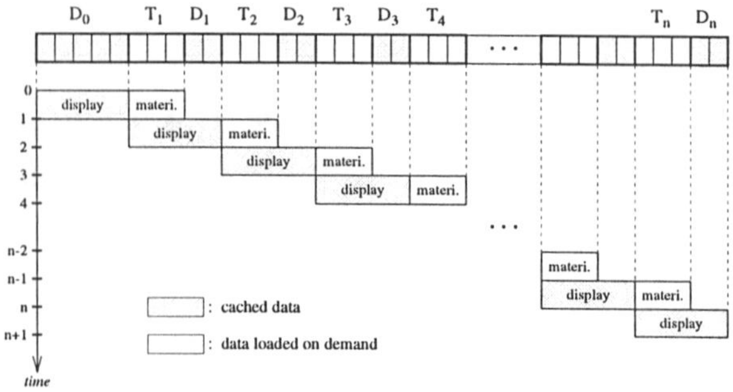

Figure 1. BiHOP pipelining technique.

and D_i should be equal to the elapsed time of materializing T_{i+1} for $i > 0$. Mathematically, we can express the above requirements as follows:

$$\frac{Size(T_1)}{B_M} = \frac{Size(D_0)}{B_D}, \quad and \tag{1}$$

$$\frac{Size(T_{i+1})}{B_M} = \frac{Size(T_i) + Size(D_i)}{B_D} \quad \text{for } i > 0, \tag{2}$$

where B_M and B_D denote the materialize rate of an object from tertiary devices to disks and the transfer rate of data from disks to a display station, respectively. We make the sizes of the fragments more uniform by letting $Size(T_i) = T$ and $Size(D_i) = D$ for $i > 0$; and $Size(D_0) = T + D$. Substituting the values T and D into Equation (2), we have:

$$\frac{T}{T+D} = \frac{B_M}{B_D} = PCR,$$

where PCR (*Production Consumption Rate*) is defined as the ratio of B_M to B_D. The size of the entire object X can then be computed in terms of T and D as follows:

$$Size(X) = (n+1) \cdot (T+D).$$

Let S_D and S_T represent the accumulative size of all the D-fragments and the accumulative size of all the T-fragments, respectively. S_D and S_T can be computed as follows:

$$S_D = \sum_{i=0}^{n} D_i = T + (n+1)D \qquad S_T = \sum_{i=1}^{n} T_i = nT.$$

If $T \ll Size(X)$, we have the following approximation:

$$\begin{aligned} S_D &\approx (1 - PCR) \cdot SIZE(X) \\ S_T &\approx PCR \cdot SIZE(X). \end{aligned} \tag{3}$$

The equations derived above serve as the foundation for the subsequent discussions.

We note that unlike the data fragments in PIRATE and SEP which are monotonously decreasing in size, there are only two types of fragments in BiHOP. Its regular design makes it possible to pipeline in either forward or reverse direction. We will discuss the implementation of VCR functions in details later.

2.2. Space Optimization

With the new pipelining scheme, we must load all the D-fragments into the disk system before the display can start. We note that the size of S_D is equal to the size of the HEAD (i.e., X_0) in PIRATE and SEP for a given file. In BiHOP, D-fragments (disk-resident fragments) are kept in the disk buffer for as long as possible. We will discuss the replacement policy in the next subsection. For the moment, let us focus on the space required by the staging buffers to retrieve the T-fragments from the tertiary devices.

There are two ways to implement the staging buffers:

Double Buffer: We maintain two buffers, one for reading and one for writing. While the data of fragment T_i is being transferred to the display station from one buffer (consumption buffer), the tertiary device writes T_{i+1} into another buffer (production buffer). These two buffers switch roles when the current consumption buffer is exhausted. Obviously, the size of these two buffers is T, and the total space required by this scheme is $2 \cdot T$.

Single Buffer: This approach uses a circular buffer shared by both the consumption and production procedures as illustrated in Figure 2. The space requirement for this approach is $T + 1$.

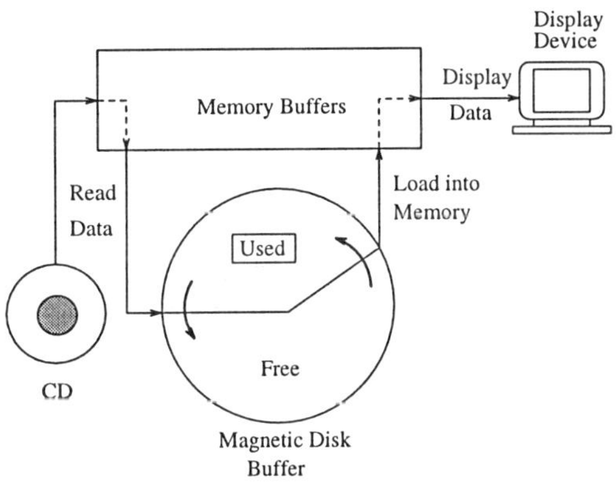

Figure 2. Circular staging buffer.

When either approach is used, we should minimize T to keep the size of the staging buffer minimal. Equation (2.1) is repeated below:

$$\frac{T}{T+D} = \frac{B_M}{B_D} = PCR < 1.$$

We can reduce the fraction $\frac{T}{T+D}$ to its irreducible form $\frac{p}{q} = \frac{T}{T+D}$, such that p is prime to q. Thus, the minimum size for the T-fragments is p blocks, where *block* is an efficient unit for I/O operations and display. Accordingly, the size for D-fragments, except the first one, should be $q - p$. The size for the first D-fragment is $T + D$ or q blocks. For instance, if $PCR = 0.6$, we have $p = 3$ and $q = 5$. The sizes of D-fragments and T-fragments, therefore, are 2 blocks and 3 blocks, respectively. This example is illustrated in Figure 1. Let a block be 4 KBytes. The size of the staging buffer is $2 \cdot p$ blocks or 24 KBytes if double buffering is used, and is $p + 1$ blocks or 16 KBytes if circular buffering is used. SEP would have required a staging buffer as large as 363 MBytes. PIRATE does not use a staging buffer. In this case, it would have required a disk space of 907 MBytes in order to retrieve the TAIL of the object. Obviously, the savings due to BiHOP are tremendous.

The tiny size of the staging buffers used in BiHOP offers many benefits:

- Since the size is so small, the staging buffer can be implemented in the memory. This approach allows the pipelining to bypass the disk subsystem leaving all the disk bandwidth to the replacement activities of the D-fragments.
- Since the staging buffers require no disk space, the disk space saved can be used to support more users, and therefore improve the throughput of the system.
- A smaller staging buffer translates into a lower admission cost. Users, therefore, will experience better access latencies.

We note that one can consider using the technique proposed in [7] to manage the in-memory staging buffers. This scheme takes advantage of the fact that each staging buffer shrinks as its data are being forwarded to the display station. Since the storage subsystem must multiplex its bandwidth to refresh these buffers in a round-robin fashion, the space released by the shrinking buffers can be given to the ones which are being refreshed. Since staging buffers take turns to use the same memory space, reduction in memory requirement is possible. The performance study in [7] shows that up to 50% savings in memory space is achievable.

2.3. Replacement Policy

As we have mentioned, pipelining is done through the memory system bypassing the disk units. The disk buffer is used exclusively for caching the D-fragments. The replacement policy for the D-fragments is presented in Figure 3. The following notations are used in the algorithm:

$SIZE(X)$:	Size of the requested object X in block.
$DISK(X)$:	Size of the disk-resident portion of object X.
$HEAT(X)$:	Access frequency of object X.
$\mathcal{D}$:	The set of disk resident objects not currently displayed.

Algorithm *BiHOP_Reserve* is based on Equation (3). For each video object requested, it computes the additional

```
Algorithm: BiHOP_REPLACE(X : mmobject)
 reserved_space = BiHOP_RESERVE(X)
 needed_space = reserved_space - free_disk_space
 if (needed_space > 0) then
   repeat
     victim ← the object (≠ X) with lowest HEAT in D
     if (victim is null) then return(failure)
     else
       if (DISK(victim) ≥ needed_space) then
         DISK(victim) = DISK(victim) − needed_space
         free the last needed_space amount of victim's space for X
         needed_space = 0
       else
         displace victim to make room for X
         remove victim from D
         needed_space = needed_space − DISK(victim)
   until (needed_space = 0)
 Allocate reserved_space amount of free disk space for object X
 return(success)

Algorithm: BiHOP_RESERVE(X : mmobject)
 if no D-fragments of X is disk resident
   then reserved_space = ⌈(1 − PCR) · SIZE(X)⌉
   else reserved_space = ⌈(1 − PCR) · SIZE(X) − DISK(X)⌉
 return(reserved_space)
```

Figure 3. BiHOP replacement algorithm.

amount of disk space required to load the D-fragments not currently in the disk buffer. Once this has been determined, Algorithm *BiHOP_REPLACE* tries to satisfy this requirement by using as much of the free disk space as possible. If there is not enough free disk space, it casts out as many objects as necessary to make room for the request. We note that the unit for replacement is a D-fragment, not a whole object. Thus, some of the disk-resident objects may have some, but not all, of its D-fragments in the buffer. We note that LRU policy can be used to select victims for replacement. Alternatively, access frequencies of video objects are usually known beforehand [2]. This information can also be used to select victims. Without loss of generality, the latter approach is used in the presentation of Algorithm *BiHOP_REPLACE*.

3. Simulation Model

In the previous sections, we have analyzed the advantages of BiHOP in terms of disk space utilization. Although this metric has the most direct impact on the system performance, it is still worthwhile to investigate the ultimate performance metrics, namely access delay and system throughput. To do this, we decided to use a simulation model since it becomes too complex to do it analytically. The simulation environment is presented in the following. We will examine the simulation results in the next section.

Our simulation model is similar to the one used in [8]. The *Request Generator* generates requests for multimedia objects and submits them to the *Waiting Queue*. The *Scheduler* examines the requests in the queue in a FCFS manner. When bandwidths become available to serve the pending request at the head of the queue, the scheduler forwards the request to the *Serving Unit*. Serving Unit then allocates a playback stream to serve this request. Serving Unit simulates a hierarchical storage system and the playback mechanism. The buffer manager was implemented using the replacement policies presented in Figure 3. We note that the requests arriving at the Waiting Queue can be viewed as coming from different users. Our simulator allows multiple requests to be served simultaneously by different playback streams. This model is different from the single-user environment modeled in [4], which does not allow concurrent playback of several video files.

In terms of the workloads, each user request is characterized by an interarrival time and choice of object. User request interarrivals were modeled using a Poisson process. The access frequencies of objects in the database follow a Zipf-like distribution [5, 6, 9]. Let n be the total number of requests for a simulation run. The number of requests for each object O_i is determined as follows:

$$R_i = \frac{n}{i^z \cdot \sum_{j=1}^{v} 1/j^z},$$

where v is the number of objects in the system, and $0 \leq z \leq 1$ is the skew factor. A larger z value corresponds to a more skew condition, i.e., some objects are accessed considerably more frequently than other objects. When $z = 0$, the distribution is uniform, i.e. all the objects have the same access frequency. This Zipf-like distribution is similar to the distribution used in [2]. Each workload consists of 20,000 requests. A workload, called a *job sequence*, is generated for each skew condition. For each simulation run, the same sequence is used for both SEP and BiHOP. Thus, the Request Generator does not really generate requests on the fly. Instead, it keeps a database of these request sequences. For each simulation run, it scans the appropriate sequence, and appends the next request from the sequence to the Waiting Queue when the corresponding inter-arrival time is up.

Without loss of generality, we assume that all client display devices have the same display rate (i.e., B_D is constant). B_M is determined from the PCR. The default values for the system and workload parameters are given in Table 1. In our experiments, many of these parameters were also varied to perform various sensitivity analyses.

In this study, the system throughput is computed by dividing the number of requests in the job sequence (i.e., 20,000) by the total simulated time (i.e., the time it takes to serve the 20,000 requests). The average latency is computed as the mean of the 20,000 individual latencies. To avoid the buffer warm-up effect, we actually ran another short sequence of requests to fill up the disk buffer before the actual run takes

Block size	4 KBytes
Disk space	$13,500,000$ blocks
B_D	100 blocks/sec
B_M	80 blocks/sec ($PCR = 0.8$)
Zipf factor	0.7
Requests per minute	30 (average interarrival time is 2 sec)
Number of objects	600
Minimum object size	$100,000$ blocks
Maximum object size	$200,000$ blocks
Number of requests	$20,000$

Table 1. Simulation parameters.

place. The requests in the short sequence were randomly selected from the long sequence to ensure that the data initially cached in the buffer (to simulate the steady-state condition) were relevant and truthfully reflected the distribution of the requests in the workload (long sequence).

4. Simulation Results

We present the simulation results in the following subsections.

4.1. Effect of Request Rate

The effect of the request rate on BiHOP and SEP is plotted in Figures 4(a) and (b). In this experiment, the size of the disk buffer was set at 15% of the database size. We gradually increased the request rate from 20 requests/minute to 50 requests/minute, and observed how well these two schemes could sustain the faster request rates. Figure 4(a) shows that BiHOP consistently provides better average latency than SEP can. The savings range from 300% (under 20 requests per minute) to 1,000% (under 40 requests per minute). In terms of system throughput, although both schemes perform comparably under slow request rates (less than 30 requests per minute), only BiHOP can continue to extend its good performance beyond 30 requests/minute. When the request rate is 50 requests/minutes, we see that BiHOP outperforms SEP by 54% in terms of system throughput. The improvement on system throughput is really a lot more significant because applications normally have requirements on the maximum access latency. Let us say that the required average access latency for some video-on-demand application is two minutes. Under this condition, SEP can handle no more than 20 requests/minute. This limits its performance to less than 1,200 services/hour. On the contrary, BiHOP can sustain request rates well beyond 40 requests/minute. This allows BiHOP to offer substantially better system throughput. For instance, if we let BiHOP operate at 40 requests/minute while SEP is constrained to 20 requests/minute, the difference in system throughput is more than double. Obviously, much better throughput is achievable by further increasing the request rate for BiHOP. We note that the dramatic improvement, due to BiHOP, observed here is consistent with the analytical results discussed previously.

4.2. Effect of Space Ratio

We define the space ratio, *Space Ratio*, as the ratio of the disk size to the database size. In this experiment, we want to investigate the effect of this ratio on the performance of the two disk-buffer designs. A good technique should be able to achieve good performance using a reasonably small buffer. In other words, we want to keep the Space Ratio as small as possible without compromising too much performance.

The results of this study is plotted in Figures 4(c) and (d). We varied the space ratio from 10% to 30%. Figure 4(c) shows that BiHOP consistently outperforms SEP by a significant margin for practical buffer sizes (i.e., space ratio is less than 15%). For instance, the average latency of BiHOP is more than eight times better than that of SEP when the space ratio is 15%. In terms of system throughput, the performance difference is not significant under this workload because the performance of BiHOP is unfairly constrained to the 30-requests/minutes request rate. We decided not to run this experiment under a higher request rate, say 40, because the average latency for SEP would have been too high for most applications. This issue was discussed in the last subsection.

4.3. Effect of Access Skew

Although movie-on-demand and many multimedia applications are known to have a skew factor of around 0.7 (which is used in the above experiments), other applications can have very different access patterns (i.e., different skew factors.) We investigate this effect on BiHOP and SEP in this subsection. The results of this study is shown in Figure 5. We varied the skew factor between 0.0 (a uniform pattern) and 1.0 (a severe skew condition). It shows that the performance of SEP and BiHOP improves as we increase the skew factor. This behavior is due to the improvement in the temporal locality of reference causing the hit ratio of the disk buffer to improve. In comparison, we observe that BiHOP tremendously outperforms SEP in terms of average access latency. BiHOP is around 50% better than SEP in terms of system throughput when the workload is uniform. The differences in system throughput are not significant under the severe skew workload due to the same reasons explained in Section 4.2.

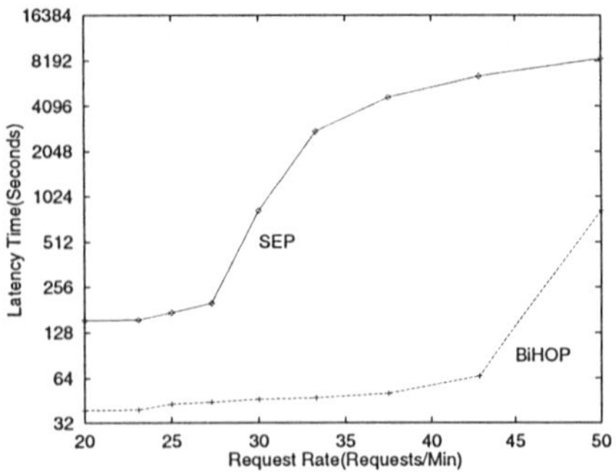

(a) Latency times for different request rates.

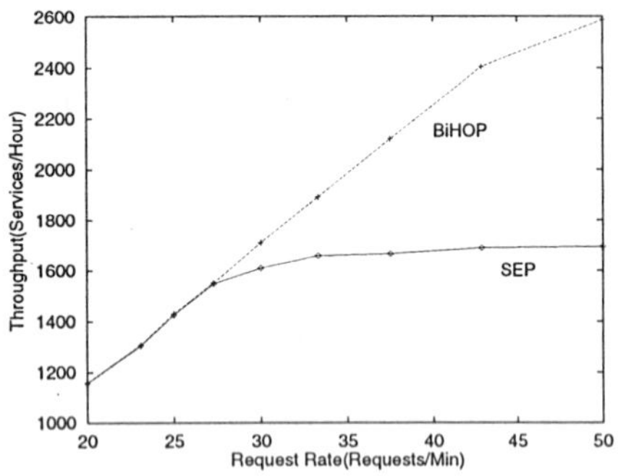

(b) Throughputs for different request rates.

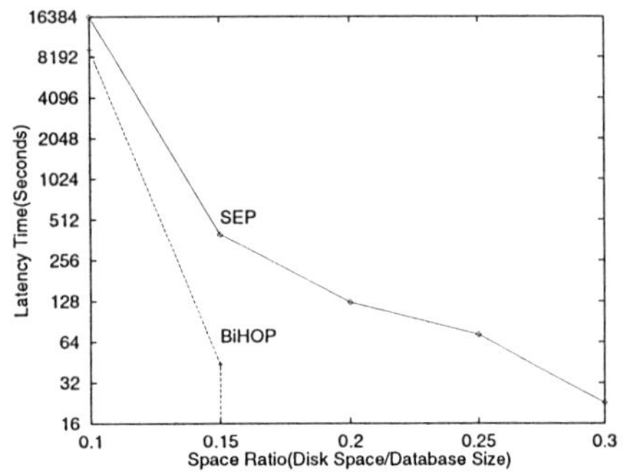

(c) Latency times for different space ratio.

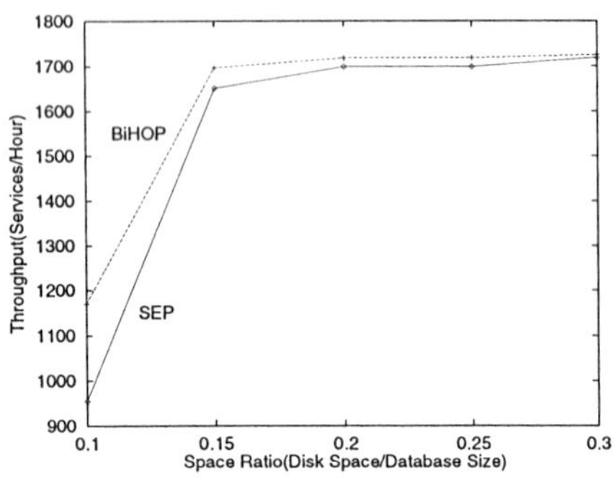

(d) Throughputs for different space ratio.

Figure 4. Performance comparison.

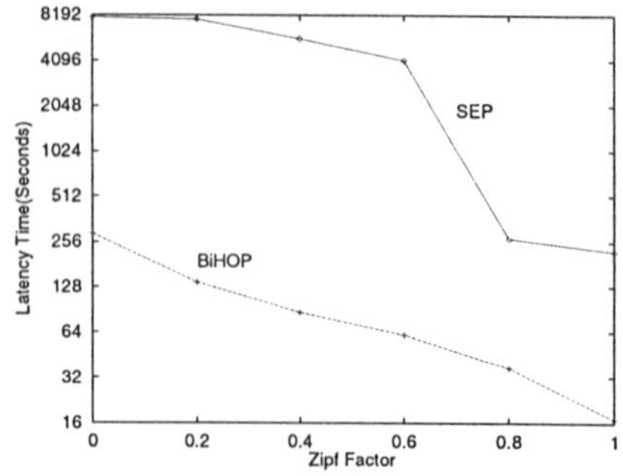

(a) Latency times for different Zipf factors.

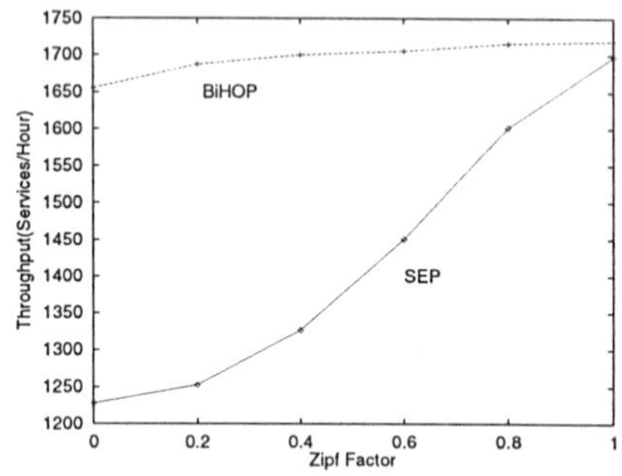

(b) Throughputs for different Zipf factors.

Figure 5. Skew effect on performance.

5. Support VCR Functions

Another important feature of the BiHOP approach is its efficient support for VCR functions, such as random access, fast-forward and fast-reverse. We discuss these features in the following subsections.

5.1. Random access

Let us first examine PIRATE and SEP. Since both of these techniques cache the HEADs in the disk buffer, let us consider the case when the HEAD of the object being used, say X, is already disk resident. If the random access starts at some point P in the HEAD, then the delay time for setting up the pipeline is equal to the time it takes to display the portion D in front of P (see Figure 6). This is due to the fact that the duration for playing the HEAD starting from P will not be long enough to eclipse the time it takes to materialize the entire X_1. The time difference is the playback time of D. Thus, we have to spend that amount of time (i.e., the delay) to load the leading blocks of X_1 (i.e., M in Figure 6) before the pipelining can start. Hence the delay is computed as follows:

$$Delay = \frac{x \cdot Size(X)}{B_D}, \tag{4}$$

where x $(0 < x \leq 1 - PCR)$ denotes the fraction of the data file preceding the start point P. For instance, $x = 0.5$ if one starts the playback at the middle of the file.

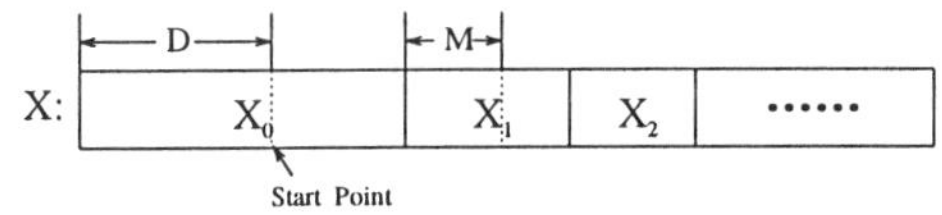

Figure 6. Random access in the HEAD under PIRATE and SEP.

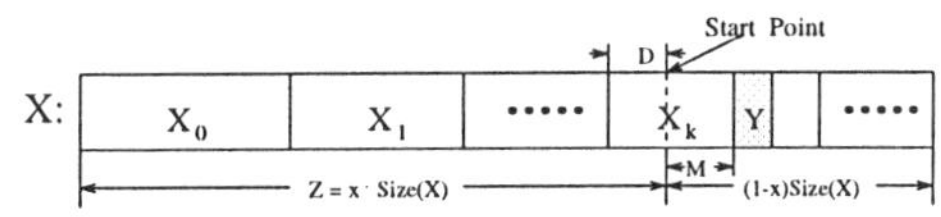

Figure 7. Random access in the TAIL under PIRATE and SEP.

Now, let us consider the case of starting the playback at some random point P in a non-HEAD fragment X_k. As illustrated in Figure 7, the delay for setting up the pipeline is equal to the time to materialize the portions M and Y. To ensure a continuous playback, we must have the time to materialize the portion Y equal the time to play back the portion D. Thus, Delay time can be computed as:

$$\text{Delay} = \begin{cases} \frac{x \cdot S}{B_D} & \text{for } 0 \leq x \leq 1 - PCR \\ \frac{(1-PCR)\cdot(1-x)\cdot S}{PCR \cdot B_D} & \text{for } 1 - PCR \leq x \leq 1. \end{cases} \quad (5)$$

Let $\mathcal{T}$ be the total playback time of the entire video file, i.e., $\mathcal{T} = \frac{Size(X)}{B_D}$. Substitute $\mathcal{T}$ into Equation (5), we have:

$$\text{Delay} = \begin{cases} x \cdot \mathcal{T} & \text{for } 0 < x \leq 1 - PCR \\ \frac{(1-PCR)\cdot(1-x)\cdot \mathcal{T}}{PCR} & \text{for } 1 - PCR \leq x < 1. \end{cases} \quad (6)$$

If every point in the object is equally likely to be accessed as the starting point, the average delay for random access can be computed as follows:

$$\begin{aligned} \text{Average Delay} &= \int_0^{1-PCR} x \cdot \mathcal{T}\, dx \\ &\quad + \int_{1-PCR}^{1} \frac{(1-PCR)\cdot(1-x)\cdot\mathcal{T}}{PCR}\, dx \\ &= \frac{1}{2}\cdot(1-PCR)\cdot\mathcal{T}. \end{aligned} \quad (7)$$

Assuming $PCR = 0.6$, the delay is about 20% of the playback time of the whole file. Thus, if a movie is 1 hour long, the average delay for random access will be 12 minutes. This is certainly not tolerable by most viewers.

Let us now turn our attention to BiHOP. If the starting point is in a T-fragment, the delay for setting up the pipeline is the time to materialize areas 1 and 2 as illustrated in Figure 8. We need to materialize area 1 because the data is not yet in the disk buffer. After area 1 has been materialized, the duration for playing this area and the next D-fragment is not long enough to eclipse the time to materialize the next T-fragment. The time difference is the time to materialize area 2. Let the size of area 1 be $T - t$, where t is the portion of the T-fragment excluded from the playback. The size of area 2 can then be computed as follows. To ensure a continuous playback, the following relationship must hold:

$$\frac{Size(Area2)}{T} = \frac{t}{T+D} \quad \text{or} \quad Size(Area2) = \frac{T \cdot t}{T+D}.$$

Thus the delay time is:

$$\text{Delay} = \frac{T - \frac{t \cdot D}{T+D}}{B_M} \leq \frac{T}{B_M}. \quad (8)$$

That is, the maximum delay time cannot be longer than the time to materialize a T-fragment which is only a few blocks.

If the starting point is in a D-fragment, the delay time is the time to materialize the portion t in the next T-fragment as shown in Figure 9. To ensure a continuous playback, we must have the following relationship:

$$\frac{t}{T} = \frac{T+d}{T+D}.$$

Thus the delay time is:

$$\text{Delay} = \frac{\frac{T+d}{T+D}\cdot T}{B_M} \leq \frac{T}{B_M}.$$

Again, the maximum delay time cannot be longer than the time to materialize a T-fragment.

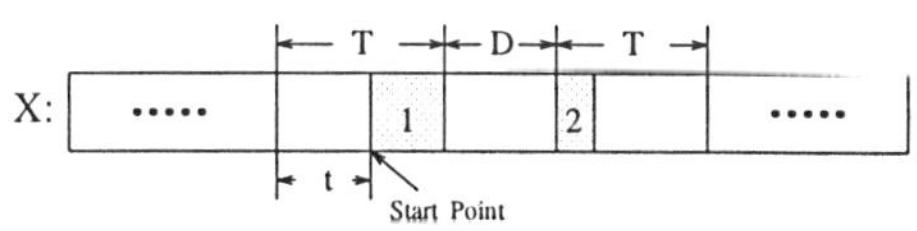

Figure 8. Start the playback in some T-fragment.

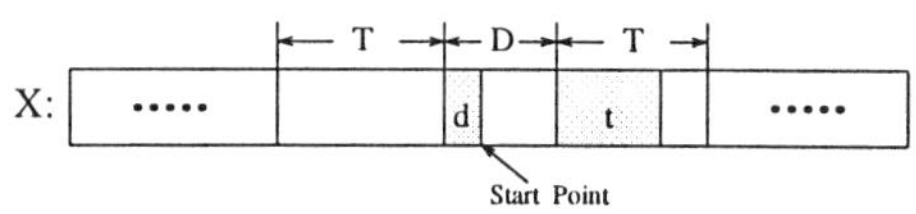

Figure 9. Start the playback in some D-fragment.

We have shown that the delay is only a few blocks for BiHOP independent of where one wants to start the playback of a file. Such a tiny delay is generally unnoticeable.

For instance, let us consider a 1-hour MPEG-2 video with $PCR = 0.6$ and a block size of 4 KBytes. The average delay, in this case, is less than 0.05 second. The average delay would have been 12 minutes if PIRATE or SEP were used.

5.2. Fast-Forward/Reverse

Although normal playback is the most important function for all multimedia applications, providing the user with VCR capabilities such as fast-forward and fast-reverse is also highly desired. Several approaches have been proposed for implementing these special functions [3, 1]. The most straight forward technique is to retrieve and transmit the multimedia stream in higher speed, say n times the normal playback rate. It is apparent that this simple scheme requires n times the system resources. Obviously, all PIRATE, SEP and BiHOP will not be able to avoid these extra costs if this approach is used. Alternatively, the Loss scheme in [3] or the Frame Skipping scheme in [1] can be used to reduce the requirement on system resources. The idea behind these methods is to skip forward or backward through the video file showing one out of several blocks. This strategy is not suitable for PIRATE or SEP due to their unidirectional nature. For instance, neither PIRATE nor SEP can efficiently support a fast-reverse soon after a random access. In this case, some of the data needed might not be in the buffer, and reverse pipelining is not an option for these techniques. We note that this sequence of two operations is very commonly used to search in a video file. Although fast-reverse during a normal play is possible with PIRATE, this function is provided at the cost of retaining all the data in the buffer until the end of the session. If the normal play is resumed after a fast-forward, this sequence of operations has the same effect as a random access. The intolerable delay as discussed in the last subsection is inevitable for either PIRATE or SEP. On the contrary, the methods presented in [3, 1] are natural for BiHOP because it also skips through the file and caches in the disk buffer only every other fragment, i.e., skipping T-fragments and caching D-fragments. Interestingly, when all the D-fragments are disk resident, the symmetrical nature of BiHOP allows fast-forward and fast-reverse be done without even involving the tertiary devices. If one needs to resume the normal play after a fast-forward or fast-reverse, the delay is essentially unnoticeable since this can be treated as a random access.

6. Conclusions and Future Studies

This study focuses on disk space management of hierarchical storage in multimedia systems. We have proposed a novel technique called *Bidirectional Highly Optimized Pipelining* (BiHOP). Our simulation results indicate that BiHOP significantly outperforms a recently proposed technique called SEP. This result can be attributed to our caching technique which caches every other data fragment of the multimedia file, rather than caching consecutive fragments as in traditional practice. This new approach allows us to use tiny staging buffers for pipelining. Their small sizes allow them to be implemented in the server memory to conserve disk bandwidth. The whole disk space, therefore, can be dedicated for caching purposes to improve the hit ratio.

Another important benefit of BiHOP is its bidirectional nature. While the sizes of the data fragments are nonuniform in existing techniques, the symmetrical file organization (i.e., uniform pattern) of BiHOP allows it to pipeline in either forward or reverse direction with the same efficiency. This unique feature, not possible with other schemes, makes BiHOP natural for implementing VCR functions.

In this study, we focused our attention on disk space management. Other scarce resources include the transmission bandwidths between different levels of the hierarchical storage. We are currently investigating techniques to make more efficient use of these resources. Admission control is another issue needed to be studied more carefully. Our simulator does not currently implement an admission-control policy. Instead, each request is automatically "accepted."

References

[1] M. Chen, D. Kandlur, and P. S. Yu. Support for fully interactive playout in a disk-array-based video server. In *Proc. of ACM Multimedia*, pages 391–398, 1994.

[2] A. Dan, D. Sitaram, and P. Shahabuddin. Scheduling policies for an on-demand video server with batching. In *Proc. of ACM Multimedia*, pages 15–23, October 1994.

[3] J. K. Dey-Sircar et al. Providing VCR capabilities in large-scale video servers. In *Proc. of ACM Multimedia*, pages 25–32, October 1994.

[4] S. Ghandeharizadeh and C. Shahabi. On multimedia repositories, personal computers, and hierarcical storage systems. In *Proc. of ACM Multimedia*, pages 407–416, October 1994.

[5] K. A. Hua, C. Lee, and C. M. Hua. Dynamic load balancing in multicomputer database systems using partition tuning. *IEEE Trans. on Knowledge and Data Engineering*, 7(6):968–983, December 1995.

[6] D. E. Knuth. *The Art of Computer Programming, Volume 3: Sorting and Searching*. Addison Wesley, Reading, Massachusetts, 1973.

[7] R. T. Ng and J. Yang. Maximizing buffer and disk utilizations for news-on-demand. In *Proc. of the 20th VLDB Conference*, Santiago, Chile, 1994.

[8] J. Z. Wang, K. A. Hua, and H. C. Young. SEP: a space efficient pipelining technique for managing disk buffers in multimedia servers. In *Proc. of the IEEE int'l Conf. on Multimedia Computing and Systems*, Hiroshima, Japan, June 1996.

[9] G. K. Zipf. *Human Behavior and the Principle of Least Effort: An Introduction to Human Ecology*. Addison-Wesley, Reading, Mass., 1949.

Performance of Congestion Control Mechanisms in Wormhole Routing Networks

CHRISTIAN ROCHE PRASASTH PALNATI MARIO GERLA
FABIO NERI EMILIO LEONARDI

UCLA Computer Science Dept.
3732H Boelter Hall
Los Angeles, CA 90095, USA.
email: roche@cs.ucla.edu

Abstract

In order to minimize latency in high-speed interconnection networks, the wormhole routing *technique can be employed. With this technique, a switch transmits an incoming message as soon as it receives it, without waiting for the entire message. The problem then is that a message stretches over several links and locks network resources, thus making a contention situation possible. Two principal congestion control mechanisms can be considered,* backpressure flow control *and* deflection routing. *The performance of these mechanisms depends both on the traffic characteristics and on the network topology. In order to compare them, we study analytically the behavior of a wormhole routing network model with random input traffic under both policies. We estimate the probability of collision between messages and express the average message transit delay as a function of the offered load. Simulation provides a good confirmation for the analytical results. This study gives us an understanding of the behavior of the system under different resource management policies.*

1 Introduction

An important concern for time-sensitive applications such as distributed computation over interconnected supercomputers or real-time data processing is the latency of the interconnection network. Since these applications require large amounts of data to be transmitted within short periods of time, the reaction time of the underlying communication system must be minimized. Connection-oriented techniques like ATM may not be best suited to this kind of application because the connection establishment and cell segmentation phases may introduce non-negligible delays in the transmission of the data. In order to minimize the latency of the network, the *wormhole routing* technique can be used [1, 2]. An example of a commercially available wormhole routing LAN is Myrinet [3]. Myrinet LANs use source routing and 8-bit wide data transmission to achieve data rates of up to 640 Mb/s. Their geographical reach is currently limited to a maximum link length of 25 meters. The ARPA-sponsored Supercomputer SuperNet (SSN) project at UCLA extends the reach of Myrinet LANs to campus area networks via an optical backbone network [4].

With wormhole routing, the data units are variable-length messages. A switch that receives the head of a message immediately forwards it if possible to the next switch on its path. It does not wait to receive the whole body of the message as with the classical *store-and-forward* policy. Thus, the latency associated with buffering the message is eliminated and the transit time of a message can be reduced to a minimum [4]. However, a message can be blocked by another message currently being transmitted on the desired output port.

Several approaches can be used to handle blocking. With *cut-through routing*, a buffer large enough to store a whole message is provided at each input port [5]. If a message cannot be transmitted it is buffered while waiting for the output port to become available. This reduces message loss but basically leads to the same type of congestion encountered in store-and-forward networks [2, 6].

A second approach consists in using a hop-by-hop *backpressure flow control* mechanism [7]. When

0-8186-7780-5/97 $10.00

the desired output port is unavailable, a message is blocked; a STOP signal is propagated upstream. This prevents the risk of buffer overflow but causes a lock up of network resources (i.e., buffers and switch ports). Under high load conditions, second and third order blockings and ultimately *deadlocks* occur.

A third approach is to use a *deflection routing* mechanism [7]. With such a mechanism, a message which finds the preferred output port busy is deflected to another port. Thus, messages may travel on longer paths and consequently suffer longer delays, but will not be lost due to buffer overflow. Most importantly, network resources are not locked up. An alternative to pure, asynchronous deflection routing is *delayed deflection*: a blocked message is temporarily buffered while waiting for its preferred output port to become available.

The performance of backpressure flow control depend on traffic characteristics, in particular message length. In contrast, the performance of deflection routing depend essentially on the network topology. Simulation results have been presented in [7]. Our goal in this paper is to evaluate and compare analytically the performance of these mechanisms.

This paper is organized as follow: in Section 2 we describe the different congestion control mechanisms. In Section 3 we present the network model and the modeling assumptions. We estimate the collision probability in Section 4 and assess the performance of the system under each policy in Section 5. Section 6 validates the theoretical results against simulation results and compare the respective performance of the mechanisms. Section 7 concludes the paper and indicates possible directions for future research.

2 Congestion control mechanisms

2.1 Backpressure flow control

The concept of backpressure flow control is illustrated in Figure 1. When a message is blocked, a *choke packet* is sent upstream to stop the transmission. A portion of the message is stored in a small *slack buffer* associated with the input port. When the link becomes free, a *release packet* is sent to resume transmission.

In order to be able to send the control packets, the backpressure flow control mechanism requires bidirectional links. Also, the switch must provide a small slack buffer to store the fraction of the message that is "in flight".

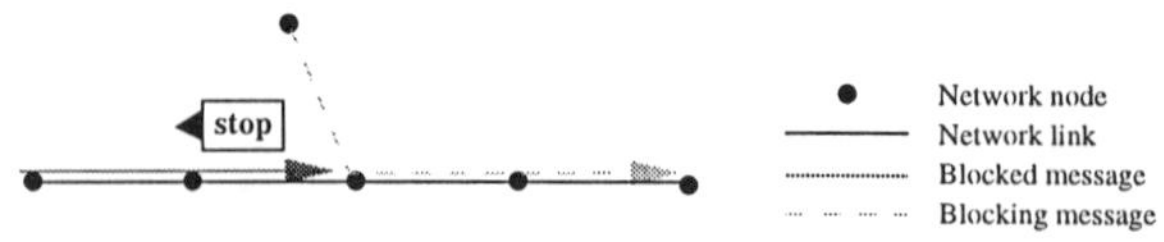

Figure 1: Backpressure flow control.

A critical problem of backpressure flow control is the occurrence of *deadlocks*. Several deadlock avoidance mechanisms have been proposed, including acyclic routing, timeouts and dynamic detection/resolution [8, 9]. In Myrinet, a type of acyclic routing called *Up/Down routing* is used [3].

2.2 Deflection routing

The concept of deflection routing is illustrated in Figure 2. When a message arriving at a switch finds its preferred output port busy, it doesn't wait. Rather, it is deflected from its shortest path and immediately transmitted on another available link. Thus, it takes a detour, which increases its path length and transit delay.

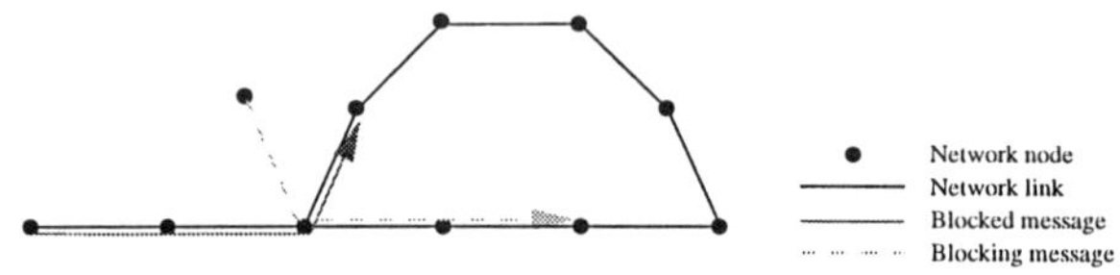

Figure 2: Deflection routing.

Deflection routing requires that there always exist an available output link. This can be achieved if the network has a *regular topology*, i.e., if each switch has as many inputs as outputs. Note that this condition is automatically met when the links are bidirectional. A drawback compared to backpressure flow control is that the message sequencing may not be preserved, since messages are randomly deflected [2, 7].

With deflection routing, deadlocks are not possible since messages are not blocked. However, *livelocks* can occur, i.e., situations where some messages are deflected indefinitely and never reach their destinations. As with deadlocks, such a situation must be detected and resolved. One possible solution is to limit the maximum number of hops that a packet can make. However, this poses the problem of choosing a suitable upper bound. As another approach, slotted networks use random choices of output ports to probabilistically break livelocks. In an asynchronous, unslotted case like ours, however, in overload conditions only one output port is free. Thus, random choices does not work. Some form of synchronization or message alignment may be desirable.

We consider the *delayed deflection* message alignment technique. When the head of a message arrives at a node and the preferred output port is unavailable, the node checks whether the message can be buffered in the input buffer until the preferred output port becomes available (i.e., until the remainder of the message using that port is transmitted). If the input buffer would overflow, then the message is deflected through another output port. Otherwise, the message is buffered and deflection is delayed. It is possible that by the time the output port becomes available, other messages waiting for the same output port may have arrived. One of these messages is then randomly chosen and the output port assigned to it. This message alignment mechanism introduces more choices of output port selection, thus resolving livelocks and improving the overall efficiency.

3 Network model

In order to evaluate the performance of the different congestion control mechanisms described above, we consider a simplified model of a wormhole routing network. The model is depicted in Figure 3.

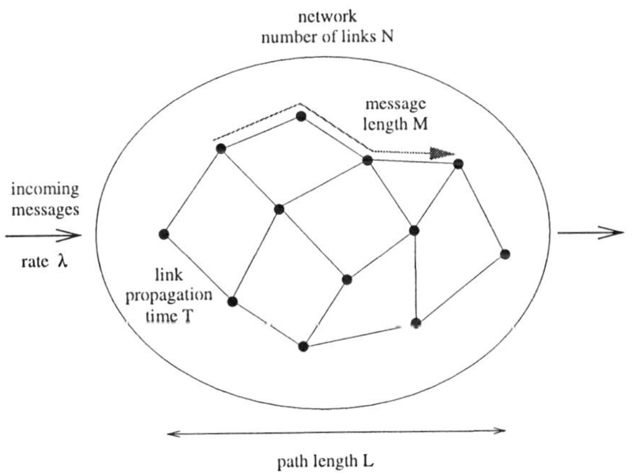

Figure 3: Wormhole routing network model.

The network we consider is composed of N unidirectional links with identical propagation times T and transmission capacities C. This model accommodates the case of bidirectional links by modeling each bidirectional link as two independent unidirectional links. There are H hosts communicating through the network. The messages are of fixed length M and cross the network along paths of length L, where L is the number of links. Time is expressed in link propagation time units. Likewise, M is expressed in number of links. More precisely, if b is the messages size in bits, then M is given by

$$M = \frac{b}{CT}. \qquad (1)$$

In the deflection model, a key performance measure is the *average deflection cost* K. This quantity is strictly dependent on the topology and represents the average increase of the message path length introduced by a single deflection.

For the sake of simplicity, we make the following assumptions:

- We do not take into account the propagation delay of control packets in case of backpressure flow control, i.e., we assume that the messages are stopped instantaneously.
- We assume that the input traffic pattern is uniform and the network topology is such that the total load is evenly distributed throughout the system. All the links carry the same amount of traffic.
- We assume Poisson message arrival distribution with parameter λ.

In the following, we consider the system described above in a stationary regime under a given input load. We first derive the probability of collision and then the average message delay for various schemes.

4 Collision probability

We first introduce the dimensionless total input load z, defined as the ratio of the total incoming data rate to the nominal rate C of a link. This quantity can be viewed as the average number of hosts simultaneously transmitting. The theoretical maximum value of z (the saturation load) is H. From (1) we find

$$z = \frac{\lambda b}{C} = \lambda M T. \qquad (2)$$

Next, we define m to be the average number of message headers in the system. From Little's result:

$$m = \lambda t, \qquad (3)$$

where t is the average header transit delay (i.e., the time elapsed from the moment the first byte enters the network till the moment the first byte exits the network).

Recall that message length M was expressed in link segments. Thus, the average arrival rate expressed in link segments is $M\lambda$. Hence, the average number Λ of link segments in the system (i.e., the number of busy links) can be obtained by using Little's result again, provided that we know the average time that a link segment spends in the system.

In the case of pure deflection routing, each segment spends the same amount of time in the system, namely t. So the average number of busy links is simply

$$\Lambda_{\text{defl}} = M\lambda t = Mm. \tag{4}$$

This relation also holds for the case of delayed deflection as long as the probability of blocking remains small. This is the case when the size of the deflection buffer is small compared to the size of the messages.

Next, we consider the case of backpressure flow control. Note that once the head of a message has made its way through the system, the rest of the message crosses without blocking. In particular, the average transit time of each segment is a function of its position in the message, as shown on Figure 4.

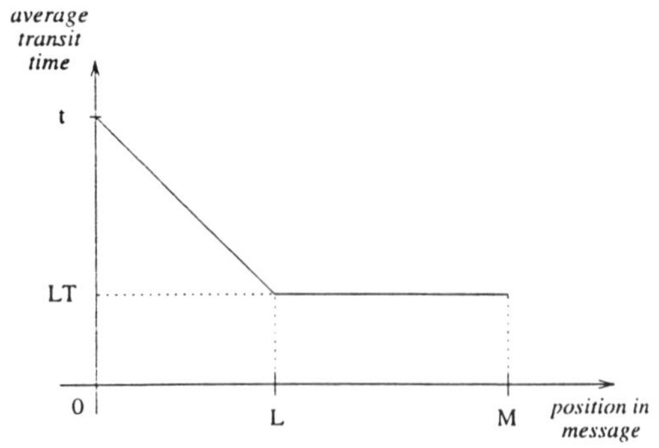

Figure 4: Transit time of each part of a message.

In the simple case of constant message length M and path length L, the average transit time of a segment can be evaluated as $\xi t + (1-\xi)LT$, with

$$\xi = \begin{cases} 1 - \frac{M-1}{2L} & \text{if } M \leq L, \\ \frac{L+1}{2M} & \text{if } M \geq L. \end{cases}$$

So in the case of backpressure flow control we have

$$\Lambda_{\text{back}} = M\lambda\left(\xi t + (1-\xi)LT\right). \tag{5}$$

Next, we define the link collision probability p as the probability that the next link on a message path is busy. In order to derive p, we first assess the probability p_0 that any given link is busy. By definition, p_0 is the ratio of the average number of busy links to the total number of links, that is

$$p_0 = \frac{\Lambda}{N}. \tag{6}$$

The collision probability p depends on the time distribution of the message arrivals. In this study we consider the case of Poisson arrivals, which means that the probability of observing k arrivals in a time interval of length τ is

$$P_k = \frac{\omega^k}{k!}e^{-\omega},$$

where $\omega = \lambda\tau$. In order to evaluate p, we use for τ the characteristic time interval for message interaction. A message is present in the system (head to tail) for a time $t + MT$, so we set $\tau = t + MT$. Let us assume that during this time interval the message occupies an average of μ links, where $\mu \leq L$. Using Little's result, we can write

$$\Lambda = \mu\lambda\tau = \mu\omega.$$

We now consider a time interval of length τ on which there are more than one arrival and calculate the probability that a message be blocked by any message other than itself. Ignoring dependencies, p is given by the fraction of links occupied by other messages. Formally, this can be written

$$p = \frac{1}{N}\frac{\sum_{k=1}^{\infty}(k-1)\mu P_k}{\sum_{k=1}^{\infty} P_k}.$$

The numerator in this expression is the average number of link segments in the system belonging to messages other than the message in question. We finally obtain the following expression for p:

$$p = \frac{\mu}{N}\left(\frac{\omega}{1-e^{-\omega}} - 1\right) = p_0\left(\frac{1}{1-e^{-\omega}} - \frac{1}{\omega}\right). \tag{7}$$

5 Analysis of the mechanisms

5.1 Deflection routing

Let us first consider the case of pure deflection routing. We denote by l the average path length of the messages expressed in number of links. The minimum path length of a message is L and is increased by K each time the message experiences a deflection.

The collision probability is p, which means that on a path of length l a message experiences on average lp deflections. Hence, we have the relation

$$l = L + lpK,$$

which yields

$$l = \frac{L}{1 - pK}.$$

Since in the case of pure deflection routing a message is never blocked, its transit time is directly proportional to the average number of links it crosses, that is

$$t = \frac{LT}{1 - pK}. \tag{8}$$

Equations (7) and (8) form a system of two equations in the two unknown p and t, with z defined in (2) playing the role of a parameter. This system is non-linear and cannot be solved in closed form. However, we can use numerical techniques to solve it for different values of the load z, as shown in Section 6.2. Also, we can use approximations to linearize the system for small values of z, as shown in Section 6.3.

5.2 Backpressure flow control

In the case of backpressure flow control, the average path length is fixed and is equal to L. So, a message experiences an average of Lp collisions. In order to evaluate the waiting time upon blocking, we define the *average progress rate* (in links per sec) of a message as

$$v = \frac{L}{\xi t + (1 - \xi) LT}.$$

On average, a message is blocked in the middle and must therefore wait for the blocking message to travel $M/2$ links. Thus, the average waiting time upon blocking can be written as

$$w = \frac{M}{2} \frac{\xi t + (1 - \xi) LT}{L}.$$

Hence, we can write

$$t = LT + Lp \frac{M}{2} \frac{\xi t + (1 - \xi) LT}{L},$$

which gives

$$t = LT \frac{1 + (1 - \xi) pM/2}{1 - \xi pM/2}. \tag{9}$$

5.3 Delayed deflection

In the case of delayed deflection, each node has on each input port a buffer of size B, with $0 < B < M$. When a message experiences a collision, its time to wait is estimated and the message is deflected only if the wait exceeds the available buffer. So if we denote $\gamma = B/M$, we have upon each collision:

With probability	γ	$\rightarrow$	buffering,
With probability	$1 - \gamma$	$\rightarrow$	deflection.

In order to evaluate the average path length of the messages, we can use the result of Section 5.1 with a reduced probability of deflection $p' = (1 - \gamma)p$. Thus, we obtain

$$l = \frac{L}{1 - (1 - \gamma) pK}.$$

Now when a message is blocked, its average waiting time is $BT/2$, so we can write

$$t = lT + l\gamma p \frac{BT}{2}.$$

Finally, we obtain

$$t = LT \frac{1 + \gamma^2 pM/2}{1 - (1 - \gamma) pK}. \tag{10}$$

6 Numerical results

In order to verify the validity of the analytical model, we compare in this section the analytical results against simulation.

6.1 Simulation model

For the simulation runs we use a 64-node bidirectional network with *torus* and *shuffle* topologies [2]. The connectivity of the network with both topologies is 4, which means that there are four bidirectional transit ports per node. The corresponding number of links in the analytic model is $N = 4 \times 64 = 256$. The dimension parameters of the simulation model are gathered in Table 1.

The average deflection cost K is defined as the increase in path length that a message experiences when it is deflected from its shortest path. This value is averaged over all source/destination pairs and is weighed by link traffic. The computation of K can be made exactly for a given topology with a given input traffic pattern. It does not depend on the assumptions made in this study.

Symbol	*Quantity*	*Shuffle*	*Torus*
T	Propagation time on a link	1	
H	Number of hosts	64	
N	Number of links	256	
M	Message length	12	
B	Deflection buffer size	1.2	
L	Average path length	3.429	4.063
K	Average deflection cost	1.385	0.942

Table 1: Dimensions of the simulation model.

The network uses shortest-path routing, i.e., a message is always transmitted when possible on a link that brings it closer to its destination. If several links are possible, one is chosen at random. Each node sends with the same average rate to all the other nodes.

It is interesting to note that with this uniform traffic pattern, the total load is equally distributed on all the links in the case of the torus topology but not in the case of the shuffle topology. In this latter case, there is a ratio of 2 to 3 between the traffic rates at the least and most loaded links. Also, even though we carried the analysis considering paths of fixed length L, the simulation runs are conducted with paths of different lengths. Now L represents the average path length under the considered traffic pattern.

We will see below that, in spite of these differences between the analytic and simulation models, the simulation results still provide a very satisfying match with the analysis. This confirms the validity of the analytic model when these simplifying assumptions are relaxed.

6.2 Simulation results

Figures 5 shows the curves obtained by simulation with the above system configuration in the case of backpressure flow control and pure deflection routing, and compares them with the theoretical results obtained using numerical techniques. These curves depict the average transit time t of the messages as a function of the total input load z. We see that the analytical model provides quite a satisfying approximation of the system performance.

The deviation that can be observed at higher loads (above 15% of capacity) comes from the fact that when the system's load increases, deadlocks and livelocks occur more often. Then the corrective measures that must be undertaken to resolve these situations (essentially destroying the corresponding messages) steer the real system's behavior away from the ideal behavior described by the analytical model. When the offered load exceeds 20% of capacity, the network becomes unstable and its performance collapses, due to the number of deadlocks or livelocks that the system suffers. This shows that the simplest operation mode, with unrestricted routing and with no input control, is not applicable in a real situation. This issue will be further discussed in the next section.

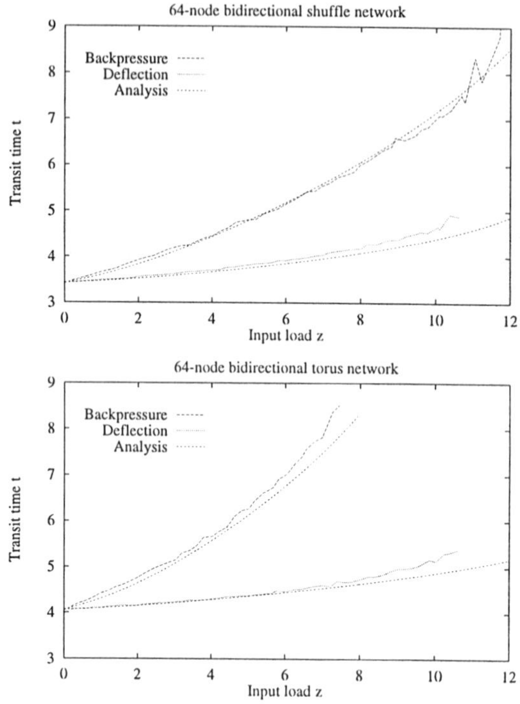

Figure 5: Backpressure flow control *vs* pure deflection.

Figure 6 compares the pure deflection and delayed deflection mechanisms with $\gamma = 10\%$. We see that, although we cannot distinguish quantitatively between the two mechanisms, the analytical model still captures the general shape and respective position of the curves.

6.3 Performance comparison

In order to be able to compare the performance of the mechanisms, we need to define a simple performance criterion. One possible choice is the slope of the curve $t(z)$ at $z = 0$. This quantity captures the respective position of each curves and thus the relative performance of each mechanism, at least at low load. To evaluate this quantity we approximate the expression of the collision probability given by equation (7)

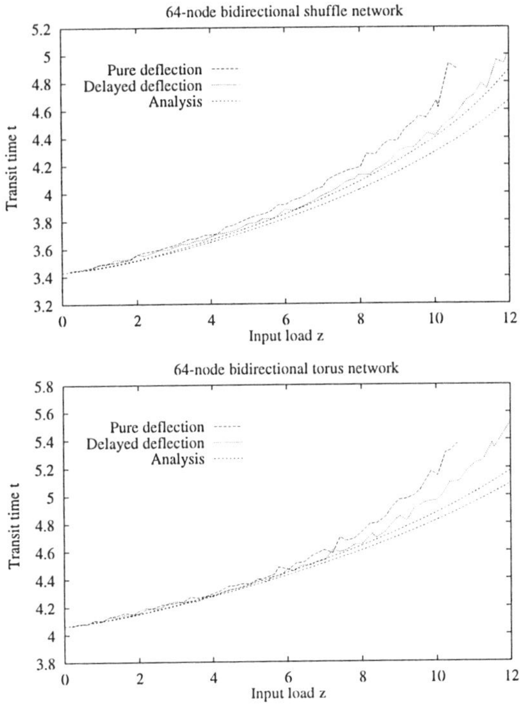

Figure 6: Pure deflection *vs* delayed deflection.

to the first order, hence

$$p \approx \frac{p_0}{2}.$$

Then t appears in each case as the solution of a second-degree polynomial in z and can be expressed in a closed form. To compute the slope of this polynomial at the origin is then straightforward. The resulting quantity is the exact expression of the desired performance criterion. In the case of pure deflection routing, we have

$$\left.\frac{dt}{dz}\right|_{z=0} = \frac{TL^2K}{2N}.$$

In the case of backpressure flow control, we obtain

$$\left.\frac{dt}{dz}\right|_{z=0} = \frac{TL^2M}{4N}.$$

We can see that these two expressions are similar, with K and $M/2$ playing an equivalent role. This shows that the relative performance of backpressure flow control compared to pure deflection routing depends essentially on the average message length compared to the average deflection cost. If $M/2$ is greater than K, then deflection routing will exhibit better performance. On the other hand, if it is smaller, the backpressure flow control will exhibit better performance.

6.4 Extensions of the model

The analysis so far was conducted using a simplified wormhole routing network model. The maximum offered load was limited due to deadlock and livelock. In [7], a more detailed model of a Myrinet network is studied through simulation. It includes deadlock avoidance mechanisms such as Up/Down routing and virtual channels and considers variable-size messages. The interested reader will find a detailed description of the simulator along with an extensive presentation of results in [7]. In this paper, we limit ourselves to reporting the transit delay results for the 64-node bidirectional torus network (see Figure 7).

In this figure, the x axis indicates the average host load (i.e., z/H). The y axis indicates the average message transit delay, measured from the time the first byte enters the network to the time the last byte is delivered to the destination (i.e., $t+MT$). This quantity is measured in byte transmission times. The considered 1 km links at 640 Mb/s represent 400 byte times (i.e., $T = 400$). Several policies are considered, namely deadlock-free virtual channels (VC), deflection routing with different deflection buffer sizes (DF) and Up/Down deadlock-free restricted routing (UP). The message length is geometrically distributed with an average of 5000 bytes (i.e., $M = 12.5$) and a upper limit of 10000 bytes.

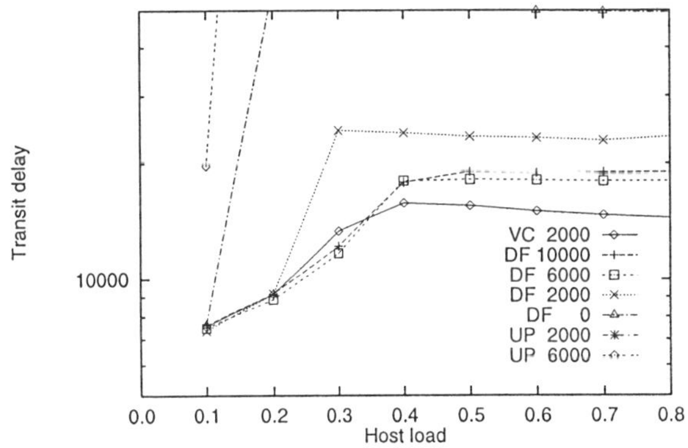

Figure 7: Average message delay *vs* host load.

These curves can be compared to those in Figures 5 and 6 in the case of torus topology. We note that pure deflection delay for load .1 (7,000 byte times) is consistent with the value in Figure 5 (namely, $(4.5+12)\times 400 = 6,600$). The backpressure delay with Up/Down routing (for deadlock prevention) is somewhat higher due to the longer paths and link loads compared to shortest path routing.

The most interesting information provided by Figure 7 is that higher loads can be achieved by employing suitable deadlock and livelock avoidance mechanisms. Therefore, the analytical models developed in this paper can be profitably extended to incorporate the behavior of more complex flow control strategies. This extension is considered as a direction for future research.

7 Conclusion

Wormhole routing is a promising technique for low-latency, high-speed interconnection networks. However, this technique introduces challenging problems including resource contention and deadlock occurrence. Two principal mechanisms can be employed to alleviate congestion in wormhole routing networks, namely backpressure flow control and deflection routing.

In this paper, we analyzed and compared the performance of these mechanisms in a general network configuration. By estimating the probability of collision in the system for a given input load, we are able to express the average message transit time as a function of the offered load. Simulation results show a good match with the analytical results.

This study allows us to compare the respective performance of the mechanisms and decide which one is best suited to a given network configuration. It also helps understanding the influence of the system dimensions on its overall performance and thus predict how the system will scale.

Several research directions can be considered from here. One direction consists in refining the model and relaxing some assumptions in order to get a closer match to a real system. Another interesting issue would be to apply the analytical techniques developed here to other networking techniques and compare them with one another. Also, work is currently in progress in developing the analytical model in order to capture the behavior of different deadlock/livelock avoidance mechanisms.

References

[1] L. Li and P. McKinley, "A survey of wormhole routing techniques in direct networks," *IEEE Computer*, vol. 26, no. 2, pp. 62–76, Feb. 1993.

[2] C. Baransel, W. Dobosiewicz and P. Gburzynski, "Routing in multihop packet switching networks: the Gb/s challenge," *IEEE Network Magazine*, vol. 9, no. 3, 1995.

[3] N. Boden, D. Cohen *et al.*, "Myrinet: a gigabit-per-second local-area network," *IEEE Micro*, vol. 15, no. 1, Feb. 1995.

[4] L. Kleinrock, M. Gerla *et al.*, "The Supercomputer Supernet testbed: a WDM based supercomputer interconnect," *IEEE JSAC*, vol. 14, no. 6, June 1996.

[5] P. Kermani and L. Kleinrock, "Virtual cut-through: a new computer communication switching technique," *Computer Networks*, vol. 3, no. 3, pp. 267–286, Sept. 1979.

[6] R. Jain, "Congestion control in computer networks: issues and trends," *IEEE Network Magazine*, vol. 4, no. 3, pp. 24–30, May 1990.

[7] E. Leonardi, F. Neri, M. Gerla *et al.*, "Congestion control in asynchronous, high-speed wormhole routing networks," *IEEE Communication Magazine*, Nov. 1996.

[8] W. Dally and C. Seitz, "Deadlock-free message routing in multiprocessor interconnection networks," *IEEE Transactions on Computers*, vol. C-36, no. 5, pp. 547–553, May 1987.

[9] P. Palnati, M. Gerla and E. Leonardi, "Deadlock-free routing in an optical interconnect for high-speed wormhole routing networks," in *Proceedings of 1996 International Conference on Parallel and Distributed Systems*, Tokyo, June 1996.

Re-routing in Circuit Switched Networks

Eric W. M. Wong, Andy K. M. Chan

Department of Electronic Engineering
City University of Hong Kong
Tat Chee Avenue, Kowloon, Hong Kong
Email: ewong@ee.cityu.edu.hk
kmchan2@ie.cuhk.edu.hk

Tak-Shing Peter Yum

Department of Information Engineering
The Chinese University of Hong Kong
Shatin, Hong Kong
Email: yum@ie.cuhk.edu.hk

Abstract

Dynamic routing has been adopted in many circuit switched networks in many parts of the world. A number of dynamic routing schemes have been designed and studied with the aim of maximizing the network throughput. The Least Loaded Routing (LLR) is simple and efficient, while other more elaborate routing schemes can only provide marginal throughput gain over that of LLR. Re-routing is the practice of routing calls on alternate paths to direct paths or other less congested alternate paths. It allows the continuous re-distribution of network loads so that the congestion on direct paths can be relieved. In this paper, we study a re-routing scheme based on LLR. An original analysis of re-routing is performed and numerical examples confirm the significant throughput gain over LLR routing.

1 Introduction

The basic idea of dynamic routing in a circuit switched network is to increase throughput by routing calls to alternate paths when the direct path is blocked. However, the use of alternate paths usually consumes more network resources as the path length, in hops, is usually longer. Therefore, indiscriminate use of alternate paths could lead to the decrease of the network throughput and even network instability, as many of the previous research studies have shown [17, 2, 23, 22].

In recent years, a variety of approaches to alternate routing networks have been developed. AT&T has used a decentralized non-hierarchical routing strategy, called Dynamic Nonhierarchical Routing (DNHR) [3] for a number of years. DNHR is a time-dependent routing scheme that increases network efficiency by taking advantage of the non-coincidence of busy hours in a large-toll network. Dynamically controlled routing (DCR), a routing scheme developed by Bell Northern Research, uses a central processor to track the busy-idle status of network trunks and determine the best alternate route choices based on status data every 10 seconds [7, 6]. Dynamic alternate routing (DAR) was developed by British Telecom and uses a simple decentralized learning approach to adaptive routing [12, 24]. When the direct trunk group is busy, the two-link alternate path used last time is used for the overflow call. If the alternate path is busy, the overflow call is blocked, and a new alternate path is selected at random for the next overflow call. Taking advantage of the fact that it is feasible to monitor channel occupancies and make routing decisions on a call-by-call basis, AT&T recently adopted a new routing scheme called Real-Time Network Routing (RTNR) [4]. In RTNR, if a direct path is blocked, the call will be routed to the least loaded two-link alternate path. It was shown that this practice can improve the network connection availability while simultaneously reduce the network costs.

One major focus of dynamic routing research is to determine the "right" choice of alternate paths for overflow calls [22] The idea is to balance the traffic load among the alternate paths as much as possible while not loading any of them into congestion. Over the years, researchers have learned that the simple Least Loaded Routing (LLR) with trunk reservation can provide significant throughput gain over fixed routing while other more elaborate approaches (e.g. Markov Decision Process) can only provide marginal throughput gain [14, 15]. No wonder LLR was chosen as the basis of RTNR in AT&T Switched Network.

In this paper, we study the further throughput gain of LLR by incorporating re-routing. Re-routing is also called call crankback and call repacking in the literature. Previous studies by simulation can be found in [1, 13, 16, 26, 11, 18]. One purpose of re-routing is to re-distribute network load from time to time so as to

0-8186-7780-5/97 $10.00 © 1997 IEEE

free up more capacity for direct path calls. For example, if a channel has just been free up in link AC due to a call departure (Fig. 1), then a call on an alternate path (path ABC) can be re-routed back to link AC. Doing so would free up one channel each on links AB and AC and thus throughput can be increased. The focus of this paper is on an original analysis of a specific re-routing rule in a symmetrical fully connected network. This analysis is based on the Erlang fixed-point model first applied to state-dependent dynamic routing by Wong and Yum [27], in which LLR was analyzed. While significantly reducing the computational effort, the model was shown to be quite accurate. Subsequent application of this method appeared in [19, 20, 21, 5, 8, 9, 28, 29, 25, 30, 10]. This method has also been applied for analyzing a real network [5]. Two assumptions were made in these models and remain used in this paper: link independence and Poisson overflow traffic. As before, verification by computer simulation is done here as well.

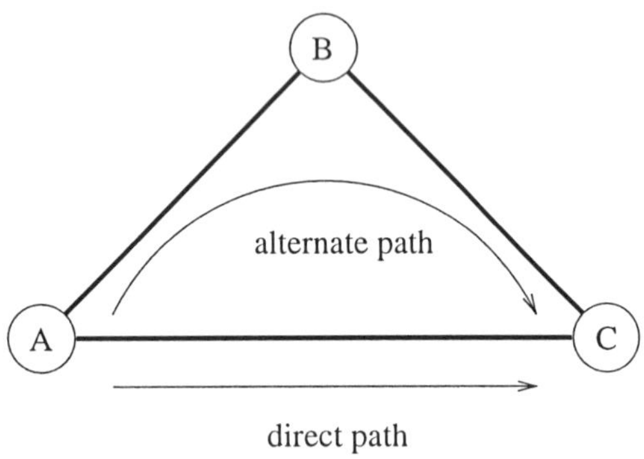

Figure 1: An alternate path of a node pair.

Many versions of re-routing is possible. Our focus is on a very simple one as follows: When a new call arrives finding the direct link blocked, an alternate call on this link, if any, is picked at random and gets re-routed back to its direct path (if not blocked) to make room for the new call. If re-routing is not possible, the overflow call is routed to the alternate path with the maximum number of free circuits as in LLR routing. If all alternate paths are full, the call is blocked.

The implementation of re-routing in a network requires the making of routing decisions on a call-by-call basis. And this has been shown to be feasible by the AT&T's RTNR [4] using stored-program control switches interconnected through a common channel signaling (CCS) network. Aside from a slightly more complicated software control and more signaling traffic, no hardware modification to the switching system is envisaged.

2 Analysis of Re-routing

Consider an M node fully connected and uniformly loaded network where all links consist of N channels. Let $\mathbf{n} = (d, a)$ be the loading state of a link where d and a are the numbers of direct and alternate calls on a link, respectively. Let $P_{\mathbf{n}} = P_{d,a}$ be the state probability. Let λ_D be the rate of direct-route offered traffic to a link and λ_O be the rate of overflow traffic from a link to other links. Let both these traffic streams be Poisson processes and let the call service time be exponentially distributed with mean equal to one time unit. We restrict our choice of alternate paths to those of two links only. The total number of such two-link alternate paths, denoted as m, is equal to $M - 2$ for the fully connected network under consideration. It is well-known that, if no suitable control is taken, the number of alternate path calls may dominate, resulting in significant reduction of network capacity [23]. It is also well known that trunk reservation, i.e. reserving the last r unoccupied channels in a link for direct route calls only, is an effective means of maintaining the network in the high capacity mode. Let Ω, Ω_D and Ω_A be the state space, the set of direct call blocking states, and the set of alternate call blocking states, respectively,

$$\Omega = \{\mathbf{n} : d, a \geq 0,\ a \leq N - r,\ d + a \leq N\} \quad (1)$$
$$\Omega_D = \{\mathbf{n} : \mathbf{n} \in \Omega, d + a \geq N\} \quad (2)$$
$$\Omega_A = \{\mathbf{n} : \mathbf{n} \in \Omega, d + a \geq N - r\} \quad (3)$$

Consider a particular alternate path. Let the number of occupied channels on the first link be i and that on the second link be j. Then, the number of available circuits k on that path is $k = N - \max(i, j)$. When the direct path is full, the LLR routing will direct the call to the alternate path with the maximum number of free circuits or with maximum k. When there are more than one such paths, choose one at random.

The overflow traffic from a link with rate λ_O consists of two components. The first component represents new calls finding all channels on the direct link being occupied by direct path calls. The second component comes from new calls finding a (> 0) alternate path calls and $N - a$ direct path calls but the direct paths of these a calls are all full. Under this situation, these a alternate path calls cannot be rerouted to their direct paths to make room for the new calls and these new calls have to overflow onto their alternate paths. Let H_a be the probability that all the direct paths corresponding to the a alternate path calls are full, then the overflow rate λ_O can be expressed as

$$\lambda_O = \lambda_D P_{N,0} + \lambda_D \sum_{a=1}^{N-r} P_{N-a,a} H_a \quad (4)$$

2.1 Deriving H_a

Consider a tagged link carrying a alternate calls. Let $\xi_{a,k}$ be the event that the a alternate calls come from k direct paths. At first sight, this is equivalent to the classical combinational problem of finding the probability that k boxes are occupied when a balls are thrown into $2m$ boxes at random. But a closer observation reveals that the balls are less likely to fall into empty boxes. Let us see why. We can distinguish two types of direct paths contributing to the alternate path traffic. The first type, denoted as *ordinary* direct paths, are those which do not currently have alternate path calls on the tagged link. These corresponds to the empty boxes. The second type, denoted as the *overflow* direct paths, are those currently having alternate path calls carried on the tagged link. These corresponds to the occupied boxes. It is apparent that these a alternate calls have some kind of *self-aggregate* property in the sense that the overflow calls are more likely to come from those overflow direct paths. Therefore, some modification to the urn problem is needed to capture this self-aggregate effect. We start from the following recursive argument by relating the case of a alternate calls to that of the $a-1$ alternate calls as follows:

$$\begin{aligned}\Pr[\xi_{a,k}] &= \Pr[\text{the additional alt. call comes from an overflow direct path} \mid \xi_{a-1,k-1}]\Pr[\xi_{a-1,k-1}] \\ &\quad + \Pr[\text{the additional alt. call comes from an ordinary direct path} \mid \xi_{a-1,k}]\Pr[\xi_{a-1,k}] \\ &= \frac{(2m-k+1)\lambda_O/\lambda_D}{k-1+(2m-k+1)\lambda_O/\lambda_D}\Pr[\xi_{a-1,k-1}] \\ &\quad + \frac{k}{k+(2m-k)\lambda_O/\lambda_D}\Pr[\xi_{a-1,k}] \end{aligned} \tag{5}$$

where λ_O/λ_D is the probability that an ordinary direct path is chosen to join the existing set of the overflow direct paths for the additional alternate call. This equation can be solved using the initial condition $\Pr[\xi_{1,1}] = 1$ and $\Pr[\xi_{1,k}] = 0$ for $k \neq 1$.

Returning from the definition of H_a, we have

$$\begin{aligned} H_a &= \Pr[\text{all direct paths corresponding to the } a \text{ alt. path calls on the tagged link are full}] \\ &= \sum_{k=1}^{\min(a,2m)} \Pr[\text{all } k \text{ direct paths are full} \mid \xi_{a,k}] \\ &\quad \times \Pr[\xi_{a,k}] \end{aligned} \tag{6}$$

Let $\beta_{a,k}$ denotes the probability that a particular direct path L corresponding to one (or more) of the a alternate paths calls on the tagged link are full given that there are k such direct paths. Assuming that the link occupancy statistics of these k paths are independent, H_a can be further expressed as

$$H_a = \sum_{k=1}^{\min(a,2m)} (\beta_{a,k})^k \Pr[\xi_{a,k}] \tag{7}$$

To derive $\beta_{a,k}$, let us consider the re-routing of alternate calls back to the direct path link L. Note that when a re-routing attempt occurs, the direct link is more likely to be in a high occupancy state, as otherwise alternate routing would not take place in the very beginning. Therefore, the direct link occupancy as seen by a re-routing attempt is no longer $P_{\mathbf{n}}$. Here, for simplicity, we choose to approximate it to be

$$P^*_{d,a} = \begin{cases} \dfrac{P_{d,a}}{\sum_{i+j=N-1}^{N} P_{i,j}} & d+a \in \{N-1, N\} \\ 0 & \text{otherwise} \end{cases} \tag{8}$$

by assuming the occupancy is always at either $N-1$ or N. Simulation results in all cases we tried did show that $N-1$ and N are the two most probable states as seen by re-routing calls. The steady state trunk occupancy distributed, however, is observed to be quite different. Therefore, we have $\beta_{a,k} = \sum_{i+j=N} P^*_{i,j}$.

2.2 Overflow rate at state n

Consider a particular link AC as shown in Fig. 1. If this link is full, the overflow calls of rate λ_O will be routed randomly to one of the LLRs. Let there be a total of α such paths. Then the alternate path load of AC that falls on a particular LLR, say path ABC, is λ_O/α. Let Z_i be the probability that a two-link alternate path has i or more occupied circuits. Then, assuming the two links are independent, we have

$$Z_i = 1 - \{\sum_{\forall \mathbf{n}: n < i} P_{\mathbf{n}}\}^2 \tag{9}$$

where $n = d + a$.

Given that path ABC has i occupied circuits, the probability $f(\alpha \mid i)$ that $\alpha-1$ other alternate paths also have i occupied circuits each **and** each of the remaining $m-\alpha$ alternate paths has more than i occupied circuits is given by

$$f(\alpha \mid i) = \binom{m-1}{\alpha-1}(Z_i - Z_{i+1})^{\alpha-1} Z_{i+1}^{m-\alpha} \tag{10}$$

where $Z_i - Z_{i+1}$ is the probability that an alternate path has exactly i occupied circuits. Therefore, given that path ABC has i occupied circuits, the amount of traffic y_i that gets routed from AC to alternate path ABC is

$$\begin{aligned} y_i &= \sum_{\alpha=1}^{m} \frac{\lambda_O}{\alpha} f(\alpha \mid i) \\ &= \frac{\lambda_O}{m}\frac{Z_i^m - Z_{i+1}^m}{Z_i - Z_{i+1}} \end{aligned} \tag{11}$$

Given that link AB is in state $\mathbf{n} \in \Omega \setminus \Omega_A$, where $A \setminus B$ denotes set A minus set B, the total overflow rate at state $\mathbf{n}$, denoted as $A_\mathbf{n}$, can be obtained by removing the condition on the second link to be

$$A_\mathbf{n} = 2m \sum_{\mathbf{i}\in\Omega\setminus\Omega_A} y_{\max(n^{(AB)}, i^{(BC)})} P_\mathbf{i} \tag{12}$$

where $x^{(y)}$ represents the number of calls in link y at state $\mathbf{x}$.

2.3 Re-routing transition rate at state n

If a new call between nodes A and B finds link AB full but has in it one or more alternate calls, i.e. the link is in state $(N-a, a>0)$, then it will cause an alternate call to be re-routed to its direct path if there is a vacant channel in that direct path. In this way, the new direct call can be accommodated on link AB. This occurs with probability $1-H_a$. Therefore, the corresponding transition rate $\psi_\mathbf{n}$ from $(N-a, a)$ to $(N-a+1, a-1)$ is

$$\psi_\mathbf{n} = \begin{cases} \lambda_D(1-H_a) & \mathbf{n} \in \Omega_R \\ 0 & \text{otherwise} \end{cases} \tag{13}$$

where $\Omega_R \equiv \{\mathbf{n} : \mathbf{n} \in \Omega,\ a>0,\ d+a=N\}$ is the set of re-routing states. As far as link AB is concerned, one direct call comes in and one alternate call departs, leaving the total number of calls unchanged.

2.4 Direct-route rate at state n

The re-routed traffic from alternate paths represents "extra" direct-route traffic in a link. Assuming the alternate calls for re-routing are randomly chosen, the re-routing rate ψ in a link is simply $\psi = \sum_{\mathbf{k}\in\Omega_R} \lambda_D(1-H_a)P_\mathbf{k}$. There are two issues to note. First, when a re-routing occurs, the direct link is also more likely to be in a high occupancy state. Therefore, the direct link occupancy as seen by a re-routed call is no longer $P_\mathbf{n}$. Here, for simplicity, we choose the distribution seen by a re-routed call to be

$$P^{**}_{d,a} = \begin{cases} \frac{P_{d,a}}{\sum_{i+j=N-1} P_{i,j}} & d+a=N-1 \\ 0 & \text{otherwise} \end{cases} \tag{14}$$

by assuming the occupancy is always at $N-1$. This is an approximation and is justified by the simulation results showing that the most probable state is indeed $N-1$ for all the cases we tried. Under this approximation, the states for which re-routing can take place are $\{(d,a) \mid d+a=N-1\}$. Therefore, the effective re-routing rate ψ' seen by these states is

$$\psi' = \frac{\psi}{\sum_{i+j=N-1} P_{i,j}} \tag{15}$$

Second, the extra direct traffic in a link comes from $2m$ possible links. But each of these $2m$ links also has $2m$ possible links for re-routing or has a probability $1/2m$ to choose the tagged link. Therefore, the total direct-route rate at state $\mathbf{n}$ is

$$D_\mathbf{n} = \begin{cases} \lambda_D + 2m(\frac{1}{2m})\psi' & d+a=N-1 \\ \lambda_D & 0 \le d+a < N-1 \\ 0 & \text{otherwise} \end{cases} \tag{16}$$

2.5 Service rate at state n

The re-routing of alternate calls in a link, say AB, (due to new call arrivals on that link) causes "extra" departures in another link, say BC, since an alternate call lies on a two-link alternate path. However, since link BC has $2m$ possible alternate path traffic on it and its companion link such as AB also has $2m$ possible links on which its alternate paths can possibly lies, the service rate $\mu_\mathbf{n}^{(A)}$ for alternate calls at state $\mathbf{n}$ is increased to

$$\mu_\mathbf{n}^{(A)} = a + 2m(\frac{1}{2m})\frac{\psi}{\sum_{j\neq 0} P_{i,j}} \tag{17}$$

where $\psi/\sum P_{i,j}$ is the normalized rate of "extra" departures due to re-routing under the condition $a \neq 0$. As a check, $\sum_{a\neq 0}(\mu_\mathbf{n}^{(A)} - a)P_{d,a} = \psi$ as it should be. The service rate of direct calls at state $\mathbf{n}$ is simply $\mu_\mathbf{n}^{(D)} = d$.

Therefore, for state $\mathbf{n} \in \Omega$, the global balance equation is given by

$$(\mu_\mathbf{n}^{(D)} + \mu_\mathbf{n}^{(A)} + D_\mathbf{n} + A_\mathbf{n} + \psi_\mathbf{n})P_\mathbf{n} = \mu_{d+1,a}^{(D)} P_{d+1,a} + \mu_{d,a+1}^{(A)} P_{d,a+1} + D_{d-1,a}P_{d-1,a} + A_{d,a-1}P_{d,a-1} + \psi_{d-1,a+1}P_{d-1,a+1} \tag{18}$$

with the understanding that $P_\mathbf{n} = 0$ for $\mathbf{n} \notin \Omega$.

Let Λ denote the set of $A_\mathbf{n}$ and $\mathcal{P}$ denote the set of $P_\mathbf{n}$. Then (12) and (18) can be expressed in the fixed point model form [22]: $\mathcal{P} = f_1(\Lambda)$ and $\Lambda = f_2(\mathcal{P})$. The $P_\mathbf{n}$'s can be computed by the Successive Over-Relaxation (SOR) method with the set of alternate traffic rates obtained from (12) in each iteration.

Finally, the call blocking probability is given by [23] as

$$P_B = \lambda_O/\lambda_D[1-(1-\sum_{\mathbf{n}\in\Omega_A} P_\mathbf{n})^2]^m \tag{19}$$

3 Discussion

We study the performance of re-routing by numerical examples. Computer simulation results are also obtained and compared. The 95 percent confidence intervals have all been set to a size smaller than the marks on the figures (by varying the duration of simulation) and are therefore not shown. The results of

LLR without re-routing based on the model in [27] are presented for comparison. For simplicity, we use D to represent the direct-route offered load λ_D. Figure 2 shows the performance of re-routing as a function of D on a 5 node ($m = 3$) and a 10 node ($m = 8$) symmetrical fully connected networks with $r = 3$ and $N = 20$. It is seen that the analytical result matches well with the simulation results both for LLR and re-routing. It is also seen that the performance of LLR can always be improved using re-routing. Figure 2c shows the re-routing rates against D. It is found that in both $m = 3$ and $m = 8$, re-routing rate increases with network load.

Figure 3 shows the overflow traffic rates at different trunk occupies, i.e. the number of calls in a link. It is shown that re-routing can reduce the amount of overflow traffic. Figure 4 shows the call blocking probabilities as a function of r. It is seen that re-routing can maintain network stability without trunk reservation. In fact, minimum blocking probability occurs at $r = 0$. Figure 5 shows the re-routing rate as a function of r. It is seen that as r increases, re-routing rate drops since there is less and less alternate calls in a link available for re-routing.

Figure 6 shows the call blocking probability of re-routing as a function of network size M with trunk size $N = 20$, $D = 19$, and $r = 3$ for LLR routing and $r = 0$ for re-routing. It is found that as M increases from 5 to 12, call blocking using re-routing is reduced at fixed loading while for LLR routing the blocking probability is nearly constant. This shows that re-routing has the added advantage of "sizing efficiency" in addition to trunking efficiency.

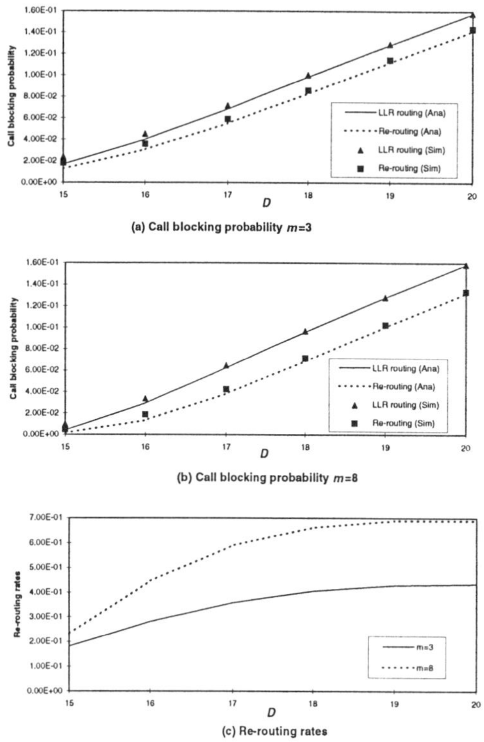

Figure 2: Performance of re-routing against D.

4 Conclusions

A simple re-routing scheme based on Least Loaded Routing (LLR) was studied in this paper. Numerical results showed that re-routing can provide a significant throughput increase over LLR under all conditions. More interestingly, re-routing is shown to be an effective means for maintaining the stability of the network under dynamic routing. Therefore, using re-routing, trunk reservation is no longer needed and for which additional throughput gain can be obtained. The approximate analysis is shown to be accurate and computationally efficient.

References

[1] M.H. Ackroyd, "Call repacking in connecting networks," in *IEEE Trans. on Commun.*, Vol. 27, No. 3, pp. 589-591, March 1979.

[2] J.M. Akinpelu, "The overload performance of engineered networks with nonhierarchical and hierarchical routing," *AT&T Bell Labs Technical Journal,* 63:1261-1281, 1984.

[3] G.R. Ash and E. Oberer, "Dynamic routing in the AT&T network – Improved service quality at lower cost," in *Proc. IEEE Global Telecommun. Conf.*, Dallas, Texas, Nov. 1989.

[4] G.R. Ash, J.-S. Chen, A.E. Frey, and B.D. Huang, "Real-time network routing in a dynamic class-of-service network," in *Proc. Thirteenth Int. Teletraff. Congr.*, Copenhagen, Denmark, June 1991.

[5] G.R. Ash, and B.-S.D. Huang, "An analytical model for adaptive routing Networks," *IEEE Trans. on Commun.*, vol. 41, no. 11, pp. 1748-1759, Nov. 1993.

[6] BNR, Special Issue: "Dynamic Network Controller Family," *Telesis Mag.*, 1986.

[7] W.H. Cameron, J. Regnier, P. Galloy, A.M. Savoie: "Dynamic routing for intercity telephone networks," *ITC-10*, Montreal, 1983.

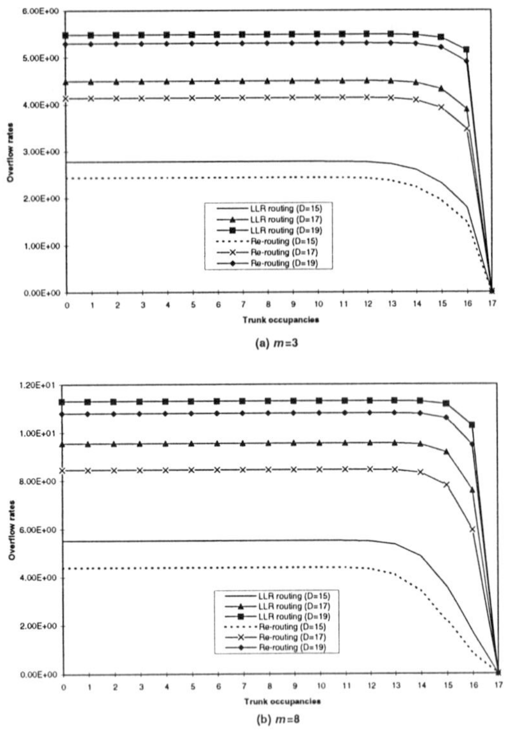

Figure 3: Overflow rates against trunk occupancies.

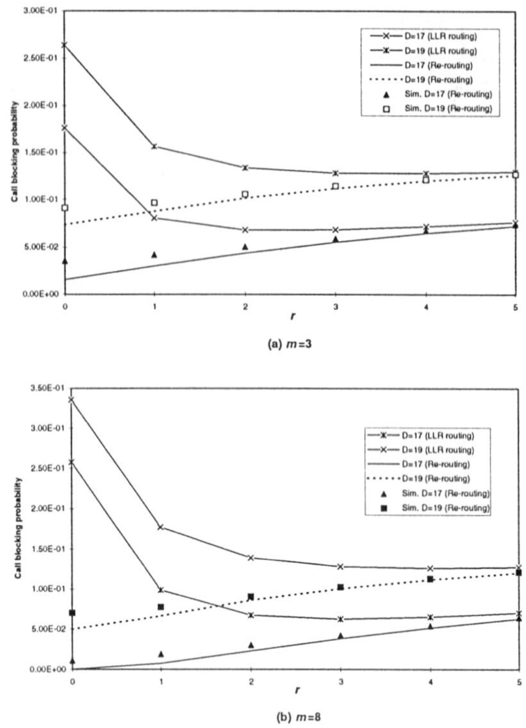

Figure 4: Call blocking probability against r.

[8] K.M. Chan and T.S.P. Yum, "Analysis of adaptive routing schemes in multirate loss networks," *Proc. IEEE Globecom 93,* 1993. Also in *Telecommun. Systems.*, vol. 5, pp. 341-359, 1996.

[9] K.M. Chan and T.S.P. Yum, "Analysis of Least Congested Path routing in WDM lightwave networks," *Proc. IEEE Infocom 94,* 1994.

[10] K.M. Chan and T.S.P. Yum, "Comparative analysis of call admission policies with adaptive routings in multirate loss networks," submitted to *Proc. IEEE ICC '97.*

[11] R. Cohen, "Smooth intentional rerouting and its applications in ATM Networks," in *Proc. IEEE Infocom 94,* pp. 1490-1497, 1994.

[12] R.J. Gibbens, "Some aspects of dynamic routing in circuit-switched telecommunications networks," *Statist. Lab.*, Univ. Cambridge, Jan. 1986.

[13] A. Girard and S. Hurtubise, "Dynamic routing and call repacking in circuit-switched networks," in *IEEE Trans. on Commun.*, Vol. 31, No. 12, pp. 1290-1294, Dec. 1983.

[14] R.H. Hwang, J.F. Kurose and D. Towsley, "MDP routing in ATM networks using the virtual path concept," in *Proc. IEEE Infocom 94*, pp. 1509-1517, 1994.

[15] R.H. Hwang, "LLR routing in Homogeneous VP-based ATM Networks," in *Proc. IEEE Infocom 95,* pp. 587-593, April 1995.

[16] R.H. Hwang and J.F. Kurose, "On virtual circuit routing and re-routing in packet-switched networks," *Proc. IEEE ICC'91*, pp. 1318-1323, 1991.

[17] R.S. Krupp, "stabilization of alternate routing networks," In *Proceedings of International Communications Conference*, Philadelphia, 1982.

[18] K.C. Lee and V.O.K. Li, "A circuit rerouting algorithm for all-optical wide-area networks," in *Proc. IEEE Infocom 94*, pp. 954-961, 1994.

[19] D. Mitra, R. J. Gibbens and B.D. Huang, "Analysis and optimal design of Aggregated-Least-Busy-Alternate Routing on symmetric loss network with trunk reservations," *13th International Teletraffic Congress,* 1991.

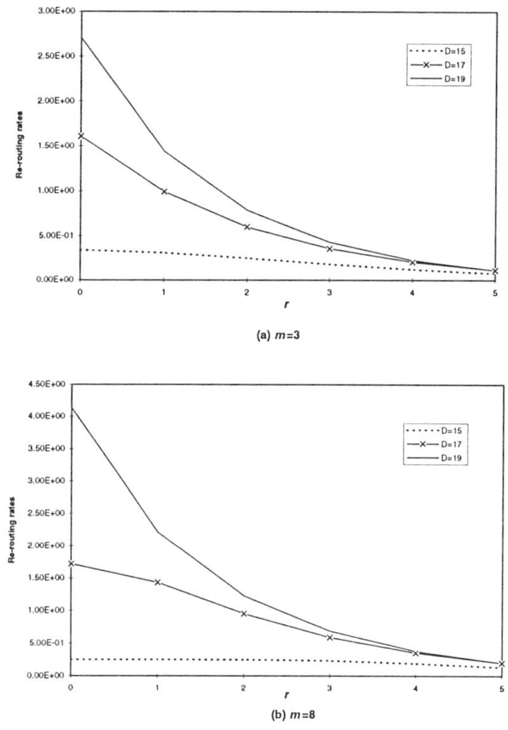

Figure 5: Re-routing rates against r.

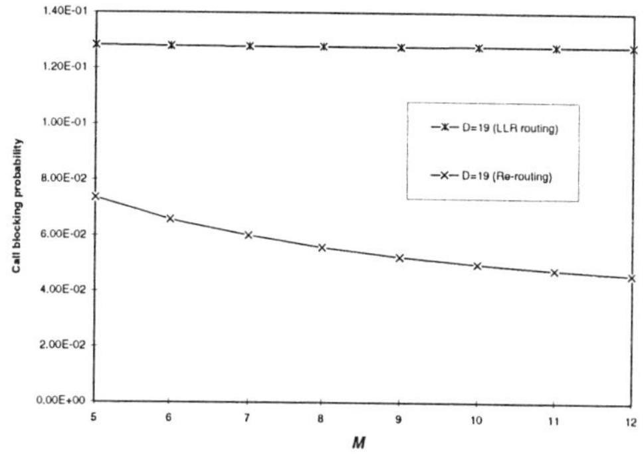

Figure 6: Call blocking probability against network size M.

[20] D. Mitra and R.J. Gibbens, "State-dependent routing on symmetric loss networks with trunk reservations, II: Asymptotic, Optimal Design," *Ann. Oper. Res.*, 35:3-30, 1992.

[21] D. Mitra, R.J. Gibbens, B.D. Huang, "State-dependent routing on symmetric loss networks with trunk reservations, I," *IEEE Trans. on Commun.*, vol. 41, no. 2, Feb. 1993.

[22] K.W. Ross, *Multiservice loss models for broadband telecommunication networks,* Springer, Chapter 7, 1995.

[23] M. Schwartz, *Telecommunication Network: Protocols, Modeling and Analysis,* Addison Wesley, 1988.

[24] R.R. Stacey and D.J. Songhurst, "Dynamic alternative routing in the British telecom trunk network," in *Proc. Int. Switching Symp.,* Phoenix, AZ, Mar. 1987.

[25] C. Vargas, M.V. Hegade, M. Naraghi-Pour, and P.S. Min, "Shadow Prices for LLR and ALBA," *IEEE/ACM Trans. on Networking*, Vo. 4, No. 5, pp. 796-807, 1996.

[26] B.R. Venkatraman and R.E. Newman-Wolfe, "Performance analysis of a method for high level prevention of traffic analysis using measurements from a campus network," *Proc. 10th Annual Computer Security Application Conference*, pp. 288-297, 1994.

[27] E. W.M. Wong and T.S. Yum, "Maximum free circuit routing in circuit-switched networks," *INFOCOM '90*, pp. 934-937, 1990.

[28] E. W.M. Wong, T.S.P. Yum, and K.M. Chan, "Analysis of the M and M^2 routings in circuit-switched networks," *European Transactions on Telecommunications*, Vol. 6, N0.5, pp. 613-619, Sept.- Oct. 1995.

[29] E. W.M. Wong, K.M. Chan, S. Chan, and K.T. Ko, "Bandwidth allocation and routing in virtual path based ATM networks," *Proc. IEEE ICC'96*, June 1996.

[30] E. W.M. Wong, K.M. Chan, S. Chan, and K.T. Ko, "VP formulation and dynamic routing in ATM networks," *Proc. IEEE GLOBECOM'96*, Nov. 1996.

IP Multicasting for Point-to-Point Local Distribution*

George Xylomenos George C. Polyzos

{xgeorge,polyzos}@cs.ucsd.edu
Computer Systems Laboratory
Department of Computer Science and Engineering
University of California, San Diego
La Jolla, CA 92093-0114, U.S.A.

Abstract

While support for IP multicasting continues to spread enabling new applications, an increasing number of hosts connects to the worldwide Internet via low bandwidth Point-to-Point links, such as wireline or wireless telephone lines. In this paper we discuss existing proposals for local and wide area IP multicasting and their implications for Point-to-Point links, identify problems with their integration in this environment, and propose alternative special purpose mechanisms to solve these problems. The main problems are overhead due to IGMP **leave latency** *and unnecessary continuous probing of potentially power constrained hosts. Our solution is an alternative to IGMP mechanisms based on* **join/leave** *messages for tracking group membership over PtP networks. After presenting the implementation requirements of our proposed and the existing mechanisms, we compare them with respect to performance, interoperability, robustness and implementation complexity, demonstrating that our* **join/leave** *protocol is uniformly superior.*

1 Introduction

The traditional modes of communication in computer networks are *unicasting* and *broadcasting*, where data are sent to one and all hosts in a network, respectively. *Multicasting*, where data are sent to an arbitrary set of hosts referred to by a *single* identifier, can be viewed either as an intermediate case, or as a generalized mode encompassing both unicasting and broadcasting as extreme cases. Multicasting eases communication with a *logical* set of hosts that may implement distributed or replicated services or may participate in group communication applications. Broadcasting also uses a single identifier for communication with multiple entities, but is wasteful of host and network resources. Alternatively, multicasting delivery semantics may be achieved by multiple unicasts, but the sender must keep track of intended recipients, while independent unicasts cause data duplication whenever paths to separate recipients share links. As multicasting offers a useful addressing abstraction and the potential for bandwidth savings, it is a desirable service for both local and wide area networks.

*This research was supported in part by a National Semiconductor Corporation Graduate Fellowship, a DDR&E Focused Research Initiative under ARO Grant No. DAAH 04-95-1-0248, and the UC MICRO program.

On the Internet, the *Internet Protocol* (IP) has been used for many years to achieve interoperability among heterogeneous technologies at the network layer, forming a single wide area internetwork that presents a common service interface to end-to-end layers. IP extensions that support multicasting have been proposed and implemented, leading to the development of the *Mbone*, a wide area multicasting testbed [1]. The MBone has been used for audio and video conferencing, following the general trend towards integration of various modes of digital communications in a single network. For these applications multicasting is used due to its potential for bandwidth savings. On the other hand, its increased flexibility compared to broadcasting is important for resource discovery and automatic host configuration applications, which are becoming more important as host mobility is introduced in IP. The next version of IP will integrate support for multicasting from the beginning with the goal of replacing broadcast based with multicast based services.

Although IP multicasting has evolved from mechanisms available in shared medium broadcast LANs, IP itself is an internetworking protocol that achieves interoperability among different technologies. In recent years the Internet has been expanded by incorporating emerging or existing *Point-to-Point* (PtP) local distribution mechanisms, such as *Asynchronous Transfer Mode* (ATM) networks and serial lines. Many end hosts are connected to Internet service providers via telephone links, either analog or digital, wireline or wireless, effectively forming PtP link LANs with the provider's equipment as the hub of a star topology. These PtP networks are sufficiently different from shared medium LANs to warrant closer examination of the implications of transplanting the existing IP multicasting model to them. By separating *models* from *mechanisms*, we examine in this paper the problems that emerge when existing mechanisms are used in PtP networks and propose alternative optimized mechanisms that remain compatible with the IP multicasting model.

In Section 2 we describe the IP multicasting model, its supporting mechanisms and their origins, as well as their potential problems when used for PtP local distribution. In Section 3 we examine alternative approaches to solving these problems and identify a *join/leave* mechanism as the most promising one. In Section 4 we describe the modifications to existing mechanisms required to implement this approach. In Section 5 we evaluate our approach by com-

0-8186-7780-5/97 $10.00 © 1997 IEEE

paring it to existing ones with respect to performance, interoperability, robustness and implementation complexity. In Section 6 we examine quantitatively the performance of all proposals discussed in the paper under two sets of assumptions. We present our conclusions in Section 7.

2 IP multicasting and Point-to-Point local distribution

2.1 IP multicasting model

The basic concept in IP multicasting is the *host group*, an arbitrary set of network hosts identified by a single, class D, IP address [2]. Hosts can *join* or *leave* a group at any time. Group members receive all datagrams addressed to the group, while *any* host can send datagrams to a group, regardless of its membership status. Multicast IP datagrams are distinguished from unicast ones by their destination address only. To achieve multicasting in a wide area network, we need a mechanism to keep track of the dynamic membership of each group and another mechanism to route the multicast datagrams from a sender to these group members without unnecessary duplication of traffic. IP multicasting implements these mechanisms in two parts: *local* mechanisms track group membership and deliver multicasts to the correct hosts within a local network, and *global* mechanisms route datagrams between local networks. Distinguishing local from global mechanisms is appropriate for IP since it is an internetworking protocol: each local network can use mechanisms appropriate to its technology, while co-operation among networks is achieved by hiding local differences behind a common interface.

In each local network, at least one host or router acts as a *multicast router*. A multicast router keeps track of local group membership and is responsible for forwarding multicasts originating from its network towards other networks, and for delivering multicasts originating elsewhere to the local network. Multicast delivery of either externally or locally originated datagrams to local receivers, as well as reception of local multicasts by the router for subsequent propagation to other networks, depend on the underlying network technology. Accordingly, the information needed within the local network regarding group membership in order to achieve local multicast delivery may vary. In contrast, co-operation among multicast routers with the purpose of delivering multicast datagrams between networks is based on a network independent interface between each local network and the outside world. The information needed in order to decide if multicasts should be delivered to target networks is whether at least one group member for a destination group is present there. A multicast router uses the information for each of its attached local networks along with information exchanged with its neighboring routers to support wide area multicasting. Irrespective of the group membership information tracked by a multicast router for local purposes, *the interface between local information and global routing is a list of groups present at each attached network*. Based on this interface, alternative algorithms can be used for routing among networks, without affecting local mechanisms. Conversely, as long as this interface is provided by the local mechanisms, they can be modified without affecting routing.

2.2 IP multicasting mechanisms

Since in IP multicasting global and local mechanisms are decoupled, any combination of mechanisms supporting the group membership list interface described above can be employed. A variety of global, wide area multicast routing, mechanisms exist, with the earliest and most widespread being the *Distance Vector Multicast Routing Protocol* (DVMRP). DVMRP v.1 [3] is a variant of *Truncated Reverse Path Broadcasting* [4]. Routers construct distribution trees for each source sending to a group, so that datagrams from the source (root) are duplicated only when tree branches diverge towards destination networks (leaves). Each router identifies the first link on the shortest path from itself to the source, i.e. on the shortest *reverse* path, using a distance vector algorithm. Datagrams arriving from this link are forwarded towards downstream multicast routers, i.e. those routers that depend on the present one for multicasts from that source. A *broadcast* distribution tree is thus formed with datagrams reaching all routers. Since each router knows which groups are present in its local networks, redundant datagrams are not forwarded by *truncating* the tree. DVMRP v.3 [5] implements the improved *Reverse Path Multicasting* [4] mechanism, which *prunes* tree branches leading to networks that have no members, and *grafts* them back when members appear, thus turning the group distribution tree to a real multicasting one.

Another proposal is the *Multicast Open Shortest Path First* (MOSPF) [6] protocol, which uses a link state algorithm: routers flood their membership lists among them, so that each one has complete topological information concerning group membership. Shortest path multicast distribution trees from a source to all destinations are computed on demand as datagrams arrive. These trees are real multicast ones, but the flooding algorithm introduces considerable overhead. A radically different proposal for multicast routing is the *Core Based Trees* [7] (CBT) protocol, which employs a *single* tree for each group, shared among all sources. The tree is rooted on at least one arbitrarily chosen router, called the *core*, and extends towards all networks containing group members. It is constructed starting from leaf network routers towards the core as group members appear, thus it is a multicast tree composed of shortest reverse paths. Sending to the group is accomplished by sending towards the core; when the datagram reaches any router on the tree, it is relayed towards tree leaves. Routing is thus a two stage process which can be sub-optimal. The first stage may propagate datagrams away from their destinations until the tree is reached, thus increasing delay, and in addition, traffic tends to concentrate on the single tree rather than being spread throughout the network. Another proposal, the *Protocol Independent Multicast* (PIM) [8] protocol, employs either shared or per source trees, depending on application requirements.

Networks supporting IP multicasting may be separated by multicast unaware routers. To connect such networks, *tunnels* are used: tunnels are *virtual* links between two endpoints, that are composed of a, possibly varying, sequence of physical links. Multicasts are relayed between routers by encapsulating multicast datagrams within unicast datagrams at the sending end of the tunnel and decapsulating them at the other end. The MBone [1] is a virtual network composed of multicast aware networks bridged by such tunnels. Multicast routers may choose to forward through the tunnels only datagrams that have *Time to Live* (TTL) values above a threshold, to limit multicast propagation.

Routing mechanisms are concerned with multicast propagation on a mesh of PtP links, the typical topology for an internetwork backbone. The end points of this mesh are local networks served by their local multicast routers. Global routing mechanisms are able to function correctly as long as a group membership list for each local network is maintained and made available by local routers. This interface enables global routing to deal with networks as single entities, thus reducing routing calculations and tables to manageable magnitudes, while hiding local details from the outside world. Multicast routing protocols that employ multicast sources in addition to destinations (DVMRP and MOSPF), also view sources as source *networks* rather than as source *hosts*.

In contrast to global mechanisms, only a single set of local mechanisms exists. These local multicasting and group management mechanisms were based on shared medium broadcast networks such as Ethernet, and this is evident on some of the design decisions made. Delivery is straightforward on these LANs, as all hosts can listen to all datagrams and select the correct ones. If a LAN supports multicasting as a native service, class D IP addresses may be mapped to LAN multicast addresses to filter datagrams in hardware rather than in software. Multicasts with local scope do not require any intervention by the multicast router, while externally originated multicasts are delivered to the LAN by the router. The router also monitors all multicasts so that it can forward to the outside world those for which receivers exist elsewhere. Both unicasts and multicasts are physically broadcast on these LANs, so the only issue for the router when delivering externally originated multicasts is whether at least one member for the destination group exists in the network. The router only has to keep internally a local group membership list, which coincides exactly with the information on which global multicast routing is based.

Both versions of the *Internet Group Management Protocol* (IGMP) provide a mechanism for group management well suited to broadcast LANs, since only group presence or absence is tracked for each group. In IGMP v.1 [9] the multicast router periodically sends a *query* message to a multicast address to which all local receivers listen to. Each host, on reception of the query, schedules a *reply*, or report, to be sent after a random delay, for each group in which it participates. Replies are sent to the address for the group being reported, so that the first reply will be heard by all group members and suppress their own transmissions. The router monitors all multicast addresses, so that it can update its membership list after receiving each reply. If no reply is received for a previously present group for a number of queries, the group is assumed absent. In steady state, in each query interval the router sends one query and receives one reply for each present group. When a host joins a group it sends a number of unsolicited reports to reduce *join latency* for the case where it is the first local member of the group. No explicit action is required when a host leaves a group, as group presence times out when appropriate.

In IGMP v.2 [10] a host must send a *leave* message when abandoning a group, but only if it was the *last* host to send a report for that group. However, since this last report may have suppressed other reports, the router must explicitly probe for group members by sending a *group specific* query to trigger membership reports for the group in question. It can only assume the group absent if no reports arrive after a number of queries. All IGMP v.2 queries include a time interval within which replies must be sent: general queries may use a long interval to avoid concentrating reports for all groups, while group specific queries may use a short interval to speed up group status detection. The time between the last host leaving a group and the router stopping multicast delivery for that group is called the *leave latency*.

2.3 Point-to-Point vs. broadcast LANs

The query/reply mechanism has two peculiarities: first, it periodically repeats the same cycle of queries and replies, and second, joining and leaving a group normally takes effect after one or more cycles are completed. Join latency is reduced by the, possibly redundant, unsolicited reports. In contrast, after all hosts leave a group, it will not be assumed absent for a number of cycles. During this period redundant multicasts will be delivered to the network. Even if *every* host did multicast a leave message when abandoning a group, the router would still need to decide whether other members of the group still exist locally, by further probing for group status. IGMP v.2 requires members to send leave messages only when they were the last to send a membership report: in all other cases, at least one other group member existed locally a while ago. The reason that leave messages are not enough to determine group status is that routers keep a list of present groups rather than a list of member hosts for each group. The simple group list is sufficient for making delivery decisions in broadcast LANs, but then group absence can only be determined by the absence of membership reports and not by leave messages alone. In a LAN with plenty of bandwidth, this approach trades off bandwidth overhead due to query/reply cycles and leave latency, for simplified group management at the router. The duration of the query interval is a compromise between management overhead and delivery overhead after a group disappears, hence the decision in IGMP v.2 to support distinct intervals for each query at the price of complicating somewhat the router protocol. Although the periodic queries add robustness to group management, they also add complexity to hosts, which have to continuously set up timers for replies and suppress or send periodic reports.

When end hosts are connected to a router via Point-to-Point links, some of these assumptions do not hold. While bandwidth may be plentiful in ATM LANs, hosts connected to the Internet via telephone links are currently quite bandwidth constrained, and will continue to be so if these links become wireless. Wireless mobile hosts have additional battery power and processing constraints that urge for simplified local mechanisms. Thus, local mechanisms that reduce the leave latency and periodic group management overhead of existing mechanisms would be preferable. IGMP v.2 can reduce overhead compared to IGMP v.1 by using different intervals for general and group specific queries, but still some query/reply cycles are needed to detect group absence, thus management and leave latency overhead cannot be completely eliminated. In addition, the periodic queries disturb mobile hosts that could otherwise employ *sleep mode* to conserve battery power. Fortunately, we can take advantage of the fact that only one host is at the end of a PtP link. Group presence on such a link is equivalent to the host being a member of this group, solving the problem of distinguishing between individual and collective group membership. This means that both join and leave messages can be interpreted unambiguously as indications of group presence and absence, respectively. Therefore, periodic queries are not needed to detect group absence. To take advantage of PtP links, the router needs a group presence list per link, the same information kept by existing mechanisms. We will show how these lists may be simply aggregated to present all local PtP links as one local network for routing purposes. Multicast delivery from the router to end hosts is trivial, as is reception by the router of local multicasts that need to be forwarded to the external world. Local multicasts are *not* automatically received by other local receivers; they must be relayed to them via their PtP links by the router.

3 Supporting Point-to-Point networks

3.1 Extending local mechanisms

Existing implementations of the IP multicasting extensions treat each physical interface of a multicast router as an entry point to a distinct network, including local PtP links. Note the distinction between backbone and local PtP links; global routing mechanisms are used in the former, while local delivery and group management mechanisms are used in the latter. The router executes an instance of the IGMP protocol for each local PtP link, treating it exactly the same as a broadcast LAN. In DVMRP v.1 each multicast reaches all routers, so the only local decision is whether to deliver it locally. This decision is based on the individual membership lists. If however the routing protocol limits multicast propagation to only those areas containing group members, information must be summarized. MOSPF routers have complete knowledge about membership in all networks, so summarizing this information across all local links is the only way to avoid routing explosion. DVMRP v.3 prunes and grafts distribution trees based on aggregate membership lists at each router [5]. It is advantageous for last hop routers to keep aggregate group membership lists spanning all their local PtP links, since routers serving telephone links can be expected to have numerous PtP interfaces. IGMP processing and group membership aggregation across these links places a considerable overhead to the router, but per link group membership information is necessary to avoid delivering multicasts that have only one local receiver over *all* links.

Routers can periodically update their aggregate group membership list by combining individual lists across all PtP links. The problem is that existing IGMP mechanisms are not very well suited to PtP links as discussed earlier. IGMP v.2 leave messages attempt to reduce leave latency but they are not authoritative indications of group absence in broadcast LANs, so the router must send group specific queries to determine group status. To guarantee robustness, multiple such queries are required. In a broadcast LAN, if the group is not absent, unnecessary messages are exchanged, but if it is absent leave latency is reduced. To compensate for this overhead, general query intervals may be increased, but not too much, as group absence *cannot* be noticed via this mechanism in some cases. For example, when the last host to send a membership report crashes and all other hosts leave the group before the next query, no leave messages will appear, making the general queries the only way to determine group absence. In contrast, leave messages over PtP links are authoritative; since only one host is connected to the link, they are definite proof that the group is absent. Since only one host uses the link, it will always be the one that sent the last reply for the group, thus IGMP v.2 reduces leave latency without requiring any changes for PtP links. Even though this solves the problem of detecting group absence, the protocol still goes through periodical general and group specific query/reply cycles that are largely redundant, as we will show.

An alternative treatment for PtP links would be to view them as backbone PtP links, by turning each end host into a multicast router and extending the area covered by global routing. Even though multicast routing works well over a mesh of PtP links, moving all end hosts into the backbone is impractical, due to scalability problems. DVMRP v.1 broadcasts each multicast to all routers, so multicasting would effectively turn into broadcasting all the way to the end hosts. DVMRP v.3 starts in a broadcasting mode until the distribution tree is pruned, and periodically reverts to broadcasts, so it would have similar problems at a lesser scale. MOSPF would face routing table explosion, since each router would have to keep information on all end hosts. Only core based protocols (such as CBT or PIM) could work with this approach, as they explicitly construct distribution trees without ever employing broadcasts and routers make forwarding decisions based on local information only. Regardless of the routing protocol used, extending global mechanisms to local PtP links violates the IP distinction between internetworking and local networking. Local mechanisms should be used to address issues at a network characterized by common physical attributes so that optimizations can be taken advantage of, rather than forcing global internetwork mechanisms on dissimilar networks. Thus, extending local mechanisms to best support PtP links is the only viable approach.

3.2 The Join/Leave mechanism

As already discussed, on both PtP and broadcast links one group membership report is enough to indicate membership presence on that link. Furthermore, for PtP links one leave group message indicates group absence from the link. Thus, periodic group membership queries and replies can be eliminated completely from a PtP link by employing simple *join* and *leave* messages to unambiguously determine the membership status of the end host. The leave message obviates the need to periodically reconfirm membership, while the (unsolicited) join message immediately indicates group presence. General group queries, which serve as synchronization points for the randomized timers in broadcast networks, as well as their corresponding replies, are redundant. The group specific queries of IGMP v.2 are also redundant on a PtP link. Since the periodic queries and the group presence timeouts enhance robustness with IP, which only offers unreliable delivery, join/leave messages should be *confirmed*, that is, they should be explicitly acknowledged by the router and retransmitted if an acknowledgment does not arrive before a timer expires. The join/leave mechanism is similar to the proposal for tracking multicast group membership in the IP multicast over ATM case [11], although there connectivity between the *multicast server* and end hosts is over virtual circuits rather than physical PtP links, and the delivery mechanisms differ. The join/leave mechanism is based on the observation that in PtP links the periodic queries result in end hosts sending repeatedly their *complete* state. By only transmitting the state *difference*, we end up with the join/leave messages, since it is these actions only that result in state changes.

Because only one end host is attached to the PtP link, there is no need to synchronize random timers to avoid multiple reports, in turn making periodic queries redundant. This mechanism eliminates join and leave latencies between the local router and end hosts since there are no waiting periods for group timeouts, potentially eliminating overhead from redundant multicast transmissions. Similarly, periodic queries and replies are also eliminated, reducing group management overhead, but not always minimizing it (see Section 5). The join/leave mechanism is end host initiated, with changes to membership state being transmitted as they occur rather than periodically. As a result, mobile wireless hosts would have to wake up only when absolutely necessary, to process either join/leave messages that they initiate, or multicasts that they want to receive. There is no need for periodic per group timer management to handle replies to queries, although per join/leave event timers are still required for retransmissions of the (acknowledged) join/leave messages. The multicast router has always updated information on local membership by modifying its tables whenever join and leave messages arrive rather than periodically. It can also immediately aggregate group information across all local PtP links, as we will see below, in order to present to other routers the image of a single local network, by using a single group list.

4 Implementing the Join/Leave mechanism

In this section we describe the implementation of the join/leave local multicasting mechanisms in order to facilitate comparisons with existing mechanisms (see Section 5). To clarify both differences and similarities between the join/leave and query/reply mechanisms, we describe a proposed implementation as a set of modifications to existing query/reply ones. We assume that the link layer notifies the network layer multicast module when the state of the PtP link changes either due to the peer rebooting or due to a *cell handoff* in a cellular network, where the end host changes its point of attachment to the network. This may be achieved by an upcall to the network layer whenever the link layer re-establishes its PtP connection.

Multicast transmission between end hosts and the router uses the same primitives as normal unicasts, so the multicast router automatically receives all multicasts that may have to be forwarded to other networks. The router maintains per link group membership lists in order to deliver both local and external multicasts only to group members, treating each PtP link as a separate interface and using the same data structures employed by existing mechanisms.

From the viewpoint of end hosts, group management is considerably simplified. Processes join and leave multicast groups, and the host keeps a reference count for membership in each group so that it can notify the multicast module when a group is initially joined or finally abandoned, similar to existing mechanisms. These notifications however lead directly to acknowledged join and leave IGMP messages; the host must retransmit these messages after a timeout if no acknowledgment arrives. Acknowledgments and retransmissions are used as a substitute to the automatic recovery from lost messages provided by the periodic queries and replies in existing mechanisms. The timer bookkeeping overhead is reduced since instead of one timer per group that has to be set and reset continuously, only one timer per join/leave operation is required. The host does not need to remember if it sent the (nonexistent) last membership report, so eliminating the local leave latency using leave group messages is achieved considerably easier. Since with join/leave group management consists of isolated rather than continuous periodic actions, in periods of network inactivity battery powered hosts can employ sleep mode.

From the viewpoint of the multicast router, query timers, general queries and group specific queries, are completely eliminated. In the join/leave approach, the router *never* initiates any messages, its only responsibility being to acknowledge join/leave messages from end hosts. Queries and their associated timers are redundant because in PtP links both join and leave messages are authoritative. Updating per link membership lists consists of adding the group when a join arrives and deleting it when a leave arrives. For the aggregate group membership list, join actions cause adding elements to the list, if needed, but leave actions in one link do not necessarily mean that there are no members in other links. One approach for simple aggregate list management is to use reference counts for each membership entry, updating them based on join and leave actions for each per link list. Reference counts, if used, should be updated only the *first* time that a join/leave is received, and not for its retransmissions, by ignoring, for reference counting purposes only, join/leave messages that do not modify the per link list. Using these mechanisms, both per list and aggregate group membership lists are immediately updated, eliminating leave latency incurred overhead.

The proposed join and leave messages can employ the same format as existing ones, with new type numbers. IGMP messages already contain a group address field which is the only data that join/leave messages need. For fixed networks, router and end hosts could be expected to use the same IGMP variant, so existing messages could be used (*report* and *leave*) without causing interoperability problems. For mobile wireless hosts however, it is not guaranteed that all systems (routers and hosts) would agree on IGMP operations, so an initial negotiation phase is needed. As a minimum, all systems should implement, and be able to fall back to, the standard query/reply mechanism. Since in the join/leave approach routers do not initiate any transactions, the mobile host could initiate operations by sending a join message for an arbitrary group: if the router acknowledges the message, the join/leave mechanism is supported, and the host can send a leave for the group, else, if after a number of retransmissions there is no response, the mobile should use the standard mechanisms. The router should start in standard mode to cater for hosts using standard mechanisms, and switch to join/leave mode for a *specific* PtP link only after receiving a join.

When an end host reboots, the router should empty its link membership list and the host will re-establish this state as its applications are restarted, while when the router reboots, the host should retransmit a join for each of the groups that it participates in to re-establish its link membership list. For mobile hosts, when a handoff is detected, the host acts as if the router on the other end is rebooted in order to re-establish its link state, while the old router serving the mobile empties its link membership list, as if the end host had rebooted. These events are communicated to the multicast module by the link layer whenever the link state is changed from connected to disconnected and back.

5 Evaluation of the Join/Leave mechanism

As discussed in Section 3, the join/leave mechanism is a simplified form of the query/reply mechanism that takes advantage of PtP link properties to optimize operations. In this section we will present a more detailed comparison between the two models with respect to performance, interoperability, robustness, and implementation complexity. The generic performance analysis presented in this section is taken further in Section 6 with two examples showing the tradeoffs involved under specific assumptions on protocol parameters and application behavior.

Concerning performance, in IGMP v.1 the parameter that determines the balance between group management and leave latency incurred transmission overhead is the query interval. It is impossible to eliminate both types of overhead with a single query interval value and it is also impossible to make reasonable tradeoffs based on individual group behavior as periodic queries trigger reports for *all* groups. In IGMP v.2 leave latency is reduced due to the leave messages, but subsequent group specific queries are needed to guarantee that a group is absent (ignoring the case discussed in Section 3.1 where group absence is determined by general queries) and to guarantee robustness multiple queries are needed. In PtP links leave messages do not cause unneccessary overhead as they are always authoritative, even though the protocol does not know it. By adjusting the group specific query interval the leave latency can be reduced. Thus, with respect to transmission overhead the zero local leave latency of the join/leave mechanism is superior to the query/reply mechanisms. When messages are lost, all mechanisms recover after additional messages, but while join/leave timers can be tight as they only have to account for round trip and processing delay, query intervals should be large enough to make randomization effective in suppressing duplicate reports, even though they are impossible in PtP links. Thus, even when messages are lost, the join/leave mechanism remains superior. The added accuracy in tracking group membership may also reduce transmissions among routers when a non broadcast based routing protocol is employed.

Group management overhead, as measured by IGMP messages, is more complicated. Membership in a group in the query/reply model requires one report per interval, but leaving *any* number of groups in the same interval leads to *all* groups being detected as absent after some queries. Assuming messages are not lost and a large number of groups (so that the cost of queries can be ignored) the join/leave mechanism is superior to the IGMP v.1 when *membership to any group lasts for at least four consecutive intervals*. The justification is that membership to a group in the join/leave model for *any* period of time costs four messages: a join, a leave, and their acknowledgments, which is the cost of four periodic replies, as a separate report is sent for each group. As the number of groups that a host participates in at the same time is reduced, the join/leave mechanism becomes more favorable since the group queries are amortized among fewer reports. The cost for leaving a group in IGMP v.1 is small as its detection is automatic and it does not depend on the number of groups present. In the presence of lost messages the costs are harder to compare as they depend on the exact messages lost. To reduce join latency, IGMP requires hosts to immediately send a number of reports upon joining a new group. In IGMP v.2 we also have leave messages sent on PtP links with only one receiver. Routers respond to each such message with a number of group specific queries. When these mechanisms are taken into account, even when each message is only sent once, the four mandatory messages of the join/leave mechanism are balanced in IGMP v.2 *after only one query interval*: one initial report, one report after the first query, one leave message, and one group specific query. Thus, protocol message overhead for the join/leave model is usually lower than any version of IGMP, while leave latency transmission overhead is always lower. For battery powered mobile wireless hosts, in addition to the reduced transmission and protocol overhead, we should also take into account the advantages arising from the receiver initiated nature of the join/leave mechanism. As the join/leave mechanism is simpler in operation than existing mechanisms, due to fewer timers, a simpler protocol state machine and easier aggregation of membership state, its processing requirements are lower.

Interoperability among different versions of IGMP can be achieved using the procedures described in Section 4. Routers using join/leave mechanisms locally can participate in multicast routing based on the present groups list, which remains the interface between local group membership information and multicast routing. An optimization over existing IGMP versions is the automatic aggregation of all PtP link information as if a single LAN interface was present. Deployment of the join/leave mechanism should be direct for fixed networks, while for mobile wireless networks both variants should be implemented in a common module for backward compatibility. Since all mechanisms share the same data structures, dual implementations should not be considerably larger than existing ones.

Robustness in join/leave is achieved by acknowledged messages, while with query/reply recovery is provided by the periodic queries. An advantage of the join/leave mechanism is that the explicit acknowledgments to joins are a positive indication to end hosts that they are members of the group, while in the query/reply model a host cannot distinguish between group inactivity and lost reports. Conversely, absence of replies to periodic queries may mean either group absence or lost reports, while in the join/leave case leave actions are explicit and authoritative, and the protocol knows it.

A sample implementation has been described in Section 4. Since most structures and operations are based on existing implementations, join/leave mechanisms are easy to implement, while shared data structures mean that dual implementations will be compact. The only significant addition is the initial handshaking used to discover the version of IGMP supported by the peer. In most aspects, including timer management, mapping process actions to messages, and mapping messages to state updates, the join/leave mechanism either simplifies existing mechanisms, as is the case with timers, or eliminates them, as is the case with group specific queries. A pure join/leave implementation could be developed by deleting code from existing implementations and adding join/leave handling and retransmission timers, resulting not only in easier maintenance, but also in simpler protocol operation, which in turn affects performance. Even when multiple protocol variants are implemented for compatibility, only join/leave will be executed when supported by both peers.

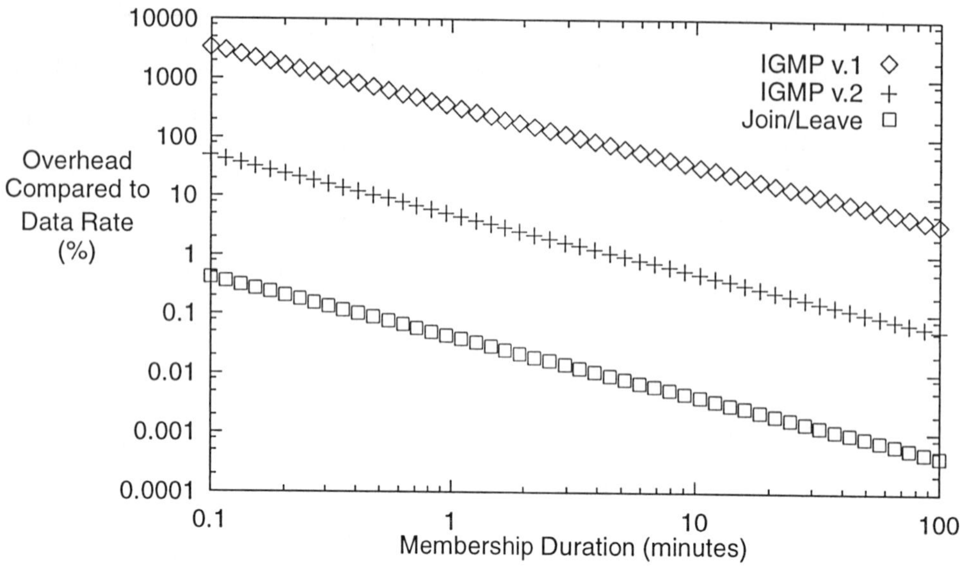

Figure 1: Overhead as a percentage of data rate for a 128 Kbps videoconference as membership duration varies.

6 Quantitative performance examples

To supplement the analysis of Section 5, we examine the exact overhead involved when the two IGMP versions and our join/leave mechanism are used in two scenarios. Note that on a PtP link, when an IGMP v.2 host leaves a group it always sends leave messages. We use the timer, query interval and repetition values specified in the draft specification of IGMP v.2 for both IGMP versions [10]. We assume that IGMP messages, regardless of mechanism, are 256 bits long on the link, which includes 20 bytes for the IP header, 8 bytes for the IGMP payload, and 4 bytes for link layer overhead. We also assume that no messages are lost. Under these assumptions, the overhead can be analytically computed.

The first scenario is a video conference which uses a total of 128 Kbps for one audio and two video streams, each using a separate group. This is the bandwidth of two ISDN B channels, although in practice we would use the 128 Kbps to accommodate both data and overhead rather than only data. In this example group membership lasts as long as the host participates in the conference, so the host joins and leaves each group exactly once. We compute protocol and leave latency overhead as a percentage of data rate, as membership duration varies from 0.1 to 100 minutes. IGMP sends two unsolicited reports when joining a group and queries are sent every 125 seconds. In IGMP v.1 two query intervals plus 10 seconds are needed to notice group absence: assuming that the host leaves the group halfway between two queries, it continues to receive data for about 200 seconds. In IGMP v.2 when a host leaves a group it sends one leave message and the router replies with two group specific queries, so datagrams for the group stop being forwarded after only 3 seconds. Join/leave only sends one acknowledged join and one acknowledged leave message per group, regardless of membership duration. Figure 1 shows total protocol and transmission overhead as a percentage of data rate for the videoconference example. We ignored the impact of query messages, which is negligible on this busy high speed link. Scales are logarithmic, to show the differences in overhead despite the wide range of numbers involved and to clarify the effects of membership duration. IGMP v.2 and join/leave are close, although for short membership intervals IGMP v.2 has significant overhead, while join/leave drops immediately below 1%. IGMP v.1 causes considerable overhead, with very high values for short conferences and significant values for longer ones. Overhead in this link is mainly due to leave latency, as the high data rates dwarf the group management overhead. IGMP v.1 is slow in detecting leave events, so it performs very poorly until the conference duration is long enough to amortize the 200 seconds of wasted transmissions. IGMP v.2 is much faster in detecting group absence due to leave messages and their short timeout interval of 3 seconds. Over longer intervals, IGMP v.2 is only marginally worse than join/leave due to the periodic reports. For join/leave the cost is constant and small, so overhead percentage quickly approaches zero. Thus, when membership duration is extremely short, join/leave has a definite advantage over IGMP v.2, which vanishes for longer membership durations. Similar results hold when the aggregate bandwidth is varied from 16 Kbps to 1 Mbps: join/leave performance is slightly affected since its fixed cost is amortized slower or faster.

In the second scenario, the host participates in an arbitrary set of groups that emit 64 bps data streams, e.g., an 8 byte message every 4 seconds, including IP and link layer overhead. This could be a wireless host receiving low data rate streams, such as messaging services. Since we assume the same data rate for each group, we analyze them separately. The formulation is as in the first scenario, the only difference being that each group has a 64 bps data rate and we need the overhead as a percentage of that rate. Membership duration varies independently for each group. We ignore the query overhead as it is again much less than the data rate, although periodic queries prohibit wireless hosts from entering sleep mode. The results are shown in Figure 2, again using logarithmic scales. Here the periodic

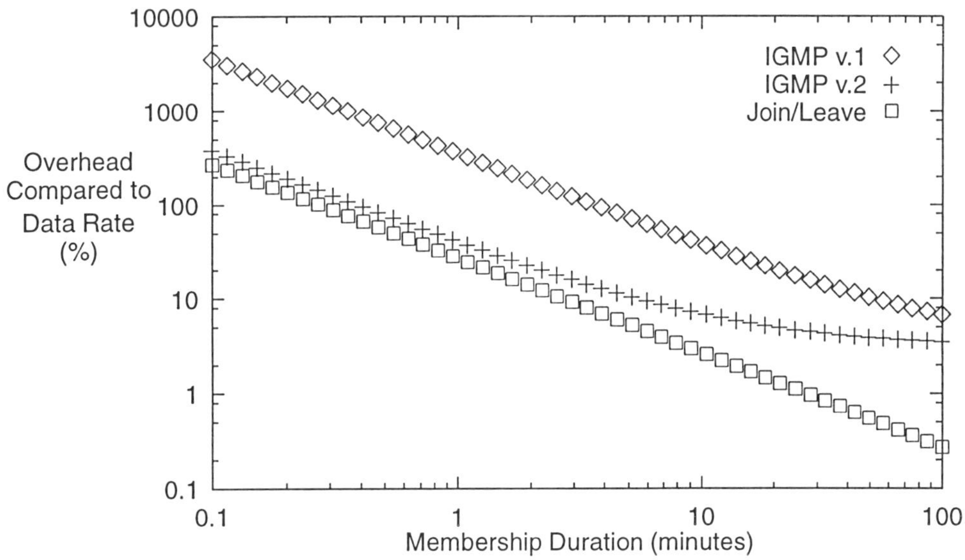

Figure 2: Overhead as a percentage of data rate for a 64 bps group as membership duration varies.

group management overhead is much more important than before, due to the low data rates. For the same reason, leave latency has a smaller effect. As membership duration increases, join/leave amortizes its fixed total cost with the overhead eventually approaching zero, while for short membership periods the overhead is significant, due to the low data rate. Similarly, both IGMP versions start with a significant overhead, and amortize it as membership duration increases. However, periodic IGMP costs, which are the same for both versions, make both curves eventually approach the same asymptote, away from join/leave. Thus, even though IGMP v.2 and join/leave start close, as membership duration increases join/leave overhead approaches zero while IGMP v.2 overhead never falls below a certain level, making join/leave a superior choice. Similar results hold for data rates between 8 bps and 512 bps, i.e. the relative positions of the curves do not change.

7 Conclusion

We have presented some problems that existing implementations of IP multicasting extensions face when deployed in networks with Point-to-Point (PtP) local links, such as wireline or wireless telephone lines, and identified as their cause the orientation of local IP multicasting mechanisms towards broadcast LANs. After considering the alternatives, we proposed a *join/leave* mechanism for tracking group membership over PtP networks. We then presented an implementation outline for this mechanism by modifying existing mechanisms, showing that the join/leave mechanism considerably simplifies operations. We also compared the join/leave approach with the standard query/reply mechanism with respect to protocol performance, as measured by transmission overhead, as well as interoperability with existing implementations, robustness and implementation complexity. Based on this comparison we conclude that the join/leave mechanism is superior to existing ones for any type of PtP link, while being easy to implement and deploy. When bandwidth or processing power are limited, as in battery powered mobiles using cellular telephone links, our proposal could lead to significant improvements.

References

[1] H. Eriksson, "MBONE: The multicast backbone," *Communications of the ACM*, vol. 37, no. 8, pp. 54–60, August 1994.

[2] D.R. Cheriton and S.E. Deering, "Host groups: A multicast extension for datagram internetworks," in *Proceedings of the 9th Data Communications Symposium*, September 1985, pp. 172–179.

[3] S. Deering, C. Partridge, and D. Waitzman, "Distance vector multicast routing protocol," Internet Request For Comments, November 1988, RFC 1075.

[4] S.E. Deering and D.R. Cheriton, "Multicast routing in internetworks and extended LANs," *ACM Transactions on Computer Systems*, vol. 8, no. 2, pp. 85–110, May 1990.

[5] T. Pusateri, "Distance vector multicast routing protocol," Internet Draft (Work in Progress), September 1996.

[6] J. Moy, "Multicast routing extensions for OSPF," *Communications of the ACM*, vol. 37, no. 8, pp. 61–66, August 1994.

[7] A. Ballardie, J. Crowcroft, and P. Francis, "Core based trees (CBT) — An architecture for scalable inter-domain multicast routing," in *Proceedings of the ACM SIGCOMM '93*, October 1993, pp. 85–95.

[8] S. Deering, D. Estrin, D. Farinacci, V. Jacobson, C. Liu, and L. Wei, "An architecture for wide-area multicast routing," in *Proceedings of the ACM SIGCOMM '94*, October 1994, pp. 126–135.

[9] S. Deering, "Host extensions for IP multicasting," Internet Request For Comments, August 1989, RFC 1112.

[10] W. Fenner, "Internet group management protocol, version 2," Internet Draft (Work in Progress), October 1996.

[11] G.J. Armitage, "Multicast and multiprotocol support for ATM based internets," *Computer Communications Review*, vol. 25, no. 2, pp. 34–46, April 1995.

Application-Layer Anycasting

Samrat Bhattacharjee, Mostafa H. Ammar, Ellen W. Zegura
Viren Shah, Zongming Fei

Networking and Telecommunications Group, College of Computing,
Georgia Institute of Technology, Atlanta, GA 30332
{bobby,ammar,ewz,viren,fei}@cc.gatech.edu

Abstract

The anycasting communication paradigm is designed to support server replication by allowing applications to easily select and communicate with the "best" server, according to some performance or policy criteria, in a group of content-equivalent servers. We examine the definition and support of the anycasting paradigm at the application layer, providing a service that maps anycast domain names into one or more IP addresses using anycast resolvers. In addition to being independent from network-layer support, our definition includes the notion of filters, functions that are applied to groups of addresses to affect the selection process. We consider both metric-based filters (e.g., server response time) and policy-based filters. An expanded version of this work can be found as a technical report.[1].

1 Introduction

The Internet is increasingly being viewed as providing services, and not just connectivity. As this view becomes more prevalent, it becomes important to provide, within the Internet, explicit support for the efficient delivery of networked services. An important consideration in the provision of networked services is the ability to meet the demands of a large number of geographically wide-spread users. It is also important that the user-perceived quality of service (e.g., response time, throughput, reliability) be maintained at an acceptable and (in the case of commercial services) competitive level. This is often referred to as the *scalability* of the service.

There have been several approaches proposed for improving the scalability of a networked service. These include server replication [1], caching [2, 3], batching of requests at the server [4] and multicasting of server responses over the network [5, 6]. We investigate the *anycasting* communication paradigm which has been proposed [7] to support server replication.

As originally defined [7], anycasting provides:

> "a stateless best effort delivery of an anycast datagram to at least one host, and preferably only one host, which serves the anycast address."

In this definition, an *IP anycast address* is used to define a group of servers that provide the same service. A sender desiring to communicate with only one of the servers sends datagrams with the IP anycast address in the destination address field. The datagram is then routed using anycast-aware routers to at least one of the servers identified by the anycast address.

In our work we adopt a more general view of anycasting as a *communication paradigm* that is analogous to the unicast, broadcast, multicast communication paradigms. In particular, we differentiate between the anycasting *service definition* and the *protocol layer* providing the anycasting service [2]. The original anycasting proposal [7] can, therefore, be viewed as providing the anycasting service definition *and* examining the provision of this service within the IP layer.

In this paper we examine the definition and support of the anycasting paradigm at the *application layer*. Our motivation derives from the fact that network-layer-supported anycasting has the following limitations:

- Some part of the IP address space must be allocated to anycast addresses. For IPv4, several ways to allocate anycast addresses have been suggested [7].These include designating some existing addresses as anycast (e.g., within Class C) or creating a separate class of addresses. IPv6 proposals [9] do include a specific address space allocated to anycasting.

- The use of anycast addresses requires router support. Routers must recognize anycast addresses

[1] ftp://ftp.cc.gatech.edu/pub/coc/tech_reports/1996/GIT-CC-96-25.ps.Z

[2] For example multicasting as a communication paradigm represents a desire to send the same message to a group of receivers. The multicast paradigm can be supported using multicast routing at the network layer, or it can be supported above a unicast-only network or transport layer by using multiple unicasts. This latter approach was how many multicast problems were addressed in early system designs (e.g., the original ISIS distributed system [8]). There is clearly a distinction between multicast as a communication paradigm and how this paradigm is supported.

0-8186-7780-5/97 $10.00 © 1997 IEEE

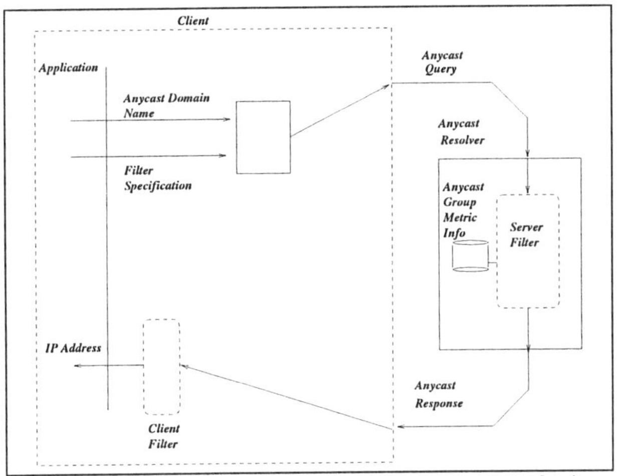

FIGURE 1: Anycast Name Resolution Query/Response Cycle

and forward packets properly. Routers must coordinate with one another to ensure that delivery is usually made to exactly one host.

- The selection of the server to which an anycast datagram is sent is made entirely within the network with no option for user selection or input.
- Consistent with the stateless nature of IP, the destination is determined on a per-datagram basis. Thus, two successive datagrams sent to an anycast address may be delivered to two different hosts that serve the address. Protocols that require all datagrams be delivered to a single host may use anycasting for discovery of a satisfactory host; but use standard IP for subsequent transmissions.
- The network layer is able to efficiently determine shortest paths, thus it is well-suited for an anycasting service that selects the closest server based upon a shortest path metric such as hop count. An application layer approach is better suited at handling a variety of other metrics such as server throughput.

Whereas network-layer support hinges around the use of anycast IP addresses, our application-layer support makes use of *anycast domain names* (ADNs). The function of an application-layer anycasting service is to map an ADN into one or more (multicast or unicast) IP addresses. An important feature of application-layer anycasting is that it does not require modifications to network layer operations.

This paper focuses on the design of an infrastructure to provide an application-layer anycasting service. Our design centers around the use of *anycast resolvers* to perform the ADN to IP address mapping. Clients interact with the anycast resolvers according to a basic query/response cycle illustrated in Figure 1: a client generates an *anycast query*, the resolver processes the query and replies with an *anycast response*. A key feature of the system is the presence of *metric databases* containing performance data about servers. The performance data is used in the selection of a server from a group, based upon user-specified performance criteria.

2 Related Work

The server or resource finding problem has been the subject of much investigation for over a decade. Initially, with low to moderate server loads, the problem was how to find the desired resource over the network knowing only its name or property. Techniques were proposed and investigated, including: 1) the use of multicast or broadcast communication to "touch" all the locations where the resource may reside in an attempt to find it (e.g., [10, 11]) , 2) the use of various name server architectures in order to lookup the location of the resource (e.g., [12, 13, 14]), 3) the use of caching of a resource's location (not content) at sites where the resource is frequently accessed [15]. The case of a mobile resource was addressed through interesting techniques such as the use of forwarding addresses [16]. More recently, the Service Location Working Group of the IETF is considering the design of the Service Location Protocol which allows a user to specify a set of service attributes which can be bound to a server's network address in a dynamic fashion [17].

The Internet has experienced a dramatic growth in the use and provision of information services such as `ftp`, `archie`, `gopher`, and more recently the World Wide Web. This has resulted in heavy demands being placed on servers and the desire to replicate (or mirror) servers. This adds a new dimension to the server-finding problem: it is now important to find the "best" server from among many content-equivalent servers. Two notable studies in this area are: 1) the original work by Partridge, Mendez and Milliken [7] proposing the idea of anycasting and discussing its network-layer support and 2) a recent study by Guyton and Schwartz [18] which addresses the problem of locating the nearest server. The latter work also presents a classification of "best"-server location schemes. The work is related to earlier work on the `Harvest` system [19] which provides a set of tools for gathering information from various servers and efficiently indexing and searching through this information.

To avoid the scalability problems inherent in probing for performance, we explore the idea of having the server "push" onto the network its own locally generated performance observations. This is related to the *Push Caching* idea [20] where servers are in charge of pushing the desired information onto remote caches and the *server push* mechanism [21] implemented in Netscape browsers.

Finally, anycasting is related to the technique used to build scalable HTTP servers [22]. In such a scheme multiple servers are clustered and appear to the outside world a single logical server. Modifications to the DNS resolution mechanisms are made to allocate the load among the servers.

3 Generalized Anycasting

In this section we describe the definition of application-layer anycasting as a communication paradigm. Later sections are concerned with issues relating to the realization of this paradigm.

3.1 What Is a Replicated Service

An anycast domain name (ADN) is used to identify a particular network service that can be provided by multiple locations on the network. We say that two servers *replicate* each other if they contain equivalent content and/or functionality from an *application perspective*. It is true that servers with identical content or functionality are considered replicas of each other, though in our definition replicated servers do not necessarily have to be identical.

The Network Time Protocol (NTP) is an example of a simple service that is widely replicated, where all servers provide identical functionality. On the other hand, whereas the many web news sites (e.g., CNN Interactive, Time Magazine and USA Today) carry different information, they, nevertheless, can be construed as being replicated servers for some applications.

We also extend our notion of service to include more general functionality than information content, e.g., *compute servers*. In this case the user is interested in finding a server on which to run a particular computation. The set of available hosts can then be made to form an anycast group. A performance measure of interest to select the best server might be CPU load. An interesting variation occurs if the user has a parallel program to run that requires the use of multiple hosts. This is an instance of multiple hosts providing a single instance of a service; making the anycast group a collection of pre-formed multicast groups each containing enough hosts to execute the parallel program.

3.2 Anycast Groups

An anycast domain name (ADN) uniquely identifies a (potentially dynamic) collection of IP addresses, which constitutes an *anycast group*. An anycast group can be made up entirely of unicast IP addresses or entirely of multicast IP addresses [3]. In the former case the anycast group represents a group of servers and in the latter it represents a collection of multicast groups. In both cases, the anycasting service provides a mapping from the ADN representing the group to the "best" address in the collection according to some criteria.

The motivation for collecting a set of unicast IP addresses into an anycast group is straightforward and derives from the original motivation of the anycasting paradigm. Each of the IP addresses in the group represents the address of one of the replicated servers providing the service. Reaching any one of them is acceptable (as far as service content and functionality is concerned), and the anycasting service makes a decision based on performance and/or policy metric.

We allow a collection of multicast addresses to form an anycast group in order to support classes of quorum consensus applications [23, 24, 25, 26]. For these applications, it makes sense to define multicast groups made up of subsets of the set of all coordinators, assign each subset a multicast address and collect the multicast addresses into an anycast group. The application then would use the ADN associated with this group to refer to the coordination service. The anycasting implementation would map the ADN into a multicast group with the desired quality (e.g., least average coordinator load or distance from client).

It is also possible to define an anycast group as a collection of server domain names or aliases [4]. In this case the anycasting service provides a mapping from an ADN into a host domain name or alias. Obtaining the IP address in this case requires an additional DNS server lookup. On the other hand, knowing the domain names that make up an anycast group may facilitate the process of selecting from among the group members as will be discussed later.

3.3 Anycast Domain Names

The issue of the structure of anycast domain names influences the operation of the anycasting system in general, and the anycast resolver architecture in particular. We propose an approach in this paper that is derived from the Internet naming and directory service architecture. Such an approach makes it straightforward to integrate our anycasting architecture into the

[3] Although the general case of a mixture of unicast and multicast addresses is possible, we do not consider it in this paper since we cannot conceive of an application that would use it.

[4] As there is no existing convention for naming multicast groups, currently this only makes sense if the anycast group is a collection of hosts and not a collection of groups of hosts.

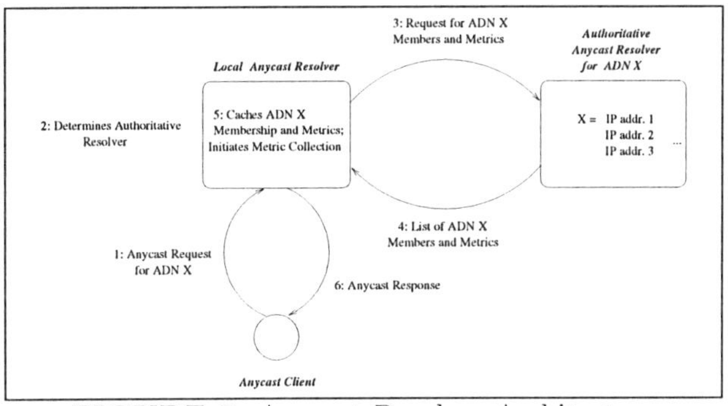

FIGURE 2: Anycast Resolver Architecture

existing Internet infrastructure.

We prefer to view the anycast resolver as logically distinct from other name servers like DNS [12], allowing us to consider issues related to anycast resolver design separately from other name service issues. In reality, the functions of an anycast resolver could be integrated with the operation of DNS.

We propose that an anycast domain name (ADN) be of the form `<Service>%<Domain Name>`. Such a name will typically be used as an argument to a library call that invokes the anycasting service and results in the mapping of this ADN to an IP address. The `Domain Name` part of the system indicates the location of the *authoritative* anycast resolver for this ADN. The `Service` part of the ADN identifies the service within the authoritative resolver.

The anycast resolver architecture is shown in Figure 2. Each network location is preconfigured with the address of its local anycast resolver in the same way local DNS servers are configured. An anycast client makes its initial anycast query to its local resolver. If the resolver is authoritative for the ADN in the query or if it has cached information about the ADN, it can process the query immediately and return the appropriate response. Otherwise, the local resolver determines the address of the authoritative resolver for the `Domain Name` part of the ADN and obtains the anycast group's information which is then cached in the local resolver. Determining the address of the authoritative anycast resolver for a particular domain can be done using the same technique used for DNS to determine an authoritative name server [12].

This hierarchical naming allows users to define their own anycast groups and maintain such groups in local anycast resolvers. Propagating the ADN of a locally-defined anycast group (including the name of the domain in which its authoritative resolver resides) allows others to make use of this anycast group.

An anycast resolver maintains the information necessary to perform the mapping from ADN to IP address. This information includes:

1. The list of IP addresses that form particular anycast groups. Authoritative resolvers maintain the definitive list, whereas local resolvers cache this information.

2. The metric information associated with each member of the anycast group. This information is maintained independently at each anycast resolver that has the ADN group membership information cached. Because of the local significance of the metric information, metrics maintained at the authoritative resolver are, in general, of little value to other resolvers. The authoritative resolver may provide its locally maintained metric information whenever it receives a request from another resolver for the anycast group member list for a given ADN. Local resolvers can use this information as "hints" initially as they begin to gather their own metric information.

4 Interacting with Anycast Resolvers

An anycast resolver is consulted through the use of *anycast queries* and the resolver responds with *anycast responses*. The basic anycasting query/response cycle is illustrated in Figure 1. First, the anycast client generates a query that is passed on to the anycast resolver. After processing the query, the resolver generates a response which is sent back to the client. In general, an additional processing step is performed at the client to yield the final IP address. Another message exchange may be required between a local resolver and an authoritative resolver. A separate (but straightforward) protocol needs to be defined for such an exchange.

4.1 Filtering and Decision Making

In our proposed approach the anycasting service is accomplished through a set of filters that are applied to the information maintained about the anycast group to obtain an IP address. We distinguish between three basic types of filters: content-independent filters, metric-based filters and policy-based filters. We further distinguish between two locations for filtering: within the resolver and at the user. (See Figure 1.)

Content-independent filters can be used to specify a selection of anycast group members based solely on membership information and not based on any other criteria maintained or known by the server. Examples of such filters include: 1) the selection of any member at random, 2) the selection of all members of the anycast group, or 3) the selection of a subset of the anycast group of some given size.

Metric-based filters specify selection according to the values of one or more metrics associated with the members of the anycast group. The following variations are of interest:

- Select the best anycast group member(s) according to a single criterion.
- Select the best anycast group member(s) according to a function of one or more metrics. For example, a weighted sum of metrics can be used, allowing a client to control the importance of each metric in the overall evaluation of an anycast group member.
- Select the best anycast group member(s) resulting from the sequential application of filters. By composing filters in series, one can specify a strict priority in the selection process. In the case of two filters, the first metric is given top priority and the second metric is used to further refine the selection set. For example, one might first select a web location that has the fastest response time, and then (amongst the fastest) choose the location that is the least number of hops away.

Policy-based filters are not based on measurements of performance, but rather encompass the broad range of other criteria that might affect the selection of an address. Policy filters are likely to be boolean, in the sense that an address either meets or fails the policy criteria. Applying policy filters may be easier if the membership of the anycast group is known by domain names rather than just IP address. If the anycast group members are maintained by IP address, mapping these addresses into domain names (e.g., through the use of DNS Pointer Queries) may be required before the application of a policy filter.

Related to the issue of the *order* in which filters are applied is the issue of the *location* where they are applied. In our generalized version of anycasting, the anycast service may provide the anycast client with a *list* of addresses that meet the specified criteria. Thus there are two locations for filters: in the anycast resolver and at the anycast client. The resolver begins with the set of anycast group members and applies filters to produce a list. The client can take the resolver list and further apply filters to select a single member.

A sequence of filters applied to the set of anycast group members is *successful* if the number of addresses produced is acceptable to the client procedure. In all cases the return of exactly one IP address for an application to use should be an acceptable outcome. Ideally, the application procedure that invokes the anycasting service should also be capable of dealing with the case where multiple or no addresses are returned. This is because, in general, it is not always possible to know *a priori* the outcome of the application of a set of filters to an anycast group. In the case where multiple addresses are returned from the anycast service invocation, the application can arbitrarily pick one of the returned addresses. This is equivalent to applying yet another (content-independent) filter. In case the anycast service invocation returns no addresses, a fall back position needs to be programmed into the application procedure. For example, it could retry with another set of filters or a content-independent filter asking for any group member at random.

4.2 Filter Specification

Local filters are relatively easy to deal with since they are typically conceived, specified and applied in the same location. Resolver filters, on the other hand, are specified at a client but are run by the resolver, which adds complexity to their specification.

We envision two types of filter specifications. In the first case, the client desires to use a filter that is already built into the resolver. In this case all the client has to do is refer to this filter using some agreed upon identifier. We expect that many popular filters will be available this way through well-known identifiers. In the second type of filter specification, the client provides a procedural description of the operation of the filter. This can be in the form of a function of metrics or a procedure describing a sequence of filter applications.

Another important issue is where and how filter specifications are made. We explore two alternatives. In the first, a new application layer interface (API) function call is provided, that can be used by an application to invoke the process of ADN to IP address mapping. Arguments to this call can be used to specify the filtering desired, either by identifying a built-in filter or by pointing to some local function or procedure to be communicated to the server. An example of this in the context of the Sockets API is the definition of a (new) `getanyhostbyname()` function call that can be used to invoke the anycasting service in a manner similar to how the `gethostbyname()` function call typically invokes the DNS service.

An alternative method for specifying filters is to use *Metric-Qualified* Anycast Domain Names (MQ-ADN) to convey the desired filter as part of the ADN being sent to the anycast server. A metric-qualified ADN is of the form `<Filter-Specification>.<ADN>` where `Filter-Specification` provides informa-

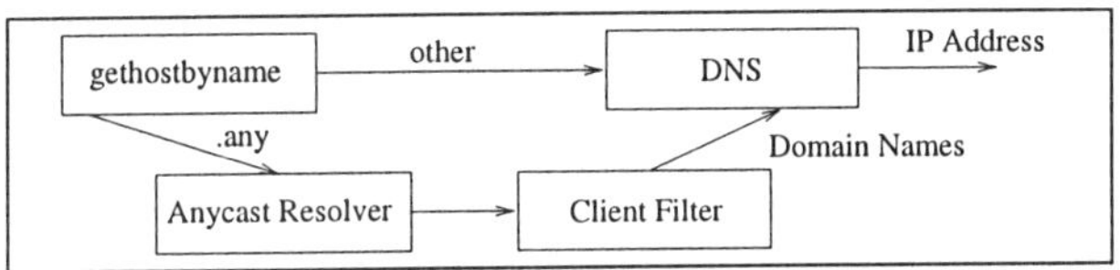

FIGURE 3: Implementation using Metric-Qualified ADNs

tion about the filter to be used by the server. This is relatively straightforward if a built-in filter is being specified. For example, the name `ServerLoad.wwwnews%cc.gatech.edu` could convey to the resolver the desire to use the ServerLoad built-in filter on the anycast group represented by the `wwwnews%cc.gatech.edu` ADN.

MQ-ADNs can be enhanced to allow existing API calls to be left intact, thus existing applications need not be rewritten. Many of these applications take domain names as input; one would simply need to substitute a MQ-ADN instead, to allow the application to make use of the anycasting service. In this case, the MQ-ADN is augmented by the suffix ".any".

4.3 Implementation Using MQ-ADNs

In our implementation (shown in Figure 3) we intercept calls to the `gethostbyname()` library[5] call and check if the argument is an ADN (i.e., ends with the `.any` suffix). If that is the case, then an anycast resolver query is formulated, after parsing the name to obtain the resolver filter specification. This query is sent to the anycast resolver which returns a set of host domain names. The set is passed through a client filter to reduce it to a single host domain name. This name is then used as input to the original `gethostbyname()` procedure to return the desired IP address. If the `gethostbyname()` argument is other than an ADN then the usual procedure is called directly. This allows us to use traditional applications without modification and gives the option of using them with or without the anycasting feature [6].

5 Metrics and Metric Determination

The use of metric-based filters in the anycasting service requires the ability to measure performance metrics with "reasonable" accuracy, without unduly loading the network or the servers. The measurements need not be perfectly accurate; the anycast mechanism relies upon *relative* ordering to determine the best server, rather than absolute metric values. Further, the performance penalty associated with out-of-date or slightly inaccurate metric data will not typically be severe; rather than selecting the "best" server, the service may identify a "nearly-best" server.

5.1 Metrics

To better understand how anycasting will perform, we have used four specific metrics: 1) server response time, 2) server-to-user throughput, 3) server load, and 4) processor load [7]. We focus on these metrics because they are likely to be of interest to clients in selecting from a set of replicated servers. Further, they represent diversity in the components (server, path, client) involved in determining the metric value and diversity in the time scale on which the metric value changes. We envision that additional metrics (e.g., packet loss, delay jitter) would also be of interest to certain types of applications.

The use of metrics to identify the "best" server is predicated on the assumption that there are significant differences across servers at various times, otherwise the selection of a server could just as well be random. Further, the variation in a metric must occur on a time scale that is practical to track using measurement tools.

Detailed experiments, results, and perfomance analysis are presented in the technical report [27].

5.2 Metric Collection Techniques

We now consider how to efficiently and accurately maintain databases of the metric values. We have identified four possible approaches to maintaining replicated server performance information in anycast servers' database:

1. *Remote Server Performance Probing:* In this technique, probing agents are in charge of periodically querying the replicated servers to determine the performance that will be experienced if a client were to actually request service. Each probing agent acts as a proxy for a set of clients. These probes need to be designed to mimic (as much as possible) the parts of the network and the server that the client request will "exercise". We have experimented with this technique in our implementation [27].

2. *Server Push:* It may be advantageous in some circumstances to have the replicated servers send (or push) the relevant local performance information onto the anycast servers. The primary advantage

[5] SunOS 4.1.3

[6] Use of this technique on existing applications requires dynamic linking of the application code to our own library. We successfully used this technique to augment many applications with anycasting capabilities, including the Mosaic web browser.

[7] The original anycasting proposal [7] was primarily concerned with a server distance (hop count) metric; measuring server distance has also been studied extensively by Guyton and Schwartz [18].

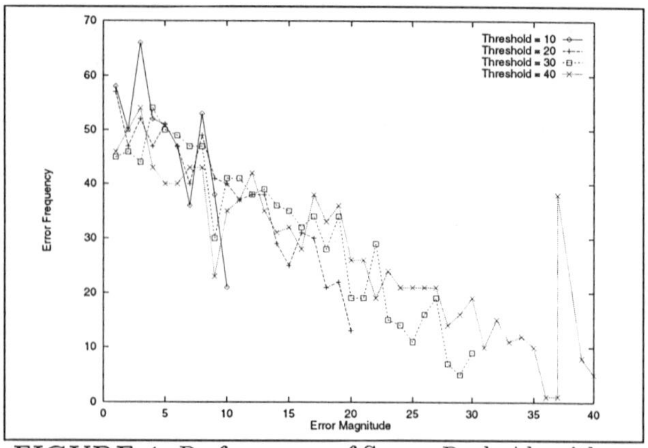

FIGURE 4: Performance of Server Push Algorithms

Update Threshold	Max. Interval Between Updates	Average Error	Number of Updates
10	5	1.53	939
10	10	1.64	922
20	5	4.21	682
20	10	4.69	643
30	5	6.87	537
30	10	7.74	464
40	5	9.21	445
40	10	10.45	360
50	5	10.82	291
50	10	12.68	379

Table 1: Load and Accuracy of Server Push

of this technique is scalability: it allows the server to update its performance information only when interesting changes are observed. Further, the update information can be (network layer) multicast to all anycast resolvers that maintain information about the server. The anycast resolvers can join well-known multicast groups for each server that they are interested in, allowing the servers to disseminate performance information without knowing the identities of the resolvers.

3. *Probing for Locally-Maintained Server Performance:* Another possibility is to have each replicated server maintain its own locally monitored performance metrics in a globally readable file. Remote probing locations can then read the information in the file (as opposed to attempting to exercise the server) to obtain the desired information. In a sense, this is a hybrid between the probing-for-performance and the server-push techniques. Since probes merely read from a locally-maintained file, they may represent less of a burden on the server than the probing-for-performance approach.

4. *User Experience:* The last technique is motivated by the observation that users currently make server access decisions based, in part, on past experience. That is, if one finds a particular server to be unreachable, that server is likely to be avoided for a period of time. Collecting information about past experience offers a coarse method of maintaining server performance. The primary advantage of this method is that the information is collected for free; no additional burden is placed on the server or the network. The quantity and accuracy of the information can be increased by sharing of experience among clients. For example, a gateway into a campus might maintain server performance information based on the experience of all clients on the campus.

5.3 Example: Server Push

To discuss the performance of the server push technique, we must first define the algorithm that the server will use to determine what information to push and when. In general, we want the server to push state information whenever the state has changed sufficiently to be "interesting" with some constraint on the maximum frequency of updates so as to bound the overhead of the updating mechanism.

Note that the task of updating link state in a distributed routing environment has precisely the same criteria. We have adopted the link state update algorithm used in the ARPANET [28] and experimented with the performance and overhead with a variety of parameters. The update algorithm is parameterized by a measurement interval I, a maximum threshold T and a reduction factor R. The algorithm maintains a current threshold C, initialized to T. The server measures its state over each interval I. If the state changes from the previous measurement by at least C, the state is pushed and C is reset to T. If the state does not change by at least C, C is reduced by R. (Note that when C becomes 0, the state will be pushed and C will be reset to T.) The algorithm will send updates at least every T/R time units and at most every I time units.

We have implemented this server push algorithm for an HTTP server, where the measurement quantity is the number of connections initiated in the measurement interval. In our experiments we use

	Net Load	Server Mod	Server Load	Exercises Net Path	Accuracy
Probing	$2PT_p$	No	Moderate	Yes	Moderate
Server Push	T_s	Yes	Low	No*	High
Reading Server Log	$2PT_p$	Yes	Low	No*	High
User Experience	None	No	None	Yes	Low/Varies

(* See note in text)

Table 2: Comparison of Metric Collection Techniques

$I = 1$ minute. We process HTTP server logs to determine the pushed values for varying T and R.

In Figure 4 we examine the accuracy of the updating mechanism as a function of T. At each one minute interval, we compare the value of the server load based on the pushed information to the true value of load extracted from the logs. We record the magnitude of the difference between the estimate and the true value, and plot a frequency distribution of error magnitudes for each threshold value. Thus, the plots represent the error distribution for different values of T, and each data point is the number of times the estimate had an error of the corresponding error magnitude. In Figure 4 we used $R = 5$ minutes and varying T; we also collected data for $R = 10$ minutes.

Table 1 gives the average value of the inaccuracy and the number of update messages, for various values of T and R. The number of update messages generated is a measure of the load placed on the network by the mechanism; the average value of the inaccuracy summarizes the performance data given by the frequency distribution. The tradeoff is clear: a more accurate algorithm also incurs a larger overhead. Interestingly, increasing the maximum interval between updates from 5 to 10 has relatively little effect on the accuracy for a constant update threshold.

5.4 Comparison of Techniques

Which technique is most appropriate will depend on a number of factors, including the time-scale on which the metric varies, the components (server, network path, client) that determine the metric value, the desired accuracy of the information, and the cost of burdening the network and/or the server.

Table 2 summarizes the four techniques based on performance and cost dimensions. The first three columns are measures of system overhead. The Net Load column represents the number of messages generated per unit time to obtain the metric data from one server, where P is the number of proxies, T_p is the period of proxy probing, T_s is the period of server push. Note that the Server Push messages are multicast rather than unicast. The Server Mod column indicates whether the server must be modified to allow the metric to be collected. The Server Load column expresses (relatively) how much additional load is placed on the server by the collection of the metric data. The last two columns are performance measures, indicating whether the method exercises network path, and (relatively) how accurately the method is able to maintain the metrics that it can evaluate. Note that the Server Push and Server Log methods can be made to exercise the network path by measuring hop count or latency for the metric update message.

6 Concluding Remarks

We have explored the implications of an anycasting service supported at the application layer. Specifically, we have developed and evaluated an implementation based on the use of anycast servers to map anycast domain names to one or more IP addresses. Via metric and policy filters, we explicitly provide for considerable user control over the selection of a specific server from a group, while preserving the spirit of the anycast definition. That is, clients control the selection by specifying desired properties of the server (e.g., fastest response time), and need not know which specific servers are able to satisfy the request.

We believe that one advantage of our application layer support is its ability to operate with current network layer implementations. Further, our work is complemented by other efforts in resource discovery and efficient indexing of information.

In the area of metric determination, our results suggest a number of avenues for future work. Collecting proxy and user experience data from a larger set of sites would allow us to better determine how accuracy varies with proxy, server, and base machine locations. It would also be interesting to explore methods for applying base-machine-specific transformations to the proxy or user-experience data to improve accuracy. We have examined a simple class of server push algorithms; more work is needed to optimize these algorithms, and may require metric-specific techniques. Our results on throughput indicate that there may be metrics (e.g., hop count) that are easier to measure accurately and still correlate well with end-user perceived performance.

7 Acknowledgements

We would like to thank Yusuf Goolamabbas for his involvement in the original implementation of Application-Layer Anycasting.

References

[1] P. B. Danzig, D. Delucia, and K. Obraczka, "Massively replicating services in wide-area internetworks." Tech. Rep., University of Southern California, January 1994.

[2] P. Danzig, R. Hall, and M. Schwartz, "A case for caching file objects inside internetworks," in *Proceedings of SIGCOMM 93*, pp. 239–248, 1993.

[3] J. Pitkow and M. Recker, "A simple yet robust caching algorithm based on dynamic access patterns," in *Proceedings of 2nd WWW conference*, 1994.

[4] A. Dan, D. Sitaram, and P. Shahabuddin, "Scheduling policies for an on-demand video server with batching," in *Proceedings of ACM Multimedia 94*, pp. 15–23, 1994.

[5] D. Gifford, "Polychannel systems for mass digital communication," *Communications of the ACM*, vol. 33, pp. 1847–1851, February 1990.

[6] R. Clark and M. Ammar, "Providing scalable web service using multicast delivery," in *Proceedings of 2nd IEEE Workshop on Services in Distributed and Networked Environments*, pp. 19–26, 1995.

[7] C. Partridge, T. Mendez, and W. Milliken, "Host anycasting service," *RFC 1546*, November 1993.

[8] K. Birman and T. Joseph, "Reliable communication in the presence of failures," *ACM Transactions on Computer Systems*, vol. 5, pp. 47–76, February 1987.

[9] R. Hinden and S. Deering, "IP version 6 addressing architecture," *RFC 1884*, December 1995.

[10] J. Bernabeu, M. Ammar, and M. Ahamad, "Optimizing a generalized polling protocol for resource finding over a multiple access channel," *Computer Networks and ISDN Systems*, vol. 27, pp. 1429–1445, 1995.

[11] D. Oppen and Y. Dalal, "The Clearinghouse: A decentralized agent for locating named objects in a distributed environment," *ACM Transactions on Office Information Systems*, vol. 3, pp. 230–253, July 1983.

[12] P. Mockapetris, "Domain names – concepts and facilities," *RFC 1034*, November 1987.

[13] I. Gopal and A. Segall, "Directories for networks with casually connected users," in *Proceedings of INFOCOM 88*, pp. 1060–1064, 1988.

[14] A. Birrel, R. Levin, and M. Schroeder, "Grapevine: An exercise in distributed computing," *Communications of the ACM*, vol. 25, pp. 260–274, April 1982.

[15] D. Terry, "Caching hints in distributed systems," *IEEE Transactions on Software Engineering*, vol. 13, pp. 48–54, January 1987.

[16] R. Fowler, *Decentralized Object Finding Using Forwarding Addresses.* PhD thesis, University of Washington, 1985.

[17] J. Veizades, E. Guttman, C. Perkins, and S. Kaplan, "Service location protocol," *Internet Draft (work in progress) draft-ietf-srvloc-protocol-13.txt*, June 1996.

[18] J. Guyton and M. Schwartz, "Locating nearby copies of replicated Internet servers," in *Proceedings of SIGCOMM 95*, pp. 288–298, 1995.

[19] C. M. Bowman, P. Danzig, D. Hardy, U. Manber, M. Schwartz, and D. Wessels, "Harvest: A scalable, customizable discovery and access system," Tech. Rep. CU-CS-732-94, University of Colorado - Boulder, 1995.

[20] J. Gwertzman and M. Seltzer, "The case for geographical push caching," Tech. Rep. 34-94, Harvard University, 1994.

[21] M. Humes, "Netscape's server push, client pull and CGI animation." http://www.emf.net/mal/animate.html.

[22] E. D. Katz, M. Butler, and R. McGrath, "A scalable HTTP server: The NCSA prototype," *Computer Networks and ISDN Systems*, vol. 27, pp. 155–164, 1994.

[23] L. Lamport, "The implementation of reliable distributed multiprocess systems," *Computer Networks*, vol. 2, pp. 95–114, 1978.

[24] D. Gifford, "Weighted voting for replicated data," in *Proceedings of 7th Symposium on Operating Systems*, pp. 150–162, ACM, 1979.

[25] M. Ahamad and M. H. Ammar, "Performance characterization of quorum-consensus algorithms for replicated data," *IEEE Transactions on Software Engineering*, vol. 15, pp. 492–496, April 1989.

[26] D. Barbara and H. Garcia-Molina, "Mutual exclusion in partitioned distributed systems," *Distributed Computing*, vol. 1, pp. 119–132, 1986.

[27] S. Bhattacharjee, M. Ammar, E. Zegura, V. Shah, and Z. Fei, "Application level anycasting," Tech. Rep. 96-25, College of Computing, Georgia Institute of Technology.

[28] E. C. Rosen, "The updating protocol of ARPANET's new routing algorithm," *Computer Networks*, no. 4, pp. 11–19, 1980.

Virtual LAN Internetworking over ATM Networks for Mobile Stations

Nen-Fu Huang*, Yao-Tzung Wang*#, Bo Li+, and Te-Lung Liu*

* Department of Computer Science, National Tsing Hua University, Taiwan 30043, Republic of China
# Computer & Communication Research Laboratories, ITRI, Taiwan 30043, Republic of China
+ Department of Computer Science, Hong Kong University of Science and Technology, Hong Kong
E-mail: nfhuang@cs.nthu.edu.tw

Abstract

One of the most attractive features of the virtual LAN (VLAN) is the capability to group users into broadcast domains, which are independent of their locations on the physical network. This paper deals with the VLAN services using ATM LAN emulation technology which operates on a client/server model. The focuses are on the issues of supporting transparent VLAN services and internetworking among VLANs for mobile stations. A mobile VLAN (MVLAN) architecture is proposed, perhaps for the first time, to efficiently maintain multiple VLAN broadcast domains over a single ATM network even when the VLANs contain mobile stations. The proposed solution 1) ensures that layer 2 frames between a mobile station and any station, either static or mobile, that belongs to the original registered VLAN can be exchanged transparently, 2) provides transparent communications between VLANs using layer 2 bridging approach, and 3) handles excessive server-to-server traffic efficiently, including the broadcast/multicast frames. The proposed MVLAN architecture brings one step closer towards facilitating the mobility management in an ATM network while conforming to the emerging LAN emulation standard.

1. Introduction

Virtual LAN (VLAN) over ATM networks has attracted much attention recently across the networking industry [3], [9]-[10]. Its main characteristics is to allow a virtual LAN segment to co-exist across the whole ATM network without being bounded by the actual physical location. This has a major advantage over the real physical LAN segment where the overhead involved in manual reconfiguration for station movements. Note that a major difference between existing LANs and ATM networks is that LANs are connectionless, whereas ATM natively supports only connection-oriented services, i.e., data may not be sent until a virtual channel connection (VCC) is established. Thus, an important function for a LAN emulation service is to be able to support the shared broadcast nature of a LAN over ATM. The process of mapping shared broadcast to point-to-point communication is the so-called ATM LAN Emulation (LE) service developed by the ATM Forum to be standard [1].

The ATM Forum's LE service is based on a client-server architecture. The components of an emulated LAN network include LE clients (LECs), an LE server (LES), and a broadcast and unknown server (BUS) [1]. (The term "emulated LAN" is the terminology of the ATM Forum specification. It supports only ATM-attached devices, while VLANs are defined for both ATM and non-ATM network devices. VLANs can be seen as supersets of emulated LANs. In this paper, we treat them as the same.) The LEC is the entity within ATM workstations or ATM-LAN bridges, which performs data forwarding, address resolution, and other control functions. The LES provides a facility for registration and resolving MAC addresses to ATM addresses. The BUS handles data to broadcast address and to any multicast address. It may also handle initial unicast data which are sent by a source LEC before a direct virtual connection to the destination LEC is setup. Stations within the same emulated LAN are connected to the same LES/BUS pair, and stations belonging to different emulated LANs are attached to different LES/BUS pairs. In this respect, a multicast frame is first sent from an LEC to the BUS, which then relays it to all the LECs on the emulated LAN, but not forwarded to other emulated LANs. This result is a secure *broadcast domain* or known as a *virtual LAN*. For an LE-based VLAN, the membership of a station is primarily determined by the LES/BUS pair to which it is connected, not by its physical location.

The VLAN, in our opinion, is potentially more rewarding in wireless environment where constant moving of the mobile stations are highly anticipated. This issue is similar to the problem of supporting mobility throughout the Internet using IP layer (mobile IP) rerouting strategies [4], [7], [11]. Nevertheless, it is still not clear the mobility impact on the VLAN service when there are multiple VLAN segments on an ATM network. A mobile virtual LAN (MVLAN) architecture that endeavors to provide transparent communications for large number of mobile terminals belonging to the same VLAN on an ATM network has been proposed in [6]. In the proposed MVLAN architecture, servers for different VLANs are interconnected into a hierarchical structure through permanent or signalling (dynamically established) virtual connections. The membership tracking would be maintained and determined based on the interconnection structure. The servers are partitioned into groups and formed a variety of trees. To avoid traffic concentration around the root nodes, a hypercube over tree (HOT) structure is used for the MVLAN operation. Thus, the roots of these trees are linked in a hypercube manner, in which each link is a virtual connection. The hypercube virtual connections provide direct and redundant paths between trees. As a result, the HOT structure offers smaller diameter and more balanced traffic pattern.

In this paper, we extend the MVLAN system to achieve the goal of providing communications between different VLANs' (mobile) members. Typically, the inter-VLAN communications could be furnished via the routers. This paper considers another approach to achieve this by the LAN Emulation technology. Also we evaluate the search and inform overheads of the HOT

0-8186-7780-5/97 $10.00 © 1997 IEEE

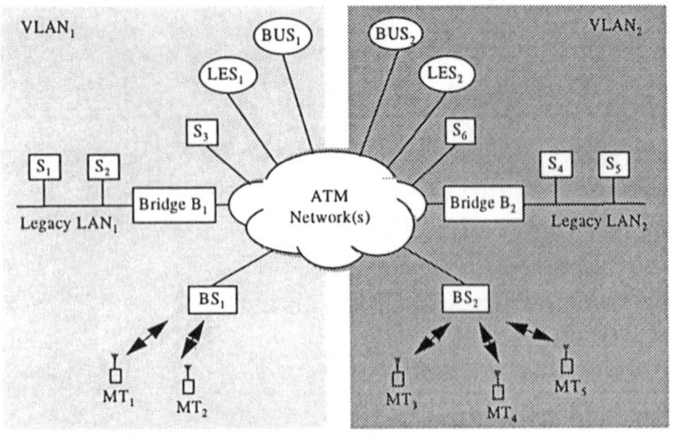

Fig. 1. ATM-based VLAN Architecture.

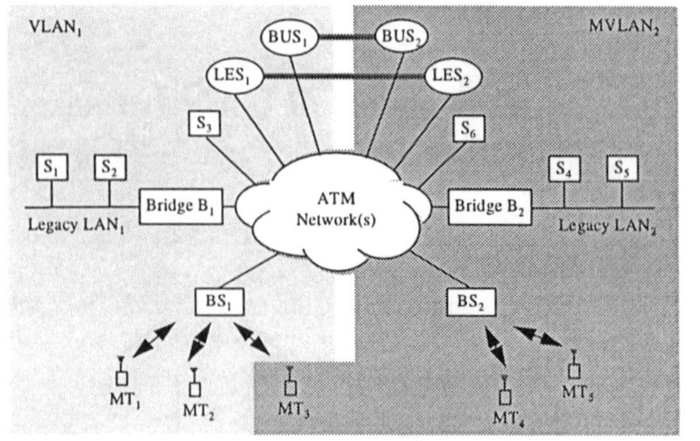

Fig. 2. The territory of $MVLAN_2$ after the mobility of MT_3.

structure in a mobile environment and compare it with a typical pure tree one.

The rest of the paper is organized as follows. In Section 2 we describe an LE-based MVLAN model on an ATM network. The mobility tracking procedures and the broadcast frame forwarding algorithm based on the HOT-based server interconnection topology are considered in Section 3. A short example about the MVLAN operation is given in Section 4. The simulation model and simulation results for analyzing membership maintenance cost under different server interconnection structures (tree vs. HOT) are reported in Section 5. Finally, some concluding remarks are given in Section 6.

2. Mobile VLAN architecture

2.1 The two-VLAN model

A typical network configuration of VLANs on an ATM network is shown in Fig. 1. MTs, such as MT_1, gain access to the ATM infrastructure via base stations (BSs), such as BS_1. Static stations, such as LAN stations S_1 and S_2 on legacy LAN_1, acquire access to the ATM backbone through ATM-LAN bridges, such as B_1. Other static stations, such as S_3, are directly attached to the ATM network. Note that both BSs and bridges implement the LE service and act as a proxy ATM station for MTs or LAN stations. In Fig. 1, there are two VLANs, $VLAN_1$ and $VLAN_2$ which related to different shaded regions. Moreover LES_1/BUS_1 and LES_2/BUS_2 pairs are responsible for the provision of address resolution and multicast/broadcast services to $VLAN_1$ and $VLAN_2$, respectively. It is possible to have multiple physical LES/BUS pairs within a single VLAN for scaling and resiliency issues [5]. Such distributed LAN emulation services or known as the LNNI functions are still being defined by the ATM Forum [2]. Without loss of generality, we assume that each VLAN has only one physical LES/BUS pair.

Consider the algorithm of transferring frames with a unicast or multicast/broadcast MAC address from ATM stations to LAN stations, but the LAN stations are mobile. In this case, we need to track the station mobility and extend the VLAN broadcast domain, i.e., the delivery of unicast and multicast/broadcast frames to and from MTs, even when the MT has already moved to another VLAN coverage area. This creates the architecture of the mobile VLAN (MVLAN). One of the most important goals of the MVLAN is to ensure that layer 2 frames can be exchanged between 1) the MT and any static station that belongs to the originally registered VLAN, and 2) any mobile stations that belong to the originally registered VLAN.

For simplicity, we illustrate the message transfer algorithm based on the two-MVLAN configuration as depicted in Fig. 1. Further assume MT_3 moves from the coverage area of BS_2 to BS_1 which are (virtually) connected to LES_2/BUS_2 and LES_1/BUS_1, respectively. Thus an inter-VLAN mobility is occurred, as shown in Fig. 2. The shaded region $MVLAN_2$ denotes the MVLAN domain which still desirable to maintain MT_3 on $VLAN_2$. Following is the example of transferring message from ATM station S_6 to mobile MT_3.

1. When ATM station S_6 has a frame for transmission and the corresponding ATM address of the destined LAN is unknown, it issues an ARP request to LES_2.
2. Through the handoff procedure, LES_2 would know that MT_3 has moved out. Then the ARP request is forwarded to LES_1 through a predefined VCC. LES_1 re-broadcasts this request to all $VLAN_1$'s ATM-LAN bridges, including BS_1.
3. In order to transmit the frame as soon as possible, while S_6 is waiting for a response from LES_2, it sends the frame to BUS_2. Like the condition as LES, BUS_2 will forward the frame to BUS_1 via a preestablished VCC. Eventually, the data frame is broadcast to all $VLAN_1$'s stations, including MT_3.
4. After receiving the ARP reply from LES_2 (via intermediate LES_1), S_6 establishes a virtual connection to BS_1. Finally, the frames can be transmitted from S_6 to the ATM network to BS_1 and then to MT_3.

From the above descriptions, the following observations can be made. The mobile membership maintenance is via the servers cooperation. After the location of an MT is found even it is on another VLAN, a point-to-point virtual connection is setup between pairs of LECs (e.g., S_6 - BS_1) for later communications. In the following subsection, we will generalize the two-VLAN model to multiple VLANs.

2.2 Hypercube over tree (HOT) server node organization

According to the proposed MVLAN system, the LES/BUS server nodes, one for each VLAN, are organized into a hypercube over tree (HOT) structure [6]. Each tree includes a

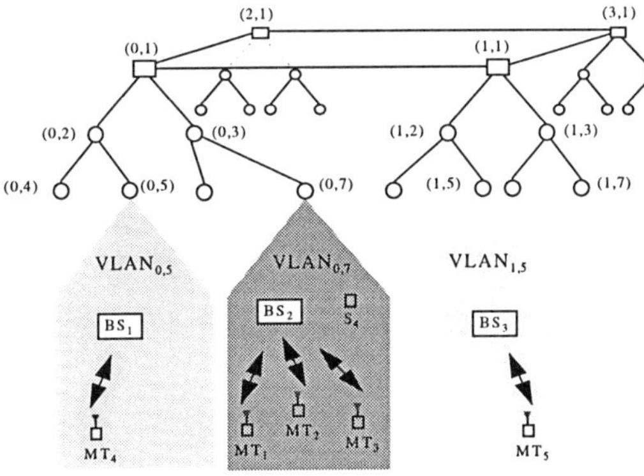

Fig. 3. An example of MVLAN operation (before mobility).

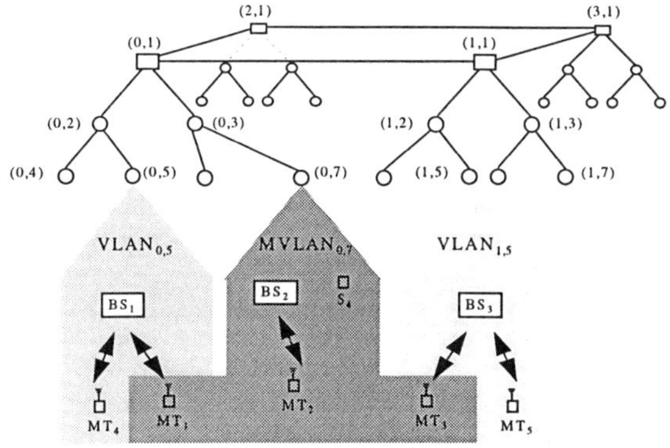

Fig. 4. An example of MVLAN operation (after mobility).

root server (LES/BUS pair) node and non-root server nodes. The former is referred to herein as "inter-tree" server node and the latter are referred to as "intra-tree" server nodes. Each tree is assigned a unique integer. Within the *i*-th tree, the inter-tree server node is assigned a label as the pair of integers (i, 1). The intra-tree server nodes are also assigned as labels, unique pairs of integers (i, j); where j=2, 3, 4, ...

Each VLAN is assigned a unique identifier indicating the location of the VLAN in the HOT organization. For sake of convenience, the identifier assigned to the VLAN is the same pair of integers (i, j) used to label the LES/BUS server node on the VLAN.

Fig. 3 illustrates the organization of server nodes in a HOT structure. Illustratively, four binary trees 0, 1, 2 and 3 are formed and their inter-tree server nodes (0, 1), (1, 1), (2, 1) and (3, 1) are formed into a two-dimensional hypercube (square) structure. The $Tree_0$ includes server nodes (0, 1), (0, 2), (0, 3), (0, 4), (0, 5), (0, 6) and (0, 7). The $Tree_1$ includes server nodes (1, 1), (1, 2), (1, 3), (1, 4), (1, 5), (1, 6) and (1, 7). As shown, three VLANs are depicted, namely, $VLAN_{0,5}$ and $VLAN_{0,7}$ on $Tree_0$, and $VLAN_{1,5}$ on $Tree_1$. On $VLAN_{0,5}$ are BS_1 and MT_4 (in communication with BS_1). On $VLAN_{0,7}$ are S_4, BS_2 and MT_1, MT_2, MT_3 (all in communication with BS_2). On $VLAN_{1,5}$ are BS_3 and MT_5 (in communication with BS_3).

Next as shown in Fig. 4, MT_1 moves from the coverage area of BS_2 to that of BS_1. A handoff procedure is executed so that BS_2 deregisters MT_1 and ceases to provide services for MT_1. Likewise, BS_1 registers MT_1 and begins to provide services for MT_1. Furthermore, MT_3 moves from the coverage area of BS_2 to that of BS_3. As shown, BS_2 ceases to provide frame communication for MT_3 and BS_3 begins to provide this for MT_3.

Although BS_2 does not serve the MT_1 and MT_3 directly due to their movements, it is still desirable to maintain MT_1 and MT_3 on the same $VLAN_{0,7}$. This is achieved as described below.

3. Mobile VLAN operations

In this section, we discuss the MVLAN solution in more details by first describing some databases for tracking the movement of MTs, then the mobility tracking procedures followed by a detailed frame forwarding algorithm. Initially, assume that each MT is served by a BS on the same VLAN. Each BS is presumed to maintain a registration database which records information regarding the serving MTs. In particular, the registration database should contain the VLAN identification of each MT, denoted herein as VLAN-ID(MT). Such information could be obtained during the handoff.

3.1 Membership tracking databases (MTDs)

Each intra-tree server node maintains two databases for tracking the movement of MTs, namely, the OUT-MTD and the IN-MTD. The OUT-MTD is simply a count {*Out-Count*} of the number of MTs moved out from this VLAN. In Fig. 3, the OUT-MTD for each of the $VLAN_{0,5}$, $VLAN_{0,7}$ and $VLAN_{1,5}$ is zero. In Fig. 4, the OUT-MTD for the $VLAN_{0,7}$ is two.

The IN-MTD is used to record the information of MTs moved into this VLAN. Table 1 shows an illustrative IN-MTD.

Table 1. IN-MTD

VLAN-ID	In-Count	ATM address of BS	VCC to BS
(1,2)	1	$ATM(BS_k)$	$VCC(BS_k)$
(3,4)	4	$ATM(BS_k)$	$VCC(BS_k)$

In Table 1, VLAN-ID is the identifier of a VLAN. *In-Count* is the number of MTs came from the VLAN with identifier VLAN-ID. Each entry also stores the ATM address of, and the VCC to, the local BS. Table 1 illustrates a local BS, BS_k, is serving one MT comes from the $VLAN_{1,2}$ and four MTs come from the $VLAN_{3,4}$.

Each inter-tree server node also maintains the above two MTDs. In addition, it maintains an Inter-Tree-MTD. The Inter-Tree-MTD indicates the number of MTs from each VLAN that are serving by the BSs in each tree. Table 2 illustrates an example of Inter-Tree-MTD.

Table 2. Inter-Tree-MTD

VLAN-ID	Count($Tree_0$)	Count($Tree_1$)	Count($Tree_2$)
(1,1)	1	15	2
(2,1)	0	2	10

As before, VLAN-ID is the identifier of a specific VLAN. *Count*($Tree_j$) is the total number of MTs from the VLAN with VLAN-ID, which are serving by the BSs of $Tree_j$. Thus, for $VLAN_{1,1}$, one of its MTs is served by a BS on $Tree_0$, 15 MTs are serving by BSs on $Tree_1$ and two MTs are serving by BSs on $Tree_2$. For $VLAN_{2,1}$, two of its MTs are serving by BSs on $Tree_1$, and 10 MTs are serving by BSs on $Tree_2$.

Initially, each server node initializes its OUT-MTD to be zero and IN-MTD to be empty. Each inter-tree server node initializes its Inter-Tree-MTD to keep the total number of MTs in each VLAN in the associated tree. The ways to construct and update these tables are described in more details below.

3.2 Mobility tracking procedures

In order to track the movement of each MT, some mobility messages are transmitted by the moving MTs, the BSs and the server nodes. Illustratively, three types of mobility messages are designed as follows:

- **Mobility Message type I (MM_I).** This message is transmitted by the BS that currently serves the MT (BS_{orig}) to the server node of the VLAN ($VLAN_{orig}$). The MM_I message is used to update the OUT-MTD or/and IN-MTD, and contains the *VLAN-ID(MT)*, the identifier of $VLAN_{new}$ and the ATM address of BS_{orig} ($ATM(BS_{orig})$).
- **Mobility Message type II (MM_{II}).** This message is issued from an intra-tree server node when an MM_I message frame is received and the $VLAN_{new}$ and $VLAN_{orig}$ belong to different trees. The MM_{II} is forwarded up along the tree until it is received at the inter-tree server node. This is to notify the inter-tree server nodes to update their Inter-Tree-MTDs to reflect the movement of the MT from an original tree ($Tree_{orig}$) containing $VLAN_{orig}$ to a new tree ($Tree_{new}$) containing $VLAN_{new}$. This message frame contains the *VLAN-ID(MT)*, the identifier of $Tree_{orig}$ and the identifier of $Tree_{new}$.
- **Mobility Message type III (MM_{III}).** This message is transmitted by BS_{new} to a server node on $VLAN_{new}$ for the purpose of updating the OUT-MTD and/or IN-MTD thereat. It contains the *VLAN-ID(MT)* and the ATM address of BS_{new} ($ATM(BS_{new})$).

Now we describe the procedures for handling a mobility from $VLAN_{orig}$ segment to $VLAN_{new}$ segment. The MTDs in the relevant corresponding servers should be updated to reflect this mobility. The actions taken in the $VLAN_{orig}$ and the $VLAN_{new}$ are stated as follows.

A. $VLAN_{orig}$ actions upon mobility

A process executed by the moving *MT*, BS_{orig} and the server node on $VLAN_{orig}$ is illustrated below.

For each move, the *MT* issues a handoff message to BS_{orig} for deregistration. The handoff message contains the identifier of $VLAN_{new}$. The BS_{orig} determines if the two VLANs are the same, i.e., $VLAN_{new} = VLAN_{orig}$. If so, then the server nodes do not modify their MTDs. Otherwise, the BS_{orig} deregisters the *MT* and additionally transmits an MM_I to the server node on $VLAN_{orig}$.

The server node on $VLAN_{orig}$ receives the MM_I and extracts the contents thereof. It then determines if *VLAN-ID(MT)* is the same as $VLAN_{orig}$. If so, then the *MT* on the same $VLAN_{orig}$ is moving into another VLAN. In such case, the server node increases the *Out-Count* in its OUT-MTD. On the other hand, if *VLAN-ID(MT)* is not the same as $VLAN_{orig}$, then the *MT* is not on the same $VLAN_{orig}$ as the server node. In such case, the server node uses the *VLAN-ID(MT)* and $ATM(BS_{orig})$ as indexes to retrieve the corresponding entry of its IN-MTD. The server node then decreases the *In-Count* value of the retrieved entry.

The server node then determines whether the tree identifier of the $VLAN_{new}$ ($Tree_{new}$) is identical to that of $VLAN_{orig}$ ($Tree_{orig}$). If it is, the server node simply drops the MM_I and the process ceases. Otherwise, the Inter-Tree-MTDs of each inter-tree server node must be updated. The server node then issues an MM_{II} to its inter-tree server node (for $Tree_{orig}$) along the tree. Using *VLAN-ID(MT)* as an index, the inter-tree server node retrieves the corresponding entry from its Inter-Tree-MTD and increases the count for $Tree_{new}$ by one and decreases the count for $Tree_{orig}$ by one. The inter-tree server node then transmits a copy of the MM_{II} to each of the other inter-tree server nodes which update their Inter-Tree-MTDs accordingly.

B. $VLAN_{new}$ actions upon mobility

The action to be done by the moving *MT*, BS_{new} and the server node on $VLAN_{new}$ is illustrated below.

When the *MT* moves to the coverage area of BS_{new}, it issues a handoff message, contains the identifier of $VLAN_{orig}$, to BS_{new}. The BS_{new} registers *MT* and transmits an MM_{III} to the server node on $VLAN_{new}$ if $VLAN_{new}$ is not the same as $VLAN_{orig}$.

When the server node on $VLAN_{new}$ receives the MM_{III}, it checks whether the *VLAN-ID(MT)* is identical to that of the $VLAN_{new}$. If so, then the *MT* has simply returned to the original VLAN. In such case, the server node simply decreases the *Out-Count* value in the OUT-MTD by one. Otherwise, the MT comes from another VLAN and the IN-MTD must be updated. In this case, the server node uses the *VLAN-ID(MT)* and the $ATM(BS_{new})$ as indexes to retrieve a corresponding entry from the IN-MTD. For the first MT moved from a VLAN, the server node creates a new entry for this VLAN with *VLAN-ID(MT)*, $ATM(BS_{new})$ and the VCC of BS_{new}. The *In-Count* value of the retrieved or created entry is then increased by one.

3.3 Broadcast frame forwarding algorithm

The broadcast frame routing in each of the interconnected server nodes is described as follows. Since it is possible that frames from different VLANs has to be sent to mobile members, which are scattered around anywhere, a uniform frame format for distinct VLANs is desirable. For our discussion below, a VLAN header, includes the destination VLAN identifier (DVLAN-ID) and the source VLAN-ID (SVLAN-ID), is added at the head of the conventional LE frame.

The frame forwarding algorithm differs slightly depending on whether the frame is to be broadcast by a BUS or an address resolution is to be performed by a LES. The discussion below uses the BUS as an example.

A. BUS receives a frame from a BS

A process executed by a BUS in routing a broadcast (or an unknown) frame on a VLAN is given below.

Assume that an *MT* transmits a broadcast frame. Such a frame is received at the BS that serving the *MT*. The BS transmits the received frame to its BUS. Next, the BUS receives the broadcast frame and determines if the DVLAN-ID is the same as that of the VLAN of the BUS. If so, the BUS then broadcasts the frame to all nodes on the VLAN. Next, the BUS retrieves the OUT-MTD and determines if the *Out-Count* is zero. If so, then no MTs on this VLAN have moved out. Otherwise, at least one MT on this VLAN has moved out. In this case, the following operations will be done, which depend on whether the type of BUS is an intra-tree or inter-tree BUS.

The BUS will retrieve all entries of the IN-MTD indexed by the DVLAN-ID in the received frame. If no entry exists, the BUS transmits the frame to all connected parent and child BUSs. Otherwise, the BUS transmits the frame to the BS indicated in each retrieved entry. Each BS then transmits the frame to the MTs on the destination VLAN.

If the BUS is an intra-tree BUS, it then transmits the frame to each child BUS and parent BUS on the same tree. Otherwise, it transmits the frame to each child BUS. Furthermore, the inter-tree BUS retrieves from its Inter-Tree-MTD the entry for the DVLAN-ID and determines which trees are serving MTs moved from the same VLAN. The inter-tree BUS then transmits a copy of the frame to each of these inter-tree BUSs.

B. BUS receives a frame from an interconnected BUS

A procedure for a BUS where a frame is received from another BUS is given below.

The BUS determines if the DVLAN-ID is the same as the VLAN of the BUS. If so, the BUS transmits the frame to all nodes on the VLAN of the BUS. Otherwise, the BUS checks all IN-MTD entries indexed by the DVLAN-ID. If there exists at least one entry, the BUS transmits the frame to each BS indicated in each retrieved entry.

For an intra-tree BUS, it also transmits the frame to all connected parent and child BUSs, except the one where the frame came from. If the BUS is an inter-tree BUS and the received frame is from another inter-tree BUS, then the frame is transmitted to each child BUS. Otherwise (the frame is received from an intra-tree BUS), the inter-tree BUS retrieves from its Inter-Tree-MTD the entry for the DVLAN-ID and determines which trees are serving MTs moved from the same VLAN. The inter-tree BUS then transmits a copy of the frame to each of these inter-tree BUSs. The inter-tree BUS then further transmits the frame to each child BUS, except the one where the frame came from.

From the above procedures, we have the following observations. When a BUS receives a broadcast (or an unknown) frame for the same VLAN, it transmits the frame to each node on the VLAN. Otherwise (the frame is received from another VLAN), the BUS transmits the frame to its BSs where at least one MT from the VLAN has moved into. The BUS also transmits the frame to its parent BUS and child BUSs so that they can perform the same routing. Inevitably, the frame reaches the inter-tree BUS at the root of the tree. The inter-tree BUS transmits the frame to each inter-tree BUS where at least one MT from the VLAN has moved into. Each of the inter-tree BUSs then performs the same procedure to forward the frame in the tree.

4. An example of MVLAN operation

In this section, an example is illustrated to show the operations of the MVLAN. Consider the HOT-based interconnection topology shown in Fig. 4. The shaded region of $MVLAN_{0,7}$ denotes the MVLAN domain which extends over the ATM network and includes $VLAN_{0,7}$ segment, MT_1 on $VLAN_{0,5}$ segment, and MT_3 on $VLAN_{1,5}$ segment. The way to update the MTDs for these mobilities is described as follows. As part of handoff procedures, BS_2 first compares the new location ($VLAN_{0,5}$) of MT_1 with its original location ($VLAN_{0,7}$) and concludes that it is an inter-VLAN mobility. It then issues the $MM_I\{VLAN\text{-}ID(0,7),\ VLAN_{0,5},\ ATM(BS_2)\}$ to $LES_{0,7}/BUS_{0,7}$ for membership tracking operation in addition to removing MT_1 from its registration database. Upon receiving the MM_I, $LES_{0,7}/BUS_{0,7}$ increases the *Out-Count* value by one in the OUT-MTD. Furthermore, it checks the new location ($VLAN_{0,5}$) of MT_1 and finds that the MT_1 is still under the same tree area ($Tree_0$), which implies that the update process is completed and the MM_I is dropped without forwarding to other inter-tree LESs/BUSs. At the same time, BS_1 adds MT_1 to its registration database and sends the MM_{III} $\{VLAN\text{-}ID(0,7),\ ATM(BS_1)\}$ to $LES_{0,5}/BUS_{0,5}$ which then creates an entry for MT_1 in the IN-MTD. Table 3 is the contents in the IN-MTD of $LES_{0,5}/BUS_{0,5}$.

Table 3. IN-MTD of $LES_{0,5}/BUS_{0,5}$

VLAN-ID	In-Count	ATM address of BS	VCC to BS
(0,7)	1	$ATM(BS_1)$	$VCC(BS_1)$

On the other hand, the mobility of MT_3 to $VLAN_{1,5}$ is an inter-tree mobility. The $LES_{0,7}/BUS_{0,7}$ updates the *Out-Count* value (now the *Out-Count* value is two for MT_1 and MT_3), BS_3 adds MT_3 to its registration database, and $LES_{1,5}/BUS_{1,5}$ creates an entry for MT_3 in the IN-MTD. Table 4 is the contents in the IN-MTD of $LES_{1,5}/BUS_{1,5}$.

Table 4. IN-MTD of $LES_{1,5}/BUS_{1,5}$

VLAN-ID	In-Count	ATM address of BS	VCC to BS
(0,7)	1	$ATM(BS_3)$	$VCC(BS_3)$

The $LES_{0,7}/BUS_{0,7}$ also issues the MM_{II} $\{VLAN\text{-}ID(0,7),\ Tree_0,\ Tree_1\}$ to the root node $LES_{0,1}/BUS_{0,1}$ of the tree which then broadcasts it to all the other inter-tree LESs/BUSs. As a result, the inter-tree LESs/BUSs will create an entry for MT_3 in the Inter-Tree-MTD. Table 5 is the part of contents in the Inter-Tree-MTD.

Table 5. Inter-Tree-MTD

VLAN-ID	Count($Tree_0$)	Count($Tree_1$)	...
...	...	...	...
(0,7)	2	1	...
...	...	...	...

Consider what happens when MT_4 (belongs to $VLAN_{0,5}$) sends a frame with a destination MAC address to $VLAN_{0,7}$ segment. Now the DVLAN-ID and the SVLAN-ID are $VLAN_{0,7}$ and $VLAN_{0,5}$, respectively. This is a communication between VLANs (VLAN internetworking). When base station BS_1 receives the frame and finds the record $\{\ VLAN\text{-}ID(0,7) \rightarrow MT_1\}$ in its registration database, it then sends the frame to MT_1. Also BS_1 recognizes that the destination VLAN of this frame is remote, it will forward the frame to $BUS_{0,5}$. Next the frame will be broadcast on $Tree_0$. In this example, the intermediate BUSs on $Tree_0$ do not perform the forwarding operation due to no entry for $VLAN_{0,7}$ members in their IN-MTDs. Eventually, $BUS_{0,1}$ forwards it to the inter-tree $BUS_{1,1}$ on $Tree_1$ according to the record for MT_3 in the Inter-Tree-MTD. Based on the tree broadcasting operation, $BUS_{0,7}$ and $BUS_{1,5}$ surely received this frame. $BUS_{0,7}$ sends the broadcast frame to all members on $VLAN_{0,7}$, including BS_2 and S_4. BS_2 then further forwards the frame to MT_2. As to $BUS_{1,5}$, it will perform the forwarding operation to BS_3 based on the record in the IN-MTD. BS_3 then forwards the frame to MT_3. Note that in this example the rest intermediate BUSs on $Tree_1$ just relay the frame without performing the forwarding operation.

Following the similar operations, it can be easily applied to the unicast communication between VLANs. Now the frame forwarding decision for interconnected LESs or BUSs are based on the record of destination VLAN members in the MTDs. In other word, an unknown unicast frame should be forwarded to all members belonging to the destination VLAN even though they may have moved into another VLAN segment.

Finally, consider what happens when MT_3 moves back to $VLAN_{0,7}$ segment. As part of handoff procedures, BS_3 will find that this is an inter-VLAN mobility, and then issues the MM_I {$VLAN\text{-}ID(0,7)$, $VLAN_{0,7}$, $ATM(BS_3)$} to $LES_{1,5}/BUS_{1,5}$ in addition to removing MT_3 from its registration database. Upon receiving this MM_I, the $LES_{1,5}/BUS_{1,5}$ takes a lookup at the IN-MTD according to $ATM(BS_3)$ and decreases the corresponding *In-Count* by one. Thus, the IN-MTDs of $LES_{1,5}/BUS_{1,5}$ are empty now. Furthermore, $LES_{1,5}/BUS_{1,5}$ recognizes that the new location ($VLAN_{0,7}$) of MT_3 is within a different tree area ($Tree_0$), it then issues the MM_{II} {$VLAN_{0,7}$, $Tree_1$, $Tree_0$} to the root node $LES_{1,1}/BUS_{1,1}$ which then broadcasts it to all the other inter-tree LESs/BUSs. As a result, the entry for MT_3 would be removed from each of the Inter-Tree-MTDs. In the mean time, BS_2 adds MT_3 to its registration database and issues the MM_{III} {$VLAN\text{-}ID(0,7)$, $ATM(BS_2)$} to $LES_{0,7}/BUS_{0,7}$. Since MT_3 originally belongs to $VLAN_{0,7}$, $LES_{0,7}/BUS_{0,7}$ decreases the *Out-Count* value by one (now the *Out-Count* value is one for MT_1 only).

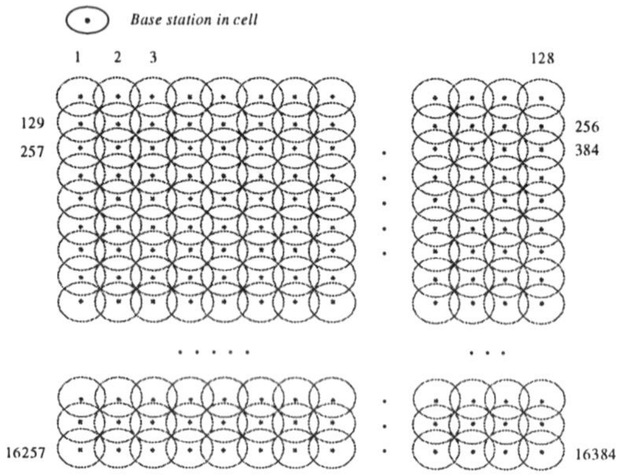

Fig. 5. A 128*128 Manhattan-style wireless network.

5. Simulations

5.1 Experimental design and assumptions

In order to evaluate the effectiveness of the proposed HOT-based membership tracking scheme, an experimental test was implemented. The experiment is implemented by the C++ programming language on an Intel Pentium personal computer. A Manhattan-style wireless network model is considered as shown in Fig. 5. The coverage area of the wireless network is divided into cells with a size of 128*128. We randomly select 32 cells to form a VLAN segment. As a whole, there are 512 VLANs associated with responsible LESs/BUSs. These LESs (or BUSs) will be randomly partitioned into four or eight equal groups ; each of them forms a binary tree. The roots of the four (or eight) trees are shaped into a two-dimensional (or three-dimensional) hypercube. Hereafter we will call them the HOT-dim2 and HOT-dim3 based MVLAN architecture, respectively.

The above 512 LESs (or BUSs) can also be interconnected as a pure binary tree structure. Upon an inter-VLAN move, location informing takes place in all the LESs (or BUSs) located on the shortest path from the original LES (LES_{orig} or BUS_{orig}) to the new LES (LES_{new} or BUS_{new}). As to searching process, if a given LES (or BUS) does not have any record for the destination VLAN of a frame, it forwards the frame to the next higher level LES (or BUS) on the path to the root. This process repeats until one LES (or BUS) which serving at least one MT of the destination VLAN is reached. Then the frame is forwarded to all the members of the destination VLAN. Such informing and searching strategies are similar to that of [8]. Hereafter we will just call it the Tree based MVLAN architecture.

Assume that there are totally 32,768 mobile terminals uniformly distributed over the wireless network, i.e., two mobile terminals per wireless cell. For simplicity, initially the MTs within one cell area are assigned to the same VLAN and the served BS is connected to the responsible LES/BUS over ATM backbone network. A roaming terminal must either roams to up, down, right or left cell (randomly determined). The time interval between the movements of an MT is assumed to follow an exponential distribution with a mean M.

5.2 Cost metrics

In order to compare the performance of the HOT-based MVLAN architecture with the Tree-based one, the inform/search costs and the size of database for membership maintenance are investigated. Here we use hop counts and entries number as the basic cost metrics. The inform (search) cost is the number of servers along informing (frame forwarding) path, including the servers really updating their MTDs (forwarding frames) and the servers only relaying mobility messages (frames). In our experiment, the search cost is measured by the broadcast cost. That is, one static station on a VLAN sends broadcast frames to all the members belonging to the VLAN even though they have already moved into another VLAN segment. The time interval to generate broadcast frames is assumed to follow an exponential distribution with a mean B.

For considering the mobile membership (inform + broadcast) cost and the consumed membership tracking database (MTD) size, we define the total MVLAN cost as

$$totalMVLANcost = (inform\ cost + broadcast\ cost) \times MTDs\ size.$$

The rationale for this formula is illustrated as follows. If the mobile membership cost is 50 and the MTDs size is 20, the *totalMVLANcost* is then 1,000 (50×20). In another case, the mobile membership cost is 20 and the MTDs size is 50, the *totalMVLANcost* is still 1,000. In our view, the above two cases are with the same performance. The more network resources used (reflect to MTDs size), the less mobility overheads produced (reflect to inform and broadcast costs).

5.3 Experimental results

The simulation results are depicted in Fig. 6 which shows the average mobile membership cost (Fig. 6 (a)) and the total MTDs size (Fig. 6 (b)) versus time in the compared server interconnection topologies for M = 15 and B = 25. From Fig. 6 (a) we can see that the Tree-based MVLAN architecture has an extremely higher inform cost than the HOT-based one. It will result in a very long transient time due to terminal mobility. The HOT-based (either HOT-dim2 or HOT-dim3) MVLAN system provides a much better trade-off between the broadcast and inform overheads. Meanwhile, we can observe that both the inform and broadcast costs of the HOT-based structure are approximately laid in the middle area between the two costs of the Tree-based one. This means that the HOT-based MVLAN system furnishes the good property of 50-50 load sharing but with the same mobile membership cost as the Tree-based one. On the other hand, Fig. 6 (b) depicts the total MTDs size used in the HOT structure is only about 50% of that in the Tree one. In summary, the HOT-based MVLAN architecture takes less network resources but owns better performance.

Fig. 7 shows the total MVLAN cost of the compared architectures as we increase the broadcast mean time B for different values of M. The time interval for performance observation is 1,500 time units. In all cases, the HOT-based structures take less MVLAN cost. For example, for $M = 15$ and $B = 30$ the total MVLAN costs of the Tree structure are two and three times larger than that of the HOT-dim3 and HOT-dim2 ones, respectively. It is also clear that for the Tree-based structure, higher the mobility frequencies (smaller M) produces more full cost. For instance, when the value of M is decreased from 25 to 15 under $B = 30$, the total MVLAN cost of the Tree-based system is increased significantly by almost 60%. On the contrary, that of the HOT-based structure is just increased by 25-35% under the same condition. Thus the HOT-based architecture lessens the mobility impact on the VLAN service. Note that in our experiment the HOT-dim2 MVLAN structure always performs better than the HOT-dim3 one. This is because the contents of the Inter-Tree-MTDs must be replicated for all roots of trees. In some extreme cases, the total MTDs size of a HOT-dim3 structure would be twice of that of a HOT-dim2 one.

6. Conclusions

This paper has taken a step in the direction of designing an MVLAN system on an ATM network using LAN emulation technologies. The mobile membership tracking operation based on the HOT-based LES/BUS interconnection structure is proposed. We also demonstrated that implementing an intelligent frame forwarding scheme in BUS is well-suited to conditionally filter excessive inter-BUS traffic. In this sense, an intelligent BUS becomes a virtual bridge/router in the MVLAN system. Simulation results show that the HOT-based architecture provides a moderate trade-off between the search and inform costs in a mobile environment and significantly lessens the mobility impact on the VLAN service. The major contribution of the proposed MVLAN system is to provide transparent communication between the same or different VLAN members (VLAN internetworking) in spite of whether the members are static or moved to the other VLANs.

Acknowledgments

This work is supported by the R.O.C. Ministry of Economic Affairs under contract number MOEA85-EC-2-A-15-0146, and by the R.O.C. National Science Council under contract number NSC85-2622-E007-009.

References

[1] ATM Forum, "LAN Emulation over ATM Version 2-LUNI Specification," Dec. 1995.

[2] ATM Forum, "LAN Emulation over ATM Version 2-LNNI Specification," Dec. 1995.

[3] R. B. Bellman, "Evolving Traditional LANs to ATM, " *Bus. Commun. Rev.*, pp. 43-48, Oct. 1994.

[4] P. Bhagwat, C. Perkins, and S. Tripathi, "Network Layer Mobility: An Architecture and Survey," *IEEE Pers. Commun.*, vol. 3, no. 3, pp. 54-64, June 1996.

[5] E. W. Gray and O. C. Ibe, "ELAN Scaling and Resiliency Issues," ATM Forum/95-0351.

[6] N. F. Huang, Y. T. Wang, B. Li and T. L. Liu, "Mobility Management of Interconnected Virtual LANs over ATM Networks," *Proc. IEEE GLOBECOM*, pp. 1156-1161, London, Nov. 1996.

[7] J. Ioannidis, D. Duchamp and G. Q. Maguire Jr., "IP-Based Protocols for Mobile Interworking," *Proc. of ACM SIGCOMM'91*, pp. 235-245, Sep. 1991.

[8] P. Krishna, N. H. Vaidya and D. K. Pradhan, "Location Management in Distributed Mobile Environments," *3rd Int'l Conf. on Parallel and Distributed Information Systems*, pp. 81-88, Los Alamitos, CA, 1994.

[9] B. Li and P. Vankwikelberge, "Virtual LAN (VLAN) Configuration and Address Resolution in an ATM Network," *2nd Int'l Symp. on Interworking (INTERWORKING'94)*, pp. 179-190, Sophia Antipolis, May 1994.

[10] J. P. Morency, "Do VLANs Really Deliver ?," *Bus. Commun. Rev.*, pp. 39-43, July 1995.

[11] B. V. Patel, P. Bhattacharya, Y. Rekhter, and A. Krishna, "An Architecture and Implementation toward Multiprotocol Mobility," *IEEE Pers. Commun.*, vol. 2, no. 3, pp. 32-42, June 1995.

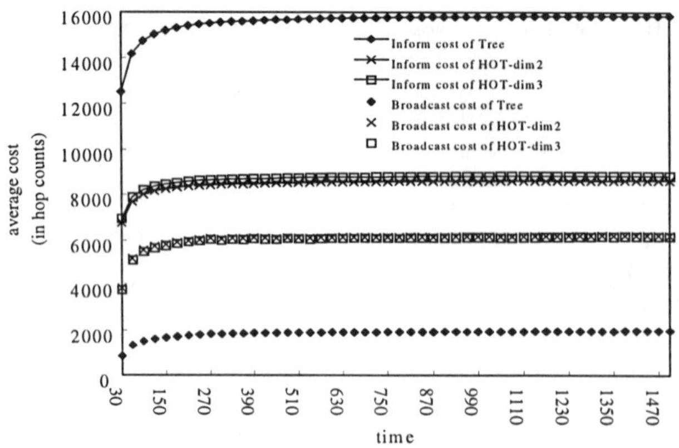

Fig. 6 (a). The average mobile membership cost for different LES/BUS interconnection topologies.

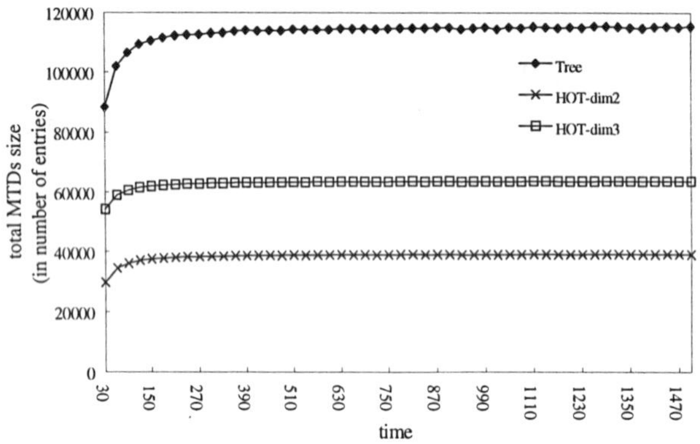

Fig. 6 (b). The total MTDs size for different LES/BUS interconnection topologies.

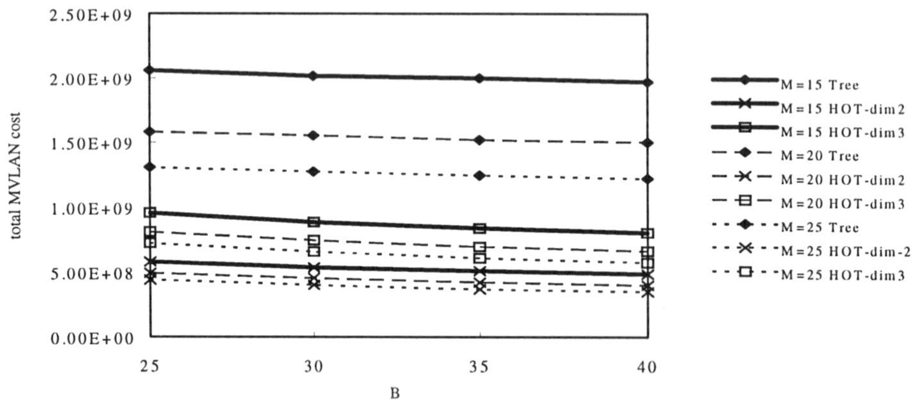

Fig. 7. The total MVLAN cost under various values of *M* and *B*.

A Highly Adaptive Distributed Routing Algorithm for Mobile Wireless Networks

Vincent D. Park[a] and M. Scott Corson[b]
[a]*Naval Research Laboratory, USA*
[b]*University of Maryland, USA*

Abstract

We present a new distributed routing protocol for mobile, multihop, wireless networks. The protocol is one of a family of protocols which we term "link reversal" algorithms. The protocol's reaction is structured as a temporally-ordered sequence of diffusing computations; each computation consisting of a sequence of directed link reversals. The protocol is highly adaptive, efficient and scalable; being best-suited for use in large, dense, mobile networks. In these networks, the protocol's reaction to link failures typically involves only a localized "single pass" of the distributed algorithm. This capability is unique among protocols which are stable in the face of network partitions, and results in the protocol's high degree of adaptivity. This desirable behavior is achieved through the novel use of a "physical or logical clock" to establish the "temporal order" of topological change events which is used to structure (or order) the algorithm's reaction to topological changes. We refer to the protocol as the Temporally-Ordered Routing Algorithm (TORA).

1.0 Introduction

We consider the problem of routing in a mobile wireless network as described in [1]. Such a network can be envisioned as a collection of routers (equipped with wireless receiver/transmitters) which are free to move about arbitrarily. The status of the communication links between the routers, at any given time, is a function of their positions, transmission power levels, antenna patterns, cochannel interference levels, etc. The mobility of the routers and the variability of other connectivity factors result in a network with a potentially rapid and unpredictably changing topology. Congested links are also an expected characteristic of such a network as wireless links inherently have significantly lower capacity than hardwired links and are therefore more prone to congestion.

Existing shortest-path algorithms [2] and adaptive shortest-path algorithms [3-9] are not particularly well-suited for operation in such a network. These algorithms are designed for operation in static or quasi-static networks with hardwired links. If the rate of topological change in the network is sufficiently high, these algorithms may not be able to react fast enough (i.e. to maintain routing) and flooding will be the only recourse. Furthermore, most of these algorithms provide only one path for routing between each given source/destination pair which exacerbates the link congestion problem. While link-state algorithms provide the capability for multipath routing, the time and communication overhead associated with maintaining full topological knowledge at each router makes them impractical for this environment as well.

Some existing algorithms which have been developed for this environment include the following: the Gafni-Bertsekas (GB) algorithms [10], the Lightweight Mobile Routing (LMR) protocol [11], the Destination-Sequenced Distance Vector (DSDV) routing protocol [12], the Wireless Routing Protocol (WRP) [13], and the Dynamic Source Routing (DSR) protocol [14]. While these algorithms are better suited for this environment, each has its drawbacks.

The GB algorithms exhibit instability in portions of the network which become partitioned from the destination. During the period of instability, nodes will non-productively transmit both control packets and message packets until such time that the network is re-connected. This results in inefficient use of the available bandwidth and is unacceptable, since partitioning is expected to be common in a mobile wireless network.

The LMR protocol also exhibits some unwanted behavior which is most prevalent in partitioned portions of the networks. The protocol can result in temporary construction of invalid routes through "false reply" propagation. While it was shown that all invalid routes would be erased in a partitioned portion of the network (with probability one), no finite bound could be placed on the time required.

DSDV is limited in that it provides only a single path for routing between each given source/destination pair. Furthermore, the protocol requires selection of the following parameters: periodic update interval, maximum value of the "settling time" for a destination and the number of update intervals which may transpire before a route is considered "stale". It is difficult to assess the

0-8186-7780-5/97 $10.00 © 1997 IEEE

impact that selection of these parameters will have on performance, but we believe good parameter selection may be critical. These parameters will likely represent a trade-off between the latency of valid routing information and excessive communication overhead. To further complicate the problem, good parameter selection will likely be dependent on the networking environment (i.e. the size of the network, rate of topological change, etc.)

While WRP is described as providing only single path routing, nodes maintain sufficient information to perform multipath routing. However, there is potentially a significant amount of overhead associated with maintaining the shortest-path spanning tree reported by each neighbor and reactions to failures may be far-reaching (i.e. every node which includes the failed link in its shortest-path spanning tree must participate in the failure reaction).

DSR is also desribed as providing only single path routing; although, it could be amended to support multipath routing. More significantly, it suffers from a scalability problem due to the nature of source routing. As the network becomes larger, control packets (which collect node addresses for each node visited) and message packets (which contain full source routing information) also become larger. Clearly, this has a negative impact due to the limited available bandwidth.

In our view, a routing algorithm well-suited for operation in this environment should possess the following properties:

- Executes distributedly
- Provides loop-free routes
- Provides multiple routes (to alleviate congestion)
- Establishes routes quickly (so they may be used before the topology changes)
- Minimizes communication overhead by localizing algorithmic reaction to topological changes when possible (to conserve available bandwidth and increase scalability)

Routing optimality (i.e. determination of the shortest-path) is of less importance. It is also not necessary (nor desirable) to maintain routes between every source/destination pair at all times. The overhead expended to establish a route between a given source/destination pair will be wasted if the source does not require the route prior to its invalidation due to topological changes.

We have developed a routing algorithm which is tailored for operation in this highly dynamic network environment. The algorithm is based, in part, on the work presented in [10] and [11]; however, it does not share their undesirable characteristics associated with network partitions. The protocol is designed to *minimize* reaction to topological changes. A key concept in its design is that it *decouples the generation of potentially far-reaching control message propagation from the rate of topological changes.* Such messaging is typically *localized* to a very small set of nodes near the change without having to resort to a dynamic, hierarchical routing solution with its attendant complexity. A possible enhancement to the protocol (to be discussed later) would be to imbed far-reaching control message propagation into the protocol as a secondary mechanism. This propogation would occur periodically at a very low rate—independent of the network topology dynamics—and would be employed as a means of infrequent route optimization and soft-state route verification.

The algorithm is distributed in that nodes need only maintain information about adjacent nodes (i.e. one hop knowledge). It guarantees all routes are loop-free, and typically provides multiple routes for any source/destination pair which requires a route. Like LMR, the protocol is "source initiated" and quickly creates a set of routes to a given destination only when desired. Since multiple routes are typically established, many topological changes require no reaction at all as having a single route is sufficient. Following topological changes which do require reaction, the protocol quickly re-establishes valid routes. This ability to initiate and react infrequently serves to minimize communication overhead. Finally, in the event of a network partition, the protocol detects the partition and erases all invalid routes within a finite time.

2.0 The Protocol

2.1 Notation and Assumptions

We model a network as a graph $G = (N, L)$, where N is a finite set of nodes and L is a set of initially undirected links. Each node $i \in N$ is assumed to have a unique node identifier (ID), and each link $(i, j) \in L$ is assumed to allow two-way communication (i.e. nodes connected by a link can communicate with each other in either direction). Due to the mobility of the nodes, the set of links L is changing with time (i.e. new links can be established and existing links can be severed). From the perspective of neighboring nodes, a node failure is equivalent to severing all links incident to that node. Each initially undirected link $(i, j) \in L$ may subsequently be assigned one of three states; (1) undirected, (2) directed from node i to node j, or (3) directed from node j to node i. If a link $(i, j) \in L$ is directed from node i to node j, node i is said to be "upstream" from node j while node j is said to be "downstream" from node i. For each node i, we define the "neighbors" of i, $N_i \in N$, to be the set of nodes j such that $(i, j) \in L$. For the subsequent discussion, we assume the existence of a link-level protocol which ensures that each node i is always aware of its neighbors in the set N_i; although the logic of the protocol remains the same if this is not the case—i.e. there may be an arbitrary delay in the time between a link status change and subsequent protocol notification of the change. We also assume that all transmitted packets are received correctly and in order of transmission. Finally, since existing networks of this type typically employ omnidirectional antennas, we have assumed that when a node i transmits a packet, it is broadcast to all of its neighbors in the set N_i,. The rules of the protocol described herein reflect this assumption; however, only slight modifications to the rules would be required to make it work in networks where only a subset of the neighbors receive a transmission—i.e. those which incorporate Space Division Multiple Access (SDMA) techniques.

2.2 Foundation and Basic Structure

A logically separate version of the protocol is run for each destination to which routing is required. For the following presentation, we will focus on a single version running for a given destination.

The protocol can be separated into three basic functions: creating routes, maintaining routes, and erasing routes. Creating a route from a given node to the destination requires establishment of a sequence of directed links leading from the node to the destination. This function is only initiated when a node with no directed links requires a route to the destination. Thus, creating routes essentially corresponds to assigning directions to links in an undirected network or portion of the network. The method used to accomplish this is an adaptation of the query/reply process described in [11], which builds a directed acyclic graph (DAG) *rooted at the destination* (i.e. the destination is the only node with no downstream links). Such a DAG will be referred to as a "destination-oriented" DAG. Maintaining routes refers to reacting to topological changes in the network in a manner such that routes to the destination are re-established within a finite time. By this we mean that its directed portions return to a destination-oriented DAG within a finite time. Two GB algorithms, which are members of a general class of algorithms designed to accomplish this task, are presented in [10]. However, the GB algorithms are designed for operation in connected networks. Due to instability exhibited by these algorithms in portions of the network which become partitioned from the destination, they are deemed unacceptable for the current task. We have designed a new algorithm in the same general class, which is more efficient in reacting to topological changes and capable of detecting a network partition. This leads to the third function—erasing routes. Upon detection of a network partition, all links (in the portion of the network which has become partitioned from the destination) must be undirected to erase invalid routes.

The protocol accomplishes these three functions through the use of three distinct control packets: query (QRY), update (UPD), and clear (CLR). QRY packets are used for creating routes, UPD packets are used for both creating and maintaining routes, and CLR packets are used for erasing routes.

2.3 General Class of Algorithms

It is beneficial at this point to briefly review the GB algorithms. Consider a connected DAG with at least one node (in addition to the destination) which has no downstream links. We shall refer to such a DAG as "destination-disoriented." The following excerpts from [10] loosely describe two algorithms designed to transform a destination-disoriented DAG into a destination-oriented DAG.

Full Reversal Method: At each iteration each node other than the destination that has no outgoing links reverses the direction of all its incoming links.

Partial Reversal Method: Every node i other than the destination keeps a list of its neighboring nodes j that have reversed the direction of the corresponding links (i, j). At each iteration each node i that has no outgoing links reverses the directions of the links (i, j) for all j which do not appear on its list, and empties the list. If no such j exists (i.e. the list is full), node i reverses the directions of all incoming links and empties the list.

These two algorithms are subsequently re-stated in the context of a generalized numbering scheme which we will summarize here; however, much detail will be left out. For a thorough understanding, one should review the original paper. Essentially, a value is associated with each node at all times, and the values are such that they can be totally ordered. For example, in the full reversal method, a pair (α_i, i) is associated with each node where i is the unique ID of the node and α_i is an integer. The pairs can then be totally ordered lexicographically (e.g. $(\alpha_i, i) > (\alpha_j, j)$ if $\alpha_i > \alpha_j$,or if $\alpha_i = \alpha_j$ and $i > j$). Let us refer to the value associated with each node i as its "height" and denote it h_i. Now, assume that we assign an initial height to each node in the destination-disoriented DAG such that node i is upstream from node j if and only if $h_i > h_j$. Then it is clear that node i has no downstream links when, measured by its height, it is a local minimum with respect to its neighbors, $h_i < h_j$ for all $j \in N_i$. To achieve the desired behavior in the full reversal method, node i must select a new height such that it becomes a local maximum with respect to its neighbors, $h_i > h_j$ for all $j \in N_i$. Node i simply selects a new value $\alpha_i = \max \{\alpha_j \mid j \in N_i\}+1$ and broadcasts the value to all of its neighbors. The partial reversal method can neither be viewed conceptually nor explained as easily. Again, a node selects a new height only when it is a local minimum, but it does not always become a local maximum. To reverse only some of its links (i.e. partial reversal), a node selects a new height which is higher than its own previous height and the height of some of its neighbors, but not higher than all of its neighbors.

Further details of these two algorithms are not relevant to the development and discussion of our protocol. What is relevant is that [10] goes on to describe a general class of algorithms based on a generalized numbering scheme. This class of algorithms is shown to be loop-free, and terminate in a finite number of iterations to a destination-oriented DAG. Furthermore, only nodes which have lost all downstream paths to the destination react to a given failure. These properties all apply to the new algorithm as it is a member of this class. The new algorithm is similar to the partial reversal method in that it often reverses only some of its links. However, the rules for the selection of a new height are significantly more complex, in order to provide its partition detection capability. These rules are discussed in detail in section 2.4.2.

The basic idea is as follows. When a node loses its last downstream link (i.e. becomes a local minimum) as a result of a link failure, the node selects a new height such that it becomes a *global* maximum by defining a *new* "reference level". By design, when a new reference level is defined, it is higher than any previously defined reference levels. This action results in link reversals which may cause other nodes to lose their last downstream link. Any such node executes a partial reversal with respect to its neighbors that have heights already associated with the newest (highest) reference level. In this manner, the new reference level is propagated outward from the point of the original failure (re-directing links in order to re-establish routes to the destination). This propagation will only extend through nodes which (as a result of the initial link failure) have lost all routes to the destination. Any node, which prior to the start of this reaction had only downstream links, may experience link reversals (as a result of the same initial link failure) from all its neighbors. Any such node must select a new height such that it becomes a local maximum. This is accomplished by defining a higher sub-level associated with the new reference level, which we refer to as the "reflected reference level". This node essentially "reflects" this higher sub-level back toward the node which originally defined the new reference level. Should this reflected reference level be propagated back to the originating node from all of its neighbors, then it is determined that no route to the destination exists. The originating node has then detected a partition and can begin the process of erasing the invalid routes.

2.4 Detailed Description

At any given time, an ordered quintuple $H_i = (\tau_i, oid_i, r_i, \delta_i, i)$ is associated with each node $i \in N$. Conceptually, the quintuple associated with each node represents the height of the node as defined by two parameters: a reference level and a delta with respect to the reference level. The reference level is represented by the first three values in the quintuple while the delta is represented by the last two values. A new reference level is defined each time a node loses its last downstream link due to a link failure. The first value representing the reference level, τ_i, is a time tag set to the "time" of the link failure. For now we will assume that all nodes have synchronized clocks. This could be accomplished via interface with an external time source such as the Global Positioning System (GPS) [15] or through use of an algorithm such as the Network Time Protocol [16]. As we will discuss in section 2.5, this time tag need not actually indicate or be "time," nor will relaxation of the synchronization requirement invalidate the protocol. The second value, oid_i, is the originator-ID (i.e. the unique ID of the node which defined the new reference level). This ensures that the reference levels can be totally ordered lexicographically, even if multiple nodes define reference levels due to failures which occur simultaneously (i.e. with equal time tags). The third value, r_i, is a single bit used to divide each of the unique reference levels into two unique sub-levels. This bit is used to distinguish between the original reference level and its corresponding, higher reflected reference level. When a distinction is not required, both original and reflected reference levels will simply be referred to as "reference levels." The first value representing the delta, δ_i, is an integer used to order nodes with respect to a common reference level. This value is instrumental in the propagation of a reference level. How δ_i is selected will be clarified in a subsequent section. Finally, the second value representing the delta, i, is the unique ID of the node itself. This ensures that nodes with a common reference level and equal values of δ_i (and in fact all nodes) can be totally ordered lexicographically at all times.

Each node i (other than the destination) maintains its height, H_i. Initially the height of each node in the network (other than the destination) is set to NULL, $H_i = (-, -, -, -, i)$. Subsequently, the height of each node i can be modified in accordance with the rules of the protocol. The height of the destination is always ZERO, $H_{did} = (0, 0, 0, 0, did)$, where did is the destination-ID (i.e. the unique ID of the destination for which the algorithm is running). In addition to its own height, each node i maintains a height array with an entry $HN_{i,j}$ for each neighbor $j \in N_i$. Initially the height of each neighbor is set to NULL, $HN_{i,j} = (-, -, -, -, j)$. If the destination is a neighbor of i (i.e. $did \in N_i$) node i sets the height entry of the destination to ZERO, $HN_{i,did} = (0, 0, 0, 0, did)$.

Each node i (other than the destination) also maintains a link-state array with an entry $LS_{i,j}$ for each link $(i, j) \in L$, where $j \in N_i$. The state of the links is determined by the heights H_i and $HN_{i,j}$ and is directed from the higher node to the lower node. If a neighbor j is higher than node i, the link is marked upstream (UP). If a neighbor j is lower than node i, the link is marked downstream (DN). If the neighbors height entry, $HN_{i,j}$, is NULL, the link is marked undirected (UN). Finally, if the height of node i is NULL, then any neighbor's height which is not NULL is considered lower, and the corresponding link is marked downstream (DN). When a new link $(i, j) \in L$ is established (i.e. node i has a new neighbor $j \in N_i$), node i adds entries for the new neighbor to the height and link-state arrays. If the new neighbor is the destination, the height entry is set to ZERO, $HN_{i,\,did} = (0, 0, 0, 0, did)$; otherwise it is set to NULL, $HN_{i,\,j} = (-, -, -, -, j)$. The corresponding link-state, $LS_{i,\,j}$, is set as outlined above. Nodes need not communicate any routing information upon link activation.

2.4.1 Creating Routes. Creating routes requires use of the QRY and UPD packets. A QRY packet consists of a destination-ID (*did*), which identifies the destination for which the algorithm is running. An UPD packet consists of a *did*, and the height of the node i which is broadcasting the packet, H_i.

Each node i (other than the destination) maintains a route-required flag, RR_i, which is initially un-set. Each node i (other than the destination) also maintains the time at which the last UPD packet was broadcast and the time at which each link $(i, j) \in L$, where $j \in N_i$, became active.

When a node with no directed links and an un-set route-required flag requires a route to the destination, it broadcasts a QRY packet and sets its route-required flag. When a node i receives a QRY it reacts as follows. (a) If the receiving node has no downstream links and its route-required flag is un-set, it re-broadcasts the QRY packet and sets its route-required flag. (b) If the receiving node has no downstream links and the route-required flag is set, it discards the QRY packet. (c) If the receiving node has at least one downstream link and its height is NULL, it sets its height to $H_i = (\tau_j, oid_j, r_j, \delta_j + 1, i)$, where $HN_{i,\,j} = (\tau_j, oid_j, r_j, \delta_j, j)$ is the minimum height of its non-NULL neighbors, and broadcasts an UPD packet. (d) If the receiving node has at least one downstream link and its height is non-NULL, it first compares the time the last UPD packet was broadcast to the time the link over which the QRY packet was received became active. If an UPD packet has been broadcast since the link became active , it discards the QRY packet; otherwise, it broadcasts an UPD packet. If a node has the route required flag set when a new link is established, it broadcasts a QRY packet.

When a node i receives an UPD packet from a neighbor $j \in N_i$, node i first updates the entry $HN_{i,\,j}$ in its height array with the height contained in the received UPD packet and then reacts as follows. (a) If the route-required flag is set (which implies that the height of node i is NULL), node i sets its height to $H_i = (\tau_j, oid_j, r_j, \delta_j + 1, i)$—where $HN_{i,\,j} = (\tau_j, oid_j, r_j, \delta_j, j)$ is the minimum height of its non-NULL neighbors, updates all the entries in its link-state array LS, un-sets the route-required flag and then broadcasts an UPD packet which contains its new height. (b) If the route-required flag is not set, node i simply updates the entry $LS_{i,\,j}$ in its link-state array. The section on maintaining routes discusses the additional reaction that occurs if (b) results in loss of the last downstream link.

An example[1] of the route creation process is depicted in Fig. 1. The respective heights are shown adjacent to each node and the destination for which the algorithm is running is marked DEST. A circle around a node indicates that the route-required flag is set. Recall that the last value in each height is the unique ID of the node, and that lexicographical ordering (where $0 < 1 < 2...$ and $A < B < C...$) is used to direct links. Note that the height selected for node B in Fig. 1(e) reflects an arbitrary assumption that node B received the UPD packet from node E prior to the packet from node D. Had node B instead selected a height in response to the packet from node D, the direction of link (A, B) in Fig. 1(f) would have been reversed.

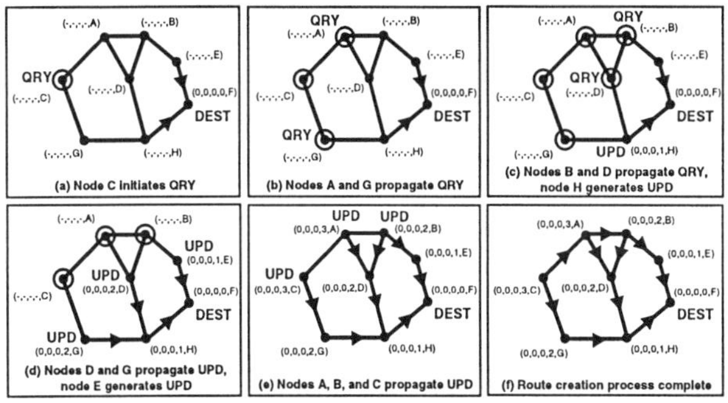

Fig. 1 Creating routes

2.4.2 Maintaining Routes. Maintaining routes is only performed for nodes which have a height other than NULL. Furthermore, any neighbor's height which is NULL is not used for the computations. A node i is said to have no downstream links if $H_i < HN_{i,\,j}$ for all non-NULL neighbors $j \in N_i$. This will result in one of five possible reactions depending on the state of the node and the preceding event. Each node (other than the destination) that has no downstream links modifies its height, $H_i = (\tau_i, oid_i, r_i, \delta_i, i)$, as follows.

Case 1 (Generate): Node i has no downstream links (due to a link failure).

$(\tau_i, oid_i, r_i) = (t, i, 0)$, where t is the time of the failure.

$(\delta_i, i) = (0, i)$

In essence, node i defines a new reference level. The above assumes node i has at least one upstream neighbor. If node i has no upstream neighbors it simply sets its height to NULL.

[1] While the algorithm is designed to operate asynchronously, the examples depict the algorithm executing synchronously with transmissions occurring at fixed points in time.

Case 2 (Propagate): Node i has no downstream links (due to a link reversal following reception of an UPD packet) and the ordered sets (τ_j, oid_j, r_j) are **not** equal for all $j \in N_i$.

$$(\tau_i, oid_i, r_i) = \max\left\{(\tau_j, oid_j, r_j) \mid j \in N_i\right\}$$

$$(\delta_i, i) = \left(\min\left\{\delta_j \;\middle|\; \begin{array}{l} j \in N_i \text{ with } (\tau_j, oid_j, r_j) \\ = \max\left\{(\tau_j, oid_j, r_j)\right\} \end{array}\right\} - 1, i\right)$$

In essence, node i propagates the reference level of its highest neighbor and selects a height which is lower than all neighbors with that reference level.

Case 3 (Reflect): Node i has no downstream links (due to a link reversal following reception of an UPD packet) and the ordered sets (τ_j, oid_j, r_j) are equal with $r_j = 0$ for all $j \in N_i$.

$$(\tau_i, oid_i, r_i) = (\tau_j, oid_j, 1)$$

$$(\delta_i, i) = (0, i)$$

In essence, the same level (which has not been "reflected") has propagated to node i from all of its neighbors. Node i "reflects" back a higher sub-level by setting the bit r.

Case 4 (Detect): Node i has no downstream links (due to a link reversal following reception of an UPD packet), the ordered sets (τ_j, oid_j, r_j) are equal with $r_j = 1$ for all $j \in N_i$, and $oid_j = i$ (i.e. node i defined the level).

$$(\tau_i, oid_i, r_i) = (-, -, -)$$

$$(\delta_i, i) = (-, i)$$

In essence, the last reference level defined by node i has been reflected and propagated back as a higher sub-level from all of its neighbors. This corresponds to detection of a partition. Node i must initiate the process of erasing invalid routes as discussed in the next section.

Case 5 (Generate): Node i has no downstream links (due to a link reversal following reception of an UPD packet), the ordered sets (τ_j, oid_j, r_j) are equal with $r_j = 1$ for all $j \in N_i$, and $oid_j \neq i$ (i.e. node i did not define the level).

$$(\tau_i, oid_i, r_i) = (t, i, 0), \text{ where } t \text{ is the time of the failure}$$

$$(\delta_i, i) = (0, i)$$

In essence, node i experienced a link failure (which did not require reaction) between the time it propagated a reference level and the reflected higher sub-level returned from all neighbors. This is not necessarily an indication of a partition. Node i defines a new reference level.

Following determination of its new height in cases 1, 2, 3, and 5, node i updates all the entries in its link-state array *LS*; and broadcasts an UPD packet to all neighbors $j \in N_i$. The UPD packet consists of a *did*, and the new height of the node i which is broadcasting the packet, H_i. When a node i receives an UPD packet from a neighbor $j \in N_i$, node i updates the entries $HN_{i,j}$ and $LS_{i,j}$ in its height and link-state arrays. If the update causes a link reversal which results in node i losing its last downstream link, then it modifies its height as outlined in the cases above. Fig. 2 summarizes these five cases in the form of a decision tree, starting from the time a node loses its last downstream link. In the event node i loses a link $(i, j) \in L$ which is not its last downstream link, node i simply removes the entries $HN_{i,j}$ and $LS_{i,j}$ in its height and link-state arrays.

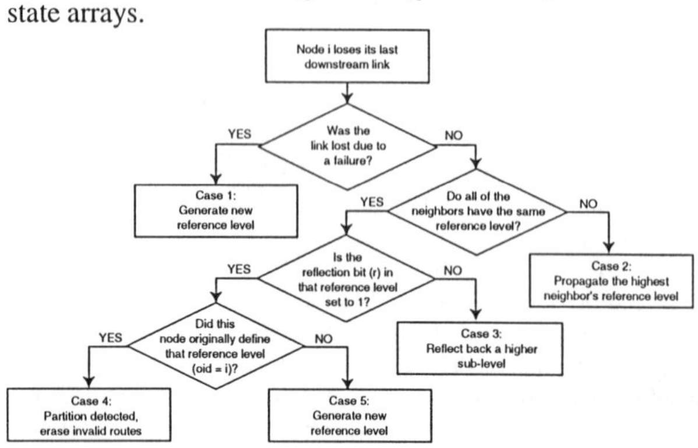

Fig. 2 Maintaining routes decision tree

The following examples illustrate how the algorithm works. Fig. 3 provides an example where no reaction is required. The network is first depicted as at the end of Fig. 1, with the addition that link (B, E) is marked as failing. Since all nodes still have downstream links following the failure, no transmissions are required. The significance of this is greater for networks which are highly connected. If a given node in the network on average has degree k (i.e. k adjacent links), then one could estimate the average number of downstream links for a given node to be (k/2). This implies that a node could tolerate (k/2)-1 downstream link failures without requiring any reaction. Fig. 4 provides an example where a reaction is required. The network is first depicted as at the end of Fig. 3, with the addition that link (D, H) is marked as failing.

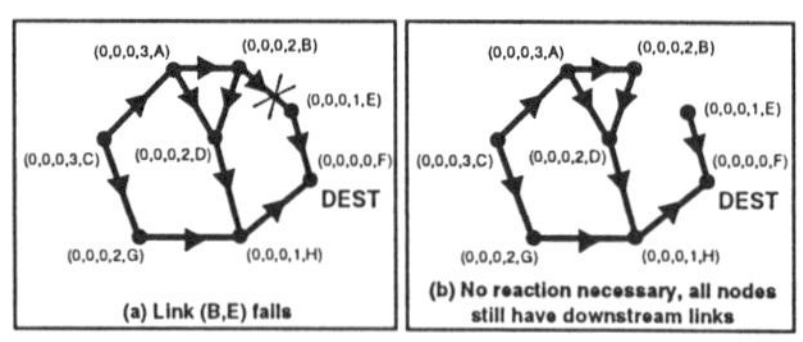

Fig. 3 Link failure with no reaction

2.4.3 Erasing Routes. Following detection of a partition (case 4), node i sets its height and the height entry for each neighbor $j \in N_i$ to NULL (unless the destination is a neighbor, in which case the corresponding height entry is set to ZERO), updates all the entries in its link-state array *LS*, and broadcast a CLR packet. The CLR

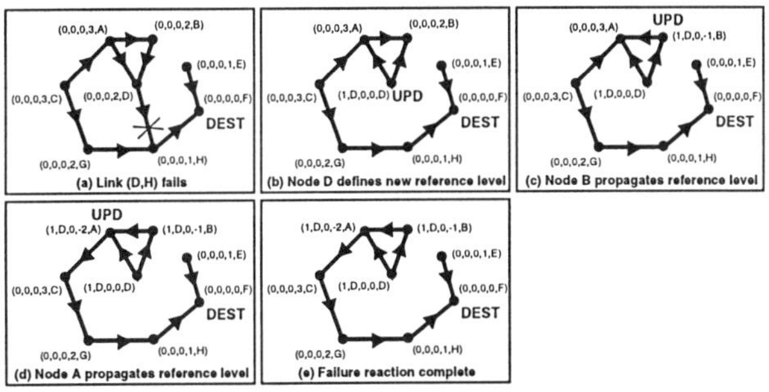

Fig. 4 Re-establishing routes after failure of last downstream link

packet consists of a *did* and the reflected reference level of node i, $(\tau_i, oid_i, 1)$[2]. When a node i receives a CLR packet from a neighbor $j \in N_i$ it reacts as follows. (a) If the reference level in the CLR packet matches the reference level of node i; it sets its height and the height entry for each neighbor $j \in N_i$ to NULL (unless the destination is a neighbor, in which case the corresponding height entry is set to ZERO), updates all the entries in its link-state array *LS* and broadcasts a CLR packet. (b) If the reference level in the CLR packet does not match the reference level of node i; it sets the height entry for each neighbor $j \in N_i$ (with the same reference level as the CLR packet) to NULL and updates the corresponding link-state array entries. Thus the height of each node in the portion of the network which was partitioned is set to NULL and all invalid routes are erased. If (b) causes node i to lose its last downstream link, it reacts as in case 1 of maintaining routes. Fig. 5 provides an example which demonstrates partition detection and erasing of invalid routes. The

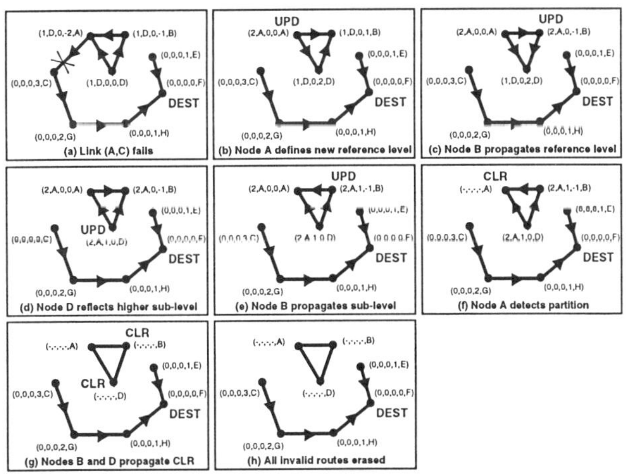

Fig. 5 Erasing invalid routes after a failure which partitions the network

[2] In actuality the value $r_i = 1$ need not be included since it is always 1 for a reflected reference level.

network is first depicted as at the end of Fig. 4, with the addition that link (A, C) is marked as failing.

It is advantageous to define the CLR packet with an additional one bit field, which we will refer to as a query flag. When a node would normally broadcast a CLR packet immediately followed by a QRY packet, the node sets the query flag and broadcasts only the CLR packet . Consequently, reception of a CLR packet with the query flag set is processed as if a CLR packet was received first and then a QRY packet was received.

We will summarize the results illustrated by the examples. When a failure causes a node to lose its last downstream link, the node will re-establish a route to the destination in one pass of the set of nodes affected by the failure (provided that a path to the destination exists). If a path to the destination no longer exists, the node will detect the partition in two passes of the set of affected nodes, and all invalid routes will be erased in three passes of the set of affected nodes.

2.5 Effect of Time Tag Errors

The effect of clock errors is difficult to bound analytically, or to determine quantitatively without simulation. The following is a general discussion regarding the effects of clock errors on protocol correctness and efficiency.

By using the assumption of synchronized clocks and time tagging the reference levels that are created each time a node loses its last downstream link, we are establishing the temporal order of these events. Because the algorithmic reactions are structured in this manner, we refer to the protocol as the Temporally-Ordered Routing Algorithm (TORA). If time tags are created by some other method, such that the relative ordering of the time tags still matches the temporal order of the corresponding events, the algorithm will function exactly as described thus far. For example, to evaluate the results of three link failures which occur at times 1, 2 and 3, it would not matter if the corresponding time tags were (1, 2, 3), (5, 6, 7), (10, 20, 30), or (4, 80, 900); the results would be the same. An excellent analysis on the ordering of events in a distributed system is provided in [17]. While the details will not be covered here, suffice it to say that simply establishing the order of events does not require the use of physical clocks. Such an ordering can be accomplished with "logical clocks" which can be implemented by counters with no actual timing mechanism.

Now, let us consider the effect of time tag errors such that the relative ordering of the time tags associated with a sequence of events does not agree with the actual order in which the events occurred. First, note that time tag errors do not exclude this algorithm from the general class; thus, all of the class properties are retained. What is lost, in some cases, is the efficiency with which routes are re-established.

Let us now consider how this applies to a practical implementation of the algorithm. If statistics are known about the rate of topological change in the network, one could use this information to determine a desired clock synchronization accuracy. For instance, if the average time between link failures is on the order of minutes, then achieving a clock synchronization on the order of seconds is very likely sufficient. While this would not guarantee preservation of the correct ordering of all events; intuitively, it seems unlikely that events would be incorrectly ordered very often.

3.0 Performance

There are no comparitive simulation results available at this time, although such work is underway. Instead, we present a comparitive summary of worst-case protocol complexities, augmented with a discussion of basic operation of several major protocol classes.

The complexities of TORA, along with an Ideal Link-state (ILS) algorithm, the DUAL family of algorithms, the GB full reversal algorithm, the LMR protocol, the DSDV protocol, and the WRP protocol are shown in Table 1. We borrow the complexity computations of ILS, and DUAL from [7] to which the reader is referred for details. The ILS protocol assumes that each network topology change must be sent to every node. DUAL is the lowest complexity, distance-vector, shortest-path algorithm known.

Table 1 Complexity Comparison

Protocol	TC	CC
ILS	$O(d)$	$O(2\|L\|)$
DUAL (link failure, cost increase)	$O(x)$	$O(6Dx)$
DUAL (link addition, cost decrease)	$O(d)$	$O(\|L\|)$
DSDV (link failure)	$O(x)$	$O(Dx)$
DSDV (periodic update)	$O(l)$	$O(\|L\|)$
WRP (link failure, cost increase)	$O(h)$	$O(Dx)$
WRP (link addition, cost decrease)	$O(d)$	$O(\|L\|)$
GB (connected, postfailure)	$O(2l)$	$O(lDx)$
GB (disconnected, postfailure)	∞	∞
LMR (connected, postfailure)	$O(2l)$	$O(2Dx)$
LMR (disconnected, postfailure)	$< \infty$ w.p.1	$< \infty$ w.p.1
TORA (connected, postfailure)	$O(2l)$	$O(2Dx)$
TORA (disconnected, postfailure)	$O(3l)$	$O(3Dx)$

In making comparisons, we make the same assumptions as [7]. We assume that the protocols execute synchronously. We compare the Time Complexity (TC), defined as the number of steps required to perform a protocol operation, and the Communication Complexity (CC), defined as the number of messages exchanged in performing the operation.

The complexity parameters are the number of network links $|L|$, the network diameter d, the number of nodes in a network segment materially affected by a topological change x, the length of the longest directed path in the affected network segment l, the height of the routing tree h, and the maximum nodal degree D.

The comparison shows that TORA's worst case complexity is generally better than the algorithms to which it is most closely related. In many cases, TORA would actually require only a single pass with TC $O(l)$ and CC $O(Dx)$ to react to a link failure, further improving its performance. Additionally, like GB and LMR, it has no explicit reaction to link additions further reducing its complexity relative to ILS, DUAL and WRP.

Having written this, we still refrain from placing much emphasis on worst-case complexity comparisons as they have limited value. Unfortunately, they are fuzzy and imprecise as it is difficult to compare algorithms with differing functionality in a precise, fair and meaningful fashion. For example, the number of nodes denoted by x is potentially different for each protocol, and the variables l and h are specific to given protocols. Rather, what is important is the protocol's average performance which is only obtainable via simulation.

We feel TORA has the potential to perform well relative to existing approaches based on the following reasoning. Existing approaches can be categorized into several broad classes which we now discuss. Link-state algorithms have the property that changes in link status, such as a failure, must be propagated to *all* nodes in the network. This is an example of "far-reaching" message propagation mentioned previously. Distance-vector approaches entail propagation of distance update information to a potentially large set of nodes, depending on the location of the change, in furtherance of a distributed shortest-path computation. Path-finding algorithms have characteristics of both link-state and distance-vector approaches, and seek to combine the best aspects of each into a hybrid protocol. Still, depending on the location of a change, a large set of nodes may be included in a shortest-path computation. The link-reversal mechanism of TORA forgoes propagation of link-state or distance information and, consequently, is able to *localize* its reaction to topological changes much more than the preceding classes. Its operation is best suited for relatively dense networks in which only several nearby nodes are typically involved in a reaction.

The effect of this localization is that the *scalability* of the protocol is greatly increased. Scalability, rather than being constrained by communication and time complexity, is now limited primarily by storage complexity, which only grows linearly with the number of nodes in the network.

4.0 Conclusions

We have proposed a highly adaptive distributed routing algorithm that is well-suited for operation in mobile wireless networks. It quickly creates and maintains loop-free multipath routing to destinations for which routing is required, while minimizing communication overhead. It rapidly adapts to topological changes, and has the ability to detect network partitions and erase all invalid routes within a finite time.

As mentioned earlier, the protocol is designed to decouple (to the greatest extent possible) the generation of far-reaching control message propagation from the dynamics of the network topology. Consequently, there is no distance estimate or link-state information propagation. A negative effect of this design choice is clear; viz. over time, as the link reversal process proceeds, the destination-oriented DAG may become less optimally directed than it was upon creation.

That is, upon route creation (before any subsequent link reversals), the DAG is formed and the fourth element of each node's height δ_i essentially contains the distance in hops from the destination over the path traveled by the UPD packet to the node (recall Fig. 1f). This distance information can be used, if desired, to favor routing over links with shorter distances; although—under heavy traffic conditions—we would not advocate routing all packets over a single path due to the congestion-enhancing effect of single-path routing [2]. As links are reversed in reaction to a failure, this distance information is lost in these "reversed" network portions (as δ_i no longer denotes distance to the destination when the reference level is not zero).

A possible enhancement to the protocol would be to periodically propagate refresh packets outwards from the destination, reception of which resets the reference level of all nodes to zero and restores distance significance to their δ_i's. The usage of periodic, destination-initiated, route optimization was mentioned as a possible routing enhancement in [18] and, later, a similar technique was developed as the major mechanism for route adaptation and maintenence in [12]. Besides serving as a routing enhancement, the periodic refresh guarantees that router state errors—resulting from undetectable errors in packet transmissions or other sources—do not persist for arbitrary lengths of time. Any router state which is not explicitly refreshed will eventually time-out and be deleted (i.e. returned to a NULL value). Thus, the periodic optimation also serves as soft-state confirmation of route validity.

This refresh process permits introduction of far-reaching control message propagation into the protocol in a fashion that is independent of network topology dynamics. The refresh interval is controllable, and the refresh procedure is expected to occur at a very low rate—it can be viewed as a secondary, background mechanism. The refresh overhead only grows linearly with the number of destinations in the network.

References

[1] M.S. Corson, S. Batsell and J. Macker, Architectural considerations for mobile mesh networking, working draft, May 1996, available at http://tonnant.itd.nrl.navy.mil/mmnet/mmnetRFC.txt.

[2] D. Bertsekas and R. Gallager, *Data Networks* (Prentice-Hall, 1987).

[3] P. Merlin and A. Segall, A failsafe distributed routing protocol, *IEEE Trans. Commun.* (September 1979).

[4] J. Jaffe and F. Moss, A responsive distributed routing algorithm for computer networks, *IEEE Trans. Commun.* (July 1982).

[5] P. Humblet, Another adaptive shortest-path algorithm, *IEEE Trans. Commun.* (June 1991).

[6] J.J. Garcia-Luna-Aceves, Distributed routing with labeled distances, *Proc. IEEE INFOCOM '92*, Florence, Italy (1992).

[7] J.J. Garcia-Luna-Aceves, Loop-free routing using diffusing computations, *IEEE Trans. Networking* 1(1) (1993)

[8] J.J Garcia-Luna-Aceves and S. Murthy, A loop-free path-finding algorithm: specification, verification, and complexity, *Proc. IEEE INFOCOM '95*, Boston, MA (1995).

[9] J.J Garcia-Luna-Aceves and J. Behrens, Distributed, scalable routing based on vectors of link states, *IEEE Journal on Selected Areas in Commun.* (October 1995).

[10] E. Gafni and D. Bertsekas, Distributed algorithms for generating loop-free routes in networks with frequently changing topology, *IEEE Trans. Commun.* (January 1981).

[11] M.S. Corson and A. Ephremides, A distributed routing algorithm for mobile wireless networks, *Wireless Networks* 1 (1995).

[12] C Perkins and P. Bhagwat, Highly dynamic destination-sequenced distance vector routing (DSDV) for mobile computers, *ACM SIGCOMM*, (October 1994).

[13] S. Murthy and J.J. Garcia-Luna-Aceves, ``An Efficient Routing Protocol for Wireless Networks," *ACM Mobile Networks and Applications Journal*, Special issue on Routing in Mobile Communication Networks, 1996.

[14] D. Johnson and D. Maltz, Dynamic source routing in ad hoc wireless networks, T. Imielinski and H. Korth, eds., *Mobile computing*, (Kluwer Academic Publ. 1996).

[15] NAVSTAR GPS user equipment introduction, MZ10298.001 (February 1991).

[16] D. Mills, Network time protocol, specification, implementation and analysis, *Internet RFC-1119* (September 1989).

[17] L. Lamport, Time, clocks, and the ordering of events in a distributed system, *Comm. of the ACM*, (July 1978).

[18] M.S. Corson, A. Ephremides, A Distributed Routing Algorithm for Mobile Radio Networks, *Proc. MILCOM '89*, Boston, MA, (October, 1989).

Dynamic Global Packet Routing in Wireless Networks

Nabil Kahale Paul E. Wright

AT&T Labs-Research
Murray Hill, NJ 07974
{kahale,pew}@research.att.com

Abstract

We consider schemes for reuse-efficient packet access in wireless data networks. We show that computing the maximum ergodic packet arrival rate is NP-hard. We give an upper bound on the maximum ergodic throughput in terms of the eigenvalues of matrices related to the path-gain matrix. We present simple, practical heuristic algorithms which exhibit good throughput and packet delay and report on results of preliminary simulations. More sophisticated algorithms that yield optimal throughput are also presented. A recent result of McKeown, Anantharam and Walrand on scheduling of input-queued switches is obtained as a byproduct.

1. Introduction

This paper addresses schemes for reuse-efficient transmission in wireless packet data networks. Particular attention is paid to recent proposals (see for example [19]) for wireless data packet networks in which the medium access (MAC) layer protocol is:

(i) deterministically scheduled.

(ii) has good delay performance.

(iii) provides near-optimal channel capacity in a single channel (i.e. is reuse-efficient).

References [11, 10] provide an overview of some of the salient themes and constraints of particular relevance in the design of wireless packet data networks. Because of the limited availability of the spectrum, *interference management and power control* are crucial to obtain optimum system capacity in wireless networks. Routing in a wireless network involves both *spatial* and *temporal* allocation of resources to meet given service demands while respecting *quality of service* (QoS) constraints such as maximum packet delay. Such QoS guarantees are part of ATM (Asynchronous Transfer Mode) contracts. An additional concern in wireless data networks is *fading*, i.e. the degradation of received signal power at the receiver. Due to the nature of the channel, the deliverable payload of a wireless data channel is not all that high. Current estimates lie in the range of 1 to 10 Mbps, in the optimistic case.

Throughput can also be severely limited by the fact that multiple users are trying to use a given channel at the same time. This is well known from experience with ALOHA and the Carrier-Sense-Multiple-Access CSMA protocols typically used in wired and wireless local area networks (LAN's). ALOHA suffers from poor throughput while CSMA can be sensitive to thresholds for collision detection as well as the choice of methods for collision-resolution [18, 1].

We study in this paper an alternate approach to ALOHA and CSMA in which multiple stations with packets ready to transmit can determine ahead of time whether the signal-to-interference ratio (SIR) required for adequate bit-error-rate (BER) is obtainable in the next transmission interval. Thus channel access is conflict-free with good BER performance. However the scheduling of stations must be done carefully to get good throughput as well. This approach can be applied to either a time-division multiple access (TDMA) system or a channel-division multiple access (CDMA) system.

Related scheduling problems have been studied for input-queued switches (see [14] and references therein). Scheduling problems where requests that cannot be served are *blocked and cleared* rather than being queued have been analyzed in [7, 15, 6].

2. Contribution

This paper presents new bounds on the available throughput in a fixed wireless data network. It is

 0-8186-7780-5/97 $10.00 © 1997 IEEE

shown that the problem of determining the maximum stable throughput for a system with unbounded buffers is NP-hard. However, we address this problem by considering a variety of practical algorithms which obtain good throughput, good signal-to-interference protection and are easy to implement, even for systems with hundreds of links for which simultaneous access is desired (a *link* is an ordered pair of stations, the first of which is the *transmitter*, the second being the *receiver*). Our algorithms might be adapted to cases where there are mobile terminals moving within a service area but, for simplicity, we only consider a wireless network in which all the terminals are fixed. We study the case of a single channel; extension of ideas presented here to multiple channels is possible.

We consider two modes of operation. In the first, discrete interference relationships between every pair of links are determined before transmission and are assumed to remain constant. That is, the interference constraints are represented by an undirected graph in which the nodes are *links* and any edge between two links exist if both links may not be in simultaneous operation. In the second mode, *aggregate interference* is taken into account and the controller has detailed information on the propagation path losses between any station pair; *power control* may or may not be used. With power control, transmitter powers may be varied in order to alter the interference environment and influence the SIR's. It is known that in the case where power control is possible significant capacity gains may be realized, though at the cost of a more difficult interference management problem. Our theoretical results on the maximum stable throughput apply in either context.

We assume that all scheduling is done by a central controller; distributed implementations are currently under study. The central controller is aware of all routing requests and packet queue states at every instant, and all conflict relationships between links or the actual path-gains. This model is quite reasonable for a moderate number of stations (100 - 200), as is the case for current systems. Indeed currently deployed AMPS (Advanced Mobile Phone Service) wireless systems integrate the management of up to 200 stations (cell sites) in a single service center known as a mobile switching center (MSC).

Our algorithms can also be used for other scheduling problems in which multiple requests contend for the same resources. In particular, using a Lemma in [14], we note in Section 6 that a recent result of McKeown, Anantharam and Walrand [14] on scheduling of input-queued switches follows from our Theorem 6.1. Our proof is similar but simpler than [14].

3. The Graph Model

Let $\mathbf{G} = [G_{ij}]$ denote the path-gain matrix, where G_{ij} equals the path-gain from the transmitter of link i to the receiver of link j. At a given time-step, let p_i be the power level of transmitter of link i (in general p_i is a function of the *link* i, not only of the transmitter of link i): $p_i > 0$ if and only if link i is active. Thus, the interference signal received by the receiver of link i is $\sum_{j \neq i} G_{ji} p_j$, and the power received by the receiver of link i from the transmitter of link i is $G_{ii} p_i$. Let m be the number of links, γ_i be the required signal-to-interference ratio (SIR) for link i, and $\Gamma = diag(\gamma_1, \dots, \gamma_m)$ be the diagonal matrix with the γ_i's on its diagonal.

Let N be any real matrix with nonnegative off-diagonal entries. It follows from the theory of nonnegative matrices [17] that one eigenvalue of N that has the largest real part is real (and uniquely determined). It will be denoted by $\lambda_0(N)$.

Let $\mathbf{G}' = [G'_{ij}]$ where $G'_{ij} = G_{ij}/G_{ii}$ for $i \neq j$, and $G'_{ii} = 0$. A set of links S can be activated (i.e. is *feasible*) at a given time-step if and only if there exists a power vector $\mathbf{p}$ whose support is S (i.e. $p_i > 0$ if and only if $i \in S$) such that $\Gamma \mathbf{G}' \mathbf{p} + \nu \leq \mathbf{p}$, where ν is a noise vector, and element-wise comparison is implied. In other words, the SIR at any active link is above the SIR threshold. Assuming that the power vector can be arbitrary (i.e. there is no upper constraint on the transmitter power), this is equivalent (see [16, 20] and references therein) to the condition $\lambda_0(\mathbf{G}'_S - \Gamma_S^{-1}) < 0$, where $\mathbf{G}'_S$ is the submatrix induced by the elements of S. Let $H = \{S_1, \dots, S_h\}$ be the collection of feasible subsets of the links. Note that any subset of a feasible set, including the empty set, is feasible.

Each link i has a queue associated with it. We assume that packets arrive at link i according to a Poisson distribution of rate r_i. When a packet arrives at link i, it is appended to the tail of the queue at that link. When a set of links S is scheduled at a time-step, the head of the queue of each link in S gets removed from the queue.

4. Stability

Let $a_i(t)$ be the number of packets generated at link i at time t, and $a(t) = (a_i(t))$ be the arrival vector. Let $r = (r_i)$ be the vector of arrival rates.

Theorem 4.1. *If there is a scheduling algorithm for which the system is ergodic, then r is strictly dominated by a convex combination of the characteristic vectors of the S_k's. Conversely, if r is strictly dominated by a convex combination of the characteristic vectors of the S_k's, then there exists a scheduling algorithm for which the system is ergodic.*

Proof Assume first that there exists a scheduling algorithm for which the system is ergodic. Let $q_i(t)$ be the queue-size of link i at time t, and $q(t) = (q_i(t))$ be the vector of queue-sizes. Let $S(t)$ be the feasible subset scheduled at time t, and $\chi_{S(t)}$ be its $0-1$ characteristic vector. We have

$$q(t) = a(0) + a(1) + \cdots + a(t-1) - tv, \qquad (4.1)$$

where $v = \frac{1}{t}(\chi_{S(0)} + \chi_{S(1)} + \cdots + \chi_{S(t-1)})$. Since v belongs to the set C of convex combinations of the characteristic vectors of the S_k's, so does its expected value. Thus, it follows from Eq. 4.1 that $r - \mathrm{E}[q(t)]/t \in C$. By taking the limit as t goes to infinity, we conclude that $r \in C$, since C is a closed set.

We now show that r is strictly dominated by a vector in C. The total arrival at link i during the interval $[0, t-1]$ has a Poisson distribution with mean $r_i t$. Let B_i be the event that it exceeds $r_i t + \sqrt{r_i t}$. The probability of B_i is at least an absolute constant c. If follows from Eq. 4.1 that

$$\mathrm{E}[q(t)|B_1, \ldots, B_m] \geq tr + \sqrt{t}\sqrt{r} - t\mathrm{E}[v|B_1, \ldots, B_m], \qquad (4.2)$$

where $\sqrt{r}$ is the vector $(\sqrt{r_i})$. The left-hand side of Eq. 4.2 is upper bounded by $\mathrm{E}[q(t)]/c^m$, which is bounded by a constant independent of t. By choosing t sufficiently large, we conclude that r is strictly dominated by the vector $\mathrm{E}[v|B_1, \ldots, B_m]$, which belongs to C.

Conversely, we show that if $\mathrm{E}[a]$ is strictly dominated by a vector in C, then there is a scheduling algorithm for which the system is ergodic. Assume that $(1+\epsilon)r \leq \sum_{k=1}^{h} \alpha_k \chi_{S_k}$, with $\alpha_k \geq 0$ and $\sum_{k=1}^{h} \alpha_k = 1$. At each time-step, schedule subset S_k with probability α_k. Then the system is ergodic and the expected queue-size of each link is $O(1/\epsilon)$. This is because the arrival rate at link i is r_i and the departure rate, when link i is nonempty, is at least $(1+\epsilon)r_i$. Our claim then follows from standard queuing theory [8]. ■

Corollary 4.2. *For general G, (γ_i) and r, determining whether there is a scheduling algorithm for which the system is ergodic is NP-hard.*

Proof If G is the adjacency matrix of a graph K, and if $\gamma_i = 1/2$ for all i, then the feasible subsets are the independent sets of K. If $r_i = s$ for all links i, then Theorem 4.1 implies that there is a scheduling algorithm for which r is ergodic if and only if $1/s$ is greater than the fractional chromatic number of K. The fractional chromatic number of a graph is the minimum sum of nonnegative coefficients $\beta_1, \cdots, \beta_h$ such that, if we assign β_k to independent set S_k, the sum of values assigned to the independent sets containing w is at least 1 for each vertex w. The fractional chromatic number of a graph is known to be NP-hard to compute [13]. ■

5. Upper bound on the maximum ergodic throughput

We give in this section a necessary, but not sufficient, condition to determine whether there is a scheduling algorithm for which the system is ergodic. This condition can be checked in polynomial time.

The eigenvalues of any real symmetric $m \times m$ matrix M are known to be real, and will be denoted by $\lambda_0(M) \geq \lambda_1(M) \geq \ldots \geq \lambda_{n-1}(M)$.

Theorem 5.1. *If there is a scheduling algorithm for which the system is ergodic, then*

$$\lambda_0(R - \frac{1}{\lambda_{n-1}(R^{-1}B)}B) \leq 1,$$

where R is the diagonal matrix representing the vector r, and $B = (\min(G'_{ij}, G'_{ji})) - \Gamma^{-1}$.

Proof Since the matrices B and $G' - \Gamma^{-1}$ have nonnegative off-diagonal entries and B is dominated by $G' - \Gamma^{-1}$, $\lambda_0(B_S) \leq \lambda_0(G'_S - \Gamma_S^{-1})$ for any subset S of links [17]. In particular, $\lambda_0(B_S) < 0$ if S is feasible. As noted before, $r = \sum_k \alpha_k \chi_{S_k}$, where the α_k's are nonnegative and sum up to 1. Let $x = -1/\lambda_{n-1}(R^{-1}B)$, where $\lambda_{n-1}(R^{-1}B)$ is the smallest eigenvalue of $R^{-1}B$. Since the diagonal elements of B are negative, $x > 0$. Let f be an eigenvector corresponding to the largest eigenvalue of $R + xB$, and f_k its projection on S_k. That is, the ith coordinate of f_k is equal to the ith coordinate of f if $i \in S_k$, and is equal to 0 otherwise. The smallest eigenvalue of $I + xR^{-1}B$ is 0, by definition of x. The matrices $I + xR^{-1/2}BR^{-1/2}$ and $I + xR^{-1}B$ have the same eigenvalues since $I + xR^{-1/2}BR^{-1/2} = R^{1/2}(I + xR^{-1}B)R^{-1/2}$, and so $I + xR^{-1/2}BR^{-1/2}$ is positive semi-definite. Hence the matrix $R + xB$ is also positive semi-definite, since $R + xB = R^{1/2}(I + xR^{-1/2}BR^{-1/2})R^{1/2}$. It follows that the quadratic form $< g, f >= g \cdot (R + xB)f$ is positive semi-definite. The Cauchy-Schwartz inequality with respect to this positive semi-definite form implies that $< g, h >^2 \leq < g, g >< h, h >$, for any m-dimensional real vectors g and h. Taking $g = R^{-1}f_k$ and $h = f$ we get

$$\begin{aligned}
&(R^{-1}f_k \cdot (R + xB)f)^2 \\
&\leq (R^{-1}f_k \cdot (R + xB)R^{-1}f_k)(f \cdot (R + xB)f) \\
&= (f_k \cdot R^{-1}f_k + xR^{-1}f_k \cdot BR^{-1}f_k)\lambda_0(R + xB)||f||^2 \\
&\leq (f_k \cdot R^{-1}f_k)\lambda_0(R + xB)||f||^2.
\end{aligned}$$

The third inequality follows from the inequality $\lambda_0(B_{S_k}) < 0$, and thus $R^{-1}f_k \cdot BR^{-1}f_k \leq 0$. But

$$\begin{aligned}
R^{-1}f_k \cdot (R + xB)f &= \lambda_0(R + xB)R^{-1}f_k \cdot f \\
&= \lambda_0(R + xB)R^{-1}f_k \cdot f_k.
\end{aligned}$$

Together with the preceding equation, this implies that

$$(f_k \cdot R^{-1}f_k)\lambda_0(R + xB) \leq ||f||^2.$$

Since

$$\begin{aligned}
\sum_k \alpha_k(f_k \cdot R^{-1}f_k) &= \sum_k \alpha_k(f_k \cdot R^{-1}f) \\
&= Rf \cdot R^{-1}f \\
&= ||f||^2,
\end{aligned}$$

we conclude that $\lambda_0(R + xB) \leq 1$, as desired. ■

Corollary 5.2. *If all arrival rates are equal to r and if the system is ergodic, then*

$$r \leq \frac{\lambda_{n-1}(B)}{\lambda_{n-1}(B) - \lambda_0(B)}. \quad (5.1)$$

Remark. The above inequalities hold when B is any non-null symmetric matrix such that $0 \leq (B + \Gamma^{-1})_{ij} \leq \min(G'_{ij}, G'_{ji})$, for all i, j. This is because this condition implies that $\lambda_0(B_S) \leq \lambda_0(G'_S - \Gamma_S^{-1}) < 0$. In our experiments, we have chosen $B_{ij} = (\min(G'_{ij}, G'_{ji}, (\gamma_i\gamma_j)^{-1/2})) - \Gamma_{ij}^{-1}$.

When r is constant across links and we consider only pairwise interference, i.e. when the feasible subsets are the independent sets of a graph K, Eq. 5.1 is a slightly stronger version of Hoffman's bound (see [2], and [9] for related work) on the chromatic number. Indeed, we can model this case by setting G' to be the adjacency matrix of K and setting $\Gamma = \epsilon^{-1}I$, where $0 < \epsilon < 1$. By letting ϵ tend to 0, we get the bound

$$r \leq \frac{\lambda_{n-1}(K)}{\lambda_{n-1}(K) - \lambda_0(K)}. \quad (5.2)$$

Using results from [12, 4], it can be shown that the bound in Eq. 5.1 can be off by a factor of at least $\Omega(m/2^{O(\sqrt{\log m})})$ from optimal, for general G and Γ, even if B is chosen optimally. However, in the simulations we performed, the bound given by Eq. 5.1 was off by only a small multiplicative factor from optimal, as discussed in Section 7.

6. Algorithms and Heuristics

In a real-life application, time slot lengths are likely to be in the range of 10's of msecs. This places a bound on the complexity of algorithms for practical implementation. A natural algorithm is to schedule a largest feasible subset at each time-step. However, there are simple examples (i.e. when the interference graph is a large star and the arrival rates are slightly smaller than .5) where this algorithm yields sub-optimal throughput and some stations may be starved for long periods. Consequently packet delays will be high.

We present below two algorithms that yield optimal throughput with good delay performance. However, they are difficult and impractical to implement. The remaining algorithms achieve good (albeit, in general, sub-optimal) throughput with good delay performance. Furthermore, they are relatively easy to implement.

Algorithm Max-Weight: at each time-step, schedule a maximum weighted feasible subset. The weight of a link can be its queue-size (s-Max-Weight), the waiting time of the oldest packet in its queue (w-Max-Weight), or any other potential function. By convention, the waiting time at time t of a packet generated at time s is $t - s + 1$.

We show that both Algorithm s-Max-Weight and Algorithm w-Max-Weight give the optimal stable throughput. Furthermore, the ergodic delay under Algorithm w-Max-Weight if off from the optimal ergodic delay by a factor of order m plus an additive factor (see Theorem 6.2 for a detailed statement.) For typical networks, however, we suspect that the behavior of Algorithm w-Max-Weight is much closer to "optimality" than what is implied by Theorem 6.2. The proof of these results for Algorithm w-Max-Weight is omitted in this abstract for lack of space, but will appear in the journal version of the paper. We note that, unfortunately, it is NP-hard to find a maximum weighted feasible subset in general.

Let $S_{k(t)}$ be the subset scheduled by Algorithm Max-Weight at time t, and $q'(t) = q(t) + a(t)$.

Theorem 6.1. *If r is such that there is an algorithm for which the system is ergodic, then algorithm s-Max-Weight achieves ergodicity.*

Proof By Theorem 4.1, $r < r' = \sum_{k=1}^{h} \alpha_k u_k$, where $u_k = \chi_{S_k}$, $\alpha_k \geq 0$ and $\sum_{k=1}^{h} \alpha_k = 1$. For any time-step t, $q(t+1) = q'(t) - u_{k(t)}$.

$$\begin{aligned} ||q(t+1)||^2 &= ||q'(t) - u_{k(t)}||^2 \\ &= ||q'(t)||^2 + ||u_{k(t)}||^2 - 2q'(t) \cdot u_{k(t)}. \end{aligned}$$

On the other hand, by definition of the algorithm, $k(t)$ is chosen so that $q'(t) \cdot u_{k(t)}$ is maximum. As a consequence,

$$\begin{aligned} q'(t) \cdot u_{k(t)} &\geq \sum_{k=1}^{h} \alpha_k q'(t) \cdot u_k \\ &= q'(t) \cdot r'. \end{aligned}$$

Combining the two preceding equations yields

$$\begin{aligned} &||q(t+1)||^2 \\ &\leq ||q'(t)||^2 + ||u_{k(t)}||^2 - 2q'(t) \cdot r' \\ &= ||q(t)||^2 + ||a(t)||^2 + 2q(t) \cdot a(t) + ||u_{k(t)}||^2 \\ &\quad -2q'(t) \cdot r' \\ &\leq ||q(t)||^2 + ||a(t)||^2 + 2q(t) \cdot (a(t) - r') + m. \end{aligned}$$

Taking expectations and noting that $q(t)$ and $a(t)$ are independent, it follows that

$$\begin{aligned} \mathrm{E}\left[||q(t+1)||^2\right] &\leq \mathrm{E}\left[||q(t)||^2\right] - 2\mathrm{E}\left[q(t)\right] \cdot (r' - r) \\ &\quad + \mathrm{E}\left[||a(t)||^2\right] + m, \end{aligned}$$

and so

$$\begin{aligned} &2(r' - r) \cdot \mathrm{E}\left[q(t) + q(t-1) + \cdot + q(0)\right] \\ &\quad \leq (t+1)\left(\mathrm{E}\left[||a||^2\right] + m\right). \end{aligned}$$

Since $r < r'$, this implies that the expected value of $(q(t) + q(t-1) + \cdots + q(0))/(t+1)$ is bounded, and thus the system is ergodic. ■

Theorem 6.2. *If r is such that there is an algorithm for which the system is ergodic, then Algorithm w-Max-Weight achieves ergodicity. The ergodic waiting time under algorithm w-Max-Weight is off the ergodic waiting time under any algorithm for which the system is ergodic by at most a multiplicative factor of order m plus an additive factor of order $m/r \cdot 1$.*

Proof Omitted for lack of space. ■

The results in this section also apply for other scheduling problems where the feasible subsets are drawn from a given collection H. In particular, for input-queued switches, H consists of all matchings. It is shown in [14] that for *admissible arrival rates*, the algorithm that schedules a maximum weighted matching (where the weight is the queue-size) achieves 100% throughput (see [14] for details). The maximum weighted matching coincides with Algorithm s-Max-Weight in this setting. Thus, the result in [14] follows from Theorem 6.1. This is because, as shown in Lemma 1 in [14], an admissible rate vector is a convex combination of characteristic vectors of matchings. It follows from Theorem 6.2 that the maximum weighted matching algorithm where the weights are the waiting times of the oldest packet in queue also achieves 100% throughput.

Note that if the vectors r and (γ_i) and the matrix G are known in advance, it is possible to find a vector $r' \in C$ that strictly dominates r using linear programming. For general G and (γ_i), this might take an exponential amount of preprocessing time, though. Since H lies in a vector space of dimension m, r' can be written as a convex combination of at most $m+1$ characteristic vectors of feasible subsets. These $m+1$ subsets can be determined using an exponential amount of preprocessing time. Once these subsets are determined, it is easy to run a variant version of Algorithm Max-Weight by choosing the subset of maximum weight among these $m+1$ subsets. Theorems 6.1 and 6.2 also hold for this version of Algorithm Max-Weight.

An exponential bound with a small decay rate can be shown to hold on the tail of the distribution of the queue-sizes of Algorithms s-Max-Weight and w-Max-Weight. We show below that, for a suitable weight function, a variant of Algorithm Max-Weight gives an exponential bound on the tail of the distribution of the queue-sizes with a better decay rate. This algorithm assumes that, for a given $\epsilon > 0$, there is a scheduling algorithm for which the system is stable under the arrival vector $(1+\epsilon)r$. An algorithm of similar flavor has been considered [6] for routing in ATM networks.

For fixed $\alpha = \Theta(\epsilon)$ to be determined later, let $\phi(x) = e^{\alpha x}$ and $\Phi(q) = \sum_i \phi(q_i)$.

Algorithm Exp-Weight: At time step t, schedule a feasible subset so that $\Phi(q(t+1))$ is minimized.

As in the case for Algorithm Max-Weight, Algorithm Exp-Weight is NP-hard to implement.

Theorem 6.3. *Assume that r is such that there is an algorithm for which the system is ergodic under the arrival vector $(1+\epsilon)r$. Then Algorithm Exp-Weight achieves ergodicity, for a suitable $\alpha = \Theta(\epsilon)$. Furthermore, the tail of the ergodic queue-size distribution at any link is exponentially decreasing with a decay rate $\Omega(\epsilon)$.*

Proof Since $q_i'(t) = q_i(t) + a_i(t)$ and $q_i(t)$ and $a_i(t)$ are independent,

$$\begin{aligned} \mathrm{E}\,[\phi(q_i'(t))] &= \mathrm{E}\,[\phi(q_i(t))]\mathrm{E}\,[\phi(a_i(t))] \\ &= e^{r_i(e^{\alpha}-1)}\mathrm{E}\,[\phi(q_i(t))]. \end{aligned}$$

Since there is an algorithm for which the system is ergodic under the arrival vector $(1+\epsilon)r$, $(1+\epsilon)r = \sum_k \alpha_k \chi_{S_k}$, where the α_k's are nonnegative and sum up to 1, as shown in Theorem 4.1. Given the vector $q'(t)$, assume that we schedule S_k with probability α_k at time t. If link i is nonempty, $q_i(t+1) = q_i'(t) - 1$ with probability $p_i = (1+\epsilon)r_i$. Thus,

$$\begin{aligned} &\mathrm{E}\,[\phi(q_i(t+1))] \\ &\leq (1 - p_i + p_i e^{-\alpha})\phi(q'(t)) + 1 \\ &= (1 - p_i + p_i e^{-\alpha})e^{r_i(e^{\alpha}-1)}\mathrm{E}\,[\phi(q_i(t))] + 1. \end{aligned}$$

A simple calculation shows that, for a suitable $\alpha = \Theta(\epsilon)$, the coefficient of $\mathrm{E}\,[\phi(q_i(t))]$ in the above equation is at most $1 - \Theta(r_i\epsilon^2) \leq 1 - \Theta(r_{\min}\epsilon^2)$, where $r_{\min} = \min_i r_i$. It follows that, if S_k is chosen with probability α_k,

$$\mathrm{E}\,[\Phi(q(t+1))] \leq (1 - \Theta(r_{\min}\epsilon^2))\mathrm{E}\,[\Phi(q(t))] + m. \tag{6.1}$$

The left-hand side of Equation 6.1 is a convex combination of the expected values of $\Phi(q(t+1))$ that we would have obtained by scheduling deterministically each of the S_k's. This implies that Algorithm Exp-Weight maintains the invariant in Eq. 6.1. We conclude that

$$\mathrm{E}\,[\Phi(q(t))] - O\left(\frac{m}{r_{\min}\epsilon^2}\right),$$

for all t. As a consequence,

$$\Pr[q_i(t) \geq B] \leq \frac{m}{r_{\min}\epsilon^2}e^{-\alpha B},$$

as desired. ■

We have experimented with the following heuristics. The first one was suggested in [19].

Heuristic Sequential: Initialize the subset S to be scheduled as the empty set. Order the links according to their weight and scan them in that order. If $S \cup \{i\}$ is feasible, let $S = S \cup \{i\}$.

Heuristic R-Sequential: Initialize the subset S to be scheduled as the empty set. For each remaining link i, let $R(i)$ be the set of remaining links j such that $S \cup \{i, j\}$ is not feasible. Add to S the remaining link i such that $w(i)/w(R(i))$ is maximum. Delete the remaining links j such that $S \cup \{j\}$ is not feasible.

Proposition 6.4. *When the feasible subsets are the independent sets of a graph K, the weight of the independent set obtained by Heuristic R-Sequential is at least the total weight divided by $1 + \lambda_0(K)$.*

Proof In the case where the feasible subsets are the independent sets of a graph K, the set $R(i)$ is the set of remaining links that are adjacent to i in K. Let s be the maximum ratio $w(i)/w(R(i))$ obtained in the first iteration. Thus, $w \leq sAw$, where A is the adjacency matrix of K. This implies that $s \geq 1/\lambda_0(K)$. The same bound holds in subsequent iterations, since the largest eigenvalue of a subgraph of K is upper bounded by $\lambda_0(K)$. Thus, the weight of the independent set I obtained by Heuristic R-Sequential is at least the weight of $K - I$ divided by $\lambda_0(K)$. This concludes the proof. ■

7. Implementation results

We present in this section the results of preliminary simulations of some of our algorithms. The mean delay is plotted versus offered traffic for each algorithm, under either the fixed discrete conflict graph model or with power control.

The graphs in Figures 1 through 4 are labeled using the following simple scheme:

(i) A leading s- indicates that the queue-sizes were used as the weights in the heuristics **Sequential** and **R-Sequential**, while a leading w- indicates that the waiting times were used.

(ii) A following pc- designation indicates that power control was employed, while a following ci- designation indicates that in the algorithm no power control was employed but the actual cumulative interference was determined using the path-gain matrix and assuming that all transmitter powers were identical.

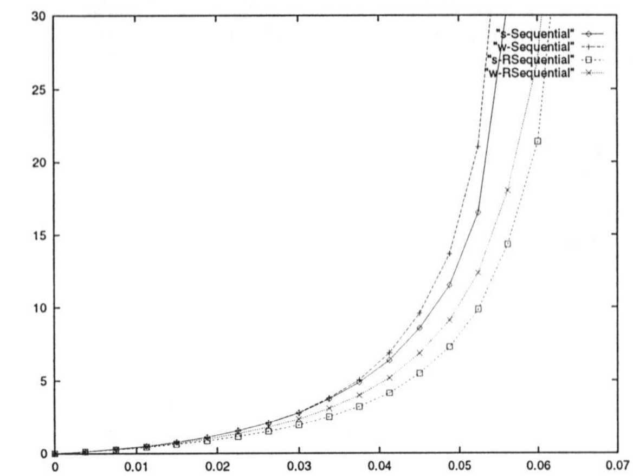

Figure 1: Mean delay versus offered traffic for 25 station, 150 link network at 1800MHz (PCS) in a large urban environment (discrete link conflict graph model).

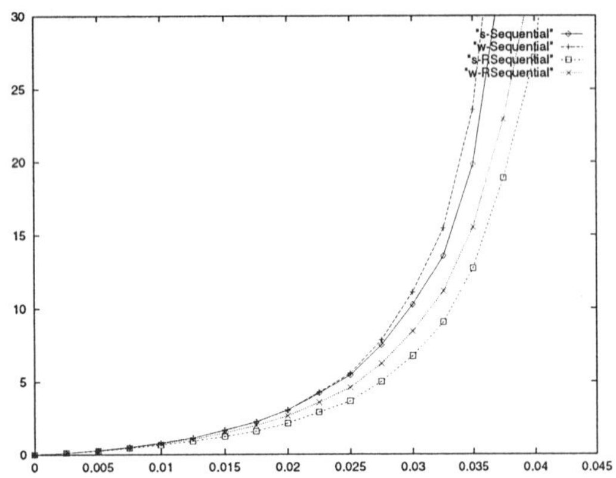

Figure 2: Mean delay versus offered traffic for 25 station, 150 link network at 900MHz (cellular) in a suburban environment (discrete link conflict graph model).

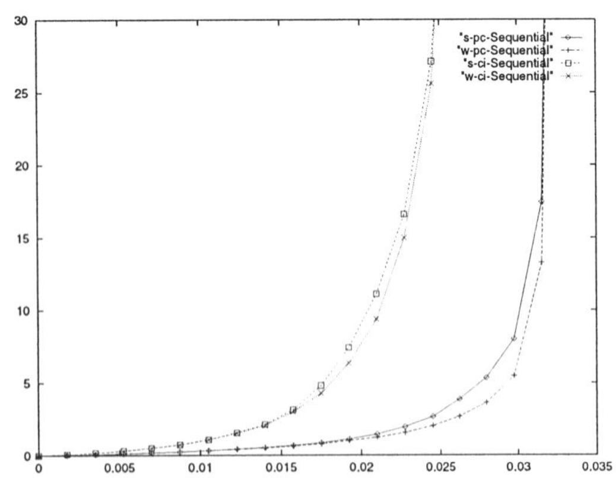

Figure 3: Mean delay versus offered traffic for 25 station, 150 link network at 900MHz (cellular) in a suburban environment with power control.

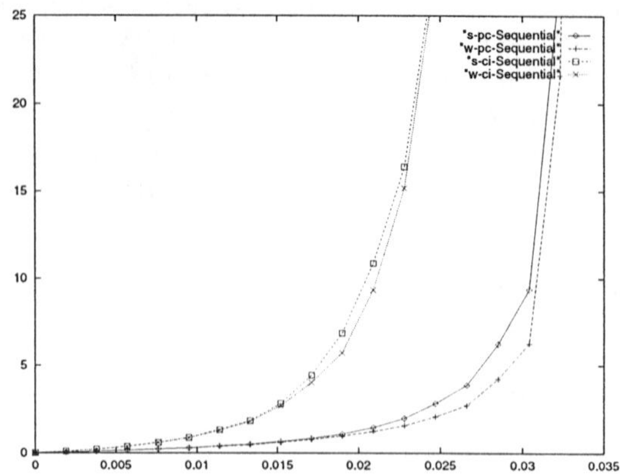

Figure 4: Mean delay versus offered traffic for 25 station, 150 link network at 1800MHz (PCS) in a suburban environment with power control.

Generally, our heuristics outperform those suggested in [19] in terms of mean delay. Disappointing results, in terms of mean delay, were obtained using the power control based algorithms versus the algorithms based on the discrete interference model. This can be explained by the fact that the latter algorithms, by simplifying the interference model, give worse signal-to-interference protection in general. The SIR losses of the conflict graph based algorithms need to be studied to quantify this effect.

7.1. Simulation model

We implemented the following simulation model:

1. 25 station locations were chosen at random points within a square area, 100 km per side.
2. Terrain models (urban for large, medium and small cities, suburban for open rural and quasi-open rural) were those of Hata [5, 3].
3. The average link length was in the 10km range. Links larger than 20 km were not considered due to the excessive path loss. This resulted in 150 links between pairs of stations.
4. Log-normal shadow fading with a standard deviation of 4dB was modeled as well but no multipath propagation effects were included in the study.
5. The conflict graph was constructed by assuming that a pair of links, i and j, could not operate simultaneously if $\min(G_{ij}, G_{ji}) <= 24$ dB.
6. In the case where actual path gains were used, a set of links was considered infeasible if the receiver on any link had an SIR less than 24 dB.

7. The arrivals at each link had independent identical Poisson distributions.

Because we consider here a single-channel system, in the conflict graph based model, a single station was explicitly ruled out from simultaneously transmitting to multiple sites.

7.2. Eigenvalue bounds

For the system corresponding to Figure 4, the eigenvalue bound technique of Section 5 yielded a bound of 0.244165 on the maximum stable packet arrival rate at each link. The over-estimate over the apparent maximum stable arrival rate under **Sequential** was by about a factor of 7. However it is not known how well the latter algorithm is performing compared to the optimum scheduling policy. The choice of the matrix B was not optimized for this calculation. The corresponding bounds for the systems illustrated in Figures 1 through 3 were 0.166932, 0.139353 and 0.244165 respectively.

References

[1] D. Bertsekas and R. Gallager. *Data Networks.* Prentice-Hall, 1987.

[2] N. Biggs. *Algebraic Graph Theory.* Cambridge University Press, 1974.

[3] Y. Okumura et. al. Field Strength and its Variablity in VHF and UHF Radio Service. *Rev. Elec. Comm. Lab., NTT.*, 16:9–10, 1968.

[4] U. Feige. Randomized graph products, chromatic numbers, and the lovász θ-function. In *27th Annual ACM Symposium on Theory of Computing*, pages 635–640. ACM Press, 1995.

[5] M. Hata. Empirical Formula for Propagation Loss in Land Mobile Radio Service. *IEEE Trans. on Vehicular Tech.*, VT-29(3):317 325, 1980.

[6] A. Kamath, O. Palmon, and S. Plotkin. Routing and admission control in general topology networks with poisson arrivals. In *Proceedings of the 7th Annual ACM-SIAM Symposium on Discrete Algorithms*, pages 269–278. SIAM Press, January 1996.

[7] F. P. Kelley. Blocking probabilities in large circuit-switched networks. *Adv. Appl. Prob.*, 18:473–505, 1986.

[8] L. Kleinrock. *Queueing systems*, volume I. Wiley, New York, 1975.

[9] D. E. Knuth. The sandwich theorem. *The Electronic Journal of Combinatorics*, 1(A1):48pp., 1994.

[10] J-P. Linnartz. *Narrowband Land-Mobile Radio Networks.* Artech House, 1993.

[11] J-P. Linnartz. *Wireless Data Networking.* Artech House, 1995.

[12] L. Lovász. On the Shannon capacity of a graph. *IEEE Transactions on Information Theory IT-25*, pages 1-7, 1979.

[13] C. Lund and M. Yannakakis. On the hardness of approximating minimization problems. *J. ACM*, 41:960–981, 1994.

[14] N. McKeown, V. Anantharam, and J. Walrand. Achieving 100% throughput in an input-queued switch. In *Proceedings INFOCOM'96*, pages 296–302. IEEE, 1996.

[15] D. Mitra. Asymptotic Analysis and Computational Methods for a Class of Simple Circuit-Switched networks with Blocking. *Adv. Appl. Prob.*, 19:219–239, 1987.

[16] D. Mitra. An asynchronous distributed algorithm for power control in cellular radio systems. In *Fourth WINLAB Workshop on Third Generation Wireless Information Networks*, Rutgers University, 1993.

[17] E. Seneta. *Non-negative matrices and Markov Chains.* Springer-Verlag, 1981.

[18] A. S. Tannenbaum. *Computer Networks.* Prentice-Hall, 1988.

[19] J. Whitehead. Global Packet Resource Allocation (GPDRA) for Wireless Networks. Technical report, AT&T, 1996.

[20] J. Zander. Performance of optimum transmitter power control in cellular radio systems. *IEEE transactions on vehicular technology*, 41:57–62, 1992.

A New Hierarchical Routing Protocol for Dynamic Multihop Wireless Networks

Ian F. Akyildiz * Wei Yen * Bülent Yener, †

Abstract

The routing techniques used in conventional packet radio networks are not suitable for dynamic multihop wireless networks because of their unique architecture. In this paper, a new hierarchical multihop routing algorithm is introduced which balances the cost of location-update and path-finding operations by partitioning the terminals and mobile base stations to produce a virtual topology. *Based on the* virtual topology, *each network entity stores a fraction of the network topology information and maintains the routing efficiency. Finally, the performance of the hierarchical multihop routing algorithm is investigated through simulations.*

Key Words: Dynamic Wireless Networks, Location Update Operation, Mobile Base Stations, Multihop Routing Algorithm, Path Finding Operation, Virtual Location Area, Virtual Cell, Virtual Topology.

1 Introduction

Dynamic wireless networks are more reliable and efficient than conventional packet radio networks because (1) they save bandwidth for communications between remote terminals by providing routes through the wired part of the network, and (2) multihop wireless links are used between terminals close to each other. In general, the dynamic wireless network distinguishes itself from the packet radio networks by its unique architecture which can be used for, but not limited to, exploring and provisioning dangerous zones, military, and journalism applications [4, 7].

Since dynamic wireless network is a relatively new architecture, there are a lot of open research issues to be addressed. One of these issues is the routing problem. In this paper, we introduce a new hierarchical multihop unicast routing protocol. First, we briefly review the related work regarding routing protocols in various network environments.

The routing algorithm used in ARPA and SINCGARS packet radio networks is the distributed version of the Bellman-Ford algorithm (DBF)[1][1]. In the DBF, each node in the network updates its routing table by exchanging routing information with its immediate neighbors periodically. Therefore, a network topology change caused by mobility requires very long time to be noticed by all nodes as the message exchanges "ripple" through the network. In other words, the DBF algorithm fails to accommodate the terminals with high mobility, because it does not converge quickly enough.

Another algorithm commonly used in packet radio networks is the flooding mechanism which creates a loop-free broadcast tree to carry packets from a source to all nodes in the network [6]. In general, the flooding mechanism can accommodate high mobility because network entities are not required to keep up with the network topology changes due to the broadcast nature. However, the broadcast approach used in this algorithm consumes excessive bandwidth which is especially intolerable in a wireless environment.

In [2], a routing algorithm containing three types of control messages is proposed for packet radio networks. This algorithm divides the communication period into two phases, construction and maintenance phases. A multipath route is established by using *query* and *reply* messages during the construction phase. Later, as the network topology changes, the route is updated by using *failure* and *reply* messages during the maintenance phase. Although this algorithm only has local effects when reacting to a topology change in the maintenance phase, it involves all nodes in the construction phase of each communication, even if the source and destination are immediate neighbors. Thus, the message complexity of this algorithm might be too high in some cases. Furthermore, as pointed out in [2], this algorithm cannot accommodate high mobility. The network topology should not change too frequently such that the multipath route obtained during the construction phase remains valid.

In [5], a *wireless routing protocol* (WRP) is introduced for packet radio networks. The WRP uses the concept of *predecessor* to reduce excessive update messages resulting from network topology changes. However, compared to the routing algorithm in [2] and the flooding mechanism [6], the WRP requires a large memory space to store various routing information. In particular, the storage complexity of the WRP increases with the number of nodes in the network. Thus, the WRP might not be suitable for large networks.

In summary, we believe the existing multihop routing algorithms for packet radio networks have significant drawbacks which may not be overcome easily. Besides, the performance of these multihop algorithms when applied in the dynamic wireless networks is unknown. For example, in a dynamic multihop wireless network, only mobile base stations (MBSs) can communicate with their peers, i.e., with other MBSs. On the other hand, mobile terminals (MTs) cannot communicate with other MTs. Thus, the existing multihop rout-

*Broadband and Wireless Networking Laboratory, School of Electrical and Computer Engineering, Georgia Institute of Technology, Atlanta, GA 30332, {ian,wei}@ee.gatech.edu, Tel:(404)894-5141 Fax:(404)894-0035

†Department of Computer and Information Science, New Jersey Institute of Technology, Newark, NJ 07102-1982, yener@cis.njit.edu, Tel.:(201) 596-2666

[1]SINCGARS stands for the primary Single Channel Ground and Airborne Radio System which has been widely adapted in the Army and Navy.

0-8186-7780-5/97 $10.00 © 1997 IEEE

ing protocols [2, 5, 6] may be applicable on the MBS level. However, they cannot handle the mobility of the MT because a MT can move from a MBS to any other MBS.

The remaining of this paper is organized as follows. In Section 2, we describe the network model of the dynamic wireless network. Then, we explain the proposed hierarchical multihop routing protocol in Section 3. In Section 4, we investigate the performance of the proposed algorithm through simulations. Finally, we conclude this paper and point out possible future research in Section 5.

2 System Description

We assume that the dynamic wireless network consists of (i) a wired backbone network, (ii) a collection of fixed *switching centers* (SCs) that are connected to the backbone nodes, (iii) a collection of *mobile base stations* (MBSs) linked to the SCs (although we use the name "BASE stations", our so-called "base stations" are highly mobile) and (iv) *mobile terminals* (MTs) that can communicate with mobile base stations as shown in Figure 1. More specifically, we have four levels of hierarchy

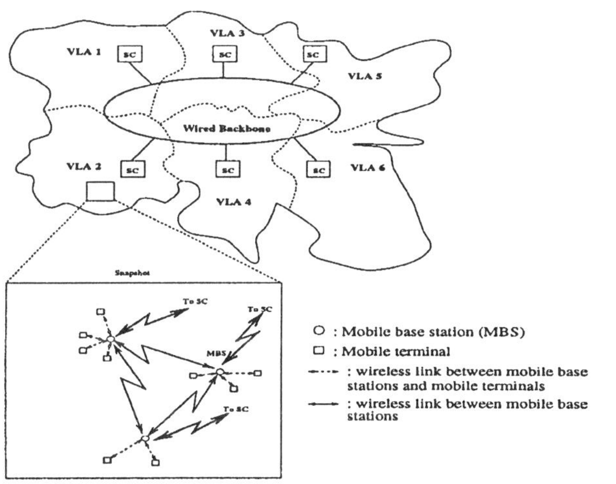

Figure 1: Network Model

in our architecture:
HIERARCHY 1. A wired backbone network represented as an undirected, connected, simple graph G=(V,E) with an arbitrary topology.
HIERARCHY 2. Each switching center is connected to at least one backbone node through physical links. We assume that each backbone node can serve up to S SCs.
HIERARCHY 3. Each SC can support at most B MBSs using wireless connections. Furthermore, two MBSs can communicate with each other without going through SCs. Note that we assume an underlying mechanism which assures each MBS can directly communicate with one and only one SC at any time instance. Since the scope of this paper concentrates on the routing issues, this assumption is reasonable in the sense that it prevents us from considering physical layer problems.

Next, we define a virtual location area (VLA) as the collection of MBSs which are supported by a single SC. Those MBSs that reside within the same VLA can communicate with a *virtual topology* as we will explain in Section 3. The topology in this level is determined by choice and it is called virtual since there is no physical link between them but instead a routing table entry between connected MBSs.
HIERARCHY 4. Each MBS can support at most T mobile terminals (MTs). The communication between an MBS and MTs in the same virtual cell are made via broadcast medium. However, no communication among MTs is allowed even if they are in the same virtual cell. We assume that *each MT is supported by exactly one MBS at any time instance.*

We assume parameters S, B, and T are given, thus, the total number of MTs in the system is $N = S \cdot B \cdot T$. In the next section, we explain the basic concept of the new hierarchical multihop unicast routing protocol.

3 The New Multihop Routing Protocol

In dynamic wireless networks, routing cannot be achieved if we fail to (i) locate the destination MT or to (ii) find a feasible path between the source and the destination. In other words, we need a location update and path finding procedures to address these two problems. In this section, we will demonstrate a distributed database structure (Sections 3.1 and 3.2) which allows us to perform the location update (Section 3.3) and path finding (Section 3.4) procedures effectively.

3.1 Partitioning the MBSs

As will be shown in Section 3.2, the distributed database structure requires partitioning of the MBSs within a VLA into disjoint *Breadth First Search* (BFS) trees [3] with diameter at most D and size at most Δ, where $\Delta \geq D$. Each tree is rooted at one unique mobile base station. In brief, if a BFS algorithm wants to add a node to a existing tree, then it will select from those nodes which do not increase the diameter of the existing tree. In other words, if the situation allows the BFS algorithm tends to maintain the maximum distance (hop count) from the root to leaves on the tree. Note that the tree induces a virtual topology since an edge between two bases in the tree corresponds to a directory entry in each end point. In Section 3.4, we show that the virtual topology of the BFS trees allows us to determine the routing cost.

We present the following procedure to partition the MBSs in a VLA:

1. Initially, all the MBSs are unmarked.
2. While there is an unmarked MBS, perform the following steps.
   - 2.1 Choose a root MBS b from the unmarked MBSs to build a new BFS tree.
   - 2.2 Expend the BFS tree by adding an unmarked MBS adjacent to that BFS tree.
   - 2.3 Repeat step 2.2 until the tree is saturated, i.e., at least one of the following conditions is violated.
     - *Condition 1.* The size of the BFS tree cannot exceed Δ.
     - *Condition 2.* The diameter of the BFS tree cannot exceed D.
   - 2.4 Mark all the MBSs in this tree and go to step 2.

Note that each VLA only invokes the partition algorithm once during the network setup. Therefore, the overhead incurred by this partition algorithm is negligible.

3.2 Distributed Database for Location Tracking

In this section, we demonstrate a distributed database which maintains the location information of the partitioned MBSs and MTs as shown in Figure 2. This distributed database achieves low storage complexity by only requiring involved network entities to store partial topology of the entire network. Furthermore, when combining with the location update and path finding procedures, this distributed database architecture provides a very attractive routing solution to the dynamic wireless network. In the following, we specify the involved network entities and the information they maintain in detail.

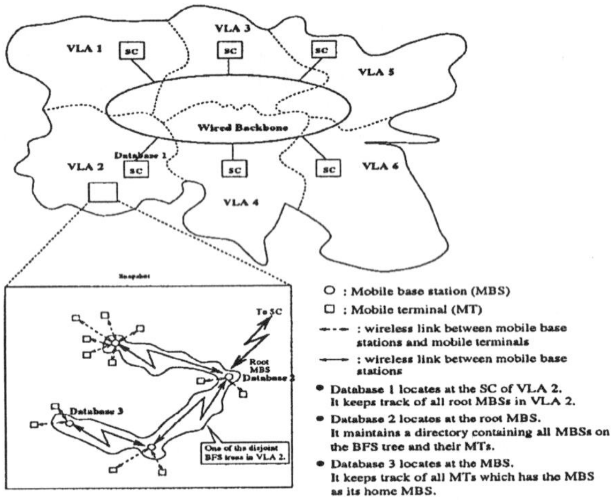

Figure 2: Trees, Directories etc

1. Each switching center (SC) maintains an entry only for the root MBSs in its VLA. The directory size is at most B/D, where B and D the maximum number of MBSs in a VLA and the maximum diameter of a BFS tree, respectively.

2. Each MBS in a BFS tree is a unique *home* to $O(T)$ mobile terminals (MTs) residing in its virtual cell. The MBS has to maintain a directory for these MTs. We call such an MBS as the **home MBS** and the corresponding BFS tree as the **home tree** of these MTs.

3. Each root MBS (selected at step 2 in the partition algorithm) of a BFS tree knows all the MTs covered by the MBSs on this tree. Thus, each root MBS has a directory in the size of $O(T\Delta + \Delta)$.

4. Each MBS in a BFS tree knows the topology of that tree which requires $O(\Delta)$ entries. Thus, the total directory size in an MBS (except the root MBS) is $O(\Delta + T)$ where T is the maximum number of MTs allowed in a virtual cell.

Given the distributed database architecture, we can calculate the total directory size, or storage complexity, in a BFS tree is $O((T\Delta + \Delta - 1) + \Delta - 1(\Delta - 1 + T)) = O(\Delta^2 + T\Delta)$. In addition, the total directory size in a VLA is $O(B/D(1 + \Delta^2 + T\Delta))$.

3.3 Location Update Procedure

The location update procedure is invoked to let the SCs and MBSs to detect and record any change occurring in the virtual topology, e.g., VLAs and virtual cells. In particular, suppose that t is an MT which has its home-MBS b in the home-tree T_i whose root MBS is denoted by r_i. Let b' be the new MBS of the MT t at the time of update. In the following, we consider several possible cases. Note that the proposed algorithm, in its current state, prohibits an MBS or MT leave its own VLA. This is a realistic assumption in various applications. For example, in a digital battlefield scenario [4, 7], a VLA may be a large area. The MBS and MT, corresponding to armored vehicles and foot soldiers, usually stay within their respective VLA.

- *Case 1:* $t, b, b' \in T_i$. i.e., the move is local to the home tree of the terminal.

- *Case 2:* $t, b \in T_i$ and $b' \in T_j$ where $j \neq i$. i.e., the move causes a home tree change.

  In Cases 3 and 4 we consider the mobility of the MBS.

- *Case 3:* Let $t, b' \in T_i$ and $b \in T_j$ where $j \neq i$. Thus, in this case, the MT t moves to a new VC on the same home-tree. However, the previous home MBS of t moves to a different tree.

- *Case 4:* $t, b, b' \in T_j$. Here both terminal and the home base move to a new tree.

As explained shortly, the location update procedure responds differently to each one of these cases. However, before we discuss the exact steps how the location update procedure reacts in these different cases, we will determine the size of the update message exchanged among network entities at the update time. An $UPDATE$ message is a quadruple: $< type, terminal\_ID, home-MBS\_ID, tree\_ID >$. Since there are at most T mobile terminals in each MBS and B MBSs in a VLA, the total number of bits, ζ ,in an update message is[2].

$$\zeta = 3 + logT + logB + \log(B/D). \qquad (1)$$

The field "tree_ID" contains the ID of the root MBS in that tree. Now we explain how the location update procedure handles the previously mentioned four cases.

3.3.1 Case 1: Tranquil Home MBS and Moving MT are in the Same Home-Tree

1. Upon moving to a new MBS (i.e., detecting a stronger MBS) b', the MT t sends an $UPDATE(000, t, b, r_i)$ message to b'. The type field of that update message indicates that it is originated from an MT.

[2] We assume that there are, at most, 8 types of update messages. In other words, the type field needs 3 bits to represent the update message types.

2. Upon receiving that update message, the new MBS b' informs the home MBS b of the MT t.

3. Since both b and b' are on the same tree, the MBS b remains to be the home MBS for the MT t.

Cost: Note that the cost of this location update procedure is the diameter of the tree because the new MBS b' needs, at most, that many wireless links to reach the MBS b.

3.3.2 Case 2: Tranquil Home MBS and Moving MT are in Different Trees

1. The MT t, upon moving to a new MBS b', sends an $UPDATE(000, t, b, r_i)$ message to b'.

2. Upon receiving that update message, the MBS b' compares the tree_ID field with its tree_ID, e.g., r_j, and decides that the MT is a visitor which comes from a different home-tree. The MBS b' makes an entry in its directory for the MT t.

3. The MBS b' requests to *takeover* this visiting MT t using the following **reliable** protocol with explicit ACKnowledgment.

   3.1 b' sets the type field to 001 and forwards the $UPDATE(001, t, b, r_i)$ message to r_j. This type field indicates that this is a takeover request from new base b'.

   3.2 Root r_j forwards this message to the SC since it does not maintain routing information for the other trees.

   3.3 SC S forwards the message to the tree rooted at r_i.

   3.4 Root r_i informs the home MBS b.

   3.5 The MBS b *handover* MT t by sending back $UPDATE(011, t, b, r_i)$ message to the new base b' and deletes the entry for t in its directory.

4. Upon receiving the $UPDATE(011, t, b, r_i)$ message, root r_i, root r_j and new base b' update their directories accordingly.

Cost: In addition to the update message sent by MT t, each takeover request costs 4 messages, $b' \rightarrow r_j \rightarrow SC \rightarrow r_i \rightarrow b$, and each hand-over ACK costs another 4 messages in a reverse order. Thus, the reliable protocol is expensive. However, it may be argued that the ACK phase can be dropped.

3.3.3 Case 3: Moving Home-MBS and MT in Different Home-Trees

Since our architecture permits MBSs to change their locations, here and also in the next sections we consider the mobility of an MBS. There are important questions which need to be answered first:

- How does an MBS decide which tree it belongs to after it moves?
- What happens to the MTs that it was serving?
- If the MBS moves to a different tree than its home-tree, how does it get inserted to the new tree?

In the following we address these issues.

1. The moving MBS b broadcasts an $UPDATE(100, NULL, b, r_i)$ message whenever it suspects that its connection to the associated BFS tree is no longer valid.

2. Each adjacent MBS b' on tree rooted at r_j (note that it is possible that $i = j$) that hears this message, broadcasts the $UPDATE(110, b', b, r_j)$ message. Note that the MBS b' copies its ID to the NULL (empty) field in the update message received from b.

3. Upon receiving the $UPDATE(110, b', b, r_j)$ message sent by b', the moving MBS b uniquely identifies that this message is directed to itself (this is important if multiple MBSs change their home trees).

4. Note that the moving MBS b may receive some $UPDATE(110, b', b, r_i)$ messages and some $UPDATE(110, b', b, r_j)$ messages. The question is *how it decides which tree it belongs to.* The moving MBS b makes the decision by applying the *majority function* to these messages. In case that the numbers of two update messages are the same, the moving MBS b randomly selects its new home tree.

5. After deciding which tree it belongs to, the moving MBS b chooses the MBS with the minimum ID (among the MBSs which sent the $UPDATE(110, b', b, r_j)$ message) as its parent in the tree rooted at r_j. The moving MBS b further informs its new parent MBS b' of this decision by sending $UPDATE(111, b', b, r_i)$.

6. Upon receiving $UPDATE(111, b', b, r_i)$ message, the MBS b' forwards this message to the root r_j if $i \neq j$. Root r_j informs all MBSs in the tree T_j.

7. Root r_j also informs root r_i via the switching center.

8. Root r_i informs all MBSs on tree T_i about the topology change. (We omit the maintenance of the tree, since it is a well-studied problem.)

9. Regarding those MTs that the moving MBS b used to serve, we assume that those MTs are distributed among the neighboring cells. Thus, the root MBS r_i which knows the global view of the tree T_i does it in a centralized way. For example, a tranquil MT used to be served by b may initiate a location update procedure as explained in Case 1. However, the root MBS r_i intercepts the message sent by the new MBS b' to the old MBS b (Case 1, step 2) and assigns b' the new home MBS of that tranquil MT.

Cost: In this case, the moving MBS b initiates the location update procedure by sending a broadcast message. As we described, it receives $O(\Delta)$ replies from its adjacent MBSs which hears its update message. Then the moving MBS b sends a message to its new parent MBS

b', which, in turn, sends another message to its root, r_j. The root MBS r_j, then, is required to inform the old root MBS r_i about the departure of the moving MBS b. Finally, all MBSs on both the old and new home trees of the moving MBS b is informed and updated by $O(\Delta)$ messages. Thus, total number of messages in this case is still $O(\Delta)$.

3.3.4 Case 4: Moving Home MBS and MT in the Same New Home Tree

The location update procedure for this case is very similar to that for Case 3. However, since the home MBS and MT move to the same new home tree, the location update procedure will be transparent to MT t. In other words, in Case 3, the MTs used to be served by the moving MBS may need to initiate a location update procedure as explained in Case 1 while it is not necessary in this case.

Note that in all four cases discussed above, the location update procedure never requires network-wise broadcast. All the location updates are achieved by modifying the corresponding entries in the distributed databases of the adjacent network entities. Due to this desirable characteristic, the distributed database converges very quickly in response to network topology changes. In other words, the new hierarchical multihop routing protocol can accommodate the very high mobility.

3.4 The Path Finding Procedure

In this section, we present a novel path finding procedure which distributes the complexity and overhead among the MBSs and SCs. In particular, we consider the following four cases.

3.4.1 Case 1: Source and Destination are in the Same Tree

In this case, there are two possibilities: source and destination both reside in (i) the same cell, or (ii) in different cells. Since the first one is trivial, we elaborate the second one. Since the root MBS of a BFS tree knows all the directories of the MBSs on this tree, the MBS of the source routes the packet to the root MBS which in turn forwards it to the MBS of the destination on the tree.

Cost: The routing length will be bounded by twice of the depth of the tree, or, $O(D)$.

3.4.2 Case 2: Source and Destination are in Different Trees but in the Same VLA

Since the information kept in each tree is local to the members of that tree, inter-tree routing operations are performed via the switching center that coordinates the roots of the trees in the same VLA. In the following, we specify the path finding procedure for this case.

1. The MBS of the source, forwards the packet from the source MT to the root MBS of its tree.

2. The root MBS of the source tree does not have the information about the destination since its knowledge is also limited to this tree. Thus, it forwards the packet to the SC.

3. The information kept in an SC is only for the root MBSs of the BFS trees, thus that SC does not know the location of the destination MT. Consequently, the SC broadcasts the packet to all the root MBSs in its VLA. Assuming that broadcast is a unicast to each tree, the cost of this broadcast is B/D messages, since there are, at most, that many roots MBS.

4. Only one root MBS will forward the packet to the destination MBS which serves the destination of the packet. This is true since each root MBS knows all MTs residing in this tree.

Cost: In this case, we need two multihop routes[3] and a broadcast between an SC and the root MBSs in its VLA. Therefore, the message complexity is $O(B/D)$ which is primarily contributed by the broadcast overhead.

3.4.3 Case 3: Source and Destination are in Different VLAs

The fixed part of the dynamic wireless network plays an important role in this type of communication. Since the source and destination may be far away from each other, it is unreliable and inefficient to solely use multihop routes as shown in Figure 3. Therefore, we utilize the fixed part of the network to achieve better reliability and share the load in the wireless part of the network. The detailed path finding procedure for this case is given in the following.

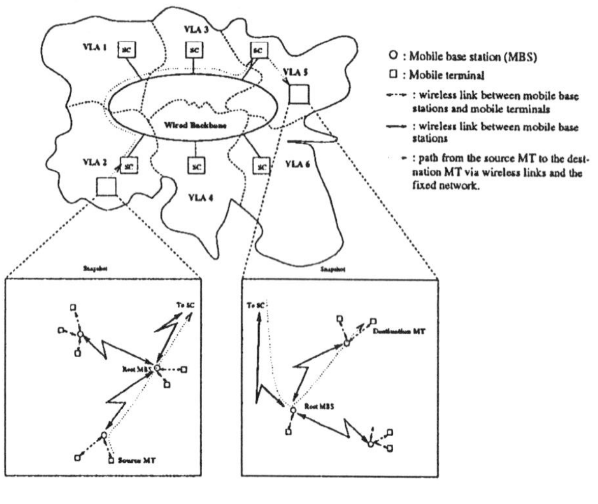

Figure 3: Source and Destination in Different VLAs

The packet from the sources gets routed over the wired-backbone. Upon receiving the packet, an SC performs the following operations.

1. The SC forwards the packet to all the root MBSs in its VLA.

2. Since each root MBS knows the MTs and their bases in its tree, only one root forwards the packet down to the destination tree and, then, to the destination base.

[3](source → source root MBS) and (destination root MBS → destination).

Cost: The cost of this path finding procedure is equal to the sum of that in Case 2 and the cost of routing on the fixed backbone network.

4 Performance Evaluation

Here we evaluate the performance of the proposed algorithm through simulations. In particular, we, first, describe our simulation model including the network topology generation, mobility model, and traffic model. Then we demonstrate and discuss the simulation results.

4.1 Simulation Model

In the simulation, a square-shaped area is divided into nxn unit squares where n is an input parameter and could be any positive integer. We place an SC in the center of each unit square so that the small square becomes the VLA of the SC[4]. Within each VLA, we generate a set of MBSs and MTs based on a uniform distribution. These MBSs and MTs have their own mobility parameters, denoted by m_{MBS} and m_{MT}, respectively. In each time unit, we first determine how many MBSs and MTs move according to their mobility parameters and then generate their movement vectors. A movement vector has x and y elements derived from a uniform distribution between $[0, 1)$. If a moving MBS or MT obtains a movement vector leading outside the VLA from one side of the unit square, we assume that the MBS or MT comes in from the opposite side of the VLA as shown in Figure 4. In this example, a node moves across a VLA boundary, i.e., both its x and y coordinates are larger than 1. Then, according to our mobility model, we reduce both coordinates by 1 so that the new location of the node falls within the VLA area.

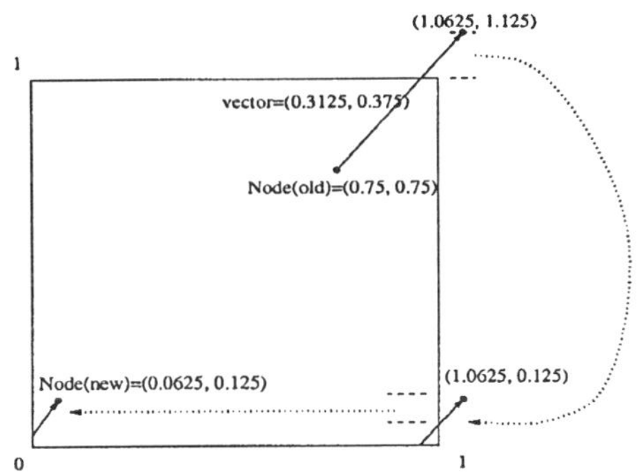

Figure 4: Movement Leading Outside the VLA

In our simulation, we do not assume any particular underlying MAC (medium access control) protocol as well as no specification on the wireless link capacity. Instead, we assume that within each time unit an MBS can transmit a message, if it desires. Thus, we believe that the simulation results will not loose their significance when various network models are considered.

Since an MBS residing at a VLA can directly communicate with the SC of that VLA, we know that the VC of the MBS has a radius of, at least, $\frac{\sqrt{2}}{2}$. Therefore, there exists a wireless link between two MBSs as long as their distance is less than the radius of their VCs, or $\frac{\sqrt{2}}{2}$ in our simulation. However, the MBSs within a VLA are divided into multiple trees using the BFS algorithm introduced in Section 3. An MBS records only its wireless links in the BFS tree. In the beginning of the simulation, an MT may reside in the overlapped region of several VCs. However, the MT selects the nearest MBS as its home MBS. Once the MT selects its home MBS, this MT is considered as being at the same VC until it moves outside of the VC.

[4] In practice, a VLA may have an irregular shape and the location of an SC is not necessarily at the center of its VLA.

Messages generated in the simulation can be divided into two categories, the control and data messages. The control message results from the MBS or MT mobility as described in Section 3. Hence, the control message generation is implied by the mobility model. On the other hand, the data message is generated by the source MT. In our simulation, each MT has probability p to generate a data message destined to an arbitrary MT for each time unit. Both the control and data messages are transferred to their destinations by the MBSs in the network. We assume each MBS has an infinite buffer to accommodate incoming messages and can transmit only one message in each time unit. Furthermore, each MBS will not serve the data messages before it finishes serving all control messages in its queue.

Due to the mobility, an MBS may be isolated because i) it does not have any wireless link to the other MBSs, or ii) it cannot join a BFS tree without violating the size and depth restrictions stated in the BFS algorithm. If an MBS is isolated, it drops all messages it receives. Similarly, an isolated MT can neither receive nor transmit data messages.

4.2 Simulation Results

Here, we start with a single-VLA scenario where all messages are generated by and destined to the MTs in the VLA. In other words, in the single-VLA scenario, only the wireless links are used which either connect the SC and root MBSs or connect the MBSs in the BFS trees. The performance we obtain from the single-VLA scenario is equivalent to a more general nxn-VLA case, if intra-VLA traffic is considered. This feature is a direct result of our proposed routing algorithm, i.e., limiting the mobility of the MBS and MT to their respective VLA. Note that the inter-VLA traffic in the nxn-VLA case affects the average routing cost performance which is also evaluated and will be presented as what in follows.

In the single-VLA scenario, we use the following simulation parameters. We generate 40 MBSs and 200 MTs. Then, we divide these MBSs into several BFS trees according to the algorithm introduced in Section 3.1. We find for each MT its home MBS. The diameter D of these BFS trees is 2 while the size Λ of BFS trees is an input variable. The mobility parameters of the MBS and MT are 1 and 2 per time unit, respectively. The message arrival probability p is another input variable ranging between [0.005, 0.03] message/MT/time unit. Note that the p value could depend on various factors such as the MAC protocols and the link capacity.

In Figure 5 (a), we show the throughput performance λ which is obtained by

$$\lambda = p\,\frac{\alpha}{\beta}. \qquad (2)$$

where α is the number of messages received by their destinations during the simulation time while β is the number of messages generated by the MTs/MBSs during the simulation time.

By inspecting Figure 5 (a), we note that i) the throughput decreases as the offered load, controlled by the parameter p, increases, and ii) the throughput decreases as the size of the BFS trees increases. The first result is obvious but the latter needs an explanation. In our proposed routing algorithm, the root MBSs are responsible for all messages generated by and destined to the MTs stored in its directory. An increasing BFS tree size means that the root MBSs have to maintain more MTs in its directory and handle their according messages. Consequently, the root MBS quickly becomes a bottleneck as the offered load increases. Therefore, we suggest to use a smaller BFS tree size, e.g. $\Delta = 5$ to avoid possible congestion at root MBSs. Furthermore, all three throughput curves in Figure 5 will decrease and, finally, approach zero with increasing p.

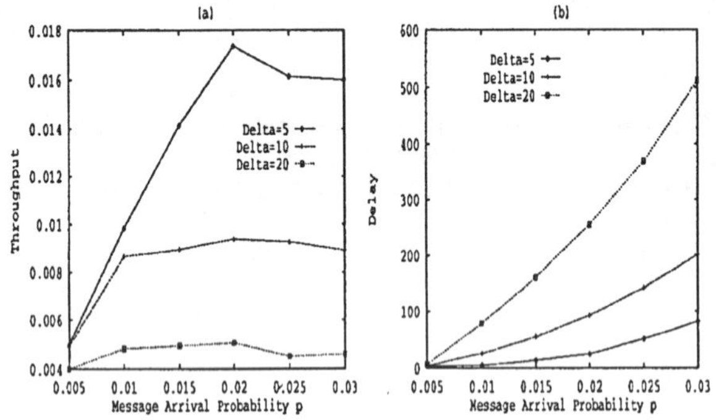

Figure 5: Single-VLA Scenario (40 MBSs, 200 MTs, $D = 2$, MBS mobility=1/time unit, MT mobility=2/time unit) (a)Throughput; (b)Delay

In Figure 5 (b), we show the delay results for three different BFS tree sizes. The delay value takes the average of the delay experienced by all messages transmitted successfully during the simulation period. As expected, the delay performance becomes worse when the BFS tree size increases reflecting the degraded throughput performance.

By assuming that each MBS has a small buffer size for only two messages and using the same simulation parameters as in Figure 5, we show the percentage μ, defined in equation (3), of dropped messages in Figure 6.

$$\mu = \frac{\gamma}{\beta} \tag{3}$$

where γ is the number of dropped messages and β is the number of messages generated by MBSs/MTs during the simulation time.

It can be observed in Figure 6 that our proposed routing protocol does not discard messages when the offered load is low. However, as the offered load increases, the number of dropped messages of the curve with $\Delta = 20$ increases drastically. The curves with $\Delta = 10$, 5 also increase as the offered load keeps increasing. The three curves in Figure 6 gradually approach 100%, i.e., the root MBS becomes a bottleneck, especially for larger BFS trees.

In Figure 7, we show the average number of MTs which move from their currently residing VC (virtual cell) to another VC in each time unit dependent on the

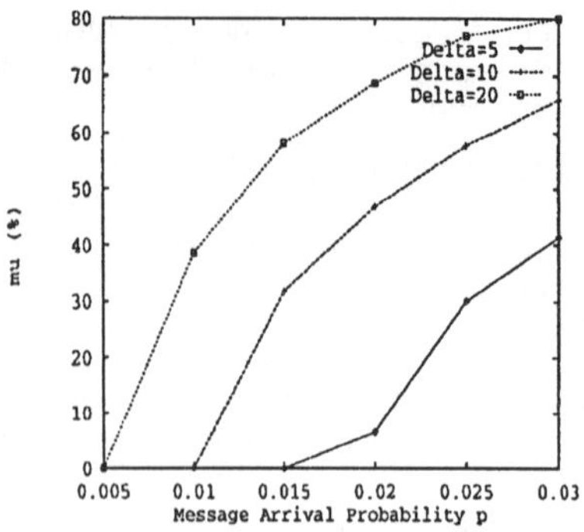

Figure 6: Percentage of Dropped Messages in the Single-VLA Scenario (40 MBSs, 200 MTs, $D = 2$, MBS mobility=1/time unit, MT mobility=2/time unit)

mobility parameter. The average number represents the overhead of control messages caused by MTs changing VCs. The three curves in Figure 7 have MBS mobility m_{MBS} equal to 0, 5, and 10, respectively, while the other simulation parameters remain the same as in the previous experiments. The curve with $m_{MBS} = 0$ (tranquil MBS scenario) increases linearly to the MT mobility m_{MT}. This behavior is expected because, as m_{MT} increases, more MTs can move and, hence, can increase the possibility that they leave their according VCs. In the cases where the curves with m_{MBS} not equal to zero, a tranquil MBS may change to a different VC because the MBS of its currently residing VC moves. In other words, given the same m_{MT}, the curves with higher m_{MBS} values increase faster than those curves with smaller m_{MBS} values. However, as the m_{MT} keeps increasing, the three curves gradually converge to the same value because all MTs move in each time unit regardless of whether their corresponding MBSs are tranquil or moving.

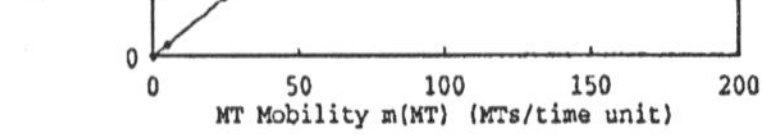

Figure 7: Percentage of Dropped Messages in the Single-VLA Scenario (40 MBSs, 200 MTs, $D = 2$, MBS mobility=1/time unit, MT mobility=2/time unit)

Note that nxn-VLA scenario has same performance behavior as the single VLA scenario. However, the routing costs in nxn-VLA scenario become a significant component. Therefore, we want to compare the average routing costs of our proposed routing protocol and the flooding mechanism[5], denoted by $c_{r,p}$ and $c_{r,f}$, respectively.

First, we define

- c_1 is the cost for an MBS to send a message,
- c_2 is the cost to broadcast a message to all root MBSs via the fixed network in the proposed protocol,
- c_3 is the cost to broadcast a message to all MBSs and MTs using the flooding mechanism, and
- c_4 is the cost of using a wireless link between a MBS and a MT.

In the nxn-VLA scenario, we have

$$c_{r,p} \leq 2(D\ c_1 + c_4) + c_2 \qquad (4)$$

where D is the maximum diameter of a BFS tree. In the worst case, the source and destination MTs are in the leaves in VCs (virtual cell) of two BFS trees which belong to two different VLAs. If the flooding mechanism [6] is used, then we

$$c_{r,f} = c_3 \leq M\ (c_1 + c_4) \qquad (5)$$

where M is the number of MBSs in the network. In the worst case of the flooding mechanism, all MBSs transmit the message once. For example, for a network with a virtual bus topology where $\max c_{r,p} \leq \max c_{r,f}$, then we obtain[6]

$$c_2\ <\ (M - 2D)c_1 + (M - 2)c_4. \qquad (6)$$

Equation (6) must be satisfied to apply our proposed routing protocol. In fact, given M = 160 MBSs distributed in 2x2 VLAs with $D = 2$, c_1=5 , and $c_4 = 1$, the bound for c_2 is 938 according to equation (6) which, we believe, is far larger than the actual c_2 value in the real world dynamic wireless networks. In Table 1, we show our simulation results of the average routing costs for a 2x2-VLA dynamic network with various c_1 and c_2 values while c_4 is set to 1. Each VLA has 40 MBSs and 200 MTs with BFS trees of $D = 2$ and $\Delta = 5$.

In the last column of Table 1, we include the maximum (worst case) value of $c_{r,f}$ for comparison. According to our simulation, the proposed routing protocol achieves one or two orders better routing costs than those obtained by the flooding mechanism.

	$c_2 = 1$	$c_2 = 2$	$c_2 = 5$	$c_2 = 10$	$\max c_{r,f}$
$c_1 = 1$	5.708	6.496	8.85	12.851	320
$c_1 = 2$	8.627	9.418	11.777	15.724	480
$c_1 = 5$	17.375	18.176	20.488	24.474	960
$c_1 = 10$	32.003	32.754	35.175	39.092	1760

Table 1: Average Routing Costs with Various c_1 and c_2 Values

[5]We use the basic flooding mechanism for the worst case comparison.

[6]Equation (6) is derived from equations (4,5) and $c_{r,p} \leq c_{r,f}$.

5 Conclusion and Future Work

We introduced a new multihop routing algorithm for dynamic wireless networks in this paper. This algorithm partitions the MBSs (*mobile base stations*) of a VLA (*virtual location area*) into multiple virtual trees. A message originated from a source MT (*mobile terminal*) is transmitted to its destination via those virtual trees and, sometimes, the fixed network.

Using the concept of the *virtual topology*, network entities store a small fraction of the network topology information. Therefore, if an MBS or MT moves, only a few of involved network entities have to update their directories. The inexpensive location update allows the dynamic wireless network to actually route messages rather than blindly broadcast them. Furthermore, the hierarchical structure of the proposed algorithm effectively shares the load on the multihop links with the fixed network. Roughly speaking, the traffic between remote source MT and destination MT pair involves the fixed network.

Regarding the future research, we plan to relax the constraint stated in Section 3.3 which requires MBSs and MTs to stay in their VLAs. We also plan to improve the survivability of the proposed algorithm by creating a backup scheme for the root MBS which stores the critical information for its BFS (*breadth first search*) tree. In addition, we will experiment with another virtual topology to remove the bottleneck at the root MBS produced by the virtual tree topology.

References

[1] R. E. Bellman, "Dynamic Programming," *Princeton University Press*, Princeton, N.J., 1957.

[2] M. S. Corson and A. Ephremides, "A Distributed Routing Algorithm for Mobile Wireless Networks," *ACM/Baltzer Journal of Wireless Networks*, Vol. 1, pp. 61-81, 1995.

[3] R. K. Ghosh and G. P. Bhattacharjee, "Parallel Breadth-First Search Algorithms for Trees and Graphs," *International Journal of Computer Mathematics*, Vol. 15, No. 3-4, pp. 255-268, Jul. 1984.

[4] R. B. Mouldin and P. A. Young, "Wireless Battlefield Tactical Networking Supporting C2OTM and C4I for the Army Warrior," *Proc. of Milcom '94 Conference*, 1994.

[5] S. Murthy, J. J. Garcia-Luna-Aceves, "A Routing Protocol for Packet Radio Networks," *Proc. of ACM Mobicom '95 (Mobile Computing and Networking Conference)*, Berkeley California, Nov. 13-15, Nov. 1995.

[6] W. Stallings, *Data Communications*, Fourth Edition, McMillan Publ. Co., 1995.

[7] T. J. Wheeler, J. D. Richardson, M. Rosenzweig, and D. Cummings, "Designing a Tactical ATM Network Integrating Performance Engineering and Design," *Proc. of Milcom '94 Conference*, 1994.

Author Index